■ The Origins of the World's Mythologies

The Origins of the
World's Mythologies

E.J. Michael Witzel

OXFORD
UNIVERSITY PRESS

OXFORD
UNIVERSITY PRESS

Oxford University Press, Inc., publishes works that further
Oxford University's objective of excellence
in research, scholarship, and education.

Oxford   New York
Auckland   Cape Town   Dar es Salaam   Hong Kong   Karachi
Kuala Lumpur   Madrid   Melbourne   Mexico City   Nairobi
New Delhi   Shanghai   Taipei   Toronto

With offices in
Argentina   Austria   Brazil   Chile   Czech Republic   France   Greece
Guatemala   Hungary   Italy   Japan   Poland   Portugal   Singapore
South Korea   Switzerland   Thailand   Turkey   Ukraine   Vietnam

Copyright © 2012 by Oxford University Press, Inc.

Published by Oxford University Press, Inc.
198 Madison Avenue, New York, New York 10016

www.oup.com

Oxford is a registered trademark of Oxford University Press.

Library of Congress Cataloging-in-Publication Data
Witzel, Michael, 1943–
The origins of the world's mythologies / E.J. Michael Witzel.
p.   cm.
Includes bibliographical references and index.
ISBN 978-0-19-536746-1 (hardcover : alk. paper)
ISBN 978-0-19-981285-1 (pbk. : alk. paper)
1. Mythology.   2. Myth.   I. Title.
BL312.W58   2011
201'.3—dc22   2010050957

Printed in the United States of America
on acid-free paper

For: Yayoi
     Manabu
     Meimei

> Most interesting findings usually result
> from . . . hypothesis formation
> based on preliminary data analyses.
> C. C. RAGIN

On a cold February night in 1990, I rushed down a steep Japanese hill to bring fire to the world of the living. Along with some 2,000 men, all dressed in white and carrying burning torches, I ran down some uneven 500-odd steps to bring fire, Prometheus-like, to the women assembled below in the small town of Shingu in Wakayama Prefecture. This was a men-only affair: that day, women were forbidden to go up to the Kamikura Shrine, where a Shintō priest kindled the first fire of the lunar new year and distributed it to us. The town's men, stray acquaintances, whom I had asked for help, were somewhat surprised about the foreigner who wanted to participate. They nevertheless accepted and embraced me warmly, helped me to buy the special clothes and dress up properly, tying the thick straw cord around my waist, getting my *taimatsu* torch inscribed with traditional good wishes. Like other small groups, loudly greeting each other and clashing our torches, we roamed the town during the afternoon, accepting all-white food like radish and rice from the town's women, who had put up stalls along our path, and fortifying ourselves in various pubs with a lot of rice wine— so as to strengthen us for the ordeal. The crowded run downhill, my companions said, was very dangerous: some people break their legs each year. I got away with a little singeing of my ceremonial dress.

The experience was moving: the mad rush downhill in a community of men with the same purpose, and their friendliness toward a stray stranger who had merely dropped in from his sabbatical at Kyoto. Our small group included a number of men who had come home from far away for the *otō-matsuri* and its rites. Our task of delivering the new fire accomplished, we continued to an all-male bathhouse and on to a private dinner party in one of my new friend's houses. Next day, back at the shrine, I interviewed the priest who had performed the churning of the new fire, and he readily answered, even though he was busy with an elaborate private ritual. His counterquestion was whether I had felt *pure* the evening before.

Then, there was the stirring feeling of participating in an archaic ritual that, people say, had been performed for some 1,400 years, always on the sixth day of the first lunar month. It was like taking part, as a Westerner like me would think, in a pre-Christian ritual that symbolized the bringing of fire by Prometheus (see §3.5.3) and the simultaneous delivery of the sun deity, Amaterasu, from her year-end and primordial rock refuge (§3.5.1).

By 1990, I had been playing with fire for quite some time: for some 25 years, I had been involved in the study of ancient Indian and Iranian religious and ritual texts, many of which deal with the sacred fire. I had read a lot of the ancient-most Indian mythology found in the Veda, and I had witnessed many Vedic and Buddhist fire rituals during my nearly six years in Nepal in the seventies.

The first, traditional Vedic fire ritual that I saw there was a secluded and secret affair. The *agnihotra* ritual was carried out by a Brahmin priest whose family had done so for the Nepalese king for the past 200 years. After that first experience I managed to witness many other solemn rituals. Active participation, however, is not allowed for those not born as Hindus. It was deeply moving to see the *agnihotra* performed exactly as our 3,000-year-old Sanskrit texts tell us. Its priest, living in a compound next to the national temple of Paśupatināth just east of Kathmandu, was very friendly and allowed me and even our NTV film crew ready access. The film then helped me greatly in comparing ancient texts and modern performance.

***

However, next to my experience of archaic Indian rituals, I had also read, since my student days, some Japanese texts dealing with the oldest myths and rituals of Japan. For this reason, I was interested in Japanese fire rituals and made an effort to witness a number of them, both Shintō and Buddhist, during my year-long stay in Kyoto.

However, the one at Shingu is special: it is the ritual enactment of an ancient myth, a combination that I had often encountered in Vedic rituals. A month earlier, we had made a tour to Shio no Misaki, the southernmost promontory of the Kii Peninsula, to greet the first sun of our (common calendar) New Year, on January 1. Again, there was a throng of people who had come to watch the first rising of the sun.

During my year at Kyoto, I had many other occasions to see the close interrelation between ancient Japanese myth and current rituals, performed by supposedly irreligious (*mushinkyō*) modern citizens. Observing them rekindled my long-standing interest in the oldest Japanese mythological texts of the early eighth century. I was especially interested in the myth of the delivery of the sun (see §5.3.1). It is found in the oldest, originally oral text, the Kojiki, which was written down by imperial order in 712 CE. The myth has a very close resemblance to the Old Vedic one of the delivery of sunlight from a cave of the Dawn, Uṣas.

I had noticed that correlation a quarter of a century earlier, as a graduate student, but I did not seriously pursue it as I then saw no solution as to the historical relationship between both myths, at least not one according to the methods of philology and historical linguistics that I was trained in. We were used to explanations such as immigration, whereby certain tribes brought their language, religion, and rituals with them. Pouring over ancient Kashmiri birch bark manuscripts and discussing the fine details of the migration process in the seminars of my late teachers Paul Thieme at Tübingen and Karl Hoffmann at Erlangen, and much later F. B. J. Kuiper at Leiden, the pattern of the "Aryan migration" was foremost in our minds. That means the movement of Indo-Iranian (Ārya) tribes speaking the language ancestral to both Old Iranian and Vedic, moving southward from the steppes around the Ural Mountains. Even allowing for some migrations from the continent into early Japan, however, the country is very distant from India and Iran, and its language belongs to a completely different linguistic family. A close relationship seemed excluded.

Nevertheless, the impressions gained from my training and especially the experience of rituals and living myths in Nepal and Japan encouraged me not to forget my earlier observations and to follow up on the topic of the underlying myths from time to time, over the next decades, even though I did not publish anything on this problem. This book, thus, has slumbered in my cabinet for many long years.

▨ ABOUT THE DISCOVERY OF LAURASIAN MYTHOLOGY

As mentioned, the first beginnings of the present study go back some 40 years. As a graduate student I noticed a number of surprising correspondences between the oldest Indian myths of the Ṛgveda (c. 1000 BCE) and those of Old Japan (written down in 712/720 CE). But I did not follow up on this topic for the simple reason that connections between India and Japan, via Buddhism, were established only in the mid–first millennium CE. By then, it was too late for any transmission of archaic, long-lost Vedic Indian traits. I concluded that, somehow, common origin, a long-range relationship, may have been the source of such similarities, but I could not explain how and thus left the question open. It surfaced again when I noticed many similarities between major Eurasian mythologies in the early eighties, while I was working on rebirth and cosmogony and the Milky Way,[1] but again I did not pursue it in detail, though I thought that common origin in southern Siberia was possible.

However, during a year-long blissful stay, in 1989–90, at the Institute for Research in Humanities (Jimbun Kagaku Kenkyujo) of Kyoto University, I could make many observations of living Japanese myths and rituals that were fruitful in thinking about their roots. This was greatly helped by earlier observations of living South Asian myths and rituals, made during my long stay in Nepal (1972–78), which I combined with studies of the most archaic Indian texts, the Vedas. Returning to Europe after this long stay, I saw many "Christian" rituals and local myths in a completely different light: in many cases, it was relatively easy to discern their pagan roots. After these various experiences and studies I drew up, in early 1990, the first scheme of comparative mythology that included texts from Iceland to Egypt to Japan. As appears from the description given above, this model was not based on the work of M. Eliade and others like him; rather, it emerged from actual comparisons of texts (and rituals). Like Eliade, however, I may have been influenced, initially, by the several accounts in Old Indian texts of the Four Ages and of a story line extending from the creation of the world to its destruction. However, this background had only heuristic value, as soon as I discovered similar models elsewhere, far from India.

A first overview of my new Eurasian theory was presented in a talk at the Jimbun Kagaku Kenkyujo of Kyoto University on June 30, 1990. At the time, I was convinced that Japan represented one outlier, and Iceland, the other one, in a common Eurasian scheme of myths. On my return to Boston, in late 1990 and early 1991, my scheme was unexpectedly supported by several then published popular accounts of recent advances in genetics and linguistics that delineated a division between African, Out of Africa, and later Eurasian populations.[2] The latter conveniently overlapped with my proposed Eurasian/Laurasian scheme of mythology.

Since then, I have been working on and off, in between other pressing work, on the details of the proposed Eurasian scheme. It soon was expanded to the Americas (Laurasia), and I noticed that the Laurasian scheme differed from the rest of the world (Gondwana Land). It was only during this process that I consciously applied the model of *historical and comparative* studies—such as linguistics—to the initial Laurasian model: it gained additional strength from learning what has been successful in historical comparative linguistics and similar historically oriented fields such as population genetics and from applying this consistently to myth studies. For this very reason some space will be given in chapter 4 to human population genetics, archaeology, and linguistics: they, in addition, sustain the results of the Laurasian model.

Finally, another pleasant year-long sabbatical at the Asia–Africa Institute of the Tokyo University of Foreign Studies (2004–5) rekindled my interest and provided me with the opportunity to concentrate on the theory and its implications. It was during the last months of my stay at Tokyo that the materials for this book could finally be collected. It is therefore due to both these kind invitations that a rough draft of the present book could written.[3] I am very grateful to my friends and colleagues of both Japanese institutions for giving me this chance.

In the course of the investigations carried out in 2005, it became clear that the seemingly seminal connection between Old Japanese and Old Indian myth represents but *one* aspect of Laurasian mythology, emanating from a Central Asian center around 2000 BCE.[4] This link is similar to the Japanese–Indo-European (Greek, Scythian, etc.) parallels that A. Yoshida has been drawing up for some decades.[5] Some aspects of the older form of the Laurasian theory (1990–2005) were, accordingly, adjusted or given up, something that is commonly necessitated by newly emerging materials, as Ragin points out so clearly.[6] The Indian–Japanese connections therefore turn out to be merely an interesting intermediate central Eurasian interlude but no longer a major fundament of the theory, which spans all of Eurasia, Polynesia, and the Americas. In short, not all of the results of this study are exactly those that I expected when I first began it.

First results of my investigations were printed in Japanese in 1990 in *Zinbun*, and a brief overview of the theory was published in *Mother Tongue* in 2001.[7]

***

This book, consequently, deals with a neglected method in the study of myth— the combined *historical* and *comparative* approach. Its aim is to trace back in time not just single myths, such as the Oedipus or Orpheus one, but the *complete* mythology of a people, say, the Greeks or Mayas, *and* to compare it with the mythologies of other, neighboring and distant peoples. This has not been done so far, at least not systematically and certainly not in a historical fashion.

There are well-known similarities between individual myths belonging to various traditions worldwide. However, once complete mythologies are compared across space and time, this soon leads to the discovery of an underlying structure—that of a *story line*, extending from the creation of the world to its final destruction. This narrative system, however, is not found globally. It is certainly widespread but not universal: the mythologies of the Aborigines of Australia, the Melanesians of New Guinea and its neighboring islands, and most populations of sub-Saharan Africa lack it.

Due to its wide spread in Eurasia and the Americas, I will call this mythological system the "Laurasian" one, following established geological and biological usage. The Afro-Australian system, again using a geological term, I will call "Gondwana."

The bulk of this book deals with establishing the Laurasian framework and comparing it with the Gondwana one. It is thrilling to observe that the Laurasian system can be traced back, step by step, to the later Paleolithic, some 40,000 years ago, when aspects of it first appear in cave paintings (§4.4.1). Conversely, the Gondwana scheme must have been that of our African ancestors: a small group of them ventured "out of Africa" some 65,000 years ago and followed, by "quick train," the coastline of the Indian Ocean via Arabia, India, and Sunda Land to Australia. They became the ancestors of all non-African people. A subset of them developed the Laurasian mythological system that became increasingly dominant after the last two ice ages, some 50,000 and 20,000 years ago.

A comparison of both systems leads to the discovery of certain commonalities that indicate how the Laurasian system developed out of the preceding Gondwana one. Even more astonishingly, this close comparison also allows us to sketch a few traits of a still earlier form of mythology, the one that humans had at the time of the so-called African Eve of the geneticists, some 130,000 years ago.

The current project thus enables and facilitates the discovery of increasingly older forms of mythologies that have been shared by our ancient ancestors inside and outside of Africa. It opens a window into their mind that cannot be delivered by other approaches such as archaeology, linguistics, or genetics. We will see that early humans were confronted with the same eternal questions that we still struggle with: why are we here, where do we come from, and where do we go? It is moving to see how millennia after millennia, humans have tried to answer these fundamentally human questions. They did so in following the Laurasian and Gondwana pathways, be they the ways of traditional local mythology or the paths of current major world religions, which all build on Laurasian myth.

However, the present investigation also has a lesson for us today: as most of us are still engaged in the same eternal human project, we should take a look at it from outside the inherited framework, think outside our box of Stone Age path dependencies. Is emancipation in sight? The repeated 20th-century use of inherited mythologies and the eternal deliberate creation of new variants by political forces, from the pharaohs to Kim Il Sung, demonstrate the inherent danger of the hardwiring of humans for myth and religion. The recent resurgence of the great world religions, too, seems to indicate that we still are dominated by Stone Age myths and their 2,000-year-old descendants. The power of myth is with us, and we better understand it.

▪ LIMITATION OF INVESTIGATION BY ONE PERSON

As a philologist of ancient Indian texts, I am well aware of the limitations and pitfalls of the present undertaking. Numerous texts in many languages are involved, from Iceland to Tierra del Fuego, and it is impossible for any one person to have sufficient command over the languages and the intricacies of the ancient and modern texts involved. One has to rely on recent, hopefully good translations. Frequently, it is not clear to the outsider where the real problems and hidden difficulties of the individual field of study may lie. Obviously, one cannot even attempt to read up on all published criticism of, say, Maori or Sumerian texts and their translations. In short, the present book may contain some misjudgments caused by lack of familiarity.

Occasionally, however, even an outsider gets a glimpse of the individual philological situation, not just by comparing the—frequently widely differing—translations but when one is actually able to do a limited countercheck. This is the case with the translation of the 500-year-old mythological text of the Quiché Mayas, the Popol Vuh.[8] Here, we have an early edition by Schultze Jena of the Maya text based on a single old manuscript accompanied by a German translation and a detailed word index with grammatical notes and discussion.[9] These tools allow one to critique, in some critical passages, the recent translation by Tedlock,[10] who frequently draws on *modern*

Maya beliefs, while Schultze Jena, in philological fashion, compared various *old* Mesoamerican texts.

In most cases, however, I had to rely on recent translations that I occasionally may have misunderstood or overinterpreted. I crave the indulgence of specialists if I have used outdated translations or have misunderstood specific points in their respective fields and ask for their corrections. This fact may jeopardize or even invalidate some of my incidental comparisons, but I am convinced that the major features of the method and theory discussed below will stand the test.

A follow-up to the present investigation should therefore be carried out in close cooperation between specialists in the various philologies and in the anthropology of various populations without written traditions. A special problem is presented by the texts that have come down to us only in oral form or have only recently been recorded by anthropologists, whose work is frequently affected through the filtering by one or even two levels of translators, not to speak of missionary and colonialist bias. I have always marveled at how early 19th-century anthropologists witnessed a certain ritual or the telling of a myth for one night and then proceeded to give a lucid account of it—obviously with the help of translators. But how much of it is correct, and how much is their interpretation or that of their assistants?[11]

These technical problems apart, much more work should be done in what I will here call the Gondwana mythologies of sub-Saharan Africa, New Guinea, and Australia, for the simple reason that they are least known and because many of them are highly endangered now and are in urgent need of proactive protection, documentation, and recording. This precious inheritance of humanity must not be lost due to the economic forces of globalization that drive traditional societies farther and farther into a few precariously remaining pockets. Unfortunately, the process is intensified by the concurrent missionary onslaught of the major world religions on small communities and tribal populations.

The same is true, obviously, of the endangered remnants of Laurasian mythologies, precariously surviving among the various smaller populations of Eurasia and the Americas, such as the Kalasha in northern Pakistan; the Toraja in Indonesia; the Koryak, Chukchi, and Gilyak in eastern Siberia; the Ainu in Japan; the Inuit; and many Amerindian tribes from Alaska to Tierra del Fuego. Just as there now exist some large research projects for the description and preservation of the many endangered languages of the globe, we urgently need a project for the preservation of endangered mythologies.

Concurrently, it is also very relevant to take a close look at the mythology of the major, increasingly dominant world religions through the lens of Laurasian and Gondwana mythology (§8). Their kinds of myth are surprisingly persistent and ever more relevant in many parts of the world: a good example is the close connection that exists between the Zoroastrian-inspired last book of the Christian Bible, Revelation, and American politics.

***

In the project of comparative mythology, cooperation is required, not just by philologists and linguists but also by colleagues in the sciences, such as archaeology and population genetics (§4). Recent advances in these fields, notably in population genetics, allow us to record parallel developments in these fields and to draw conclusions about the historical development of mythology. To enhance such scholarly cooperation we have held round tables at Harvard and elsewhere for nearly a decade,[12] ran a three-year pilot project on myth (Harvard Asia Center),[13] and founded the International Association for Comparative Mythology.[14] Our association held its first conference at Edinburgh in August 2007 and will continue to do so at other locations during the following years.

I warmly invite colleagues in the concerned fields to take part in the large-scale undertaking of historical comparative mythology, and of Laurasian and Gondwana mythologies in particular. A dedicated website has been created,[15] where announcements, contributions, and discussions by serious scholars will be posted. In addition, our small database of worldwide myths will gradually be expanded.[16] My friend Yuri Berëzkin at St. Petersburg has collected a huge amount of data on world mythology that is available at his website.[17] Another database, mostly devoted to folklore, is maintained by Prof. Junichi Oda at the Asia–Africa Institute of the Tokyo University of Foreign Studies.

***

I hope that this book will stimulate some interesting discussions, agreement, pointed criticism—or a reasoned refusal of the proposed theory. That is, after all, why theories are heuristically built and proposed—to be tested.[18] The current proposal likewise remains just that: a solidly heuristic model offering a solution that can be changed or disproved by adducing new facts and their interpretation.

In sum, I hope for the participation of colleagues, the educated public, and, perhaps, a philanthropist in expanding the current project so that we will be able to make significant progress.[19] The eventual aim should be to establish a larger project or institution for the kind of enduring, wide-ranging interdisciplinary research in the humanities and sciences envisaged in this book. It is required for comparative mythology, just as it is for the early history of language as now carried out at the Santa Fe Institute or population genetics as currently under way by the National Geographic Society.

Such major backing is required to follow up thoroughly on the current proposal of early human mythologies, be they Laurasian, Gondwana, or Pan-Gaean—in other words, to allow us to pursue the exiting story of early humans and their spirituality and its long history since the Stone Age (and record some of their currently very much endangered versions among smaller ethnicities worldwide). Only then will we be able to make lasting progress.

▓ ACKNOWLEDGMENTS AND THANKS

A few words of sincere thanks are due to all who have helped me in this book project. First of all, I thank all my friends in Japan whose invitations made writing this book possible. They have arranged invitations for three sabbaticals at Kyoto and Tokyo: my warm thanks go to my old friends Yasuke Ikari of Kyoto University and Peri Bhaskararao and Hideaki Nakatani of the Tokyo University for Foreign Studies.

Then, I thank my wife, Yayoi, who has discussed many aspects of Japanese mythology and this book with me over the years, vividly and incisively. Actually, we had originally planned an earlier, more Japan-centered version (*Japanese Mythology Seen from the Outside*), which will hopefully follow after the completion of the present work.

For administrative and financial support, my thanks are due to the Harvard Asia Center, especially its executive director, Ms. Deirdre Chetham. The center gave me several grants (a three-year project and conferences at Kyoto in 2005, Beijing in 2006, and Edinburgh in 2007) that assisted greatly in letting this project take shape.

Likewise, I thank my old friend Professor Toshifumi Gotō (Tōhoku University, Sendai) for organizing his Sendai conference on monotheism and polytheism in February 2005, where some of the issues dealt with in this book could be discussed with eminent Japanese colleagues. I warmly thank my friend Professor Hideaki Nakatani (Tokyo University of Foreign Studies) for organizing the first of his *sciences géneralisées* conferences at Tokyo in March 2005, including a mythology section. He also invited me for another sabbatical stay at his university, in fall 2008, to follow up on the global social implications of Laurasian mythology.

I am very grateful to Professors Toshitaka Hidaka and Toshiki Osada of the Research Institute for Humanity and Nature, Kyoto, for organizing our round table at Kyoto in June 2005 and likewise, to Professors Duan Qing and Liu Shusen of Peking University for organizing a conference on comparative mythology at Beijing in May 2006. I thank Professor Emily Lyle of Edinburgh University for organizing the first international conference of our International Association for Comparative Mythology—"The Deep History of Stories"—at Edinburgh in August 2007, Professors Wim van Binsbergen and Eric Venbrux for organizing our second conference at Ravenstein in the Netherlands in August 2008, and Professor Kikuko Hirafuji for organizing our third conference in Tokyo in 2009.

***

My warm thanks are due for discussions on Japanese materials with Professors Atsuhiko Yoshida, Kazuo Matsumura, and Kikuko Hirafuji, who have also provided me with rare books and papers on Japanese mythology. The late Shintō scholar Iwao Kinoshita kindly sent his revived German translation of the Kojiki—the manuscript had been burned in an air raid on Tokyo in 1944—to my Kathmandu home in 1976. Mr. Mikio Yotsuya of the Jinja Honchō at Tokyo helped to arrange for a visit to one of the main Shintō shrines of Japan, Izumo Taisha. There, Mr. Kazuhiko Senge, priest and researcher, graciously received us in 1999 and showed us this very ancient Shintō shrine, where his family has been officiating for more than 80 generations. The shrine and its priests were first impressively described by Lafcadio Hearn more than a century ago; it has since gained additional prominence due to extensive excavations that revealed an unusual archaic, very tall shrine, accessible only by a steep stairway. In the same way, I thank the people of Shingu on the Kii Peninsula who let me participate and included me in their *otō-matsuri* (fire ritual) in 1990. The priests of the Torigoe Jinja in Kanda, Tokyo, did so for an impressive *ōharae* expiation ritual, carried out from boats in the midst of Tokyo Bay, in June 2005.

I am also very grateful to my former student, Professor Huang Pochi (National Chengchi University, Taipei), and Professor Hsia Li-ming (of National Taitung University, Taiwan) for arranging a visit to the Aborigine Ami, Rukai, and Puyuma tribes at Taitung (Taiwan) in October 2005, which allowed me to gain insight into their history and current customs. Likewise, my warm thanks go to many persons in Nepal and India, too numerous to be named individually, and to the people of Nepal, Orissa, Kerala, and Kashmir. They have received me warmly and helped me greatly during my long stay and many visits to their respective homelands in my studies of their history and mythologies. They have permitted me to freely observe and record their rituals and festivals.

***

I also extend my thanks to my Harvard colleagues, especially Joseph Harris and Gregory Nagy, with whom I had many conversations on mythology. This also includes members of the Harvard Shop Club, as well as my friends in our weekly Faculty Club tabula: the late Willard Van Quine, Carl Smith, and Ihor Ševčenko, as well as Michael McCormick, Eduard Sekler, Prudence Steiner, Dante della Terza, and Lilian Handlin. The latter kindly read and critiqued my book summary. My thanks also go to my graduate students who actively participated in several classes on Eurasian comparative mythology while this book was hibernating. Over the years I could discuss with some of them many aspects of this project.

***

Since 2001, scientists from neighboring or related fields have discussed and helped me in the many areas that are not my own, to begin with the geneticists Professors Paolo Francalacci (of Sassari University in Sardinia), Richard Villems (Tartu University, Estonia), and especially Peter Underhill (Stanford). Peter has read the genetic section (§4.3) and saved me from some embarrassing mistakes. My friend Richard Meadow (Harvard), who has co-taught with me classes on oldest South Asia since 1990, has gradually introduced me to the intricacies of current archaeology. Another friend, the mythologist Yuri Berëzkin (Museum of Anthropology and Ethnography, St. Petersburg, Russia) has liberally provided me with his papers and valuable maps, some of which are included here with his permission, and another friend, Wim van Binsbergen (Leiden University), has discussed mythology with me since we met at the Leiden conference on mythology in December 2003.

I am also very grateful to those who have helped me with our mythology web-sites: my students David Blakeslee and Natasha Yanchevskaya. I also thank my son Leonard, who has assisted me in many computer-related questions and problems, and my friend, the Sanskritist and computer scientist John Robert Gardner, who has freely given me technical advice and provided for *Web drilling*.

Last, but certainly not least, I warmly thank my friend, the comparative historian Steve Farmer (Palo Alto). We have collaborated on several projects since 1999, such as on correlative thought, and have had many conversations about this book and his own one dealing with history and the brain, which will take off where I leave the question: with the emergence of early states. He has read and extensively critiqued an earlier draft of this book.

For the kind permission to use their materials liberally I warmly thank Yuri Berëzkin (Figures 2.1–2), Carol Cusack (Australian Association for the Study of Religion, for excerpts from Strehlow 1978), Jim Harrod (for various excerpts from his Originsnet.org website), Toomas Kivisild and Peter Underhill (Figures 4.12–14), Colin Masica (Figure 4.1), Mait Metspalu (maps from his 2006 essay), Peter Robinson (Editor, Bradshaw Foundation, for Figures 7.1–2), Merritt Ruhlen (Figures 4.6–7), Peter Underhill (Figures 4.7–8), and Dan Te Kanawa (http://www.maori.org.nz/korero/, for several excerpts from the "Stories of Old" pages).

***

In the end, my warm and sincere thanks are due to my family, who had to endure my virtual mental absence, especially over the past few years. To them this book is dedicated. Needless to say, in spite of all the help and constructive criticism that I have received from my friends over the years, all remaining flaws of this book are mine.

Newton (Mass.), Dies Solis Invicti MMVII
(Mahāvrata, Laukika Samvat 5083)

■ POSTSCRIPT

Since this foreword was written, more than three years ago, I have experienced the hospitality and friendship of other ancient populations. I thank the Atayal and Ami of Taiwan, the Hopi of Arizona, the shamans of Miyako (Okinawa, Japan), the Yi of Yunnan (China), and the Toda of the South Indian Nilgiri Mountains for their kindness in allowing me to watch their rituals and listen to their myths.

I also thank my colleagues in genetics, David Reich (Harvard) and Nick Patterson (MIT/Broad Institute), for their participation in our round tables and for frequent discussions. Some of these concern some recent intriguing developments that touch on topics covered in this book.

One of them is the discovery of a small strain of Neanderthal genetic material in anatomically modern humans after they had moved out of Africa. It must have occurred close to Neanderthal territory, somewhere in the Greater Near East. Another is the discovery of a tenuous new strain of early humans (c. 41,000 BP), the Denisovans of the Altai Mountains of southern Siberia. They too have left a few genetic traces in *part* of the post-exodus humans, curiously in inhabitants of distant Melanesia.

Both discoveries, however, do not contradict the theory presented in this book, though they may ultimately shed some light on the northern Eurasian bear cult. However, the text of this book has not been updated to reflect these discoveries or other developments after late 2007.

June 14, 2011

■ CONTENTS

■ The Origins of the World's Mythologies

1 Introduction

▨ §1.1. WHAT IS MYTH, AND HOW DO WE STUDY AND COMPARE IT?

The children's rhyme "Eeny meeny miny moe," known to most of us, was first recorded in England in the early 19th century.[1] However, it is found in many other European languages, where it is a simple rhyme that decides who is "in" or "out" in a game. As such, it is free of the racial undertones that it acquired in England and America.[2] In German, for example, we can find it as "Ene mene timpe tu,"[3] and it appears in many similar versions across the continent.[4]

However, it is much older than the 19th century. The first testimony comes from a c. 1,500-year-old Central Asian Buddhist manuscript that has the invocation mantra:[5] "Ene mene daṣphe daṇḍadaṣphe," which is closer to the German version. The largely meaningless line must have originated in India a few centuries earlier and arrived in eastern Central Asia (Xinjiang) along with Buddhism.[6] However, it is not recorded earlier,[7] nor does it appear in later Indian texts, except for some modern jingles that might as well be due to recent British influence on Indian education.[8] The wide distribution of the rhyme opens up a large vista,[9] in time and space, from England to Central Asia and northern India.

We are led to ask many questions: was India the sole origin of the jingle, or did it arise independently in Western Europe? Did it spread from India to Europe, like so many Indian fairy tales and fables, just as it spread to Central Asia through the vehicle of Buddhism? Why is there a change in meaning from a religious verse to a mere children's jingle?[10] Or is the actual rhyme much older than its application in Buddhism?[11] Why are there so many variations of the rhyme after the first two words?[12] The surprising fact, certainly, is the wide spread of the rhyme, which can be explained by *diffusion* from a center in northern India or by *independent* origination, that is, the faculty of small children to (re-)create simple rhymes, songs, and games.

It is precisely these kinds of questions that are the central theme of the present book: can the many worldwide similarities, overlaps, congruences, and identities of myths be explained by *diffusion* from an unknown center? Or is this due to the innate quality of the human mind to create similar myths, based on Jungian *archetypes*, anywhere and anytime? Or do these similarities *go far back into prehistory*, even back to the Stone Age? May they ultimately come from an original stock of myths of the geneticists' "African Eve"?[13] In this book we will explore, carefully and step by step, the latter possibility.

***

Even a casual reader is struck by the fact that many myths of origin are very similar to each other, even when they are found in distant parts of the globe and often separated from each other by long periods of time. One is struck by the constant reoccurrence of very similar themes in the religious and spiritual lore of various populations around the world. In the traditional Polynesian myths of origin we hear of a beginning of the world that is very much like that of the medieval Mayas and Icelanders, the ancient Romans and Greeks, Bronze Age Indians, Mesopotamians, Egyptians, and Chinese. To quote just three cases (details in §3):

> When on high the heaven had not been named,
> firm ground below had not been called by name,
> naught but primordial Apsu, their begetter,
> (and) Mummu-Tiamat, she who bore them all,
> their waters commingling as a single body; ...
> Then it was that the gods were formed.
> (Enuma Elish, Mesopotamia, early second millennium BCE)[14]

> There was neither "being" [sat] nor "non-being" [asat][15] then, nor intermediate space, nor heaven beyond it. What turned around? Where? In whose protection? Was there water?—Only a deep abyss.[16] ... Darkness was hidden by darkness, in the beginning. A featureless salty ocean was all this (universe). A germ, covered by emptiness, was born through the power of heat as the One. (Ṛgveda 10.129, India, c. 1000 BCE)[17]

> Before there was any light there was only darkness, all was night. Before there was even darkness there was nothing. ... It is said in the *karakia*, at the beginning of time there stood the *Kore*, the Nothingness. Then was *Te Po*, the Night, which was immensely long and immensely dark. ... The first light that existed was no more than the glowing of a worm, and when sun and moon were made there were no eyes, there was none to see them, not even *kaitiaki*. The beginning was made from the nothing. (New Zealand, Maori, contemporary)[18]

The three myths selected here have much in common: accounts of the origin of the universe and the world, the idea of primordial chaos, darkness and great waters, and the initial absence of heaven and earth (and also, the power of the spoken word in naming parts of the universe). These accounts, myths, are understood in this book as highly regarded, nonsecular tales dealing with questions of the origin, nature, and ultimate destiny of the world and its human beings, including that of their societies, rituals, and festivals.

How could people from Iceland to Polynesia and Mexico agree on so many points, though they were not in direct contact, separated as they were from each other by tens of thousands of miles and by some 5,000 years in time? An answer to these questions will be attempted in this book.

The standard answers given during the 20th century were either that of a worldwide *diffusion* from an ancient cultural center such as Egypt or that of *universal innate* characteristics of the human psyche, such as the archetypes that create similar myths anytime and everywhere. As we will observe, both proposals are not nearly correct or comprehensive enough to explain such widespread concurrences. It is difficult to imagine an early, Bronze Age spread of many important myths across vast continents and wide oceans. It has often been assumed but not yet proved that archetypes employed in the myths mentioned here are universally human and are indeed found all across the globe. These two points will be discussed in some detail (§1.4–5).

However, both approaches will find their correct place with *certain* instances in the reconstruction of the earlier mythologies pursued here. Cases in point include the diffusion seen in myth exchanges (§2.5.3–4) between some societies of the periods after the exodus from Africa at c. 65,000 years ago, such as those of the Greater Near East or Mesoamerica, or the eventual detection of certain universal mental characteristics and common myths in pre-exodus times, in the reconstructed Pan-Gaean mythology (§6).

***

Instead of the two standard approaches of diffusion and universals of the human mind, a *new approach* is proposed in this book that recognizes the congruities in myths and looks into their individual origins.[19] It will be done by tracing them back, step by step, ultimately to the stories told by early *Homo sapiens sapiens* or, to use the now popular term, to the period of the *African Eve* who lived some 130,000 years ago.

The approach proposed here thus looks for a *common* origin but certainly not for one found in some monotheistic religions such as in the Adam and Eve myth of the Bible. Instead, it aims at establishing a cladistic (family) tree of a host of mythological tales—just as botanists, zoologists, paleontologists, geneticists, linguists, and philologists habitually construct from their data. As it looks for *origins*, this approach is unabashedly "romantic"—in the sense of the early 19th century, when scholars were fascinated by looking for (common) origins of languages and "peoples."[20] But the proposed approach also aims to be strictly scientific: it proposes a hypothesis and puts it through several rigorous tests, which involve the theory as a whole as well as its details. The approach of this book is, after all, heuristic. If extensive counterchecking (§2.6, §§5–6) should turn up serious objections to the hypothesis, it will have to be given up, like any other scientific theory. I have tried to disprove it over the past 15 years or so. Obviously, no serious objections, also by others, have surfaced so far; otherwise the present book would not have been written.

***

The quest for the origins of individuals and their families,[21] for the early stages of a certain population, as well as for the (common) origin of all humans, is something that is near universal.[22] Ultimate answers are given in the many myths across the globe that deal with the eternal question of humankind: "who am I, where do I come from, why am I here, and where do I go?" They are given in tales clearly perceived by the various populations that tell them as nonsecular, not intended as popular stories or meant for the amusement of children. Myths are also different from hero or adventure stories, from "how so" tales that explain various small features of our surroundings, and from fairy tales (*märchen*), though the latter may retain "sunken" mythological materials.[23]

The three creation myths that were briefly quoted above originate from the ancient Near East, Asia, and Polynesia. They try to answer the perpetual questions about origins. Modern myths (and religions) continue trying to do the same, each in its own way, for example, in currently popular science fiction stories. Back then in Mesopotamia, just as in the present time, the prominence in many religions and the sciences of these questions and answers keenly points to the importance we attach to *ultimate origins*.

Similarities such as those quoted from Eurasia and Polynesia also appear in many myths other than those of primordial creation. These include tales about the subsequent four generations (or "ages") of deities, of an age of monsters and semidivine heroes, of the emergence of humans, even of the origins of certain (noble) lineages, and of many aspects of local cultures. They frequently conclude with a violent end to our present world, sometimes with the hope for a new world emerging from disaster. Ultimately the universe is seen, in the myths of Eurasia and beyond, as a living body, in analogy to the human one:[24] it is born from primordial incest, grows, develops, comes of age, and has to undergo final breakdown and death.

Importantly, any systematic comparison of myths as carried out here soon leads to the recognition of a shared common *narrational* scheme. It encompasses many myths ranging from the ultimate origins to the very end of the world. Mythologies such as the Mesopotamian, Vedic Indian, Chinese, Polynesian, and Maya ones share more than just similar contents (individual myths with the same or with very similar motifs). They also are arranged in the same or in very similar fashion. In other words, they share a common *story line*. Therefore, the comparisons carried out in this book involve whole systems or *collections* of myths belonging to individual populations; and comparisons are not merely between single myths, as has commonly been done so far.

The common story line thus recovered can be found in most of the mythologies of Eurasia, North Africa, Polynesia, and the Americas. Close comparison allows us to reconstruct a coherent early mythology that will be called "Laurasian,"[25] after the well-established geological term derived from *Laurentia* in Canada, and of Greater *Asia* and the northern parts of the original Pan-Gaean supercontinent[26]—admittedly of much earlier times than the emergence of humans. This book will therefore deal with the establishment of the Laurasian story line and its major myths and also with their subsequent geographical and historical spread and development over time.

Even though this undertaking is, prima facie, a large-scale project that would necessitate the participation and assistance of many specialists of various individual cultures, the undertaking cannot end even here. Initial exploration, carried out over the past few years, indicates that Laurasian mythology is not the only type in existence and that it is not isolated among the other existing types.

***

The mythologies of the aboriginal Australians and Papuas as well as those of most of sub-Saharan Africa represent distinct types that are very different from the Laurasian one. I will call them *Gondwana* mythologies—again, using a geological term that indicates the southern parts of the original supercontinent that existed long before the emergence of humans.[27]

It is significant that certain motifs are missing in the "tropical" Gondwana belt. Examples include the lack of creation myths that tell of the origin as well as the end of the world, as well as the preference for improvised magical spells that disregard the power of "true," well-formulated, secretly transmitted magical poetry, so typical of much of Laurasia. Instead, Gondwana mythologies generally are confined to the description of the emergence of humans and their culture in a preexisting world. The geographical isolation of some Gondwana mythologies helps to securely establish and date these various types, especially those of Australia and the Andaman and Tasmanian islands, as well as highland New Guinea.

***

Still, the implications of the current project do not come to an end here. Initial exploration indicates that certain individual motifs and myths occur across all four major types of mythology, the sub-Saharan African, Laurasian, Papuan, and Australian ones. What is significant about these truly universal motifs is not just their worldwide spread; rather, it is the fact that these "universals" are *isolated* in Laurasian myth. They often go against its grain or are "superfluous" variants of topics comprehensively and systematically treated elsewhere in Laurasian mythology. Mostly, they are not part of the "official" local story line but occur as isolated myths, generally in the form of folktales or *märchen*.

What we thus observe, worldwide, are the fragmentary remnants of a tradition that precedes the major types of mythology enumerated above. Laurasian mythology is, in fact, merely an offshoot, a reformulation of the older Gondwana type underlying the sub-Saharan African and Papuan/Australian mythologies. Based on these types, a still earlier stage, Pan-Gaean mythology, can be reconstructed, albeit in rather sketchy outline that is entirely heuristic. Pan-Gaean myths are those of the "African Eve" and her contemporaries. They deal with the creation of humans by a distant, otiose god of the sky, with the hubris and misdeeds of early humans, and with the emergence of death that looms large in all human (and ape) experience. I hasten to add that this reconstruction does not imply the *ur*-monotheism of W. Schmidt.

***

In short, Laurasian mythology is our *first novel*, and the Pan-Gaean motifs are the oldest tales of humankind. At any rate, they are the oldest that can actually be discovered, barring new insights about Neanderthal speech and ritual. And this is their fascination. The Laurasian and Gondwana projects will take us back beyond all written and oral literatures of the past 5,000 years and also beyond the cultural data encapsulated in the vocabulary of recorded languages and that of their reconstructed predecessors. It also surpasses the scattered (and frequently "unreadable") traces of human cultures discovered by archaeology (§4.4, §7). It will enable us to take a glimpse at the human condition as experienced by our distant ancestors, before and after they moved out of Africa, some 65,000 years ago.

▦ §1.2. DEFINITION OF MYTH AND ITS STUDY IN THE PAST

Before delving further into the subject, a more explicit definition of the topic at hand is required. The common perception of "myth" is that of an unlikely account or an untrue story, secular or otherwise.[28] Expressions such as "climate change is a myth" or "the myth of a classless society in America,"[29] that of "social security," of "male superiority," of the "Aryans," of "a future, just society," of "a united world," of "the tooth fairy," of "supermundane forces," or of "(the existence of) God,"[30] are frequently met with. Myth is "mere myth."

Different from such common perceptions, myths are not inherently unscientific, fantastic, and hence untrue "fairy tales" about aspects of human life and nature, nor are they intentionally invented, misleading, and supposedly untrue stories about topics otherwise important to us. Rather, myths deal with questions of the origin, the nature, and the ultimate destiny of the world and its human beings.

Myths are part of the larger realm of religious thought that is characterized by symbolism. This point has been stressed repeatedly in past decades.[31] Eliade justifiably goes so far as to state that the human being is "a homo symbolicus, and all of his activities comprise symbolism, therefore all religious acts necessarily have a symbolic character."[32] The same applies, per force, to *homo symbolicus's* religious and mythological narratives. In addition, language itself is a system of mutually agreed signs and symbols (as first stressed more than a century ago by de Saussure)[33] that indicates a reality beyond the mere sounds produced. Surpassing the use of language in commonplace daily interactions, myths and whole mythologies are *systems of symbols*. Anatomically modern humans, as *Homo narrans* or *Homo fabulans*, a narrating and fabulating being, have created them by pointing to supernatural facts and beings and to primordial times that are no longer directly accessible to humans—manifestations such as Australian Dreamtime excepted.

A comprehensive definition, largely following a recent one by W. van Binsbergen,[34] would define myth as a narrative

- that is told or recited at certain special occasions
- that is standardized (to some extent)
- that is collectively owned and managed (often by specialists)
- that is considered by its owners to be of great and enduring significance[35]
- that (whether or not these owners are consciously aware of this point) contains and brings out such images of the world (a cosmology), of past and present society (a history and sociology), and of the human condition (an anthropology) as are eminently constitutive of the life society in which that narrative circulates, or at least where it circulated originally
- that, if this constitutive aspect is consciously realized by the owners, may be invoked (etiologically) to explain and justify present-day conditions
- and that is therefore a powerful device to create collectively underpinned meaning and collectively recognized truth (regardless of whether such truth would be recognized outside the community whose myth it is)

Individual myths are structured, like all narratives,[36] in certain distinctive ways, for example, the Russian folktales studied by V. Propp,[37] the Indian Rāmāyaṇa, and the hero tales analyzed by Lord Raglan.[38] Myths are built on individual *motifs*, such as that of the origin of fire, of death, or of a particular animal. A large-scale collection of motifs has been undertaken by Stith Thompson in his 1932–36 *Motif Index*.[39] However, wide ranging as it is, this collection remains heavily tilted toward Europe, the Near East, Asia, and the Americas. Sub-Saharan Africa, New Guinea, and Australia, not to speak of isolated but important locations such as the Andaman Islands, are much less represented. When using Thompson's data, this limitation has to be considered and must be counterbalanced, as will be done here, by a wide-ranging overview of these largely neglected areas of the globe (§5).

A related term, coined by Lévi-Strauss, is that of *mytheme*. It refers to the several individual smaller items and units that make up a myth. To take up a well-known example, the myth of the creation of humans in the Bible includes the mythemes of human origin from clay, the insertion of breath or spirit, the creation of the first woman from the man's rib, the initial lack of sexual shame, their primordial mistake or sin, and so on.

***

Myths have been studied for a long time, in fact since antiquity, and comparatively so for some 200 years. However, such comparisons have not yet yielded a cogent system of mutual relationships, the task prominently undertaken in this book.[40] There is a long list of interpretations of myths. They range from G. Vico's allegorical and euhemeristic views to Max Müller's (and now Barber and Barber's) disguised nature myths and astral mythology, from ritual-based myths to Malinowski's social charter, from Freud's theories of repression to Jung's universal psychic archetypes, from myth as disguised history to Lévi-Strauss's binary structural analysis.[41] A brief overview and discussion of previous interpretations of myth is given at the end of this chapter (§1.5). However, as this book is built on the principles of the comparative (and historical) method, a discussion of it is in order first.

■ §1.3. COMPARATIVE MYTHOLOGY

Similarities, whether found in myths or in other human creations, such as the children's jingles mentioned above, can be explained by a restricted number of possible scenarios: common origin, borrowing and diffusion, convergence, or derivation from the shared structural characteristics of the human mind. This would also include incidental combinations of some of these scenarios, as will be argued in some sections of this book (for a detailed discussion, see §2).

However, interpretations and comparisons of myths have usually been restricted to one myth (or variants of it). If similarities between particular myths found in various cultures were noticed, they were explained in a limited number of ways, the two most current and popular ones being that of diffusion from a known or assumed center and that of archetypes as a feature of the psychic inheritance of *Homo sapiens sap.* Both approaches are difficult to sustain when studied comprehensively.

§1.3.1. Diffusion

Diffusion entails that the similarities between widely distributed myths are due to a gradual dispersion of individual motifs from a certain geographical center. In particular, one thinks of an ancient civilization such as that of Egypt or Mesopotamia, from where it would have spread around the globe by gradual dispersal.[42] Historically well-attested cases of dispersal are those of Judeo-Christian-Islamic and Buddhist mythologies that have swept large parts of the globe, well before the age of European "discovery" and worldwide expansion that, beginning around 1500 CE, disrupted or destroyed many local communities and their mythologies.

A more recent example is the phenomenally quick diffusion of the Ghost Dance and its mythology, which spread among the Native Americans of the western United States across tribal and linguistic boundaries at the turn of the 20th century.[43] It was a religiopolitical reaction against the American conquest of Native American lands. Consequently, the ritual was forbidden by the government for decades. A still later, well-attested case is that of the New Guinea cargo cult,[44] which originated during World War II when Americans landed their planes on small airstrips in the hinterland of New Guinea and were taken as messengers and cargo deliverers of the gods. This new religion and mythology have survived the postwar and postcolonial period; in fact, some if its leaders are in government now.

In most other cases, however, we cannot closely follow the diffusion of individual myths or myth complexes. For example, classical "Siberian" shamanism, with its myth of the shaman's death, the recomposition of the body, and the shaman's ascent to the heavens, is spread over a wide area, from northern Siberia to Nepal and Borneo and from Lapland all the way to the tip of South America.[45] But we do not know how it spread and when or whether it really was the predecessor of some other current mythologies and religions in Eurasia. The same holds true for individual myths such as the Orpheus myth that is found in several versions in Greece, Japan, India, and North America.[46]

Such diffusionary spread has been studied by Stith Thompson and his school. Thompson holds that motifs and "tale-types" with the same motifs arranged in the same order have spread from a common center. It is therefore necessary to collect all variants of a tale and to analyze individual traits. Their frequency and distribution then allow us to trace the motif's history and geographical spread. Similarly, Bierhorst, in his work on North American Amerindian myths,[47] traces some North American myths back to Siberia and Northern Europe, as those of Stone Age hunters and gatherers who crossed the then dry Beringia land bridge that existing until c. 11 kya.[48] More recently, Yuri Berezkin has collected an enormous amount of such data from the Americas, from Siberia, and by now also from the rest of the world.[49] He has arranged them according to individual motifs and has presented them in a large number of maps.[50] Close study indicates some obvious spread of single motifs, for example, from various parts of North and Central Asia to the Americas.[51]

The classical form of the diffusion theory, however, goes back to the German anthropologist and Africa specialist L. Frobenius (1873–1938).[52] He explained the worldwide similarities in myth via diffusion that spread from the great ancient civilizations, wave after wave,[53] across the wide areas of still more archaic, "archemorph" hunter and gatherer cultures. Diffusion has been aptly described by Kroeber as "the direct origin of a cultural trait are other cultural traits."[54] Differently from the diffusionists, however, some scholars rather assume that certain (unnoticed) metamorphoses have taken place in tropical and subtropical horticulture societies.[55]

A recent representative of the diffusionist view was Frobenius's student H. Baumann (1902–72),[56] who perceived a "world myth"[57] that existed around 3000 BCE. Its roots are in the village communities that preceded advanced "archaic high cultures" between the Nile and the Indus and whose influence spread from there up to Iceland, China, and Peru.[58] It is characterized by the parallelism of heaven/earth, the correlation of microcosm/macrocosm, "bisexual" (androgynous) myths, megaliths, and so on.[59]

Baumann's assumed "world myth" is

> not a contiguous myth continuum (*Mythenzusammenhang*) that has moved and dif-
> fused with one single ethnic group at a certain time, but as a complex that has spread
> in thousands of years of separate migrations, with the effect of superimposition by
> individual and border line acculturation.... It will have spread, in many waves, from a
> few centers between Nubia–Libya and China.[60]

Baumann traces several of these myths and connected rituals across the globe, including those of the sun deity, the heavenly twins, the world egg, the primor-dial giant, and so on (see Figures 1.1–1.2). He does not see a problem in deriving Chinese and Mesoamerican agriculture and mythology from the "archaic" Middle Eastern center of c. 3000 BCE.[61]

Diffusion,[62] thus, envisages that the similarities found in widely distributed myths are due to a *gradual* dispersal from a known or assumed center.[63] In that sense, it has not only a "horizontal" (geographical), and often synchronic, but also a "vertical" (historical) axis. One cannot overlook the formidable obstacles that speak against the diffusion of an entire myth complex across large sectors of the globe, especially across the Pacific or Atlantic ocean, while a polar, Ice Age route is obviously excluded for (sub)tropical mythologies.[64] Though mari-time contacts have been alleged, usually supported by weak evidence,[65] it is dif-ficult to conceive of sustained transoceanic connections and of a society borrowing a large set of myths or an entire mythology based on such incidental contacts.

We actually have occasional evidence of contact, such as a tale of a Japanese shipwreck in 13th-century Hawai'i preserved in traditional accounts or sightings of Japanese ships on the west coast of North America around 1700.[66] However, the impact on local mythology is negligible. Some incidental, accidental pre-Columbian trans-Atlantic or trans-Pacific traffic may have occurred, but it was not significant enough to affect local mythologies in any serious way.[67] Further, such transfer depends on the prevailing ocean currents and winds, which often are not in favor but opposed to assumed transfers, say, for regular maritime con-nections between Jōmon-time Japan and Ecuador, as pottery suggests to some

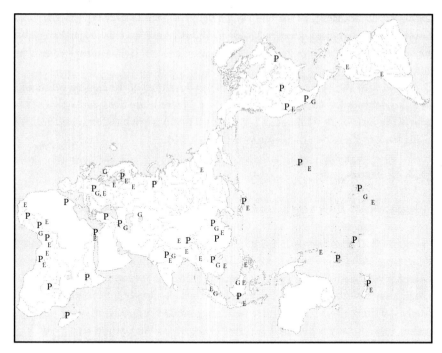

Figure 1.1. A diffusion model of the spread of mythological features: data for World parents (P), primordial giant (G), and primordial egg (E), after Baumann 1986.

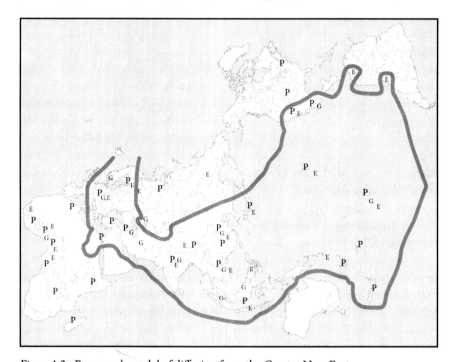

Figure 1.2. Baumann's model of diffusion from the Greater Near East.

scholars.[68] In addition, as we will see later (§4.3), the lack of typical East and Southeast Asian human genes in Meso- and South America clearly speaks against sustained movement of people and diffusion of cultural traits through extensive contacts.

Just as with the competing concept of universalities of the human mind and its subconscious forms, to be discussed next, I leave aside the question of diffusion in the introductory chapters (§§1–2) as I first have to build my case. We will come back to these two concepts later (§5.1.4, §6).

§1.3.2. Archetypes

Nowadays many if not most scholars follow the psychological explanation of C. G. Jung and assume that similarities found in myths the world over are due to common, universal features of the human mind that forever produce the same images or "archetypes" anywhere in the world. Actually, this approach was pioneered several decades earlier by A. Bastian.[69] He used the term *Elementargedanke* (basic, fundamental thought),[70] which he saw independently appearing across vast reaches of the globe, in areas where such ideas could not have spread through diffusion. Instead, they were based on "the homogeneousness of human psyche."[71]

This concept is similar to what C. G. Jung and his followers such as Joseph Campbell maintain: certain mythemes or complex motifs, the archetypes, are universally human.[72] In Jung's version of Freud's "repressed or forgotten contents,"[73] such content of the unconscious mind "is not individual but universal [collective]," with "contents and modes that are more or less the same everywhere and in all individuals.... The contents of the collective unconscious [are the] archetypes."[74] Archetypes "are those psychic contents which have *not yet been submitted to conscious elaboration.*"[75] Importantly, this would disqualify them as *directly* dealing with myth. Myth is therefore seen as the *secondary elaboration* of archetypes. Common archetypes include the (Great) Mother, the Father, the Hero, the Eternal/Miraculous Child, the Youthful Maiden, the Seductress, the Wise Woman, the Old Man, the Crone, and the Shadow. Campbell has devoted a large work to one of them, the "monomyth" of the typical American hero, the "lone rider who dispels evil."[76]

Since archetypes are generally human, they can appear everywhere and anytime in dreams, visions, and myths. This occurs even in areas where such archetypes have not been prominent for a long time. One example would be the lack of an overt image of the mother deity (the Goddess)[77] in some northern and northwestern European societies. However, this analysis conveniently overlooks both the pre-Christian and early Christian, pre-Protestant myth of Maria, mother of Christ, her ubiquitous images, and her fervent worship prominent in Christian Europe for some 1,500 years before the Reformation took hold. She appears, to modern thought quite contradictorily, as mother, immaculate virgin, heavenly bride, and ruler of the world—all under the guise of a very prominent Christian saint. The power of the image has recently been reinforced by alleged miraculous visions and by some actions of the Catholic Church; it even affects non-Christians, such as Hindus who now make pilgrimages to Mary of Lourdes or worship her in India.[78]

More importantly, if the Jungian explanation by archetypes were correct, we would expect that individual archetypes would indeed turn up in *all* parts of the globe. This, however, is debatable: not all of the supposed archetypes do indeed turn up worldwide. While we may grant that the human psyche has a universal biological substrate in the cortex that *may* produce similar images worldwide,[79] it is, however, unclear how far this actually underlies local manifestations in myth, art, ritual, or certain stereotypes of behavior and how far such similarities can be explained by a monolateral metatheory such as that of Jung.[80] At any rate, archetypes do not result directly in elaborate structured tales and certainly not in long sequences of such tales, the story line that is discussed in this book.

Archetypes are supposed to be balanced in an individual's mind, as their contradictory forces can overwhelm people. When elaborated into "eternal images," the archetypes "are meant to attract, to convince, to fascinate and to over-power...[and their] images have become embedded in a comprehensive system of thought that ascribes an order to the world."[81] Laurasian mythology would then be one such elaboration. It makes use of a powerful structuring device (§2.4) that is markedly different from those of other (Gondwana) mythologies.

However, archetypes are often employed by some scholars as a comfortable escape route. They refer to them each time a particular motif is encountered in two very distant locations. We all certainly are members of the *Homo sapiens sapiens* species, and one might therefore expect congruities, but our individual backgrounds and histories vary a great deal. Thus, the all-powerful mother figure is not (or not yet again) important in Protestant Europe and much of largely Protestant North America, while the father figure is absent or much less important in the few truly matriarchal societies, such as those of the Minangkabau in Sumatra or the Khasi in the Assam hills of northeastern India. Laurasian mythology usually has a rather patriarchal bent (which opens the question as to whether we have, as, for example, in most of Australian myth, just the male version).[82]

One example of taking an opportune way out of the dilemma posed by archetypes and diffusion is seen in the work of the very popular J. Campbell. He conveniently employs both concepts whenever they are expedient. Most of the time he prefers Jung's archetypes,[83] but occasionally, when he comes across two very similar myths or customs in far-flung locations, he assumes some kind of diffusion, even if the idea spans huge expanses of space and time.[84] For example, he compares the custom of palanquin bearers of divine chieftains that is found in Spanish-period Florida, medieval Rome, and recent Polynesia.[85] This kind of facile toolbox approach randomly selects from various "methods" to "explain" the stubborn facts.[86] It may still be fashionable at present, but it sheds at best just some stray, arbitrary, postmodern light on complex issues. Such critique has its uses, however merely heuristic ones: it aids in counterchecking the so-called facts, assessing their reliability, exposing possible motives of their raconteurs and collectors, and finally taking into account our own "personal *māyā*"—our own educational background and our unconscious assumptions. Beyond that, we have to record counterchecked, verifiable facts and then weigh the accumulated evidence, in other words, try to be *objective* in an almost positivist fashion.

In contrast to Jung's and Campbell's approaches, it is *not* the aim of this book to explain the psychic background or ultimate neurological basis of individual myths but, rather, to establish how ancient and contemporary myths are ordered and interpreted in Eurasia and beyond. (Nevertheless, the question of the meaning of important Laurasian myths will be taken up in §8 and that of universal, Pan-Gaean myths in §6.)

***

Related to the Jungian approach is Campbell's use of the respective environment that would have motivated certain human responses in their myths. Speaking of the Pygmies of the Central African rain forest and of the San (Bushmen) of the South African semidesert, he maintains,

> These...are two contrary orders of life, determinant of the life styles, mythologies and rites of the most primitive men known: one, of the wide-spreading animal plains [of the Khoi-San], the other of the sheltering forest [of the Pygmies]. They were not arrived by reason, but are grounded in fundamental experiences and requirements touching very deep levels of the psyche. In contrast, such questioning as "who made the world"? "why"? "how"? and "what happened to make life so difficult"? belongs to a plane of consciousness much closer to the surface of things than those deeps from which the controlling images of these two orders of life arose, not reasoned but compelled.[87]

This is inspiring prose, but it is intriguing why the distinction between the "reasoned" classical, ancient Near Eastern (and Laurasian) mythologies and the "primitive" one of the Pygmies would put them at a "lower," deeper level of consciousness: it assumes that certain ethnic groups of modern *Homo sapiens sap.* lived or still are living at differing levels of consciousness! But all anatomically modern humans can look back to some 130,000 years of psychic and religious development. Significantly, the systems of mythology as found with the Pygmies (§§5.3.5) are also encountered elsewhere with people who are not interested in (or are socially forbidden to tell about) the ultimate origins of the universe. Curiously, this includes the hunter-gatherer Khoi-San (Bushmen) of Campbell's own examples or even the mythology of the food-producing Maori with regard to their primordial deity Io.[88] In sum, it is not differing levels of consciousness but the physical *and* social environment as well as the position and importance of local spiritual leaders (shamans, priests, *kahuna*, etc.) that condition local systems of mythologies.

It is indeed true that there are many mythologies that do not deal with ultimate origins, as will be seen immediately, and that several of them are found in (sub)tropical areas of the world. However, one cannot simply ascribe the lack of creation or origin myths to the environment: people living in tropical Africa as well as people living in open steppe and desert lands, such as the San (Bushmen) of southern Africa and the Aboriginals of Australia, equally lack them. Conversely, peoples with Laurasian mythology that is characterized by myths of the origin of the world live in all climes: in polar ice deserts, temperate forest belts, steppe and desert zones, and tropical and rain forest areas. But they still retain versions of the original origin and creation myths (§3).

In view of this, it is methodologically interesting to note that Campbell,[89] just like Doniger,[90] had all the necessary facts before him to arrive at another explanation than that of archetypes. But Campbell and Doniger failed to perceive the answer, as they were bound by mental pathways established a hundred years earlier. These pathway dependencies reinforced the strength of their ultimate *belief* in psychological explanations (whether Jungian with the first or Freudian with the latter).[91] The possibility of common origin was not envisaged or even denied out of hand.[92]

In sum, both currently fashionable explanations cannot explain the extraordinary amount of global similarities and congruities of myth (§3), whether such explanations suppose diffusion (Frobenius, Baumann, S. Thompson), psychic archetypes (Jung, Campbell), or bare-bones, binary structures of mental arrangements (Lévi-Strauss).[93] Such congruities are found in large areas of the world, but they are neither *evenly distributed* nor *found* on all continents.

▓ §1.4. LAURASIAN MYTHOLOGY: ESTABLISHING THE COMMON ORIGIN OF THE MYTHOLOGIES OF EURASIA AND THE AMERICAS

Psychic universals and diffusion fail to address the central problem dealt with in the present book: the mutual comparability of large indigenous collections of myths—in written or oral texts—in other words, the comparability of *whole systems* of myths. As far as I see, such comparison has not been carried out so far. However, it will be observed below not only that complete mythologies, such as the Greek, Mesopotamian, Egyptian, Japanese, and Maya ones, have similar contents—individual myths with similar motifs/archetypes—but that these are also arranged in closely similar or even identical fashion: many myths are arranged in a *common story line.*

In establishing this scheme, I will maintain a currently still quite unfashionable stance.[94] I will try to show that a large number of present and past mythologies (though by no means all) go back to a *single* source, from which they have branched off in various directions and have developed in their own way through certain innovations. Still, the descendant mythologies maintain enough similarities to allow the discovery, enumeration, and description of common, original features. They will become increasingly visible as we proceed with this study.

The proposed approach, thus, does not depend on the gradual *diffusion* of certain myths from population to population all over the world, which started out from a Bronze Age Near Eastern or a (sub)tropical center, as Frobenius and Baumann have proposed. My approach also does not rely on the assumption of general human archetypes, creating spontaneously the same types of myths everywhere and at any time (Jung, Campbell). Nor does it rely on an unstructured, omnicomparativist style of study that randomly selects isolated data from various populations across the globe, as was done by the early comparativists a century ago to fit their monolateral, universalizing, and sometimes indeed monomaniacal theories (Frazer, Max Müller, etc.).[95]

***

Instead, the present approach is based on the mutual comparison of a sufficiently large number of mythologies of Eurasia, Polynesia, and Native America *over time*. In other words, the approach is both comparative and historical:[96] it involves the axes of time and space; it works by collecting individual myths and analyzing their underlying structure, importantly including that of their arrangement in a myth collection.

Indeed, the main problem of the earlier types of explanations proposed so far is that they fail to address what I regard as the central but *unnoticed* problem briefly delineated earlier:[97] the comparability of *whole systems of myths*. To use a linguistic simile, this entails something alike to the comparison of complete grammars of various languages, not just of particular words, forms, declensions, conjugations, or syntactical features. We are not merely comparing small mythological items such as mythemes; nor do we study just some archetypes such as the attempted return of a beloved person from the world of the dead (Orpheus and Eurydike); we also do not compare, even worldwide, single myths such as that of the Great Flood. Instead, we will investigate something held in common by all the mythologies studied: a structure or framework, indeed an underlying *system* that is shared by most Eurasian and American mythologies. This is an important characteristic that has not been observed so far.

The structure common to these mythologies is a well-arranged and well-constructed narrative framework, a *story line* extending from the original creation of the world to its destruction. It underlies the original form of many mythologies of Asia, the Americas, and Europe. It can be recovered, I believe, through collection of the congruities of many or most of these mythologies, followed by an evaluation of their individual adherence to the original story line. It will then be seen that most mythologies of the three continents, including Polynesia, share the same mythological structure.

As mentioned earlier, I will call this original form *Laurasian*.[98] This originally geological and paleontological term is derived from *Eurasia* and *Laurentia*, the ancient Cambrian landmass of northeastern Canada, which I use here to represent all of the Americas (see Figures 1.3–1.4).[99] Alternatively, one could simply call Laurasian mythology the "northern" (or septentrional/boreal) one,[100] as I may indeed do occasionally. However, the term is too vague.[101]

The new comparative and historical approach as well as the steps undertaken to establish it are similar to the well-tested methods of historical linguistics.[102] As in linguistics, the present approach, however, is first and foremost descriptive and *comparative*: it aims at establishing the story line and the structure of the Laurasian mythologies, in contrast to that of the Gondwana.

Second, it is *historical* in ascertaining the "family tree" (stemma, cladistic arrangement) of human myths. It *must* be historical, as humans and their myths have evolved over many tens of thousands of years, from Paleolithic to modern times. In pursuing these goals, the method is value- and theory-free and does not set out to achieve a certain goal. Once a family relationship (such as the Laurasian

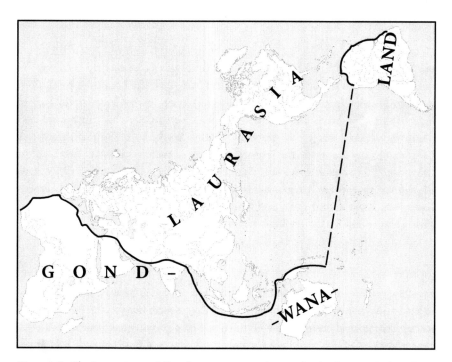

Figure 1.3. The Laurasian and Gondwana supercontinents that broke up c. 250–150 million years ago.

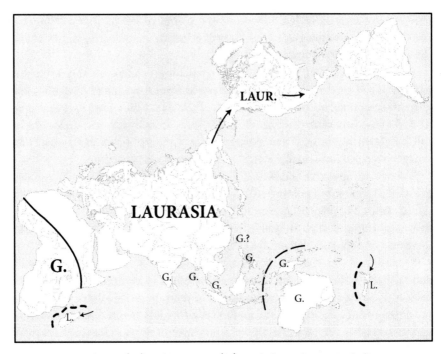

Figure 1.4. Gondwana (G.) and Laurasian (L.) mythological areas, including remnant Gondwana areas in Asia.

one) has been ascertained, however, these findings can be used to flesh out the details of the inherent connections and to distinguish the Laurasian mythological family from non-Laurasian (Gondwana) ones. In the same vein, Puhvel maintains in his book about Indo-European mythology that "historical and comparative mythology," as practiced in this book, is in the last resort not beholden to any theory on the "nature" of myth or even its ultimate "function" or "purpose."[103] However, in the final chapter (§8) of the present book, I differ from Puhvel in attempting to capture the *meaning* of the reconstructed Proto-Laurasian, Proto-Gondwana, and Pan-Gaean mythologies, at *each* of their historical stages and for the civilizations involved.[104]

***

Invoking methodologies from related fields has proved to be a successful strategy in many disciplines of the humanities over the past century. In the present case, just as in historical comparative linguistics, first a provisional, heuristic general reconstruction of the complete mythological structure is attempted. It is based on the observation of a large number of obvious similarities. Second, account is taken of the structure and actual extent of the various local mythologies. Finally, while looking at all such common features, the reconstruction of a coherent original mythology is established. However, this is not yet the place to go into detail, which will be done later (§§2–3).[105]

All Laurasian mythology, then, can be traced back to a *single source*, probably in Greater Southwest Asia, from where it spread across Eurasia, long before the immigration of the Amerindian populations into North America and before the Austronesian colonization of the Indonesian archipelago, Madagascar, and the Pacific.[106] That latter expansion actually provides a perfect case, as the somatic (genetic traits; §4.2), cultural (Lapita archaeological culture; §4.4), and linguistic developments (various subbranches of Polynesian spreading out from Fiji/Tonga; §4.1) closely match the evidence of Polynesian mythology, which includes even parts of the well-preserved lineages of gods and chieftains.[107] The historical and comparative method thus applies well in all these sciences, just as it did when it was pioneered for Indo-European linguistics, poetics, religion, mythology, ritual, and material culture over the past two centuries.

However, the Polynesian expansion comprised the colonization of new, previously unsettled territories, and it was achieved in a vacuum that was not disturbed by later immigration and influences until the arrival of the Europeans. Such ideal conditions normally do not occur. Even the similar case of the settlement of the Americas after c. 20,000 BCE, which expanded all the way to Chile in less than 10,000 years, cannot be compared at the same level. Later immigration of Na-Dene-speaking tribes (Athapascans, Navajo, Apache) from Siberia and the introduction of their mythology have slightly disturbed the original picture, as has the movement of other Amerindians *within* the Americas, so that North, Central, and South America now show a patchwork of some large stretches of major linguistic groups, interspersed by pockets of older ones, especially at the fringes of the continent. Worse, the study of the development and historical levels of Amerindian mythologies has hardly even been attempted beyond the synchronic, descriptive stage.[108]

***

The Laurasian mythologies include the ones of the populations speaking Uralic, Altaic, Japanese, Afro-Asiatic, Indo-European, Tibeto-Burmese, and Austric (South Asian, Southeast Asian, and Polynesian) languages (§4.1). They obviously also include the old written mythologies of the Egyptian, Levant, Mesopotamian, Indian, and Chinese peoples. The Inuit and American Indian mythologies (Athapascan, Navajo-Apache, Pueblo, Algonkin, Aztec, Maya, Inca, Amazon, Guarani, Fuegan, etc.) are closely related as well.

As briefly mentioned, the structure of Laurasian mythology is characterized by a narrational scheme that encompasses the ultimate origins of the world, subsequent generations of the gods, an age of semidivine heroes, the emergence of humans, and later on in time, even the origins of "noble" lineages. It frequently includes a violent end to our present world, sometimes with the hope for a new world emerging out of the ashes. Ultimately, as will be discussed later (§3, §8), the universe is seen as a living body, in analogy to the human one: it is born (sometimes from primordial incest), grows, develops, comes of age, and has to undergo final decay and death.

But the Laurasian structure is missing in the rest of the world's mythologies, including those of Australia, New Guinea, most of Melanesia, and many parts of sub-Saharan Africa.[109] For convenience, I will call them and their area of spread by the counterpart of *Laurasia*, the geological term *Gondwanaland*.[110] In Gondwana mythologies the world is regarded as eternal, and Laurasian-style cosmogony does not appear, just as an account of the end of the world as well as many other Laurasian features are missing.

The Laurasian arrangement of mythological tales represents our *earliest* "historical novel." It also is the story of a large section of early humanity itself, telling us how early humans saw themselves and interpreted their existence. Laurasian mythology offers us a glimpse of early humankind's concepts and of their frame of mind that made this complex composition possible. However, before going into these and further details, we need to take a brief look at other, earlier and more recent interpretations of myth.

■ §1.5. EARLIER EXPLANATIONS OF MYTH

Myths have been discussed since times immemorial.[111] In Greece, Euhemeros (c. 330–260 BCE) was a seminal early discussant. He regarded the Greek gods merely as representations of famous, deified human beings; myths therefore incorporated elements of historical facts. His ideas were picked up and developed by Roman and later by European writers. However, he was preceded by some others who already around 500 BCE questioned mythological beliefs.[112]

This critical attitude is not restricted, as is often believed, to the Greeks. Even the oldest Indian text, the Ṛgveda (RV, c. 1200–1000 BCE), once asks whether the god Indra, the great warrior and king of the gods, really exists.[113] The great early skeptic Kautsa (c. 400 BCE?) thought that the foundational RV text itself has no meaning, which amounts to saying that all its myths are meaningless. On the other hand, Yāska (c. fourth century BCE), who reports Kautsa's opinion, composed a long text, the Nirukta, in which he discussed the meaning of RV stanzas and the "difficult" words occurring in them, often using pseudo-etymologies (as also seen in Plato's Kratylos and beyond).

In early China, on the other hand, myths were thoroughly demythologized by Confucius (549–479 BCE) and his school,[114] such as Mencius, in a fashion parallel to that of the similarly practically minded Romans: the deities of the creation period, as well as early demiurge and trickster figures that established human culture, were "historicized" and turned into early monarchs—the early Roman kings and the first Chinese "emperors."[115]

In more recent times, the innovative Italian polyhistor G. Vico (1744)[116] still regarded myths as allegorical and used "hieroglyphs" (heraldic and similar symbols) as well as etymology to establish a rational order of Near Eastern and classical mythological and historical accounts, which indicated to him that history moved in repeating cycles. Some more recent scholars have taken similar attitudes when they understand myths as etiological:[117] they explain the cause and the nature of entities in heaven or on earth. Thus, Frazer, in his famous work *The Golden Bough*, which stresses the ritual killing of an aged king, thought that the basis of myth lies in the superficial use of correlations and identifications made in magic. In this myth and ritual theory, according to him, magic and its use in ritual constitute a primitive "science" that can evolve rationally: when a belief was proved to be wrong it would disappear; in the end, all superstitions of mythology would finally be superseded by science.[118] It has to be noted, however, that Frazer's data are concentrated on food-producing and agricultural societies, that is, a stage of the development of human culture that set in only around 10,000 BCE, after aeons of hunter-gatherer cultures.

Another kind of identification was made by the founder of modern comparative mythology, the Oxford scholar Max Müller. He understood myths—in typical overstated 19th- and 20th-century universalizing, monolithic, or rather *monolateral* explanation[119]—as the simple tales of early humankind that originally explained meteorological and cosmic phenomena.[120] His nature mythology is based on the inherent changes in tales over time, especially linguistic changes in the transmitting language, which he famously called a "disease of language." These processes did not allow later generations to understand the simple tales of nature, especially those about the sun. Therefore they invented elaborate myths to explain the enigmatic older, fossil-like tales. This approach has been reinvented and reiterated, to some extent, by Barber and Barber,[121] when they insist that many myths reflect the memory of certain natural or astronomical phenomena or some striking occurrences in nature,[122] such as volcanic activity and poisonous caves ("dragons"). A more complicated case is the observation of the gradual changes in the rising point of important stars (precession). Myth therefore is a storage device in Stone Age societies without script. Similarly, Lévi-Strauss believes that myths are the means to retain such knowledge.[123]

A somewhat different approach is that of the historical school: echoing Euhemeros, myths reflect history,[124] though they may have been remodeled over time, creating, for example, the "national" cycle of myths of Greece.[125] For these, Nilsson thinks of a remodeling through epic poetry,[126] a creation of a heroic age, and thus makes a clear distinction between divine and heroic mythology.[127] A more recent example that incorporates the "myth as history" approach is that of Barber and Barber,[128] who maintain that myths reflect actual occurrences that took place in historical times. This is not excluded, for example, in the case of the Black Sea flood (c. 5600 BCE) or the Toba explosion and its tsunami (c. 77,000 years ago).[129] They might present a case for the flood myth. But the worldwide distribution of this myth (say, in West Africa, Australia, the Americas) clearly speaks against (uni)local origin conditioned or caused by a natural event. This "historical" explanation remains a monolateral one (see §3.9, §5.7.2).

Another form of the historical approach, somewhat akin to the one discussed at length in the present book but much more restricted in scope, is that of the historical-geographical method of Stith Thompson and his school.[130] If a set of motifs is found in the *same sequence* in a number of tales, he calls it a "tale-type." (This concept resembles the Laurasian scheme, but on a much more limited scale.) Motifs and tale-types are collected, with all their variants, and their individual traits are analyzed. Their frequency and geographical distribution allow us to trace the history and spread of the myth in question, such as from Siberia to the Americas.[131] Single-motif tales must be present in many versions with separate traits to be of significance for this approach.

The social aspect of myth was stressed in the 19th-century myth and ritual school.[132] Myths are derived from rituals or at least associated with rituals (for example, as spoken parts of rituals). The original proponents of this functionalist school were W. R. Smith, Tyler, Frazer, and Durkheim, followed with various models and at various levels of application by Malinowski, Gluckman, Leach, Eliade, Raglan, and Burkert.[133] The latter sees ritual, originally that of the early hunting societies, as an "as if" behavior, acting as if hunting, which protects against the hunter's guilt and cements relationships within hunter bands (see §7.1–2).[134] Ritual has since been adapted for food-producing societies (which are dominant in Frazer's explanations) and continues to this day (§8).

Early in the 20th century, Malinowski saw myths as "pragmatic charters," as justification for beliefs, customs, or social institutions. In his functionalist approach, myth is closely related to social needs, and myths replicate and validate the customs, beliefs, and patterns of local society. These can be observed in the field, especially in the performative aspects of rituals and their real-life outcomes. The actions of gods and humans long past are the charters for present actions and validate them.

Similarly, Eliade saw the aim of myth as to reestablish a long-past, primordial creative era (*in illo tempore*), to re-create and thus increase its power.[135] Myth thus is both charter and creative. For example, the first beings of primordial Australian Dreaming still exist in eternal Dreamtime and can be accessed in rituals.

A cogent summary of the development of the myth and ritual school has been given by R. A. Segal,[136] who expresses the hope, with G. Nagy,[137] that anthropologists will, in future, concentrate on investigating the *continuum* between (performed) myth and ritual, to which we may add the aspect of play(fulness).[138]

***

Explanations given by many prominent scholars of the 20th century are, however, based on the psychic quality of myth. For them, the ultimate reality of myth lies in the human psyches that manifest themselves as symbols in dreams, art, and texts.

Freud saw the unconscious working in dreams. They reshape (and reinterpret) our experiences in symbols and images, as does myth. Myths thus are *public* dreams, shaped by consciousness to make them less dangerous. This is achieved by "condensing the material of daytime experience, displacing the elements, and representing it in symbols and images."[139] Like Frazer, Freud thought that they would eventually be supplanted by science.[140] However, as we know now, new myths emerge all of the time, today just as in the past (see §§7–8). In reality, Freud's psychology is and has itself worked as a modern myth,[141] for example, by explaining humans to modern humans and by removing one's feelings of guilt while transferring it to early childhood experiences, for which one is not responsible.[142]

Nevertheless, the psychological approach to myth has been very prominent over the past hundred years, especially in the form it took with Freud's younger contemporary, C. G. Jung. For Jung, too, myths are psychic representations, though not individual ones (through dreams), as with Freud, but those of a *collective unconsciousness*. Myths represent its fundamental symbols, which are "more or less the same everywhere and in all individuals." These are the historically inherited *archetypes*, "those psychic contents which have not yet been submitted to conscious elaboration,"[143] and they continue to supply us with key symbols. Through archetypes, humans keep in touch with their inner, unconscious processes; consequently, they are positive and life-furthering. However, similar to Freud's ideas, archetypes are not a *direct* creation of the unconscious but appear in "literary" form, which is also seen in folktales and other stories with happy endings.[144] Differently from Freud, however, archetypes and myths are never to be replaced by science[145]—as they indeed have not been, up to today (see §8).

Archetypes include those of the Father, the (Great) Mother, the Hero, the Ogre, the Wise Woman, and so on. These are adapted by the various cultures to local forms of deities and demons, and they tend to form local ordered patterns, a *Weltanschauung*. If Jung's analysis were correct, the archetypes would constitute, taken together, a brief history of the human mind, not unlike the many *seemingly* prehuman (amphibious etc.) stages that an embryo seems to go through in its development.[146] However, by now, all anatomically modern humans alike share a history of at least some 130,000 years. This includes the original creation of myth, though admittedly, we know very little of the development of the human mind for most of that period. If, for argument's sake, the origin of myths and its motifs *originally* resided in the dreams and beliefs of the "African Eve" and her "Adam," these primitive motifs would have been transmitted by humans ever since and would now be part of our collective subconscious. As such, they would spontaneously come up constantly and would thus be universal, since we all have, more or less, the same (Stone Age) history of mind.[147] However, as will be incidentally seen below (§3, §5), some archetypes are neither evenly nor generally distributed all over the world (§1.3, 1.5), such as the assumed worship of the generative power of a universal Mother.[148] Nor does an archetype lead to a full-fledged myth and even less so to a well-structured mythology, and certainly not to one with a story line, such as the Laurasian one. For these reasons, I will leave aside this concept and theories about the universal unity of the structure of the human mind, its subconscious state, and their productions and first make the case of Laurasian and Gondwana mythologies, before coming back to some shared universal traits (§6). The same applies to the competing concept of diffusion, as I first have to build my case.

In addition to the question of archetypes, there is a process that may be called *secondary elaboration*. Every culture has subjected older myths to continuous reshaping and reinterpretation (§7.2), but, again, we do not know what has occurred for much of the period under discussion, so that we do not have access to the "original" forms of Jung's archetypes of Paleolithic times—that is, unless we study the development of Laurasian and other major mythologies, as is done in this book.

Other prominent 20th-century scholars who have employed psychological approaches include Kerényi, Dundes, and Campbell.[149] In his popular book *Myths to Live By*,[150] Campbell clearly states that myths are not of historical nature but, rather, a human universal, a feature of psyche. Though influenced both by Jung's psychology and by diffusionism, his own contribution is, like those of his predecessors, a monolateral one. It stresses the underlying archetype of the Hero, which he saw and formulated as the (American) monomyth. It follows the standard features of the Hero,[151] his quest and various inherent tests, but it also stresses his outsider quality, his return home, his tragic end, or just his "riding off into the sunset." Campbell's closeness to current American mythology in film and fiction has been reciprocated by his sustained influence on these art forms.[152] For him, they are "living mythology."

***

Structuralism, too, is ultimately based on a psychological approach to myths and their supposed deep, binary structure.[153] The main protagonist of this approach has been the French scholar J.-C. Lévi-Strauss.[154] Like most structuralists (such as those in linguistics, beginning with de Saussure in the late 19th century), he is very skeptical of historical explanations.[155] Instead, he stresses the tendency to organize human experience in binary sets of opposites that appear in many societies, where they are mediated in myth, ritual, and society. He sees in this a characteristic of these societies to "polarize experience, to divide it for the purpose of understanding into sets of opposites."[156]

The analytic method is applicable to all myths and texts. Incidentally, this binary tendency does *not* reflect our bicameral mind, as Lévi-Strauss stresses in his latest book, but, rather, is the choice of the societies involved,[157] and as such, it affects local social structures. Since he mostly has dealt with Amerindian, and once with Greek, myth, this choice could be an important characteristic of Laurasian myths.

These structures are—somewhat like features of language in the work of another structuralist, N. Chomsky—inherent in humans and their languages, so that "myths think themselves without humans' awareness."[158] The binary sets of opposites are reflected in complex but, unsurprisingly binary tales that are intended to establish the norms of society and solve its inherent conflicts. It important to collect *all* variants of a myth, including obvious inversions, in order to analyze it and understand its ultimate structure.

However, like most structuralists, Lévi-Strauss says little about the actual content and "meaning" of myths beyond stating that they solve the inherent problems of a given society by overcoming the binary structures. As Hübner complains, "In the end, of a myth only its dry bones remain...there is too much syntax and too little semantics."[159] Indeed, structure apart, myths are of deep meaning to those who tell, enact, perpetuate, and change them.

***

Continuing with the observation of influences between the various fields of the humanities, it is interesting to observe that both modern structuralism and historical comparativism in linguistics and mythology have received an important stimulus from ancient Indian works,[160] that is, those of the grammarians beginning with Pāṇini (fourth century BCE?). In some 4,000 very brief, quasi-algebraic rules, Pāṇini described the forms and syntax of Sanskrit in a system that is still dominant in India today. However, unlike the classical Greek and Roman authors who spoke about "inflection" or changes in forms, he systematically analyzed the (admittedly more regular) forms of Sanskrit verbs and nouns by separating them into roots, suffixes, and endings. This provided an important analytical tool for early Indo-Europeanists like Rask and Bopp (§4.1), who began to compare Sanskrit with Greek, Latin, Gothic, Church Slavic, and so on and thus quickly constituted the Indo-European family of languages. This discovery, in turn, inspired Max Müller's comparisons of Indo-European myths, as described above.

On the other hand, the very analytical (and synchronic) structure of Pāṇini's grammar inspired the 19th-century linguist de Saussure, and later on Chomsky, to look at language as a system of signs agreed to by society and to describe this system, without the use of historical developments, in synchronic fashion. This, in turn, gave rise to structuralism in its various forms, culminating in Lévi-Strauss's ultimately linguistically inspired work.

These long-range geographical and deep chronological relationships have profoundly influenced the course of modern thought, while traditional Indian pandits remain quite unaware of the effects that their scholarship has had on the worldwide studies of language, mythology, and texts in general.

We will observe the same cross-fertilization and long-range effects in mythology (§§5–6).

***

The tendency to classify motifs and mythemes and to arrive at an objective scheme according to which certain texts are structured is also seen in the work of V. Propp.[161] He analyzed Russian folktales and found that they are typically structured according to 31 functions or mythemes that are characteristic of hero tales with happy endings. The same structure has recently been established by M. Ježić for the great Indian epic,[162] the Rāmāyaṇa, which is unsurprisingly still the most beloved Indian text (§8) and is frequently regarded as literally true "scripture."[163]

Another unwitting forerunner of structuralism in the study of mythology is G. Dumézil. He too introduced the idea of *structure* in the study of myth, especially Indo-European myth, though he combines this, just as in Indo-European linguistics, with the study of historical developments. The late F. B. J. Kuiper successfully used a similar structural (but not structuralist) method to analyze ancient Indian and Iranian myths.[164] Dumézil stressed that similarities are found at both the *substantive* and *structural* levels (cf. below, §2.1). Such observations, often from widely dispersed areas of the Indogermania region, led him to establish his theory of a tripartite setup of Indo-European myth, echoing that of Vedic and Indo-European society.[165]

One may add another famous 20th-century mythologist, M. Eliade, as far as he stresses the binary opposites of sacred and profane and the opposition between archaic and modern humans (echoing the concerns of Frazer, Malinowski, etc.). As mentioned, modern people can return to their blissful origins (*in illo tempore*) through the vehicle of myth. Curiously, this idea resembles some aspects of Australian Dreamtime.[166] However, the pursuit of such concepts is not the aim of this book (nor does it arrive at similar conclusions). Rather, it aims at the *exploration* of the actual (reconstructed) myths of that distant time in human history.

Finally, one may also mention some metatheories, such as those of E. Cassirer,[167] who looked for the origins of human knowledge in mythological consciousness, largely without the presence of "objective spirit."[168] The various cultural forms would derive from this type of consciousness. This approach is also seen in the works of anthropologists and philologists contemporaneous with him, such as L. Lévi-Bruhl, S. Lévy, M. Granet, H. Oldenberg, and S. Schayer.[169]

■ §1.6. UR-FORMS, HISTORY, AND ARCHAEOLOGY

There are two contemporary scholars whose ideas are diametrically opposed to the reconstruction of early stages of mythology, one of them working on mythology itself and the other on early, Stone Age religion. Their views need to be discussed at some length before we can proceed with the main task envisaged for this book.

Since at least 1991,[170] the Indo-European mythologist B. Lincoln has added a new twist to the study of the reconstructed mythology of the Indo-Europeans.[171] No serious scholar, including Lincoln himself, denies that the language of the Proto-Indo-Europeans has been reconstructed well or that even many aspects of the Indo-Europeans' poetical language, including some actual phrases such as "imperishable fame," have been ascertained. So why not their mythology?

It has been well known since the 1850s that the Indo-Europeans had deities such as Father Heaven and Mother Earth (§4.1). Lincoln had worked on aspects of Indo-European mythology earlier in his career. However, in c. 1990, frustrated that he did not succeed to reconstruct a particular mytheme, Lincoln began to question the whole theory of reconstructed Indo-European mythology. Such incidental mythemes may, however, never be ascertained in any linguistic or mythological reconstruction. So why throw out the baby with the bathwater? Lincoln now rather stresses the *variations* in actually attested myths that have taken place over time and space. These he regards as the most fundamental feature, as *"the problem."*[172] Such variations certainly are routinely observed and have their own special value (§2.2.4–2.3), but what speaks against reconstructing an *ur*-form for a language group such as Indo-European? Simply that Lincoln no longer *likes* it, as he thinks that reconstruction aims

> to reverse the historic processes and recapture the primordial (and ahistoric) moment of unity, harmony, and univocal perfection.... Such research is [itself]...a species of myth and ritual, based on the romantic "nostalgia for paradise."

Writing on mythology is just writing (modern) "myths with footnotes."[173]

This may have been so in the 19th century, but as the discussion in this and the following chapter shows, reconstruction never aims at a "primordial (and ahistoric) moment of unity, harmony, and univocal perfection." Rather it brings up, time and again, earlier and earlier forms of myth (see §§5–6) that are not pristine either—just like reconstructed languages—and actually never reach unity, harmony, or perfection. Every reconstruction leads to an earlier one and, like any other reconstructed stage, even the hypothetical Pan-Gaean myth (§6), is not "unitarian" or "harmonious," and certainly not paradise-like;[174] it will have had its rivals told by other early bands of humans whose inheritance may not have come down to us, neither in genetics nor, perhaps, in mythology.

All of this is well known to Lincoln from one of his own fields, linguistics: Proto-Indo-European is reconstructed as the ancestral language of the Indo-Europeans, but linguists usually state that even Proto-Indo-European had its dialects and was preceded by historically older forms. For example, we can easily notice such variations, based on older forms, as are preserved in the (Indo-European) genders of the number 2 in English: *twain* (in marine use) and *two*;

they correspond to German *zween* (masculine gender, archaic, found in Luther's Bible), *zwo* (feminine, now employed only when talking on the telephone), and the usual (neuter) *zwei*. Their current use no longer makes sense in contemporary speech, but it reflects a lost gender distinction seen in Sanskrit, Greek, and so on.

Instead, Lincoln, inspired by the sociological and Marxist approaches of Durkheim and Gramsci, now defines myth as "authoritative narratives that can be used to construct social boundaries and hierarchies," as "narratives that have both credibility and authority."[175] This obviously is a very narrow description of myth (see the much wider definition above, §1.1) that leaves out all spiritual aspects. We will not be deterred any further by this fashionable but too restricted approach.

***

Then, there is the concern for properly incorporating the *prehistorical* (and archaeological) parameter in the interpretation of myth, especially that of early myth, which is the major objective of the present book. Myths have continually been changing to a smaller or larger degree, and this process was and still is closely related to the prevailing situation of the societies involved.[176] However, "the archaeology of religion, regardless of type, is in fact a relatively new and still somewhat underdeveloped concern."[177] Nevertheless, as described in some detail (§1.4 sqq., §2.2), the present book follows a comparative *and* historical approach that pays close attention to the historical situation in which the respective myths emerged (see especially §7).

This approach is particularly appropriate in adjusting our interpretations of early myth and religion to the then prevailing type of society and its way of life, consecutively hunter-gatherer, horticulturalist, agriculturist, nomadic, early state society, and so on. These types of society were already proposed by Montesquieu and elaborated by Durkheim.[178] Starting out from Enlightenment ideas about societies and religions, and from the Hegelian and (recent) Western concept of a continuous "progress" of society, this typology has been further developed by Bellah.[179] He gives a very general definition of evolution and wants to see his proposal as heuristic in assuming a series of stages in religious development since the Paleolithic.[180] According to Bellah, there are five distinct types (or stages) of early religions. Even the earliest religions could "transcend and dominate [the natural conditions] through [the human/primate] capacity for symbolization."[181]

First, the "primitive" religions of the pre-Neolithic stage, best seen in Australia,[182] were characterized by a mythical worldview that links them directly to the features of the physical world, with mythical human or animal ancestors as the highest beings. (This idea, however, is contradicted by the High God of some southeastern Australian and African hunter societies, such as the Khoi-San,

Pygmies, etc.; §5). The ancestors and their actions prefigured all human action in the Dreaming (Dreamtime). The mythical figures possess a rich repertoire of *unconnected* myths (which is somewhat similar to my Gondwana and Pan-Gaean proposal; §§5–6). The primitive worldview is acted out in rituals that repeat "creation" time, such as in Australian Dreamtime, which through actual dreams furthers change and innovation. (Bellah's "constant revision and alternation" apart, basic changes in Gondwana myths are contradicted by the comparative study of these myths; §5.) The structure of ritual, which Stanner and Bellah limit to initiation rituals, is similar to the "later" one of sacrifice (§7.1.2): offering, destruction, transformation, and return "communion."[183]

Such societies do not yet have a division of labor, and hence, there are no priests (but note the Gondwana type of early shamans; §7.1). Bellah admits the existence of shamans or medicine men for "archaic" religions (below) but does not regard their presence as necessary. Some restrictions in ritual may apply, based on sex and age, but political dominance of a certain group or clan does not exist.

However, even such early religions already possess a complex worldview that incorporates both nature and society.[184] They would include those of the Paleolithic, Mesolithic, and early Neolithic: from hunter and gather cultures to incipient food-producing cultures. The most typical case, according to Bellah, would be that of the pre-Neolithic Australian cultures. However, his procedure "privileges" two of the three major types of Australian mythology (§5.3.2) and neglects the evidence of other pre-Neolithic hunter and gatherer societies such as the Pygmies, San (Bushmen), and so on that possess some features, such as deities, that Bellah attributes only to the next stage, his "archaic" religions.

Second, "archaic" religion possesses actual gods, priests, ritual, sacrifice, and occasionally even a divine king. The previous mythical beings have become gods, who have more individual characters, and their mutual relations as well as their individual spheres of dominance are defined better. Divine order includes the cosmos as well as nature and humans, in which all beings have their appropriate positions. Humans act according to social norms that reflect divine order, which is reinforced by sanctions.[185] I refrain from a detailed critique as this would lead too far.[186]

However, Bellah's assertion that through priests and their writing, "a relatively stable symbolic structure ... transmitted over an extended period of time" "may become the object of critical reflection and innovative speculation which can lead to new developments" is contradicted by nonliterate societies such as the Vedic Indian one, where all these features were present *without* written texts, a case apparently similar to that of the Celtic Druids. Just as in the case of "primitive" religions, the boundary lines are much more flexible than assumed by Bellah.

Third, these stages are followed by those of the historic, early modern, and modern religions that do not concern us here.

It is obvious that Bellah's scheme is one of historical speculation based on the observation of modern, surviving hunter cultures and of early state societies. Nevertheless, the archaeologist I. Wunn underlines the value of this classification,[187] which she accepts as the basis for her detailed investigation of Stone Age religions. She thinks that it allows a correlation of these and later, archaeologically attested religions with a certain type of economy and society (it also allows us to fill in gaps in attestation).

However, the combination of Bellah's evolutionary classification with archaeological data merely remains a deductive process. It relies on the (more or less incidental) attestation of archaeological remains that are thought to be prognostic for the social relationships as well as the assumed setup of the particular early society under study. Nevertheless, relying on this theory, Wunn necessarily concludes that the lack of social stratification and the existence of a simple (hunters' etc.) economy *predict* a religion of "primitive" type.[188] By the same token, the Australian Aborigines or the South African San, both without social stratification, would appear to a future archaeologist to be people without religion, as they leave very little tangible, archaeologically visible evidence of their religion and rituals— were it not for their magnificent rock art. The future archaeologist would depend on the lucky find of such art to "discover" religion with them.

***

However, as another test case, Wunn's archaeologically based predictions could be compared with the detailed study by F. Barth of a group of linguistically and culturally closely related, only recently contacted Neolithic populations in New Guinea.[189] The Ok exhibit a great diversity of religious beliefs and practices. But archaeologists would notice, if such a lucky find were indeed made upon incidental excavation, only a very small fraction of this diversity, and one would not be able to detect the great differences in local religion. For example, members of one of the Ok groups place a male skull in their sacred hut, while some neighboring ones put a female head on the altar or a number of skulls (cf. §2.2.3, below; also see §§5.3.4, §7.2). Another typical case that indicates the unreliability of arguing from archaeological remains, so far discovered, and further argumentation ex nihilo, is indicated by the so far unique find of a late Paleolithic ivory figure of a human that had been interred in a grave at Brno (Czech Republic).[190] Had this figure not been discovered, Wunn would have argued that human figures were *not* used as grave goods, as figures of spirits or deities did not exist then, in her view. Similarly, due to the absence of remnants of early Australian religion and ritual, she would argue that the early immigrants did not yet have a religion—were it not for some late Paleolithic rock paintings of at least 17,000 years ago.[191]

Returning to the Ok, the great diversity in the myths of various villages, and certainly their complete absence in other villages, would go unnoticed. At best, one would detect some kind of skull cult. (The underlying beliefs obviously would remain rather obscure.) Similar statements have been made for another part of New Guinea, where the populations of one large river valley had a fairly similar material culture but differed greatly in language and religion.

This teaches us the useful lesson of how far the combined evaluation of restricted, incidental archaeological discoveries linked to Bellah's evolutionary model may mislead. A direct link between (lucky) incidental archaeological finds and the spiritual world of the population that produced them can be made neither easily nor at all times.[192] The absence of archaeological finds, even in large numbers, also does not count, as the Brno discovery indicates.

***

A similar kind of argument from absence would apply to the early Laurasian and Gondwana mythologies treated in this book. As per Wunn's scheme, they simply cannot exist, because Paleolithic representations of the myths of the Laurasian story line have not been detected in art or excavated. But then, how to explain the more or less contemporaneous appearance of such myths in Tierra del Fuego and Siberia, in Australia and Africa? By rather quick diffusion? By the identical underlying structure of the human mind? When answering in this fashion, we would be thrown back to our initial question: why and how similarities in myth exist in distant parts of the globe.

In short, even Wunn's generalizations—incidentally, restricted to European materials—conceived through a broad overview of Upper Paleolithic archaeological materials as well as by the use of Bellah's theory can be misleading. They may easily be overturned by the very next excavation, such as the 32,000-year-old figure of a lion-man at Hohlenstein in the Lone Valley of southwestern Germany. Another case in point is the recently discovered, extraordinary case of Stone Age art using an early form of perspective at Chauvet in France (c. 32,000 BCE) or the unusual Magdalenian deposition of decapitated heads at Ofnet in southern Germany.[193]

Wunn's scheme may, however, serve as a useful hermeneutical tool against the all-too-common overinterpretation of archaeological finds.[194] In contrast, we may carry out a counterexperiment: how can Gondwana and Laurasian mythology (respectively, at minimally c. 50,000 and 20,000 BCE) be explained? In doing so, we must leave the absence of evidence apart. That means leaving aside the (current) absence of archaeological data that could indicate certain aspects of Laurasian mythology, such as the four generations of deities. Conversely, which archaeological evidence then would actually speak *against* it? This would be difficult to show: for example, how would Australian Dreamtime be indicated, perhaps except for the painting of some totem animals—which would say nothing to the uninitiated observer. Some such points will be taken up later (§4).

***

Bellah's main points, however, can be neglected here as they are speculation based on an evolutionary scheme of economic development that is closely linked to a supposed spiritual one; it does not provide *proof* that both are indeed always closely connected. For instance, examples taken from modern hunter and gatherer tribes cannot automatically be applied (as Wunn also admits).[195] Modern hunter tribes share with other modern humans some 10,000–65,000 years of spiritual development and the same fundamental intellectual faculties. These long time periods surely did not pass without *any* change in the worldview of the cultures involved, and current hunter cultures cannot automatically be equated with and used as explanations for their ostensible prehistoric likenesses. (Cf. below, §4.4.1, §7.1.)

Further, if, following Wunn, "real" religion did develop only during the late Upper Paleolithic and especially during the Mesolithic, how can it be explained that even remote tribes in South America (the Yanomami in the Amazon or the Fuegans) share at least some aspects of Laurasian mythology that are common in Eurasia? Even more significantly, how can the Australians and Tasmanians (§5.3.2) have traits that are very similar to those found in sub-Saharan Africa? In the first (Amerindian) case, the date of immigration is around 20,000 BCE, but in the second (Australian) one, it is c. 50,000 BCE. For both, this evidence is way too early for Wunn's "late Paleolithic" scheme for the development of religion and mythology.

It is useful, in this context, to take a closer look at the complicated population history after the initial peopling of the Americas and Sahul Land (§5.3.2–3). Australia and New Guinea were first settled around 50 kya, and Tasmania around 35 kya; there has been little demographic disturbance since, except for a Papua migration into Arnhem Land/Kimberleys some 30 kya ago, when New Guinea and Australia were again connected by a land bridge during the Ice Age. This is reflected in both genetics (§4.3) and myth (§5.3.2) but not directly in language. However, in spite of some early Papuan influence in northern Australia, areas of southeastern Australia and Tasmania indicate older traits. Tasmania, too, was linked to Australia from c. 38 to 12 kya. In sum, Sahul Land myth indicates some older (maximally 50 kya) traits that are different from neighboring Southeast Asia and must be old: the same is indicated by linguistics (Papuan, Australian, and Tasmanian languages etc.) and genes.[196]

The situation is similar in the Americas, even if we take into account the later population movements by Na-Dene and Inuit (Eskimo) speakers. South America, in particular, preserves some archaic traits, as Berezkin has shown,[197] that must go back to the time of initial settlement that is attested, even for distant Chile, at 12.5 kya.

In sum, both the Americas and Sahul Land have preserved mythologies that are clearly pre-Mesolithic and that according to Bellah and Wunn could not yet have developed. But then, how can they agree with the rest of Eurasia,

Australia, and Africa? Independent local emergence of transcontinental and transoceanic motifs, and in the case of Laurasian mythology, of the complex Laurasian story line, cannot be posited just because *current* archaeology does *not yet* indicate their existence. *Absence of evidence is not the evidence of absence.* Instead, the very existence of Laurasian myths in the Americas is proof of a pre-Mesolithic mythological tradition. The limitations of a purely archaeo-logical model for the interpretation of the spiritual world of *any* early culture are conspicuous.

In other words, the archaeology/ethology/religion-based theoretical method of Bellah and Wunn shows only what can actually be *seen* in archaeological remains, not what was actually present in the *mind* of Stone Age people. This narrow window of evidence is, in fact, the general problem of archaeology (§4.4): without texts, recovered archaeological finds are open to multiple inter-pretations that in many cases can recover only a small part of the worldview, religion, and mythology of their originators.

Conversely, the existence of complicated late Paleolithic mythologies is *sustained* by the proposed mythological scheme (Laurasian :: Gondwana) and by a few archaeological remains so far.[198] A detailed discussion will be given later (§7).

***

In sum, a complex religion must have existed already around 50,000 BCE, brought by immigrants to Australia, New Guinea, and so on, or around 20,000 BCE at the latest (Americas). Both forms are pre-Mesolithic. The independent origin of Gondwana motifs in Africa and Australia is excluded by the great number of similarities found on both continents (§6). So is independent origin of the Laurasian story line in Eurasia and the Americas. In short, the Bellah/Wunn scheme is contradicted by comparative, geographical, and historical evidence. There is more to religion than meets the eye.

Finally, I believe that we have to reckon with more than just the two stages of "primitive" and "archaic" religions that Bellah posits (§7). They are exemplified as the Pan-Gaean (§6) and as the various Gondwana and Laurasian stages (§3, §5) that were present in hunter and gatherer groups, early food-producing societies (such as horticulturalists), early agriculturalists, and state-based societies and that are found in still later outcomes, such as well-organized, missionary religions (Buddhism, Jainism, Christianity, Islam)—all of them movements that began after 500 BCE (see §7.1 for details).

■ §1.7. SUMMARY

In balance, all the great scholars mentioned in the last and the preceding section (§1.5) appear to have grasped, in common human fashion, only part of the complete picture. As the famous Indian elephant simile—similar to Plato's cave myth—has it: some blind men in a dark chamber touch different body parts of an elephant and give completely different accounts of what they have experienced.[199] However, the present approach of historical comparative mythology adds another facet to the emerging picture.[200] Myths, like poems, paintings, and rituals, reflect reality in a creative fashion that captures its salient features for a contemporary audience and offers explanations and deeply felt meaning.

Specifically, myth tries to make a significant statement about human life itself: "where do we come from, why are we here, where do we go?" Just like Gauguin's enigmatic painting, myth artistically combines many motifs into a meaningful whole, modifying the older (even the reconstructed original) layout according to individual local conditions. As shown by Farmer et al., such modifications are additionally conditioned by path dependencies;[201] that is, they are based on earlier cultural stages that strongly inform contemporary social and religious conditions. Myth still binds humans to their natural habitat and social background; it provides people with reasons for the cyclical seasons of nature, for festivals, rituals, and social strata; myth also tells of a deep underlying meaning of human life itself, satisfying basic spiritual needs (§8).

***

Many if not most of the various interpretations and approaches enumerated and briefly discussed above suffer from the general problem inherent in unilateral, monolithic, or even monomaniacal theories[202]—that they try to explain reality by using just *one* principle or cause. In the end, some of the explanations given above are better than others, though some, such as nature mythology or M. Müller's "decay of language," are clearly too one-sided. However, the current general disdain for the 19th-century explanations is not called for: the 20th century clearly produced many similar fallacies, and I am sure that late 21st-century scholars will have much to say about currently fashionable approaches.

However, the evaluation of past interpretations must not necessarily lead us to general despair,[203] agnosticism, or eclecticism, such as the currently somewhat fashionable "toolbox" approach that entails selecting whatever *seems* fit to "explain" a certain myth. In the end, we rather have to follow a holistic, not a haphazard, eclectic, or monolateral, approach, as G. S. Kirk put it already more than 30 years ago: "Like any tale, a myth may have different emphases or levels of meaning. ... Analysis of a myth should not stop when one particular theoretical explanation has been applied and found productive."[204]

Still, we might expect more "explanations" of myth to emerge, especially coming from the promising field of neurobiology.[205] Though silence has reigned in the prominent center of new theories, Paris, for the past decade or two, occasionally we may come across new explanations and theories, such as, hopefully, the Laurasian one.[206]

In the final chapter (§8), I will try to capture the *meaning* of the reconstructed Laurasian, Gondwana, and Pan-Gaean mythologies. Obviously, the latter point is not something that can be carried out fully, nor can justice be done to it within the pages of this book. Other questions, such as the inevitably interwoven nature of personal psychic experience, dreams, tribal memory, and imagination, as well as social pressure for the justification of customs, rules, and beliefs, can be mentioned only in passing.[207] However, the question will be put (§8) and, hopefully, answered: why was the *story line* created at all? And finally, why myth at all?

***

To sum up, in this chapter, the definition, scope, and past investigations of myth have been explored: a "true" narrative that tells of cosmology and society as well as of the human condition and that is frequently employed to explain and justify social circumstances. Worldwide similarities between individual myths are habitually explained by diffusion or by common human psychic traits (Jungian archetypes). However, the current Laurasian proposal supersedes these approaches as it involves a whole *system* of myths, notably one characterized by a narrative structure (story line) from the creation of the world to its end. This mythology has been spread not by diffusion but above all by the constant advance of humans: after their exodus out of Africa into northern Eurasia and beyond after the past two ice ages, respectively (c. 52,000–45,000 BCE and 10,000 BCE).

The Laurasian scheme also supersedes the Jungian proposal because the actual formulation of myths and their arrangement in a complex narrative system are located on higher planes than that of the archetypes. The current approach is, at present, not interested, involved, or concerned with the ultimate psychic basis of mythemes, motifs, and myths. It does not intend to explain their assumed ultimate psychic or neurological background. It is, moreover, independent of any theory that accounts for the creation of a certain myth, whether by archetype (Jung), by the mnemotechnical mechanics of myth formation as storage device of Stone Age "scientific" knowledge,[208] or based on an underlying binary mental structure.[209]

Rather, the artistic arrangement of myths in Laurasia (and beyond) is explored and traced back in time to the Mesolithic or Upper Paleolithic period. Finally, the history of the Laurasian scheme is sketched, from the Paleolithic until today.

However, the comparative aspect of the current project necessitates, first, a discussion of the methodologies involved with comparison as such; this is undertaken in the next chapter.

2 Comparison and Theory

■ §2.1. THEORY AND PRACTICE OF COMPARISONS

Any comparison involves the linking, correlation, or identification of two items on (roughly) the same plane of existence or thought.[1] It is obvious that each culture has its own set of classifications that usually are not consciously recognized. For example, the Zoroastrian texts classify hedgehogs as dogs and include in this category also the otter and the porcupine.

Other, linguistic classifications sometimes play tricks on our mind, such as German and Dutch *Walfisch* and *walvis*, which automatically classify the whale as a fish, though we should know better. Whorf went so far as positing that if speakers of the Hopi language had developed a detailed analytic philosophy, it would look quite different from the Western one,[2] as the Hopi language classifies items quite differently. Or Indo-European languages usual confuse "being" (living, existing, the verb "to be") with the mere indication of objects or beings ("there is," "2 + 2 = 4," etc.). Similar cases could be brought up from Chinese or from Bantu (e.g., with eight noun classes in Swahili).[3] Western philosophy had a certain advantage in that Indo-European languages have a neuter gender and thus do not need to classify things as male/female only. Other languages distinguish animate/nonanimate. Yet all such categories will influence our way of thinking, though we can overcome such restrictions when reflecting properly.

These difficulties apart, humans correlate certain items, objects, things, beings, and their characteristics when perceiving, describing, and classifying them. Importantly, such mental activity is based on certain neurological factors of our brain, which has a predilection for correlating any two items, as explained in some detail by Farmer et al.[4] Casting aside artificial boundaries, sets, and frames that are culturally built into our mind, we have to see how we can proceed objectively.

Multivariate and principal component analysis

An important recent method of comparison has been multivariate analysis. This is a complex method, involving statistics and other mathematical techniques. It has been explained in accessible form by the prominent geneticist L. L. Cavalli-Sforza in his characterization of principal components analysis,[5] following the methods H. Hotelling developed in the 1930s. It entails the calculation of averages for a large number of observations.[6]

If we were to apply this method to comparative mythology, it would necessitate a collection and a map of the geographical spread of many mythemes, motifs, and myths, such as has been done for the myth of the earth diver by R. Villems,[7] or of the Milky Way,[8] or of the flood myth,[9] and by J. Oda for motifs in folklore.[10] One would have to create distribution maps, such as Y. Berezkin has done for a number of mythemes, as well as maps for the important foundational myths,[11] such as the origin of the world from Chaos or the origin of humans from deities, stones, clay, or plants.

Berezkin (and Oda)[12] has, in addition, used the method of principal component analysis (see above and §4.3) to arrive at several principal components (PCs) of worldwide myths. Just as in some of the early results of human population genetics,[13] such calculations have global results that are very informative in determining the general geographical layout and spread of the myth or motif in question, and they indicate a trend while the actual geographical origin of a trait remains unclear.

However, just as in genetics, interpretations of the actual spread of particular myths have to be provided "from the outside," that is, by fields other than descriptive mythology (or folklore), such as archaeology, which Berezkin employs, or genetics; they will help to determine the point of origin. It is precisely here that comparative *historical* mythology can step in in a major way: the Laurasian model provides firm coordinates and "archaeological" historical levels for the interpretation of such distributions.

When collapsing many such maps of myth distribution as elaborately constructed by Berezkin into a single one we would generate a "dialect map" of myths that would provide clues for the origin and spread of certain clusters of myths and of the Laurasian and the other mythologies (see Figure 2.1). Such a map would be similar to Berezkin's map of the first PC, but it would also go beyond its generalizations. Like composite dialect maps, it would show more details of specific myths, the individual boundaries of their spread, and not just a depiction of their mathematical average. Further specification of mythemes within such myths would allow for additional statistical data: how many mythemes do exist, and in which order are they present locally and regionally? Examples could include, for example, the type of the world diver animal or how many divers appear; or for the Milky Way (Figure 2.2),[14] as what kind of path or animal is the Milky Way regarded, how many parts does it have, what do they represent, and so on; or again, for the flood myth, how does the flood originate, how far does it spread, how are people saved, why did it begin in the first place, what retribution or revenge (§5.2.7) was involved, and so forth.

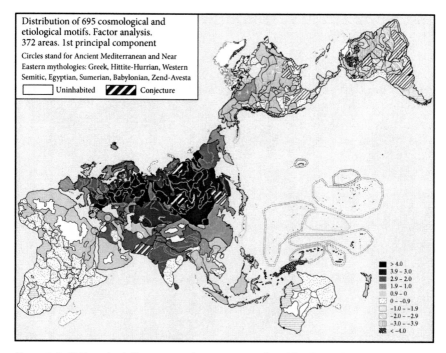

Distribution of 695 cosmological and
etiological motifs. Factor analysis.
372 areas. 1st principal component

Circles stand for Ancient Mediterranean and Near
Eastern mythologies: Greek, Hittite-Hurrian, Western
Semitic, Egyptian, Sumerian, Babylonian, Zend-Avesta

☐ Uninhabited ▨ Conjecture

■ > 4.0
■ 3.9 – 3.0
■ 2.9 – 2.0
▨ 1.9 – 1.0
▨ 0.9 – 0
▨ 0 – -0.9
☐ -1.0 – -1.9
☐ -2.0 – -2.9
▨ -3.0 – -3.9
▨ < -4.0

Figure 2.1. Y. Berezkin's first principal component of worldwide myths. Note the low
level of occurrences in South America and New Guinea.

***

Another item important for multivariate analysis would be the "path dependency" of each group/culture.[15] By this, I mean the set of *foundational* topics in
each civilization that have exercised extraordinary influence on all its subsequent
stages. Compare, for example, the idea of primordial sin in Christianity,[16] and of
the role of Eve, in contrast with that of primordial obligation (*ṛṇa*) in India or the
avoidance and casting off of primordial "evil" (*tsumi*) in Japan in the myth of
Izanami/Izanagi and their child, Hirugo (Kojiki 1.4).[17] They have persisted for
several thousands of years.

Such path dependencies can play havoc with the straightforward development
of particular myths or of myth complexes as they forcefully shape the way a
particular culture looks at its traditionally received (Stone Age) myths. Certain
ideas are foregrounded, and others are not: *sin* plays no role in India or East Asia,
and most of what ensues from this concept in the Christian Bible and Western
culture has no impact on, or similarities with, these civilizations. The concept of a
divine savior from primordial sin is alien to them (before Mahāyāna Buddhism);
and the facile way *tsumi*, guilt, and even political misdeeds are cast away by the half-
yearly Japanese *ōharae* ceremony may look "too easy" to Westerners[18]—just as the
Catholic confession and forgiveness of misdeeds and sins may look to Asians.

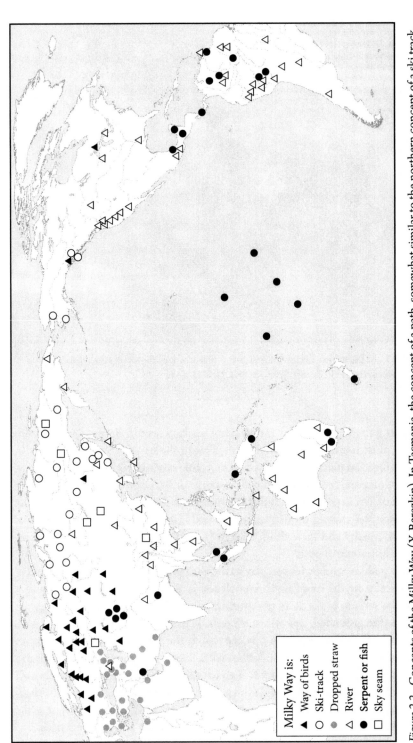

Figure 2.2. Concepts of the Milky Way (Y. Berezkin). In Tasmania, the concept of a path, somewhat similar to the northern concept of a ski track, existed before the extinction of Tasmanians in the first part of the 19th century.

Milky Way is:

▲ Way of birds   △ River
○ Ski-track   ● Serpent or fish
● Dropped straw   □ Sky seam

Obviously such attitudes, inherited by pathway dependency, shape many myths; they force cultures to leave out others (there is no myth of an end of the world in Shintō Japan), and they foreground or create new myths. The inclusion of this principle in multivariate analysis will provide a powerful tool that will counterbalance mere geographical spread and simple inheritance patterns. It must be said, however, that as far as I know such a mathematical analysis has never been attempted. The mere enumerations by Stith Thompson are not enough,[19] though one could begin with his materials (incomplete and biased toward Eurasia and the Americas as they are) and expand them by Berezkin's collections. In addition, the data and listings by Gusinde and Wilbert for South America as well as the collection and database of folktales created by Junichi Oda could help a long way;[20] however, such detailed work cannot be carried out in the present context.

Challenges

There has also been some recent discussion on the method and validity of the comparative approach as such.[21] A few relevant points will be discussed here.

As mentioned, a potential obstacle to comparisons of Stone Age myth and religion is presented by Wunn,[22] who, however, relies just on the material testimony discovered by archaeology to decide on the type of religion present at the time.[23] Another interesting "challenge" has been posited by a prominent American scholar of religion, J. Z. Smith.[24] He presents an outline and critique of four approaches to comparison—ethnographic, encyclopedic, morphological, and evolutionary—and attempts to give "a survey of some 2500 years of the literature of anthropological comparison."[25]

However, the commonly-met-with, inherently Eurocentric problem of his approach is obvious: the question of comparison is treated as if there were nothing to be found before the "Greek miracle." But other ancient civilizations have made their own comparisons, attested ever since we have written records. For example, various cultures make clear the distinction between insiders and outsiders, such as the *ārya/dasyu* in early Vedic India and the people of the Middle Kingdom and various "outsiders" (usually called "barbarians" in translations) in China; similar distinctions exist in Mesopotamia (the "black-haired people" versus the desert and mountain outsiders)[26] and with the ancient Egyptians, who clearly distinguish themselves, even in color, from outsiders such as the Levantine Hyksos, Hittites, Nubian Africans, and Pygmies. However, Smith concludes that each such comparison is unsatisfactory and that each new proposal is a variant of an older one. There being "nothing easier than the making of patterns," he regards this problem to be solved by "theories and reasons, of which we have had too little." He feels that we still are left with the question, "How am I to apply what the one thing shows me to the case of two things?"[27]

This characterization is much too simple. Structuralism apart, scholars normally do not establish simple, binary comparisons. We rather employ multiple categories and sets of data, which may emerge to be *structured* as soon as we notice some initial patterning.[28] Items fitting the underlying *structure* will then be added, and the scheme will be expanded, and one tends to wind up with a finely meshed theory.

It is certainly true that the "making of patterns" or comparing (and correlating) any two entities is easy and indeed is frequently done. Undeniably, it has been an inherent part of the human understanding of the world.[29] However, ancient peoples did so with an underlying theory, whether expressed or not.[30] One might therefore reverse Smith's statement and say that there have not been too few but, instead, all too many theories explaining the world by patterning and by the subsequent correlation of items. They can be found from ancient India, to Chinese and Greek philosophical systems, to recent ones, underlying the *Weltanschauung* and systems of thought of many populations without written traditions. Worse, Smith explicitly denies the possibility of historical comparisons: "comparison does not necessarily tell us how things "are" (the far-from-latent presupposition that lies behind the notion of the "genealogical" with its quest for "real" historical connections)."[31]

Obviously, it has been an ancient human quest to approach one's origins, their true nature, in other words: how things were and therefore supposedly still are. But this endeavor is quite different from modern scientific comparisons, be they of languages, skeleton structure, or genes. In making such comparisons, scientists attempt to find, if possible, the antecedents or even the original ancestor of the items they study and to indicate how its descendants evolved: in other words, the "true nature" of the items they study, based on their descent. However, this is done while not neglecting incidental external influences and resulting changes. Usually, comparativists know very well about the tenuous, theoretical structure of their constructs, and they are elated if they can occasionally be confirmed by the discovery of intermediate stages or even of *missing links*. In short, a reconstructed item must not always coincide fully with a real, once-existing specimen, whether this is a plant, animal, or human being or a language, custom, ancient literary text—or Laurasian mythology.

Surprisingly, however, a few years later Smith admitted that historical and genealogical comparisons have indeed been successful in comparative anatomy, historical linguistics, folkoristics, and archaeology,[32] each one of which fulfills, he maintains, the preconditions of a strong theoretical interest and a thick dossier with micro-distinctions. Even then, however, he neglects mutual dependency, individual development, and mutual influence of systems but nevertheless concludes for the comparison of religions that "at present, none of these [preconditions] are fulfilled in the usual comparisons of religious phenomena, but there is nothing, in principle, to prevent their successful deployment."[33]

All of which would be carried out by the present Laurasian (and Gondwana) theory of historical comparative mythology.[34] In religion and myth, according to Smith we would be back to square one: inquiring about the validity of the comparative and historical method that actually has been rigorously tested in several sciences over the past 200 years. Scholarship in many fields, from paleontology to genetics, from manuscriptology to linguistics, has shown differently.

***

Of much greater theoretical importance for the current project is the "qualitative comparative method" discussed by C. C. Ragin, who looks at the comparative method "beyond qualitative and quantitative strategies."[35] The qualitative comparative method has been used for comparing just a few items up to hundreds of cases.[36] Ragin regards it as an alternative to multivariate statistical analysis; it breaks cases into parts and variables, and therefore this method allows for (multiple) constellations, configurations, and conjunctures: "It is especially well suited for... outcomes resulting from multiple and conjunctural causes—where different conditions combine in different and sometimes contradictory ways to produce the same or similar outcomes."[37] This procedure is particularly apt for certain situations in comparative mythology, where individual mythemes and motifs that may be geographically very distant from each other have coalesced in a very similar or identical fashion.

Pertinent examples would include the potent case of widely dispersed items, such as the appearance of the rainbow snake in India,[38] South America, Australia, and sub-Saharan Africa. One may speculate that natural surroundings have inspired the motif, as is indeed the case in India with the Mundas.[39] However, social conditions are very different in all the areas concerned: tribal food-producing societies with the Indian Munda, state societies in Africa (with the king ascending the rainbow), Stone Age hunter and gatherer societies in Australia (with the shaman ascending), and horticultural food-producing tribal societies in South America.

Other cases could include the motif of human origins from a tree (Iceland, sub-Saharan Africa, Taiwan,[40] Japan, Australia); or the cosmological sand paintings found among the Navajos and Tibetans;[41] or the same or similar colors of the directions of the sky used in Chinese, Iranian, Navajo, Hopi, Aztec, and other Amerindian myths; or the motif of the Four/Five Ages and the colors applied to them by the Greeks and Navajos; or cattle herders' age groups, rituals, and claim of sole possession of cattle (found with the Vedic Indians of 1000 BCE and with the present Maasai people of East Africa). Such incidental resemblances and congruities may not have the same origins, but they share similar outcomes and therefore could be analyzed by Ragin's method, if enough samples are found. A suitable database is found in the work of S. Thompson, Y. Berezkin, and J. Oda.

However, Ragin's theorizing is "not restricted to the field of comparative sociology and political science. Essentially, I address metatheoretical differences between approaches generally called qualitative (or case-oriented) and quantitative (or variable-oriented)."[42] To which we may add the materials and theory of comparative mythology.

***

As for the actual procedure of comparisons in mythology, K. Tuite has made the following important observation regarding the comparison of isolated congruities in ethnology and linguistics:

> Dumézil noted that a comparison... is convincing to the extent that similarities are found at both the *substantive* and *structural* levels. As in historical linguistics, where genetic groupings... [are made] more probable by striking, functionally *unmotivated* similarities in grammatical features, so hypotheses... [are] strengthened by such correspondences in both the form and structural contextualization of symbols[, such as]... Dumézil's... discovery of paired one-eyed and one-handed gods or heroes, associated with magic and justice.... [T]his... "bizarrerie"... [makes common origin] all the more likely.... What I propose here is the application of a similar procedure of substantive and structural comparison of symbols of two speech communities for which historical linguistics has not yet conclusively proven a relationship. The two bodies of comparative data—ethnological and linguistic—taken together provide a stronger case for historical linkage than either would do on its own.[43]

The same can be said about historical comparative mythology in general and the present approach in particular. As Puhvel has formulated for comparative Indo-European mythology:

> What does it take to reconstruct an Indo-European protomyth? It means recapturing via the comparative method a piece of the onetime living religion of a hypothetical protosociety. The procedure is to evaluate in relation to one another such survival versions as can be judiciously isolated and identified. Naturally, the least-changed varieties would best reflect the prototype.[44]

To which should be added that, when surpassing the narrow confines of a linguistic family, the method must be the "substantive and structural comparison" of mythemes, myths, and systems of myths of two or more "speech communities for which historical linguistics has not... conclusively proven a relationship."[45]

The procedure proposed in this book thus closely echoes that of comparative linguistics: isolated and unmotivated similarities found in widely separated areas usually are indicators of an older, lost common system, higher on the structural level and cladistic tree; their nonmotivatedness makes them stand out in the individual culture and marks them as a (functionally) unexplained item or a strange relict. Examples would include, for example, the weeping and crying of the separated parents Father Heaven and Mother Earth (Maori, Ṛgveda) and the showing of bare breasts as a sign of friendship (Ṛgveda and Gilyak in the Amur area).[46]

Similarly, in the related field of ritual behavior, one many compare many widespread items of current ritualistic conduct (such as tipping one's hat, military salute, bowing, scratching one's head, laughing with bared teeth, hiding one's teeth when laughing, etc.), some of which even go back to our prehuman ancestors. In the comparatively little-studied field of children's culture, there are also jingles (such as "ene, mene, …"), melodies, string figures, and games that are widespread across the globe; all of them cannot be investigated here (§4.5).

***

As far as comparisons of similarities in mythology (and its practical basis, language) are concerned, we must distinguish between several possibilities. The linguist M. Ruhlen distinguishes three reasons for such similarities:

> When one identifies similarities among molecular structures, plants, human societies, or stars, the origin of such similarities can be explained only by one of three mechanisms:
>
> (1)   common origin
> (2)   borrowing
> (3)   convergence.
>
> To demonstrate that two languages (or language families) are related, it is sufficient to show that their shared similarities are not the result of either borrowing or convergence. As regards convergence—the manifestation of motivated or accidental resemblances—linguists are in a more favorable situation than biologists. In biology, convergence may be accidental, but it is more often motivated by the environment; it is not by accident that bats resemble birds, or that dolphins resemble fish.[47]

We may add that nature has produced several "reincarnations" of "sharks," and wolflike predators among the marsupials of Australia, over the course of natural history. We will see that many such resemblances will appear in the comparison of myths as well: we have borrowing (diffusion), and we have convergence, especially when climatic and social conditions conspire to necessitate explanations of cultural features (such as deities of grain and other agricultural products or their birth, death, and rebirth).

The range of major possibilities for the explanation of similarities includes

- common origin (as proposed in this book)
- diffusion: spread by incidental word of mouth, such as in trade; by direct or osmosis-type contact of the concerned cultures, which proceeds

further in domino fashion or back and forth in ping-pong style. Diffusion was furthered by periodic climatic changes during the Stone Age, followed by postglacial expansion and later on by economic exchange in early "world systems."[48]

- a characteristic of human nature: that is, the neuro-correlative functioning of the brain,[49] by inherent archetypes, specifically during a presumed universal "axial age"; or "resonance" by which cultures develop according to universal laws; or "Indra's net" (*indrajāla*), which interconnects all phenomena with all others in mutual fashion (and thus, also cultures)
- independent origin (again, based on inherent human nature)
- convergence of independently developed traits

W. Doniger, in her review of Carlo Ginsburg's book on witches, uses most of the same categories:. "Given cultural convergences the theoretically possible explanations are: (a) diffusion, (b) derivation from a common source, (c) derivation from structural characteristics of the human mind." She adds that Ginsburg rejects a common source (genealogical tree) as a Romantic, pre-Positivist model.[50]

It is, however, exactly the rather prematurely and rashly shunned model of common origin,[51] of the family tree, that is, of the cladistic arrangement of the data of historical comparative mythology, that will be pursued in this book—and for the same good reasons that have been used in comparative linguistics, paleontology, and genetics.[52] The historical comparative approach is not one of old-fashioned Romanticism looking for and speculating on distant *ur*-situations, but it is the cladistic procedure also used by genetics, human anthropology, archaeology, linguistics, and philological manuscript research (§4): all of them present pedigrees or stemmas of subsequent historical layers and their interrelations, filiations, or branchings.

Precisely when the cladistic model made a strong reappearance in the popular mind due to the advances of genetics, Doniger and Ginsburg still rejected it, as they were unwittingly bound by the path dependencies firmly embedded in the Western mind by early 20th-century psychologists such as Freud and, ironically, Jung. Conversely, as just mentioned, a number of sciences have established "family trees" that lead back to a common ancestor. Paleontology and genetics deal with historical descent, with the development of living organisms, and establish their pedigree. Others, such as philology, deal with the development of traditions and texts that have come down in direct descent from earlier ones, their "ancestors." Some of the descendants share a common innovation (or mutation) that distinguishes them from their ancestors and other relatives. Further examples include the study of inanimate entities, such as the family trees of manuscripts that have been continuously copied from each other, again with certain "mutations." Their comparative study results in a pedigree (stemma) of copying efforts that create mistakes (by eye or ear) similar to those occurring in copying genetic features in our DNA.[53]

Then there is the pedigree of descent of current human languages derived, again, by innovations (mutations) from older forms, their "ancestors," which is studied by historical linguistics. Examples are the various "daughter" languages that derive from Proto-Indo-European, Proto-Sino-Tibetan, Proto-Bantu, and so on and ultimately, from the hypothetical speech of "African Eve" herself.[54]

***

The comparative method employed in all these sciences proceeds from obvious similarities of the items compared (say, since Linné in biology, giving birth from the uterus by mammals) to a more structured investigation that establishes sets of regular correspondences between the items compared (as mammals, suckling babies, etc.). Such regular correspondences must reappear in further items that are taken up for comparison (being warm-blooded, being vertebrate with an internal skeleton, etc.). The various sets of regular correspondences lead to a well-structured body of links and correspondences that govern nearly all of the cases involved (i.e., the establishment of Linné's various *typologically* and synchronically distinguished animal and plant groups).[55] The comparison continues with a *historical* analysis that accounts for the innovative changes and developments (mutations) seen in the several sets of regular correspondences (mammals versus reptiles versus fish etc.) and that finally results in a pedigree of the entities involved (paleontological tree, cladistic arrangement).

Historical comparative reconstruction

Historical comparative studies have established pedigrees of the development of *Homo sapiens*, of most human languages, and of human DNA (female mitochondrial DNA and the nonrecombinant male Y chromosome) from the "African Eve" to that of all modern humans. In all cases, the descendants of a certain parent along the line of descent are characterized by *common mutations* or as called in linguistics, by *shared innovations*. The same comparative and historical method will be used in this book for the reconstruction of earlier forms of mythology.

In a nutshell, the features of one particular generation, form of language, genetic setup, or contemporaneous mythological system are compared not just with other "neighboring" ones but also with their (reconstructed or actually attested) *older* forms. These, in turn, will be compared with still older forms and where these are not available, with a reconstruction based on later materials.

Time depth in mythological reconstruction is thus built up step by step, just as in linguistics and the other sciences. Earlier and earlier synchronical mythological systems are reconstructed (e.g., Indo-European, Nostratic, Eurasian, Laurasian), finally leading to the period of the exodus from Africa and of the "African Eve." The method is described and discussed below in some detail (§2.2.2 sqq.).

***

At each earlier level, however, materials get scarcer, again just as in the sciences. Yet comparisons with various other mythological systems (of Australia, sub-Saharan Africa, etc.) and use of the results of archaeology and human population genetics help: we can distinguish Australian and Amerindian myths by their migration times (at c. 50,000 and c. 20,000 years ago).

The same result can be expected from mythological comparisons, that is, if such comparisons indeed establish a set of sustained correspondences and underlying structures. This possibility will be demonstrated in the following sections and chapters, step by step, moving from similarities to regular correspondences and finally to a family tree of mythologies.

The new approach of *historical comparative* (Laurasian, Gondwana) *mythology* and the steps taken in its establishment consequently are quite similar to the well-tested methods of the other sciences mentioned. As mentioned, comparisons with archaeology and genetics allow us to distinguish early migrations, and hence that of their accompanying mythologies, even if these sciences do not directly attest to the individual details of mythology or the *Weltanschauung* of the bearers of the cultures involved (§4). It is the aim of this book to ascertain and present similar pedigrees for the development of human mythologies.

***

However, there exist some potential objections against the methods sketched in this section (§2.6; cf. §5.2, §6). They may include the methods used in deciding whether similar myths in distant regions are derived from common ancestral myths or have developed independently due to neurobiological invariances and similarities in ecological conditions.

As far as similarities are concerned, this question has been answered above (§2.1), also by pointing to unmotivated fragments preserved in isolated areas (§2.2). After the reconstruction of the preceding stage of mythology, they turn out to be a relevant part of the earlier system. This is frequently seen in comparative historical linguistics, and we may assume the same relevance in comparative historical mythology.

The occurrence of similarities due to similar or near-identical ecological conditions can also be answered effortlessly. For example, the ancient pastoral Ṛgvedic society of northwest India of c. 1000 BCE shares many items with the pastoral Maasai society of contemporary East Africa, such as the belief of having been divinely ordained to own *all* cattle and the institution of age classes. But their mythologies have little in common and actually belong to the two major different systems of Laurasia and Gondwana.

Or, for example, the occurrence of horse sacrifice in Northeast Asia,[56] among the Indo-Europeans, and, quite unexpectedly, among Amerindians of Patagonia in recent centuries is only a case of superficial resemblances. The Indo-European horse sacrifice is closely connected with the elevation of a tribal leader to supreme ruler (Vedic India, Ireland; cf. also the October horse in ancient Rome),[57] and similarly, so is Chinese horse sacrifice.[58] But the Patagonian one, reported by Charles Darwin,[59] has none of these characteristics. It was performed by a tribal society that had only recently acquired the horse from the Spaniards, and it functioned merely as a substitute for earlier offerings at a pole, stand-in for the world tree in the treeless and featureless southern Argentinean steppes. Again, the mythologies of the three areas are clearly distinct from each other.

It may be pointed out that the hunter populations of the Congo, Borneo, and South American tropical forests may share items such as blowpipes and so on, but their mythologies again belong to two different systems. In sum, similar ecological and economical conditions do not result in similar or identical mythologies.

On the contrary, Laurasian mythology exists in a variety of climates, from polar ice regions to tropical jungles, and from the hunter-gatherer stage to modern state societies. It should be obvious that, even though certain aspects of mythology will be influenced by habitat and economic and cultural conditions, the basic features of the reconstructed Laurasian and Gondwana mythologies are independent of such conditions.

One may point to fairly similar flood and destruction myths that are found in many early river- or ocean-based societies and seem to be independent of long-range transmission. However, as the investigation (below, §5.7.2) indicates, the flood myth is one of the oldest ones still present. It is found in many areas that are *not* threatened by oceanic floods or large riverine inundations (such as mountainous Hawai'i and dry central Australia). It occurs in virtually all parts of the globe and thus is not likely to have been transmitted by late diffusion from an unknown cultural center. This is especially obvious in the combination of the mytheme of the sky falling down connected with the flood, as is seen in Central Africa as well as in Polynesia.

While such close analysis of the details of widespread myths often allows us to distinguish cases of inheritance versus diffusion, the methods required to do so have been made explicit above and will be further pursued in this chapter. The main methods include the checking of adherence to the Laurasian or Gondwana mythological schemes and their various macro- and subregional forms (§2.3), their fit with such schemes or their complete isolation, the establishment of clear cases of regional loan relationships, and the like. (For further discussion of possible objections to the Laurasian theory and historical comparative mythology in general, see below, §2.6.)

Once the framework of comparison and its method have been set up, we can begin with the actual reconstruction of Laurasian mythology, starting out from observing simple and obvious similarities and proceeding from there to the various higher levels of comparison described just now. (The matter is summed at the end of §2.3.)

▪ §2.2. RECONSTRUCTING LAURASIAN MYTHOLOGY

The present investigation starts out and takes its inspiration, as mentioned, from the observation that current explanations of the widespread similarities in myth, such as by archetypes and diffusion,[60] cannot explain the extraordinary amount of similarities and congruities across the globe. They also fail to address a central characteristic aspect, the comparability of *whole systems of myths*, that is, inherent aggregates or intentional collections of the myths of one population.[61] Therefore, a new comparative approach is proposed here that looks at common origins.

As outlined above (§1.4), it proceeds systematically in several steps:

- first, obviously common features of various mythologies around the globe are spotted and listed;
- second, account is taken of the complete aggregate extent and internal structure of the various local mythologies—especially of their story line;
- third and finally, a coherent ancestral mythology is reconstructed for much of Eurasia, North Africa, and the Americas. As indicated earlier, its designation, *Laurasian mythology*, is derived from the area that it covers: it makes use of the geographical term *Laurentia* in Canada for the Americas and of *(Eur)Asia* for Greater Asia (and its North African extension).[62]

***

The new approach as well as the steps taken in setting it up are quite similar, as mentioned, to the well-tested methods of historical and comparative linguistics or the biological sciences. A detailed comparison of both methods is not intended here. Suffice it to say that commonly made comparisons of individual myths would correspond in linguistics to those of particular words, that is, their outward shape (phonetics) and their forms (declension, conjugation; see Table 2.1). Further comparisons may entail some structural features (Lévi-Strauss's mythemes, binary structure) corresponding to the formal and abstract syntactical features of sentence structure (word order within a sentence etc.). But even the discovery of such structures does not lead to an *understanding* of a particular mythology, much less of a set of mythologies. In the words of the linguistic simile, that would mean the discovery of the structures and the establishment of the *complete* grammar of all parts of speech of a particular language and all its relatives. The next step is the reconstruction of earlier forms of the language(s) at hand. Without this kind of comparison, we would never have arrived at the reconstructions made in comparative linguistics (Indo-European, Semitic, Bantu, Amerindian, etc.) of earlier forms of the languages in question, just as, without such wide-ranging comparisons, we would not arrive at the story line and general structure of Laurasian mythology.

The next step in the comparison is the evaluation of the actual *content* of the texts. In comparative linguistics, this would correspond to the studies going

TABLE 2.1. *Parallels between linguistics and mythology.*

LINGUISTICS	COMPARATIVE MYTHOLOGY
Phonetics	Mytheme
Forms (declension, etc.)	Motif, other structural elements
Word order	Myth: Propp's "syntax" and
Complete grammar	Lévi-Strauss' binary structure
Comparative grammars	Comparative mythology
Historical analysis	Historical analysis
*Reconstruction of macro-families	*Reconstruction of Laurasian & Gondwana families
*First language	*First myths

beyond single sentences to the investigation of *texts*, in other words, the structure (and interpretation) of the texts concerned. In mythology, this would amount to the description of certain quasi-syntactical features, such as Propp's theory of the 30-odd constituents of Russian folktales.[63] However, comparisons of whole mythologies, corresponding in linguistics to that of, say, the Latin, Greek, Sanskrit, and beyond, the Egyptian, Sumerian, and Nostratic languages and so on, are missing even now. In other words, we lack truly comparative and historical mythology, whose parallel has existed in linguistics since the early 19th century. This book is an attempt to fill that gap.

Finally, there is the semantic aspect of linguistics, which involves the multi-faceted meanings of words, sentences, and texts. This, too, is largely missing in comparative mythology, where it would correspond to the *meaning* of mythemes, motifs,[64] myths, and, finally, the meaning of whole mythologies and of the reconstructed Laurasian mythology as such (see §8).

Procedure

In actual procedure, when carrying out the Laurasian project, we have to start by stating obvious similarities between myths, sets of myths, and whole mythologies. As a matter of principle and procedure, one needs two or three identical or similar items, best those distant from each other in time or space, to establish a common ancestral element. Comparisons of items found only in adjacent cultures are discouraged as they may be due to borrowing, but widely distant, remote mythologies (for example, those of Polynesia and ancient Israel, Scandinavia, or Greece or those of the Maya and Greeks) are especially useful. Pursuing these investigations, the Laurasian mythological model will gradually emerge and take shape.

Obvious similarities are necessarily those that heuristically appear as such to the investigator. Whether they are indeed historically linked will only become apparent in the course of the investigation. This process will sometimes lead to a reformulation of parts of the theory (see §2.1, §3.9, §5.1.1). Some surface similarities are due, just as in linguistics, to a number of factors. In mythology, they include a certain amount of convergence due to similar natural and social environments, such as seen between totally unrelated Maasai, Toda, and Vedic cattle lore or in the interpretation of the rainbow as a snake in Africa, Australia, and South America, mentioned above (§1.6, §2.1).

A shortcut in the investigation of correspondences and the establishment of the Laurasian scheme is quite often provided by discovering isolated archaisms in geographically and temporally widely dispersed areas. They can immediately lead on to the right track and reveal the underlying structure—the Laurasian story line—that may be partially hidden by later developments elsewhere.

The result is that, just as in linguistics, as soon as we actually have established a family tree, any comparison of individual items, and of whole mythologies, attains a new, higher level of perspective: it provides a new point of view to certain isolated items. Through the evaluation of disparate but widespread fragments found in the nooks and corners of Eurasia and all of Laurasia, such items will lose their uniqueness and isolation and will add up to an unexpected scenario: a lost myth is recovered, or mutual explanation of one fragment by another is achieved, or links are established between an ancient myth in one region and a corresponding ritual in another. All these include elements that have so far remained unexplainable.[65] The successful comparison of such items can lead to substantial "filling in" of the initial reconstruction of Laurasian myth.

Immediate benefits include the inherent reevaluation of certain aspects of a particular mythology that might otherwise seem to be of no importance or might appear as quaint local developments. Upon the discovery of some corresponding items in other parts of Laurasia, they may even assume a dominant role in the reconstruction. Notable are such isolated terms as the epithet *arm-strong* in Vedic and Japanese myth (§3.5.1) and the "weeping" Father Heaven and Mother Earth in Vedic and Maori myth (§3.3). In sum, the evaluation of the various bits and pieces of local myth will always be enhanced. Conversely, this will add to the extent and quality of the reconstruction.

***

Once the basic outline of Laurasian mythology has been established (see §2.5) we can turn around and make use of the model and try to fit in the isolated items mentioned above as well as take account of developments in the individual mythology of a given population. In doing so, one can, so to speak, move "up and down" the reconstructed family tree, informing local myths by the reconstructed Laurasian one and informing the Laurasian one with elements of the local ones.

***

Finally, obvious gaps in the reconstruction that occur due to the attrition of transmitted materials over time (just as in linguistics) may be filled in by informed guesses based on *internal reconstruction*. For example, if we establish the deities Father Heaven and Mother Earth for Proto-Indo-European mythology, then they are expected to turn up, say, in oldest Vedic myth. However, we find only Father Heaven and "the (female) broad one," that is, Earth. Reconstruction of the deity "Mother Earth" is required, and she has indeed recently been found in the Ṛgveda (1.89.4, 1.164.33, 1.191.6, 5.42.16, 5.43.15, 6.72.2, 8.103.2, 10.62.2, 10.70.5)[66] and in a neglected early post-Ṛgvedic text, the Khila, that provides a welcome list of Ṛgvedic mythological topics.

In the next sections, the individual steps undertaken in historical comparative mythology will be discussed in some detail.

§2.2.1. Similarities

First, thus, the obvious similarities between the motifs and myths found in many mythologies are assembled.[67] This is the one area of comparative mythology that has been studied well, but it has also led to numerous, often mutually exclusive claims. A typical case is the Oedipus myth, dealt with by many specialists, including Lévi-Strauss.[68] Other topics include the prominent motif of the hero or the flood myth,[69] which has produced a veritable deluge of publications, most of which overlook its quasi-worldwide distribution.[70] However, once closer attention is paid to the actual distribution of such similarities, it will be recognized that they are *not* evenly spread worldwide,[71] and important conclusions will have to be drawn from this distribution.[72]

The initial collection and comparison of certain mythological motifs allow us to establish a number of obvious similarities, including, among others, such widespread and well-known myths as those of

- the origin of the universe and our world;[73]
- the several generations of deities;
- the creation of light;[74]
- the killing of the dragon (or of a similar monster);
- the emergence of humans, along with their faults;
- the involvement of the gods in human affairs;
- a Great Flood and the reemergence of humans;[75]
- an age of semidivine heroes, often overlapping with
- the origins of local shamans or the later "noble" lineages and, as such, of local human "history"; and
- a violent end to our present world.[76]

In addition, we can isolate many seemingly disparate topics, such as the origin of death and the recovery and revival of a departed wife (or other relative) from the netherworld,[77] the theft of primordial fire for the gods and/or humans, the emergence of shaman-like persons, the first institution of rituals and sacrifice, the origin of sacred drink, and the very establishment of human society, including mutual exchanges, agreements, marriage, and so on.

§2.2.2. Regular correspondences and establishment of a unified narrative scheme

The gathering of these and other topics, mythemes, and motifs leads to the insight that they are not only common to the mythologies investigated but also more or less arranged in a particular order, often very similar to the one just given above (§2.2.1). Their sequence is one of consecutive, gradually progressing mythical time, which takes shape as a kind of "mythical history."[78]

There is a first beginning, followed by a "logical progression" of most of the events listed above. For example, one cannot expect the flood to take place before humans have behaved in a way not pleasing to the gods, whether this occurs in Hawai'i, in Vedic India, or in the Hebrew Bible. And the killing of the dragon clearly must take place after the emergence of the first sexually distinguished deities (usually, Heaven and Earth), simply because the dragon is one of their descendants. Frequently, but not universally so, this "historical" progression comes to a predictable end,[79] with the destruction of our (current) world.

In other words, the initial collection and subsequent linear arrangement of motifs result in a "history" of the world, the gods, humans, and individual bands, tribes, or peoples. The underlying "historical" framework entails that mythology (encompassing the individual items mentioned here) is characterized by an *inherent narrational scheme* that records, in succession, all events from the creation to the end of the world.

In other words, the scheme has a recognizable pattern, it follows a *red thread*, it has a distinct *story line*.[80] Even if we were to assume that Maya priests, Japanese courtiers, or Greek poets individually constructed this framework, the evidence all over Laurasia (§3) is too strong to sustain independent origination: they must have built on already-present story line materials that they transformed into the existent literary forms.

Individual chapters of the story line aggregate can be told separately,[81] as the occasion arises: for example, the tale of the theft of fire or of killing the dragon, which appears independently in hero tales of various cultures (such as St. George and the Dragon) or even turns up as a folktale.[82] But the chapters normally are part and parcel of complete sets of mythologies, such as the Japanese Kojiki, Hesiod's *Theogony*, the Icelandic Edda, the Mesopotamian Enuma Elish, the Maya Popol Vuh, and the large oral Dayak or Hopi corpus, where they appear at their proper, predictable place.[83]

In sum, Laurasian mythology, reconstructed along these lines, represents *our oldest complex story*. It is a *novel* of the creation, growth, and destruction of the world, of divine and human evolution and decay, from birth to death, from creation to destruction. It is this particular narrational device that unifies the many individual motifs and presents listeners with a comprehensive and intelligible view of the world, an ancient *Weltanschauung*. Laurasian mythology is, like others, ideology in narrative form.[84] According to this worldview, the universe is ultimately regarded as a living body, not surprisingly in analogy to the human one: it is born, grows, and finally dies (see §2.5, §3, §8). Human analogies play a great role in ancient and modern correlative thought: animals, trees, rocks, and so on are viewed as similar to humans and are attributed human characteristics, feelings, thought, and speech (such as the indistinct speech of mountains and trees in Susa.no Wo's story in the Kojiki 1.14, Nihon Shoki 1.29).[85]

Before entering into the wider ramifications and effects of the narrational scheme and its applications, such as the establishment of a pedigree of mythologies (see §2.2.5, 2.3), a comprehensive look at several details of the method employed is advisable.

§2.2.3. Oldest texts to be used

In establishing the wide-ranging correspondences and, ultimately, the outline of the Laurasian scheme, we must rely on all materials at our disposal. Their range includes the oldest recorded versions, beginning at c. 3000 BCE in Egypt and Mesopotamia, mid-second-millennium Hittite Anatolia, Vedic India, and China, as well as, significantly later, medieval Europe, Japan, and Mayan Mesoamerica; but we must also include texts that were only recently recorded with populations that do not have a written tradition,[86] such as the Dayak, with their c. 15,000 pages of oral texts. Initially, however, it is best to rely on the oldest texts available in each region.

For Eurasian myths this is possible from a fairly early time onward. As mentioned, the earliest materials directly attested in writing are found in ancient Egyptian pyramid texts and the Mesopotamian texts of the Sumerians, from around c. 3000 BCE onward. They are amplified by some slightly later Near Eastern texts (Hurrite, Hittite, Ugaritic, Eblaic, Hebrew, etc.) that are recorded from c. 1600 BCE onward and belong to various peoples speaking a host of often unrelated languages. These early testimonies are further expanded by early Indian and Iranian initially oral texts (Veda, Avesta) from c. 1200 BCE onward. At the other end of Eurasia, early Chinese texts (tortoise shell inscriptions) set in, tentatively, around 1200 BCE as well. However, the earliest American texts (of the Maya, Mixtec, Aztec, Inca) are much later (mid–second millennium), though the decipherment of the Maya script and recently found paintings now allow us to place some isolated elements of Maya myth hundreds of years earlier.

***

The reason for using the oldest and geographically widespread texts available for a particular civilization is as simple as it is obvious. We can hope, first, that in this way we do not rely on materials "contaminated" by medieval and modern developments.

To take the example of India: if we were only to study the extensive medieval mythology of the Purāṇas (c. 320 CE onward) or of the slightly older epics that apparently were first assembled about 100 BCE and were finally redacted around c. 500 CE, we would arrive at a picture of early Indian mythology that is completely different from that presented by the multitude of the extremely well-preserved oral Vedic texts (c. 1200–500 BCE). Early Vedic mythology is still largely recognizable as Indo-European, but even epic mythology has been fundamentally restructured, and the Purāṇic version has been further developed and is basically close to what we hear and see in India today. There are, thus, at least three successive and widely different forms and layers of attested Indian mythology.

Since we are interested in the older versions of Eurasian myth and aim at establishing their Laurasian predecessor, it is therefore prudent to begin with the oldest available versions. The process is similar in other cultures: many layers of text accretion can be found in the 3,000 years of attested Egyptian and Mesopotamian history.[87]

It must be observed, however, that these "frozen" accounts of early mythologies frequently are locally or even politically motivated versions that have gained prominence due to their very recording. They must be compared with other versions, if available. For example, in ancient Egypt, we have four major successive mythologies that are tied to the capitals of the period during which they were codified. The common ground and "original" version of ancient Egyptian mythology can only be ascertained by their comparison. Obviously, it would be a mistake just to use the oldest attested Egyptian version. Nevertheless, due to its relative age, it gains a certain prominent position against which the three later ones can be evaluated. Similarly, Sumerian, Akkadian, and later versions must be compared and evaluated to reach a common Mesopotamian mythology. The case of Japan, with many different versions of its eighth-century mythology recorded in the Kojiki and Nihon Shoki, is similar. Again, Greek mythology appears in an early but very fragmentary Mycenaean form and then in Homer's epics, Hesiod's "chronological" rendering in the *Theogony*, and many local variations.[88] The major figures and motifs, however, are the same.

These examples alone indicate that local mythologies are not as stable as their earliest written version may let us assume. F. Barth has shown how much the orally transmitted mythology of the Ok,[89] a recently contacted tribal population in the central New Guinea highlands, has changed in the various villages involved. However, just as the written Egyptian, Mesopotamian, Japanese, or Greek sources indicate multiple versions of local mythology but also many major underlying common traits, so does Ok mythology (see §2.6). In a first comparison of similar mythemes, myths, and strings of myths it would be a mistake to use the argument of local "instability" against the employment of the earliest attested versions.

The small oral, illiterate cultures of Laurasia must not be neglected. Detailed investigations such as that of the myth of the hidden sun (§3.5.1) indeed show that these cultures (such as that of the isolated Kekchi Maya) can retain important archaisms (in this case, those shared by Indo-European, Central Asian, and Japanese mythologies). Obviously, the very *isolation* of these motifs speaks to the survival of archaic traditions, as, for example, with the Kekchi of Mesoamerica,[90] who were surrounded by the literate culture of the Maya. These traditions could be altered by later, agriculturally and technologically more advanced societies, such as the major Maya groups. To be prudent, we have to take into account *all* geographically dispersed versions of a motif or myth and balance them against our oldest sources.

A second reason for using the oldest preserved texts is that they may still be comparatively little affected by the omnipresent local substrates: these reflect the beliefs of the population(s) that lived in the area before a particular population entered that brought in a (sub)type of Laurasian mythology. Cases in point are ancient Greece, India, and Japan (see below, §2.3). The earliest Indian text, the Ṛgveda, is still largely free of the (later) typical Hindu deities and myths, and it is much closer to its Old Iranian counterpart (Avesta) as well as other ancient Indo-European texts. Conversely, the gradual upscale movement into prominence of local substrate mythology in later texts can be used—with caution—to reconstruct the lost mythology of, in the present case, pre-Ṛgvedic India.

Third, even the form of the myths available in the oldest written texts necessarily represents already *local* forms, as writing goes back only to c. 3000 BCE while Proto-Laurasian mythology is several tens of thousands of years older. To arrive at the latter necessarily involves employing the method of careful, step-wise reconstruction (§2.3), starting out from the oldest versions locally available. This is carried out by reconstructing the common mythology of a particular language family, say, Indo-European, and comparing it to other reconstructed ones, always while taking into account local and regional developments (§2.3).

Some objections

An objection could be that even these oldest recorded texts of humankind are simply not old enough to reconstruct the situation of late Paleolithic mythology at 40,000–60,000 years ago. In other words, this concerns the level of reliability that can be assigned to the reconstruction of very ancient prehistoric myths based on much later written (and still later, only orally transmitted) texts.

Theoretically, the relative stability of myths that we find in written sources, such as those enumerated above, may provide an unrealistic idea about the stability of myths in prehistoric eras, especially among migrating peoples living in a succession of radically different environments. However, the stability of Laurasian mythology and its story line is evident in cultures from the polar regions to the tropical jungle, while Gondwana mythologies have their own constancy, from Africa to Australia.

This basic stability is evident even if we take into account that a lot of local variation may occur, within a small territory, such as that of certain Papua tribes studied by F. Barth. However, just as Egyptian, Greek, and Japanese myths appear in a large variety of forms, they still have their own common, culture-specific central themes and motifs. The same is true for Barth's Ok culture; variations are visible just on the surface, so to speak, while the underlying mythology remains largely the same for all variations. This situation applies to literate as well as to oral societies, as the examples mentioned above indicate. Though literate societies may have a written dominant form of a particular myth or sequences of myths, the various derived local forms persist.

The very possibility of a Gondwana and Laurasian mythology (detailed in §3 and §5) should be indication enough that some of their *patterns* have not changed much over tens of thousands of years, in spite of all local innovation. For example, the Lakota (Sioux) have incorporated, over the past thousand years after leaving their eastern agricultural habitat, the buffalo and finally the horse in their myths, and their mythology is close to that of their neighbors. And the Saami (Lapp) in northern Scandinavia and the Ainu at the other end of Eurasia both have preserved the Stone Age bear cult (§7.1.2), irrespective of local developments and general cultural surroundings. Finally, the mythology of the three Abrahamic religions retains the old Laurasian structure from beginning to end, even though the idea of a single supreme deity has been introduced—obviously from Zoroastrian Iran—only around the mid–first millennium BCE (§7.2, §8).

In sum, it is not correct to assume that the myths of nonliterate societies (like those Barth studied) that developed no complex mnemonic methods (as in ancient Indian Vedic society) changed more quickly than those of literate ones. Individual change may be driven by many factors, such as influences from important cultural centers nearby (§2.3); however, the basic features have remained, due to path dependency.

Examples of extreme conservatism appear both in the Laurasian mythologies from Iceland to Tierra del Fuego (§3) and in the Gondwana mythologies from Guinea to Tasmania (§5), both preserving basic features of their respective original forms and content: the Laurasian story line and its myths, such as original creation from chaos or darkness, the creation of sunlight, and human descent from a solar deity; and the Gondwana area, with myths about human descent from a distant *deus otiosus* and of the Great Flood due to the bleeding of a wound. In turn, both being descendants of the proposed Pan-Gaean mythology of the African Eve (§6), they retain certain features of this early mythology, including the Great Flood and trickster figures that bring human culture.

Not surprisingly, it is only at this very early level that truly universal, pan-human features apply. The rest is due, in the first place, to path dependency;[91] only secondarily to migration and the immigration of others, and to some extent to later regional diffusion (§2.5.3–4); and third, but only in a surprisingly minor way, to societal change (§§7–8).

***

A second objection against the reliability of the comparisons may be based on the relatively late date of the myths collected from nonliterary societies. Especially in the case of Gondwana myths, we have only comparatively late, often just contemporary materials collected by current anthropologists. The oldest accounts of the religion and mythology of sub-Saharan Africa go back no further than the Portuguese explorers on the West African shores at the end of the 15th century (and some Arab travelers to Timbuktu). The situation is similar for New Guinea and Australia. Many accounts are those of missionaries who saw the world through their particular Christian lens. Their reliability thus can be doubted. However, these drawbacks can be overcome by more, wide-ranging comparisons. Just as indicated below in the case of the Hawai'ian myths about the creation of humans (§3.7), some versions will show clear Christian overtones while others remain free of them. The same is true for individual motifs as such. Suspected direct or indirect introduction of motifs by Muslim or Christian missionaries in Africa will stick out like the proverbial sore thumb, just as in the Hawai'ian case, if neighboring, related mythologies do not have that motif and if it is absent from the rest of the area.

For example, the "biblical" mytheme of the building of a tower is limited to an area along the Zambezi (and thus perhaps due to Portuguese influence or rather that of the Lemba tribe in Zimbabwe, who seem to have Jewish ancestry);[92] it stretches farther west into the southern Congo as well as into Tanzania and western Uganda. In a related form, with the *pande/lungu* designs indicating chieftainship,[93] it even is found in the neighboring, clearly non-African, Austronesian traditions of western Madagascar.[94] Clearly, the motif is isolated, and its occurrence in Africa must be explained. By such wider-ranging comparisons, the objection based on late attestation can be overcome, even involving other Gondwana areas.[95]

***

These cases point to the practical procedure and outcome: we must take into account both the most ancient texts (as to avoid later contamination) and orally transmitted texts, especially those that are found in isolated nooks and corners of Laurasia or Gondwanaland. In addition, there also is the method of subsequent reconstruction of increasingly earlier stages, to be employed in addition to the mutual comparison of the very few oldest texts (Egypt, Mesopotamia, India, China, etc.). Both taken together yield considerable insight into the state of development of Laurasian mythology at c. 3000–1200 BCE and then, through subsequent reconstruction, of much earlier periods and ultimately back to the "African Eve" of the geneticists. Such reconstructions have to follow the cladistic (family tree) model described above (§2.2).

　For example, some of our oldest, though admittedly reconstructed materials are based on the comparison of the various Indo-European mythologies that are recorded by Homer and Hesiod,[96] in some Hittite records, in the Avesta and Veda, in the Edda, and so on. Common Indo-European mythology (with items such as "Father Heaven") may go back as far as 3000–4000 BCE.[97] This is the approximate time period when an Indo-European-speaking population first developed along with their own typical view of the world—or, to put it differently, when the Indo-Europeans split off from other old, postglacial Eurasian groups, such as those speaking Uralic or Caucasian languages.

　The latter ancient populations and many others are now perceived by some linguists as having spoken *Nostratic* languages.[98] In the opinion of researchers such as Illich-Svitych, their languages all go back to a common ancestor, Nostratic, "our [language]" (§4.1). Its descendants include the Indo-European, Uralic (Finno-Ugrian etc.), Dravidian, Altaic, Kartvelian (Georgian etc., in the Caucasus), and Afro-Asiatic (or "Hamito-Semitic" etc.) language families. Nostratic languages thus cover most of Europe, Iran and India, and North and Northeast Asia, as well as North and much of East Africa. The existence of their ancestor, Proto-Nostratic, at more than 12,000 years ago,[99] may be regarded as highly likely.[100] Therefore, some of our linguistic reconstructions in individual language families, such as Indo-European, may now be further backdated by many thousands of years,[101] and the (few) religious items reconstructed so far for Nostratic allow us a first glimpse into the mythology of those distant Stone Age times.

　Examples include words for spirit, wolf/dog,[102] fire, and water. The words for fire and water are particularly interesting, as Indo-European posits the "elements" fire and water, which have neuter gender (Greek *pūr*, Hittite *peḫur*, German *das Feuer*; Greek *hudōr*, Hittite *watar*, German *das Wasser*).[103] Indo-European distinguishes them from their deities, which are of male and female gender, respectively (Sanskrit *Agni*, Latin *ignis*, Lithuanian *ugnis*, Old Church Slavic *ogn'*; Sanskrit *Āp[aḥ]*, Tocharian *āp*, Old Prussian *ape*, Latin *aqua*, German river names: Ache, Aa, etc.). The same male/female distinction is made in some Altaic languages, which, however, do not have grammatical gender.[104]

　However, Nostratic is a field that still is in its infancy as far as such content-based comparisons are concerned.[105] Therefore, not much of its *structured* mythology could be reconstructed so far, when compared with what we could establish for Indo-European (Father Heaven/Mother Earth, Sons of Heaven, Dawn, primordial incest, etc.) or even for Altaic (Heaven/Earth, Fire, etc.).

　The comparison of the early records of other diverse early linguistic groups or of the reconstructions of their mythologies would yield important insights into the older form of Eurasian myth. These languages include Chinese, Sumerian, Elamite, Hattic/Hurrite (North Caucasian), Semitic (Akkadian, Ugaritic, Eblaic, Phoenician, Hebrew), Afro-Asiatic (Berber, Egyptian, Semitic), and some Amerindian languages such as Maya and Aztec.

To achieve reasonable completeness, however, the oldest recorded texts from more regions and language families have to be added, even when they stem only from the first or second millennium CE. From Nostratic, they include those of Old Tamil (Sangam texts of South India), Old Turkic (Orkhon inscriptions), Old Japanese (Kojiki, Nihon Shoki), Koguryo, Korean (traditional history, in Samguk Yusa),[106] Mongolian (Secret History), South Arabian (early inscriptions), Old Slavic (Igor's Tale), Baltic (missionary records, Latvian Dainas), Germanic (Edda, Beowulf, etc.), Celtic (Old Irish and Welsh epics, Gallic inscriptions), and Italic (Roman annals, Umbrian inscriptions). Those outside Nostratic include Tibetan (early inscriptions and Dung Huang texts), Cambodian (early inscriptions), Vietnamese (traditional history), Indonesian (Dayak in Borneo [with some 15,000 pages of unrecorded texts][107] Toraja in Sulawesi, etc.), and Polynesian (genealogies, the Hawai'ian Kumulipo, Maori texts). Not all of these data, especially from the later versions, could be made use of in this book.

***

Importantly, the early (medieval) texts from Meso- and South America can significantly aid in reconstructing the original Laurasian mythology. They include Aztec, Mixtec, Olmec, Maya, and Inca texts that were written down only in the mid–second millennium CE and, unfortunately, often merely in Spanish translation. However, these mythologies are very distant in place and time from the Eurasian ones. They have long been isolated from Eurasia, after the initial immigration from northeastern Siberia, for at least some 11,000 years.[108] Therefore, following the typical pattern also observed in comparative linguistics, these isolated members of the family have preserved many items that are lost in Eurasia or that were superimposed by later developments (see §2.2.4). Examples include the myth of the hidden sun (§3.5.1), the Orpheus myth, shooting down the Sun, the various Amerindian forms of shamanism (§7.1), and the "aberrant" forms of the myth of the Four Ages (§2.5.2).

Obviously, in addition to the oldest written myths, all other available individual Laurasian mythologies, distant in time and space from those just mentioned, must be compared as well. They range from those documented only over the past two centuries in parts of Africa, South Asia, Siberia, Southeast Asia, and Polynesia to those of the Americas: from the Inuit (Eskimo) and Athapascans in the north to the now extinct Neolithic inhabitants of Tierra del Fuego in the extreme south.

The date of Amerindian immigration, now put at c. 20,000 BCE (and thus at a date similar to Nostratic) allows wide-ranging comparisons. They lead back into the Middle Paleolithic and to the beliefs of early Crô Magnon/*Homo sapiens sapiens* humans, which will help us to understand how many of our common concepts are rooted in very old customs and beliefs.

§2.2.4. Geographically dispersed items

Apart from achieving the desired time depth, the comparisons of widely distant mythologies (as, for example, those of Polynesia, ancient Israel, and Scandinavia or of the Americas and the ancient Near East) are especially useful, as premodern contact can virtually be excluded in such circumstances.[109] In the case of Polynesia, such topics may be taken up as the flood (overturning of Mataaho), the fixing of the sun at a certain position in the sky (Maui, perpetual solstice as seen in Joshua), and the role of a reptilian creature (Mo'o, Mo'opelo) at the time of the "mistake" of the "fallen chief" (Kumu-Honua, the biblical Adam), taking place in mythical Savaiki (Hawai'i) at the world tree or at the tabooed breadfruit tree (Ulu-Kapua-a-Kane, Yggdrasil, etc.; cf. Job's ladder). A detailed investigation of their constituent mythemes and motifs, their role, and their relative narrative positions in the tales of the mythological persons involved has to follow.

When comparing, for example, Scandinavian, Greek, Hebrew, Japanese, and Polynesian myths, it is obvious that there has not been any contact between these groups and their myths until the coming of the Europeans to Polynesia a few centuries ago. Furthermore, we now know that the Polynesians moved out from their intermediate,[110] mythical "homeland," Savaiki, in Vanuatu/Fiji—we still have derivative names such as the island Sava'i in nearby Samoa and, of course, Hawai'i. This took place already by 1200/1000 BCE and is seen in the distinctive Lapita archaeological culture.[111] The Polynesians then spread over the whole Pacific, up to New Zealand, Easter Island, and Hawai'i.[112] Their mythologies, just like their languages, still are closely related. Those traits in their mythology that they share, for example, with Japanese mythology (such as dragging up an island with a hook, several asexual stages in earliest creation), or with Laurasian mythology in general (Father Heaven/Mother Earth, their separation, etc.), must have been *inherited*. Yet, even a long time before 1200 BCE, there had not been any direct sustained contact with people living near to or between Polynesia and Japan, such as the Southeast Asians or Chinese; significantly these populations do not share these myths in the form preserved in Polynesia. Other items that the Polynesians share with the Hebrew Bible or with Scandinavian myth, in various divergent forms, must belong to the common Eurasian stock of myths. Even if a prima facie suspicious motif such as the reptile and the "mistake of fallen chief at the [world] tree" is perhaps not found anywhere else outside the Bible and once in West Africa,[113] the motif is widely spread in Polynesia and firmly embedded in local myth and poetry,[114] so that it is not likely to have been taken over from 18th- and 19th-century missionaries (see further discussion below, §3.5.2). Indeed, an antecedent is found with a related Austronesian people, the Dayak of Borneo, who live fairly close to the area from which the Polynesians spread eastward.[115] As has been pointed out (§2.2), it is the occurrence of such isolates that frequently presents us with a shortcut in the reconstruction of Laurasian mythology.

***

As has briefly been indicated initially (§1), the accumulation of such similarities leads to the hypothesis of a common source of these myths. This source is not to be sought in ancient Babylonia or Egypt, as some thought at the beginning of the 20th century, due to the then still very limited archaeological background information. According to diffusionists like Frobenius or Baumann, these early civilizations produced much of global mythology and culture. Instead, we have to look for a Eurasian source in an unknown area of Stone Age times.[116]

The common stock of Laurasian mythology must have existed well *before* any of the early written evidence from Egyptian, Mesopotamian, or Chinese sources.[117] Because of the congruence between Amerindian and Eurasian mythemes, myths, and whole mythologies, it must even be older than the Amerindian immigration, put at c. 20,000 BCE.[118] For example, many aspects of the myths concerning the first mortals, the first evil deed, and the improper behavior of humans are very similar in ancient Indian, Iranian, Hebrew, Polynesian, Japanese, and Amerindian myths; they mostly result in punishment such as by a flood.

***

However, the Laurasian mythological scheme (as explained in §1.4 and in more detail in §2) should be regarded as a *working hypothesis* that is to be subjected to serious, severe countercheck. The scenario achieved through this theory should be compared with the portrait of early humanity that results from other approaches (§4) and then be compared with the remaining myth families of the world (§§5–6).

§2.2.5. Reconstruction of the Laurasian common story line and individual myths

After comparing many myths across Laurasia, based on the oldest and/or geographically most distant versions, and listing them in the order of the reconstructed Laurasian story line, we arrive at their probable initial stage, the *ur*-form of Laurasian mythology. Its story line includes some 15 major mythological themes, as briefly hinted at (§2.2.1), from creation to the destruction of the world. This inventory is arrived at by a comprehensive listing of the most important "ingredients" of the major mythologies involved, from Iceland to Tierra del Fuego. .

Some major myths and the story line

These motifs may slightly vary in number or order from one individual mythology to another, but they are present, as a set, in the Laurasian mythologies studied. See Table 2.2.

Laurasian form of major myths

Proceeding further to individual myths, the *original Laurasian form* of each particular myths is to be established first. We must then discuss the major stories, mythemes, and motifs that deviate, say, in Greek, Egyptian, Indian, Chinese, Japanese, Maya, and Inca mythology. To be comprehensive and so as not to overlook less "privileged" versions, *all local variants* of a myth, now both ancient and modern, have to be compared, as the "official" versions sometimes obscure ancient traits. Subsequently, we must closely compare such parallel versions in various Laurasian mythologies in order to find out any (expected and probable) regional and local influences on the version studied (details in §3).

For example, Japanese mythology often seems to be much closer to Indian, Greek, or Germanic mythology than to Chinese mythology, except in the rare cases where early Japan has directly taken over some myths and concepts from China,[119] such as the Tanabata myth,[120] the polestar, and Buddhist ideas. In some other cases, however, Japanese mythology is closer to Malayo-Polynesian, Southeast Asian, Central Asian (Altaic), and again, Indo-European mythology. Therefore, the investigation of Japanese mythology must focus, as the case may be, on a closer comparison of Vedic Indian and Japanese mythology (the hidden sun; §3.5.1), or on that of Japanese and Polynesian mythology (dragging up islands), or again, on that of Japanese and East Asian mythology (the story of the Inaba Hare, formerly thought to have been derived from India).[121] The same

TABLE 2.2. *A provisional list of major mythemes in Laurasian mythology*

1	primordial waters/chaos/'nonbeing'
2	primordial egg / giant
3	primordial hill or island
4	(Father) Heaven/(Mother) Earth and their children (4 or 5 generations / ages)
5	heaven is pushed up (and origin of Milky Way)
6	the hidden sun light revealed
7	current gods defeat or kill their predecessors
8	killing the 'dragon' (and use of heavenly drink), fertilization of the earth
9	Sun deity is the father of humans (or just of 'chieftains')
10	first humans and first evil deeds (often, still by a demi-god), origin of death / the flood
11	heroes and nymphs
12	bringing of culture : fire / food / culture by a culture hero or shaman; rituals; spread of humans / emergence of local nobility / local history begins
14	final destruction of humans, the world (and) the gods (variant of the Four Ages theme)
15	(a new heaven and a new earth)

applies to the constituent parts of all other local mythologies, whether those of Iceland (Edda), Greece (Hesiod's *Theogony*), Mesopotamia (Enuma Elish), or Mexico (Popol Vuh).

In proceeding with this kind of investigation, we constantly have to move "up" and "down" the provisionally established Laurasian pedigree, the cladistic family tree of Laurasian mythology. This is done in order to understand the countless variations it has undergone and the various forms that it has taken during its spread and development, both regionally and locally.

***

In sum, once the story line, structure, and main outline of Laurasian myth have been determined, the results can be compared with what we actually encounter in the various versions belonging to the many populations compared. It will then appear that the individual forms in major myth traditions (Egyptian, Mesopotamian, Indian, Chinese, Mesoamerican, etc.) differ to some degree from the established, *reconstructed* Proto-Laurasian myths and story line. The obvious reason is the long time span that intervened between the original Laurasian composition, probably around c. 40,000 BCE after the end of an earlier ice age (§2.2.4, 2.5.2; §7.2), and the written form in which the individual texts have come down to us, from c. 3000 BCE onward (§2.2.3). When including reconstructed forms, such as the Indo-European linguistic ones, their mythological "texts" are earlier merely by some 1,000–2,000 years, and in their entirely vague Nostratic forms by some 7,000–9,000 years. It its therefore important to take a closer look at the post-40-kya, regional and subregional variations of Laurasian myth that have shaped local mythologies.

■ §2.3. ENHANCING THE RECONSTRUCTION: LOCAL, REGIONAL, MACRO-REGIONAL, AND SUBCONTINENTAL VARIATIONS

Macro-regional variations

First, local forms of Laurasian myths are in part due to the *several layers* that intervened between Proto-Laurasian mythology at c. 40,000 BCE, its reconstructed American version at c. 20,000 BCE, and its early local manifestations after c. 3000 BCE. The earliest written codifications consist of the Mesopotamian Enuma Elish, the (four major) Egyptian cosmogonies, the oral but—due to extremely faithful oral transmission—virtually "tape-recorded" Vedic corpus, the Greek *Theogony* of Hesiod, the Japanese Kojiki, the Quiché Mayan Popol Vuh, the Hawai'ian Kumulipo, and not to forget, the Torah, the Hebrew Bible. Frequently, it appears that one of the intervening layers, which cover some

35,000 years, includes a number of myths that seem to be extraneous to the local mythology. On further investigation they soon turn out to be thematically, historically, and linguistically unrelated to the local one in question.

A typical case is the ancient Near Eastern conglomerate, or "myth family,"[122] that connects *several* aspects of the Mesopotamian, Hurrite, Hittite, Ugaritic, Eblaic, Hebrew, Phoenician, and Greek mythologies.[123] Other mythology macro-regions include the mythologies of ancient East Asia (China, Korea, Japan), of ancient Central Asia (to be discussed in §3), and of Mesoamerica (Olmec, Toltec, Pueblo, Aztec, Maya).

Obviously, because of their intermediate position between Proto-Laurasian and local mythologies, such regional or subcontinental complexes will differ in certain specific ways both from the reconstructed Laurasian scheme and from its individual written local manifestations. Macro-regional features must constantly be considered when evaluating a particular local mythology, say, that of ancient Japan or Greece. Their influence is clearly visible, as a local myth does not correspond to the form the reconstructed ancestors of Japanese or Greek mythology and so on would predict.

Comparing linguistic procedure again, intrusions into Indo-European mythology correspond, in the case of Greece, to the intrusion of locally preexisting loanwords into Old Greek texts. Just as these words do not fit the appearance of standard Greek words, neither do Near Eastern myths in the context of inherited Indo-European myths fit in early Greek mythology, for example, the myth of killing one's divine father by castration.

We can then proceed in several successive ways. Taking note of the macro-regional varieties and comparing them with reconstructed Proto-Laurasian mythology, several intermediate stages intervening between local and Laurasian myths can eventually be identified. If we follow, for argument's sake, standard but controversial "Long-Range" linguistic comparison,[124] we might call these intermediate stages Nostratic, Macro-Caucasian, Dene-Caucasian, Sino-Tibetan, Austric, and Amerindian. A *hypothetical* model for the ancient Near Eastern macro-regional mythologies might then look like the one given in Table 2.3.

Against the main outline and geographical extent of Laurasian mythology, such secondary macro-regional clusters stand out like the proverbial sore thumb, as they frequently overarch several distinct linguistic and cultural units in the geographical area they share.[125] The spread of myths belonging to such macro-regional clusters may be compared with the spread of Christianity all across the Roman Empire or of Buddhism across South Asia, before both religions and their mythologies expanded even farther.

These macro-regional complexes, their mutual interrelations, and their mutual secondary influences upon each other cover areas of considerable extent, such as the ancient Near East (including Anatolia and Greece); or Egypt, including Nubia and surrounding areas; or East Asia, or Mesoamerica.

TABLE 2.3. *Some macro-regions within Laurasian Mythology*

```
*Laurasian mythology


*Nostratic level            *Dene-Caucasian          *Amerind.
   |        \                    |                      |     |
*Indo -Eur. *Afro-Asiatic,   *Macro-Caucasian, Na-Dene |     |
             etc.                 |                     ▼     |
                             *North Caucasian         *Uto-  (others)
                                                       Aztec |
                                 (Hurrite)                   |
   |            ...               |            ...     ...    |
...              ...              ▼ ...        ...      |     ▼
   |              |          [Near Eastern macro-region]   [Pueblo/Aztec/Maya
   |             ╱▐  ▐            ▐          ▐              macro-region]
   |          ╱ ▐  ▐            ▐          ▐  ▐
   |      ▼  ╱Hittite,  Hurrite, Levant, etc., Mesopotamian,etc.
   ▼      ╱                              |
Greek  mythology                  Sumerian, Akkadian mythology
   |                                      |
local Greek variants              local Mesopotamian variants
(Attica, Crete, Arcadia, etc.).
```

Among them, the correspondences and differences between Eurasian and Mesoamerican myths are methodologically very significant. In spite of regional and local variations, the many shared features of both macro-regions indicate the existence of the early Laurasian myth complex at or before c. 20,000 BCE (based on the date of immigration into the Americas). Notwithstanding local developments, the Amerindian macro-region serves to countercheck the state of development of Laurasian myth in early Eurasia before that date. For example, the Vala/Iwato cave myth can be found in at least three different regional varieties (§3.5.1), and similar features emerge for the dragon myth (§3.5.2).

After having explored such macro-regional variations and clusters (including the largest ones, the pan-Eurasian and Amerindian ones), the next stage is to set up sections of a refined Laurasian family tree that incorporates such sub-groupings as well as the myths and myth complexes that were mutually trans-ferred inside such macro-regional clusters.[126] Once established, they can obviously be *ruled out* as constituting the *original* Proto-Laurasian mythology. For example, the particular regional shape of Laurasian myth found in the Near East obviously is *not* the original Laurasian one but represents a compar-atively late development that gained prominence from around c. 3000 BCE onward due to the cultural prestige of the Fertile Crescent in the areas neigh-boring it.[127] A provisional scheme of several Laurasian mythological subre-gions appears in Table 2.4. All such macro-regional subgroupings obviously

TABLE 2.4.   *Laurasian Macro-Areas and myth complexes*

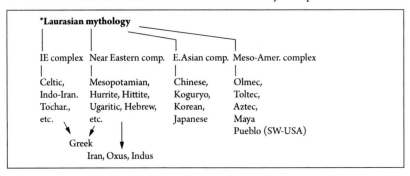

take an intermediate position between reconstructed Proto-Laurasian mythology and the individual, regional, and locally attested ones such as the Greek or Mesopotamian ones.

Moving from macro-areas up to Laurasian mythology

Second, after such macro-regional versions of Laurasian mythology have been established, the next step can be taken: a "backward" comparison of an individual macro-regional version with the Laurasian prototype. As will be seen in the discussion of Mesoamerican myth (§2.5), there is a clear distinction in the appreciation of the Four (or Five) Ages and generations of gods as found in Greece/ the Near East and in Mesoamerica. The Greek view is one of pessimism, of declining quality of the Four Ages, while the Pueblo and Mesoamerican one supposes the increasing quality of each subsequent "creation," or rather, emergence or "Sun." The Mesoamerican interpretation, separated by millennia and tens of thousands of miles from the Greek one, either may be an innovation or may represent the older Laurasian view that has been obscured in the Near Eastern version.[128]

From macro-regional to local mythologies

Third, as has been indicated (§2.2.5), we may also take the opposite step and investigate the development of Laurasian mythology "down" along the family tree to its local forms. That is, we can "descend" to the level of actually attested, individual local mythologies and investigate it by concentrating on a particular extant version (say, the Greek *Theogony* by Hesiod), exploring how far it agrees with the observed Subcontinental/macro-area type, how far it represents the reconstructed Laurasian one, and what it misses of the latter. Further, we may

TABLE 2.5. *Development of Greek mythology*

```
Laurasian mythology
 |            ↓
... ... ...   (Near Eastern influences)
 ↓            |
early Greek mythology           |
 ↓                              |
Mycenean        |               |
(1200 BCE)      ↓               |
            Ionian:            |
            Homer              |
            (~700 BCE)         |
                    \     ↓
                    Attic
                    (Hesiod's Theogony)
                    (~700 BCE)

    many local variants, rituals, festivals, etc.
```

reconstruct, by internal comparison of fragments available in the particular local (e.g., Pan-Hellenic) mythology, what the early (e.g., pre-Mycenaean) form of the local (Greek) mythology might have looked like (Table 2.5).

The procedure can be tested against early written evidence, for example, available in archaic and ancient Egypt. As is well known,[129] we have some four major variants of Egyptian myth, codified by the priests of Heliopolis, Memphis, Hermopolis, and Thebes at different stages in history. In all four cases, a local deity was propagated as the major deity for certain periods of the Egyptian kingdom. This necessarily involved reformulating and rewriting certain aspects of older pan-Egyptian mythology, reinterpreting the functions of certain other gods, merging local deities with the currently dominant one(s), and so on. A comparison of the four major variations (and of some fragments of other local traditions) will result in the reconstruction of a Pan-Egyptian mythology from which local tendencies can be clearly distinguished.

Just as is the case with Laurasian mythology in general, it is the regular correspondences among the (four) versions compared that lead to their original (e.g., Egyptian) form, and it is the subsequent comparison of this "archaic" version with local ones that clearly shows the various individual innovations that occurred in certain local centers—whether under priestly influence or merely by popular and individual shamanic rethinking.[130] As the comparable case of linguistics has shown (§2.2, §4.1), such two-way reconstruction ("up and down the family tree") is a powerful tool in establishing the original state of things but also in then explaining the local variations. In addition, the procedure allows us to reconstruct the several stages in between the attested local one and the reconstructed parent form.

Local variations

Fourth, after having defined and demarcated the influences on a local mythology from surrounding and culturally important macro-areas, their influence can be contrasted with secondary, purely local changes. For example, the Near Eastern influence on Greek myth,[131] visible in the idea of the Four Ages,[132] can be contrasted with the purely local development of the great bow shooter Apollo into a Sun deity and with further local differences found in various Greek myths, say,[133] from Attica. Such local variants will have to be taken into account and evaluated so as to define original Greek mythology, which must be *reconstructed* from such sparsely attested but quite diverse data.

Local myths and Laurasian mythology

Fifth, at this stage, the procedure can still receive additional help, difficult as it is,[134] from the constant comparison with reconstructed Proto-Laurasian mythology as such. Again, one can and must constantly proceed up and down the mythological pedigree and adduce relevant materials found at the various levels, as required.

Local mythologies and substrates

Sixth, the influence of the local substrate on the local mythology will be prominent. In the Greek case it is that of the "Pelasgian" (as Plato called it) or Aegean area, which is represented by the c. 70 percent of non-Indo-European loanwords in Greek. They include such important names as Athena (Mycenaean *atana potinija*), Apollo, and place-names in *–ss–* or *–nth–* such as Knossos and Korynthos.[135] In the so-called Pelasgian creation myth,[136] creation begins with a female deity, arisen from Chaos, who creates a great serpent, her lover, and gives birth to the world egg out of which sun, moon, the earth, and so on emerge (see below, §3.1). This is quite different from Hesiod's version and must be compared with the mythologies of other peoples, from Old Egypt to East Asia (see Table 2.6; §3).

Internal reconstruction

Seventh, after filling in details of influences from neighboring macro-regions and of local developments, including the local substrates, one can proceed with an *internal reconstruction*, say, the Greek one. This reconstruction is another step in filling the gap between the reconstructed Indo-European and Near Eastern macro-branches and the individual local mythology of the Greeks (or similarly that of the Sumerians or Hurrites; see Table 2.7).

A case in point, taken from another region, that of early India, is the fire deity, Mātariśvan. His original nature would remain rather obscure if only Indian

TABLE 2.6. *Greek mythology and influences from the Near Eastern macro-region*

Substrate and local influences on Indo-European mythology in Greece

* **Indo-European mythology**

Local substrate   ***early Greek mythology**   Near Eastern complex

Mycenean
(~1200 BCE)

Ionian
Homer
(~700 BCE)

Attic

(Hesiod's Theogony)
(~700 BCE)

various local variants, local festivals, etc.
(Attica, Arcadia, Delphi, Ionia, Crete, etc.)

mythology were consulted. While his origin as fire deity is rather unclear in Vedic literature, he gets confused and amalgamated, in the epic, with the deity of the wind, as Mātalī (Ṛgveda 10.14.3)/Mātālī; both are "cleansers": that of the earth by fire and that of the atmosphere by wind. However, the distant Japanese mythology (Kojiki) provides the necessary clue. The original Japanese fire (*hi/ho*) deity Ho-musubi grows (*musubu*) in his mother, Izanami, just like Mātariśvan grows or "swells" (*śū–/śva–*) "in his mother" (*mātari*; Ṛgveda 3.20.11). During his birth, Ho-musubi kills his mother by excessive burning and is therefore punished by his father, Izanagi, with beheading. We do not know about the fate of Mātariśvan, as his name, "(Fire) growing inside his mother," is merely an archaic and isolated fragment of Laurasian myth inside Vedic mythology. He may have

TABLE 2.7. *Greek and Near Eastern mythologies*

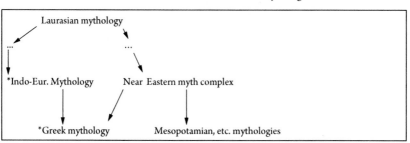

had a similar fate, possibly reflecting the myth of fire "growing" in water. The comparison of the Indian and Japanese motifs may be another case of close Proto-Indo-Iranian and Koguryo/Yamato mythology that existed in Central Asia between c. 2000 and 1000 BCE.[137] The observations in this section (§2.3) will be amplified with concrete examples in a later section (§2.5).

Further variations

It can further be noticed (and this may be tempting as possible counterargument) that quite a number of *unexplained* variations and deviations from the general Laurasian scheme can be found in the individual mythology of a particular population. A typical case is found in Egyptian myth, where Father Heaven does not lie on or arch above Mother Earth, as he does in Eurasia; in fact, the exact opposite takes place. The motif is prominently displayed on the inside of the lids of many Egyptian sarcophaguses, where Mother Earth (Tefnut) is bending over the deceased male, who lies prostrate in the coffin.[138] However, Egyptian mythology otherwise employs a large number of Laurasian themes such as Heaven/Earth, the primordial hill emerging from the ocean, the dragon fight, and so on.[139] It therefore remains unclear why it would have developed this deviation. However, the arching "Earth" is depicted against the background of a starry night sky. This seems appropriate for the situation of the deceased male who is now descending into the dark netherworld,[140] approaching the ruling that Ma'at will make about his future fate.[141]

The reversed position may be further elucidated by a comparison with Vedic myth. In daytime, the sky arches over the earth, like Father Heaven, stemmed up by Indra from the prostrate Mother Earth. But at night, the situation is reversed: Earth and the primordial hill or rock, on which she rests, have turned upside down and overarch the now prostrate Heaven as the "stone sky" of Iranian, Indian, Hawai'ian, and Pueblo myth.[142] This image is clearly reflected in the image of the world tree that grows,[143] in daytime, from the netherworld and earth upward to heaven (Germanic Yggdrasil, Irminsul), while at night it is turned upside down (Ṛgveda, Bhagavadgītā).[144] The reversed position is precisely that of the deceased (pharaoh identified with the Sun, Father Heaven) and the nighttime sky (Tefnut, Mother Earth) found on the Egyptian coffins.[145]

The prima facie divergent Egyptian motif turns out, in the end, to be a remnant of an old Laurasian mytheme, that of the inverted nighttime sky—just like the isolated idea of the fire deity in India and Japan described above. Thus, when we notice such seemingly divergent or aberrant forms, they may just be the prima facie view that will be explained as soon as we compare a wider range of the diverse Laurasian texts.

Deviations from reconstructed Laurasian mythology may also be due to, or may have been influenced by, previous local substrate populations, as has been pointed out for Greece. The Hittites of Anatolia (c. 1900/1600–900 BCE) supply a good example. Their Indo-European mythology has undergone quick admixture and change, due to the dominant influence of the original inhabitants, the Hatti people, so much that the Caucasus language, Hattic, was used as hieratic language next to Hittite. The deviations were increased by subsequent adstrate influence from their southern neighbors of the Mitanni realm of northern Iraq and northern Syria, the Hurrites, who spoke a North Caucasian language related to that of biblical Urartu and modern Chechen. Many Hittite myths, such as the emasculation of Kumarbi,[146] which was also imported into Greece as the mytheme of Kronos's cutting off the testicles of Ouranos, are in the end Hurrite and ultimately, Mesopotamian mythemes.[147]

Or we may take the case of the relatively isolated archipelago of Japan, at the easternmost rim of Asia. One may expect the influences of immigrants from outside, and they are indeed visible in the various genetic and archaeological layers that make up the present Japanese people and their culture: they are represented by the early Stone Age, Jōmon, Yayoi, Kofun, and other archaeological strata. Using the oldest version of Japanese mythology, the Kojiki and Nihon Shoki, and comparing the early account in the Chinese imperial Wei history (*Wei-Shu*,[148] post-280 CE, written 551–554; Jpn. *Gishiwajinden*), we cannot always be completely sure whether to allocate certain myths to the "true," "original" Yayoi mythology (c. 1000 BCE–400 CE) or to the intrusive Kofun mythology of the early first millennium CE[149]—that is, the form in which it must have been introduced from the mainland and transmitted all over the archipelago.[150] However, we may be fairly sure that most of the items in the Kojiki represent the interests of the nobility, especially those of the emerging imperial court, and not those of the older strata of local rice farmers and of the still older Jōmon-time hunter-gatherers and incipient food producers (who seem to have survived in certain areas).[151]

***

In some cases, however, we may suspect substrate influence, for example, in the isolated myth of the origin of food from the bodily excretions (tears, snot, urine, feces, etc.)[152] of the food goddess Ōgetsu. The agricultural content and the position of the myth within the Kojiki do not make sense as a constituent part of its narrative framework, which closely follows the Laurasian model.[153] As in many other food-producing cultures, the myth appears to be a "new" development that seeks to explain the origins of agriculturally produced food. A famous example is the Melanesian Hainuwele myth.[154] Singular myths like the Ōgetsu one are also found in the isolated and rather artificial late Vedic account (Vādhūla Sūtra)[155] of the origin of rice and barley and in the several Pueblo and Mesoamerican myths about the origin of the all-important maize (see also §7.2 on the development of mythologies from hunter-gatherer to food-producing and state societies).[156]

At the same time, by concentrating on the oldest Japanese texts (Kojiki, Nihongi), we can eliminate later, medieval changes and innovations, such as the addition of an indigenous god of war, Hachiman, who is based on a historical personality, or that of Benten, goddess of riches and of merchants, who was introduced via Buddhism only after the middle of the first millennium CE. Her role as protector of riches is a local development and very distant from her origins as the Indian goddess Sarasvatī, deity of the heavenly river (Milky Way),[157] of a river northwest of Delhi, and of speech, poetry, and learning. In short, local variations of the types discussed here may represent the many subsequent local layers that have to be peeled off, so to speak, before coming close to the original Laurasian form of the mythology in question. In some cases, however, one or several of the layers may represent something completely different, a pre-Laurasian stage (that will be taken up in detail later, §§5–6).

Summary: Method and procedure of reconstruction

As has been repeatedly stressed, the comparative method in mythology starts out from similarities found in various sets of evidence (myths). Such comparisons are normally carried out in random fashion, across space and time. They are not performed systematically or in historical fashion; in other words, the application of the *historical comparative* approach, as employed in the present book, is an entirely new method.[158]

So far, comparativists have stopped at a rather general level of comparison (whether Jungian or diffusionist), and in many cases, they have resorted to the facile omnicomparativist approach: anything in myth, anywhere and anytime, was compared with anything else. However, as has been stressed above, the historical parameter adds a significant vector to the analysis of myths and to comparative mythology in general. Just like the parameter of space (the geographical vector), it raises the level of analysis and argumentation to a *higher level* that allows a much wider vista than the "flat" atemporal one. Historical comparative mythology makes use of both time and space parameters in its procedures and analyses. It transcends the common comparative approaches of omnicomparativism and diffusionism, not to speak of the atemporal and nonspatial approach of Jungian archetypes.

Instead, historical comparative mythology proceeds from the simple observation of similarities and to the establishment of regular correspondences (such as the Laurasian story line), and to the reconstruction of the preceding "original" mythological system (i.e., Proto-Laurasian mythology).

Once this has been done, the method can be reversed, and the differences between the reconstructed ancestral ("original") protoform and its individual descendants (local myths) can be studied. Further comparisons result in establishing several layers (Near Eastern, Amerindian, etc.) between the original reconstructed *ur*-form and the individual local ones (Egyptian, Maya, etc.).

The changes involved are always characterized by individual innovations (or mutations) that are shared by the descendants of a common ancestor. Such *shared innovations*—just as in biology or linguistics—clearly distinguish the new forms from their ancestral ones (which may or may not have survived in our records, for example, Maya versus Amerindian versus Laurasian mythology). A cladistic arrangement and a "family tree" emerge.

The several successive layers of descendants of the original ancestor that give rise to further "generations" are always indicated by individually developed *innovations* ("mutations"), by which they are distinguished from the earlier ancestor generation(s). These successive layerings bridge the gap between original Proto-Laurasian mythology and its oldest written (or otherwise recorded) forms.

The procedure has been tested for some 200 years in linguistics and has also been powerfully used in the stemmatic study of handwritten manuscripts, in paleontology, and in genetics. In some cases, the missing links mediating between levels have been found, for example, the archaeopteryx in biology, mediating between reptiles and birds, or Mycenaean language between Homeric Greek and Indo-European.

In short, whether changes concern biological descendants of an original parent (mutations of a gene, plant, animal) or culturally created "children" of a "parent" text (in myths or manuscripts), the descendants of this parent are characterized by individual, *shared innovations* (mutations). Tracing them allows us to establish a family tree that leads back to the original ancestor—which is exactly what is attempted in this book.

■ §2.4. RECONSTRUCTING THE LAURASIAN MYTHOLOGICAL SYSTEM AND INHERENT PROBLEMS

As pointed out earlier, even a brief comparative listing and account of Laurasian myths (see §1.4 and immediately below) rapidly results in a large number of obvious similarities and correspondences, hinting at the identity of the underlying mythological structure. Once such close comparisons of myths and their arrangement have been carried out (details in §3), one can easily notice that complete mythologies, such as the early Indian (Vedic), Mesopotamian, Greek, Japanese, and Maya ones, have similar contents—that is, they contain individual myths with similar motifs. Further, these myths are also arranged in similar or identical order, which means that they have a common narrative structure. Just as in the linguistic simile, the Indo-European languages have a common structure, with inflected nouns and verbs arranged in sentences with a subject–verb order, all features that distinguish them from language families such as Austric, Bantu, and Amerindian. A large number of mythologies in Eurasia and the Americas (Laurasia) exhibit such common features, most prominently the narrational scheme of a *common story line.*

Structure

The items arranged by the common story line are dominated by creation myths that answer the question: how did the world and human beings originate? These accounts include, in succession, the following major steps. They begin with primordial creation or rather, emergence, and lead via four generations of deities to early semidivine heroes and to the origin of humans. They continue with the establishment of a sustained human biosphere (*oikumene*) and culture. They frequently include a violent end to our present world, sometimes with the hope for a new world rising from its remains.

The most prominent individual topics (cf. §2.2.1) include primordial waters/chaos/nonbeing/egg/giant/hill or island; Father Heaven, Mother Earth, and their children (four generations/ages); the pushing up of heaven; incest between Heaven and his daughter; revealing the light of the hidden sun; the current gods defeating their predecessors; killing the dragon; the Sun deity as the father of humans (especially of chieftains); the first humans and first evil deeds; the origin of death/the flood; heroes and nymphs; the bringing of fire/food/sacred drink and so on by a culture hero; the spread of humans and later, in actual, if legendary, history, of local noble (subsequently, royal) lineages and the beginning of local history; the final destruction of humans, the world, and the gods; and sometimes the hope for a new heaven and a new earth. Frequently, the list of common topics also includes exclusively human-related motifs such as human conception and birth; the initiation of boys (and girls); sacred speech, rituals, and shamanism; marriage and children; growing up and emancipation (hero tales); aging and death; ancestor worship; and rebirth.

The story line of Laurasian mythology

The emergence and development of the world are commonly,[159] but wrongly, called "creation" in Judeo-Christian-inspired common parlance. Emergence can be described for Laurasian mythology in some initial detail as follows. It takes place in several progressions: mostly beginning with primordial "creation" out of primordial chaos, darkness, and/or the salty ocean, via Four Ages or generations of gods, to the origin of mankind and early semidivine heroes.

Actual creation occurs in a number of forms:[160] there is the killing and dismemberment of a primordial giant, whose body parts then constitute the universe, such as his skull becoming the heaven above us (Ymir in the Edda, Puruṣa in Vedic India, Pangu in South China).[161] Or, somewhat similarly, the universe develops from a primordial egg, the upper half of its shell becoming the sky.[162] There also are the primordial salty waters,[163] from which the earth emerges as a primordial hill in Egypt and Vedic India or as brought up by an earth diver.[164] A more abstract version begins with primordial darkness (*Po* in Polynesia, Maya

Popol Vuh),[165] or with Chaos (in Greece, *Kore*; "void, negation" in Polynesia), or, most "philosophically" expressed, with primordial "nonbeing" (*asat* in the Veda, emptiness in China).

Some of these concepts of creation also appear in combination, such as in early Japan (§3.1.7) or in the 19th-century Finnish version (Kalevala 1), where the daughter of sky floats on the primordial ocean, and a duck lands on her knee and lays seven eggs, from which High Heaven, sun, moon, stars, Mother Earth, and so on develop. Which one of these several versions of creation is the oldest, how far they all can be combined (as in the Kalevala), and which ones are later, quasi-philosophical shamanic or priestly speculation will be investigated below (§3.1.7).

Emergence: A summary

In a variety of ways, the emergence of the world continues after the primeval stage that gives "birth," or rather, from which emerge the first male/female entities, Heaven and Earth. They are frequently described or depicted as a pair in primordial intercourse,[166] such as in Old Indian, Greek, and Polynesian (Maori) myth. They are the ancestors of the several generations of deities (the Greek Titans and Olympians, the Indian Asura and Deva, the Japanese Ama.tsu Kami and Kuni.tsu Kami) and ultimately, of humans.

After the universe has emerged, there is the need to firmly establish the earth and its *oikumene*. In early Indian myth, the earth, just risen from the bottom of the ocean, still is an unstable island, floating on the ocean. A demiurge, Indra, has to fix the earth (to the bottom) with mountains.[167] This deity also is the actor in the major creation myth, found from Greece and India to Japan and Hawai'i and to the Maori of New Zealand: stemming apart heaven and earth and pushing up the sky. This is typically called "prop, pole" (*toko*) in Polynesia; he is Atlas in Greece or the heroic Indra in India, who pushes up the sky with both hands.[168] Polynesian myth describes his action as necessary since the children of Heaven and Earth had no space to live in, in the darkness between the two parents. The two are thus forever parted, and Heaven now cries bitter tears (the rain; cf. Vedic *rodasī*, "heaven and earth," from *rud*, "to cry"). In Egyptian myth, the opposite is seen: the female night sky overarches a reclining male;[169] however, as pointed out (§3.2), this is the nighttime version, a reversal of the same underlying day-time concept.

After the separation of Heaven and Earth, other actions are necessary to turn the young world into a livable space (*oikumene*). First of all, light. We are perhaps most familiar with the biblical account of *fiat lux!* by which the Elohim/Yahweh created light, but the same is expressed in many other mythologies in a similar way. In the Popol Vuh of the 16th-century Quiché Mayas, primordial semidarkness hovers above the ocean, just as in the Bible. However, in Vedic India, in Iran, in the

Hindu Kush (Kafirs), and in Old Japan, the hidden light (dawn or sun), depicted in myth by the semipastoral Indo-Europeans as a reddish cow, has to be released from her primordial rock prison.[170] The myth of the release of the hidden sun is also found in many forms (release from a house, basket, etc.) elsewhere in Southeast Asia and in the Americas, from the Inuit (Eskimo) to the Amerindians of North, Central, and South America (in the conservative Grand Chaco; §3.5.1).[171]

Still, the new earth is not yet ready for living beings. It has to receive moisture, whether water or the blood of a primordial creature. In many traditions, it is the latter. The primordial gods' children, the Greek Titans, Indian Asuras, or Japanese Kuni.no Kami (gods of the earth), are depicted by their younger and victorious cousins, the Olympian gods, the Indian Devas, and the Japanese Ama.no Kami (heavenly gods), as monsters who have to be slain or at least subdued (for the time being, for a year). Most prominent in these fights is the slaying of the primordial dragon by the Great Hero, a descendant of Father Heaven. In India, it is Indra who kills the three-headed reptile, just like his Iranian "cousin" Θraētaona kills a three-headed dragon and their distant counterpart in Japan, Susa.no Wo, kills the eight-headed monster (Yamata.no Orochi). In the West we see the same: in England it is Beowulf, in the Edda it is Sigurd, and in the medieval Nibelungen Epic it is Siegfried (a theme used by Wagner for his opera) who performs this heroic feat. We may also compare Herakles's killing of the Hydra of Lerna.[172] In Egyptian myth the "dragon of the deep" (Apophis) is slain by the victorious sun when it passes underground, each night, from its western setting point toward the east, to rise again. There are even echoes as distant as recent Hawai'ian (Mo'o),[173] earliest Chinese, Navajo,[174] Old Mexican, and Maya myth.[175] In sum, it is only after the earth has been fertilized by the dragon's blood or water released by him that it can support life.

Now it is time for the humans to emerge as well. Normally, they are somatic descendants of the gods themselves, in most Laurasian mythologies those of the deity of the sun.[176] This is found from Egypt to India, Japan, and Hawai'i and farther east with the distant Mayas and Incas. In some cases, such claims of descent have, in historical times, been restricted to the ruling lineage only (Egypt, Japan, Polynesia, Incas, etc.)[177]—a development conditioned by the respective evolving societies; the topic will be investigated below (§3.8).

***

But with the first humans, evil and death enter into the world as well. Very frequently death is paradoxically attributed to the giver of life—a primordial woman—and to her curiosity (Bible,[178] but importantly, also in non-Laurasian areas such as Melanesia; §5.3.3).[179] This should tell us something about the mind-set of the (male) originators of this mytheme.[180] We must not forget that all too often we only have the male version of mythology. As female anthropologists have discovered in aboriginal Australia, each moiety of society may not know of or does not share the other's myths;[181] however, both male and female ceremonies have the same underlying mythology,[182] though male and females actors may stress different aspects and events.

Evil, or the inherent hubris of humans, is taken care of in different ways.[183] Often, a great all-devastating flood (Greece, Mesopotamia, Bible, Vedic India, Mesoamerica, etc.; §3.9)[184] is connected with the origin and spread of evil among early humans or with their hubris (importantly, also in non-Laurasian areas; §5). The many recurrent attempts to find the origin of flood myths in natural phenomena is immediately disproved by the extremely widespread, indeed global, occurrence of these myths,[185] from sub-Saharan Africa throughout Eurasia, Australia, and the Americas (§3.9, §6.7.2). They seem to belong to a very old, generally human inheritance (§6).[186]

After the Great Flood a new generation of humans emerges,[187] followed by a second spread of humankind (Gilgamesh, Noah, Manu's flood, Pyrrha and Deukalion, etc.) and by the establishment of human culture and society. The latter acts involve gods or tricksters and great heroes, who fight various demons and monsters, such as the dragon, or, in Chinese myth, personified monsters such as inundation (§3.5.2). These are left over from the third generation of gods, the immediate children of Heaven and Earth, such as the Greek Titans, Indian Asuras, and Japanese Kuni.no Kami. Usually, the heroes still are demigods, sometimes with one human parent (such as Zeus's son Herakles), or viewed as "quasi-incarnations" of deities, such as Yamato Takeru in Japan.[188] Frequently, they are the progenerators of the first noble lineages (later "royal" dynasties) of their individual mythological areas. Such heroic tales and their protagonists can, but must not necessarily, overlap with traditional epics. Examples include the Anglo-Saxon hero Beowulf, the Old Norse Sigurd, the Siegfried of the Nibelungen Epic, the Mahābhārata enemies (Pāṇḍava), the heroes of the *Iliad* and *Odyssey* (Achilles, Hector, Odysseus, etc.),[189] the first "kings" of Rome (Remus and Romulus)[190] and of early China (such as Nugua; or Yu, who killed Gong Gong; or the archer Yi),[191] some biblical heroes such as David, Gesar in Tibetan and Yamato Takeru in Japanese myth (Kojiki), Maui in Hawai'i,[192] Xbalanque in Maya myth, and so on (§3.10). In some versions, the heroic age leads to accounts of the early history of the population in question (Mahābhārata, Kojiki, Bible, Roman "kings" in the *Annals*, early Chinese "emperors," local Greek lineages, Hawai'ian and other Polynesian lineages, etc.).

Finally, there is the prophecy or the expectation of a final destruction of our world.[193] It may take place as a final worldwide conflagration: the *Götterdämmerung* or Ragnarök in the Edda, molten metal in Zoroastrian myth,[194] Śiva's destructive dance and fire in India, fire in Munda myth, fire/water and so on in Maya and other Mesoamerican myths, and Atum's final destruction of the earth in Egypt.[195] However, the end also takes other forms such as ice/winter (in the Edda, Yima's underground world in Zoroastrian myth) or, again, a flood.[196] (Many more details of such destructions and their rearrangement into the myth of the Four or Five Ages appear in Mesoamerican myth; see §2.5.1.) The final destruction is often coupled with the hope for a new and perfect world to rise from the ashes (Edda, Christian Bible, Zoroastrian myth about the final judgment, various Maya and other Mesoamerican versions, etc.).[197]

This kind of reconstruction obviously remains heuristic; details can and will change as more data become available.[198] However, the major lines of this reconstruction are expected to stand.

***

In sum, Laurasian mythology presents us with a detailed, well-structured account of the origins and end of the world and of its humans. It is the earliest, quasi-historical "novel" that we have, but it also is a mythical description of, and the justification for, human existence in this world (§8). Ultimately, as will be discussed in some detail below (§6.2, §8), the universe is seen as a *living body*, in analogy to the human one.[199]

▨ §2.5. STRUCTURE AND CONTENT IN SOME MACRO-AREAS OF LAURASIAN MYTHOLOGY

It is instructive and very useful to take a closer look at some of the early macro-regional features that Laurasian mythology developed long after humankind spread out from Africa around 65,000 BCE and after it originated and spread, apparently from Greater Southwest Asia, perhaps around 40,000 BCE. As has been briefly indicated earlier (§2.3), investigations of such macro-regions will facilitate a better grasp on and increasing control of the hundreds of mythologies involved in the Laurasian scheme. This investigation will also address some of the concerns about possible ways of comparison (§2.1) and the underlying structures of myths: diffusion, human psyche, and mono-origin. However, before proceeding to the actual reconstruction of Laurasian creation myths, a few important details will have to be discussed, such as the macro-regional (Eurasian/American) distinctions found in the myths of the Four (or Five) Ages of the world or the generations of the deities, the changes that occurred in the later macro-regional centers (such as the ancient Near East), and those that occurred due to still later borrowings.

§2.5.1. Macro-areas

As has been stressed earlier (§2.3), on a more theoretical level, the ancient reconstructed Proto-Laurasian mythology was not passed down to local mythologies in a "straight line" without any intervening stages. Many thousands of years have passed; many amalgamations of clans, tribes, and larger populations have occurred; and many migrations across the continents have taken place between the time of the exodus out of Africa, the birth of the innovative Proto-Laurasian mythology, and our first extant local mythologies, whether they are attested in writing (around c. 3000 BCE) or have been recorded as oral texts only over the past 200 years or so. In short, we have to reckon with a *series of stages* between Laurasian and, say, Old Japanese, Old Greek, or Maya mythology.

For example, in the case of Japanese mythology, these can be summed up as indicated above (§2.3, 2.5), echoing the parallel linguistic development: subsequently, the Laurasian, Eurasian, Nostratic, Altaic, Eastern Altaic, Japonic, Pre-Japanese, Yayoi, Yamatai (Yamato), Kofun, and Kiki (Kojiki/ Nihon Shoki) stages of mythology.[200] Old Japanese mythology has also seen substantial substrate influences, on Japonic from local cultures in Manchuria and the Korean Peninsula,[201] as well as on Japanese from the preceding local Jōmon culture.[202] In addition, there were various adstrate influences: from the Koguryo culture on the Korean Peninsula, the half-mythical Tsuchigumo,[203] the Ezo or Yemishi (Ainu) of northern Honshu and Hokkaido,[204] and the Austronesian Aborigines (Takasago) of Taiwan—all people of the archipelago and its immediate continental and southern neighbors.

Similarly, to use a perhaps more familiar scenario, that of Greek mythology, we would have to reckon with Laurasian, Eurasian, Nostratic, Indo-European, Western Indo-European, Pre-Greek, early Greek (Mycenaean, at c. 1400/1200 BCE), and various early forms of Greek myths (Doric, Attic, Ionian, etc.), along with very considerable local Aegean ("Pelasgian") substrate influences, before common Greek mythology emerged with Homer (c. 700 BCE) and a little later on, with Hesiod.

Again, in the case of Old Indian mythology, we would have to distinguish Laurasian, Eurasian, Nostratic, Indo-European, Eastern Indo-European, Indo-Iranian, Pre-Indo-Aryan, early Indo-Aryan (Mitanni texts in Mesopotamia, at c. 1400 BCE; Ṛgveda, c. 1200–1000 BCE), later Vedic, Epic, Purāṇic, and medieval and recent Neo-Hinduism stages (after c. 1800 CE). Indian mythology, too, has substrate and adstrate influences: first from Central Asia (Bactria-Margiana Archaeological Complex, c. 2400–1600 BCE), when speakers of Indo-Iranian passed through the area, and then from the Hindu Kush (by non-Indo-Aryan people such as the Burusho), from the Panjab (Indus civilization, 2600–1900 BCE), from other local post-Indus cultures, and finally, from many other Subcontinental cultures (Munda, Dravidian, etc.) when Vedic religion and mythology spread throughout the Subcontinent, after c. 1000 BCE.

***

It is useful, therefore, to distinguish reconstructed Laurasian mythology in the strict sense (*Proto-Laurasian)[205] from its subsequent stages (*Proto-Eurasian, *Proto-Nostratic, *Proto-Altaic,[206] etc.) as well as from its various *regional* forms, such as the areal versions found in the East Asian macro-region, which includes

China, Koguryo, Korea, and Japan, as well as other local populations such as the Ainu in northern Japan/Sakhalin and the Austronesian tribes of Taiwan. Although all these mythologies belong to quite diverse branches of Laurasian mythology and have been preserved by speakers of quite diverse language families, the East Asian area represents, as indicated (§2.3, 2.5), a particular regional (*EAsLaurasian) subvariety. It is the result of the various *secondary* interchanges that have taken place in the region only over the past few thousand years. They follow a number of trends that are quite distinct from those of other areas, such as the Greater Near East (*NELaurasian), early Central Asia, and Pueblo-Central America (§2.3, 2.5).

To provide a practical example, the geographically relatively isolated Japanese mythology is looked into here in some detail. We may have to assume, first of all, a post-Laurasian Nostratic branch (*NosLaur) that precedes it. It would comprise the ancient populations that spoke and still speak the languages belonging to the Indo-European, Uralic, Kartvelian (Georgian), Afro-Asiatic, Dravidian, and Altaic families in North Africa and Eurasia.[207] For this large group, one can (but must not necessarily) assume a mythology that was still fairly similar among all of these incipient branches; it was almost directly derived from Proto-Laurasian mythology and probably still very close to it. Research into this question would depend on the acceptance and further fleshing out of details of the (controversial) linguistic Nostratic superfamily. As far as we can see at present, the mythology of the Nostratic family seems to stress, like the Indo-European one, the ultimate genesis from water, the opposition between Father Heaven and Mother Earth, the solar origin and descent to earth of chiefs (or "kings"), a strong role of shamanism, and so on. However, such information is derived *not* from linguistic comparisons (which only yield a few items such as "spirits" so far; see §4.1) but from a comparison of *historically attested* myths found in the various Nostratic branches, just as has been done for Indo-European.

Further down the Laurasian pedigree, we have to reckon with a separate Altaic branch (*AltLaur),[208] to which the Japanese language and much of its mythology belong. A common Altaic mythology has not yet been reconstructed,[209] as even the definite establishment of Proto-Altaic linguistics, though first proposed in the 19th century, is of fairly recent date and is again controversial these days.[210] Even so, some general observations can be made and compared with Japanese mythology.

Altaic mythology, as attested in its linguistic subfamilies, seems to stress, like the Nostratic and Indo-European ones, the primordial deities Heaven and Earth, shamanism, the divine descent of chiefs, and so on. The shamanistic traits are most typically found in Siberia (see §7.1) but also in Japan and Korea, as well as, for example, in the non-Altaic-speaking Tibeto-Burmese Himalayas. Here we come across both male and female shamans,[211] while in Japan and Korea female shamans are more important.[212] Other typical traits include the role of the world tree and the way the descent of the first Japanese "emperor" from heaven is described in the Kojiki and Nihongi.[213] The latter is similar to mythemes of the Mongols and Tibetans.[214] Further indications come from preserved Koguryo (Kōkuri) myth.[215] Koguryo was a Koguryo-Japonic-speaking kingdom of the early first millennium CE in Manchuria and North Korea. Its founding myth presents us with an interesting mix of Laurasian, Central Asian, and "Indian" features: a woman, daughter of a river god, is impregnated by the rays of the sun,[216] gives birth to an egg, and produces the first king of Koguryo. This myth has many echoes of Indo-Iranian myth (Mārtāṇḍa/Gayō Marətan, son of the Sun deity, born from a dead egg;[217] neighboring Chinese myths of royal origins, Shang/Zhou)[218] or the Finnish Kalevala myth (Ilmatar, daughter of the Air, swimming in the ocean, giving birth to seven eggs; see §3.1.7).

The myth is told in Chinese sources as that of the Fu-tü people on the Gulf of Pohai (Bohai), east of Beijing. It is recorded in the Wei history (Wei-Shu, written 551–554 CE) as "The history of Kao-kou-li" (Jpn. Kōkuri, Korean Koguryo):

> Kao-kou-li was founded by the Fu-yü, who called their ancestor Chu Meng. Chu Meng's mother was a daughter of Ho-po (Lord of the Yellow River). Imprisoned in a room by the king of Fu-yü she was touched by the sun's rays. Whenever she moved away from the sunlight, it followed her. Soon she became pregnant and gave birth to an egg, which was so large that it could have held nearly five pints. The king gave the egg to the dogs, who refused to eat it. It was given to the pigs, who would not eat it either. It was then thrown on the road, and cattle and horses walked away from it. It was thrown out into the wilderness, but the birds flew down to cover it with their feathers. The king Fu-yü tried to cut it with a knife, but could not. He finally gave it back to his mother. The mother wrapped it and sheltered it in a warm place, and baby boy broke the shell and emerged. After he grew up he was named Chu Meng.[219]

This myth can be compared, as indicated, with some other Eurasian myths (Mārtāṇḍa/Gayō Marətan)[220] and a Kekchi Maya myth (detailed in §3.5.1). We then arrive at the scheme in Table 2.8 for much of Eurasia, including Finland (Kalevala), India (Ṛgveda and Yajurveda Saṃhitās), Iran (Avesta), Koguryo and Japan (Kojiki/Nihon Shoki), Old China (Shang/Zhou dynasties), and even Mesoamerica.[221]

The diverse, multiple relations between the Finnish (Kalevala, recorded in the 19th century), the c. 2000/1000 BCE Indo-Iranian,[222] the sixth-century CE Koguryo,[223] early Japanese (712 CE), and modern Mesoamerican myths are obvious: they include the role of a secluded young woman connected with water/ocean, her relationship with the sun as father or her child, and her giving birth to a "dead" egg that splits and whose issue becomes the Sun deity and ancestor of mankind (Indo-Iranian) or of a particular kingdom (China, Koguryo); the latter's language is closely related to that of early Japan.[224] The Mesoamerican version is more distant, but it still fits the general scheme once all the various details are taken into account: the connection of the woman with

TABLE 2.8. *The marriage of Sun and Moon across Laurasia*

Finland	India/Iran	Koguryo	Japan	Kekchi (Guatemala)
(Kalevala)	(Hoffmann)	(see § 2, n.227) (K.C. Chang)	(see §2, n.225 (Kojiki 2,106)	(Bierhorst 1990)
daughter of Heaven	Aditi	daughter of River god	woman	weaver woman, daughter of "King"
swimming	---	shut up in a room; rays of sun come through window	shut up in a room visited by a god through keyhole	shut in kitchen/on ocean throws maize water visited as humming bird / they leave through keyhole
bird touches/ lands on her knee	gets pregnant by eating rice before male relatives		touched by rays of the sun (or; while taking nap at a swamp)	slept with humming bird he = hunter = **Sun**),
becomes pregnant, gives birth	becomes pregnant, gives birth	becomes pregnant, gives birth	becomes pregnant, gives birth	she gets pregnant, killed by father, transformed to blood on waters;
to 3 eggs	3x2 Ādityas, then to Indra & "dead egg," thrown away,	to a big egg thrown away,	to red jewel	blood changed to small snakes, etc.; put in small 'bottles' (calabashes?), are left behind; one
one splits, and becomes the **sky**	then is carved to become the **Sun** deity: Mārtāṇḍa / Gayō Marətan	splits, and becomes baby boy, **king** of the Kao-kou-li emerges	turns into beautiful woman	opened after 14 days, revived small weaver woman stepped over, emerges as real woman/**Moon**

maize water; exposing her pregnant remains (blood) on water and keeping this in some sort of receptacle ("bottles," or gourds); her seclusion in a locked chamber that is entered by the hunter (a form of the sun) as a hummingbird/man through the keyhole, and so on.[225]

The original Laurasian form of this myth needs to be investigated in much more depth.[226] It seems to contain the motifs of the male Sun as male hunter or cowherd—the hunter being the historically older form—and that of the female Moon as a weaver woman (cf. the Iwato myth below, §3.5.1);[227] further, note their separation by the woman's father and their reunion after getting through a small opening or across a narrow bridge; the pregnancy of the (weaver) woman, giving birth to an egg (symbol of the round sun or moon) or gourds ("bottles"); and the reshaping of the egg or an emergence out of the gourd in human form or as deity of the Sun (or Moon).

To return to Japanese mythology as such: the Japanese language belongs to the Eastern (Tungus/Ewenki-Manchu-Japonic) group of Altaic languages. In the view of some linguists, such as S. Martin, it belongs to a subcategory with Ryūkyū and Korean,[228] called "outer Altaic" languages by R. A. Miller. Or it belongs, along with Koguryo, to Japonic,[229] which Martin does not see as connected to the (in that view unsubstantiated) Altaic family. It will therefore be necessary to specify how far Ryūkyū (Okinawan), Koguryo, and actual Korean mythology are related to Japanese (Kiki) mythology and further, whether some elements in Korean myth stem from Koguryo domination in the first few centuries CE and therefore are due to long-lasting regional contacts with their pastoral neighbors in the north and west.[230] Elements derived from the nomadic cultures might include the descent from heaven (probably non-Korean but Koguryo),[231] the male pillar (*onbashira*) and stone deities, and perhaps also the mytheme of women becoming pregnant by the sun's rays (see above) and the idea of the soul box.[232]

From the Japonic level (languages of Koguryo, the Ryūkyū Islands, Old Japanese) we also have to take into account the "pre-Altaic" populations of Manchuria/Korea and especially those of Japan: these long-established cultures include the highly developed prehistoric Jōmon culture (c. 11,000–1000 BCE), which may (or may not) reflect Laurasian mythology: it is rather difficult (but not impossible) to interpret the pictorial representations on Jōmon pottery and their clay figurines.[233] The exact composition of all these substrate populations and their prehistoric languages is still difficult to fathom. However, we can determine, for early (pre)historic times, several populations on the Korean Peninsula,[234] including the para-Japanese Koguryo straddling the Manchuria border, and we must suppose several others for the archipelago, such as the Tsuchigumo, Ainu (Ezo),[235] or those of the Jōmon civilization.

As mentioned, the latter civilization, in spite of the ubiquitous remnants of its magnificent art, remains difficult to interpret because we do not have written documents or a coherent transmitted mythology. Instead, we have to rely on its—always—enigmatic and ambiguous figurines and other depictions that are frequently open to several interpretations. What to make, for example, of the *dōgu* figurines, illustrating (pregnant) women that for the most part have been deliberately scratched and, in the common interpretations, seem to be intentionally disfigured or destroyed(?).Naumann finds a new explanation:[236] the scratching representing the lifeline that stretches from the navel upward (cf. §4.4.2, §7.1).[237]

In sum, whether in Japan or elsewhere, we have to distinguish many subsequent historical levels in Laurasian mythology. Consequently, the interpretation of a single local mythology is a difficult undertaking. It should not be undertaken by bringing into play simplistic oppositions, such as Indo-Aryan (Vedic, Indo-European) :: local Indian ("Dravidian") myths, or Indo-European Greek :: Pelasgian ones,[238] or "northern" :: "southern" elements in Japanese myths. Instead, more complex situations, such as the additional influence of the Near Eastern orbit on Greek myth, are seen, for example, in the way the father of the current gods is killed. In Mesopotamia, Marduk killed his father, Anshar (and also killed and dissected Tiamat). But the very mytheme of castration is missing outside the Mesopotamian *Kulturkreis* (e.g., in India).[239] This is a useful and exemplary case for regionalism that set in only after the spread of Laurasian mythology.

As was stressed in the initial summary exploration of the various historical stages in Laurasian mythology (§2.3), detailed comparative regional investigations, transgressing the myths that are restricted to just one language family, help to bridge the gap between the original Laurasian and the various extant local mythologies. Among the several important features of the Laurasian story line that may help us considerably to disentangle the various post-Laurasian stages is the myth of the Four Ages, which often overlaps with that of four generations of deities.

§2.5.2. The Four Ages in the Eurasian and Mesoamerican macro-areas

This myth frequently implies the change of "rule" from one divine generation to the next one. The process is, first of all, a biological one: the generations of descendants of Father Heaven and Mother Earth biologically follow each other. However, the change from one generation to the other often involves a certain amount of violence, as in real life. For example, we have frequent examples of violent takeover of rule in some societies such as the Shilluk, Dinka, and Bunyoro.[240] This is indeed reflected in local myth, for example, in the Vedic myth of the appropriation of the wealth of the older Manu, the ancestor of humans, by his sons or that of King Lear by his daughters and so forth. But nowhere does this process take the violent form found in the Greater Near East. In the well-known Greek myth, Kronos, the son of the primordial Ouranos (later on the god of the ocean) and Gaia (Earth), kills and castrates his father, cutting off his testicles with a sharp sickle. In the closely related Near Eastern version (Hurrite/Hittite), the son (Kumarbi) even bites off and swallows the testicles of his father and thus becomes pregnant.[241]

In India, there is a hint of violent succession in the killing by Indra of his father (Ṛgveda 4.18), which may be due to the prehistoric contacts between the ancestors of the Indo-Aryans in the Central Asian steppes and the peoples of the ancient Near East or with their North Caucasian (Hurrite etc.) neighbors.[242] This contact is in fact also seen in some isolated linguistic features (wine, copper, ox wagon, and its parts).[243]

Prima facie, there is no connection with Frazer's theory of regicide (heavily stressed in his *Golden Bough*) that occurs, for example, in parts of Africa. When the king ages and is no longer able to function as embodiment of (vegetational) power he is to be killed. The custom is widespread in the Nilotic area and beyond. If we assume that this is what ultimately underlies the tales of "killing the father," we must assume the influence of the early Near Eastern farming societies that were also transmitted southward along the Nile and the Sudan to Uganda (by c. 500 BCE).[244]

There also is no link to the myth of the killing of the primordial giant (Ymir, Puruṣa, Pangu, Remus, etc.). Freud, of course, would give quite another explanation of this myth, which, however, may be nothing but another, modern myth linked to his interpretation of the Oedipus myth: killing one's father and sleeping with one's mother.

Instead, the myth of killing the "ruler" of the previous generation of gods is part and parcel of another (Near Eastern?) characteristic, that of the Four Ages.[245] In this myth, we find not only four generations of gods but also four increasingly evil ages. These are the famous golden, silver, bronze, and iron ages, vividly described in Greece in Hesiod's *Theogony* for the first time. Because of the overt absence of the Four Ages in Homer, one may speculate on Near Eastern influences on Greek myth,[246] though the details are not yet clear.

The concept is indeed older with the Mesopotamians, at least as one of four generations of deities, seen in Babylonian myth (Enuma Elish) that was transmitted to the Hurrites and Hittites, who know of it in the form of a succession of the deities Alalu–Anu–Kumarbi–Weather God.[247] It is also found in Zoroastrian texts right from the start,[248] and it can be observed, if vaguely so, in early Vedic Indian texts.[249] Also, there is the later Zoroastrian account (Vīdēvdād 2) of the creation of the world by Ahuramazdā and its expansion three times (cf. Varuṇa' s actions in R̥gveda 4.42), which represents the Iranian version of the Four Ages.[250] The combination of these features indicates the possible Indo-Iranian age of the motif around 2000 BCE.[251] However, the myth of Four Ages is very prominent in the later Indian epic and other texts.[252]

The underlying pessimistic outlook from a golden to an iron age may indeed be ascribed to the influence of the Near East, specifically that of the "pessimistic" Mesopotamians or that of their neighbors.[253] The history of the concept, traceable so far, indicates that after the Sumerians and early Babylonians, it is found after c. 1600 BCE in Hittite, at c. 1000 BCE in Vedic and Zoroastrian texts, but only at c. 700 BCE in Hesiod's *Theogony*, as well as elsewhere, for example, in Celtic myths as summed up by Rhys.[254]

However, on closer inspection, there are actually *five* ages both in Greece and in Mesoamerica.[255] In addition to the well-known Four Ages, Hesiod assigns an extra age to the Greek heroes. In Mesoamerica, too, there are five ages, as we have to include that of the counterparts in Maya myth of the Greek heroes, the twins Xbalanque and Hunahpu. We now live in the "Fifth Sun," a recast of the Four Ages motif (§3.6).[256] In both cases, the heroes do not fit in well into the system of Four Ages and get haphazardly inserted, early on. In Aztec mythology, too, various "protohumans" were produced during each of the four ages called "Suns,"[257] and each new age was reigned over by a different god.[258] After the destruction of the Fourth World, the gods assemble in Teotihuacán to remove darkness once more and to re-create humankind for the Fifth World.[259]

The apparently old concept of Four Ages is retained even with the neighbors of the Pueblo/Mesoamericans, the Navajo, late immigrants from the Arctic north. They belong to the speakers of the Na-Dene group of languages, concentrated in the American Northwest (Alaska, Yukon), which is distinct from all other Amerindian languages. These populations seem to be one of the latest groups to have entered the Americas from Siberia.[260] The Navajo have a myth about the Four Ages that exactly reflects the Greek color-coded one: a golden age is followed by a silver- and a copper-colored one, and we now live in the black age.[261] It may, however, be questioned whether they have taken over the idea, like much of their mythology, from their Pueblo neighbors.[262] The relevant South American myths have been discussed by L. E. Sullivan;[263] with the Incas, too, the previous Four "Suns" have been followed by the present one, the fifth.[264] Importantly, *four* different catastrophes are found with the isolated Gran Chaco tribes as well,[265] and parts of this scheme are found as far south as Tierra del Fuego, with the Yamana.[266]

The occurrence of this concept all over the Americas constitutes a powerful test case for the age and nature of the idea of Four Ages and/or of four generations of deities in particular and of Laurasian mythology in general. Its occurrence in the Near East *and* in Mesoamerica confirms a date before c. 20,000 BCE for the age of the myth.[267] Rather, if the construct of a Dene-Caucasian language family should hold,[268] which, according to some linguists,[269] stretches from the Basque to the Navajo,[270] this would indicate its (partial) origin with people speaking this early Eurasian protolanguage. Their respective dates are those of the immigration of the early Europeans from Southwest Asia, the probable ancestors of the Basques, at c. 40,000 BCE; that of the Na-Dene people, ancestors of the Navajo, probably after the last Ice Age around 10,000 BCE; and further that of the Amerindians, the ancestors of the Mesoamericans, by c. 20,000 BCE.[271] This would indicate an early date for the common Laurasian origin of the concept. According to recent theories the early Amerindians, on arrival from Beringia and Siberia, passed through a narrow corridor between the Arctic ice shield and that of the coastal Cordillera in Alaska and British Columbia before it closed up for some 10,000 years. It opened up again only c. 11,500 BCE and allowed other groups (such as those represented by the Clovis culture) to pass southward to the Great Plains and beyond. If so, the ancestors of some Amerindians would have lived south of the ice shield for all of that time and would have preserved the myth of the Four/Five Ages in the Pueblo and Mesoamerica areas.

In sum, the great distance and the long-standing isolation of Mesoamerica from the ancient Near East do not allow for a direct influence of Near Eastern concepts on America. The same is likely for the eastern Siberian area of origin of the Amerindian and Na-Dene populations. The Sumerian, Dene-Caucasian, and Amerindian myth is, in other words, an early Eurasian/Amerindian one: it belongs to the basic stock of Laurasian mythology (§2.4, §3). In stark contrast, it is missing in non-Laurasian, Gondwana mythology (§5).[272]

***

Nevertheless, as mentioned, the character of the Four, or rather, Five, Ages in Mesoamerica represents the *opposite* of the pessimistic views found in early western Asia. The Mesoamerican process is one from an imperfect primordial age—via three (or four) additional, increasingly perfect stages—to the age of present-day humans. How to account for the difference in the West Asian and Mesoamerican outlooks? If Kramer called the Mesopotamians pessimistic,[273] the Mesoamericans certainly were even more obsessed with death, as the imagery of Mexican festivals still shows,[274] and they were equally preoccupied with the renewal of divine, solar power through blood offerings and human sacrifice. Worse, the end of certain of their calendar cycles was an ever-looming threat, as clearly felt at the time of Cortez's invasion of Mexico. The end of the current Fifth World is predicted for an exact date (2012). If the historical scenario sketched here is correct, people in Mesoamerica would have had at least 10,000 years to develop the new Amerindian version of the myth.

But how to account for the difference in outlook? May we regard the Mesoamerican version, isolated from the Near Eastern one by 8,000 or several more thousands of years, as the original one? It would make sense, for Laurasian mythology, at least as I see it, is an optimistic one: development of the world and its improvement all the way up to *our* current divine "generation," that of the present gods and humans, who in this scheme will face decay and death only much later in their common destiny. Even in the Eurasian West, all previous divine generations or "ages" just lead up to us: from primordial chaos; to Heaven and Earth; to the generation of "monsters" (Titans, Asura, the dragon); to that of their cousins, the current gods; and finally to *us*. We are the descendants of the gods themselves, who think (or used to think) of themselves, as Goethe let his Dr. Faust say in 1808, with typical Western hubris: *wir, die es so herrlich weit gebracht* ("we, who have progressed so much"). Pueblo and Mesoamerican myth actually presents this sentiment and its five stages as stepwise *improvements*, where each age of dumb (proto)humans is destroyed and followed by a more clever and intelligent race.

Conversely, the seeds of the Near Eastern version are also contained in this view: humans are, after all, just a few steps "down" from the primordial and current generations of gods, that is, from their ancestor, the sun deity. Though they are no longer immortal, are afflicted by various illnesses and ailments, and certainly are much less powerful than the gods, there is an inherent optimism in many mythologies that lets things get periodically restored to an optimal state, especially at the beginning of a new annual *mini-cycle*, at New Year. However, the inherent yearly decay of cosmos and society can easily be recognized in this scheme, too. If it is stressed *more* than in the annual (optimistically viewed) renewal in nature, time, and society, it results in the pessimistic Mesopotamian and Greater Near Eastern frame of mind.[275]

The closeness of such ideas to those of Zoroaster is notable. He lived in the northeastern parts of the Greater Near East, probably in the border area of Bactria (Balkh, northern Afghanistan) and Margiana (Merw, eastern Turkmenistan). He started out from the old Indo-Iranian concept of the renewal of time and society at year's end, but he transposed it to the final period of one's own life and that of the world. He stressed the inevitability of the choice during the fight of two opposing forces at year's end that was commonly made at this critical time: one had to choose between righteousness (aša, Vedic ṛta) and evil (druj, Vedic druh; cf. Engl. be-tray; German be-trügen, Trug). The obvious, natural choice was the one for the yearly auspicious restoration of universal order (aša, ṛta), based on truthful action. The decision was made *before* the onset of this yearly repeated, dangerous period of dissolution of order in the universe and in society. In Zoroaster's new worldview, the choice is to be made "now," in every human's life; the outcome would lead one, via the Cinṭuuaṇt bridge, to Ahuramazdā's Heaven—or to "hell"—"falling from the bridge into molten metal." This is the ultimate origin of the Christian and millenarian American ideas of heaven and hell,[276] conceived about a thousand years before Jesus—an idea that, due to path dependency, still is extremely powerful in the modern West, especially in America.

As for reconstructed Laurasian myth, however, we may have to be content, for the moment, with stating that there was a mytheme of the Four (or Five) Ages and generations of deities that was open to subsequent interpretations (§3.6, 3.11).

§2.5.3. Later centers of innovation

Some prominent myths have, however, spread only in still more recent historical times, such as the spread of the Near Eastern myth of the castration of the divine father figure to Greece, or Buddhist and Christian mythology worldwide. These are *secondary* developments that have gained considerable geographical (and chronological) extent but that have neither Laurasian distribution nor Laurasian time horizon.

Among such local changes, certain individual myths are only more or less datable. To use some Japanese examples, the motif of the diver bird (Kojiki 1.37)[277] is widely spread in Siberia and North America and in one form even in Australia;[278] the churning of the ocean by Izanami and Izanagi in the Kiki is also found in post-Vedic India; the role of the twins in creation is found in the Kiki but also with the Austronesian Ami and Atayal of Taiwan, with the Indo-Europeans (Yama–Manu, Ymir/Tuisto–Mannus, Romulus–Remus), with the Mundas of India, and with some South Americans (emergence from an egg; cf. §3.1.6); the role of the messenger bird in the myth of the hidden sun is found in late Vedic India, Southeast Asia, and Kiki Japan;[279] the characterization of the Sun deity as "curious" in the same myth is seen also with the northeastern Indian Naga and Khasi;[280] and—if not a reflection of the ancient Ymir/Puruṣa/Pangu myth—the myth of the Japanese goddess of food has parallels elsewhere.[281] In all these cases, however, Japanese mythology may have diverged somewhat from the original Laurasian topics, while the *basic structure* of the "official" imperial

Japanese (Kiki) mythology—like that of other Laurasian mythologies—is not affected: the *story line* remains the same.

On the other hand, even the few, still somewhat superficial investigations of certain major motifs and myths, as proposed in this section, allow us to discern intrusive elements. They may be derived from the local substrate or may have entered from the outside as adstrates, that is, from neighboring cultures and dominant regional civilizations. In such cases, the basic features and the structure of local (in this case, Japanese) mythology can and should be further clarified and its basic Laurasian structure reconfirmed.

***

Outside influence in Japan is visible, for example, in the Chinese Tanabata and some other myths,[282] in the motif of looking for the "apples/peaches of paradise," and later on, in the introduction of many Buddhist motifs and myths. Here, just as in the Greater Near East (§2.3), early great civilizations have become *secondary centers of mythological innovation*, whose impact spread far and wide beyond their original homelands. Among them were the various centers of the Neolithic agricultural revolution and innovation:[283] the Fertile Crescent (from 9000 BCE), the Greater Indus Valley (6500 BCE), northern China (7000 BCE), southern China (7000 BCE), New Guinea (7000 BCE), Sudan (3000 BCE), and Meso-/South America (3000 BCE). Each early dominant civilization subsequently spread its individual, new *agricultural ideology* all over its zone of influence. Such instances can be admitted within the Laurasian theory as a secondary *diffusion* of myths, by osmosis or by domino effect (§2.5.3).

To name but one conspicuous example, there are clear indications of pre-Columbian influence by Pueblo and Mesoamerican agricultural societies and their religions on North American tribes, up to North Dakota and New York State. Their influence is obvious in local agriculture-related myths. They are isolated within the original local mythologies.[284]

Many of such agriculturally inspired myths include that of the yearly decay, death, and rebirth of an (agricultural) deity, as discussed by Frazer for the killing of the king,[285] for example, with the Shilluk and the myths of Persephone, Isis, and Osiris; of the annual exhaustion and reconstitution of the post-Ṛgvedic India creator god Prajāpati; of Mayan deities; and so forth. Not unexpectedly, these agricultural myths take a somewhat different form in non-Laurasian cultures, such as those of Melanesia (Hainuwele myth; §5.3.3)[286] and of sub-Saharan Africa (see §§5–6).

As for the pre-agrarian Laurasian mythology, to be discussed at some length in the sections on archaeology (§4.4; cf. §7.1.2), these developments originate from and then further expand on an ancient, Paleolithic Laurasian myth: that of the killing of the hunted animal and of the primordial giant,[287] their dismemberment, and their eventual reconstitution from their bones, carefully preserved during slaughter and dismemberment—they are the "life possessing bones," as Zarathustra still says.

***

The process of further continuous development of Stone Age myth by agricultural societies (§7.2) was still being repeated when early state societies emerged. Frequently, human origin from the sun deity was appropriated by the emerging elites and nobility and ultimately, by the supreme chieftain or king. Typical cases are those of the Egyptian pharaoh, the Indo-European higher classes and their "kings," the Chinese and Japanese emperors, the Amerindian rulers (Aztec, Maya, Inca), and the Polynesian chieftains. In some cases, such as in the highlands of central Mexico, the increasing stratification and emergence of central rulers can be traced archaeologically (see §7.2) even in the absence of early textual sources.[288]

Narrowing down the focus of solar descent on chieftains and kings had serious implications for the individual structure of local Laurasian mythologies. While a deceased king was deified in Polynesia,[289] this process brought about spiritual disappropriation of all who were not noblemen (Haw. *ali'i*, Maori *ariki*). They were supposed to loose their soul upon death: their spirits just went to the western edge of their island and jumped off the cliff into nothingness.[290] Surprisingly, in Egypt the opposite development gradually took place over the course of some 3,000 years of recorded history. At first, only the pharaoh was reborn, like the victorious sun is each morning, but progressively others, too, were granted that privilege, built more or less extensive graves, and got mummified after death. In India, by contrast, only the three upper classes retained the privilege "to go to heaven," while the mass of the population, the Śūdras, were excluded (and due to path dependency still are, according to traditional Vedic ritual).

Still later, such socially conditioned reshaping of original Laurasian mythology is to be observed in the spread of missionary religions and of their distinctive mythology. These include, most importantly, Buddhism, which spread over most of Asia, followed by the Christian religions and still later by Islam in Africa and Asia. The three Abrahamic religions combined include more than half of humanity now. Their respective myths and overarching mythologies (or "doctrines") have overlaid if not overrun much of the original mythologies of Europe, North Africa, the Near East, and parts of India and Southeast Asia, as well as Australia and the Americas. However, they had a fairly limited impact in East Asia, where the old religions (Daoism, Shintō, Shamanism) have continued side by side with Buddhism. In certain ways, the spread of "missionary" myths continued with the secondarily derived 20th-century totalitarian movements and their utopian ideologies (Fascism, Communism).[291]

The current, quasi-missionary incarnation of these global ideologies is universally widespread. It is a mixture of American secular and Christian ideologies

(§8) that come with unlimited consumerism and concurrent globalization, as well as with a strong missionary drive by a number of Protestant Christian organizations.[292] However, like all such ideologies, they have but a temporally limited appeal, especially when the prophesied "end" fails to arrive.

Just as can be observed in the historically attested spread of the myths of powerful religions, doctrines, and ideologies, one may also expect a similar, earlier spread of certain new myths, mythologies, and religions. They can occur in pre-state societies, some of them even at a still earlier, Neolithic level.[293] The rise, just a century ago, of the Amerindian Ghost Dance movement, based on the vision of a Paiute man called Wovoka in 1889, is a case in point.[294] It started out as a reaction against the American expansion westward into the Rocky Mountain areas and quickly spread across linguistic and cultural boundaries to a large number of Amerindian tribes, before it was suppressed by the American government. Similarly, the New Guinean *cargo cult* (cf. §1.3) began in a Neolithic environment, though likewise within cultures that were in contact with modern Western state societies. Before and especially during World War II, the ready availability of cargo brought on ships and airplanes spawned the desire in Melanesians to get to that cargo that originally belonged to their own ancestors, ideas that are actually quite similar to those of modern chauvinism (Hindutva) in India. The Melanesians did so by attracting cargo and airplanes in their rituals, by sympathetic magic;[295] Indian chauvinists do so by "reappropriating" the Vedas, where they claim to find all modern technology—in late Bronze Age texts—however, without actually *employing* these supposed manuals outside of some traditional Vedic fire rituals. Similar movements were spawned by Christian missionary activity in Africa; they have led to many new syncretistic African religions.

We know of such development only because there was close contact with literary civilizations that kept a record of such cults. However, one can easily extrapolate and imagine similar religious movements to have taken place in the distant past, for example, in contact situations between agricultural societies and hunter-gatherer ones or between state societies and those of Neolithic farmers. In the absence of written documents, it is obviously very hard to trace such influences. However, the clear clustering of macro-regional mythologies outlined above (§2.3) plainly points to such "hidden" influences in the past.

They can frequently be detected when they are confronted with the reconstructed Laurasian mythology and its subsequent incarnations (Eurasian/Amerindian, Near Eastern, Indo-European, etc.) or with the reconstructed Gondwana mythology. If this is done, the extraneous influences from neighboring cultures, or new developments, can often be detected, as they stick out like the proverbial sore thumb.

For example, many of the Austronesian Aboriginals of Taiwan have a prominent flood myth. However, when visiting the Catholic Church at Taitung in southeastern Taiwan, one will find it surrounded by a wall with wood carvings that depict Noah's flood and his ark.[296] The casual observer would be led to assume that these carvings were inspired by the biblical myth. However, on closer observation it becomes apparent that the missionaries selected this myth—not, for example, the crucifixion—because it chimes in with the local tradition of a Great Flood that brought the Aborigines to the area. They depicted it in traditional carving style, adding small touches such as Noah's ark, instead of a simple boat as in the local myths. The case serves as a useful example of how local myth develops and incorporates extraneous influences.

§2.5.4. Late borrowings (diffusion)

It is with historical processes such as missionary Buddhism, and now the Americanism spread by powerful media, that the principle of diffusion and its effect on original Laurasian mythologies comes into play most visibly. Even then, though, diffusion occurs to a rather limited extent as far as the main topics of previously existing local mythology are concerned. The diffusion of individual myths, seen, for example, in the incidental mutual influence of the mythologies of the Near East and of eastern Asia, has already been mentioned (Tanabata myth, emasculation of father figures). It is a priori not improbable that the populations of ancient eastern or western Asia have been in prolonged contact with each other, ever since prehistoric times,[297] and that they not only have exchanged valuable trade goods but have also shared some of their "more interesting" beliefs and individual myths.

Any investigation of regionally spread myths will reveal a number of such migrating topics.[298] To restrict the discussion to eastern Asia, a very clear case is the well-attested move of the Tanabata myth, which has already been repeatedly mentioned. Typically, this myth, which is first attested outside China in Korean wall paintings of c. 400 CE and as Japanese court ritual in the eighth century CE, is quite *isolated*. It is only told as a folktale. As a late Chinese import, it has not been included in the "official" creation myths of the Kiki (Kojiki and Nihon Shoki) as recorded in 712/720 CE.

Another case of intrusion, this time included in the Kiki, is the Japanese story of the Hare of Inaba, usually traced back to Indian origins. As such, it could have come with Buddhism via Korea, in the sixth century CE. Nevertheless, it was surprisingly included in the Kiki, which would be due to a certain amount of importance or popularity. Instead, the transmitting agent probably was not Buddhism but the strong cultural influence on Kofun-time Japan by the Koguryo realm of North Korea and Manchuria, which has a similar myth.[299] However, it has now also been explained as Chinese influence.[300]

Further, scholars usually have included among such intrusions the very beginning sections of the official Japanese mythology in the Nihon Shoki, with its "philosophical" series of creation stories. Some are rather abstract and remind one of similar Chinese accounts. However, not *all* of these accounts are late and foreign (see, in detail, §3.7). Admittedly, when the creation story is told in terms of Yin and Yang (Japanese *In/Yō*), this is clearly due to Chinese literary influences: the Nihon Shoki has after all been influenced by the style of Chinese "mythical" historiography and is actually written in Chinese. But the basic creation myths of the Kiki are rather old and very similar to those of Polynesia, eastern Central Asia, and Laurasia in general (§3).[301]

Clearly, all such regional features are only of secondary importance for the development of Laurasian mythology, as the original Eurasian and Laurasian system has largely been maintained (for details, §3.1.6). However, regional features that stand out must be observed closely, as they may cloud the picture of the available Laurasian evidence and the reconstruction of its mythology. The preceding examples indicate that we have to establish, very carefully, the several historical levels that go before the actual attestation in extant written texts, until we reach the original Laurasian one (§2.4).

***

In sum, by following the processes discussed in the preceding sections, we can establish a many-faceted, geographically widespread, and historically leveled view of the origin and development of Laurasian mythology. This complex enterprise will lead us back to the Stone Age and to the beliefs of early *Homo sapiens sapiens* (Crô Magnon; §§6–7). Conversely, understanding the underlying pattern of Laurasian mythology will help us, ultimately, to understand how many of our current "modern" concepts are still rooted in the ancient customs and beliefs of Paleolithic people (§8).

Moreover, even though the Laurasian project is a large-scale undertaking, possible only with the help of many specialists of the individual cultures involved, we cannot stop here. Instead, initial explorations, carried out over the past few years, have indicated that Laurasian mythology, though it now covers large, if not most major parts, of the globe, is not the only one in existence. Rather, it is just one among the several other still existing types. The most prominent ones are to be found in sub-Saharan Africa, the Andamans Islands, New Guinea, and Australia,[302] as well as in smaller refuge areas of Asia. These are the *Gondwana* mythologies,[303] which are to be discussed later (§5).

▪ §2.6. SOME OBJECTIONS TO THE APPROACH OF HISTORICAL COMPARATIVE MYTHOLOGY

There are a number of points that could be raised as objection to the theory laid out in this chapter, especially with regard to the Laurasian theory and its establishment (§2.1). They need to be clarified before we can progress further.[304]

As mentioned, one basic objection against the comparative method in mythology includes the sociologically and Marxist-inspired one made by Bruce

Lincoln,[305] who regards the writing of comparative mythology as that of new "myths with footnotes."[306] However, in spite of being a student of Indo-European linguistics, he fails to apply the methods and results of that discipline consistently, due to his new, sociologically based approach, to comparative Indo-European mythology. Instead, he draws some erroneous general conclusions based on his rather narrow approach to myth (§1.6, §2.6).

Another major objection would concern the results of Stone Age archaeology. As discussed above, Ina Wunn would implicitly deny the possibility of any theory such as the Laurasian one.[307] While assemblages of stone tools, and later on of pottery, are datable by a number of methods, the interpretation of Stone Age art is open to dispute.[308] If Wunn's basic *assumption* could indeed be made of a consistent correlation between art objects and their underlying, more or less evolved culture and society, the insights of ethology, and the assumption of continuous material and spiritual progress, then Stone Age art might indeed correctly reflect ancient religion. However, Wunn closely links Bellah's evolutionary theory of the continuous evolutionary development of religion since Paleolithic times with the (always lacuneous and incidental) finds of archaeology.[309] This procedure results in the virtual *absence* of religion in late Paleolithic times (§1.4), that is, precisely when Laurasian (and Gondwana) myth originated according to the thesis discussed in the present book. As has been pointed out and as will again be taken up in detail later (§7.1), Wunn's approach is too simplistic: early art reflects only certain limited aspects of Stone Age life, especially hunting and fertility. The potential argument against Paleolithic religion and, by implication, against the reconstruction of Laurasian mythology is a classic case of evidence from absence, a typical ex nihilo argument, but *the absence of evidence is not evidence of absence* (§1.5).

***

Other incidental objections to the comparative method in mythology have also been discussed and rejected earlier (§2.1, end). They include the assertion that myth could have developed independently due to neurobiological invariances (as Jung would have it; §1.5) and that similarities in ecological conditions would have occasioned similar mythologies, which is contradicted by the multiclimate reach of Laurasian mythology. A more specific objection would be the insistence that similar flood and destruction myths of river- or ocean-based societies are independent of long-range transmission, which is contradicted by their existence in many areas far distant from such natural conditions.

Further, among several reasons applied in this discussion is that pointing to isolated, unmotivated fragments of myth preserved in remote, out-of-the-way areas (§2.1, end; §2.2). They represent fragments of an older *system*, which means that ecological and climate factors do *not* play a great role in the specific local occurrence of such fragments of myths; instead, such factors only result in superficial similarities, not major structural features.

In addition, it is important to stress from the outset that certain aspects of the sciences discussed later (§4) contain as yet undecided and even some untestable features. As in all fields of the humanities and sciences, there are certain areas that still are under discussion and positions that are out of the (current) mainstream or are mere proposals. They have been indicated as such in the relevant sections of this book. Some of the less common proposals (such as superfamilies of languages and Long-Range studies) are favored here as they seem to coincide with the results from archaeology and genetics.

Some objections, however, are very basic ones. For example, population genetics depends partly on so-far-untestable assumptions about rates of genetic drift that have not yet been firmly established (§4.3). The field also is dependent on calculations based on the assumed split of the ancestral line of chimpanzees and humans, which results in an Out of Africa date of either c. 60 kya or 77 kya.[310] However, the dates provided by this method are very good as far as *relative* chronology is concerned, if compared with the equally problematic, absolute, but generally accepted relative dates for linguistic change (§4.1). In future, systematic comparisons of results from *ancient* DNA may help to narrow down such dating uncertainties.[311] At any rate, the difference of 17,000 years does not matter very much as far as ancient Gondwana and Laurasian mythologies are concerned.

Similarly, the assumptions about the speed of linguistic shift (as used in glottochronology) are equally vague, especially when employing the original Swadesh model.[312] However, the method has since been updated by the late S. Starostin.[313] According to him, the rate of replacement for the most common 100 words has come down from 14 to about five–six words per millennium. Also, the reconstruction by Long-Range linguists of superfamilies that go beyond the universally accepted families such as Indo-European, Uralic, and so on has not yet been accepted by traditional (mostly Indo-European) linguists. Their rejection includes even the superfamily of Nostratic and that of Eurasiatic, which is in competition with the Nostratic one (§4.1). Both are too easily, if not superficially, rejected by traditional linguists. Only patient and careful comparisons of sound correspondences and grammar, following the traditional, well-established Indo-European model, will lead to further clarity here. However, very few scholars are involved in this field, and progress will be slow unless some major funding is received.[314]

***

Other problems involve many types of contamination that affect the quality of the genetic, linguistic, archaeological, and mythological data used in such reconstructions. Some of them are routinely handled by the involved scientists, for example, disturbance of archaeological layers or in linguistics, the dialect as well as substrate and adstrate influences that disturb regular reconstructions. However, the reconstructed meanings of some important words will remain under discussion. Linguistic archaeology, or rather, linguistic paleontology, has its closely circumscribed limits: we cannot be sure that a certain reconstructed word actually meant *exactly* the same thing in prehistoric times (does the Indo-European word for cow refer to a domesticated animal only, and since when?).[315] Caution is advised.

In the same way, in historical comparative mythology, many similarities in myths and story lines may be attributed to contamination and would then not be reflections of ancient shared myths. However, as will be pointed out below (in §5.1–2, §6) such perceived influences are just based on prima facie impressions. They can be corrected by other, uncontaminated evidence of neighboring peoples or by large-scale comparisons covering extensive areas. These will readily allow us to pinpoint individual contamination. Nevertheless, it is always appropriate to be alert to the possibility of contamination.

Another variety of contamination is that we do not know how far the relatively recently recorded African, South American, Polynesian, and similar nonliterate sources have been affected by missionary activities and influences (see §§5–6). That means, in particular, how their recording by missionaries or colonial officials has slanted these accounts, as they could see the world only through their own, Christian categories. Related problems are the poor quality of our early records caused by intermediate translations and by the retelling by scholars or laymen of some of the myths of nonliterary societies. A telling example from the Andaman Islands is found in Radcliffe-Brown's account of the original text and his own retelling of the myth about the theft of fire involving the Kingfisher.[316]

Influences by literary traditions on orally transmitted mythologies would fall into the same category. This applies to the spread of motifs from dominant ancient cultures to surrounding areas (§2.2.4) as well as those (classical, European, Christian) ideas that (potentially) influenced the early reporting by colonial officials, missionaries, and anthropologists. In both cases, however, *mass comparison* of related mythologies in the same general area will allow us to pinpoint, again, where such influences or interpretations have been made and will easily isolate Eurocentric reporting and interpretation.

***

A related problem is the possibility that some key characteristics of early recorded Laurasian mythology may owe part of their similarities, such as the story line, not to their common descent from a shared protomythology but to transformational forces operating in manuscript traditions over long periods, in other words, that are the result of compilational tendencies in literate traditions, which commonly lead to this kind of comprehensiveness. This includes, primarily, the steadily increasing accretion of myths. Frequently, such syncretic accretion is the result of superimposing various local mythologies and setting them up in a comprehensive (written) framework (such as in ancient Egypt or India).

This scenario is, however, excluded for comparative mythology on two counts. There are indeed cases where separate and inclusive written traditions are clearly visible, as in Old Egypt but interestingly, not (yet) in the extant Sumerian texts. Wider comparisons across cultures indicate that the direct influence of written traditions on myth collection cannot be generalized. For example, a direct comparison of Mesopotamian and Old Indian data is not possible, as the Vedic Indian tradition was altogether oral and *written* accretion is simply not found. The earliest Indian texts constitute a large aggregation of mythological and ritual data that was entirely oral but was not organized like the Egyptian data or the Babylonian Enuma Elish. The direct impact of written Mesopotamian tradition on the neighboring Indian oral one is also not seen: incidental similarities between India and Mesopotamia (such as in the respective versions of the flood myth; §3.9, §5.3.3) must be explained differently, for example, as oral myths transmitted through early trade contacts.[317] Or to use another example, Mayan and Near Eastern traditions both have "manuscript" traditions, but this does not establish a general model of gradual accretion of data from manuscripts or literary traditions as such. Nonliterary traditions continued side by side with written ones.

Available evidence indicates that prima facie composite schemes, such as that of the Four/Five Ages (§2.5.2, §3.6), are also found in areas that were *never* influenced by the old centers of literate culture. The myths of the Amazonian Yanomami, the Gran Chaco Amerindians (with four kinds of catastrophes), and the Fuegans are cases in point. Further, complicated frameworks, including that of the Laurasian story line, are found in many nonliterate societies (such as the Dayak), even those that have not been in any contact with literary cultures (again, such as the distant Fuegans).[318]

The only open question, then, would be whether nonliterate societies could have developed a comprehensive oral text that includes the major motifs of the Laurasian story line (or of Gondwana collections). This merely depends on historical accident. As Schärer points out,[319] the Dayak of Borneo have myths and ritual texts that would come to some 15,000 pages in print. However, not all myths are always present in the mind of one and the same shaman. All that was needed, thus, was something like a tribal council that collected the available myths, as happened in the collection of Ṛgvedic hymns around 1000 BCE.[320] Another kind of political impetus is evident in the collection of Old Japanese myths (Kojiki, Nihon Shoki) by the early Japanese imperial court in 712 and 720 CE, which was made on the basis of traditional bardic or shamanic recitation. However, the Nihon Shoki intentionally lists many variants to the official "national" myth given in the "imperial" Kojiki. Another case is that of the preliterate Hawai'ian text Kumulipo, whose compilation apparently also was due to local politics around 1700 CE.[321]

Still other motivations include the reaction to outside pressure, such as the collection of Winnebago myths that were told in comprehensive form just when it was obvious that this tradition would soon disappear.[322] The point clearly is that in the said traditions most or all myths of the story line existed, even if they were not always collected in one oral "text."

***

In related fashion, one may also claim that the apparent lack of comprehensive story lines in Gondwana myth (§5) may simply be a function of the more fragmented presentation of myths (as seen in Dayak myths). This is typical of preliterate societies that developed complex mythologies. The case would therefore be similar to the one discussed just now: a tribal society and its shamans or priests would have stored in their memory individual tales but not a unified, comprehensive account "from the beginning to the end." In the Gondwana case that means: from a primordial High God and his creation of humans to their (mis)deeds (§5) and to current conditions.

This scenario, likewise, is contradicted by available evidence. Comprehensive myths, though not a unified story, were found even among the long-isolated Stone Age society of the Tasmanians. They moved about in small bands, numbering altogether some 900 people, who spent extensive periods of time in retelling their myths (§5.3.2.1). From the fragments that have been preserved, we can reconstruct a mythology that accounted for the creation of humans, animals, and current conditions. A similar case involves the rather complex account of the creation of humans by the central Australian Aranda (§5.3.2), which amounts to some eight pages in Strehlow's (rather compact) retelling.[323] He functioned, so to speak, as a local shaman who collected all available creation myths. Just as in the case of the nonliterate Laurasian Dayaks, all that was needed was such a shaman. Whether this happened or not is a function of local conditions, rivalries between shamans, and so on. The situation varies, obviously, from tradition to tradition.[324]

***

One may therefore assume that even in nonstratified hunter-gatherer cultures the forces of the gradual accretion of myths could have been due to local retellers and shamans and to their interactions. These may have been at work over the many millennia, since Paleolithic and Neolithic times. However, as we do not have any indications or proof that this was indeed the case, it is easier (and more elegant) to assume that the many congruences in Gondwana and Pan-Gaean myth collections (§§5–6) were *inherited* from their Paleolithic ancestors instead of having independently developed in exactly parallel fashion since then.

Available materials, however, indicate that the development of the Laurasian story line was precisely such an accretion: it is based on earlier Pan-Gaean and Gondwana collections (§§5–6), to which the typical Laurasian features were added, such as creation myths, the end of the world, and most importantly, the coherent underlying story line.

Finally, it is important to point out that this scenario of the Laurasian story line and its heuristically assembled contents (§2.2, 2.4) may receive some modification by a reevaluation of some of Y. Berezkin's extensive materials.[325] Certain clusters of motifs show a close correspondence between Sahul Land and South American myths. Berezkin correctly interprets this as *survival* of older motifs in South America. These were first introduced at the time of the first immigration into the Americas at c. 20 kya.[326]

This would mean that many aspects of North American myths are *late* introductions from Siberia (which is obvious for the Na-Dene [Athapascan/Navajo/Apache] languages). It has to be investigated, however, how far this late influx impacted Mesoamerica or rather, vice versa, how far the strong influence of the mythology of the Pueblo and Central American maize cultures (a clear case of a Viennese *Kulturkreis*) have overlaid older Na-Dene mythology,[327] as can readily be observed in Navajo myths.[328]

■ §2.7. CONCLUSION

In this chapter, the general and theoretical background of comparisons has been explored, drawing on recent work by scholars such as C. Ragin and others. Subsequently, the various theories and methods used in the comparison of myths were spelled out. Ultimately, any comparison is heavily dependent on the structure of the human mind, which favors binary combinations, as explored by Lévi-Strauss.[329] It uses analogies based on experience and the anthropomorphization of nature.

Following these general observations, the characteristics of the proposed scheme of Laurasian mythology, and of various mythologies in general, have been discussed at length. It has been indicated how the Laurasian scheme can be built up, step by step, by observing a large number of similarities between mythologies worldwide while focusing on their *regular correspondences* across time and space. The comparison is crucially enhanced by the discovery of a *fixed structure* underlying most mythologies in Eurasia and the Americas: the narrative scheme of Laurasian mythology, that is, the *story line* from original creation to the end of the world. Some 15-odd major motifs appearing in the Laurasian story line have been enumerated heuristically.

In the subsequent discussion of this model, it was argued how to proceed with the actual reconstruction: it makes use of the oldest available texts, as to avoid contamination by later developments. Then, the process moves further back in time to various reconstructed levels of mythology (such as the Near Eastern, Eurasian, or Amerindian ones). Ultimately, reconstruction aims at going back to the Proto-Laurasian stage. The various individual local mythologies then appear to be mere branches of the complex family tree of Laurasian mythologies. Conversely, the reconstructed original Laurasian mythology can then be compared with the actual mythologies attested locally. Incidentally, this also serves as a countercheck on the validity of the reconstruction.

The changes that occurred between these early stages are due to local thinkers working with the inherited materials available to them. Other changes and additions clearly indicate certain insertions into the Laurasian scheme, as well as the relative time frame in which they occurred. Some such insertions and changes have taken place in early Bronze Age, regionally important cultural centers, which in turn have influenced neighboring local mythologies, such as the ancient Near Eastern one (Anatolia and Greece) and the Pueblo and Mesoamerican one (Mexico, southwestern United States, etc.). In all such cases, this development took place because of the cultural prominence of early nuclei of civilization. Examples discussed here include the two versions of the Four Ages scheme (§2.5.1) in Eurasia and the Americas. Their mutual differences are very important for the Laurasian reconstruction. Due to their long separation in space and time, at least some 20,000 years, they lead back to early Laurasian times.

A purely synchronic comparison of myths cannot achieve these dimensions. Historical comparison adds several layers of evidence and provides additional strength to the model of comparative mythology in general and to the Laurasian proposal in particular.

***

We can now turn to the reconstruction of the various stages of Laurasian mythology (mentioned in §2.5) and to their representation in individual mythologies, as available in old texts as well as in important modern oral traditions. As mentioned, I prefer to begin, as a matter of principle, with the oldest evidence available (see §2.2.3). The reason has already been discussed (§2.1). This procedure offers us the chance to avoid wrong reconstructions that are based on more recent (modern, medieval, classical, and occasionally even some incidental archaic) written attestations and distributions of individual items.[330]

This concerns especially those that have been influenced by the increasing stratification, reinterpretation, and ensuing syncretism of competing local mythologies within organized early state civilizations,[331] features that are additionally driven by the written transmission of texts and commentaries to them. As has been indicated, a typical case is that of Old Egypt. Its myths can be studied in great detail, revealing the reformulations that took place over three millennia.[332] Such changes were often aligned with shifting political centers and their priestly elites, such as those of Heliopolis, Memphis, Thebes, and so on. Clearly, the "oldest" Egyptian mythology does not exist as such in written form but has to be reconstructed first, just like the rest of Laurasian mythology.[333] Ancient Vedic and medieval India offers a similar scenario: it is based on texts between c. 1500 and 500 BCE and shows multiple changes, ultimately leading to modern Hinduism.

Even these early written traditions, however, are quite "late" with respect to original Laurasian mythology, and many changes and reshapings will have to be accounted for that intervened between both stages (see §2.3). But this is the best we can do under existing circumstances.[334]

On the other hand, the oldest written versions of myths in ancient civilizations must necessarily be contrasted with much more recent ones, collected from populations spread all over Laurasia that did not or do not possess written traditions. An objection to the use of the less "organized" and often quite late oral traditions may be that such traditions are much more diverse than those of the first civilizations with written traditions.

However, it has to be recognized that this is not exactly true. While we have early collections and summaries of local mythologies, such as the Mesopotamian Enuma Elish, Hesiod's *Theogony*, the Japanese Kojiki, and the Mayan Popol Vuh, they by no means represent the *sum* of indigenous tradition. A look into R. Graves's *Greek Myths*, the major versions of Egyptian myth,[335] early Indian myths from various Vedic texts,[336] and Japanese myths (with early variants as recorded in the Nihon Shoki) immediately indicates that local traditions differ, often widely, from the "official" version, as the preface to the official collection of Japanese myths in the Kojiki freely admits (712 CE). In other cases, such comprehensive collections have not even been attempted, for example, in ancient China and Rome.[337]

Moreover, the bulk of oral tradition of one particular population, say, of the Winnebago,[338] the Hawai'ians (Kumulipo), or the Dayak of Borneo, can run into hundreds, even tens of thousands, of pages.[339] These traditions merely lacked a local shaman or priest who would have collected and redacted all traditions, as has been done in Egypt, Mesopotamia, Greece, and so on. If we would have had, say, a medieval Dayak writer or compiler, this mythological collection and system would have been just as impressive as those of the ancient civilizations. As will be seen, *some* of these often geographically isolated oral traditions have preserved very old Laurasian traits.

***

After the lengthy, but necessary, initial deliberations found in this chapter, we therefore begin with the detailed discussion of Laurasian myths, stressing some of the most prominent ones, the *emergence myths* (of "creation"; §3.1.1–7). It is useful to begin detailed comparisons by taking a closer look at the global forms that the first stage of Laurasian mythology, the emergence (creation) of the world, takes in the individual versions. The following chapter thus is the mainstay of the book: a large number of creation myths in Eurasia and beyond are compared. In each instance, for example, the world's creation from water, relevant data are brought to bear upon the central narrative. Related materials from non-Laurasian mythologies are also mentioned in preparation for a later discussion (§5, the countercheck).

Frequently we will find, initially rather surprisingly, if not disconcertingly, *several* creation myths next to each other or even within a single mythology. Laurasian mythology identifies a number of actual "creations" that account for the world's emergence from water or chaos, sometimes with the help of an earth diver. This mythology also recognizes creation by the cutting up of a primordial giant, bull, or egg. In some versions these strands are combined, occasionally in a "logical" order, while others stand apart as alternative myths of origins.

It is an intriguing question whether all of them are of equal age or whether some of them, such as the dismemberment account of the primordial giant, are older. The problem will be addressed in the following chapter (§3.1.7), and the enigma of the coexistence of such divergent myths will be resolved in §§5–6, once non-Laurasian myths have been compared. Nevertheless, as we will see, the prima facie mysterious and potentially troubling factor of multiple creation myths in the reconstruction of Laurasian mythology does not disturb its story line.

Then, after having dealt with these foundational myths, we will proceed along the "timeline" of the Laurasian narrative arrangement and select some important mythemes: the creation of a habitable environment for humans, their actual creation, their mythical "history," and the (final) destruction of the world.

3 Creation Myths: The Laurasian Story Line, Our First Novel

Mundi origo.
Before the ocean and the earth appeared—
before the skies had overspread them all—
the face of Nature in a vast expanse
was naught but Chaos uniformly waste....
　　As yet the sun afforded earth no light,
nor did the moon renew her crescent horns.

—P. OVIDIUS NASO, *METAMORPHOSES*[1]

Before there was any light there was only darkness, all was night. Before there was even darkness there was nothing.... It is said in the *karakia* [invocations], at the beginning of time there stood *Te Kore*, the Nothingness. Then was *Te Po*, the Night, which was immensely long and immensely dark.... The first light that existed was no more than the glowing of a worm, and when sun and moon were made there were no eyes, there was none to see them, not even *kaitiaki*. The beginning was made from the nothing.

—MAORI, CONTEMPORARY[2]

▩ §3.1. PRIMORDIAL CREATION

Myths about the beginning of the universe and the earth are the most prominent feature in Laurasian mythology.[3] They constitute the very beginning of "mythic time." The Laurasian stress on cosmogony, however, is entirely absent in Gondwana mythologies (§5).

Original creation, or rather, more correctly, "emergence," is often shrouded in mystery. The eternal human question about ultimate origins is common and persistent; compare, for example, Gauguin's *D'où venons-nous? Que sommes nous? Où allons-nous?* (Where Do We Come From? What Are We? Where Are We Going?) or Kant's both theoretical and practical *"drei Fragen: 1. Was kann ich wissen? 2. Was soll ich tun? 3. Was darf ich hoffen?"* (three questions: 1. What can I know? 2. What shall I do? 3. What may I hope?).[4] These questions have been answered by many Laurasian peoples in very similar ways. Most of them agree that, in the beginning, Heaven and Earth were "created"; however, they also tell about a preceding stage of the initial emergence of the universe in several, sometimes surprisingly diverse ways.

***

For example, in ancient India, the oldest text,[5] the Ṛgveda (c. 1200–1000 BCE),[6] contains several approaches to the question, made by its many poets. Some of them assume that the world and humankind have sprung out of "nothing" ("there was neither being nor nonbeing" [Ṛgveda 10.129]), or out of a great void or darkness, or out of a great, featureless salty ocean. However, if they indeed speak of creator gods, then these deities were not even present from the beginning or they originated from the primordial void. Thus, the Ṛgveda (10.129) asks whether the gods were in existence at the time of the first creation or whether even they do not know about it—as they came only later.

***

Yet these types of myths do not represent the only solution to the question about ultimate origins. Surprisingly, there actually are a number of additional answers given within the area covered by Laurasian myth (primordial giant, egg, etc.; §3.1 sqq.). How they are related to each other will be discussed in the later sections of this chapter, and a solution to the disturbing aspect of their seemingly mutually exclusive coexistence will be presented later on (§5).

Thus, next to the emergence of the world from "nonbeing," archaic Indian myth also contains the somewhat isolated idea of a primordial giant,[7] from whose cut-up body the various parts of the universe were formed.[8] A slightly later Vedic Indian text adds the idea of the shaky young earth floating on the waters and the mytheme of a diver animal that first had to bring it up from the bottom of the sea.[9] In India it is not a bird, as usual in northern Asia, but a primordial boar. Later on, this turned into the boar incarnation of the great Hindu god Viṣṇu. Finally, another early Vedic text speaks of an egg with a golden germ.[10] One cannot maintain that all of this is just late Ṛgvedic priestly speculation, as some do, because these motifs are much older than this text (§3.1.1 sqq.).

These diverse mythemes, in fact, constitute the aggregate of most creation motifs found in the various Laurasian mythologies. In short, we not only find various creation myths in individual Laurasian mythologies but even encounter *several* creation myths within *a single* Laurasian tradition. The reason escapes immediate understanding.[11] This not inconsiderable diversity may appear to pose a problem for the Laurasian theory. However, there are avenues to proceed beyond this and reach the form of creation myths as they must have been present in earliest Laurasian mythology (§3.1.7; §5, 5.7; §6).

The various major forms of Laurasian cosmogony include six prominent sets of motifs:[12] primeval chaos, water, diver and floating earth, giant, bull, and egg, as well as combined versions (§3.1–7). These will now be taken up in this order.

§3.1.1. Chaos and darkness

To begin with, there is a fairly widely spread, quite abstract notion of the primordial emergence of the universe out of primordial darkness,[13] out of chaos,
or even out of "nonbeing," as seen in the Rgvedic and Maori cases.[14] In some
versions it is connected with primordial waters, as can be seen below. We
begin with the oldest attested versions, a practice to be followed, wherever
possible, throughout this chapter. As mentioned, the most abstract version,
chaos and *nonbeing*, can be found in India, in the Rgveda (c. 1000 BCE). Interestingly, this version appears among the late "philosophical" and speculative
hymns:

> There was neither "being" [*sat*] nor "nonbeing" [*asat*][15] then, nor intermediate space,
> nor heaven beyond it. What turned around? Where? In whose protection? Was there
> water?—Only a deep abyss.[16]
>
> There was neither death nor immortality then, nor was there a mark of day and
> night. It breathed, windless, by its own determination, this One. Beyond this, there
> was nothing at all.
>
> Darkness was hidden by darkness, in the beginning. A featureless salty ocean was
> all this (universe). A germ, covered by emptiness, was born through the power of heat
> as the One.
>
> Desire arose then in this (One), in the beginning, which was the first seed of mind.
> In nonbeing the seers found the umbilical cord [relationship] of being, searching (for
> it) in their hearts with planning.
>
> Obliquely stretched out was their cord. Was there really "below"? Was there really
> "above"? There were the ones bestowing seed, there were "greatnesses" [pregnancies].
> Below were (their) own determinations, above was granting.
>
> Who then knows well, who will proclaim here, from where they have been born,
> from where (came) this wide emanation [*visrsti*]? Later than its emanation are the
> gods. Who then knows from where it developed?
>
> From where this emanation developed, whether it has been created or not—if
> there is an "overseer" of this (world) in the highest heaven, he alone knows it—or
> (what) if he does not know? (RV 10.129; my translation)[17]

The last verse is a clear addition, as a concept of a "creator" (Prajāpati, "Lord of
the descendants, children, creatures") emerged only in the late Rgveda. The
mentioning of primeval desire is remarkable; we will again encounter it in
Greece. In Old China,[18] too, there is frequent mention of primordial waters but
also one of Chaos or emptiness:

> In a time when Heaven and Earth still were without form, was called the great
> beginning. The *dao* began in the immense emptiness.... Then "breaths" were born
> from space and time. What was light moved and formed the sky (easily); what was
> heavy, the earth ... this process was difficult. (Huainan zi)[19]

A similar version is that of Old Greek mythology: First there was *chaos*, in it Nyx (female "Night") and Erebos (her brother) were found; the force uniting them was *love* (echoed by the Indian account of primordial *desire*). Erebos descends and liberates Nyx, who spreads and becomes the wide sphere; they separate like two parts of an egg and give birth to Eros (Love),[20] as well as to Heaven (Ouranos) and Earth (Gaia); Eros binds the two together closely. In Hesiod's *Theogony* this is told as follows:

> Verily at first, Chaos [void] came be, but next wide-bosomed Earth, the ever-sure foundation of all…and Eros (Love), fairest among the deathless gods.…From Chaos came forth Erebus [darkness] and black Night; but of Night were born Aether and Day, whom she conceived and bare from union in love with Erebus. And Earth first bare starry heaven, equal to herself, to cover her on every side.[21]

In another version, Earth is directly born from Chaos, emptiness, with help of Eros; or Chaos gave birth to Night, which itself gave birth to Aether, the first brilliant light, the purest fire, the Day. The so-called Pelasgian version, as reconstructed by R. Graves, begins with Chaos and a primeval egg, too:

> In the beginning, Eurynome, the Goddess of All things, rose naked from Chaos, but found nothing substantial to rest for her feet on, and therefore divided the sea from the sky, dancing lonely on the waves.…She caught hold of the north wind, rubbed it between her hands and behold! the great serpent Ophion.…Ophion grown lustful, coiled about those divine limbs and was moved to couple with her.…So Eurynome…got with child. Next she assumed the form of a dove, brooding on the waves and in due course of time, laid the Universal Egg. At her bidding, Ophion coiled seven times about this egg, until it hatched and split into two. Out tumbled all the things that exist: sun, moon, planets, stars and the earth.[22]

The Romans, heavily influenced by Greek literature and thought, follow suit closely. In the poetry of Ovid's *Metamorphoses* quote above: "was naught but Chaos."

***

Turning to more recent and modern myths, another Indo-European-speaking people, the northern Germanic Icelanders, agree. In Old Norse mythology recorded in the Edda (c. 1177 CE),[23] there was chaos at the time of the beginning of the world, "a yawning abyss" (*gap var ginnunga*; Vǫluspá 3). Then the sea was created; as were Niflheim, the land of clouds and fogs in the north, and Muspelheim, the southern land of fire. Through the contact of ice from the north and the warm breezes from the south, a first being, the primordial god Ymir, was created:[24]

> Once there was the age when Ymir lived.
> There was neither sand, nor sea, nor salty waves,

not was Earth found, not Upper Heaven,—
a yawning gap, and grass nowhere. (3)
Until Bur's sons scooped up the lands,[25]
they who created mighty Midgard.[26]
The sun from the south shone on the rocks
and from the ground green leeches greened. (4)
I know an ash (tree), called Yggdrasil;[27]
white fog wets the high tree;
from there comes the dew which falls into the valleys,
Evergreen it stands above Urd's spring. (Vǫluspá 19)[28]

Far away from the Indo-Europeans and Chinese, the Polynesians, an Austric people whose ancestors had emerged from South China around 4000 BCE,[29] speak of primordial emptiness and darkness, too. In the Maori version, negation or nothingness (*kore*) gives birth to chaos or darkness (*po*), and this, to *rangi* (heaven or sky;[30] see the introduction to this chapter). Another version, involving a primordial deity, Io, has the following account:

Io dwelt within the breathing space of immensity.
The Universe was in darkness, with water everywhere.
There was no glimmer of dawn, no clearness, no light.
And he began by saying these words—
That he might cease remaining inactive:
"Darkness become a light-possessing darkness."
And at once light appeared.... [31]
Then (he) looked to the waters which compassed him about, and spake a fourth time, saying:
"The waters of *Tai-kama*, be ye separate.
Heaven be formed." Then the sky became suspended.
"Bring forth thou *Tupua-horo-nuku*."
And at once the moving earth lay stretched abroad.[32]

Normally, the descent of the gods is listed as negation (*kore*) developing into –> chaos/darkness (*po*) –> *rangi* (heaven, sky). The supreme deity Io, known only to some specialized priests,[33] had escaped the Western mythographers for quite some time and thus is not listed in the older accounts of the myths of New Zealand:[34] "unknown to most Maoris.... cult was esoteric... ritual in the hands of the superior priesthood... no form or sacrifice was made to Io, no image ever made... [there was] no *aria* (form of incarnation) such as inferior gods had."[35]

As a useful exercise in the comparison of the closely related Polynesian mythologies, and so as to indicate how local mythologies can develop from a common ancestor, we may compare the famous Hawai'ian version, the Kumulipo. It has undergone, as we know, some editing by powerful clans since c. 1700 CE. The Kumulipo only has this:

At the time when the light of the sun was subdued
To cause light to break forth
At the time of the night of Makalii (winter)
Then began the slime which established the earth,
The source of deeper darkness,
Of the depth of darkness, of the depth of darkness,
Of the darkness of the sun, in the depth of night,
It is night, so it was born.[36]

However, the Tahiti version is more explicit. Here the creator is the god Ta'aroa (Maori Tangaroa, Takaroa; Haw. Kanaloa), who apparently existed before actual emergence:

He existed, Taaroa was his name,
In the immensity.
There was no earth, there was no sky,
There was no sea, there was no man.
Taaroa calls, but nothing answers.
Existing alone, he became the Universe.
Taaroa is the root, the rocks.
Taaroa is the sand.
It is thus that he is named.
Taaroa is the light. Taaroa is within.
Taaroa is the germ. Taaroa is the support.
Taaroa is enduring. Taaroa is wise. He erected the land of Hawaii.[37]
Hawaii the great and sacred,
As a body or shell for Taaroa.
The earth is moving.
O, Foundations, Rocks,
O sands, hither, hither,
Brought hither, pressed together the earth.
Press, press again. They do not unite.
Stretch out the seven heavens,[38] let ignorance cease
Let immobility cease.
Let the period of messengers cease.
—
It is the time of the speaker.
Completed the foundations.
Completed the rocks.
Completed the sands.
The heavens are enclosing.
The heavens are raised.
In the depths is finished the land of Hawaii.[39]

Or in still another version, recorded twice between 1848 and 1922,

> Ta'aroa was the ancestor of all the gods; he made everything....
>
> He was his own parent, having no father or mother....
>
> Ta'aroa sat in his shell (*pa'a*) in darkness (*te po*) for millions of ages....
>
> The shell was like an egg revolving in endless space, with no sky, no land, no sea, no moons, no sun, no stars.
>
> All was darkness, it was continuous thick darkness (*po tinitiniia e te ta'ota'o*)....
>
> But at last Ta'aroa gave his shell a fillip which caused a crack resembling an opening for ants. Then he slipped out and stood upon his shell... he took his new shell for the great foundation of the world, from stratum rock and for soil for the world. And the shell... that he opened first, became his house, the dome of the god's sky, which was a confined sky, enclosing the world (*ao*) then forming....
>
> Ta'aroa made the great foundation of the earth (*te tumu nui o te fenua*) to be the husband, and the stratum rock (*te papa fenua*) to be his wife... and he put his spirit into it, which was the essence of himself, and named it Ta'aroa-nui-tumu-tahi, Great-Ta'aroa-the-first-beginning.
>
> Ta'aroa dwelt on for ages within the close sky... he conjured forth (*rahu*) gods (*atua*), and they were born to him, in darkness (*i fanau i te po*)....
>
> ...It was much later that man (*ta'ata*) was conjured [forth] when Tu was with him.[40]

The Polynesian myths, in spite of some local developments, thus agree on primordial chaos or "nothingness," which was transformed by a creator (Io, Ta'aroa) deity into our present world.

In Amerindian myth, too, we find several versions of primordial darkness or chaos. The oldest recorded ones are found in Mesoamerican texts. They speak of origins in darkness or semidarkness, before the sun rose.[41] According to the medieval Quiché Maya text, the Popol Vuh, in the beginning,

> all was in suspense; all was calm and silent; all was motionless and all was quiet, and wide was the immensity of the skies.... The face of the earth was not yet to be seen; only the peaceful sea and the expanse of the heavens... for as yet naught existed.... Alone was the Creator, the Maker, Tepeu, the Lord, and Gucumatz, the Plumed Serpent, those who engender, those who give being, alone upon the waters like a growing light.... It is then that word came to Tepeu and Gucumatz... and they spake and consulted and meditated and joined their words and councils.[42]

The Hebrew Bible,[43] too, has primordial darkness, though it occurs only *after* the initial creation of heaven and earth by the gods (*elohīm*, notably, *not* a single God),[44] when the wind moves about the waters. Incidentally, it is important to note, again, the role that speech plays in the Vedic, Icelandic,[45] Maya, Maori, and biblical and other Laurasian texts; we will return to the topic of the power of formulated speech and of naming things.[46] According to the Hebrew Bible, "As to origin, created the gods [*elohīm*] these skies (or air or clouds) and this earth....And a wind moved upon the face of the waters" (Genesis 1.1–2).[47] However, in the traditional Christian version this reads quite differently (King James translation),[48] here quoted at length:

> (1) In the beginning God created the heaven and the earth. (2) And the earth was without form, and void; and darkness was upon the face of the deep. And the Spirit of God moved upon the face of the waters. (3) And God said, Let there be light: and there was light. (4) And God saw the light that it was good: and God divided the light from the darkness. (5) And God called the light Day, and the darkness he called Night. And the evening and the morning were the first day.
>
> (6) And God said, Let there be a firmament in the midst of the waters, and let it divide the waters from the waters. (7) And God made the firmament, and divided the waters which were under the firmament from the waters which were above the firmament: and it was so. (8) And God called the firmament Heaven. And the evening and the morning were the second day.
>
> (9) And God said, Let the waters under the heaven be gathered together unto one place, and let the dry land appear: and it was so. (10) And God called the dry land Earth; and the gathering together of the waters called the Seas: and God saw that it was good.[49]

Another version (Genesis 2.4sqq) has an abbreviated creation myth:

> In the day that the Lord God made the earth and the heavens, when no plant of the field was yet in the earth...a mist went up from the earth...and watered the whole face of the ground—then the Lord God formed man of dust from the ground.[50]

Also to be compared is Psalm 104.2 sqq., which reads like a Ṛgveda or Avesta hymn (Yasna 43):

> 1. Praise the Lord...2. you spread heaven like a curtain (or tent)...5. who has laid the foundations of the earth so that it should never be shaken...8. The mountain arose [from the ocean]...19. You made the moon...20. You made the darkness.[51]

In sum, whether in our earliest or even in late versions, the world emerges from an undefined state of chaos, by itself; in some later versions it does so with the help of a creator god. However, the similarity between the Vedic Indian, Greco-Roman, and Polynesian versions, with a time gap of some 3,000 years and at a distance of tens of thousands of miles, is remarkable and did not escape even early British observers in New Zealand.[52]

§3.1.2. Water

The idea of primeval waters is closely connected with that of primeval darkness or chaos and therefore has already come up several times in the preceding section. Chaos is often identified with a watery waste.[53]

In North Asia/North America and the Near East, the emergence of the earth from the waters seems to be the standard myth, transmitted in several versions (often involving the earth diver bird; see §3.3). The myth of primordial waters is very widely spread, especially in northern Europe,[54] Siberia and the Americas,[55] the Near East,[56] India,[57] and Southeast Asia/Oceania.[58] It is "logically" linked to the myth of the floating earth (see §3.3), as it provides the background for bringing up the earth from the bottom of the primordial waters and subsequently, the floating earth (§4.3.4). To begin with one of the older attestations, in India there is a frequently repeated myth with slightly varied wording, usually summed up as "In the beginning there was (only) salt water" (*agra idam sarvam salilam āsīt*); there are similarly old accounts in Egyptian, Mesopotamian, Greek, and Chinese mythologies.

One of the oldest, the Mesopotamian version, is of interest: it does not start from an undifferentiated primordial ooze but, rather, from a union of salty (ocean) waters and sweet (river) waters, which perfectly reflects the southern Iraqi marshland situation. From the (female) waters Tiamat and (male) Apsu, two generations of ancestors of the sky god Anu emerged: Tiamat, the primordial (sea) waters, and Apsu, the primordial (fresh) waters, are found in the beginning. They give birth to Lahmu and Lahamu, who in turn give birth to Anshar and Kishar ("Father of gods, king"). His son is Anu (the sky god); note again the role of speech:

> When on high the heaven had not been named,
> firm ground below had not been called by name,
> naught but primordial Apsu, their begetter,
> (and) Mummu-Tiamat, she who bore them all,
> their waters commingling as a single body....
> Then it was that the gods were formed within them.
> Lahmu and Lahamu were brought forth, by name they were called.
> For aeons they grew in age and in stature.
> Anshar and Kishar were formed, surpassing the others.
> They prolonged the days, added on the years.
> Anu was their son.[59]

The contemporaneous and even older Egyptian mythology has four basic versions of the creation myths,[60] formulated in successive religious centers that became large temple cities. The mythology of Heliopolis (Vth Dynasty) is the most "orthodox"; then there is that of Memphis, the capital of united Egypt; that of Thermopolis, itself with four variants; and that of Thebes, the capital of the New Kingdom (1570–1085 BCE).

The beginning, the time of the gods, is called "First Time," a golden age when the gods lived on earth and justice reigned.[61] The universe was just a vast ocean (Nun) with no surface and is compared to an egg.[62] It is typical for Egyptian myth that the earth arose out of these waters in the form of a hill,[63] similar to what may be seen in the floating earth (§3.3). It was fixed to the bottom of the ocean. According to the Heliopolis myth, the bisexual god Atum, the "Complete one,"[64] created himself by his own will, or he was thought to be a child of Nun, the primordial waters, who is the self-created father of the gods. As there was no place to stand on, Atum created a hill at the place of his first appearance, and he is sometimes regarded as the hill itself. He sat on it as it arose out of the waters of chaos (Nun) and brought the first gods into being:[65]

> The Lord of All, after having come into being, says: I am who came into being as *Khepri* ("the becoming one"). When I came into being, the beings became into being, all the beings came into being after I became. Numerous are those who became, who came out of my mouth, before heaven existed, nor earth came into being.... I being in weariness was bound to them in the Watery Abyss. I found no place to stand. I thought in my heart, I planned myself, I made all forms being alone, before I ejected Shu, before I spat out Tefnut.[66]

In another version, creation took place in the primordial waters (that is, the male Nun, father of Re); there was no place to stand,[67] and other texts speak of the primordial hillock. Re/Atum came into being as Khepri (Morning sun/scarab). Re masturbates or spits out Shu (Air), Tefnut (Moisture), Nun ("the eldest god...the father"), and Atum/Re and so on.[68]

The Hebrew Bible has an account of primordial waters, though existing at the same time as the creation of the earth: "the earth was without form, and void; and darkness was upon the face of the deep. And the Spirit of God moved upon the face of the waters" (Genesis 1:2, King James trans.).

Farther east, the Old Indian (Vedic) myth of a primordial salty ocean has already been discussed above. A later Vedic text (Bṛhadāraṇyaka Upaniṣad 3.6) puts it in a way vaguely recalling the biblical account: "Then Gārgī Vaicaknāvī asked him: 'Yājñavalkya, as all of this (universe) is woven, warp and woof, in the waters, in what then are the waters woven, warp and woof?'—'In the wind...'" (my translation).

Chinese myth also speaks of the primordial waters, indicating that when the earth was covered with water, the heavenly Lord sent down one of his subjects to prepare it for habitation, that is, Gun battling the waters (Shanhai jing 18). Their southern neighbors, the Tai-speaking people of northern Indochina, who are part of the great family that speaks Austric languages,[69] also regard the earth as a flooded terrain, and "this concept fits well the cosmology of a continental population."[70]

The primordial waters are also found in Siberia, for example, with the Tungus (§3.3)[71] or with the Ainu of North Japan and Sakhalin:

> In the beginning the world was a big swamp. Water was completely mixed up with earth...there was no life...god created the wagtail bird and sent it down from heaven to bring forth the earth.... It flew about, tread on the swamp and beat its tail up and

down.... Dry earth emerged on these spots.... The earth grew more and more, finally emerged from the waters and swam on it. That is why the Ainus call it *moshiri* "swimming earth."[72]

According to Ainu myth, the sun, the moon, and the stars are ships (*shinta*) traveling in the sky; the *shinta* is also used when the gods, such as the son of the thunder god or a dragon god, visit Ainu land (an idea similar to that of Old Japanese mythology). Such culture heroes descended to different regions, often to the top of mountains,[73] such as that of Nibutani, where the god Okikurumi landed.[74]

***

Not surprisingly the Amerindians have concepts similar to those of their Siberian homeland across the Bering Strait. The oldest records are those of the Aztecs and Mayas. However, in their mythologies as well as in many other Amerindian ones, the origin of the world from primordial waters is not as clear as in Eurasia proper, as it is part of the myth of the Four Ages, which results in a fourfold creation that existed before our age.[75] The last one, however, was swept away by the Great Flood.[76] The Aztecs, for example, have an account of Four Ages preceding our times, "the Four Suns." The Mayas, too, speak of a fourfold creation. According to their Popol Vuh, in the beginning,

> the face of the earth was not yet to be seen; only the peaceful sea and the expanse of the heavens.... Then... (Tepeu and Gucumatz)...spoke: "Let it be done. Let the waters retire and cease to obstruct, to the end that earth exist here, that it harden itself and show its surface."[77]

Other Amerindian tribes, whose myths have been recorded only relatively late, agree.[78] The Omaha, for example, tell,

> At the beginning all things were in the mind of Wakonda. All creatures, including man, were spirits.... They descended to the earth. They saw it was covered with water.... Suddenly from the midst of the water up rose a great rock. It burst into flames and the water floated into the air in clouds. Dry land appeared.[79]

The Maidu of California have a myth that agrees more with the Siberian version and the earth diver motifs (see §3.3):

> In the beginning there was no sun, no moon, no stars. All was dark and everywhere there was only water. A raft came floating on the water. On it were Turtle (A'nóshma) and Father of the Secret Society (Pehē'ipe). Then from the sky a rope of feathers... was let down and down it came Earth-Initiate.... (Turtle then dove into the water four times, each time bringing up a little more earth.) The fourth time... it was as big as the world, the raft was aground and all around were mountains as far as he could see.[80]

Finally, the South American Chibcha tell that humankind was created by a common mother,[81] Bachue, who came out of a swamp together with a small boy of three years on her arm. Grown up, he married her. Many children were born from this couple, four–six at a time: they are the ancestors. When the two grew old, they disappeared into the swamp and became snakes. A similar myth is told in Amazonia and among the Inca (§3.7).[82]

§3.1.3. Earth diver and floating earth

In "logical" continuation of the mytheme of the primordial waters, many mythologies envisage the earth as floating on the ocean,[83] from whence it has been brought up by the "earth diver."[84] This figure is prominently found in Asia and North America as a diver bird or a muskrat.

However, in South Asia, it is another animal that roots in mud, the boar. This version is found in early post-Ṛgvedic texts,[85] thus shortly after c. 1000 BCE. Mud brought up from the bottom of the ocean by a boar forms the new, still shaky (*śithira*) earth,[86] floating on the ocean. Later on, the motif developed into the famous Hindu myth of Viṣṇu's boar (Vārāha) incarnation. However, the concept may be much older in South Asia, as boar worship is found in the isolated Andamans and in the Subcontinent. Andaman archaeology indicates a boar cult already at c. 3000 BCE,[87] and there are echoes of it in the Ṛgveda.[88]

Its "logical" outcome is the very common mytheme of the earth floating on the primordial waters. As indicated, the oldest preserved version, perhaps, is again found in the Ṛgveda and in some early post-Ṛgvedic texts:[89] the earth was *śithila* (shaky), and Indra fixed it with flying mountains,[90] whose wings he had cut off.

Among the Siouan-speaking Winnebago of Wisconsin, the repeated creation by Earthmaker resulted in the Fourth World, which "would not remain quiet." Earthmaker created four Island-Anchorers with his own hands and placed them in the four corners of "island-earth."[91] This motif is very similar to the Vedic Indian one of fixing the still shaking or moving earth with mountains. In the Winnebago version, however, this action is followed by the forming of water spirits, spirit-walkers, a large sacred woman, and four large trees that finally keep the earth down.[92]

In other versions, peoples in Siberia, India, Indonesia, and South America see the earth as floating on the primordial ocean.[93] Among the Tungus, the myth has incorporated some of the Christian figures of their Russian neighbors:

> In the beginning there was no land, and god, the holy Nicolas, and a dog were on a float [raft]. . . . The devil wanted to drag god from the float, but the more he dragged the bigger the float became . . . it became the immense earth.[94]

Their northeast Asian neighbors, the Ainu, tell of a bird, the wagtail, that helps in spreading out the emerging earth (see above). In North America, among the

Omaha, we have a version that reminds one of Old Egypt: "Suddenly from the midst of the water up rose a great rock. It burst into flames and the water floated into the air in clouds. Dry land appeared."[95] Another, somewhat aberrant version is found in Polynesia and in Japanese myth: the gods bring out the earth or some of its islands with the help of fishhooks.[96]

Or the lands of the earth are churned by the gods out of the primordial sea, for example, in Japan (Kojiki 1.6) and in India (Rāmāyaṇa 1.45.15–25), where this primordial churning is closely connected with the antigods, the Asura, who help in the undertaking, and it results in the birth of various (semi)divine beings. This myth first appears in Vedic Indian mythology, where we have the enigmatic sentence about the birth of the earth through an action of the gods who stood in a flood and foam was splashing off them (as if they were dancing; RV 10.72.6). In later Indian myth (Rāmāyaṇa epic), the gods took Mt. Mandara (Meru), reversed it, and put it on its top; wound the world snake Śeṣa around it; and churned the ocean to extract the drink of immortality (*amṛta*). The action is represented, in gigantic form, at Angkor Wat. We can compare this with an archaeological find in Jutland (western Denmark):[97] an inverted tree was put into a stone mill and set into a pile of stones,[98] which describes a movement that has astronomical significance as well.[99] In sum, in most cases, Earth (and Heaven) arose out of a void, of chaos, which is often identified with a watery waste, from which the earth was fished by some other aquatic animal.

***

However, as indicated, we find myths relating creation out of a primordial being that was dismembered or from a primordial egg that split up. Again, in the case of India, we find all of these myths already in the Ṛgveda or immediately after it; in Finland they have even been amalgamated into a single story (see §3.7).[100]

§3.1.4. Giant

In addition to the emergence of the world from darkness and primordial waters there also are the seemingly aberrant versions of a primordial giant or egg. The giant was in existence before the world emerged: he was somehow killed and carved up, and the various body parts became the origin of heaven and earth and even of humans.

The well-known prototype is the Germanic Ymir, who is slain, and from his skull heaven is made; from his ribs, the mountains; and so on. In the parallel version of Old India, it is *puruṣa* (man) from whose body the various parts of heaven and earth are created, including even humans (Ṛgveda 10.90). In Old China, there is the quite similar myth of Pangu (P'an ku), which seems to derive from southern Austric neighbors.[101] One can also compare some Greek and Near Eastern variants: the Greek myth of the spilling of Kronos's blood so as to fertilize earth or the Mesopotamian creation of man from mud and blood—the gods decided that one of them, Kingu, was to be killed so that humans could be created from his blood.[102]

The longest and oldest version of this myth is found in the Ṛgveda, where the primordial Puruṣa (man) is carved up:[103]

> 7....the gods, the Sādhyas, and the Ṛṣis (Seers, poets) offered him (Puruṣa) for themselves....
>
> 11. When they portioned out Puruṣa, in how many parts did they fashion him? What are his mouth, arms, thighs, and feet called?
>
> 12. His mouth was the Brahmin, his arms were fashioned (into) the nobleman (Rājanya), his thighs were the Vaiśya, from his feet the Śūdra was born.
>
> 13. The moon has been born from his mind, the sun was born from his eye; from his mouth was born Indra and Agni, and from his breath the wind.
>
> 14. From his navel there was the intermediate space (atmosphere), from his head developed heaven, from his feet the earth, from his ears the cardinal directions. Thus they fashioned the worlds.
>
> 16. With sacrifice the gods offered to sacrifice. These were the first forms (of sacrifice). (RV 10.90.7 sqq.; my translation)

The same myth occurs in the Old Norse Edda (Grimnismāl 40, c. 1000 CE), where the primordial giant Ymir is carved up:

> From Ymir's flesh the earth was created,
> from the sweat the sea;
> from the bones the mountains, from the hairs the trees,
> from the skull, Heaven.[104]

The corresponding Old Indian hymn from the Ṛgveda (10.90), quoted above, often reads like a translation, or vice versa. The correspondence opens up the possibility that this is an old, Indo-European idea.[105] This is strengthened by the closely related Old Norse myth of the god Odin, who hung himself on the Yggdrasil tree for nine days and nights as an offering *by himself to himself*.[106] This again has a Vedic parallel, in that "the gods offered the sacrifice with the sacrifice" (Ṛgveda 1.164.50, cf. 10.90.16, above).[107]

***

There also are a number of local South Asian reminisces of this myth, for example, in Nuristani (Kafiri) myth in northeastern Afghanistan and in Kashmir;[108] or by others in Rome, by the killing by Romulus of his brother Remus (< *Yemus, representing the Indian Yama);[109] and in the Hebrew Bible, by Cain's slaying of his brother Abel.[110] However, the myth is also found in southern China, from where it has entered the standard Old Chinese texts (late first millennium BCE). It thus is originally an Austro-Thai myth.[111] According to this version, the primordial giant Pangu was cut up in similar fashion.[112] The first version (below) has close similarities with the Tahiti myth of Ta'aroa (§3.1), which is not surprising, given that both the Austro-Thai and Austronesian language families originated in southern China:

(1) First there was the great cosmic egg.[113] Inside the egg was Chaos, and floating in Chaos was P'an ku, the undeveloped, the divine embryo. And P'an ku burst out of the egg...with an adze in his hand with which he fashioned the world....He chiseled the land and sky apart. He pulled up the mountains on the earth and dug the valleys deep, and made courses for the rivers. High above ride the sun and moon and stars in the sky where P'an ku placed them; below roll the four seas....[114]

(2) The world was never finished until P'an ku died....[F]rom his skull was shaped the dome of the sky, and from his flesh was formed the soil of the fields; from his bones came the rocks, from his blood the rivers and seas; from his hair came all vegetation. His breath was the wind; his voice made thunder; his right eye became the moon, his left eye the sun. From his saliva or sweat came rain. And from the vermin which covered his body came forth mankind.[115]

Related is the Borneo and Filipino myth of the origin of animals from different parts of the body of a slain giant.[116] In Japan, dismemberment is not a feature of primordial creation, but it occurs after the violent death of Izanami, that is, after she was severely burned while giving birth to the fire god Hi.no yagi-haya-wo.no kami (Kojiki 1.7).[117] From her body were created the eight thunders.[118] Later, from the blood of the fire god, killed by her mate, Izanagi, various gods were created, a general trend that is continued by the creation of many other gods from the various polluted parts of the dress and body of Izanagi, at his great purification upon his return from the netherworld.

However, different from the other Eurasian myths, the various parts of Izanami's body do not become parts of the universe. In fact, most of the constituent parts of the universe, especially all the islands of Japan as well as many deities of the sea, the waters and rivers, the wind, the mountains, the plains, the land, and so on, had already been born by Izanami, and even when about to die, she still gave birth to various gods from her vomit, feces, and urine.[119] The case of the killing of the Fire god (Kojiki 1.8) and the birth of various gods from his blood is closer to the myths reported above from Greece and the Near East.

A somewhat aberrant version of the myth of the primordial giant is the Hittite (originally Hurrite) version in which Ullikummi stands on a primordial giant of stone, Upelluri,[120] with which the Austronesian story (Taiwan, Polynesia) of a preexisting rock may be compared.[121] In Japan, the large rock pillar at Shingu (Kii Peninsula), representing Izanagi, is worshipped rather than the deities in the adjacent Shintō shrine.[122] Note also that in Chinese myth, Yü, the first king of the Hsia (Xia) dynasty, was born from his father, Kun (Gun), who had turned into stone. This happened after his execution by the High God, because he had stolen the magic "swelling mold" from him, by which one could build dams to stem the flood. Yü was born when his father's belly was cut open after three years.[123] Similarly, Ch'i (Qi),the son of the first Hsia king, was born from his mother, Tu Shan (Du Shan), who had changed into a rock when frightened by her husband, Kun, who had changed into a bear.[124]

***

In sum, there is fairly widespread evidence for a Laurasian myth that entailed the origin of the world from a preexisting giant, sometimes made of stone. The carving up of the primordial giant may represent a very old stage of (Laurasian) mythology, going back to Stone Age hunter times.[125] The giant would then be a reflection of the hunted or killed animals that were carved up in a similar way, one that could be seen until recently in the northern European (Saami), North Asian, and Ainu bear sacrifice (§3.7, §7.1.2).[126] The bones of such animals must not be cut and were preserved intact as to allow their rebirth (in heaven or in this world).[127]

While the Germanic and Vedic myths of Puruṣa and Ymir may thus go back to Indo-European mythology,[128] the southern Chinese (Austric), Austronesian, Polynesian, and Hittite versions represent other traditions. However, in all these cases they were no longer told by ancient hunters and gatherers but by food-producing societies;[129] in sum, they were reminiscences of an earlier stage of culture—and presumably, of mythology.

§3.1.5. Bull

This motif is further developed in the closely related version of a late Stone Age animal sacrifice (§3.6, §7.2), mostly that of a bull. It appears as the second Indo-European version,[130] which does not feature a giant or a hunted animal but a primordial bovine. Cases in point are the primordial Icelandic cow Audumla in the Edda and, more importantly, the Iranian primordial bull.[131] The same idea is also found in a Vedic passage and,[132] importantly, in the Old Irish Tain Bo Cuailnge (4854–4919), telling of the great battle between two bulls. The victorious one, Denn Cuailnge, spread the remains of the other one, Finnbennach, all over Ireland. And, not to forget, Zeus in the form of a bull pursues Eurōpē, whose name means "the broad," just like Vedic pṛthivī (earth). Its Greek linguistic counterpart, *Plataiai*, is a famous place-name in northern Greece, which area is also called Eurōpē and has given its name to the continent Europe.

The idea of bull sacrifice (cattle or buffalo) seems prominent in the Mediterranean, Indian,[133] and Austric world; its appearance in early Indo-Iranian texts may be due to such southern influences. If, however, this mytheme was already Indo-European,[134] it could represent a *later* version of the myth of the primordial giant: it would be the preferred one of a largely pastoral people, such as the early Indo-Europeans. It is, then, not surprising that in Icelandic myth, a primordial cow (Audumla) licks the primordial giant (Ymir) out of the eternal ice, and her milk nourishes him (cf. Vǫluspá 3; Vafϸrúnismál 21). The Indo-European myth has been reconstructed by Lincoln:[135]

> There were a bull and two men, the twins Manu, first priest, and Yemos, first King. Manu sacrificed and dismembered Yemos, with whose body parts he formed the world; likewise, from the bull he created edible plants and domestic animals. Yemos became King of the realm of all Dead.[136]

This Indo-European "myth of creation" changed, as per Lincoln and Rafetta, with the various Indo-European peoples, until it became almost completely "disguised" by folklore and religion. Rafetta improbably maintains that this proto-myth underlies "all" Indo-European cosmologies, creation myths, and sacrifices, which she regards as an act of reunification of the divided cosmos.

In other parts of the globe, primarily in Southeast Asia and parts of eastern and Central India, it is the buffalo that plays this role.[137] However, one may add that buffalo sacrifice and putting up the offered animals' horns on temples are also found with the Tibeto-Burmese Newars of the Kathmandu Valley, and the customs are more widely spread in the Himalayas. Finally, the old Mediterranean tradition of bull chasing, sport, and sacrifice has to be taken into account (Neolithic Çatal Höyük, ancient Crete, and modern Spain). It is found in a wide belt, via the Nilgiris and Yunnan, up to Okinawa in Japan.

As will be discussed in more detail below (§7.1.2), emerging food production, especially agriculture, by necessity brought about certain shifts in the mythological system. The hunted animal of late Paleolithic Laurasian times was substituted by the slaughter of a domesticated animal, the bull. Therefore, it is not surprising that a Ṛgvedic hymn (3.38) can refer to the Great Bull in a cosmogonic context. This hymn was later assigned to the demiurge and war god Indra, who is often metaphorically described as a bull. In this hymn, the androgynous "older bull" (*vṛṣabha*) Asura, also called the "great hoary" bull, gives birth to or creates the world. He is in part identified with Heaven and Earth (Rodasī). The (younger) bull, Heaven/Sun, is called Asura Viśvarūpa.[138]

§3.1.6. Egg

Still another version of creation is that of a primordial egg;[139] it represents a vague, "round," undefined, and at the same time limited shape. The motif is more widespread than that of the giant.[140] The universe is created by splitting up an egg; its upper half becomes the vault of the sky, and the lower part, the earth.[141] The mytheme of the eggshell becoming the sky is closely related to that of using the primordial giant's skull for the vault of heaven;[142] in fact, the words for skull and cup or bowl often are the same.[143]

An old version is again found in Vedic myth:[144] Jaiminīya Brāhmaṇa 3.360–61 speaks of the primordial nothingness (quoting Ṛgveda 10.129), the great salt ocean, from which an egg arose; it split, after a hundred divine years, into an upper part (heaven) and a lower one (earth).[145] Similarly, Śatapatha Brāhmaṇa (11.1.6)[146] has the primordial waters and then an egg, from which the creator god Prajāpati burst forth after a year; he created the worlds by speech and then the gods and the antigods (Asuras) from his breath. Another late Vedic text, Chāndogya Upaniṣad 3.19, echoing Ṛgveda 10.129, has a similar version but without a creator:

> In the beginning this (world) was only nonbeing. It was existent. It developed. It turned into an egg. It lay for the period of a year. It split apart. (Its) two eggshells became a silver and a golden one. That which was the silver one became the earth, what was the golden one became the sky. What was the outer membrane (amnion) became the mountains. What was the inner membrane (chorion) became cloud and mist. What were the veins became the rivers. What was the water within became the ocean. (my translation)

An older version, found in Ṛgveda 10.121.7–9, speaks of a golden embryo (*hiraṇyagarbha*)[147] in the midst of the "high waters" from which all developed: the (Himalayan) snow mountains, the ocean, the great stream Rasā, the directions of the sky, Heaven and Earth, the Sun and the Sky. This is similar to the Old Egyptian idea of the vast primordial ocean (Nun) with no surface that was compared to an egg.[148]

However, the myth is also found in Greece, Finland, and China;[149] with the Naxi in southwestern China;[150] and in Indonesia, Hawai'i, and New Zealand.[151] An aberrant version, from Borneo,[152] linked to the myth of the earth retrieved from the bottom of the ocean, is that of the earth recovered by a bird as an egg, again, from the bottom of the ocean. Other versions of this myth have even the humans develop from it.[153] It is found with the Munda (Santals)[154] and also with the Khasi. Since both peoples speak Austric languages, it is not surprising that a similar version is also found in non-Han southern China, where both Austric and Miao-Thai/Kadai language families are found:

> When the great flooding of the Yellow River devastated the land, it killed all mankind. Only a brother and a sister survived by grabbing hold of a big tree trunk. They ended up on a mountain top when the water finally receded. In order to repopulate the land, the brother made the sister pregnant. But she gave birth only to a large, white egg. When the brother wanted to throw it away, the sister protected it with her life.[155]

A related story, again connected with the flood, is found in another area with an Austric language, in Vietnam. The Vietnamese (or Yue) lived in South China well into the first millennium BCE. In the tales of the *Viet Dian U Linh* and *Linh Nam Chich Quai* we have a myth about a primordial egg as origin of the universe and of humans. It is related to the traditional account entitled "The Dragon Lord of Lac [the People]" that tells of Sung Lam, the Dragon Lord, as a trickster who taught the people agriculture and so on but finally returned to his underwater kingdom from where he only emerged, as *deus otiosus*, when specially petitioned. At one time, he appeared as a handsome young man who married the Chinese princess Au Co, who gave birth to 100 children, the Vietnamese. The modern retelling of the myth has the universe emerging from eternal darkness through two eggs, a red one that gave birth to a golden crow (the sun, related to the black crow in the sun in Chinese and hence, Japanese myth) and an ivory one that turned into a swan (the moon). The fierce sunlight shone up to the 36th heaven and made the goddess An Co and her sisters visit the lands below the sun. Eventually An Co met the Dragon Prince, who had come in human form from his undersea palace. Their children, emerging from a large sack of eggs, are half-Nāga and half-divine, the humans. Finally the Dragon Prince returned to his father's undersea palace.[156]

The latter part of the myth has echoes in the Old Japanese myth of Ho-wori's visit to the undersea palace (Kojiki I 43–45) and his marriage to the daughter of the sea deity. Ho-wori is a god but already born on earth after the descent of the sun deity's (Amaterasu) descendant Ninigi. After three years Ho-wori returns to dry land; his wife, in *wani* (crocodile?) form, gives birth and then returns to the sea. Their child becomes the ancestor of the first "emperor," Jimmu. The Japanese myth thus combines origin from the sun deity with that from a reptile-like creature (which, after all, lays eggs). We can establish a web of closely related mythemes reaching from Manchuria and Japan to Vietnam.

However, the motif involving the half-snake Nāga, who can change shape between their human and reptile forms, is also frequently found, in the Indian epic (Mahābhārata) and throughout recorded history from Kashmir to Cambodia, where it is typical for the ancestry of kings. Further, the myth of the origin from an egg is also found in Oceania, Indonesia, and South America.

A variant is that of the origin of humans from an egg. It is found in Old China, especially along the eastern seaboard (whose southern part was Yue territory); but it also is told about the origin of the first Shang king as well as the para-Japonic-speaking Koguryo;[157] an egg as origin of humans in general is found in Munda and Khasi myth (see above).

***

The question may now be put whether the myth of the origin of the world (and secondarily, of gods and humans)[158] from an egg can be linked with that of the primordial waters. After all, "water" is a prominent part of the contents of an egg. Inside these fluids the primeval germ was created, generating the contents of the egg. The two halves of the egg are also linked to the skull of the primordial giant, as already noted. In sum, though the number of mythemes of world creation is not completely reduced, several of them are "logically" related, not in the least by the typical human faculty of establishing links and correlations.[159]

***

Evaluating the evidence presented in this section, we may posit a "logical" development: chaos/darkness –> primordial waters –> (diver myth) floating earth or primeval hill(/egg/giant) –> emergence of heaven and earth. In most cases, only certain sections of this scheme have been preserved in the various Laurasian mythologies.

Further, as has been pointed out above, the mytheme of the primordial giant does not fit well into the Laurasian scheme. This topic is not found in all or even in most Laurasian mythologies, and the question must be asked why the motif has persisted in geographically widespread areas, from Iceland to South China. As indicated, it may well go back to much older, Stone Age ideas of carving up hunted animals,[160] and it may have been inserted into the story line when the new Laurasian mythology was created about 40,000 years ago (§7.1.2). Depending on the evaluation of a few diver myths that are found in Australia and Papua,[161] we may have to expand the range and age of this mytheme beyond the Laurasian sphere and classify it as an "Out of Africa" myth, but one that was formed well *before* the creation of the Laurasian story line.

Using this kind of evidence together with that of the flood myth (which is found in Laurasia but also in Africa, the Andaman Islands, Papua, and Australia; §5.7.2), this discovery leads to a further layering of the development of Laurasian and other mythologies:

• Pan-Gaean myths: the primeval giant, flood myth, etc.
• Out of Africa myths: the earth diver myth etc.
• Laurasian mythology: incorporation of both mythemes into its story line (§6)

If this is correct, we would arrive at the formation of the original Laurasian creation myth. It envisaged primordial darkness hovering over primordial waters; out of this, the earth emerged as primordial hill, or it was fished up, floating on the ocean. It had to be stabilized (§3.1.3) and to be separated from heaven (§3.3).

As an afterthought, we will now look into several versions of these myths that creatively combine many or most of the six versions discussed above.

§3.1.7. Combined forms

In the national epic of Finland, the Kalevala,[162] we find a story that reflects a joining of two motifs, that of the birth of the earth from water, with the help of a bird, and a second one, the birth of the earth and heaven from a primordial egg. The following is summarized from the first canto of the Kalevala:

Luonnotar, "the daughter of the winds" [*ilmatar*], let herself fall from the celestial regions into the sea and floated about until the sea made her pregnant. Having floated about for seven centuries, an eagle (or a duck) searching for a resting place, sat down on her knee and built a nest on it. Luonnotar felt a pain in her knee and the moved it so that the bird's eggs fell into the sea. Their lower part became the earth, and their upper part heaven, their yolk the sun, their white part the moon, their spotted fragments the stars and their black fragments the clouds.

The South American Chibcha people,[163] too, have a fairly confused mythology. Next to a version featuring the creator Chiminigagua, father of all, especially of Sun and Moon, there also is another version according to which mankind was created by a common mother, Bachue. She came out of a swamp near Iguape with a boy of three years on her arm. Grown up, he married her. Many children were born from this couple, four to six at a time; they are the ancestors. When the two grew old, they disappeared into the swamp and became snakes.

Similarly, some Amazon peoples believe that the Milky Way first fertilized the Sun and that the first mother emerged from a river, followed by the first human couple and by the prototypes of the animals and plants. In pre-Colombian Inca belief, Huiracocha created the sun, and the people first emerged from lakes and rivers.[164] With the Incas, the Milky Way was regarded as a river in the sky. In the Inca Empire, a pilgrimage quite similar to that along the Sarasvatī River in Vedic India existed in the Cuzco area of Peru,[165] where the Vicanota River was identified with the Milky Way. Annually, priests used to follow it from Cuzco up to La Raya. This, however, was more than the mere

> renewal of the Sun and the Inca. It was a re-enactment of the creation of the Universe by Huiracocha. The journey was equal to a walk along the Milky Way to the point of origin of the universe. The river was perceived as a mirror of the Milky Way.[166]

Finally, there is the complex case of early Japanese mythology.[167] Early Japanese myths about the primordial unity of Heaven and Earth are not necessarily derived from Chinese influence, as many interpreters of the Kiki (Kojiki and Nihon Shoki) maintain, who normally compare only Chinese texts.[168] It is true that the influence of Chinese culture was strongly felt by the time the Kiki was first written down in the early eighth century.[169] However, the Eurasian background of the Kiki explains the many versions found in these texts in much better fashion.[170]

As has been pointed out above at length, there are several similar variants of the creation myth. All of them are found with just *one* relatively small population in the eastern Nepalese Himalayas, the Rai. Here, Chinese influence is definitely to be excluded; one would expect Tibetan or Indian influence. Such variation is in fact very common in all oral cultures,[171] as can be observed, for example, among the Iroquois people of North America, who have been studied for some 400 years.[172] Thus, if several variants appear in the Kiki, especially in the Nihon Shoki, which makes a point of recording as many as possible, this is not to be marveled at. If, then, one or two versions seem to agree with Chinese mythology, even these may theoretically go back to the older, common Laurasian source. Just their wording may have been influenced by the then-dominant Chinese written culture of the time period that the Nihon Shoki was compiled and put to writing, nota bene, not in Old Japanese but in Chinese.

Actual creation in the Kiki starts from the primordial waters and is described in various versions (Nihon Shoki 1.1–3; cf. Kojiki 1.1):

> The divine beings were produced between them (heaven and earth).... "When the world began to be created, the soil...floated about..."; ...in one writing it is said, "when heaven and earth began, a thing existed in the midst of the void..."; another, "of old, when the land was young and the earth young, it floated about..."; another, "when heaven and earth began, there were deities produced together..."; another "before heaven and earth were produced, there was something...a cloud floating over the sea,[173] a thing was produced shaped like a reed shoot[174] existed in the midst of the void...the soil of the young earth floated about..."; or "when heaven and earth began, a thing was produced in the midst of the void."

And in the Kojiki 1.1 we find:

> At the time of the beginning of heaven and earth, there came into existence in Takama. no hara a deity called *Ame.no Minaka-nushi.no Kami*, next *Taka-mi-musubi.no Kami*, next *Kami-musubi.no Kami*. These three deities all came into existence, as single deities, and their forms were not visible. Next when the land was young, resembling floating oil and drifting like a jellyfish, there sprouted something like reed-shoots [*ashi-kabi*].[175]

It is important to note that the three first gods of the Kojiki creation myth are invisible and worshipped in the Imperial Palace but otherwise only at Ise and in some minor shrines,[176] as well as in those of ancient esoteric sects, especially in Kyushu.[177] However, the ancient prayer (Norito) texts of the period reveal that there are two gods who existed even before all other creation, the male Kamuro-gi and the female Kamuro-mi.[178] Interestingly, these two (apparently very secret) primordial gods occur only in ritual and are never mentioned even in the Kojiki and Nihon Shoki. However, they survive in Norito, in ōharae purification rituals, and in worship at Ise and other shrines. They may represent the primordial pair, in Indo-European terms, Father Heaven and Mother Earth, who are otherwise missing in the Kiki. Their names obviously contain the word for "god," kamu/kami, and the male/female suffixes –gi/–mi, which are also seen in *Izana-gi/Izana-mi*.

That these two deities are not mentioned outside the Norito is not surprising either. The ultimate, primordial gods often are surrounded by a veil of secrecy. They are only known to a few initiated specialists. This is the case, for example, with the Polynesian primordial god Io, the supreme being, ancestor of Io-rangi and his son Tawhito-te-raki.[179] Normally the descent of the Polynesian (Maori) gods is listed as Negation (Kore) –> Chaos/Darkness (Po) –>

Rangi (Heaven or sky). The supreme god Io, known only to some priests, escaped early mythographers for quite some time and thus is not listed in the older accounts of New Zealand mythology.[180] As we have seen (§3.1.1–6), in many other mythologies these early divine generations are as vague as they are in Japan.[181]

The question of the ultimate origin of the world is thus solved in the Kiki in an admirable way. First, it states, matter-of-factly, "There was *something* at the beginning." The rest devolves from this, first by asexual and then, successively, by bisexual creation.[182] There is an inner logic in this. The account begins with the most amorphous, simplest form of life, a "breath," "something" of unknown gender, and gradually, the more "developed" gods take shape. Like their Polynesian neighbors, however, the Old Japanese have given a lot of thought to these very primordial generations. They were not content with just a few of them, like the Greeks, but they must explain and *list*, in great detail, what these "generations" of gods were. As we cannot discuss these stages in great detail here, a list, with my current interpretation, may suffice (Table 3.1).[183]

However, the Ainu of North Japan have a different myth, in which a bird plays the role of creator of the earth out of water, just as in some Siberian and North American Indian myths. In Japan, this recalls the creation by churning of a reed shoot out of the ocean by Taka-mi-musu-bi.no kami or Kami-musu-bi.no kami and Kami-musu-bi-(oya).no mikoto. It also recalls that of all of Japan by Izanami and Izanagi, who churned the ocean with a spear. The latter reminds one of the

TABLE 3.1. *The first stages of the world in Old Japanese mythology (Kojiki, Nihon Shoki)*

0. Primordial state	Primordial ocean, and appearance of: *Kamurogi/Kamuromi* (= Heaven/Earth?)	INTERPRETATION 0. PRIMORDIAL STAGE
1. Polar Star	(*Mi-naka-nushi*)	1. SYMBOL OF STEADINESS
2. Heavenly "pestle"	(*Taka-mi-musubi*)	2. PRIMORDIAL PRODUCTION
3. Earthly "mortar"	(*Kami-musu-bi-[oya]*)	FROM GENERAL MALE / FEMALE INTERACTION
4. Reed shoot	(*Umashi-ashi-kabi-hiko-ji*)	3. (POSSIBILITY OF) VEGETATIVE LIFE
5. Heavenly prop	(*Ame.no toko-tachi*)	4. DUALITY OF COSMOS / GODS
6. Earthly prop	(*Kuni.no toko-tachi*)	
7. Rain god	(*Toyokumo*)	5. ORIGINS AND POSSIBILTY OF VEGETATIVE LIFE
8. Wet Earth (m.) Wet Earth (f.)	(*U-hiji-ni*) (*Su-hiji-ni*)	
9. Door Post (m.) Door Post (f.)	(*Tsunu-guhi*) "germ integrating" (*Iku-guhi*) "life integrating"	6. PRINCIPLE OF POSSIBILITYOF ASCENT TO HEAVEN(?)[194]
10. Male Gate (m.) Fem. Gate (f.)	(*Oho-to.no ji*) "great place" (*Oho-to.no be*) "great place"	
11. *Omo-daru* (m.) *Aya-kashiko-ne* (*f*)	"Face/surface-complete" "Oh how awsome, ah."	7. PRINCIPLE OF INDIVIDUALIZATION IN ANTHROPO-MORPHIC FORM
12. Izanagi (m.) Izanami (f.)	"Inviting male" "Inviting female"	8. PRINCIPLE OF HUMAN(-LIKE) SEXUAL PROCREATION

Indian epic, where the ocean is churned with a big mountain, Mandara. The Fins combine nearly all these versions in a single story.

The Japanese creation myth thus is positioned somewhere between a rather old Indo-European and Near Eastern version (primordial sea) and the widespread motif of a shaky, floating earth found with some Siberian, American Indian, Chinese, and Indian myths. However, it is *not* very close to the particular form the creation myth takes in China, with the "breaths" separating and thus forming heaven and earth; or to the Ainu myth of a bird creating the earth; or to the Polynesian myth of a primordial god Io, who begins the sequence. However, all versions, including the "typical Japanese one" of churning the ocean, are present in Old Indian mythology.[184] The actual start of the creation sequence, thus, is difficult to establish.

Yet it is methodologically important that some of the spatially and temporally very distant mythologies, such as those of Polynesia, Egypt, and Israel, as well as those of the Omaha and Maya, agree more with each other than with those of their neighbors. This observation is *significant*. Just as in the spread of languages, certain motifs that are seen in individual myths and in Laurasian mythology in general have been preserved at distant, diverse ends of the world; frequently, it is *not* the immediate neighbors that are most closely linked, whether in myth or in language.[185] As discussed earlier, isolated, "bizarre" features found in two distant areas usually are a sure hint at something old, an older, now lost structure, myth, or mytheme.[186]

It must be underlined, again, that the mythologies of sub-Saharan Africa, the Andamans, New Guinea/Melanesia, and Australia do not contain most of the creation myths discussed above, especially that of the initial creation of the universe,[187] which is very important in view of the basic similarities and agreements in Laurasian mythologies and their common origin. The motifs and myths discussed in §3.1.1–6 will be taken up again in a wider context, that of the Gondwana and Pan-Gaean mythologies (§§5–6).

■ §3.2. FATHER HEAVEN, MOTHER EARTH

After the emergence of the earth, dealt with in many variations in the individual mythologies, Laurasian mythology had to explain that of Heaven, who overarches her. There are innumerable variations of this topic from Iceland to Tierra del Fuego. However, the emergence of heaven and earth from a primordial close (sexual) union is a clearly established feature among most Eurasian mythologies. The concept clearly is old and may even be represented in late Paleolithic Stone Age rock carvings.[188]

To quote the Maori version of the mytheme, Rangi and Papa were in permanent sexual union, so that their children were kept in permanent darkness between them—a variation of the motif of primordial darkness before creation—until both were pushed apart permanently by a prop (*toko*):

Darkness (*Po*) evolved from the void, negation (*Kore*). Heaven (*Rangi; Wakea* in Hawai'i) and earth (*Papa*) lay in close embrace, so intertwined that their children dwelt in darkness in this narrow realm. The children resolved to rend their parents apart, several attempted in vain, until Tane-mahuta, Lord of Forests,[189] forced heaven upwards from the breast of his wife and let in the light of day....Heaven (Rangi) became content in the sky, only casting down his tears (at night, dew) towards his loving separated wife.[190]

The myth closely fits the distant Indo-European one. Here, Heaven is identified as a male deity, and Earth as female, as "Father Heaven" and "Mother Earth." The Greek *Zeus pater* and *Demeter*, the Latin *Iu-ppiter*, the Ṛgvedic *dyaus pitā* (Father Heaven) and *pṛthivī mātā* (the broad [= earth] Mother),[191] the Germanic **tiu* (as in *Tue's*-day), and so on contain the words *father heaven* and *mother earth*, collocations that can actually be reconstructed for the Proto-Indo-European parent language at c. 3500 BCE:[192] **dieus ph₂tēr* and **dheg'hōm mātēr*, Father Heaven and Mother Earth. The same ideas are reflected in many individual myths of the populations speaking early Indo-European languages. The Greeks have a Homeric hymn to Earth (No. 30),[193] and the Vedic Indians have one to the "broad earth" in the early post-Ṛgvedic Atharvaveda (12.1). However, hymns to Heaven and Earth are fairly rare in the Ṛgveda itself.[194] They were no longer the focus of religious attention, which had moved to gods such as Indra, Agni, and Mitra-Varuṇa.[195]

Similar ideas can be found in the various Altaic languages and religions (Turkic, Mongolian *tngri*)[196] and Korean,[197] as well as in Chinese myth (*di*, "Heaven, god").[198] Heaven is created from the (male) *yang*, and the Earth, from the (female) *yin*; for example, "Heaven was established before earth was fixed. The essences from the sky formed the Yin and Yang."[199] (The myth is remarkably different, however, with a remnant population of Northeast Asia, the Ainu.)[200] In Indonesia or Polynesia,[201] as mentioned above, we find in the same pair, Rangi, the god Heaven, and Papa, the goddess Earth. A modern Maori version reads as follows:

Then Ranginui, the sky, dwelt with Papatuanuku, the earth, and was joined to her, and land was made. But the children of Ranginui and Papatuanuku, who were very numerous, were not of the shape of men, and they lived in the darkness, for their parents were not yet parted. They sky still lay upon the earth, no light had come between them. The heavens were 12 in number, and the lowest layer, lying on the earth, made her unfruitful. Her covering was creeping plants and rank low weed, and the sea was all dark water, dark as night. The time when these things were seemed without end.[202]

However, the matter is interestingly different at the Near Eastern rims of the Eurasian mythological continuum, where killing and dismemberment are stressed. According to the Enuma Elish of Mesopotamia (§3.1.2), in the beginning, the gods of salty and sweet water (Apsu and Tiamat) have several sons, who reside, similar to the case in Polynesia, *inside* her body. Among them is the sky god Anu,[203] who has the child Nudimmud (Ea), an earth/water god. Ea marries Damkinu, and they have a son, Marduk, who eventually becomes the king of the gods (after slaying the great monster Tiamat and creating the world from her body).[204]

The myth of heaven and earth is also somewhat different in Egypt, where it is the *female* sky who covers the *male* earth. This image is prominently found on the lids of sarcophaguses. As mentioned earlier, and as will be discussed later on (§7.1), this merely represents a nighttime version of the same myth: at night, heaven and earth are turned upside down, as is most clearly observable in Vedic myth.[205] Even this perceived aberration reflects Laurasian myth, and the item cannot be attributed to African influence, though clearly, Egypt is on the geographical fringe of Eurasian mythology, and its mythology seems influenced by its original African neighbors and by a local pre-Afroasian ("Hamito-Semitic") substratum.[206]

On the other end of Laurasia, the Amerindian versions must go back to c. 20,000 BCE. They demonstrate many comparable features. Again, we find the typical opposition between a male god of heaven/sun god—as in Eurasia, often identified with fire—and a female goddess of the earth (or reflections of it). For example, the Aztecs know of four creations,[207] in the last one of which all beings are born from the pair Ome-tecuhtli (Earth) and Ome-ciuatl (Fire). They give birth to the gods, and the gods give birth to the world and the sun ("the new fire"):

> The gods assembled at Tenochtitlan, in darkness; they light a big fire and one of them, the smallest, Nanhuatzin, his body covered with pustules of illness,[208] jumped into the brazier. He re-emerged as the bright day time star. The sun and the earth are called *intotan intola Tlaltecuhtli tonatiuh* "our Mother and our Father, the Earth and the Sun."[209]

Among the Maya, the creator god Hunab produces a son, Itzamna, lord of heavens. He is called on in the New Year festivals, and his cult is often associated with that of Kinch Ahau, the sun god. For the Columbian Chibcha of South America, the creator Chiminigagua is the father of all, especially of the Sun and Moon, who create warmth, dryness, or rain. In this mythology, the Moon is the wife of the Sun. Similarly, the Kagaba (Columbia) tell:

> (She is the) mother…of all men, of thunder, streams, trees, all things, the world, older brothers (the stone people),[210]…of fire, the Sun and the Milky Way…of the rain, the only mother we possess.[211]

Still farther south, the Inca's hero Huiracocha, too, is seen as creator and sun god, and the Inca emperor is seen as his descendant. However, there also is a weather god, Illapa, and an earth mother, Pachmama. Closer to Eurasia, the idea of (Father) Heaven is prominent with many native North Americans (and eastern Siberians), among whom he is identified with the sun or the sky (like in Indo-European myth) or with various animals and human figures.[212]

Interestingly, as mentioned, the first two (very secret) gods of Japanese mythology, Kamurogi and Kamuromi, may represent the primordial pair Father Heaven and Mother Earth, though they are not named as such in the Kiki.[213] That both are not mentioned outside the Norito prayers is not surprising. As mentioned, the ultimate, primordial deities are often surrounded by a veil of secrecy. They are only known to a few initiated specialists, as is the case with the Polynesian primordial god Io, the supreme being of the Maori.[214]

In sum, we find a Laurasian-wide spread of myths of the pair Father Heaven/ Mother Earth, a second generation of deities after the primordial "creation," or rather, emergence, out of a featureless void. As we will see later, the non-Laurasian Gondwana religions do not have this pair, except for a few well-explained cases in sub-Saharan Africa,[215] where, at best, a distant and shadowy figure (*deus otiosus*) in heaven sends down his son or others to create the world we live in. (In Australia this is further diversified.)[216] This "dualism" led, in some cultures, to an express division between two segments of society as "male/female" moieties, which can be found in Laurasian as well as in Gondwana societies.[217]

The continuation of this myth is to be found in the detailed accounts of how land was created and shaped, which is a tale quite different from the primordial emergence of (Mother) Earth as such. The new land had to be fashioned in various ways so as to make life on it possible (§3.4).

▪ §3.3. SEPARATION OF HEAVEN AND EARTH, THE PROP

When Heaven and Earth emerge, they are at first lying flat on each other in continuous sexual union, as indicated earlier. They had to be separated,[218] as is perhaps best described in the Maori myth quoted above. The separation is often carried out by a special deity, such as Tane-mahuta and the *toko* pole in Polynesian,[219] Indra in Indian, Atlas in Greek, and Shu in Egyptian mythology.

The propping up of the sky is brought about in various ways that sometimes overlap with each other: by a pole or pillar, a tree, a mountain or giant, and exceptionally even the Milky Way.[220] To begin with, in what seems to be an outcome of the myth of the primordial giant, it is the stone giant, Upelluri, who carries heaven, earth, the ocean, and the hero Ullikummi in a Hittite myth.[221] Geographically close by, in Greek myth we find another giant, Atlas, the son of the Titan Iapetos, who carries Heaven on his shoulders. He has given his name to the Atlas Mountains in Morocco, though Atlas was at first the name of the Kyllene Mountains in the Peloponnese.[222] Just as in the case of Kronos's emasculation, the similarity in concept may be due to influences from the Near Eastern subregion of Laurasian mythology, already noted above (§2.3).

However, the mytheme is also found much farther afield, in Old China: there are eight poles or posts that prop up the sky, or the Buzhou/Kunlun Mountains. When the northwestern mountain was taken away, the sky tilted to the northwest.[223] The story is best told by the Polynesians. The Maori contemporary version, as seen above, is quite elaborate:[224]

> Ranginui, the sky, dwelt with Papatuanuku, the earth, and was joined to her, and land was made. But the children of Ranginui and Papatuanuku, who were very numerous, were not of the shape of men, and they lived in the darkness, for their parents were not yet parted. They sky still lay upon the earth, no light had come between them....
>
> At length the offspring of Ranginui and Papatuanuku, worn out with continual darkness, met together to decide what should be done about their parents that man might arise. "Shall we kill our parents, shall we slay them, our father and our mother, or shall we separate them?" they asked...they decided that Ranginui and Papatuanuku must be forced apart, and they began by turns to attempt this deed....
>
> So then it became the turn of Tanemahuta. Slowly, slowly as the kauri tree did Tanemahuta rise between the Earth and Sky.... [H]e placed his shoulders against the Earth, his mother, and his feet against the Sky. Soon, and yet not soon, for the time was vast, the Sky and Earth began to yield.... Far beneath him he pressed the Earth. Far above he thrust the Sky, and held him there.... As soon as Tanemahuta work was finished the multitude of creatures were uncovered whom Ranginui and Papatuanuku had begotten, and who had never known light.[225]

We may find some occurrences of such myths also in Gondwana mythology and with Munda beliefs about the rainbow snake.[226] At any rate, this version of the prop of the sky seems to be rather old and as such, was incorporated into Laurasian mythology.

The tree

A more common version of the heavenly prop is that of a pole or tree.[227] The world tree is usually thought of as reaching down with its roots into the netherworld and reaching up with its top branches into heaven. It is widespread in northern Eurasia.[228]

For example, the Germanic Yggdrasil of the Edda is described in exactly these terms: the leaves on its upper branches are eaten by the goat Heidrun, and its roots pierce through Niflhel, the netherworld. The three Norns sit at its roots, next to the netherworld spring Hvergelmir, from where the primordial rivers emerge. Similarly, in Japanese myth, there are the eight "ugly females of Yomi,"[229] found at Nihon Shoki 1.19. In one version, in a curious variation, Izanagi, when pursued by the eight Ugly Females of Yomi, "urinates against a large tree, which at once turned into a great river."[230]

Under this tree there also are two wells:[231] one, situated under the root of Yggdrasil, which pierced through the land of the Giants, is the fountain of Mimir,[232] which contains all wisdom. The other one, situated under the third root of Ygg-drasil,[233] was the fountain of the Norns.[234] One of them watered the world tree with its water each day, ensuring its eternal life and perpetual growth. Another version of a subterranean well connected with the tree is found in the Kiki myth of Hohodemi's visits to the palace of the Sea god, where he hides in the large, thousand-branched tree at the gate, above the well.[235]

***

This idea provides the link with the specific Indian idea that the sky or sun is sup-ported by the Milky Way.[236] It can easily be understood, as the Sarasvatī, the river on earth and in the nighttime sky,[237] emerges, just as in Germanic myth, from the roots of the world tree. In Middle Vedic texts, this is acted out in the Yātsattra (pilgrimage-like series of sacrifice) along the Rivers Sarasvatī and Dṛṣadvatī (northwest of Delhi),[238] up to the Plakṣa Prāsravaṇa tree (the "forthstreaming Plakṣa tree") that grows in the foothills of the Himalayas, where one finally reaches Heaven. The texts leave no doubt: "One span north of the tree is the center of the earth viz. the centre of heaven."[239] The connection of the (world) tree with heaven is readily seen in many other instances: note that the bones of dead persons are buried in an urn at the roots of a tree (Kauśika Sūtra 82.32), obviously so as to reach heaven: an archaic practice reminiscent of the burial at the roots of the central pole of a Buddhist *stūpa*.[240]

Like Yggdrasil, the sacred pole at the national shrine of Ise in Central Japan is said to be one-third underground. This feature is also found with the central pole of the Indian *stūpa*, originally a kurgan-like grave mound for the Buddha.[241] In some early sculptures, the pole still is represented with branches and leaves sprouting from its top, just above the dome of the *stūpa*. The pole rises from below the ground, where it is supposed to stand in water,[242] through the dome of the *stūpa*, to its top part, a "box," where it is normally crowned with umbrellas repre-senting the worlds of the gods.[243] The dome-shaped *stūpa* clearly is an image of the three worlds (remember that the sky is created out of half an eggshell or skull; see §3.6). Interestingly the image is maintained in medieval Nepal, where the central *stūpa* of Svayambhūnāth is said to rise above the "ocean," that is, the myth-ological (in fact, geologically real) lake that once covered the Kathmandu Valley, while its pole would reach down into the waters below that lake.[244]

Returning to the tree itself, one may add the fairly early description (c. 1000 BCE) of the two birds in the Ṛgvedic riddle hymn (1.164.20–23). Two birds sit on the branches of an immense tree, that is, the world tree that supports heaven. At night, the god Varuṇa holds it, upside down, its branches pointing down-ward,[245] a concept also found in Indonesia and Micronesia. A similar idea seems to be depicted in some archaeological finds in Jutland (western Denmark).[246]

Such images of the world tree are indeed found well outside India,[247] for example, prominently in the northern Laurasian belt: in the Baltic lands and

Finland,[248] in Siberia, and in the Americas.[249] In Polynesia, the Marquesans mention such a tree in their paradise, "the tree of life, firmly rooted in heaven above, the tree producing in all the heavens the bright and sprightly sons."[250] Note that the tree is rooted in *heaven*, not unlike Varuṇa's upturned tree at night. Again, in Old Chinese myth,[251] a tree grows on top of a mountain sustaining the sun (or rather, the original ten suns).[252]

Even the aboriginal (*bumiputra*) Negritos of Malaya, the Semang, who otherwise follow the Gondwana pattern, have this myth, which raises the question of whether influence for neighboring Austronesian populations is to be assumed. A giant rock, Batu-Ribn, is found at the center of the world above the Netherworld. It is also thought of as a stone pillar that penetrates the sky, into a world where the souls and spirits live and rejoice.[253] The tree plays an important role in Australian ritual, however.[254]

***

Ultimately, for an explanation of this stress on the world tree one must also look back to shamanistic beliefs and practices (§7.1.1), especially those of North Asia. In shamanic belief and ritual, a tree connects the netherworld, this world, and heaven, and it is used notably in the initiation ceremonies of shamans. At this time they climb a tree, symbolizing the ascent to the nine heavens, to sit there for some nights, not unlike the Old Norse Odin in his shaman-like offering of himself to himself.[255]

The tree is well represented in ritual, either as tree or as pole (see below). Examples from burial rituals have already been given; in addition, in India the Vedic offering pole even today has remnants of its original branches left at its curving top (*caṣāla*) as seen in a 2,000-year-old specimen found at Isapur near Mathura (and also in some old sculptures showing *stūpas*). In Japan, the world tree is represented by the *himorogi* tree, on which the gods descend during the ceremony, or by other sacred trees such as the sacred sakaki tree, universally planted at Shintō shrines. They are the mundane representation of the heavenly sakaki growing in Heaven on Mt. Kaguyama.

The pole or pillar

A pole or a pillar appears in many mythologies as the representation of the world tree, especially in northern Eurasia but also in such cases as the *toko* pole, in Polynesia,[256] and as Herakles's pillars on the Atlantic.[257] In the Vedic creation myth it is personified as Indra, who stands up and stretches out his arms to stem apart and support the sky, as does his comrade Viṣṇu (Ṛgveda 1.154.1) and his rival, the ruler of the Universe, Varuṇa (8.41.10). This scene was represented in Vedic ritual by a pillar that is perpetuated by the *indradhvaja* pole at the Indra festivals (*indrajātrā*) in Nepal. Further, we find it in the eastern extension of Siberia, in the Americas:[258] as the tribal pole of the Lakota (Sioux) or as the pole around which the four Mexican *voladores* descend down to earth.[259] In western Eurasia, it appears as the Yggdrasil in Old Norse myth and as Irminsūl in eighth-century Germany, a feature continued to this day in the May Pole festival in many Germanic-speaking countries. In Japan the pole is important as the pillar that the Japanese primordial deities Izanami and Izanagi circumambulated before they procreated to bring about the gods and other living beings,[260] or as the churning pole with which they created the Japanese islands, or as the sacred pole at Ise (see below).

The pole at the center becomes the axis mundi when it is positioned in an azimuth–nadir position. This is evident during the Vedic *vājapeya* ritual, when husband and wife must climb a pole that has a wheel at its top. The pole represents the world tree/world axis[261]—doubtless a reminiscence of Central and northern Asiatic shamanistic ideas—and the wheel at its top is the world of heaven, which turns—as do the Mexican voladores—in the course of the year with the sun and with the turning of the nighttime sky around the polestar. However, in Vedic India the pole is most prominently known as "the pole of Indra," the god who propped up heaven from the earth at the beginning of times. It was erected once per year in Vedic times (*indradhvaja* festival), and this still is retained in modern Nepal at the *indrajātrā* festival in late monsoon as well as at the current Hindu New Year in April.[262]

Since the pole or world tree establishes a direct connection with the gods in heaven, sacrificial animals are slaughtered at its base: this why we have the Vedic offering pole (*yūpa*) and its modern versions in Nepal and India.[263] Most interestingly, there is a strange small rite, otherwise not recorded in Vedic ritual, which is provided by the late Vedic etymologist Yāska. A widow has to climb a pole if she wishes to conceive offspring from her deceased husband: in this way she is closer to him, in his heavenly abode, in the worlds of the fathers.[264] A similar idea is expressed in the Vedic death hymn in connection with the grave.[265] The image of a *sthūna* or *vaṃśa* pole used here is close to that of the world tree. There also is the very clear symbolism of the pole (*yaṣṭi*) found in the center of a Buddhist *stūpa*, mentioned above.

The May Pole in Europe and the *indradhvaja* in modern Nepal and in Vedic India are clear representations of the original prop, that is, the world tree by which heaven was stemmed up. Even current German versions show on the artificial horizontal "branches" of the tree the various levels of life on this earth and of the heavenly regions; they represent all classes of people, with the pope and the emperor on the high branches. It still is a custom to climb the tree and to bring down from its top, which is crowned by a round wreath (like the wheel in the Indian Vājapeya), some delicious food or some other prize. The custom must originally have symbolized a climb to heaven, not unlike that in the Vājapeya and in the actual shamanistic trip to the various stages of heaven. These ascents took or take place, whether in Vedic India, or in Siberia, or with the

Kham Magar tribe of Nepal, on the higher branches of specially cut trees. The feature is also retained in the idea of the Tree of Life, evergreen like the Nordic Yggdrasil or the latter-day Christmas tree.

Similar symbolism of the pole can be found with such diverse groups as the Indonesian Toraja people in Sulawesi (Celebes) and the Lakota (Sioux) Indians, whose sacred Pole symbolizes their tribe and has a life of its own.[266] Here belong also the props used to stem up the sky in Polynesian mythology (toko), briefly discussed earlier (§3.2).[267] When heaven and earth were separated, they were kept apart through props (toko-mua, toko-roto, toko-pa, and rangi-potiki and going by many different names). Sometimes there are two outside and two inside props—or even seven. As described earlier, Tane tore apart the parents to allow daylight to enter the world. Tane alone was able to do so. He is described, like the Indian Indra, as a creator and demiurge god. He spread out the ocean and spread out the stars on the breast of his father, Rangi. He also prepared the Living Waters.[268] He also fought two evil deities, just like Indra fights the Asuras. They are the Tu and Rongo; Tane threw them out of Heaven, into the netherworld darkness of Kaihewa.[269]

At the Totonac New Year festival in Mexico, a large pole is erected, with a square contraption at the top, from which four persons (voladores) are suspended at their feet by strings. Hanging upside down, they slowly descend, turning around 13 times—symbolizing the months and weeks of the year—while unwinding the strings that are wound around the pole. This old custom, used since Aztec times, symbolizes the course of the sun during the Four Ages.[270]

Finally turning to Japan again, the sacred pillar found in the national shrine of Ise cannot be seen by ordinary people but only by particular priests and some young and very old women.[271] There are some other representations of the world tree or pole that can be found at various places. A curious case is that at the Kamikura Shintō shrine on a hill above Shingu on the Kii Peninsula, where, as mentioned, a large, roughly phallus-/pillar-shaped stone is found, which points to a survival of rock worship,[272] which has been incorporated into Shintō worship.[273]

Such cases are different from that of two gods in the Kiki account of original creation: first, Ame.no toko-tachi.no kami (Heavenly eternally standing deity), one of the first gods, emerged. His early position in mythological "history" supports the interpretation of his function as the prop supporting heaven and separating heaven and earth,[274] just like the Polynesian toko or the Indian Indra. Interestingly, he has a counterpart, most probably in the night sky, Ame.no mi-naka-nushi.no kami (Master of the august center of heaven). The center of Heaven at night is not the zenith but the polestar, around which the sky revolves.[275] Naming it the "master of the center of heaven" is appropriate for this nighttime counterpart of the daytime "heavenly eternally standing deity."[276]

A variation of the pole/pillar mytheme is that of the sky being supported by four pillars or by five,[277] as in Old China. These versions are found among the

Aztecs and in Greece, India, Old Egypt,[278] and beyond.[279] Just as Atlas is replaced by the pillars of Herakles, so the four world pillars are replaced by various gods (India, Aztec, Chibcha) or even dwarfs (Edda).[280]

World mountain

A close relative of the stone pillar motif is that of actual mountains.[281] The most well known is that of Atlas.[282] The motif is also found in northern India since Ṛgvedic times: Indra used the mountains to fix the still shaking earth. They flew around, and so he cut off their wings.[283] The world mountain, known since late Vedic as the Meru Mountain, is still found in Chitral in northwestern Pakistan as Tirich Mir. Meru or Sumeru has become the center of the Indian world,[284] which is why the gods' home is often sought on high mountains such as the Himala-yas.[285] The Mongols, Buryats, and Kalmyks know of it as Sumbur, Sumur, and Sumer—all loans from India (via Buddhism), but the concept is older: with the more isolated Altai Turks, it is Bai Ülgän, who sits in the middle of the sky on a golden mountain; it has from three to seven stages, depending on the individual mythology.[286]

***

The mountain is represented later on by pyramids such as in Mesoamerica and coastal Peru, by the mythical primordial hill and the step pyramids of oldest Egypt,[287] and by similar structures in Mesopotamia (ziggurat) and in nearby Iran. Further, a topic related to that of the world tree, pillar, or mountain is the other kind of connection with heaven: a ladder of various kinds.[288] The motif of a stone pillar, a wooden pole/tree, or a world mountain is firmly established in Laurasia and seems to have sparked off many important developments (from shamanic trees to pyramids).

■ §3.4. CREATION OF LAND

After the permanent separation of heaven and earth, creation continues with the actual formation of land (cf. §3.3). Usually this is done with the help of a demi-urge, such as the Vedic Indra, who created land some time after he had stemmed apart Heaven and Earth: the Earth, floating on the ocean, was shaky still. As mentioned, Indra cut off the wings of the mountains that used to fly around and sit down here and there. Once the mountains sat down permanently, the Earth became fixed.[289]

In China, where primordial actions of the deities have been turned into political history (as in Rome),[290] it was Nügua,[291] the second of the primordial "emperors," who accomplished this when the new earth was still in a chaotic state:

The four extremes [quarters of the sky] and the nine provinces were dislocated....Heaven did not cover earth completely....Fire transgressed everywhere without being mastered, water accumulated without being dispersed. Beasts devoured men, rapacious birds took away the old and weak. Nugua purified the fire of the stones of all colors, killed the black dragon...accumulated the ashes of reeds to stop the overflowing waters....She cut the feet of the grand tortoise in order to fix the four extremes....Then, men could live on earth. (Huainan zi)[292]

In Japan we have two versions of the creation of land, told one after the other and both connected with the early goddess Izanami. In the Kiki, seven generations of gods emerge after the initial creation;[293] the last ones are Izana-gi.no kami (Divine male who invites) and Izana-mi.no kami (Divine female who invites). They were commanded to solidify the drifting land. Standing on the floating bridge of heaven (Ame.no Uki-hashi) they put down a spear into the ocean and churned it, creating the island of Onogoro.[294] The other version is connected with Izumo, the northwestern counterpart of imperial Yamato (in Central Japan).[295] A command is given to the god Ō-kuni-nushi (Kojiki 30.5), and Ō-namuji and Sukuna-biko-na solidify the land. Other versions speak of poles or nails driven into the earth to fix it.

The motif of stabilizing the shaky earth is found in several other traditions, already discussed in passing, such as those of the Ainu.[296] It is also connected with the idea of the underpinning or support of the earth on some sort of base, in China and later on in post-Vedic India. In both traditions, the support surprisingly is the same, a giant turtle. The idea may go back to the Austric substrates in both cultures.

This idea differs from that seen in Egypt and in Vedic India, where the earth emerges from the bottom of the ocean as primordial hill (or is brought up by some animal). In these cases, the earth does not need any stabilizing, just separation from the overarching sky. It may be that the idea of an unstable earth is Siberian and hence, Vedic, while that of a stable primordial hill is Mediterranean/Indian—a matter that cannot be pursued here in detail.[297]

■ §3.5. THE DEMIURGE OR TRICKSTER

Apart from stemming apart heaven and earth and the fixation or stabilization of the land, there are several other themes in cosmogony that take place before the emergence of humans. They tell of the creation of a bright and fertile land that is required for the human environment, the *oikumene*. Such preparations are usually carried out by a demiurge or, as this being is usually called in Amerindian studies, a trickster.

They include the original concealment of the sun/dawn in a cave or inside the earth, its release, the killing of the dragon, and the fertilization of the land with its blood or by releasing sweet waters. Then follow the creation of humans and the associated evil that was attracted by the ancestor of humankind. Human life further requires the acquisition of fire and of the sacred drink. At this stage, too, follow the flood and the repopulation of the world, as well as the origin of human (later, "noble") lineages and their exploits, leading to the histories of individual populations, ending in many traditions with the destruction of the world and its human populations.[298]

§3.5.1. Creation of light

A crucial creation myth is that dealing with the emergence of light.[299] It belongs to one of the stages after the emergence of heaven and earth. More specifically, it deals with the emergence of the light of the sun, which makes life in this world possible. Even a brief look into Stith Thompson's *Motif Index* brings up many forms of this topic: from the well-known biblical version (*fiat lux*) to tribal ones that have the sun shut up in a box or somewhere underground.[300]

As an initial, more detailed exercise of comparison, the close similarity of Old Japanese and Old Indian myth is investigated here (cf. above, foreword). In ancient Japanese myth of the sun deity Amaterasu-ō-mikami hiding in and re-emerging from the Iwato Cave is first recorded in the Kojiki and Nihon Shoki (712/720 CE).[301] The Indian version, the myth of Indra opening the Vala Cave and his release of the "first dawn," is found in the oldest Indian text, the Ṛgveda (c. 1200–1000 BCE).[302]

Both versions are *unlikely* to have influenced each other directly.[303] A diffusion to Japan of this myth from early India around 1000 BCE or even from Buddhist Central Asia around 500 CE is extremely unlikely. When Indian mythology (in Buddhist form) entered Japan via Korea around 500 CE, the Vala myth had virtually disappeared from Indian and certainly from Buddhist consciousness. Even the great Indian epic, the Mahābhārata (assembled c. 100 BCE), knows only of a "demon" Vala who figures in some brief references that have little similarity to the Vedic myth.[304] The many congruences and similarities between the Vedic and Japanese myths that we will encounter in the present section, therefore, must be explained differently. Prima facie, situated at two ends of Asia, they seem to be a good test case for the Laurasian theory. Beyond this, several versions are found in Vedic Indian, Greek, Japanese, Ainu, Southeast Asian, and Amerindian sources and in an aberrant version with the Hawai'ians.

***

The myth relates the disappearance of the sun,[305] or the deity of the sun, in a cave or some other enclosure and its reappearance (often as Dawn) after the intervention of a group of gods (and others), creating or restoring light and prosperity to the world.[306] Its classical Indo-European form is found in the Veda (Ṛgveda). The early morning sun, as dawn, is regarded as a beautiful young woman (Uṣas,

"Dawn").[307] As the "first" Uṣas she was hidden in a cave found on an island in the middle of the stream Rasā at the end of the world. The cave is opened by the strong warrior god Indra,[308] who is accompanied by poets and singers, the Aṅgiras.[309] They recite, sing, shout, and make a lot of noise outside the cave, which is blocked by a robust lock (*phaliga*). The "strong-armed" (*tuvi-grabha, ugra-bāhu*) god Indra smashes the gate with his weapon (*vajra*). He is helped by the recitations and the noise made by his Aṅgiras friends. Through their various combined efforts, he opens the cave, and the "first dawn" emerges, illuminating the whole world. It brings with it not only life but also riches in the form of cattle, the reddish cows. These are identified with the reddish dawn and with ritual poetry,[310] which, in the Ṛgvedic conception, holds this world together. Hence, both cows and poetry are highly coveted by early Indian poets and priests (*brahman*).

The typical hymn, Ṛgveda 3.31, sums up the actions of Indra: light or the dawns (v. 4) are imagined as cows (v. 4), but they also appear as real cows; the repetition of Indra's primordial deed is carried out in today's ritual and poetry (vv. 5, 9), described for past and present times.[311] Indra's exploit is preceded by the explorations of his bitch, Saramā (v. 6), and he is helped by his friends, the Aṅgiras poets and priests (v. 7). All are joyous about the winning of the cows (dawns, cows, poetry; v. 10).

At the time of winter solstice people wondered whether the sun would ever start moving again or whether the dark and cold winter would remain forever. With proper rituals, such as horses races around a turning point, staged fights, and verbal competitions,[312] the sun indeed was moved to return toward its northward course, late in December.[313] This yearly event is referred to by the Ṛgveda, in the context of cosmogony, as having occurred at the *beginning* of time. The initial, primordial act is repeated each year during the dangerous period around winter solstice and year's end,[314] when nature and society dissolve.[315] The reasons for the sun's initial disappearance are not immediately clear in the Indian context, but they are both inside and outside Indo-European myth.[316]

The closest parallel to this foundational myth comes from the other end of Eurasia, from early Japan. If one reads the Veda in comparison with the Kojiki or Nihon Shoki,[317] one will be strongly reminded of the myth of the sun goddess Amaterasu hiding in the cave of the heavenly river (Kojiki 1.15). The cave is mirrored here on earth at Ama.no Kaguyama in the Yamato Plains south of Kyoto and at Amaterasu's shrine at Futami.ga Ura opposite Ise in Central Japan. *Amaterasu* literally means "(She who) shines from heaven."

She hides in the Iwa(ya)to (Stone [house] door) Cave, as she had been insulted in many ways by her unruly younger brother Susa.no Wo (originally the god of the ocean) after he had climbed up to heaven.[318] Amaterasu enters the cave and slams its rock gate shut behind her. The world is thrown into darkness, and the gods assemble at the bed of the heavenly river Ame.no Yasu-Kawa to deliberate what to do. They decide to use a trick. They prepare a ritual and festival in front of the cave, complete with music and dancing. One goddess, Uzume, dances an erotic dance, lowering her garments and exposing her genitals. This makes the other gods shake with laughter. Amaterasu is plagued by curiosity, opens the gate a crack, and peers out. She is shown a mirror, Snow White–like,[319] and sees a "more eminent" deity than herself. This competition makes her come out of the cave. The god Ta-jikara (Arm-strong), hiding next to the door, immediately seizes her, and another god, Futo-tama, puts a string (*shimenawa*)[320] behind Amaterasu so that she cannot go back into the cave. The world is saved from eternal darkness.

As in Vedic India, this myth is told in the context of early cosmogony. The connection with New Year, however, is obvious in Japan as well. The *oho-nihe/daijōsai* (first fruit offering) festival in the 11th month precedes the major New Year rituals, the *chinkonsai* (or *tama-shizume, tama-furi,* "spirit pacifying") and the *mitama-shizume.no ihahi* (spirit enshrining), held in the 12th month. These rituals can be linked to the Iwato myth and indeed have often been linked by Japanese scholars. The sighting of the first sun (*hatsu-hi.no de*) on New Year's Day still is celebrated today.

The details of the two myths cannot be treated here at length; for this an earlier long article on the topic may be compared.[321] Some of the salient features and the surprisingly large degree of overlap between the two versions, as well as in all of Laurasia, can be gleaned from an earlier, more extensive version of this section.[322] We will return to the surprising congruences in both the Japanese and Indian myths after having taken a closer look at corresponding myths of other Indo-European, Eurasian, and Amerindian peoples.

Other Indo-European myths of the hidden sun

The oldest sources for Iranian religion (Avestan texts, c. 1000–500 BCE) contain a similar myth. In Vīdēvdād 2, the first mortal, Yima (Ved. Yama) builds an underground cave functioning as an "ark of Noah," helping humans and animals survive the long cold winter at the beginning of human time. It substitutes for the well-known flood myth, which is not found in Old Iranian texts. The creation of the world and its expansion three times by Ahuramazdā (cf. R̥gveda 4.42.4: Varuṇa)—clearly the Iranian version of the Four Ages (§2.5.2, §3.6)[323]—are followed by a fierce winter that resembles the Germanic Fimbul winter of the Edda and that of Mesoamerican myths, where the Four Ages preceding our present one are marked by successive destructions. Yima's fortress has interior light,[324] as well as stars, moon, and sun and living beings. They all reemerge from the fortress, and human history begins with descendants of the god Yima, the first mortal.

Another version of this Indo-Iranian myth is found with the third Indo-Iranian branch, the fierce Nuristani (formerly called Kafiri) in the mountains of northeastern Afghanistan. Imrâ (Ved. Yama Rājā) was one of their major gods before the recent Islamization (1895).[325] In their myths, a fortress or a house contains light, the sun and moon, water, fields, and so on. The gods engage in various preparations to release the sun, which had been captured by a demon. A track of light leads to the house. It can be entered through a crack in the door or by direct attack from outside: the door is broken, and the gods regain the sun/moon and a horse.

In all Indo-Iranian versions, the basic outline of the myth is retained, even after the 3,000 years that have passed since the time of the oldest sources: the Sun is shut up in a cave, an underground fortress, or a house. A young hero finds its location, smashes the gate or enters the place of the Sun's confinement by trickery, and releases it, along with some women, animals, and plants that make human life sustainable. The Indo-Iranian cave myth thus provides a classical case, albeit one very little used in comparative mythology.

The Baltic languages have preserved many data that are closely related to Indo-Iranian, and some of their myths are well preserved in the Latvian *daina* songs, where some evil character (Velns) captures the Sun's daughter, as in the Indo-Iranian cave (Vala/Vara). Both Slavic and Baltic myths have indeed preserved more vague reminiscences of the Vala myth itself.[326] The Lithuanian god Vēlinas/Vélnias/Véls is the god of the netherworld, and the Old Russian Velesu/Volosu is a god of riches and thus of cattle. Velesu is often seen in opposition to the "striker" deity (Lith. Perúnas, Russ. Perun'), an epithet often used for Indra, who opens the Vala with his *vajra* weapon. The opposition between Velesu and Perun' is still represented in place-names of Slavic Dalmatia.[327]

The Latvian *daina* songs speak of the wedding of God's son (*Dieva dels*) or the Morning star (Auseklis) or the Moon (Mēness) with the Sun's daughter (*Saules Meitas*). Another god, Pērkons (Lith. Pērkunas, Russian Perun', Ved. Parjanya), a relative of the bride or of the groom, strikes the golden oak, the tree of the Thunder god. Probably this is an exorcism meant to expel evil spirits, such as Velns (Ved. Vala), who hide there.[328] There is a close correspondence between the idea of the Sun's daughter, or Dawn, or Sūryā (Ṛgveda 10.86) being married to another god and the opposition of the thunder god (like the Vedic Indra).

Further, in a Lithuanian tale,[329] the hero seeks Aušrine (Dawn):[330] one of the three brothers went to search for the second of the Saule (Suns), that is, Dawn (Aušrine), who presides at dawn and dusk. The ensuing abduction of Dawn reminds one of the shutting up of the dawns (= Vedic cows) in the Vala. Further, Aušrine, just like Uṣas, has a mortal lover. The dawn/sun goddess emerges from the cave and brings light and posterity—and, as in India, also cows—into the world. Even closer to the Vedic myth, as late as 1432 CE, there still was a group of Lithuanian sun worshippers who had a myth about the onetime capture of the sun and its release.[331]

The Latvian *daina* songs deal at length with the (female) sun deity. Her journey takes place in a ship,[332] on the sea (just like the Japanese gods move about in their stone ships or like Herakles in Apollo's cauldron, see below).[333] At night, the Sun moves back by boat, not unlike the Egyptian sun, *under* the earth, toward her rising point in the east. She dances at night on a rock in the middle of the sea, which agrees with the mytheme of the Sun's island in the Rasā in Indian myth as well as with that of the meeting place of Japanese gods on the River Ame.no Yasu-Kawa, where the Sun's alter ego, Uzume, dances her erotic dance.

The related western Indo-European myths from Greece and Rome echo the tale of Indra freeing the cows/dawns from the Vala Cave. However, they seem to deal with the exact opposite of the morning/winter solstice release of the sun, that is, its release from the evening/summer solstice.

According to Greek myth, Geryoneus owned a great heard of cows on the island of Erytheia (Redland),[334] situated in the ocean at the western end of the world. As one of his 12 great "works," the great hero Herakles crosses the *okeanos* in the golden beaker of the sun god Apollo, kills Geryoneus, and drives the cows back eastwards toward Greece.[335] Obviously, the cows of the west, of sunset, are the exact opposite of the cows in the Vala Cave of the east, of sunrise. The island of the cows, Erytheia, has long been understood as the horizontal "other world" in or beyond the world ocean.[336] Herakles, who often looks like a Greek Indra, is a son of Zēus Patēr, "Father Heaven," and he therefore has the same genealogical position in myth as Indra in India and Susa.no Wo in Japan.[337]

However, a myth missing in many Indo-European tales,[338] the abduction of Persephone, provides the background for the disappearance of light. Persephone is the daughter of Demeter (Mother Earth).[339] She is abducted by Hades and becomes his wife. Her angry mother, the earth goddess, no longer produces any food. Everyone starves, and Zeus tells Hades to send back Persephone. But she had already eaten from Hades's granite apple, which ties her to the Underworld forever.[340] Therefore she spends one-third of the year in the Underworld as wife of Hades and two-thirds of the year with the gods on Mt. Olympus. The abduction of Persephone echoes, to some extent, shutting up Amaterasu and Uṣas in caves.

In the Roman version of the Herakles myth, the hero (Hercules), on his way back to Greece, approaches the cave of Cacus near Rome,[341] along with the herd of cows he had taken away from Geryoneus. Cacus, a son of Volcanus, pulls in a number of the cows by their tails.[342] Herakles hears their bellowing, enters the cave, and kills Cacus.

In sum, the Indian winter solstice myth (dawn, eastern position) has been moved in Greece and in Rome, along with the reddish cows, to an evening (dusk/western) setting, while the effect of the disappearing winter sun on the earth, that is, the lack of agriculture produce, is met with in the various Persephone myths.

Other Eurasian mythologies

In other parts of Laurasia, similar myths, or echoes, are found in abundance. Only some of their bare outlines can be listed here. The Ainu, along with the

Koryak, Kamchadal, and other northeastern Siberian peoples, tell that the sun goddess was taken captive and all the deities and human beings died from excessive sleep.[343] Among the peoples of Southeast Asia, the Miao (Hmong) speak of the "long crying birds" (just as in the Kiki), the roosters that were made to cry to summon the sun at dawn, after she had concealed herself for two years.[344] Or they tell that an archer shot down nine of ten suns,[345] so that the sun concealed herself. On hearing the rooster cry, she became curious and went to look for it from an eastern summit, and the world became bright again. This myth has several similarities with the Japanese Kiki myth (curiosity of the sun, rooster); however, the archer myth is close to the southern Chinese version.[346] The motif of sending out animals to find the sun, too, closely matches the Indian versions.

Similarly, for the linguistically unrelated Khasi and Nāga in Assam, the Sun goddess hides in a cave. The Angami-Nāga stress that the rooster made the sun move up to heaven and shine on the whole world, and the Khasi tell of a beautiful young woman hiding in a cave until a boy showed her flowers, slowly pulled her to the opening, and married her.[347] This myth adds the Japanese motif of drawing out the Sun goddess: not by force, as in the Indo-European myths, but by temptation.

Clearly, Japanese myth takes an intermediate position between the Indo-European and the Southeast Asian versions of this myth. The motif of opening the gate of a cave is found in all versions, but the methods differ: force or treachery in the Indo-European versions and stirring the Sun's curiosity in Southeast Asia and in Japan, where some "Indo-European" echoes have been added (opening of the gate of the cave by a strong male deity, sexual exhibition by a female deity in a carnival outside the cave—as in the Vedic Mahāvrata ritual, the sun's retreat into the cave because of sexual assault by a relative).

***

An important point of method and procedure is that the comparison of the Old Indian and Old Japanese myths of the hidden sun evidently indicates that these myths (and related rituals) share many more features with each other than with those of the surrounding Eurasian area. This points to an especially close relationship. A. Yoshida has looked for precisely such a relationship to Japanese myths in Greek and Scythian mythology as well as for possible intermediate links[348]—which are largely missing in Central Asia. However, the Vedic evidence detailed above and its reconstructed Indo-Iranian predecessors provide just that missing link.

The early Indo-Iranian area has to be located, around 2000 BCE, somewhere in the central Eurasian steppe belt close to the homeland of the Uralic speakers (Finnish, Estonian, Hungarian, etc.) as well as that of the Yeneseian language family (Ket, etc.). Early Uralic and Yeneseian loanwords, such as the word for the group of gods, the Asura,[349] indicate a close, early geographical relationship among the speakers of these three language families.[350] The Indo-Iranians thus lived south of the Eurasian woodlands (taiga), in the Eurasian steppe belt. It stretched from Hungary and Rumania all the way to eastern Manchuria, where the speakers of the Koguryo (Kōkuri) language lived, which is most closely related to Old Japanese.[351] Further, the intrusive Yayoi culture that was introduced into Japan via the Korean mainland is now dated back to 1000 BCE.[352] Somewhere between the Tien Shan Mountains and Manchuria, the Pre-Koguryo-Japonic and Pre-Vedic speakers could have been in contact before c. 1500–1000 BCE, that is, before the western and, in part, the Xinjiang steppes took on an Iranian character. The Vala-Iwato myth may be one of the earliest cases where a particular mythological regional area (Central Asia) can be traced, similar to the one that existed, around 1500/1000 BCE, in Greece and the Near East (seen, for example, in the myth of castrating and killing the last king of heaven by Kronos/Zeus).

In short, in terms of method, the Laurasian myth of the hidden sun functions both as a proof of unexpected long-distance relationships, similar to those between Old Icelandic and Vedic in linguistics, and as an example of an equally unexpected ancient subgrouping—facilitated by the Central Asian mythological macro-region—comparable to that of the easternmost Indo-European language, Tocharian in Xinjiang, with the closely related western Indo-European *kentum* languages such as Greek, Latin, Germanic, and so on. It must be underlined that in all these cases, mythological or linguistic, it is *isolated archaisms* (§2.2) that lead on to the right track and soon reveal the underlying structure, the Laurasian story line. The same can be said about the Amerindian manifestations of this myth.

Amerindian mythologies

The Americas are a continuum of Eurasia, having been settled out of Northeast Asia in several waves only fairly recently, beginning at c. 20,000 BCE.[353] The Amerindian myths, notwithstanding some local developments, therefore offer a welcome means of countercheck for the period before that date. In the Americas, the Vala/Iwato Cave myth can be found in at least three different varieties: the sun is hidden in a box or basket, an (underground ceremonial) chamber of the Sun or the first dawn (in the so-called Emergence myths), or marriage of Sun and Moon (several suns are brothers).[354]

Inuit (Eskimo) mythology is still very close to that of northern Asia; they tell a rather long story about the culture hero/trickster Raven, who found the sun in a house. The Crow and the Amerindians on the northwest coast of Canada have similar tales; in other North American myths, the sun is hidden in a sack. The Cherokee tell a long, involved myth about the Daughter of the Sun.[355] Its motifs are familiar: the sun is shut up in a house/box, the Orpheus myth, the sun is too hot in the beginning, Redland is the evening home of the sun, and also the flood myth. The grieving of the sun about the death of her daughter was only appeased when young men and women amused her by dancing, reminding one of the Japanese version, in another faint echo of Uzume's dance in front of the cave.[356]

In these North American myths, the sun is often hidden in a box instead of a cave or house. However, the ancient Eurasian correlation or even identification of sun and fire is repeated.[357] The Cherokee myth adds the feature of the redbird as the (daughter of the) Sun, a theme we will again encounter in South America. The redbird contains the soul of the sun enclosed in a box, an idea that is rather close to Korean, Japanese, and Dayak ideas about a "spirit box."[358]

The method used to get the sun out of the box or its chamber is the familiar one of trickery, just as in Japan and Nuristan. An Inuit boy tricks the owner of sunlight; Raven tricks Sea Gull in the Crow myth; and the Seven Men of the Cherokee bring back, by a trick, the daughter of the sun from Ghost Land (the netherworld, as in the Orpheus, Persephone, and Indian Sāvitrī myths). Interestingly, the Cherokee myth ties in the (re-)creation of sunlight, descent from solar ancestors, the emergence of death, and the Great Flood in one single, long myth.

Echoes are also found in South America, where the sun often has several brothers, which is reminiscent of the Chinese myth of the ten suns.[359] For example, the tale of the origin of day and night of the Yabarana on the Upper Orinoco occupies a curious position, with a mixture of North, Central, and South American motifs:[360] The sun was caught in a basket; birdsong was heard from it, but when the box was opened the Sun bird flew out and night descended (cf. the Cherokee myth). Another bird put it back into the basket; it rose again to the sky, moving about and standing still only momentarily at the solstices.

Meso- and South America

In Mesoamerica, the stress is on the emergence of the sun from the earth, from *below*. The emergence takes place after a series of "trial creations," during which the gods unsuccessfully tried to create the world, light, and human beings. These ages surprisingly correspond, sometimes even in name, to the Four Ages or four generations of the Indian, Near Eastern, and Greek mythologies.

In Aztec mythology, after the destruction of the Fourth World (or "Sun"), the gods assemble in Teotihuacán to remove darkness once more.[361] They select a certain spirit, Nanahuatl, who jumps into the flames of a "spirit oven" and becomes the Sun; another spirit following him lands in the ashes and becomes the pale Moon.[362] But the new Sun was merely tumbling along, from one side to the other.[363] The Sun declared, "I am asking for their blood, their color, their precious substance." The collective self-sacrifice of the assembled gods, and the human sacrifice to the Sun by the ancestors of the Aztecs,[364] made the sun move regularly through the sky.

Their neighbors, the Mayas, have left us a detailed account in the 16th-century Popol Vuh of the Five "Suns":[365] after the creation of the world the sun did not yet rise; there was only "blackness, early dawn."[366] Then, the bright bird Seven Macaw usurped the position of Sun and Moon and was shot down by two hero boys, Hunahpu and Xbalanque,[367] which again reminds one of the Chinese and Miao myths of shooting down the nine *extra* suns. The boys went to the netherworld and went headfirst into the oven, where they died; on the *fifth* day they reappeared as handsome boys and tricksters and ascended as sun and moon.[368]

However, there is also a brief episode that recalls Indra releasing the cows (dawns) and other important beings from the Vala Cave.[369] Lehmann speaks about Huracan,[370] who splits the mountain with a lightning strike: in this mountain, maize was hidden,[371] just as in the local adaptation of the Vala myth, Indra splits the mountain to reveal a rice dish.[372] The independent appearance of this mytheme may point to old Siberian sources of this Maya tale.

The Kekchi of Guatemala tell a long story about the courtship of Sun and Moon.[373] Again, the future moon, a weaver woman and daughter of a "king," was shut up in a room and then released by a deer hunter (the sun). While both escaped from there, the hunter in bird form, the weaver woman was killed by volcanic fire. Both were reborn as sun and moon. The tale revolves around the marriage of the Hunter and the Weaver girl. However, in the end, Hunter and Weaver girl are again separated when they become Sun and Moon. This evokes many Eurasian echoes, aspects of Greek, Indian, Japanese, and Chinese myth, which will be discussed in detail (§3.5.2).

Mesoamerican mythology thus has transformed some features, apparently due to individual local environment, new social and economic configurations, and especially with emerging large chiefdoms and states, the stress on maize agriculture and the origins of humans from maize.

***

From the point of comparative method, it is remarkable how well some minute aspects of Eurasian myth have been retained, some 10,000–20,000 years after the migration into the Americas. The extant variations, however, provide a good test case, even a prime example, of what can happen to ancient Laurasian myth, how it can be transformed independently, but also how we can retrieve many old features once we start comparing data all across Laurasia. The myth also serves as another useful reminder of the fact that a small, illiterate culture (the Kekchi) can retain important archaisms, while neighboring literate cultures (in this case, the Maya) may have altered, reinterpreted, and reassembled the old myths and motifs so as to fit their advanced, agriculture-based city civilization. In the end, we have to take into account *all* versions of a tale, as we cannot predict which trait or mytheme will become important.[374]

TABLE 3.2. *The myth of the hidden sun in Eurasia and the Americas*

–	sun/dawn/light has not <yet> appeared /	W. Eurasia	E. Eurasia	Americas
–	is hidden, often out of 'greed' of older gods	W. Eur.	E.Eur.	Americas
	<or as the present sun is not yet created			Americas
	or as it is the last surviving sun>			
	or as it is annoyed, due to sexual molestation	W. Eur.	E.Eur.	
–	the gods try to remedy the situation, often in	W. Eur.	E. Eur.	
	association with early humans			
–	they send animal (sometimes human-like)	W. Eur.		Americas
	messengers to explore, to entice keeper			
	of sun (light)			
–	they approach place of the sun & use magic,	W. Eur.	E. Eur.	
	poetry, tricks to get the sun out			
–	the cave/chamber/box of the sun is opened	W. Eur.	E. Eur.	Americas
–	the sun comes out	W. Eur.	E. Eur.	
	(often, out of curiousness)		E. Eur.	Americas
–	is hindered of going back, or only periodically		E. Eur.	Americas
	(days, seasons)			
–	sun light appears; life becomes possible	W. Eur.	E. Eur.	Americas
–	keepers of sun/dawn, offenders punished	W. Eur.	E. Eur.	
	or some sort of exchange is arranged			Americas

***

Again, from the point of view of method, what is important here is the difference between *first emergence* of the sun in Mesoamerican myth and the *(re)emergence* of the sun/dawn in the myths of the Indo-Europeans, Japanese, Miao, and so on.[375] There is either

- emergence, in Central America, with the increasingly *positive* nature of each of the succeeding four/five worlds,[376] or
- first dawn, with the Indo-Europeans and in the Near East/Greece, with the increasingly *negative* aspects of declining "goodness/righteousness" of each of the Four Ages.

Further, we can now take several steps beyond the well-reconstructible Indo-Iranian myth, detailed above, and can begin to describe its *earliest traceable* form (and some of its very early variants). The Laurasian myth of the hidden sun can be summed up as seen in Table 3.2. Myth combines all these features into a meaningful whole, according to the individual local (pre)conditions, path dependencies,[377] and the social and religious background, and it tries to make a significant statement about human life (see §7).

§3.5.2. The slaying of the dragon

Even after the initial creation of the universe, of the earth, and of light and sun-shine,[378] the new earth is not ready for living beings. It has to receive moisture, whether (sweet) water or the blood of a primordial creature. In many traditions, it is the latter. It is only after the earth has been fertilized by a giant reptile's blood that it can support life.

Frequently, (Father) Heaven and (Mother) Earth are the primordial gods. Their children are the Greek Titans, Indian Asuras, or Japanese Kuni.no Kami (Mundane gods).[379] Their younger, victorious cousins are the Olympian gods, the Indian Devas, or the Japanese Ama.no Kami (Heavenly gods), who depict their older cousins as enemies or monsters who have to be slain or at least be subdued.

Most prominent among these fights is the slaying of these early monsters, including the primordial dragon by the Great Hero, a descendant of *Father Heaven*. In India, it is the great Indra who kills the three-headed reptile, just like his Iranian counterpart Θraētaona kills a three-headed dragon and as their distant match in Japan, Susa.no Wo, kills the "eight-forked" dragon (Yamata.no Orochi).[380]

The same is echoed at the other end of Eurasia. It is Beowulf in England, Sigurd in the Icelandic Edda, and Siegfried of Wagner's opera and of the medieval Nibelungen Epic who perform the heroic feat of slaying the "worm."[381] We may also compare Herakles's killing of the Hydra of Lerna. Herakles is the mortal son of the king of the Olympian gods, Zeus. Herakles not only kills various monsters but also finds the cows, or dawn—in other words, he acts just like Indra.

Closely related with the latter topic is the Slavic myth of the hero's fight with Veles (whose name is closely connected with the Avestan Vara and Ved. Vala, both terms for an underground fortress or cave that contains the "cows" [dawn] and the sun and moon as well as goods desired by humans [and in Nuristani myths, "the house near heaven"]). The dichotomy is between Slav. Veles (Lithuanian Vēlinas, Vélnias; Latvian Véls) and Perun' (Lith. Perkúnas,[382] still seen in place-names, even in such relatively late Slavicized areas as Dalmatia).[383] The Indo-European myths have recently been studied by C. Watkins.[384]

Further afield, in ancient Egyptian myth, the victorious Sun (Re) slays the dragon of the deep (Apophis, "With a knife on his head") each night when he passes underground on a boat back toward the east so as to rise again. Even Apophis's bones are destroyed; there is total destruction—no shadow and so on is left.[385] In ritual, Apophis is burned daily *in effigie* at dawn and dusk, an action that reminds of the Vedic *agnihotra* ritual, which also keeps the fire and the sun alive overnight.

In Mesopotamia, Marduk's killing of Apsu is a related theme (see below). The earliest Chinese mythology has the "black dragon" killed;[386] the dragon was not yet regarded then as a beneficial being, as it was later on. There are even echoes as distant as in Hawai'i (Mo'o).

To begin with Japan for a more detailed discussion: the dragon Yamata.no orochi lives on the River Hi in Izumo,[387] the land of Susa.no Wo, originally the lord of the Ocean. In Nihon Shoki 1.51, "he had an eight-forked head and eight-forked tail; his eyes were red like the winter cherry; and on his back firs and cypresses were growing."[388] As it crawled it extended over a space of "eight hills and eight valleys."[389] Susa.no Wo gets the dragon drunk with sake and cuts off one head after another,[390] and tearing him apart, he finds a sword (*kusa-nagi.no tsurugi*) in the dragon's tail, which is to become important later on in the Kiki. The dragon's blood makes earth fertile. It must be investigated in detail why this myth is so close to Indo-Iranian and Indo-European traditions. The case of the creation of light (§3.5.1) points to a common, regional (western) Central Asian origin.[391] This also seems to be the case with this version of the dragon motif, which had spread to the ancestors of the continental Proto-Japanese mythology before entering Japan.[392]

In Iran and India, the dragon-slaying motif is of Indo-European origin, but it has undergone some significant local influence. The dragon is the primordial guardian of productive forces or of riches, and the divine hero Indra (very common in the Ṛgveda) or the Iranian hero Θraētaona or Kərəsāspa is his slayer.[393]

It is one of Indra's main deeds to overcome Vṛtra, originally "Resistance,"[394] who was imagined in Indo-Iranian tradition as a dragon or as a giant snake, lying on the primordial mountain or in the ocean. However, there is also archaeological evidence from southern Central Asia, an area where the speakers of Vedic and Avestan must have passed through.

In the representations of the dragon in the Bactria-Margiana Archaeological Complex [BMAC], an early south Central Asian Bronze Age culture (2400–1600 BCE), the dragon mainly appears as an ugly, scaled, human-headed, standing man carrying a water vessel.[395] In most Indo-Iranian descriptions, however, the dragon is seen not in human form but as a giant reptile, killed by Indra, Θraētaona, or Kərəsāspa, who was resting and cooking on it. However, the reptile also appears, with local Indian and Hindu Kush adaptations, as a giant cobra (*vyaṃsa*).

In the BMAC area, the Eurasian motifs have thus evolved into a typical, local variety. Many of the similarities between the Indo-European and BMAC motifs, however, are due to the general, underlying paradigms of Eurasian myth, found from Ireland to Japan and beyond; they may differ in details as they represent local variations. Interaction between the BMAC and steppe peoples is now clearly visible. By a comparison of Indo-European and BMAC mythological systems, it appears that the old Indo-European myth of dragon slaying has been adjusted in the Avesta under the influence of the BMAC or its successor cultures. Several Avestan texts were composed precisely in the BMAC area. We find not only the killing of the dragon but also Tištriia's fight with the demon of drought, Apaoša, and the generation of clouds and rain, reflecting what Francfort has reconstructed, based on archaeological evidence, for the BMAC belief system.

It appears, then, that the old Indo-European myth of slaying the dragon reflects the influence of the BMAC. Some of these influences, however, are still visible in the Ṛgveda, much farther southeast, in the Panjab. Indra is not just the dragon slayer but also closely connected with releasing the waters. The Ṛgvedic giant cobra, *vyaṃsa*, surrounds the (Pamir and Himalayan) waters and must be killed—at least temporarily—to let them flow.[396] The Indo-Iranian myth, however, lacks the Old Japanese episode of freeing a young woman from the clutches

TABLE 3.3. *Slaying the dragon in Germanic, Indo-Iranian and Japanese mythology*

Germanic	Indo-Iranian	Japanese
Siegried/Sigurd Beowulf	Indra	Susa.no Wo
(mead)	Soma	Sake
	invigorates Indra	is given to dragon, gets drunk, is killed
dragon is slain	dragon *ahi/aži*	*yamata.no orochi*
(cf. Fenris wulf/midgard snake)	is slain	is slain
> releases riches	> released water makes land fertile for cattle herding	> his blood makes land fertile

of the dragon, a motif that is found in later Iranian texts and that has spread from there to Armenia (myth of Mher),[397] the Caucasus, and Europe, mostly as the medieval Christian legend of St. George.[398] The relationships between the dragon and the heroes are summarized for the Indo-Iranian, Germanic, and Japanese areas in Table 3.3.

In another part of Eurasia, in ancient Greece, the motif is first found in the "Homeric" hymn 3.179 ff., where the sun deity, Phoibos Apollo, kills a female snakelike dragon (Python) in a way that in many respects echoes the slaying of the female Tiamat by Marduk and that of the male Vṛtra by Indra (Ṛgveda 1.32):[399]

> Apollo...with his strong bow, the son of Zeus killed the bloated, great-she-dragon,...cruel Typhaon,...a plague among men...until the lord Apollo, who deals death from afar, shot a strong arrow at her. Then she, rent with bitter pangs, lay drawing great gasps of breath and rolling about that place...and so she left her life, breathing forth in blood. The Phoebus Apollo boasted over her: "Now rot here upon the soil that feeds men!"...and darkness covered her eyes.[400]

In this version of the myth, however, nothing is said about fertilizing the earth or providing water for it. We can also compare the myth of Kadmos and the dragon.[401]

Still older is the Hittite myth of Illuyankaš (Eel-snake), which tells of the fight of the Storm God with this giant snake, who steals the god's heart and eyes but is finally killed:[402] similar to Japanese myth, Inara prepares a great festival with drinks and lures the dragon to it. He eats and drinks until he is no longer able to descend to his lair. The human hero Hupasisas binds him with a rope, and the Storm God kills him. The Hittite myth is similar to a Hurrian one, but it is preceded in age by the account of the Mesopotamian text Enuma Elish (tablet IV), which was recited at New Year. The gods elect Marduk as their leader and tell him:

> "Go, and cut of the life of Tiamat!"
> He fashioned a bow, designated it as his weapon,
> Feathered the arrow, set in the string.
> He lifted up a mace and carried it in his right hand,

> Slung the bow and quiver at his side....
> The lord spread his net and encircled her....
> He shot an arrow which pierced her belly,
> split her down the middle and slit her heart,
> vanquished her and extinguished her life.
> He threw down the corpse and stood on top of her....
> The Lord trampled the lower part of Tiamat.
> With his unsparing mace smashed her skull,
> Severed the arteries of her blood,
> And made the North wind carry it off as good news.[403]

The story continues, in the fashion of the Ymir–Puruṣa–Pangu myth (§3.1.4), to explain how the world was fashioned out of her bones.

***

In China, a dragon myth belongs to the oldest strata of local mythology, for example, in Li-ki (Liji), chap. 9, Li-yün, the dragon (*lung*) is one of the four fabulous beings.[404] Nügua,[405] the second of the primordial "emperors," accomplishes the work of dragon slaying. As in the beginning, the earth was still in chaos, and some heroes must put it in order. As quoted above,

> The four extremes and the nine provinces were dislocated.... Nügua purified the fire of the stones of all colors, killed the black dragon.... She cut the feet of the grand tortoise in order to fix the four extremes [quarters of the sky].... Then, men could live on earth. (Huainan zi)[406]

Here the topic of establishing the *oikumene* is most clearly expressed, and killing the dragon is one of its requirements.[407] Another version has, for the first time, also a peaceful, beneficial dragon, as habitually found in later Chinese myth:

> Gonggong [Kung Kung] extended the flood for 22 years.... His son Yu emerged in the form of a horned dragon. Gun's body also transformed into a dragon at that time and thenceforth lived quietly in the deeps.... Yu led other gods to drive away Gonggong, distributed the Growing Soil to remove most of the flood, and led the people to fashion rivers from Ying's tracks and thus channel the remaining floodwaters to the sea.[408]

Another early Chinese dragon-slayer myth focuses on the legendary Hsia (Xia) dynastic anthropogenic figure of Emperor K'ung-chia (Gung Jia).[409] Southern China is home to a large number of Austro-Tai peoples. In one of their myths, coming from Sichuan, the ancient land Pa (Ba):[410]

> The Pa serpent is said to have a black body and a green head. It is so gigantic and greedy that it could swallow an elephant whole. Downstream east lay the Grotto Court Lake, and the Pa serpent also lurked in the waters there and did harm to many fishermen.

Archer I (Yi), the hero of the I people in the east, killed this Pa serpent in a big battle. There is a small hill by the side of Lake Grotto Court that is called the Pa Mound. It is located at the southwest of Yueh-yang, Hunan province. It is where the bones of this gigantic Pa serpent were supposed to have been piled up after Archer I had killed the monster.[411]

Finally, in Polynesia, where we do not expect any dragons—Hawai'i has no snakes or *waran* reptiles like the Komodo dragons—we still hear of them in the form of large lizard gods,[412] who also appear in many other, smaller shapes. They are prominent in the Hawai'ian creation story, which seems superficially influenced by Christian motifs. However, the very similar Maori version has some old verse lines mentioning them.[413] We find a "fallen chief," the lying lizard Ilioha, at the tree with the forbidden fruit of Kane (Maori *Tane*). The myth resembles one that is found closer to the original home of the Polynesians, in Borneo (§2.2.4, §3.5.2), and has correspondences not just in the Bible but also in Greek myth (the serpent at the foot of the tree of the Hesperides, in a garden in the Far West, bearing golden apples; see Table 3.4).[414]

The eagle eating the snake is also prominent in the myths of the Oxus culture (2400–1600 BCE [BMAC]), in Vedic and later Indian myth (Garuda bird in India and Indonesia), in Navajo myth,[415] and in Aztec myth,[416] from where it is preserved in the Mexican state seal, as well as with the Maya (Dresden codex).[417] Occasionally, it is also found outside Laurasia.[418]

We could stop here and regard these stories as myths that deal with doing away with the monsters that populate the newly emerged earth that need to be overcome so as to allow life on earth—frequently, even before humans emerge. However, a closer look at these myths reveals that they are part of a grander mythological

TABLE 3.4. *The slaying of the dragon across Eurasia*

EGYPT	MESOPOT.	GREECE	INDIA/IRAN	JAPAN	CHINA
Seth (god of thunder) attacks	Marduk	Apollo (sun god)	Indra (thunder god)	Susa.no Wo (ascending heaven noisily)	Nüwa
	attacks Apsu	attacks Python (dragon)	attacks dragon	Yamata.no	Black
dragon of the deep; killed & dismembered each night (Apophis)	& monsters: dismembered		ahi/ *aži, is* slain, dismembered	orochi slain, dismembered	Dragon killed
	\<New Year\>		\<New Year/Spring: brings flood / water\>	\<after year-end, Spring\>	\<dragon/water re-emerge in Spring\>
dragon gets drunk by red beer			Soma invigorates Indra	Sake is given to dragon; gets drunk,	
			[Iran/Georgia] [St. George / saved virgin]	is killed virgin Kushinada Hime is saved	

and ritual scheme that is connected with the two solstices, the winter solstice (emergence of the sun or of light; see §3.5.1) and the summer solstice (with the killing of the dragon). A detailed investigation has been carried out elsewhere.[419] Here, the mere results are presented in tabular form (Tables 3.5–3.6).

Methodologically speaking, the correspondences between Eurasian and Meso-american myth are, again, very significant. They testify to the Stone Age prevalence of this myth complex, well before c. 20,000 BCE. This adds significantly to the emerging, large body of rather old data for Laurasian mythology (cf. §2.3). Summing up, the motif of killing the dragon and that of releasing the light of the sun are old Laurasian motifs that can be dated to well before 20 kya, due to their import into the Americas by the first immigrants crossing Bering Land.

§3.5.3. The theft of fire and of the heavenly drink

Fire

The classic locus for the theft of fire is the Greek myth of Prometheus,[420] who steals the fire from the Olympian gods, for the benefit of humans, and is punished by Zeus:[421] he is chained to a rock in the Caucasus, where an eagle daily eats his liver, until he is eventually freed by Herakles (Hesiod, *Theogony* 526). The very name of Prometheus is derived from the Indo-European verbs **meth$_2$* (to snatch away) and **pro-meth$_2$* (to steal). The verb is in active use in the Vedic texts, where *pra-math* means "to steal." However, in Vedic myth, the theft of fire is not carried out for the benefit of humans but for that of the current generation of gods,[422] who originally lived on earth before they ascended to heaven. Among other things, such as the method of sacrifice (apparently executed for the benefit of the primordial deities),[423] they also needed the benefit of fire, which is used in many rituals.

At any rate, we can speak of an Indo-European myth of the theft of fire.[424] However, it is also found in Japan,[425] in many other areas of Laurasia, such as among the Uralic and most Austric speakers (Indonesians, Micronesians, and Polynesians), and in the Americas (Inuit, Amerindians).[426] A close variant of the topic is the mytheme of fire as a gift of a deity.[427] As fire and sun are identified or at least correlated in many Laurasian traditions,[428] the theft of fire is often seen related to that of the theft of light or of the sun. From the Ha-ni ethnic group in western Yunnan of today's China comes this myth of fire (Ah-cha):

> In the beginning, there was no fire and mankind lived in dread of cold and darkness. A young man named Ah-cha determined to obtain fire from the monster who had it in his possession. While the monster was asleep, he stole the fiery pearl that was embedded in the middle of its forehead…and swallowed it.…At home, took a bamboo knife, and cut open his chest so he might release this fire ball within. The pearl rolled out and brought light to the world, but Ah-cha died from the severe burn.[429]

TABLE 3.5. *Sun and Moon and the solstices in Eurasia and Central America*

WINTER Reconstructed for Laurasia	India	China	Japan	Kekchi [1st part/myth]
Winter solstice	Mahāvrata solstice Ritual; New Year Śunāsī-rīya ritual for Indra		(great expiation on December 31) (New Year rituals)	
Sun's daughter/Dawn pursued by own Father (Heaven)	Uṣas pursued by Father Heaven	–	Amaterasu	[Hunter and Weaver woman]
(cf. Greece: Orion and Pleiades)	in antelope form (= Orion) & shot at by Rudra (Sirius)		– –	
she has sexual relation	Uṣas attacked	–	A. & Susa.no Wo	[Hunter & Weaver
with her brother	by her brothers		are siblings: S. violently ascends to A.'s heavenly realm; attacks her & weaver women	Woman probably are siblings]
	Uṣas enclosed in Vala cave	(Weaver woman enclosed in divine village = Vega)	she dies of wound caused by weaver shuttle	Hunter approaches her and dies
	emerges from cave after liberation by Indra		gets revived after liberation from cave by Tajikara	Transforms to humming bird
gets married to a violent god, (of moon, ocean)	marriage of Sūryā, RV 10.85, to Soma (moon?) – Urvaśī 'married' to descendant of Sun: Purūravas (10. 95)	Weaver woman gets married to Cowherd (Altair)	– no overt sexual union between Amaterasu and her brother Susa.no Wo (god of ocean); stand-in for Moon	Weaver woman unites with deer Hunter (Sun)
	[Dawn & Night are weavers (Ṛgveda)]	she neglects her weaving; father separates them by Milky Way	S. & A. produce children: chewing & spitting out, across Milky Way	unite in kitchen; father is 'jealous', separates them on stretch of water
SUMMER				[2ⁿᵈ part of myth]
Summer solstice	Viṣūvat day of year long Gavām Ayana; Varuṇapraghāsa ritual for Varuṇa		(great expiation on June 30)	
Sun's daughter has several lovers	nymph Urvaśī is promiscuous with Gandharvas	–	–	–
Sun's daughter is married to a violent god (of moon, ocean)	Urvaśī is 'married' to Sun's descendant, Purū-ravas for 3 years; Sūryā married to Soma (moon?)	Weaver woman is married to Cowherd	Divine weaver, Sun goddess, A. is in ambiguous rela-tion with her bro-ther Susa.no Wo	Weaver woman (Moon) meets and unites with dear Hunter (Sun)
deities are jealous of sexual relation between the siblings	U.'s sexual partners (Gandharvas) are jealous of union with Purūravas	Heaven is angry (due to exessive sex with Cowherd and neglect of weaving)	–	father is 'jealous' of this union
they violently sepa-rate the two lovers	Gandharva violentlly separate them by sending a flash of lightning	Heaven separates them by Milky Way	first separated by Milky Way; later by gods' punish-ment & expulsion	he separates them on stretch of water & sends flashes of volcanic fire after

(Cont.)

TABLE 3.5. (*Continued*)

WINTER Reconstructed for Laurasia	India	China	Japan	Kekchi [1st part/myth]
			of Susa.no Wo	them
love in separation: two lovers separated by Milky Way	P. roams about madly in mundane Milky Way area (Kurukṣetra) for10 lunar months	Both cannot meet as they live on two sides of Milky Way, as Vega and Altair	both are separated; live in heaven / Yamato or mundane world / Izumo	Hunter roams near stretch of water, for 2 weeks (half lunar month)
(Greece: Orion and the Pleiades)	Uṣas flees her father to the east of Milky Way (= a Pleiade)	–	–	Weaver woman flees her father to a stretch of water
	P. &. U. meet again at lake of mundane Milky Way, in Kurukṣetra	Vega & Altair meet again at MilkyWay bridge	–	Hunter & Weaver meet again at stretch of water
	U. accompanied by 6 other Apsaras as ducks = Pleiades (Kṛttikās)	made of magpie's wings (Cygnus)	–	Weaver is accompanied by snakes, dragon flies
they can meet once per year, near Milky Way	P. meets U. at pond in Kurukṣetra;	(meets at Milky Way)	–	Hunter meets revived Weaver at stretch of water
(on full moon day near Summer solstice?)	they are allowed to meet once per year	they are allowed to meet once per year	–	after 'rebirth' from bottle; (they had previously united for one night only)
Midsummer's Night	On Summer solstice day (Viṣūvat); (by a ritual: bringing Gandharva fire to humans)	On 7th day of 7th month (~ August)	–	–
	U.(?) & Apsaras appear in bird form	by crossing Milky Way on wings of a magpie/crow	–	on water (they had succeeded before to meet in bird form)
final separation as Sun and Moon	P. offered a stay in heaven after death; or in Gandharva world after a one year ritual	year-long separation repeated forever	both separated as deities of heaven/ south/ Yamato and of earth/north/ Izumo	both go their separate ways as Sun and Moon

TABLE 3.6. *Slaying the dragon and freeing the sun across Laurasia in the course of a year*

WINTER SOLSTICE

Indra, Sun disappear	Re-emergence of
dawn's retreat into cave	Sun, Indra
universe becomes dark	new Dawn
Varuṇa takes over	Varuṇa agrees to overlordship of Indra
(Amaterasu in cave; Kekchi Weaver	(Amaterasu reappears; weaver woman
in locked 'kitchen' at night)	released by hunter; they flee)
- - - - - - - - - - - - - - - - - - equinox - - - - - - - - - - - - -	- - - - - - - - - - - - - - - - - - equinox - - - - - - - - - - - -
water captured by dragon/snake	killing of dragon by Indra, Susa.no Wo,
(India, BMAC, Japan, etc.)	(India, BMAC: scaled dragon, Japan),
draught reigns supreme	world becomes fertile

'princess' imprisoned by dragon	princess freed by hero; they marry;
Purūravas & Urvaśī separated, after lightning strike, for 3 years, united only for one night per year, through Gandharva fire;	
Weaver girl (China) separated/Milky Way united by magpie bridge only for 1 night;	
Weaver woman (Kekchi) 'imprisoned' in water bottle, after volcano strike	woman delivered from bottle; reborn as moon; again separated: move to sky as moon and sun

SUMMER SOLSTICE

The famous Polynesian version is that of the great hero Maui, here quoted from a long contemporary version:

> Maui thought that he would extinguish the fires of his ancestress of Mahu-ika. He put out the fires left in the cooking-houses of each family in the village.... At last, Maui said to his mother: "Well, then I will fetch down fire for the world; but which is the path by which I must go?"
>
> His parents... said to him: "If you will go... you will at last reach the dwelling of an ancestress of yours; and if she asks you who you are, you had better call out your name to her, then she will know you are a descendant of hers; but be cautious, and do not play any tricks with her...."
>
> Then he went, and reached the abode of the goddess of fire.... At last he said: "Oh, lady, would you rise up? Where is your fire kept? I have come to beg some from you."... "Oh, then," cried she, "you are my grand-child; what do you want here?" He answered: "I am come to beg fire from you."...
>
> Then the aged woman pulled out her nail; and as she pulled it out fire flowed from it, and she gave it to him.... [He extinguished it again and again.] And thus he went on and on,... until she had pulled all the fingernails out. Then out she pulled the one toe-nail that she had left, and it, too, became fire, and as she dashed it down on the ground the whole place caught fire.
>
> And Maui ran off,... but the fire followed hard after him...; so he changed himself into a fleet-winged eagle,... but it almost caught him.... The forests,... and the earth and the sea both caught fire too, and Maui was very near perishing in the flames.
>
> Then he called on his ancestors Tawhiri-ma-tea and Whatitiri-matakataka, to send down an abundant supply of water... and Tawhiri-ma-tea sent heavy lasting rain, and the fire was quenched; and before Mahu-ika could reach her place of shelter, she almost perished in the rain.
>
> In this manner was extinguished the fire of Mahu-ika, the guardian of fire; but before it was all lost, she saved a few sparks which she threw, to protect them, into the Kaiko-mako, and a few other trees...; hence, men yet use portions of the wood of these trees for fire when they require a light. (www.maori.org.nz/korero)

The origin of fire in Gondwana traditions is seen differently. Frequently, it is not stolen but is derived, similarly to the feat of Mahu-ika, from a person's body.[430] It remains to be investigated how far other Gondwana myths are related.[431] In isolated Tasmania, however, we find a legend of the origin of fire that links it with the stars.[432]

The heavenly drink

The origins and the acquisition of sacred drink are an important topic in many traditions.[433] The exact nature of the inebriating or stimulating drink does not seem to matter that much, though local tradition is always shaped by its effects. Apparently, humans everywhere were quick to explore and discover the stimulating or mind-changing effect of certain drugs contained in plants or their derivative, most notably in drinks. These plants include the fly agaric, ephedra, hashish, bhang, betel, peyote, coca, tea, coffee, and cocoa. An animal derivative is the important fermented honey (mead), and plant derivatives include Indo-European and Near Eastern wine, Tibetan and Newar rice beer (chang), and Tibetan barley beer; northeastern Indian (Arunchal Pradesh) fermented rice itself and its derivatives, such as toddy and sake;[434] and further, Polynesian kava and South American chewed and fermented plants, such as coca, and their derivatives, such as potato-based alcohol. Somewhat later in time, distilled drinks arrived on the scene:[435] such as whiskey, vodka, arrack, rakshi, brandy, cognac, and so on. Many if not most of them have been used in various ritual and shamanistic practices, notably the fly agaric and the soma plant. Their original use seems to have been as mind-altering drugs in shamanistic practices, but people everywhere were quick to discover their mundane pleasures. However, the myths connected with such plants clearly point to a nonmundane origin and often attribute the sacred drinks to the deities, who used it as their own drink.[436]

The classical Greek case is that of the theft of ambrosia from the mountain by an eagle.[437] *Ambrosia*, literally "immortality" (*am-brotos*, "immortal"), is fermented honey (mead). Honey, due to its golden, sunlike color and nondecaying quality, has been a symbol of immortality with many Laurasian peoples. The underlying magical idea is that a nondecaying drink confers nondying—immortality, as its other name, *nectar*, indeed indicates. It is derived from Indo-European *nek'* (to perish) and the suffix *ter*, which indicates instrument or means: *nectar* is the "means (to overcome) death."

The same idea is conferred by the Vedic Indian word *a-mṛta* (nondead, immortal), which refers to the Indian version of the sacred *mead*, which is linguistically equivalent to Skt. *madhu* (sweet). The gods seek it by churning it out of the primordial ocean, according to the epic tale found in the Rāmāyaṇa. The older India texts, the Vedas, however, elaborately speak of another drink, soma, which they call *madhu* (sweet). This apparently is a remembrance of the Indo-European *medhu* (mead). The famous soma (Old Iranian haoma) was stolen by an eagle from a mountain, just like mead in Greek myth, and brought to the gods, especially Indra. More about soma below.

However, mead also was the sacred drink of the Germanic peoples. Caesar has a tall tale to tell in his *Gallic War*: in winter people habitually drank large amounts of mead (and beer). In Germanic myth, mead was first stolen by none other than Odin himself,[438] who needed it because it enabled him to create sacred poetry—just as soma does in India.

Soma indeed is the sacred Indo-Iranian drink par excellence:[439] it inspires poets, it keeps them awake in the long rituals, it is invigorating, and it makes Indra strong enough to face the terrible dragon Vṛtra (§3.5.2) and has the same effect on human warriors. Its identity still is shrouded in mystery. Previous theories such as those by Wasson (fly agaric) do not fit the biological and psychopharmic data: we must look for a small plant with branches (but apparently without leaves) that can be pressed out—*soma* is derived from *su* (to press out)—to yield a bitter fluid that must be sweetened with milk and that still is called, in the pathway tradition of the Indo-Europeans, *madhu* (sweet). It is clear that it was incorporated by the ancestors of the Vedic Indians and Old Iranians into their ritual practices and mythology in Central Asia. This should have occurred close to the high Tien Shan and Pamir mountains, as the best soma/haoma grows, according to the Ṛgveda and the Avesta, on the high mountains.[440] Ephedra seems to be a good possibility. (It is found in westernmost Xinjiang, eastern Afghanistan, and Kalash Land.)[441] A complex cult with very elaborate rituals (both Indian and Zoroastrian) has developed around soma/haoma.

In China, the drug of immortality was stolen from Xiwangmu by Chang'e, the wife of the great archer Yi, and brought to the moon, where Chang'e (or Heng'e) now lives in the form of a toad.[442] In Japan, sake, or *miwa*, has played a comparable role, and it still is first brewed for and used in Shintō rituals.[443] In Polynesia the sacred drink is kava.[444] Beer played a similar role in Egypt and Mesoamerica.

In the Pontic and Near Eastern area, it is wine that played a similar role. The well-known biblical account of Noah getting drunk has been emblematic for much of Judeo-Christian religion. However, wine plays a significant part even in Christian ritual (as the blood of Christ in the Mass) and also in the Greek mystery cult of Dionysus,[445] who is regarded as its "inventor."[446] When Alexander came across vines in the eastern Hindu Kush, he immediately concluded that this area must have been that of Dionysus. Indeed, the inhabitants of Nuristan and Kashmir (both before Islam) and of the modern pagan Kalash Land (northwestern Pakistan) still grow vines and press and ferment their grapes each fall. The new wine is still dedicated to Indra:[447] it has been locally substituted for the once prominent soma, though ephedra grows in the higher Kalash valleys. It can be shown linguistically that the origin of wine is in the Greater Near East: Indo-European *woino– is derived from something like Semitic *wajn, and the Georgia region was one of its early centers. Other tales of the original acquisition of wine are told from India to China and beyond.[448]

▨ §3.6. GENERATIONS, FOUR AGES, AND FIVE SUNS

After the initial creation of the world, further mythological "history" evolved in four or five ages. The concept of the Four Ages (golden, silver, bronze, iron) is well known in occidental mythology. It has been discussed to some extent above (§2.5.2). In the Occident it is first found in Hesiod's *Theogony*, from where it has entered medieval and modern parlance. The same divisions also occurred in various related versions in the ancient Near East, such as in Hurrite and Mesopotamian myths. However, the myth is also widespread in the ancient Indo-European-speaking areas. Importantly, it is also found well beyond this in Eurasia and even in the oldest sources we have from the Americas.[449] Consequently, it must be older than c. 11,500 BCE, the latest date agreed to for the settlement of North America from Siberia; in fact, it must be older than c. 20 kya as new data indicate.

1. Chaos

Most mythologies start with a period of chaos, darkness, or just infinite primordial waters enveloped in darkness. This stage has been discussed in detail earlier (§3.1).

2. Heaven and Earth

Out of chaos arises, sometimes directly, sometimes via some intermediaries, the primordial pair Heaven and Earth (§3.2). This "archetypical pair" is known in occidental (Greek) myth as Ouranos and his wife, Gaia; Ouranos is the father of the Titans, the Cyclopes, and the Hekatonkheires—thus of all gods. Similarly, in India, we have the generation of Father Heaven and Mother Earth (the latter is mostly called the "broad" one). The other Indo-European, Near Eastern, and Amerindian variations of this mytheme have already been discussed earlier (§3.2).

In Japan, however, the sequence of ages and generations begins with some obscure and rarely mentioned deities: (1) Kamurogi and Kamuromi, primordial deities, perhaps representing Heaven/Earth. However, there also are Taka-mi-musu-bi.no kami/Kami-musu-bi.no kami/Kami-musu-bi-oya.no mikoto, who churn the primordial ocean and create a reed shoot. The matter becomes clearer with the emergence of (2) Izanagi and Izanami, who, again, churn the sea and create the Japanese islands. Their children (3) Susa.no Wo and Amaterasu create six male and female deities; one becomes the ancestor of the imperial line, among whom is (4) Ho-Wori.no Mikoto, who marries Toyo-tama Hime, a sea goddess. They establish the use of land and sea and are the ancestors of (5) transitional figures like the Greek heroes: the first "emperor," Jimmu, and his brother, who was to die, like Remus, in the process of the establishment of the Yamato realm. Greek or Germanic-style Titans are absent, however, except for the omnipresent local and mundane gods, the Kuni.no Kami.

3. "Titans"

The primordial deities (Father Heaven/Mother Earth)[450] have two sets of children: the Titans and the Olympians, to use the Greek names in the following discussion. The "demonic" Titans (Kronos etc.) take the same genealogical and functional position in the evolution of the gods as the Germanic giants, the Japanese Kuni.no Kami (Mundane deities). They oppose the "Olympian" gods, such as Zeus, the German Æsir gods of Asgard/Valhalla, or the Japanese Ama.no Kami (Heavenly deities).[451] (In the Bible, too, the *elohīm* [gods] have humans as their children, "in their likeness," both good and evil.)

A variation of this theme involves the Germanic gods of Asgard and Vanaheim—Æsir/Vanir—or the Indian Asura/Deva, two moieties in constant competition who nevertheless also cooperate periodically.[452] The children of Heaven and Earth also cooperate to stem both apart (§3.3)[453] as they were enclosed in the dark space between the two primeval lovers, their parents.

Subsequently, in Greek myth, the Cyclopes and the Hekatonkheires were banned by Ouranos to the Underworld (Tartaros). Angry about the banishment of her children, Ouranos's wife, Gaia, incited her youngest son, Kronos, to rebel. Kronos castrated his father with a sickle and took over the rule of the universe.[454]

The same motif is found in ancient Near Eastern mythology, as, for example, in the Hurrite myth of a succession of the gods Alalu–Anu–Kumarbi–Weather God.[455] But the castration mytheme is missing outside the Near Eastern/Greek *Kulturkreis*. This fact may serve as a useful, exemplary case for the secondary regionalism as an areal feature that emerged after the initial spread of Laurasian mythology (§2.3).

In ancient India, for example (Ṛgveda 4.18.12), the leader of the present gods,[456] Indra, kills his father but does not castrate him. He merely slays him, grabbing his foot. Castration seems to be a Near Eastern predilection. The spread of this particular mytheme confirms something that has long been suspected, namely, that Greek myth was heavily influenced by Greater Levant beliefs. This was in fact a feature well known to the Greeks themselves, for example, in the myth of the abduction from Lebanon to Crete of Eurōpē. No need for an imagined "Black Athena."

While the motif of several generations of gods, one succeeding to the earlier one, is thus widespread—from Iceland and Ireland to the Aztecs and Mayas—the mytheme of castration is not. On the other hand, Kronos's slaying has been compared with the ritual killing of old kings that is found in Africa (as detailed in Frazer's *Golden Bow*). Freudian interpretations apart, the killing of the deity, the father, indeed overlaps with the killing of a reigning "monarch" in the case of Greek, Near Eastern, and Nilotic myth (Shilluk, Dinka, etc.).[457]

In sum, we can establish an old Laurasian myth about the succession of the several generations of deities. We now live in the evil period of the fourth generation and age or rather, as we shall see, in the Fifth Age or "Sun," according to Mesoamerican tradition.

***

In addition, there also are myths of primordial incest between twins (Yama/Yamī),[458] by closely related beings (Izanagi/Izanami, Adam and Eve) or siblings (Indra and Uṣas, Amaterasu and Susa.no Wo),[459] and by Father Heaven and his daughter Dawn.

***

In Japan, the motif of a contest between two groups of deities is present as well, though it is usually claimed that they reflect the incorporation of an important political center at Izumo (on the Sea of Japan in the northwest) into the Yamato state that emerged in the Asuka/Nara region of Central Japan. It is also often thought that, at the same time, Izumo mythology was taken over, too, and superficially incorporated into the official Kiki texts. The events related in Izumo myths precede the descent of the children of Amaterasu to this earth and are of great importance for the understanding of Kiki mythology.[460]

However, against the background of Eurasian mythology, the contest between two sets of deities looks quite different. In various mythologies we have the event, called a "(land-)ceding" process in Japan, taking place between two groups of gods, such as the Greek Titans and Olympians or the Indian Asura and Deva. This competition between cousins—descendants of Father Heaven and Mother Earth—is built into Laurasian mythology, and it is not one instigated by mysterious earlier settlers or Aborigines and their religion. This holds for Japan as well as for other areas. The opposition of two groups of gods and their fight and ultimate agreement in sharing power are not limited to India and Japan. The situation is similar in Old Greek and Germanic mythology. The Germanic-speaking areas, with their Æsir and Vanir deities, or Mesopotamia, with the generation led by Marduk and the earlier ones such as Tiamat, indicate the same kind of opposition. The Greek Titans, children of Father Heaven, have to fight their cousins and even their own descendants, Zeus and the other gods, for supremacy. The leader of the Titans, Kronos, is killed by his own son Zeus. Both groups, however, also intermarry.[461] One may also compare the complex relationships of the Maya deities, as depicted in the Popol Vuh.

In the Kiki, Ō-kuni-nushi and his son give up the land of Izumo to the messengers (i.e., the descendants) of the sun deity Amaterasu.[462] It is important that the Izumo gods are descended from Susa.no Wo, Amaterasu's brother, which perpetuates the Laurasian conflict between cousins, a fight for supremacy between close relatives. Similar to the Germanic myth where Æsir and Vanir have interaction but sometimes remain in separate locations, the son of Ō-kuni-nushi later moves from Izumo and settles on Mt. Miwa in Yamato, the heartland of the emerging Japanese realm. In other words, the two groups of deities are now closely associated in the early center of Japanese power, the Asuka region in southern Yamato.[463] Like the Indian Deva and Asura, both are needed for a balanced *oikumene*; they periodically challenge each other, at New Year, when time and order break down.[464]

4. "Olympians": The competition between Olympians and Titans

The leader of the third generation of Greek deities, Kronos, had many children with his wife, Rheia, whom he devours immediately after their birth, such as the great god of the Ocean, Poseidon. Zeus alone escapes, as he is substituted for by a stone wrapped in diapers. As mentioned, these deities, of the Fourth Age, will be called Olympians here, again following the well-known Greek specimen of Laurasian mythology.

The Olympian gods, with Zeus as their leader, fight for supremacy with their elder brothers, the Titans and their various offspring, usually monsters. The leader of the Titans, Kronos, is defeated by Zeus. Grown up, he forces his father to vomit out his siblings and to concede the reign to him. Just like Zeus or his double Herakles, the Japanese great hero Susa.no Wo and Indra killed various Titanic monsters or drove them to the very rims of the *oikumene*.

***

Both groups, however, intermarry; and thus, the infighting among the two groups reflects the typical relationship between members of a large joint family…who fight for supremacy (Vedic: the rival, *bhrātṛvya*, is derived from the word for "brother"). Of course, in mythology, there is more to this than just rivalry: the structure of the world, and of society, is reflected in this strife as well.

The situation of strife between cousins is found in the oldest Indian mythology (of the Ṛgveda), in clear form. Two groups, the Devas and the Asuras (viz., Āditya), fight for supremacy. Both are descendants of the earlier gods (Pūrve Devāḥ, the Sādhya). The Asuras are defeated, but one of them, the most important god, Varuṇa, joins the Devas and takes over the position of "spiritual" ruler (Varuṇa *rājan*) next to the military leader of the gods, Indra (Indra *rājan*). Varuṇa, however, governs by *ṛta* (active truth, truthful behavior, [universal] law and order). He resides in the ocean in the daytime and in the night sky (Milky Way) at night. The sun and the stars are his spies.

Similarly, in Old Japan, the fight between the "Olympians" and "Titans" takes place after the descent from heaven of the grandchild of the sun deity Amaterasu. As mentioned, it has often been claimed that this strife reflects the incorporation of an important political center at Izumo into the Yamato state, as well as parts of the Izumo mythology into the Kiki.[465] However, against the background of Eurasian mythology, this has to be understood differently, as we find the same, built-in conflict between two groups of gods in various mythologies.

In Japan, Ō-kuni-nushi and his sons give up the land (of Izumo) to the descendants of Amaterasu. However, both groups are closely related. Just like the Indian Asura are cousins of the Devas, the Izumo gods descend from Susa.no Wo, Amaterasu's brother.[466] We thus have a fight for supremacy between relatives, descendants of the siblings Amaterasu and Susa.no Wo,[467] just like the ones seen all over Eurasia. The actual descent of Amaterasu's "grandchild" to reign on earth takes place after the "victory" over the Izumo gods, in the third (Ninigi) to fifth (Jimmu) generation after Amaterasu,[468] on Mt. Takachiho in southern Kyushu—interestingly not in Izumo or Yamato.

Henceforth, while the deity Ōkuninushi goes to the "other world," to Hades (*tokoyo*), and rules over "secret" things, Amaterasu's imperial descendants rule over worldly affairs. Ōkuninushi made it a condition that he was to be worshipped (Kojiki 1.37), and he set down the rules: he established the shrine, the fire drill that is still used in the Izumo shrine, and the offering plates whose clay was brought by him in the form of a bird from the bottom of the sea. The same foundational procedures are later reported about Emperor Jimmu, worshipping at the central hill of the Yamato realm, Ama.no Kaguyama, south of Nara.

It is important to note, however, that in India the supremacy of the "Olympian" gods is temporal only: it lasts for most of the year, but at year's end, Varuṇa joins the Asura group again, and chaos spreads.[469] This feature is retained even today, though it has been shifted, along with the beginning of the year, to the monsoon period when Viṣṇu goes to sleep under the earth for the four months of the rainy season: then, all the demons are let loose and appear as various illnesses and in ritual, as masked demons (such as the Lakhe in Kathmandu). Around the local New Year, carnival-like bouts and diachotomic competitions still take place, for example, in the conservative Kathmandu Valley, or around winter solstice among pagan Kalasha of westernmost Pakistan,[470] when the gods (*devalok*), led by Indr (Balumain), come to the valley from the outside as typical temporal *marebito* visitors and assemble for the main rituals. (In Hawai'i, Captain Cook was welcomed at one such festival as the archetypical outsider but was killed later on.)

***

The opposition of two groups of gods, their competition and fights, and their ultimate agreement on sharing power are thus not limited to Greece, India, and Japan. Instead, the situation is similar in Old Germanic mythology, where the Old Norse Æsir and Vanir fight among themselves. They are descendants of the Giants, but they also intermarry. They may even live in different places, such as the sea gods and Freya, but not in Asgard, the home of the current gods.[471]

Similar dichotomies can be deduced for old Central Asian populations. The influence of the early Indo-Iranians with their Asura/Daiva dichotomy is seen with the Yeneseian and Uralic speakers.[472] Such opposing groups are widespread in Siberia, if only under local names. Farther afield, the early Chinese celebrated similar spring/fall festivals with opposing groups.[473] The Dayaks of Borneo even have a two-month period of upheaval at the end of their year.[474] This is similar to that of the Polynesians, where a god visits them, just as the Japanese *marebito* deities assemble at the Kamiarisai festival at Izumo in November—interestingly not in Yamato. Indra (Balumain) and other deities (*devalok*) visit the Kalasha of the Hindu Kush, at New Year, before order is restored. In Polynesia, the Hawai'ian god Kanaloa creates humans and things destined for humans,[475] while his opponent, Kane (otherwise called Suq, Marawa the spider),[476] always get things wrong—just like the Indian Asuras do in their ongoing struggle with the gods whenever they try to imitate them, which is reported in the post-Ṛgvedic Brāhmaṇa texts.

As has been pointed out (§3.5.1), in Mesoamerica the situation has developed in a somewhat different way.[477] Granted, there are several generations of deities, for example, in the Quiché Maya Popol Vuh: the Plumed Serpent (Cucumatz) and Tepeu, then the "grandparents" Xpiyamoc and Xmucane, their sons including Seven Hunahpe, and finally their grandsons, the hero boys Hunahpu (sun) and Xbalanque (moon), who act before Dawn rises and humans are created. As true "Olympians" they defeat the Lords of the Netherworld. Other opponents, such as Seven Macaw, appear earlier than the successful gods of our times. Seven Macaw tried, with "self-magnification," to be the sun when there was no sunlight yet after the flood. He was shot down by one of the two Maya heroes, Hunahpu.[478]

However, the matter has been tied to the five re-creations of the universe, the Five "Suns." The present (fifth) phase of the universe began when the dawn of the fifth sun appeared, after the previous *Four Suns* had failed. In these "trial creations" the gods had unsuccessfully tried to create the world, light, and human beings. The Four Suns correspond, sometimes even in name, to the Four Ages or four generations of the Indian, Near Eastern, and Greek mythologies. The Navajo name their eras with the same colors as the western Eurasians: the Greek gold, silver, bronze, and iron ages become their golden, silver, red, and black ages.[479] The myth is also found in South America, with the Incas. W. Sullivan (over) interprets it in astromythical fashion,[480] followed by Barber and Barber.[481]

That we indeed are dealing with an ancient myth of Four Ages also appears from the confusion in Maya myth about the proper position in the mythical sequence of the great heroes Xbalanque and Hunahpu. With the addition of these heroes, we now live in the "Fifth Sun." This is a point that also confused Hesiod in his *Theogony*; he has the famous Four Ages but also adds an extra one for the Greek heroes, usually sons of gods, such as Herakles as a son of Zeus, "Father Heaven." Similarly, though the Maya hero Hunahpu clearly is a god, he has attracted many of the heroic features of such semidivine characters as Herakles.[482]

***

In all the mythologies discussed so far, some of the defeated gods leave the inhabited center of this world, but, for example, in India, they (at least Varuṇa) receive worship by the "official" religion and are integrated with the victorious gods. The rest of the defeated, earlier gods become a group of "demons" (Asura, Titans, etc.) or, like the Japanese "mundane deities" (Kuni.no Kami), little more than good or evil local spirits.[483]

***

Comparing the Eurasian and Mesoamerican schemes of four/five generations of deities and Four/Five Ages, the question arises whether the concept of three/four previous worlds is the original one or whether it is a unique local development of Mesoamerica.[484] The concept may have radiated from this important agricultural and political zone to some neighboring areas. Yet we have independent, individual myths of the world's destruction by water, fire, darkness, and cold even with the isolated tribes of the Gran Chaco—whose mythology is not a derivate of distant highland Inca myth—and similarly with the Fuegans.

Moreover, we can find some traces of the Mesoamerican concept of the Five Suns even in Eurasia, though it appears in a different garb. There is the southern Chinese (Miao/Hmong) myth of several, usually ten suns that existed once, before they were eliminated so that only the present sun remained. The Miao and hence the Chinese tell about these ten (the Atayal of highland Taiwan of two) previous suns that made the world too hot; thus, all but one of them had to be shot down by a great archer (Yi, in China).[485] Obviously, there existed ideas about previous suns, not just two or three or four but, frequently, ten.[486] Note that in Maya myth, too, the hero Hunahpu shot down the earlier sun, Seven Macaw.

Apparently, the ancestors of the Mesoamericans and their original, Stone Age Eurasian neighbors, the Miao (and hence, the Chinese), as well as the Austronesians, have combined the myth of the four generations of deities and of the Four Ages (Greece, India, Iran, Navajo, etc.) with that of the ten (or three, or two) suns. As pointed out, Iranian myth has three previous ages before the current one, when the sun and all living beings retreat into the cave-like fortress of Yima. Another related trans-Laurasian feature, the color names of the Four Ages, has already been discussed.[487]

Consequently, the Mesoamerican scheme of the Five Suns is just one outcome of the widespread Laurasian scheme of isolated destructions of the world by the Great Flood, by a great fire, by ice and snow, by being devoured by a monster,[488] or even by "darkness." These have usually, but not always—Iran differs due to its new Zoroastrian ideology—been positioned early on in the mythical time line or at the end of time. The Zoroastrian and Mesoamerican scheme has them in succession, so as to lead to our current "Sun."

***

As discussed earlier, within the general framework of the Laurasian Four Ages,

– either there are increasingly *negative* aspects of declining "goodness/righteousness" in each of the successive Four Ages (with the Indo-Europeans and in the Near East/Greece)
– or there is an increasingly *positive* aspect of each successive world (in Central and South America).[489]

▪ §3.7. THE CREATION OF HUMANS

Semidivine characters such as the Indian Manu, the Greek Herakles, the Japanese Jimmu, the Mayan heroes Hunahpu and Xbalanque, the Inca hero Huiracocha, or the Polynesian Kumu-honua (in Hawai'i; Maori Ko-honua) represent the beginning of humankind on earth and of their subsequent lineages. Many such early lineages have been preserved in the ancient texts (§3.8). The divine ancestors of Greek, Indian, and Germanic princes are well attested.

Interestingly, many lineages trace their origins back to a sun deity, as briefly indicated above (§2.3). This particular belt of origin tales stretches from Old Egypt via Mesopotamia and India to China, Japan, and Polynesia and, farther, to the American offshoot of Laurasia: the great Aztec, Maya (Popol Vuh),[490] and Inca civilizations.

Some have seen, in this distribution, a diffusion out of the ancient Near East.[491] However, this is only an artifact of literary attestation. The question, then, would be: "when, and how?" As some of the occurrences of sun origin are quite old (in Egypt c. 3000 BCE), Frobenius et al. assumed an Near Eastern origin. The question remains (§2.2), however, how the spread should have taken place, especially the assumed one via the Pacific to the Meso- and South American cultures. Reliable evidence for early sustained trans-Pacific travel is slim.[492] On the contrary, in certain well-defined areas such as highland Mexico, we can observe a gradual emergence of village chieftains and leaders of state societies, who then took on the title of sun-derived kings.[493] In short, the spread of solar origin myths is not limited to contiguous areas and those that are connected by wide stretches of ocean, from Egypt to Peru.[494] Their individual occurrence must be explained otherwise. The most obvious solution, it would appear by now, is to assume an older Laurasian version that sees human origins in some solar deity.

***

Individual examples include the following. The Egyptian pharaoh is the son of the solar deity Atum/Amon-Ra;[495] in Mesopotamia, the weather god Marduk is the son of Ea and thus like a "cousin" of Indra.[496] Likewise, the Chinese emperor, always dressed in golden sun's clothes, is the son of Heaven and the human representative of the gods, just as in later Indian myth the king is a living incarnation of the great god Viṣṇu.[497]

In oldest India, however, the "earlier gods" (Pūrve Devāḥ) or the primordial god Tvaṣṭr and his wife, Aditi, have several children.[498] Among them is Vivasvant, the "wide-shining" sun (= Iran. Vīvaŋhuuant). He was actually aborted, in the form of an unshaped "dead egg" (mārtāṇḍa). Vivasvant has one divine, though mortal, son, Yama (Iran. Yima), and another son, Manu, who becomes the ancestor of humans (while it is Yima in Iran).

The idea is also found in other Indo-European areas: we have, through the Roman witness Tacitus, a western Germanic ancestor figure called Mannus, the son of Tuisto (Twin), while Mannus's original sibling Ymir (= Yama) is subsequently found in medieval Iceland, but much earlier in mythical time, as the primordial giant. The motif of *Manus and *Yemos thus is a Proto-Indo-European one,[499] though their solar origin is not that clear. A faint echo is also seen in Rome: the mythological founder of Rome, Romulus, had a brother, Remus (derived by alliteration from Indo-European *Yemos, "Twin"). He was subsequently killed, like Yima in Iran (Spitiiura sawing him up; Yt.19.46) or like the biblical Abel by his brother Cain. Note also that Itsuse.no Mikoto, the elder brother of the first Japanese "emperor," Jimmu, was killed (in battle) before Jimmu reached Yamato on his eastward march, establishing the empire of Yamato (Kojiki I 48).

***

In Vedic India as well as in later Iran, Yama/Yima have a sister (Yamī, "Twin"; Middle Iran. Yimeh). In Iran, where close-kin incest marriage was encouraged, she gave birth to the humans. Yamī was not allowed to do so in India, where Manu had to fashion himself a substitute wife, made of clarified butter (ghee), so as to have children.[500]

Similarly, in Greece, humans are created through a side line of the deities, via the Titans: Ouranos and Gaia → Okeanos → Iapetos → Prometheus/Epimetheus and Pandora → humans Deukalion and Pyrrha, who procreate with stones, the bones of Mother Earth, after the Great Flood.

Perhaps clearest, in Old Japan, the sun deity is descended from the primordial pair, Izanagi and Izanami, who produce three children (among many others, the Sun deity Amaterasu, the god of the ocean and storms Susa.no Wo, and the Moon deity [who soon disappears from the tale]). However, Amaterasu and her brother Susa.no Wo produce children not sexually but, while standing on opposite sides of the Heavenly River, by chewing and spitting out certain substances. As in India and Greece, some of these early generations are not generated sexually. In India and Japan this is done so as to avoid incest—which is another one of the several congruences (creation of light, killing the dragon, etc.) that seem to go back to a common source in the prehistorical Central Asian subregion of Laurasian mythology, c. 2,000 years ago.

***

Somewhat related is the Ainu myth of the origin of humans. They are the children of the Fire goddess Chi-kisa-ni-kamuy (We make firewood [with elm]), who was the first *kamuy* (deity) to descend to earth. Therefore the Fire deity is worshipped first in all rituals.[501] Like the Indo-European and Vedic fire god, she transports human wishes to the gods.[502] Given the typical Eurasian identification of the fire with the sun, the Ainu may have preserved another version of the Laurasian myth of human origins from the Sun deity. Indeed, the Fire goddess is thought of as representing the rays of the fire and of the sun and is depicted as such: holding a fan with sunlight on one side and fire on the other.[503]

The first man in Polynesian myth, Kumu-honua/Kohonua, also is derived directly from the gods, through the goddess of dance, Laka, among others.[504]

***

Across the Pacific, solar origin is seen as well. With the Aztec, the Sun (Tezcatlipoca) produces, in the form of a serpent, together with the Female Sun (Tonacacihua), two children, a male and a female, from whom humankind descends. With the Inca, their emperors are children of the sun, too. Their ancestor is the Inca hero Huiracocha.[505] But the same is true for other Amerindian tribes living outside these empires. The Cherokee myth about the hidden sun ties together the (re-)creation of sunlight, the descent from solar ancestors, the emergence of death, and the Great Flood in one long myth.[506] Echoes are also found in South America, where the sun often has several brothers, which reminds one of the Chinese myth of the ten suns.[507]

***

In comparing the various Laurasian versions, it seems that divine beings become mortal one or two generations down from the solar divinity. For example, in the (reconstructed) Indo-Iranian culture of c. 2000 BCE and therefore in both Old India and Iran, Yama/Yamī and Manu are mortal while their father, Vivasvant (the sun), still is a god, even though he was aborted and born misshaped.

Second, the brother of the founding figure usually must die: Remus in Roman myth, Ymir in Germanic myth, and Yama in Indo-Iranian myth. The same is true for Abel, the brother of Cain of the Hebrew Bible, and Itsuse, the elder brother of the first Japanese emperor, Jimmu.

***

One of the two primordial Japanese deities, too, dies. However, it is not Amaterasu or her brother Susa.no Wo but one of their parents, their mother, Izanami, who dies when giving birth to the fire god Ho-musubi. Her brother, Izanagi, then followed Izanami to the netherworld. She asked him,

> "Pray do not look upon me!"... [Izanagi finally] broke off one of the large end-teeth of the comb... lit [it as] one fire, and entered as to see.... Izanami said "he has shamed me!" (Kojiki 1.9–10)[508]

The Nihon Shoki (1.25) is more detailed:

> He said: "I have come because I sorrow for thee." She answered and said "We are relations. Do not look on me!"... Izanagi... continued to look on her.... Izanami said "You have seen my nakedness.... Now I will in turn see yours." Then Izanagi was ashamed and went away saying: "our relation is severed."[509]

This is one of the many cases where a certain motif has been moved up or down the "family tree" of primordial deities. For example, Ymir is no longer the brother of the western Germanic Mannus, the ancestor of humans, but has become the primordial giant. A similar case is that of Father Heaven and the Thunder god, the Greek Zeus, who corresponds in India to Father Heaven's (Dyaus Pitā's) grandchild, the Thunder god Indra, and in Germanic myth to Thor.

***

In some cases, claims of solar descent have been restricted, in historical times, to the ruling lineage only (Egypt, Japan, Polynesia, Incas).[510] This is a development conditioned by the respective evolving societies; the topic will be investigated further later on (§3.10, §7.2, §8). In such cases, human descent from a (sun) deity has been supplanted by the *restricted* descent of just the nobility from the solar deity. This is prominent even in some Neolithic societies, such as those of Polynesia, where a clear distinction existed among nobles, common men, and slaves; in addition there are the—very prominent—priests (Haw. *kahuna*) as a fourth class. They could paralyze society by declaring a certain taboo (Haw. *kapu*). All these societies have myths about the solar origin of their chieftains.[511] The special position of noblemen is further accentuated by the fact that in many parts of Polynesia only the nobles (*ali'i*) have permanent souls, get permanent burials, and proceed to the otherworld after their death. When common people die, they move toward the western end of their island and just "jump off the cliff"—into nothingness. While similar restrictions were seen in oldest Egypt, where only the pharaoh was reborn, these were subsequently relaxed so as to allow regular people a rebirth.

***

There are some motifs in Gondwana myth that seem superficially related (§5). In such cases, however, humans do not descend from a Sun deity but are heavenly beings (though with tails) from heaven. Or they were created through the agency of an otiose High God;[512] frequently a primordial human pair is found.[513] Or, in southeastern Australia, humans were even created by a trickster-type High God right on earth (§5.3.2). In these myths humans are normally not somatic descendants of the High God, or only indirectly so, via his son or some other descendant or totem (§§5–6). In all cases, however, the myth differs from the Laurasian one, in that humans are not descendants of a Sun deity. Baumann regards such myths, where a High God creates humans from clay, mud, wood, fat, a jawbone, and so on, as extremely old (§5.3.5.2); on the other hand, he thinks that the ultimate origin of the idea is "unclear; it might also have originated from another African or non-African population."[514]

However, human origin from the sun deity is not the only version found in Laurasian mythologies either. There are a number of differing myths, most notably involving origin from clay, from an egg/gourd, or from a tree. They will be dealt with in more detail in the discussion of "southern" (Gondwana) mythologies (§5). However, a brief overview is given below.[515]

From earth

Stories of the creation of humans from clay are widespread: in ancient Egypt (with the help of beer),[516] in Mesopotamia,[517] in the Hebrew Bible, in a very similar version with the Bassari in West Africa,[518] and in the Nuristani version of ancient Indo-Iranian myth. Further, humans were created from clay in China,[519] with the Dayak,[520] and in Polynesia with the Maori and in Hawai'i, where the creation story seems superficially influenced by Christian motives. However, the Maori version has old verse lines with similar motifs.[521] In this version, we find a "fallen chief" and the lying lizard Ilioha at the tree with the forbidden fruit of Kane (Maori Tane). According to Fornander's Hawai'ian version:

> Man (Haw. *Kumu-honua*, Maori *Ko-honua*) is formed out of earth, after the image of Kane. The Gods give him a garden in "the land that moved off," with pig, dog, *mo'o* of many sorts, and a *tapu* (taboo) tree: with sacred apples that cause death if eaten by strangers, and *tapu* cloth that is only used by chiefs. The gods make a wife for him from his right side. He breaks Kane's Law, and is then called "the god who fell because of the law" (*Kane-la'a[kah]uli*). The great white albatross of Kane drives both out of the garden. Kumu-honua retreats eastwards, dies and is buried there.[522]

However close this maybe to the Bible, other versions are more original,[523] but they, too, also have Kane molding Kumu-honua out of wet clay: he is a chief, along with his wife, until she meets a great seabird and is seduced to eat the sacred fruit of Kane. His wife goes mad and becomes a seabird; the bird carries them away; the trees close in after them: therefore, their original home is the "hidden land of Kane"—apparently the original *Savaiki. The Maori version is quite detailed and is again given here as a specimen of local living myth in its contemporary version:

The time had come for the human form to be produced. Urutengangana was anxious that the earth should be provided with the element of *ira tangata* [human beings]. He encouraged his siblings to search for the female element to enable the creation of woman. Urutengangana knew that the *ira tangata* needed would only come from the earth and not just from himself or siblings as they were of *ira atua* [divine]....

They journeyed to Kurawaka and here they found the red clay that Papatuanuku had spoken of. The siblings shared in the creation of woman....After this was completed, Tanematua put the breath of life into her mouth, nostrils and ears. The eyelids opened, the eyes lit up, breath came from the nostrils, hot breath from the mouth, and the living body sneezed. *Tihei Mauri Ora!* [Carrying heart and life!] It is important to note that although Tanematua supplied the breath, Rehua, the head *mangai* of Io, following the instructions from Io Matua, implanted the thoughts and the living spirit (*hau*) into her.[524]

Even in distant South America, echoes of this myth of human creation are found.[525] In the Inca myth of origin, the ancient, pre-Inca site of Tiwanaku on Lake Titicaca was used to underline the divine nature of the Inca.[526] At Tiwanaku, the creator deity Huiracocha formed the first people and then the Inca, whom he then sent northward—underground—to Cuzco to found the empire.[527]

From a tree

Further, we have a number of myths that specify the origin of humans from trees. They are found, occasionally but widely spread, from Iceland (Askr and Embla, licked by a cow out of the primordial ice), Greece (from ash trees), Armenia (Vahagn, the Indo-Iranian Vṛtrahan [from a reed]),[528] and Taiwan (in several versions)[529] to Japan, where this motif appears only in folktales (Kaguyahime, *ki. no mata*) and is not part of the official cosmogony in the Kiki.

However, the motif is much older, as we shall see later (§5.3.6; 5.4).[530] It is prominent in Africa, Melanesia, and Australia. It also occurs in the Waq-Waq Islands known from the *Arabian Nights*; and it is indeed found in the well-known Hainuwele myth of the island of Ceram in eastern Indonesia. Hainuwele was born from the fork of a branch and the stem of a tree.[531]

From maize

A variant of the latter, agriculturally inspired motif is that of origin directly from food products, such as with the Maya. According to the Popol Vuh, humans were created in the present fifth generation of beings, after the deeds of the two heroic boys, Hunahpu and Xbalanque, in the netherworld and after their move to heaven as Sun and Moon: by the use of the new ears of yellow and white maize.[532] This is similar to the motif found in Egypt, where wheat beer is used.

From an egg

Reverting to the origin of the Indo-Iranian Sun deity Vivasvant, this kind of direct or indirect human origin from an egg-shaped form or from an actual egg is widespread.[533] It is presaged by world origin from an egg (§3.1.6) in Egypt, India, Tibet,[534] Oceania, Indonesia, and South America. Apart from this generalized theory of origin, humans are born from an actual egg, for example, in Old China, especially along the eastern seaboard, as well as in the origin myth of the first king of the Shang dynasty as well as that of Koguryo.[535] We also find the origins of humans in general from an egg, in Munda and Khasi myths.[536]

A variant of this motif is the origin of humans, not from the world egg floating in the primordial ocean but more indirectly, from the "great pond." An animal that lays eggs, the stork, carries the new humans, as babies, toward their future mothers. The myth is still alive among the Germanic-speaking peoples, with their motif of the pond as the origin of babies, from where they are brought by a stork (cf. end of §8)—as any look at cards congratulating a new birth readily indicates. In Vedic India, this is the śaiśava ("baby" pool) in the bend of the river Ganges. Similarly, among the Amerindians of the Northwest Coast, there is a baby land, where unborn children play and live before birth.[537]

From a gourd

Another close variant of the birth from an egg is that from a similarly shaped object, a gourd;[538] this is found with many agricultural peoples, for example, in the Chinese myth of the origin of the Chou (Zhou) clan and dynasty, Ch'i (Qi). The "abandoned one" or Hou Chi (Lord Millet) was born when his mother, Lady Yuan, stepped on the big toe of a footprint left by Sheng Min,[539] a distant descendant of the High God ("she trod on the big toe of the God's footprint, and so became pregnant"). He was abandoned but saved several times.[540] Grown up, he started farming and specialized in millet, beans, and other plants; he also was the first sacrificer.[541] In another myth the origin of human beings is likened to that of spreading gourds:[542] "Long drawn out are the stems of the gourds when (our) people first was born" (from the poem "Mien" [Mian], from Shih Ki [Shiji]).[543]

Some late Vedic texts (Taittirīya Āraṇyaka 2, Kaṭha Brāhmaṇa) contain a similar story about the Vātaraśana Ṛṣis, who emerge, naked, from a patch of gourds. Many stories about the origin of certain humans from gourds are also found in the Mahābhārata.[544] Though this is usually very much hidden, it can be traced back through the etymology of the words involved. These myths go back to aboriginal Austric ones,[545] which are represented by Indian (Munda) myths of northern India, the Na-Xi, Miao (Hmong) myths of southern China, and the Kammu myths of northern Thailand.[546] This kind of tale is also found in the myths of the isolated, pastoral, Dravidian-speaking Toda tribe of the South Indian Nilgiri Mountains. Here, Kwoto/Meilitars is born from a gourd.[547]

***

What do we have to make of this great variety of myths about human origins?[548] For sure, they are indeed all found in Laurasian areas, though some of them merely survive in the form of folklore and are not found in official myth collections. The answer to this paradox will be found, just as in the case of the primordial giant (§3.1.4), in a comparison with the non-Laurasian-type myths, the various Gondwana mythologies in sub-Saharan Africa and Australia (see §5).

■ §3.8. DESCENT OF "NOBLE" LINEAGES

While the creation of humans in some cases seems to take place here on earth, especially when they are made from clay, in many others their arrival on the earth is described as a descent from heaven. This is especially clear in the many cases where humans directly descend from the sun deity.[549] This automatically leads to the establishment of local (noble) lineages. It must be clearly understood and *strongly underlined*, however, that this development could take place only *after* the emergence of more complex societies, such as those of food producers in Neolithic times.

One of the clearest cases is the descent of the Japanese deities from heaven, which results in the establishment of the imperial dynasty. It is discussed here at some length. The actual descent of Amaterasu's children to reign on earth takes place after the victory over the Izumo gods (§3.1.7),[550] as mentioned, only in the third (Ninigi) to the fifth generation (Emperor Jimmu)[551] after Amaterasu (her included). It happens on Mt. Takachiho in Hyūga (Kyushu), literally the country "facing the sun" (*hi-muka*). Interestingly, the descent does not occur in Yamato, the heartland of the realm. Jimmu's progress toward Yamato is detailed in Kojiki I 47–52.[552] Why the Yamato elite had to point to Kyushu as their place of origin is an unsolved riddle of Old Japanese mythology and history. It is further complicated by the fact that the Kiki says that Mt. Takachiho is "opposite" of Kara (Korea). If we want to read history into the myth, it may well be the case that cultural influences from the Japanese-speaking Kaya states of South Korea, as well as from the para-Japanese-speaking Koguryo realm in Manchuria and North Korea,[553] are remembered here.

Similar to Japan, the descent of the Indian gods' children to "reign" on earth takes place only in the third generation after the sun god: Aditi's son Vivasvant has as children Yama (who becomes lord of Hades) and Manu, the first real man. Manu's son Nābhanediṣṭha (Closest to his [Manu's] navel) is a shadowy figure, but his grandson Purūravas is well known in mythology as a great fighter who is temporarily "married" to a nymph, the Apsaras Urvaśī (§3.5.2), who leaves him after three years, having produced a son.[554] Similarly, Ninigi, after his descent, marries a lovely young woman whom he met at Cape Kasasa; she is the daughter of Ō-Yama.tsu mi-no kami, a local deity (Kuni.no Kami), a child of the primordial pair Izanagi/Izanami.

Note again the parallel: both Ninigi and Purūravas are married to non-Olympians, a local deity or a nymph. These and other parallels in Indian and Japanese myth are in need of deeper investigation as they point to a shared Central Asian inheritance.[555] Thus, both marry outside their group, while their children become the first in the local lineages. Purūravas in fact is told that he will ultimately go to heaven, to his ancestor, and that his son will go on to "fight for the gods." The son, Āyu, has become the ancestor of all future Indian kings (āyava), of what is later called the "solar line" (sūryavaṃśa).

Another interesting feature, apparently limited to Central Asia and Japan, is that the deity descending to earth is rolled up in a carpet or blanket (Jpn. *fusuma*), which is still used in the Japanese "coronation" ritual,[556] reminding us (of the myth?) of the delivery of Cleopatra to Caesar.

The descent of the Japanese deities taking place on a mountain has been compared with Korean and Altaic mythology.[557] However, we should not forget that the Indian Manu also descends from a mountain—though this takes place after the Great Flood, as does Noah's descent in the Bible. Manu's "touching down (his) boat" and the "stepping down of Manu," as the Śatapatha Brāhmaṇa and Nīlamata Purāṇa say, take place in the Himalayas. This is still known to the Kashmiris as having taken place on the southern mountain range of Kashmir, the Pīr Pantsāl.

The flood story seems to be missing in Japanese mythology.[558] However, the descent of Ninigi from heaven to Mt. Takachiho is quite parallel to the Manu story. The gods, including Ninigi, travel by (stone) boat.[559] Ninigi touches down on a high mountain and descends to earth from there. Just as in the other Japanese myths dealt with above (hidden sun, slaying of the dragon; §3.5.1–2), there is no question of direct Mesopotamian or Vedic Indian influence on Kofun-time Japan. This particular motif, too, must have been transferred to a pre-Japonic population from a common place of origin in Central Asia.[560]

However, a still better case may be that of Itsu.no wo-ha-bari.no kami, who dwells at the upper reaches of the River of Heaven, the Ame.no Yasu-Kawa, which he dammed up, thus blocking the way of other deities. This god was sent down to earth, like Ninigi, and his son was sent to Izumo. As mentioned, the major Japanese deities come down to earth in (stone) boats, so it is perhaps not surprising if it is put in the context of the dammed-up heavenly river,[561] which can actually be seen to touch down on earth each night and which is represented as such in Old Indian mythology:[562] as the heavenly and mundane River Sarasvatī.

In sum, Ninigi coming down in a boat from heaven to Mt. Takachiho clearly reflects the old Eurasian story of a descent of the first man, the ancestor of all living kings (and their subjects), by boat on a high mountain: from the biblical account of Noah to that of Manu. It is possible to add many more accounts of this motif (§3.9, §5.7.2), such as the reemergence of humans after the flood with

Pyrrha and Deukalion, who create humans by throwing stones over their heads or from seeds thrown overhead after the flood.[563]

***

In areas that do not have a heavenly descent, other methods of delivering the first chieftain or king are found. Nevertheless they are linked to the origin of humans from a mother deity (like the Indian Aditi) who gives birth to the Sun god. In this tale, Aditi, the wife of an unnamed group of gods, prepared food for the "earlier deities" (Pūrve Devāḥ), who in the Indian scheme of things must be either her husbands or, more likely, their ancestors. She always ate a remnant of this food—as Indian women must still do today as they are not allowed to eat before their husband and male relatives. After eating the remnant, she always got pregnant and gave birth to several pairs of twins, the Ādityas (Varuṇa, Mitra, Aryaman, etc.). However, finally, she ate *before* handing over the food, and her new pair of twins, Vivasvant and Indra, were more powerful than the elder brothers and were aborted by them. Nevertheless, as they were so magically powerful—derived as they were from untasted food—they continued to live: Indra just stands up and walks away, but Vivasvant is born as a round "dead egg" (round like the sun). The older gods take pity on him and carve him into human form, hence his name, Mārtāṇḍa, "Stemming from a dead egg"—the Sun deity, Vivasvant, the father of Yama and Manu, the ancestor of humans.[564]

This myth has a close parallel in China, where the ancestor of the Hsia (Xia) dynasty, Yü, is conceived by his mother after eating some grains of Job's tears (*coix lacryma-jobi, yi-ssu*): hence the name of the Ssu clan who founded the dynasty.[565] K. C. Chang adds that these are some of the oldest domesticated crops in Eurasia.

However, Hsieh (Xie), the ancestor of another early dynasty, the Shang, was born after his mother had become pregnant by eating an egg dropped by a dark bird.[566] Chang adds,[567] correctly, that the myth of birth from an egg is widespread in the coastal areas of China, as well as for the para-Japanese-speaking state of Koguryo at the borders of Manchuria and Korea.[568] There, it is attested in a stele on the Yalu River, dated 414 CE, that describes the birth of the founder of the Koguryo dynasty. We may further add that it also is prominent in South Asia (Munda, Khasi; see above, §3.1.6).

***

Any historian, however, will readily and justifiably object to the preceding descriptions of the divine origin of nobles, chieftains, and kings as these did not exist in late Paleolithic times, the setting of Laurasian mythology. At that time we can only reckon with small bands of hunter-gatherers who made their way out of Africa.

However, their shamans may already have claimed a link with the celestial spirits and deities—as they still do in Siberia today by experiencing an ascent to heaven and subsequent descent back to this world (§7.1.1). The same is repeated in Vedic Indian ritual, where the priests moved up to the sun/sky and back. Apart from shamans, all humans descend from the Sun deity, as, for example, in Cherokee myth.[569]

That some emerging local chieftains, from Neolithic times onward, claimed heavenly descent solely for themselves is a development (cf. §2.5.3, §3.7) that cannot obscure the original "ideology" of divine origins of all humans. Incidentally, the concept may have had long-standing, pre-Laurasian antecedents: descent from a remote divine figure in heaven is found both in sub-Saharan Africa and in Australia. This point will be investigated further below (§5).

▪ §3.9. THE FLOOD

The motif of actual descent from heaven or from a high mountain (§3.8) is often connected with that of a primordial flood that wiped out nearly all early humans.[570] It is best known from the biblical story of Noah's flood and from the ancient Mesopotamian Gilgamesh Epic (Utanapishtim's tale, tablet XI),[571] the oldest attested written version in world literature.[572] The early Indian version telling of the flood of Manu is found only in a later Vedic text,[573] the Śatapatha Brāhmaṇa. It is of roughly the same time period as the composition of the biblical myth.

All these versions agree that a Great Flood covered all lands and only a few humans survived on a boat. When the flood receded it got stuck on a certain mountain (Ararat in the Caucasus; Mt. Niṣir in eastern Mesopotamia; Naubandhana, "Tying up the boat," in southern Kashmir), and the survivors stepped down from the mountain to repopulate the earth. This congruence of tales has led to widespread speculation, usually based on limited comparisons only. However, from the point of view of Laurasian mythology, these three tales would merely constitute another example derived from the secondary Laurasian subregion of the Greater Near East (§2.5).

The biblical version stresses the flood as punishment for an evil deed. Likewise, the Mesopotamian gods grew restless because of the constant noise of the bustling humans and decided to kill them.[574] The element of retribution or revenge by a deity (or exceptional human such as a shaman-like figure)[575] is indeed a frequent and outstanding feature of this myth wherever it is found. It may, again, be best summarized by a Polynesian version, that of the Maori (with some Christian overtones):

> Puta preached the good doctrines to the wicked tribes in the name of Tane. Mataaho or Matheo was the most obstinate unbeliever of all the skeptical race. Puta prayed to Rangi (heaven) to upset the earth; then the earth turned upside down and all the people perished in the deluge. Hence the flood is called "overturning of Mataaho."[576]

The Polynesian Marquesas' version of the myth is closest to that of the Bible too.[577] However, there are various versions of the myth with other Polynesians and even another version with the Maori, such as the contemporary one that follows:

> Up to the present time Ranginui, the Sky, has remained separate from his wife, the Earth. But their love has never diminished....At length, lest all the land be lost, a party of the other children of Ranginui and Papatuanuku resolved to turn their mother over, so that she and Ranginui should not be always seeing one another's grief and grieving more. This was done and is called Te Hurihanga a Mataaho....When Papatuanuku was turned over by Mataaho, Ruaumoko was still at her breast, and he remained there and was carried to the world below. To keep him warm there he was given fire. He is the guardian of earthquakes, and the rumblings that disturb this land are made by him as he walks about.[578]

The motif of a great flood is found all over the Laurasian area,[579] according to S. Thompson's *Motif Index* (A1010),[580] from Ireland and Old Egypt to Siberia, China,[581] India,[582] Indo-China,[583] Indonesia, Polynesia, and the Americas: it is found with the Inuit and North, Central, and South American tribes, including the isolated Amazon and Fuegan tribes. It can also be found in many tribal areas of the Philippines and in Taiwan,[584] whose Austronesian tribes have several versions of the flood myth. Some of them have now been appropriated by the Christian missionaries.[585]

The Neolithic Selk'nam hunter-gatherers of Tierra del Fuego have transmitted, among the now exterminated Yamana tribe, the myth about a flood that covered all land,[586] except for five mountains (just like a Navajo tale, which ironically comes from a different language group, the non-Amerindian Na-Dene). It is an example of ultima Thule tales, which are not likely to have been transmitted by diffusion from such centers as the Maya or Inca civilizations:[587]

> Once, when spring was approaching, an Ibis was seen flying over someone's hut and people shouted "the Ibises are flying. Spring is here."...However, the Ibis herself...took offense at all that shouting, and, in revenge, let it snow so hard and long that the whole earth was blanketed. The sun came out, the snow melted, and the earth was flooded. People hurried to their canoes, but only the very lucky reached one or another of the five mountain peaks that remained above the waters. When the flood subsided, these came down, rebuilt their huts along the shore, and ever since that time, women have been ruled by men.[588]

Based on incomplete evidence, I have previously claimed that the myth was missing in Africa and Australia.[589] The handbooks provide almost exclusively Laurasian entries, for example, Stith Thompson's *Motif Index* (A1010); Frazer's large collection of flood myths seemed to indicate that it is absent in Africa and China;[590] and Dundes—like most mythologists since Frazer—maintains the same,[591] while adducing one flood myth from the Sahel belt of northern Cameroon and one from Australia. Yet it can be shown (§5.7.2) that the few African flood stories known to me then cannot simply be explained, as I thought, as intrusions from the Sahel belt or from northern sections of the East African

"North–South Highway" (§5.3.5.3–4)—that is, the savanna and steppe belt stretching from Uganda/Kenya to South Africa. Nor are the Australian flood myths to be derived from missionary tales, as the Aranda myth in Dundes's book clearly is, at least in its current form, which has Noah's ark.[592]

Instead, the flood motif is so widespread and universal that it must be very old and must have been taken over from the original tales of the "African Eve."[593] This will be investigated below (§5.7.2).

If so, both the Laurasian and the Gondwana (African, Australian, etc.) flood myths go back to a time well before the last Ice Age. Consequently, naturalistic explanations must be excluded, such as a flood caused by the meltdown of the great ice sheets or the recently popular story of the fairly quick flooding of the Black Sea, out of the Mediterranean. It also means that we can safely exclude diffusion from Near Eastern (Mesopotamian) origins, a theory that was popular earlier on.[594] Instead of an assumed Near Eastern areal feature, there have been innumerable other, often quite fanciful explanations of this myth, ranging from a diffusion of the biblical or Mesopotamian motif to such inventive psychological explanations as that of A. Dundes connecting men's wish to give birth and the salty floods with a nightly vesical dream, an urge to urinate.[595]

***

It now is clear that my original claim of a purely Laurasian origin of the flood myth was not correct, based as it was on limited evidence only,[596] and that we have to rethink the problem. Importantly for the Laurasian theory, this apparent "setback" is not as crucial as it may look initially. As will be discussed below (§5.1.2; cf. §2.1 sqq.), like any developing theory, the present one, too, will initially contain a few items that are unimportant, insufficient to sustain the theory, or just plain wrong. As Ragin has it,

> Most interesting findings usually result from … hypothesis formation based on preliminary data analyses. In other words, most hypotheses and concepts are refined, often reformulated, after the data have been collected and analyzed. Initial examinations of data usually expose the inadequacy of initial theoretical formulations, and a dialogue, of sorts, develops between the investigator's conceptual tools for understanding the data and the data analysis itself. The interplay between concept formulation and data analysis leads to progressively more refined concepts and hypotheses. Preliminary theoretical ideas may continue to serve as guides, but they are often refined or altered, sometimes fundamentally, in the course of the analysis.[597]

The case of the flood myth belongs to the latter category, that of refinement of theoretical concepts, of reformulation "after the data have been collected and analyzed." Though it is present in many, if not most, Laurasian mythologies as part of the original story line, it apparently did not originate with the ancient Laurasian shamans. It seems to be much older, and it was artfully incorporated as a "popular" motif that could be used to explain many things that have gone wrong (see the biblical or Yamana myths).

However, this readjustment of the theory also means that the Laurasian theory itself cannot be dismissed or obliterated simply by the appearance of this African and Australian motif. The theory merely has to be fine-tuned and amended. As the flood myth, in consequence, takes such a crucial position in pre-Laurasian mythology, it will be treated at great length in the section dealing with comparison with Gondwana and Pan-Gaean myth (§5.7.2).

■ §3.10. HEROES

The important but extensive motif of heroes cannot be treated here at any length.[598] Let it suffice to point out that heroes often are of divine or semidivine origin and as such overlap with trickster figures, the culture heroes of many traditions.

Many traditions do not quite know where to put them in their scheme of the subsequent Four Ages. As heroes have at least one divine parent, they often appear at one of the three stages that follow primordial creation; they necessarily must precede the establishment of the present *oikumene* that makes life on earth possible for humans. Yet, as mythic persons who frequently have one human parent, they can overlap with early humans, as is seen in the case of heroes like the Greek Herakles. Greek myth, as depicted by Hesiod, puts them in an extra age, in addition to the well-known four; Maya myth likewise inserts its two heroes, Hunahpu and Xbalanque, at an early stage among the Five Suns.

Typical heroes include the following: Gilgamesh, Osiris, Herakles, Achilles, Hector, and Odysseus; the Iranian Θraētaona (Firdausi's Feridun), who is divine in India (Indra); the Indian Rāma, Kṛṣṇa, and the five heroes of the Mahābhārata; the Japanese Yamato-Takeru; the Roman Aeneas; the English Beowulf; the Nordic Sigurd (Siegfried); and the eastern Central Asian Gesar (from: Kaisar, Caesar) in Tibet, Mongolia, and Hunza. In many cases they overlap with (semi-)historical figures, about whom (half-)mythical tales are told. Cases in point include the Macedonian Alexander, whose exploits have spawned a multitude of medieval adaptations in Europe and the Near East, with echoes as far afield as the Tibetan Gesar epic and, further, the medieval Japanese tale of the Heike and of Benkei, the Old Turkish Dede Korkut, the Mongolian Secret History, and the Franks' Roland.

In some cases, hero tales are a part of current folklore, as, for example, in Russian fairy tales. These have been subjected to detailed investigation and criticism by the Russian scholar V. Propp,[599] who distinguished 31 recurring elements in them that, incidentally, are also found in the Indian epic Rāmāyaṇa.[600] (This accounts for its continuing great popular appeal [as opposed to the Mahābhārata].) Finally, Lord Raglan has compared the figure of Jesus under this rubric;[601] one might add other moral reformers.

▪ §3.11. THE FINAL DESTRUCTION

As frequently discussed earlier (§2.5.2, §3.6; cf. §5.7.2), Laurasian mythology also tells of the destruction of our world.[602] It may take place as a final worldwide conflagration—the Götterdämmerung or Ragnarök in the Edda, Śiva's destructive dance and fire in India;[603] by molten metal in Zoroastrian myth or by devouring the world;[604] or by fire and water in Maya and other Mesoamerican myths; or as in the Old Egyptian tale of Atum's destruction of the earth.[605] However, the end also takes other forms, such as ice and long-lasting winter, for example, in the Edda, or in Iran with Yima's underground world, or again, a flood.[606] Many more details of such destructions appear in Mesoamerican myth, where they are arranged, however, as the myth of the Four, or rather, Five, Ages, discussed earlier (§2.5.1).

The final destruction is often coupled with the hope for a new and perfect world to rise from the ashes, as in the Edda, in the Christian Bible, in Egyptian and Zoroastrian myth,[607] and in various Mesoamerican versions.[608] Examples include the world of the new Æsir gods after the destruction, Ragnarök, in the Edda (Vǫluspá), or the end of the world, judgment of humans, and emerging paradise in Zoroastrian myth, from which the Christian belief in the "end," the final judgment, and paradise are derived, as seen in the last book of the Christian Bible, Revelations.

Such "new worlds" must be kept separate from the reemergence of the world out of the Great Flood, as found in the Bible, Mesopotamia, Greece, Vedic India, Polynesia, and so on (§3.9, §5.7.2). Both the reemergence from the flood and a new world after the final destruction must also be kept separate from and contrasted with periodic re-creation in medieval Indian myth (Purāṇas)[609] and similarly, the four preceding creations in Maya myth. Aztec texts, too, presuppose the destruction of the age we live in, the "Fifth Sun."[610]

Earlier "Suns" were just trial creations in which the successive attempts at creating human beings were met with little success (§3.6). As the "end," then, is just intermediate in these traditions, they insert the flood or the great fire and the repopulation of the world as one of these successive "Suns," while the origin of noble lineages and their exploits leading to the history of the individual populations obviously must come at the end of the process. Nevertheless, the current Fifth Sun must end, according to the Maya calendar, with the destruction of the world and its human populations,[611] in 2012.

***

As appears from the brief survey given above, the ultimate destruction of the world in some mythologies (Zoroastrian, Indian, Germanic, Egyptian, etc.) is the final act of the Laurasian story line and its "novel," while it is merely a recurrent theme in Mesoamerican mythologies. The destruction by a flood is built into the story line as a punishment of humans, for example, in Greece, Mesopotamia, the Bible, and Polynesia and even in some Gondwana myths (§§5, 5.7.2). In contrast, destruction is a *recurrent* occurrence in Mesoamerican and later Indian myth, due to the failure of trial creations. Regular series of destructions are also found with some ethnic groups in what is now China,[612] which may hint at the ultimate Asian origin of the Amerindian versions. In other words, we have

> onetime final destruction :: cyclical destruction by various means
> Eurasia :: Amerindians, later Indians

The opposition between recurrent destructions or a single one occurring early on in mythic history indicates that the former is an old motif that preceded the immigration into the Americas around 20 kya (§2.5.2). It also indicates that the motif of recurrent destructions cannot have independently developed in South Asia and in Meso- and South America while their local civilizations evolved.[613] The model preexisted: there are various myths of destruction, by water, fire, ice, devouring the world, darkness, and so on.

To use them for local *newly invented* schemes of the Four (or Five) Ages would have involved *recasting* of preexisting but separate, local myths about floods and so on and of *whole mythologies* involved with them: this would have resulted in a "higher," layered, syncretistic system of four–five successive ages while ironing out differences between various stories of catastrophes. What occurred, instead, was that a correlation was made of the preexisting generational scheme of the Four Ages of the gods with the motif of various world catastrophes.[614]

For the fact remains that we have a widespread series of destructions: on the one hand, individual mythologies put one near the very beginning of mythic time (second creation of humans after the flood) and, on the other, the final one takes place at the very end of the world. For other mythologies, these two(?) destructions are just part of a larger scheme of imperfect creations (Meso-/South America) that required repeated destructions of misshapen worlds, so as to make room for a new trial. However, the first version (second creation after a flood) implicitly also *includes* the theme of trial creation. Both types are widespread. In other words, the germs of *serial* creation and destruction can be found in both Eurasia and the Americas and must go back to Laurasian times.[615]

Therefore, it cannot be argued that the myth of the Five Suns has developed in the great civilizations of Meso- and South America as a mere priestly layering of traditions. If it were indeed so, the new prestigious scheme would have influenced neighboring cultures, just as the myths connected with maize agriculture have done in large parts of North America (§7.2). But we do not find much of such concepts in neighboring cultures, and where they occur, such as with the Pueblo people (Hopi etc.), they are markedly different from the Mexican versions. Further, the occurrence of the Four(!) Ages with the Navajo has been discussed earlier (§2.5.2): their myth exactly reflects the Greek color scheme of golden, silver, copper-colored, and black ages.[616] It *may* go back to early Eurasia, as the Navajo, like the other Na-Dene peoples, are late immigrants from the north, though heavily influenced by the Pueblo mythologies. Similarly, the Inca scheme of Five Suns is not found influencing their neighbors,[617] say, the Yanomami in the Amazon or the Fuegans; the Yamana, who have both the fire and the flood myths;[618] or, closer by, the Gran Chaco tribes, who even have *four* destructions. The Mesoamerican and Inca schemes thus are merely well-preserved priestly accounts of an *underlying* Laurasian scheme of serial creations and destructions that is found in Eurasia as well as in the Americas.

In the end, we have to reckon with a series of several types of destructions (flood, fire, ice, winter, devouring, darkness, etc.), from which the local destruction myths have developed: two destructions (flood, end of the world) with Four or sometimes Five Ages in western Eurasia, but four or more destructions in the Americas, with Five Ages (Suns) and sometimes even more, still future ones (as with the Hopi, Navajo).

▪ §3.12. SUMMARY

The multitude of creation myths that have been discussed in this chapter, including that of humans and their early mythic "history" from all areas and periods of Laurasian mythology, sustains the initial reconstruction of the Laur-

TABLE 3.7. *Combined table of major Laurasian myths and mythemes*

Creation from nothing, chaos, etc. Father Heaven/Mother Earth created
Father Heaven engenders: two generations ('Titans/Olympians')
Four (five) generations/ages: Heaven pushed up, sun released
current gods defeat/kill predecessors: killing the dragon, use of sacred drink
Humans: somatic descendants of (sun) god; they (or a god) show hubris are punished by a flood
Trickster deities bring culture; humans spread, (emergence of 'nobles')
local history begins
final destruction of the world
new heaven and earth emerge

asian story line (§2; see Table 3.7). Their (more or less) detailed study has made it sufficiently clear that we are indeed dealing with a widely spun web of tales that agree with each other in content, form, and order, in spite of individual local developments (as is clearly apparent). They form the core of Laurasian mythology. This proposal will be tested (§5) against the remaining types of mythology—mainly those of Africa, Melanesia, and Australia—and the unique Laurasian features will be debated further (§6).

Some cases in Laurasian mythology that, at first impression, seem to represent doubtful instances, serious exceptions, or contradictions to the theory have also been noted. They, too, will be discussed in detail in the next chapters (§§5–6). Some such myths will turn out to be remnants of earlier pre-Laurasian stages (such as the motifs of the primordial giant and the flood); others reflect human evolution and spiritual changes since the late Paleolithic period, such as the shift from a general human descent from the Sun deity to a restricted one only for nobles and kings (§7.2).

The ultimate value of the comparison made in this chapter, however, does not lie in the specific reconstructions. They are proposed heuristically and can be expected to be modified somewhat by future empirical findings. Their value rather lies in the novel means proposed here for reconstructing protomyths in general, which is, I believe, firmly established.

In addition, other disciplines and the natural sciences provide further support. For once the general Laurasian framework and some of its constituent features have been established and sustained by a multitude of examples, conversely, ways and means can be sought that either confirm or contradict the theory. Like any other theory, that of Laurasian mythology must be subjected to rigorous tests: we must investigate whether the theory can be contradicted, demolished, and obliterated or not.

The following chapters (§§4–6) will be devoted to this task. In chapter 4, the data and theories available in linguistics and in the natural sciences will be evaluated. Not unexpectedly, perhaps, these sciences are historical in the sense that they deal with data from several subsequent time levels. Linguistics, physical anthropology, population genetics, and archaeology all present a history of events. As far as the present work is concerned, they all deal with the development of humans along a *time line* beginning with the emergence of *Homo sapiens sapiens*. They also employ both long-range and close comparison, just as does the present undertaking, and so does stemmatic philology (now enhanced by biological computer models). In sum, these sciences use the same stemmatic and cladistic approach as historical comparative mythology.

In chapter 5 the evidence from other, non-Laurasian (Gondwana) mythologies will be compared and considered. As will be seen, the data in both chapters sustain the Laurasian theory.

In chapter 6, the next logical step that suggests itself will be taken: a comparison of both Laurasian and non-Laurasian mythologies. The result is the albeit sketchy reconstruction of some fragments of a still earlier mythology. It precedes both Laurasian and Gondwana types. Likely, it was that of the "African Eve" and her relatives, including male shamans.

We begin, however, with the materials available for testing both in the humanities and in the natural sciences.

4 The Contributions of Other Sciences: Comparison of Language, Physical Anthropology, Genetics, and Archaeology

If the reconstruction of Laurasian (and some Pan-Gaean) myths as proposed in the preceding chapters is valid, it must be reflected in some other traits of humans, whether physical or psychical. Given that all myths are told by humans using a particular language, the most obvious area to look for comparative evidence is language itself. One can expect that the traditional telling of myths within any population group—be it an extended family, a clan, a tribe, or a people—would reflect a certain style, a manner of telling, or recitation, using a more or less ancient segment of the language employed to tell the myths in question.

In other words, myths—just as poems, epics, or fairy tales—form a large part of the traditional oral literature of the population in question. As such they are intrinsically linked to the history of the language used in telling them. It is a well-known fact that certain types of prose tales or poems are preserved in older or archaic forms of the language, whose older stages are commonly compared by linguists. During the past 200 years, they have arrived at the reconstruction of the earliest stage of the language in question and of that of their close relatives in other languages.

In addition to language, the material output of artifacts, in implements or art, of a certain population can be studied over time. A constant danger, however, is to conflate such material culture with a population, their language, or in our case, their mythology. People everywhere use the computer now, or have been using the printing press, the plow, or the bow for more or less long periods of time, but they do not agree in their cultures, religions, and mythologies. One clearly must avoid reification of such data, though this still is commonly done by professionals in the fields involved as well as lay writers.

Archaeologists have extensively investigated cultural and human remains of particular sites and cultures for nearly two centuries and have established links with other cultures. Many of the representations in ancient art, thus recovered, can be linked to mythology. Similarly, the relationship between the bearers of a mythological tradition, their particular language, and the physical traits they embody can be investigated, whether these are overtly, somatically visible in their phenotype (bones, teeth, skin; §4.2) or are hidden in their genes (§4.3).

However, an automatic correlation between cultural products and various human somatic features is fraught with difficulties. Obviously, speaking a certain language does not necessarily make one adhere either to a particular archaeological culture or to a particular phenotype or certain genetic makeup. A look at current "multiracial" or multilingual societies found within a larger area (North America, India) or a smaller space (Switzerland) is enough to convince of the opposite. Similarly, spiritual and physical culture obviously are independent of somatic features. Again, it is very dangerous to reify such data, as has been done with the greatest damage with regard to somatic phenotype features, so-called race (§4.2).

All such features overlap only to a certain degree and for certain distinctive periods of time, especially in the early Stone Age, when humanity existed only in small bands of hunter-gatherers that carried their particular set of language, myths, genes, and artifacts with them. The most obvious, convincing cases of such overlap are the initial immigration into the Americas and into Polynesia and, though more difficult to establish, the migration out of Africa along the northern shores of the Indian Ocean. In all these cases, genes, language, and culture went together. In later times, given the constant crisscrossing of the continents by migrations and subsequent domination by certain populations, such relationships are much harder to disentangle. Nevertheless a beginning has been made by one of the pioneers of human population genetics, L. L. Cavalli-Sforza,[1] who worked closely with one of the more daring comparative linguists, M. Ruhlen.[2] It is now time to evaluate such early results and to take a closer look at the parameters that should be used.

▪ §4.1. LINGUISTICS

The link between a given mythology and a certain language can be much closer than those covered by the other sciences just addressed, for the simple reason that a myth must be told in a particular language, normally that of one's own group. Undoubtedly, certain myths and even complete mythologies may have been transmitted by speakers belonging to several languages.[3] However, in late Paleolithic and Mesolithic times, among more or less isolated bands of hunter-gatherers, the overlap between tribal language and tribal mythology will have been much closer than what we can occasionally still obverse today (e.g., in New Guinea or Australia).[4]

In other words, certainly not every one of the c. 6,000 languages that are still spoken today has its own mythology. However, before the large number of populations that began to adhere to one or the other of the major religions today, the overlap must necessarily have been much closer in the past. Ancient records, such as those of the first few great Near Eastern civilizations, some 5,000 years ago, the Greco-Roman ones, and the classical Indian and Chinese authors indicate the same. Based on this plausible assumption, we can take a closer look at the languages involved and subsequently compare and correlate language and mythology.

The question of the origin of human language has been on the mind of people for millennia. Leaving aside the well-known myth of the Tower of Babel,[5] one of the earliest instances of this quest is the case of the Egyptian pharaoh Psammeticus, who, according to Herodotus II 2, isolated two children from the time of birth and concluded from the first word (*bekos*, "bread") they spoke to each other that the original language of all humans was Phrygian, an Anatolian language.

Significant advances in comparing languages could be made only when the structural analysis of Sanskrit made by the great Indian grammarian Pāṇini (c. 350 BCE) was used in the analysis and comparative study of the various languages of Europe, Iran, and India. Franz Bopp,[6] following the initial though over-stated announcement of a close relationship of these languages made by Lord Monboddo at c. 1770 and William Jones in 1786, actually proved the case. Most of these languages go back to a common source, originally termed Indo-Germanic or, later on, (Proto-)Indo-European (PIE), which is used here at length as a model for comparative historical linguistics and, by extension, mythology.

The comparative method relies on the—almost always—regular changes that occur in all languages over time. If two or more languages are related, certain sets of such regular sound changes (*lautgesetze*) occur in a particular word of the same meaning in each of the related languages involved. One of the first securely established items of Indo-European mythology, "Father Heaven," is a good case in point (nominative and accusative):

Sanskrit	*dyāus pitā(r)*	*pitaram*
Greek	*zēus patēr*	*paterem*
Latin	*iu-ppiter*	*patrem*
Germanic	*tiu* (+ Goth. *fadar*), Engl. *Tues-(day)*, (+ *father*)	

Thus, in reconstructed Indo-European we have:[7]

| PIE | **diēus ph₂tēr* | **ph₂terem* |

Here certain sounds of Sanskrit, Greek, Latin, and Germanic are found in a regular relationship (*p/f, e/a*, etc.) that is normally met in (nearly) all other words of the languages involved.

Superficial similarity of words does *not* constitute proof at all. On the surface, Armenian *hair*, Irish *athir*, and English *father* have fairly little in common when compared with the more "regular" Latin *pater* (French *père*), Greek *patēr*, Sanskrit *pitā(r)*, and Tocharian *pācar/pacer*, but they are closely related by regular sound correspondences. Conversely, two similar-looking words such as English *heart* and Sanskrit *hṛd* (heart), or Greek *theos* and Aztec *teo* (god), or German *kaufen* and Japanese *ka(h)u* (to buy) are historically unrelated. It has often been said that one can find 50 words in any two languages of the world that look somewhat similar and have a similar meaning.

In any such comparison, the meaning of the words compared should be the same or must be semantically closely related, such as seen in English *dog* :: German *dogge* (bloodhound)[8] or in English *queen* :: Gothic *qvino* (woman). However, if two reconstructed words differ more or less in meaning, this must be explained plausibly (as in *queen* :: *qvino*); otherwise, the two words are not related.[9]

Exceptions from regular correspondences in sound and close ones in meaning can often be explained by borrowing from dialects, analogies, or some particular development in one of the languages involved, such as the *–pp–* in Latin *Iuppiter*.[10]

Next to regular sound change, another principle is the regular structure of the ancestral grammar. For example, in the case of PIE *father*, the nominative case has no ending, but the accusative has *–m*. Building on these two principles, by the late 19th century, the structure and much of the vocabulary of Indo-European had been reconstructed. Obviously these initial steps in reconstructing the parent language are parallel to those taken in comparing mythemes, motifs, and (ancient) collections of mythology (§2).

Although doubts have occasionally been voiced as to the possibility, correctness, and reality of such reconstructions, the simple observation of some cases, such as the particular grammatical pattern of the present tense of "to be" that remains in use today, should remove such doubts. This PIE verb[11]—and many others of its class—has a marked difference between the singular forms (h_1es-) and the vowelless plural forms (h_1s-):

	"he/she/it is"	"they are"
Indo-Eur.	*$h_1$és-ti*	*h_1s-énti*
Sanskrit	ás-ti	s-ánti
Greek	es-ti	–(eisin)
Latin	es-t	s-unt
French	es-t	s-ont
German	is-t	s-ind
English	is	–(are)

In addition, many of the early reconstructions have been subsequently reconfirmed, for example, the laryngeal (h_2) in ph_2ter (father), by the discovery of a previously undeciphered language, Hittite, where this "lost" sound is actually written; there are other cases in recently deciphered Mycenaean Greek that have preserved some pre-Homeric sounds. The result of systematic comparison is the establishment of the ancestral Proto-Indo-European vocabulary and grammar.

As the mythologies of individual Indo-European-speaking peoples overlap with Laurasian mythology, the reconstruction of Proto-Indo-European is of significance: first, it allows us to push back certain myths and mythemes to a specific Bronze Age culture, estimated at c. 3000 BCE. Second, the Indo-European pattern has become, by and large, the template for the establishment of other language families.

**

Employing the same method, similar reconstructions have been made for a number of other language families that were established during the past two centuries: Afro-Asiatic (including Semitic), Uralic (Finno-Ugrian), Altaic, Austronesian (Malayo-Polynesian), Austro-Asiatic, Sino-Tibetan (Tibeto-Burman), and Bantu and in the Americas, a whole slate of families ranging from Eskimo-Aleut to Uto-Aztecan, Caribbean, Ge, and Guarani. Establishing a family relationship for language groups without old written records, such as for the Amerindian and African languages, has been more difficult, and the same is true for languages with few or no apparent affixes (prefixes, suffixes, etc.), such as Chinese. Procedures thus slightly differ in these individual subdisciplines, but the underlying principle of regularity of sound changes over time (*lautgesetze*) and of a common core of grammatical elements is undisputed. With the establishment of these principles in the late 19th century, many earlier, unsystematic attempts at comparison have been rendered fruitless: they turned out to be random listings based on superficial similarity.

In order to link language families, reconstructed for c. 3000–5000 BCE, with early Laurasian mythology, we have to undertake the next logical step, that is, progressing further back in time and comparing the reconstructed families with each other. The reworked, well-established language families included, by the mid–20th century,

- Indo-European in Europe, Armenia, Iran, North India, and Sri Lanka[12]
- Hamito-Semitic (now: "Afro-Asiatic, Afrasian") in the northern half of Africa and the Near East[13]
- Uralic (including Finno-Ugrian) in northern Europe and Siberia[14]
- Altaic (Turkish, Mongolian, Manchu, and Ewenki, including now also Korean and Japanese)[15]
- Sino-Tibetan (Tibeto-Burmese/Burman and Chinese)[16]
- Austric, including Austro-Asiatic,[17] in Central and East India, the Nicobar Islands, Burma, Malaya, Cambodia, and Vietnam; as well as Malayo-Polynesian/Austronesian in Taiwan, the Philippines, Indonesia, Madagascar, and the Pacific;[18] and, in addition according to some, Tai-Kadai or Austro-Tai
- Papuan (with some 700 largely still unexplored languages in New Guinea) and Melanesian[19]

- Australian[20]
- Nilo-Saharan (in the Sahel and Sahara belt of North Africa)[21]
- Niger-Congo (including Bantu in Central, East, and South Africa)[22]

These also include a host of a priori mutually unrelated language families in West Africa and a multitude of languages in the Americas. In West Africa these are Wolof, Aka, Yoruba, Mande, and so on, and in the Americas these are Na-Dene (Athapascan, Navajo/Apache), Uto-Aztecan, Andean, Caribe, Guarani, Ge, Quechua, Fuegan, and so forth. Only a few languages remained totally isolated, such as Basque, the extinct Etruscan, and the various Caucasian languages (Georgian, Cherkes, Chechen, etc.) in Europe; Burushaski, Kusunda, and Nahali in the hills and mountains of South Asia; Ket in central Siberia; Ainu in Japan and Sakhalin; Khoi-San (Bushmen) in South Africa; Inuit (Eskimo) in North America; and so on.

This family scheme was known, by and large, already by the end of the 19th century. Occasionally, scholars have tried to compare individual language families with each other, such as Semitic and Indo-European (Möller) or Uralic and Indo-European (Collinder, Joki). Such efforts usually were discarded by specialists, classified as "too early to try," or dismissed as "trying the impossible: the time depth involved is to big": or they were simply classified, like many amateurish efforts, as "omnicomparativist."

Interfamily comparison, thus, was at an impasse, and the field of comparative linguistics then would be entirely useless for Laurasian mythology. While important and often detailed work had been carried out for the individual language families, the possible interrelationship between the families had been largely neglected. The last few decades, however, have seen important advances, first of all, the recent Russian effort of establishing a Nostratic superfamily. Due to the large number of language families represented in the territory of the former Soviet Union, some Russian linguists, such as V. M. Illich-Svitych, A. Dolgopolski, V. A. Dybo, and V. Sheveroshkin, have systematically studied the relationships between a number of Eurasian language families. Illich-Svitych, following up on an earlier idea of H. Pedersen, developed the concept of an ancestral Nostratic family ("our [language]"). It includes Indo-European, Afro-Asiatic (in North and East Africa, Near East),[23] part of Caucasian (Kartvelian, such as Georgian, in the South Caucasus Mountains), Uralic (Finnish, Estonian, Hungarian, Samoyed, etc.), Dravidian (in South India), and Altaic (Turkic, Mongolian, Tungus, Korean, Japanese). In short, Nostratic is a superfamily that covers most of Europe and northern Africa, as well as western, southern, northern, and northeastern Asia. One might just as well have called it *Eurasian* or *SaharAsian.*[24]

The method used by the Russian scholars is the classical "Indo-European" one: comparing words, establishing the rules of regular sound changes, and finding common grammatical features. In other words, the reconstruction is based on the same kind of principles as those used in all "traditional" comparative linguistics. Even the casual observer can establish some such grammatical relationships, for example, a close relationship between the root of the first-person singular (m) in pronominal and verbal morphology and the possessive case marker (n) and the accusative marker (m) in Indo-European, Uralian, and Altaic, resulting in such forms as Engl. *mi-ne*, Finnish *mi-nä*, Mongolian *bi-n*, and Old Japanese *wa-nö*.

Yet the Nostratic theory has not been accepted by most traditional linguists, as they claim that we cannot reconstruct languages beyond a—completely arbitrarily set—limit of 6,000 years before the present. Other arguments include that Indo-European, Uralic, and Semitic linguistics work with actually attested languages, while Nostratic often takes a shortcut and starts out from the reconstructed forms of the individual language families, which increases the rate of uncertainty. A tacit reason, however, is that few linguists can handle all the languages involved, from ancient Egyptian and Mesopotamian (Akkadian) to the classical Indo-European languages, Old Tamil, Old Turkic, Old Japanese, and Georgian.

***

Once we accept the reconstruction of Nostratic, we can establish the natural habitat, the material culture, and the *Weltanschauung* and mythology of the Nostratic population by employing linguistic archaeology,[25] as has been done for PIE. It then appears that the Nostratic-speaking tribes lived in an area that had mountains and rocks, snow and hoarfrost; the area was close to a sea or another large water tract and had swamps. Of the flora we know of the ash tree, perhaps the poplar, and the willow. The animals known include the wolf/dog: the two species are not yet distinguished. Thus, Nostratic seems to be older than the domestication period of c. 15,000 years ago.[26] Notable too is the absence of (domesticated) cows, sheep, and horses, though the word for "cattle," *$pek\Lambda$, is attested in Indo-European and Altaic, as well as that for "sheep," both of which still referred to the wild forms. Other animals known are the jackal, marten, fox, antelope, and bees and their product, honey. Just as in the later Indo-European, many of these animals are those of a temperate climate: the lion and tiger do not make an appearance. The words used for animals and for "herd" indicate still undomesticated animals and the prevalence of hunting. There was no agriculture or horticulture yet, but there is a word for (autumn) gathering, collecting, and harvesting, apparently of wild grasses and the like. As far as material possessions are concerned there is a word for some kind of "building," but the word seems to have been taken from "fastening" or from "arranging" and thus seems to indicate a tentlike structure; some kind of settlement is indeed well attested. Among the implements and products we find words for "vessel" and "weaving." Words for killing, violence, and some simple weapons are well attested. We thus obtain a glimpse of Nostratic nature, flora, fauna, and material culture in the late Paleolithic or Mesolithic period.[27]

However, as far as abstract concepts are concerned, we find only a few so far, such as "name." There definitely was a word for "spirit," and this allows us to speculate on the prevalence of shamanism at the time, a supposition that is supported by archaeological and pictorial evidence (see §4.4, §7.1). In addition, it is clear that fire was regarded as a male deity in Indo-European and Japanese, and probably in Nostratic (Nostr. *Henkʌ > Sanskrit agni, Latin ignis; *p.iɣwa > Jpn. hi/ho), and that water was thought to be female (*ɣakʌ > Latin aqua; German Ache, Aa; Skt. ap). However, the "elements" fire and water are clearly marked in PIE by an innovative Indo-European device, the heteroclitic neuter endings in –r/n, such as in *wetʌ > Engl. water, Greek hūdōr, Skt. udan/udr–, and Hittite watar/weten–. This PIE suffix is still missing in Altaic and so on.[28]

Interestingly, the words for "sun," *dila, and "fire," *dulʌ, may ultimately be related, derived from a protoform, **dvlv. This does not surprise in view of the widespread identification in Eurasian myth and ritual of the two entities. The same may apply to other words for "fire" and "water": *Henkʌ and *ɣakʌ < **hʌnk/hʌkʌ, again two entities often seen in close connection.[29] This kind of relationship is not as strange as it may seem. In Australian languages, for example, words expressing opposite concepts often are freely substituted because of taboos. Similar substitution patterns are known from Black English (bad for good) and London Cockney (bread for money). That taboo actually was at work in PIE as well as in Nostratic can be noticed by a close study of words such as those for "tongue" and "bear," which was a highly regarded animal, an incarnation of a god in wide stretches of northern Eurasia (§7.1.2).

***

It has been noted (§2.3) that some of the language families (such as Nostratic) overlap with the post-exodus regional centers established for post-Laurasian mythologies, for example, the early hunter cultures of Eurasia and of North America and those of the Bronze Age ancient Near East and of Mesoamerica. Comparative linguistics helps in distinguishing between the Laurasian features typical for a particular local mythology and a regional one; it also does so for the extensive areas (such as the Americas) that have transmitted mythologies that evolved from the Proto-Laurasian scheme at two well-defined points in time, c. 20,000–10,000 years ago.

A curious feature related to the Nostratic reconstruction is the large array of Asian areal linguistic features that unite northern, northeastern, western, and southern Asia.[30] This area forms a clear, large subset of the Nostratic family. There even is an additional connection between South Asia and Ethiopia, which establishes a link with a part of the Afroasiatic (Southern Semitic) subfamily of

Nostratic, which moved into East Africa at a comparatively late date. At present, it is unclear, however, exactly how old these areal features actually are.[31] They go back at least several thousand years (§4.3) but must be very deep and persistent, as they transgress many language boundaries and even several linguistic families: Uralic, Altaic (including Japanese and Korean), Indo-Aryan—but much less so Iranian—Dravidian, and highland Ethiopian. In other words, we seem to perceive a reflection of the language(s) of some early group(s) that moved out of Africa (§4.3, 4.4) around 65,000 years ago and then moved northward after an earlier ice age, around 40,000 years ago. It is notable that Andamanese shares a few characteristics as well.[32] Most of the same area is dominated by the genetic features of mitochondrial DNA (mtDNA) haplogroup M, as opposed to N in other parts of Asia (§4.3). This theory should be tested by a comparison of Papuan and Australian languages, which seem to have other characteristics.

However, while a connection of this regional linguistic phenomenon, or part of it, with areas of Gondwana mythology can be made, the comparison mainly applies to large areas with Laurasian mythology, which developed out of Gondwana mythology (§6). If correct, the largely Nostratic, pan-Asian linguistic area would reflect the language (Figure 4.1) and mythology of some of the early speakers of the second "Laurasian" exodus northward, c. 40 kya, from southern regions along the shores of the Indian Ocean, as well as their genetic data.

***

Be that as it may, in many cases certain myths and motifs or (parts of) a mythology can "jump" the language barriers and move from one culture to the next. This is well known with respect to the ancient Near East, and it has been demonstrated for early Central Asia (see immediately below; cf. §2.5.1).[33]

Just as certain isolated remnants (archaisms) seen in comparative linguistics go back to more ancient systems, so do Laurasian motifs that have been transmitted in individual languages or language families but do not make sense in isolation. Some of them match, some transgress language families. The latter situation is a good indicator for cultural transfer, such as the one between the (western) Central Asian steppe cultures and early Japan (§2.5.1, §3.5.1). In such situations, certain words connected with a particular myth have been taken over as well, as is well known for the transfer from the Near East of certain Greek mythological names.

However, in other cases we might discover the same mytheme or even the same epithet, though they are not linguistically related (such as Japan and western Central Asia).[34] Comparative linguistics greatly helps to clarify such details. For example, in the historically unconnected mythologies of Old Japan (Kojiki) and earliest India (Ṛgveda), the male deity who opens the primordial cave is described as or even named by the same (though linguistically unrelated) semantic terms. He is called "arm-strong": Old Japanese *ta-jikara*, Vedic Skt.

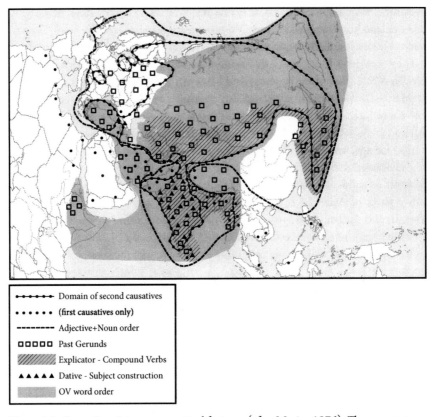

```
•-•-•-•-•   Domain of second causatives
• • • • •   (first causatives only)
- - - - - -   Adjective+Noun order
□□□□□   Past Gerunds
/////   Explicator - Compound Verbs
▲ ▲ ▲ ▲ ▲   Dative - Subject construction
          OV word order
```

Figure 4.1. Some Pan-Asian grammatical features (after Masica 1976). They suggest the spread of speakers of Nostratic languages, including Semitic in Ethiopia. Note the absence of these features in China, Southeast Asia, and New Guinea.

tuvi-grābha, ugra-bāhu (Indra).[35] Further, in both mythologies the deities of fire are male and those of water are female (and grammatically so in Indo-European).[36]

Other incidental, isolated, and unexpected details and poetic motifs may be adduced, such as the congruence of the Vedic Indian fire god Mātari-śvan (Growing inside the mother; Ṛgveda 3.20.11), whose name has remained unexplained so far, and the archaic Japanese fire god Ho-musubi (Growing [as] fire [inside his mother]), who at birth burned his mother, Izanami, so severely that she died. Then, there are such isolated motifs as that of the Vedic deity Uṣas exposing her breasts as a greeting to her close friends (the poets),[37] a feature also found with the historically unrelated Gilyak of the Siberian Amur region. Finally, there is the isolated name Rodasī of "Father Heaven" and "Mother Earth" in the Veda. It has been explained as the "Two faces/crying ones(?)." The name may easily be explained by taking recourse to the Maori myth, already mentioned (§3.3), that describes Heaven as constantly crying because of his forceful separation from Earth after they had been stemmed apart by the *toko*. Sometimes, however, such correspondences are the clear result of areal influences, such as that of the mythology of the Pueblo peoples on that of the latecomers from the Athapascan north, the Navajo and the Apache—or that of Near Eastern mythology on the Greeks, Greek mythology on the Etruscans, and Etruscan mythology on the Romans.

***

It is obvious that the items just discussed transgress what we can establish by straightforward linguistic comparisons, and evaluation comes down to a comparison or straightforward translation of motifs and mythemes. It is also evident that the more we go back in time trying to reconstruct the mythology of the Nostratic or Eurasian periods, the less we can depend on direct *linguistic* relationship. Even the reconstructed Proto-Nostratic yields few items, so far, as we have just seen.

While Nostratic seems to be a good candidate for a late Paleolithic hunter and gatherer society that may have overlapped with a *large part* of the area of Eurasian or Laurasian mythology, the problem of establishing other earlier linguistic superfamilies involved in Laurasian mythology has much less prospect. The various "Laurasian" languages involved have diverged very far from each other over the many millennia after the initial exodus from Africa some 65,000 years ago. They include (mostly) the language families of northern Africa, Eurasia, Polynesia, and the Americas. These are, on the surface, completely unrelated languages and language families.

***

The linguistic investigation would be left at this inconclusive stage were it not for some important recent developments: enter the late Joseph Greenberg (1915–2001). Looking at the multitude of language families in Africa, and comparing their vocabulary across the board, by mass comparison, he established just two superfamilies: Nilo-Saharan and Niger-Congo, which includes all West African and the Bantu languages. After some initial resistance, his ordering was accepted by Africanists some decades ago.

Next, he tried to unite the languages of New Guinea and the surrounding Melanesian areas with those of the Andaman Islands and Tasmania.[38] He called this family Indo-Pacific. The proposal has received much less attention but was recently highlighted when Whitehouse and Usher added Kusunda, an isolated language in the Nepalese Himalayas.[39]

In the nineties Greenberg proceeded to establish a superfamily for the Americas. Instead of some accepted 150 language families—a priori, a bizarre situation for populations that arrived only some 10,000–20,000 years ago—he reconstructed only three: first, Inuit-Aleut (Eskimo); second, Na-Dene (Athapascan in Alaska/Yukon, Navajo/Apache); and third, the large Amerindian family covering the rest of the American continents.[40] Like his African proposal initially, the current one still is under intense discussion and has received severe if often petty criticism from specialists.

Greenberg's last work, on Eurasiatic,[41] unites most languages of Europe and northern Asia, including the Paleo-Siberian languages Eskimo-Aleut, Chukotian (Chukchi, Kamchadal), and Nivkh (Gilyak) but also Korean-Japanese-Ainu, Altaic, Uralic-Yukaghir, Indo-European, and Etruscan in one superfamily, Eurasian.[42] However, different from Nostratic, it excludes Dravidian and therefore only partially overlaps with the Nostratic proposal.

In sum, Greenberg has singlehandedly established some major superfamilies, though some of his proposals are decried by traditional linguistics. Nevertheless they have *heuristic* value and can be used as long as they have not been supplanted by better-founded theories. As will be seen, they fit in with much of the genetic and mythological data.

The problem with most African and American languages is, as indicated, that they hardly have records that are older than a few hundred years, so time depth, so important in the reconstruction of Indo-European and Semitic, is altogether lacking. In the latter two cases, we have records, "archaeological" layers of language that date back up to c. 3000 BCE. Thus, it is easily observable that the earlier a word or grammatical form is actually attested, the closer it is to the reconstruction. For example, the Indo-European laryngeal (h with the varieties h_1, h_2, h_3) was purely a reconstruction until, early in the 20th century, one of them (h_2) was discovered as written in the newly deciphered Hittite records of c. 1600 BCE. In his reconstructions of most African and the American languages, however, Greenberg had to rely not on such archaeological layers but on the "surface" finds of these languages as they present themselves now (or in the very recent past).

Yet the establishment of most of Greenberg's large superfamilies may be taken heuristically, just as the initial establishment of the Indo-European, Semitic, and Polynesian families was readily accepted once it was proposed. The many difficult (and tedious) details of reconstruction will follow, and the ultimate shape and content of the new superfamilies will only resemble to some 50–70 percent, as has happened with Indo-European, ever since 1816, just as Ragin has described all newly developing theories.[43] Such superfamilies should be welcome in our undertaking, as, just like the Nostratic one, they would allow us to access the Stone Age spiritual world embodied by the vocabulary of the language superfamily in question.

What Greenberg did was not different, in principle, from what Bopp and others had originally set out to do for Indo-European: to compare some words that looked similar and had the same or closely related meanings and only then proceed to correspondences in sounds and grammar. Indeed, Greenberg achieved his classifications by mass lexical comparison, which means merely a comparison of similar words (with the same or closely related meanings) across the broad regions he studied. As indicated, this is certainly legitimate as a *first* step in setting up a new language family. However, it can only be a first step, a broad, sweeping look at similarities in sound and meaning. The discovery of regular sound correspondences and of identical grammatical features had to follow to validate the investigation in the same way that Indo-European, Semitic, and Uralic were validated.

Greenberg thus committed, in the eyes of the traditional historical linguists (mostly Indo-Europeanists), two cardinal sins: he did not establish, or hardly utilize, regular sound correspondences between the various languages involved, and his method does not involve historical reconstruction of protostages and uses little of common ancestral grammar. Greenberg's method therefore cannot directly be compared with that of the Nostraticists. This does not entail that he is wrong, it is just that many of the actual internal relationships still have to be worked out and proved. At the present moment, we only know that Amerindian languages are somehow closely related as opposed to Eskimo or Na-Dene or Ainu or Sino-Tibetan. For that reason, his results indicate macro-level relationships, which are very useful for the study of the early stages of human expansion, in Paleolithic and Mesolithic times—including comparative historical mythology.

While the macro-families discussed above are variously accepted or (frequently) disregarded by linguists, as the case may be, some scholars have tried to advance even beyond these large macro-families and have proceeded to establish several levels of hyperfamilies. Notably, J. Bengtson has tried to establish some wide-ranging relationships, beginning with Basque, North Caucasian, and Burushaski (Macro-Caucasian),[44] which he and colleagues have linked with Ket (central Siberia), Chinese, and Na-Dene (in North America), in a superfamily called Dene-Caucasian.[45] J. Bengtson and M. Ruhlen even compare the dozen resulting hyperfamilies to arrive at 27 words of the original "Proto-World" language,[46] or Pan-Gaean, as I would call it. It was spoken by our *Homo sapiens sapiens* ancestors, for example, by the mitochondrial Eve reconstructed by geneticists, a language of c. 130,000 BCE.

Much less than Nostratic, the few fragments of a reconstructed "Proto-World" language can (yet) provide clear-cut materials about the designations of deities, creation, and other myths and motifs. It is here that comparative mythology can help out, precisely *because* it is independent of reconstructed language families and thus transcends language comparison and linguistic archaeology.

As mentioned, the Nostratic group of languages would partly cover a large part of the area and many of the populations that have transmitted Laurasian mythology. It remains to be seen, however, whether populations speaking non-Nostratic languages and still adhering to Laurasian mythology can be linked geographically and by "family descent" with the mythology of the Nostratic-speaking areas. Candidates would include the Dene-Caucasian group comprising Macro-Caucasian, Ket, Chinese, and Na-Dene.[47] The question to be answered by mythologists is whether the Dene-Caucasian group originally reflected Laurasian mythology or whether its speakers accepted it only later on. Solving the question would involve extensive study of the few remnants of Basque, North Caucasian myths and so forth, which cannot be undertaken here. The problem, however, should be kept in mind (§4.3). In addition, the still controversial Austric super-family,[48] that is, the Austronesian (Malayo-Polynesian) group along with its Southeast and South Asian relatives (Austro-Asiatic), must have formed part of the Laurasian group (§4.3.5),[49] as well as, not to forget, the Amerind languages.

It is precisely while trying to answer this question and those of long-range, Pan-Gaean comparativist linguistics that Laurasian mythology, archaeology, and genetic studies can step in, involving the most recent methods, and aid in establishing the exact relationships between these and other language families and early populations (see Figure 4.2).[50]

***

If the relationship of the major language families referred to above can indeed be convincingly demonstrated eventually, the Laurasian theory will find a close parallel in their dispersal all over Eurasia and the Americas. However, many of the macro-families mentioned in this section have not (yet) been accepted by mainstream linguists working on individual language families. Further, some of the proposed macro-families may change in nature and extent, once more comprehensive and systematic comparisons have been made; this will involve the establishment of regular sound changes and of corresponding grammatical features. Such work is plainly not progressing much due to strong resistance from mainstream linguists and because of the small number of scholars working in this field (not to mention the lack of funds)—all in spite of the promising vista that sustained investigation offers.

At this moment, therefore, the very tentative linguistic reconstructions available for the late Paleolithic and Mesolithic period do not yet allow us to achieve a clear view of the contents of their vocabularies,[51] and less so their religious and mythological terms. Yet the *spatial* distribution of the various language families involved provides important indications for the spread of their original speakers and about the relative age of their spread.

The typical pattern, worldwide, is that of the sweeping advance of a particular language group, religion, or archaeological culture, just like that of certain plant and animal species. Such spread is contrasted by pockets of survival of earlier populations, languages, and so on, which allow us to reconstruct an earlier pattern disturbed by the new arrivals. A typical example would be Basque, North Caucasian, and Burushaski, which are spoken in the Pyrenees, Caucasus, and Pamir mountains. The spread of this Macro-Caucasian family probably goes

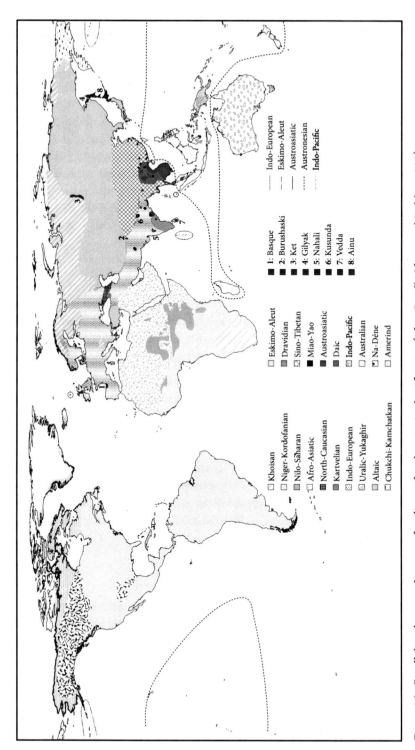

Figure 4.2. Parallelism between language families and early genetic classification (after Cavalli-Sforza and Ruhlen 1988).

back to the northward expansion at c. 52–45 kya, after an earlier ice age.[52] Incidentally, this scenario is echoed by genetic evidence (§4.3),[53] and there are indications of shared early mythology as well (discussion in §5.6.1). In similar fashion, other linguistic data will serve as supplementary evidence for the spread of Laurasian mythology—especially once its homeland can be determined more securely than is possible at this instance.

For the time being, however, it is tantalizing to observe the recent developments in the field, which—hopefully—are progressing to include regular sound correspondences and analyses of grammatical (morphological) features.[54] Correspondingly, it will be very fascinating to see whether Afro-Australian (Gondwana) mythology can be matched by a closer relationship between the African, Andamanese, Papuan, and Australian languages as well. However, as pointed out, genes, languages, and mythologies may very well, but not *necessarily*, have spread together even in those early times.

As R. McMahon put it recently:

> We are at a particularly important point in understanding the relationships between languages, genes and populations; we are close to being able to provide "a unified reconstruction of the history of human populations" ... but to get there will require a good deal of interaction between linguists and geneticists in the design and implementation of future research strategies.[55]

The same applies to their mutual relationship with mythology.

The combination of well-tested linguistic methodology with modern technological means (such as a maximum number of comparisons by supercomputer) will lead to clear and convincing results[56]—and to the rejection of some previous proposals. If pursued well, the results will establish whether we can (ever) ascertain the remnants of a one-world *ur*-language (Pan-Gaean). This will be of immediate interest for theories regarding the development of early mythology, for comparisons of the genetic distribution, and for the evolution of paleontological and archaeological records. These data will be discussed in the next sections and evaluated with regard to the Laurasian theory.

▓ §4.2. PHYSICAL ANTHROPOLOGY

Moving on from a somato-cultural product, language, to our very physical nature, we will now take a brief look at physical anthropology, paleontology, and in a more detailed fashion, our genetic makeup (§4.3), in order to determine how far such data overlap with the proposed mythological theory. Skeletal and other somatic records, especially anthropometric data derived from the shape of the head, facial features, and skin color, have frequently been used and abused over the past two centuries to establish the so-called racial features. But all such features are rather superficial and recent; they do not allow us to divide humankind into separate "races" for whose existence no scientifically acceptable set of criteria can be established (see below).

These types of data must be clearly distinguished from genetically encoded ones, such as blood groups, proteins, mtDNA, and so on.[57] As Cavalli-Sforza puts it in his great summary:

> External body features, such as skin color, and body size and shape, are highly subject to the influence of natural selection due to climate.... [I]t is risky to use these features to study genetic history, because they reveal much about the geography of climates in which populations lived *in the last millennia* and little about the history of fissions of a population.... [I]t will not tell us *when* the people separated, nor *from* which preexisting peoples they descended.[58]

Many somatic features in the narrow sense thus are dependent on the comparatively recent history of their bearers.[59] In sum, "the genetic tree...can tell us more about the history of descent, i.e. of common ancestry, while the anthropometric data [tell] us about climate."[60]

In other words, we all are "African under the skin," but we look quite different from each other now. For example, "white" skin color is a rather recent development, a genetic mutation that has occurred twice independently, in Europe and in East Asia.[61] Restricting the current focus to human anthropology in its narrower sense of body features, it is nevertheless possible to take advantage of some recent studies. They include the study of various features of the skeleton, especially that of the skull and teeth, which have been subjected to multivariate analysis.

Multivariate measurements considerably improve on the old method of measuring just one or two items of the human skull,[62] such as just its breadth and length. This kind of measurement resulted in a *doliocephalic* or longer head and a broader, *brachycephalic* shape, with an index of at least four-fifths breadth as against the length of the skull. A much larger number of measurements are now employed,[63] coming from a sizable sample of a population. They include such items as teeth shape, which seems to be a rather good indicator of relationships, and fingerprint patterns (see below).

Present-day anthropologists seem to agree that the results of such measurements are reasonably correct,[64] bearing in mind, however, that they reflect fairly *recent* responses to climatic conditions, not ultimate origins. For example, rounder heads with smaller noses are believed to be more adapted to colder climates, as they preserve body warmth more easily than longer-shaped ones with larger noses. This would throw some interesting light on and point toward the Ice Age location of early East Asians and their trans-Pacific descendants as compared with early Europeans.

Even restricted multivariate data, taken only from the human head or just the teeth,[65] can deliver several sets of data that can be mapped. Kennedy's and

Sergent's South Asia– and Europe-centered tables,[66] when plotted in a single diagram (Table 4.1), result in a good representation of some characteristics. Not surprisingly they agree, by and large, with the respectively northern or southern locations of the populations involved as they reflect data that are ultimately based on the adjustment to local climate. (Sergent, however, takes them as absolute, and he stresses, for example, the close association of Vedda, Dravidian, and Bronze Age Indus data, where the Sri Lankan Veddas are situated between the Tamils and the Indus people.)

The table only tells us that the people who lived in the area of the Indus civilization (2600–1900 BCE), and thus "typical" South Asians, fall somewhere in the middle between "Africans" and "Europeans." Given what we now know from genetics (§4.3), this is not very astonishing, as the Africans would by necessity constitute one pole from which the first emigrants, moving along the shore of the Indian Ocean, have diverged to some extent. Some of their descendants are the "Indus people." Further, the late immigrants northward, the Europeans, have

TABLE 4.1. *Some major anthropometric features in Africa and Asia, after B. Sergent, Genèse de l'Inde, 1997: 42 (br.= Bronze Age, V. = Vedda)*

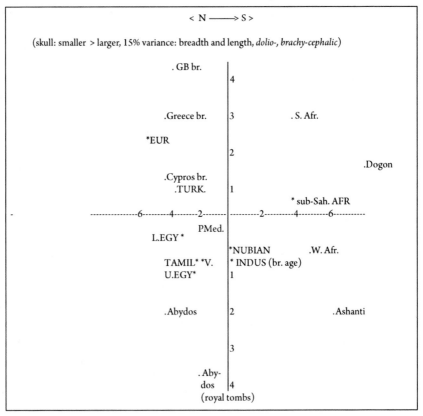

diverged even more. It is not surprising, then, that the Nubians and "Dravidians," both geographically close to the East African area of origin of all non-African humans, occupy similar positions in the chart. At the same time, this example shows that such charts can only produce relative positions, not detailed answers: they cannot indicate that, say, the Dravidians originated from the area of or from the "Nubians" and so on. The rest of the individual data reflect this in more detail. The influence of climate is also visible (see immediately below).

Purely on the basis of paleoanthropological data, it is difficult to establish the track, number, and importance of the human movements into South Asia and beyond, to the rest of Asia and Europe.[67] W. W. Howells's statistical data indicate that Table 4.1 merely reflects a general north–south gradient,[68] that is, the influence of climate.[69] As for the Dravidians, it is important to note that, in *recent* history, the speakers of Dravidian languages shared a geographical location closer to that of the Proto-Mediterraneans, Nubians, Upper Egyptians, and Somali-Galla, rather than to the West Africans, including the famous Dogon of Burkina Faso. This underlines the close, still very enigmatic relationship of areal linguistic features that exists between South Asia and highland Ethiopia.[70]

Further multivariate measurements of human skeletons, especially those of the skull, reveal a number of interesting specifications. For example, for the vexed question of an influx of Indo-Aryan (that is Indo-Iranian, late eastern Indo-European)-speaking populations into South Asia, physical anthropology can add an interesting sidelight, *the absence of "Indo-Aryan bones."*[71] That is something that linguists and textual scholars have long assumed, as the impact of Indo-Aryans was mostly cultural, not necessarily strongly somatic.[72] However, such scenarios, when purely based on paleontology, are difficult to sustain even for the relatively late period presently under discussion. In addition, it must be noted that the Indus sample is very restricted—a few hundred skeletons that were all taken from a very limited area of this widespread civilization. Any lucky find of the remains of an immigrating pastoral community would seriously change this "unified" picture. The same kind of scenario is by now obvious in another area of Eurasia, in Yayoi/Kofun-period Japan (1000 BCE–400 CE), which saw the influx of a continental Iron Age culture, along with a (small?) horse-riding population, both of which exercised an immense influence on early Japan and its culture. The cases of ancient Greece and early England are similar.[73] All of this has nothing to do with "race," though this has been maintained perpetually in such discussions.

As the powerful, but faulty, concept of "race" has consistently been brought into any discussion of human spread and differences over the past 150 years or so, a brief discussion is in order. As mentioned, any scientific basis for the concept has been rejected over the past decades. The reason is that "the classification into races has proved to be a futile exercise.... Humans races are still extremely unstable entities in the hands of modern taxonomists, who define from 3 to 60 or more races."[74]

Cavalli-Sforza sums up that the differences between humans are very small. However, as we are accustomed to noticing variations in skin color or facial structure, we usually assume that the actual differences between us, whether Europeans, Africans, or Asians, are significant. However, these differences in us result from genes that have reacted to climate and thus

> influence *external features*.... [W]e automatically assume that differences of similar magnitude exist below the surface, in the rest of our genetic makeup. This is simply not so: the remainder of our genetic makeup hardly differs at all.[75]

The traditional definition of race, however, wrongly insists on these features as being constant and thus transmittable—we should now add "genetically." But

> for almost all hereditary features, the differences found between individuals are much greater than those between racial groups....In short, the level of constancy is not high enough to support the current definition of *race*....Each classification is equally arbitrary.[76]

Though the term is still much used (e.g., unfortunately in official American census documents and in the press), the definitions of the perceived races are very vague, and the differences within one "race" are greater than those between any two races. The old classifications of groups such as the "Australoid" or "Negrito" races as "primitive," in the sense of the development of modern humans, have long been given up in favor of a staggered migration from the homeland of *all* present-day humans (*Homo sapiens sapiens*) inside Africa and out of East Africa, and in favor of a subsequent adjustment to local surroundings. After all, humans of all races mutually reproduce with fertile offspring, something that is not the case even between the various apes or the equids (horse, ass, hemione, and zebra).

In sum, our present differences are often due to adaptation to colder or to more tropical climates. The original African and Asian emigrants, for example, the European Crô Magnons, seem to have been darker than their present-day descendants. The change was due, just as in the parallel development in northern East Asia, to mutation of a gene responsible for skin color.[77] In view of such data, any correlation between "race" and mythologies is clearly ruled out. There is no "black" or "white" mythology—except in politically inspired modern myths *about* the "white race" or *négritude* and the "Black Athena."

***

The somatic, "racial" theory was that of the late 19th and early 20th centuries, but it has altogether been given up since. Biologists now maintain, instead, that "our skeletal series does not sort into 'types' along biological, linguistic, or cultural lines because we are looking at adaptive processes to stresses in different ecological settings over time."[78] That means, they responded to the same "stresses in different ecological settings over time" and reacted with adaptive processes. All of which has little to do with the development of culture and language. Early South Asians, for example, simply took over Indo-Aryan pastoralism and its culture (language, poetry, and religion) in order to survive under worsened ecological and changed social conditions of the northwest of the Indian Subcontinent.

***

In comparison with archaeological, linguistic, and mythological data, the evidence from somatic features such as bones, skin, hair, and so on is rather meager—perhaps with the exception of tooth shapes, such as the typical Sundadont shape in Southeast Asia and the Sinodont in East Asia. Again, most of these data point to recent adaptations to local climate. Therefore, the use of such data for a comparison with mythological ones seems rather limited. Undoubtedly, one can make use of some data coming from fairly recent immigrants into a certain area that do not agree with those of an older population. Such results will reinforce, rather than independently indicate, important cultural movements brought about by migrations.

Apart from the general problem of linking somatic features to language, texts, or mythology, paleontology thus retains an auxiliary role, at best, with regard to the establishment of Laurasian mythology and can largely be disregarded for the present purpose. The situation is much more promising, however, with regard to the study of inherited human genetic traits. They can be used for comparisons with the linguistic and mythological data found with a given population. Unlike the paleontological data, they can be tied much more closely to the parameters of temporal and spatial spread and therefore to the development of both the Laurasian and Gondwana mythologies.

■ §4.3. GENETICS

Most of human DNA that encompasses the information of our genetic inheritance is found in 23 pairs of chromosomes totaling 46 chromosomes of the nucleus of each cell. Gender is dictated by the apportionment of males having one Y chromosome they inherit from their father and one X from their mother. Females have two X chromosomes since they inherit one from each parent. The rest of the heritable information is located on the remaining 22 pairs, the nonsex autosomal chromosomes. Within each human reproductive gamete (egg and sperm), only half of the genetic complement (23 chromosomes) is present, allowing a fertilized egg to be reconstituted with 46 chromosomes.

With the exception of most of the Y chromosome, during reproduction this information gets recombined and scrambled when the two half-complements of chromosomes provided by the parents join and get copied, leading to the uniqueness of each human individual. The consequences of recombination in reproduction depend on whether a certain trait within the autosomal constitution inherited is dominant or recessive or neutral, typically resulting in the kind of outcomes first discovered by Gregor Mendel in 1866.

§4.3.1. Recent advances in human population genetics

There is abundant information found on the male sex Y chromosome in the cell nucleus. Such nuclear DNA is comparatively frequent,[79] with some 25,000 genes, and it offers much material for comparative study.[80] The reason is that the Y chromosome is inherited unchanged by the male offspring, as it does not recombine with the female gene: in short, it is nonrecombinant. It is transmitted in a manner similar to the way surnames are passed from generation to generation. Still, occasional copying changes can occur during reproduction at incidental locations on the chromosome.[81] They lead to small unnoticed or to marked changes in male offspring. If these changes do not reduce reproductive fitness, then the changed nonrecombinant Y (NRY) version is transmitted intact, as such, to all future male generations, eventually creating a "family tree" (gene phylogeny) of mutations. Due to the low rate of nuclear mutation, each mutation traces its occurrence to a single unique event (molecular ancestor), creating a robust phylogeny. Improved phylogenetic resolution within the NRY phylogeny that is often closely correlated with geography can provide reliable information on the movement in time and space of multiple genes (i.e., populations).[82]

***

A similar process is seen in females. However, it does not involve the cell nucleus and its female X chromosome but, rather, the mtDNA that is found in *all* cells outside the cell nucleus. Mitochondria carry their own genetic information in their DNA. They have their own nonrecombining chromosomal genome, with just 37 genes; it differs markedly from the nuclear one. It is smaller, circular, and very compact, and it has a high number of copies in each cell, about 1,000 times more than the nuclear one.

Mitochondrial DNA is inherited just from the mother and is not affected by scrambling as in autosomal gene reproduction. Thus, all children (female *and* male) of a particular woman (and her female siblings and immediate relatives) carry her mtDNA, barring mutations. However, only daughters can transmit it to succeeding generations. Again, over time certain copying mistakes occur and are then inherited by subsequent generations. This, again, leads to a *family tree* of mtDNA variations. Their mutation rate is five to ten times that of nuclear genes, occurring at a certain rate over time.[83] This allows us to estimate the date of our ultimate common female ancestor (popularly called "African Eve"), some 130 kya. It is only her genetic material, not that of other females then alive, that is present in all living humans. All surviving female human lineages of today carry her mtDNA, while her neighbors' offspring has died out. These two haploploid nonrecombining systems, mtDNA transmitted only through the female line and its counterpart NRY in males, provide unique insights as to gender-specific roles in human evolution.

Compared with the large number of autosomal recombining genes, the nonre-combinant mtDNA and NRY genes are comparatively fewer and very sensitive to incidental changes, drift, and results from (repeated) founder effects and bottle-necks. As in all other investigations involving "family trees" (paleontology, lan-guages, manuscripts) we have to reckon with the disappearance of certain lineages over time, so that the reconstruction remains lacuneous just like those in linguis-tics, archaeology, and so on.[84] Nevertheless, the two family trees, that of NRY and mtDNA, can be compared in their structure, origin, and development, thus even-tually leading back to our ultimate ancestors and providing the background for the populations that have transmitted the Gondwana and Laurasian mythologies.

***

Generally speaking, populations living in a certain well-circumscribed area have evolved certain typical, local characteristics that are due to a network of frequent intermarriages. Nontypical features are derived from incidental local changes ("drift"), especially in isolated populations, or they are due to import of genetic features from outside, such as by incidental movement of males in trade, migra-tion, conquest, and so on ("gene flow"). Similar processes occur when females marry outside their area, as is the custom with many patrilineal societies.

In addition to the geographic feature of location and development over time, a third parameter, that of climate, plays a great role, as explored in more detail below (§4.4.). People moved south during the last two ice ages (52–45 and 25–15 kya) or adapted locally in certain refuge areas,[85] which eventually led to further genetic changes. During each ice age, populations were isolated from one another in refugia, where they continued to diverge (drift) genetically. Following subsequent climatic improvement there was a spurt of range expansion to areas that became habitable or farther north or away from inhabitable areas, such as in the expanding great deserts.

Finally, the appearance of food production (especially cereals) since c. 10,000 BCE increased reproduction rates enormously, which has led to further genetic diver-sification as rare variants are often preserved (rising tide raises all boats). In some cases it has led to demic expansion and impetus for migration.

It is obvious that the development of mythology parallels that of other human developments and dispersals. A closer look into genetic inheritance therefore will provide useful data that can be compared with those of mythology, linguis-tics, archaeology, and so on.

***

Over the past two decades, it has become well known that anatomically modern humans (*Homo sapiens sapiens*) can be traced back to a single woman in Africa who lived well over 100,000 years ago. We all share derivatives of her mitochondrial genetic features (mtDNA), while that of her female contemporaries has been lost. The date of our ultimate common female ancestor can be estimated at some 130,000 years ago.

Two derivative versions of her mtDNA endure in two major types (haplogroups L1a and L1b) in Africa,[86] while all other humans descend from the East African subgroup, L3. These people departed Africa around 65,000 BCE,[87] crossed the then much narrower Strait of Aden, moved eastward along the Indian Ocean shore (the "southern route"),[88] and reached Southeast Asia and Australia within a few thousand years. Based on studies of bottlenecks in the gene pool, it is believed that initially only some 10,000 or even as few as 2,000 migrants were involved. Over the next 40,000 years, these hunter-gatherer and beachcombing groups continued to spread from their outposts along the shores of southern Eurasia all across the rest of the world, as will be discussed later.

The early migrants surely brought with them their version(s) of an original African language and mythology. However, as indicated in the preceding chapters, Laurasian mythology is *not* identical with that exported from Africa, and it is limited to groups *other* than those now speaking Australian, Melanesian (Papuan etc.), and Andamanese languages with populations that are descendants of the earliest migrants.[89] Genetically speaking, too, the DNA of the Sahul Land populations (New Guinea and Australia)[90] and of refuge areas, such as the Andamans,[91] differs markedly from that in the rest of Eurasia, where *later* derivates predominate.[92] These are by and large restricted to Eurasian and American populations speaking Nostratic, Sino-Tibetan, Austric, and Amerindian languages, while their DNA is limited to populations with the early derivatives of the L3 mtDNA haplogroup, M and N, which are dated at c. 54 kya and probably belong to the same demic migration.[93] As for the parallel male Y chromosome (NRY), these are haplogroups C, F, and so on (further details below).

This brief overview of the Paleolithic period indicates that human population genetics, like linguistics, can provide a template for the emergence and spread of Laurasian mythology. Obviously, there are no inherent and automatic links among genetic features, languages, and mythology: both language and beliefs are acquired by children from their parents and surroundings, and those conditions can drastically change even over a few generations. However, only a small number of Paleolithic humans moved out of Africa, and still relatively few Eurasian and Sahul people lived around 65,000–40,000 years ago. This allows one to assume still close links between, on the one hand, their particular genetic features and, on the other, the languages and mythological texts that they brought along. In other words, for this early period—the Paleolithic—the results of genetics, archaeology,[94] and comparative mythology,[95] as well as comparative (Long-Range) linguistics, make a good fit.[96]

It should, however, be observed that the absolute dates calculated for these early genetic data have error bars of quite a few thousand years.[97] While the absolute dates thus are imprecise, their *relative* age provides a reliable temporal framework (again, just as in comparative linguistics). This feature is not as crucial for the Paleolithic period as for more recent periods: we are still only dealing with just a number of small bands of hunter-gatherers gradually moving along the shores of the Indian Ocean—apparently at a rate of a kilometer per year—and not yet with the major populations shifts of the Stone Age and (proto)historic periods.

***

De facto close connections among languages, genes, and mythology can indeed be observed under certain conditions. There are indications that relatively minute mythological developments in Siberia are closely echoed and reflected in the genetic setup of certain populations.[98] This is no doubt due to the seclusion of the group in question, which has transmitted both their genes and their myths in relative isolation. On a wider scale, close overlaps among languages, genetics, and myths can be observed in the typical cases of the peopling of Australia, the Americas, and Polynesia (below, §4.3.3).

It is nearly impossible to observe such scenarios in later times, due to frequent remixing of populations and therefore of genes, myths, and certain traits of languages. However, more secure genetic results for these later periods will be attainable through a newly developed method that allows us to test ancient DNA extracted from buried human remains (even though there are only relatively few preserved early samples).[99] Some tests have already shown that Neanderthals are not closely genetically related to modern humans and that their genes apparently do not survive in ours, if interbreeding had indeed taken place.[100] More genetic research will further differentiate the subcategories mentioned above, and it will facilitate mythological analysis relying on the broad patterns plotted earlier (§4.1–2). At this instant, it is important to note that the transmitters of Laurasian mythologies stem from certain descendants of the ex-Africa language families and from certain derivates of the above mentioned genetic subclades, both of which differ from Sahul and Andaman derivatives of the early migrants from Africa.[101]

Already in 1991, that is, at the onset of the rapid development of human population genetics, L. Cavalli-Sforza and M. Ruhlen noticed certain overlaps in the genetic pedigrees and the linguistic ones resulting from wide-ranging comparisons of the major human language families.[102] Ruhlen was then engaged in reclassifying all human languages and in investigating their linguistic families and macro-families. His study resulted in some 15 major families (§4.1).[103]

Ruhlen's and Cavalli-Sforza's discussions at Stanford persuaded the latter to posit a close relationship between his genetic classifications and the linguistic ones made by Ruhlen, resulting in the heuristic tables in Figure 4.3. They show the perceived correspondences between language families and genetic sub-groupings of humans.[104] As mentioned, during the Paleolithic, humans, language, and genes could still spread in tandem, as this involved only small bands of people. Several of the major language families and a number of isolated languages are remnants of such early movements.[105] Importantly, several later movements of language families have overlaid much of the early ex-Africa languages (Figure 4.4; cf. Figures 4.18, 4.13).

Importantly, even at this early stage in the comparison of population genetics and Long-Range linguistics, a trend toward an all-encompassing scheme was established that will ultimately unite the "family trees" of genetics, linguistics, mythology, and archaeological cultures in one "superpedigree." By 1990, the new insights appeared even in journals appealing to the general public.[106] However, conclusions for mythology were not drawn then and in fact, have not been drawn even now. In the meantime, the picture of human population genetics has become much more involved: a brief overview is necessary.

§4.3.2. Overview of recent developments

In human genetic studies, various items of the cell structure are investigated.[107] Early in the 20th century, only such studies as that of blood groups (A, B, AB, O) and, subsequently, of the Rh factor were possible.[108] Over the past few decades, the investigation of proteins and enzymes followed, and recent technological advances have allowed studying the genes themselves,[109] including that of mtDNA and the male (Y) chromosome.[110]

As mentioned, mitochondrial DNA indicates a unilocal origin of more recent humans (*Homo sapiens sapiens*) in Africa some 130,000 years ago. The originators of this theory include W. M. Brown,[111] Allan C. Wilson, Mark Stoneking, and Rebecca E. Cann. Already in 1987, they studied the mtDNA of 147 people from all continents and found 133 types, with the greatest diversity of mtDNA in sub-Saharan populations. According to this early scenario, mtDNA changes at a rate of 0.57 percent,[112] resulting in our common ancestor, the "African Eve," living between 140,000 and 290,000 years ago.[113] Since then, mtDNA studies have taken great strides.[114]

The mtDNA scenario was subsequently expanded considerably by the study of male genes, taken from the cell nucleus, in other words, from the non-recombinant Y chromosome. In 1995, Robert L. Dorit of Yale, investigating the Y chromosomes of 38 males from all continents, originally calculated that a single male ancestor of all living humans had lived some 270,000–27,000 years ago, which indicates the problem involved with the assumed rate of

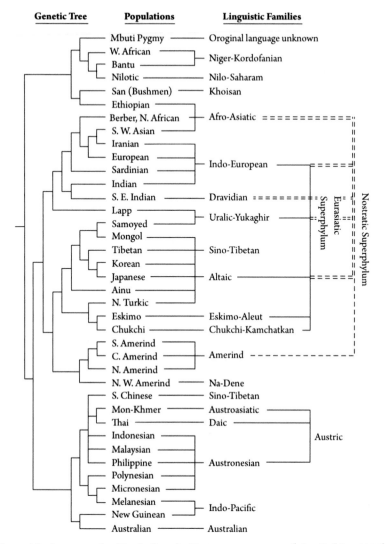

Figure 4.3. Language families before the European expansion (after Ruhlen 1987).

mutation, the "chromosome clock." However, he could not yet convincingly establish where his "Adam" could have lived. Since various parts of the Y chromosome mutate at different speeds, this question has subsequently been addressed at great length.

John Armour then detected that the great diversity of sub-Saharan mtDNA is paralleled by an even greater diversity of male NRY DNA. As is the case with mtDNA, all non-African male DNA is only a subset of a much greater pool of lineages inside Africa. The split between African and non-African NRY was originally estimated to have occurred only some 770 generations ago, much too late

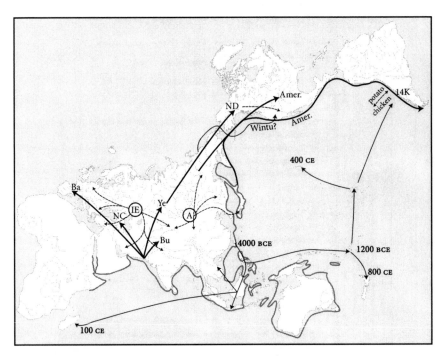

Figure 4.4. Some late movements of language families (general direction, not exact route, is indicated):

- Amerind: languages of North, Central, and South America
- Dene-Caucasian: Macro-Caucasian (Basque [Ba], North Caucasian [NC], Burushaski), Yeneseian (Ye: Ket), Na-Dene (ND: Athapascan, Apache, Navajo)
- Austronesian, c. 4000 BCE–100 CE
- Indo-European (IE), c. 3500 BCE
- Altaic: Turkic, Mongolic, Tunguse, Korean, Japanese

for all other comparative models based on language, archaeology, and so on. However, here, too, much progress has been made since. As mentioned, some 47,000-year-old nonhuman DNA has been analyzed, and in recent years Neanderthal DNA has been extracted.[115]

As in mtDNA, NRY cladistic family trees thus go back to Africa, and by now many secondary movements have been documented, based on the changes in the various (sub)branches of the cladistic arrangement. The currently available information on our NRY ancestry, the main features of its cladistic "family tree" (phylogeny), is by now well established globally.[116] Future work will have to concentrate on sublevels, the subcladistic geographic diversification patterns that led to the current distribution of NRY types worldwide.[117] This allows us to trace certain populations, among which a particular trait is prominent, back in time to their probable location and ancestor. As indicated earlier, geographical features are typically involved in the NRY landscape. In future work, the discovery of new subclades and research in the fast-changing microsatellite ("short tandem repeats") will lead to further insights. A comprehensive comparison of mtDNA and NRY phylogenetic trees that indicates the several subsequent levels of genetic changes since c. 65 kya has recently been published by Underhill and Kivisild.[118]

***

In the early stages of genetic comparisons, classical, mitochondrial, and many other genetic data were analyzed by a complicated mathematical procedure, *principal component analysis.* This

> allows to summarize large quantities of data…and discover the trends and patterns common to many genes that are the outcome of events influencing their geographic distribution.… [R]andom oscillations [are] overcome by calculating averages from a large number of observations.[119]

Cavalli-Sforza's calculations resulted in a high percentage of the most common group of genes (the "first principle component," PC) found in a certain area and lesser amounts farther away from that center. Other clusters of genes (the second, third, etc. PCs) are increasingly less frequent in percentage even in their very center of clustering. After the fifth or sixth PC, they are of limited value. It must be underlined that concentration in a particular area does not necessarily mean that this was an area of origin or original expansion; it also can be one of implosion, of a remnant group surrounded by newer traits, a feature Cavalli-Sforza calls *impansion.*[120] Such remnant groups are often found in relatively inaccessible areas, such as the high mountain chains (Pyrenees, Alps, Caucasus, Himalaya, New Guinea, etc.). The situation is very similar to that of isolated languages, such as Basque or Burushaski, whose earlier, much more widely spread traces across Eurasia can still be detected in place-names.[121]

Comparison of the various PCs showed that there is a split between Africa and the rest of the world, which has subsequently been confirmed by mtDNA and male chromosome analysis.[122] Several of the PCs are linked to geographically conditioned influences of climate, especially the second and also the sixth. This is also the case with the first climatic PC (due to maximum temperatures) and the fourth PC with the second climatic PC (due to humidity). Skin color as an adaptation to local climate is clearly linked to geographical latitude;[123] it is darkest in sub-Saharan Africa, East and South India, Papua, and Australia, while the relatively recent immigrants to tropical climates, the Amerindians, have not yet reached these levels, even in equatorial America.[124]

The much more detailed discussion of genetic traits that is to follow will include the major results based on the study of mitochondrial DNA and male Y chromosomes.[125] However, the establishment of the spread of a single mtDNA (or NRY) trait does *not* indicate the descent of the population in question or, worse, its adherence to a particular so-called race, such as the "Mediterranean," "Caucasian", "Nordic," "Australoid," "Veddoid," "Mongoloid," and so on or whatever these old-fashioned but sometimes still persistent designations have been. By now, more than a decade after Cavalli-Sforza's pioneering summary based on classical genetic data, the ongoing work on mtDNA and NRY chromosomes has largely refined the scenario of early *Homo sapiens* and provides an excellent background for historical comparative mythology in general and for the development of Gondwana and its derivative, Laurasian mythology in particular.

§4.3.3. Out of Africa

The data derived from both the female mtDNA and the male NRY point at a spread out of Africa around 65,000 BCE.[126] The exact absolute date depends on the rate of mutations, discussed above. It can, however, be confirmed by the discovery of ancient bones of modern *Homo sapiens sapiens* outside Africa. The earliest are found in Australia and dated around 40,000 BCE or by some even at 65,000 BCE. Indeed, already Cavalli-Sforza summed up the evidence then available as seen in Table 4.2.[127]

These early general results have been generally held up by more recent mtDNA and NRY studies. The ultimate background of the migrations seems to have been the following:[128] The ancient *Homo sapiens sapiens* spread to the Levant (where they partially overlapped with Neanderthals) was only of a temporary nature. This occupation disappeared with deteriorating climatic conditions after 90,000 BCE (§4.4). However, it is now clear that there were two major stages in the expansion of humans from Africa. First, there was the original "Out of Africa" exodus and the subsequent migration trailing the shores of the Indian Ocean.[129] Second, after the waning of an earlier ice age (52,000–45,000 BCE), there was a second migration into the central and northern parts of Eurasia,[130] including East Asia, the Near East, and Europe.[131]

The initial migration out of Africa to the Levant still presents a problem, as far as the coexistence with Neanderthal populations in that region is concerned.[132] The rather late evidence of *Homo sapiens* outside Africa and the Levant is intriguing.[133] As mentioned, the population emigrating from Africa eastward to

TABLE 4.2. *Overview of the genetic distance between the continents (Cavalli-Sforza et al. 1994)*

Separation of peoples	Date	Genetic Distance
Africa and rest of world	100,000 years ago	100
Southeast Asia and Australia	55–65,000 years ago	62
Asia and Europe	35–40,000 years ago	48
Northeast Asia and America	15-35,000 years ago	30

South Arabia must have been a rather small group that descended from a population that itself was fairly restricted when compared with earlier evidence for modern humans in Africa. As C. Stringer and R. McKie have it: "Our mitochondrial DNA's remarkable uniformity [is] a certain sign of a recent bottleneck.... [T]his numerical compression occurred about 100,000 years ago.... Our African recovery seems to have begun first, perhaps 60,000 years ago."[134] It is now indeed generally assumed that the move out of Africa took place some 60,000 years ago.[135] At the present state of research, modern humans are not attested along the emigration path in South Asia by skeletons or, indirectly, by contemporary stone tools before c. 30 kya,[136] as their route is now covered by the Indian Ocean. On the other hand, anatomically modern humans had already entered Australia at about 50 kya (or even earlier).[137]

The Negritos (Andamanese, Semang in Malaya, Negrito in the Philippines, etc.)[138] might be remnants of the early exodus. However, they all speak, like the Central African pygmies,[139] various languages adopted from their neighbors. The only exception are the Andamanese.[140] They have, in Cavalli-Sforza's view,[141] less intermixture with other populations and may represent remnants of groups on the track of beachcombers eastward out of Africa. This opinion has recently been confirmed by two genetic studies.[142] Importantly, all these remnant groups have or show signs of the original Gondwana mythology (§5).

This exodus from Africa at c. 65,000 years ago was thus followed by a quick spread to Sunda Land (insular Southeast Asia) and onward to Sahul Land (Australia, New Guinea) as well as to South China (Figure 4.5). It led to strong regional variation (West Asia, South Asia, Southeast Asia/East Asia, Australia, New Guinea), creating new autochthonous branches.[143] However, even today, certain sections of the initial populations, left behind intermittently along the exodus path, do not show close links with later genetic traits and have, instead, preserved major elements of the original Gondwana mythologies.[144]

As for the other populations, for example, in South Asia, their maternal lines (mtDNA) go back, by and large, to the *initial* immigration out of Africa, around 65,000 BCE: mostly, but not universally, haplogroup M2, from which they developed further. This is true both for North Indians speaking Indo-Aryan languages and for Dravidian-speaking South Indians. The picture thus is fairly static,[145] just as in other regions, such as Southeast Asia, New Guinea, and Australia that were settled during the first expansion. There, other derivative haplogroups dominate or are found as well: N, R, P, Q, and so on.

The picture is, however, markedly different when it comes to male lineages. The seminal papers by Semino et al. and Underhill established ten paternal nonrecombinant Y chromosome lines (I–X)[146] that have by now been expanded and renamed as A–R.[147] For individual areas, the situation is very complex, for example, for Europe or for South Asia:[148] not just the initial Out of Africa lineages (haplogroups IV, V = D, C) are represented, but many others are as well,

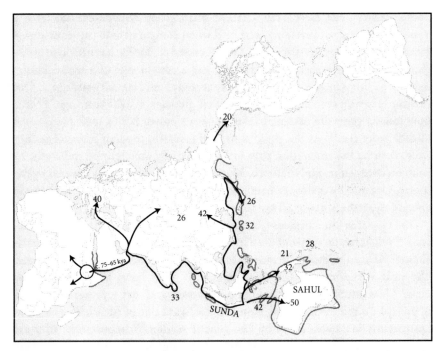

Figure 4.5. Spread of anatomically modern humans along the initial southern (coastal) route out of Africa, c. 75–65 kya. Only by c. 40 kya had anatomically modern humans moved farther north into the Eurasian inland during a warm period. For Eurasia/Australia the coastlines of the colder period of c. 75–65 kya are indicated.

such as III (E), VI (F, K, prominently found in North Asia, North Africa, and Europe), and X (P, R$_1$, which is typical for the Americas) and even some of the East Asian haplogroups (VII = O etc.).

Over the past few years, thus, both the mtDNA and NRY scenarios have become much more sophisticated and complex. Whether we have to reckon with a second, much later post-exodus expansion eastward is a moot question. If it really occurred, it would coincide with the spread of Laurasian mythology (§4.3.5).

As mentioned, the dates for recent movements of people still have error bands that are too wide, for example, the one into South Asia around 10 kya that is probably due to West Asian farmers and is reflected by recent haplogroups.[149] These error margins are typically as wide as some 3,000 years plus/minus, on either side (thus giving possible dates at 13 kya or as late as 7 kya). Thus, they are not of any immediate use for studies of absolute dates in recent population history, during the (pre)historical period. However, they provide reasonable *relative* dates, such as those for pre- and post-exodus, the subsequent migration into Sahul Land, Europe, or the Americas. Along the same lines, the R1a1-M17/

M198 marker that was originally quoted as the one pertaining to the Indo-Aryan immigration into India occurs both in South Indian tribes and with Indo-European speakers. It has by now been split into several subgroups, some early,[150] some later, some of South Asian origin, some not.[151] However, the picture of R1a1 in South Asia is still too vague (though it is most prominently found in the northwest), and R1a1 must first be further resolved in order to indicate population movement(s) out of or back into India or both.[152]

The current picture: mtDNA

The current picture of mtDNA indicates that all non-African people descend from the African mtDNA haplogroup L3 with the prominent branches M and N and their descendants R, B, U, and so on.[153] This indicates a quick spread of humans to South, Southeast, and East Asia and to Australia/New Guinea (Sahul Land)[154] that overlaps with the spread of the oldest forms of Gondwana mythology. During the opening stages of human movement out of Africa, the earliest offshoots of haplogroups M and N were rapidly segregated into several regional variants:

West Asian: e.g., R –> JT, R –> U
South Asian: e.g., M2, N5, R5, U2a, b, c
East Asian: e.g., M –> D, M7, M8, N9, R9 –> F, R –> B
and further into the
Australasia-specific ones (Sahul): N –> S, O; R –> P, M –> Q[155]

These became the sources for the autochthonous, local mtDNA diversification in their respective regions, with Gondwana mythologies. However, admixture among the four basic Asian mtDNA domains has been surprisingly limited ever since. It is important to note that Central Asia appears as the largest admixture zone (Figure 4.6),[156] where the mtDNA pools of West and East Asia, and to a very much lesser extent of South Asia, met and mixed.[157]

The development of Asian mtDNA, following Metspalu as well as Underhill and Kivisild,[158] can be summed up as seen in Tables 4.3–4.4. From the point of view of Laurasian and Gondwana mythology, the scheme shown here corresponds well to the original spread of Gondwana mythologies out of Africa via South Asia to Sahul Land; however, it cannot yet easily explain the spread of Laurasian mythology that developed some tens of thousands of years later as an offshoot of Gondwana myth and thus, of mtDNA haplogroups M, N/R. But which later descendant haplogroups exactly? Given the relatively stable status of female DNA, it is more advantageous to take a closer look at the evidence from the male chromosome (NRY), as men always have been more mobile and tend to intermarry with preexisting local populations. In addition, much of mythology has been transmitted by men;[159] and the link between NRY and available myth texts can tell more about the early stages of mythology than the few fragments of truly "female" myths.

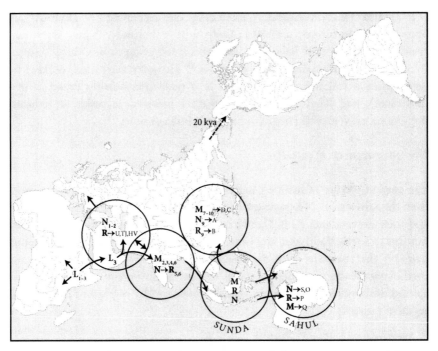

Figure 4.6. Spread of early mtDNA haplogroups out of Africa: L3, M, N, R, and their derivatives (based on Metspalu et al. 2006, http://www.springerlink.com/content/h007402m82331750/fulltext.pdf).

The current picture: NRY

Studies of the male nonrecombinant Y chromosome often allow for more refined evaluations. They agree, however, with the general outline provided by mtDNA. A few years ago, Semino et al. and Underhill counted ten original male lineages (I–X);[160] not all of them, obviously, developed at the same time. These lineages

TABLE 4.3. *MtDNA lineage Major genetic groupings (mtDNA) after the Out of Africa movement (Note that the divergence of R is early)*

MtDNA				
SW. Asia	**S. Asia**	**SE. Asia**	**E. Asia**	**Sahul Land**
Africa →	75/65 kya	55/42 kya	42 kya	50/45 kya
N	M, N (R$_5$)	M, N	M, N, (R$_9$)	M, R N→S
|	subgroups	some		| |
R	diversified	subgroups		Q P
	in situ	not transmitted		
← M$_1$ ← ←		to E.Asia		

TABLE 4.4. *Female mtDNA ancestor ('Eve') and her descendants, simplified (after Kivisild & Underhill 2007)*

```
Africa            Out of Africa

female
ancestor
("African Eve")

    LO/L1

              L2    L3 (c. 65 kya)

              M       N

                        R

              SW/S. Asia → rest of Eurasia/Sahul Land (c. 50 kya);
              northward expansion (c.45 kya);
              finally to the Americas (c. 20 kya), and
              Polynesia/Madagascar (2000–1200 BCE)

        Current worldwide distribution of MtDNA lineages
```

have now been renamed by the Y Chromosome Consortium,[161] amplified, and further subdivided as the NRY haplogroups A–R.[162] A summary has been given by M. A. Jobling and C. Tyler-Smith as well as by Underhill and Kivisild.[163]

Of these lineages, only NRY haplogroups I and II (= A, B) have remained in Africa; the haplogroups III/E, IV/D, and V/C moved out to South and Southeast Asia early on. The haplogroups VI–X (F/K) and out of these, successively, P, O, N, R, Q, N, M, and L developed only later on. See Table 4.5 and Figures 4.7–4.8 for a summary.

TABLE 4.5. *The 18 Y chromosome haplogroups (A – R) have evolved from a common male ancestor (an "African Adam") via just two branches: from M91 to haplogroup A (I), and from M42 to the rest, that is haplogroup B (II) and haplogroups C-R (III-X).*

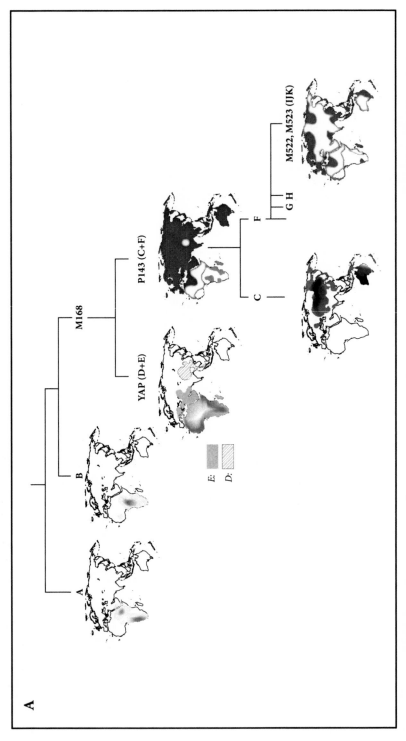

Figure 4.7. Early spread of NRY haplogroups (NRY I–X are now renamed A–S; after Chiaroni et al. 2009; from the 2004 article by Metspalu et al. in *BMC Genetics*, http://www.biomedcentral.com/content/pdf/1471-2156-5-26.pdf).

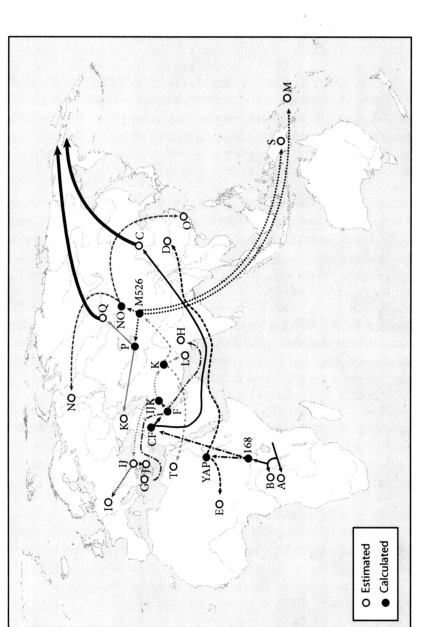

Figure 4.8. Spread of NRY subclades (after Chiaroni et al. 2009).

NRY

The 18 Y chromosome haplogroups (A–R) have evolved from a common male ancestor (an "African Adam") via just two branches: from M91 to haplogroup A (I) and from marker M42 to the rest, that is, haplogroup B (II) and haplogroups C–R (III–X). The descendants of the male ancestor lineage M42 all are "Asian" (haplogroups C–R), except for haplogroup B (M146, M182), which stayed in Africa. The history of M168 thus more or less corresponds in the migration scheme to mtDNA L3. Both are the common ancestors of all humans that moved out of Africa. They had the "Asian" mtDNA "daughters" M and N and NRY "sons" C–R, with C, F, and K as the founder lineages (see Figures 4.9–4.11). As mentioned, the Out of Africa migration first reached West and South Asia, and people spread from there both eastward to Sahul Land and the southern sections of East Asia (c. 60 kya) and (north)westward toward the Near East and Europe (c. 40 kya).

Of special interest for mythology as well as for the early spread toward East Asia is the fact that haplogroup D (IV) moved all the way,[164] from South Asia along the then expanded sea coast of Indonesia up to East Asia. In Japan, it still is strongly represented (some 25–50 percent, depending on area), while it has virtually disappeared elsewhere, except for Tibet.[165] It has also been discovered among the linguistically isolated Andamanese and with two Indian tribes, the Rajbanshi on the Bengal/Nepalese border, who now speak Indo-Aryan, and the Kurumba in the South Indian Nilgiri Hills, who now speak Dravidian. In this context, it is worth mentioning that there are a few indications that the Ainu language of North Japan and Sakhalin represents that of these early immigrants: some of its words are still found in India with the Nahals.[166] Note also the relatively isolated genetic data of Japan,[167] where NRY D-M55 clearly is an early leftover from the exodus; this is also represented at lower numbers in mainland Japanese and with the Okinawans but is absent in the East Asian neighborhood, while D is also found in Tibet and some refuge areas of India.[168] These neglected facts of early spread are in need of further research. If further corroborated, it would indicate a perfect overlap of the genetic and linguistic data of early human expansion throughout Asia. Unfortunately, it is much harder to demonstrate mythological connections. The Nahals have been more or less Hinduized over the past thousand years, and the Ainu share many features of the northeastern Asian and Siberian mythology, including shamanism (§7.1) and the bear cult (§7.1.2).

Of special interest for the Laurasian theory, obviously, is the split between the Gondwana (African, Toda, Andaman, Semang, some tribes of highland Taiwan,[169] Papua, and Australian) mythologies, on the one hand, and, on the other, the rest of Eurasian mythology. To put it in simplified terms, haplogroups NRY I–V (A, B, E, D, C) *seem* to overlap with the Gondwana type of mythology, while VI–X (F/K, P, O, R, etc.) generally have the Laurasian one. This point will

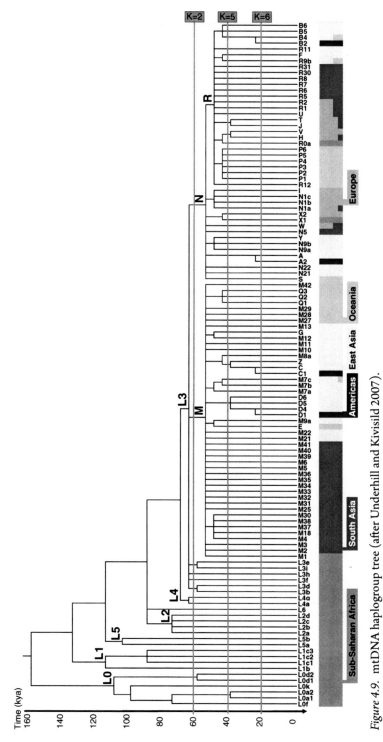

Figure 4.9. mtDNA haplogroup tree (after Underhill and Kivisild 2007).

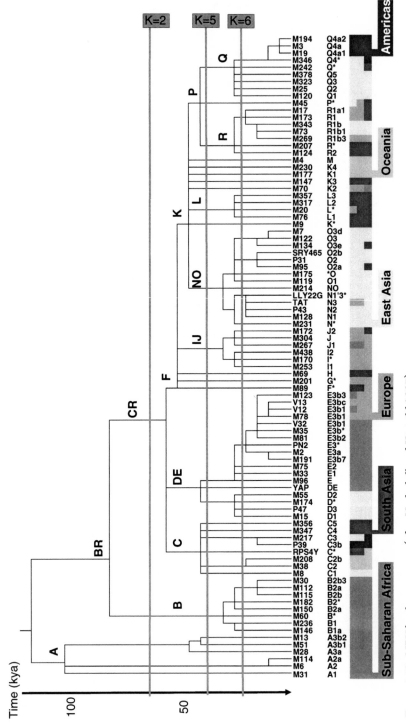

Figure 4.10. NRY haplogroup tree (after Underhill and Kivisild 2007).

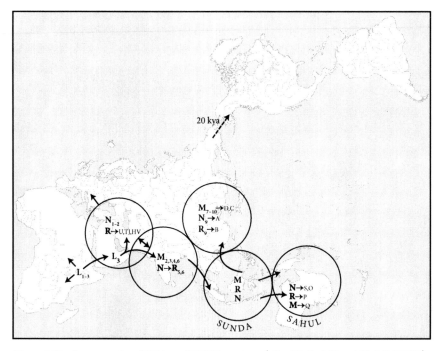

Figure 4.11. Autosomal, mtDNA, and NRY locations (after Underhill and Kivisild 2007).

be taken up in more detail below; first, however, it is necessary to review in some detail the distribution of the individual NRY and mtDNA data points during the post-exodus periods.

§4.3.4. Movement northward after the last two ice ages

The post–Out of Africa developments, after the initial spread of c. 65,000 BCE, may be summed up as shown in Figure 4.12. The spread northward of humans from their initial habitats scattered along the Indian Ocean and Sunda Land was furthered by congenial climatic conditions that persisted during the long inter-glacial period from c. 50 to 25 kya.[170] It saw the emergence of many new sublin-eages of mtDNA and NRY all over Eurasia. The period also witnessed the development of new hunting techniques (§4.4) and the much discussed "explosion" of symbolic thought around 40 kya.[171] This also includes the development and spread of Laurasian mythology during the late Paleolithic period and much of early rock art (France/Spain, Sahara, South Africa, Central India, Timor, New Guinea, Australia, and Tasmania; §4.4.1).

All of Eurasia was eventually occupied, and the areas to the north of the original coastal spread were covered by populations who were descendants of the haplo-groups mtDNA M, N, and R and NRY C–R. Working backward from attested

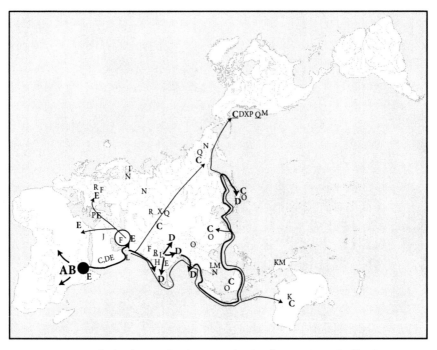

Figure 4.12. Spread of early NRY haplogroups (C, D, E). Later spread of haplogroup F and its derivatives G –> R, S.

and reconstructed forms, it appears that they mainly spoke ancestral forms of the Dene-Caucasian, Nostratic, Sino-Tibetan, and Austric languages and followed a form of Laurasian mythology.[172] It is this expansion that brought Laurasian mythology to northern Asia and Europe. Rare residual pockets of this immigration are still visible in the remnant languages of the high mountains, from West Europe to the Pamirs.[173] Their mythologies must be studied at length, a rather complicated project that cannot be carried out here, as both the Basque and North Caucasians as well as the Burushos in the southern Pamirs have changed their original religions to Christianity or Islam. Their older religion and mythology can only be reconstructed from folktales and certain rituals.[174] It is significant that Long-Range linguists such as J. Bengtson have now definitely linked the Basque language with Northwest and Northeast Caucasian (Cherkes, Chechen, etc.) and with Burushaski, spoken in the isolated corner of Hunza in northernmost Pakistan.[175] The Macro-Caucasian language family has left some faint traces in western Central Asia as well.[176] Interestingly, Burusho and Basque genes share some features,[177] which agrees well with their linguistic connections—some 40 kya after the westward migration of the ancestors of the Basques; we will briefly return to their mythology below.

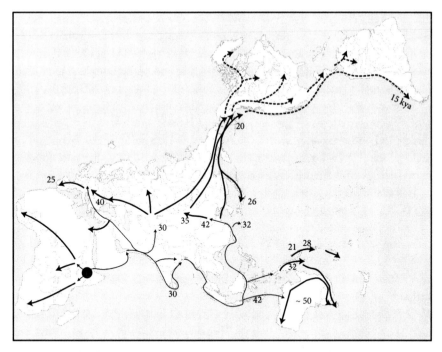

Figure 4.13. Northward spread during the interglacial warm period, c. 45–25 kya (gray lines) and from 25 to 22 kya (bold lines).

The first human expansion across northern Eurasia must be studied along the same lines (Figure 4.13). Here, again, the situation has been disturbed by later movements of peoples and by the spread of new belief systems. The Ket in western Siberia are one such remnant population. They have been linked to Macro-Caucasian and to the Na-Dene-speaking peoples of North America.[178] Northeastern Asia harbors some other old remnant populations that are isolated linguistically (Koryak, Chukchi, Gilyak/Nivkh, Ainu, etc.) and in part also genetically.[179] They have been influenced by classical Siberian shamanic beliefs (§7.1). The older strata of their mythology must be distilled through comparison with the original Laurasian one. This, again, is a subproject that cannot be covered by the present book.

Last Glacial Maximum

The extraordinary, long warm period that enabled the spread of anatomically modern humans all over Eurasia was followed by the Last Glacial Maximum (LGM) of 25–15 kya. It forced many populations to retreat to warmer climates farther south and into small, isolated northern refuge areas that were climatically favored.[180] Many of the expanded populations that lived in northern and central Eurasia were thus restricted to a few areas of refuge, such as in Spain/southwestern

France,[181] the Balkans, East Asia south of the line of permafrost,[182] some small pockets in central and northeastern Siberia/Bering Land,[183] and subsequently some small areas of North America.[184] From these restricted pockets, the wide areas north of them were only resettled after the end of the last Ice Age around 10,000 BCE.[185] Consequently, the genetic traits of the Basque (mtDNA H, V)[186] and Sardinians,[187] for example, stand out against much of Europe. Many of the recent, new genetic developments in East Asia and Europe took place during this period and even later, such as the change in skin color or the formation of regional centers in Laurasian mythology.[188] After the LGM, humans quickly spread across all currently settled regions. (Cf. Figure 4.14.)

It is also important to note that during the extremely cold and dry period of the LGM, wide areas of southern Europe, Central Asia, and North Africa were by and large separated from South Asia and East Asia by great deserts, extending uninterrupted from the Gobi to the Sahara. This increased the localization of genetic developments in Africa, Europe, South Asia, Southeast Asia, East Asia, and Africa that had set in after their initial settlement, as already referred to earlier.[189]

There was, however, some possibility of contact between East Asia and South Asia via a savanna and scrub belt in Bengal-Assam-Burma-Sichuan, along the steep but passable route (much later on, the so-called Southern Silk Road, which

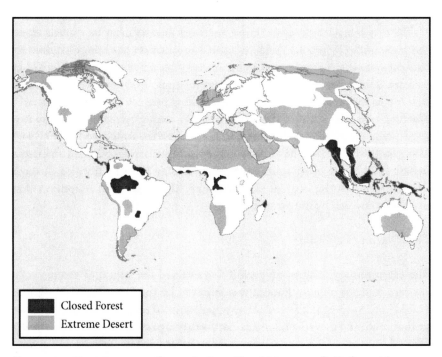

Figure 4.14. Vegetation cover during the Last Glacial Maximum (LGM), c. 18 kya.

allowed only travel on foot and sometimes by pack animal).[190] Sub-Saharan Africa, too, was open to interchanges across its widespread scrub, grassland, and savanna belts, from the Sahara southward to the tip of South Africa. The gradual movement southward to Tanzania and beyond of the Khoi-San-speaking people falls into this period;[191] they arrived in South Africa only by c. 6000 BCE.[192] Notably, they have a mythology that differs from that of the surrounding populations (§5.3.5.1).

Finally, northern Australia and southern New Guinea were connected via a grassland belt (now submerged) that allowed for cultural and genetic influx. It can be clearly detected in Papuan influences on northwestern and northeastern Australian mythology (§5.3.2),[193] while the genetic influence is less prominent.[194] South Australia was separated from the north by a large central desert, while scrub covered the northern two-thirds and as well a long north–south belt in the east of the continent. The resulting relative isolation of the southeast might be reflected in the differences between southeastern myth (and to some extent, some features of their languages) and that of the rest of the continent (§5.3.2). Tasmania, too, was connected to Australia by a land bridge. In many respects, it therefore functions as an extension of the archaic traits of southeastern Australia (§5.3.2.1), whose mythology is related, though the languages of both areas are not.[195] Genetic studies (mtDNA) of the survivors of the Tasmanians (with female Tasmanian and paternal British lines) have only yielded limited results so far,[196] mainly in a fast-mutating area of the genome; current results indicate a distant relationship with the Australian mainland.

However, the first entry of humans into the Americas at c. 20 kya falls in the period of the last Ice Age.[197] It was facilitated by lower sea level and the consequent exposure of Bering Land between Siberia and Alaska. The migrants brought Eurasian genes and Amerindian languages as well Laurasian mythology with them.[198] All of them developed on their own in the western hemisphere, which was soon to be isolated again by the melting ice cap (after c. 11,500 BCE). The mythological data, especially those from the first migration into the Americas,[199] can function as a welcome countercheck to developments in Eurasia, as most parts of the Americas have been isolated by now for some 13,000 years.

Importantly, the severe climatic conditions during the last Ice Age reinforced the isolation of some of the populations in the areas discussed, in their genetic development (such as drift) as well as in mythological developments, to which we now return at some length.

§4.3.5. Genetics, language, and mythology

Once we combine the evidence of male NRY and female mtDNA lineages, such as has recently been done by Underhill and Kivisild,[200] a picture emerges that largely overlaps with that of major language families and, importantly for the present undertaking, with mythologies (Table 4.6). A current, heuristic scenario of these three fields may therefore be hazarded here. It remains open to adjustment, correction, or even abandonment, upon the discovery of new data. It must be underlined again that the scheme presented here is heuristic; details of the combined family tree of genes, languages, and mythologies may change any time that new facts or new haplogroups are discovered.

TABLE 4.6. *Combined, Simplified table of mtDNA, NRY haplogroups and mythologies*

mtDNA   "EVE"   NRY

L0, L1,L2   A= I
(African)   L3   (Afr.)

                                 B = II (African)

PAN-GAEAN and
AFRICAN MYTHOLOGY

                                                                        c. 65 kya

EXODUS

   M   N   YAP   RPS4Y   M89
(Asian) (Asian)   (Asian)
GONDWANA MYTHOLOGY

          R

                                                            52–45 kya ICE AGE

C,Z,G, S,A, P,H,V,   E=III   D=IV   C=V   F = VI-X   K
Q   Y,W,   T,U,F,   NEAR   Ainu   Asia, Siberia   (M9)
             B   EAST,   Nahali?   Ainu
                      AFRICA   Andam.   Sahul Land
                      EUROPE   India,   Amer.   GOND. MYTHOLOGY
                      GOND.   GOND.   → LAURASIAN
                      MYTH.??   MYTH.?   MYTHOLOGY
                                         F=VI, I-J   K = SAHUL
                                                        L, N-R (S) :
                                         NEAR   N-O,
                                         EAST   S.E.
S,O,P,Q (Sahul Land)   MEDIT.   ASIA /
                                         EUROPE   L
Z, B, C, D (Asia, Americas)   S.ASIA /
G (Asia)   BASQUE,   P >R, Q
                                         SUBSTR.   E.Asia,
A,Y,B,F (East Asian, Americas)   LANG.S   S.Asia
                                         of Europe   Europe
X,I,Y J,T U>K H,V,W,T   America (Q)
    (European/West Asia)

                                                    25–15 kya ICE AGE (LGM)

§4.3.6. Summary and outlook

For historical and comparative mythology it is important to take note of the early emergence of regional genetic domains that developed soon after the exodus from Africa. This favored the development of regional centers in mythology as well, as already described (§2.3). The oldest ones are those in sub-Saharan Africa; others are those outlined by Metspalu:[201] the Greater Near East (Southwest Asia), South Asia, Southeast Asia, and East Asia. There also is the separate Indo-Pacific area (Andamans, New Guinea, Tasmania, and Australia). Further, secondary centers developed in Europe, Central Asia, Northeast Asia, and the Americas.[202]

Some of them overlap with Laurasian mythology, and others, with Gondwana mythologies. As mentioned, Laurasian mythology is generally restricted to Eurasian and American populations that speak Nostratic, Macro-Caucasian, Sino-Tibetan, Austric, and Amerindian languages, while their DNA is restricted to populations that predominantly have the haplogroups mtDNA M and N. This includes those of their descendants: R, A, Y, F, B, C, G, Z, E, and D in East Asia and the Americas; M, N, R, and U in South Asia; and N, W, X, I, R, U, and M in West Asia and Europe.[203] These populations share the NRY haplogroups descending from F (G–R = VI–X) and perhaps also E (V = YAP, M145, 203), which descended from the same common ancestor P14/M89/M213.

In sum, the first migration included the founder lineages mtDNA M, N –> R as well as NRY C, D, and F.[204] Their areas broadly overlap with Near Eastern, South Asian, and Southeast Asian languages but with both Gondwana and Laurasian mythology.

***

Of special interest for the Laurasian theory is the early split between, on the one hand, African, Toda, Andaman, Semang, highland Taiwan, Papua, and Australian mythology, and their respective languages and genes, and on the other, the rest of Eurasian genes and mythologies. In simplified terms, haplogroups NRY I, II, and IV (A, B, D), perhaps V (C), and probably III (E) seem to represent the Gondwana type of mythology (see Figure 4.15), while VI–X (F and descendants, especially K) represent the Laurasian one. The problem of NRY haplogroup E is in need of further study, especially insofar as its relationship with Macro-Caucasian languages and myths is concerned. At this stage it is unclear whether the ancestors of these populations adhered to Gondwana or Laurasian mythology.

The developments of the post-exodus period, after the initial spread out of Africa at c. 65 kya, have been detailed earlier and may briefly be summed up as follows. The spread of humans to large parts of Eurasia took place during the warm period between the second-to-last ice age (c. 52–45 kya) and the last one (c. 25–15 kya). It seems to have overlapped with the development and spread of

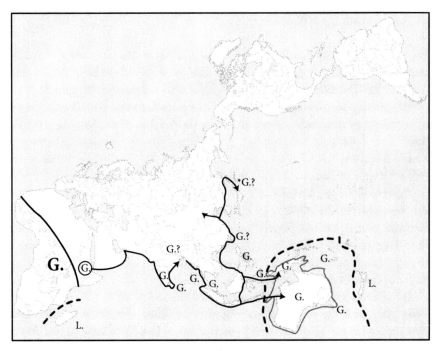

Figure 4.15. Spread of Gondwana mythologies (including residue areas). Uncertain spread is indicated by G.?; *G indicates originally Gondwana area.

Laurasian mythology. This is sustained by archaeological finds: there is some overlap with early rock art found in France/Spain, the Sahara, Central India, and Timor but also in South Africa, New Guinea, and Australia (§4.4.1, §7.1.2), which needs to be explained. Yet apparently "new" human symbolic creativity did not stop at the "Laurasian border" but included populations with both types of mythologies.

However, the Last Glacial Maximum of 25–15 kya restricted many of these expanded populations to a few areas of refuge.[205] The severe conditions reinforced the isolation of many populations, in genetic exchange as well as in mythological developments. Only after the LGM, humans again spread across all currently settled regions, reinforcing the spread of Laurasian mythologies from the glacial refuge areas in Asia and Europe.

The spread of Laurasian mythology

The major question that must remain in the balance for the time being is: *which spread* exactly, *when*, and by *which population*?[206] We can observe its results in the first written texts (Egypt, Mesopotamia, etc.) and extrapolate the intermediate stages (§2.2.5–3), but we cannot yet be sure about the exact trajectory. Did Laurasian mythology spread from an original refuge center somewhere in

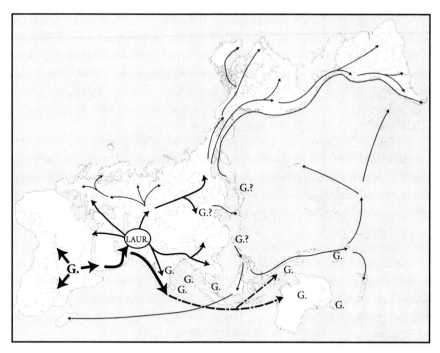

Figure 4.16. Development and spread of Gondwana and Laurasian mythologies. Later spread (Austronesian, Amerind) is indicated by thin lines.

Greater Southwest Asia eastward toward South Asia and Southeast and East Asia as well as, at the same time(?), north- and westward to western Central Asia, Europe, and North Africa?

The question then arises how exactly Laurasian mythology moved from Southwest Asia to Southeast and East Asia. Did it already spread northward during the warming period between c. 52 and 45 kya after an earlier ice age?[207] For example, was it brought into what is now China by the ancestors of the Tibeto-Burmese speakers (including pre-Shang/Zhou Chinese)? Or did it arrive from the north, post-LGM, from the glacial refuges of central Siberia,[208] and then spread south to the Tibeto-Burmese and Tai-Kadai/Austric language areas?[209] (See Figure 4.16.)

The Na-Dene migrations

The link provided by the hypothetical Dene-Caucasian linguistic family, which also includes Chinese according to the classifications of Long-Range linguists, may supply a hint. This language family nowadays extends from Basque via the Caucasus and Burushaski in the Pamirs to Yeneseian (Ket), Chinese, and Na-Dene (Athapascans, Navajo, Apache) in North America. Obviously, it includes populations that, on the surface, seem to belong to quite separate genetic groups.

However, apart from a possible language shift, phenotype appearance is a misleading factor, and as the case of Burushaski indicates, it may just be a superficial initial impression. As mentioned, the Burushos have both linguistic and genetic links with the Basque people at the other end of Eurasia.[210] In addition, the Na-Dene-speaking peoples are known to be late "Siberian" immigrants into North America,[211] who may have spread into the continent only after the postglacial flooding of Bering Land around 11 kya.[212]

In sum, if the eastern section of the Dene-Caucasian group had retained an *early* foothold during their assumed pre-LGM migration, in Siberia and northern East Asia and then a limited refuge during the last Ice Age,[213] Laurasian mythology could have spread from there to all of East Asia, and later on to Southeast Asia, forming an overlay over earlier peoples with Gondwana mythology.

It all would depend on the answer to the question of whether the speakers of early Dene-Caucasian still had a Gondwana mythology or already had the Laurasian one. Detailed investigation of the few surviving Dene-Caucasian myths is required, which, as mentioned, cannot be carried out here as it involves a large project of studying Basque and Caucasian tales, the remnants of Burusho and Ket spiritual culture, and Na-Dene mythology, all of which have been seriously influenced by their more recent neighbors.

Two routes out of Africa?

The scenario sketched above would agree with the hypothesis of two migration routes out of Africa: an earlier one along the sea coast to southern East Asia and a later, Upper Paleolithic one from the Levant through Central Asia and southern Siberia/North Asia. This is the so-called pincer model.[214]

However, this model should have resulted in a genetic pattern in which individual, localized post-40-kya Central Asian developments are visible:[215] in short, a well-defined central Asian domain. This is *not* the case,[216] as no unique Central Asian and North Asian lineages exist that are *not* derived from the southern-track ones and as the Ket/Na-Dene spread was postglacial. We are therefore left with an *ultimate* late Paleolithic origin of northern, Siberian lineages from Southeast Asian ones; the recent find at Zhoukoudian (42–39 kya) agrees with such a scenario.

The scenario of a spread of Laurasian mythology from Southwest Asia must be linked to the spread of *descendants* of the mtDNA haplogroups M/N and NRY F (G–R). However, both M and N, dated at c. 65 kya,[217] belong to the general Out of Africa movement that is closely linked with *Gondwana* mythology. The idea that Laurasian mythology spread eastward just with people of the mtDNA haplogroup N (and R) can be excluded, as they are of basically the same age as M (and also U2), whose bearers are expected to have adhered to Gondwana mythologies.[218] As Metspalu and colleagues have outlined,[219] the various postexodus centers in Eurasia are very stable with regard to later admixture, and the

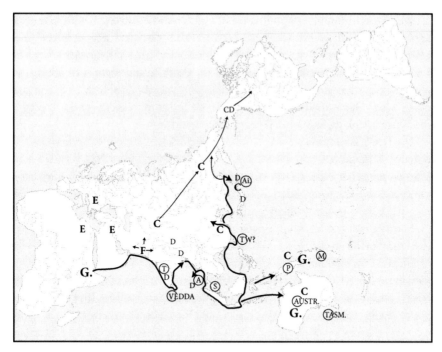

Figure 4.17. Spread of Gondwana mythologies and of early Out of Africa NRY haplogroups (C, D, E).

T. = Toda, A. = Andaman, S. = Semang, P. = Papua, M. = Melanesian, TW = Taiwan Aboriginals, Ai. = Ainu

descendants of M and N mostly are local developments, likely to have possessed Gondwana mythologies (Figure 4.17).

NRY lineages and shamanic transmission

Thus, the maternal lineages may indicate little or nothing about the actual spread of Laurasian mythology. As pointed out in detail below (§6.1, §7.1), it is more likely that the actual myths and their story line were propagated and transmitted by *male* Paleolithic shamans (§7.1). Males usually are more mobile than females, as countless examples from history attest.

It should also be noted that mythology, while being similar with both the males and females of a given population,[220] is frequently transmitted in an organized fashion by the spiritual leaders, shamans, or priests of that society. In other words, the male lineage (NRY) can be correlated with (Laurasian) mythology, "grandfathers' tales," while the females may tell "grandmothers' tales."[221]

One may therefore take a closer look at the spread of post-exodus male (NRY) genetic traits. The NRY haplogroups represented by and descended from F (G–R = VI–X)[222] would make good candidates for Laurasian mythology. Do we actually have to think, along the lines of Forster and Renfrew,[223] with a limited second spread of anatomically modern humans eastward across South and Southeast Asia (their "weaker garden of Eden" model)? At the present stage of research it is prudent to take a minimalist position and state that Laurasian mythology superseded the then prevalent Gondwana mythology in Southeast Asia, which nevertheless is still preserved in some refuge areas (Nilgiri, Andamans, Malaya, highland Taiwan, Sahul Land).

The DNA haplogroup NRY E, a brother clade of the very early East Asian, Indian/Andamanese, and Tibetan D, is found only in sub-Saharan Africa and Europe. Its occurrence seems too early for Laurasian mythology. It may have involved some early migration to Europe, such as that of the Crô Magnon ancestors of the Basque—in that case, probably still with a different mythology.

Another major remaining question concerns DNA haplogroup NRY C (V). It is found on all continents, except Africa, and it is old, a non-YAP brother clade of DE. Its bearers therefore are unlikely to have carried Laurasian mythology with them on arrival in all of their ex-African locations. Note that bearers of early NRY C also lived too early to reach Europe around 40 kya ago: they are mainly South Asian, Australian, and East Asian (and thus American). Perhaps they still reflected Gondwana mythology that was overlaid in some areas by Laurasian mythology (such as in India, East Asia, and the Americas). This point, again, must be left open at the moment, awaiting more detailed interdisciplinary research in genetics, linguistics, and mythology.

Instead, a glimpse of the early post-40-kya settlement of Eurasia and a possible link with Laurasian mythology is provided by the overlapping areal linguistic features studied by Masica for South, Central, North, and Northeast Asia.[224] However, it cannot be excluded either that the vast spread of linguistic features outlined by him was a post-LGM feature only and thus too late for a correlation with early Laurasian mythology. Perhaps one should rather take a closer look at the spread of mtDNA R (derived from N), whose descendants are found all over Eurasia.

In pursuing this scenario, the following observations are of importance. The mtDNA haplogroup M is slightly more frequent in South Asia, North Asia, North China, and Japan. Certain old linguistic patterns cover exactly the same area.[225]

On the other hand, mtDNA N (and its derivative R) is more typical for Southwest Asia and eastern Eurasia, while the N/R domain does not overlap with the M domain. We thus have two separate areas, Southwest and East versus South, North, and Northeast Asia[226]—just as seen in linguistics with the Nostratic languages.[227] Nevertheless, a *direct* link between this scheme and Laurasian mythology cannot yet be established: it would fit most of these Nostratic areas and that of mtDNA M, but it would genetically and linguistically exclude much of East and Southeast Asia.

A facile solution would correlate Laurasian mythology with mtDNA N/R. In this case, South Asia, where we find remnants of Gondwana mythologies and ancient language groups in refuge areas such as the Andamans and Nilgiris, would simply have retained the major post-exodus mtDNA genetic traits (mtDNA M) while adopting Laurasian mythology at a later time. However, this scenario is contradicted by the relative age of N/R, which is more or less contemporary with M.

Southeast and East Asia

For East and Southeast Asia, the scenario of the separate M and N/R domains would coincide with the post-40-kya spread of several language families, especially the move into East Asia from what is now South China of first the ancestor of Austric and then Tibeto-Burman. In other words, the northern lineages derive from the southern ones.[228] This agrees with the established southern route of early anatomically modern humans along the shores of the Indian Ocean to Southeast and East Asia and to Sahul Land.

Another, more complex scenario would attribute the first appearance of Laurasian mythology in East and Southeast Asia to the spread of Sino-Tibetan from the eastern Himalayas to Sichuan and northward into present-day North China, if G. van Driem's Tibeto-Burman model is correct.[229] In this case, Laurasian mythology could have been present with pre-Austric speakers in northern South Asia as well as in northernmost Southeast Asia since c. 40 kya;[230] it would subsequently have been brought northward and spread farther after the end of the Ice Age.

Notable in this context is the relative absence of chicken and pigs in other forms of Laurasian mythology (§5.1.3), as both animals are indigenous to Southeast Asia, where they are prominent in myth and ritual. The matter thus may have some bearing on the discussion of when and how Laurasian mythology was introduced to Southeast and East Asia.

The northward spread after c. 40 kya may also have included some cultural influx into present-day South China (the ancestors of the Miao/Hmong, Tai-Kadai languages).[231] However, all of this was followed by a subsequent, well-attested reflux from the north into Southeast Asia by speakers of Austric languages and by still later, medieval arrivals (Burmese, Thai, etc.).[232]

In order to decide the question of whether Laurasian mythology arrived in Southeast Asia from the north or the (south)west, there is an urgent need to further differentiate the various movements of people carrying the haplogroups described above, as well as their relationship to the spread of archaeological cultures, languages, and mythologies. As far as the latter are concerned, we need more intensive work in Southeast Asia that must rely on the broad patterns plotted above (§2, §3). Especially, we are in need of closer study of the populations of southern China and Southeast Asia, both genetically and mythologically. (The language situation, too, is still lacunose.)[233] To what extent was Gondwana mythology present in this area, and how much of it survived not just among the

Semang of Malaya but also with the Miao/Hmong or, more likely, in highland Taiwan?

This tangled question can only be solved by detailed investigations of many individual populations and by placing them in their relevant genetic, linguistic, and mythological position in a cladistic as well as regional framework (§2).[234] As far as Southeast Asian groups are concerned, the mythology of the relatively isolated aboriginal tribes of Taiwan, the Dayaks of Borneo, the Malagasy of Madagascar, and the Toraja of Sulawesi, who all belong to the Austronesian language family, may be used to define the original, reconstructed Austronesian mythology, if they have not become Muslims, Christians, or Buddhists. The result is then to be compared with the mythology of the other Indonesian, Philippine, and mainland Southeast Asian populations and their DNA.

For example, it has recently been shown that a subgroup of mtDNA B (B4a1a),[235] which is found in Taiwan Aborigines, is the origin of further lineages in Polynesia. This is not a surprising result, as it has long been pointed out by linguists that the Formosan languages are the most archaic ones in the Austronesian language family and this indicates Taiwan to be the homeland of Proto-Austronesian. These populations also share similar versions of the flood and other creation myths. In this particular case, archaeology (Lapita culture spreading eastward into the Pacific around 1300 BCE), genetics, linguistics, and mythological studies opportunely agree. (However, some of the aboriginal Taiwan tribes—most notably isolated mountain tribes such as the Atayal and Bunun—have preserved very archaic, Gondwana mythological traits as well.)[236]

This particularly strong set of evidence is helped by the fact that Polynesians settled in previously unpopulated areas and thus provide unadulterated evidence, which makes investigations, at least for the eastern branch of Austronesian languages, much easier than in many other parts of the world. Only when such investigations, including the other Austric populations, have been completed can we reach a better understanding of early Southeast Asia and South China after the initial settlement around 60 kya, of which the various Negrito groups seem to be remnants.

***

At this instant, it seems that we can restrict Laurasian mythology to several subclades of NRY F. Notably, in these groups, sub-Saharan Africa is hardly present, while these clades are found in Asia, America, and Europe (and, only as far as K and M are concerned, in "Oceania"; K2 is also marginally found in Africa).

Generally speaking, at the present stage of our knowledge, it is sufficient to note that the populations that have transmitted Laurasian mythology belong to the ex-Africa language families and genetic subgroups mentioned above. Laurasian mythology's ultimate area of origin and the individual tracks of its spread must be kept in balance for the time being, due to a lack of sufficient pertinent interdisciplinary information. It is likely, though, that it originated on the borders of Greater Southwest Asia and spread eastward and to Europe some 40 kya.

Once extensive comparative studies have been carried out, we may combine, on a global scale, the facts derived from archaeology (below, §4.4), paleontology, genetics, linguistics, and comparative mythology and try to arrive at a grand "unified theory" of the spread of early humans and their belief systems in Eurasia and beyond. A tentative, heuristic model has been given in this section (§4.3.6).

However, as already pointed out (§2.2 sqq.), the reconstruction of Laurasian mythology importantly does *not depend* on, though it can be *aided* by, linguistic and genetic comparisons. Nor does it depend on the unlikely assumption that myths, languages, and genes *always* spread together. There are many clear cases that would contradict such a general statement. (One may think of the joint occurrence of English and Christianity in modern America, the concurrent spread of Latin and of the Iranian Mithras cult in the Roman Empire, or the spread of the Bantu language Swahili and of Islam in premodern eastern Africa.)

At the current state of our knowledge, a combination of the data represented by genetic haplotypes, language families, and mythology types is heuristically promising, especially for the *early* stages of human expansion to South, Southeast, and East Asia as well as to Sahul Land, during which those populations were carrying Gondwana myth. Close conformity of these data can also easily be observed during the initial settlement of uninhabited lands, such as Iceland, Madagascar, Polynesia, and the Americas. But as mentioned at the outset of this chapter, matters become much more complex in Neolithic times, due to the constant crisscrossing movements of populations involving whole continents and because of the macro-regional spread of cultural influences involving language, spirituality, and material culture as well as ritual and mythology. In this complex situation, archaeology can play an important role in distinguishing some of the later and more localized trends.

▪ §4.4. ARCHAEOLOGY

Still another type of human data, those uncovered by archaeology, tells a parallel story. At the outset it should be noted, however, that archaeology can trace human remains as well as human cultural products, as far as both have been preserved under favorable conditions—and importantly, as far as they have been discovered so far. The archaeological record thus is *always incomplete*, and it is more so in certain little-studied parts of the world. Conclusions drawn from lack of (presently available) evidence must be avoided, in this field just as in others. *The absence of evidence is not evidence of absence.*

Furthermore, archaeology cannot directly reconstruct the belief system of a given population, unless there are written documents to sustain such interpretations. A large data set will be helpful to compare the remains of a given culture with similar ones nearby or elsewhere, and certain patterns of religion and beliefs can be *inferred* from recorded sources. However, this always remains a matter of *interpretation*, not of the facts of "hard science." All too frequently, speculation and flights of fancy abound. Problems resulting from local politics and funding deepen the dilemma.

Though archaeology usually cannot directly attest to the beliefs of a population, historical comparative mythology and archaeology not only reconstruct parallel scenarios; both are actually linked by the archaeologically, paleontologically, and genetically attested evidence of early *Homo sapiens sapiens* at c. 65,000 BCE. Due to the small number of emigrants out of Africa—estimated between 2,000 and 10,000 people—it is entirely unlikely that their archaeological and skeletal remnants and the traces of their DNA do not correspond to the data provided by mythologies of the Gondwana type. This situation still applied to the immediate aftermath of the exodus (and maybe down to the emergence of Laurasian mythology), before further migrations set in. For the early period, however, and thus for the spread of the various Gondwana mythologies, both archaeology and genetics—literally—march side by side, along with the development of mythology from Africa to Australia and to the northern Eurasian continent. Later on, things became much more complex, due to migrations and secondary diffusion, as will be seen below, for example, in the difficult search for the original locus of Laurasian mythology. Another close correlation can be established, in spite of certain problems of interpretation, between reconstructed Laurasian mythology and early (late Paleolithic) cave paintings of France and Spain and between the early cave art of Australia and Gondwana myth (§4.4.1, §7.1.1).

That said, though skeletal remains and tools can be traced even before *Homo erectus*, it is anatomically modern humans (*Homo sapiens sapiens*) who have left a sketchy but identifiable trail of tools and skeletal remains, enabling the reconstruction of their spread both inside and out of Africa. The data of genetics, of Long-Range linguistics, and of the Laurasian theory are fully borne out by the early surviving archaeological record.

An early form of humans, *Homo erectus*,[237] was widely spread in Africa. It is also found later on in Asia (Peking, Java Man); now the "hobbit" (*Homo floresiensis*, 70–12 kya)[238] has joined them. In Europe such early humans are known as Neanderthals,[239] or as *Homo neanderthalensis*, which developed from *Homo heidelbergensis* and existed by 370,000 BCE;[240] while archaic *Homo sapiens sapiens* first appears in African fossil remains some 160,000 years ago.

Recently, some Neanderthal DNA has been found and analyzed;[241] it shows comparatively little genetic variation with *Homo sapiens*: they are 99.5 percent identical.[242] However, Neanderthal DNA has so far *not* been found in modern humans. If any interbreeding between Neanderthals and *Homo sapiens sapiens* had taken place their descendants must have died out (but, see now this book's postscript in the Foreword).

Ofer Bar-Yosef maintains that the earliest Crô Magnon or *Homo sapiens sapiens* appeared in the Levant already about 90,000–100,000 years ago (Qafzeh

Cave),[243] where modern humans were contemporaries of Neanderthals.[244] Sometimes they even occupied the same cave sites (though at different times). For the current purpose, that of tracing mythology development and transmission, Neanderthal faculty of speech,[245] if any, would be of interest.

While modern humans and Neanderthals share 99.5 percent of their genes, Neanderthal anatomy suggests to Bar-Yosef that Neanderthals could also speak:[246] a skeleton excavated at Kebara II in 1983 (60 kya)[247] has a hyoid bone, which is necessary for humanlike speech. This bone (with attached muscles) allows the tongue to modify the space in the throat that is needed for proper articulation.[248] The question of Neanderthal speech rests on the specifics of the Neanderthal larynx,[249] which has not survived in fossils. However, available skeletal remains indicate that the Neanderthal larynx was apparently not in the right position to produce our type of fully vocalized human speech. (The recent discovery of a primate variant of the FOXP2 gene in ancient Neanderthal DNA only points to general speech ability, as this gene is only marginally linked to its development.)[250]

In addition, apparent trade exchange between *Homo sapiens* and Neanderthals, seen at Vindija in Croatia,[251] may point at rudimentary speech. There also is a find in France of Neanderthal remains with *Homo sapiens*–type (Upper Paleolithic)artifacts that were either made by Neanderthals or simply exchanged by (silent) trade.[252]

Some remnants of rituals found in graves,[253] too, indicate symbolic thought, which is necessary for speech. Neanderthal burials in Shanidar (northern Iraq) indicate a clear perception of death and the intent to preserve the life force of the deceased by putting ochre color (though not flowers) on the body.[254] These and a number of widely dispersed other finds point to some Neanderthal religious or mythical concepts of an afterlife.[255]

Some concepts may have even been taken over by *Homo sapiens sapiens* (if not already present since the pre-*sapiens* ancestors). There is the curious fact of the worship of the cave bear and related rituals. Early finds of bear skulls separated from their bodies, with leg bones inserted, are present in the Neanderthal areas.[256] The same kind of ritual appears with certain recent and modern northern European, Siberian, and Northeast Asian populations, such as the Saami and Ainu (see §7.1.2). The common (shared?) appearance of a form of the bear cult in both human communities may be an indicator that some customs or ideas have been transmitted,[257] even if there apparently is no clear indication, so far, of interbreeding[258] (but see now the postscript in the Foreword).

***

Whether there was any substantial transmission of ideas (and myths?) from the Neanderthals to anatomically modern humans would depend on the existence of speech. However, for current purposes, all of this is ultimately irrelevant. Even if Neanderthals indeed had more or less developed speech enabling them to transmit their ideas, for example, about bear worship, to their newly arrived Crô Magnon neighbors, this could have occurred *only* in Europe and adjacent areas in the Levant and westernmost Asia. The bear cult, however, is found in over a wide range of northern Eurasia, from northern Scandinavia to northern Japan. In almost all of these areas, except in the west, there existed no Neanderthal population, and we know even less about the linguistic abilities of *Homo erectus*, which preceded *Homo sapiens sapiens* in Asia. In short, the question is moot and irrelevant for the story of Laurasian mythology (§7).[259]

***

Be that as it may, the spread of early, pre-*sapiens* humans into Europe and western Central Asia at c. 700,000–375,000 BCE led to the development of *Homo heidelbergensis* and then *Homo neanderthalensis*.[260] This form endured in Europe until well after the arrival from Asia of *Homo sapiens sapiens* (Crô Magnon), at c. 40,000 BCE.[261] Neanderthals first disappeared from southeastern Europe some 40,000 years ago but remained in outlying areas until much later: in the North Caucasus a skeleton has been found that is 29,000 years old. In some refuge areas, such as in Spain, Neanderthals survived for another 10,000–20,000 years,[262] where they overlapped with Crô Magnon settlements. As mentioned, no clear evidence is found of interbreeding with modern humans, either in anatomy or in DNA.[263]

Between c. 200,000 and 130,000 BCE, Rhodesian Man evolved in Africa into current, anatomically modern humans (*Homo sapiens sapiens*, called Crô Magnon in Europe). Early *Homo sapiens sapiens* is found in various parts of Africa, although mostly in the east, where other early forms of hominids also emerged. Their outward spread across the globe can be tracked fairly well by finds of human bones and artifacts, though at first mostly by their stone tools.

Homo sapiens sapiens is well attested in the Middle Awash Valley of northeastern Ethiopia (Afar area), with a transition of *Homo erectus* skeletons from 1,000,000 BCE (Daka), to 500,000 (Bodo) and 160,000 (Herto) years ago. The Herto find represents the first modern humans.[264] A current summary of finds includes the ones in Table 4.7.[265] Based on these data one may think of the emergence of *Homo sapiens sapiens* around 200,000 BCE, if one takes the Kabwe (Zambia) skeleton at 250/150 kya into account, or even later if one takes the Herto (Afar, Ethiopia) skeleton of 160 kya as the earliest representative of anatomically modern humans.[266]

As mentioned (§4.2, 4.4) there is evidence of an early spread of *Homo sapiens sapiens* into the Levant (Qafzeh etc.) around 100 kya, where they overlapped with Neanderthals for several tens of thousands of years, often at the same locations but at different time periods;[267] we do not yet know of any

TABLE 4.7. *Development of Homo Sapiens sap., Anatomically Modern Humans (after H. Fleming 2003)*

Herto	Afar, Ethiopia	165 kya	H. sapiens idaltu
Kabwe	Zambia	125	H. rhodesiensis, or 250 kya H.erectus/sapiens
Ngaloba	Tanzania		
Singa	Sudan		
Eliye Springs	Kenya		
Omo Kibish	Ethiopia	3 to 125 kya	Most like Herto. also called Omo I
Jebel Irhoud	Morocco	125 kya?	Most like Herto. also Jebel Ighoud
Qafzeh	Israel	90–115 kya	Most like Herto
Skhul	Israel	same?	Most like Herto
Border Cave 1	South Africa	49–115 kya	Much disputed dates, sap.
Florisbad	South Africa	38–41 kya	Disputed taxon. H. helmei H. sapiens?
Crô-Magnon	European sites	25–40 kya	Homo Sapiens sap.

interbreeding. However, due to deteriorating climate, these early *Homo sapiens sapiens* populations disappeared from the record, until a new exodus from Africa began around 65,000 years ago,[268] which was strongly influenced by climatic factors (Table 4.8).[269]

As detailed in the section on population genetics (§4.3), there are two competing theories about the spread of anatomically modern humans out of East Africa, involving different time lines. They have been succinctly summarized by P. Mellars.[270]

The most common scenario has the ancestors of all non-African *Homo sapiens sapiens* emerge from eastern Africa, cross the narrow straits of Aden (Bab el Mandab), and expand rapidly[271]—at a rate of at least one kilometer per year— along the coasts of Arabia,[272] India, and Southeast Asia (Sunda Land). They reached the Andamans and Malaysia by 55 kya, perhaps even by 65 kya.[273] At the famous Niah Cave in Sarawak (Malaysia), we have dates from 41 kya, including a skull from 40 kya,[274] and on Flores we have a date of 42 kya.[275] From Sunda Land, the emigrants turned northward toward China (Zoukoudian, 42–39

TABLE 4.8. *The influence of climate (Ice Ages) on human spread*

130-110 kya	Eemian interglacial	(gradual cooling until 25-15 kya:Last Glacial Maximum, LGM)
110- 70 kya	Heinrich events	(warmer and cooler periods)
70-50 kya	**Glacial Maximum**	(stage 4 : Early Wisconsin/Würm glaciation, similar to LGM), followed by a warmer period
65 kya	Sea level much lower than today:	boats necessary to cross the shortest distance between Timor and Australia: c. 170 km between 70-65 kya, sea level c. 80 m lower than today; (by 50 kya, 220 km, sea level at -40 m); similarly for the Andaman and Solomon Islands
50-25 kya	Warmer, but highly variable, until LGM; less dry	Open green passage between Arabian Sea and Levant (Zagros corridor). Deserts (C. Asia, N. Africa) remain a difficult habitat
25-15 kya	**Last Glacial Maximum**	(LGM, Tioga/late Würm); maximum at 18 kya

kya)[276] and Okinawa (at 32 kya)[277] or crossed over several narrow straits in eastern Indonesia until they reached Timor.[278] From there, they traversed a wider expanse of ocean to reach Australia (Sahul Land) by (at least) 45 kya.[279] A similarly wide gap separated easternmost Sunda Land near Sulawesi from New Guinea.[280] (See Table 4.5. We will return to the details of this scenario later.) This agrees with the scenario of the spread of modern humans according to genetic markers (§4.3).[281]

The exodus out of Africa had lasting effects:[282] it resulted in the permanent spread of humans around the globe. This distribution can be correlated well with the spread of Gondwana-type mythologies from Africa to Australia, New Guinea, and areas along the Indian Ocean (where they are preserved by some tribal peoples of the Nilgiris, Malaya, and Philippines; §5). Gondwana mythology will be discussed in detail later on (§5).

***

Another version of the theory has the Out of Africa event occur already at c. 77 kya.[283] Oppenheimer wants to see modern human settlements in Malaysia before the massive explosion of the Toba volcano in Sumatra at 74 kya,[284] which is in need of archaeological support.[285] Recently, excavations in South India,[286] establishing dates of c. 75 kya, have indicated that humans lived there *before* and *after* the Toba supereruption that delivered a gigantic layer of ash in other areas. That means that shortly after the allegedly all-annihilating Toba explosion, human life continued undisturbed in South India. Further, the similarity in tool style in South India at 75 kya and in South Africa (Howieson's Poort)[287] at 70–60 kya adds further proof to the theory of a southern expansion along the shore of the Indian Ocean, perhaps even earlier than usually estimated.[288]

***

However, there also exists a competing theory that has *Homo sapiens sapiens* migrating northward along the Nile, toward the Sinai Peninsula and the Levant (where human remnants have indeed been found around 100 kya).[289] From there, these populations would have spread, according to archaeological and genetic data, to Southwest Asia and eventually to Central Asia and Europe (to the latter by 45–40 kya). This "northern" group of migrants had a different stone tool technology than the southern one of the "Express Train to Australia" (microlith blades).[290]

Some geneticists also favor this theory.[291] It has, however, come under scrutiny recently and is denied on the grounds of the available evidence by others.[292] Their argument is based on the diminishing diversity of human DNA as the early groups moved forward due to a series of founder's events. Archaeology seems to concur when the similarities between Indian and East/South African stone tools of the migration period are taken into account.[293] The striking lack of such "advanced" tools in early Australia is explained by a concurrent founder effect in the lack of full technology transmission as well as the lack of local availability of stones and the lack of necessity to produce stone tools in a maritime habitat.[294]

***

If the northern Eurasian route is to be abandoned, this would present somewhat of a problem for the spread of Laurasian mythology, as has been indicated earlier (§4.3.6). Indeed, in an earlier publication,[295] I had still retained this scenario. If it does not apply, we will have to account for the spread of Laurasian mythologies into Southeast and East Asia with a different scenario—for example, a purely hypothetical second wave of migration via India to Southeast Asia or a post–Ice Age reflux into Southeast Asia from what is now China by speakers of Tibeto-Burmese and Austric languages, whose ancestors had arrived there at c. 40 kya. In sum, the archaeological picture can be seen in Table 4.9. Many of the first fossils of modern humans found in southern Eurasia and Australasia thus occur relatively late, probably because most of such remains are buried under water, outside of the current coastline, as the sea level was up to 150 meters lower during the past two glacial periods.[296]

However, this spread was followed by the transition from Middle to Upper Paleolithic, the so-called Upper Paleolithic revolution, which occurred some 40,000–50,000 years ago: hunting and gathering continued, but the number of

TABLE 4.9. *Archaeological and genetic dates for human spread outside Africa*

75 kya	Tamil Nadu, S. India, archaeological finds, but without human remains
62? - 40 kya	human remains in Borneo & Australia (at Lake Mungo); (suggested dates, 50 ~ 62 kya)
55 kya	Andamans, Malaysia (perhaps 60 kya)
42 kya	Flores
41 kya	Niah cave, Sarawak, Malaysia; a skull of 40 kya
42-39 kya	Homo *sap.* at Zoukoudian near Beijing
30 kya	Inner Mongolia
32 kya	Okinawa
32 kya	New Guinea
28 kya	Salomon Islands
33-28 kya	First human remains in S. Asia: Sri Lanka
30 kya	S. Asian Upper Palaeolithic, not found before this time; coexisted in India with Middle Palaeolithic for 10 ky.
50 kya	Upper → Middle Palaeolithic transition in southern Near East
47 kya	archaeological remains in the Zagros Mountains
47 kya	archaeological remains in Central Europe, N. Spain
45-37 kya	human remains in Europe: Romania
43-39	archaeological remains in the Altai, Baikal area
30-32 kya	archaeological remains in the Caucasus
18 kya	archaeological and skeletal (teeth) remains, Upper Palaeolithic artifacts

human bands increased rapidly, and new artifacts such as the spear-thrower appeared.[297] The transition may have been triggered by new hunting techniques, probably in East Africa and in the Nile Valley. The event is also related with the explosive development of complex art as preserved in rock, cave, and plastic art (§4.4.1, §7.1.2 sqq.); this seems to coincide with the evolving Laurasian mythology and its spread northward into Eurasia during the interglacial period after c. 50 kya.

***

The exodus out of East Africa and the early immigration into South and Southeast Asia are now commonly dated,[298] as mentioned, around 65,000 BCE;[299] humans rapidly reached Australia,[300] by 45,000 BCE at the latest.[301] Just as the genetic evidence and the Laurasian theory predict, the earliest and most copious remains of *Homo sapiens sapiens* are found inside Africa, while only a few early artifacts and skeletons have been retrieved along the exodus path. Part of the reason is that the sea level was some 50 meters lower around c. 65,000 BCE than it is today.[302] Remains are therefore mostly found inland from the ancient coastlines of the Indian Ocean.

Significantly, they also occur along one major inland route, the Narmada Valley corridor, which transverses Central India from the west coast to a small strip of land that divides the broad Narmada Valley from the Son Valley and leads to the Gangetic Plains near Patna. Many ancient remains and copious rock art have been found in this corridor, especially at Bhimbetka.[303] Some of its rock art can be dated (proved by subsequent sealing of the cave floor).[304]

The further spread into Sahul Land is attested by early finds in Australia (at Mungo Lake in southeastern Australia).[305] The voyage across some 150 kilometers of open sea between the then extended continental shelf of Australia and Timor must have been made before 43,000 BCE,[306] as many early finds in all parts of Australia (and Tasmania) testify.[307] There was another possible passage, with a similar distance, from eastern Indonesia to New Guinea,[308] which then was part of the Australian continent.[309] New Guinea and New Ireland were settled by 32 kya, and the distant Solomon Islands, by 28 kya.

Gondwana mythology is likely to have been introduced into Sahul Land by these early immigrants, while Laurasian mythology developed only somewhat later, probably around 40 kya, and therefore could not yet reach Australia. Due to geographic isolation, the Gondwana type of early mythology has been well preserved in all parts of Sahul Land, in its earliest form probably in Tasmania (and nearby southeastern Australia; §5.3.2.1).

However, the ultimate breakup of the Indonesian Sunda Land and the New Guinea–Australian Sahul Land at the end of the last Ice Age is dated only around 10,000–6000 BCE, which allowed for some movements and exchanges between the two Sahul groups of peoples. For example, the recently exterminated

Tasmanians are believed to have been somatically close to the Papua inhabitants of New Guinea and to have left earlier traces in eastern Australia (§5.3.2.1). Tasmania was first settled at 35 kya, perhaps from Melanesia.[310]

Late impacts on Australia include the import of microliths, which set off a revolution in the use of stone tools.[311] This occurred around 3000–1000 BCE, and the introduction of the dingo dog from Southeast Asia occurred around 1500 BCE;[312] both were too late to allow their introduction into Tasmania. Here also belongs, it seems, the spread of the X-ray style of painting, which is well preserved and still executed in northern Australia; it is dated to c. 2000 BCE in Arnhem Land, while it appears much earlier in India, Europe, and Africa. There also have been speculations about a linguistic connection between Australian languages and Dravidian in South India.[313] Late exchanges persisted, for example, several hundred years of seasonal contact by Austronesian traders from Makassar with northern Australian Aborigines, which ended only in 1907. In sum, not all of (northern) Australia was as isolated as is generally thought.

It is, however, unclear how far such contacts could have influenced Australian mythology. For example, the Makassar contacts resulted only in a few Austronesian loanwords in Arnhem Land,[314] and I do not detect typical traits of Laurasian mythology in the area.[315] Nevertheless, anthropologists usually discern earlier Papua influences that must have occurred during the Last Glacial Maximum,[316] until c. 8000 BP (§4.3, §5.3.2).

***

Leaving apart Sahul Land, the first immigration northward into the central and northern sections of Eurasia is now believed to have taken place around 52–45 kya, after the end of an earlier ice age.[317] Europe was reached via the Near East, and early *Homo sapiens sapiens* (Crô Magnon) coexisted for a while with Neanderthals.[318] Similarly, northern China, Mongolia, Siberia, Korea, and Japan were first settled then, as has been confirmed by the discovery of a 42,000- to 39,000-year-old skeleton at Zoukoudian near Beijing.[319] However, Central Asia, different from a recent theory,[320] is an area that was settled only comparatively late, from the east as well as from the west.[321]

Immigration into the Americas is now believed to have occurred in three waves from c. 20,000 BCE onward, via or along the Aleutian land bridge (Bering Land). There are early dates by now for Chile (Monte Verde, at 12,500 BP), as well as for the east coast of the United States, in Pennsylvania, Virginia, and South Carolina.[322] However, the last major immigration must have occurred before the breakup of the Aleutian land bridge at c. 11–7 kya. It is believed that this immigration brought the Na-Dene-speaking groups into North America, which would have allowed for the last major influx of eastern Siberian types of mythologies. Geneticists concur (§4.3), as do linguists like Joseph Greenberg

(§4.1). They see the Amerindians move in first, followed by the Na-Dene group in Alaska and Yukon (Athapascans), with an offshoot in the southwestern United States, the Navajo-Apache, who were heavily influenced by the preexisting Pueblo mythology.[323] Some later regional mythological diffusion (especially from Central America; §2.3) and the spread of cults, such as the Sun Dance and, more recently, the Peyote cult, have complicated the picture.

Similarly, in Sahul Land, late movements and influences such as that from New Guinea into Australia during the Last Glacial Maximum may have disturbed the Gondwana and Laurasian mythological picture somewhat,[324] but they did not change the basic pattern. On the other hand, some forms of Siberian and circumpolar culture (such as Inuit mythology) have penetrated into North America; to be noted, too, is the enigmatic resemblance between northwestern American and Chinese-like dragon head motifs,[325] as well as Aurignacian or rather Solutrean (European) tools in Pennsylvania, Virginia, and South Carolina.[326]

***

In passing, it may be mentioned that in the wake of "New Archaeology" over the past few decades an "isolationalist" view of the development of archaeological cultures has emerged and, to a large extent, has dominated discussions:[327] cultural changes are preferably explained by strictly *local developments*. Outside influence and migrations are hardly accepted, at best, as diffusion of some cultural traits, such as by trade. Curiously, this was also the official Marxist stance in the former socialist countries, but the pattern as such has found many adherents in the West and, for example, in India,[328] curiously echoed by the stance of others of a multilocal origin of anatomically modern humans.[329]

This type of scenario, however, has been severely disturbed by the recent evidence for early (Middle/late Paleolithic) and later (Neolithic and later) movements of humans across the globe, along with the movement of their genes, languages, cultures, and mythologies. A clear case is that of the Austronesians, who spread from Taiwan up to Madagascar, Hawai'i, New Zealand, and Easter Island (and maybe even South America).[330] It seems that the pendulum in archaeological fashion is swinging back in the other direction again.

***

In sum, there are a number of inferences to be drawn from archaeology for the study of myth. First, the exodus out of Africa resulted in the spread of humans around the globe, initially with the exception of the Americas and the Austronesian Pacific. They brought along their early mythology, the Gondwana type. It spread from Africa along the shores of the Indian Ocean to Australia and New Guinea, where it persists. In the subsequent surge of later Laurasian mythology that has swept all of Eurasia, a few "islands" of Gondwana mythology remain, such as among the tribal peoples of the South Indian Nilgiris, in Malaya, and in the Philippines (§5). Other population retreat areas (highland Taiwan, Sakhalin/Hokkaido, Pamir, Caucasus, Pyrenees, etc.) need to be studied in detail—and urgently. Due to geographic isolation, the Gondwana type of early human mythology has been well preserved in all parts of Sahul Land—in its earliest form probably in Tasmania (and nearby southeastern Australia; §5.3.2.1).

Second, while Gondwana mythology is likely to have been introduced into Sahul Land by early migrants, Laurasian mythology could not yet reach Australia and New Guinea as it developed only somewhat later, probably around 40 kya. There was no later migration into this area, except a limited one from New Guinea into northern Australia during the last Ice Age, indicated by genetics and mythology alike (§5.3.2).

The development of Laurasian mythology seems related to that of new technologies (spear-thrower and later, the bow).[331] More important for our purpose is the development of symbolic thought, demonstrated by what has been called the explosive development of complex art that is preserved in rock, cave, and plastic art (§4.4.1, §7.1.2 sqq.). This again reflects, to some extent, the evolving Laurasian mythology as it spread northward into Eurasia during the interglacial period after c. 50 kya.

Third, as the northern Asian route of the early spread of humans after c. 65 kya is to be abandoned on genetic and archaeological grounds,[332] the spread of Laurasian mythology eastward has to be explained in a different fashion (§4.3.6). It could be explained by a hypothetical second wave of migration via India to Southeast Asia, or by the effects of the Na-Dene migrations, or by some late backflow from eastern Central Asia and southern China toward Southeast Asia, along with the Tibeto-Burmese- and Austric-speaking populations and the related archaeological complexes such as the Hoabinhian, Dongson, Lapita, and so on.

Fourth, later population movements and diffusionary influences, such as that from New Guinea into Australia during the LGM or the still later, very significant spread of the Austronesian-speaking peoples, have disturbed the geographical extent of both the Gondwana and Laurasian mythologies as well as that of individual myths to some degree,[333] but they could not change basic myth patterns (§2.3). However, some forms of circumpolar culture have penetrated into North America, which may include Solutrean (European) spread into the eastern United States during the last Ice Age.[334]

In sum, the available archaeological evidence largely agrees with that provided by genetics, linguistics, and comparative mythology (§4.3.4). It closely follows the two geographically and ultimately climate-based migration patterns of Middle and Upper Paleolithic humans: first, around 65,000 BCE, an early exodus out of Africa up to Australia along with Gondwana mythologies; then, another—largely "Laurasian"—move northward, during the favorable interglacial period around 40,000 BCE, and into the Americas after c. 20,000 BCE. The exact location of the origin and the various individual trails of the spread of Laurasian mythology remain to be determined. Archaeology would be unlikely to assist in this particular enterprise, were it not for Stone Age art, especially the complex cave paintings and the plastic art of Africa, Europe, India, and Australia.

§4.4.1. Cave paintings and plastic art

The appearance of complex symbolical thinking, which is required for the creation of myths, is a very important indicator of anatomically modern humans. While even the Neanderthals used some grave goods,[335] made necklaces, and used nearly 3,000 beads in the case of the man from Sungir,[336] it is the sudden emergence of complex Stone Age art, especially cave paintings, that points to complex symbolic thinking and thus, the production of myths.[337] Keeping in mind the distribution of archaeological finds, discussed above, the spread of some aspects of such art is another important tool to track Laurasian mythology.

The best-known examples of Stone Age art stem from southern France and Spain (e.g., Lascaux, Altamira) and the Sahara;[338] recently Upper Egypt has been added.[339] However, there are equally old paintings from the Urals (Belaya River),[340] Central India (Bhimbetka area),[341] New Guinea,[342] Australia,[343] and eastern and especially southern Africa (as well as, later on, from the Americas).[344]

All of these examples of Paleolithic art appear on the scene rather suddenly, after several millions years of human development, including *Homo erectus* and *H. neanderthalensis*. This breakthrough has been called a "creative explosion." It occurred at c. 40,000 BCE and was without genuine predecessors.[345] The phenomenon also extends to other forms of art such as sculpture (see below). In older publications, including popular books such as those of J. Campbell, this "explosion" is described as if first attested in and originating from late Paleolithic (Crô Magnon) Europe.[346] However, this impression is merely a by-product of the history of exploration. More recently, similar finds have been made in South Africa, pointing to possible African origins of the phenomenon. In addition, it is altogether unclear whether the lost art of tropical areas may not have preceded such available testimony. The moist climate of the rain forest and savanna has destroyed the traces of artwork done in wood, as some have suggested earlier.

Indeed, several indications have turned up recently that rather point to the *gradual* beginnings of symbolic representation in early art. The earliest perhaps is the one reported for Pinnacle Point on the cape of South Africa, at 164 kya. It concerns shells, tools, and pieces of red ochre cemented in the wall of a cave that did not, however, yield human bones. It also has complex stone bladelets and ground red pigment, both items that are usually regarded as indicators of modern behavior.[347] Further, early shell beads have been found at Shkul in Israel and at Oued Djebbana in Algeria, both at locations remote from the sea; they point in the same direction. The Shkul shells date from c. 130 to 100 kya.[348]

Similarly, early geometric designs occur at the Blobos Cave at 75 kya and at Howieson's Poort on the Klasier River, both in South Africa, where X-like crosshatching designs have been found that are dated at 65–60 kya.[349] These are quite similar or even identical to the designs found 30,000 years later, well after the exodus, at Patne in West India and Batodomba-lena (34–30 kya) in Sri Lanka. Finally, there are eggshell beads from Enkapune ya Muto (Kenya) at 40 kya.[350] In sum, to quote Mellars: "There is certainly much more to the emergence of cognitively 'modern,' symbolically constructed behavior than the production of typically Upper Palaeolithic stone tools."[351]

***

Nevertheless, it seems that the "artistic explosion" traveled *independently* from the general Out of Africa movement,[352] along the general trail of anatomically modern humans:[353] such art occurs in Australia,[354] eastern Timor,[355] and India from early on.[356] The nature of sub-Saharan rock art is in urgent need of further investigation. If it moved, along with the Khoi-San-like people,[357] from northern, once-verdant Saharan locations southward, via Tanzania (where the Hadza/Sandawe survive still),[358] it would fit the expansion pattern just described. If, however, the early art of tropical Africa has disappeared due to the impact of climate, only to emerge with later San and Bantu paintings in eastern and southern Africa, the emergence of art would be already Pan-Gaean. Its lacuneous distribution, as described above, is merely due to the current state of archaeological knowledge. We may, again, be surprised by the ingenuity of early *Homo sapiens sapiens.*

***

As against such more or less generally accepted assumptions of Stone Age art and religion, it is essential to discuss in some detail the recent critical work put forward by Ina Wunn,[359] which summarizes earlier approaches and advances new ones. Her work has been briefly discussed above (§1.6). Unfortunately, her voluminous book only deals with the Near East and Europe. Wunn starts out (§2.6)[360] from the evolutionary premise in Bellah's early work that there was progress of religious knowledge,[361] just as is seen in the progress in tool manufacturing techniques. According to Wunn, religious development reached a preliminary culmination point in the Neolithic. Its predecessors in the late Paleolithic and its very first beginnings in the Middle Paleolithic are *therefore* supposed to have been much simpler than the developed religion of the Neolithic. As has been stressed above (§1.6), this approach is based on the availability of actually recovered archaeological objects and on Bellah's evolutionary theory, the combination of which can be challenged.

In addition, always according to Wunn,[362] it is not possible to reconstruct Paleolithic religion with the aid of *uncritical* ethnographical comparisons, as is commonly done. Even if certain characteristics in material culture would suggest such a comparison, today's hunters and gatherers are separated from Paleolithic humans less by fundamental differences in intellectual faculties than by several tens of thousands of years of historical developments (§1.6). Instead, Wunn proposes new approaches based on ethology and comparative art (see below).

The somewhat predictable result of her detailed investigations covering nearly 500 pages is that the beginnings of *differentiated and developed* religion first appear only in the Middle Paleolithic,[363] as is seen in burial rituals. Speculative thought appearing in art and ritual indicates highly developed cognitive faculty and a long period of development. The first signs of such abstractions are handprints and the burial sites of the late Paleolithic.[364] Religion was at first domestic, taking place in open-air rituals, and the famous Paleolithic caves were no sanctuaries.[365] Further, according to Wunn, initially there still was a lack of deeper symbolic understanding; nor was there an explicit beginning of art or of utensils that transgress practical use, though Wunn sees the beginnings of a sentiment of beauty. (Of course, this must now be contrasted with reports of much earlier, Middle Paleolithic art objects.)[366] Wunn also cannot discern any superhuman, transcendental figures or a death ritual involving maceration, the cutting away of flesh from bones. Only the secondary burials of the Upper Mesolithic (in Europe, 35 kya) may indicate the wish to preserve the deceased intact as far as possible; therefore the custom was to place the dead in caves. This may presuppose a belief in existence beyond death, bound to the continuing existence of these body parts.[367]

According to Wunn,[368] it is thus only in the Upper Paleolithic that one can discern many innovations that began in Africa and the Near East and that were perhaps instigated by language use. They are seen in material culture and especially in the sudden appearance of art. Even then, she is extremely cautious about symbol consciousness: symbols have been used but cannot function as proof for religion.[369]

As preconditions for the development of religion Wunn lists not just a more developed economy but also a symbol system, which was important, and maybe necessary, to manage contingency. She regards it as possible that late Paleolithic humans could think in certain abstract ways, though different from ours, and that this was the result of culture.[370] As is readily seen, this assessment would agree with the emergence of mythology as such, but the late dates Wunn proposes for the emergence of religion are in clear contradiction with reconstructed Gondwana and Laurasian mythology.

***

In our specific context, Wunn's observations on the relationship of late Paleolithic and early Mesolithic art and religion are of interest.[371] Late Paleolithic art has so far only been investigated in isolation, and it was not compared with its immediate Mesolithic successor, though a clear development toward greater abstraction can be observed. Further, Paleolithic art does not yet show signs of picture composition, which alone can tell stories. (However, note the discussion below of the famous, late Paleolithic Lascaux painting of a wounded bull and a prostrate shaman-like figure.)[372] Only beginning with the Mesolithic, Wunn maintains, were humans and animals seen as (frequently rather abstract) *types*, and only in the Mesolithic do we find actual scenes of hunting, war, dancing, and other common human activities.[373] However, differently from Wunn, one should not infer that such scenes *could not* be produced or *were not* present in Paleolithic imagination: the interest of the early cave painters was elsewhere, quite obviously in depicting hunted, wounded, and procreating animals.[374]

In this respect, Wunn proposes a new evaluation of hunter's magic, and it is only at this point that she brings in ethnographic comparison that "might help" in the interpretation of cave art.[375] She speculates that perhaps the animals depicted were "soul catchers" that were used in the ritual preparation of larger hunting trips. We will see below (§7.2) how far this agrees with a sustained historical and comparative reconstruction of early shamanic religion.

It is in this light, Wunn insists, that archaeological data, especially those of Stone Age cave art, have to be counterchecked.[376] Three recent prominent interpretations, those of Henri Breuil,[377] André Leroi-Gourhan,[378] and Mircea Eliade, are investigated, disputed, and largely rejected.[379] Eliade saw parallels to Paleolithic art in the simple hunter's economies that allow for hunting magic and for a "sanctuary,"[380] but, as Wunn criticizes, he used only one painting to illustrate this art: Breuil's much discussed sketch of a painting at Trois Frères,[381] that of the shaman-like "Great Sorcerer" of c. 14,000 BCE.[382]

Similarly, the famous Lascaux painting already mentioned, of an ithyphallic man lying in front of bison,[383] has found various interpretations: as hunting magic, or as the memorial of a wounded or slain hunter,[384] or as a shamanistic séance.[385] Shamanism in cave art has also been asserted by Dickson and Mithen (see the discussion in §7.1.2).[386]

Since the seventies, however, the pendulum has swung to ethnographic comparison, further including, if still hesitatingly, elements of art history (Panofsky) and the psychology of human development (A. Warburg). Prominent, too, is the interpretation of schematic and abstract signs, especially for Australian art, by Peter Ucko.[387] However, at least some of the frequently used dots may also be interpreted as representing particularly effective acoustic spots,[388] and the "reading" of geometric signs is equally problematic.[389] Various explanations have also been sought for apparent doodling and macaroni-like lines.[390] Even the arrangement (subjected to structuralist interpretation) of multiple animals in cave paintings remains unclear.[391] In some such structuralist interpretations (Leroi-Gourhan), individual compared animals that supposedly make up elaborate schemes are in fact separated in artistic creation by hundreds, if not thousands of years.[392]

Another line of approach follows the work of the art historian E. Panofsky. He underlines that we can recognize only what we know already; our interpretation rests on personal experience, and unknown objects cannot be identified. Indeed, at first scholars could easily recognize only human and animal forms, including even the so-called sorcerer of Trois Frères, who has human and animal elements. The experience of cave art specialists indeed highlights that they could only gradually discern certain designs, figures, and animals among the multitude of drawn lines that have been superimposed on each other in the course of millennia.[393]

However, some of the linear or geometric depictions that Wunn associates with playfulness may instead be due to the entoptic phenomena that occur in altered stages of consciousness,[394] such as those of shamans.[395] Another recent explanation for the dot patterns in cave art is, as mentioned, that they seem to reflect locations that were particularly suited to create sonar effects (resonance, echoes, etc.).[396] Clearly, more explanations are to be explored.

Summing up her observations reviewed so far, Wunn maintains that in order to understand abstract Paleolithic art, we have to begin from a new, the *only* starting point: as we cannot use our established canons of abstractions, we have to approach the repertoire of forms gradually, and we have to try to understand them by employing the "psychology of human expression."[397] This is done by including the insights of ethology and by looking for traces of *typical* human behavior that have *always* been repeated throughout human history.[398] This includes certain typical artistic expressions, produced on the spur of the moment.[399] Essentially, they are little more than play, and young humans or primates do not show any interest in their art after its creation. This would then be the reason for Paleolithic doodling and "macaroni" lines.[400]

Another step would involve categorization and interpretation, the search for regularity and order, as humans are predisposed to automatically neglect irregularities.[401] This resulted, for instance, in the schematic, simplified human representation in Paleolithic art. Some of the earliest art forms and some of the unidentified designs belong here, such as "arrows," schematic female bodies,[402] and hand positives and negatives (which might indicate warding off and taboo). This also includes the depiction of other common "gestures" like the erect penis, presenting the vulva and so on. Human ethology shows that such depictions are very archaic art forms, without predecessors, and little shaped by local culture.

Wunn further believes that even the depiction of mixed human/animal beings also belongs here: they too are expressions of spontaneous art, "without secondary meaning."[403] Such depictions of composite beings would indicate speculation about the nature of human beings and their difference from animals, as well as the relationship between hunter and prey. Though this line of thought comes close to what San, Australian, and other shamans think about the hunt (§7.1.2), Wunn still maintains that late Paleolithic composite human/animal figures, so typical for the shaman costume,[404] do *not* represent shamans.[405] She summarizes:

The [preceding] catalog of judgments [about the reconstruction of prehistoric and early historic relics] is scientifically justified and intersubjectively testable. Ideally, any attempt at the reconstruction of the worldview of an unknown culture should progress in several steps, building on each other.... The essential precondition for any interpretation, then, is the knowledge of the lifestyle, without which wrong interpretation can hardly be avoided. To use the vocabulary of the study of art: first, the actual sense [use] of an object must be understood before one can ask for its underlying symbolic meaning. In a next step, the meaning of the object within its mental context has to be elucidated: what is represented, which symbolical meaning is attached to the depicted item, and which aim does the piece have? These questions can only be clarified with the help of human ethology. However, only the classification of the material emanations of a particular religion and their specific task in a socioreligious context allow insight into the larger context.[406]

Taking all of the above into account, Wunn insists that cave art[407]—including the so-called Mother Goddess figures[408]—must now be explained differently. The latter are not cult idols; these are only found in later religions.[409] Indications of ritual (such as burials) would be more important for the reconstruction of archaic religion. The importance of certain types of rock art would thus be much reduced as an indicator of Stone Age religion and myth, which, as indicated, would contradict the existence of Laurasian (and Gondwana) mythology at the point in time when some of these concepts appear in rock art (§7.1). However, according to Wunn, this overview of Stone Age art allows just one answer about Paleolithic religion: "There are no clear examples for religious practices of late Paleolithic humans that can be connected with cave art. Neither sorcerers nor shamans were depicted, nor clashes between totemistic clans."[410]

This theory and archaeology-based conclusion should, however, be contrasted with the careful methodology proposed by J. Harrod,[411] which includes the following 18 plus eight steps (here abbreviated):

1. Select objects of secure archaeological provenance and dating.
2. Identify that the object is a human-made artifact or art.
3. Determine what survived and what did not.
4. Accurately determine material features and context.
5. Rule out background noise, such as carnivore marks, natural fractures, and so on.
6. Examine if marks are restricted in number, repeated, paired or otherwise associated, set in binary oppositions or correspondences, or have iconic potential.
7. Identify indications of semiotic operators such as "nonutilitarian" aspect or comparative markings on related objects or sites.
8. If the subject appears semiotic, identify whether code, icon, or signal.
9. Further identify whether metaphor or similitude.

10. Reconstruct, decode, and decipher the overall "semiotic competence," that is, meaningful narrativity and discourse, including conceptual, thematic, semantic, pragmatic, syntactic, and glyphic deep structure.
11. Decipher "meaning" or "message," "for them" and "for us."
12. Consider limits of interpretation, amplifying meaning "for them" and "for us."
13. Explore amplification of archetypal symbols as a poetic performative presencing of supernatural beings, spiritual principles, or divine powers.
14. Attempt to systematically reconstruct tentative prehistoric beliefs, rituals, or myths; criteria may include
    a. Coherence, consistency, and comprehensiveness of accounting for the semiotic evidence.
    b. A rigorous critical method, such as mythic group-theoretic structure or set-theoretic inclusion/exclusion dialectics.
15. Check adequacy and validity of the decoding.
16. Check the reconstruction against the evolutionary, stage-specific model of mind inferred from the archaeological and "cognitive archaeological" context.
17. Scan for precursors or survivals of the decoding—a further check on validity.
18. Amplify and check via ethnographic and mythological analogies, restricting analogies by factors such as geographic, cultural, and genetic propinquity.

A second basic method for reconstructing prehistoric religions is to extrapolate from archaeological findings coherent sets of technological or subsistence strategies. According to Harrod, these (abbreviated) steps roughly follow:

1. Identify a particular, coherent, paradigmatically related set of subsistence and/or technological strategies (modes).
2. Deduce a hypothetical mental template for generating that set.
3. Identify later mythological or ritual forms that refer to the invention of those subsistence and/or technological sets.
4. Determine if these mythic forms are structurally interrelated and thus may be survivals of the particular prehistoric culture.
5. If so, then reconstruct a hypothetical religious template compatible with the hypothetical mental template.
6. Decode the psychological message of the religious template.
7. Test the mythological set's meaningfulness as a coherent religious form.
8. Test the hypothetical religious template against archaeological and paleoanthropological evidence.

***

Comparing the two well-considered approaches of Wunn and Harrod, it is clear that we must deal, in the first place, with the critical evaluation of archaeological finds and their interpretation. These were practically the only materials available before the reconstruction of mythologies offered in the present book. The Laurasian and Gondwana materials can now be contrasted with the data and theories presented so far. The results are quite different from what has been supposed by Bellah, Wunn, and Herbig.[412]

Second, some amount of circularity is involved in Wunn's proposal: archaic lifestyles are determined and described by using input from current-day hunter or horticultural societies and by making use, in the same comparison, of the cultural anthropology of modern religions. (Wunn only objects to "uncritical" use of such ethnological data.)

Third, the whole exercise is based, as underlined before, on an evolutionary view of the development of culture and religion,[413] which is not applicable in its full exact and literal form, as no one actually knows whether and how much a particular archaic Stone Age religion differed from its immediate successors or from current, similar-looking forms. To use the (current) absence of certain archaeological data to prove a more "primitive" state of religion in Paleolithic times is not proof at all: absence of evidence is not evidence of absence. We are dealing with *spiritual* data, *not* their incidentally preserved archaeological record, remnants, or monuments. Many religions and rituals, for example, in Australia, use perishable materials or simple lines on the ground. Thus, we would be hard pressed to characterize, say, Pygmy, San, or Australian religion based on the few remnants they leave behind (obviously, with the exception of rock paintings).

Therefore, it is not exactly surprising that Wunn ended up in reconstructing a comparatively simple Paleolithic and Mesolithic religion—there are few remaining archaeological artifacts that would sustain the image of a more "developed" one with elaborate mythologies and rituals. Again, we do not know much of what Neanderthal and early *Homo sapiens sapiens* actually *thought*—unless we try to reconstruct their mythologies (and languages), as is done in the present book. In other words, the available evidence of early myths (and languages) is understandably missing in Wunn's important book; the present reconstruction was not yet available to her. Her work is, nevertheless, *heuristically* important, as it allows us to approach and judge the evidence presented by archaeology much more carefully than normally done so far.

***

Wunn's correlation of Bellah's evolutionary scheme and her insistence on archaeological objects, discovered so far, disregard the evidence from language and mythology. In this situation, some of the major archaeological evidence of art must again be taken up and discussed in some detail.[414]

Early rock art mostly depicts, not surprisingly, the local animals of the Stone Age hunt and later on, from the Mesolithic onward, also humans in the act of hunting, dance, daily life, and war. We also find some composite human figures, spirits, or deities (especially in Australian art). Importantly, for our purpose, there are some early paintings (especially at Lascaux) with depictions of a figure that has been variously interpreted as a shaman or "sorcerer" who is involved in the magic of the hunt.[415] It is such shamans that would have transmitted the Laurasian myths to their pupils and the population at large.

Apart from rock art, whether engraved, drawn, or painted, there also exist some examples of early sculptures and plastic art (30,000–34,000 BP),[416] often at the same locations. In Europe they are found in ice-free areas from Spain to the Urals.[417] An important instance is a rock engraving found at Laussel (France) that has been interpreted as showing a rare early example of a depiction of sexual intercourse.[418] Based on the Laurasian myths described above (§3.1.6, 3.2), it could depict combined androgynous beings or the primordial union (for details, see §7.1).[419] Then, there is the female figure at Laussel of c. 20,000–18,000 BCE,[420] depicted in a large rock sculpture with a horn in her hand. Interestingly, the horn seems to have 13(?) incisions, which is close to the 14-day cycle of the moon from new to full and from full to new (see §7.1).[421]

There also are widespread sculptures of the (erroneously) so-called Mother Goddess. This includes small statues of the "Venus" type that are very common in Europe (Willendorf in Austria, Desna, Don River) and beyond, for example, in central Siberia.[422] Some of them are typically corpulent, and others, rather slender. As they commonly lack feet, they must have been inserted into the ground or in some other kind of pedestal or niche (such as at Kostienki on the Don) and would then be classified as cult objects. Their interpretation as "mother goddesses" is, however, very much open to question.[423]

In addition, we also find a few clay sculptures of bison, in the caves of Montespan and Tuc d'Audoubert in France, in one case showing a copulating bison couple.[424] This may have been intended for the procreation of bison herds. It is clear that much more must have existed that has been lost or has not yet been found. Examples are the recently discovered Chauvet Cave and the underwater cave complexes at Cosquer.[425] Incidentally, the carvings stand in contrast to the cave paintings, which are mostly interested in animals, much less so in humans.[426] We have the occasional sculpture showing two copulating bisons and such mixed beings as the enigmatic lion man from the Vogelherd Cave (c. 32,000 BP),[427] which appears in an already fully developed art form.[428]

Apart from painting and sculpture, and music—seen, for example, in the bone flute from Geissenklösterle[429]—complex counting systems provide another aspect of the complex symbolic mentality of early modern humans. A. Marshak has indicated that systems of counting,[430] sometimes as simple tallies,[431] have been attested for some 30,000 years.[432] Others have pointed to designs on bones that indicate all 27 or 28 days of a lunar cycle.

There also has been some discussion, as mentioned, of still earlier Paleolithic art around 160 kya in South Africa and 90 kya in Algeria (and even earlier).[433] However, such early finds do not yet express the complex ideas found later in rock art. The same applies to some vestiges of Neanderthal art,[434] such as some Neanderthal grave goods and of the use of ochre. A Neanderthal(?) necklace made of pierced bones has been found at Arcy-sur-Cure (France); it was made some 40,000–35,000 years ago.[435]

***

In short, both rock painting and early sculpture provide some inkling of Stone Age thought, myths, and rites. However, some scholars such as Wunn and Herbig are rather pessimistic about the endeavor:

> The investigation of the art of the Stone Age hunters cannot deliver the answer sought for. These works carry symbolic, encoded messages; for their understanding we would have to know the myths and rites of Ice Age humans. But these traditions, transmitted in language, song, dance, and gestures, have disappeared forever.[436]

The present book endeavors to provide precisely these early myths.

In sum, conclusions such as Herbig's or Wunn's are based only on available archaeological and anthropological observation, as there are no Stone Age texts. However, we can recover a considerable part of the meaning of this early art through an investigation of its correlation with Laurasian mythology (cf. §6).[437] Clearly, renewed study of Mesolithic and Neolithic art, carried out in conjunction and comparison with research into Laurasian and Gondwana mythology, is required. This correlation may remarkably enrich this contested field as it furnishes, for the first time, Paleolithic "texts" or, to be precise, the summary-like texts we can distill in reconstructions. The study of Stone Age art can overcome, in this fashion, the structuralist, religious, evolutionist trends that have dominated it so far. Further elucidation can be achieved through a careful comparison of the rituals, customs, and myths of modern hunter-gatherer societies,[438] always bearing in mind that current hunter societies are as distant in time from their Paleolithic ancestors as we are. Care should thus be taken, with Wunn and against Eliade, not to mechanically compare modern hunter-gatherers with their ancestors many thousands of years ago. The few hunter-gatherers remaining today are, like us, *modern* humans with a long history, and their current state of mind cannot automatically be projected back to 50,000 years ago or to more recent times. If some of the ancient patterns have been maintained by their myths better than in other mythologies, this must be the object of additional, detailed study (§7).

Nevertheless, the sudden "explosion" of complex art (§4.4.1)[439] around 40,000 BCE—including even some early examples of the use of perspective[440]—seems to coincide, but does not entirely overlap geographically, with the emergence of Laurasian mythology, which took place around that time.[441] This suggests that the contemporaneous emergence of the complex Laurasian mythology is *just one* of several important developments in human culture. They probably started in Africa and the Greater Near East and are related to the expansion of symbolic representations at this time.[442]

The spiritual world of Paleolithic and early Mesolithic people is accessible only through their art (Wunn's position) *and* through the reconstructed Laurasian mythology.[443] The archaeologically limited evidence of art supports the worldview envisaged by Laurasian mythology, though such evidence apparently represents only a fraction of reconstructible Stone Age religion. For this art is mainly related to hunting and the role of shamans. It is important to recognize and underline these limitations.[444]

Judging from rock art and Paleolithic and Mesolithic hunting techniques, their respective belief systems were dominant in all areas of Africa, Eurasia, and Sahul Land that were occupied by then. However, it is the role of the shamans that is important for the Laurasian system. Both economic activities—at least of males—and what we know of presently current shamanistic beliefs agree with Stone Age art (§4.4.1, §7.1–2) to a remarkable degree. (Details will be discussed below, §7.2.)

The early shamans were, as some paintings in France seem to indicate, the facilitators of a spiritual connection with the animals and probably with the Lord/Lady of the Animals.[445] As such, and by teaching their secret lore, shamans played an important role in the formulation and preservation of Laurasian mythology (§5, §7).

Unfortunately, as mentioned, the extant rock paintings provide only limited access to the spiritual world of Paleolithic and early Mesolithic people; the rest must be looked for in the reconstruction of Laurasian (and Gondwana) mythology. Rock art encompasses just a certain fraction of the reconstructible data, mostly those related to hunting, the life and rebirth of hunted animals, the role of the shaman, and so on, but there is little else on creation, cosmography, the role of other spirits or deities, and so forth. Nevertheless, whatever can be gathered from these restricted materials does *not contradict* but, instead, *supports* the worldview envisaged by Laurasian mythology. One of these early features involves hunting and sacrifice, dissecting the prey, and the primordial being (§3.1.4).

§4.4.2. Sacrifice in late Paleolithic art

The original (late Paleolithic) form of Laurasian mythology underwent several stages of development while the people adhering to it spread inland from the shores of the Indian Ocean. In the interglacial period (after c. 50 kya) before the last Ice Age (25–15 kya) anatomically modern humans dispersed all across

Eurasia, resulting in the regional mythological and language groups (and further DNA branches). At the same time, new techniques, tools, and hunting methods were developed, for example, the spear-thrower, bow and arrow, and so on. The spiritual world developed as well, as can be noticed in the development of sha-manism from its initial African forms still seen in Africa (among the San) and Australia to later, "classical" forms, such as that of Siberia (§7.1). It includes the offering of animals (§7.1.2). Sacrifice seems still to be absent in Australia, though some scholars want to see it reflected by certain initiation rituals,[446] in which elder participants offer their blood to the young initiates. Some of the young men are killed by exhaustion,[447] not as planned sacrificial victims. The offering of animals, however, plays a great role in most later religions including those of New Guinea.

Sacrifice seems to have developed from an early connection with shamanic hunting magic that developed in both Laurasian and Gondwana cultures (New Guinea, Africa),[448] though not all of them. Its early forms can be detected in late Paleolithic art; its connections with mythology and shamanism will be discussed at length below (§7.1.2). The development from hunting animals to offering them in ritual is traceable in both myth and art. Among the paintings at Lascaux, there is a scene that seems to refer to a Stone Age tale or myth that can be dated at c. 17,000–12,000 BCE.[449] A bison bull is looking back at the spear that has transfixed him, from anus to penis. Below him lies an ithyphallic man and a spear-thrower; further below there is an upright stick, crowned by a duck-like bird. This painting has been interpreted by some as hunting magic or an offering (details in §7.1.2). As modern hunter-gatherer cultures seem to indicate, some parts of hunted and killed animals—obviously not the best ones,[450] which were eaten by humans—were offered.[451]

In such Paleolithic rock art, certain (hunted) animals are frequently depicted, others rarely, and certain animals seem to form pairs, such as horse and bison/ox, and mammoth and bison.[452] While it will probably remain difficult to pene-trate this system, Laurasian mythology may aid us, in the future, to solve this and other mysteries (§1.6, see especially §7.1.2).

§4.4.3. Food production

There were further changes in myth and ritual coinciding with the onset of Neolithic food production around 10,000 BCE. The sacrifice of hunted animals (e.g., as still seen with the Ainu) was substituted by that of domesticated ones. However, the ancient pattern as such was perpetuated: it was continued even by early state societies, by pastoralist tribes, and by the major monotheistic (Abrahamic) religions. Examples include cattle sacrifice in the Second Temple of Jerusalem before its destruction by the Romans; animal sacrifice at the Islamic festival of Id; and in thinly disguised and reinterpreted form, in each Christian mass, the sacrifice and partaking of the "lamb," that is, Christ.

Underlying the Neolithic developments is the fact that the late Paleolithic technical and "artistic explosion" around 40,000 years ago was followed by another revolution: that of the development of agriculture and horticulture, some 30,000 years later.[453] The change took place about 10,000 BCE, at first, it seems, in the western Fertile Crescent. It was caused by the dryer climate of the Younger Dryas (11,000–9600 BCE). Grains of barley, rye, and wheat where increasingly eaten. This resulted, on the one hand, in major changes in human body size and, on the other, in more fertility in women, better infant survival rates, and thus, population growth.

The new economic system was carried forward rapidly in a northwestern direction by population expansion,[454] while it spread more slowly southwestward and eastward by cultural transmission (acculturation). It took 2,000 years to reach the Nile Valley, and it was halted at the eastern end of the Iranian Plateau and in the dry climate of the Indus Valley for another 2,000 years, which were needed to develop plants that fit the South Asian climate.[455] On the other hand, rice was domesticated separately in the Yangtze River area at (increasingly) early dates,[456] and there seems to have been another area of agricultural development in the Ganges Valley.[457]

Agriculture spread rapidly around the end of the Dryas, at the beginning of the Holocene (about 11,000 years ago).[458] This can also be shown in linguistic data.[459]

As will be discussed at some length later on (§7.2), the transition from hunting and gathering to food production caused some far-reaching changes in Laurasian (and Papuan, African) mythology. However, the basic Laurasian outline of creation myths, story lines, and so on was maintained. The same apparently occurred in Africa, where the old Gondwana myths of a High God and his creation of humans were maintained (see §5.3.5).

During the Neolithic period, it becomes increasingly easier to trace mythological developments in archaeology, in art as well as in other artifacts, such as decorated utensils.[460] A discussion would lead too far here but is briefly attempted below (§7.2). Recently Ina Wunn has undertaken to investigate these topics at length,[461] however, without a study of ancient mythologies as such (see §1.6).

Typically, deities and rituals connected with food production are calqued on the earlier offering of the primordial giant or a large hunted animal (§4.4.3),[462] and they still stand out in the mythologies of societies that did not predominantly have agriculture but relied on pastoralism (§4.4.5). Examples include the abrupt explanation of the origin of rice and barley from a series of slaughtered animals and fish in late Vedic texts;[463] and that of the Old Japanese goddess of food, Ōgetsu, who appears quite out of context in the Kojiki;[464] and the Mayan maize deity. These developments will be discussed in detail later on (§7.2).

§4.4.4. Domestic animals and pastoralism

The history of Laurasian mythology from shamanic to early food-producing societies, as outlined in the preceding sections, can now be discussed in conjunction with another important economic development, that of domesticated animals and how they figure in early and later Laurasian myth. Obviously, all of them postdate the postulated date of Laurasian mythology, after c. 40,000 BCE, as seen in the cave paintings of Africa, Europe, India, and Australia. The earliest domestication of animals (goats, sheep) occurred east of the Levant (Zagros and also in the Taurus Mountains), from where it spread around the end of the Dryas (c. 10,000 BCE).

However, the date for the earliest domesticated animal, the dog, is difficult to establish even for the Nostratic language family: dog and wolf are not clearly differentiated in Proto-Nostratic (or even in the northern Eurasian version of it, in Greenberg's Eurasiatic). This should perhaps not surprise, as even this oldest domesticated animal was derived from wolves only around 15,000 BCE.[465] In fact, while our own original word for "dog" (Indo-European *kuon, Engl. *hound*) is found in many of the language families of the world, the meaning of the word frequently, but not unexpectedly, is just "wolf," "hyena," or similar, as Ruhlen (with some cases added) indicates (see Table 4.10).[466]

TABLE 4.10. *The spread of the word for 'dog' (from Ruhlen (1994: 302, with some additions).*

**kuan 'wolf/dog'*	
Nostratic/Eurasiatic	
Nostratic	*kujn
Indo-European	*kwon, Engl. hound
Uralic	*küjnä 'wolf'
Altaic	~ qan/qin : O.Turkic qančiq 'bitch', Mong. qani 'wild dog' Tunguse *xina, Japanese inu, Korean ka
Eskimo	Sirenik qanaγa 'wolf'
Gilyak	qan 'dog'
Afro-Asiatic:	*k(j)n 'dog,wolf'
Dene-Caucasian	
Basque	(haz-)koin 'bear-dog, badger'
Caucasian	*xHĕje
[Burushaski	huk]
Yeneseian	*kün 'wolverine'
Sino-Tibet.	*qhʷīj; Archaic Chin. *kʰiwən, Tib.-Burm. *kwiy
Amerind	
Hokan	kuān 'silver fox'
Yurimanui	kwan 'dog'
Popoloca	kuniya
Esmeralda	kine
Ge	okong, hong-kon, etc.
Austronesian	*nkaun
[Austric:	*asu/atsu, PAA *suq, acuq, PAN: *asu: L.V. Hayes]
Indo-Pacific	Pila kawun, etc.
Khoi-San	!gwāi, gwĩ, etc. 'hyena'
Bantu	*bua
Australia	[the dingo is a late import]

Clearly, the oldest meaning of the apparently onomatopoetic word **kuan*, probably in East Asia,[467] seems to be "wolf-like creature." Its spread is nearly Pan-Gaean, but some areas are missing, such as sub-Saharan Africa[468] and Australia, where the dingo appeared late. Consequently, we have to judge the occurrence of dogs in mythology with some caution. The dog thus *cannot* occur in original, old versions, such as Gondwana or Pan-Gaean stories. It can be expected to occur in the later versions of Gondwana myths of peoples in East and Southeast Asia and, obviously, in Laurasian myths.

The raven often follows animals and in this fashion becomes a guide for hunters.[469] The same role can be played by other opportunistic birds such as crows and vultures, which will have led early hunters to killed carnivore prey. The dog, once domesticated, took over this role, and it added value in tracking fresh prey and animals wounded in the chase. Consequently, it occurs in Laurasian myth most prominently in a tracker and guardian function or as a messenger and guide. It is prominent in Siberian shamanic myth, where it leads the shaman to heaven or, like the bitch Saramā, is a guide for its human counterpart, the eager Indian trickster deity Indra.[470]

The guarding aspect that is most prominently met with in extant Laurasian myths is that of guardian of the Netherworld or of the gates of "hell."[471] The Greek Kerberos is well known; its Indian relatives are the two old Vedic hellhounds, the Śabala, sons of the bitch Saramā, who is a key figure in the myth of releasing the sun from the Vala Cave (see §3.5.1). In another version of this story, she acts after another messenger, a *suparṇa* bird (vulture), has failed. Both kinds of animals act as messengers.[472] The Vedic and Avestan hellhound is a horrifying creature with "four eyes," that is, the two bright spots above the eyes of a Tibetan-style mastiff or Near Eastern dog. A recent paper treats the role of Saramā as the *psychopompos* of a shaman.[473] Indeed, this role is still found in many shamanic myths of northern Eurasia. Just as the Sārameya dogs guard the path downward to the Netherworld, so, too, do they guard the way to heaven. Drawings show how a dog leads the shaman on his ascent.[474] The eastern Siberian Chukchi and Koryak also offer their best dogs.[475] D. Anthony's excavations at Samara, west of the Ural Mountains, have brought to light a very large number of elaborate dog sacrifices.[476]

The same role is played by the bear in Ainu mythology. Indeed, the bear is often regarded in northern Eurasia as the "dog" of the gods. The bear, an Ice Age human prey, has been dealt with above. In southern areas, such as the Hindu Kush, it has been substituted by the fox.[477]

The spread of other animals, domesticated still later, adds important facets to the study of Laurasian subbranches and of interactions with other mythologies. The aurochs continued to be hunted and figures as a wild, dangerous animal in many myths. It was domesticated in various areas of Eurasia,[478] and bovids were substituted as the sacrificial animal par excellence in some southern cultures such as those of Egypt, early Israel, and Mesopotamia. It even was sanctified, as seen in Eurōpē's bull, the Cretan Minotauros, the Apis bull in Egypt, the bull (and its sacrifice) in the art of the Indus civilization, and so on. The fascination with the bull hunt still is enacted in modern Spain and South America, in the yearly bull chase through the streets as well as in bull fighting.[479] Competition involving bulls is seen in paintings of the Minoan civilization of Crete of the second millennium BCE. The role of the aurochs is played by the water buffalo in large areas of Southeast and South Asia.[480]

The goat was domesticated fairly early in the eastern areas of the Fertile Crescent, in the Zagros Mountains, around c. 9700 BCE. It took over the role of the sacrificial animal par excellence in some areas such as Mehrgarh (southwestern Pakistan), at 6000 BCE, or in Vedic religion and in all of later India. However, its important role is also visible in the early Sahara engraving at Djebel Bes Seba in Algeria,[481] where it is the carrier of a solar disk with five or seven rays emanating from it. Actual rams and the ram deities Khum, Harsaphes, and Amon (hence the biblical golden ram) were worshipped in Egypt;[482] in India the ram is connected with the fire god Agni.

Another substitute for the primordial sacrifice, the boar,[483] has also been treated above. It is found early on in the Andaman Islands, at c. 3000 BCE, and as earth diver in early Vedic texts.[484] The later Indian boar incarnation of the great god Viṣṇu is a typical case of the takeover of an older (muskrat/bird earth diver) myth into a local framework and subsequent elevation to high status.

Similarly, the widespread offering of horses substituted for the animals listed above, after horse domestication in the steppes of the early Bronze Age. It is especially prominent in Indo-European but also in some other Eurasian traditions.[485] Interestingly, the horse is a (linguistic) newcomer in Indo-European, while the words for cows and sheep (in addition to the Near Eastern import, the goat)[486] belong to older strata. However, due to its new, high status in Indo-European society as draft animal and its resultant economic prominence, horse sacrifice was more highly valued than that of cows, sheep, or goats (while pig sacrifice is virtually absent from older strata, though it is found in Rome).[487] Horse sacrifice was also prominent in Central and eastern Asia, where it is attested since Shang times.[488] The old form of the horse sacrifice (by suffocation),[489] prominent among the Vedic tribes, was still performed by the Altai Turks around 1900.

Consequently, the horse has been included in many Eurasian myths and also, as a latecomer, in Lakota (Sioux) mythology.[490] As the horse was absent in pre-Columbian America, its inclusion in Amerindian myth, after its import by the Spanish conquistadors, must have happened sometime after 1500 CE. This instance provides a useful test case for the adaptation of items such as new domesticated animals into an already existing mythology. In the present case, Lakota mythology was dominated by the buffalo, the major prey of the prairie Amerindians.[491] A similar, late addition to Amerindian ritual is known from Patagonia.[492]

The older Laurasian mythologies also do not know of chicken or of the rooster that cries to greet the dawn. Chicken apparently were domesticated in South Asia (from the Bengal jungle fowl)[493] and made their way westward only fairly slowly. The morning cry of the rooster appears in the Later Avesta (*kahrka*, "call of the rooster," "rooster") and in Later Vedic (*kṛka-vāka*, '*kṛk*-sayer, "rooster"). It reached Greece in the eighth century BCE, and a rooster was offered to Asklepios by Socrates, 399 BCE.[494] Farther east, the announcement of dawn by crying roosters, so important in various versions of Laurasian myth,[495] is found from the Tibeto-Burmese Nagas all the way to Japan's Kojiki ("the long-crying birds of dawn"; §3.5.1).

However, nothing of this is seen in the oldest South Asian text, the rather conservative Ṛgveda (c. 1000 BCE)—situated very close to the homeland of chicken domestication.[496] Indeed, in the older western Eurasian (Indo-European) mythologies, the role of the rooster was played by dogs or by geese (in Republican Rome when under attack from the Celts). There even is a myth about the mutual enmity of dogs and chicken (though the myth comes from Africa).[497] The spread of chicken across the Pacific has recently been traced (along with that of sweet potatoes and cotton).[498]

As with many domesticated animals and plants, this seems a clear case of cultural diffusion from eastern South and Southeast Asia westward to Europe and eastward up to South America (where, however, a different species is found).[499] Chicken were one of the few items that Polynesians brought along on their long trek from their western homeland, the mythical Sawaiki.[500] But exactly how chicken got into South America still is unclear.[501]

Further archaeological data such as megaliths, pyramids, and ziggurats or various forms of graves could be added for discussion of their underlying mythologies; however, these items mostly fall into the historical period, and a detailed investigation would lead too far here. But some relatively neglected features of human culture, gestures in the widest sense, should be added to the current chapter. They, too, reflect archaic origins, regional variations, and probably also diffusion, which could be linked with other cultural traits (such as mythology) over time. They provide more resolution to the story of human cultural development, including facets of religion and mythology.

■ §4.5. OTHER ITEMS OF COMPARISON: CHILDREN'S SONGS AND GAMES, ANCIENT MUSIC AND REGIONAL STYLES, USE OF COLORS, AND GESTURES AND THEIR REGIONAL VARIATIONS

As a corollary, we can also investigate other facets of human culture that have a more or less direct relationship with mythology as some of them clearly show limited regional spread, while others are more widespread. These features include, notably, Pan-Gaean(?) children's games, rhymes, and songs but also typical regional styles of music and even variations in such seemingly innate features as gestures. Each one of these items would be suitable and desirable for a detailed—and fascinating—study that cannot be undertaken here. Instead, just a few interesting highlights will be mentioned.

Small children are known to form a highly conservative group that transmits the games, rhymes, and songs of their predecessors faithfully. Such groups include children from the ages of, say, four–ten and therefore constitute very short-lived "generations." Extreme faithfulness in tradition is exacted by small children who insist on exact reproduction of the wording and actions of games and stories. Variation is shunned and loudly protested against, as any parent can easily notice with their own children. So, it is not surprising that the first few words of the English rhyme "eeny meeny miny moe" turn up in Germany as "ene mene timpe tu" and in a Buddhist mantra (*dharaṇī*), found in Central Asia, as "ene mene daṣphe daṇḍadaṣphe"[502]—which have been invoked at the outset (§1). As is the case with other rhymes and tales, it is especially the beginnings ("Once upon a time, there was…") that are preserved well.[503] Nevertheless, like all cultural products, such verses do get changed and reinterpreted over time. Sometimes the corrupted (perseverated) versions of such "mantras" offer an idea of the time of change, for example, when the German children's rhyme ending in *empolen*, a nonsense word that has nothing to do with Poland (Polen), now has a reference to "Pomerania that has been burned down," which can only refer to the Thirty Years' War (1618–48) or the Napoleonic wars. Or, among other traditional items, games such as making cat's cradles and stairways to heaven[504]—a clearly mythical theme—apparently have a worldwide spread, whose actual extent must be studied.

Further, the melodies used in such games are equally archaic, often consisting only of two or three notes (like the English "nana nana nā na"). Obviously, such games and songs should be compared worldwide, and it would be interesting to see whether they belong, as expected, to Pan-Gaean traditions. Frequently, they may represent forms of older "sunken" traditions that adults no longer adhere to or to forgotten myths that may appear in fairy tales.[505]

The music of adults, too, represents another important traditional cultural trait.[506] Though modern and recent regional styles have been studied to some extent, we still miss, as far as I see, a comprehensive comparative study of all extant variants.[507] Major regional styles are well known, for example, the Arab, Indian, and Chinese ones, and we may add styles such as East African (of Sudan, Ethiopia, Somalia), Southeast Asian, or some five African ones. However, the predilection for pentatonic melodies in the Americas, East Asia, Southeast Asia, and the Urals/Hungary and folk traditions of India, Iran, and western Central Asia or among the Berbers points to a rather old phenomenon that may perhaps be linked to the spread of populations during the warm period around 40 kya.[508] Obviously, this wide area overlaps with linguistic data only in part (§4.1), but genetic data would agree more (§4.3). The spread of various other tonal systems, such as the recent tempered 12-half-tone European style, the older Greek and Near Eastern ones, or the 22- or 24-quarter-tone style of Arabia and India, may be among some other, though much later, important features that indicate old cultural provinces that partially overlap with linguistic and mythological ones.

Similarly, the predilection of sub-Saharan African music for complicated rhythms is another regional feature. They often acquire a intricate, fugue-like character, just like Bach's melody-based one. Singing in harmony, so typical for recent European music, is another feature that is also found in the Caucasus and far beyond.

***

Even the selective use of colors is clearly regional. Most of us will be used to the rather simple scheme of white, red, blue, and black, as well as the additional colors of yellow, brown, and green. All these are in use by many folk cultures, as is readily seen in their costumes or body paint. Pastel colors add to the scheme but are more "refined," and their names are not always known to the average person. Such names then tend to be easily borrowed from other languages. However, a largely unstudied feature is the combination of two or more colors. The simple red/white/blue scheme is found in most older European flags (some-times substituted by red/white/green)[509] and costumes.[510] In Asia, things look different. Non-Indians will be visually shocked by the "garish" colors combined in the Subcontinent, such as a brilliant light green with an equally bright light red. This combination is not allowed, for example, in Japan, where a complex code of which colors may be combined has been in existence for at least a millen-nium. Again, comparative study is in order to define ancient regional differences and how far they may go back. Clearly, most of the color combinations are culture related and have an emblematic character, such as green in Islam, or red and saffron in Hinduism, or black as the color of mourning in some cultures, white in others. Such features may have only some limited congruence or overlap with the various areas of ancient mythology, but they need to be investigated.

Art provides additional important clues for ancient cultural areas. Compara-tively recent regional styles, however, are very obvious. Contrast, for example, any Japanese or Chinese Zen-inspired painting—with much empty space left to the imagination of the viewer—with the crowded pictures or temple facades of the Indian cultural area (India, Angkor in Cambodia, Borobodur in Indonesia, Bali), where every available bit of space is filled in. Earlier art styles, before the (re)introduction of perspective,[511] tend to show simplified approaches to depict spatial relationships, and Egypt stands out with its fixed and rigid tradition (§4.4.1), which was only briefly abandoned under Akhenaton.

However, the invention and spread of the so-called X-ray style are marginally important for the current undertaking. It can be found in Mesolithic art in Europe from c. 8000 BCE onward and apparently spread far and wide from an unknown center, as to reach Africa, South Asia, and Australia (by c. 2000 BCE). This looks a clear case of an early diffusion of a cultural feature, interestingly one that occurred several tens of thousands of years after the Out of Africa event. Otherwise, how did people come up with the same idea of showing the interiors of animals and humans? Or, more likely, did the concept predate its appearance in Stone Age art? Its apparent Pan-Eurasian and Sahul spread may be compared with that of megaliths that are clearly related to religion—both items that cannot be pursued here.

Some of these features will be due to cultural diffusion, while others are not: just as we see in mythology. Possible overlaps between these two fields of study should be investigated at length.

***

Surprisingly, not all of the "fundamentally" human gestures are in fact universal;[512] instead, they show—pace Aboudan and Beattie[513]—many regional differences. Anybody who has shaken his or her head in a restaurant in Greece will know: the waiter will bring exactly the item just refused. The "Greek way" of saying yes by shaking one's head is a gesture employed in the Greater Near East and India and is found down to Botswana,[514] though it apparently is not met with in intervening Bantu territories such as in Tanzania. (I am not sure, so far, about its exact spread.) Most Eurasians will use the gesture of shaking their head to say no.

Other well-known items include greeting gestures such as the Inuit touching of noses, the Tibetan projection of the tongue, the San projection of one's elbows, the Indian (and ancient Bactria-Margiana's, prehistoric Japan's) joining of one's palms, and East Asian (and residual European) bowing. Another potentially ancient gesture is that of a closed fist with the index and little finger stretched out, pointing at a dangerous or hated object and warding off its effect.[515] It is found in the magic of Lascaux caves on a "wizard beast,"[516] in magic as horns tied to the heads of Australian dancers,[517] and in reverse form also with the San,[518] but it is symbolized as a hand gesture in the Indo-Mediterranean area as the *corna* gesture in Italy or as the *tarjanī-mudrā* (threatening hand gesture) in India. A formally related Hawai'ian form (shaking the fist left and right, thumb and little finger pointing outward), however, is a form of friendly greeting. Such observations may be expanded to establish ancient cultural provinces of gestures, and this may also be useful in comparing archaic and local mythology.

Obviously, there also are panhuman forms of behavior and gestures, such as laughing while showing one's teeth in mock aggression, which we have inherited from our prehuman primate ancestors. It is made even less aggressive in India (since Vedic times) as well in Japan and China by covering the mouth with one hand, especially in the case of women. Then there are the complex meanings of kissing and the gesture of scratching one's head as a sign of embarrassment or uncertainty.

The topic of ancient gestures has recently been explored for early art and religion by Wunn based on the recent results of ethology.[519] A fairly comprehensive list of panhuman gestures, most derived from our primate ancestors, include the following ones that are independent of language: pacifying smile, threatening baring of teeth, and staring ("evil eye"). Further, there is the demonstration of the erect penis as a threat and power gesture or its modern American variation of raising the middle finger. It is derived from the imitation of mock sexual intercourse between primate males, which itself is connected with the exposure of the female posterior as an invitation to sex and as a demonstration of submission. However, the presentation of the vulva, knees raised and spread out, is a gesture of female dominance (also of mocking).[520] The demonstration of female breasts is a pacifying gesture.[521] Finally, the presentation of a raised palm is used as sign of denial (and as a protecting device, such as in the Indian *abhaya mudrā*, e.g., of the Buddha). Such gestures are found in the art of all peoples and times, where they have had a long, individual transmission with inherent changes that lead from clear representation to abstraction and finally, to mere ornaments, such as the M design.[522]

Again, the exact spread of panhuman and regional gestures must be investigated so as to show their reach and age as well as their potential overlap with the geographical spread of early humans and their corresponding mythological areas. Some of them may cover the same areas as Laurasian or Gondwana mythology.

Obviously, the individual worth of the items discussed in this small additional section is only of relative value for the study of ancient mythology, perhaps with the exception of children's rhymes. However, such items can add interesting facets about the early spread of human culture that can adumbrate those of mythology.

■ §4.6. CONCLUSIONS RESULTING FROM THE COMPARISON OF THE SCIENCES INVOLVED

The "historical" sciences adduced in this chapter—linguistics, archaeology, and genetics—concur with the findings of historical comparative mythology. This makes its claims much stronger and points the way to future interdisciplinary research.[523] As has been described earlier, sub-Saharan Africa and Papua/Australia, as well as several areas in between, were covered by the old Out of Africa, Gondwana type of mythology. But something new, the Laurasian mythology, developed, apparently in Greater Southwest Asia, around 40,000 BCE.

When I first noticed, back in 1990, the basic structure of Laurasian myth, I soon observed the split between this and the Gondwana type of mythology, but I could not explain where, when, and how this development had come about. I merely surmised that Laurasian mythology had developed later on somewhere in the Middle East or western Central Asia. It now turns out that Central Asia and Europe were settled only fairly late, during the warm period between the second-to-last (c. 52,000–45,000) and the last Ice Age (c. 25,000–12,500 years ago). During this time period, Laurasian mythology developed among some Out of Africa populations that had remained somewhere in the Greater Southwest Asian area and that later spread toward the Near East and Europe as well as to Central Asia.[524] The ancestors of the Dene-Caucasian as well as the Nostratic language families seem to have been involved, the latter at a slightly later point in time. However, the pattern of spread in Southeast and East Asia remains enigmatic for the time being (see below).

If we correlate the emerging picture of Laurasian mythology and its evolving subregions (Near East, East Asia, Central Asia, Mesoamerica, etc.) with the origin and spread of major genetic haplogroups (mtDNA M, N, R; NRY F*) and their respective localized subclades, as well as that of language families (Nostratic, Austric, Sino-Tibetan, Amerindian, and their later descendants), the scenario depicted in Figure 4.18 emerges.[525]

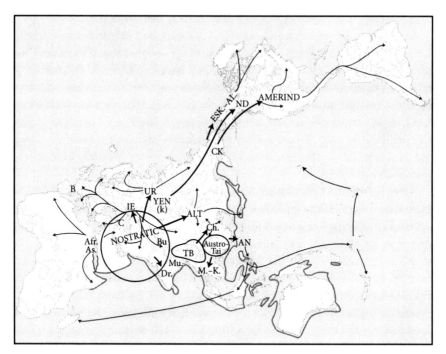

Figure 4.18. Interglacial and postglacial spread of major language families (black lines). Later spread of language families is indicated by thin lines. (Arrows do not indicate the exact track of spread, just the general direction.)
Dene-Caucasian: B (Basque), C (Caucasian), Bu (Burushaski), K (Ket), ND (Na-Dene); IE: Indo-European; UR: Uralic (Finno-Ugrian); Dr.: Dravidian; Mu.: Munda; M.-K.: Mon-Khmer; AN: Austronesian; TB: Tibeto-Burman; Ch.: Chinese; CK: Chukchi–Kamchadal; Esk.-Al.: Eskimo (Inuit)–Aleutian.

The quick spread of *Homo sapiens sap.* out of Africa can be followed, by a trail of tools and skeletal remains, all the way from Ethiopia to Southeast Asia (Borneo) and South and North China (Zhoukoudian) as well as Sahul Land, with early sites between c. 40,000 and 60,000 BCE. In addition, archaeology indicates some of the spiritual concepts of late Paleolithic humans. The "artistic explosion" in rock art, of c. 40,000 BCE, that is found all over Africa, South Asia, Europe, New Guinea, and Australia has left us with precious indications of otherwise lost mythology and ritual, for both the Gondwana and Laurasian versions.

The contemporaneous emergence, at c. 40,000 BCE, of Laurasian mythology as an expressive form of symbolic representations of the late Paleolithic allows us to put the archaeological discoveries into a firm narrative context, and the myths themselves can provide some interpretations (see above, §4.4.1–2). Caution is certainly advised in all interpretations of art.[526] This is especially the case when abstract signs are involved. They frequently turn out to have unexpected, surprising meanings when and where we can actually check them. For example, in contemporary West Africa the ubiquitous Indian, Buddhist, Jaina, Amerindian, and so on *svastika* sign has no relation to the course of the sun, as it does in many other cultures, but, rather, indicates... *monkey's feet.*

In the end, archaeology, paleontology, genetics, and linguistics sustain the Laurasian theory in varying degrees. Archaeology supplies some "hard facts" of early *Homo sapiens sap.* skeletons, tools, and later on, artwork. Paleontology interprets human remains and establishes broad patterns for our early ancestors up to the emergence of modern humans, the bearers of Pan-Gaean, Gondwana, and Laurasian mythologies and associated rituals. It also can provide rough data (by multivariate analysis) for further regional subdivisions, for example, along the lines of teeth shapes (Sinodont and Sundadont), though hardly for connections with mythology.

More importantly, human population genetics has provided us with increasingly finer classifications of all humans according to their maternal (mtDNA), paternal (NRY), and autosomal inheritance. The early spread of humans out of Africa up to Australia, and later to the rest of Eurasia and the Americas, is matched by genetic details that indicate increasingly less overall general variation, but much secondary splitting up of lineages, the farther east humans moved: the Americas being a subset of East Asia, East Asia derived from Southeast Asia, this from South Asia, and the latter from the first emigrants, themselves just a subset of all African lineages. Some of the then developing sublineages, notably those that spread into northern Eurasia around 40,000 BCE, coincide in time and place with the perceived sudden emergence of pictorial art. This suggests that the contemporaneous emergence of Laurasian mythology embodies just one of many other, worldwide forms of symbolic representations.

Linguists, at least those innovative if daring individuals active in the emerging Long-Range studies,[527] tend to agree as well. While Africa has retained the Niger-Congo and Nilo-Saharan language families—just as it has retained the genetic haplogroups mtDNA L1 and L2 and NRY A and B—the expansion out of Africa brought the ancestors of Andamanese-Papuan (Indo-Pacific) and Australian languages to the ends of Asia. After 40,000 BCE during an interglacial period, a second great migration produced the widely spread Dene-Caucasian language group (from the Basque country to the Yenesei, Yukon, and the Navajos). Somewhat later, the same movement spawned the huge Nostratic superfamily that is now found in most of North Africa, Europe, and much of Asia. It also led to the development of Austric languages in the southeastern Asian sector as well as to that of Sino-Tibetan in the southeastern and eastern Asian area. A clear echo of this is the development of the great DNA clade NRY F*, which has spread, with its subclades G–R, over all the same areas. The development of several subclades of the immediate descendants of the African emigrants, the female haplogroups mtDNA M and N, led to the emergence of further haplogroups, of A, C, D, H, J, T, U, V, W, X2, and Z, in Asia and Europe. The same is again shown in autosomal locus 5.[528]

These data and those of the language families are echoed by special regional developments of Laurasian mythology, such as those reaching from northern Europe via Siberia to North America (shamanism, bear cult) or those of the southern regions (bull/buffalo sacrifice).

The late spread of humans into the Americas around 20 kya is echoed by that of Amerindian languages,[529] later added to by Na-Dene and Eskimo-Aleut. As even a brief look at Bierhorst's composite tables of myth motifs in the Americas indicates,[530] these two major Amerindian groups also have different mythologies, both of the hunt and of food production, though some overlap is seen in the circumpolar region and due to the secondary influence of Pueblo mythologies on the Navajo and Apache, derived from Mesoamerican influences; they constitute another case of Laurasian macro-regions (§2.3). The latter is characterized by the emergence myths of Mesoamerica and the spread of this tradition northward up to the Dakotas and southern Canada, along with maize agriculture. The composite Table 4.11 tries to capture some of the main traits of all the developments discussed in this chapter.

***

However, it must again be emphasized strongly (§6) that the various details of the above results are of a heuristic nature and can be changed (or even overturned) by new evidence. Certain small changes in the present (heuristic) state of the theory can be expected. For example, some recent evidence seems to point to an earlier exodus from Africa than supposed so far.[531]

Another such case may be briefly highlighted. There is some indication that the comparative data collected by Y. Berezkin in his great project may point to *an earlier version* of Laurasian mythology that has been preserved in Mesoamerica and especially in South America.[532] Certain clusters of motifs

TABLE 4.11

ARCHAEOLOGY, PALAEONTOLOGY GEOLOGY	GENETICS	LINGUISTICS	MYTHOLOGY
125 kya Homo Sap. sap. remains (E. / S. Africa)	'African Eve' mtDNA; male NRY	Pan-Gaean mother tongue: → pre-African: Niger-Congo, Nilo-Saharan, Khoi-San	**PAN-GAEAN** mythology → pre-Afr. **GONDWANA** mythology
115-90 Qafzeh/Skhul (Levant, died out)	mt L0-L3 NRY A, B	?	
70-50 Glacial Maximum Borneo, Australia, Andamans	mt L3→M, N, R NRY C, D, E, F/K, P, R/S (SW, S, SE, E Asia; Sahul: mt Q, P)	S/E. Asian substrate languages, Austral. Indo-Pacific; Borean/pre-Nostratic, pre-Dene-Caucasian	Out of Africa- **GONDWANA** mythologies (Andaman, Australia. etc.)
50-25 Warmer period Beijing, Okinawa, New Guinea, S. Asia	mt M7-10, D, C, N9, A; R9, B NRY C, D, F	ancestor of Asian languages: Sino-Tib., Austric; Nostratic; Dene-Caucasian	Gondwana type mythologies retained in these areas?
40-25 "Crô Magnon" Zagros, Romania, rest of Europe Northern Eurasian expansion	NRY E/F/G-J/R; mt N1-2, X, U1-3, R4-5,7-8, HJT, HV	Macro-Caucasian: (Europ. substrates: pre- Basque etc.) N. Nostratic; pre-Ket, pre-Amerind;	**LAURASIAN MYTH.** develops, expands in SW/S/E/N/Asia, Europe
25-15 Last Glacial Maximum retraction to southern and isolated retreat areas; migration to N. America		pre-Basque, Caucas. immigr. of Amerind; Na-Dene	(Gondw. myth?) Amerind version of Laurasian myth.
10- final global expansion of humans		development of current language families: Afrasian, Indo-Eur., Uralic, Altaic, Tibeto-Burman, Bantu, Polynesian, etc.	global expansion of Laurasian mythology & world religions

show a closer correspondence between Sahul Land and South American myths. Berezkin correctly interprets this as the survival of older motifs in South America that were introduced there at the time of the first immigration into the Americas at c. 20 kya,[533] rather than as the result of later transoceanic transmissions by boat. Such incidental visits, indicated by the pre-Columbian spread of Polynesian chicken to South America and of the sweet potato, however, did not lead to a wholesale (mutual) takeover of myths, mythologies, or even the structure of the Polynesian version into South American Laurasian mythologies.[534]

However, following up on Berezkin's discussion, it is clear that certain aspects of North American myth are late introductions from Siberia and Bering Land, by speakers of the Na-Dene languages (Athapascan/Navajo/Apache). It has to be investigated, however, how far this late influx has also impacted the rest of North America or, as is evident, whether the maize *Kulturkreis* has overlaid their influence in the Navajo/Apache area.

If correct, Berezkin's observation would explain some of the correspondences seen in Melanesia and South America: both simply have preserved older traits than those prominent in the Neolithic form of Laurasian mythology in Eurasia and North America. Even then, it must be underlined that Laurasian mythology as such stands: Melanesian mythology, being Gondwana, is quite different from the various Laurasian versions found in South America. This again requires a detailed investigation that cannot be carried out here and must be postponed to a future occasion.[535]

Second, though the problems listed above (§2.1, 2.3, 2.6, etc.) seem to create some uncertainty, we can be confident that overlapping results from the various fields involved (as detailed in §§2–6) point in the right direction. For example, the confidence exhibited by population geneticists originated in the mid-nineties when they noticed that linguistic and archaeological data showed overlapping results. In the present case we have the overlapping results from the four fields of mythology, genetics, archaeology, and linguistics.[536] However, the basic assumption made in this book, namely, that we can establish parts of humankind's earliest stories by using reconstructive methods similar to those used in comparative and historical linguistics, remains an attractive proposal that I have not yet been able to argue against (see above, and below, §§5–6).

In consequence, the development of Laurasian mythology, with its myths added to the preceding Gondwana myths, as well as its underlying story line, which unifies them, seems to have taken place during the transition to the Upper Paleolithic, which occurred some 40,000 years ago. At this time, new artifacts (such as the spear-thrower) appeared, and the number of human bands increased rapidly. This event also seems related to the explosive development of complex art as preserved in rock art (§4.4.1, §7.1.2 sqq.).[537] It also coincides in time with the spread northward of anatomically modern humans into Eurasia during this interglacial period.

In sum, archaeology, linguistics, population genetics, and studies of paleoclimate all present scenarios overlapping with or very similar to that assumed by comparative historical mythology and by Laurasian mythology in particular. They point to Laurasian mythology as an offshoot of the earlier Gondwana mythology of the peoples of the exodus out of Africa. It is to their Gondwana mythology that we now must turn for closer study and for a countercheck of the Laurasian theory.

5 The Countercheck: Australia, Melanesia, and Sub-Saharan Africa

■ §5.1. POSSIBLE WAYS TO COUNTERCHECK

All scientific theories must be tested, and the Laurasian theory can be submitted to such tests, like any other theory. If its reconstruction is correct, it can and must be subjected to counterchecks of all available evidence. There are several requirements for doing so.

First it must be shown that the present reconstruction is typical for Laurasian mythology and that it does not have correspondences in other (types of) mythologies. Contradiction and negative proof would thus hinge on success-fully showing that the underlying principle of Laurasian mythology, its story line arrangement from the creation to the destruction of the world, is found outside the Laurasian area. The prediction is that a full-blown story line cannot be found, say, in Central Africa or southeastern Australia. Or to come to the level of details, it can be predicted that Siberian-type shamans did not exist in Australia, New Guinea, or (originally) sub-Saharan Africa or that the Eurasian-type secret sacred speech (of shaman-like) specialists, such as with the Indo-Europeans, Himalayan shamans, or Taiwan's Ami priests, was not found in the Gondwana areas.

The problem in historical comparative mythology, just as in other historical fields, obviously is that we cannot make predictions of the type that physicists can pronounce about nature, nor can we predict future outcomes (say, next cen-tury's American mythology). But we can make predictions about which particular facts must have existed at certain stages in the past, as has been done successfully in historical comparative linguistics (§4.1). I assume the same can eventually be done for mythology, even though script and written texts earlier than c. 3000 BCE will hardly emerge to prove my case. Early human art, however, such as some cave paintings (§7), which present their own difficulties in under-standing, may indicate whether I have been right or not.

The investigations carried out so far in the preceding chapters, as well as those performed in this chapter, indicate that there are several other types of mythologies, notably the Gondwana mythologies of sub-Saharan Africa, New Guinea/Melanesia, and Australia. They differ substantially from each other and, importantly, especially so from Laurasian mythology. Their characteristics and mutual similarities, correspondences, and differences will be discussed in this chapter.

As stressed, the typical story line of Laurasian mythology is absent in the Gondwana mythologies. This is a critical feature: it constitutes a crucial test to indicate that the non-Laurasian mythologies possess the same or a very similar type of story line (something that could not be shown by me or by others). So far, the Laurasian theory stands.

***

Second, on the other hand, if conversely some individual motifs or developments of Laurasian mythology should be observed in non-Laurasian mythologies, this does *not* serve as negative counterproof, as individual motifs and even small myth cycles can drift and travel. Therefore, demonstration of disagreement with the theory in *incidental* points is not a sufficient condition for abandonment of the proposal: such incidental points will not be enough to scuttle the theory.

A case in point is the flood myth. Based on insufficient materials,[1] I originally thought that it was not typical for Africa, Melanesia, and Australia.[2] However, as discussed at length below (§5.7.2), the myth is actually widespread on all continents.[3] Such incidental corrections in theory building in progress are typical for any development of new theories, as will be pointed out presently (cf. §2).

***

Third, as will be shown below (§6), certain motifs that appear in both Laurasian and non-Laurasian mythologies may belong to an *older* stratum, one of pre-Laurasian, Gondwana mythology. They are isolated relics that have accidentally been retained in both Laurasian and non-Laurasian mythologies. (This is especially the case with some of the "creation" myths, such as humans emerging from trees, from clay, etc.)

Further, as we will see, there are some typical examples of motifs that spread *after* the creation of the Laurasian mythology (§5.6). In sum, as long as it can be shown that the reconstructed story line is something typical for Laurasian myth and that its typical creation mythemes are lacking in non-Laurasian myths, the theory will stand.

§5.1.1. Method

Testing a theory usually begins with the discovery of one or more exceptions to the theory. Subsequent investigation frequently provides sufficiently convincing explanations of such exceptions, merely resulting in a minor shift in (sub)sections of the theory (as in C. C. Ragin's admission, below). However, if substantial accumulations of exceptions occur that cannot be explained in reasonable fashion, and if this involves those critical to important parts of the theory, this will have to result in the abandonment of the theory. In the present case, such an argument would involve the existence and wide spread of a clearly structured, detailed story line outside the Laurasian area and secondarily, the existence of myths dealing with creation from chaos or "nothing" or an end to the present world.

The old maxim that "exception proves the rule" is not really a useful concept here; rather, exceptions must be employed creatively: "exceptions test the rule."[4] Such exceptions to the rule are frequently encountered by researchers when developing a new theory. Ongoing work on a theory usually reveals that

> no...intentional gulf between hypothesis or concept formation and data analysis usually exists. Most findings, at least most *interesting* findings, usually result from some form of grounded concept and hypothesis formation based on *preliminary* data analyses. In other words, most hypotheses and concepts are refined, often reformu-lated, after the data have been collected and analyzed. Initial examination of data usu-ally exposes the inadequacy of the investigator's conceptual tools for understanding the data and the data analysis itself.
>
> The interplay between concept formation and data analysis leads to progressively more refined concepts and hypotheses.[5]

The present theory, too, has gone through several stages and avatars (between 1990 and 2008). I started out with the aim of clarifying the extent of a perceived common Laurasian mythology. The scope of the investigation was soon expanded to take into account what emerged as non-Laurasian, common Gondwana mythology. Finally, putting both early types of mythologies in perspective, a framework appeared for the description of the common traits among all types studied. Consequently, early Pan-Gaean myths, our oldest tales, were brought into focus.

To use the linguistic simile again, this is like what we have been doing in com-parative historical linguistics for some 200 years. The "initial" proposal by William Jones (1786) still excluded Irish, as well as Celtic in general, and he could not yet know about Mycenaean, Hittite, and Tocharian. All of these lan-guages (and a few more) have been added since. Importantly, the initial theory of the beginnings of the 19th century has been altered,[6] expanded, and refined by the Neogrammarians around 1870 and by latter-day scholars.[7] Consequently, the original proposals look quite different from today's state of the art: witness the early imaginative "reconstruction" of an Indo-European tale by Schleicher and its more recent versions. There is a clear shift from Sanskrit-looking forms to uniquely Proto-Indo-European ones, increasingly looking like a Caucasus language.[8]

Be it an initial idea, or flash of insight, or incidental daydreaming, or for some scholars even an actual dream—connections made consciously or unconsciously can lead to a new theory. In my case, it was triggered by the comparison of Japanese mythology with the Vedic one—an insight that is still largely echoed, though much altered, in the discussion provided above (§3.5.1) of the myth of the hidden sun. The theory was conceived, as described at the start of this book, due to renewed exposure to Japanese myth and ritual during a sabbatical at Kyoto in January 1990; since then, the main thesis, that of a Laurasian story line, has remained unaltered in spite of some adjustment.[9]

A theory built on an initial insight normally involves a number of inconsistencies, some plainly wrong facts, and even some wrong ideas that have to be ironed out subsequently, as explained by Ragin. Or as one of my teachers, the late Paul Thieme, put it in his classes in the sixties: "Of course, I do not publish *how* I found it." Well, here I did so.

As has been pointed out above (§2.1), there has been some recent discussion on the method and validity of the comparative approach by J. Z. Smith.[10] But, as indicated above, while Smith is still inquiring about the validity of the comparative and historical method, we have successfully been carrying out such comparisons in fields like linguistics, paleontology, zoology, botany, and now population genetics for some 200 years.

§5.1.2. Criteria for testing the theory

The issue of the validity of comparative studies apart (§2.1), the present theory—just like any other one—is only valid as long as it can be tested by stringent counterchecking. Any theory that does not allow for testing and countercheck represents just a *probability*, a *possibility*, or at worst, plain fantasy.

The probability and the methods for comparison have been addressed above (§2, §5.1.1). In the case of myth, they include common origin, diffusion, convergence, and the underlying structure of the human mind. Preference has been given in this book to common origin. In this light, we need to assess the theory, possibility, and weight of any counterchecks and reasonable doubts in testing the Laurasian theory.

It has been shown above (§2) that the present theory can *predict* certain developments in religion in the general Laurasian area (due to path dependencies);[11] it can also predict that certain typical Laurasian features, as established by theory, will not be found in the non-Laurasian (Gondwana) areas. The latter items can serve in a *countercheck*, a test of contradictions within the theory and of possible arguments or reasonable doubt against it.

If counterchecking and testing bring up valid cases, either the theory must be adjusted (obviously, with good reasons only) or, if such counterevidence strikes at the heart of the theory, it must be abandoned, and the matter must be rethought along other lines. The present theory has, like any other one, only heuristic value. If new facts are discovered that confirm it, they are included;

however, if others emerge that seem to cast reasonable doubt or contradict it, they must be explained within reasonable limits, or parts of the theory have to be adjusted.

To look for such counterexamples is, in my view, the duty of all individual scholars. They must test their new theory *themselves* and take into account any possible and probable objection. To take a shortcut, that is, to simply propose a (nonverifiable) thesis without countercheck, may be good publicity, but it is irresponsible. A new theory may have great appeal or allure, but one should not "enjoy" its fame or notoriety—as long as it lasts—and simply wait for the inevitable indication of negative proof or denouncement by others who can show, painfully, how wrong one has been. (Such caution and painstaking countercheck-ing have delayed this book for several years.)

In the present case, however, one has to make a clear distinction between the main theory (the Laurasian story line) and incidental components (the flood myth, witches, the importance of the power of the word,[12] magic, human origins, the rainbow, and the like). The main feature, the story line approach, cannot and must not be abandoned; it is central to the theory.

As mentioned, if someone could point out either that the model of a continuous Laurasian story line from creation to destruction is wrong or that it is not unique for Laurasian myth but also found in the rest of the (Gondwana) world, I would consider myself proved wrong. For that purpose, we will scrutinize below some of the non-Laurasian mythologies of Gondwanaland, that is, those of the African, Andamanese, Papuan, and Australian areas (§5.2 sqq.). The few rudimentary, abbreviated series of myths or short story lines found in some of these mythologies (§5.3.6, 5.7) cannot produce *reasonable doubt* and do not serve as counterproof: they are limited to the emergence of humans and civilization. The typical Laurasian story line from the creation of the world to its destruction is missing. In other words, the typical accumulation of hard Laurasian data is missing in the non-Laurasian mythologies: that is, the compilation of certain myths such as the creation out of chaos and so on next to the descent of humans from a solar deity and the creation of light, all of which are typical for Laurasian mythologies (even when seen irrespective of the story line).

As indicated above (§5.1.1 sqq.), disagreements in *incidental* points, such as the quasi-universal spread of the flood myth, will not be sufficient to obliterate the theory, which is predicated on the *story line* from creation to destruction of the world (and, only secondarily, its major constituent parts). Even a certain amount of accumulation of such circumstantial counterevidence does not suffice to bring down the theory: for example, if someone were to show that certain individual items (diver, flood myth) are in fact also found in sub-Saharan Africa or in Papua/Australia, I would not concede: the main pillar of the Laurasian theory, the story line arrangement, and myths of primordial creation and impending destruction, would still stand.

***

If one were to maintain, as I mistakenly did (2001) based on limited materials, that the flood myth is a typical Laurasian feature (for details, §3.9), the expectation would be that it would *not* be found in the Gondwana areas. This claim seems to be contradicted, on the surface, by the fact that the comprehensive volume on the flood myth by A. Dundes contains one flood myth from Africa (northern Cameroon) and one from Australia.[13] However, on closer observation, it appears that the Cameroon myth (flood from a calabash)[14] is found in the northern Sahel belt, close to, or overlapping with, Laurasian mythologies that have shaped the mythologies north of sub-Saharan Africa. The Australian case is even more obvious: the myth from the Kimberleys area in western Australia includes a rock formation showing...the ark of Noah.[15] Further, Frazer's large collection of flood myths indicates that it is absent in Africa and China.[16] (Similarly, very little is found about these areas in Stith Thompson's *Motif Index*.)

However, a closer investigation (including some fairly early publications)[17] indicates quite a number of flood myths from Africa/Papua/Australia.[18] Even Baumann (in 1936) could already discuss 24 for Africa. As the discussion above (§3.9) indicates, this wealth of Gondwana flood stories requires a typical, heuristic adjustment of theory, as referred to above. As secondary diffusion of the myth to Australia and all parts of sub-Saharan Africa is unlikely, it now seems that the flood myth preexisted the origin and development of Laurasian mythology, which took place well after the exodus out of Africa. However, it is important to note, again, that the present testing and countercheck of an early claim does not destroy the theory as such:[19] the Laurasian story line can exist well without a general flood; however, the flood is indeed incorporated into many of its extant versions.[20]

***

In similar fashion, all other indications of reasonable doubt, proposals of contradictions or counterevidence, and suggestions of apparent negative proof have to be followed up and checked with Stith Thompson's and other more recent indexes.[21] Apart from these items, we also have to reckon with some Gondwana elements in Laurasian myth, by whatever process they may have arrived. This item will be discussed in some detail below (§5.6.1). In sum, while having looked out, since c. 1990, for individual items of contradiction and negative proof, I have so far not been able to find a striking case that would force me to abandon the theory. (As indicated, the case of shorter and more simple Gondwana series of tales will be discussed below; §5.3, §6.)

***

The reliability of such comparisons, as far as (enormous) time depth and (late) attestation are concerned, has been discussed above (§2.2.3), and it has been indicated that wide-ranging, mass comparison itself is a good safeguard against incidental comparison of isolated features that superficially appear to be connected (as carried out in diffusionist theories). This argument is also relevant for the following section.

§5.1.3. Diffusion versus genetic relationship

Diffusion of myths has played a major part in the discussion of theoretical models (see above, §1). As this model is diametrically opposed to that of common origin, the model proposed in this book, the evidence subsumed under diffusion can be used as a countercheck against the Laurasian theory.

Of great theoretical interest is the question of the close interlinking, or the side-by-side existence, of "genetically" transmitted mythologies (that is, via a parents-to-children type of pedigree) and of those that have arrived by diffusion.[22] Both can occur side by side within one and the same local mythology.

For example, one could try to understand large parts or maybe even the basic structure of Japanese or Chinese mythology as imports from Central Asia. They would be "texts" that arrived with and under the influence of the nomadic pastoral peoples: early on in Chinese history (c. 1200 BCE) and fairly late in Japanese history (c. 400 CE). In this case, the Central Asian influence on Shang and Zhou China might be due to direct or indirect Indo-European impact or the result of diffusion from the (Greater) Iranian area to Central Asian populations that then spread this mythology farther into China.[23] As examples, one might quote such materials as the horse and the chariot and the corresponding idea of the Sun horse, the idea of "(Father) Heaven," or the idea of the dangerous dragon that is killed early on in the mythical past,[24] which is to be contrasted with the later, beneficial dragon so typical for Chinese mythology.[25] If this proposal were true, Chinese mythology would be largely mixed with Central Asian elements. However, only a detailed comparative investigation—not one limited to Chinese materials—of the earliest evidence written on oracle bones and preserved in the oldest texts will bring about a solution to this problem; this line of questioning cannot be pursued here in any detail.

In similar fashion, if larger parts and even the basic structure of Japanese mythology were attributed to late (Kofun, c. 400 CE) horse-riding immigrants from Korea, Koguryo, and ultimately Central Asia—as has traditionally been done so far—one would have to call the Kojiki and Nihon Shoki (Kiki) ulti-mately Central Asian texts with some admixture of pre-Kofun Japanese mythology.[26] However, a sustained comparison immediately indicates that many typical East and Southeast Asian themes and topics permeate the Kiki,[27] such as those detailed in the myth of the hidden sun (§3.5.1): the crowing of roosters and so on, the contest between the fisher and hunter gods, the drawing up of land from the ocean by a fishhook or a fishline, the myth of the origin of food emerging from the body of the primordial goddess Ōgetsu (as if from a primordial Pangu/Puruṣa/Ymir), and so forth.

To illustrate this by a thought experiment: if we were ignorant of ancient European mythology and history, we might think of the various Christian myths and legends as typically European and wonder about their close relationship with those of Israel and the Near East. One might regard the Near East as an outlying area, not the actual center of diffusion. Nevertheless, we would be surprised by the large number of items in European folksongs, customs, and fairy tales that do not fit biblical topics at all, for example, the multifaceted role of the "devil." Much of their individual background would quickly be "explained" as being secondary explanations of natural phenomena and the like, which occur in other etiological tales. Many other figures, such as Jack and the Beanstalk, Jack and Jill (as an image of the sun and moon in Norse mythology), Snow White, and so on, however, do not occur in the biblical lore at all. Then, there are tales about the Milky Way as the path of the dead or the lambs, the threatening figure of the "Wild Hunter and his troop" at Christmas, and so forth.

Pursuing this kind of imagined investigation, we would, however, quickly be led to conclude that these are remnants of an older level of European myth. Biblical myth would thus be revealed as constituting a later level, irrespective of local developments and the way it had entered. It would, nevertheless, be difficult to interpret the figure of Christ. Perhaps one would think of a solar or lunar figure (resurrection); perhaps of a hero-like figure, as Lord Raglan actually proposed;[28] or of an independent European development. The general assumption would certainly be correct: that we are dealing here with several levels that could be sorted out, even without knowledge of the New Testament and older European mythology.

This sort of thought experiment (here controlled by our knowledge of actual historical facts) indicates that we will ultimately be able to discover several levels even in those mythologies for which we do not have written texts preceding the presently available information. To be sure, in such cases, it is difficult to sort out the various levels, but that, too, can be done if we look at mythology not as a haphazard collection of diffuse myths but as embedded in a well-structured story line from creation to final destruction. Within each local mythology, we must expect several opposing groups of gods as well as an opposition between gods and demons and, furthermore, several levels of beings, such as humans, spirits, and gods. If this is done, to return to Japanese myth, its diverse elements, such as the goddess of food (next to the creation of animals etc. in the early chapters of the Kiki) or the idea of pulling up land with a fishhook (next to the creation of land by Izanagi/Izanami), will clearly stand out from the rest of the texts.

If, in this way, Laurasian mythological structure is compared with the individual structure of a certain mythology, the "foreign," new, or pre-Laurasian elements (see below, §5.2 sqq., §6) will stand out.[29] Some such later additions will now be discussed.

§5.1.4. Later additions

One such case is that of the dog in Indo-European and Chinese mythology, where it appears as hellhound, while it is not very prominent in Amerindian mythology.[30] This would indicate the relative and absolute age of common Laurasian traits, to which the hellhound theme was added in Eurasia, at a time later than the migration to the Americas (c. 20,000 BCE). The matter can be closely linked to the domestication of the dog at c. 15,000 BCE (§4.1, 4.4.4).[31] If the former case holds, dogs could not have been part of pre-domestication Laurasian mythology.[32]

Similarly, the case of the "sun horses" is Eurasian—but obviously not in American (and Polynesian) myths. The mytheme of the horses drawing the chariot of the sun is prominent in Greek and early Indian myth. Horses were domesticated around the fourth millennium BCE and used for drawing vehicles even later: heavy wagons existed in Europe around 3500–3000 BCE, and spoke-wheeled chariots were invented only at c. 2000 BCE. The seminomadic Central Asian tribes and then the Near Eastern people added the horse to their mythology around that time—just as some American Indians of the steppes did much later, in the later half of the second millennium.

Clearly, we cannot expect the horse to be an important part of original Laurasian mythology. However, it could be introduced at any later stage, as soon as it became important, a prestige animal. As mentioned, the horse was even introduced into Native American mythology, for example, that of the Lakota (Sioux), even though the main animal in their myth is the buffalo. Its introduction into Lakota myth clearly happened after the actual import and spread of horses through the prairies in the 16th and 17th centuries. Nevertheless, the myth of the hidden sun, children of the Sun, and so on (§3.2 sqq., 3.8) is found—without the horse—even in the Americas and in Southeast Asia and thus is much older than c. 10,000–20,000 BCE.

Another surprising item is the relative absence of chicken and pigs in Laurasian mythology.[33] True, they occur in some local mythologies or rituals,[34] but they are not central to these mythologies at all. If Laurasian mythology indeed arose in the Greater Near East or in West Asia, one would not expect them to be represented, as both animals clearly stem from Southeast Asia. Indeed, they are prominent in southeastern Eurasian and Melanesian myth and ritual. In sum, they do not fit the Laurasian scheme. The matter may have some bearing on the discussion of when and how Laurasian mythology was introduced to Southeast and East Asia (§4.3.6).

In this way, several layers of the development of Laurasian mythology can be discerned that may help in developing the general scheme as well as the core and minor additions to it. It is important to investigate such details in a study of regional subsets of Laurasian mythology (§2.3).

Some of the items discussed in this section clearly spread by secondary diffusion and were integrated into Laurasian mythology. As such, they can be regarded as additional materials within the framework and theory of Laurasian origins. The same principle applies to secondarily spread materials found in Gondwana mythology, which will be discussed next.

■ §5.2. BEYOND LAURASIA: GONDWANA MYTHOLOGY

This section will attempt to show in some detail that sub-Saharan Africa, Australia, the Andaman Islands, and New Guinea do not participate in Laurasian mythology. Therefore, various Gondwana mythologies are explored, starting with the most isolated ones, those of Australia and Tasmania (§5.3.2 sqq.); we will then proceed with those of Melanesia, including New Guinea, the Solomon Islands, and so on. The isolated Negrito tribes of the Philippines, Malaya, and the Andaman Islands as well as the Vedda in Sri Lanka and the Todas of the South Indian Nilgiri Mountains can only be briefly mentioned here.[35] Finally, the extensive mythologies of sub-Saharan Africa will be reviewed in some detail.

Before even beginning to do so, however, one may object that reconstructing mythology for such long time distances is virtually impossible. For example, in the related field of comparative linguistics, some orthodox Indo-European linguists maintain that it is impossible to reconstruct languages from more than 6,000 years before the present, due to the increasing uncertainty of the limited number of reconstructed sounds (and meanings) involved and due to the steadily increasing number of incidental correspondences. Similarly, one may object that mythological reconstructions are equally difficult to prove, as they are made on the basis of disparate myths found over a large area and as they require a common ancestral mythology transmitted over several tens of thousands of years.

However, in both cases, the proof of the pudding is in the eating. If some linguists can show—by employing standard Indo-European tools of comparison—that very early, pre-Indo-European language families (such as Afro-Asiatic and Macro-Caucasian) *do* exist, there is no reason to stick to the artificially imposed time limit of 4000 BCE. Similarly, reconstructions of early mythologies that precede the Indo-European, Semitic, and Austronesian ones and so on (§2.2–3) by 10,000 or more years can be made probable by detecting their common motifs, their structures, and eventually, their narrational frameworks. Such a case will be presented below for Gondwana mythology; it can be tested for consistency and comparability with Laurasian myth.

To return to the aim of this section: in the spirit of testing and counterchecking the theory proposed in this book, we have to peruse the collections of Gondwana myths and ascertain whether they contain the basic structure and elements of Laurasian mythology or not. If these indeed exist, we have to determine whether they are intrusive (coming from Eurasia; see §5.7)[36] or whether they may represent archaic forms of certain Eurasian myths: that is, whether they are part, together with the Eurasian substrata, of a still older Gondwana or even Pan-Gaean layer of myths (§6).

As will be readily seen, the mythologies of these areas differ so much from Laurasian ones that they cannot be included in the Laurasian scheme. Most notable is the highlighted absence of myths of primordial creation and final destruction. The question of how the universe and the world came into being is simply not asked.[37] This has recently been expressed eloquently, as quoted above (§3), by H. Hochegger:

> Congolese creation myths do not seek to explain, for example, the creation of heaven and earth (cosmology).... There is hardly any notion here of an ancient source of all things, placed at the beginning of a long history.... The focus of mythological interest is on the concrete questions of human life.[38]

In other words, Congolese and other sub-Saharan African mythologies have made the choice to see the world and the universe in human terms only, as related to the emergence and sustenance of human beings. This particular trait is not limited to Africa. Laurasian mythology, too, insists on homologies between the fate of the world and that of human beings. However, the African way of looking at the world is special, in that it is not interested in ultimate origins, while the Laurasian one expressly is.

Similarly, Melanesian mythology does not tell of creation of the world but of that of the surroundings and of humans. In Leenhardt's words: "The original order of the world is generally attributed to these benevolent gods [*bao*]. It is not a matter of creation ex nihilo. The *baos* created the islands."[39]

Hochegger's view is echoed by several other scholars dealing with all of African mythology, such as Bauman and Bastide.[40] They stress that African mythology is characterized by a lack of distinction between profane and religion; the whole of human existence, all actions in life and culture, is integrated into myth.[41] Myth is reflected in society and civilization at every step. It is taught to initiates as a symbolic, complete theory of knowledge.

Melanesian myth has a similar function. It

> is rather lived than considered and it is less a system of symbols than the totality of factors that act between humans and nature, between woman and totem...as if the individuals were still embedded in entities, as if they had not yet been separated from society and cosmos.[42]

Or as Leenhardt puts it:[43]

> The Melanesian's mythic view. He is not aware of what we call "myth." ... He creates identifications by means of representations... [such as] the identity of structure and substance between the plant kingdom and the self.[44]
>
> The Melanesian projects himself into this world. He does not distinguish between reality and his own psychic life, between his self and the world.[45]
>
> He plays a quasi-cosmic role.[46]

> The Melanesian myth is lived before it is formulated, fixed into a mythology, and revivified by ritual.[47]
>
> Myth is always at the surface of their daily life. Though they may not be able to tell it in stories, it is lived.[48]

I believe it is here that we can observe the roots of the differences between Gondwana and Laurasian mythology. Laurasian myth seeks to explain the *origins* of things, gods, and humans as a means to understand them fully. (As we all know, even small children tend to ask endless questions such as, "Why is the sky blue?") The ultimate questions on *first origins* are not asked in Gondwana myths; one is interested, at best, in the origin of one's land or of humans and their condition.[49]

In Laurasian myth, however, the (typically shamanic) belief is that knowledge of origin establishes power over the item in question. (Other requirements are its name and form, *nāma* and *rūpa* in early Sanskrit; the word and naming things are important in Mesopotamia, the Bible, Old Egypt, Old Japan, the Mayan Popol Vuh, etc.) One can establish verbal and material equivalences and correlations between all entities and use them in magic and sorcery,[50] as typically practiced in the Laurasian area.[51]

In Melanesia, by contrast, there is no distinction, according to Leenhardt,[52] among word, thought, discourse, and action; all are expressed by *no*, "the word," which emerges from the heart and the intestines. It is enduring, a solid reality.[53] Yet identifications between the plant kingdom and the self are made (see above).

Correlations, however, are also found in African mythology: this always puts "distance between the various levels of reality: there exists a mimesis between the cosmic, sociological and individual, as if the world was divided into several well-cordoned off layers which, nevertheless, are analogous due to their mutual correspondence."[54] Everything can become a symbol, which takes its place in certain series. A multiplicity of correlations and analogies ensues.

Though the use of correlations is thus a general human trait,[55] nevertheless the way they are employed and the use they are put to differ in the two regions. For example, African sorcery lays greater stress on objects used, "fetishes,"[56] as seen in Caribbean Voodoo. Little care is given to the actual wording employed in sorcery. The use of the fetish struck even the first, Portuguese observers in West Africa of the 15th century.

Conversely, Laurasian magic prominently employs the power of the word,[57] the magical formulas establishing correlations, along with the pertinent actions, whether in the Trobriand Islands, in India, with the Austronesian Ami in Taiwan, or in ancient Japan. The power of (well-formulated) speech is very important, as has appeared time and again.[58] Not just the Christian account of creation stresses that "in the beginning, there was the word." In the Vedic Indian and Zoroastrian theory of ritual (implied in the texts), thought, speech, and action must concur to be effective (Ved. *manas*/Avestan *manah*, *vāc*/*vāc*, *karman*/*šiiaoθna*). The same concept is also found in Christian thought (no doubt copied from the Zoroastrians). Word and action thus must concur in ritual and in sorcery,[59] while the role of the object involved as "mediator," for example, a figure representing an enemy, is less important.

Keeping these differences in mind will help us to better understand the great divide between the two mythological regions, Laurasia and Gondwana. Unlike Laurasian insistence on the "word" of origins, on the secret or sacred tales of origins (often known only to initiates), the Gondwana stress is on remembering the first ancestors in ritual, to use the Australian term, on Dreamtime, and on charter myths for humans living now.[60]

There also is a difference in time scale. The Indo-Pacific area is of great importance as it has preserved, in the Andamans and in Australia, Stone Age hunting societies and, in Papua New Guinea, an archaic form of food production, horticulture. Among these populations, the highland Papuas, the Andamanese, and the Australians were least influenced from the outside, that is, until colonization. (As we will see, sub-Saharan Africa has been much more disturbed by influences coming from the north of the continent.)

***

The Sahul Land populations also provide some welcome *absolute dates*.[61] Immigration into Australia is currently put at 40,000 (or even 60,000) BCE, based on archaeological remains (see §4.4) and increasingly so also on the time line provided by genetics (§4.3). The Andamans, too, were settled early. Archaeology and genetics have recently shown that the Andamanese belong to some of the early emigrants from Africa who reached the South Asian subcontinent.[62]

In contrast, the Amerindian myths reflect the Laurasian scheme. While some of them, such as the Dene/Navajo in North America, and the Inuit/Eskimo represent late intrusions from Siberia, the bulk of the Amerindian population is older, providing a date (*ante quem*) for the origin of Eurasian mythology. It must be older than the first immigration at c. 20,000 years ago (or, at minimum, at 11,500 BCE).[63]

This means that certain aspects of all Out of Africa mythology must have been present at 40,000 BP, while those of Laurasian mythology must have been present by 20,000 BP at the latest but probably much earlier. A heuristic scenario may be (§7) that Laurasian mythology evolved—probably in Greater Southwest Asia—around 40,000 BP, the time of the great "artistic explosion," but it did not reach Australia, whose early immigrants had moved to Southeast Asia and Sahul Land well before. Entry into Australia at 60,000–40,000 BP precedes the spread of Laurasian mythology.

▪ §5.3. GONDWANA MYTHOLOGIES

§5.3.1. Sub-Saharan Africa, the Andamans, New Guinea, and Australia/Tasmania—An overview

In the four areas to be surveyed here in brief form, we must expect very old materials. However, our enthusiasm must unfortunately be tempered, first, due to the purely oral way that mythology has been preserved there and, second, due to the complicated histories of initial and subsequent settlement of the individual areas—as far as it been detected so far by archaeology and now increasingly also by genetics.

All these regions have some of their own problems in the attestation and development of their mythologies. A few of them are rather limited, such as a certain amount of Papua influence on northwestern and northeastern Australian mythology, while the southeast (and Tasmania) are more isolated and archaic in this respect.[64]

Similarly, the Melanesian mythologies have been isolated for many thousands of years (especially those in the New Guinea highlands, in the Solomons, and beyond), though on their fringes, the Polynesian languages and their version of Laurasian mythology have exerted some influence. The juxtaposition of Laurasian-influenced mythologies with typical Melanesian ones clearly indicates the differences between the two types. In addition, anthropologists have recently shown that even the "isolated" highland tribes are connected by trade, directly or indirectly, with the coastal areas and therefore are prone to potential outside influences. Caution is thus advised in judging each of the items to be discussed.

The Andaman Islands, too, have been isolated for long spells of time. There may have been a passing period of direct continental influences by Laurasian, Austro-Asiatic-speaking groups around 3000 BCE, as is clearly seen with their Nicobar neighbors, who speak Austro-Asiatic. However, Andaman mythology has reverted to typical non-Laurasian themes that survive on some islands until today; even now, some tribes have never been contacted, such as the Sentinel and until very recently, the Jarawa. (In addition, there are the little-studied Shompen, a non-Austronesian tribe in the Nicobars.)

Africa, finally, poses special problems. The sub-Saharan part of the continent has not been as isolated as the areas discussed above. Anthropologists such as Frobenius and Baumann have long pointed out that the various cultures of West Africa, from Guinea to Nigeria and Cameroon, have experienced varying degrees of influence from the Sahel steppe belt. One can therefore expect, and will indeed find, numerous cases of impact by the Laurasian mythologies of the Sahel cultures. However, just as in the Melanesian case, the juxtaposition of "typical" (original?) African mythologies (à la Frobenius)[65] with those influenced from the north is very instructive.

This situation is quite similar to that of the extended East African belt stretching from Kenya southward to Zimbabwe and the eastern parts of South Africa, where communication was facilitated by a savanna-like landscape. Here, too, northern mythologies have heavily influenced the sub-Saharan ones. The Kenya–South African belt may be called the East African "North–South Highway" (§5.3.5).

All these problems will be discussed in some detail in this chapter. At the outset, it is important to point out that we cannot expect completely "pristine" mythologies even in the relatively isolated parts of the globe. Nevertheless, the bulk of the accumulated and mass-compared evidence will allow us to define original themes and motifs from those acquired later on.

***

As indicated, the first major problem encountered is the shallow attestation of the mythology of these areas. Most of it has been recorded only over the past 200 years or even less. Many of our records are only contemporaneous. This compares poorly with the ancient traditions of the Near East, India, and China and even those of the Americas (Aztec, Maya, Inca, Iroquois, recorded shortly after 1500 CE). However, in some areas, this deficiency can be counterbalanced by the testimony of early rock art (North, East, and South Africa; India; New Guinea; and Australia; see §4.4, §7.1). Though such art does not come with a label and its interpretation frequently is tenuous, it still provides some insights into the world of belief of these early populations.

***

The other problem we have to deal with is the history of the peopling of these areas. One would assume that Australia is the perfect case for an isolated mythology, descended from that of the first immigrants at c. 40,000–60,000 BCE. But, in reality, the continent was intermittently linked and finally severed from New Guinea only after the end of the last Ice Age, around 6000 BCE. Some late influx of Papua populations and their ideas may therefore be expected. Recent genetic and linguistic data have further muddled the picture.[66] The connections between Australian and Indian traits have been attributed to the influence of or an influx of an "Indian" population from Southeast Asia only some 5,000 years ago, which may be linked to the introduction of small tools and later, of the dingo dog. Redd et al. assume a mid-Holocene common ancestry of aboriginal Australians and populations of the Indian Subcontinent at a time that corresponds with changes between 5,000 and 3,000 years ago, such as the introduction of the dingo,[67] the Australian Small Tool Tradition,[68] the appearance of plant-processing technologies, and the (assumed) date for the expansion of the Pama-Nyungan language in most of Australia.[69] They note that, while there is no anthropological consensus, "the former three changes may have links to India, perhaps the most relevant of which is the introduction of the dingo, whose ocean transit was almost certainly on board a boat." In addition, they refer to the linguist Dixon,[70] who (like others before and after him) has pointed to similarities between Dravidian and the Pama-Nyungan languages.[71] Redd et al. conclude that "the combined genetic (Y chromosome and mitochondrial DNA) and anthropological evidence supports Holocene contact between the Indian subcontinent and Australia."[72] This connection is now explicitly denied by Hudjashov (see below).[73]

Further, the extermination of the Tasmanians by British settlers, carried out in the 19th century, has robbed us of the chance to investigate their mythology and language in any detail. This would have been very important as the isolated island was finally severed from Australia by c. 5000 BCE, at the latest. There are many indications that the inhabitants of Tasmania were different from those of the Australian mainland. Likewise, some linguists see connections between Tasmanian and the Indo-Pacific language group established by J. Greenberg. It includes Papuan, Andamanese, and, as some now claim, also the isolated Kusunda of central Nepal.[74]

All of the above archaeological, genetic, and linguistic evidence apart, there also is the fact that specialists have divided Australian mythology into three areas: first, the north (Arnhem Land), which supposedly saw Papua influence; second, the southeast and also Tasmania, both of which are markedly different;[75] and third, the rest of the continent, where we have to reckon with multiple crisscrossing movements over the past tens of thousands of years.[76]

Dixon even maintains that Australia was an early continent on its own,[77] a large linguistic area that was *not* influenced by Papuan languages (except in the Torres Strait). This is remarkable, as Australia was finally separated from New Guinea only some 10,000–7,000 years ago;[78] ideas may have crossed language boundaries here too (§2).

The north is the homeland to languages clustered around Arnhem Land, while the rest of the continent has been covered by the Pama-Nyungan language family.[79] In Arnhem Land, the languages are bundled most closely, a fact that generally points to original habitat.[80] (A typical example is the dense packing of a large variety of English dialects in Britain, as opposed to just a few in the recent spread zones in America, South Africa, Australia, New Zealand, and South Asia.) Fortunately, Arnhem Land has preserved some degree of autonomy so that the Aboriginals may survive there as a people, along with their culture and languages, helped by the mineral wealth of the area.

The same kinds of problems of spread and secondary overlay are encountered in New Guinea, the Andamans, and especially Africa. As we will see below, in the case of Africa, they range from difficult to surmountable. Obviously, in all the cases mentioned so far, the Laurasian traits have to be carefully "subtracted" from what we find in Gondwana myths. This can best be done by starting out from the rich mythologies of isolated areas, such as highland New Guinea or the backwoods of Central Africa.

***

The subsequent evaluation indicates that the four major types of non-Laurasian mythologies mentioned share a certain amount of data in common, notably the lack of true creation stories and the lack of a continuous story line. (On the other hand, they agree in some individual motifs, such as human origin out of trees.) Keeping these questions in mind, we will first take a look at the three mythological areas of Australia and Tasmania.

§5.3.2. Australia

First, in Australia, the origin of the world is rarely described: only the central Australian Aranda (ironically) tell that the earth gradually grew out of a large ocean. As this is an isolated occurrence (just like some rather new introductions such as an ark in the western Australian flood myth),[81] the question arises whether this mytheme is old with them and whether it indeed represents a remnant of an old Afro-Australian layer that can also be found in Eurasia. This clearly needs more detailed research that cannot be pursued here but will be touched upon in this chapter.

However, of the three major cultural areas mentioned, the southeast (and apparently, Tasmania)[82] stresses origins from a heavenly All-Father—now seen as the star Altair—called Mungan-ngaua, Mani-ngata (Our father), Bunjil (Eagle hawk),[83] Bajaume/Baiame,[84] Daramulun, or Nurunberi.[85] In the north and northwest, by contrast, we find an All-Mother, the Rainbow snake (Ngalijod or Wallaganda), for whom West Papuan influence is seen.[86] In central Australia, however, the ancestors and totems of the patrilineal clans are the focus of emergence myths; for them, eastern Papuan influence has been assumed.

These claims are in need of detailed study, preferably on a broader comparative basis, such as that of the proposed Gondwana mythology. Even now, however, we can say that Papuan influence cannot be correlated with that of the *original* settlement by speakers of Australian languages that are altogether different from New Guinea languages.

As mentioned, New Guinea and Australia have been linked by land bridges on and off during the past 60,000 years. Serious Papua influences must be of a late date, most probably occurring during the Last Glacial Maximum, when Australia was connected with New Guinea from c. 26,000 until 10,000–7,000 years ago; similarly, land bridges with Tasmania existed between 22,800 and 8,000 years ago. The western land bridge with New Guinea across the Arafura Sea flooded around 8000 BCE, leaving western Papuan languages stranded in Timor and also leaving genetic as well as religious influences in northwestern Australia. The eastern land bridge across the Torres Strait flooded only around 8000–5000 BCE,[87] leaving some eastern Papuan religious influence in the northeastern and subsequently, the central parts of Australia.[88] Clendon now argues that the split between the northern languages (Kimberleys, Arnhem Land) and the rest of the continent (Pama-Nyungan languages) is due to their origin in widely separate regions of Sahul at an early time.[89] After the last Ice Age, c. 9,000 years ago, Pama-Nyungan is proposed to have spread inland from a northeast coast refuge, while the northern languages moved in from the now flooded Gulf of Carpentaria.[90]

On the other hand, if aspects of the southeastern Australian and Tasmanian languages and myths have preserved the older state of things, their spread southeastward must be dated to the original dispersal, probably out of Arnhem Land, after c. 60–40 kya.[91] As mentioned, Tasmania was linked with Australia by a land bridge around 38,000 years ago,[92] settled around 35,000 BCE, and finally separated from Australia after the last Ice Age, between 12,000 and 5000 BCE.

In all these areas mutual influences in Stone Age times can thus be assumed, extending until fairly recently. However, outside influence, for example, the one assumed from India since Huxley,[93] including the introduction of the dingo by new human arrivals from India at c. 4,000–3,500 years ago,[94] along with new stone tool types (small tools with backed blades),[95] is still disputed.[96] Hudjashov expressly denies any recent genetic influence from India,[97] both for mtDNA (which has only old M- and N-derived lineages) and for NRY, which shows a new marker, M347, that distinguishes all Australian NRY C types from Asian ones. All such migrations are considerably older than that of speakers of the Pama-Nyungan languages. They spread nearly all over the continent, except for the north (Arnhem Land, Kimberleys). The spread is traditionally put around 4000 BCE or, according to Clendon, much earlier, after the last Ice Age at c. 9000 BCE.[98]

The mythological scheme sketched above, if correct, would have some southeastern Pama-Nyungan groups, opposite Tasmania, preserve the original Australian mythology, which elsewhere was gradually influenced and even superseded by myths from Papua lands, while preserving some underlying traits.[99] Indeed, the southeast also differs in some linguistic features from the rest of the continent.[100] In studying "original" Australian mythology, the southeast thus acquires great importance. Unfortunately this is also the area that was earliest settled by Britons and where many tribes have disappeared.

Second, a comparison with Tasmanian myths is important, due to their repeated isolation from the rest of the continent, the final one after c. 8000–5000 BCE. The southeastern myths about a high god, "our Father," Mungan-ngaua or Bunjil, are only told during secret initiation rituals, which would vouch for the antiquity of the mytheme: it cannot be attributed to early British influence.[101] The belief may also be reflected in Tasmanian myth (§5.3.2.1). At any rate, even the southeastern myths do not constitute a cosmogony of Laurasian type as the first stages of creation are missing. Mungan-ngaua was a trickster-type deity on earth, and his son and his wife are the ancestors of humans, after a great fire or flood had killed the humans who came before. (A similar situation is found in

Tasmania.) Mungan-ngaua then left the earth for heaven. His cult is found in the southeast, below a line from Murray River to Cardwell in Queensland.[102]

With other tribes, the earth opens, and the Aborigines emerge,[103] a motif found also in Meso- and South America as well as in Indian myth.[104] Yet, even though southeastern Australian mythology vaguely resembles the Eurasian one in having a primordial trickster god or hero,[105] there is no stress on cosmology.

In contrast, in Arnhem Land, the original deity is an All-Mother, the Rainbow serpent Ngalijod or Wallaganda (who is also identified with the Milky Way).[106] Inside her, she carried her children, who became the ancestors of the Aborigines. It should be noted that the mytheme of the rainbow snake is widespread in East and South Africa, Iran, India (Munda), Burma, Sumatra, and even South America and may belong to the original Pan-Gaean level.[107] As in many Gondwana mythologies, it is clearly stated in Arnhem Land that sky and earth existed in the beginning.[108] However, there also is a tradition about Ungud (Snake), *the* ultimate cause or being.[109]

Third, there is central and northeastern Australia (Queensland), and again, these are areas exhibiting some linguistic differences from the rest of the continent. They are supposed to have undergone mythological influence from eastern Papua New Guinea. Here, the Aranda and other tribes have a strongly patrilineal social setup, which ultimately points both to an All-Father-type myth as in southeastern Australia and to the northern Australian Ungud snake.[110] Some of the detailed, and perhaps best-known, central Australian mythology of the Aranda is presented here as an extensive specimen.[111] It should be kept in mind, however, that this is the retelling of a scholar, combining information gathered from many informants and over a long period of research. It is unclear whether the myth, as told here, was ever related by an Aranda shaman in this comprehensive form; the case is similar to that of the extensive oral texts of the Dayak that have never been collated by local priests (§6.1):

> Throughout the Aranda area it was generally believed that both the sky and the earth were eternal, and that each of them had its own set of supernatural beings.... [T]he sky [was] inhabited by an emu-footed Great Father (*kŋáritja*),[112] who was also the eternal youth (*altjíran ṇḍítja*). The Great Father had dog-footed wives and many sons and daughters—all the males being emu-footed and all the females dog-footed. They lived in an eternal green land[113]... through which the Milky Way flowed like a broad river.... All these sky dwellers were as ageless as the stars....
>
> The power of death was limited to the earth, and men only had to die because all connections had been severed between the sky and the earth. Traditions about "broken ladders" were found at many ceremonial sites....[114]
>
> Two Ntjíkantja brothers, like the sun, the moon, the Seven Sisters and the evening star, had once emerged from the earth and had wandered about on its surface like all other earth-born totemic ancestors...who remained on earth after completing their labors finally grew old, returned into the ground, and sank back into

ever-lasting sleep. Their fellows who rose into the sky, on the other hand, changed into ageless celestial bodies that knew neither decay nor death.... The original sky dwellers[, however,] took no interest in anything that happened on the earth beneath them. Hence the true sky dwellers were not honored in song or in ritual.... [I]t would be impossible to regard the emu-footed Great Father in the sky of western Aranda mythology as a supreme Being in any sense of the word.... Nowhere were the links between human Time and changeless Eternity stronger in religious thought than in Central Australia.... [I]t was the very strength of these links that explains the complete absence of formal prayers and sacrifices for the propitiation of deities....

The earth like the sky had always existed...and had been the home of supernatural beings. At the beginning of time the earth had looked like a featureless, desolate plain.[115]...It was covered in eternal darkness, lit only by the distant fires bordering the Milky Way; for the sun,[116] the moon, and the Evening Star, too, were still slumbering under the earth's cold crust.[117]...[A] vague form of human life existed in the shape of semi-embryonic masses of half-developed infants...[at the later] salt lakes or waterholes.... Only below the surface of the earth did life exist in its fullness, in the form of thousands of uncreated supernatural beings that had always existed; but even these were still slumbering in eternal sleep.

Time began when these supernatural beings awakened from their sleep.[118] They broke through the surface of the earth; and their birthplaces became the first sites on the earth to be impregnated with their life and power. The earth was flooded with light for the first time: for the sun rose out of the ground.... The supernatural beings...varied greatly in their appearance. Some rose in animal shapes, resembling kangaroos, emus, and the like. Others emerged...like perfectly formed men and women. Both sexes were represented among them.... Those beings that looked like animals...generally thought and acted like humans; conversely, those in human form could change at will into the particular animal with which they were invisibly linked. Only plant shapes were unknown.... [T]he ancestors and ancestress linked with them were invariably visualized as beings human in form.[119]

After emerging...these..."totemic ancestors" moved about on the surface of the earth[120] [and] brought into being all the physical features of the Central Australian landscape.... [T]here was not a single striking physical feature which was not connected with an episode in one of the many sacred myths, or with a verse in one of the many scared songs...[that] were accepted as compositions by the supernatural beings themselves. Similarly, all ritual...was believed to have been instituted by [them]. Hence among the Aranda, the sacred songs...the body decorations worn by the actors impersonating the totemic ancestors, and all sacred ritual, were regarded as eternal and unalterable.

Some of the totemic ancestors assumed the functions of "culture heroes." Among the most important of these were the personages who first liberated the semi-embryonic masses of humanity into the fullness of life, and then taught the[m] the most important things necessary for their survival.... [They] taught men how to fashion spears and shields, how to make fire, and how to use it for cooking food. Numerous other non-sacred traditions existed about [them].

After the[y] had accomplished their labours and completed their wanderings, overpowering weariness fell upon them.... [Their newly shaped] world...was that mythical Golden World.... They were personages living in a world where the human notions of good and evil had but shadowy meaning.... [but] not beyond the reach of all moral laws. The slaughter[121] of the grim Eagle Brothers... by the Mice Men and the annihilation of the bloodthirsty and cannibalistic Bat Men...by a single honest champion who lived...in the Northern wastelands...showed that...there still existed some indefinable, nameless Force which was capable of bringing about the final downfall of even the most powerful supernatural beings....

There was one further limitation to the[ir] might and power.... [T]hey were subject to age and to decay. They could be hurt and wounded, and they knew the meaning of pain. [But] they were immortal, and even those who had been "killed" by other totemic ancestors still lived on in the form of *tjúrunga*. All of them, however, in the end, sank back into their first state of sleep...and their bodies vanished into the ground...or turned into rocks, trees, or *tjúrunga* objects. [Such sacred places] could be approached only by initiated men, and only on special ceremonial occasions.... Death had been brought into the world by the acts of some of these supernatural beings. The sun, the moon, and the rest of the earth-born celestial bodies now rose into the sky and the world of labour, pain, and death that men and women have known ever since came into being.[122]

The question, put earlier, about the relationship between Stone Age art and Laurasian mythology (§4.4.1) must now be asked again, in a more refined version: does Australian mythology (or the three versions of it) reflect the early migration from Africa (via India), with incipient, "partial" Laurasian characteristics? Or have the Australians just preserved a late stage of Pan-Gaean mythology, which already had, for example, a world tree?[123] To answer this question would depend on a secure dating of the (so far not yet) reconstructed pan-Australian mythology, as based on its three major varieties, and on the date of the entry of the speakers of ur-Australian into the continent (c. 40,000–60,000 BCE) and influences, now genetically confirmed, from New Guinea during the last Ice Age.

These immigrants came along the beaches of the Indian Ocean, bordered by the evergreen tropical forests of Southeast Asia that persisted even through the Ice Age, when much of Asia was desert, steppe, or tundra. The ancestors of the Australians must have been people of an environment like the one still seen in the Andaman Islands, with the Semangs in Malaysia, and among other Southeast Asian Negrito tribes.[124] While we do not have archaeological remains of the early artistic expressions of these populations, Australian rock art belongs, by all accounts, to a fairly early stage of post-exodus art (40 kya, 17 kya in the Bradshaw area of the northwestern Kimberleys).[125] Nevertheless, once in Australia, the immigrants' newly evolving steppe and desert hunting culture (as detailed above) is close, due to climatic conditions, to that of parts of Africa, that is, of the San (Bushmen), Hadza, and Sandawe.[126]

§5.3.2.1. Tasmania

In view of the isolated nature of Tasmania, an additional, somewhat extensive sketch must be added that deals with the few scattered notes that we have of Tasmanian religion and ritual. As all Aboriginals on the island were exterminated by white settlers or died of disease during the first half of the 19th century, and only the Anglicized descendants of unions between white men and aboriginal women survive, it is hard to present a clear account of the religion of the nine (or more) major tribes of the island. Our records are based on the observations of the few early French and British expeditions in the late 18th and early 19th centuries and the more extensive records, of varying quality, of the 19th century.[127]

Tasmania is of special importance because of its early settlement and subsequent isolation from the Australian mainland. As mentioned, Tasmania was separated from Australia after the last Ice Age by the Bass Channel, c. 7,000 or 8,000 to 14,000 years ago.[128] However, the first settlements are dated at 35,000 BP.[129] The latest land connections between Australia and Tasmania existed between c. 22,800 and c. 8,000 years ago, via two land bridges at the western and eastern ends of the Bass Straight. This would have allowed for some influence from the conservative southeastern Australian region. Tasmanian culture and religion thus might also provide a glimpse of parts of (southeastern) Australian religion and culture as they existed some 8,000 years ago, notwithstanding some subsequent local Tasmanian developments, also visible in late Pleistocene (and later) rock paintings (hand stencils).[130] There exist quite complex petroglyphs (of unknown meaning) on the west coast, at Marrawah, and simpler ones on the east coast. Some of these designs were also found on the inside walls of bark huts erected over graves,[131] and some of them were used in the scarring of people's skin. The east coast petroglyphs are much simpler, merely branched lines. The earliest remains of human designs found so far are handprints in deep caves and rock shelters.

Tasmanian culture was in many ways simpler than that of Australia. There were no bows or spear-throwers, just wooden spears and clubs. There were none of the more complex microliths that arrived in Australia only some 5,000–3,000 years ago but, instead, simple flake tools, such as stone choppers, scrapers, and so on made by flaking technology, especially of spongolite. Also, there were no hafted stones (as used in axes), or boomerangs, or wooden dishes.[132] The dingo that arrived in Australia about the same time as the microliths is missing as well. However, there are a number of similarities with southeastern Australia, such as in basket weaving, the practice of cremation and subsequent burial of the ashes, and, sometimes, putting the dead body in a hollow tree before cremation (see §5.4).

One may add that the southeast of Australia is sometimes linguistically separated from other areas as well, though there is little resemblance between the Australian and Tasmanian languages that goes beyond the phonological system.[133] However, some southeastern Australian languages have (retained?) initial consonant clusters that are typical for Tasmanian,[134] and there are some words that are common between these southeastern languages and Tasmanian that may not necessarily be due to late (19th-century) migration of a few Australian Aboriginals into Tasmania.[135]

However, T. Usher has now shown that the Tasmanian languages correspond closely to the Solomonic branch of Melanesian.[136] He assumes a migration by boat, as was necessary to settle the distant Solomon Islands.[137] Earlier, Tasmanian had already been included by the late J. Greenberg in his Indo-Pacific language family,[138] which ranges from the Andamans to New Guinea and now also includes the isolated Kusunda in central Nepal.

We do not know much about the prehistory of the Tasmanians on the mainland before their separation after the Ice Age; however, it has been proposed that a certain pygmoid Australian tribe (Yidinj)[139] in the Cairns Rain Forest in northern Queensland would be of "Tasmanian" physical type.[140] Such features, too, would link Tasmanian with New Guinea.

***

Tasmanian Aboriginal religion has often been described by 19th-century British authors—no doubt due to lacuneous information—as devoid of "the idea of a supreme being" or being devoid of "any rites or ceremonies" and even of "any religion." However, the Tasmanians clearly distinguished between good and evil spirits (called "devils" by the British).[141] W. Schmidt lists just one name for the (supreme?) beneficial spirit, Tiggana Marrabona,[142] whom his source defined as a "spirit of great creative power."[143] He does not list the names of other good spirits such as Moihernee or Parlede (or Parledee,[144] Párllerdé), the "superior being" who lives in the sky.[145] The good spirit was also called Tyerenoyerpanner (Ben Lommel area)[146] or Pluckerteeburrer (Little Swanport);[147] Plomley in addition lists the following:[148] Loihanner (eastern area), Loinermurergartar (north), Moonerlowndeender, Moreretenner, Nareter, Noihenner,[149] and Nounedooppenner.[150]

It appears that two male spirits or stars in the Milky Way were active at the time of the creation of the "land" (Tasmania), the islands, and humans.[151] The two spirits are named Moihernee and Droemerdeene but also go by many other, in part regional, names as well.[152] Droemerdeener is the bright star in the south (apparently, Canopus), who appears "out of the sea."[153]

The two spirits Moihernee and Droemerdeene fought in heaven, and Moihernee was hurled or fell down from the sky and landed on Louisa Bay (Coxes Bight) where he is represented by a large stone; apparently he looked like

an Aborigine. He fought many evil spirits at Togee Law.[154] His wife soon followed him but entered the sea. Rain falling from the sky impregnated her, and
they had many children. Moihernee/Moilnee is apparently also seen as Laller, a
small ant, who is involved in the creation of humans (which, again, looks like a
totem ancestor). Moihernee or Moilnee created humans and kangaroos "out of
the ground" (from clay?). It seems that there was not much difference between
the two, as the early human had no legs but a kangaroo tail and a joint leg. The
other spirit, Droemerdeene, saw it and helped out the first human (Parlevar) by
cutting the tail and furnishing him with legs that have joints, so that he could
stand up and walk.[155]

The creation of humans is otherwise attributed to the two stars in the Milky
Way, Pumpermehowle (or Pumperneowlle) and Pineterrinner ("stops a long
way off," apparently in the sky).[156] Laller, an ant-like form of Moilnee/Moihernee,
also "first made natives" and "perforated the penis."[157] This limited information
nevertheless reminds one of Australian totemistic myth and the circumcision or
subincision practiced in central Australia (that is said to have eastern Papua
influences).

Moihernee or Moilnee is also credited with the creation of the big and small
rivers, which he cut out of the land, as well as of the island of Tasmania itself.[158]
Apparently, as in Gondwana myth in general, the earth and the ocean already
existed.

Droemerdeene also created the kangaroo rat. The story is quite similar to that
of the creation of the badger by the otherwise unknown Droegerdy.[159] This
action involved fire as well.[160] The bringing of fire is otherwise attributed to the
two star spirits or Pumperneowlle and Pineterrinner,[161] but not so by the Bruny
people.[162] It is also attributed to Parpeder (or Parledar),[163] while an Aborigine "of
Macquarie Harbour said that fire was first obtained from a *numer*, i.e. the white
man [= a spirit], who appeared among them and coughed it up his throat. The
subject was discussed among them with much vehemence."[164]

***

There are a number of names for stars and constellations:

> They are quite at home on the subject, that is, they have names for the stars and con-
> stellations and are aware that they revolve.... They call the black spot in the Milky
> Way or Orion's Belt a stingaree and say the blackfellows are spearing it [Coal Sack in
> the Southern Cross?]. The natives of the south call it *Larder*, which is their name for
> this fish, and the natives of the east call it *Larner*.... They spoke on the subject of the
> stars with great zest.[165]

Most of the constellations were seen as humans or other figures, such as
Aborigines fighting or courting, a husband and wife, or men's legs and limbs.[166]
The Bruny and Cape Portland Aborigines "said that the two stars in the Milky

Way are two men and that Mars is his foot, and that the Milky Way is his road."[167] A certain group of three stars, perhaps part of the Southern Cross, was seen as mother, father, and child, the mother being the largest one: "They are called by the Brune natives Pur, by the western tribes Lone'erten, by the northern natives Noego, and by the natives of Oyster Bay Parngerlinner."[168]

There also existed a myth about the sun and the moon.[169] The female moon, Vetaa, originated from the islands offshore and "stopped" at Oyster Bay (in the east). She was a woman (*looner*)[170] who got partly burned on her side when she was roasting muttonfish (hence her dark spots). After this, she rolled into the sea and moved up into the sky (*warrangerly*) to join her husband, the Sun, Parnuen. The rainbow represents their children.

Other beneficial spirits, those of deceased ancestors, were called *warawah*.[171] The human soul was thought to exist in the left breast. The northern tribes thought that it moved, after death, to the Bass Strait Islands,[172] where there were "many" departed.[173] Dead bodies were cremated and then buried in a grave under a tent-like construction made of bark strips. Sometimes the dead body was put in a hollow tree before cremation, as in Australia.[174] Parts of cremated bodies were used by their relatives as "amulets" (similar to the Andamanese). The spirits of the dead were thought to be white—the opposite of humans, a common feature. They live in a pleasurable world, on the terrestrial islands or in the stars.[175] Robinson reports, "Today observed Racedunupe, the widow of Tybuner, in deep conversation with the amulet, i.e. the ashes of her deceased husband[,] which was made into an amulet called by the Brune natives *roideener*, and by the west coast natives *numremurreker*."[176] Robinson continues to state that on the death of a relative, Tasmanian mourning behavior includes breaking of spears and necklaces, throwing away of kangaroo skins, cutting of baskets, and avoidance of putting on red ochre; in sum: "they are quite neglectful and mourn."[177]

The good spirit, Moihernee or Parledee,[178] governed the day, and the evil spirit, Wrageo-Wrapper,[179] the night.[180] He was thought to be white colored (like the spirits of the dead) but otherwise looks just like a Tasmanian, though he is big and ugly. Wrageowrapper was also called by other names: in the east he was called Kalepenunne or Karpennooyouhener; by the Cape Portland Aborigines, Kormtennerkarternenne; and by those of Oyster Bay, Markaneyerlorepanener.[181] He is also called Prarmmeneannar,[182] who is a strong, black spirit who lives in the bush, and also Wyerkartenner.[183] He is quick like the wind and appears at night, but before daylight he goes away like a swift wind.[184] He is heard whistling.[185] He is often described in the literature as "devil."

P. W. Schmidt lists a large number of divergent forms for the evil spirit(s) that in part overlap with those given above.[186] Some such evil spirits were thought to dwell in rocks, forests, and so on. Still other evil spirits (Kal-, Kar-, Mar-) or "devils" live in a "blue" fire (not the normal fire),[187] hence the obvious connection, made by the West Point and Cape Grim Aborigines, with thunder and lightning. As they are seen as evil they are called by the same name as evil spirits, *nowhummer.*[188] There also was a belief that "there are flying snakes.... [T]hey had been seen in the forest and mountainous country inland and in the neighbourhood of Mount Norfolk."[189]

The creation myth, from the Bruny Island group (south of Hobart), has been summarized as follows: the Tasmanians, the animals, and the landscape were made by ancestral beings (which is not unlike certain aspects of Australian myth). These beings were called

> Moihernee and Droemerdeener. These two beings fought in the heavens, and Moihernee fell from there and dwelt on the land at Coxes Bight, his wife coming after him to dwell in the sea. When Moihernee died he was turned into a stone which stands at Coxes Bight. Moihernee was associated with the star Canopus. Other stars were associated with men and animals.[190]

In the myths of another tribe, that of Cape Portland in the northeast, "certain stars of the Milky Way were said to have given fire and to have made rivers."[191] Moihernee also is a trickster deity:

> Moihernee made the first black man, Parlevar,[192] who had a tail like a kangaroo,[193] and no joints in his legs so that he could not sit down. The great star spirit Droemerdee [*sic*], saw this and cut off his tail, rubbed grease over the wound to cure it and made joints to his legs. Parlevar sat down and was well pleased. Moihernee also made all the rivers and cut the riverbeds, made the islands and the mountains. He was then hurled from heaven and turned into a big stone which stands at Cox Bight.[194]

It is notable that this totem-like myth has some similarities with central Australian myth, while the existence of two primordial spirits reminds one of the Andamanese, whose language has been linked by Greenberg, Whitehouse, and Usher with Papuan and Tasmanian.[195] The several connections between the stars and the spirits also are remarkable.

***

In sum, it is important to stress that the Tasmanians shared a number of concepts with other Gondwana groups. There seems to be a vaguely conceived High God, though his name(s) and functions remain very obscure. More clearly described are the two opposing deities (similar to Andaman myth) of the day and the night. Some of the good spirits who originally were stars also act as trickster deities. Moihernee creates the features of the landscape and humans, while Droemerdeener assists in creating humans out of a kangaroo (totems?). Like many other Gondwana tricksters, Moihernee falls down from heaven, which might signal, as elsewhere, the end of the primordial golden period. Unfortunately our meager sources do not allow further elaboration. However, souls and an afterlife on a horizontally situated Otherworld on some islands are clearly attested.

These few recorded remnants of Tasmanian mythology thus fit in exactly where they "should." They generally are of Gondwana type, closely related to both Andaman and southeastern Australian myth and, by language, as per J. Greenberg and Usher, also with the rest of Indo-Pacific (Andamanese, Papuan, Kusunda)—as will be seen below (§6).

§5.3.3. Melanesia

Much of Melanesian mythology has been isolated for many thousands of years, as briefly discussed above. It is extremely difficult to generalize about the accounts of this vast region—New Guinea and its islands, the Solomons, Vanuatu (New Hebrides), and New Caledonia—which has more than 100 major tribal societies and more than a thousand languages. However, a few points can be made.

Just as in Australia, the world is not created, nor does it emerge. Instead, it was already present, a desert on which eternal light shone, when the sea had no tides. As Leenhardt defines it:

> It is not a matter of creation ex nihilo. The *baos* created the islands, for example by wrapping some land in a taro leaf and throwing it into the sea, and so forth. They were the possessors of fire. On occasion they stole it from each other.[196]

Trompf sums up:

> beings (of human form and qualities but with super-human powers and abilities) were abroad in the land during primordial time, bestowing on a given group's ancestors "the skill of warfare, food production and other technologies," and even establishing certain features of the environment. These figures then went away, or died, although…they may return or be re-contacted.[197]

The universe includes a world of sky people and settlements where the spirits (of the dead) live just like living humans do.[198]

There are several types of Melanesian deities, such as local spirits, nature gods, and specialized deities (of war etc.). Some of them are barely distinguished from ancestor spirits.[199] On Banks Island (Vanuatu) such a *vui* spirit is described: "It lives, thinks, has more intelligence than a man; knows things which are secret without seeing; it is supernaturally powerful with *mana* [spirit effect], has no form to be seen; has no soul, because itself is like a soul."[200] Totems are attested as well, as Trompf summarizes:

> Totems…or specific series of objects in the cosmos on which clans (or other specific groups defined by blood ties or activity) place sacred meaning or tabus to identify themselves, are usually already part of the "known order."[201]

In some societies, the role of the demiurge or trickster deities, called Dema, is much stressed. The classic account is that of Paul Wirz of the Western New

Guinea (Irian) tribe of the Marind-Anim,[202] whose clan- and age-based society derives from the totemic Dema ancestors of primordial times.[203] The Dema are totem ancestors in plant, animal, and mostly human shape. They set the world and all its beings in order.[204] These beings at first were still very much like the Dema themselves; they were a group of intermediaries between the original Dema and the current humans but gradually lost their Dema characteristics and turned into the current beings and objects. The primordial time of the Dema is reenacted (and apparently revived) in yearly, sometimes heavily sexually accented festivals that involve elaborately masked men as representations of the Dema.[205]

However, there also is some evidence about a primordial first being, as in southeastern Australian and perhaps in Tasmanian religion. For example, on Bonarua there is the belief in a supreme being in the sky, Yabwahine,[206] and in Roku (Trans-Fly region), there is just

> one great spirit (apart from sky-dwelling ancestors),—the originator and cosmic Serpent, Kampel, and, though he gave birth to a son ("the heavenly rainmaker") and other beings, these could all be prayed to as the one "Primordial" (Gainjan) now in the sky.[207]

A similar *deus otiosus*, Jabar, is found with some northern Papua tribes. He created the stars, the earth, and humans but takes no further interest in them.[208]

In the Biak and Numfor islands of Geelvink Bay, the snake is regarded "as prototype of the primordial chaos" that led to the dualism of the dead and the living—note that it is sometimes said to have two heads and a double name—and it is closely related to initiation.[209] All of which reminds much of some Australian concepts, and perhaps not without good reasons, as Papua myths and genes influenced parts of northern Australia during the last Ice Age (see above). Many myths tell of a primordial victory over the man-eating snake. In one version we even find the (Japanese-like) trait of getting the snake drunk first.[210] Such features open the question of possible Austronesian influence on these cultures, emanating from the coast.

In another myth, the killed snake becomes the ancestor of humans, and therefore snakes and snakelike beings are taboo and cannot be eaten.[211] A former hunter-gatherer tribe, the Seragi of southeastern Papua, who had been moved in colonial times to lower elevations, tell:

> A snake was captured.... [T]he adults hung it in a net bag.... The serpent turned into a proud dancing warrior, who warned the children that once [it] was cooked, a great catastrophe would occur so that [the children] should persuade their parents to flee to the mountains. Only one family heeded the warning, however, and when the snake was cut and placed in the (earthen) oven, "there was a thunderous landslide" which carried the hamlet and the surrounding land away...destroying all people with it.[212]

In southern Melanesia (New Caledonia), there is worship of both mountains and nature, next to that of ancestors, which some local traditions assert was late on some islands.[213] In addition, some parts of Melanesia, such as the New Hebrides (Vanuatu), have undergone heavy influences from Polynesian mythology (§3.9).

***

In Melanesian myth, a primordial spirit (not a god), who was born from a rock, created the living beings: men and women were carved from a tree. Or man was created from clay, and woman from a tree. In those days, old people could shed their skin, like snakes, and enter a new life.[214] This idea is strongly present in western New Guinea as well, for example, with the highland Dani,[215] for whom the faculty of rebirth was lost through a mangled message delivered by the snake Kalije and the Sibine bird (the hornbill). As in the Hainuwele myth, the Saa people (Solomon Islands) believe that their ancestors emerged from two sprouts on a sugarcane plant.[216] Among the Marind-anim, however, humans emerged from a hole that had been dug by a Dema. At first, they were just bamboo pieces that floated on water. A stork(!) demon fished them out; they were put next to a fire, which made them split and develop arms and legs; when splitting further with a big bang their mouths opened and they could speak.[217]

Dead bodies were predominantly exposed to decompose so that the skull or a bone could be obtained that would be hung around the neck.[218] (These customs are similar to those of the linguistically related Andamanese and Tasmanians but also found in Australia.)[219] The deceased are generally perceived as moving on to another, usually pleasurable world, though this sometimes depends on one's moral standing; from there, one may be reborn again.[220]

***

If the very complex situation in Melanesia can be summarized at all,[221] it may be stressed that in Melanesia, as in the rest of Gondwana mythology, the earth already existed when the primordial totemistic deities (Dema) created or shaped the predecessors of current beings. There are also indications of a High God,[222] who is, however, imagined in snake form in some of the western areas of Melanesia. From there, the concept spread eastward into the Solomons and also southward into northern Australia, when a land bridge existed during the last Ice Age.[223] Some vestiges of the totem cult may even be preserved in Tasmania, where they could have arrived during the last Ice Age at the latest.

§5.3.3.1. Negritos and other southern remnant populations

The Negritos of Malaya believe that the world was brought up from below by Taheum, the dung beetle, as some kind of powdery substance. Kawap, the bear, stamped on it, not to fix it as in other mythologies but to keep it from rising up further: it would have reached the sky.[224] The supreme deity is variously called

Tapern, Tak/Ta' Tapern, or Ta' Pönn. Apparently he is a deified ancestor.[225] He and his wife, Jalang, appear in a myth about a war between various kinds of monkeys, and he has a father, Kukak, and a mother, Yak Takel, as well as a grandmother. She lives below the earth at the foot of Batu Herem, a stone at the center of the world. It supports heaven and pierces it; beyond it is a dark region called Ligoi. From the top of the pillar four strings extend to the four corners of the world. Their ends are weighed down by stones on earth.[226] There also is water below the earth that may rise to the surface to punish people.[227]

Tapern and his wife use a ladder made from darts shot by Tapern's blowpipe to climb up to heaven, where he reigns over the many Chinoi spirits, who act as his messengers. Nothing is said about the creation of the universe, which can be assumed to preexist as in other Gondwana mythologies. The sun was a house of two persons that later became birds. One of them moved the house upward, where it became the sun.[228] The rainbow is a two-thread fishing line used to catch fish for a king of dragons.[229] Others think of it as two snakes. All animals were once humans[230]—as in Australia—and the Malays were wild pigs. Animals change shape in the myths, and so do some plants. A certain fruit turns into a child or a tiger.[231]

There is, however, the story of a Great Flood that occurred when some Negrito children imitated a Sagwong bird. Thunder and lightning and a Great Flood ensued, in which all drowned but one shaman.[232] The flood was caused by the three "grandmothers" of Tapern and his wife—Yak Leleph, Yak Manoid, and Yak Takel—by raising the waters below the earth.

The souls of the dead leave the body through the big toe and go to the western edge of the world. After seven days they cross a bridge made out of fern to an island called Belet that is situated in the northwest. They are led there by a giant guardian, Mampes. There, the dead reach their deceased relatives and friends staying under a Mapik tree. These break all the bones of the newly arrived and turn their pupils inward, changing them into spirits (*kemoit*). They are now allowed to take the flowers of the Mapik tree or eat its fruits, which are the common food on earth. The tree also has breasts that give milk. The evil dead, however, live in another place near to the Mapik tree, from where they unsuccessfully call for help.[233]

The Negritos have shamans (*halak*) who perform inside small medicine huts (*panoh*). The shaman sings short chants while others, women and children outside, repeat his words. The hut shakes, announcing the arrival of the shaman's familiars,[234] usually many Chinois.

***

The Aeta pygmies,[235] of the mountainous regions of the Philippines, have adopted, like the Malaya Negritos, Veddas, and Pygmies, the languages of their neighbors. They have a High God called Magbaya or Apo Namalyani, next to lesser gods and spirits of nature (*anito, kamana, taglugar*, etc.). The Veddas of Sri Lanka have retained traces of their own isolate language;[236] however, we would like to know more about their Yakka religion.

***

The Dravidian-speaking,[237] pastoral Toda of the high South Indian Nilgiri Mountains have preserved a religion that differs completely from ancient and recent southern Hinduism.[238] Their High God, Ön (Intöw), and his wife, Pinakurs, have a son, Püv (Püf), who accidentally drowned in a spring. Ön then took leave of all Todas, their buffaloes, and even the trees and followed Püv, which is reminiscent of the common Gondwana theme of the distant High God. Püv now rules the netherworld (Amnòdr, Önnodr, or Inor) and sends messengers to tell humans their duties.

The important female deity, Teikirzi (or Tirshti), who perhaps is the (elder?) sister of Ön, created and now rules all Todas as well as their cattle, the buffaloes. Elaborate rituals are performed with the buffaloes and their milk.[239] There also is a large number of additional deities;[240] nothing is said about the creation of this world. Toda religion should be urgently scrutinized against the background of Gondwana mythology and compared with that of isolated Dravidian-speaking jungle tribes such as the Orāon (Kurukh) and Malē (Malto) of North India,[241] which can be done here only briefly.

***

The northern Dravidian-speaking tribes have superficially Hinduized names for their deities; however, it is clear that they worship Heaven or the Sun (Dharmē) and Earth, who are sometimes, as with their southern Dravidian neighbors, the Goṇḍ, regarded as having been in close sexual union and pushed apart by human action.[242] Their marriage is celebrated annually. The Kandh see it as a struggle between Būṛhā Pennu, the god of light, and his wife, Tarī, the earth goddess, which leads to the creation of humans and other beings.[243] The Orāon (Kurukh) retain a myth about slaying the dragon and a catastrophe by rain or fire from which only one boy and one girl escaped by hiding in a crab shell.[244] There also is an elaborate epic among the Goṇḍs of their hero Lingo. It is obvious that these Dravidian data reflect general Laurasian mythology and are very different from the myths of the relic tribe of the Toda in their mountain refuge.

§5.3.4. Andaman Islands

The Andaman Islands have always been cut off from the Asian mainland just like Australia and New Guinea, though during the glacial maximum the channel between an extended southern Burma and the Andamans was not very wide. However, archaeology and genetics tell us that the early inhabit-ants[245]—now believed to have arrived there by at least 55 kya from Africa via South Asia,[246] as linguists and geneticists have discovered[247]—have not always been completely isolated since then. Early excavations have shown basically three layers:[248] first, an early one on arrival, one without any pottery, as is expected for Paleolithic peoples. By 3000 BCE pottery suddenly appears, though it then quickly disappears.[249] Also, the pig, now running wild, was introduced about 2,200 years ago. However, much of such pottery stems from foreign visitors searching for bird nests, as later excavations made clear.[250] Osteology indicates that all early Andamanese skeletons have the same fea-tures as today, and recent genetic data indeed confirm that the Andamanese are a very early South Asian split-off from the original African gene pool dating back some 60,000 years.[251]

Taking some contacts with mainlanders into account when studying Andamanese mythology,[252] we may expect *some* continental admixture.[253] Early works by Man and Radcliffe-Brown provide details, though during the latter's stay (1906–8) most myths already had to be collected from laypeople as sha-manism was already on the decline. Now, a century later, more data may be forthcoming from the little-contacted Jarawa tribe and, one day, from the still completely isolated Sentinelese.[254]

There is no creation story, no cosmology: in the beginning, the time of the ancestors, two gods still lived on earth;[255] they represent the northeast and southwest monsoons. The northeast monsoon, often called Puluga, Biliku, or similar, is sometimes regarded as the creator deity and at other times as a trick-ster figure.[256]

Humans emerge from a split bamboo;[257] women then are fashioned from clay.[258] In one version, the first man died and went to heaven, a pleasurable world.[259] The blissful primordial period ended, however, as with the Australian Aborigines, the Pygmies, and the Bassari of West Africa, because of the breaking of a food taboo and an ensuing catastrophe. It was caused by the eating of some forbidden vegetables of the creator deity,[260] who then went to heaven or the northeast.[261]

Another version of the catastrophe has a flood story, told by H. Man. It occurred at the time of Kolwot, grandson of Tomo, the first man, when the world was overpopulated and people disregarded Puluga's rules. In this flood, sent by Puluga, only four people survived, but they had lost their fire. It was retrieved by Kingfisher, the animal spirit of one of the drowned. Non-Andamanese, too, were regarded as spirits (*lau*) of the dead (as in Tasmania). According to one myth the first deceased person was buried several times, finally in a tree, and then had access to the spirit world.[262] Hunted animals, too, are transformed men.[263]

There are some 20 versions of the myth of fire theft.[264] It should be noticed, however, that the myths are told in extremely short, abrupt (paratactic) sentences that usually are "filled in" by the reporting anthropologists.[265] Radcliffe-Brown gives one such example in an extremely literal translation (imitating also the word order):

> Sir Prawn makes fire; yam leaf catches fire; yam leaf is dry; that one he burns; he makes fire; Sir Prawn slept; Sir Kingfisher takes; he fire with he runs away; Sir Kingfisher makes a fire; Sir Kingfisher fish (food) cooks; his belly in he sleeps; Sir Dove runs away taking.

This, he translates freely as:

> It was Sir Prawn who first produced or obtained fire. Some yam leaves, being shriveled and dry by reason of the hot weather, caught fire and burnt. The prawn made a fire with some firewood and went to sleep. The kingfisher stole the fire and ran away with it. He made a fire and cooked some fish. When he had filled his belly he went to sleep. The dove stole fire from the kingfisher and ran away.[266]

Unfortunately, many of our sources for world mythology from oral sources are of the second type, making it impossible for us to check on the original wording—with problems of intermediate translation (as also in Radcliffe-Brown's case) adding to the poor quality of the data.

Another important point in the study of Andamanese mythology is that the main transmitters, the local shamans, tried to outdo each other, tried to please their audience, and therefore varied their myths to some extent while keeping the main outlines intact. As in other Gondwana (and also in oral Laurasian) traditions there was no "standard" mythology; many variants existed even within the same tribe.[267]

Returning to the motif of the theft of fire, this is usually carried out by early animals, as with the Tasmanians. One may think of them as being similar to the Australian totem animals because they figure prominently in various creation myths, including some dealing with the origin of humans.[268]

***

Some myths, however, rather look like adaptations from Laurasian mythology: there is the typical separation of Heaven and Earth and an axis mundi.[269] The catastrophe, in the form of a Great Flood,[270] was created by excessive rain. People take refuge in a tree and come down from there via a creeper. Finally, there is a curious connection between the mythology of the moon and the boar,[271] which is found all over Eurasia due to the similarity of the shape of boar tusks and that of the waxing moon.[272] The connection is clearly found on the mainland with Southeast Asian planters and pig raisers.[273] Yet it is observed in the early ritual use of an Andaman boar's head, found in an excavation,[274] which indicates that the ritual functions of the Andamanese pig hunt ultimately stem from mainland cultures, like the people themselves.

However, whatever may have transpired briefly some 3,000 years ago, the archaic lifestyle of the Andamans seems to have taken over again, and little of this influx has remained. Perhaps some motifs in mythology are reflections of this early influence. These may include the myth of the separation of Heaven and Earth and perhaps the mytheme of an axis mundi, topics that would have to be explored in detail with worldwide mapping such as that by Y. Berezkin.[275] We may hold out the hope that future anthropologists will retrieve more of Andamanese mythology from the (shamans of the) so far little- or not yet contacted tribes of the Jarawa and Sentinelese.

§5.3.5. Africa

Moving farther west, to the original home of anatomically modern humans, Africa, we encounter the same problems of late contamination of original mythologies as we have seen with the Australians, Melanesians, and Andamanese. To acquire a greater degree of certainty about this problem, we begin with two groups that are not part of the dominant sub-Saharan peoples. In linguistic terms, the latter include the Nilo-Saharan- and the Niger-Congo-speaking populations that spread, during the African Iron Age, out of Cameroon (or an adjacent northern area, such as northeastern Congo).[276] The majority are Bantu-speaking peoples of Central, East, and South Africa, as well as their more distant West African relatives. The two major exceptions from this near-universal spread are the Khoi-San or San (Bushmen), along with their distant Hadza and Sandawe relatives in central Tanzania, and the Pygmies of the Greater Congo Basin, though the latter—like other relict tribes such as the Toda and Negritos— have adopted the languages of their neighbors and speak Bantu now. As the Pygmy substrate language has not yet been studied in any detail, we cannot form an opinion about their original language. Both groups are also of great genetic interest. It has been shown that the San and Hadza-Sandawe belong to the oldest layers of human populations. Some, however, claim that Hadza are as distant from San as other Africans (but closer to the Pygmies), which may be due to the fact that geneticists have tested only just the so-called Black Sandawe but not yet the Yellow Sandawe,[277] who seem to be much closer to the San.[278] The last common ancestor of the Hadza/Sandawe and San (Jun/wasi) lived at c. 40 kya.[279]

The San, the Pygmies, and the older Bantu-speaking peoples (in Cameroon, Congo) thus provide two separate avenues that allow us to determine the nature of older African mythology. All were fairly isolated from the rest of the continent. This was less the case with the Eastern and Southeastern Bantu, who could be influenced by peoples and ideas coming down the eastern steppe and savanna corridor stretching from southern Ethiopia and Kenya to Zimbabwe, Namibia, and South Africa and possibly by early oceanic contact along the Kenya–Mozambique coast.

§5.3.5.1. Remnant populations: San and Pygmies

1. San

The San (or !Kung San, Khoi-San, or Ju/'hoansi) are the remnants of pre-Bantu populations of southern Africa. That they once must have settled much farther north is obvious because of their genetic and linguistic relatives, the Hadza and Sandawe of central Tanzania, who like them speak click languages.[280] All of them are typical hunters and gatherers. Their ultimate origin may have been in the fertile Sahara grasslands of the Neolithic, where the ancient rock art has some characteristics that are also found in that of early South Africa. The earlier San habitat can be shown to have been in Tanzania; they spread south only about 6,000 years ago.[281]

It may therefore well be the case that these late arrivals in South Africa brought with them a northern, steppe/savanna-type hunter and gatherer mythology that was closer to that of other hunter-gatherer cultures, such as the early "Out of Africa" Gondwana groups. Their mythology indeed is characterized by the absence of Laurasian-type creation myths. However, there is a primeval High God, a feature also seen with some other more or less mixed groups in southern Africa, the Hottentots, the Damara, and the latecomers, the Herero.[282] The San creator god is called Kaggen (/Kaggen or !Kung, like the people themselves). He created the world and all its beings,[283] though there was no distinction between animals and humans (which recalls Australian animal totems); in reality, both were human. However, again similar to some Australian, Tasmanian, and Andamanese ideas, during the second stage of creation humans and animals were differentiated, as they are today.[284]

The life-giving creator lives in the eastern sky, with the rising sun, and is more powerful than Gauwa of the western sky, of the setting sun. Gauwa is both a typical trickster deity but also the one who gives death. Beyond this duality, there are a number of less powerful animal and ancestral spirits who can be benevolent or the opposite.[285] The San believe, again similar to Tasmanians, that they were "animals" (eland, springbok) of primordial times and were changed into current humans by the power of the mantis, a form of Kaggen. The spirit of a San lodges itself in the body of an animal as it leaves for the eternal world to join the ancestors, called (in Dutch) *bokveld*.[286] Some of this can be observed in South African rock art, especially in the rich paintings of the Drakensberg Mountains.[287]

To create the wall paintings, the blood of the bull eland is used; the animal also dominates the paintings; it has been interpreted as a form of the creator and trickster, Kaggen. The "flying bucks," with their combination of human and animal (antelope) features, and the combination of birds and antelopes, are interpreted as elements of shamanistic lore. Most typical are the combined figures of beings with faces, hooves, and forelegs of antelopes but human torso and rear legs. They show the bent-over and arms-back posture of San shamans in trance, and like them they bled from the nose.[288]

Apparently, their distant linguistic relatives, the Sandawe of central Tanzania, share some of the religious concepts of the San. Most notably, they venerate, like the San, the mantis, which is regarded as a divine messenger that appears only for specific reasons and is commonly consulted as a medium. Like the San, they also have a rather distant High God, Warongwe. Like other African forms of *deus otiosus* he is so remote and unrelated to human well-being that he is only rarely invoked, prayed to and sacrificed to in great emergencies. Other deities include the moon, the stars, and the seasons. The moon is connected with fertility, especially the cycle of fertility in women, and it brings rain. The Sandawe retain a large repertoire of songs and rituals for harvest and courtship, as well as rituals including the possession dance, in which lions are imitated to combat witchcraft. Connected are the shamanistic healing rituals involving trance (Dempwolf 1916).

Similarly, the Damara of southwestern Africa tell of the High God Gamabin, who lives in heaven, above the sky, together with the souls of the dead who have reached him there via a deep abyss and now live there under the shade of the heavenly tree, all of which is very reminiscent of Eurasian myths.[289] The Herero, another Namibian nomadic people, have been influenced much by Bantu mythology. They have a High God, but for them, the first man is more important (as it is with the neighboring Zulu or with the distant Nilotic peoples). However, in all these cases we miss an account of original creation, a cosmogony that is prominent in Laurasia.

Baumann describes the mythology of still another pastoral people of Namibia, the Hottentot, as characterized by their High God Tsui-Goab, who has some functions of a creator as well.[290] Apparently there also existed a primordial ancestor, an old bush demon called Heitsi-Eibib or Heiseb (Big tree?), who has become the national hero of the Nama Hottentot; he shares some characteristics with a similar deity of the San. At the same time he is the grandfather and a great sorcerer. Gaunab (or Gamab of the Mountain Dama tribe), his opposite, is a demon that is associated with wind, lightning, and thunder, who has more ghost-like features with the Hottentot. Some of the deities of the San, Dama, Hottentot, and Herero have influenced each other and even carry similar names.

2. Pygmies

The Pygmies are physically very small people (of c. 150 centimeters or 5 feet, or even less). They are scattered all over the Central African rain forests.[291] They may have entered these areas relatively late, as they are shown (as dancers) on ancient Egyptian reliefs and must then have lived closer to Egyptian trade routes.[292] Knowledge of them must have come from the Sudan or East African coastal areas.

The Pygmies, too, have a High God, Tore (Man of the forest), whom they also call "our father/grandfather."[293] They have a clear concept of a primordial age, "the age of the beginning" when their High God created everything,[294] and a blissful period ensued. This is, however, unlike the Laurasian idea of first origin, and Pygmy mythology lacks the Laurasian story line from the beginning to the end of the world.

Humans are sent down from heaven by the High God, or he himself forms them from clay.[295] In one myth, his human son joins him. He also functions as a culture hero, from whom fire originated;[296] or a woman stole it from the forest spirit.[297] Due to a mistake of his human daughter, he leaves the world "downstream," not to be seen again;[298] death also originated as a result. In another myth, the blissful primordial period is ended when a pregnant woman craved a certain fruit of the Tahu tree that the creator had forbidden to be eaten. As a result, humans now have to die.[299]

Like the Australians, the Pygmies have a concept of a rainbow serpent.[300] However, Baumann regards this motif,[301] as well as some others,[302] as having drifted in from their neighbors.

Some scholars such as Campbell think of Pygmy mythology as "rain forest mythology," as it is so clearly geared to their natural surroundings. Pygmies indeed do not feel at ease once they leave the rain forest. Campbell, however, (over)stresses this psychological factor,[303] as quoted earlier,[304] in Jungian fashion. He makes the Pygmies somehow live in close union with their collective consciousness, as if they were more "primitive" than other populations. However, given the similarity of basic myths of the Khoi-San, Pygmies,[305] and Australians, this is both a simplification and an overinterpretation. All humans are no doubt influenced by their surroundings, and their mythology, too, may take on a very local color. However, the basic structure of mythology of these three widely dispersed Gondwana populations, whether desert/steppe or rain forest people, is surprisingly similar. They all have no interest in the origin of the world but, instead, in that of humans, and they also share the concept of a distant High God (*deus otiosus*). They also have the concept of some sort of primordial misdeed that resulted in the end of the primordial period, often by a flood (see above, §3.9, §5.7.2) or a similar catastrophe.

§5.3.5.2. Sub-Saharan Africa

After briefly surveying these remnant peoples of Africa, it is time now to turn to the major population groups, first those speaking the Niger-Congo languages, whose territories stretch from Senegal to Kenya and southward to South Africa. In East Africa, there also are scattered groups of Nilo-Saharan-speaking populations; farther north we find their Nilo-Kordofian subgroup (cf. below, §5.3.5.5).

For reasons that have been mentioned before (§5.3.1), we must begin with those populations that are fairly isolated from, on the one hand, the influences of the northern Sahel belt stretching from Senegal eastward to Sudan and, on the other, the influence radiating out of the East African steppe/savanna "highway" between Kenya and South Africa.[306]

Anthropologists such as Frobenius and Baumann have pointed out for a long time that the various cultures of West Africa, from Guinea to Nigeria and Cameroon, have undergone varying degrees of influence from the Sahel steppe belt in the north, along many of these western north–south highways.[307] One can therefore expect, and will indeed find, numerous cases of impact by the Laurasian mythologies of the Sahel cultures all over West Africa, from Guinea to Cameroon. However, just as in the Melanesian case, the juxtaposition of "typical" (original?) African mythologies with those influenced from the north is very instructive.

The situation is quite similar in the extensive East African belt, stretching from Kenya southward to Zimbabwe, Namibia, and the eastern parts of South Africa, which was facilitated by a savanna-like landscape. Here, too, northern mythologies have heavily influenced the sub-Saharan ones; this belt may be called the eastern North–South Highway.

In addition, we have to reckon with several waves of movements within sub-Saharan Africa itself. The Bantu wave of advance out of Cameroon, or a region east of it, is well known; it reached South Africa only during the past few hundred years. Linguistic data, too, indicate some three successive levels of Bantu occupation in the Congo, including that of the Bantu-speaking Pygmies.[308]

***

Obviously, in the cases mentioned so far, the Laurasian traits have to be carefully "subtracted" from what we find in Gondwana myths. This can best be done by starting out from the mythology of isolated areas, such as the "backwoods," literally speaking, of Central Africa. We therefore begin with the central Bantu peoples of the Congo Basin, who were fairly isolated due to their habitat within the rain forest.

Central African mythology is characterized as *not interested in creation myths*. This feature has been stated by scholars who could not yet know of the present theory.[309] In the summary of his book, Baumann formulates in general and rather stark terms:

> [These myths] are indeed much less colorful.... They lack the speculation of nature philosophy of the Polynesians and some Amerindians, the close intertwining of human fate with the astral word as found with the Amerindians, and the grotesque fantasy of the Eskimos. The center of African myth is occupied by a creation principle that in most cases is identical with the High God, and the First Man, who has been begat, formed or brought forth by him. How this first man came to earth, how he lived and what he experienced is the topic of almost all African mythology. Next to this, the myths are almost insignificant of the emergence of heaven and earth, of the stars, and of supernatural beings that occupy a large portion of the mythology of other continents.[310]

More recently,[311] H. Hochegger, a scholar whose specialization is Central Africa, has described the situation as follows:

> Congolese creation myths *do not seek to explain*, for example, *the creation of heaven and earth* (cosmology). Nor do they tell us about how man and women were made. *The focus of mythological interest is on the concrete questions of human life.* ... What, in the end, is creation? ... [I]t is simply the beginning of the concrete situation that continues into the present. There is *hardly any notion here of an ancient source* of all things, placed *at the beginning* of a long history understood in linear fashion.[312]

In the mythology of the wide area from southwestern Cameroon to mid-Angola, and from the Atlantic to central Congo, as well as on the Upper Zambezi,[313] we find a distant High God, variously called Nyambi, Yambe, Ndyambi, Nzambi, Zambi, or Zam.[314] With the Fan (Pahouin), for example, the name of this distant High God, Nzame,[315] is closely connected with the names (*mbi/mba*) of other, lower gods. The etymology indicates that they, too, were creator gods, apparently, demiurges and trickster deities.[316]

Nzame created the first man,[317] Fam, the lord of all beings, who was, however, banned into a hole because of his haughtiness. The second created man,[318] Sekumeh, is mankind's ancestor; his wife was created from a tree.[319] Paradoxically, women are often thought of, as in Melanesia and Australia, as responsible for death.

Nzame's son Bingo, who was born from a human wife, was subsequently thrown out of heaven and became a culture hero here on earth. This sort of stepwise creation is found with many peoples of the area. The retreat to heaven of the creator High God usually is due to some mistake of the humans and is a widespread phenomenon.[320] After his ascent, he remains a distant *deus otiosus*.[321]

However, a western Sahel people, the Bambara of Senegal and Mali, still have a similar mythology that stresses consecutive creation: all things emerged from the "voice of emptiness" at a time when the earth already existed. The primordial spirit dropped a small ball on the earth from which developed, successively, a tree stump, then water, and then Faro, who continues the creation and the creation of man. Note also the extensive lore of the Dogon about origins,[322] though the substance of the accounts of Griaule have been criticized by now.

Baumann sums up the culture of this region that he calls, in line with then prominent *Kulturkreis* theory, the "Old African" or "Old Sudan" culture, as one with hoe agriculture, patriarchal society, and a "manistic" (ancestor-centered) religion.[323] Leaving this theory apart, his description of its mythology still holds: the primordial ancestor is at the center of the world, and all life grows from it. Heaven and stars are not very important. Instead of "creation" we find "emanation" or "calling forth" of the mundane beings, animals, and humans.[324] Frequently, the primordial ancestor or all ancestors have been turned into deities who may have pushed the old High God aside. The chief or priest, a rainmaker, can become a living deity (as is typical in the feudalistic, younger Sudan cultures). In addition, we have a strong cult of the earth and nature (trees, coves, stones, swamps, etc., which are regarded as children of the earth deity). The earth is also the dwelling place of the ancestors, who are reborn from it. Many items of culture, such as fire, are retrieved from the netherworld.

Later on, the sub-Saharan cultural complex was amplified by iron use and myths about smiths. In the mythology of the peoples of the central and eastern sub-Saharan area,[325] the heroes as ancestors, and also the joker as culture hero, are central. Occasionally, we find remnants of a sky god who sent men down to earth. Here, again, the earth existed already from the beginning.

§5.3.5.3. Northern influences: The western North–South Highway

However, among the peoples who live near the Sahel belt, we frequently find northern influences, for example, with the Dogon in Burkina Faso (Upper Volta).[326] In general, the sub-Saharan peoples of the Volta/Niger region have a mixed mythology, with older sub-Saharan traits such as the veneration of the Earth and Neo-Sudanic traits such as god kings. All of this was further influenced by Islam.[327]

As studied by Griaule and Parin,[328] the Dogon have the High God Amma, who created the Earth and married her. They had several sons, that is, Jurugu and later the Nommo twins (male/female). The first son committed incest with his mother, and she gave birth to the evil bush spirits. Amma then created the first men without the help of the Earth. Amma's son Nommo sent a culture hero, the first smith, who descended by boat along the rainbow. Many of the tales of divine descent and incest sound suspiciously like Eurasian mythology.

Due to such strong northern influences, exercised, for example, by Ful and Mosi-Dagomba immigration and conquest since c. 1000 CE, even peoples in the rain forest belt stretching along the Guinean and Nigerian coast have similar Sahel-like mythological traits and systems. It is unclear, thus, how far the West African peoples' mythology, as we have it now, reflects the original one of this area. The Sahel influence has long been noticed by anthropologists, ever since Frobenius pointed to shamanistic influences from the north and northeast of the continent.[329] It has now been put into historical context by W. van Binsbergen.[330] (Further, there is the possibility of some European influence along the coasts, ever since the 15th century.)

For example, the Ashanti (Ghana, Ivory Coast) have a sky god Nyameh (Energy, vital force), who is the typical *deus otiosus*: he is impersonal and distant.[331] An earth mother and goddess of procreation, Asase Ya, is his wife.[332] They have four children, such as the thunder god Tano. However, there also is Ananse, the spider (which is also found with the Zande in the eastern Sudan).[333] Taking the form of a bird, he creates the sun, the moon, the stars, day, and night. A culture hero, the first king, marries the daughter of the sky god. Ananse is likely the original creator god (like the *mba/mbi* deities in Central Africa),[334] and the idea of Father Heaven and Mother Earth may well be due to northern influence. Occult power resides in "fetishes," charms worn on bodies, which were prominently recorded by the first European sailors in the area, 600 years ago.[335]

Another Guinea people, the warrior-like Fon (in Togo, Dahomey, Benin), have a mixed mythology, too: a father of the gods and his twin children—a male (heaven, sun, power/might) and a female principle (earth, moon, fertility)—a culture hero, and many other gods are worshiped as well. Farther east, in Nigeria, the Yoruba have a High God, Olurun (Owner of the sky),[336] who typically is not worshiped. In the beginning, below him was only water, the sea called Olokun. Both unite and have two sons. The oldest, Obatala, was let down to the sea in order to create the earth; but he got drunk and slept. The younger, Odudua, took sand and a chicken; he dropped the sand, and the chicken scratched it: this became the earth. This looks like an echo of many northern (Laurasian) and Australian myths about a bird as originator of the first dry land.[337]

In another myth, Obatala is Heaven and Odudua is Earth. Heaven covers the Earth; their union creates a second pair: dry earth and wet earth. Then, there is incest of wet earth with her son: from this, the 16 gods of the pantheon, such as Shango, Ogun, and so on, are born. This myth looks even more like an echo of Eurasian mythological topics.

It must be stressed that this kind of mythology goes along with state formation and god kings, both among the Yoruba and the Ashanti. We will detect this pattern with other African peoples as well.[338]

The checkered distribution of mythologies similar to the Laurasian type in West, East, and South Africa is counterbalanced by large chunks of territories with the original sub-Saharan African mythology in between, notably in relatively inaccessible areas such as the Congo but also in the jungle belt of West Africa. This type of distribution points to intrusion, and not an original development, of a "Laurasian"-type mythology in West, East, and South Africa.

§5.3.5.4. The eastern North–South Highway

The rest of sub-Saharan Africa is even more difficult to evaluate, as it was open to northern influences all along the East African corridor of steppe and savanna lands, stretching from Kenya to Zimbabwe and South Africa.[339] The major deliverers of northern mythology in East Africa were the Nilo-Saharan-speaking peoples, from southern Libya to Tanzania. Their eastern, Nilotic branch mainly is settled in southern Sudan, Kenya, and Uganda. Nilo-Saharan speakers include the Kanuri, Nubian, Shilluk, Nuer, Dinka, Luo, Maasai, and so on. The speakers of the local Niger-Congo (Bantu) languages, however, can be expected to follow more originally sub-Saharan traits.

East Africa, thus, is part of the sub-Saharan as well as of the Afro-Asiatic (formerly, "Hamitic") cultural areas; the latter is represented in the region by the

Omotic speakers in the northeast and the Cushitic/Somali-speaking populations.[340] Among the Nilotic-speaking peoples, we can again discern several historical levels of mythology, for example, among the Shilluk and the Dinka of
Sudan. Both have a High God and original ancestor(s) of men; the dog functions
as culture hero.

Another non-Bantu group are the Nilotic, pastoral Maasai. They live in Kenya
and northern Tanzania, in the midst of Bantu-speaking people. They, too, have a
High God, Ngai, and in some versions a goddess of the earth, Neiterogob.[341] As
with other Africans, the earth already existed when the ancestors of the Maasai
were created as children of the "black" or "blue" god in heaven and stepped
down to earth, along with their cattle. In another myth, there was a single man at
the beginning; on a visit to the sky, he married the daughter of the sky and then
returned to earth. Death is brought into this world at that time, as so often, by
mistake.

The ancestor of the chiefs, too, descended from heaven as a boy with a tail; he
later on killed a monster, the dragon (*endiamassi*) Nenaunir (Thick stick), with
the help of his daughter. The blood of the dragon made the earth fertile—all of
which reminds one very much of the Japanese version of the Laurasian dragon
myth.[342] The first humans lived in this mundane "paradise" (*kerio*) until the High
God returned to heaven by a ladder.

***

Turning now to the Eastern Bantu, many populations in this area are mixed
with Nilotic or Afro-Asiatic immigrants and their myths. For example, the
Bahima have a High God, Wamara, whose mother, Nyante, is the Universe; he
has no father. His four sons are the gods of the sun, moon, and water and a
hero, Kagoro. The son of the Moon, Hangi, carries the sky, very much as in
Laurasian myths. This High God has many distinctive names: with the Baganda
(in Uganda) he is called Katonda;[343] with the Kikuyu (Kenya), Murunga; and
likewise, Murunga or Mulungu by some 25 other populations of East Africa or
Kalunga in the western parts of Central Africa.[344] With the Leza (Tanzania,
Zambia, Upper Congo) his name means "To cherish," and in Tonga (Zambia),
"First cause."

The Ila people live on the Kafue River,[345] in the northern hills of central
Zambia. They are a matrilineal people but have male chiefs; they have been influenced by the kingdoms of southern Congo and Zimbabwe. Their deities are
characterized by a supreme male/female dichotomy that is in charge of war,
herding, hunt versus the earth, and farming (with hoe). This division is typical
for segmentary societies in Zaire and the Central African savanna but also for
Cameroon, eastern Nigeria, and the Voltaic people of Ghana and the Ivory
Coast.[346] The supreme deity is the central figure in Ila regional cults, unified by

regional shrines. There also is a Titan-like being, the *itoshi* monster that lives in rivers and lakes.[347] He belongs to a past when deformed monsters roamed the earth, before the culture heroes established order. In sum, he is ancestor, culture hero, nature spirit, and water beast. The Itoshi is a transformed chief or a trickster, who rules the dead living in villages below the water.

The same pattern continues in the southern areas of East Africa as well as in South Africa, for example, in the Monomotapa realm of Zimbabwe and among the Zulu. The Southern Bantu have partly been influenced by San mythology. They have a High God and a male ancestor who developed from a bed of reeds. Among the Zulu, this is the "lord of heaven, chief in the sky," and Unkulunkulu, "God, great one, old one."

If we did not take into account northern, Afro-Asiatic, and Nilotic influences, many of the features discussed in this section would align much of sub-Saharan African mythology with the Laurasian system. Typical is the pastoral cattle/spear cultural continuum reaching down from East Africa into Central Africa and the strong influence of intralacustrine cultures with possession trance ideology.[348] Such influences, again, have been pointed out since long ago.[349]

***

In sum, with most sub-Saharan Africans we find a supreme being,[350] a distant High God, such as with the West African Ashanti and Yoruba, and in the Congo, and with the East African Baganda and Kikuyu, and all the way down to the Zulu in South Africa. Usually, the High God lives beyond the sky and does not receive regular worship.[351] There was a golden age or paradise that came to an end by a woman's mistake (hitting the sky with a stick etc.);[352] now the High God is far away. The many, actually worshipped deities are those of nature or local spirits.[353] This results in fully developed polytheism. Ancestors play a great role,[354] and the rulers are divine.[355] However, there also are kingless societies,[356] such as those of the Ibo, Ewe, and Kikuyu (as well as the Nuer and Maasai), that represent the older sub-Saharan form of society and religion, before northern influences arrived.

§5.3.6. Summary

An evaluation of the data supplied by the four major types of (modern) non-Laurasian, Gondwana mythologies indicates that they lack a certain amount of myths, particularly "true" creation stories (emergence out of nothing/chaos), and lack a continuous story line (from creation to destruction). The Gondwana mythologies share some individual motifs, such as human origin from trees[357]— who in many Laurasian myths formerly could talk—or from rocks and that of an ultimate, if otiose, High God and his descendant, a trickster or totem deity.

However, if such motifs are ordered by observers, something like an incipient story line of Gondwana myth would emerge, as is obvious in the Aranda case quoted above, though the story is not told as such anywhere: there is no creation; the earth already exists. There is an otiose High God who moves to heaven, from where he sends down his son (or other beings) to create humans. These show hubris and are therefore punished by a flood. Trickster deities bring culture to them. There is no final destruction of the world.

If much of this sounds like the biblical account, it may have deeper, underlying sources in the Levant region that should be explored in detail, which can only be pointed at (cf. §5.4) but cannot be done here. The most salient features of the Gondwana traditions are listed in Table 5.1. These features can be summarized as in Table 5.2. The relationship of this scheme with the Laurasian one will be discussed below (see Table 5.3; §5.7).

TABLE 5.1. *Major Gondwana myths*

AFRICA (sub-S.)	ANDAMAN	MELANESIA	AUSTRALIA
In the beginning: Sky and earth / (or ocean) preexist		earth and sea preexist	heaven and earth preexist (or from ocean: Aranda; or from Ungud snake: Northern tribes)
High God is common with Pygmies, Khoi-San; Nilo-Saharan peoples; Rainbow snake (Pygmies)	Puluga? (also 2 deities on earth: NE/SW monsoon)	First spirit from a rock	High god "Eagle Hawk" = Father in heaven (SE); fem. Rainbow Snake = Milky Way; Mother (N, NW); totem animals (C.)
but: lower gods (mbi,mba) show independent character as creator gods (Centr.: Congo)	rainbow snake		(E: deities, as daughters of the Sun)
stepwise creation of earth, living beings, men and earth	separation of heaven	(NB: earth is desert with eternal light, the sun, and a vast sea, without movement)	heaven and earth preexist (N) <Aranda: (C.): vast ocean; *axis mundi*; earth grows gradually>
end of primeval period by flood	primordial period ends with broken taboo and catastrophe		flood, usually because of some mistake/evil deed
Son of god/*mbi* = often trickster, or joker = culture hero (descends by rainbow)			(E: deities, partly daughters of sun) SE: All-Father; trickster on earth; goes to heaven after flood

				C: totem ancestors create landscape, rituals, etc.
humans created by High God; or from tree stump: → woman or:	humans from tree: split <u>tree</u>; from clay;	men, women woman then carved from tree (or: man	(tree & cycle of life)	
man from clay; women often from tree (or: directly created by High God)	or from Lady Crab	from clay)		SE: children of gods; or from underground;
				C: from totem animals
< first man banned into a hole>				no eschatology <but totem well>
Evil: son of High God is thrown out of Heaven (incest) or:				C: <u>evil deed</u> brings end of Golden Age: primordial beings die
human haughtiness, or woman's <u>mistake</u> leads to catastrophe	broken <u>taboo</u>: catastrophe death arises	death due to some broken <u>taboo</u>: before that, mere change of skin and 'rebirth'		

TABLE 5.2. *Major stages and motifs in Gondwana 'cosmogony'*

- in the beginning: heaven and earth (and the sea) already exist
- a High God lives in heaven, or on earth, or ascends to heaven later
- series of lower gods, often children of High God, act as tricksters and culture heroes
- primordial period ended by some evil deed of son of High God (or by humans)
- humans are created from trees and clay (or rock); occasionally, descend directly from the gods/totem ancestors
- humans act haughtily or make a mistake; punishment by a great flood; humans reemerge in various ways
  (an end to the world is missing)

TABLE 5.3. *Comparison of major stages in Gondwana and Laurasian cosmogony*

GONDWANA mythology	LAURASIAN mythology
—	**Creation from nothing, chaos,** etc.
Earth, Heaven, sea **preexist** **High God** in/toward heaven, sends down his son, totems, etc.	Father Heaven/Mother Earth **created**, separated **Father Heaven** engenders:
—	Two generations ("Titans/Olympians"):
—	Four (five) generations/ages
—	heaven pushed up, sun released
—	current gods defeat/kill predecessors
—	killing the dragon/sacred drink
... to **create humans**: from tree/clay they show **hubris**, are punished by a **flood**	**humans: *somatic* descendants of Sun god** they (or a god) show **hubris**, are punished by a **flood**
Trickster deities bring culture — (local tribes)	**Trickster** deities bring culture humans spread, emergence of "nobles" local history begins
— —	**final destruction of the world, new heaven and earth emerge**

■ §5.4. INDIVIDUAL GONDWANA MYTH TYPES AND THEIR COMMON CHARACTERISTICS

In conclusion, it must be underlined that the brief investigation of Gondwana mythology presented above (§5.3) could only provide a sketch; much of it clearly is in need of detailed investigation. Several additional smaller traditions across Eurasia could and should be added, such as those of the Todas of the South Indian Nilgiri Mountains, the Aeta in the Philippines,[358] the Semang of Malaysia, the Austronesian Aborigines of highland Taiwan, and so on.

Each of each of the four major Gondwana areas, as well as the various subregions (such as West Africa, southeastern Australia), must be explored further. We also have to look into some special cases of aberrant Gondwana elements in Laurasian myths and conversely, some surprising Laurasian elements in Gondwana myths (§5.5.6.1–2), such as the separation of heaven and earth by an axis mundi in Andaman myth.

***

The schemes given above (§5.3.6; Table 5.4) clearly indicate that we have to reckon with the concept of a High God in all Gondwana areas. This is a *deus otiosus* who is often regarded as living in (or having ascended to) heaven. He may take some divergent forms, such as Eagle Hawk among the southeastern Australians or as a spirit born from a rock with the Melanesians. Though he is involved in "first things," this typically does not include the creation of the earth or of the universe. He remains a rather distant deity who has no special forms of worship but is very occasionally invoked by modern populations if a special threat emerges.

In some cases the position of the High God has been taken over by the Rainbow Snake, who may be his wife. With the northern/northwestern Australians she has developed into an All-Mother who is identified with the Milky Way.[359] She carries her children inside her. She, or more commonly the High God, is the direct or indirect originator of humankind. However, there also are a number of additional deities, notably the creator gods (*mba*) found in Central Africa, the two gods of the Andamans and Tasmania, and the many totem animal ancestors of humans in central Australia.

***

In all Gondwana traditions studied above, the earth, the sky, and the sea typically already exist, though the earth occasionally rises out of the ocean—even with the landlocked Aranda of central Australia—or is created by strewing out some sand (Africa). These cases (with the Dogon, Yoruba) seem to be due to northern influences on African mythology. There even is a faint trace of the

TABLE 5.4. *Detailed summary of Gondwana myths*

Topic	AFRICA	Khoi-San/Damara/Herero/Hottentot	Pygmies	Nilgiri	ANDAMANS	Semang	Taiwan Highland Tribes	NEW GUINEA, MELANESIA	TASMANIA	AUSTRALIA
1. Primordial time	*Sub-Saharan Africa: not interested in "creation" myths* Bambara (Sahel: Senegal and Mali):: all things emerged from the "voice of emptiness" (but earth already existed) [same with central and eastern sub-Saharan peoples] Maasai: the earth already existed sub-Saharan peoples of the Volta/Niger region have a mixed mythology	— All miss account of original creation, cosmogony (absence of Laurasian type creation myths)	Primordial "age of the beginning" (lacks Laurasian story line from beginning to end of world)	(Ōn?)	— (no creation story, no cosmology)	World brought up from below by Taheum, the dung beetle Kawap, the bear, stamped on it as not to let it rise up to sky	— (Isolated mountain tribes (e.g., Atayal, Bunun) - preserve some archaic mythological traits; while some of low land tribes (Ami) have closer links with typical Austronesian mythology. Also, they maintain special (Laurasian) language reserved for gods and priests (Ami)	Bonarua Isld.: primordial supreme being; Yabwahine in the sky Trans-Fly: Roku; Originator, cosmic Serpent Kampel, prayed to as the "Primordial" (guinjan) in sky. Biak and Numfor, Geelvink Bay: snake prototype of primordial chaos: leads to dualism of dead and living New Caledonia: worship of mountains and nature, and of ancestors (late on some islands)	?	

(continued)

TABLE 5.4. *Continued*

Topic	AFRICA	Khoi-San/Damara/ Herero/Hotentot	Pygmies	Nilgiri	ANDAMANS	Semang	Taiwan Highland Tribes	NEW GUINEA, MELANESIA	TASMANIA	AUSTRALIA
	Bambara: earth already existed but: The primordial spirit dropped a small ball on the earth from which successively, a tree stump, then water, then Faro developed, who continues the creation and the creation of man. Yoruba: In beginning, only sky and water: the sea, Olokun				—		—		?	Central: Earth grows out of large ocean (Aranda). Earth desolate, eternally dark, no sun, moon, and stars yet North: only sky and earth in beginning (Arnhem L.) // Ungud snake as ultimate origin.
High God	"center of African myth is occupied by a creation principle that in most cases is identical with the High God, and the First Man, who has been begat, formed or brought forth by him" — *hardly any notion here of an ancient source of all things, placed at the beginning of a long history* "Instead of "creation" we find "emanation" or "calling forth" of the mundane beings…" with distant High God Nyambi, Yambe, Ndyambi, Nzambi, Zambi, Zam Fan: Distant high god, Nzame Dogon: High God Amma who created the earth and married her.	High God, Kaggen created the earth and its beings, lives in the eastern sky San creator god, called Kaggen (/Kaggen, or !Kung, like the san Created the world and all its beings — Damara: High God also with the Hotentot, Damara and Herero: Damara: Gamabin in heaven, with souls of dead, under shade of heavenly tree Herero: first man, high god (influenced by Bantu)	High God *Tore*, "man of the forest"; also "our father/ grandfather" — rainbow snake	Two deities: Ön and sister Teikirzi; Ön married to Pinakurs; Teikirzis's son Kora-teu born from her afterbirth	Two deities = NE/SW monsoon in beginning, time of ancestors, two gods lived on earth = NE/ SW Monsoon (Puluga) (after a broken taboo, he went to heaven/ Northeast)	High God, Tata Ta Pedn/Tapern; spirits (*chenoi, cenoi*) are mediators, Tata Ta Pedn or: Kari/Karei "lightning" in heaven beyond sky (*ligoi*); not venerated: only blood offer when storming			High God(?) Tiggana Marrabona Good spirit Moihernee, or Parlede(e)/Parllerdé is "superior being," lives in the sky	C.: Heaven and earth eternal; Aranda: sky and the earth eternal; emu-footed Great Father (*kyáritja*) lives in Heaven, green land along Milky Way, with wives, children; also: eternal youth (*altjira ṇḍitja*): males emu-footed, females dog-footed; both age-less SE: "our Father" Mungan-ngawa or Bunjil N: All-Mother, the Rainbow serpent Ngaljod or Wallaganda (identified with the Milky Way)

Shilluk and Dinka:
Both have a High God and original ancestor(s) of men; the dog functions as culture hero

Maasai:
High God, Ngai

—

E. Bantu: Bahima:
High God, Wamara, whose mother Nyante is the Universe; no father.

High God with: Baganda: called Katonda; Kikuyu: Murunga,

By 25 other tribes: Murunga or Mulungu

Leza: "to cherish", Tonga: "first cause"

Ila: supreme deity, unified by regional shrines

Southern Bantu:
High God.

Zulu: "Lord of heaven, chief in the sky", Unkulunkulu "god, great one, old one."

Hotentot: High God Tsui-Goab, who has some functions of a creator

a primeval high god, a feature also seen with some other more or less mixed groups in Southern Africa, the Hotentot, Damara and the late comers, the Herero

creator lives in the eastern sky, with the rising sun, and is more powerful than Gauwa of the western sky, of the setting sun.

TABLE 5.4. *Continued*

Topic	AFRICA	Khoi-San/Damara/Herero/Hotentot	Pygmies	Nilgiri	ANDAMANS Semang	Taiwan Highland Tribes	NEW GUINEA, MELANESIA	TASMANIA	AUSTRALIA
Pre-Creation stages							World not created or not emerged: present as desert with eternal light; sea has no tides	?	<u>C</u>: Earth desolate, eternally dark, no sun, moon, stars <u>C</u>: embryonic life under the earth, to emerge as supernatural beings
Early stages Creation of life	<u>Fan</u>: *mbi/mba* lower gods as creator/trickster gods <u>Ngombe</u>: the creator acts like a potter (Congo) — <u>Bambara</u>: primordial spirit dropped small ball on earth, a tree stump, then water, then the Faro developed who continues creation, also of man. <u>Dogon</u>: High God Amma creates earth and marries her. They had several sons, i.e. Jurugu, and later the Nommo twins (male/female). First son committed incest with his mother and she gave birth to the evil bush spirits. — <u>Ashanti</u>: sky god, Nyameh, "energy, vital force": *deus otiosus* married to earth mother, Asase Ya	<u>San</u>: duality; there are a number of less powerful animal and ancestral spirits who can be benevolent or the opposite <u>Hotentot</u>: Gaunab (or Gamab of the Mountain Dama tribe) is the opposite deity, a demon that is associated with wind, lightning and thunder, who has more of ghostlike features		Ön's son Püv, and Anto/Önteu			*Baos* created islands, by wrapping some land in taro leaf and throwing it into the sea *Bonarua*: one great spirit (apart from sky-dwelling ancestors), is originator and the cosmic Serpent, Kampel, gave birth to son ("heavenly rainmaker") and other beings (all are prayed to as one "Primordial" (Gainjan), who is now in the sky) <u>Melanesia</u>: several types of deities local spirits, nature gods, specialized deities (of war, etc.) Some barely distinguished from ancestors	two male spirits or stars in Milky Way active at time of creation of land and humans Droemerdee(ner) is bright star in south: "out of sea" D. fought in heaven, Moihernee was hurled from heaven or fell down M.'s wife followed, entered the sea; rain falling from sky impregnated her. they have many children	<u>C</u>: embryonic life emerges, light appears: embryos take form of animals and as men/women (can change to animals; no plants) move about, create landscape, names, rituals, songs <u>SE</u>: All-Father: Mungan-ngawa or Bunjil "eagle hawk," Bajaume, Daradulum, Nurunberi

An earth mother and goddess of procreation, Asase Ya, is his wife

Ashanti

(Ghana, Ivory Coast) have a sky god, Nyameh, "energy, vital force" who is the typical *deus otiosus*: he is impersonal and distant

(Fon in Togo similar)

Yoruba:

high god Olurun "owner of the sky"; marries the sea, Olokun

or: Obatala is Heaven and Odadua is Earth. Heaven covers the earth; their union creates a second pair: dry earth and wet earth.

E. Africa:

High God; many names: Baganda (in Uganda) he is called Katonda, with the Kikuyu (Kenya); Murunga, and likewise Murunga or Mulungu by some 25 other populations of East Africa (or Kalunga on the western parts of Central Africa, Baumann 1936: 80–90); with the Leza (Tanzania, Zambia, Upper Congo) his name means "to cherish", in Tonga (Zambia) "first cause".

Dema:

demiurge, trickster deities, totem ancestors of primordial times in plant, animal, mostly in human shape

they gave a group's ancestors: skill of warfare, food production, other technologies; created features of environment then, went away or died

primordial time of Dema is reenacted and revived in yearly, (sexual) festivals with masked men as Dema

Mungan-ngawa: a trickster on earth, his son and wife = ancestors of humans; after great fire/flood killed them; Mungan-ngawa left earth for heaven

N/NW:

All-Mother/Rainbow snake (Ngalijod /Wallaganda = Milky Way (from W. Papua?)

Ngalijod /Wallaganda, identified with Milky Way, carried her children inside her; they became ancestors of Aborigines.

C.

ancestors and totems of patrilinear clans (from E. Papua, like All-Mother from W. Papua?)

(continued)

TABLE 5.4. *Continued*

Topic	AFRICA	Khoi-San/Damara/ Herero/Hotentot	Pygmies	Nilgiri	ANDAMANS	Semang	Taiwan Highland Tribes	NEW GUINEA, MELANESIA	TASMANIA	AUSTRALIA
	Bahima have a High God, Wamara, whose mother Nyante is the Universe; he has no father. His four sons are the gods of sun, moon, water and a hero, Kagoro. The son of the Moon, Hangi, carries the sky									
	The Ila people live on the Kafue river, in the northern hills of central Zambia. Deities are characterized by a supreme male/female dichotomy that is in charge of war, herding, hunt vs. the earth, and farming (with hoe). This division is typical for segmentary societies in Zaire, the C. African savanna and for Cameroon, E. Nigeria, the Voltaic people of Ghana and the Ivory Coast									
	— NILOTIC									
	Maasai: High God, **Ngai**, and goddess of the earth, **Neiterogob**									
	the earth already existed									
	Maasai. They live in Kenya and N. Tanzania, in the midst of Bantu speaking people. They have a High God, **Ngai**, and in some versions, a goddess of the earth, **Neiterogob**									

End of golden age: catastrophe	Ancestors of the Maasai were created as children of the "black" or "blue" god in heaven and stepped down to earth, along with their cattle. The ancestor of the chiefs, too, descended from heaven as a boy with a tail, who later on killed a monster (the dragon (*endiamassi*) Nenaunir "thick stick", with the help of his daughter. The blood of the dragon made the earth fertile or: a single man at the beginning; on a visit to the sky, he married the daughter of the sky and then returned to earth Yoruba: Heaven covers the earth; their union creates a second pair: dry earth and wet earth. Then, there is incest of wet earth with the son: from this, the 16 gods of the pantheon are born, such as Shango, Ogun etc. E. and S. Bantu: golden age ended by woman's mistake (she hit the sky with a stick, etc.); now God is far away	Püv accidentally dies in water; Ön takes leave of all Todas, follows him to Netherworld (Amnödr) = western Lowlands	Separation of heaven and Earth; *axis mundi* period ends with broken food taboo and flood catastrophe myth of fire theft (by early animals)	Batu Herem/ Batu Ribn:world mountain/ rock/ pillar, supports world at its center, above Netherworld; penetrating the sky into pleasant world (Ligoi) for souls and spirits	One sun is shot down (Atayal)	Moihernee fell down to earth after a fight	SE: All-Father is trickster deity on earth, goes to heaven after flood

(continued)

TABLE 5.4. *Continued*

Topic	AFRICA	Khoi-San/Damara/ Herero/Hotentot	Pygmies	Nilgiri	ANDAMANS Semang	Taiwan Highland Tribes	NEW GUINEA, MELANESIA	TASMANIA	AUSTRALIA
2. son / daughter	**Dogon:** High God's son Jurugu etc.; Nommo twins (male/female) Amma who created the earth and married her. They had several sons, i.e, Jurugu, and later the Nommo twins (male/female). The first son committed incest with his mother and she gave birth to the evil bush spirits. — **Fan:** Nzame created the first man, Fam, the lord of all beings who was, however, banned into a hole because of his haughtiness. The second created man, Sekumeh, is mankind's ancestor; his wife was created from a tree — **Ashanti:** Sky god Nyameh and Asase Ya have four children, e.g. thunder god Tano. **Fon:** warrior-like (Togo/Benin) have a mixed mythology, too: a father of the gods and his twin children: a male (heaven, sun, power/might) and a female principle (earth, moon, fertility); a culture hero and many other gods are worshipped as well **Yoruba:** two sons of Sky God: oldest, Obatala, let down to sea to create earth; got drunk and slept; younger son, Odudua, took sand and a chicken, chicken scratched sand: became the earth.			Püv, etc.	The "nephews" of gods: Chinoi / cenoi spirits seen as ancestors		birth of a son ("the heavenly rainmaker") and other beings (Trans-Fly) *bao* deities as creators/ tricksters	Sons(?): 2 spirits: Moihernee and Droeerdeen(er) Moihernee/Parledee = Canopus, Good spirit, governs the day Droemerdeener / Wrageo-Wrapper, evil, governs the night Moihernee/Moilnee is also seen as Laller, a small ant, involved in the creation of humans Moon got partly burnt in fire, rolled into sea and moved into sky to join husband, the Sun, Parnuen; rainbow = their child	Sky deity sends animal totems

						SE	C
Or: Obatala, Heaven, covers Odadua, Earth: a second pair is born: dry earth and wet earth. Incest of wet earth with son: 16 gods of pantheon are born: Shango, Ogun, etc. E. Africa: Bahima: four sons: gods of sun, moon, water and a hero, Kagoro. Son of Moon, Hangi, carries the sky S. Africa: Southern Bantu have a High God, and a male ancestor who developed from a bed of reeds; they are partly influenced by Khoi San mythology. Among the Zulu, this is the "lord of heaven, chief in the sky" and Unkulunkulu "god, great one, old one". Zulu: male ancestor who developed from a bed of reeds;							All-Father: trickster deity on earth, goes to heaven after flood : ancestors move about, create landscape, names, rituals, songs; some culture heroes: shape embryos, create weapons, fire

		High god	Creation of	Bringing of fire		SE	C
Tricksters	Fon: Nzame's son Bingo, thrown out of heaven, became a culture hero Dogon: Nommo sends culture hero, first smith, descends by boat along the rainbow Bambara: The primordial spirit dropped a small ball on the earth from which successively, a tree stump, then water, then Faro developed, who continues the creation and the creation of man.	setting sun, Gauwa, is both a typical trickster deity but also the one who gives death	High god: He also functions as a culture hero from whom fire originated.	Creation of Buffalos by Ọn or his son Anto/ Ọn-teu Kwoto/Meilitars (born from a gourd) binds the sun with stone chain	Bringing of fire by theft	bao deities as creators/ tricksters	Moihernee/Moilnee created fire, rivers (cut them out of the land), islands, mountains Droemerdeene also created the Kangaroo Rat: fire Or: bringing of fire by two star spirits Pumper-neowlle and Pineterrinner	

(continued)

TABLE 5.4. *Continued*

Topic	AFRICA	Khoi-San/Damara/Herero/Hotentot	Pygmies	Nilgiri	ANDAMANS	Semang	Taiwan Highland Tribes	NEW GUINEA, MELANESIA	TASMANIA	AUSTRALIA
	Central and eastern Sudan: the heroes as ancestors, often joker as culture hero (and remnant of High God)								Or:fire first obtained from *numer* = "white man" [= spirit], appeared among people and coughed it up:	*Aranda*: death was limited to the earth; men had to die because all connections were severed between sky and earth; traditions about "broken ladders"
	Fan: *mbi/mba* lower gods as creator/ trickster gods								Black spot in Milky Way or Orion's Belt: a stingaree	—
	Ashanti: spider, Ananse; in form of bird, creates sun, moon, stars, day, night. As culture hero, first king, marries daughter of sky god								constellations seen as humans including Aborigines; two stars in Milky Way are two men and Mars = his foot; Milky Way = his road	Two Ntjikantja brothers, like the sun, the moon, Seven Sisters and evening star, emerged from earth, wandered about, like all earth-born totemic ancestors;
	Shilluk and Dinka: Both have a High God and original ancestor(s) of men; the dog functions as culture hero								sun and fem. moon, Vetaa, form islands;	grew old, returned into ground, sank back into ever-lasting sleep
	Maasai: single man at the beginning; on visit to sky, marries daughter of sky, returns to earth: ancestors of the Maasai were created as children of the "black" or "blue" god in heaven and stepped down to earth, along with their cattle. The ancestor of the chiefs, too, descended from heaven as a boy with a tail, who later on killed a monster (the dragon (*endiamassi*) Nenaunir "thick stick", with the help of his daughter. The blood of the dragon made the earth fertile								Moon got partly burnt in fire, rolled into sea and moved into sky to join husband, the Sun, Parnuen rainbow = their child good spirit, Moihernee/Parledee govern the day; evil spirit, Wrageo-Wrapper, the night	but those who rose into sky, got into ageless celestial bodies A vague form of human life existed as semi-embryonic masses of half-developed infants, at salt lakes or waterholes.

Totem Animals	<<Ashanti: spider, Ananse (that is also found with the Zande>> Ila: Itoshi monster, in rivers, lakes, from a distant past, before culture-heroes. He is he is ancestor, culture hero, nature spirit and water beast, often Itoshi a transformed chief, or even a trickster/culture hero	The San believe that they were "animals" (eland, springbok) of primordial times and were changed into current humans by power of the mantis, a form of //Kaggen.	<<a concept of a rainbow serpent: from neighbors?>>	Ôn or his son Anto/Ôn-teu creates buffaloes	all humans were once animals		Dema totem deities: totems or objects with sacred meaning or taboos used by clans, bloodlines, or people bound by shared activities: as part of "known order"; baos = possessors of fire; they stole it from each other	Parledee with kangaroo feet (> human); flying snakes, seen in forest and mountains; C: Distinguished between good and evil spirits	C: ancestors and totems of patrilinear clans; behave like humans; also some humans who can change into animals; C: supernatural beings awakened from sleep, broke through surface of earth; earth has light for first time: sun rose out of the ground
HUMANS created	Humans created: from clay (Baumann 1936: 203): wood, 205; from trees, 224; tree grave, 235; from heaven, 206; from excrements, 214 etc.; humans as center, 215; from termite hills, from caves and rocks, 219; from knee, 221 Fan: Nzame creates 1st man, 2nd; Sekumeh, mankind's ancestor; his wife created from tree; Nzame created the first man, Fam, the lord of all beings who was, however, banned into a hole because of his haughtiness. The second created man, Sekumeh, is mankind's ancestor,	Khoi San were animals (springbok), changed into humans by mantis = Kaggen Created all its beings no distinction between animals and humans, during the second stage of creation, humans and animals were differentiated, Herero: first man is important: Bantu influence Hotentot: a primordial ancestor, an old bush demon, called Heitsi-Eibib or Heiseb, national hero, and a great sorcerer	Humans are sent down from heaven by the High God Or high god forms them himself.	Teikirzi or Tirshti) creates all Todas and rules Man follows buffaloes on his tail Woman born from one rib	Humans emerge from split bamboo; women made from clay (or by cutting off male genitals) or: from root of tree; from SW monsoon, or from Lady Crab	Humans emerge from rock (Atayal) or from a tree (then, arrive by boat after the flood)	men and women carved from a tree; Or: men created from clay, women from a tree. (Banks I.) first spirit (not a god), born from a rock, carved men and women from a tree. Or, man created from clay, woman from a tree	Parledee made 1st man, Parlevar, from the ground Moihernee/Moilnee created humans, also kangaroos, "out of the ground" first human (Parlevar) had kangaroo feet and tail and a joint leg; Droemerdeene cut the tail and gave him legs with joints	SE: Mungan-ngawa's son and wife, ancestors of humans, after a great fire or flood had killed humans N/NW: All-Mother's (snake's) children become humans others: earth opens and Aborigines emerge C: totem animals change to humans: "totemic ancestors" moved about on earth, created all physical features of landscape

(continued)

TABLE 5.4. *Continued*

Topic	AFRICA	Khoi-San/Damara/Herero/Hotentot	Pygmies	Nilgiri	ANDAMANS	Semang	Taiwan Highland Tribes	NEW GUINEA, MELANESIA	TASMANIA	AUSTRALIA
	Bambara: The primordial spirit, then Faro developed, who continues the creation and the creation of man. Dogon: Amma creates humans with help of earth — Zulu: male ancestor who developed from a bed of reeds — Maasai: ancestors of the Maasai were created as children of the "black" or "blue" god in heaven and stepped down to earth, along with their cattle. The ancestor of the chiefs, too, descended from heaven as a boy with a tail, who later on killed a monster (the dragon (*endiamassi*) Nenaunir "thick stick", with the help of his daughter. The blood of the dragon made the earth fertile first humans lived in "paradise" (Kerio) until the High God returned to heaven by a ladder.							At first, old people shed their skin, and entered a new life faculty of rebirth is lost through a mangled message, delivered by snake Kalije and the Sibine bird (hornbill). spirits of dead live as sky people with settlements like humans — Or: primordial killing of man-eating snake, becomes ancestor of humans; therefore snakes are taboo, cannot be eaten	or: humans created by two stars in Milky Way, Pumpermehowle /Pumperneowlle /Pineterrinner	Some totemic ancestors, culture heroes, do age and decay, but immortal; even when "killed" live on in form of *tjúrunga* implement (used in initiation) (sun, moon, and earth-born celestial bodies rise into the sky)
From Trees	From tree, reeds				Tree		Tree	Tree	(tree burial)	(tree burial)
clay	Clay				Clay		Rock (Atayal)	Clay		

3. EVIL	Nzame's son Bingo, born from human wife, thrown out of heaven, became a culture hero **Dogon:** High God's son Jurugu has incest with mother; gives birth to evil bush spirits **E. and S.Bantu:** golden age ended by woman's mistake	San: setting sun, Gauwa, is both a typical trickster deity but also the one who gives death			?	Droerdeen(er) as evil spirit ?
Punishment, by Flood and death	Flood (widespread) mostly as punishment; (no retribution) Rainbow serpent	Flood from tree, <rainbow serpent>	Catastrophe: great flood through excessive rain; people rescued on a tree and come down by creeper	water below earth rises due to actions of grandmothers of Tapern; or: flood occurred when children imitated a bird; all drown except one shaman	Flood Myth: escape by boat (Puyuma arrive by boat in Taiwan) Curious woman spoils rebirth of deceased from their graves (old people shed their skin, and entered a new life)	SE: after a great fire/flood had killed human, repopulated by Munganngawa's son and wife C: Evil deed (killing) brings end of Golden Age; origin of death:
Death	Bushmen: soul in body of animal when leaving for eternal world (rock art, too: flying bucks) The spirit of a San lodges itself in the body of an animal as it leaves for the eternal world to join the ancestors, (in *bokveld*). -Damara: souls of dead, in heaven; no more children; eat dead persons' bodies	Maasai: Death brought to earth after a single man married a daughter of heaven: through a mistake	Souls travel via bridge guarded by watchman, to tree on island and eat its fruit; are reborn(?) as small children		Soul, in left breast After death goes to (Bass Strait) islands (with "many" departed) and "jump up" "white man" = a spirit	primordial beings on earth must die death was limited to earth because all connections severed between sky and earth: "broken ladders"
Ritual	moon and boar: ritual function too				?	broken ladders: tree, spear, at many ceremonial sites
Sorcery	Use of materials (fetish), lack of sorcery formulae. No sacred speech? Ashanti: Occult power in "fetishes", worn on body	shamanism	shamanism	shamanism	Some secret spells ? in exist in New Guinea; shamanism	shamanism

Eurasian diver myth, in that a chicken scratches sand and the earth emerges. In some of these cases, the earth and other items are created by a stepwise progression (Africa, Tasmania). This is also visible in Australia, though in a different fashion: it is through the actions of the totem ancestors that the world finally takes shape in its current form.

***

As has been emphasized, the interest of Gondwana mythology clearly lies with the origins of humans. The first man and woman are sometimes created by the High God (Africa); however, in many other cases they simply emerge from trees:[360] a split tree, a tree stump, or a bamboo.[361] Even where this is not clearly stated, such as in Australia, it is symbolized in ritual, where the tree plays a great role in initiation and in burial; this is also seen in Africa.[362]

There exist some important variations on the topic, insofar as women (or sometimes men) are created from clay. Both motifs exist next to each other in some African, Andamanese, and Melanesian mythologies and may therefore be assumed to be original. Both motifs are also found, here and there, in Laurasian territories as well: clay origin is seen most obviously in the Bible, but it is also found in northeastern Afghanistan (Nuristan) and in ancient Egypt. Curiously, the tree motif is found in Laurasia, too: it occurs in Iceland (Edda), in the Philippines, in Austronesian Taiwan, in Japanese folktales (Kaguyahime), and in Mesopotamia;[363] and there are indications of a tree burial, similar to Australian, Tasmanian, Andaman, and African customs,[364] in ancient India (Veda) and North America. We will return to this topic later on (§5.7, §6). Curiously, southeastern Australia also has a tradition of the origin of humans from below the surface of the earth, a motif that is prominently found in the Americas and sporadically elsewhere (ancient India).[365]

Finally, most of the Gondwana traditions share the motif of the primordial misdeed or hubris of the early humans. Usually a broken food taboo leads to the origin of death. This can occur early on and is then compounded by a son of the High God who commits incest with his mother. More commonly, it is the humans who show hubris or misbehave. Sometimes the guilt is put on a woman (Africa, Melanesia),[366] but in most cases it is individual men who commit some action that invites punishment.

In many instances, such punishment is a Great Flood (or occasionally fire). This motif, however, is attested worldwide and will therefore be investigated in detail below (§5.7.2). At this instance it is important to underline that the motif of the Great Flood is not part of a scheme of the Four or Five Ages as in Laurasian mythology but remains a onetime affair. A few humans emerge from the Great Flood, either because they had taken refuge on a tree or mountain or in a boat or because the gods re-create them (southeastern Australia). As expected in a myth of worldwide distribution, these very mythemes are also found in Laurasian myth.

Death not caused by the Great Flood but affecting all human beings is prominent in all traditions. In some, guilt is laid at the feet of a curious woman (Melanesia) who wanted to find out how the deceased were reborn, out of the ground. In most traditions, however, the guilt is of a more general nature: it is due to the violation of certain taboos. For example, in Australia, the evil deed of killing certain totem animals by one of their comrades brings about the end of the Golden Age; from this instance onward, even the original totem beings must die, and so do humans.

Many of the Gondwana myths and mythemes are remarkably close to certain myths in the Hebrew Bible.[367] Gondwana origin cannot really be expected for them, as the ancient Hebrews formed part of the Semitic Near East, an area clearly following Laurasian mythology. The opposite, late biblical influence on various distant populations in Africa, Asia, and Sahul Land, is also not very likely: the motifs are too widely spread even among little- or not yet contacted populations and form part and parcel of their mythologies. For example, the myth of Adam and Eve's expulsion from Paradise is very close to that of the West African Bassari tribe in Togo and of the Pygmies (§5.3.5.1).[368] Interestingly, the paradise motif is found as far afield as among the Polynesians, where it is an ancient part of their myths and has an Indonesian parallel. These problems are worth a detailed separate investigation that cannot be undertaken here.

In spite of such common Gondwana and some isolated Pan-Gaean motifs, it must be emphasized that Gondwana myth does not share the Laurasian story line from creation to destruction: it misses the account of original creation and the final destruction. Instead, its focus is the origin of humans. In sum, the reconstruction as given for Laurasian mythology in the preceding chapters (§§2–3) is confirmed by its "antipode," Gondwana mythology.

***

If we want to characterize, in a more general fashion, the early, unattested levels of Gondwana mythology beyond the listing of the various mythemes involved, we have to take into account, first, the differences between the African myths and those of the Australian and Melanesian subgroups. African mythology is deeply interested in dualism (see §5.4). Nature and society are both split into two groups. This anticipates (or parallels?) the strong Laurasian penchant for dualistic structures that some see present already in Stone Age rock art.[369] Sub-Saharan African myth further divides the world into several layers that are linked by symbolism, which again is a feature that has close parallels in the Laurasian system of correlations.[370]

On the other hand, this sort of arrangement is not typical for Australia and Melanesia (Sahul Land).[371] In the Sahul system, life and myth form an immediate, close union and less a *system* of thought, as scholars like Leenhardt underline. It is said to be less organized and structured and provides for a direct "explanation" of existing customs, rituals, or features of nature. The system, however, may just remain unexpressed and unspoken in myth and ritual, though it in fact underlies them.[372] Australian mythology stands out for its well-known feature of Dreamtime (the Dreaming) in certain rituals, a characteristic found in this particular form only in Australia.

The Papuan/Melanesian system must be investigated separately in much more detail, especially as the highland Papuas developed a form of food production (horticulture) at a very early time (c. 7000–6500 BP)[373] and can be expected to have worked out complex new ritual structures and worldviews then. One would expect new agriculture-based items in their myths, for example, in comparison with Australian myths. Indeed, Jensen's Hainuwele myth provides precisely such data.[374] Hainuwele and other humans are born from the fork between the tree stem and its branches, as if these were the spread thighs of a woman giving birth.

■ §5.5. SECONDARY INFLUENCES ON GONDWANA MYTHOLOGY

As mentioned, a major problem that affects the evidence found in Africa, Melanesia, New Guinea, and to some extent Australia is not just the late attestation of these mythologies but also the possible mutual influences of Gondwana and Laurasian mythology. In some coastal areas of New Guinea we have Micronesian and Polynesian influences that must carefully be distinguished from the original common Papua/Melanesian pattern of mythology. The same kind of external influence is perhaps true, to a minor extent, in the case of Papua influence on Australia (see §4.3.2, §5.6). However, these areas, especially Australia, have been isolated from the rest of Asia for a long time. As is well known, the only well-attested influx from Asia to Australia may have been the *dingo* dog, which was imported 5,000–3,000 years ago.[375] It may have been introduced from Sunda Land,[376] which also brought a new stone tool technology. For the rest, the Australians Aborigines developed in an undisturbed and isolated fashion.[377]

In Africa, however, such isolation was not possible, in spite of the formidable Sahara Desert. It actually was much less an obstacle to human survival and travel at certain times in prehistory, for example, during the Mesolithic and Neolithic. Until c. 3000 BCE the Sahara was much wetter, a wide belt of steppe grassland, as the Sahara rock paintings indicate (see §4.4). Contact of "sub-Saharan" populations with the Berber and Egyptian ones north required much less effort than during the last 5,000 years or so.

In addition, another zone of contact existed, as described earlier, from Ethiopia and Somaliland via all of East Africa down to Zimbabwe, Namibia, and South Africa, areas that have been settled by Bantu-speaking Africans over the past 2,000 years.[378] Agriculture spread south from Kenya after c. 500 CE.[379] In this savanna and steppe belt, one could quickly bypass the impenetrable jungles of the Congo Basin (also settled by Bantus). It is precisely along the East African corridor that we see northern influences penetrate deeply into the south.[380] (Baumann also detects Indian influences by trade across the India Ocean.)

Another area of impact, discussed already, is the steppe area south of the Sahara that is partly settled by Berber and other Afro-Asian-speaking peoples such as the Hausa, as well as by Niger-Congo- and some Nilo-Saharan-speaking Africans. The Sahel belt has deeply influenced the Guinea coast. Interestingly, however, more remote areas, such as those of the Bantus of the Gabon and Congo areas, do not show northern influences (except in northernmost Congo, where we have evidence of some influences from the powerful, well-organized Azande). The Bantu-speaking peoples who now settle in all of Central, East, and South Africa from Cameroon to the Cape are believed to have emigrated from their original homeland in Cameroon or nearby areas about 2,000 years ago.

***

By separating such relatively isolated areas in Africa, the Andamans, Papua, Australia, and Tasmania from zones of potential contact, we can establish the older forms of the Gondwana belt of mythology. Most cases of secondary influences can be explained by subsequent interaction with Laurasian mythologies. In the Andamans, interestingly, the suggestion of secondary influence was first made by an archaeologist.[381] The same is true for the West African "mixed" mythologies, where the explanation of Sahel influence has long been asserted by anthropologists such as Frobenius. In both cases, these conclusions were reached long before the Laurasian theory was first conceived or proposed.[382] Incidental Gondwana influences on Laurasian myth have been discussed in preceding chapters, passim, whenever they came up (§2, §3, §6.1).

In other words, there are some cases of secondary diffusion that have affected both the Laurasian and Gondwana areas. They will be taken up next.

▪ §5.6. CONFLICTING MYTHS IN GONDWANALAND

§5.6.1. Gondwana elements in Laurasian myth

As indicated, there are a number of special cases where certain isolated items of the earlier, Gondwana and Pan-Gaean mythologies have succeeded in being included in the Laurasian scheme. To be precise, they were occasionally inserted not just into "folktales" but into the very story line. A case in point is that of human origin from trees. It is found in Japan, in Taiwan, and in another version in Iceland's Edda (where Askr and Embla, "Ash and Elm" trees, are ancestors). Such occurrences are not entirely unexpected, if Laurasian mythology emerged from mythologies belonging to the "Out of Africa" movement that took place around 65,000 BCE.

To use the linguistic simile: just as a few isolated archaic (pre-Indo-European) forms remain in the reconstructed (Indo-European) "mother" tongue, so do a few mythic archaisms remain in the reconstructed Laurasian mythology. Other cases may include many tales that are now classified as folktales ("Jack and Jill," "Jack and the Beanstalk," etc.) and certain creation myths discussed earlier (§3.4), such as the flood (§3.9, §5.7.2) and the origin of the universe from a primordial giant or a rock or stone pillar.

***

In the margin, the complicated case of an early, hypothetical Dene-Caucasian or Macro-Caucasian mythology and its influence on Laurasian myth may be taken up briefly. The ancestors of the peoples who speak Macro-Caucasian languages (Basque, Northern Caucasian such as Cherkes or Chechen, Burushaski in the Pamirs) migrated into these areas probably during the warm period at c. 40 kya (§4.3, 4.4). The genetic situation—NRY C—is complex (§4.3), though some evidence points to a link of the Burusho with the Basque.[383] However, it is entirely unclear so far whether these peoples also shared a common mythology, whether this mythology was already the Laurasian one, or whether it was a predecessor that was still close to the Gondwana one. The problem is compounded by the fact that all three populations have become Christian or Muslim, so that their original mythology is obscured and can only be reconstructed based on legends and rituals. This must be set up as a detailed study, requiring good knowledge of the languages and cultures involved, and it is therefore something that cannot be carried out here.

However, there is growing evidence that facets of the Macro-Caucasian myths can be recovered. The Caucasus specialist K. Tuite has drawn attention to correspondences between the mythologies of linguistically unrelated high mountain peoples, such as the Svan (whose language belongs to the Southern Caucasus family of Kartvelian/Georgian) and the Burusho in the Pamirs (who speak a Macro-Caucasian language to which Basque and *Northern* Caucasian belong). This also includes the pre-Hindu religion of the Indo-Aryan-speaking Kalasha of Chitral in northwestern Pakistan. They share the same mythical structure involving the pure high mountains, where a Lady of the Animals lives, a *potnia thērōn* who rules over the mountain goats, ibex, and the like. She is opposite to the low, impure villages of the valley, and the two realms are mediated by goatherds and hunters.

Details of this scheme, seen both in the Caucasus and in the Hindu Kush, can be observed by contrasting the accounts of K. Jettmar for the Pamirs and K. Tuite for the Caucasus.[384] Such "mountain systems" clearly are not restricted to the Macro-Caucasian languages; they have also heavily influenced the mythologies of their neighbors, or rather, these have taken over many aspects of Macro-Caucasian mythology. In the Caucasus this applies to various peoples such as the non-Dene-Caucasian Kartvelians, and in the Hindu Kush, to the Indo-Iranian Nuristani and Indo-Aryan Kalasha; even in the early Vedic texts (c. 1000 BCE) there are many traces of such "mountain" beliefs and myths.[385]

The remnants of Basque myths (as well as those of neighboring Asturians and Cantabrians)[386] should also be compared. A first indication of old, underlying connections is that the main goddess (*lamia*) of the Basque, the beautiful Mari, is a deity of the high mountains, who occasionally leaves her cave and moves along the mountains, producing hail and storms. Mortals such as shepherds are not allowed to come close to her cave, a feature she shares with the "fairies" of the Hindu Kush and Pamirs.

Certainly, a single myth such as that of the Lady of the Animals and associated customs and rituals cannot decide the existence of an old, assumed Macro-Caucasian mythology from the Pyrenees to the Pamirs, and even less that of a possible Dene-Caucasian one. However, this is an intriguing beginning whose lead should be investigated further.

§5.6.2. Laurasian elements in Gondwana myth

Conversely, the occasional intrusion of some Laurasian features into Gondwana mythologies speaks *for* the validity of the theory. The complex situation in sub-Saharan Africa can be explained, as indicated above, by northern and northeastern African influences. As also indicated earlier (§5.3.4–5), the impact by northeastern African (Afro-Asiatic and Nilotic) mythology can be seen all along the "East African Highway" from Kenya down to South Africa. This impression, based just on mythological evidence, is now confirmed by that derived from agriculture and linguistics. Myths were transported south by Bantu agriculturalists who started to move out from southernmost Kenya at c. 500 BCE.[387] The wide belt of wooded savanna between East Africa and the lands south of the Zambezi is infested by the tsetse fly and thus home to trypanosomiasis and other livestock diseases. The Bantus' cattle adapted to this only later and finally reached South Africa.[388] Northeast influence is especially evident when certain myths are connected with ritual kingship.[389]

***

In the following, I quickly review the motifs that can be suspected to be of Laurasian influence or of predating the formation of both current African and Laurasian myths. They are typically isolated among surrounding, "true" African motifs and can be regarded (a) as isolated survivals of older (Pan-Gaean) motifs that have survived in other Gondwana and Laurasian traditions or (b) as intrusive material that entered sub-Saharan Africa from the Sahel north or the northeast via Uganda, Kenya, and so on. The matter is further complicated in that we only have very recent materials for this vast region, often collected by Christian missionaries or colonial officials who may or may not have (even unconsciously) been influenced by or added from their particular religious background. These theoretical possibilities apart, it will be seen that the isolated items listed below are due to northern/northeastern influences. The most prominent among them include the following.

1. Primordial ocean.[390] This mytheme has been described above (§3.1.2) as typical for Laurasian myth. Baumann clearly identifies Egyptian and Asian origins for this mytheme. It is found with the Baule, who live west of the Akan on the Ivory Coast, and who are indeed within the range of Sahel influences (§5.3.4.5);[391] similarly, it is found among the Ibo on the Lower Niger, whose royal ancestors descended on termite hills in the midst of water. This is again clearly reminiscent of the Egyptian primordial hill. Other myths about primordial mountains are not connected.[392]

   A version reminding one most of Laurasian myth is that found with the Bushongo (Kuba) in western Congo, who are connected culturally with the "Yoruba-Benin cultural area":[393] in primordial half-light only the giant god Bumba existed on the waters, until he vomited, in Egyptian fashion, the stars. Similarly the Konde (on Nyasa Lake) talk of "prehuman spirits that were in the world when the earth was covered with water."[394] All these cases are found in the areas of Sahel and northern East African influences (§§5.3, 5.4 sq.), if we can indeed include, with Baumann, the Bushongo in this scheme.

2. Fishing up the floating earth and spreading it. As described above in §3.1.3, this motif is found with the Yoruba and the Edo in Benin. They tell of a bird that spread the earth on the primordial waters.[395] Closely connected is the mytheme of the soft, unstable earth.[396] It is found in the southern Congo area,[397] the Songe in northeastern Congo on the Lomani River, the Bemba in southeastern Congo, the Zulu, the Baule, and so on—again in areas that are within the range of northern and northeastern influences.

3. The world egg.[398] This mytheme is found with the Pangwe in the northwestern Bantu area, who immigrated from the Upper Sangha and Shari rivers, "areas of predominantly Sudan culture."[399] The earth is derived from a mushroom "like an egg." The upper half of the egg became heaven, and the lower one, the earth. From both halves developed the sun, stars, trees, animals, and the primordial Mother, who gives birth to further items including the High God and father of humans. Baumann again derives most of this myth from the "high civilizations and their derivatives."[400] The motif is also found with the Pygmies living just east of the Pangwe and with some remnant population on the coast of Gabon, where the two halves became man and woman.

4. Creation of light (cf. §3.5.1). By exception, the Yoruba and Vili-Fote (Loango in Congo) even have the typical Laurasian motif of heaven lying on earth: light appears only after they have been separated.[401]

5. Primordial waters are guarded by a monster.[402] Apart from some motifs that are close to flood myths,[403] there are exceptional motifs among the Remba of Mashona Land that tell of water being guarded by an eight-headed snake(!) that demanded a young woman as payment. This is very close to the Japanese version of the myth. The snake, however, is killed by two friends, a young lion and a bull. Similar myths are found with the Ila of Zambia (*itoshi* monster), the Kulia (Lake Victoria), and the Nyaruanda; in western Sudan with the Fulse of Yatenga; and in derived versions elsewhere, for example, with the Maasai, Nama (Hottentot), Kikuyu, and so on. Again, almost all the populations mentioned are (or were) located within the areas of influence of the northern (Sahel) and northeast African mythologies.

6. Father Heaven/Mother Earth. Some areas in West Africa, a few small pockets in the Congo–Zambezi area, and a narrow strip from Uganda to southern Ethiopia have the myth of the world parents, which comes close to the Laurasian motif of Father Heaven/Mother Earth. Baumann has explained them as influences from the Sudan (Sahel belt) and others as influences that came with the India trade (via the Kenya coast).[404]

In West Africa, the motif is found in the area south of the Niger bend in Mali, down to the Guinea coast, stretching from the Ivory Coast to western Cameroon, and further, in eastern Nigeria from the Lower Niger area and northeastward toward Lake Chad. Baumann attributes the spread of these features to the influence of the Yoruba, Edo, Mossi, and Baule. He tentatively suggests their import from these areas to a small pocket east and west of the mouth of the Congo as well as to another small pocket near the Upper Zambezi (Luyi/Rotse).

Another major area of this motif extends from the east coast of Lake Victoria toward southern Ethiopia, with a small pocket near the coast in southeastern Kenya. Baumann thinks of late influence due to trade with India and laments that more work should be done on Indian influence in East Africa.[405] We now know that trade between the Indian Subcontinent and Africa goes back to at least c. 2000 BCE, when millet was exported from Africa to India and the zebu bull was brought to Africa (and 500 BCE when bananas were brought, indirectly, all the way from Papua to Africa).[406] However, as we do not know much about Indian religions at the time and just have some pictorial motifs of the Indus civilization, nothing definite can be said. The Indo-European motifs of Father Heaven and Mother Earth can be expected only after c. 1000 BCE, when the landlocked Vedic civilization seems to have developed some maritime trade.[407]

Theoretically, the spotty attestation of this motif could also be explained as the survival of a widespread myth, more or less overlapping with the

"Niger-Congo" language family from West Africa to the Kenyan coast and to the Upper Zambezi. However, that would leave unexplained why the motif is not found more widely in most Bantu-speaking areas. The scenario is unlikely.

In sum, these Laurasian motifs in Africa are isolated and can be explained as intrusions from areas that have Laurasian mythology.

Australia

Similar cases of "contamination" may be observed in Australian myth. An investigation must take into account the claim by some anthropologists of outside influence emanating from the Papuas during the last Ice Age.[408] There seems to be some indication of this influence in language and clearly so in genetics.[409] We may further also suspect some impact from the early British settlements in Australia on southeastern Australian mythology.[410] The most important countercheck to be carried out in this particular context may be that of studying the few relics of Tasmanian beliefs, recorded before British settlers exterminated the Tasmanian tribes around 1835 and their few survivors died by the end of the century.[411]

Sahul Land and South America

Another means of counterchecking the two great mythological traditions of Laurasia and Gondwana is the comparison of a number of mythemes found both in Sahul Land and in South America. The two areas, one belonging to Gondwana and the other to Laurasian mythology, should show clear distinctions.

However, a comparison of the prominent motifs of both areas has been carried out by Y. Berezkin, who has amassed, over the last two–three decades, large amounts of materials from Asia, the Americas, and now also Europe and Africa.[412] At first sight, this overlap may be regarded as a counterpoint to the Laurasian theory: items found with the Amerindians should only be derived from southern and eastern Siberia, and not from Sahul Land. However, once the current Out of Africa theory is considered, the concurrence no longer surprises.[413] Both Australia/ Papua and South America reflect refuge areas, where old myths have survived later population movements. In North America, these could be due to the later Siberian immigration by the Na-Dene (Athapascan, Navajo/Apache)-speaking peoples and their mythologies. Indeed, Berezkin has found a large degree of congruence between Siberian and North American myths but much less with South American myths. In that case, South American myths may represent remnants of the myths of the first migration into the Americas, now generally put at c. 20,000 BCE.

If correct, overlapping Australian/Melanesian and South American myths may indicate original Gondwana and *early* Laurasian mythology. Reconsidering this evidence may help in the reconstruction of the earliest form of Laurasian mythology, in the same way as a comparison between Mesoamerican and Eurasian myths of the Four (or Five) Ages (§2.5.2) effectively does.

Isolated items, again

However, one has to be extremely careful with isolated items, say, the motif of Father Heaven/Mother Earth, which is exceptionally found also in sub-Saharan Africa.[414] If taken at face value, the isolated "dot" on one of Y. Berezkin's maps would indicate a very ancient, Pan-Gaean origin of the concept, while specialists have long pointed out that such items are an import from the north.

Here, the principle of "isolated survivals" (§2.3) and that of local historical development including diffusion (§1.5) are in conflict. Initially, we may simply state the occurrence of such data, but we will have to leave the resolution to detailed, individual studies. At any rate, such *isolated* features cannot be used to deny the validity of the Laurasian theory, a point that is taken up next.

▪ §5.7. COUNTERCHECKING LAURASIAN MYTHOLOGY BASED ON GONDWANA MYTHOLOGY

After having established the structure and major items of the original, Proto-Gondwana mythology as well as those of the individual African, Andaman, Melanesian, and Australian mythologies, the reconstructed Proto-Gondwana mythology can be used for a mutual countercheck of both the Gondwana and the Laurasian schemes. If reconstructed Gondwana mythology contains items or major motifs that are supposed to be Laurasian, they may be due either to the influence of neighboring Laurasian mythologies, or to later influx through migrations, or to (individual?) diffusion. Such items must be explained as intrusions within a reasonable range of probability. Otherwise, the item in question can no longer be attributed to Laurasian influence and must have originated under different conditions, which remain to be explored. For example, these items could derive from still earlier stages of Out of Africa mythology, as is suggested by some overlapping mythemes found in Australian/Papua and South American mythologies.[415]

The Laurasian theory is not affected by such individual cases, but it would be obliterated, as discussed earlier (§2.6), if its typical structure (story line from creation of the universe to its death) could be shown to be attested in Gondwana mythology as well. So far such evidence has not appeared.

However, a brief incipient, if different story line can be noticed in reconstructed Gondwana mythology. It has been summarized earlier (§5.3.3) and in Table 5.2.

§5.7.1. Essential features of Gondwana and Laurasian mythology

Some parts of the outline of Gondwana mythology may be compared with reconstructed Laurasian mythology. (Essential features are listed in Table 5.3, p. 323.)

The development of Laurasian mythology, with its added myths and the underlying story line that unifies them, may have taken place during the transition from the Middle to the Upper Paleolithic, which occurred some 40,000 years ago when the number of human bands increased rapidly and new artifacts appeared. The event may also be related to the "explosive" development of complex art (preserved in rock art; see §4.4.1, §7.1.2 sqq.) and, according to some, even the development of true human speech.[416] It also coincides with the spread northward of anatomically modern humans during this period, effectively establishing Laurasian mythology in most parts of Eurasia.

***

As an excursus—intended as a paradigmatic undertaking of Laurasian/Gondwana overlaps and origins—a somewhat detailed study of the global flood myths will follow.

§5.7.2. The flood myth in worldwide perspective

A Gondwana myth—and beyond

As has been discussed in some detail above (§3.9), the flood myth is widespread in Laurasian mythology,[417] as well as in Gondwana areas. It will therefore be treated here at some length, as a countercheck to the Laurasian theory. This is based on relatively well-attested mythemes connected with the flood myth. It is intended as a specimen of investigations that should be carried out for all major myths involving both Gondwana and Laurasian mythologies.[418]

In both, the flood myth has the distinct aspect of retribution or revenge, regardless of details: it does not matter whether the flood emerges from heaven, from the ocean, or just from a calabash (a mytheme also found outside Gondwanaland). In most Gondwana myths, the flood is retribution for or the result of a mistake. It frequently originates from rain or from a rain spell. Some divine creature is involved, either the rainbow snake (only in Australia) or a deity of heaven or of the mountains.

Australia

To begin, we take a closer look at Australia, as this region was settled early (c. 60,000–40,000 BCE) and thus offers the possibility for relatively undisturbed preservation of old data. Most typical for all of Australia is the idea of the rain spell. It is common in all areas, the southeast, the northeast, and the north. As has been explained above (§5.3.2), the latter two areas are suspect of later intrusions of people,[419] concepts, and motifs from New Guinea. It therefore is best to keep these areas separate in the following investigation. Also, while the flood as retribution or as the result of a mistake is very common, the involvement of the rainbow snake is found only in the north, while that of a creator deity is present only in the southeast. As the latter is also found in Africa (§5.3.5, and see below), this is of importance.

Southeastern Australia

The southeast exhibits other phenomena of retention, such as some linguistic features and some indications of genetic peculiarities, spelled out above (§4.3, §5.3.2).[420] It also has relative homogeneity in the etyma of tribal names, favoring those in *Gu*–. From the point of view of religion, the southeast is the only area in Australia that knows of a *deus otiosus*, a distant creator god, which may also be assumed for Tasmania (§5.3.2.1). An earlier occupation by Tasmanians may be the basis of these facts. The individual flood mythemes involved are the following:[421]

(1) Flood covering all land, all people die, except some
(2) Flood as *retribution* by creator for evil deeds of humans, emerging from ocean
(3) Flood as *retribution* for specific evil deed of (a) man, emerging from frog
(4) Flood as solution for *overpopulation* (by animal clans), emerging from *rain spell* (all old features comparable with Laurasian mythology)

Northeastern Australia

The northeast is regarded as a separate myth zone, with some eastern New Guinea influence; it has an extension to the southern and western parts of Australia, again a feature with some linguistic backing (area of nonbound pronouns, see above). The major mythemes involved are the following:

(1) Flood covering all land, few survive on *mountain*
(2) Flood from *rain spell*, all die
(3) Flood from water bag, covering land, stopped by tree
(4) Flood from misdeed/mistake of rainmaker, covering all land
(5) Flood from *spell*, reaches canoe on top of mountain
(6) Flood with boat carrying people
(7) Flood from saltwater in footsteps, as retribution
(8) Flood from river kills half of mankind

North(west)ern Australia

The northern part of Australia, especially Arnhem Land and the Kimberleys, is regarded as the original home of the languages not from the large Pama-Nyungan language family that covers the rest of Australia. Typically, the north has a large number of densely packed languages. The area is also typical for its prefixed bound pronouns, which are only found here in this particular way, excluding even those parts of Australia that have bound pronouns (southeast, much of the central and western areas). The mythological facts tend to agree with the concept of the north and northwest as a separate region, though some secondary Western New Guinean influence during the past glacial maximum has been proposed and proved by population genetics.[422]

As far as the flood myth is concerned, the following mythemes are typical, including the Rainbow Serpent's involvement in the flood (mythemes 1–8), a typical intrusive Papua feature of this area:

(1) Flood from rainbow serpent's *rain spell*, as high as tall serpent
(2) Flood from rainbow serpent's flooding, children drown
(3) Flood from *crying*, people die, rainbow serpent eats them
(4) Flood from rain rock, Rainbow Snake *urinates*, people drown[423]
(5) Flood from *crying*/breaking rainbow snake's eggs, becomes rock
(6) Flood from killing snake, woman drowns and is eaten by snake
(7) Flood from killing Rainbow Snake, women drown and are eaten by snake
(8) Flood from tree falling into creek, all drown
(9) Flood from felling tree, people drown
(10) Flood from wounds, people drown to dream world
(11) Flood from wounds/*rain spell* and *crying*/tears, people washed away
(12) Flood from honey bag, people turn into birds

In spite of some regional differences, nearly all of Australia is characterized by having flood myths that involve rain or rain spells and sometimes also boats by which one can flee to mountains or other areas. Another universal motif is that of retribution for some sort of mistake or evil deed: by a creator deity in the southeastern myths and by a rainbow snake in the northwest. Some of these motifs, such as the rainbow snake, will also be met with in other areas of Gondwanaland (and even in Laurasian India and South America).

***

Summing up, in all of Australia, we can discern the following main motifs:

(1) Flood covering all land, few survive on mountain
(2) Flood from water or honey bag, covering land, stopped by tree
(3) Flood from misdeed/mistake of rainmaker, covering all land
(4) Flood from saltwater in footsteps, as retribution
(5) Flood from (rainbow snake's) *rain spell*, all die
(6) Flood from *spell*, escape by boat, on top of mountain
(7) Rainbow serpent's flooding (from rain rock), children/people drown
(8) Flood from *crying*, Rainbow Snake eats people

(9)   Flood from killing the Rainbow Snake, woman eaten by snake
(10) Flood from tree falling/felled into creek, all drown
(11) Flood from wounds and rain spell/crying tears, people drown, go to dream world

New Guinea and the other Melanesian islands

The vast island of New Guinea and the other Melanesian islands stretch in a wide arch all the way from Indonesia to Fiji and New Caledonia, from the equator to the Tropic of Capricorn. Unlike Australia, a vast area of hunter and gatherer cultures, Melanesia has preserved, largely until today, early food-producing societies of a horticultural type. They are interesting as societies with the mythologies of early food-producing people that are quasi-frozen in time (though obviously the Melanesians are modern humans, just like everybody else). The type of flood myths found in Greater Melanesia matches those in Australia to some extent. A simplified list has these four major items:[424]

(1)   General flood covers all, except a mountain
(2)   Creator/other god destroys humans
(3)   Flood as retribution for killing of culture hero, some people escape
(4)   Flood as retribution for other mistakes, escape on raft or canoe

In the following, some of the important variants are given in some detail.

Atá (Philippines)

Water covered the whole earth, and all the Atás drowned except two men and a woman, who were carried far to sea. They would have perished, but a great eagle offered to carry them on its back to their homes. One man refused, but the other two people accepted and returned to Mapula.[425]

Andaman Islands

The Andaman Islands have been isolated for very long periods in history, basically until the arrival of the British in the mid–19th century. Their people, who speak isolated languages (connected by Greenberg to Papuan), carry a very old strain of DNA (NRY D), as early South Asian descendants of the move out of Africa.[426] Interestingly, their mythology has retained some very ancient traits as well (§3.5.3.4). Their flood myth, too, fits the pattern of the Papuan and Australian flood myths: it is one of the flood as retribution for early human misdeeds and an escape by boat (note that this is a retold version, like most Andaman myths, including Radcliffe-Brown's):

> Some time after their creation, men grew disobedient. In anger, Puluga, the Creator, sent a flood, which covered the whole land, except perhaps Saddle Peak where Puluga himself resided. Of all creatures, the only survivors were two men and two women

who had the fortune to be in a canoe when the flood came. The waters sank and they landed, but they found themselves in a sad plight. Puluga re[-]created birds and animals for their use, but the world was still damp and without fire....

After the people had warmed themselves [at the fire newly created by Puluga] and had leisure to reflect, they began to murmur against the Creator and even plotted to murder him. However, the Creator warned them away from such rash action, explained that men had brought the flood on themselves by their disobedience, and that another such offense would likewise be met with punishment. That was the last time the Creator spoke with men face to face.[427]

The biblical echoes of flood and covenant, again, are striking in this isolated population. However, it is against the emerging Andaman/Melanesian/Australian pattern that we must evaluate the flood myth as per the complicated evidence of sub-Saharan Africa.

Africa

While North Africa and the northern parts of East Africa clearly belong to the realm of Laurasian mythology, the vast lands south of the Sahara present a complicated picture that has been discussed above (§5.3.5). Anthropologists have long expressed the view that, like in Australia, there are several areas that have undergone influence from the north, especially from the Sahel belt and from the northern part of the East African area.[428] The data presented below will therefore be subdivided along these lines: (a) the core area, sub-Saharan Africa; (b) possible influence of the Sahel belt; and (c) northern East African influences.

In all areas, the flood myth is basically seen as an act of retribution;[429] it often originates from rain (or a vessel); and it is caused by some heavenly deities or mountain spirits. We begin with the area that has most likely retained the most

TABLE 5.5

GONDWANA mythology	LAURASIAN mythology
---	**Creation from nothing, chaos,** etc.
Earth, Heaven, sea **preexist**	Father Heaven/Mother Earth **created**, separated
High God in/towards heaven,	**Father Heaven** engenders:
sends down his son, totems, etc,	Two generations ('Titans/Olympians'):
---	Four (five) generations/ages
---	heaven pushed up, sun released
---	current gods defeat/kill predecessors
---	killing the dragon / sacred drink
... to **create humans**: from tree/clay	**humans:** *somatic* **descendants of Sun god**
they show **hubris**,	they (or a god) show **hubris**,
are punished by a **flood**	are punished by a **flood**
Trickster deities bring culture	**Trickster** deities bring culture
--	humans spread, emergence of 'nobles'
(local tribes)	local history begins
--	**final destruction of the world,**
--	**new heaven and earth emerge**

Comparison of major stages in Gondwana and Laurasian cosmogony

TABLE 5.6 *Laurasian and Gondwana, and Pan-Gaean flood myths*

Gondwana flood myths	Laurasian flood myths
(1) General flood covers all except a mountain	
Gondwana myths: Pygmy, Melanesia, Australia.	Laur. Mythology: Near East, India, Siberia, Taiwan, S.E. Asia, Americas, etc.
(2) Flood as retribution by god(s)/spirits & destruction of humans:	
Melanesia, Andaman, Africa	Laur. : Near East, Polynesia, Americas, etc.
Escape by boat (worldwide)	
Details:	
(2a) as retribution for killing of culture hero/ rainbow snake: Mel., Aus.	
(2b) by mistake or spell of rainmaker/rainbow snake, some humans eaten by snake: Aus. only cf. rainbow after flood (Hebrew Bible)	
(2c) as retribution for other mistakes: Mel. Aus., Laur. (human noise, etc.)	
(3) Flood from vessel, calabash, water/honey bag:	
Aus., Afr.	by rain (Near East, etc.), overturning of heaven/earth (Polynesia)
(4) Flood caused by someone's wounds or sores:	
Aus., Afr.	--

Pan-Gaean myths
(1) General flood covers all except a mountain
(2) Flood as retribution by god(s)/spirits, destruction of humans, escape by boat
(3) Flood from vessel/heavenly water store
(4) Flood caused by someone's wounds or sores: Aus., Afr. (but likely old)

original features, the central core area stretching from West Africa to the Congo and South Africa.

The African core area

The central sub-Saharan area exhibits some seven major mythemes. For practical reasons, the Pygmies are included here, though their mythology goes back much beyond any Bantu settlements in the area:

(1)   flood and first humans, flood emerging from tree
(2)   flood as retribution, from god's granddaughter
(3)   flood from sun/moon fight, and first/later humans
(4)   flood from a vessel, retribution for killing
(5)   flood as retribution, from sores
(6)   flood from sores
(7)   flood as retribution, by spell

West Africa

The areas in West Africa that are closer to the Sahel belt and that are prone to influences from the north exhibit these major mythemes:

(1) flood from calabash
(2) flood from calabash, and stones creating rivers/flood
(3) flood as retribution by a god
(4) flood, from rain, as punishment, escape
(5) flood, of village, broken clay pot as marriage sign
(6) flood, friend of sun and moon, rise to sky

The East African belt

As indicated above, the eastern belt of Africa, stretching from Kenya to South Africa, has been subject to influences from the Nilotic and Omotic areas. It exhibits the following major mythemes of the flood myth:

(1) flood from pot on top of house
(2) flood, from rain, retribution for murder; boat, rainbow
(3) flood from rain, retribution by spirit on mountain
(4) lake created by mountain spirits

***

In sum, the sub-Saharan African evidence suggests the following major mythemes within flood myth traditions:

(1) flood and first humans, flood emerging from tree, no retribution (Pygmy)
(2) flood (from rain) as retribution by a god, god's granddaughter, or mountain spirits
(3) flood from sun/moon fight, first and later humans
(4) flood from vessel or calabash, retribution for killing
(5) flood as retribution and sores, or by spell

It is remarkable that a specific item, such as the connection with wounds (5), reappears in Australia (see above) but not in Laurasian mythology.

Summary

Finally, by a general comparison of Gondwana myths, involving the African, Andaman, Melanesian, and Australian flood myths, we arrive at the flowing simplified scheme that seems older than any Christian or Islamic influence in the regions concerned:

(1) General flood covers all except a mountain (Pygmy, Melanesian, Australian) ~ Laurasian myth
(2) Flood as retribution by god(s)/spirits, destruction of humans (escape by boat) (Melanesian, Andaman, African) = Laurasian

(2a) Flood as retribution for killing of culture hero/rainbow snake (Melanesian, Australian)

(2b) Flood by mistake or spell of rainmaker/rainbow snake, escape by boat to mountain, some eaten by snake (Australian only)[430]

(2c) Flood as retribution for other mistakes (Melanesian, Australian) = Laurasian

(3) Flood from vessel, calabash, water/honey bag (Australian, African) = Laurasian (rain)

(4) Flood caused by someone's wounds or sores (Australian, African)

The last item, the "wound," may ultimately refer, as Wim van Binsbergen suggested to me,[431] to women's menses (regarded as polluting in many cultures).

In sum, both the Laurasian (§3.9) and the Gondwana flood myths share the topic of retribution by a divine or superior human being (see Table 5.5). It often is caused by some sort of mistake made by one or more early humans and is executed by excessive rain. Some people escape by float or boat, usually to one or more high mountains. In some cases, a new race of humans evolves from the saved primordial persons. In view of these major correspondences, we have to regard the flood myth as an early myth that is indeed panhuman and that belongs to the Pan-Gaean period, before the expansion of *Homo sapiens* out of East Africa.

If this is correct, a preexisting (Pan-Gaean) flood story has been intelligently inserted into the structure of Laurasian mythology. This took place at a node in the story line where it does not disturb its flow. Instead, it dovetails well with the separate myth of a (three- or fourfold) re-creation of the world and the reemergence of humans as told in Mesoamerican and Eurasian mythology.

Employing this example, we can further extrapolate how Laurasian mythology developed out of earlier forms of Gondwana mythologies. It appears that Laurasian mythology is just *one* offshoot of an earlier form that was close to the various Gondwana mythologies. Comparing them and Laurasian mythology, we can try to establish their common ancestor (Table 5.6), which was prevalent long before the exodus from Africa, in other words, at the time of the "African Eve": early, global (Pan-Gaean) myth. This will be attempted in the next chapter.

6 First Tales: Pan-Gaean Mythology

Now that the Laurasian scheme has been reconstructed (§§2–3) and its counterparts in Gondwanaland have been described and analyzed (§5), we can proceed and take the next logical step in reconstruction: investigate, as has just been done for the flood, whether Laurasian and Gondwana mythologies have common characteristics that allow us to reconstruct a common ancestor.[1]

***

As in the case of reconstructed Gondwana mythology, one may object that reconstructing mythology over such long time distances and time spans is virtually impossible. However, as has been pointed out above (§5.7), the consistency of the reconstruction can be tested by checking common motifs, structures, and narrational frameworks.

This is precisely the case that will be made here: one can detect some major common themes of both the Laurasian and Gondwana mythologies. The most salient features have been listed earlier (§5.7) and as seen again in Table 6.1.

The actual occurrence of some major common motifs in both mythologies indicates a very old common substratum of human thought. It is here that truly human universals emerge, as imagined and postulated by Jung and his followers (§1.3).

For example, in the discussion of Laurasian mythology it has appeared, from time to time, that certain motifs simply do not fit its common story line. One case is the origin of humans from trees (Iceland, Japan, Taiwan) and clay (Egypt, Bible, Nuristan, Polynesia). These now turn out to be typical Gondwana features. The manner of intrusion into Laurasian myth is a priori unclear, especially in areas so distant from Gondwana mythology as Iceland. Others include some common Pan-Gaean motifs such as the flood myth (§5.7.2) and the ubiquitous trickster figures that bring human culture, such as Prometheus ("the thief" of fire),[2] or Indra, or the early Roman "kings" and early Chinese "emperors."

Other, historically late examples include the several planters' myths, for example, that of the Japanese food deity Ōgetsu, or the myths about the origin of rice and barley in later Vedic Indian texts.[3] On the other hand, we have, among early food-producing societies such as those of the New Guinea area, myths about the origin of food and humans from plants (Hainuwele type).[4] Obviously the latter myths cannot be older than c. 10,000 BCE when food production first took hold worldwide, though the originators of these myths seem to have taken their cue from older hunters' myths about the re-creation of killed animals from

TABLE 6.1. *Comparison of major stages in Gondwana and Laurasian cosmogony*

GONDWANA mythology		LAURASIAN mythology
---		{Creation from nothing, chaos, etc.
earth, heaven, sea preexist		{Father Heaven/Mother Earth created
High God in/toward heaven,	→	{(Father) Heaven engenders:
sends down his son, totems, etc,	→	Two generations ('Titans/ Olympians'):
---		{Four (five) generations/ages
---		{heaven pushed up, sun released
---		{current gods defeat/kill predecessors
---		{killing the dragon /sacred drink
to create humans: from tree/clay	→	Humans: somatic descendants of (sun) god
they show hubris		they (or a god) show hubris
are punished by a flood		are punished by a flood
Trickster deities bring culture		Trickster deities bring culture
--		humans spread, (emergence of 'nobles')
local tribes emerge		local history begins
--		{final destruction of the world
--		{new heaven and earth emerge

{ indicates new items in Laurasian mythology;
→ indicates development from Gondwana to Laurasian mythology

their preserved bones. Nevertheless, some of these myths have impacted neighboring Laurasian areas. They have to be kept separate from early myths such as those mentioned above (humans from trees).[5]

Stimulated by several conferences on the topic of comparative mythology, the Africanist W. van Binsbergen has recently presented several long lists of "universal" myths,[6] based on his comparison of African topics with those from the rest of the world. He has now narrowed them down to 20 motifs of various time periods.[7] Many or most of them do not originate in the same period but emerge in "contexts of intensified transformation and innovation," "in a spasmodic and far from mechanical or unilineal process."[8] Theoretically, this is in agreement with the Gondwana and Laurasian proposals of the present book. However, as van Binsbergen's method is not based on a cladistic, phylogenetic, and tree-like analysis and as it neglects the Laurasian story line, our results differ widely. Similarly, the anthropologist Y. Berezkin has now pointed out very ancient links among African, Australian, and South American myths that would either precede the spread of Laurasian mythology or preserve ancient Gondwana mythemes and myths in South America that have subsequently been lost in Eurasia and North America due to post–Ice Age spread.[9]

However, the approach followed here is, in my view, situated at a higher level. I do not just compare occurrences of individual motifs, as S. Thompson did while mostly limited to Eurasia and the Americas and as now van Binsbergen and Berezkin do on a worldwide scale (§1.2).[10] Instead, I compare *sets* of myths that appear in both Laurasian and Gondwana mythologies.

As briefly discussed earlier (§5.6.1), many myths stand out among the common Laurasian ones that clearly mark them as archaisms, as residues of

Gondwana and Pan-Gaean times. They have not been integrated well into Laurasian mythology. Here, however, I will argue on the level of reconstructed Laurasian and Gondwana mythology, not on that of individual motifs that— always—can have traveled and diffused. In other words, I compare myths at a level that is several historical stages removed from their first appearances in antiquity or in our myth collections. Again, I compare whole mythologies and their structures, not single myths or motifs, as is commonly done.

The aggregates of Gondwana myths and of Laurasian myths have more to tell than any isolated individual myths. That makes the present comparison more meaningful and powerful than those of single, current myths, for which we do not know how they emerged or arrived in the areas concerned. A more detailed exploration will follow in this chapter (§6.2).

▪ §6.1. BEYOND LAURASIA AND GONDWANA: COMMON MYTHS

As briefly indicated in the introductory chapter (§1.3–5) and has increasingly become apparent, I hope, in the ensuing discussion of Gondwana mythologies (§5), we can now list and reconstruct some of the motifs and myths that are known to all of humankind. These are likely to be our oldest tales and must be appreciated and studied with the attention they deserve. In this context, questions about the universality of the human mind and of diffusion (§1.3) will have to be asked again.

Starting out from Pan-Gaean tales and the initial ex-Africa or Gondwana form they took, the author(s) of the complex Laurasian story line made a selection of some older Gondwana tales and added some other significant features (see Table 6.1). However, all humans, whether belonging to the Laurasian or the Gondwana populations, look back to a common history of more than a hundred thousand years. The Gondwana myths have retained the pre-Laurasian, largely unstructured, loose arrangement as well as much of the content of the original Pan-Gaean tales (§6.2). Even then, *all* post-exodus groups involved have made use of a large amount of prior mythology, selected certain items, stressed others, and (re-)created certain (new) features and structures to fit their own time period and cultural patterns.[11]

The reconstruction of a truly Pan-Gaean mythology is therefore only possible along the lines of a family tree (cladistic) arrangement of the motifs found in Laurasian mythology compared with Gondwana myths. As mentioned, when some Gondwana motifs actually do appear in the proper Laurasian story line, they stand out as archaisms that can easily be isolated and compared with various Gondwana myths; therefore they are old, ex-Africa (Proto-Gondwana) or indeed Pan-Gaean myths. The same applies to Laurasian intrusions onto Gondwana mythologies. The residues, the commonalities pointed out earlier (Table 5.3, §5.7), reflect Pan-Gaean myth. The following items stand out as common to both mythologies.

High god

Among the common Gondwana motifs, there is the concept of a High God. It is somewhat similar to what P. W. Schmidt had attempted to show from a Christian perspective.[12] However, the Gondwana High God is a *deus otiosus* who has retreated into heaven and is little occupied with humans and therefore is hardly venerated. In Laurasian mythologies, however, a High God is rarely seen; only occasionally there is one primordial deity that might fit the description, such as the Maori god Io, or the Indian, Icelandic, and Miao primordial giant who rather looks like an archaic Gondwana remnant (see §3.1.4). Either the Gondwana High God lived on earth at first and then went to heaven,[13] or he was present in heaven from the start,[14] from where he sent down his son, other intermediate deities, or totem animals to create humans.[15]

This ancient Gondwana motif seems to have been further developed by those that conceived the Laurasian scheme. The High God has been transformed into "Heaven" or "Father Heaven," who is very similar to or identical with the daytime sky but also has a mythological personality of his own. He frequently is a *deus otiosus* who does not or does no longer care about the earth and its humans—though not in Greece, where he shares many characteristics with his son, the Indian Indra or Greek Herakles. In Laurasian myth this motif has been incorporated into the system of Four Ages and four divine generations. The last age is the one in which humans emerge as children of the Sun deity, not as descendants of the Gondwana High God or his intermediaries, such as totem ancestors.

At the beginning of the 20th century, Pater W. Schmidt discussed the "universal spread" of the mytheme of a High God at great length.[16] The concept is indeed found in many populations, from Africa to Australia and the Americas. Schmidt saw in its wide spread the remnants of an *original* belief in a Judeo-Christian-like almighty God. (Obviously, this neglects the complicated—then already well known—history that the concept of Elohīm, Yahweh, El, Adonai, and so on has undergone in the Hebrew Bible and the fact that the emergence of the biblical single god and creator took shape only during the second part of the first millennium BCE, clearly under Zoroastrian Persian influence.)

Instead, it is important to observe that neither the Gondwana High God, nor the Eurasian (Father) Heaven, nor the Amerindian Great Spirit is a *creator* god: they do not create the universe or the world, and they leave its establishment to later demiurge deities. In parts of sub-Saharan Africa, these are the very active local deities (*mba/mbi* in Central Africa), while in the Indian Nilgiris, in the Andamans, and apparently also with the Tasmanians, *two* deities seem to exist from the beginning.[17] In Melanesia and Australia, however, a primeval god or spirit was born from a rock.[18] In Laurasia, a demiurge and other deities assist in the initial creation, for example, the Indian Indra, who delivers light and water and kills the dragon.

For the Laurasian case we may therefore conclude that the original Pan-Gaean motif of the High God was copied into Laurasian mythology but was reshaped as (Father) Heaven and repositioned to the second age, after initial creation (or "emergence"). It was thus clearly built into the new, much expanded story line scheme. In other words, the "rewriting" of a Pan-Gaean topic was deemed necessary, while the idea of a High God was kept alive, if altered and somewhat diminished in the new Laurasian scheme. What we see here is one of the oldest path dependencies of human myth, reasserting itself from Laurasian times until today: "one nation under God."

Creation

The Pan-Gaean situation is quite different as far as the actual creation of heaven and earth is concerned. In Gondwana myth, both heaven and earth as well as the ocean are clearly preexistent. Nobody created both time and space; actually the question is never asked, with very few exceptions. For the Bambara in Senegal and Mali, living close to the Laurasian area, all things emerged from the "voice of emptiness," which seems to echo the typical Laurasian scheme of creation from nothing or chaos, but they also say that the earth already existed.[19] Obviously, among the people of the Sahel belt, some Laurasian influence is felt. The Pygmies, too, speak about the primordial "age of the beginning," but they also have the typical Gondwana High God, the "man of the forest" who is also called "our father" or "grandfather."

In Gondwana myth, thus, the earth already existed and was a hot, dry, and sometimes dark place. The only question that is of interest for Gondwana myth is how the earth can be shaped properly so as to make human life possible. This is reflected in the actions of both Gondwana and Laurasian demiurge or trickster deities.

Laurasian myth, in contrast, is characterized by the myth of the original emergence (or "creation"), though how that took place is left unclear to some extent or shrouded in mystery. The various "competing" origin myths clearly point to ancient shamanic discussions about the origin of the universe, as they are still found in the oldest Indian text, the Ṛgveda. All following stages, however, are emanations or creations from the previous ones.

The universe first emerged, as has been discussed at length (§3), from "nothing," chaos, darkness, primordial waters, and so on. Laurasian mythology also seems to have incorporated some suspected Gondwana myths, such as origin from a primeval giant or rock or egg. It is noteworthy that the origin of the universe is frequently seen as an "emergence," often not gender-specific, out of a primordial nothing or chaos or a great ocean. The concept of the primordial ocean is perhaps not surprising, when taking in account the long stay and the long wanderings of pre-Laurasian populations out of Africa close to the beaches of the Indian Ocean. Not surprisingly, the world ocean surrounding the livable world (*oikumene*) is very prominent in all myths that were to come, even those of landlocked people such as the medieval Mongols and Bronze Age Ṛgvedic Indians.

Another potentially very old remnant of Pan-Gaean myth is the motif of a primordial giant made of stone and the accompanying worship of large stones, rocks, and stone pillars. The stone giant is seen in Melanesia and with the Austronesian-speaking Dayak, in Old China,[20] in Hittite (Upelluri and Ullikummi), and in Old Norse myth. Actual stone worship, such as that of the primordial parent Izanagi as a phallus-shaped rock pillar at Shingu (Kii Peninsula, Japan), is found in many Laurasian regions but also in Australia (Uluru or Ayers Rock). These mythemes seem to be remnants of Gondwana mythology inside the Laurasian one, where it is represented, for example, by Deukalion and Pyrrha, who procreate, after the flood, by throwing stones.

***

In some Gondwana myths we find the motif of a stepwise creation of the earth and its various beings and humans (Bambara: via Faro; central Australia: via totem beings; cf. §5.2 sqq.). These motifs need further consideration as they partially overlap with the later, Laurasian idea of a series of world ages or of trial creations. The motif is, in all likelihood, not an original Gondwana one and therefore hardly a Pan-Gaean motif.

Humans

Quite the opposite is the case with the universal motif of the creation of humans. Here, we can clearly distinguish a very archaic trait, the emergence of humans out of a tree. The motif is found in the "undisturbed" parts of Central Africa, the isolated Andaman Islands, Melanesia, and Australia (in ritual). But it is also found several times in the Laurasian area, such as in Indo-European Iceland (Edda), in Austronesian Taiwan, and in Japanese folktales (Kaguyahime).

It takes two or three forms.[21] Its basic variety appears in the more isolated areas of Central Africa, where humans, especially women, come from a tree stump (while men are sometimes formed from clay). In Melanesia, too, humans are carved from a tree (and sometimes are made from clay).

In the Andamans, Austronesian Taiwan, and Japan humans emerge from a split bamboo, such as in the Japanese folktale of Kaguyahime (which is not part of the official mythology). The small child found there later turns out to be the princess of the moon. A similar motif is also found in the Icelandic Edda (Askr and Embla).

However, Australia has a somewhat divergent version. Here the relation of humans with the (world) tree is visible in initiation ritual (pole, *tjurunga* board) as well as in burial.[22] Just as in their myths, the Aborigines often bury or keep their dead inside hollowed-out trees (also in Tasmania). In other words, there is rebirth for a young man in initiation and again after death;[23] both involve trees. A related motif in Laurasia may be one of the four forms of Ṛgvedic burial, that is, the burial below a tree or exposure on a tree (or on a wooden scaffold, as also in North America). This custom is found next to cremation, actual burial in the ground, and simply "throwing away" the dead body, typical for early humans and tribes on the move.

A related topic is that of the emergence of humans from underground. It is prominently found in Mesoamerica and neighboring areas but also in southeastern Australia and the Trobriand Islands, where it takes place as emergence from a cave. This is also seen in Vedic India (Jaiminīya Brāhmaṇa 3.233–35), where nymphs (Apsaras) emerge, together with cattle, from a cave opened by Indra. Related is the myth of Amaterasu's emergence from the rock cave.[24] In Mesoamerica and with the Pueblo populations, however, humans emerge into this world from underground through the inside of a big tree (or reed).

In all likelihood, the motif of human emergence from a tree is a very old Pan-Gaean concept, found in various regions of the globe, whether Laurasian or not. Its surprising survival in Laurasian myth is probably due, as in Japan, to the telling of fairy tales, thus "grandmother's tales," as opposed to the shamanistic Laurasian version ("grandfather's tales"), for which see further below.

***

The rivaling concept of creation of humans from clay poses an interesting problem. Both the origin from clay and that from trees frequently occur next to each other,[25] such as in Africa, the Andamans, and Melanesia. Again, the concept is likely an old one. It certainly was inspired by the frequently made observation that humans turn to mere bones—many peoples exhumate their dead after some months—or eventually turn to clay after decomposition and burial in the ground.

However, there are several composite versions that incorporate both the tree and clay motifs. They offer a new view on the biblical motif of Adam's creation from clay and Eve's from his rib (which surprisingly is also found in the Andamans). The two versions seem interchangeable: sometimes men are created from trees and women from clay, sometimes it is the other way round. The biblical myth may be a latter-day version of the African and Melanesian motif of creating women from trees (where men are created, as in the Bible, from clay).[26] Wooden humans do occur in Mesoamerican myth, though as one of the failed creations that precede our present one.

Definitely to be compared is the famous Hainuwele myth found on Ceram (Seram) Island in eastern Indonesia—a non-Laurasian territory.[27] According to this myth, humans are born out of the partition between the tree stem and its branches. Apparently, the motif made its way, as a tall tale of sailors, into the

Arabian Nights as the story of the Waq-Waq Islands. The latter case may serve as an interesting warning post indication of how certain interesting, *isolated* motifs can travel halfway around the globe through commercial contact. In sum, the motif of human origins from trees (and clay) seems to be a very old, Pan-Gaean motif.

***

A related topic is that of a reservoir of souls. In Australia, there is the belief in a well of souls. As the origins of clan totem animals are important for the Aborigines, we find many myths concerned with these items. The souls of unborn children are believed to come from certain totem wells. This is a motif that is also found in Laurasian Europe, India, and Japan, for example, in the still current Germanic belief about babies coming from "the big pond" (from where they are brought by a stork) and the Indian motif of *śaiśava*, the "baby (and rejuvenation) pool" situated in a bend of the Ganges River (Vedic: Jaiminīya Brāhmaṇa 3.120–28). The "well of souls" apparently is not just a Eurasian myth; with the Australian evidence added, it represents a much older level of mythical thought. Again, this motif is not found in the "official" Laurasian mythologies but appears in folktales and legends (such as typically, in the Jaiminīya Brāhmaṇa, the *Brāhmaṇa fabulans* par excellence, as Karl Hoffmann has called it: "ein *Märchenbuch*").

The motif is in all likelihood an ancient Pan-Gaean one. Without doubt, many more incidental motifs and mythemes will turn up, once the extant Gondwana mythologies are extensively and properly compared with Laurasian materials.[28]

***

In both types of mythologies, humans are described as by nature being full of hubris. In Gondwana mythology their arrogance usually leads to the origin of death. It is due to some misdeed or mistake, often one committed by a woman. Ironically, the bearer of life, woman, is often made responsible for its inevitable end, death. Frequently, hubris or (deliberate) mistakes also lead to a Great Flood that eliminates almost all humans. In Laurasian myth, these motifs have again been incorporated into its general story line. Even the first mortal and/or human—the Indian Yama, Adam, the Polynesian Kumu-Honua—or his wife, commits some sort of offense that is not always specified. In any case, the first humans are punished by being expelled (Hawai'i, Bible, Andamans, Bassari in Togo)[29] from their original habitat and become mortal (Manu and Yama in ancient India); this deed or some other mistake leads to the Great Flood.

The emergence of death, thus, is another important Pan-Gaean motif. As the Melanesian version puts it, humans at first did not die, they just changed their skins (like snakes do). However, a woman broke the taboo of not looking at this process, and since then humans must die. The linking of life-giving women with death is widespread. In many areas, it is the result of a primordial mistake or the breaking of a taboo. The list is long: the famous biblical story of Eve seducing Adam to eat of the forbidden fruit in Paradise is closely echoed by a Polynesian myth that basically says the same (see §3.7). There also is a myth of the Bassari in Togo, outside Laurasia, and other African and Andaman versions assert the same breaking of a taboo or speak of human haughtiness directed toward the gods. Because of its importance for comparisons, especially in relation to the biblical story, the Bassari version is given here at length. It tells of Unumbotte, High God and creator of beings:

> Unumbotte (god) made a human being. The Man was Unele (man). Then, Unumbotte next made Opel (antelope...). Then, Unumbotte made Ukow (snake...) named Snake. When these three were made there were no other trees but one, Bubauw (oil palm...). At that time, the earth had not yet been pounded (smooth).... Unumbotte said to the three: "...You must pound the ground where you are sitting." Unumbotte gave them seeds of all kinds, and said: "plant these." Unumbotte went (away).
>
> Unumbotte came back. He saw that people had not yet pounded the ground, but had planted the seeds. One of the seeds had sprouted and grown. It was a tree that had grown tall and was bearing fruit. The fruits were red.... Now, every seven days Unumbotte returned and plucked one of the red fruits.
>
> One day Snake said: "We too would like to eat these fruits. Why must we be hungry?" Antelope said: "But we don't know this fruit." Then Man and his wife (...who had not been there at first...) took some of the fruit and ate it. Then, Unumbotte came down from Heaven. Unumbotte asked: "Who ate the fruit?" Man and Woman answered: "We ate it." Unumbotte asked: "Who told you that you should eat of it?" Man and Woman replied: "Snake told us." Unumbotte asked: "Why did you listen to Snake?" Man and Woman said: "We were hungry."
>
> Unumbotte questioned Antelope: "Are you hungry too?" Antelope said: "Yes, I am hungry too; I'd like to eat grass." Since then Antelope has lived in the bush, eating grass.
>
> Unumbotte then gave Idi (...sorghum) to Man,...yams and...millet....And since then people have cultivated the land. But Snake was given by Unumbotte a medicine (Njojo) so that it would bite people.[30]

It is remarkable that, differently from the Bible, this myth does not speak of primordial guilt, or of an expulsion from paradise, or of a punishment of the snake. It merely assigns roles to the living beings and specifies the food they will have to live on. The only punishment one can discern in this tale is that of humans, who have been victims of snakebite ever since (and presumably die).

An echo of this myth is also found in the Quiché Mayas' Popol Vuh,[31] when Xquic, the virgin daughter of Cuchumaquic, visits the famous tree that carries the talking head of Hun-Hunahpu in its branches. It was forbidden for its fruits to be plucked. The head and the virgin talk with each other, she puts out her hand to pluck a fruit, and the head lets saliva drip into her hand, by which she becomes pregnant.

In sum, the motif again seems to be rather old. In stark terms, it may be characterized as the search for the origin of death and whom to blame for it. The experience of death is fundamental, as recent investigations into primate (and elephant) behavior seem to indicate. Much of mythology deals with the wish to overcome death in one way or another, as is still seen in the most important world religions of today. It therefore is not surprising that Laurasian, Gondwana, and apparently already Pan-Gaean myth chose to deal with it.[32]

***

In many mythologies, the breaking of a taboo leads straight to retribution or to punishment by a Great Flood, again a topic that is found in both Gondwana and Laurasian mythology (see above, §5.3 sqq., §6).

Demiurge

Both mythologies also share the concept of some demiurges or tricksters who bring various features of culture to humans. We have already noted a typical Laurasian incarnation, the Indian god Indra, who not only stems up heaven, thus creating room for humans, but also liberates light,[33] kills the dragon—thus fertilizing the earth—and releases the waters. Other trickster-like persons (such as Prometheus) bring fire (§3.5.3). The motif is prominently found in Amerindian myths and also with Tasmanian and African tricksters or jokers. These usually are the sons of the High God—apparently also in Tasmania—while in Australia, they are totem animals (or daughters of the sun, in eastern Australia). They come down from heaven and produce the present landscape and humans.

While the motif of the trickster or culture hero seems to be very old, and obviously Pan-Gaean, its use in Laurasian mythology is a peculiar one. The motif seems to have been inserted into the story line at various occasions. For example, the Indian god Indra is a deity belonging to the last generation of gods. Prometheus, the bringer of fire to the humans, is likewise a descendant of a Titan, the third generation of gods. The Mayan twins Hunahpu and Xbalanque are the sons of Hun-Hunahpu and grandsons of the divine grandparents Xpiyacoc and Xmucane.

These "heroes" and tricksters, thus, are not the sons of Heaven as in Gondwana myths but belong to a later generation, that of the grandchildren of Heaven. Their appearance at this stage makes more sense, as they have to deal with the world that emerged at the time of their grandparents, Heaven and Earth. They, however, have to make it inhabitable, an *oikumene*.

***

Finally, differently from Laurasian mythology, in Gondwana myth there is no explicit eschatology of eternal return, though the Andaman, Australian, and many African rituals connected with death and burial point in that direction. It cannot yet be safely established whether this was a Pan-Gaean trait. The idea of an afterlife, however, is a very old one, as even some Neanderthal burials indicate (see §4.4), though it seems quite difficult to establish the related myths. Clearly, we need more comparative research, which cannot be attempted and included here; it must be referred to another, more detailed account.

Ritual

Briefly turning to ritual, always a close companion of myth (see introduction, §§1–2), it may be observed that animal sacrifice is present in most of the Pan-Gaean mythologies and rituals. As has been discussed (§4.4, §7.1.2), the archaic Stone Age ritual connects the preparation for the hunt of large beasts and the feelings of guilt and apprehension of the hunters. Testimonies of the ritual and the hunt are found in the ancient rock paintings of Africa, Europe (Lascaux), India, and Australia. Vestiges of it are still present in the few surviving Stone Age hunter societies that even now include, or very recently still included, the San (Bushmen), Pygmies, Hadza/Sandawe, Andamanese, Australians, Samoyeds, Chukchi-Koryak, Ainu, Inuit (Eskimo), and many Amerindian tribes such as the Haida and Fuegians.[34]

The development of sacrifice (§7.1.2) would include a Pan-Gaean Stone Age stage, with a shamanistic religion of hunters' societies that had the primordial sacrifice of the primordial deity (Pangu, Tiamat, Puruṣa, Ymir, etc.), as still seen in many Laurasian mythologies (§3.1), or of its human correspondent, man. He was substituted in some (later) societies by large local animals. In some societies the animals to be eaten are transformed men,[35] while in some (recent) Melanesian, Polynesian, and African societies actual people were or still are sacrificed and consumed.

Closely related to hunting magic and sacrifice is the institution of a sha-man-like figure (or witch doctor), which will be discussed in some detail below (§7.1). This figure is first seen in some cave paintings in France (Les Trois Frères, Le Gabilou, Lascaux), at c. 14,000 BCE, in typical professional dress consisting of animal skins. As discussed in detail (§4.4, §5.3 sqq., and §7.2), the shaman appears in various forms with the San, Andamanese, and Australians. They all mention the difficulty of mastering the force inherent in the calling, which often manifests itself as heat that rises up the spine. Obviously this is a very old Pan-Gaean trait: the concept of shamanic heat, and the careful management of this "power," which (snakelike) moves up the spine, is a fact still known to Yogic practitioners. In its simplest form, it is found with the San, Andamanese, and Australians.[36] It has its most prominent outcome in the various forms of Indian yoga that have been developed, ratio-nalized, and discussed in more than 2,000 years of oral and written Indian traditions.

The "classical" Siberian form of shamanism, with offshoots in northern Europe and South and Southeast Asia, as well as Korea, Japan, and the Americas,[37] has some additional characteristics, such as an elaborate costume and the circular frame drum. In many traditions, women can be shamans as well as men. The raven frequently is the shaman's messenger.[38]

Individual Mythemes

A few individual, early, and persistent myths and mythemes, unconnected with each other by a story line, may be listed in addition to those already mentioned; the following are given on a provisional, heuristic basis. Some of those mentioned here may turn out not to be typical on further investigation (especially if we include *all* African occurrences).

First of all, there is the flood myth, which is indeed universal (§5.7.2).[39] Then, the underground origin of humans (or animals, or gods), either from beneath the earth, or from caves (Vala etc.), or as an emergence upward through a hollow tree stem (Americas), may belong here. This motif is found worldwide and may belong to Pan-Gaean mythology, just like some forms of stone worship, with remnants even inside the Laurasian myths.

The same may be true for the Orpheus myth, which is very widespread in Europe, North Asia, India, and America and is also found in Melanesia.[40] In its simplest form, a husband goes westward to search for his deceased wife, and he becomes a ghost himself, takes her home from the land of the dead, and thus breaks a rule; sometimes this is the origin of permanent death.

The Laurasian concept of a world axis or tree has vague echoes in Melanesia and Australia (pole, double *tjurunga*) and must be investigated at length, which cannot be undertaken here. More Pan-Gaean myths and mythemes may be gleaned from Y. Berezkin's extensive collections and comparisons,[41] such as those of the reviving moon/mortal people, death and shed skin, lost and found eyes, lecherous parent, false burial, moon spots, Milky Way as serpent, Rainbow Snake, arrow ladder, and perhaps the chthonic canine.

***

In sum, many of the details discussed in this section indicate that Laurasian mythology is an offshoot of the older Gondwana type that underlies the sub-Saharan African, Andaman, Papua, and Australian mythologies. Based on these types, the still earlier *Pan-Gaean* type may be reconstructed for the period *before* the Out of Africa event at c. 65,000 BCE. It includes a distant otiose High God, his direct or indirect creation of humans, their hubris, and their punishment by mortality and a Great Flood, as well a series of demiurges or tricksters that establish human culture.

This only fragmentarily preserved scheme has been extensively altered and expanded by Laurasian mythology, in which the High God is substituted by

(Father) Heaven. However, he is preceded by the primordial creation of the universe, and he thus is just part of four generations of deities. Humans are the descendants of one of his children, the sun deity. He, or other late-born deities, functions as a demiurge and killer of monsters. An end of the world also is frequently envisioned. In short, a long and complicated story line has been added to and supersedes the loosely arranged, disparate Pan-Gaean tales.

***

Pan-Gaean mythology would then include most of the topics mentioned in this section. We must keep in mind, however, that they have been collected from isolated pockets among the peoples of the tropical belt, with no old attestations in writing, which is, anyhow, only some 5,000 years old. However, such plot lines are usually not "compiled," even in societies that have complex and fixed oral traditions (Vedic India) or incipient written traditions.

For example, in Greece we have the mythology embedded in Homer's *Iliad* and *Odyssey*, but it took Hesiod to compile and narrate it comprehensively. Still, local traditions continued unabated, as witnessed by the many variants collected by R. Graves.[42] Similarly, the various traditional mythological accounts, orally transmitted by professional *katari-be*, and the various local traditions of Japan were collected and edited only in 712 CE, by order of the emperor, as to weed out "erroneous" versions. Nevertheless, the Nihon Shoki of 720 and the local digests (Fudōki) contain many versions of Kojiki-type myths that are local in origin and vary in many details.

Similar developments can be seen in Old Egypt: four major centers of myth collection and formulation existed, where local priests organized and fashioned the dominant mythology of their respective dynasties. In other cases, such as in oldest Sumer, our knowledge is limited by the fragmentary archaeological finds of their tradition. We have found (so far) only individual myths, such as those of Gilgamesh, but not a continuous collection as in the somewhat later Babylonian Enuma Elish. Whether a Sumerian equivalent ever existed or not cannot be said right now. In still other cases, such as the Edda, the collection was only prompted by the increasing influence of Christianity on Iceland and the wish to preserve ancient lore and its poetics.

In evaluating all such attempts it must be remembered that even seemingly "primitive" tribes, as one used to say, such as the head-hunting Dayaks of Borneo, have myths and ritual tales that, according to Schärer,[43] amount to some 15,000 pages, once collected.[44] Schärer notes that not *all* these myths were known to *all* Dayak shamans.

However, even then, a comparative study of the variants of such "national" or tribal mythologies indicates that they follow a certain underlying pattern, of which they are but individual variations (§2.3). The same is true even for the quickly evolving "myths in the making" in parts of New Guinea,[45] where, again, variants go back to an underlying pattern (see §5.3.3). This underlying pattern is even the same where it has been alleged, such as in Australia, that men and women have developed their own (versions of) myth.

The only question remaining, then, is whether a certain population undertook, or not, to collect all their lore in one "book" (like Hesiod's *Theogony*) or an oral collection (like the Hawai'ian Kumulipo).[46] For example, the Indian Ṛgveda (c. 1000 BCE) has a clear mythology that is in many respects similar to that of Old Iran and Nuristan, but it was not collected in one text that told it *consecutively*. Instead, we have a large collection of extremely carefully orally transmitted hymns to the deities (1,028 hymns, some 900 pages)[47] that contain most elements of Vedic mythology in incidental, short sentences or in allusions mentioning facets of it. It is only an old appended text, the Ṛgveda Khila, that gives a first, brief list of the great deeds of the god Indra and others. Even the late cosmological hymns of the Ṛgveda present but individual or local variations of the theme of creation of the world. There is no "Enuma Elish," so to say, where all data about this happening have been collected or amalgamated. Even in the post-Ṛgvedic texts, the Brāhmaṇas, this has not yet occurred, though we now find more or less extensive, even long myths—but never a complete collection of the major Vedic myths in one text. That only happened, in a much later version, in the great Indian epic, the Mahābhārata—a text that was most probably commissioned to be collected from oral sources (not unlike the Kojiki), by a late second-millennium BCE king.[48]

Again, systematic collection, "piling up" of motives, is a function of individual local conditions. This does not always amount to a construction that follows the Laurasian story line (cf. the Aranda myth given at length in §5.3.2). The myths are already there: just as with the (Laurasian) Dayaks, they simply "await" collection and redaction.

We may therefore also interpret all the minor, isolated topics of Pan-Gaean mythology mentioned above as representing the rudiments, the very beginnings, of an *incipient story line*. It would include the motif of a High God creating humans, their hubris and punishment, and the creation of civilization by tricksters. All of this still amounts to much less than the complicated Laurasian story line, and it is still missing tales of "original creation" and final destruction.

It is therefore safer to assume that Gondwana and Pan-Gaean mythologies only had the budding topics mentioned just now. The same holds for the (re)-interpretation of Gondwana myths in Laurasian mythology that sees them and their sequence in analogy to human life (see above, §5.6 sqq.; below, §7.2 sqq.).

■ §6.2. OUR FIRST TALES

The implications of the Laurasian and Gondwana projects do not stop here. Even initial exploration, as detailed above, has brought out the surprising fact that quite a number of individual motifs and myths occur across all of the four major mythology types: sub-Saharan African, Laurasian, Papuan, and Australian. While this might speak for the Jung/Thompson proposals, these facts receive a new interpretation in light of the Laurasian theory. As indicated, Laurasian myth is characterized by a coherent story line, and so are *some* of the Afro-Australian ones, if only to a very small, incipient degree. In all of the latter, the initial sections (creation, origin of the gods, the Four Ages) and the end of the world are missing.

More importantly, what is significant about the few newly emerging, truly universal motifs is not just their worldwide spread; rather, it is the fact that these universals also occur but are *isolated* in Laurasian myth. They often go against its grain and are "superfluous" variants of topics treated comprehensively and systematically in Laurasian myth.

As mentioned earlier, frequently these variants are not part of the "official" local story line but occur as isolated myths, generally in the form of folktales or *märchen*. As described above (§3.7, §5.3 sqq.), the origin of humans from trees or from tree trunks is not at all normal or common in Laurasian myth. Yet it occurs in Austronesian Taiwan, Icelandic, and Japanese myth: in Iceland as an insignificant detail of the main story line but in Japan only as folktale (Kaguyahime). The motif is otherwise found in those parts of Central Africa that are not influenced by Laurasian traits, and importantly, it is quite common in isolated Australia, which has been cut off from New Guinea since the end of the last Ice Age, some 11,000 years ago.[49] What we have here are fragmentary *remnants* of a tradition that *precedes* the four individual types of mythology briefly described above. The pursuit of the Laurasian and Gondwana projects thus takes us back beyond all written literature—which is only some 5,000 years old—and beyond most cultural data encapsulated in individual languages or reconstructed for the various language families.

Systematic comparison, as briefly discussed in §6.1, may lead to the discovery of the original, common elements in Laurasian *and* Gondwana mythology. They are *older* than even the formation of these mythologies, that is, older than the particular kinds of belief systems found both with the Laurasian peoples and with those of Africa, Australia, and Melanesia. It now appears that Laurasian mythology is an offshoot of the older Gondwana type, which underlies the sub-Saharan African, Papua, and Australian mythologies. Finally, based on a comparison of these four types, the earlier *Pan-Gaean* version that underlies all extant mythologies might be reconstructed.

In some cases, we may perhaps even access some fragmentary concepts that were already known by the Neanderthals, whether they had proper language or not, and whether we may thus regard such indications as representing myths or not. There certainly was Neanderthal ritual, as the discussion of the bear cult (§4.4, §7.1.2) and death ceremonies with ochre (but *not*, as frequently reported, with flowers; §4.4) bear out. Such indications would automatically lead us to suppose that they had some understanding of death and also some underlying thoughts or mythology. To put this question, however, is not meant to open the chicken-and-egg discussion on the origin and precedence of myth and ritual; it is merely asked here as we still do not know much about Neanderthal speech (§4.4).

The uncertain question of Neanderthal myth apart, there are a number of points that all early mythologies share. This has been discussed in some detail above (§5.4, §6.1). Among the motifs that Gondwana and Laurasian myths share there are those of an early deity, a *deus otiosus*; of humans as being full of hubris, which leads to the origin of death; and of demiurges or tricksters, as culture heroes.

These *truly first* myths must have preceded *all* those found in our texts, from Egypt to China and Mesoamerica, as well as all those presently existing. The first myths do *not yet* have the structured mythology built along a *story line* from creation to the destruction of the world, but they consist of isolated, smaller tales.

Perhaps, as mentioned earlier, we can even perceive of or reconstruct an incipient, though brief, story line: the High God, first living on a preexisting earth, moves up to heaven and sends down his child to create humans, who do some mischief and are therefore punished by a flood and/or death (see Table 6.1).[50] If we could indeed trace this "sapientian" myth, or at least some aspects of it, we would reach the original mythology of earliest humankind in Africa, well before c. 65,000 BCE, and we would obtain a glimpse of the belief system of early *Homo sapiens sapiens*. Clearly, we need more comparative research.

At this early level, we can truly speak of human universals (§1.3, §2). They could be investigated by psychologists for their underlying features in the subconscious and in dreams and for possible "archetypes" such as the Father or Trickster—again, a topic that cannot be pursued in this book.

***

However, even at this preliminary stage of our inquiry, it appears that Laurasian mythology is the *first novel* and the Pan-Gaean motifs are the *oldest tales* of humankind. At least, they are the oldest ones that actually can be discovered, barring any new insight about Neanderthal speech and ritual.[51]

And this is their fascination. The Laurasian and Gondwana projects have taken us back beyond all written and oral literature and beyond most cultural data encapsulated in individual languages or reconstructed for various language families. They allow us a first glimpse of the mind of early humans and of the human condition as experienced by our most distant ancestors, after they moved out of Africa around 65,000 BCE and before that, perhaps as far back as 160,000–130,000 BCE, the time of the African Eve.[52]

This project allows us to detect some of the joy and the sorrow, the outlook on life, and the concern about death and the afterlife of early humans. Already then, humans tried very hard to give answers in myth and ritual. Studying both, we will begin to understand the human condition as experienced by our most distant ancestors.

***

Later (§8), we will also discuss what solutions early humans imagined for the eternal questions of our origin and destiny and how they interpreted their own life and the world. We must then also try to ask such hard questions as: why myth? and why does myth persist?

First, however, a brief look is in order at the development that our various mythologies, whether Pan-Gaean, Gondwana, or Laurasian, have undergone since their inception. When their development is thus put into the historical context of archaeology, genetics, and so on, this will allow us to approach ever more closely the mind-set of our early ancestors.

7 Laurasian Mythology in Historical Development

As indicated in the preceding chapter, the very first stages of the development of early *Homo sapiens sapiens* (Pan-Gaean) mythology must necessarily remain fairly vague. We can access them only through *reconstructions* of the daughter mythologies that were already in place or began to take shape around 65,000 BCE.[1] Their form, in turn, relies on detailed reconstructions using much later texts.

Nevertheless, it may be suggested that the period from c. 130,000 to c. 65,000 BCE saw the emergence and development of Pan-Gaean myths,[2] perhaps already divided into several local forms within Africa. Future research will shed more light on this stage. These early developments, however, become clearer once a subset of early Africans had left the continent.

In other words, the innovations brought about by that small emigrant group, in myths as well as in languages and genes, stand out against the features of the populations remaining in Africa (which obviously did not remain static either). The common principle of shared innovations, made by emigrant populations, is at work here. Such innovations can be contrasted with the evidence of the (frequently) more conservative groups remaining behind. Generally, shared innovations are seen in language, manuscripts, archaeology, genetics, paleontology, and biology in general. They all can be described as and defined by tree-related, cladistic arrangements.

In the present case, the mythologies of the Out of Africa groups were retained, to a large extent, in the Andamans, Melanesia, and Australia, but they are also seen in small remnant pockets elsewhere (Toda in the South Indian Nilgiris, Semang in Malaya, Aeta in the Philippines, and perhaps in the highlands of Austronesian Taiwan). They represent several slightly aberrant, in other words, clearly innovative, versions of the original African (Pan-Gaean) myths (as dealt with in §6).

Taking a closer look at the common features of such potential early myths, one item that stands out is the importance of late Paleolithic shamanism; it will be discussed below in some detail. It is pervasive in hunter and gatherer cultures. Shamanism is found in the early male-dominated hunting segment of society, which was balanced, however, by the equally important segment of females' food gathering. As archaeology shows, both economic activities supported the late Paleolithic bands.

However, little if anything remains of the tales and rituals of early women, who, anthropologists insist, must have used language as social bond for communication on vital topics such as sources of food and on equally important social commentary, that is, gossiping. Yet an indication of their own myths and rituals may be that some of their stories have been retained even in the male-dominated hunters' and shamans' tales of Laurasian mythology. A typical example is the myth of human origins from trees, which developed into the Hainuwele myth (§§5–6) in Melanesia. We therefore have to distinguish (grand)father's tales from (grand)mother's tales, even if most of our transmitted myths and myth collections are heavily male dominated. Some peoples, such as the Tierra del Fuego Amerindians,[3] actually "recall" a mythological original dominance of women, and some scholars since Bachofen and his many epigones have reified such incidental evidence to an imagined matriarchal stage of early human culture.[4] Physical anthropology rather seems to point in a different direction: males and females are by nature heavily mutually interdependent for rearing small children.[5] Be that as it may, due to the nature of our transmitted texts, we must deal here, by and large, with reconstructed "male" mythology.

***

This sets the stage for the discussion of the development of Laurasian mythology in actual historical and archaeological perspective (§4.4) as well as that of historical anthropology.[6] The discussion must include the development of the mythology of the early hunter-gatherer stage, leading to that of early food-producing or pastoral cultures and to the emergence of state societies. At the same time, the study of these very developments serves as a powerful means to countercheck the validity of the Laurasian theory.

The great disparity of the various stages of social development found with the tribes and peoples whose mythology follows the Laurasian pattern would, according to some theories (Durkheimian, Marxist, Bellah,[7] etc.), disallow the continuation of Laurasian mythology: a new form of society would necessitate new forms of mythology. It will be argued here (and also in §8) that this theory does not hold in this extreme form. While adaptations of older myths and mythologies have been made everywhere and at any time, the basic Laurasian traits, and the "path dependency" features they have generated,[8] show up wherever this form of mythology is prevalent. Path dependency indicates the influence of early, foundational cultural features on successor cultures.[9] In the following sections a few of the successive historical stages and their individual mythologies will be investigated. If the Laurasian theory is correct, it has been able to withstand the serious challenges that the disparate stages of social development have created since its inception and still are creating.

Since Durkheim,[10] it has been assumed that society, religion, and ritual are closely interrelated, even if religion does not always account for the complete

Überbau of a given society. The simple correlative in Marxist (or Bellah's) thought between religion and social development, however, is too simplistic. Rather, instead of straightforward social conditioning of religion and myth, there exists a wide and diverse range of social developments, both historical and visible today, among the populations adhering to Laurasian mythology. As we shall see, Laurasian mythology presents a unique case of very early "path dependency." In other words, the Laurasian pattern that was set in late Paleolithic times can be shown to govern much of our current thinking about the universe and the world, as well as the role that humans and our society play in them (in detail, §8).

* * *

To begin with a brief historical overview, current general consensus has it that in late Paleolithic and Mesolithic times the outstanding feature of human religious life seems to have been that of some early form of shamanism, existing next to some sort of worship of the generative power of a universal Mother.[11] Such impressions are limited, however, by the actual evidence present in early rock and cave art as well as the incidental finds of plastic art (§4.4.1). They are influenced even more by the interpretations we give to this art. The potentially earliest indications for religion and ritual that we can find in the archaeological record, however, are some of the simple burial customs of Neanderthal humans,[12] followed by the much more elaborate record of *Homo sapiens sapiens* (Crô Magnon etc.).

We still have no clear evidence of the linguistic faculty of Neanderthals and do not know whether they had a fully developed language.[13] Yet it must surprise that they used ochre in some of their burials and, even more so, that some buried their children with small tools.[14] This clearly indicates that they wanted to equip them with the means of survival in another life, however imagined. The use of ochre in graves points in the same direction. Ochre has consistently been used as a correlative or as a substitute or symbol for life-giving blood.[15]

Both Neanderthals and early *Homo sapiens sapiens* seem to agree on some form of early bear cult.[16] Just how far ideas about death and bears could be formulated and transmitted without proper speech in (pre-)*sapiens* humans or between Neanderthals and *Homo sapiens sap.* populations remains an important point of discussion that cannot be elaborated here.[17] Given the incompatibility of genetic (DNA) traits of Neanderthals and *Homo sapiens* and the apparent lack of interbreeding between these two types of recent humans,[18] it must be regarded as highly dubious that many of the *ideas* of Neanderthals (or *Homo erectus* in general) would have been *verbally* transmitted to early *Homo sapiens sap.*[19]

* * *

It also is not yet altogether clear when early *Homo sapiens sap.* actually could produce syntactically arranged proper speech. Lieberman holds that this was possible only after c. 50,000 BCE.[20] However, this applies only to fully vocalized speech (§4.4),[21] and it is much too late if we accept that Australians moved into their continent between 40,000 and 60,000 years ago but already brought Gondwana-style mythology with them, as an offshoot of the Out of Africa movement at c. 65,000 BCE (or according to some even at 77,000 BCE; §4.4).[22]

* * *

In addition, interaction between Neanderthals or Asian forms of *Homo erectus* and anatomically modern humans could only have occurred in two or three known areas of overlap. First, there existed a possibility during the very early, temporary expansion of current humans from Africa into the Levant around 90,000 BCE. This move, however, may not have involved the actual meeting of both populations, as it rather was a sort of "interleafing" at *different* periods in time.[23]

A second occasion may have occurred when *Homo sapiens* met some *Homo erectus* populations during their expansion across Asia, after c. 65,000 BCE, and the next, much later one arose when the two kinds of humans met in Europe, after c. 40,000 BCE. The first scenario would involve the ancestors of most current humans, who moved along the shores of the Indian Ocean to South, Southeast, and East Asia as well as on to New Guinea and Australia. They may have had still other encounters with the recently discovered tiny Flores humans or "Hobbits" of c. 70–12 kya.[24] New finds indicate that these humans (*Homo floresiensis*) were apparently able to produce tools.[25] Be that as it may, folklore about "dwarfs" is found in many cultures, from Europe to the Rai of eastern Nepal, Austronesian Taiwan,[26] and Hawai'i (*menehune*).[27]

* * *

It is generally assumed that the earliest evidence for the religious ideas of current humans involves the representations found in Stone Age rock and cave art as well as some sculptures of human or humanlike figures such as the "Great Mother" and the lion-human.[28] In addition, there are some indications of early forms of shamanism in cave paintings such as those at Lascaux, which may be compared with the many comparable representations of shamans and "witch doctors" in recent and modern populations, from South Africa to Australia and from Siberia into the Americas.

■ §7.1. LATE PALEOLITHIC RELIGION

In an investigation of late Paleolithic shamanism, it is necessary, however, to recall (§1.6, §4.4.1) the correlation made by I. Wunn between archaeological data and R. Bellah's theory of the evolutionary development of religious and mythical thought.[29] This rather simplistic correlation, which is based on a theoretical assumption, has been challenged above (§1.6, §4.4.1). The additional input of ethology, art history, archaeology, and so on is certainly valuable. However, Wunn's wide-ranging conclusions, based on the correlation of incidental archaeological finds, Bellah's evolutionary scheme, Panofsky's art theory, and the insights of human ethology, can be questioned. Wunn insists that cave art must now be explained differently and that it indicates little about Paleolithic religion and myth.[30] As mentioned, she concludes: "There are no clear examples for religious practices of Late Palaeolithic humans that can be connected with cave art. Neither sorcerers nor shamans were depicted, nor clashes between totemistic clans."[31] This conclusion will be tested here against some actual data, some of which have been elaborated by Wunn herself.[32]

***

Most importantly, from a theoretical point of view as well as the factual mythological evidence available, Wunn's interpretation contradicts the scenario that is reconstructible from available global mythology. It stands in stark opposition to the central theme of the present book: that an early form of human mythology and religion can be shown to have existed around—and even before—65,000 BCE, that is, well before the late Paleolithic times (c. 32,000 BCE) that Wunn discusses.

The very existence of such early mythology is determined by the early contemporaneous existence of anatomically modern humans in Africa, Australia, and parts of Asia soon after 65,000 BCE, that is, after their exodus from East Africa. These groups cannot have *independently* developed, in their new homelands, the *closely related*, overlapping, and even identical forms of Gondwana and Laurasian mythology (§§5–6). It simply cannot have occurred independently at a time when, according to Wunn, humans were just about to begin to develop their new faculty of creating complex religion and mythology—that is, during the Upper Paleolithic, more than 20,000 years *after* the exodus. As mentioned earlier (§1.6), we cannot simply argue from the current *absence* of archaeological evidence of certain aspects of these early mythologies: *current* absence of evidence in archaeology is not evidence of absence in mythology. As mentioned, Paleolithic men(!) were much more interested in representing images of the hunt in their paintings than in depicting mythological figures or stories that were transmitted (in part, secretly) by shamans and initiated men.

***

We must revert, instead, to the actual Stone Age remains. The enigmatic rock sculpture at Laussel in France has already been mentioned (§4.4.1).[33] It is a rare case of a depiction of sexual intercourse,[34] with two halves opposing each other within an egg-like shape: the woman with pendulous breasts forming the upper half, and the (bearded?) man, the lower half. One may perhaps interpret it as an androgynous primordial union or a primordial being, like the Polynesian Ta'aroa inside his eggshell.[35] Similar images are found in some of the myths about the androgynous nature of primeval creation from an egg (§3.1.6) that split into two parts, (father) Heaven and (mother) Earth.[36] Remarkably similar pieces were found in West Africa with the Dogon in 1908 CE that were still interpreted then as the union of "heaven and earth."[37] Indeed, the Laussel piece, too, could represent the primordial union between heaven and earth, a mytheme widespread in Egyptian, Polynesian, and Indo-European myth and so on (Father Heaven and Mother Earth; see §3.2).

In addition, as Campbell correctly interprets,[38] the sculpture seems to be one of a female on top of a male figure, just as we find in the Egyptian myth and its depictions of Nut and Geb (especially on the lids of sarcophaguses). If so, this would be an image of the situation at night, when the female earth overarches the daytime sky (§3.2).

The same stress on "nocturnal religion" may have been present in another rock carving, that of a large female figure at Laussel of c. 20,000–18,000 BCE.[39] As mentioned (§4.4.1) she carries a horn in her hand that may represent the waxing or waning moon. The horn seems to have 13(?) incisions, which is close to the 14-day cycle of the moon from new to full and from full to new moon. Because of the combination of a woman with a half-moon-like object, one is tempted to interpret this as a symbol for the moon and its phases per half-month and correlate it with the menstrual cycle of 28 days. The connection between the moon and the menstrual cycle has always been well known. Though likely, it must remain open whether this sculpture represents a deity or not.

A certain stress on fertility can also be observed in the clay sculptures of bison, found in the caves of Montespan and Tuc d'Audoubert,[40] one of them a copulating bison couple.[41] As the bison figures prominently in the one possible example of a ritual killing at Lascaux,[42] it is likely that this kind of plastic art was intended for the procreation of bison herds and for successfully hunting them with the aid of shamanic rituals.

It is remarkable that, when plastic art first appears in the Aurignacian at 35–30 kya, it is in fully developed form.[43] For example, the enigmatic human figure with a (female) lion head is of that early age.[44] It points to a concept of spirits or deities that could correspond with some of the totem-like first beings seen in parts of Gondwana mythology (§5.3 sqq.).

As mentioned earlier (§4.4.1), there are many small statues of human females found all over Europe that have traditionally been classified as "Venus." As they commonly lack feet, one regards them as cult objects that were inserted into the ground. However, the traditional interpretation as "Mother Goddesses" has been challenged by Wunn and others;[45] she does not detect cult objects in the late Paleolithic.

***

Turning to cave paintings, there are some indications of late Paleolithic shamanism in some paintings in France,[46] where the shaman-like figure is seen in
his typical "professional" costume consisting of animal skins.[47] There is a
painting at Trois Frères of a shaman-with birdlike antler-headed dancer, the
"Great Sorcerer," dated at c. 14,000 BCE.[48] This was the interpretation given in
Breuil's sketch, now critiqued, first by Leroi-Gourhan.[49] A similar, bison-headed
figure also comes from Trois Frères and from Le Gabilou.[50] Not surprisingly,
Wunn again denies such an interpretation for the paintings of "shamans" at Lascaux and Trois Frères.[51] One might for argument's sake consider with her that
the drawing of the "dancer" of Trois Frères, who has both human and animal
characteristics, may be a fantastic figure that was meant, with V. Turner, to stimulate human imagination. Similarly, the drawing of Breuil's "sorcerer" at Trois
Frères might be explained in the same way.

But a detailed painting at Lascaux, of c. 14,000 BCE, does not allow for such an
easy diversion. The picture is that of a prostrate ithyphallic man, arms outstretched, with birdlike hands, and beak-like face. He lies below a wounded bison.
Below him, a bird is perched on a vertical pole. A spear-thrower lies at the feet of
the man. The huge bison bull looks back at a spear that has pierced him from anus
to penis. This has opened the bull's belly, and his intestines have spilled out and
hang down to the ground. The picture, which will be discussed in detail later on
(§7.1.2), has found various interpretations: it has been understood as representing Stone Age myth,[52] as hunting magic, as the memorial of a wounded or slain
hunter,[53] or as a shamanistic séance[54] (www.lascaux.culture.fr/x/fr/02_07.xml).

In this case, Wunn's method does not work. This is a rather realistic painting
as far as the bull is concerned; the prostrate ithyphallic man, however, is drawn
in a rather schematic way, as is common for human representations in Paleolithic
art. Thus, there is no trace in this painting of any "fantastic beings." Actually,
Wunn does not offer a new interpretation here besides mentioning and debating
earlier scholars and pointing out the fragmentary, caricature-like nature of the
prostrate man.[55] As mentioned, this feature is found in many other depictions of
humans and their faces. The style is, importantly, still prominent in Australian
rock art in the representation of ancestors.[56] Therefore, instead of breaking up,
with Wunn,[57] such paintings into various categories (fantastic beings, schematic
human depictions, etc.), it is more cogent to interpret them, with recent scholarship,[58] as representing the vestiges of a Stone Age myth involving archaic
shamanism.

***

In sum, rock painting as well as early sculpture provide some inkling of
Stone Age myths and rites. Wunn's conclusions are—justifiably—based on

archaeological and anthropological observation, as there are no Stone Age texts. However, we can now try to recover a large part of the meaning of this early art through an investigation of their correlation with Laurasian mythology (§7.1.2).[59] Further elucidation can be achieved through a careful comparison of the rituals, customs, and myths of modern hunter-gather societies.[60] Care should be taken, however, not to equate the beliefs of modern hunter-gatherers with those of their "ancestors" at 12,000 BCE or of many more thousands of years ago.

Pursuing this interpretation, we have to reinvestigate the current global occurrence of shamans and their Stone Age depictions, without being hindered by the theoretical evolutionary construct of Bellah/Wunn. This will be taken up in the next section.

§7.1.1. Late Paleolithic shamanism

Shamanism is a topic that has been under constant and controversial discussion,[61] especially since Eliade.[62] However, it will be pointed out here that his discussion of African and, in part, Australian shamanism is inadequate,[63] while his version of "typical" North Asian/Siberian and Amerindian shamanism has been reconfirmed by many scholars.[64]

Eliade nevertheless stresses the similarities between Siberian and Australian initiation rites as important for the role of shamanism and its Paleolithic origins,[65] especially the importance of caves.[66] He also compares the insertion of crystals found with the Semang, Australians, and South American Indians, which he regards as an archaic trait.[67] The same applies to dissecting of the body of the initiate in Australia and Siberia.[68] (However, Campbell's characterization of the shamanism of the Australian Aborigines as "deteriorated" is misleading.)[69]

These peoples lived (like the San, Hadza, Sandawe) close to the place of origin of anatomically modern humans in East Africa, or they otherwise lived on the trail leading east from it. Once we take into account that the latter indeed appear as remnants of the early human dispersal along the shores of the Indian Ocean, our gaze, which is focused on Siberia, must be reversed. It can be assumed, instead, that the San, the Hadza/Sandawe, the Andamanese, and the Australians have preserved a *prototype* of what later became Siberian and Amerindian shamanism. (It is to be distinguished from mere involuntary possession by a spirit, which is much more widespread, especially in Gondwana areas.)

The earlier, Pan-Gaean and Gondwana versions of shamanism have dancing, but they do not yet have the typical Siberian feature of shamanistic drumming,[70] and they do not have much of a shamanic dress. Nevertheless they share a unique perception of difficultly controlled heat that rises from the lower end of the spine upward[71]—a feature that is still retained in some forms of Indian yoga (see below).[72]

Eliade, however, regards such "heat" as a general phenomenon connected with magic, not as a typical shamanistic trait.[73]

***

The problem of defining shamanism instantly indicates that both the word *shaman* and the concept of shamanism have been employed in a multiplicity of ways in scholarly as well as in popular literature. It may be advantageous to start with a definition.[74] Walter and Fridman stress the current broad interpretation of the term *shamanism* as designating any kind of ecstatic behavior including spirit possession, witchcraft, and even cannibalism and a narrow one that stresses initiatory crisis, vision quest, an experience of dismemberment and regeneration, climbing the sacred (world) tree, spirit flight, the role of the shaman as healer, and the use of trance.[75] A comprehensive description of this narrow version is that recently given by Basilov:

> Shamanism…emerged in the period when hunting and gathering were the main means to support life.…[The] most important…beliefs [are:]
> (a) all the surrounding world is animated, inhabited by the spirits who can influence man's life;
> (b) there are general and reciprocal interconnections in nature (humans included);
> (c) human beings are not superior but equal to the other forms of life;
> (d) human society is closely connected with the cosmos;
> (e) it is possible for human beings to acquire some qualities of a spirit and visit the other worlds;
> (f) the aim of religious activity is to defend and make prosperous a small group of kinsmen.[76]

In sum, humans and spirits or deities are closely related and interact,[77] especially through the person of the shaman, who ensures the success of the clan in hunting. Basilov defines a shaman as follows:

> the peculiarities that distinguish a shaman…are
> (a) he can perform his functions with the assistance of his helping spirits only;
> (b) he is chosen, brought up, "re[-]created" and educated by the spirits themselves;[78] as a result, he possesses some supernatural qualities and knowledge;
> (c) he is able to penetrate into the other worlds in order to communicate with the gods and spirits;[79]
> (d) the shaman's contact with the gods and spirits presupposes a state of ecstasy as a form of ritual behavior;
> (e) the main ritual object of a shaman is an incarnation of his guardian spirit (or helping spirit) or his double (external) soul in animal form; this object is firmly connected with a shaman's personal professional qualities and his life.[80]

In sum, the shaman is an early form of the typical intermediary between humans and the supernatural (like later priests). He is someone that has obtained and "tamed" special powers that he exercises in trance, including the internal heat generated during initiation and performances.

Shamanism, as we know it, especially its Siberian form, has been subject to a large number of studies, including the classical, though by now criticized,[81] one of Eliade and the more recent work of Hamayon.[82] Eliade's classic study concentrates heavily on Siberian shamanism. Campbell distinguishes erroneously, I believe, between primitive (Eskimo), deteriorated (Australian), San/Bushmen,[83] and post-Paleolithic Siberian shamanism.[84] However, he correctly observes that in many tribal cultures the medicine men, the "dreamers," are the main transmitters of myths and rituals.[85] Such distinctions are based on the Siberian model and need to be redefined. On the other hand, clearly many if not most forms of African healers and witch doctors do *not* fit the criteria used by Basilov.[86]

The questions of interest in the current context of Laurasian mythology include the following. "Classical" Eurasian shamanism is found among a wide range of northern peoples, from the Saami (Lapps) of northern Scandinavia to the Chukchi in northeastern Siberia, with an extension into all of the Americas, and from the Polar Sea to the tribes of Nepal and the Dayak of Borneo.[87] We may ask: what is its relationship with the "shaman" figure attested in Stone Age paintings (§7.1.1) in southern France and elsewhere?[88] What is the relationship with similar features found among the San (Bushmen), the Andamanese, and the Australian Aborigines?[89] Further, is shamanism related to the Stone Age hunter societies of the open steppe/tundra of Eurasia, and how much could it continue among agriculturalists, for example, in modern Nepal?[90] What, then, are the stages in its development?

To what extent is the institution of shamans (whether inherited by family line or not) connected with the (possibility of) transmission of a compact *body of texts*, such as required by the complex Laurasian mythology? Is the absence of a Laurasian framework—even in areas where one would suspect it, such as Tierra del Fuego[91]—connected with the absence of shamans/priests? And is the (expected) result, then, a body of unconnected myths, stories, and fairy tales such as those of the Brothers Grimm or of medieval India and Thailand? Or is this development only due to the overwhelming impact of Christianity, medieval Hinduism (Mahābhārata, Kathāsaritsāgara), and Buddhism in these areas?[92]

Further, the indications of a supposedly old, even Neanderthal, Eurasian bear cult and of the asterism Ursa Maior,[93] as well as shamanism's relationship with the myth of the killing and dismemberment of a primordial being (Ymir, Pangu, etc.), have to be investigated as well. Is the killing and dismemberment of a bear, or the bull/boar in southern climates, a step of increasing abstraction, ultimately leading to that of creation from chaos or the waters/darkness or even from "nothing"?

***

Some of these questions will be answered below. However, given the uncertainty about the manner by which such stories might have been transmitted in Stone Age times, it is best to begin by investigating, as done earlier (§7.1.1), what testimony can be found by archaeology, in other words: of Stone Age rituals, paintings, and sculptures.[94] Such probing is even more difficult than that by the modern anthropologist, eloquently described by H. Fleming and discussed at length earlier (§4.4.1).[95]

This investigation will be followed up by a discussion of the major forms of current shamanism that are still extant,[96] following the trail of the Out of Africa migration from west to east. By comparing all major forms extant on different continents, we may be able to learn more about their mutual relationship and history.

Beginning thus in Africa, the shamans of the San know of the difficult task of mastering the internal heat (*ntum*, correctly: *n/um*, "medicine")[97] that moves up from the base of the spine and use that power for healing.[98] They have the Siberian shaman-like descent and ascent to the sky, but they do not have the "classical" dissection and transubstantiation of the shaman's body, except for the fact that the shaman can change into a flying eland antelope (Figure 7.1).

The San possess a communal dance resulting in trance collapse (*!aia, !kia*); it is accompanied by the music of various local instruments and by singing, but they do not yet have the typical (Siberian) shaman's dance accompanied by beating a circular drum. The interaction of music, singers, and dancers produces

Figure 7.1. Bushman shaman and eland antelope (Game Pass Shelter, South Africa).

heat as well: the dancers transmit heat ("boiling") to each other, and the women's singing and music, too, activate it, from which the healers may draw energy.[99] During trance they travel, like all shamans, over the earth or to the spirit world, which is often expressed as death, flying, floating, or even drowning.[100]

Early evidence for San shamanism (or its predecessors) is found in South African rock art, at 27,000 BP,[101] though archaeologists hold that the San moved into South Africa from the north only after c. 6000 BCE.[102] This rock and plastic art nevertheless shows a continuous tradition since the Upper Paleolithic.[103]

The linguistic and genetic "relatives" of the San, the Hadza and Sandawe,[104] still attest to such northern origins. Both languages, Hadza and Sandawe, use clicks, just like the South African Khoi-San languages. The Hadza and Sandawe have remained as hunters and gatherers in central Tanzania. They seem to have shamanic dancing and healing as well, though detailed descriptions still are lacking. Frank Marlowe reports for the Hadza that they

> have a cosmology and ... endless stories about how things came to be. ... Illnesses may be attributed to violation of ... rules. The most important ritual is the *epeme* dance. ... [T]his takes place after dark on moonless nights. Men wear bells on their legs, a feather headdress, a cape, and shake a *maraca* as they sing and dance ... inspiring the women to sing and dance around them.[105]

One would like to hear more about the nature of this dance, as it seems similar to the shamanic San dances. Obst, writing in 1912, said that it was difficult to find out anything about their religion beyond the fact that the sun was God and that prayers were said over dead animals. The Sandawe, too, have shamanistic curing rituals involving trance and a *simba* possession dance imitating lions to combat witchcraft.

***

Andamanese shamans are called *oko-jumu*, "dreamers."[106] The term means "one who speaks from dreams," from *jumu* (dream), and they, too, are in contact with the dangerous primordial power inherent in certain "hot" objects (*ot-kimil*); they dream, meet the spirits in the jungle, "die," and return to life, but they do not have the Siberian-style trance, nor is the community involved with dancing as with the San. Campbell, however, sees no trance and hence, no shamans. According to Radcliffe-Brown's account, their "initiation" could happen in three ways: by "dying" (or also by epileptic fits), by going into the jungle, or by meeting spirits in dreams. After initiation, shamans continue to communicate with the spirits in their sleep (dreaming). They return from such visits with their heads decorated with shredded palm-leaf fiber, put there by spirits.[107] The shamans have the power of the spirits and can cause and cure sickness. Already in Radcliffe-Brown's time (1906–8) most *oko-jumu* were dead, and only very old men (via an interpreter!) could answer about their state.

The shaman's powers include that of curing illnesses, by application of treatment, or by dispelling spirits (by using certain objects), or through his dreams, when he communicates with the spirits and asks them to help the sick person. By certain rites, he also can prevent bad weather. He also has good knowledge of the magical properties of objects, plants, and animals that he has obtained from the spirits.

Importantly for our purpose, the Andamanese shamans are skilled transmitters of traditional lore,[108] though they are always proud of being original and both carrying out their rituals and telling their tales with *small* variations, a situation that is similar to the local differences seen in the otherwise homogeneous Ok culture (§1.6, §2.2.3). The various Andamanese shamans never tell *exactly* the same story, but it retains its essence.

Shamanic "heat" is called *kimil* (hot) or *gumul*. The word carries many meanings but is connected in all cases with extraordinary states that are regarded as dangerous, such as the (state of) initiation, the result of eating certain types of "powerful" foods, illness, or the rough sea. This heat is difficult to control at first.

It is significant that the idea of internal "heat," rising up from the bottom of one's spine, where it is coiled up as "serpent power," is retained in medieval Indian Kuṇḍalinī yoga. There is further a striking similarity with the African (San) concept of how to manage this heat, which can be achieved only with difficulty and after a long period of training by other shamans. Both cultures also share the idea of a (rainbow) serpent moving up the spine or to heaven, carrying the shaman. We will see echoes of this in Australia as well. In shamanism the flying sensation is often helped by consumption of psychoactive drugs (which is reflected in myth as well; §3.5.3). Clearly the parallelism between the internal movement up the spine and the external one by flight—using the rainbow snake, a bird, or another animal—constitutes a very old concept that must go back to Gondwana times, c. 65 kya; in Siberian-type shamanism it is substituted by climbing the (world) tree.

In addition, the idea of "heat" residing in certain objects and persons has also been retained, among both Indian Hindus and Muslims.[109] "Hot" objects or persons (such as the Śivaliṅgam or the guru) must be "cooled down" by pouring water or milk on them and by other more involved methods. These are prominently featured in many myths (in Mahābhārata) and once already in a late Vedic tale (Vādhūla Sūtra), where the gods had to "cool down" an ascetic ṛṣi by letting him lose his heat in a sexual encounter with a divine nymph, an Apsaras, sent by the gods.

We can detect some very old *pathway dependencies* of Indian belief, as the Andamanese were some of the earliest settlers from the Subcontinent. It is remarkable that the San and Sandawe, who lived or still live (in central Tanzania) close to the East African origin area of the Out of Africa emigrants, all have retained early forms of shamanism, in existence well before its development into the classical Siberian type.

***

Papua shamans,[110] however, are characterized—as far as the great diversity of the Melanesian cultures involved allows us to generalize—as male (also female) medicine men or sorcerers who use dreams and soul journeys to harm or to heal the source of illnesses. Initiation does not appear to be stressed with them, and consequently, Eliade does not even classify them as shamans.[111] However, on Dobu, an island of eastern New Guinea, the shaman is clearly regarded as "burning," and his magic is connected with heat and fire. He has to keep his body "dry" and "burning" and therefore drinks saltwater and eats spicy food.[112] Similarly, on the Solomon Islands, such sorcerers are regarded as *saka* (burning).[113] It appears, thus, that the same basic concepts of heat and healing are underlying features of Papua shamans and that these are not simply connected just with magic, as Eliade believes.[114]

***

Australian shamans undergo,[115] like their Andaman counterparts, a symbolic death and descent into a cave or an ascent to heaven. Like the San shamans, they do so by riding on the Rainbow Snake.[116] In their transformation into shamans, their internal organs are removed, and a new set is inserted consisting of stones, small rainbow snakes, and crystals.[117] As elsewhere, certain spirits or personal totems, sometimes located inside the shaman's body, act as assistants. Such inserted assistants can be pulled out and travel.[118]

The most typical elements of shamanic initiation in Australia include, first, the symbolic death and ascent to heaven: the shamanic master changes into a skeleton, puts the shrunken candidate (at the size of a newborn) in his pouch on his neck, rides on the Rainbow Snake upward to the sky, and on reaching it, throws the candidate into heaven, thereby killing him. Second, in heaven, the adept's internal organs are removed and replaced by a new set made of stones. He inserts small rainbow snakes or a lizard of great power. (With the southeastern tribes it takes the form of an eagle-hawk, who represents the first deity; see Figure 7.2.)

Importantly, fractured crystals that catch the many colors of the rainbow snake are inserted into the adept.[119] Finally, he brings the adept back to earth on the Rainbow Snake, where again, crystals are inserted. He awakens him by touching him with a magical stone. The adept returns to life insane; this ends after he has painted himself, a few days later.

***

However, in classical Siberian shamanism, such as that of the Tungus,[120] the initiate shaman's flesh is cut up, and his bones are separated and eaten by the spirits;[121] finally, the spirits drink the blood of a reindeer and give the shaman

Figure 7.2. Shaman (Bradshaw, Kimberleys, northern Australia), c. 17 kya.

some blood to drink. Only after the ancestors have given up and returned his body, he begins to shamanize. With the Inuit (Eskimo), too,[122] such transformation is effected when the shaman is eaten by a bear, limb by limb. Among the eastern Siberian Paleo-Asian populations of the Koryak and Chukchi,[123] we find transvestite shamans, representing an androgynous, unified being. Therefore the Chukchi male and female shamans ritually and psychically and "to some extent even physically change their sex," usually in early youth,[124] which reminds one of Australian spiritual techniques. Similar techniques are found in the Americas and also farther south, down to the Amerindians of Tierra del Fuego, who were Neolithic hunters until c. 1900, when they were exterminated by South American ranchers.

In summary form, a comparison between these groups and the representation in Stone Age rock art can be seen in Table 7.1. There are a number of seemingly global characteristics that unite the San, Andamanese, Australian, and Eurasian shamans as well as their Amerindian offshoots. Some aspects of these characteristics are clearly, and some are likely, represented already in Stone Age rock art:

TABLE 7.1. *Features of Shamanism in Palaeolithic cave paintings and recent Eurasian populations*

Cave paintings of Upper Palaeolithic, **Gondwana** shamanism	**Laurasian Shamanism:** Tierra del Fuego Amerindians (Neolithic, c. 1900)
	INITIATION
	a. summons in solitude, from wilderness spirits
Bushmen, etc.	b. together with songs
Lascaux: 'dead' shaman & bird	c. compulsive: illness136 or death if not heeded
	d. spiritual familiar involved with call
	ASCENT
Lascaux: 'dead' shaman & bird	
Bushmen: Shaman-like ascent/ descent	
Andaman: dreams, dying/rebirth, meeting of spirits	
Australia: death, ascent, descent	
Bushmen: no dissection, but transubstantiation/eland	e. with inward physical transubstantiation
Australia: insertion of crystals, internal organs removed; *ditto*	
Semang	**POWERS**
	f. sees/moves through barriers/space
Australia: moves up/down	
Bushmen: descend/ascend	
Bushmen: in contact with 'hot' power for healing, trance	g. mediate between humans and supernatural
Andaman: in contact with hot power, dreans, but no trance	
	h. advise/guide in hunting
Bushmen: use power (*ntum*) for healing, *ditto*:	i. healing: massage, suction, flight to its heavenly source (moon, etc.);
Andaman, Australia	j. sorcery: injuring by projecting stones, etc. into enemies
	k. magic by tricks, necromancy
Bushmen: transformation from/into flying eland	l. assuming form of animals, mountain
Austr.: rainbow snake, lizard inside; eagle hawk	m. ~ power of animals, mountains, trees, etc. to shamanize
Andaman, etc,	n. ~ power to influence weather
Andaman, etc.	o. rivalry/malice between shamans
	p. schools of shamans search/foster new talents
(Laurasian story line and shamanic teaching)	q. perfected shaman initiate the young
	r. shaman relies on dreams for information and warnings
	PERFORMANCE
1. Ritual dance: dancer at Trois Frères, with bow in hand; "sorcerer" at Trois Frères	
Bushmen: communal dance resulting in trance	
2. animal costume: dancer & sorcerer, Trois Frères	
	~ d. spiritual familiar involved with call
Bushmen: no costume, but interaction with / and change to flying eland (figure 7.2).	~ l. assuming form of animals
Andaman: only plant use	~ m. power of animals, etc. to shamanize

3. identification with bird: ~ d. spiritual familiar involved with call
   'dead' shaman next to bird
   on pole, at Lascaux
   Bushmen: transformation from/   ~ l. assuming form of animals
   into flying eland
   Austr.: rainbow snake, hawk
4. ecstatic trance: ~ f. see/moves through barriers/space
   dancer, at Trois Frères
   Bushmen: ecstatic dance. Trance
   Andaman: trance after contact with spirits
   Australia: trance, moves up/down

5. master of game animals:
   dancer art Trois Frères   ~ h. advise/guide in hunting
   Bushmen: identification with
   animal (bleeding eland; its horns worn)

6. master of initiations: ~ p. shaman schools search/foster new talents
   Bushmen: go through years   ~ q. perfected shaman initiate the young
   of (self-)training, to master *ntum*
   Australia, *ditto*;
   possibly:

7. wand/ staff [with bird],   shaman's drum
   'dead' shaman with bird staff,
   at Lascaux
   shaman with music bow at
   Trois Frères

8. control of magical animal,   ~ l. assuming form of animals, etc. familiar
   supporting the shaman: ~ m. power of animals, mountains, trees, to shamanize
   Bird on staff at Lascaux?
   Bushmen: flying eland form
   Austr.: snake, hawk

9. association with animal   — —
   sacrifice

   Palaeolithic bear sacrifices;   Tunguse, Koryak, Chuckchi
   buffalo killed and offered(?)   (dog, reindeer)
   & 'dead' shaman (Lascaux)   Dog sacrifices at Samara[146]
   Bushmen: hunt itself is "sacrifice":
   eland is hunted in archaic ritual
   fashion
   Austr.: self-offering of blood in initiation
   ritual only

---

   * death and rebirth/changes inside the body
   * use of animal familiars
   * descent/ascent to the spirits or deities
   * contact with and use of supermundane powers, for healing and success
    in hunting
   * management of heat, ascending in the spinal cord
   * animal or other costume (not with San)
   * use of sacrifice in initiation (not with San, Andaman, Australians)

Unless there has been some unknown, radical change in Bushman, Australian, or Andamanese lore over the past millennia, this congruence seems to reflect an older stage of shamanism.

Importantly, several of the key shamanistic features—new body, ascent to the deities as a bird, dance, contact with powers, and connection with hunting magic[125]—are seen already in Crô Magnon paintings.[126] These are archaeologically datable, at least, to the later part of the Upper Paleolithic, from c. 27,000 to 14,000 BCE.

Further, some important features such as shamanistic dance, animal costume or shape-shifting, hunting magic, communication with spirits, and the transmission of tales present in Pan-Gaean, Gondwana, and Laurasian mythology fit quite well into early Pan-Gaean hunter societies' conceptions of shaman power. They include items such as the shaman's death and rebirth during initiation, the (parallel) rebirth of animals killed in hunting, and his ascent to heaven and return to earth.

This form of early shamanism has subsequently been further adapted along the lines seen in its Andaman and Australian forms, that is, physical change of the body of the shaman and development of the animal costume—as is later very prominent in the late Paleolithic (France etc.), in Siberia and the Americas— shamanic drumming, and so on. In addition, some mythemes underlying shamanism also appear prominently in Gondwana and Laurasian myths, such as ascent and rebirth during initiation, as well as the rebirth of an animal killed in the hunt or in sacrifice.

***

Based on these shared global characteristics, we can conclude that Paleolithic shamanism was an archaic part of Pan-Gaean and Gondwana religions, but in a less complex version of what later on developed into "classical" Siberian shamanism and its offshoots in Eurasia and the Americas. It is neither economical nor elegant, but factually impossible, to attribute the similarities among Australian, Andamanese, and San shamanism to some late diffusion—when, and from where?—or to some sort of independent local development based on Jungian "shared human characteristics" (§1.2, 1.4).

***

As briefly indicated above, the shared characteristics of early shamanic practices were of significant importance for the formation of Laurasian mythology, its composition, and its transmission across the millennia. The initiation of a shaman usually takes place after some early signs such as shaking and falling into trance. Formal initiation usually is secretive in Siberia; it is prominent and prolonged in San society as well.[127] The teachings of one or several experienced shamans involve the transmission of oral tales, beliefs, and practices that are typical for the local form of shamanism.

In the Laurasian context, these teachings and their content are highly formalized, as the development of the story line indicates. The very story line may even have been intended and used as a teaching device, an early form of a "memory palace": due to its sequential temporal arrangement, initiates could most easily posit and learn the great extent and the many facets of shamanic lore. As mentioned, Schärer estimated some 15,000 pages of lore for the Borneo Dayaks; similarly large collections have now been made, for example, by G. Maskarinec for Nepalese shamans. The shamanic teachers' texts rely on the effectiveness of sacred, frequently archaic speech.[128] They have served as the main conduit for the preservation of ancient myths and have ensured a degree of stability for them.[129] In that sense, Laurasian mythology constitutes our "grandfather's and father's tales."

Importantly, this kind of formalized transmission also favored the emergence and retention of the *very structure* of Laurasian mythology: myths are, as all oral texts, more easily learned by heart and transmitted in little changed form if they are organized according to a certain fixed pattern.[130] In the present case, it is the simple narrative structure from creation to the destruction of the world, the Laurasian story line. It represents not only the "life story" of the universe (§8), paralleling that of humans but also that of killed animals, along with their expected rebirth—that is, if their bones were preserved intact (a belief still retained by many Christians). Importantly, these beliefs reflect those about shamanic death and rebirth in initiation as well.

To put it explicitly: Laurasian mythology is the outcome of an ancient hunter ideology. It must go back all the way to that of the Upper Paleolithic shamans and to their teachings, which were continuously transmitted to their disciples. It is structured and based on the life cycle of their prey: killed and reborn animals. The process is seen as paralleling that of the fate of humans—as well as that of the reconstituted and reborn shaman—and of the world at large (§8.1). This structure would include the divine figure of a Lord (or Lady) of the Animals, who is prominently found in many later mythologies across Laurasia. The relationship between the shaman and the Lord of the Animals, as well as the shaman's intercession on behalf of his fellow tribesmen, inevitably leads to the question of hunting magic,[131] killing of animals, and sacrifice, which will be treated next.

§7.1.2. Sacrifice

The origins and development of sacrifice are related to forms of shamanism by a series of progressions,[132] from the Stone Age hunt to recent and current practices.[133] The mythology and rituals of the few surviving Stone Age hunter societies that even now include, or until very recently included, the San, Hadza/Sandawe, Pygmies, Andamanese, Australians,[134] Samoyeds,[135] Chukchi-Koryak, Ainu, Inuit

(Eskimo), and many Amerindian tribes from the Haida to the Fuegians can be tested against the postulate of a Laurasian, Gondwana, and Pan-Gaean mythology.

The shamanistic aspect of the religion of the Stone Age hunter societies presupposes, in its Laurasian version, the dismemberment and/or sacrifice of a primordial deity. Examples include that of the giant, such as the southern "Chinese" (Miao) Pangu, the Vedic Indian Puruṣa, the Old Norse Ymir, the Roman Remus, the Egyptian Osiris,[136] and the Mesopotamian Kingu (and Tiamat).[137] The giant has a human correspondent, man.[138] In many if not most societies, however, human sacrifice is substituted by that of other animals: dog, goat, bull, boar, reindeer, bear, and more recently, horse.[139] Or in the classical Vedic Indian order of "the five domestic animals": man, horse, cow, sheep, and goat, while the wild animals are not considered; this is justified in a myth reported in a late Vedic text.[140]

***

The use in myth and ritual of these animals differs widely according to their occurrence in specific geographic regions and conditions and according to the pathway dependencies of local tradition. In the Sahara or the Near East, we find depictions of large animals, such as the lion,[141] the wild bull,[142] or the antelope with the San. In tropical areas we might expect—but usually do not find—depictions of other animals, such as the ancient boar offerings of the Andaman Islands.[143] In the circumpolar regions of northern Eurasia and North America, the bear plays this role.[144] In sum, a large, important local animal is offered; the bear represents a deity, as typically seen with the Ainu and Saami (Lapp). As humans moved out of Africa, we must expect a transition from large animals like the antelope, lion, and leopard to bull, boar, and bear (and eventually to the domesticated dog, reindeer, and the horse).[145]

The dog, as our oldest domesticated animal, is still being offered in eastern Siberia and is archaeologically found, for example, in eastern Europe at Samara.[146] The goat appears in North Africa—with sun symbolism—as well as in the ancient Near East and ancient South Asia,[147] in the Id sacrifice of Islam, in the Jerusalem temple, as the lamb in ancient Mosaic religion, and as a symbol in Christian religion at each mass. The boar was offered in southern Eurasia; and pigs were sacrificed in New Guinea and across a wide belt in Eurasia up to Rome.[148] The bull ("of heaven") was offered in the Near East, in pre-Vedic India, in a derivative form in ancient Crete (dance, slaying the Minotaur), and in the modern Spanish bull fight; the male buffalo is regularly sacrificed in Southeast and South Asia.[149] The North American buffalo was hunted and offered—at least in myth—in the prairies and Rocky Mountains.[150]

The horse is a latecomer in Indo-European ritual (attested in Ireland, Rome, Vedic India, Scythia) as well as in Turkic Central Asia, Old Japan, and early China,[151] as it became a prestige animal with the invention of the two-wheeled chariot (around 2000 BCE).[152] Chicken and still later exports from India are absent in common Laurasian ritual.[153]

***

The individual choice by a particular culture of a major totem, Dema, or deified animal is another matter. For example, the use of the eland antelope in San myth is an obvious choice in the Kalahari bush,[154] while that of the little mantis as representation of their High God Kaggen is enigmatic.[155] Other enigmas of post–Stone Age developments remain: why was the wolf not chosen in Eurasia (though it is called ō-kami, "great deity," in Japan) but, rather, the bear or bull? Or note the choice of the Amerindians of the raven, hare, coyote, and so on as trickster deities instead of the rather more impressive elk, bear,[156] or buffalo. Again, why was the kangaroo not chosen in Australia? The answer must lie in the development of the individual mythology or rather, the underlying worldview and ideology of the culture in question.[157]

The animals to be killed and consumed are often seen as transformed men,[158] while in some ancient societies, such as Vedic India (occasionally) or recent Melanesia and Africa, humans were actually sacrificed and consumed.[159] In ancient Vedic Indian ritual theory (also in the Bhadāraṇyaka Upaniṣad etc.)[160] the ultimate sacrifice is that of a human (in the puruṣamedha ritual), reflecting the primordial Ymir/Pangu sacrifice. The Upaniṣad actually states that the gods like human flesh best. Some early Indian texts give a long list of substitutions,[161] from man (puruṣa) down to goats and vegetarian offerings (rice, barley).[162] However, occasionally, as the texts vividly narrate, a human being was indeed slaughtered.[163] This tradition continued, at Kāmākhyā in Assam, at least into British times (Kālikāpurāṇa).[164] Also, the flesh of the deceased still is consumed by the adherents of certain rare Indian sects, such as the Aghoris, on the haunted burning grounds.

***

Ultimately, such Pan-Gaean commonalities derive from shared historical developments. The African origins and traditions of the Stone Age hunt and sacrifice have largely been retained by the San, who originally may have lived, as their Hadza and Sandawe relatives in northern Tanzania indicate, much farther north.[165] Such traditions were further developed in the rest of sub-Saharan Africa and during the early diffusion out of Africa by the ancestors of the Andamanese and Australians,[166] around and after 65,000 BCE (cf. §4.4.3).

Thus, we find, for example, the Andamanese pig hunt. Though apparently introduced from the mainland only around 3000 BCE,[167] it establishes a close connection between the tusks of the slaughtered boar and the yellowish crescent of the moon. It can be seen in an excavated ceremonial Andaman boar head.[168]

This connection, though typical for South Asia, is found all over Eurasia and also in Melanesia.[169]

Farther north,[170] the northeastern Siberian Chukchi, Koryak, Yukaghir, and Kamchadals have a dog sacrifice, often in connection with shamanistic rituals.[171] This may continue a late Paleolithic hunting ritual (and sacrifice?) of game animals (bear, bison). Dog sacrifices have also been found in profusion in late Bronze Age southern Russian excavations by D. Anthony (at Samara)[172] and are reflected in the terminology of Indo-European rituals and dice games (Vedic śvaghnin, "the dog killer"). Next to dog sacrifice for shamans, the Chukchi also have reindeer sacrifice. This feature must have been acquired in Neolithic times, when they followed the herds northward, after the great glacier melt at the end of the last Ice Age around 10,000 BCE.

Most interestingly, in Sakhalin, Hokkaido, and Tsugaru (northeastern Japan), we encounter the archaic Ainu bear sacrifice.[173] Here, the deities are seen as visitors (cf. the Jpn. *marebito*, the Hopis' Katsina deities, or the Kalash deity Balumain), but in animal form, and the killing of the bear is *iyomante* (or *kamuy oka inkara*), his "sending away." That this form of the sacrifice has very old roots is clear from the fact that it was also found in similar form with the Gilyaks on the Amur River and the Saami in northern Scandinavia.[174] The antiquity of this practice has often been discussed, as even the Neanderthals seem to have practiced a form of a bear ceremony (though this has been denied).[175] The preservation of bear heads in grave-like caches topped by slates, or even those with their leg bones inserted into their mouths,[176] seems to point in that direction. There also is the Paleolithic exposition of their heads on "altars" in caves and the supposed attachment of a bear head to a rock that looks like his body.[177] Some details of the latter archaeological facts have, however, been criticized in recent scholarship.[178] Nevertheless, there is the clear case of a bear's head, placed on a table-like rock, in the newly discovered and undisturbed Chauvet Cave in the Ardèche region of southern France,[179] dated to c. 32,000 BCE, which is one of the oldest dated caves and has extraordinary painting (with perspective).[180]

Animal sacrifice in Stone Age art (17,000–12,000 BCE)

As has been pointed out above (cf. §4.4.3, §7.1), animal sacrifice is sometimes linked to a shaman's initiation and changes in his body, his dissection and rebirth. It can be first discerned in Stone Age rock art and in its connections with mythology and shamanism.[181] Such links have been criticized by I. Wunn.[182] As reported earlier, she sees a gradual evolutionary path in the development of religion from the late Paleolithic onward and denies direct correlation of Stone Age cave art with recent shamanism, however, with no alternative explanation and with an admission that shamanism might have existed then.[183]

Nevertheless, the following examples are evocative for early shamanism.[184] Several late Paleolithic paintings (§4.4.1, §7.1.1) seem to represent the complex animal costume of later Siberian shamans. There is the famous antler-headed shaman dancer, the so-called sorcerer of Les Trois Frères,[185] in a painting dated to c. 14,000 BCE. A similar, bison-headed figure is found at the same location,[186] and another bison-headed dancer appears at Le Gabilou.[187]

These pictures seem to represent archaic shamanistic séances.[188] Importantly, they are often found deep inside the caves, a location that may have helped the sensory deprivation typical for inducing shamanistic trance. Typically, the pictures of rarely hunted, magically powerful animals, such as lions,[189] are found in the deeper sections.[190] However, while typical shamanic dancing is found, the Siberian circular drum is still missing. But this also was the case even in the early 20th-century shamanism of the Fuegians. The lack may be due to their early immigration before shamanic drums were developed in Eurasia,[191] which again is an indication that South America was a backwater not exposed to many of the more recent imports from across Bering Land (cf. Berezkin's data, discussed in §5.6.1, §6). However, one of the dancers of Trois Frères seems to hold in his hand,[192] or he actually plays, a musical instrument (a musical bow?).

Further, as discussed briefly (§4.4.2) and in connection with Wunn's theories (§7.1.1), there is, among the paintings in the "crypt" at Lascaux and at some other locations nearby, some art that actually seems to refer to a late Paleolithic myth that can be dated at c. 14,000 BCE.[193] If we follow, *pace* Wunn, the shamanistic interpretation, we can detect some items typical for shamanism. The Lascaux painting of a bison, a rhinoceros, and a human depicts a prostrate ithyphallic man with outstretched arms, birdlike hands, and a beak-like face who lies on his back below a bison bull. To his right, below the man, a duck-like bird sits on a vertical pole, perhaps a barbed spear. A spear-thrower lies at the feet of the man.[194] All of this is drawn in a rather simplified, schematic way, while the bison and a rhinoceros to its right have been painted in typical elaborate Paleolithic style. Whether the rhinoceros, which turns its back to the scene and under whose tail there are two rows of three small strokes each, belongs to the setting is somewhat doubtful. The huge bison bull, looking backward, away from the man, is seen above and to the left of the prostrate man. He is wounded by a large (barbed?) spear that has penetrated his anal region and emerges, about one-third its length, in front of or through his penis. The penetration has opened the belly of the bull and has released a huge, sack-like agglomeration of intestines that hang down to the ground.

H. Breuil (§7.1.1) interpreted the scene as that of a slain hunter, while Campbell points to the presence of the bird and the birdlike qualities of the supine man. Birds are prominent in later, attested shamanism as messengers and vehicles of shamans. In addition, the peculiar way of killing the bison bull by piercing him along the "life line" (which is frequently seen in other rock art; see above, §4.4) points in the same direction. We may add that hunting seems to be regarded as a sexually related affair,[195] as can be seen in many Stone Age paintings of actual hunting scenes, as well as in recent Bushman myth.[196] The penis of a hunter (just like that of the supine "shaman")[197] is often shown as erect,[198] or the hunter may have horns on his head (San and Australia).[199] Wunn (for the Neolithic of Anatolia) attributes this to threatening and impressing behavior.[200] Recent research in human ethology indeed indicates that such "gestures" are those of aggression.[201] To compare a typical modern hunter society: in San hunting, the animal is wounded by a poisoned arrow and followed for hours; it is then asked for permission to be killed,[202] just as was done in rituals in ancient Greece and Vedic India and as is still being done in modern Hindu sacrifice.[203]

Campbell perceives a shamanistic scene:

> Bird-decorated costumes and staves, as well as bird transformations, are the rule in shamanistic contexts. Hence, it seems to me entirely possible that prostrate figure . . . is not a hunter slain . . . but a shaman, rapt in trance.[204]

His shamanistic interpretation is sustained by the depiction of a similar prostrate figure at Laugerie Basse near Lascaux, found on an engraved reindeer horn.[205] It has a man next to a bison marked with one stroke. Similar renderings of the scene are found in two other places, one as a sculpture at Le Roc de Sers and one painted at Villars. Campbell sums up that this is the illustration of a "crucial scene from some essential legend" of great duration,[206] as the sculpture in Le Roc de Sers is from the Solutrean, c. 17,000 BCE, some 5,000 years earlier than the paintings at Lascaux. He concludes that this is "a component of our first known (yet unknown) documented mythology, having flourished, one way or another, from c. 17,000 to c. 12,000 B.C."[207]

This kind of mythology is no longer as unknown and undocumented as Campbell still had to assume, based on his scheme of common human archetypes and diffusion of ideas—both schemes being obvious in his *Atlas*. Instead, we can try to interpret the scene in the light of Laurasian mythology. It then represents some aspects of early thought about hunting and shamans (§7.1): the death of the prey is linked to the killing and dissection of the primordial being (§3.1.4, §4.4.1) and to that of the shaman himself during initiation. In the scene, there also is a link between hunting magic and sacrifice. Both are causally related in "magical thought" due to the correlative "identification" made between the depicted animal and the hunted animal.[208] The prey is asked for permission and has to agree to its own killing—again, just like the shaman does in initiation.

We do not yet have actual proof of animal sacrifice during the Stone Age period[209]—perhaps with the exception of the Lascaux and nearby scenes of the bison bull and the "shaman"—but the same attitude toward the offering and sacrifice of bears is seen in the Stone Age plastic art of France. In the cave of Montespan,[210] the body of a bear had roughly been fashioned out of clay. It was found draped with a bear's pelt, with a bear's head still attached, while another bear's skull was found in front of this image.[211] Some sort of bear cult is also seen in the Paleolithic enshrinements of bear skulls at Drachenloch in Switzerland,[212] where the long bones of a bear were inserted into his mouth; and we can see its continuation in the (pre)modern circumpolar bear cult.

Circumpolar bear cult

The cult of the bear was (and still is)[213] found in a wide range of lands,[214] from the northern Scandinavian Saami (Lapp) to the Northeast Asian Ainu,[215] the Inuit, and some North American Indians. In all of the modern circumpolar region, we can find a great similarity of ideas related to the bear, for example, that the bear sucks his paws during hibernation.[216] The bear walks upright, like humans, and is therefore compared with them; various peoples have concepts of shape-shifting. The bear therefore has many nicknames or is referred to by euphemisms due to taboo, such as the Indo-European "the brown one" (Engl. *bear*, Dutch *bruin*, German *Meister Braun*) or "the honey-licker" (Sanskrit *madhulih*, cf. Russian *medved'*).

Secretive language is used in its hunt, a practice common for much of Eurasia.[217] When offered, he is killed with archaic instruments, a feature often found in rituals of any kind. Eurasian bear sacrificers are very apologetic about such killing, saying that it was not them but others or that it was the bear's own fault (as in the Finnish epic Kalevala).[218] Then, the offered bear is praised (as in North America), including the statement, "You were the first to die,"[219] which is clearly reminiscent of the ancient Pangu/Puruṣa myth (§3.1.4), later on reflected by the epithets of the first mortal god, Yama, in Vedic India. As mentioned, the Ainu send him back (*iyomante*) to his divine ancestors. After the sacrifice, a sacrificial meal is held that is first restricted to men and then shared by all in an "eat all" orgy, a sort of sacred communion similar to the Christian one, with the consumption of the divine messenger's blood and flesh.[220]

As further examples, we may compare the modern Gilyak and,[221] especially, the well-attested bear sacrifice of the Ainu, the *iyomante* festival,[222] as well as bear hunting (*kebokai* by the *matagi* hunters). This is performed by the Japanese-speaking but Ainu-related population of northern Honshu in Tsugaru Prefecture.[223] The rituals have many reminiscences with other old Eurasian types of rituals that will be indicated here in passing.[224]

The deities are visitors in animal form.[225] Ultimately, the animal is the same as or a substitution for sacrificed humans (cf. the Vedic *puruṣa*) as well as for the deity itself (cf. the Germanic Odin, who, according to Odin's Rune Song in the poetic Edda, hung on a tree for nine nights, offered by "himself to himself," just as the Ṛgveda says [1.164.50]).[226]

The ritual lasts overnight,[227] and the bear is slaughtered on the next day. He is strangled with logs, the same method that was used in the horse sacrifice in the Turkic Altai as late as a century ago. Suffocation is a typical (Vedic or Trobriand

Islanders') "innovation," as it avoids the spilling of blood in killing the animal. The divine "visitor" is then dismissed, which is a feature typical for all Indo-European and Indian rituals, from the Vedic period down to modern *pūjā*. He is released from his body by sacrifice, in which he is offered to himself, actually on his own pelt. As mentioned this can again be compared with the self-sacrifice of Odin and the Vedic expression: "by the sacrifice the gods sacrificed the sacrifice," *yajñena yajñam ayajanta devāḥ* (RV 1.164.50, 10.90.16).

Finally, the bear's head is set on a pole for his "sending away," with which we may perhaps compare the Neanderthal bear cult. The custom has been kept in many traditions, for example, by Herodot's Scythians putting up offered horses on poles, which is echoed by the Japanese *haniwa* clay figures of ancient burials that show the holes for such poles on their sides. Further there is the Finnish custom of depositing bear skulls on trees, and in the Himalayan Mountains buffalo horns are mounted on the walls of temples. There also were and still are some animal offerings at Japanese Shintō shrines.[228]

In sum, the recent Ainu and Tsugaru rituals point back to a time when the bear cult covered much of northern Eurasia. Many remnants of this tradition can be found in ancient and medieval European texts and customs, including perhaps the name of the Greek goddess Artemis or the Celtic Dea Artio of Bern in Switzerland (where a bear's den is still kept in the center of town).[229] Bearbaiting continued in England until 1835, and "dancing" bears are still seen in Turkey and India.[230]

The naming of some of our constellations should not be neglected either. In some Indo-European languages,[231] we still find the early Stone Age designation "Great Bear" (Ursa Maior) or "bearess" (*arktos*, with cubs, in Greece). In Vedic India Ursa Maior was at first called "the Bears" (Ṛkṣāḥ; RV 1.24.10), too, but it was soon substituted (under Mesopotamian influence?) by the "Seven Sages" (Sapta rṣayaḥ).[232] In Finland, the Great Bear appears in a Kalevala legend.[233] The ancient designation of these stars as "bear" has been substituted by the wheeled wagon, obviously only after its invention in Bronze Age times (Sumeria, before c. 3000 BCE) and its use as the asterism "the Great Wagon" (later, the Great Wain).

As mentioned, some indications of a bear cult can even be seen with the Neanderthals (§4.4.2), who set up bears' skulls in particular ways indicating worship.[234] Here, the question arises again whether there was some interchange between the Neanderthals and *Homo sapiens sapiens* in Europe and the Greater Near East (§4.4). We know for a fact that the Neanderthals copied some weapons from the Crô Magnon people newly arrived in Europe. But does the reverse also hold? Did the Crô Magnons (*Homo sapiens sap.*) in Europe, or in all of northern Eurasia, copy from Neanderthals/*Homo erectus*? Or did the ancestors of current humans already have similar concepts before their emigration from Africa or even at the time of the African Eve? An investigation into the offerings of great animals (above) indicates the latter.[235]

***

Returning to the question of early Pan-Gaean hunt and sacrifice: the bear, obviously, has to be excluded from the African hunt and sacrifice of our distant ancestors. We rather must look for local animals, such as the African antelope, or perhaps even larger ones such as the rhinoceros and elephant. San myths about the primordial god Kaggen, who creates and kills their main prey, the eland antelope, and the San hunting ritual still show that the hunter identifies with the animal that is struck by a poisoned arrow and then dies.[236] Here, we may have located the ultimate starting point of the "identification" of humans and offered animal, discussed above. In addition, the San tales indicate a close connection, correlation, or even identification of the primordial deity and the hunted/sacrificed animal (§3.1.4–5, §5.3.5.1).[237]

▪ §7.2. CHANGES FROM THE LATE PALEOLITHIC TO STATE SOCIETIES

We may therefore postulate that the primordial sacrifice in hunters' societies equals that of the primordial (androgynous) deity (Pangu, Puruṣa, Ymir, Remus),[238] who was killed and dismembered (§3.1, 3.7) and who was identified with the hunter in the hunt of large animals. The boundary line between hunter and hunted is tenuous. As mentioned, in the Andamans, for example, the animals to be eaten are transformed men,[239] especially the pig, whose meat is "hot." In Vedic India, the "five sacrificial animals" are man, horse, cow, sheep, and goat; parts of their bodies are offered and consumed, by both the gods and the participants in ritual. Just as the hunted animal is asked to agree to its killing, so is the one offered in ritual. It is a standard Indian theory, therefore, that ritual killing is not "real" killing (cf. Chāndogya Upaniṣad 8.15.1).

The mythological killing and carving up of the primordial giant as well as the parallel hunt and killing of animals were substituted, as mentioned, in various Neolithic and later societies,[240] by the killing and offering of other large or domesticated local animals, such as the bear, bull, dog, goat, boar, reindeer, or horse; sometimes, especially in food-producing societies, even humans were offered.

What is apparent in this transition is the power of Stone Age mentality, which set the pattern for all subsequent societies to come, including the Euro-American ones where Christ is the "offered lamb." In other words, the effects of ancient pathway dependencies led from killed giant and hunted animal to sacrificed domestic animals or (divine) substitutes.[241] These effects are clearly visible, even if they are no longer obvious to or recognized by subsequent societies. In sum, the fundamental concepts and customs that we have inherited from our distant Stone Age ancestors still inform and influence us today.[242]

Such archaic, if transformed sacrifice is celebrated in every Catholic and Orthodox mass as the offering and consumption of the actual blood and flesh of

Christ, the "offered lamb." Few of the active participants in this (reinterpreted) primitive sacrifice realize or will be aware of the enormity of the underlying actions.[243]

Archaic and very real animal sacrifice is still seen in various modern religions. As mentioned, there is the yearly Muslim sacrifice of sheep or cows at the Id festival. In earlier times, before the destruction of the temple at Jerusalem, animals were regularly offered there as well. Perhaps surprising to some, animal sacrifice also occurs regularly in Hinduism, for example, in many parts of India, Nepal, and Bali in the form of beheading and offering of buffaloes and other animals during the autumn festival of Durgā (Daśarātrī, Dusserah, Dasain). Surprisingly, and very much against the grain, even the a priori "nonviolent" Buddhists and Jains *indirectly* participate in this killing orgy, in which 108 buffaloes were beheaded in the compound of the old police headquarters of Kathmandu alone, in spite of some protests in 2007. Both Hindus and Jains offer certain portions of buffaloes to Bhairava (Śiva). However, these always are portions that have been bought at a local butcher's shop. In this fashion, they can avoid, just like we do when shopping, the "guilt" of actual killing and the effects of bad karma.[244] Sacrifice still is vividly enacted when Nepalese Buddhists in Kathmandu at Dasain "cut" (*kāṭne*) not a buffalo but, instead, a gourd—"with one stroke," as one enthusiastic participant told me. Animal sacrifice was also continued in China, for example, with imperial sacrifices to Heaven.

Sacrifice is perpetuated by a large number of similar rituals (or substitutions) with various other populations. For example, in Shintō, offerings of seafood are regularly made, and some substitution occurs in offering *ema* horse paintings or horses made of straw (*o-uma*), so as to get rid of evil and pollution (*tsumi*).[245] Both clearly are substitutions for earlier actual horse sacrifice.[246] Indeed, there still is occasional animal sacrifice in Shintō, such as that of hares.

Violent sacrifice is very much alive in certain other societies or was until very recently. Paul Wirz has given a detailed if explicit account of the human sacrifice practiced by the Marind-anim of southwestern New Guinea less than a hundred years ago.[247] While pig sacrifice is common on this island and is often employed in potlatch-like ceremonies of destroying and distributing wealth, the Marind-anim have a complex yearly Dema festival. It involves the construction of elaborate fences and buildings, and severe restrictions are imposed on young initiates and the rest of the population. At the culmination of the festival, a preselected, though unsuspecting young man and woman are killed by a falling wooden beam and are immediately consumed.[248] This list could be extended considerably, if we were to take into account all recent and current animal and human sacrifice worldwide, including the ritual headhunt in Borneo (Dayaks), highland Taiwan (Atayal), the Amazon, northeastern Afghanistan (Kafirs), the ritual attacking and killing of helots by young Spartan warriors, and so on.

Societies that retained human sacrifice in myth include those of Vedic (and premodern) India and Italic and Germanic tribes (Puruṣa, Remus, Ymir). These societies also carried out actual human sacrifice, such as the Vedic *puruṣamedha* ritual;[249] they used gladiators and animals in the Roman circus; and people suffocated humans in the swamps of the Germanic-speaking area and deposited heads at Celtic temples in France. These rituals were actually carried out, even if they could easily have been substituted by killing a bull, goat, and so on instead, as was done in other regular sacrifices.

Other notorious examples are those of the Aztecs,[250] Mayas, Incas, Polynesians, and Indians (at Kāmākhyā, Assam, where the practice has recently been revived).[251] Human sacrifice is still rumored to take place every 12 years at Harisiddhi in the Kathmandu Valley. Then there are the very recent cases in Idi Amin's Uganda and elsewhere in Africa, as well as the widespread occasional killing of humans whose bodies then serve as "foundation stones" for buildings.

The identification of humans with the animals to be offered may be one of the reasons for the ubiquitous appearance of animal ancestors and totem animals.[252] They are found in Laurasian well as in Gondwana mythologies and include the origin of the Old Iranians (bull) and, exceptionally, the Vedic Indians (bull),[253] the Romans (wolf), the Koreans (bear), some Chinese dynasties (egg), southern and eastern populations in pre-Han China (egg), the Munda (chicken), the Khasi (chicken), and Amerindians (humans made by Raven).[254]

Offerings to the spirits are used to placate them, or with the San and the Ngaju Dayak of Borneo (and, typically, with the Vedic Indians), "the practitioners rather than 'plead' throw themselves into combat with the gods."[255] Offerings to the spirits are considered central; they can be beads, seeds, shells, or animal sacrifice,[256] for example, a chicken with the Ngaju (Borneo) and the Wana (Sulawesi). This is still understood as a substitute for human souls, for example, with chicken or pigs in Sabah (Malaysia).[257] As pointed out, a similar ideology is seen in Vedic texts of the early first millennium BCE and other old cultures. Such offerings offer insight into the beliefs about links between humans and the spirit world as well as about local social systems.[258]

A particularly well-developed set of rituals concerns the offering of (water) buffaloes in South and Southeast Asia.[259] They are often connected with megalithic rites (erection of menhirs, dolmens, memorial poles, etc.), tribal funerary ceremonies,[260] and ancestor worship,[261] as the buffalo is regarded as the carrier of the dead's soul. His horns are attached to dwellings (or Himalayan Hindu temples)[262] that are connected with the ancestors, the Sacred Buffalo symbolizing them. In the Newar communities of the Kathmandu Valley such buffalo sacrifice is periodically enacted, especially at the Dasain festival in the fall that Hinduism has reinterpreted as the victory of the Goddess over evil.

Especially noteworthy is the case of the Australian totem ancestors. Here, the animal ancestors are "in-between beings," between the High God and the humans (§5.3.2). Actual offerings are not made,[263] but men's blood is offered to the initiates.[264] Nevertheless, in all these cases, the primordial sacrifice of a giant, some other deity, or a substitute, inherited from Stone Age times, is discernable as the ultimate substrate of these rituals.

Agricultural myths

In Neolithic post-hunting groups, from the beginnings of food-producing societies, around 10,000 BCE, sacrifice took on a different aspect. These societies developed independently of each other in the nascent centers of the great civilizations of the Old World as well as in the New Guinea highlands and a little later in Central and South America. With them, the close observation of the growing cycle, including plowing or digging the earth, sowing and planting seeds, reaping ("killing") grown plants, and replanting, led to the idea that a killed being is regenerated from or by the earth. Frazer's studies (e.g., *The Golden Bough*) deal to a large degree with these kinds of societies.

The appearance of such ideas in widely distant areas looks like the "independent" creation of new myths (seemingly sustaining the Jungian position), however conditioned by the new food-producing techniques. But, again, the "new" myths obviously are calques of some of the hunter and gatherer myths discussed above. Instead of an animal or human being, it is the plant or its deity that is sacrificed and dissected in the old Stone Age manner, and its "meat" is consumed by the participants, just like in an Ainu bear sacrifice or Paleolithic feasting on a slain mammoth. However, the new mythology goes along with actual, often quite gruesome killing and consumption of animals and even humans,[265] as described above, which are meant to reinforce the deities, Demas, or life forces involved in horti- or agriculture.[266]

The ancient texts, indeed, liken the processing of food to actual killing. In ancient Vedic Indian myth, for example, the pressing of the soma plant is seen as killing God Soma, who is then described as having a bloody head.

In Mesoamerica, we can follow the indigenous development from hunter to food-producing agricultural societies (Mexican highlands, Maya), virtually in front of our eyes, in a series of archaeological cultures.[267] The gradual development of agriculture and of social stratification is accompanied by the creation of new myths that spread north and south from Central America along with the new "technology" of maize farming.[268] Thus, the Mexican killing and offering of the earth goddess, the primordial maiden,[269] reflects the older Pangu/Puruṣa myth. Only not just the various parts of the world but also the maize plants emerge from her slain body (like out of Puruṣa). As could be expected, humans have to be killed to feed her, in reciprocity.[270] The Hainuwele myth of Ceram and surrounding areas of Sunda and Sahul Land has the same underlying ideas.

The isolated myth of the Japanese goddess of food, Ōgetsu, which sticks out like the proverbial sore thumb from the rest of the continental-oriented Kojiki myths, again confirms this scenario: various plants are created from her body's various apertures. This is described without hesitation and in gory detail at Kojiki 1.18.[271] The physical quality of the various food items matches that of her bodily excretions. The idea seems to be rather old and is datable at least to the middle part of the Jōmon period (11,000–1000/300 BCE), where representations of body secretions are prominent in figurative art.[272]

The ancient Indian myth of the creation of rice and barley stresses the substitution of grains for animal offerings and establishes a direct link between animals and grains,[273] by way of two fishes: rice had just been taken over by the Vedic people (supplementing their old cereal, barley) and had been accepted even in ritual as food for the gods. It is described here as the residue of a sacrifice, subsequently, of man, horse, cow, sheep, and goat.[274]

State societies

Laurasian myth, including that of primordial sacrifice, has even been retained by early state societies. A brief look at the extant collections of Egyptian, Mesopotamian, and Chinese myths may suffice to elucidate the connection. The Miao myth of the offering of Pangu was incorporated into early Chinese collections of myth such as that of Si Maqian (c. 145–86 BCE). The same is true for post-Ṛgvedic myth in India: just as in the first text, the Ṛgveda, the primordial Puruṣa is the origin of the four human classes and then castes, as later described, with typical path dependency, by the lawgiver Manu in the last few centuries BCE. The killing of various primordial deities, such as Kingu and Tiamat, is taken up in the Mesopotamian New Year text, Enuma Elish (§3.1.4).[275]

The same kind of adaptation that had occurred when the early food-producing societies developed took place again in the nascent state societies: the old Laurasian themes were reused by the emerging nobility as well as by their priests, who adjusted them to fit the new social conditions. Actually, there was little that had to be changed: the story line from birth to death of the anthropomorphic cosmos could be retained. It was, mainly, the origin of the noblemen and less so, of the general population that had to be adjusted: the position of noblemen, accordingly, was raised mythologically.

We can observe this development, happening almost in front of our eyes, among the Neolithic food-producing societies of the eight islands of Hawai'i. They were united under a common leader, King Kamehameha, only at the end of the 18th century. At the time of Captain Cook's visit (1778), the islands still had their own chieftains, and a clear division of classes existed: *kahuna* (priests), *ali'i* (nobles), *kanaka* (commoners), and slaves. The *ali'i* and *kahuna* guarded their rights vigorously, employing a taboo (*kapu*) system that threatened instant death for violators. It was important to link the local nobility, and especially their supreme leader, the king, with the divine ancestors. The method, or rather, the trick, used in most emerging state societies was to restrict divine ancestry and access to heaven after death to the nobility and the priests. Hawai'ian commoners were said not to have permanent souls: when they died, they would just travel to the western end of the island and jump off the cliff (*pali*)—into oblivion.[276]

A similar class system comes into view in the emerging Kuru state of post-Ṛgvedic India, around 1000 BCE.[277] Only the three upper (*ārya*) classes, that is, the mutually interdependent noblemen (Kṣatriya) and priests (Brahman) as well as some wealthy commoners (Vaiśya), had—and still have—the right to perform the solemn Vedic *śrauta* rituals that alone lead to heaven. The fourth class (Śūdra) was and still is excluded. The Śūdra had to look for other means of "salvation," such as in the later, now popular Hindu rituals. This division of society is first mentioned, as indicated, in connection with the creation from the giant Puruṣa, in the hymn RV 10.90, which has therefore been called "the first constitution of India."

This example provides another extremely long-lasting case of path dependency: it goes back some 3,000 years to the oldest Indian text and beyond that to the late Paleolithic, to the Laurasian concept of the primordial giant. Needless to say, it is a very important concept, given the number of Hindus, now about one billion. The mythically founded class (*varṇa*) and caste system is still very much in force for most people in the country, especially in the villages, where some 60 percent still live. In spite of its official abolition after Indian independence in 1947, the system remains very restrictive for individuals and outright abusive and regularly deadly in many areas for the lowest castes if they oppose it even in small ways.

In emerging state societies such as the Vedic Indian one, noblemen are traced back to the sun deity. This actually holds for all three *ārya* classes, while the fourth class, the bulk of the population, was even called *a-manuṣa* (nonhuman; as is the case in the extreme instance of the outlaw status of helots in Sparta). It seems that Indo-European-speaking peoples had and still have a knack of dividing a population into politically convenient classes, whether openly so, as is still done in Britain, or in a more hidden fashion, as in America. The system has been perfected in later India: beginning in the last centuries BCE, we notice the construction of a direct line of origin of the dominant dynasties. In a somewhat tortured way, they derive from the sun deity (Sūrya-vaṃśa), while other royal lineages are derived from the moon (Soma-vaṃśa).

In sum, a development can be observed, which started out with the equal origin of all humans from the deities and changed into an increasingly restricted system that confined this origin just to the nobility, kings, and emperors (China, Japan, Egypt, Polynesia, Incas, etc.). The early Chinese case should be investigated in more detail, as there are some indications that Zhou-time China saw an admixture of Indo-European-like religion and ritual,[278] older ideas of Heaven, and its worship involving the spirits *qi* (*ch'i*). Here, too, the stress was on social conditioning, first of all that of the relation between the current generation of noblemen and their ancestors, as well as that between them and the people.

Yet such innovations clearly are fairly recent ones when seen against the late Paleolithic origins of Laurasian mythology. There are examples of comparable contemporary, concurrent changes that produced divergent mythologies, even in relatively small, closely connected societies. F. Barth's book *Cosmologies in the Making* (§1.6) is very helpful in indicating how such societies can deal with their inherited materials. We see this *"inner conflict of tradition"* (Heesterman) in late Vedic India too: it ultimately resulted in wide-ranging changes in Indian religion and society, such as the origin of Buddhism and Jainism, which do not stress the Vedic class system or disregard it as irrelevant for salvation.

Obviously, it is very hard to detect such developments during the long periods of time that are studied here. (F. Barth expressly denounces such approaches.) But the historical and comparative method employed in the present book allows us to compare individual local results of historical developments, say, of Egyptian mythology, with the preceding stages of Nostratic, Eurasian, and Laurasian mythology, as well as with the synchronic religions of their neighbors (§2.3). We can achieve this kind of insight after having studied the variations of Laurasian mythology in Old Egyptian, Greek, Vedic, and Japanese texts and so on. In the end, the emergence of local variations is the result of the struggle between, on the one hand, materials provided by long-standing pathway dependencies and, on the other, new contemporary local thought and social pressures, as well as various internal and external influences that shape both religious and social developments. In sum, all such local developments are the outcome of the interplay of pathway dependency and innovation.

However, the underlying frame of mind, for example, that of the divine descent of humans and the resulting "filial" transgenerational relations, remained the same in all the cases quoted earlier. Identical or very similar patterns of development can be seen in Old Egypt, Mesopotamia,[279] Vedic India, China, Japan, and Polynesia as well as with the Aztecs, Mayas, and Incas. The resulting similarity of ideas about the divine origin of just the ruling classes cannot be attributed to diffusion: that would involve crossing wide stretches of ocean and land between c. 3000 BCE (Egypt) and c. 1400 CE (Incas). It would remain mysterious how such diffusion, as Frobenius and Baumann have it, would have worked: for example, by which *regular* maritime exchanges that alone would sustain the transfer of complete belief systems? For these, there simply is no consistent evidence.[280]

Instead, we must insist that *path dependencies* were at work.[281] Their long trail was established by the early shamans of c. 65,000 BCE, who emigrated out of Africa into Eurasia, carrying along their idea of human descent from a High God in heaven. It was further elaborated by their early Laurasian shaman descendants, who developed the scheme of universal human solar ancestry. Their ideology has more recently spread all over the globe, leaving apart and unaffected just some isolated pockets of Laurasia and Africa (Central and West Africa, San) as well as New Guinea and Australia.

Other later and modern forms of Laurasian myth cannot be discussed here at length (see §8). Importantly, this includes the foundational development of monotheism in Zoroastrian Iran (with Ahuramazdā as creator god) about 3,000 years ago. The Zoroastrian concept was adopted around the mid–first millennium BCE by Hebrew and subsequently by Christian religion, with major repercussions for the Roman Empire, the rest of Europe, and beyond. Finally, after the emergence of its Islamic form nearly 1,400 years ago, it affected much of Africa, the Near East, and South and Southeast Asia. The Christian and Islamic versions are the *currently* dominant forms of Laurasian myth world-wide, with about a third and a fifth of humanity adhering to them; the modern Hindu form accounts for another 14 percent; and Buddhist and Chinese religions each, about 6 percent. All together, some 75 percent are derivations of Laurasian mythology.

The Christian offshoot presents a curious mixture of the Hebrew version of Laurasian myth as found in the first chapters of Genesis, of Zoroastrian-inspired monotheism, and of Near Eastern mystery cults with a heavy dose of ancient, Neolithic theories of sacrifice (§7.1.2). In this religion, automatic physical rebirth is no longer automatic, as in Pan-Gaean (or modern West African and Indian) myth or as reestablished and reinforced by the ancient Near Eastern and Greek mystery cults. These cults employed animal sacrifice, for example, by virtually showering the initiate with the blood of the offered animal; as mentioned, animal sacrifice was also practiced by contemporary Hebrew religion. Regular, repeated animal sacrifice in Judaism was substituted in Christian religion by the onetime momentous killing of a divine "lamb" in human form, a feature that is reenacted in daily or weekly ritual. In that respect, Islam represents a more straightforward version of biblical mythology, without the Christian ritualistic amalgamations, though, on the other hand, it incorporates some of its major figures, such as Mary (Maryam) and Jesus (Isa), and it, too, perpetuates annual animal sacrifice.

***

In short, we can establish the Pan-Gaean, ultimately African origins of the myth of primordial killing and its counterpart in sacrifice. In that form, it is still retained by the (*modern*) hunting societies of the San (Bushmen), the Andamanese, and the Australian Aborigines. The myth was further developed in the rest of sub-Saharan Africa. Other developments occurred after the early diffusion out of Africa, especially after the development of early food production (c. 10,000 BCE) and after the emergence of early state societies (by c. 3000 BCE). In the latter form, Laurasian mythology remains with us today in Jewish, Christian, Muslim, Hindu, Buddhist, Shintō, and several other local forms of religion, myth, and ritual.

The powerful Christian and Islamic versions of Laurasian myth have increasingly dominated much of the globe ever since c. 313/632 CE. Their secular version, Marxism, must be included here as well. It merely turns the dependency of humans on god(s) on its head and substitutes, instead of a final destruction of the world and the individual hope for paradise, an ultimate, blissful state of society that Zarathustra and his Christian successors had reserved just for their followers. Ironically and certainly unbeknownst to its current proponents, it is precisely the Zoroastrian version, adapted in the last book of the Bible, that is prominent in a large section of the current American religious and political scene. John's Revelation includes the (Zoroastrian) end of the world with the final, now imminent judgment for all evildoers (§8).

***

In sum, Laurasian mythology has survived the numerous transformations that have taken place since the Paleolithic. It is was found with hunter-gatherers, early planters, and complex state societies such as those of Mesopotamia, Egypt, Mexico, and so on. Beyond that, it still thrives in modern societies that are characterized by its descendants: Judeo-Christian, Islamic, Hindu, Buddhist, and Shintō religion and some other belief systems.

The overall important result is that Laurasian mythology is *not* dependent on any particular form of climate, ecology, economy, or society—which militates against Marxist, Durkheimian, and Bellah's evolutionary ideas, just as it does against Frobenius's, Baumann's, and Campbell's idea of the overarching "paideumatic" influence of climate and environment. While such influences cannot be denied, they have not been strong enough to overcome the dominant Laurasian path dependency and create a *completely new*, non-Laurasian type of mythology—at least not so far.

Instead, the analysis of Laurasian mythologies indicates that its underlying themes have been kept intact, from the Bible to Polynesia, from Egypt to Japan, from Iceland to Peru—with some suitable changes carried out that were required by new environments and/or economies. For example, as mentioned, a food deity—often a goddess—was developed and typically inserted, rather secondarily, into the core of traditional Laurasian-type mythology. We find her as Ōgetsu of Old Japan, as the earth deity of the Maya,[282] and as the androgynous deity Prajāpati of Vedic India, who creates and regularly periodically re-creates by *emanation* and *regeneration*, not by hands or words.

Similarly, the myth of divine solar descent was restricted, as mentioned, to the emerging Neolithic noble and royal lineages: in Egypt, China, Japan, Hawai'i, the Inca realm, and post-Vedic India (Sūryavaṃśa). Even religions (Zoroastrian, Abrahamic) that introduced countermoves against such societal restrictions, such as the idea of personal responsibility and moral choice, are still based on the myths of a time line and of a story line that extend from original creation to the final destruction and eventual re-creation of the world. In the end, some 75 percent of humanity still fervently adhere to one form of Laurasian belief or the other—even though *they do not know it.*

▪ §7.3. DATING GONDWANA AND LAURASIAN MYTHOLOGY

Relative and absolute dating of the early Laurasian and Gondwana systems of mythology is notoriously difficult as we deal with reconstructed texts. The situation, again, is similar to that in linguistics or genetics, with the inherent difficulties of absolute dating for language families or haplogroups. However, a certain measure of certainty can be derived from the observation, discussed at length (§3, §6), that the story line is characteristic of Laurasian mythology but it is lacking in the Gondwana mythologies of Australia, Melanesia, and large parts of sub-Saharan Africa. The Gondwana area is also characterized by a lack of the typical Laurasian fascination with primordial creation; instead, the origins of one's clan or totem and of humans in general are dealt with at length. As mentioned, Proto-Gondwana mythology preserves an *earlier* stage in the development of human mythology, one that has, naturally, left many traces in Laurasian mythology. While the latter are part and parcel of Gondwana mythologies, they do not make much sense, isolated as they are, in Laurasian mythology. All of this easily establishes some points useful for *relative* dating of the various Laurasian and Gondwana mythologies.

As has been pointed out (§5), the African situation is rather complicated because of continuing contact with the Laurasian systems of the Sahel and even from beyond the Sahara, as well as with Nilotic-speaking groups in East Africa. There also are clear indications of a northern origin of San myths. They arrived in South Africa only some 6,000 years ago, via Tanzania, where their Hadza and Sandawe relatives still survive.[283]

On the other hand, the Australian mythological system has been isolated for a long time, first for some 20,000 years after initial immigration and, second, for a minimum of some 3,000 years after the last Ice Age, when Australia was finally cut off from New Guinea. Even then, Australian myth cannot be claimed to present Stone Age mythology in its *pristine* state. As with all other humans, various changes have taken place since. We deal in Australia, as elsewhere, with modern *Homo sapiens sapiens*, who have an equally long history everywhere on the globe.

When the extensive similarities of the Gondwana mythologies of Australia, New Guinea, the Andamans, and sub-Saharan Africa are taken together, they provide, along with the time frame for the immigration into the Americas, some useful *ad quem* dates for the separate existence of the two mythological systems of Laurasia and Gondwana.

Ante quem

Based on archaeological data, the earliest immigration into the Americas is considered to have occurred around 20,000 years ago.[284] While some of these early dates still are under discussion (§4.4), the existence of the Laurasian system can now be dated (*ad quem*) as existing at the time of this migration.[285] The correspondences between Eurasian and Mesoamerican and Fuegan myths (§3) indicate the existence of the Laurasian myth complex well before the traditional date of 11,500 BCE (Clovis) and more likely now, well before 20 kya. This migration also brought about the transfer of shamanism into the New World. It is found in all Amerindian populations from the Arctic to Tierra del Fuego. This distribution includes some very early South American migrants (Fuegan, Yanomami) who were not influenced by the later migrations from Siberia or Bering Land by the Na-Dene peoples (Athapascans, Navajo, Apache).[286]

The ultimate origin of Laurasian mythology may still be thousands, if not tens of thousands, of years earlier than the various migrations into the Americas. Yet, provided that the reconstruction of the Laurasian system is correct, it must have existed *at least* by 20,000 BCE, as the external data of archaeology and genetics indicate for immigration into the Americas.[287]

Amerindians, from Alaska to Tierra del Fuego, speak widely different languages that, until very recently, were typically classified as belonging to many linguistic groups and families. However, as detailed earlier, J. Greenberg united almost all of them in his bold reconstruction of Amerind, which covers all of the Americas except for the Na-Dene (Athapascan, Navajo, Apache) and Inuit-Aleutian languages.

The populations speaking Amerindian languages have mythologies that clearly belong to the Laurasian type. Some late Siberian—but still Laurasian—influence is felt too, which occurred due to the immigration of Na-Dene speakers after the submerging of Bering Land at the end of the last Ice Age.[288] However, a *late* secondary spread of Siberian motifs all over the Americas, from Alaska to Tierra del Fuego (or even a hypothetical one that would have involved *all* Laurasian characteristics), is excluded: many of such motifs cannot be traced back to the migration of the Na-Dene group but, rather, precede it.[289]

***

However, as pointed out (§6), some individual archaic motifs in South America are shared with Australia and New Guinea.[290] While they still fall within the scope of and maintain the Laurasian story line, their occurrence may force us to reevaluate the history of North, Meso-, and South American mythology to some extent. As frequently stressed earlier, the present undertaking is of heuristic nature, and new materials or analyses will be cause for some adjustment.

Berezkin's common motifs must have spread into Sahul Land early on,[291] c. 50 kya, and across Bering Land some 20 kya. They probably passed through the narrow Ice-Free Corridor east of the Canadian Rockies before it closed up during the Last Glacial Maximum and then proceeded all the way south to Tierra del Fuego. After the end of the last Ice Age some 10,000 years ago and after the concurrent reopening of the ice blockade along the Canadian Rocky Mountains, other Amerindians could spread south in the same way. The precise history of all these movements remains unclear. Among the last, coming out of Bering Land, were the Na-Dene.

The Sahul–South American mythological congruences would then be due to an early spread from Asia, around 20 kya, into the Americas down to Tierra del Fuego. This scenario has later been overlaid by (a series of) migrations from Siberia and Bering Land bringing in "Siberian" myths. The *late* overlap with Asia is especially clear in the Northwest, while many other aspects of North American myth that correspond to Siberian ones may belong to such later strata as well.[292] Again, such comparisons are heuristic and still a work in progress, which may be confirmed by future linguistic and genetic data, once both have reached deeper resolution. The preceding suppositions could not even have been attempted without Berezkin's extensive collections and his recent comparisons of pan-Pacific myths.[293]

Pan-American evidence apart, the Laurasian mythologies are attested in the art and writing of Egypt and Mesopotamia by c. 3000 BCE; then in the Indus civilization, where they are visible in mythological scenes on seals and tablets by c. 2600 BCE; and further in China by c. 1200 BCE (tortoise shell texts). Furthermore, many well-advanced food-producing communities in Eurasia are now attested at increasingly older dates, around 10,000 BCE, and may provide further pictorial data.

Early dates are now also provided by the independently arrived data of archaeology and population genetics. As discussed above, the Out of Africa event took place around 65,000 BCE, and immigration into Southeast Asia and southern East Asia as well as Sahul Land is put just a little later, at c. 60,000–40,000 BCE.[294] On the other hand, with archaeological data in the Americas and the existence of the main Y chromosome haplogroup of the Americas, X (now called P*, Q, R_1), it is put at roughly 20 kya. These relative dates are reinforced by the evidence arising from the widely spread Gondwana group of mythologies. Taken together, they share many characteristics that represent an *older* stratum than the Laurasian one (§§5–6).

***

The immigration of early Australian tribes into their continent is set at c. 60,000–40,000 BCE, with the same dates for the peopling of New Guinea. Both areas were connected during the second-to-last Ice Age (52–45 kya) and during the

Last Glacial Maximum (25–15 kya); their ultimate separation occurred at a point in time variously given as c. 12 kya or 10–7 kya for New Guinea (and 14–7 kya for Tasmania).[295] These dates offer two additional high and low parameters for the existence of these particular Gondwana mythologies. As mentioned (§5.3.2), there has indeed been some influence of Papua myth on northern Australia that must stem from this period. Recently, this has been reconfirmed by genetic studies.[296]

Nevertheless, the character of Australian mythology is quite distinct from that of the neighboring Melanesian islands, including New Guinea (§5.3.3). The question of a separate Tasmanian group, somatically as well as linguistically and mythologically, still needs to be explored in greater detail. Linguistic data indicate a connection with the Solomon Islands, an area that also seems to have preserved some older forms of Melanesian myth (§5.3.3); better Tasmanian genetic data are still awaited. The few remnants of Tasmanian myth (§5.3.2.1) point to an older Tasmanian occupation of parts of southeastern Australia, traces of which are still seen in southeastern Australian mythology (§5.3.2).[297] At any rate, early Sahul Land mythology was of partly Tasmanian, eastern Melanesian, Papuan, and Australian type. Detailed investigations will have to be undertaken in this fairly neglected field of comparison to reach better resolution.

Ad quem

However, the archaeologically attested immigration of the Australians and Melanesians at around 50 kya provides a good date *ad quem* for the last possible stage of *coherent* Gondwana mythology, stretching from Africa to Australia. This agrees well with the genetic estimates. Indirectly, it also attests to the fact that Laurasian mythology had not yet spread into the neighboring Southeast Asian archipelago—then, the large subcontinent of Sunda Land—while some linguistic and genetic data point to an earlier habitat of Proto-Australians in South India and, hence, to Gondwana presence.[298]

This scenario has been reinforced by recent genetic data, as mentioned before, for the Andaman Islanders and two tribes on the Indian Subcontinent, the (Dravidian-speaking) Kurumba in the Nilgiris and the (Indo-Aryan-speaking) Rajbanshis in northern Bengal and Nepal.[299] While the Andamanese genetic data point to an early separation from the ex-Africa lineages at c. 65 (± 7) kya, those of their Subcontinental "relatives" are younger, at c. 46/45 kya. Taken together they reconfirm an "Andamanese"-type settlement in large parts of India already by 60 kya,[300] while the south seems to have had "Australian"-type genes and linguistic substrates.[301]

Consequently, Laurasian mythology is likely to have developed—probably somewhere in southwestern Asia and on the western borders of South Asia— between 65,000 and 20,000 years ago, and judged from negative Sahul evidence for its existence then, most likely around 40,000 years ago. From there, it spread into Europe with the arrival of the first *Homo sapiens sap.* groups. They arrived via the southeastern Anatolian and eastern Ukrainian fringes around 40 kya. At the same time, Laurasian mythology also spread northward into western Central Asia, perhaps carried by early Dene-Caucasian speakers. However, the exact way Laurasian mythology reached China and eastern Central Asia is still unclear (§4.3.3). As frequently seen, language, myth, and genes must not necessarily travel together. Laurasian myth may have been transmitted into northern China by Central/North Asian hunters who spoke the Nostratic language or rather, its Dene-Caucasian predecessor; the latter group includes, according to some linguists, the ancestor of Chinese. Southern China has been occupied since c. 65,000 years ago by populations belonging to the first wave of humans that arrived from Africa along the shores of the Indian Ocean and Sunda Land, from where they moved north to China. Recent discoveries at Zhoukoudian near Beijing put the arrival of *Homo sapiens sap.* already at c. 42–39 kya.[302]

On the other hand, as discussed in detail earlier (§4.3.3), the possibility cannot be excluded, and is even hinted at by some DNA evidence, that some early immigrants into Southeast Asia may have moved in around 40 kya carrying Laurasian mythology and remained there side by side with other populations adhering to Gondwana-type mythologies, as is still seen with some residues in certain Taiwan highland tribes. This point must remain speculative and be kept in the balance for the moment. Here, too, there is need of much further, detailed field research: the genetic and linguistic history of the populations of Southeast Asia and South China must be clarified further.[303]

More importantly, some of the older Gondwana mythologies are retained, to some extent, by small, little-studied remnant populations (Andamanese, Semang, Aeta, etc.). Much of this area has been overlaid by later Austro-Asiatic and Austronesian immigrants and their myths and finally by Buddhist beliefs, though some motifs are still visible under the Buddhist veneer. Relevant investigations will result in a clearer picture of post-60-kya developments in Southeast and southern East Asia.

A brief history of mythology

Taking into account all data and features derived from several disciplines so far (§4), the development of Gondwana and Laurasian mythological thought may now be pictured as follows. First, the origin of all presently living humans is, as biologists and archaeologists maintain, to be sought in East Africa at c. 130,000 or even 160 kya. The few stories of Pan-Gaean mythology heuristically reconstructed earlier (§6) represent humanity's oldest reconstructible layer of myths.

***

Second, it seems that those myths now seen with the Andamanese, Australians, Melanesians, and so on correspond fairly closely to the oldest reconstructible version of the Gondwana emigrant groups that moved eastward from Africa at c. 65 kya. For example, the concept of shamanic generation and taming of heat, upward shamanic flight, the pursuit of animal spirits, and (Australian) Dreamtime may be very old remnants of early shamanic human thought.

On the other hand, the sub-Saharan African branch has in the meantime undergone some developments of its own.[304] These points are still lacking in the Sahul branch and with the San and Pygmies, who represent traditions other than the general sub-Saharans.

Furthermore, the African branch has undergone some secondary influences from the Eurasian branch of Laurasian mythology, via the Sahel belt and the East African savanna "highway" (§5.3.5).[305] Genetics, too, recognize some reflux out of the greater Near East into Africa.[306]

***

Third, the Laurasian branch conversely developed among some Out of Africa populations, originally as one of their subgroups. This must have been relatively early, as the Amerindian branch of "Laurasians" reached America already c. 20,000 years ago and perhaps Europe by c. 40,000 years ago. One of the main innovative features of Laurasian mythology was the invention of a continuous, coherent story line (§2.4–5). It combines certain previous (Gondwana) mythological fragments (§§5–6) into one continuous story, a "novel" that relates everything from the beginning of the world to its end.

In historical times, Laurasian mythology included the further development of the dualistic worldview, culminating in that of Zoroaster (c. 1000 BCE). This set the stage for all subsequent Near Eastern ("desert") religions—Judaism, Christianity, and Islam—and indirectly, even for ideologies such as Marxism. All of them make a sharp distinction between "good" and "evil" that was not found in earlier versions of mythologies, which allow for a large "gray" zone and shifting loyalties.

***

Based on the data discussed above, we can now think about a time line after the emergence of *Homo sapiens sapiens* after 200,000 BCE—depending on whether one takes the Kabwe (Zambia) skeleton at 250/150 kya or the Herto (Afar, Ethiopia) skeleton of 160 kya as our earliest representative.[307] (*Homo neanderthalensis* is left out here as the ability to speak is disputed.)

TABLE 7.2. *Major stages in the historical development of mythology and its relationship to the sciences*

Mythology and the sciences:

ARCHAEOLOGY, PALAEONTOLOGY	LINGUISTICS	GENETICS
c. 160/130 kya emergence of Homo *Sap. sap*.in E. Africa		
"Proto-world/Pangaia mythology"	Proto-World language (Blažek, Bengtson)	African "Eve" mother of all existing humans (mtDNA L1,2) &"Adam" (NRY A, B)
90 kya Early Homo Sap. *sap*. in the Levant & disappearance, retreat to Africa	(some doubt about existence of full language)	(some early indications of the faculty) of symbolic thought in N., S. Africa
75 kya humans in S.India, before and after Toba explosion, their fate?		
c. 65,0000 y.a. **Gondwana mythology** Out of Africa movement across S. Arabia towards S., S.E. Asia (Sunda Land), to southern E. Asia & Sahul Land (Australia-New Guinea, Salomons, Tasmania)	(theoretically: division of San, Niger-Congo/ Nilo-Saharan languages from the "Asian" rest)	mtDNA: L3 → M, N → R, U, etc.; NRY: C, D, E
Development of early Australian mythology: *The Dreaming* (no cosmogony; High God creates humans; flood, culture heroes/tricksters)	Melanesian and Australian languages & Indo-Pacific (Greenberg), (including Andamanese, Kusunda in Nepal)	mtDNA R→P, N → S Q; O, M NRY: C3 ,C4; (Andamans, S/NE India,Tibet,Japan: NRY D; India: mtDNA M)
52-45 kya: second last ICE AGE (survival of humans in the tropical belt and in certain Asian refuge areas) Further development: of the sub-Saharan branch: African branch with dualism, multiple symbolism	Ancestors of Nilo-Saharan, Niger-Congo languages	(mtDNA L; NRY A,B, etc.)
c. 40 kya: major movement northward of Asian populations; settlement of Europe: (with Laurasian mythology?)	Major language families: Dene-Caucasian (Proto-Basque), Pre-Nostratic? Pre-Austric?, Pre-Sino-Tibetan? European remnant languages: Etruscan, Pictish, Germanic/Greek, etc. substrate languages	NRY: F and sub-haplogroups (G-R)
c. 40 kya 'artistic explosion' on all settled continents, incl. S. Africa: rock and cave art		
c. 40 kya [minimum: c. 20-11.500 BCE] Development of **Laurasian mythology**, in or near S.W. Asia: invention of a continuous storyline, cosmogony and eschatology added	Pre-Nostratic? Pre-Sino-Tibetan? Pre-Austric?	
c.26 kya: movement of Jōmon population from Mongolia into Sakhalin and Japan	Jōmon language substrate in Japanese	NRY D

c. 25-15 kya: <u>Ice Age</u>: Last Glacial Maximum
northern Eurasian populations survive in a
few refuge areas in Siberia, Spain, etc;
Amerindians *ditto*, and south of the Ice in
N., C. and S. America

<u>c. 20 kya</u> (minimum: 11.500 BCE)

Earliest movements of pre-Amerindians from Bering Land into North America	Amerindian languages	
c.15 kya first domestication of the dog	dog still absent in Proto-Nostratic	

<u>After the Ice</u>: immigration of Na-Dene, part of
Dene-Caucasian family and of Inuit speakers
after submerging of Bering Land
Latest date for possible introduction of Solar
myths to the America.

<u>c. 10 kya</u>- beginning of food production
in Near East, China, New Guinea; Beginning of
domestication of animals

7 kya latest date for separation of Australia from
New Guinea, *ditto* for Tasmania. 5-3 kya
Microliths introduced to Australia, 3.5 kya dingo
dog introduced in Australia, both not in Tasmania

<u>Late movements</u>

Spread of the Afro-Asiatic branch of Nostratic in the Greater Near East and N./E. Africa	Semitic, Egyptian, Berber, Omotic, etc.	
Spread of the Khoi-San southward to S. Africa (c. 6000 y.a.)	Hadza, Sandawe in Tanzania; San in S. Africa	

c. 4000 BCE Domestication of the horse in
various northern steppe areas of Eurasia

Indo-European expansion across Europe, Anatolia, Xinjiang, Iran, N. India: largely pastoral economy;	Indo-European languages: Hittite, Vedic Sanskrit, Greek	NRY: M17? = R1a1

<u>Indo-Eur. version</u> of Laur. myth.
Solar myths reconstructed for Indo-European
("wheel of the sun")

Parallel: Uralic branch of Nostratic in the Taiga
belt of N. Russia

3000 BCE-- (Solar) myths attested in writing:
Egypt and Mesopotamia

S.A. Asians and Pacific Islanders: c. 2000 BCE: <u>Out of Taiwan move</u> by Austronesian speakers to Philippines, Indonesia, then Polynesia, Madagascar; Neolithic food production, later: full rice agriculture in S.E. Asia	Austronesian, Polynesian	mtDNA B4a1a: the "Polynesian motif"

1200 BCE Solar myths in Polynesian (reconstructed from texts) 712/720 CE solar myths in
Japanese texts (Kojiki/Nihon Shoki) 1st
mill.- Solar myths attested in Maya inscriptions
1500. Solar myths attested in Meso-S. American
texts and Descriptions

<u>1750 CE</u> – Still, lack of Laurasian type mythology
in Australia, Melanesia, Andamans, etc.

TABLE 7.3. *Dating Gondwana and Laurasian mythology*

• *post quem*	65,000 BCE	'Gondwana' Exodus	Out of Africa
• *post/ad quem*	40,000 BCE	'Gondwana' immigration	into Sahul Land
• *ad quem*	40,000 BCE	'Laurasian' immigration	into Europe
• *ante quem:*	20,000 BCE	'Laurasian' immigration	into the Americas

The developments discussed in this section may be represented in diagram form (Table 7.2), however, as stressed before, only in a heuristic way. Details can be overturned by each subsequent archaeological, linguistic, or genetic discovery.

In essence, this means that certain aspects of all Out of Africa mythologies must have been present, *at the latest,* c. 40,000 years ago (based on Australian dates), while those of Laurasian mythology must have been present by c. 20,000 years ago. Both are the lowest minimal dates. The actual existence of the Gondwana and Laurasian mythologies is probable at much earlier times.

A possible scenario is that Laurasian mythology evolved—probably somewhere in Southwest Asia or on the western border of South Asia—around 40,000 BCE, at the time of the great artistic "explosion" of the late Paleolithic. But, though Paleolithic art reached Australia, Laurasian mythology did *not.* Apparently, Australia's early immigrants moved into Southeast Asia and Sahul Land *before* the latter momentous change took place. Their entry into Australia at 60,000–40,000 BCE *precedes* the spread of Laurasian mythology into Southeast Asia. Consequently, Laurasian mythology should be dated as in Table 7.3.

A date around 40,000 years ago coincides with but was not caused by—nor is it entirely overlapping with—the influences that underlie the spread of late Paleolithic rock art. The emergence of (rock) art appears to have been a major step in the development of the symbolic functions in the human brain, though there are some indications in northwestern and South Africa of earlier, more simple art around 160/90 kya.[308] It is clear that the new wave of symbolic and artistic expression spread, from an unknown center, in equal fashion across all of Africa and Asia, irrespective of the mythologies professed. Nevertheless, this phenomenon suggests that the emergence of Laurasian mythology is just *one of several* aspects of the new symbolic representations that developed around c. 40 kya.

***

Among them, Laurasian mythology emerged as our first well-construed novel-like series of tales. Subsequently, it spread all across Eurasia, northern and eastern Africa, and finally the Americas. Nowadays, the populations believing in or otherwise following one of its latter-day versions (Christianity, Islam, Hinduism, etc.) have pushed back Gondwana mythologies into increasingly smaller areas of sub-Saharan Africa, the Andamans, New Guinea and Australia, and a few other retreat areas in Asia.

***

Further studies in archaeology and genetics will have to shed more light on both the exact source of Laurasian mythology and its spread. In addition detailed studies will have to deal with the remnants of various Gondwana mythologies, such as those of the Todas in the Nilgiris of South India, the Semang and Aeta of Southeast Asia, and various aboriginal highland tribes of Taiwan, and with the various prehistoric and local forms of southern Chinese, Korean, and Japanese myth.[309] Their particular background can then be detailed and evaluated better than could be done in the present book. Laurasian or not, such detailed studies will provide further background and specifications to the theory, and in the process we may discover more remnants of Gondwana mythology, such as seems to be the case with the Todas or some Taiwan highland tribes.

***

I hope that this book will provide the relevant materials that can be tested against such evidence. I underline, again, that the current details of the theory are heuristic; they can change as new data emerge. Yet I am confident that the outline (story line, creation and destruction myths, marriage of Heaven and Earth, etc.) will stand.

More importantly, I am hopeful that this book will provide a new vision of our oldest myths, which will contribute to the emerging new *Weltanschauung* of our global village, our rapidly shrinking world. It is important to understand that our early mythologies share the same quest for our origins, whether of humans or of the universe at large.

Though it is difficult to establish concrete numbers, a rough estimate of the remnants of Gondwana mythologies indicates that they are confined to less than 5 percent of present-day humans, mainly some of those living in sub-Saharan Africa, northern Australia, and New Guinea. Their number is still shrinking due to the continuing onslaught of Laurasian-derived religions. It is an urgent task to study and preserve whatever is left of the various Gondwana mythologies. They are an important part of our common human heritage.

As Laurasian mythology has been that successful, for millennia, we must ask, finally, what it *meant* for late Paleolithic humans—and what it continues to mean for many of us today.

8 Outlook

Like any extant mythology, Laurasian mythology should form a *meaningful* whole,[1] a *system* that made sense to its adherents. It also should not just be a simple "social reconstruction," a sort of Durkheimian social "glue" or Marxist *Überbau* that is based on an external (so-called *etic*) analysis of archaic society.[2] Much more than that is required because Laurasian mythology encompasses many disparate societies: from hunter-gatherers via horticulturists, agriculturists, and pastoralists to highly evolved town and city civilizations, early states, and modern civilizations. In short, the reconstruction should not be a simple hypostasis of society in myth and religion, as seen, for example, in Dumézil's tripartite reconstructions of Indo-European myth and society, an interpretation that is, incidentally, neither restricted to Indo-European nor always just tripartite.[3]

Nevertheless, just as the Dumézilian scheme presupposes an *ordered* system of disparate myths, so does the Laurasian one. But the Laurasian order is of a different quality. It is not based on a straightforward analysis of a pre-state society with three categories of priests, nobles, and commoners and their reflection in mythology. Rather, it is one that can be analyzed sui generis as a collection of myths and, more importantly, as a *structured* collection of such tales. As has been repeatedly stressed, Laurasian mythology has a well-developed narrative and is not a simple, disparate agglomeration of tales but, instead, a *novel* of sorts.

Ordered, logical structure

The Laurasian invention of a "first novel," with its unique *story line* from creation to destruction, produces order where in Pan-Gaean, Proto-Gondwana, and pre-Laurasian times, we had only a more or less disparate group of "first tales," such as those about a High God and about the origins of humans by sending down his son and of totem animal ancestors. The very story line, as such, expresses and underlines that *structure* is intended. But it obviously does not *explain* why there is *this* particular structure: the consistent tale of first creation and generations of gods, demigods, and humans until final destruction. We will have to investigate its inherent logic in some detail.

The inherent order is obvious in some items: a great all-covering flood cannot occur before the emergence of the earth. Other features, too, such as the generations of the gods, are arranged in an apparent and logical order: from the simple (chaos, darkness, or primordial waters) to the more complex (bisexual) creation of the later generations of gods and, finally, the descent of humans from the gods.

Once we take the complex contents and structure of the Laurasian "novel" seriously, it is obvious that it tells the story from the "birth" of the universe until its "death" (and its eventual rebirth). In other words, it takes its inspiration from something that is very close to human experience: the human life cycle from birth to death (and desired rebirth, as already seen in Pan-Gaean myth). It sums up our experience in life: growing up from childhood through teen, middle, and old age; and it expresses the ineffaceable wish for something positive to happen *after* this life—a new life or a rebirth, however it might be shaped. The Laurasian novel enumerates the gradual life stages of the world, from emergence out of chaos or darkness to the appearance of human beings and of the *oikumene*, society and culture, and the final threat to its existence.

Metaphor of human life

The Laurasian story line thus is a *metaphor* of the *human* condition,[4] of human life from its mysterious beginnings to its impending ominous end. It was the genial stroke of the creator of Laurasian mythology that it correlates and thus explains at the same time both the universe *and* the human condition:[5] *where we came from, why we are here, and where we will go.* Laurasian myth is a metaphor applied to everything around us, to the world and to the divine powers that govern it. It answers, in an encoded and shrouded way, and on a symbolic and metaphoric level, the eternal question: *why are we here?*

Viewed from the present vantage point—after detecting the Laurasian story line—Laurasian "ideology" seems to be based on a fairly simple idea, the correlation of the "life" of humans and the universe. But someone, about 40,000 years ago, had to come up with it first. As it is closely related to the concepts of the Paleolithic hunt, the rebirth of animals, and shamanism, it must have been a shaman who did so.

Apparently, the new concept was so obvious and fascinating to a large section of the contemporaneous Eurasian descendants of the Out of Africa migrants that—excluding those adhering to Gondwana mythologies—its basic idea was taken over on a large scale. Its patterns and ideology have persisted in various guises and continue to have deep resonance and meaning even for many of us today. Those who adhere to its current forms still feel—even if they do not recognize the Laurasian scheme as such—that it sums up, in large measure, our experience in life, our growth from childhood to old age. More importantly to many, this mythology expresses the wish for a positive *after*life or rebirth.

The structure and underlying metaphor of Laurasian myth have deep resonance and meaning. In various forms, we still pursue the same goal. For many, it
may be articulated as Zoroastrian, Christian, Islamic, Hindu, or even Buddhist
rebirth in some sort of blissful state or Heaven. For quite a few of us, it may now
appear as the contemporary, eager search for powerful, almost supernatural
extraterrestrial "relatives" or in looking for human origins beyond, in the cosmos
(Carl Sagan). It may be reflected by the wish to physically overcome death and
destruction through technology (cryology). Or it may be epitomized in the old
but persistent Indo-European formula of "undying fame" and the resulting wish
to preserve, at least, our personal *name*. Such desire commonly leads, in America,
to the donation of money to cultural institutions and to having one's name
"immortalized" in buildings, street names, foundations, and the like.

***

Yet there is more to the Laurasian "novel." Its myths work on *many levels*, as all
well-constructed myths and other artistic creations should indeed do.[6] Laurasian
myth

- is an *interesting story* in itself, one that people like to retell constantly and
  elaborate upon;
- is based throughout on common *human experience*, something that, due to
  common human brain structure,[7] is easily *translatable*, understandable,
  and applicable by correlation to the world around us; and
- offers an *explanation* of the human condition and of the world around us *in
  our own (human) terms*.[8]

First of all, there is the "translation" of human experience (and, importantly,
dreams) into myth.[9] Any such translation is based on similes, metaphors, analogies, homologies, and correlations: "the sky is shaped *just like* a human skull," or
"in the beginning the world *was* an egg that split open." The establishment of
such correlations has been explained in detail for China, India, and Europe (by
Farmer et al.) as an overextension of social categories to the universe, in other
words, the tendency to build anthropomorphic (or animistic) models of the
world as seen in the early mythological or religious models of the world. This is
a natural outgrowth of well-known features of brain structure and its early
development.[10]

The important, though actually banal point in this is that everything outside
of ourselves is seen, how else, through *human* eyes: birds *talk* or in the beginning
even trees and rocks *talked* (Kojiki 1.13). Poets, tellers of fairy tales, and common
people still make use of such correlations and homologies: trees whisper,
Valmiki's *krauñca* bird (in the Rāmāyana) cries and laments about the death of
its companion, the (temperate) forest *sleeps* at night, the birds in the Rgveda or
Japanese "crows" (ravens) *fly home* in the evening. The lion is the king of animals,

the owl is wise, the fox is sly, the cow is stupid (at least in Europe, though certainly not in India), bees and ants are diligent and thoughtful (in providing for the winter). The Ethiopian leopard is a Christian and fasts, while the hyena is a pagan and gluttonous;[11] in Siberian tales,[12] the hare is fearful and boastful; the fox is very clever; the goose is dignified, diligent, and thoughtful; the bear is slow in understanding and—surprisingly—also fearful. The raven, often a creator figure or demiurge, is regarded by the Chukchi, Koryak, and Itelmen as very clever but also oversexed and a thief.[13]

Laurasian myth describes the spirits and deities, too, in human terms. The gods are fashioned in the form of humans (unlike in the Bible, which says exactly the opposite).[14] They, and the animals likewise,[15] act like humans. They speak, ponder, and scheme; they create and destroy alliances among themselves; they honor commitments and take revenge; they are born, and they can die or be killed. The border line between deities, humans, and animals is vague, and many categories that we now so clearly distinguish largely overlap. In numerous myths, animals are ancestors of humans—as Australian, Tasmanian, Papua, and Austro-Asiatic totems—and so are the gods. Deities can take on animal characteristics, notably in medieval and modern India and in Old Egypt—though this is sometimes seen, as in the case of Egypt's many animal-faced deities, only metaphorically. Further, certain famous persons can *become* gods, such as the Greek hero Herakles, Roman emperors, the Indian Purūravas, and the Japanese Hachiman,[16] and they then rise to heaven. So do some animals, such as the llama seen in the Milky Way with the Incas, the archaic Great Bear with the Indo-Europeans, and the animals in many other asterisms worldwide.

Taking a closer look at the correlations made between humans and the universe, we first investigate the obvious correlations with the human life cycle.

1. Life cycle

The story of the engendering, birth, "growing up," and death of the universe closely follows that of the human life cycle: procreation by sperm and "the blood" in the mother's womb (as the ancients saw it, for example, in Old India);[17] then progressing from an amorphous (egg-like) mass, as observed in miscarriages and through animal slaughter, to an emerging fetal form and to birth; followed by infancy, childhood, and teenage; to emerge in adult life, from strong physique to diseased old age—frequently mourned by the Greeks—and inevitable death. The universe, likewise, developed from the mixture of sweet and salty waters—corresponding to blood and sperm, in Mesopotamia—to an undefined (or egg-like) shape (§3.1.6). This may have given rise to or reinforced the idea of the universe as born from an egg. It continues its "pregnancy" by giving birth to a primordial giant or to the first pair of twins(?), father heaven/mother earth.[18] The bipolar and bisexual world grew "stronger" and older with the ensuing generations of the gods. They may represent, from the point of view of the "life cycle" of the universe, the stages in life or even the age-based groups seen in some societies. The development of the world proceeds with the heroic elimination of monsters, the creation of culture, and the emergence of human beings, who have to sustain their ancestors, the gods. Yet even gods can die, and so does the universe itself: it will be burned up (like human bodies in cremation) in a final conflagration at the "end of time"—however, as held out in many mythologies, with the hope for a new life, new gods, and a new world.[19]

2. Bisexual nature of life, dualism, dichotomy

Laurasian mythology makes a clear, intelligent distinction between the first amorphous, vegetative origins of the universe and the later, structured, bisexual, dichotomy-like world of gods, nature, humans, and human culture. Just as it uses the human life cycle, it clearly makes use of the bisexual nature of observable living beings, from fish and reptiles to apes and human beings, in order to explain the nature of the universe, of humans, and, often enough, of the dichotomy of cultural constructions.

This is where Lévi-Strauss's bipolar structures of myth could come into play: they are not based on the bicameral structure of the human mind.[20] Laurasian mythology is based, instead, on the simple but brilliant culturally generated principle, used by many societies, of ordering items, beings, and people into "male" and "female" categories—or just into *any* two categories, which Lévi-Strauss has so frequently explored. These could be the north and south wind, seen with the northwestern Amerindians,[21] or the two monsoon winds, regarded as the primeval deities by the Andamanese (§5.3.4).

Many items in human experience and myth are indeed expressed in a dichotomous, bipolar fashion: that of birth/death, father heaven/mother earth, male/female sections of a clan or of a settlement;[22] that of a simple dual social structure of leaders and followers, applicable even to a basic hunter-gatherer society; that of culture versus nature (Lévi-Strauss's *cooked* :: *uncooked* or *raw*); and that of "wild" versus "civilized" (ripe/unripe or "green" in China), of "human" versus "animalistic," of gods versus "demons," and so on. However, the resulting bipolar, dichotomous structure is not enough for an "explanation" of the world or of society. It remains just a facile division of facts and a *description*, but it lacks what humans always strive for: *meaning*.

3. Family and clan

Laurasian mythology, instead, makes use of the immediate experience of the nuclear family and its surrounding small-scale society. In Stone Age times, this meant just that of small scale hunter-gatherer bands and clans. Thus, it views the development of the universe and its dominant forces by taking recourse to the family structure inherent in three-level, transgenerational societies. It therefore describes the several generations of the gods as having typical humanlike qualities, as alluded to earlier: their wheelings and dealings, their desires and animosities.

Importantly, it also views the forces of the universe as being related to each other, just as humans are. Such forces take on the form of spirits and deities, who are father/mother and their children, brothers and sisters, their grandchildren, and so on. The gods have to live and work together, interdependent just like a nuclear family, band, or clan. They have definite areas of responsibility and "work": some may gather (and later on, produce) food, such as the Greek Persephone and the Japanese goddess of food, Ōgetsu. They must be protectors and/or hunters of animals (as the "Lord/Lady of the Animals"). Others may protect the clan and guard against monsters and enemies (such as the pan-Asian "bow shooter": the archer Yi, Indra, Amaterasu, etc.). Some, often the primordial father figure, may even watch out over the rules of behavior and cooperation, over truth and keeping agreements (such as much later on, the Vedic Varuṇa etc.). On a larger scale, they watch over the orderly working of the universe as a whole (see below).

We all are the direct or less direct children of these gods, similar to them with all their good and bad traits of character, but we also are weaker than the gods and tainted by death, which, generally, is the result of or punishment for some primordial mistake made by our divine or semidivine ancestor. This "explanation" of the origin of death, satisfying as it may have been in the Stone Age, still is preserved—pathway fashion—by the major world religions today.[23] It thus shapes the outlook on life of billions of fellow humans. Needless to say, this pessimistic attitude is irrational but nevertheless persistent, and it has severe consequences for the more orthodox followers of these religions, especially for women.

During one's lifetime, be it that of a god or a human, stress is not on the modern individual "pursuit of happiness" but, rather, the pursuit of goals that are compatible with the archaic transgenerational *social contract*: of cooperation in family and clan, which is a perfect Stone Age solution for small bands of hunter-gatherers. This meant producing children (often preferably sons) for the continuation of one's lineage, gathering food and "wealth" (in hunting, later on in gardening products or cattle), and achieving "nondecaying fame," as Indo-Europeans liked to say. The benefit of "fame" is that one will be remembered for what one did, even by one's great-grandchildren, when one will long have been gone or returned (by rebirth) to one's clan. One's name will not die, as the Old Norse Edda (Hāvāmāl 76–77) sums it up: "cattle die, friends die, likewise one dies too, but never will good fame die... but I know one thing that does not die, the judgment about the dead." Such ideas are not obsolete even today: the verse was recently quoted in an interview—pathway fashion—by Iceland's president. And its repercussion in modern society—giving one's name to buildings, foundations, and the like—has been described above.

4. Four generations of gods and humans

As indicated, Laurasian mythology makes use of the general human experience of living together with several—usually three—successive generations to explain the development of the world and of its governing forces, the deities. Even today, normally only three or four generations are personally known to us.[24] And it is four (sometimes five) generations of deities, ages, or "suns" that figure prominently in Laurasian mythology (§3.6). Even this experience is symbolized in myth: there is natural decay from the age of the (great-)grandfather, from perfect primordial times—"things were better, then"—to the present, weak human condition, seen in Eurasian myths (while there is increasing perfection in Mesoamerican mythology).

As pointed out, we are descendants of the gods, usually of the sun deity. As children of the gods, we are *similar* to them, having all their good and bad traits of character.[25] The aim and the reason for our existence in this world therefore are to honor the "social contract" with our ancestors, feeding them after their death and allowing their survival in the otherworld—until they return to our family or clan, usually in the third or fourth generation.

This relationship, which necessarily includes our ultimate ancestors, the gods, is ultimately kept up in our own interest. For we will also depend on it, after our death. The scheme therefore offers, next to fame, a measure of reassurance in facing personal annihilation. In fact, it is the basis of a different and older golden rule: *"Do not do to your ancestors and the gods what you do not want to be done to you after death."* Or to put it in positive terms: honor your ancestors and *their* ancestors, the spirits or gods.[26] This transgenerational obligation includes the feeding, in ritual, of one's direct human as well as one's ultimate divine ancestors, the gods. Yet even the gods must feed their own ancestors, as is seen in Indian and Greek ritual.[27]

In sum, the world of the gods and that of the humans have wide-ranging parallels. Whatever happens in the universe (or in heaven or the nighttime sky) is mirrored here on earth in human life and society. Many rituals are based on such correlations,[28] the most notorious perhaps being the post-Ṛgvedic Indian *śrauta* ritual that linked everything with everything.[29] Some of this stance is also seen in Africa (§5.3, 5.3.5.2 sqq.).

5. The workings of society and the universe

Laurasian mythology views the workings of the universe and human society in a coherent, orderly, and harmonic way. There is a universally underlying, positive, and ordering force at work that affects humans as well as the deities and the universe.

This is an aspect that has been little studied in comparative fashion. The point of all-embracing *harmony* is especially seen in ancient China (*li*), but it is also reflected in India (*ṛta*) and apparently in several other ancient cultures, such as in the Old Egyptian *ma'at* and maybe in the Sumerian *me*. Details cannot be spelled out here;[30] however, it may be underlined that the ancient Indo-Iranian **r̥ta* (c. 2000 BCE, and its descendant, the Zoroastrian *aša*, Old Persian *arta*) is a positive force. It encompasses truth and its active aspect, the realization of truth that works in human speech acts, in keeping agreements, in the actions and commitments of the gods, and in the incontrovertible laws of the universe that govern both humans and gods. Universal, tribal, and band *harmony* is more important than personal happiness or bliss (as indicated above).

From this worldview follow many aspects of ancient customs and rites, especially the effort for a regular renewal of life in concert with the gods and the ancestors. The renewal is performed in the great yearly, seasonal, and monthly offerings, sacrifices, and festivals, especially during the dangerous period preceding the start of the new year. The important inherent bond and mutual agreement exist between, on the one hand, nature, its deities, and its seasons and, on the other hand, human society and its constituent parts. Their connection must be sustained and ensured through rituals that often include the narration of myths, such as that of the Enuma Elish at the Mesopotamian New Year. To carry these out regularly is a prerequisite for personal bliss as well as that of the clan's and of society at large, at first local amalgamations of clans and tribes and later on, the state.[31]

The concept of harmony reinforces the structure of (early) society. In Stone Age times, society did not mean much more than small families, bands, clans, and loose tribal groupings. Harmony is habitually reenforced by the voluntary sharing of food and other supplies (as still seen with the San). Yet even then *some* distinctions are made, as contemporary hunter and gatherer societies indicate: a certain man is more skillful in hunting than another and thus becomes a leader (at least on a hunt), and a successful hunter may feed several wives (Australia, San). Some others will have specialized, besides their daily hunt and search for food, in tool making, and some, most important for the study of myth, in spiritual matters. This means that they were early shamans, as can be observed in the cave paintings of southern France and elsewhere (§4.4.1)—though we must note again that shamanism is different from typical Gondwana spirit possession.[32]

In later times, when simple hunter societies developed into horticultural, agricultural, and finally state societies, social division increased. We can observe these changes in certain areas with a continuous development attested over several millennia, for example, in highland Mexico.[33] However, it is very important to note that Laurasian mythology was maintained during all of these developments, as has been detailed earlier (§7.2), which, incidentally, is another testimony to its inherent force and attractiveness. Nevertheless, such social developments caused some changes toward a more complex setup of society. Small indications of this are reflected in the Neolithic and later development of Laurasian myths.

As discussed earlier, the typical Laurasian feature that human descent from a (sun) deity has been supplanted by the *restricted* descent of *just* the nobility from the solar deity. This is prominent even in the late Neolithic societies such as that of Polynesia that have a clear distinction between nobles, common people, and slaves; in addition there are (the very prominent) priests. This is a four-class society and not a Dumézilian tripartite one. In many parts of Polynesia only the nobles have souls and go to the otherworld after their death. Common people just "jump off a cliff" at the western end of their island (§2.5.1, §3.7). In Polynesian societies, priests or shamans play such an important role that they could paralyze society by declaring certain taboos (Hawai'ian *kapu*). In many other societies, male or female shamans wielded considerable influence as they could communicate directly with the deities and ancestors (§7.1): from the shamans of the Inuit (Eskimo) to those of Amazon hunters, from those of the Saami (Lapp) or Mongol cattle herders to the Japanese female shamans of the fully agricultural, Bronze Age state society of the Yayoi period, and until today.

Where we can observe Laurasian shamanic and priestly tradition, such as among the traditional Siberian and Nepalese shamans, the Trobriand Islanders, the Ami priests of aboriginal Taiwan, and the Vedic Indian Brahmins, it puts considerable, even extraordinary stress on the power of speech.[34] Therefore, more or less fixed secret texts emerged as well as their exclusive transmission among initiates.[35] In other words, shamans formed a separate group from early on. They also guaranteed the transmission of Laurasian myth and the form of the story line from creation to destruction.

6. The explanatory force of Laurasian myth

Finally, as hinted at earlier, Laurasian mythology offers a convincing "explanation," as far as that could be done in prescientific times, of the world and its origin and of the origin and nature of humans. It thus provides a *satisfying* answer to the typical Laurasian questions of "from where, how, why?"

How can such an explanation work? Lévi-Strauss has given a cogent answer: "[In] societies without writing, positive knowledge fell well short of the power of imagination, and it was the task of myths to fill this gap."[36] (This includes the knowledge of plants, medicines, the stars, the universe, etc. as described for the Andamanese by Radcliffe-Brown.) In other words, humans knew so little of the actual physical background of the workings of nature that they needed myths to explain it, as well as to summarize all observed and known facts. Apart from myths, people have found other clever devices to "store" knowledge, such as "on the bones" of a fish in Polynesia and in the classical loci and medieval "memory palaces" of Europe and beyond.[37]

Laurasian mythology, instead, achieves this by a framework *familiar* to early humans, that of human life, of birth and death, of several generations, and of clan interaction. The human life cycle, bisexuality, family, and small-scale society are woven into a well-built structure with many levels of *meaningful* tales, a "novel" that explains our origins, and that of everything around us, in the anthropomorphic image of procreation, birth, growing up, aging, and death. Significantly, the scheme also holds out the hope, even the certainty, for rebirth, both for oneself and for the world.

The result is a well-laid-out garden of symbols: a complex, *interwoven*, "logical" structure with many levels of *meaningful* tales, a "novel" that explains our origin, nature, and culture. It is more than the "forest of tales" of Gondwana myths. It depicts our personal, psychic (and dream) experience, our tribal memory and imagination, and it provides for the social need of justification of customs, rules, and beliefs. In short, the Laurasian story line offers the individual many tales built into a composite, inherently successive, and therefore "logical" structure. It offers, in anthropomorphic form, a satisfying "explanation" of the world in which we live and of our own nature and fate.

This concept must have been of persistent appeal to many if not most peoples of Eurasia and the Americas, and we witness the constant inroads that it has made and still makes into many African, Melanesian, and other Gondwana societies. It represents a unique case of very early but persistent "path dependency" that emerged some 40,000 years ago but still holds most humans in its thrall.[38] The power of early, Stone Age mentality and imagination set the pattern for all subsequent societies to come. To repeat, we witness the lasting effects of long-term, ancient pathway dependencies that are no longer recognized by subsequent societies. This certainly includes our own civilizations: culturally acquired patterns of thought and belief normally are not obvious to their followers. Otherwise, would more than 90 percent of current humans follow the current descendants of Laurasian mythology, great world religions and their secular offspring, such as Marxism? What we have inherited from our distant Stone Age ancestors still informs us today.

▪ §8.2. BEYOND LAURASIA, GONDWANA, AND PAN-GAEA

In constructing the complex Laurasian mythology story line, its authors made a selection of much older Gondwana and Pan-Gaean tales (§6.1). However, the Gondwana mythologies of the Africans, Andamanese, Negritos, Papuas, and Australians cannot be expected to represent today, after 65,000 years or more, the original Pan-Gaean forms in pristine purity, even in isolated New Guinea and Australia, though they have retained the loose arrangement of tales and much of their content.

As detailed earlier (§6.1), the various Gondwana and Laurasian societies have made use of prior mythology while selecting features and structures appealing in their own time, following the inherent pathway dependencies of their respective cultures. This can take diverse forms,[39] such as the so-called Vedic ideas of current modern Indian myth;[40] it frequently appears as a little-studied South Asian variety of the well-known Papuan cargo cult,[41] or it can appear as various modern American myths (George Washington, Superman, Elvis, *Star Wars*, *Star Trek*, Campbell's *monomyth*). Burkert notes, with some discomfort, that "the most glaring pieces of science fiction still invariably cling to the most ancient mythical patterns of quest and combat tale."[42]

***

In all such cases, the local cultures depend on millennia of path dependencies that have shaped their modern realizations. For example, modern American myth and its social repercussions heavily rely on the ancient concept of the "hero" (§3.10; Campbell's monomyth), as earlier exemplified in medieval and classical European tales that ultimately go back to Indo-European concepts. They include those of Roland, Sigurd/Siegfried, Beowulf,[43] the *Iliad*'s heroes such as Hector and Achilles,[44] classical Greek accounts of Alexander's life by Arrian and others, Christian myths such as that of St. George and the dragon,[45] and the ever-popular god-hero Rāma in India.[46]

Many of them follow the underlying structure of fairy tales,[47] a feature that has recently also been shown to apply to the beloved Indian epic Rāmāyaṇa.[48] This or a very similar, abbreviated scheme is most typically seen in Hollywood films and television series: good always wins, even if the "lone rider" hero stays tragically aloof or leaves as soon as his feat is accomplished (Campbell's monomyth), which is a typical variant of the challenges put to the hero in traditional hero tales.[49] His incarnations in other countries with Laurasian mythology are comparable.

In contemporary India, hero tales still take the form of the typical Bollywood movie, often with mythological themes directly taken from the epics and Purāṇas or from classical poets, such as Kālidāsa. Their motifs are based on Vedic myths and tales, many of them ultimately Indo-European, if not older: and so it goes on, "turtles all the way down." The line of descent is another long-lasting effect of pathway dependency. The Indian case of dependency can be indicated clearly as it is based on still extant literature, from the Vedas down to late medieval, poetic re-creations of the same topics (Urvaśī, Śakuntalā, Rāma as hero). The most notable re-creation perhaps is the recent adaptation of the Rāmāyaṇa for a television series in the late eighties,[50] which drew huge audiences and emptied the Indian streets each Sunday for more than a year. No wonder, as the tale follows Propp's pattern of fairy tales, where good always wins over evil. The series also seems to have played a role in the rise of the nationalistic-religious cargo cult–inspired Hindutva movement, leading to India's first right-wing government (1998–2004). Interestingly, the actors portraying such mythical figures are often received in villages as if they were the very gods whom the portray, and they get elected—just like "cowboys" and other mythical "heroes" in America. Myth and politics still are closely wed, as they always have been in recorded history.

In Japan things are somewhat different. Old mythological motifs (from the Kojiki and Nihon Shoki) are rarely reproduced in films, perhaps as there is very little in the way of hero tales. The "first emperor," Jimmu, is a heroic figure, though he lacks the tragic end of traditional heroes and is said to have died peacefully at the age of 127, after having reigned in Yamato for some 73 years (Nihon Shoki). The only real hero of the Kojiki, Yamato Takeru.no Mikoto (Kojiki II 79:8, 80:13 sqq.), conquers the enemies of the Yamato realm west, north, and especially in the east. But he, too, dies of old age and fatigue (Kojiki II 87)[51] and has not become a movie hero.

However, medieval Japanese epics and early modern tales regularly do make it onto the screen, recently again the great and tragic Heike story.[52] Their heroes usually are tragic, much more so than in India or America. The underlying sentiment (or *rasa*, to use the India term) is one of Buddhist *impermanence* and that of the current "age of decline" of Buddhist teaching, *mappō*. The closest we get to the American monomyth in Japan is in the ever-popular television series of *Mito Kōmon*, where good always wins—but good is enforced by a powerful relative and agent of the reigning Tokugawa shoguns of the past few hundred years.

China, too, has a large number of series with heroic motifs from various periods of its history teaching traditional lessons about Confucian fidelity.[53] In contrast, European cinema (unlike Hollywood versions) only occasionally picks up topics from Greek mythology, Roman history, medieval legends, and tales from early modern history and myth—such as Jason, Siegfried, Robin Hood, Richard the Lionhearted, Les Trois Mousquetaires, and so on[54]—but they have relatively little popular resonance. Heroes are not much in vogue, or sought after, after the devastations of the last two world wars.

§8.2.1. Persistence of myth

We must now ask: why does myth, whether in the form of hero tales or otherwise, persist at all in modern societies? The short answer is: myth apparently is something inherently human,[55] typical for *Homo sapiens sapiens* and maybe even for Neanderthals.[56] Recent tests have indicated that humans indeed seem to be "hardwired" for religion.[57] While education plays some role in the attitude of adults toward religion, it rather depends on one's general personality whether one becomes increasingly more or less religious in later life.[58] The brief survey given below agrees with this view.

***

The inherent danger of this dependency, obviously, is that the tendency of humans toward mythological and religious explanations of reality can easily be misused by unscrupulous leaders and politicians.[59] The concept of "nation" itself is a mythical concept.[60] So what about the (recent) formulation, daily repeated and reinforced in schools, of "*one nation under God*"?

A recent example of a powerful new myth is the rise of Nazi mythology, as depicted in Rosenberg's in part Indian-inspired book *Der Mythos des 20. Jahrhunderts*.[61] Though Rosenberg was the official Nazi ideologue, Nazi politicians paid relatively little attention to his confused book and instead pursued their own versions of romanticizing "Germanic" projects. As Cassirer puts it, "[Myth] was regulated and organized; it was adjusted to political needs and used for political end."[62] Myth often has played this role, especially in all kinds of state societies,[63] and this judgment also applies to its other recent emanations.

Myth reasserts itself even in societies that propose to do away with traditional culture, such as the former Soviet Union and communist Korea and China: merely, new myths or new versions of existent myths were created. Again, in Cassirer's words: "They were brought into being by the word of command of the political leaders."[64] We have the Stakhanov myth of the successful worker in the Soviet Union (1935)[65] and the miraculous birth of Kim Il Sung on a mountain in North Korea—instead, he was born near Pyongyang—and his transformation into a war hero—instead, he stayed away from the front in the Soviet Union during World War II. Or there are various stories and picture books of the sixties and seventies about young Chinese heroes who, Mao style, overcame all natural and human-made difficulties, relying on Mao in their heart (just like others have Jesus or Rāma in their hearts). During the Chinese Cultural Revolution (1966–75), dozens of such tales were created and propagated in comic books, theater, films, and so on.

Myth also is very potent right now in the religious and political landscape of America:[66] "the end and rapture are coming," according to a myth based on a 19th-century *reinterpretation* of the last book of the Christian Bible, John's Revelation, which—ironically—has strong Iranian, Zoroastrian-based relationships.[67] This belief influences not only the thinking of a large proportion of the population but, dangerously, also that of politicians who already carry the heavy burden of other 19th-century and older American myths (the "manifest destiny"[68] of "god's own country").[69] Ever since the deist Founding Fathers of the American Republic, one semisecular myth after another has taken shape, starting with George Washington, "who never told a lie," up to the strongly myth-oriented presidency of George Bush "the Lesser," as Arundhati Roy has it: the world is divided into (Zoroastrian) *evildoers* and the rest. Environmental problems, as one of Bush's high government officials said, "will be taken care of by Jesus"—who is anyhow coming back soon, according to the current evangelical interpretation of the Book of Revelation.

Right from the start, the American self-image has been strongly myth oriented, even though the new republic emerged out of an Enlightenment background. In addition to the exceptionalism of "god's own country" and Manifest Destiny, there is the myth that "all men are created equal" (*minus* women and slaves); the myth of "everything is possible, *only* in America"; the myth of being able to become "rich and famous" and to achieve "the American dream" (neglecting the c. 40 million citizens who cannot afford health insurance and the growing lower classes); the myth of a classless American society;[70] and finally, the recent, clearly politically motivated and widely broadcast political myth of America embodying and spreading "Freedom" and/or "Democracy" *abroad*—while not taking care of its many internal problems, such as lack of food, health care, housing, and education for all of its own citizens.

The misuse of mythology for political reasons is, again, evident, just as it was in the times of the British Empire, with its "civilizing mission" due to the "white man's burden," and in the Japanese Empire, with the latter's misuse of ancient mythology and Shintō religion. Hindu myth, or rather, its very modern modifications, including the invention of a glorious past way before Egypt, Mesopotamia, and, of course, China, has been misused recently to stir up nationalistic and chauvinistic sentiments in India and beyond, in the Indian diaspora.[71]

§8.2.2. Some reasons

Why do we still need myth? One reason seems to be that even in contemporary society, "positive knowledge so greatly overflows our imaginative powers that our imagination, unable to apprehend the word that is revealed to it, has no alternative than to turn to myth again," which echoes Giambattisto Vico.[72]

Hübner saw the same inevitability already over two decades ago:[73] though it has little percolated into general consciousness, it is clear now that there is no *absolute* foundation for science, and anarchism reigns in certain sections of the sciences and humanities. Thus, one can no longer rely *just* on science as the "sole possessor of truth." Further, research over the past 200 years has shown that myth is not just the result of fantasy, though it is not foreseeable how myth (or religion in the wider sense) and science will come closer to each other.[74]

For Hübner, the question is how contemporary humans can find meaning and a sense of worth in a world seemingly governed by the laws of science (and increasingly, by unrestrained commerce and all-out competition, we may add). In this situation, he has warned against irrationalism, pessimism, and demagogues using the current crisis and increasing insecurity stemming from technological and economic "progress" as well as environmental threats.[75] The last one or two decades have proved him right: either people have increasingly turned to the traditional religions again, or they have constructed, in New Age fashion, ones for themselves. As the Dalai Lama recently said in an interview, when he was asked why Buddhism is so popular in the West now: "[it is] something new"! Or as an Australian shaman put it: "white men have lost their Dreaming."

Occidental movements back to myth and religion have been witnessed several times over the past two centuries. After the onset of the Industrial Age, the large-scale changes in society and the resulting social tensions led to a yearning for security, a harkening back to a "secure" state of affairs that was imagined to have existed during the Middle Ages. The inward-looking Romantic period ensued; it captured the newly emerged bourgeoisie for several decades.

Both world wars resulted, again, in turning to the "wisdom of the East," notably to supposedly "rational" Buddhism. Further technological advances, along with the resulting social disruptions, increasing competition within a global economy, and more recently, yearning for personal and national security, led to similar results:[76] many new belief forms, sects, and cults emerged, some of sinister character like the murderous Japanese Om sect, which combines aspects of Hinduism and Buddhism, or other doomsday cults. In other words, the unexplainable must be made immanent and visible, and myth takes over again, as Hübner (or long before him, Vico) prophesized.

***

Other reasons for the persistence of myth and mythical thinking are, first, that humans indeed seem to be "hardwired" for religion (see below) and, second, that we are heavily "preconditioned" by the predecessors of our current cultures. Cross-cultural comparison indicates that once a certain foundational, *central* motif has been established in a particular civilization, it has an enormous persistence over time.[77] Farmer et al. have called this the "path dependency" of cultural traits. The Laurasian story line that has survived several tens of thousands of years would be a primary example. Others include the following.

Over the past 2,000–3,000 years Laurasian mythology has been reformulated by the world's major religions, which now hold an ever greater sway over the majority of the world's population due to continuing inroads in areas of various tribal and Gondwana mythologies. However, Japanese Shintō,[78] numerous forms of Hinduism, and small Eurasian and Amerindian tribal religions (such as that of the Kalash of northwestern Pakistan and the Hopi of Arizona) retain the old polytheistic framework.[79] This has been overlaid, even in Hinduism, by ever more syncretistic and abstract levels of interpretation. Old spirits of nature and universal forces, personified as particular deities, lurk underneath its in part quasi-monotheistic or, rather, henotheistic and pantheistic varnish. Shintō cataloged, more than a millennium ago,[80] some 8,000 major deities and 3,000 shrines.[81] Their story is told in the first section of the "national mythology," the Kojiki of 712 CE, and they continue to be worshipped in every ward and village, next to Buddhist deities. Other, smaller and tribal religions in Asia and the Americas have likewise maintained the Laurasian story line.

***

The Laurasian narrative also holds true for the other major world religions. Among them, Zoroastrianism is the earliest monotheistic faith. Zoroaster (and his priests) abandoned the old Indo-Iranian concept of two competing groups of universal principles and deities (*ṛta* and *druh*, Deva and Asura) in favor of the supremacy of one God, Ahuramazdā, who nevertheless is opposed by the Evil Spirit (Aŋrō Mainiiu) and devil-like creatures. The Laurasian story line is central to Zoroastrian myths: Ahuramazdā creates a world that will be destroyed at the end of time, while Ahuramazdā's allies, enemies of the Evil Spirit, will live on in a world of bliss.

Judaism, too, moved from polytheistic beginnings ("no other gods next to me") to actual monotheism, reflecting Iranian influences during the so-called Babylonian captivity. All "Abrahamic" religions (Judaism, Christianity, and Islam) have replaced the ancient multiple deities with a monotheistic framework that encompasses, rather precariously, even the Christian concept of the Trinity. Yet the Laurasian narrative was retained intact: Abrahamic accounts commence with the world's creation by God (rather, *elohīm*, "the gods") and end with its destruction, mitigated by hope for a new, paradise-like world. "Paradise," again, is an echo of Old Iranian influence, where *pari-daēza* means "the walled-in [garden]."

Increasingly, Christian and Islamic versions of Laurasian myth are seriously impacting the last holdouts of polytheistic Laurasian and Gondwana mythologies in Africa, New Guinea, and many tribal enclaves elsewhere. Stiffer resistance is offered in areas dominated by the (Laurasian) Hindu, Daoist, and Shintō religions, as well as by practitioners of some new religions like the Melanesian cargo or African syncretistic cults.[82]

In all such areas we can witness various degrees of syncretism and increasingly, "new religions" that include many aspects of the local, indigenous religions: "Christian" Europe has retained many of its pre-Christian folk beliefs and festivals, from "superstition" to the classical, Iranian, and Germanic aspects of Christmas (*sol invictus*) and Easter, with Easter eggs, Easter bunny, Christmas tree, and so forth. Buddhism has included various Southeast Asian "folk" deities such as the Burmese Nat and the Thai Phi, with their spirit houses, not to forget the wholesale inclusion of the Hindu gods (Devas) in Sri Lanka and Nepal. The Buddhist coexistence and overlap with Daoism and Confucianism in China, and the same with Shintō in Japan, are other pertinent examples. Hinduism is still in the process of including "tribal" religions, for example, in Nepal and Orissa. The local deities are merely given Sanskrit names, and their rituals are "updated" according to standard Hindu forms. This, however, goes hand in hand with a tendency to "standardize" Hinduism, not least due to the influence of emigrant Hindus (nonresident Indians), who look for a Hindu "standard" in their new homelands and frequently finance Hinduizing organizations (Vishwa Hindu Parishad, Rashtriya Swayamsevak Sangh) back home. A similar tendency is observed with fundamentalizing movements in some Christian denominations and Islamic sects that want to "cleanse" their respective religions of such "folk elements."

The current tendency, together with the continuing onslaught of the Abrahamic and some other Laurasian-derived religions on tribal and other polytheistic forms of belief, puts these under great, increasing pressure, and the prospects for their survival are slim, except for the larger religions such as Shintō. Human culture will be the poorer if remaining non-Abrahamic pockets of religion, mythology, and rituals disappear. By now, the Laurasian story line and various (also secular) versions of its mythology already inform the lives of more than 95 percent of humanity.

***

Current and earlier cultural forms that precondition, through path dependency, most of humanity's adherence to the Laurasian story line also guarantee its survival. Cross-cultural comparisons indicate that, once established, motifs persist in given civilizations over enormous time spans. The Laurasian story line, a prime example of the "path dependency" of cultural traits, is perhaps the oldest of such dependencies. Others include concepts like duty (*r̥ṇa*) toward gods and ancestors as well as karma and rebirth in India, "suffering" and compassion in Buddhism, purity versus impurity (*tsumi*) in Japan, ancestor worship in China and elsewhere, the notion of "chosenness" (in Judaism, America), and monotheism (in Zoroastrianism, Judaism, Christianity, Islam).

A final reason for the survival of myth seems to be that, just like ritual, which even animals need,[83] we seem to need myth to *structure* our experience and to *explain* it. Also, it is necessary to transmit all our acquired traditional *knowledge* and all cultural trappings to our children, by way of socialization (see above, Lévi-Strauss). We still do so, whether we say, in the United States, that G. Washington never told a lie or that we are primordial and hereditary sinners who can only be delivered by Jesus;[84] or in much of Asia, that we are suffering due to our basic human condition, which we can only overcome by realizing its cause and the Buddhist way out of it; or that we merely have to retrieve our ancestors' access to "the goods," as in Melanesia and in the current, very seductive Indian cargo cult of Hindutva type; or that our conditions will be made perfect due to perpetual material "progress"; or that the future lies in an attainable, if always distant workers' paradise on earth, as was preached in the socialist countries. People may make any number of other utopian promises, in hundreds if not thousands of other, culturally conditioned and path-dependent ways.

***

Even then, what unites us all—individual politics, religions, and cultures apart—is the same old question, put in so many different ways. It is not just the typical, limited Laurasian one: "where does the earth come from?" but the truly human question: *Where do we come from, and where do we go?* The answer to this universal question has been given by all cultures, but, as the ever evolving explanations still show,[85] the question remains perpetually open. Our oldest forebears of Pan-Gaean and Laurasian times were caught by same unanswered query and quest that we still are.

It is moving to notice that they, many thousands of years ago, tried very hard to give an answer in myth and ritual. Observing and utilizing elements of their natural surroundings, they postulated that the universe and humans develop just like the animals and vegetation they saw around them. Mythological thinking, after all, develops by analogy and correlation, just like much of human thought in general and even scientific thought—though we often forget that.

■ §8.3. EPILOGUE

What, then, can we learn from this investigation? Pan-Gaean humanity, with our most ancient tales and their meaning, is very close to us, and its Stone Age way of thinking is still akin to ours. Like the still earlier Neanderthals, who buried their children with tools to help them along in the next world, our early *Homo sapiens sapiens* ancestors worried about their fate after death. They tried to explain this basic fact underlying all existence, just as we try to do today. Whatever belief system or religion people now belong to, they try to find *meaning* in their lives so as to provide some assurance that their stay here is not altogether accidental, brief, and futile, that they have a prospect to look for.

Or, in some cases, they try to find assurance that they are not alone and that the imagined extraterrestrial Others have to face the same eternal problem as we do.[86] The recent phenomenon of looking for Others in the universe also indicates that we *all*, on our increasingly small globe, feel that we belong together. In all scenarios involving extraterrestrials,[87] humans act together in a new and downright mythic undertaking, based on "the sacralization of the extra-terrestrial,"[88] which has spawned a number of new myths and cults,[89] such as those of the Raelians and the notorious Heaven's Gate.

This time, it is not the founding story of a new nation with assorted myths (Pilgrim Fathers, G. Washington's cherry tree, Manifest Destiny, etc.). It also is *not* a myth that speaks about a new, U.N.-led peaceful world.[90] Instead, the new mundane myths like those of science fiction speak about us as *humans*, united in diversity, albeit still divided by some 200-odd countries and territories, while looking for a better world without war, pollution, illness—and, maybe, death.

The first few years of the new millennium seem to provide ample examples pointing the other direction—epitomized by Huntingdon's pathway-derived American mirage of a clash of civilizations,[91] by recent wars, and by increasing religiously inspired violence. But we can also detect some convergence of beliefs. Ecologists refer to Amerindian beliefs in Mother Earth or praise Buddhist and Hindu attitudes toward all living beings. We witness increasing discussion of a new, different *social* setup, though without an accompanying myth so far.

Here, traditional East Asia can teach the Abrahamic Western world, its epigones, and its new ardent disciples elsewhere a lesson:[92] not absolute, raw capitalist competition by all means, and frequently with devastating human costs, but, rather, a combination of a socially responsible economic setup (as practiced in much of Western Europe after World War II) and the ancient quasi-religious Confucian idea of living together in society in balance and harmony.[93] This must now include the globe's many different, supposedly clashing cultures. We need something like a new Confucianism attuned to our times. This has largely been practiced—so far—in contemporary Japan, whose internalized Confucian-influenced culture stresses mutual respect, cooperation, and interdependence as well as the otherwise still widely neglected basic human rights of access to food, clothing, housing, and education.[94] So far, Japan has had an unspoken but lived mythology going along with it,[95] which is now in the process of being heavily eroded by the forces of globalization. Perhaps a new, captivating global myth is in order.

***

Looking back at the beginnings of our common mythologies in the Paleolithic, we cannot be but profoundly stirred and moved by the search of our early human ancestors for structure and deep meaning in their natural surroundings, society, and their individual lives. What they conceived—Gondwana and then Laurasian mythology—still moves and guides most of us even today. And it is not likely that this spiritual quest will abate, as was predicted during the last century. In a period of general uncertainty, the continuing, even growing strength of the Laurasian-derived otherworldly mythologies of Buddhism,[96] Hinduism, Islam, and Christianity—each now about a billion or more strong—indicates exactly the opposite. At the same time, ever new forms of mythology are constantly evolving as well.[97] As for those who are tired of the old mythologies and are looking "for something new," I am sure *someone* will come up with a new myth, supported by entirely new ideas for humanity in the global society of the 21st century—for a very simple reason: we merely have to look back at our small blue planet from outer space.

■ NOTES

■ Foreword

1. Witzel 1984b.

2. W. Allman, in *U.S. News and World Report* (1990); R. Wright, in *The Atlantic* (1991); Ph. Ross, in *Scientific American* (1991); L. L. Cavalli-Sforza, in *Scientific American* (1991).

3. This book has occasionally been referred to in my more recent papers by its working title, *Origins*.

4. Witzel 2005b.

5. Yoshida 2006; cf. also Ōbayashi 1989.

6. Ragin 1987.

7. I continued by giving graduate classes on Eurasian mythology at Harvard every five years or so. I gave overviews of my findings at a conference organized by Phyllis Granoff at McMaster University in March 1993, at the Center for the Study of World Religions at Harvard University in March 1997, in the century-old Harvard Shop Club in February 1998, and at a conference on mythology at Leiden in December 2003. I presented this line of research in two symposia, one at Tokyo in March 2005 and one at Kyoto in June 2005, the latter part of our yearly Harvard Ethnogenesis of South and Central Asia Round Tables. This evolved into a series of international conferences on comparative mythology, first held at Peking University in May 2006, at Edinburgh in August 2007, and at Ravenstein (the Netherlands) in August 2008.

8. See also Markmann and Markmann 1992: 107–19.

9. Schultze Jena 1944.

10. Tedlock 1985.

11. See the example given by Hal Fleming; §7, n. 103.

12. See http://www.people.fas.harvard.edu/~witzel/ROUND%20TABLES-2007.htm.

13. See http://www.people.fas.harvard.edu/~witzel/compmyth.htm.

14. Informally, during our Beijing meeting. It has now been incorporated in the state of Massachusetts; our website (and contact address) is found at http://www.compmyth.org, and our news list is at http://groups.yahoo.com/group/compmyth.

15. See http://www.laurasianacademy.com.

16. See http://www.people.fas.harvard.edu/~witzel/mythlinks.htm.

17. See http://www.ruthenia.ru/folklore/berezkin. Most of it is in Russian: we are in need of a small project to translate this rich store of data into English. His overview of motifs is available in English at http://www.ruthenia.ru/folklore/berezkin/eng.htm.

18. For such tests, see below, §§5–6.

19. Those inclined to get involved may visit http://www.laurasianacademy.com or http://www.compmyth.org, contact witzel@fas.harvard.edu, or phone 1-617-496-2990.

■ Chapter 1

1. "Eeny meeny miny moe" (attested 1855); "hana mana mona mike" (said to be of 1815), see Opie and Opie 1951: 156 sqq.: "Eena meena, mina, mo, catch a nigger by the toe," undoubtedly the most popular rhyme for counting out in both England and America; earlier "catch a tinker" or "catch a chicken."

2. In the British version, reference is made to the *tinker*, that is, the Roma (Gipsy) kettle smiths, and in the American version, unsurprisingly, to the *nigger*: "catch a nigger by the toe."

3. In German-speaking areas: "ene tene mone mei" (1888), "enne denne dubbe denne," "ene mene muh," "eine meine mine mu," "ene mene minke tinke," etc. See Rühmkorf 1969: 27.

4. "Ene mene dudu mene" (in Greece?); in Russia: "ene, bene, raba kvinter finter zhaba" or "eniki beniki eli vareniki" etc., with which compare the similar Czech rhyme: "enyky benyky klikly bé" or "ene bene tyky mora"; Polish: "ene, due, like, fake"; Norwegian: "elle melle deg fortelle"; Celtic: "ena dena, dahsa, doma" (1909); English: "ena dena dina do"; and Caribbean: "eny meeny makka rakka." (Thanks go to several of my students and colleagues on the Indo-Eurasian_Research list [http://groups.yahoo.com/group/Indo-Eurasian_research] who pointed out some of these instances.)

5. Discussion in Witzel 1991. The mantra (a Buddhist *dharaṇi*) "ene mene dasphe daṇḍadasphe" is found in the Bhaiṣajyavastu of the Mūlasarvāstivāda Vinaya, where it is taught to Virūpakṣa in Dasyu ("foreign") language. See Bernhard 1967; Deshpande 1999: 121.

6. The mantra rather looks like pig Latin: *ene* could be interpreted as the rare pronoun *ena–*, "they, these" (which cannot start a sentence!); *mene*, "he/she has thought"; and *daṇḍa*, "staff, punishment." *Dasphe* or its variant, *dahphe*, does not exist otherwise. And the whole line does not add up to any recognizable sentence. Buddhist and Tantric mantras have a preference for forms in *–e*.

7. It is not found in any one of the Vedic texts that precede Buddhism.

8. Hindi: "ina mina bambai bo" or "akkal bakkal/akkad bakkad bambe bo" (*akkal* is an old exclamation, going back to the Ṛgveda 7.102.3: *akhkhalī*). See F. Southworth and E. J. M. Witzel, SARVA Dictionary, entry 15: http://www.aa.tufs.ac.jp/sarva/entrance.html. An *eeny-meeny*-based rhyme is found in Indian films (Asha 1957; also in Tamil ones); see http://www.smashits.com/player/flash/flashplayer.cfm?SongIds=34644. There also is another related(?) version used in games: "ubi eni mana bou, baji neki baji thou, elim tilim latim gou"; see Nihar Ranjan Mishra's *Kamakhya, a Socio-cultural Study* (2004: 157).

9. Though the method of selecting someone in a small group of children who is to be "out" is the same in China and Japan, this rhyme does not occur there.

10. As such it would be included with the many instances where older religious beliefs and customs have become fairy tales ("Jack and the Beanstalk") or children's games (such as the Eurasian-wide hopscotch).

11. We know of adaptations of "low-level," popular beliefs and customs in early Indian Tantra (of c. 500 CE, which later on was properly "Brahmanized" to become respectable).

12. It is a typical feature of poetic lines, songs, and tales that the beginning words are standardized and unchangeable: "Once upon a time"; "es war einmal" in German; "āsīd," "there was," in Sanskrit; "mukashi mukashi, ōmukashi," "long ago," in Japanese tales; or even the Buddhist Sūtras' "At one time the Lord resided at," and the Christian Bible's "And it came to pass."

13. For example, why do people all over the world produce string designs like the "cat's cradle" (Campbell 1989: II.1: 24 sq.)? See §4, n. 355. Many similar questions could be asked.

14. Eliade 1992: 97. He usually quotes from the translations of others; the bibliographic details may be found in Eliade's book and are not always repeated in the following text. For similar worldwide collections, see Sproul 1991; Van Over 1980; and the bibliography in Sienkewicz 1996.

15. Or perhaps (with Kuiper 1983) "no organized cosmos" versus "organized cosmos."

16. Cf. Gargī's question (Bṛhad Āraṇyaka Upaniṣad 3.6): "Since all this world, is woven, warp and woof, on water, on what, then, is the water woven, warp and woof?"

17. My translation; cf. Eliade 1992: 109 sqq. (trans. A. L. Basham).

18. See http://www.maori.org.nz/korero/?d=page&pid=sp37&parent=36.

19. This new approach was first presented at Kyoto University in June 1990 and then spelled out in some detail in Witzel 2001b; cf. also Witzel 1990a.

20. Cf. for the stress on origins Arvidsson 2006: 8; see review by M. Witzel in *Science Magazine* (2007b, http://www.sciencemag.org/cgi/content/full/317/5846/1868?ijkey=vN HCuWdIhTviU&keytype=ref&siteid=sci).

21. Note the observations by J. Harrod on the quest for origins as a "fundamental principle of human consciousness" (http://www.originsnet.org/deforigins.html).

22. Notice, for example, the quest of many Americans to find their "roots" or ancestors in overseas countries, going as far as establishing their own family crests, or more recently, the use of increasingly cheap DNA analysis to pinpoint their ancestors' home in case documents are not available: see https://genographic.nationalgeographic.com/genographic/lan/en/atlas.html.

23. For a discussion of the relationship between myth and fairy tale, see Doty 2000: 426 sqq.

24. For a discussion of the cosmological human body, see Doty 2000: 314 sqq.

25. I have deliberated on a number of other possible terms but preferred, in the end, this neutral *geological* (and zoological) one. One might simply call the two major types of mythology the Northern (Laurasian) and the Southern (Gondwana) ones, but this carries political and PC overtones. Obviously *Eurasian* is too vague, and *Amerasian* stresses a secondary area, the Americas. Other geographical terms, taken from the outlying areas of Laurasia mythology, such as *Scando-Fuegan* or *Atlanto-Fuegan*," are unwieldy. One may think of *Borean*, as most of Laurasian mythology originally was concentrated in northern areas before spreading to the Americas, Indonesia, and Polynesia. The current historical extent no longer agrees with such terminology. Similarly, the Gondwana mythologies might be called "Austric" (but this term is also used for a Southeast Asian, etc., language family) or "Austro-Oceanic," "Sene(gal)-Tasmanian," or "Niger-Tasmanian." Finally, early Pan-Gaean mythology may also be called "Proto-world," "Terran," "Global"—none of which is attractive. In the end, I stay with the geological terms *Laurasian* and *Gondwana*.

A minor problem is presented by the fact that the *geological* term *Gondwana Land* also includes Madagascar, India, and South America. However, India has preserved some pre-Laurasian traits; South America, too, though clearly belonging to the area of Laurasian mythology, has preserved some archaic traits as well (Berezkin 2002). For example, the shamans of the Fuegans do not yet have the shamanic drum (§7.1), and the Yamana Fuegans, like the Tasmanians, did not even employ the bow or spear-thrower (atlatl) but used only the older weapon, the spear.

26. The term has also been used in biology (and recently even in business). The ancestors of many mammals that evolved in Laurasia (Eurasia and North America) are called Laurasiatheria. A typical dictionary definitions run like this: "The protocontinent of the Northern Hemisphere, a hypothetical landmass that according to the theory of plate tectonics broke up into North America, Europe, and Asia. [New Latin Laur(entia), *geologic precursor of North America* (after the Saint Lawrence River) + (Eur)asia]" (http://www.thefreedictionary.com, *American Heritage Dictionary*).

27. Cf. below §1, n. 98.

28. Doty 2000: 6 sqq.

29. For an amusing account of this, in fact, modern myth, see Fussell 1983.

30. Dawkins 2006, cf. 1998.

31. Eliade 1962: 3; Naumann 2000: 111.

32. Eliade 1962: 292: "L'homme étant un homo symbolicus, et toutes ses activités impli-cant le symbolisme, tous les faits religieux ont nécessairement un charactère symbolique."

33. De Saussure 1959.

34. Van Binsbergen 2003. Cf. the similarly elaborate and in part overlapping working definition by Doty (2000: 11).

35. Many populations make a clear distinction between such myths and secular "how so" tales, for example, the Xingu in central Brazil (who now have indigenous anthropologists!) or the Lakalai in Melanesia, e.g., "how the pig got its flat nose" (Trompf 1991: 18).

36. Note the literature-style approach to myths by the Anglicists Leonard and McClure (2004: 22).

37. Propp 1958.

38. Raglan 1956.

39. Thompson 1993.

40. For early pre-Socratic forerunners and early occidental mythologists, see Doty 2000: 3; Leonard and McClure 2004: 2–3; Puhvel 1987: 8; cf. Segal 2007: 1 sqq.

41. However, Lévi-Strauss (1995: 239) restricted the binary mode to *some* societies, those dealt with by him in the Americas.

42. Baumann 1986; Frobenius 1904; Thompson 1993.

43. Campbell 1988: I.2: 232 sq.

44. See Lindstrom 1993; Trompf 1991: 46.

45. See the comprehensive volume edited by Walter and Fridman (2004).

46. This myth is widespread in Europe, North Asia, India (Sāvitrī legend, in the Mahābhārata), and the Americas (with the exception of the Inuit), for example, with the Cherokee (Witzel 2005b), Comanche, and Pawnee (A. Hultkrantz, H. Gayton). It is found from Europe to the western Pacific (Puhvel 1987: 3). Baumann is, however, erroneous in stating that it does not occur in Africa etc., though some myths make a different use of the motif of a trip to the netherworld, which is found in Africa in at least 16 versions. Most, however, do not feature the death of a beloved person but deal with someone, often a hunter, following an animal to the netherworld; and with two exceptions (Nyamwezi and Budja-Shona in Zimbabwe; Baumann 1936: nos. 9, 12), they lack the motif of releasing a beloved wife (or husband) from death (Baumann 1936: 91–93).

Other candidates for diffusion could include the motifs of the Earth diver (§3.1.3), as duck, muskrat, crawfish, or other water-related animals; the widespread flood myth (and its related Central Asian version, see §3.9 and especially §5.7.2); the theft of fire (§3.5.3); and some (animal) trickster and culture hero stories; as well as the primordial tales of a distant god or (Father) Heaven. See, however, the relevant discussions in §5.7 and §6. Note also that the Orpheus myth is also found in Melanesia (Leenhardt 1979: 29; Nevermann 1957: 21, with the Marind-anim). Melanesia, however, is not free from Polynesian influences where the Orpheus motif is found, for example, Tane following his wife, Hine-nui-te-po, to Hades (Maori; the netherworld has a special smell; Leenhardt 1979: 48). In addition, weak echoes of the myth may be seen in Africa (Baumann 1936: 91 sqq.); see above.

47. Bierhorst 1986: 7 sqq.

48. For recent DNA data underlying this spread, see §4, n. 211. Cf. Goodchild 1991: ix sq.

49. See http://www.ruthenia.ru/folklore/berezkin/eng.htm.

50. To which he added a statistical analysis of the motifs, resulting in several "principal components"; for this concept, see §4.3.

51. Berezkin 2003a, 2003b, 2005a, 2005c; details in §2.1.

52. See Frobenius 1904, 1923. Anglophone diffusionists include Elliot Smith and W. Perry (who thought of diffusion from Egypt). Frobenius also was the originator of the idea of the *Kulturkreis* ("civilization circle" or region), which he first published in *Petermann's Mitteilungen* 43–44 (1897–98); it was eventually opposed by Baumann (in *Africa* 7 [1934]).

53. "Diffusionismus, ausgehend von grossen archaischen Hochkulturen (Archemorphen), von denen aus sich die Errungenschaften Welle um Welle verbreitet haben… über das weite Areal der 'archemorphen' Wild- und Feldbeuterkulturen hin" (Baumann 1986: 3). De Santillana and von Dechend's (1977: 344) idea of a belt stretching from the Celts to Egypt, China, megalithic India, and Oceania is not very distant from such concepts, though restricted to astroarchaeology and myth.

54. Kroeber 1939: 1.

55. Adapted from the introduction by Klaus E. Müller to Baumann 1986: VI sq. One should rather think of a new stratum of horticulturists and early farmers (cf. Bierhorst 1986: 18); in Central America, these prefer stories that tell of the first emergence of humans from the Earth. Farming myths spread northward with maize agriculture, up to the Hidatsa on the Upper Missouri and even to the Mohawk/Hurons. Such myths were only secondarily connected with agriculture; see, e.g., the Gondwana remnants of emergence from underground; and cf. the Pan-Gaean motifs of the emergence of light, sun, animals, or people from underground or a cave (§6).

56. He is characterized by his student K. E. Müller as "a typical German thinker of forceful philosophical ambitions, striving for 'ultimate explanations' and the will for systematic integration" ("der typische deutsche Denker mit starken philosophischen Ambitionen, dem Drang nach 'letzten Erklärungen,' und dem Willen zur systematischen Vereinheitlichung"; see Baumann 1986: VII).

57. See Baumann (1986: 250 sqq., 367), who perceives a worldwide myth (*Weltmythos*) at 3000 BCE.

58. Baumann 1986: 9, 250, 374 sq.

59. Baumann 1986: 376 sqq.

60. Baumann 1986: 252, cf. 364 sq. See his diagram of spread (1986: 372) and details in the maps following (1986: 420). Cf. also Wölfel (1951), who discusses megalith religion, the High God, and ancestor worship; see Wunn 2005.

61. Baumann 1986: 352.

62. Strangely, diffusion does *not* figure in Leonard and McClure 2004; in Doty 2000: 431, too, diffusion is very much mentioned in the margin, with regard to S. Thompson (Rumpelstiltskin tale).

63. The spread of such myths from Siberia to the Americas has been studied especially by Stith Thompson and his school and more recently by Y. Berezkin (2002 etc.).

64. Such as the European Solutrean culture types that have now been discovered at Topper in South Carolina, Cactus Hill in Virginia, and Meadowcroft in Pennsylvania, sites that are dated to c. 14,250–15,200 BP. The question is how much these supposed European immigrants could have contributed to northern Amerindian myths; the recent finding of "European" genes (X2b) with the Ojibwa (central southern Canada) may support a wider spread of these Ice Age migrants; see, however, §4, n. 198, for details on an American subvariety (X2a).

65. For an alleged case of Indian–Mesoamerican contact, see Cheek and Mundkur 1979; or of alleged Chinese anchor stones in California, Gould 1983a; or on the sighting of Japanese ships in the Seattle/Vancouver area around 1700, cf. Gilmore and McElroy 1998 and Stengel 2000, or the recent popular book *1421* by G. Menzies (2003) on alleged Chinese transoce-

anic expeditions by Zheng He (Cheng Ho). For earlier Chinese records of oceanic travel and commerce up to East Africa, see the work of Chau Ju-kua of the 11th(?) century CE (Hirth and Rockhill 1970). For a recent, detailed account of most biological transoceanic data, see Sorenson and Johannessen 2006; Storey et al. 2007.

66. On the island of Maui, with an account of their shining steel swords, see Kalakaua 1990: vii, 175 sqq., esp. 182 sqq.; cf. Beckwith 1987: 285 on Asiatic and North American driftwood etc.

67. Examples of certain (but not dated) maritime contact include the transfer of the cotton or sweet potato plant (and its name); see Campbell 1989: II.1: 13, 17 sq. However, the details and the date of transfer of the sweet potato to Polynesia and places farther west, as well as that of the Polynesian chicken, are not clearly established. For the introduction of chicken to Chile, see Carter 1971; Storey et al. 2007 (cf. §3, n. 492; §7, n. 280). Finally, there is the recent, unlikely scenario of pre-Spanish trans-Pacific slave trade (Hurles et al. 2003; cf. §4, n. 501). For an interesting spread of leopard lore, see van Binsbergen 2005. Fantastic accounts include those of the Pan-Africanist Clyde Winters, who finds African influence in ancient (Olmec) Mexico just as easily as in the Indus civilization. For a detailed study of most of such supposed transfers, see Sorenson and Johannessen 2006.

68. Antoni 1977; Campbell 1988: I.2: 195, 1989: II.1: 354 sqq.; Sorenson and Johannessen 2006. However, on chicken import from Polynesia, see Carter 1971; Storey et al. 2007; and the last note.

69. Bastian 1881, 1901.

70. Intermittently he also used the more vague phrases "peoples' thought" (*Völkergedanke* [1881]) and "humans' thought" (*Menschengedanke* [1901]); cf. summary in Bächtold-Stäubli 1987: 2: 766–77. Bastian's program is quite similar to the one proposed by me here, with the important distinction, however, that he saw Jungian-like archetypes everywhere, while I endeavor to show the common origin and inheritance for many of them (thus, not diffusion).

71. *Gleichartigkeit der menschlichen Psyche* (Bastian 1881: 177 sqq.); cf. Bächtold-Stäubli 1987: 2: 768.

72. Contra Barber and Barber, who regard archetypical human universals as "common responses to common problems" (2004: 3–4), conditioned by the handling of mythological data through language by their four principles of silence, analogy, compression, and restructuring, which all have correlates in the linguistic process.

73. Freud 1959: 3.

74. Jung 1959: 3–4.

75. Jung 1959: 5.

76. Campbell 1972: summary 193; Day 1984: 356 sqq.; Doty 2000: 240 sqq., 307 sqq.; Leonard and McClure 2004: 17; Segal 1998: xxi sq. Cf. also Lord Raglan's (1956) and Propp's (1958) analyses.

77. Note, among others, the psychological investigation by Leeming and Page (1994). Cf. Leonard and McClure 2004: 102 sqq.; and the speculative picture of the goddess in Old Europe, before the Indo-Europeans, by M. Gimbutas (1991).

78. Clooney 2006.

79. Cf. Tucker 1992.

80. Cf. J. Wallis, in Walter and Fridman 2004: 27.

81. Jung 1959: 8.

82. Note the recent female anthropologists' explorations of male conception myths in Australia. One example is given by Leonard and McClure (2004: 387–92; cf. §6.1) on "grandmother's tales." For the theoretical background, cf. Weigle 1989.

83. Segal underlines the fact that Campbell differs in his definition of myth from Jung in that he also includes noninternal, nonsubconscious features such as social harmony and that he includes the possibility of the creation of myth as required by a local community, from where it may spread (Segal et al. 1990: x sq.).

84. Actually, he acknowledges his only partial adherence to Jung himself: "I'm not a Jungian!" (Campbell with Toms 1988: 123). Cf. Segal 1990; Segal et al. 1990: xxxiv.

85. Campbell 1989: II.1: 26; see above: Storey et al. 2007.

86. Doty 2000; Leonard and McClure 2004: 23; Patton and Doniger 1996. Note, however, the warning, more than a quarter century ago, of the random use of "explanations" by Kirk: "Sometimes a myth will fulfill several … functions at once. … The important thing for the modern student of myth, in my opinion, is to be prepared to find any or all of these properties in the myths of any culture; and not to apply generalizing theories *a priori*" (1974: 83).

87. Campbell 1988: I.1: 112.

88. Campbell 1988: I.1: 91; cf. Baumann 1936: 6–21. For the reasons for the exclusion of Io, see below, §3, n. 33. Cf. also the primordial deities Kamurogi and Kamuromi, who do not even appear in the official mythology of Japan, the Kojiki (720 CE), but in old Shintō prayers, the Engishiki, etc. (Havens and Inoue 2001: 10; Philippi 1990: 72, 93).

89. Campbell 1988.

90. Doniger 1991, discussion in 1998: 138 sqq.

91. See Farmer et al. 2002.

92. Doniger 1991, discussion in 1998: 138 sqq.

93. See the critique by Kirk (1970: 61) on the concentration on Amerindian motives; and for a general critique, see Kirk 1970: 77 sqq.

94. For example, see the review of C. Ginsburg's book on witches by Doniger (1991). Obviously (Darwinian) biology and, powerfully, recent genetic advances tell otherwise (§4.3).

95. See characterizations by Doty (2000); Leonard and McClure 2004; cf. §1, n. 111.

96. For a useful discussion of the historical method in anthropology, see Bornemann 1967. The approach taken by W. van Binsbergen in his 2005 and especially his 2006 conference presentations, too, is historical and comparative, though he prefers to call it "aggregative diachronic." We have been in constant contact since late 2003, initiated by my 2001b paper on Laurasian mythology. However, our approaches differ in many major and minor details, which will be highlighted below (§2, §6, §8) as the occasion arises. First, he relies, in a major fashion, on African data that have their own, serious problems (§5.3.5) of very late attestation and conspicuous outside influence, while the present book presents both African and Out of Africa data, hopefully, in a balanced fashion. Second, I believe that the evaluation of the data presented below indeed allows us to divide world mythology, after stemmatic/phylogenetic and cladistic evaluation, into two major groups (Gondwana and Laurasia), while van Binsbergen stresses the complicated mixture of (recent and archaic) African mythology, which he calls "a relatively recent mythology that is in striking continuity (pace Witzel) with the rest of the world" (2006a: 23, cf. 26). As §5 will show, the continuity does not extend to all areas and motifs. I think he was not yet aware of my thinking about remnants of Gondwana thought in Laurasian myth and more recent Laurasian input into Gondwana myth (§5.6.1–2). Third, the cladistic (family) tree and story line aspects are missing in van Binsbergen's approach.

In a different way, Y. Berezkin, with whom I have also been in close contact over the past few years, evaluates, especially in his more recent papers (2002 to 2007), increasingly large amounts of data from world mythology in synchronic and multivariate fashion, based on published documents. Aided by archaeology and genetic studies, he goes on to draw some important historical conclusions from their distribution. His results will also be discussed below, where appropriate; cf. §2, n. 76.

97. On explanations proposed so far, see Doty 2000.

98. As mentioned earlier, the Laurentian shield, the geologically very ancient section of northeastern Canada, is used in geology to represent North America. Actually South America belongs to another landmass, Gondwanaland; still I will use the handy geological term, but due to the extent of Laurasian mythology across Central and South America, I must use it to represent all of the Americas. See §1, n. 25.

99. As mentioned, *Eurasian* is too vague, and *America-Asian* and similar coinages are too unwieldy.

100. In the same vein, one may call its counterpart, the Gondwana mythologies, the "Southern" ones (see §1, n. 25).

101. The term is also open to unintended statements of "value" and to political debate, given the current context of northern and southern economies and societies, so that it is better avoided.

102. The takeover of the methods of a neighboring field is not rare; for example, structuralism has taken over much of the linguistic approach by the ancient Indian grammarian Pāṇini of the fourth century BCE, as is evident in the late 19th-century work of de Saussure (1959). Conversely, the early comparative mythology of the 19th century was dependent on comparative linguistics ("comparative philology" as it was called then), which in turn had learned much from Pāṇini's analysis of Sanskrit words; see further details in McCrea 2008. For an approach similar to the present one, see van Binsbergen 2006a, 2006b.

103. Puhvel 1987: 19.

104. In the following, I will mostly speak of "Laurasian" and "Gondwana" mythology as a shorthand for the more correct designation of reconstructed protoforms, which cumbersomely should be called "Proto-Laurasian" and "Proto-Gondwana."

105. The various degrees of relationship between the individual Laurasian mythologies, including that of Japan, will be explained later. For example (§3.5.1), the Japanese myth of Amaterasu's hiding in the cave (Kojiki, Nihon Shoki) has an exact parallel, not used by scholars so far, in the oldest texts of India (the Vedas) and in related stories of Old Europe; there also are parallels in Southeast Asia and North America (Witzel 2005b). Based on this premise, some important features of Old Japanese mythology are then studied in detail.

106. However, the mythologies of Africa, New Guinea, and Australia (and some populations on the Eurasian continent) do not form a part of this group.

107. Tregear 1891/1969: 667 sqq.

108. For an overview, see Bierhorst 1986, 1988, 1992.

109. Some mythologies, notably in West Africa and in the eastern corridor reaching from Kenya to Zimbabwe and Namibia, share some aspects of the Eurasian/Laurasian mythology (§5.3; cf. van Binsbergen 2006a, 2006b); this is due to contact with the Sahel/Sahara, Nilotic, and Egyptian civilizations.

110. In geological usage, however, Gondwana includes not only Africa and Australia but also India, Madagascar, and South America. As it happens, even though the latter three areas belong to the Laurasian sphere, India and South America have some considerable remnants of Gondwana myths (cf. Berezkin 2002). See §1, n. 25.

111. Segal 2007: 1–20. For summaries, see Campbell 1972: 11 sqq.; Day 1984: 33 sqq.; Doty 2000; Goodchild 1991: 165 sqq.; Hübner 1985: 48–89; Kirk 1970: 1–83; Leonard and McClure 2004: 2 sqq.; Nilsson 1972: 3–10 sqq.; Segal 2007.

112. Such as the pre-Socratic Xenophanes (c. 570–480 BCE) and, earlier, Theagenes of Rhegion's allegorical interpretation, as well as Heraclitus (late sixth century BCE) and to a certain extent even Plato (427–347 BCE), who denounced traditional myths but constructed

his own "philosophical" myths (cf. Gottschalk 1979: 113 sqq., with a detailed discussion, especially of Greek myth and its contemporaneous interpretations; Leonard and McClure 2004: 3 sq.).

113. Ṛgveda 2.12.5, 8.100.3, cf. also 8.64.7.

114. Yang and An 2005: 33 sq. Those that had actually been recorded, such as in the Shanhai jing composed during the mid–Warring States and early Han period (fourth–early second century BCE), were largely burned under the Chin dynasty (221–206 BCE); some remaining documents or oral traditions were collected by Ssu-ma chien (Si Maqian, c. 145–86 BCE) in his Shiji. Another important collection was made by Wang Chong (c. 27–100 CE) in his "Critical essays" (Lunheng), which criticized contemporary myths and superstitious beliefs. Some Chinese scholars feel that Confucian rationalism was the opposite of Euhemerism, as it tended to eliminate "improbable" elements from myth and understood the remainder as historical facts (Yang and An 2005: 35). Another good collection is the Soushenji by Gan Bao (317–420 CE); see Yang and An 2005: 7, 39. On the relation between Chinese myth and "history," see also Allen 1991; Bantly 1996.

115. For Roman religion, see, for example, Dumézil's *Mythe* (1995: I: 261 sqq., 289 sqq.); he appropriately starts with a comparison of oldest Chinese mythical history. On the nature of Roman myths, cf. also Puhvel 1987: 39, 146.

116. Vico (1744/1968) mentions creative imagination, religious inspiration, impressions created by natural phenomena, and reflections of social institutions (cf. Gottschalk 1979: 120; Puhvel 1987: 11).

117. Cf. the summary in Doty 2000; Gottschalk 1979: 123 sqq.; Kirk 1974: 32 sqq.; Matsumura 2004; Segal 1996.

118. Jensen (1951: 27 sqq.) argues against this view.

119. By *monolateral* I characterize the tendency of 19th- and 20th-century mythologists to look for a single item or method that would illuminate what myth is all about. Cf. Puhvel 1987: 13 sqq.

120. Followed by the diffusionist Frobenius (1904), who saw sunrise, sunset, and the moon as the important catalysts of mythmaking.

121. Barber and Barber 2004.

122. Closely following the astute if overstated observations in archaeoastronomy by their predecessors de Santillana and von Dechend (1977) as well as those of W. Sullivan (1996) for Inca myth and ritual. Remembering some catastrophes may occur, as detailed by Barber and Barber for the American Northwest; cf. also the southern Australian tradition about the flooding of Spencer Gulf (Smith 1996: 168 sqq.).

123. Lévi-Strauss 1995: xii–xiii. See its use by Yalman (1996).

124. Cf. Nilsson 1972: 5, 31.

125. Nilsson 1972: 10.

126. Nilsson 1972: 10, 16, on popular epics.

127. Nilsson 1972: 30; cf. also Puhvel 1987: 39.

128. Barber and Barber 2004.

129. Ryan and Pitman 1998.

130. Thompson 1971, 1977: 415–40, 1993.

131. Substantiated now by the work of Y. Berezkin (2002 etc.).

132. For the ritual school of Durkheim, M. Mauss, S. Lévy, etc., see Strensky 1996.

133. For another list and relevant secondary literature, see Segal 1990: xxxiv, 1998.

134. On this connection with reenactment and play, see Jensen 1951: 61 sqq. (referring back to Huizinga).

135. Goodchild 1991: 166.

136. Segal 1998, 2001.

137. Nagy 2002.

138. Jensen 1951: 61 sqq.

139. Kirk 1974: 72.

140. Opposed, for example, by Jensen (1951: 27 sqq.).

141. This is also the opinion of James Hillmann and David Miller; see Segal 2007: 16.

142. This is the evaluation of the philosopher K. Jaspers, too, calling it *wissenschaftsaber-gläubischer Mythos* (a myth based on superstition-like belief in science). However, ethology (*Verhaltensforschung*) comes to similar results as Freudian psychology, though based on the inborn instinctive aggression of animals. See Burkert 1983; Lorenz 1963; Tinbergen 1963.

143. Jung 1959: 5.

144. Propp 1958; cf. de Vries 1954: 156; Puhvel 1987: 17 sq.

145. Cf. de Vries, in Eliade 1963: 198; Jensen 1951: 27 sqq.; Kirk 1974: 71.

146. See Mayr 2001: ill. 2.8.

147. Cf. Wunn 2005.

148. Denied by Wunn (2005: 32 sq.).

149. Cf. Patton and Doniger 1996.

150. Campbell 1972: 13 sq., 24.

151. Raglan 1956; see §3.10.

152. Such as the *Star Wars* movies etc.; cf. Leonard and McClure 2004: 17 sq.

153. Lévi-Strauss 1995: 239; cf. Puhvel 1987: 18 sqq.

154. See the critique, for example, by Kirk (1970: 7), summed up by Peter Goodchild (1991: 165 sq.) and Puhvel (1987: 19). For the semiotic structuralists in the wake of Lévi-Strauss, Jean-Pierre Vernant (1914–2007) and his colleagues, see Segal 2007: 17.

155. Lévi-Strauss (1995) barely admits that North and South American myths may be related historically. However, compare his recent essay (2002) on the White Hare of Inaba and parallels in the Americas.

156. Kirk 1974: 81.

157. Lévi-Strauss 1995: 316 sqq.

158. Lévi-Strauss 1964: 20.

159. Hübner 1985: 89.

160. Attention should also be paid to a trend in anthropology that takes historical considerations into account; see, for example, the volume edited by C. A. Schmitz (1967): it ranges from Vienna *Kulturkreis* ethnography, to Baumann's reflections on fieldwork and history, to Sapir's analysis of Amerindian views on time, to Kroeber's discussion of stimulus diffusion, to Leroi-Gourhan's study of technological evolution, to general studies on culture change. Cf. also Brednich et al. 1977– for fairy tales.

161. Propp 1958.

162. Ježić 2005.

163. See the California schoolbook debate of 2005–6 (http://en.wikipedia.org/wiki/Californian_Hindu_textbook_controversy) between scholars and Indian American Hindus, some of whom felt slighted by the depiction of early Hinduism in these books. This is just another example of the power of myth in modern society—as if we still needed proof. See further §8.

164. Kuiper 1983.

165. See the evaluation of his teacher, by A. Yoshida (2006).

166. See §5.3.2; Goodchild 1991: 167.

167. Cassirer 1946.

168. Cassirer (1946) takes his cue from Schelling's position that myth must be understood on its own, not as allegory. Similarly, see Jensen 1948: 15 sqq. Cf. also theories such as those by Nicolai Hartmann; see Harich 2000.

169. Cf. Farmer et al. 2002; Jensen 1951; Hübner 1985; Witzel 1979, 2004a. Cf. also Arieti 1967; for this allegedly earlier type of mentality that uses correlations and identifications between any two unrelated items, see Witzel 1979, 2004a.

170. See Lincoln's *Theorizing Myth* (1999).

171. Note Lincoln's earlier comparative work: *Myth, Cosmos, and Society* (1986).

172. Lincoln 1991: 123.

173. Lincoln 1991: 123; cf. Arvidsson 2006: 302 sq.

174. See Bornemann, who says exactly the same: "The *ur*-civilization, too, is the product of a development" (1967: 83).

175. Arvidsson 2006: 303.

176. Durkheim 1915, 1925.

177. D. S. Whitley, in Walter and Fridman 2004: 20; and cf. immediately below, Wunn 2005.

178. Durkheim 1915; cf. Wunn 2005: 29.

179. Bellah 1973; Wunn 2005: 30 sq.

180. Bellah 1973: 358: "A process of increasing differentiation and complexity of organization."

181. Bellah 1973: 361.

182. See Bellah (1973: 362), though he also admits it for the Navajo and some other (unnamed) New World cultures. For Australia, see also Stanner 1959, 1960.

183. Bellah 1973: 363; Stanner 1959: 118. Similarly with Navajo initiation rituals.

184. Wunn 2001: 263–84.

185. Bellah 1973: 264 sqq., 284–88.

186. These features are not present in all Neolithic and post-Neolithic societies, especially when they reverted to more simple forms of life and technology, such as some Amazon tribes etc.

187. Wunn 2005: 31.

188. Wunn 2000, 2005: 32.

189. Barth 1987.

190. Even Wunn (2005: 171) characterizes it as "unusual" and speculates that it might represent a protective spirit, as seen with early Eskimo societies (incidentally, while using an ethnological comparison that she otherwise largely avoids or warns against).

191. Many illustrations are found at http://www.bradshawfoundation.org.

192. The problem has actually not escaped Wunn's attention. Later on, however, she clearly states that "in the end, only fragments of the prehistoric worldview are accessible, in spite of all attempts of reconstruction. Prayers and beliefs do not fossilize.... Therefore only those facets of the old religions that somehow could manifest themselves materially are accessible" (2005: 413; my translation). This insight has no effect on her earlier analyses of Paleo- and Mesolithic religion.

193. Wunn 2005: 189.

194. On this topic, see also Lorblanchet 2000.

195. Wunn 2005: 71, 128.

196. Hudjashov et al. 2007.

197. Berezkin 2002, 2005b.

198. Again, this does not prove the absence of early religion, a topic constantly over-stressed in Wunn 2005. All of this indicates that the Bellah/Wunn model is insufficient to explain Mesolithic and late Paleolithic religion and myth.

199. For a similar complaint, see Kirk 1974.

200. See my website, http://www.laurasianacademy.com; for historical and comparative studies of fairy tales, see Brednich et al. 1977–.

201. Farmer et al. 2002.

202. Cf. Puhvel 1987: 13, 18, on Müller and Lévi-Strauss.

203. The current state of general insecurity about approaches and methods is reflected by the chapters in Patton and Doniger: "this leaves the mythologist…with the challenge of building a new house" (1996: 2). The same self-doubt is echoed by B. Lincoln, who regards mythography—such as the present book—as writing "myths with footnotes" (1991: 209), as he regards mythologies as mere local ideologies and our writing on them (mythography) as the outcome of our own background. This postmodern self-doubt is also found in current anthropology, where many nowadays merely write autobiographical books on the experiences of their fieldwork.

204. Kirk 1974: 39.

205. Farmer 2006.

206. Or see Segal 2001: 146, on the future of the myth and ritual theory, which approach would unite the approaches of both myth telling and performance.

207. Cf. Puhvel 1987: 19–20.

208. Barber and Barber 2004.

209. Lévi-Strauss 1995.

▪ Chapter 2

1. I leave aside those comparisons that popular speech calls comparison of apples and pears: items that are not closely linked, as it appears to the common sense of a particular culture.

2. Whorf 1956.

3. Granet 1988: 23 sq., 84 sq., 272.

4. Farmer et al. 2002.

5. Cavalli-Sforza and Cavalli-Sforza 1994: 147.

6. In genetics, the steps include (1) calculating a geographic map of many genes, (2) applying spectral analysis to the values of gene frequencies at a selected set of nodes, and (3) using eigenvectors corresponding to the highest eigenvalue to generate "synthetic" geographic maps.

7. Villems 2005.

8. Berezkin 2007; Nikonov 1980.

9. Witzel 2001b, 2006a, 2010; see §5.7.2.

10. See Oda 1984, 1995, 2001; and for details, see http://www.aa.tufs.ac.jp/~odaj/body/motif.html and http://www.aa.tufs.ac.jp/~odaj/cgi-bin/arab1.cgi.

11. Cf. Witzel 2001c on foundational, fundamental topics of various civilizations: "Out of India: Classical Values for Today and Tomorrow."

12. Berezkin 2003a, 2003b: 101, 2005a, 2005d, 2007; http://www.ruthenia.ru/folklore/berezkin.

13. Cavalli-Sforza et al. 1994; §4.3.

14. Berezkin 2007; Nikonov 1980.

15. Farmer et al. 2002.

16. Cf. Hübner 1985: 325; for the Hebrew concept of the soul's dying due to a person's own mistakes, see Hebrew Bible, Hesekiel 18.1 sqq., 20.

17. For Western and Indian ideas on evil, see Doniger's (1976) collections. Evil was created by Izanami by speaking before Izanagi in circumambulating; cf. Naumann 1971. A "nice parallel" is found in Chilcotin myth, where brother and sister have to circumambulate a high mountain in different directions (thus, see Lévi-Strauss 1995: 300, with more data on twins).

18. Cf. Naumann 1979.

19. Thompson 1993.

20. Institute for the Languages and Cultures of Asia and Africa, Tokyo University of Foreign Studies, Tokyo.

21. For a recent overview, see Michael Werner and Bénédicte Zimmermann (École des hautes études en sciences sociales, Paris; n.d., http://www.iue.it/HEC/ResearchTeaching/20042005-Spring/Werner.pdf, 4 sqq.).

22. Wunn 2005.

23. See further discussion, above, §1.3, end; §7.1.

24. Smith 2000b: esp. 27–29.

25. Smith 1982: 22 sqq.

26. For example, in Enuma Elish, tablet VII; see Dalley 1989: 272.

27. Smith 2000b: esp. 27–29. Note the praise expressed for this article in Patton and Doniger 1996: 9: "scholars have come to see that many of their comparative moves are based on gossamer like structures of flimsy identification."

28. Cf. Ragin 1987, below.

29. Farmer et al. 2002.

30. Arieti 1967; Witzel 2004a.

31. Smith 2000a: 239 n. 9, 241. Cf. also W. Doniger (1991) in the dismissal of common origins in her review of Carlo Ginzburg's book on witches.

32. Smith 2000a: 238.

33. Smith 2000a: 238.

34. First developed in 1990 without knowledge of Smith 1982. I read excerpts of his paper only in August 2003, in Mortensen 2003: 12; cf. also Brednich et al. 1977– for fairy tales.

35. Ragin 1987: x.

36. Ragin 1987: x.

37. Ragin 1987: x.

38. With the Austro-Asiatic Munda people; see Ponette 1968: 13.

39. Ponette 1968: 13: "When there are clouds portending heavy rain, the Mundas often seeing the reflected light of the sun arching like a bow, say, 'look over there! The rainbow snake has blown its breath. Now there won't be a heavy downpour, the *lur* snake has stopped it by blowing its breath.'"

40. Not surprising, as the Austronesian languages expanded, via Taiwan, from South China—an area that was settled during the first expansion out of Africa: this (Gondwana) wave of humans may have brought the tree motif. Its occurrence in Icelandic myth is more difficult to explain. However, see below. In Austronesian Taiwan the motif seems to be limited to coastal people. In the highlands we have the myth of origin from rocks (with the Atayal) or trees.

41. As stressed in Joseph Campbell's TV talks (*The Power of Myth*).

42. Ragin 1987: xi.

43. Tuite 1998: 452 sq. Cf. William Jones in 1786, in Puhvel 1987: v; see the update by Lincoln (1986: 173 n. 2).

44. Puhvel 1987: 37.

45. Tuite 1998: 452.

46. This is expanded to letting the hero drink a woman's milk from her breasts, as found in a Yakut myth from northeastern Siberia. See Holmberg 1927: 349–59. However, see Wunn 2005: 25 sq. on showing the breasts as a benevolent behavioral gesture, as studied in ethology.

47. Ruhlen 1994a: 278.

48. Sherrat 2006. In drawing up the current list I have profited from exchanges with V. Mair (2006).

49. Farmer et al. 2002.

50. Doniger 1991. Ginsburg also rejects the Jungian explanation of universal archetypal structures produced by the human mind.

51. Note also Lévi-Strauss's cry of despair: "going beyond the superficial similarities that the old comparative mythology was satisfied with, structural analysis can discover 'singularities'; however, as the habitual categories of human mind are vacillating, *one does not know any more what one is searching for*: a community of origins [as in the present book] or a structure that one *despairs* in getting hold of" (1995: 319 sq.; my translation).

52. And, not very prominently, in the study of fairy tales; see Brednich et al. 1977–.

53. Description by P. Maas (1968). On the overlap between stemmatic and biological cladistic research, see Peter Robinson, http://www.canterburytalesproject.org. It is here that van Binsbergen's and my approaches differ: I want to reconstruct, in the long run, a pedigree of global, regional, and local mythologies, while he concentrates on 20 major mythemes (representing some 200 global ones) that are variously spread and interlinked across the globe; nevertheless he tries to date them and present them, as I do, in both time and space. As indicated below, such efforts have to be undertaken but should, in the end, lead to a cladistic family tree. This phylogenetic aspect and the underlying story line are missing in van Binsbergen's approach.

54. For an overview of the method, see Anttila 1989; Hock 1986; Witzel 2001b.

55. Unlike the earlier "chain of being" or the modern biological species; see Mayr 2001.

56. Cf. Eliade 1954b: 185 sqq.; Mair 2007. Note also the offerings of horses in Old Japan and their modern substitutes, the *ema* picture tablets; cf. below, §7, nn. 245, 265.

57. Puhvel 1987: 269–76.

58. Mair 2007.

59. Darwin 1839–43.

60. See Doty 2000; cf. Leonard and McClure 2004.

61. This aspect is missing in van Binsbergen's "aggregative and diachronic" approach, as he compares 20, mostly unconnected myths and mythemes ("narrative complexes"). In contrast, I think that we can make sustained progress only if we see them in their individual framework, the underlying story line, and as part of a cladistic "family" tree.

62. Strictly speaking, we should use *"Proto-Laurasian" mythology*, as all current and past attested mythologies that belong to this family make up the group of Laurasian mythologies. However, as they will usually not be listed here as a group, and as *Proto-Laurasian* is too unwieldy, I use *Laurasian* as a shortcut.

63. Which have now also been discovered for Indian tales such as the Rāmāyaṇa (Ježić 2005).

64. Except of course for Jungian and similar analyses.

65. For examples, see §3.5.1: Vala and Iwato.

66. Witzel 2004b.

67. For a fairly comprehensive list, up to 1932, see Thompson 1993.

68. See Lévi-Strauss's *The Structural Study of Myth* (see 1967).

69. See Campbell 1972; Raglan 1956. Cf. Leonard and McClure 2004: 17.

70. For example, Dundes 1988; Etter 1989; Gonda 1978; Magnone 1999. African myths are usually missing in discussion as well as in the indexes, in spite of the extensive discussions in Baumann 1936; cf. van Binsbergen 2005, 2006a, 2006b. There also are recent euhemeristic (Judeo-Christian-inspired) explanations, such as the ever-popular attempts to find Noah's ark on Mt. Ararat in Turkey or the great Black Sea flood (Ryan and Pitman 1998). For a collection of worldwide flood myths, see the c. 100 stories collected at http://www.talkorigins.org/faqs/flood-myths.html.

71. Thompson especially noticed (see §1, n. 63) the link between Siberian and North American myths, which is not exactly unexpected, given the history of Amerindian immigration into the continent in postglacial times. See the work of Y. Berezkin (2002 etc.).

72. See §2.2.1 sqq., §5; Berezkin 1996–97, 2002, 2007, etc.

73. The various versions of these origin myths will be discussed below, §3.1–3.

74. See below, §3.5.1.

75. See collection below, §3.9, §5.1.2, 5.7.2.

76. In contrast, van Binsbergen (2006a, 2006b) lists narrative complexes that not only represent sub-Saharan African but may also include Out of Africa myths (cf. above discussion in §1, n. 96). His 20 initial narrative complexes include "1. Separation of heaven and earth; 2. The connection between heaven and earth after separation; 3. What is in heaven?; 4. The lightning bird (and the world egg); 5. The mantis; 6. The ogre; 7. From the mouth; 8. The stones; 9. The moon; 10. The earth as primary; 11. The primal waters and the flood; 12. From under the tree; 13. The cosmic/rainbow snake; 14. Fundamental duality; 15. The spider and feminine arts; 16. Shamanism, bones; 17. Spottedness and the leopard; 18. Honey and honey-beer; 19. The cosmogonic virgin and her son/lover; 20. Contradictory messages bring death." As will readily be seen only some of them are Laurasian, while some others are restricted to Gondwana myths (§5); importantly, a story line is missing.

77. Such as Orpheus/Eurydike in Greece, Satyavant/Savitrī in the Indian epic Mahābhārata, Izanagi/Izanami in Japan, the myth of the red bird of the Cherokee (see §3.5.1), and the Hawai'ian myth of Kana/Hine (Beckwith 1987: 464). Cf. also the related Sumerian/Akkadian myth of Inanna's/Ishtar's descent to the netherworld (Dalley 1989: 154 sqq.), as well as the myths of Nergal and Ereshkigal (Dalley 1989: 163 sqq.), Gilgamesh (Dalley 1989: 39 sqq.), Persephone's abduction by Hades, Väinämöinen's descent (Kalevala 16), etc.; see Thompson 1993: Motif F80-81. Journey to lower world/world of the dead.

78. Bierhorst had an inkling of this: "the term 'mythology' implies a certain unity or interconnectedness that gives stories added power. . . . Often . . . the individual who understands how to put the myths together . . . is a religious specialist" (1992: 129). However, following the pathway dependencies of S. Thompson's "motif school" (§1.5), he saw the Five Ages/Suns section of the story line that he observed in Mesoamerica merely as "myths in sequence."

79. Even if some mythologies regard time as cyclical. However, even in cyclical systems, linear time is prominent. See Witzel 1990b on Indian chronicles (Vaṃśāvali); cf. González-Reimann 2002.

80. Obviously, this theory is diametrically opposed to that of R. Ellwood, for whom "official" myths (such as Hesiod's *Theogony* or the Bible) already are "reconstructions

from snatches of folklore and legend, artistically put together with an eye for drama and meaning" (1999: 174). If we would maintain the same for Laurasian mythology, it would be a very early composition by some Paleolithic shaman(s) (§7), but this would eliminate the ultimate purpose of the new composition (§8) that transgresses Gondwana-style myth telling. For Ellwood, "real myths" would be those that are "so fresh that they are not yet recognized as 'myth' or 'scripture,' they are 'fragmentary,' imaginistic rather than verbal, emergent, capable of forming many different stories at once" (1999: 175). One wonders when such myths would have been current, at the time of the African Eve? All later ones are already conditioned by earlier myth telling, be it in small hunters' bands or in early state societies. In all such cases, the rule of "path dependency" (Farmer et al. 2002) and of constant reformulation, based on local conditions, applies (see below, §2.3, 2.5.1–3).

81. By necessity, this is the case in ritual applications, such as the use of the Enuma Elish at the Babylonian New Year or the poetry of the Ṛgvedic hymns. See Witzel 1997b.

82. Smith 1919; Thompson 1993: Motifs A162.1, B11.11. The Japanese myth of Susa.no Wo killing the dragon of Izumo (Kojiki) has many of these folktale elements—including the liberation of a "princess" from his clutches just like our later, medieval version of St. George (Witzel 2008, 2009). These hero tales fit Propp's (1958) analysis of Russian folktales closely. However, the Laurasian setup as such does not, nor does Grintser's scheme of myth/epic stories (see Ježić 2005).

83. Occasional deviations from the scheme have been mentioned above (§2.5) and will be discussed below in their regional variations (§2.3, 2.5).

84. Lincoln 1991: 207 sq. Note, in general, Lincoln on the importance of the historical and ideological situation of the particular mythology studied. This also applies to differences in the myths told by males and by females (§6) and those of shamans and other members of a particular society.

85. See below, §5, n. 360. The motif is also found in Mesoamerica with the Ixil, Lenca, Zapotec, Yaqui, and Tzotzil (grass talked); see Bierhorst 1992: 137. Plato's *Phaedrus* (275 BCE [see 1963]) has it that the "first prophecies were the words of an oak at Dodona" and that people were apt to "listen to an oak or rock, so long as it was telling the truth." Cf. §5, n. 360.

86. It may even be useful to compare modern rewritings such as the one recently attempted in China (Hu 2002), which seems motivated by the need to finally have an elaborate and "complete" Chinese account of primordial creation in its various stages (as even the Chinese newspapers criticized).

87. Ions 1990; Jacobsen 1976.

88. See Graves 1955.

89. Barth 1987.

90. See the myth of the hidden sun; §3.5.1.

91. Farmer et al. 2002.

92. Baumann 1936: 256 sqq., cf. 33. See http://www.pbs.org/wgbh/nova/israel/familylemba.html; http://www.bmj.com/cgi/content/full/325/7378/1469.

93. Baumann 1936: 259.

94. A small outlying area on the Guinea coast in southern Ghana may have a similar origin. Van Binsbergen (2006a, 2006b) does not mention this mytheme but would explain it, along with others, by transmission from Austronesian Madagascar westward into East Africa.

95. The same applies to a number of mythemes adduced by van Binsbergen (2006a, 2006b).

96. See, for example, Puhvel 1987. Other specialists such as, recently, Lincoln (1999), for different reasons, rather stress the problematic nature of many Indo-European mythological reconstructions.

97. Note the recent criticism of reconstructed Indo-European mythology by B. Lincoln (1991, 1999); cf. Arvidsson 2006: 302 sq. See, however, Witzel 2007b. Cf. above, §2.1, esp. 2.6, for objections to comparative mythology.

98. See Hegedüs and Sidwell 2004.

99. *Dog* and *wolf* were not yet distinguished in the Proto-Nostratic language. The domestication of the dog is now set at c. 15,000 BCE; see Savolainen et al. 2002; cf. http://www.harvardmagazine.com/on-line/030374.html; http://news.harvard.edu/gazette/story/2004/02/mans-smartest-friend. Surprisingly, earlier genetic data were said to provide dates as early as 100,000 years ago , which "supported the hypothesis that wolves were the ancestors of dogs. Most dog sequences belonged to a divergent monophyletic clade sharing no sequences with wolves . . . dogs originated more than 100,000 years before the present" (Caries et al. 1997, http://www.idir.net/~wolf2dog/wayne1.htm).

100. In spite of spirited if not obstinate opposition from traditional comparative linguists. See, for example, the popular account by Ph. E. Ross (1991); cf. Witzel 2001b.

101. See Ehret 1995.

102. The dog is of particular interest, as it often functions as the spirit guide for shamans. It is also offered, next to the reindeer, in shamanic sacrifice in northeastern Siberia (Campbell 1988: I.2: 175).

103. The neuter stems in –r/–n (Hitt., nominative *watar*, genitive *wetenas*) are extremely archaic in Indo-European (cf. Skt. *ahar*, *ahnas*; Latin *iter*, *itin-er-is*), but they are *innovations* from the point of view of Nostratic (see appendix in Witzel 1992).

104. For example, *fire* is male in Japan and in Mongolian; cf. Heissig 1980: 46 sq., 71–76, 569 sqq. On his mother, El/Od ɣalaqan tngri, see Heissig 1980: 55. Later, the fire god was turned into a goddess (*ɣal tngri*) under the influence of Lamaism (Heissig 1980: 72 sqq.).

105. For fanciful attempts, see Graves 1994, 1997. Cf. Harva 1938.

106. Cf. Ōbayashi 1991a; Yoshida 2006.

107. Schärer 1963.

108. Earlier dates for immigration have been assumed for Monte Verde (Chile) at c. 35,000 BCE; and cf. the question of Kennewick Man in the Columbia Basin (Washington State), with supposed Caucasoid-like antecedents. However, common opinion now tends to date Kennewick at 9,400 BP, Cedros Island (California) at 11,000, Monte Verde (Chile) at 12,500, Topper (Virginia) at 15,200, Lapa do Banquete (northeastern Brazil) at 12,700, and the previous anchor site of Clovis (New Mexico) at 11,200; note the disputed site of Pedra Furada in northeastern Brazil at 47,000 BP. Cf. §4, nn. 211, 322; §7, nn. 204, 205.

109. On premodern contacts between the Americas and the Old World, see Sorenson and Johannessen 2006.

110. Linguists and archaeologists are of the opinion that Austronesian, to which Polynesian belongs, moved out of Taiwan about 2500 BCE; see Bellwood 2000. For another view, see Oppenheimer 1998.

111. See Lynch 1998.

112. A comparison with Malagasy and Indonesian/Filipino mythology would provide more materials; see Eugenio 1993. Cf. below, §2, n. 115.

113. See Thompson 1993: Motifs A652, A878, F162.3.1, esp. C621.1. Note the "Eden" myth of the Bassari in Togo (Campbell 1988: I.1: 14, derived from Frobenius 1924: 75–76). See §2, n. 179; §3, nn. 340, 414, 523; §5, nn. 299, 368; §6, n. 30.

114. Beckwith 1987: 42 sqq.

115. Jata, the son of the supreme god Mahatara, lives in a river (or in the netherworld) and is a crocodile (or creates them). Another version has a tree of life with a crocodile at the foot of the tree and a hawk in its branches. Similar myths are found in Fiji and Micronesia (Oppenheimer 1998: 310 sq.). Cf. Schärer 1963: 28 sqq., where Jata is the daughter of Mahatala; however, there is a male and female hornbill bird (*bungai*) in the Tree of Life who fight each other (echoing other dualities in Ngaju religion; cf. for the Toradja of Sulawesi Koubi 1982: 25 sqq.); nevertheless the hornbill (*tambon*) is equated with the Tambon (water snake; Schärer 1963: 35.) Cf. above, n. 110.

116. This can now be determined by comparison with genetic studies: the migration out of Africa is set at c. 60,000 BCE, via South Arabia to South/Southeast Asia and thence to Australia and southern East Asia; see §4.3.

117. Rather at 40,000 than at 20,000 years ago; see §7.3. The similarities in North American Indian mythology could provide a date for this, as Amerindians immigrated into the Americas c. 20,000 years ago. The Na-Dene-speaking tribes arrived later, probably after the last Ice Age.

118. See the summary by Lemonick and Dorfman (2006).

119. Further elaborated by K. Matsumura's (2006b) presentation at the International Conference on Comparative Mythology, Beijing.

120. See Granet 1989: 27; Münke 1976: 203 sqq.: the Weaver Woman and the Cowherd: (K'ien)-niu(-lang)/Qiangniulang and Chih-nü/Zhinu.

121. Cf. Antoni 1982 for circum-Pacific motifs; Naumann 1988: 91 sq.; see Matsumura 2006b.

122. Including their mutual interrelations and mutual secondary influences upon each other; see §2.4.

123. For some discussion of the interrelations between the various Near Eastern mythologies and early Greek myths, see Kirk 1970: 84 sqq.; Puhvel 1987: 21–32.

124. For linguistic details, see §4.1.

125. Frequently, the same is reflected in linguistic features as well. The various Pueblo languages (Hopi, Zuni, Tewa, Taos, etc.) that belong to different language families share a mythology as well as some linguistic features. They have also influenced the mythology of the late arrivals, the Na-Dene-speaking Navajo and Apache.

126. Always keeping in mind that secondary influences may have changed the picture, as is the case with the close cultural interaction of preclassical Greece, Anatolia, and Syria-Palestine (Kirk 1970; Puhvel 1987); cf. § 2, n. 123.

127. Prehistoric Iran up to Jiroft in southeastern Iran should be included as well as its further extremes radiating into the Bactria-Margiana and Indus areas. See "Jiroft. Fabuleuse Découverte en Iran," in *Dossiers d'Archeologie* (2003).

128. Witzel 2005b; cf. also Allen 2000.

129. Ions 1990: 21–33.

130. Note the case of the isolated pre-Hindu Kalash on the northwestern border of Pakistan with Afghanistan, who lost their priests after 1929, when they were still reported by Morgenstierne (1973), and retain only a few shamans who now reinterpret the polytheistic Kalash religion on an individual basis. See Jettmar 1975; cf. Lièvre and Loude 1990.

131. This has frequently been pointed out; see, for example, Kirk 1970: 13. Cf. Burkert 1982: 80; Puhvel 1987: 23 sqq.; West 1995; see above, §2, nn. 123, 126.

132. See Morford and Leanardon 2003: 81 sqq.; West 1995. The motif is sketchily visible also in the Avesta and the Rgveda. See Allen 2000 for a discussion of the Indo-European data.

133. Similar to the Vedic Rudra, who like Apollo both sends and heals illnesses; cf. also the bow shooter myths of the Indus civilization, Iran, China, and the Mayas. Curiously enough this development is also seen in late Vedic (Kaṭha Āraṇyaka).

134. Note the many discussions on "original" Greek mythology and the disagreements about it, for example, Nilsson 1972. See Burkert 1985: 10–22.

135. See Beekes 2007.

136. Graves 1955: 27; Sproul 1991: 157.

137. See §3.5.1, Vala and Iwato, Orpheus motif, killing the dragon, Amazons, etc.

138. Note the Zimbabwe paintings of kings, killed and lying prostrate; see the illustration in Campbell 1988: I.1: 88–89, no. 158: human sacrifice, ascent by a ladder to heaven, which transforms into a lightning flash and the rain serpent. Cf. also the painting in Campbell 1989: II.1: 76, no. 160 (late: 14th–15th centuries).

139. It is another topic altogether why Egyptian myth represents many deities in animal form. The assumption is that these represent animal strength and other important character-istics (Ions 1990: 12).

140. As the Romans said: *Sit terra tibi levis.*

141. In addition the earth is seen as covering the dead (in a grave), as is clear also in Ṛgveda 10.18.8, 11–13.

142. Kuiper 1983; Witzel 1984b, 1995. There may be remnants of this idea in Greek and Germanic myth; stone weapons fallen from the sky are found from Greece to the Tibetan plains (where stray finds of Neolithic hand axes are regarded as such).

143. See discussion by Eliade (1954b: 259–26), mainly for Central and North Asia. For a detailed discussion, see his *Traité d'histoire des Religions* (*Die Religionen und das Heilige* [1949: 310 sqq.]).

144. Also seen in Germanic representations (Jutland [see Witzel 1984b]) and in North Asia; detailed listing of literature in Eliade 1954b: 259 n. 32, further 270. Cf. the world tree in Uralic and Altaic (cf. Harva 1938; Staudacher 1942), and in West Africa (Unterberger 2001) and Australia, note the *tjurunga* (Campbell 1988: I.2: 146); cf. illustration in Lawlor 1991: 75. Cf. §3, n. 248 sqq.; §7, n. 107.

145. Other nighttime images may be taken into account, such as the opening in pyramids pointing to the North Pole; the popular fantasies (propagated by TV) of G. Hancock are nat-urally to be excluded.

146. The involved generations are Alalu–Anu–Kumarbi–Weather God; cf. §2, n. 194; §3, n. 607; Kirk 1970: 217. A useful table of the Greek and Hurrian myth is given by Kirk (1970: 217), and of the Babylonian, Hurrian, Phoenician, Greek, and Old Norse versions by Barber and Barber (2004: 210). Emasculation is clearly seen in the Hurrite, Phoenician, and Greek versions only. On Oriental influence in general, see also Burkert 1982: 80 sqq.; see above, §2, nn. 123, 126.

147. For a detailed comparison of the Greek and Hurrite (Hittite) myths, see Kirk 1970: 217. He (1970: 219) concludes that neither version borrowed from the other, though the Hurrian version is earlier and cruder. He expects a Levant point of transfer.

148. See Kidder 2007; Rotermund 1988: 32–38.

149. For recent accounts of Japanese mythology, see Hirafuji 2004; Kato 1988; Matsumoto 1928.

150. Witzel 2005b. See Yoshida 2006: 236–42 on Scythian influences via Korea; on the general characteristics of Japanese mythology, see Yoshida 2006. Note now the Koguryo (Kōkuri) version of Central Asian myths, that is, of the Koguryo realm, which straddled Manchuria and North Korea in the middle of the first millennium ce. Their myth presents an

intermediate version between (Indo-European) Central Asia and Japan; see Beckwith 2004. Korean myth (as found in the Samguk Yusa) may be compared for further evidence.

151. See *Jomon vs Yayoi* 2005; further, the Japanese National Science Museum's presentation: http://www.kahaku.go.jp/special/past/japanese/ipix/3/3-12.html; Naumann 2000. For Japanese origins, see the detailed account on anthropology and linguistics in Haguenauer 1956.

152. Cf. Naumann 2000: 223.

153. See Kojiki 1.18; Nihon Shoki I 26–28, cf. I 14. Philippi 1968: 404 sqq. There are similar stories in other, neighboring food-producing cultures such as those of Taiwan and the Philippines; see Philippi 1968: 405.

154. Jensen 1978.

155. Caland 1990: 116–19; §7.

156. Markmann and Markmann 1992: 105 sqq. Incidentally, such myths spread, along with maize agriculture, northward all the way up to the Hidatsa in North Dakota and the eastern Delaware, Huron, and Iroquois in southern Canada.

157. Witzel 1984b.

158. Cf., nevertheless, the study of fairy tales; Brednich et al. 1977–.

159. "Emerged" as in the Sanskrit verb *sṛj* (let flow) or very elaborately in the first seven generations of Japanese myth in the Kojiki: they are asexual down to Toyo-Kumo-no.no Kami. Also, nothing is "created" either by speech or by manual action; instead the texts speak at first of "becoming" and later on of birth.

160. Cf. Eliade 1958.

161. Note also the killing by Romulus of his brother, Remus (from an older *Yemus), like the Indian Yama; cf. Puhvel 1987: 284–90. Further, in the Hebrew Bible, see the killing by Cain of his brother, Abel; cf. also the contest of the early Japanese gods, the brothers Ho-deri and Ho-wori (as fisher and farmer; Kojiki 1.41.17, 1.42.1–3).

162. See, for example, the late Vedic text Chāndogya Upaniṣad 3.8.19. In some versions, such as with the Munda and Khasi, humans come from such eggs (§3.1.6).

163. Sometimes, as in Mesopotamia, viewed as salty male and sweet female waters (§3.1.2).

164. By muskrat or diver bird in Siberia and North America; by boar in India (§3.1).

165. Cf. the *fiat lux* of the Bible and the nondistinction of day and night in the early Vedic text, Maitrāyaṇī Saṃhitā 1.5.12, about Yama's death and his twin sister, Yamī's, sorrow; note also the primordial half-darkness in the Quiché Maya Popol Vuh and other Amerindian myths.

166. Cf. the Stone Age sculpture at Laussel (France) of a male and female, obviously joined in copulation, their upper bodies facing away from each other, one upward, one downward (for an illustration, see Campbell 1988: I.1: 67). Virtually the same carving is found several times in Dogon Land (Burkina Faso, West Africa); see Frobenius 1998: 156 (with drawing). The composition is reminiscent of the primordial egg. Note also the ambiguous androgynous nature of many of the early creator deities, such as the Vedic Indian Puruṣa and Prajāpati.

167. Sometimes by cutting off their wings. Cf. Thompson 1993: Motif A1125: Winds caused by flapping wings. A giant bird causes the wind with his wings. The wings are cut by the culture hero so that the bird cannot flap so hard, Greece, Iceland, Babylon, India; N. A. Indian; African American (Georgia).

168. A later Indian ritual myth is closer to the Polynesian one: the late Vedic Śatapatha Brāhmaṇa 1.1.4.22 has it: "Once upon a time all these worlds were verily near and contig-

uous. (The medieval commentator Sāyaṇa adds that one can touch the sky by lifting one's hand). The gods thought, . . . how can we create space for ourselves? They breathed . . . the three-syllable word *'vítaye'* through these and caused the world to expand out."

169. This is certainly due to the nighttime setting of the myth. Note that this is found on coffin lids, representing the netherworld of the dead. In daytime, Father Heaven would over-arch a reclining Earth.

170. In Greece we have the opposite in Herakles bringing back the cows from the western "Redland" Islands in the Atlantic (§3.5.1).

171. Its opposite, typically in more southern climes, is seen in the Bible (Joshua), with the Hawai'ians (Maui), and among the Incas (sun stone at Machu Picchu). In all these cases, the wandering sun has to be fixed at one spot in the sky. In the South Indian (Toda) version, Kwoto/Meilitars (born from a gourd!) binds the sun with a stone chain (Rivers 1906: 206) and then puts it back in its place. The Aztec/Mayas effect the sun's movement by blood offerings and human sacrifice, which invigorate the young, wavering sun (cf. §3.5.1). Note also the Indian version in the tale of Yama/Yamī (Maitrāyaṇi Saṃhitā 1.5.12), where night did not exist at first and had to be created; cf. §2, n. 165; §3, nn. 306, 470.

172. On Herakles, see Burkert 1982: 77–98.

173. Cf. below, on the Mo'o (§3.5.2); Westervelt 1987: 212 sq. The Mo'o can change shape, just like the post-Vedic Indian Nāgas, between dragon and human form. Interestingly, Hawai'i is free of snakes; however, some reptiles (*Brachylopus iguanides*) have made it all the way from South America to the western Pacific, to Fiji and Tonga (see Mayr 2001: map 2.11), from which the belief in "dragons" in the intermediate Polynesian homeland (*Sawaiki) may have originated. (Note also the formidable Komodo dragon, a giant lizard, in eastern Indonesia.)

174. See the multiple heroic deeds of the twin Navajo heroes (Zolbrod 1984: 171, 183 sqq.).

175. In the form of the serpent and the eagle, since Olmec times (Freidel et al. 1993: 439) and still seen in the Mexican state seal.

176. This may be the sun itself (usually male but female in Germanic, Baltic, Japanese, and southeastern Australian traditions) or its representation: Vivasvant/Vīvaŋhuuant (m.) in India and Old Iran. The Japanese sun deity Amaterasu is female but nevertheless has many male characteristics of behavior and comes in (male) warrior's armor (see Philippi 1968; Yoshida 1961–62). Her change from a male to a female deity may have been fairly recent before the Kiki was recorded.

177. Some (very old) versions have humans produced from clay or from trees, as in the Bible and the Andaman Islands, Australia, Melanesia, and sub-Saharan Africa; or, as in Old Egypt, from clay (with beer), from clay also with the Indo-Iranian Nuristani (Kafirs), or from maize with the Mayas (Tedlock 1985: 163; see §3.7). It will become obvious below that this is a later version of agriculturalists. Similarly, the myth of human origins from trees (Kaguyahime in Japanese folktales, Askr/Embla in Iceland, with some Austronesian tribes in Taiwan) is a Gondwana time relic (see below, §5.6). There also is the old myth of human origin from rocks (Atayal tribe in Austronesian Taiwan, Melanesia).

178. But differently in Tierra del Fuego, where this is seen with two brothers. See Campbell 1988: I.2: 257, 261.

179. Done by shedding snakeskin or by stamping the dead back into the ground. However, in West Africa, the primordial man *and* his wife, deceived by a snake, eat the red fruits of the creator god's sacred tree (Bassari, in Togo; see Campbell 1988: I.1: 14; Frobenius 1924). Cf. §2, n. 113; §3, nn. 340, 414, 523; §5, nn. 299, 368; §6, n. 30.

180. "Male envy" of giving birth has taken many forms. Note, for example, the Egyptian, medieval Kashmiri, and Tibetan idea of giving birth/creating by vomiting (cf. §3, nn. 66, 68, 119) or the Greek/Indian notions of birth from the thigh of a god, from his brain, etc. Sometimes this even leads to ideas such as the Australian and Melanesian ones about lack of paternal involvement in procreation.

181. Cf. Weigle 1989.

182. Bahn and Rosenfeld 1991 (several chapters); Bell 1983: 182; Hamilton 1980: 15; Layton 1986: 45; Smith 1991: 45.

183. Note that there is no "primordial sin" in the Hebrew Bible (but punishment for an individual's "sins"); there is primordial obligation (*ṛṇa*) in Vedic India and the sending away of primordial evil in Japan, beginning with the "wrongly conceived" child of Izanami and Izanagi, Hirume. A similar expiatory ceremony of sending away accumulated "evil" (*tsumi*) is still performed in the great *ōharae* rituals on June 30 and December 31, for example, by throwing one's cutout paper images from some 50 boats into the Tokyo Bay, organized by the Torigoe Jinja of Kanda (witnessed in 2005); cf. the description at http://eos.kokugakuin. ac.jp/modules/xwords/category.php?categoryID=18. Cf. below, §8.

184. See the brief discussion of about 100 examples in §5.7.2 and by the Harvard mythology project, http://www.people.fas.harvard.edu/~witzel/mythlinks.htm.

185. Barber and Barber 2004.

186. For a mytho-astronomical interpretation, see Barber and Barber 2004: 176 sqq.; Sullivan 1996. Cf. the Black Sea flood at 5600 BCE (Ryan and Pitman 1998), Amerindian Ice Age tales in the northwestern United States, or the apparent remembrance of a volcanic eruption among the Klamath tribe at Mt. Shasta (Barber and Barber 2004: 6 sqq.).

187. Death, however, is attributed to a misstep, often that of a primordial woman. The role of human beings in the world depends on the way the relationship to the ancestral god(s) is seen and how their relation to the origin of evil in the world is defined by the individual, local mythology.

188. Yoshida 1961–62: 29–35. He compares him with Susa.no Wo.

189. See Nagy 1979.

190. See Dumézil 1995: 289 sqq.

191. See §3, nn. 256, 345, 359, 409; Yang and An 2005: 68, 74–75, 124 sqq.

192. Or Yamato Takeru in Japan, though his tale has not produced an epic but is merely told in brief form in the Kojiki 2.69, 77, 80, etc. For other persons called Takeru, see Philippi 1968: 640; discussion by Yoshida (1961–62).

193. Sometimes this is substituted by the previous four generations of the gods or the Four Ages of the world (notably in the Americas). Cf. also Barber and Barber 2004: 210. For the question of whether the myth of the final destruction is older or younger than the Amerindian version of four consecutively improved ages, see below, §3.6. And note Thompson 1993: Motif A632. Succession of creations and cataclysms. From the ruins of each earlier creation a new one is raised, Jewish, Inca, Hawaiian.

194. In the Avesta: Visprat 20.1; Sīh rōcak 1.4, 2.4; cf. Vīdēvdād 19.29–30.

195. The Book of the Dead, chap. 175; see Eliade 1992: 26.

196. Vǫluspá 57; Vafþrúðnismál 50; or the long-lasting winter and ice as in the Edda (Vafþrúðnismál 44, Fimbul winter) and in Old Iranian myth (Avesta: Vīdēvdād 2); or a world end as described in Krishna's epiphany where he devours the world (Bhagavadgītā 11); further, various types of fire, flood, etc. as recorded in Maya, Aztec, and Inca myth. (For occasional attestation in Africa, see Baumann 1936: 319.) In that light, Gilgamesh's, the biblical, and the ancient Indian (Manu's) flood are but one out of several types of destruction that are

"consecutive" in Amerindian myth (see §2, n. 193; §2.5.2) but are normally found in Eurasian myth as just *one* destruction, at the end of the world. Note also that the ancient flood myths are either Near Eastern or from adjacent areas such as Vedic India. Things are different in the Himalayas, Koran, China, and Japan (flood emerging from a lake); see Allen 1997; further details in §3.9, §5.7.2.

197. Such as the new world of the Æsir gods in the Edda (Vǫluspá 58 sqq.), the periodic creation in later Indian myth of the Purāṇas, the emergence of Noah from the biblical flood, Mesopotamia (Gilgamesh), Greece (Pyrrha and Deukalion), Vedic India (Manu), the five successive creations in Maya myth, etc. Note the Christian case of Revelation, mixed with Zoroastrian myth.

198. For example, following the handbooks, I had originally denied the existence of the flood myth for Africa (Witzel 2001b); this was erroneous, as the lists by Baumann (1936: 307 sqq.) indicate; see §5.7.2. Also see §2.1; Ragin 1987.

199. On the widely held beliefs in rebirth (but without *karma*, as commonly found in India since the Upaniṣads), see Witzel 1984a, to which one may add further occurrences in Old Egypt, Australia, West Africa, etc. See §6, n. 23.

200. Cf. Ōbayashi 1991a.

201. Cf. Ōbayashi 1991a; Yoshida 2006.

202. On their mythology, derived from archaeological records, see the cautious study by N. Naumann (2000).

203. Beckwith 2004; cf. Yoshida 2006 on Scythian influences via Korea.

204. For the Yemishi, see the account (as barbarians) in Nihon Shoki (trans. Aston 1972: 203).

205. Reconstructed forms are given, as in linguistics, with starred (*) forms.

206. See Harva 1938.

207. Cf. the similar concept of Eurasian by Greenberg (2000–2002); however, it includes Inuit while it excludes Dravidian.

208. Cf. Harva 1938.

209. See, however, books such as that by Staudacher (1942).

210. Poppe 1960. This linguistic family is again under attack now, after earlier attempts by some Turkologists such as Clauson and Doerfer; see Osada and Vovin 2003; cf. Beckwith 2004. For the opposite point of view, see Martin 1987, 1996; Poppe 1960; and decisively, Robbeets 2005.

211. Oppitz 1991.

212. Blacker 1986; Walter and Fridman 2004. Cf. Guillemoz 1983: 129 on *mudang* and *munsujaengi*, cf. 136, 209 sqq.

213. See Cahill 2003; Staudacher 1942; cf. Unterberger 2001.

214. Kings in Central Asia descend or are thrown down from heaven or are rolled in a carpet (Jpn. *fusuma*). See Ōbayashi 1984; Waida 1973.

215. Beckwith 2004; Yoshida 2006.

216. The same occurs in Japanese and Korean (Samguk Yusa) myth; or it is done by an arrow. Cf. Yoshida 2006.

217. Hoffmann 1992; cf. Colarusso 2006: 33 about Indra/Pataraz.

218. See Yang and An 2005: 37, 148–51, 186.

219. Chang 1983: 10; Beckwith 2004; cf. Chang 1983: 12 n. 8.

220. Such as the more distantly related Japanese one of the first child of the primordial deities Izanami and Izanagi. It was born misshaped because Izanami spoke first, before her husband; the child, Hirugo, was set adrift like Moses.

221. See §3.5.1; Witzel 2005b.

222. See Hoffmann 1992.

223. Beckwith 2004.

224. Beckwith 2004; Lee 1977.

225. Further links of this story can be made with the Japanese Tanabata myth and its original Chinese form (as Cowherd and Weaver Woman, Qiangniu lang/Niu-lang and Chih-nü/Zhinu). They were separated by the "ocean" of the Milky Way, until their yearly meeting, during which a magpie's wings function as a bridge (on this topic, see Witzel 2005a, 2008, 2009b). For the mytheme of conjugal visit through a keyhole, see the account in the Kojiki II 26 (cf. II 106; Chamberlain 1981: 218 sq., 321 sq.; Philippi 1968: 203 sq., 291). Cf. also the Koguryo motif of Haemosu recorded in Ku-Samguk-sa (see Ōbayashi 1984): a heavenly prince married one of the daughters of a river god, Habaek; she was kept in a room, but she became pregnant by sun rays coming from the window.

226. See some initial effort in Witzel 2008, 2009.

227. For China, see Granet 1989: 27; Münke 1976: 203 sqq.

228. See Lee 1977.

229. Beckwith 2004; Martin 1987.

230. See Ōbayashi 1991a, 1984; Yoshida 2006.

231. In Korean origin myths (Samguk Yusa), a bear is the ancestor; cf. Ōbayashi 1991a; Ye 2006. However, there are no obvious connections with Ainu myth and ritual (*Iomante*; see below, §7.1.2) involving the bear as messenger from the gods.

232. As found in the periodic ritual of rebuilding and installing the national shrine at Ise (as per personal communication from my colleague Nur Yalman, who participated in it in 1993); the soul box is also found at the top beams of Korean farmhouses, and it is carried by the Dayaks of Borneo (see Witzel 2005b). To the occurrences mentioned (Korea, Dayak) southeastern Borneo can be added: the birth ritual has a shaman store the soul of the newborn in a coconut shell, shut tight; it is hung up in the center of the house; the ceremony is repeated at each New Moon for a year. Similarly so on the Kei Islands (Jensen 1948: 129).

233. Naumann 2000.

234. Beckwith 2004; Lee 1977.

235. For their mythology, see the traditional verses of the *kumuy yukar*; see Chamberlain 1887; Munro 1963; Ohnuki-Thierney 1981 etc.; Philippi 1979; cf. Walter and Fridman 2004: 657–66. As for the acculturated Ezo/Emishi in Tsugaru, the northernmost part of the main Honshu Island, note their form of shamanism (and hunting, *matagi*); Walter and Fridman 2004: 700–704.

236. Naumann 2000: 199 sqq.

237. For the "lifeline" explanation, see Naumann 2000: 111 sqq., esp. 199 sqq. A similar idea is found in Vedic India (Witzel 2000): a "thread" (*tantu*) extends from the navel of a male person to his father, and from the father onward to his own father, etc. When one dies, the string "is cut," but a new one is established from one's son's navel to one's own, and the "lineage" is kept intact after one has joined, after a year, the other "fathers."

238. For Indo-Iranian, see Witzel 2004a; note also Puhvel 1987: 21 sqq.

239. It may perhaps be hinted at in Ṛgveda 1.32.11, where the killing and dismemberment of the (male) dragon-like Vṛtra corresponds to that of the (female) dragon-like Tiamat.

240. Frazer 1963: 348 sqq.

241. Puhvel 1987: 26 sqq. In the Hebrew Bible, there is a related but "reversed" version of the myth: Noah's sons see their naked drunken father; cf. Puhvel 1987.

242. Colarusso (2006: 35) derives the name on the great Vedic, Nuristani (and once, Avestan) deity Indra from Northwest Caucasian *yənra*.

243. Nichols 1999, cf. 1997.

244. Ehret 2002. This is different for other early food-producing cultures, such as those of Mesoamerica and China, and also for horticultural New Guinea, with its self-made "great men" (Sahlins 2004).

245. See Thompson 1993: Motifs A651. Hierarchy of worlds; A1101. The Four Ages of the world. A development of the present order through four stages or periods, the golden, silver, bronze, and iron ages, or the like. Thompson quotes the following data: "Encyc. Religion and Ethics s.v. 'Ages of the World.' Irish, Greek, Hindu, Chinese"; further, Thompson 1993: Motifs A1220.1. Man created after series of unsuccessful experiments; A1101.1. Golden age. A former age of perfection.—Hdwb. d. Abergl. III 927ff.—Irish, Icelandic, Lappish, Greek, Jewish, Persian, Hindu, Tuamotu, Aztec, Carib, Ackawoi; A631. Pre-existing world of gods above. Such a world is assumed before the real creation of the universe. Though this belief is not explicitly set forth in many mythologies, it seems to be implied in most of the North American Indian systems. See, for example, Thompson 1993: Motif A31. Creator's grandmother, Jewish, Samoa, Hawaii. There is, however, also a series of creations and destructions that agrees more with the Amerindian scheme of Five Ages (Suns): see Thompson 1993: Motif A632: Succession of creations and cataclysms. From the ruins of each earlier creation a new one is raised, Jewish, Inca, Hawaiian. See Hunger 1984; 425, s.v. *Weltalter*; cf. Witzel 2005b.

246. On Near Eastern influence here, see Burkert 1982: 80; Cahill 2003; Kirk 1970: 13 (based on F. M. Cornford); Puhvel 1987: 22 sqq. Cf. also the—overstated—case made by Bernal (1987) on Afroasiatic influences on Greek culture and note his critics, for example, W. van Binsbergen, http://www.shikanda.net/, and Bernal's (2001) subsequent answers to his critics.

247. A simplified version of the Sumerian creation myth; see Jacobsen 1976: 168 sq.

248. Yasna 32.3: *būmiiå haptaiēē*, "in (this) seventh (of the seven climes) of the world"; cf. Yt. 19.26 (Witzel 2000).

249. Such as "the earlier/later Yuga" (Ṛgveda 7.87.4).

250. For the neighboring and related Nuristani and Kalash, see Allen 2000.

251. Witzel 1985.

252. See González-Reimann 2002.

253. Kramer 1963. Cf. Herbig 1988: 447 sq. For Egypt it is implied by the golden age of Osiris; see Rundle Clark 1959: 21, 103. Cf. Herbig (1988: 445), who sees a less dangerous and more stable world of the Egyptians.

254. J. Rhys (1862), in Sproul 1991: 172–73, in a version close to the Polynesian one: Heaven and Earth with no room for their children between them; the cutting of Heaven into many pieces by a son; good and evil children of both parents, such as the Giants, whose defeated "king" went on to the land of the dead; the Great Flood, with a single pair of men saved in a ship; a new king, Father Sky, who struggles periodically with winter; he is aided by the human-born Sun hero, who also obtains the intoxicating drink from the netherworld. See Thompson 1993: Motif A1101, including a myth from China (Ferguson 33).

255. See Allen 2000 for a schema of 4 + 1 ages in Indo-European myths.

256. Similar in Pueblo myth; the Hopi have up to seven, and the Navajo even more, future worlds (Waters 1977). For the Mayas, see Lehmann 1953: 70 sq. For the Four/Five, see also Allen 2000.

257. See Bierhorst 1992: 182.

258. Similarly, with the previous four worlds in Hopi mythology.

259. Bierhorst 1992: 183.

260. Cf. the corresponding underlying genetic data; see detailed summary in §4, n. 213.

261. According to Locke (2004: 58), they have red (or black) as the color of the first world that arose in the east, blue/south the second, yellow/west the third, and black/north the fourth.

262. The strong influence of Pueblo myth on the newly arrived Navajo and Apache is well known. The Pueblo Amerindians (Hopi), however, have these colors and connect them with minerals and cardinal directions: 1. yellow/gold/west, 2. blue/silver/south, 3. red/copper/east, 4. yellowish white/mixed mineral *sikyápala*/north. For the Indo-European colors, and their connections with directions, classes of society, etc., see Lyle 1990: 3 sqq.; Witzel 1972.

263. Sullivan 1988: 49–73 sqq.

264. Sullivan 1988: 744 n. 78.

265. Flood, fire, darkness, and cold; see Bierhorst 1988: 139, 142–43, 145, and for the Inca, see 207. On the Four Ages, see §2, nn. 193, 255, 272, 275; §3, nn. 75, 602, 611.

266. A universal conflagration and the flood; see Campbell 1988: I.2: 259, based on Gusinde 1977: II: 1145 sq., 1155 sq., 1232 sq.; cf. Sullivan 1988: 49, 66–72, 81.

267. Unless one wants to invoke the extremely unlikely prospect of diffusion from the ancient Near East (after c. 2000 BCE).

268. Including Chinese; Ket, which belongs to the ancient but quickly dwindling Yeneseian language family in western Siberia; Burushaski is isolated in Hunza, in the Pamir Mountains of northernmost Pakistan (but the Burusho have genetic links with the Basque [Mehdi et al. 1999: 88 sq.; cf., however, Ayub et al. 2003; Underhill et al. 2000], probably as they are part of the move out of the Greater Pakistan area to Anatolia and Europe at c. 40,000 BCE); Northern Caucasian consisting of northwestern (Cherkes etc.) and northeastern (Chechen etc.) groups; and finally, Basque (-Aquitanian, "Vasconic").

269. Such as J. Bengtson, see http://jdbengt.net/; for some of his work, see the journal *Mother Tongue* (http://www.people.fas.harvard.edu/%7Ewitzel/aslip.html).

270. Barring Pueblo influences on Navajo mythology; see §2, nn. 115, 262; §4, nn. 106, 175.

271. See the summary by Lemonick and Dorfman (2006).

272. Two of the destructions typical for the Four Ages scheme are, however, found in Africa, as well; see Baumann 1936. First, the flood (Baumann 1936: 307) is found in Nigeria, in Gabon, on the Upper Congo, and on the southern Tanzanian coast. In a variant form connected with thunderstorms or the seasons it is found in the southern and northern Congo, on Lake Victoria, and between Ghana and Nigeria. In some localized forms or those influenced by Christian or Muslim versions it is found in West Africa, Cameroon, Uganda, Kenya, and northwestern Mozambique. Second, the great wild fire (Baumann 1936: 319) is found on the Cameroon coast, in northwestern Uganda, in northern Mozambique, and on the Zimbabwe/Mozambique border. It should be noted, however, that this concerns just two common, isolated myths (which are also found, for example, in South America); they do not yet form a scheme of Four/Five Ages. The individual myths, especially that of the flood, are much older, of Pan-Gaean age; see §5.7.2. Note the detailed discussion of the flood myth by Baumann (1936: 320 sqq.), who refutes many of the then and now popular explanations of the flood myth as vesical dream, memory of actual catastrophes, etc.

273. Kramer 1963.

274. See Bierhorst 1992; cf. Carrasco 1982; Herbig 1988: 449.

275. Compare S. N. Kramer (1961, 1963: 262) for the Sumerian and Rundle Clark (1959: 21, 103) for the Egyptian approach, and contrast the "negative" attitude in the ancient Near East toward the increasingly evil Four Ages, as compared with the "positive" one in Mesoamerica, where each age, as a trial creation, is an improvement on the earlier one.

276. See Hochgeschwender 2007.

277. The clay for Ōkuninushi's offering plates was brought by him, in bird form, from the bottom of the sea (while the first Yamato ruler, Jimmu, fashions them from local materials).

278. With a typical Indian variant, that of the diver boar; he later on became an incarnation of the great deity Viṣṇu; the diver myth is first found in the Atharvaveda (Paippalāda) 6.7 and in Kaṭha Saṃhitā 8.2 (Witzel 2004b).

279. Cf. also Noah's raven, Odin's raven, Emperor Jimmu's "crow" (actually, zoologically speaking, a raven), etc.; on the nature of ravens and their myths in Central Asia and beyond, see Mortensen 2003.

280. See also the Austro-Asiatic Khasi, the Tibeto-Burmese Naga (both in northeastern India), and the Austric superfamily, including Miao/Hmong (Benedict 1976; Blust 1996) in South China (Witzel 2005b); note that this mytheme also has a North American (Cherokee) version.

281. Though this rather seems to belong to a pre-Yayoi substrate (see §3, n. 119, 284; §4, n. 464, on Ōgetsu). In India, a related myth (Vādhūla Sūtra; Caland 1990: 416–19) is linked with the introduction of rice agriculture (and the use of rice as sacrificial offerings) into the Vedic tradition in the early first millennium BCE; see §4, n. 464; §6, n. 3; cf. §7, n. 157; Witzel 2004a.

282. Matsumura 2006b.

283. Bellwood and Renfrew 2002.

284. Such as in the isolated agriculture-related myth (Ōgetsu) in the "continental" Japanese mythology (cf. Naumann 2000: 223 on [Ōgetsu's] body secretions); or as in the rare agricultural myths in the pastoral-oriented late Vedic texts (Vādhūla Brāhmaṇa; Caland 1990: 416–19; see §2, n. 282). However the important emergence myth that is typical for the Pueblo and Mesoamericans is found as far south as with the Inca, Aymara, and Gran Chaco populations and as far north as the Hidatsa of North Dakota and the Iroquois and the Hurons of Ottawa.

285. Frazer 1963: 351 sqq.

286. Jensen 1978.

287. Cf. books by Burkert (1982 etc.).

288. Herbig 1988: 325 sqq.

289. Malo 1997: 104 sqq. The dead king was worshipped like a real god (*akua maoli*), an *amakaua*; however, some commoners, too, could be deified; cf. Beckwith 1987: 76.

290. Details in Beckwith 1987: 154 sqq. Normal humans leap into the dark pit of Milu (Lua-o-Milu), from certain jumping places (such as at the western end of the islands). Milu is an opponent of Kane (Tane) and rules the netherworld. (Cf. below, §7.2, on the development of the social class of noblemen.)

291. Visible, e.g., in Marxist rituals (October Revolution Day, funerals, marriages at the graves of heroes of the Soviet Union buried at the Kremlin wall, the May Parade, etc.) and in many forms of Nazi rituals, such as nocturnal torch parades and the like, as well as secret SS rituals.

292. Hochgeschwender 2007.

293. Cf. Colarusso 2006: 36: "The jumping [by myths] of a language boundary should cause no surprise. To speak a language is to belong to a common ethnic unit of some sort, …

but to share myth is to belong to a common cultural sphere, and this can include more than one language family."

294. Campbell 1988: I.2: 232–33.

295. See Lindstrom 1993: esp. 15–40; Steinbauer 1971 (for various areas in New Guinea, Melanesia, Fiji).

296. The Protestant and local Chinese Christian churches have nothing of this.

297. See Sherrat 2006.

298. Sometimes well hidden; see, e.g., Knauer 2006 for the "Queen Mother of the West" in China.

299. See Beckwith 2004: 29 sq.; Yoshida 2006 on Scythian influences via Korea.

300. Matsumura's (2006b) presentation at the Conference on Comparative Mythology, Beijing. Cf. for the White Hare of Inaba, Antoni 1988; Lévi-Strauss 2002.

301. For some other Chinese elements, see Matsumura 2006b; note also Kamei 1954.

302. Other remnants appear "along the way" from Africa to Australia and East Asia, in the Andamans (Radcliffe-Brown 1933), and with remnant populations in various parts of Eurasia, including the linguistically and somatically isolated Burushos of Hunza in northern Pakistan (Ayub et al. 2003; Berger 1988; Mehdi et al. 1999; Underhill et al. 2000) as well as the Kusunda of Nepal (Rana 2002; Watters 2005). Note further the linguistic substrate of Nahali in Central India (Kuiper 1962; cf. *Mother Tongue* 3 [1997]); Vedda in Sri Lanka (De Silva 1972); Toda in the South Indian Nilgiri Mountains, clearly with an older form of mythology (Rivers 1906); and some other Indian tribes. See further, the Semang, Sakai, Asli, etc. of the Malay Peninsula (Evans 1923: 185 sqq.); some remnant populations in Indonesia and the Philippines (such as the Aeta); and perhaps also some of the Austronesian-speaking highland tribes of Taiwan such as the Bunun, Atayal, etc., who seem to have preserved an older form of mythology (a case that is in need of further study; cf. Ogawa and Asai 1935; Pache 1964; Tung 1964; Yamada 2003, 2007).

303. Called so after the geological name of the early southern supercontinent, Gondwana; see §2, nn. 25, 110.

304. See the discussion above, §1.6.

305. Lincoln 1991.

306. Cf. Arvidsson 2006.

307. Wunn 2000, 2001, 2005; see §1.4, §7.1.

308. Compare, for example, the detailed methodology used by J. Harrod (2006) for analyzing early art and spirituality; and cf. his exposition at http://www.originsnet.org/gloss-meth.html.

309. Bellah 1973.

310. According to Brooks, the "oldest possible age for 'out-of-Africa' is c. 77 ky (?or 100 ky if the date of the chimp–human divergence is 7mya instead of 5mya)" (2006; cf. §2, n. 311; §4, n. 97). J. Harrod gives archaeological data for early modern humans from 195 to 100/60 kya (see 2006: 48), supported by early symbolic use of simple art, and a dispersal out of Africa at 150–130 kya (2006: 52), but he gives 60–5 kya for the Upper Paleolithic, which agrees with the *communis opinio*.

311. Culotta 2007.

312. Swadesh 1955, 1972.

313. See Starostin 2002, http://starling.rinet.ru/Texts/method.pdf; cf. http://en.wikipedia.org/wiki/Glottochronology. See also Bellwood 2000; for a brief discussion of glottochronological methods and data, see van Driem 2006: 163 sq.

314. Note the Santa Fe project (http://www.santafe.edu/) and the Rosetta Project (http://www.rosettaproject.org/); as well as the Association for the Study of Language in

Prehistory (http://www.people.fas.harvard.edu/%7Ewitzel/aslip.html and http://starling.rinet.ru/program.php?lan=en).

315. However, on linguistic grounds we know that the words for cow and sheep are older than that for horse. For the general problem, see, for example, Dolgopolsky et al. 1998; Kaye 1999a, 1999b; Renfrew and Nettle 1999; Zimmer 1990.

316. §5, n. 271.

317. Such as the early Vedic quote (Atharvaveda 19.38.2) on *guggulu* (bdellium) as maritime (*samudriya*), and thus from Arabia, as well as local (*saindhava*), from the Indus area.

318. Cf. Allen 2000, on the expansion from Four to Five Ages (in Indo-European myth).

319. Schärer 1963.

320. Witzel 1995, 1997a.

321. Beckwith 1972. For the history and a characterization of the text, see Beckwith 1987: 301 sqq.

322. Radin 1991.

323. Strehlow 1978: 11–19.

324. Among the Pirahã of Brazil, one expects that there are few myths ("sing their dreams"; Colopano 2007: 137), which has been strenuously denied by Dan Everett (2005). Cf., however, Pesetsky et al. 2007; and the popular report in the *New Yorker*, April 16, 2007, by J. Colopano. All such cases would need extensive countercheck and study by anthropologists with an interest in mythology.

325. See http://www.ruthenia.ru/folklore/berezkin; Berezkin 2002 etc.

326. See above on the c. 150 motifs that are shared by North and South American populations (Bierhorst 1988). However, there is now some evidence of contact between South America and if not Sahul Land, then at least Polynesia: chicken and sweet potato (Storey et al. 2007). This kind of occasional contact (by shipwrecked people or even incidental floating on logs) must be kept separate from wholesale transmission of myths or a complete mythology, which has *not* occurred.

327. See the discussion above. It is to be noted that North America is distinguished from South America by a number of innovations. South American myths often reflect an older stratum (Berezkin 2002) that therefore quite often overlaps with individual Sahul myths; see the discussion in §4.6 (end).

328. Zolbrod 1984.

329. Cf. A. Judge (2007, http://laetusinpraesens.org/docs00s/corresp.php#corr) on correlations and correspondences.

330. Obviously, even the oldest extant attestations can be the outcome of the early influence by certain separate traditions on each other (cf. the case of the hidden sun; §3.5.1), but the risk of running into them is considerably lower if early materials are used. Further advantages in point of time frame can be gained when we take into account the oldest attestation in Stone Age paintings and sculptures (however rarely that will be possible; §4.4, §7).

331. Farmer et al. 2002.

332. Ions 1990: 25 sqq.

333. For multiple layers of Indian stratifications, see, for example, González-Reimann 2002.

334. Excluding, for the moment, the reconstructions of some Paleolithic myths based on rock art.

335. Ions 1990.

336. Hillebrandt 1853/1980–81.

337. For accounts of Chinese mythology, see Birrell 1993; Eberhard 1968; Granet 1988, 1989; Karlgren 1946; Münke 1976; Yang and An 2005. Cf. Barrett 1995; Ting 1978. For Rome, see Puhvel 1987: 39, 146.

338. Radin 1991.

339. Schärer 1946, 1963.

▪ Chapter 3

1. Trans. Brookes (1978).

2. See http://www.maori.org.nz/korero/?d=page&pid=sp37&parent=36. On *kaitiaki*, see Tregear 1891/1969: 454, s.v. *taki-taki* (to chant recite). For other Polynesian creation myths, see Beckwith 1972: 153, 160 sqq.

3. This chapter relies, in part, on an earlier version printed as "Creation Myths" (Witzel 2006). In general, see Campbell 1988; Eliade 1958: 410 sqq., 1992; Ōbayashi 1976; Sproul 1991; Van Over 1980. For various classifications of creation myths (Eliade 1992; Long 1963; Maclagan 1977; Van Over 1980; Weigle 1989), see also Day 1984: 362 sqq.; Leonard and McClure 2004: 33. A complete list of their classifications, quite similar to the one adopted independently above, in §2.2.5 (based on my reading of creation myths), would run as follows:

1. creation ex nihilo, from chaos; emergence, secretion, accretion, or conjunction

2. from primeval abyss or water; primordial deity awakened from abyss/water; primordial deity broods over water (or two creators)

3. life created through thought, sound, sacred word by primordial deity, *deus faber*

4. division or conjugation, dividing a primordial unity, cosmic egg

5. earth diver

6. sacrifice, dismemberment of primordial being or primordial deity

7. emergence myth (from underground)

(Maclagan has a more theoretical ordering: inner and outer; horizontal and vertical; something from nothing; the conjugation of opposites; world order and the order of worlds; descent and ascent; earth body and sacrifice; death, time, and the elements.) As Leonard and McLure (2004: 33) stress, there is a finite number of motifs at work in these overlapping categories. We will see that some of these categories do not apply to original Proto-Laurasian mythology but only to mythologies of later (agricultural) societies and those of the Gondwana area.

4. Kant 1781/1956: 728.

5. For this and other Vedic myths about creation, see Varenne 1982.

6. A collection of 1,028 hymns addressed to the deities that were used during the complicated rituals.

7. Ṛgveda 10.90. For details, see Lincoln 1986.

8. This is found in later versions in the medieval Kashmirian Rājataraṅgiṇī (1150–51 CE) and in neighboring Nuristani myths of northeastern Afghanistan; see §3.1.4.

9. The RV (1.19.7, 2.11.8, 6.30.3) has the concept of an unstable earth that was fixed in place by Indra putting mountains down on her; see §3, n. 89. A very similar idea is found in North America in early 20th-century Winnebago myth and ritual (Radin 1991: 353).

10. See the late Vedic text Chāndogya Upaniṣad 3.8.19. Ṛgveda 10.121: the golden germ. See Bosch 1960.

11. One may certainly speculate that even Afro-Australian mythology originally had a creation myth and that this has been lost. If so, it could have been preserved in some accounts of Afro-Australian mythology. However, there is no trace of any such old Afro-Australian creation myth, as the earth is seen as eternal. Thus, this possibility is very vague at best.

12. According to the numbering of motifs in Stith Thompson's *Motif Index* (1993: Motifs A800–99. The earth; A800–39. Creation of the earth; A810. Primeval water; A820. Other means of creation of earth; A830. Creation of earth by creator; A840. Support of the earth). Cf. Eliade 1992: intro., with a classification similar to the one given above (§2), and that by Witzel (2004a; §1, end); note also Thompson 1993: Motifs A850. Changes in the earth; A870. Nature and condition of the earth.

13. Thompson 1993: Motifs A605.1. Primeval darkness, S. Am. Indian (Guaraní), Hawaii, Africa (Luba); cf. A605.2. Primeval cold, Iceland; A605. Primeval chaos; A115.3. Deity arises from mist, Hawaii; A115.4. Deity emerges from darkness of underworld, Mangia (Cook Is.); A115.6. Deity arises from shell of darkness where he has been for million ages, Tahiti. Primeval darkness also appears with the Tibeto-Burmese-speaking Kham Magar of central Nepal (Oppitz 1991: 24, 27 sqq.), which is, in the Magar view, part of the first of all creation myths, before that of the "blind land" (earth), the stars, primordial catastrophe, and humans.

14. In the Ṛgveda, see Kuiper 1983.

15. Or perhaps (Kuiper 1983) "not yet organized cosmos" versus "organized cosmos"; cf. above, §3, n. 12.

16. Cf. Gargī's question (Bṛhad Āraṇyaka Upaniṣad 3.6): "Since all this world, is woven, warp and woof, on water, on what, then, is the water woven, warp and woof?"

17. Cf. Eliade 1992: 110. Note that the hymn does not speak about "creating" the world, as in Old Iranian (*dā*, "to establish," in Zoroaster's Gāϑās; also in Greek; cf. Vedic Dhātar, an Āditya deity), but about "emanation"; in many other hymns, creation is seen as "birth." The question arises whether the heavy stress on "emanation," later continued with the concept of Prajāpati, the "Lord of creatures," may be due to a pre-Vedic Indian agricultural concept of the birth and death (reconstitution) of a major deity like Prajāpati; cf. §7.2. For the narrative structure "neither...nor," see the parallels in Vǫluspá 19 (below), in the Old High German *Wessobrunn* prayer, and in Greek.

18. For accounts of Chinese mythology, see Birrell 1993; Granet 1988, 1989; Münke 1976; Yang and An 2005; cf. Barrett 1995; Ting 1978.

19. Mathieu 1989: 27. The Huainan zi is an early Taoist text, c. 150 BCE. Or in a more "theistic" version: "When the earth was covered with water, the heavenly Lord sent down one of his subjects to prepare it (for habitation). He descended but found too many obstacles which let him not to succeed. The heavenly Lord sent another one...(who succeeded)" (Matsumoto 1928: 116, from Maspero 1924: 65). Cf. the motif of mishap trials, below and §1.4.1; and in the Bible (bird sent out after the flood).

20. See below, §3.1.6.

21. Translation by Hugh G. Evelyn-White (1977: 86 sq.). Cf. Ṛgveda 10.90.4–5: male *puruṣa* and female *virāj*. Note that the union of Gaia and Ouranos is as close as that in Polynesia between Rangi and Papa and has to be forcibly separated. Early British researchers on Maori myth (such as Grey 1855/1956) noticed many similarities between Greek and Maori myth.

22. Graves 1955: 27. The story continues: "Eurynome and Ophion made their home on Mount Olympos, where he vexed her by claiming to be the author of the Universe. Forthwith she bruised his head with her heel, kicked out his teeth and banished him to the dark caves below the earth. Next the goddess created seven planetary powers, setting a Titaness and a Titan over each....But the first man was Pelasgus, ancestor of all the others whom he taught to make huts and feed upon acorns, and sew pig skin tunics."

23. For a discussion of Germanic myths about creation, see Puhvel 1987: 219.

24. Who was to be dismembered like the Indian *puruṣa*. The following translation is based on those of K. Simrock and H. Kuhn (1966) and S. Nordal (1980).

25. "Bur's sons" refers to the gods, Odin etc.

26. The earth of the human beings, other than Asgard (of the gods) and Muspelheim (the world of the giants).

27. Literally, "Odin's horse"; Odin hung himself in its branches for nine days to get universal wisdom.

28. Urd is one of the three roots of Yggdrasil, the source of fate; also the Norns of the past.

29. For connections between Indian myths and those of Austric and some East Asian populations, see Sergent 1997: 369–96; for a brief linguistic overview, including putative homelands, see van Driem 2006.

30. See Tregear 1891/1969: 391. Note that the Pueblo-area myth of the Zuni Amerindians is quite similar to this, also as regards the separation of Father Heaven and Mother Earth; see Eliade 1992: 130 sqq.

31. Cf. the Bible and Maya myth; but note the old style of the passage.

32. Translation from Sproul 1991: 345, quoting Hare Hongi's "A Maori Cosmology."

33. Io (Tregear 1891/1969: 106) was never mentioned to outsiders and known only to a few initiated. (Note mention by Hare Hongi in 1907; see Eliade 1992: 86; note, however, the attempt by J. Z. Smith [1982: 66–89] to deconstruct the existence of deity before 1907). The primordial god is Io, ancestor of Io-rangi and his son Tawhito-te-raki. However, even this genealogy is not uniform. The Moriori genealogy differs: Tiki –> Uru –> Ngangana –> Io –> Io-rangi. On the similarity of Greek and Maori myths, see George Grey (1855/1956); cf. also Walter and Fridman 2004: 869.

34. Eliade 1992: 14 sqq. This view and the precise nature of Io have recently been discussed and criticized; see Head 2006: 92 sq. However, Io is also found on other Polynesian islands; see Tregear 1891/1969: 106 sq.

35. Interestingly, such myths of primordial creation are absent in Hawaii; see Beckwith 1987: intro.: Coming of the gods. The similarities between Japanese and Polynesians myths were already mentioned by Aston: "Personifications of highly abstract ideas are not unknown in myths of savages. The South Sea Islanders have personified 'the very beginning' and 'space.' Lang's 'Myth, religion and ritual,' I p.196" (1972: 5 n. 3). Cf. Philippi 1990: 92 sq., on the primordial Japanese deities Kamurogi/Kamuromi.

36. *Kumulipo* 1897. For the history and a characterization of the text, see Beckwith 1987: 301 sqq. For this and other Polynesian creation myths, see Beckwith 1972: 153, 160 sqq.

37. *Hawai'i* is the Tahitian and Hawai'ian name for *Sawaiki, the mythical home island of all Polynesians; note the Sava'i Island in Samoa. Note again the importance of speaking "the name" of beings and things—an old Laurasian trait.

38. Seven is surprising in Polynesia; on the "sacred" numbers 7 and 9, see Eliade 1954b: 263–67.

39. Campbell 1988: I.1: 15, taken from Moerenhout 1880: 419–23; translated by Fornander (1969: I: 221–23).

40. Kumulipo (Beckwith 1972: 160), based on J. Orsmond (1822 and before 1848). Cf. the shorter version quoted in Eliade 1992: 87 sq. For other Polynesian versions, see Beckwith 1987: 161–74.

41. Witzel 2005b, http://www.ejvs.laurasianacademy.com/ejvs1201/ejvs1201article.pdf.

42. Eliade 1992: 92 sqq., taken from H. B. Alexander's *Latin American Mythology*. Note that in Winnebago myth, it is mere thought that creates the world; see Eliade 1992: 83 sq.

43. Cf. Leach 1967.

44. In Genesis 2.4, to the end of chapter 3, he is called "Yahweh of the gods." The two accounts differ considerably from each other. On the development of Yahweh (as a single person), see Eliade 1958: 94 sqq.

45. Cf. Vǫluspá 6 etc.

46. Passim, §3.1, 3.2; cf. Philippi 1968: 125 n. 15 on *kotowaza*.

47. The plural *elohīm* is usually explained away as a polite form (or *pluralis maiestatis*) that is said to exist in other Near Eastern texts as well. Akio Tsukimoto has now explained to me that this may also be taken as a *plurale tantum*. Note that wind/spirit (Heb. *ruah*) has the same (expected) identification of breath and wind as seen in Ṛgveda 10.90; it has the same function as that of the air/wind separating heaven and earth in Egyptian myth. Note also the Semitic inversion of verb and subject that is also seen in the initial phrase of Indo-European tales and epics (Homer's "ennepe moi," Sanskrit "asīd rāja," German "es war einmal" in fairy tales).

48. The version by the Jewish Publ. Society is virtually the same; http://www.sacred-texts.com/bib/jps/gen001.htm#001.

49. Cf. http://www.jewishvirtuallibrary.org/jsource/Judaism/premo.html and http://www.sacred-texts.com/wmn/wb/wb03.htm.

50. Sproul 1991: 125 sq., according to the "revised standard version" of the (Christian) Bible, 1952. Sproul also gives a short overview of the well-established three authors of the Hebrew Bible: J the Jehovistic, E the Elohistic, and P, which is the work of one or more persons.

51. Cf. the Vedic texts RV I 19.7, 2.11.8, 6.30.3; Maitrāyaṇī Saṃhitā 1.10.13; Kaṭha Saṃhitā 36.7.

52. Such as Grey (1855/1956).

53. Thompson 1993: Motif A810. Primeval water: In the beginning everything is covered with water.

54. According to Thompson 1993: Finland (Kalevala), Iceland, Ireland.

55. According to Thompson 1993: Siberian, S. Am. Indian (Guarayu), N. A. Indian (Haida), (Calif.), Mixtec, Lat. Am. (Quiché) myth.

56. According to Thompson 1993: Egyptian, Babylonian, Jewish myth.

57. According to Thompson 1993: India and Buddhist myth.

58. According to Thompson 1993: Batak, Minahassa, Borneo, Marquesas, Marshall Is., Oceanic (Maori, Samoa, Society Is., Tonga, Admiralty Is.), Indonesia, Micronesia: Marshall Is., Yap.

59. Eliade 1992: 98, quoted from E. A. Speiser's *Ancient Near Eastern Texts*.

60. Ions 1990.

61. Similar to the early beginnings of the world in the Veda, when the gods first must rise to heaven themselves. (They shut the door after them.)

62. Ions 1990: 22.

63. Claimed by each of the prominent four religious centers, Heliopolis etc., as its own central place; see Ions 1990: 22. The first pyramids (such as the step pyramid at Saqqara, built by Djoser of the IIIrd Dynasty) were in this shape.

64. In the Pyramid texts he is already identified with the sun god Ra. Cf. the name of the Japanese god Omo-daru.no kami, "Face/surface-complete Deity" (Deity perfect exterior); Kojiki 1.2.

65. The primordial hill is found in any Egyptian city; see also Irwin 1982; cf. Kuiper 1983: intro. Atum brought the gods into being by naming the parts of his body: is this like the primordial *puruṣa*/Ymir?

66. Eliade 1992: 96, quoted from A. Piankoff's *The Shrines of Tut-ankh-amon*. Note the trend in Africa of letting the earth be created from the spittle/vomit of the god. This is frequently found in Gondwana myths; cf. the Bushongo (central Luanda) myth: "in the beginning, in the dark, there was nothing but water and Bumba was alone.... He retched on strained and vomited up the sun. After that light spread over everything. The heat of the sun dried up the water until the black edges of the world began to show.... Bumba vomited up the moon and then the stars... and nine living creatures... last of all came men" (Eliade 1992: 91); cf. §2, n. 180; §3, nn. 68, 119, 547. For Africa, see Baumann 1936: 423, s.v. *Menschenerbrechen*, all in the Congo area, and 79 (two women created, Kasai area), 166 (Bushongo), 169, 189 sq., 214, 246 (Kuba), 201 sq. (Kuba: animals). However, the motif is more widespread. In medieval Kashmiri Shivaism, Śiva creates the world by vomiting it; in Old Egypt, it is vomited by Atum (or created by semen put into his mouth); in ancient Tibet (in the Mani bka' 'bum) the future king of Tibet, Sron tsan sgam po, is created from the saliva of the Bodhisattva Avalokiteśvara (Rockhill 1891: 360 n. 1). Note also birth from the mouth of a snake with the Maya; see Freidel et al. 1993. As the myth is fairly strongly represented in Africa, Egypt, and India, it may belong to a very old stratum, maybe of Gondwana age (cf. §2, n. 180; §3, nn. 68, 119, 547).

67. Cf. Izanami and Izanagi's creation of the Japanese islands.

68. Memphis version, c. 2700 BCE? In a copy of c. 700 BCE, Ptah, the locally highest god, creates by conceiving the elements of the universe in his mind ("heart") and brings them into being by his speech ("tongue"). One of his forms was Ta-tenen, "the land arising" (out of the primordial waters) and also "lord of the years." Spitting out is seen with Izanagi and Amaterasu; see Thompson 1993: Motif A618.2. Universe created by spitting, Melanesia: Wheeler 66; cf. creation by vomiting (India: Śiva); A700.2. Heavenly bodies vomited up by creator, Bushongo. Cf. §2, n. 180; §3, nn. 66, 119, 547.

69. For possible connections between Indian myths and those of Austric and some East Asian populations, see Sergent 1997: 369–96.

70. Matsumoto 1928: 116, from M. H. Maspero's "Légendes mythologiques dans le Chou King" (1924: 65).

71. Findeisen 1970: 18.

72. Findeisen 1970: 18. The idea is reflected in the wagtail dress of Ō-Kuni-nushi.no Kami (Kojiki 1.30; cf. Philippi 1968: 125 n. 15).

73. The same idea is found with the assimilated Ainu of Tsugaru (Mt. Iwaki and Mt. Akakura); see Walter and Fridman 2004: 700. This is similar to Japanese ideas; note the descent of Amaterasu's grandson Ninigi to Mt. Katachihō in Kyūshū (Kojiki I 38 sqq.).

74. Following S. Tanaka, in Walter and Fridman 2004: 858.

75. Cf. Hesiod's four–five creations (Kirk 1970: 226 sqq.), the famous Four Ages, from golden to iron, plus that of the heroes (after the Bronze Age). For this number, in a pentadic scheme, see Allen 2000.

76. Soisson and Soisson 1987: 97 (*cosmogonie*).

77. Eliade 1992: 93, quoted from Alexander's *Latin American Mythology*.

78. Bierhorst 1986.

79. Eliade 1992: 84, quoted from Fletcher and La Fleche's "The Omaha Tribe."

80. Eliade 1992: 88, quoted from Roland B. Dixon's "Maidu Myths."

81. Lehmann-Nitsche 1939: 115.

82. Note however, that Thompson's (1993) Motif A810 (Primeval water: In the beginning everything is covered with water) is also found in Australia and in Africa: creation from primordial water is thus occasionally found in Gondwana areas, according to Thompson, with

the Central African Bushongo, and the Australian Arunta; cf. also Dundes 1988: 241 sqq. (biblical influence). For Africa, see Baumann 1936: 189 sqq. (mostly in West Africa and Kuba in Congo), further 433, s.v. *Urwasser/Urmeer*. For each of the African cases, it must be investigated whether its existence is due to northern (Sahel) or northeastern African influence (see §5.3.5.2–3) or not. Such intrusive cases are discussed in general terms in §5.6.2.

83. Thompson 1993: Motifs A800–39. Creation of the earth; A810. Primeval water; A811. Earth brought up from bottom of primeval water (cf. A812), India.—New Britain, New Hebrides; see http://www.sacred-texts.com/pac/om/index.htm. As the mytheme belongs to non-Laurasian myths, the New Britain version must be investigated separately. Thompson (1993), however, indicates that it is only found close to Polynesian and Micronesian areas.

84. An aberrant version combines this myth with that of the primordial egg; see Thompson 1993: Motifs A812.2. Earth from egg from bottom of sea recovered by bird, Borneo; A814.9. Earth from egg breaking on primeval water (cf. A1222), India; A701.1. Origin of sky from egg brought from primeval water.

85. Paippalāda Atharvaveda 6.7.2–3; Kaṭha Saṃhitā 8.2; see Witzel 2004a.

86. The same idea is also found elsewhere in Laurasia, for example, among the contemporary Hopi, who believe that after the "re-creation" of the earth at Winter solstice, the ground is still soft and has to be firmed up by the buffalo dances held in January.

87. Witzel 2004a.

88. Emuṣa myth; see Kuiper 1950, 1991; Witzel 1999a. According to R. Villems's "Genetics and Mythology—An Unexplored Field" (2005), the diver myth is also found in Australia, based on materials provided by Yuri Berezkin. However, the myth is actually missing in Australia according to Y. Berezkin's paper given a few years ago at Tartu: "Dwarfs and Cranes" (see 2007). Like other exceptional attestations outside the Laurasian area, this myth is in urgent need of further investigation. It may turn out to be an old, Pan-Gaean myth.

89. The mountains were fixed by Indra (Ṛgveda I 19.7, 2.11.8, 6.30.3); their wings were cut off: Maitrāyaṇī Saṃhitā 1.10.13; Kaṭha Saṃhitā 36.7.

90. A common version; see Thompson 1993: Motifs A1185. Wings cut from flying mountains. In beginning mountains have wings. They are cut off by thunderbolt, India; A964.2; A1185. Wings cut from flying mountains; A1142.4. Origin of thunder clouds: from wings of mountains, India; cf. also A1125. Winds caused by flapping wings. A giant bird causes the wind with his wings. The wings are cut by the culture hero so that the bird cannot flap so hard.

91. Cf. below, similar features in the Gondwana myth of the Semang in Malaya, about Batu-Ribn.

92. Radin 1991: 55 sq., 253 sq.

93. Thompson 1993: Motifs A813. Raft in primeval sea. Creator is on the raft and there creates the earth (cf. A812), India; Sumatra (also Siberia); A813.1. Earth in form of raft supported by spirits, S. Am. Indian (Yuracare); A813.2. Lotus-leaf raft in primeval sea, India. See the Amerindian Maidu myth above, §3, n. 80.

94. Findeisen 1970: 17.

95. Eliade 1992: 84.

96. In local Izumo tales; see Aoki 1997; cf. also Kojiki 1.30.

97. Feddersen 1881: 360.

98. Witzel 1984b: n. 103.

99. Witzel 1984b.

100. As in the case of the emergence from primordial water, there are occasional reflections of the Laurasian pattern in Gondwana territory (see §5.6.2): such as in the Andamans (Campbell 1988: I.1: 121), where a bamboo came floating on primeval water (which recalls the Hirugo myth of Japan). As there was Continental influence on the Andamans around 3000 BP (§3.3.1), the question may be moot. The African idea of the dark and empty primeval world differs (Baumann 1936: 190 sq.; see rather, §§5–6). There also is a deviating form of the diver myth in Australia (Villems 2005). Again, all such cases need detailed investigation.

101. See Aston 1972: 33 n. 2; Mathieu 1989. Recently a Chinese version of a continuous creation myth has been published: *The Story of Darkness*, compiled by Hu Chongjun (2002; cf. *China Daily*, April 3, 2002, 9). This looks like an artificial compilation, intent to provide China with a "creation myth," rather than a genuine tradition. On oldest Chinese myth, cf. David Hawkes, quoted in Barrett 1995: 72 sq.: "to arrive at some archetypal Ur-myth is a waste of time. The Eocene Age of myth is unknowable... as we work backwards... we find an even greater number of groups and... diversity." However, for methods to address this welcome diversity, see above, §2.3; and cf. Birrell 1993: 18, 22, for reconstructing older forms of Chinese myths. For major sources of Chinese myth, see Yang and An 2005: 4 sqq.

102. Jacobsen 1976: 181.

103. Cf. the discussion by Baumann (1986: 144 sqq.).

104. For the translation, see above, §3, n. 23. Linguistically, Ymir = Ved. Yama, the brother of Manu, ancestor of all humans; see below, §3, n. 109. Thompson 1993: Motifs A961.4. Mountains spring from scattered parts of slain giant serpent's body, India; A961.5. Mountains (cliffs) from bones of killed giant, Iceland.

105. For the description of the "canonical creature" visible in this myth, in sorcery (Merseburg sorcery stanzas, Atharvaveda, etc.) and also elsewhere, see Watkins 1995. For the Indo-European narrative structure of these sorcery stanzas, see Thieme 1971: 202–12: a mythological narration or poem is followed by the actual spell; Witzel 1987c.

106. Nine is the typical North Asian shamanic number, though some have compared Odin's self-offer with that of Christ, which was well known in Iceland by then (1170s CE).

107. For other Indo-European parallels (Russian, Greek, etc.), see Lincoln 1986: 1 sqq.

108. Thompson 1993: Motifs A642.1. Primeval woman cut in pieces: houses, etc., made from her body, India; A1724.1; A1724.1. Animals from body of slain person, India; however, note A969.1. Mountain from buried giant, India; A1716.1. In Kashmir, a giant Rākṣasa demon was killed, and an embankment was built from his remnants on the Vitastā River (*setu*, the modern Suth at Srinagar), using his leg and knee (see Rājataraṅgiṇī 3.336–58, cf. 1.159, Yakṣa dikes); cf. also the similar Nurustani myths and the initial section of the Finnish Kalevala (Witzel 2004a).

109. See Dumézil 1995: 289 sqq.; Puhvel 1987: 287–89.

110. The contest between the Japanese divine brothers Ho-wori and Ho-deri, farmer and fisher (Kojiki 1.42), does not have a lethal outcome. Philippi (1968: 148) compares the tale to others in Indonesia, the Marshall Islands, and the American Pacific Northwest.

111. Mathieu 1989.

112. See Münke 1976: 254 sq.; Yang and An 2005: 75, 176 sqq.

113. See another translation of a similar text dating from the third century CE, taken from San wu li chi (Sanwu Liji [Three kings and five emperors]) by Hsü Chen (Xu Zhen), in Mair 1998b: 14; cf. Yang and An 2005: 65.

114. Note the concept: four real oceans, situated in the four cardinal directions, were of course not known at the time of the composition of this myth. Cf. the "eastern, western, and *northern* sea" in landlocked Vedic India.

115. Sproul 1991: 201–2; for a similar text by Hsü Cheng, *Wu yün li-nien chi* (A chronicle of five cycles of time), see Mair 1998b: 15. Cf. also Mathieu 1989, with similar versions from the Yiwen leiju and Yishi, both referring back to the Sanwu Liji (San wu li chi) of the third century BCE. Note that Pangu's left eye became the sun, and his right eye, the moon. In Japan, too, the sun deity originated from the left eye of Izanagi; cf. Naumann 1988: 65.

116. Thompson 1993: Motif A1716.1. Animals from different parts of body of slain giant. Giant person, cow, ox, etc., Borneo, Philippines: Dixon 177.

117. Cf. in the Veda, Mātariśvan "swelling in the mother," a secret name of the Fire deity Agni. Note that Agni is born three times: in heaven, on earth (in ritual), and in the waters; Ṛgveda 3.20.11, 10.45.1 (sometimes also as *garbho rodasyoḥ*, "in the earth"). There are several fire gods in Japan as well: the one mentioned above and then several others born from the decaying body of Izanami. The first fire god is killed by Izanagi in revenge for burning her (cf. Agni's repeated death, explained as he burns up in ritual). Izanami's burning and subsequent death could then reflect the ritual production of fire by drilling it (as still done at important Shintō and Vedic rituals).

118. This is somewhat reminiscent, as Japanese mythologists have pointed out, of the myth of Hainuwele, "Coconut branch" (Ceram, New Guinea); cf. Eliade 1992: 18, studied in detail by Jensen (1948: 113 sq., 1979: no. 11 sqq.). Hainuwele had grown from a coconut tree, furthered by the blood from the wound of a man, and quickly grew into a woman; she was killed by local people during the great *maro* festival (cf. Campbell 1989: II.1: 70 sqq.) and buried in pieces; from her several graves grew various plants, especially tubers. Her arms were made into a gate: all men who could pass through it remained human; those who could not became various animals or spirits.

119. Cf. the case of the Japanese food deity Ōgetsu; Kojiki 1.18, with Philippi's (1968) additional n. 11. Note further that the body hairs of Susa.no Wo became various kinds of trees (Nihon Shoki 1.57–58). For creation from vomiting, see §2, n. 180; §3, nn. 66, 68, 547; and Egyptian and Indian Śiva myths (with the pseudo-etymology, mythologically grounded, of *bhi*, "to fear," + *ru*, "to shout," + *vam*, "to vomit" –> Bhairava = god Śiva). Cf. also Thompson 1993: Motif A700.2. Heavenly bodies vomited up by creator. See also §2, n. 180; §3, nn. 66, 68, on Egyptian, medieval Kashmiri, Tibetan, and Bushongo (Africa) myths. The motif of birth from a snake's mouth is prominent in Maya mythology; see Freidel et al. 1993: 219.

120. Colarusso 2006: 32; Gurney 1976: 192; Haas 1982; Puhvel 1987: 25 sq.

121. See Thompson 1993: Motif A644. Universe from pre-existing rocks. Originally rocks are assumed, and everything is made from them, Samoa: Dixon 17.

122. Personal observation, February 1990. On the other side if the valley there is another rock, with a vulva-like cavity, representing Izanami.

123. Chang 1983: 10; and Bodde 1961: 399.

124. Chang 1983: 10. Note the role of the bear as ancestor in Korean myth, at a mythical time of c. 2500 BCE, in Samguk Yusa.

125. There even is a slight chance that the myth may already have been a Neanderthal one (if they had speech): bear offerings, head separated, are widely found (Campbell 1988: I.1: 54 sqq.); also, a Stone Age bear figure with head attached has been found at Montespan (Campbell 1988: I.1: 62), as well as a bear skull on an "altar" in the undisturbed Chauvet Cave, dated at 32,000 BP (see §4, n. 425; §7, n. 193).

126. See the pictorial evidence in Campbell 1988: I.2: 152 sqq.; cf. Ōbayashi and Klaproth 1966 for Sakhalin.

127. For the Vedic customs, see Witzel 1987a; cf. Thor's ram, whose body is reconstituted from its bones, and similarly the role of *astuuant* (bone having [life]) in Zoroastrian

texts (Avesta). Note also the Achaemenid-period rebirth of humans from their graves in the Hebrew Bible (Daniel 12.2); see further Thompson 1993: Motifs A1724.1. Animals from body of slain person, India; A2001. Insects from body of slain monster; A2611.3. Coconut tree from head of slain monster; E610. Reincarnation as animal; E613.0.5. Severed heads of monster become birds.

128. Thompson 1993: Motifs A642. Universe from body of slain giant. Ymir; see A621.1. Iceland; A831.2. Earth from giant's body (Ymir [cf. A614.1]), Iceland, India.

129. However, they also do not represent archaic agricultural/horticultural mythology, such as seen in the Melanesian Hainuwele myth; see Hatt 1951; Jensen 1968; cf. Lincoln 1986: 173 n. 1.

130. Lincoln 1986: 39 sqq.; Dionysus of Halicarnassus, Empedocles, Herodotos 1.131 (Iran). See Thompson 1993: Motif A1716.1. Animals from different parts of body of slain giant. Giant person, cow, ox, etc., Persian, Borneo, Philippines.

131. Thompson 1993: Motifs A1791. Giant ox ancestor of all animals, Persian; B871.1.1. Giant ox. For Old Iran, see Bundhishn III.13 and XIV.1, detailing the origin of plants and animals from the bull's remains.

132. Ṛgveda 3.38 (a hymn later assigned to Indra): the androgynous "older bull" (*vṛṣabha*) Asura, the "great hoary" bull, gives birth to or creates the world; he is in part identified with Heaven and Earth (Rodasī); the (younger) bull, Heaven/Sun, is also called Asura Viśvarūpa; cf. Witzel 2004a. Heaven and Earth can also be called bull and cow; Ṛgveda 1.160.3. For post-Ṛgvedic versions of the mytheme, see Lincoln 1986: 65 sqq., esp. 73, 86. Further, on Mesopotamia and India, see Hiltebeitel 1980.

133. For connections between Indian myths and those of Austric and some East Asian populations, see Sergent 1997: 369–96.

134. Lincoln 1986.

135. Raffetta 2002, referring to the Indian Yama–Manu, the Germanic Ymir/Tuisto–Mannus, and the Roman Romulus–Remus, the latter by assimilation from the Proto-Indo-European *Yemos.

136. Lincoln 1986: 2, 66 sq., 86, following the summary by Paola Raffetta of her 2002 paper, http://www.svabhinava.org/friends/PaolaRaffetta/CreationDomesticAnimals-frame.html.

137. Brighenti 2003.

138. Cf. Witzel 2004a. For post-Ṛgvedic versions of the mytheme, see Lincoln 1986: 65 sqq. (see §4, n. 464, 281; §6, n. 3; §7, 157) and esp. 73, 86.

139. Baumann (1986: 361) sees the egg that is divided into two parts as creating the male and female part of the universe; cf. Gimbutas 1991: 213 sqq., with illustrations.

140. In the Kujiki, "Of old, the original essence was a chaotic mass. Heaven and Earth had not yet been separated, but were *like an egg*, of ill-defined limits, and containing germs. Thereafter, the pure essence, ascending by degrees, became thinly spread out, and formed Heaven" (Aston 1972: 2 n. 1).

141. Cosmology cannot be discussed here in detail. Suffice it to say that in many, if not most, mythologies the earth is flat and a vaulted sky arches over it; the world is surrounded by a mythical ocean that often is thought to exist above the sky and below the earth as well. The deities live in the sky or, rather, on top of it, where eternal light exists (beyond the sky as well as below the earth). The sun rises from the eastern ocean (or a cave nearby) and sets in the western ocean, from where it moves back to the east below the earth. Depending on the mythology involved, there are several layers of heaven, sometimes also of the netherworld. The deceased move to the other world, the sky, or the netherworld or in some

mythologies, horizontally, beyond the western ocean. Sometimes the world of the ancestors is moving, along with the Milky Way, to the top of the sky at night (Witzel 1984b). Note also the aberrant stories: see Thompson 1993: Motifs A812.2. Earth from egg from bottom of sea recovered by bird, Borneo; A814.9. Earth from egg breaking on primeval water [cf. A1222], India; A701.1. Origin of sky from egg brought from primeval water. For the oldest map of the world from Mesopotamia, see Horowitz 1988; http://en.wikipedia.org/wiki/Ancient_world_maps#Babylonian_world_.

142. Thompson 1993: Motif A701.1. Origin of sky from egg brought from primeval water.

143. Baumann 1986: 361, on the egg and the male and female part of the universe; see §3, n. 139.

144. Cf. the discussion by Baumann (1986: 143 sqq.).

145. See Hoffmann 1992.

146. Sproul 1991: 184 sqq.

147. Bosch 1960.

148. Ions 1990.

149. Yang and An 2005: 65.

150. Oppitz and Hsu 1998: 318: from a white egg a white chicken is born, and from it, nine pairs of white eggs that give birth to the major deities; this is paralleled by a black egg (etc.) that results in demons.

151. Thompson 1993: Motifs A641. Cosmic egg; A701.1. Origin of sky from egg brought from primeval water; A641. Cosmic egg. The universe brought forth from an egg, Finnish, Estonian, Hindu, Society Is., Hawaiian, Maori; A641.1. Heaven and earth from egg. They are the two halves of an egg shell. Eros escapes as they are separated, Greek, Indonesian; A641.2. Creation from duck's eggs. Upper vault from half shell, lower vault from half shell, moonbeams from whites, sunshine from yellows, starlight from motley parts, clouds from dark parts, Finnish; A655. World as egg. By exception, the motif is even found in Africa; this is in need of a special investigation. See Baumann 1936: 191 sqq.; Frobenius 1978: 119. The same qualifications as in §3.2, 3.4, apply.

152. Thompson 1993: Motif A812.2. Earth from egg from bottom of sea recovered by bird, Borneo.

153. Thompson 1993: Motifs A1222. Mankind originates from eggs, Chinese, India, Oceanic (Fiji, Torres Straits, Admiralty Is.), Indonesia, Micronesia, Sumatra, Indonesia, Marquesas, S. Am. Indian (Jivaro, Mbaya); A1261.2. Man created from egg formed from seafoam, Minahassa (Celebes). The belief is also found in contemporary Thailand.

154. In Santal myth the first humans developed from two eggs laid by a goose made of grass (Orans 1965: 5) or were created by the primordial deities (Otē Borām and Sing Bonga), put in a cave, and made drunk on rice beer to have sex and produce children (Hastings 1922–28: s.v. *Mūṇḍās* §4, Dravidians [North India], §38). On the egg from which humans develop, cf. Baumann 1986: 361 sqq., 365 sq. We can also link the Vedic Indian Mārtāṇḍa myth (Hoffmann 1992), though here it is the sun god who gets born as a round egg that then has to be shaped; however, the sun is the ancestor of the Vedic Indians.

155. From E. W. Lai, personal communication, February 29, 2004. The myth of brother/sister incest (usually without the egg motif) is widely spread in Yunnan, Taiwan, the Philippines, etc. For possible connections between Indian myths and those of Austric and some East Asian populations, see Sergent 1997: 369–96.

156. Leonard and McClure 2004: 147 sqq.

157. Beckwith 2004; Chang 1983: 10.

158. Thompson 1993: Motifs A27. Creator born from egg, Chinese; A114.2. God born from egg; A114.2. God born from egg, Tahiti, Marquesas; So. Am. Indian (Huamachuco); A114.2.1. Deity born in shape of egg, Hawaii. Cf. also the Indo-Iranian myth of the sun deity Vivasvant, who was born from a "dead egg" (Mārtāṇḍa; Hoffmann 1992) and who became the ancestor both of the lord of the other/netherworld, Yama, and of humans, Manu; cf. further Thompson 1993: Motifs A511.1.9. Culture hero born from egg, S. Am. Indian (Jivaro, Huamachuco, North Peru); A1222. Mankind originates from eggs.

159. Farmer et al. 2002.

160. The egg myth may be derived from or a variant of the myth of the killing and dissection of the primordial giant/mammal. Hunters could easily observe eggs contained inside killed birds and the various stages of bird embryos in the eggs. Such myths would then be remnants of older, Pan-Gaean ones.

161. Berezkin 2002; Villems 2005.

162. Collected in the 19th century by Lönrod from older, medieval oral traditions; see Fromm and Fromm 1985, and for the motifs, see their commentary, 387 sqq.

163. In Columbia and Ecuador, based on notes taken by the Spanish *conquistadores*; see Lehmann-Nitsche 1939: 115.

164. Sherbondy 1982: 32.

165. Witzel 1984b.

166. Jongewaard 1986.

167. See Eliade 1960: 182 sqq.; Herbert 1977; Ōbayashi 1975, 1977, 1991c.

168. Such as, early on, Motowori Noringa and Hirata Atsutane; cf. Herbert 1977: 27. But even the latest English translation by Philippi cites "products of literati familiar with Chinese culture" (1968: 397). He has native Japanese mythology begin only with Izanagi/Izanami. However, in comparison with other mythological regions, it appears that only some of the wording, such as *Yin/Yang* (*In/Yō*), has clearly been influenced by Chinese expressions and models of writing (after all, the Nihon Shoki was written in Chinese, as an official history of the realm). The multiplicity of the versions of primordial creation (such as creation out of the void, creation by Izanami and Izanagi by churning the ocean with a spear), again, is partly seen as Chinese influence, versus older Japanese concepts.

169. See Matsumura 2006b.

170. In addition, a few ancient local accounts (Fudoki) have come down to us, those of the old provinces of Hitachi, Izumo, Harima, Bungo, and Hizen; see Aoki 1997.

171. As, for example, in Indian mythology that can be followed from c. 1000 BCE onward; or in Polynesian mythology, as could be seen above, §3.1; or on a contemporary basis, with the Ok tribes in Papua New Guinea (Barth 1987).

172. See McCaskill 1987: 149 sqq.

173. Is there some Chinese influence? Cf. "Then breaths were born from space and time. What was light moved and formed the sky (easily); what was heavy, the earth" (Huainan zi); see above, §3.1.1. Cf. Naumann 1988: 58.

174. Note the story of Hirugo, the first child of Izanagi and Izanami who was set out floating about on reeds; see Kojiki I 4.

175. Translation by Aston (1972). The floating earth and the "reed shoots" have found many explanations. Hirata Atsutane thought of light that later became the sun, which rises from a cloud (cf. one of the Nihon Shoki variants); the new floating "earth" is Ama.tsu Kuni or Takama-hara. Cf. Norinaga, Kojiki-den (Wehmeyer 1997). Or a descending object that later separates from this and becomes the moon; cf. Herbert 1977: 28; note that in this version Heaven and Earth seem to exist before or at the same time as the birth of the first gods.

176. See Herbert 1977: 27, according to information provided by Harada Ken, then master of ceremonies at the Imperial Palace.

177. According to Uchida M., a Shintō priest (*gūji*) of Kōchi, in Herbert 1977.

178. Philippi (1990: 72, 92–93) translates Kamurogi (*Kaburogi*) and *Kamuromi* as "ancestral gods and goddesses" (*ro* is improbably regarded as a "word-building particle" without independent meaning). Next to Kamurogi/Kamuromi (or even Izanagi/Izanami), there are other candidates such as the mysterious Ame-yuzuru-hi-ame.no sa-giri-kuni-yuz-uru-tsuki kuni.no sa-giri.no mikoto or the shadowy god variously named Toyo-kumo-nu.no kami, Toyo-kumu-nu, or Toyo-kuni-nushi.no kami. Kamurogi/Kamuromi are also worshipped in the *ōharae* (expiation and cleansing) ceremony at Ise etc.; see Philippi 1990; further details in Havens and Inoue 2001: 10.

179. Cf. above, §1, n. 88; §3, n. 33 sq.

180. See §3, n. 179; Eliade 1992: 115.

181. Cf. Philippi (1968: 397 sq.), who regards these first generations as typical of Polynesian myths, as also noted by Matsumoto (1956: 181); otherwise, Philippi sees Chinese influence and lets Japanese mythology only begin with Izanami.

182. Cf. the discussion of nonsexual and then male–female deities by Baumann (1986: 130 sqq., 377). The Dayaks have a primordial being whose gender is ambivalent (Schärer 1946, 1963); heaven and earth are symbolized by male and female birds or a bird (male) and a snake (female) as "two aspects of the world tree." For the Maya, cf. Campbell 1988: I.2: 41, ill. 78.

183. Eliade (1960: 182 sqq.) sees eight stages: chaos; germ; brother/sister deities; marriage of deities of heaven/earth and separation of heaven and earth; sexual union and creation of the world; death of the earth mother and birth of the fire god; birth of various vegetative deities from the sacrifice of the fire deity; and creation of sun/moon/storm deities by the Sky Father, who then disappears. Cf. Ōbayashi 1975.

184. See Witzel 2004a; and note the discussion of the dragon, §3.5.2.

185. The same holds also for genetics.

186. As in historical linguistics, comparisons are made more probable by using isolated, *unmotivated* similarities (*bizarreries*), usually remnants of an older, now lost part of the Indo-European system; see §2.1 (end).

187. See, for example, Dixon 1916: 105: "Apparently one of the clearest characteristics of the mythology of the Melanesian area is the almost total lack of myths relating to the origin of the world. With one or two exceptions, the earth seems to be regarded as having always existed in very much the same form as today." Or, for Central Africa, H. Hochegger sums up: "Congolese creation myths *do not seek to explain*, for example, *the creation of heaven and earth* (cosmology). Nor do they tell us about how man and woman were made. *The focus* of mythological interest is on *the concrete questions of human life....* What, in the end, is creation? ... [I]t is simply the beginning of the concrete situation that continues into the present. There is *hardly any notion here of an ancient source* of all things, placed *at the beginning* of a long history understood in linear fashion" (2005; my italics). See below, §5, nn. 38, 312, cf. nn. 37 sq., 310.

188. At Laussel in southern France, where a pair in coitus is shown; see Campbell 1988: I.1: 180, as well as the same image in Dogon Land in West Africa (Frobenius 1998: 156). See discussion in §4.4.1 and §7.1. For the worldwide spread of the binary male/female distinction in myth, cf. Baumann 1986: 192, 345 sqq.: it involves both Gondwana and Laurasian mythologies.

189. In Mangaia it is Ru, the supporter of heaven, who raised him. Heaven is a solid arch of blue stones (for which cf. the Iranian and Vedic concept of a "stone heaven"). Maui threw

Ru into heaven, where he rotted; his bones then came down as stones. Heaven (Rangi), like Earth (Papa), has ten levels, while the typical "shamanic" number in North Asia (and the early Veda) is nine.

190. Tregear 1891/1969: 391 sq.

191. Ṛgveda 1.89.4, 6.51.5, etc.; in the early post-Ṛgvedic Ṛgveda Khila 5.5.5; AV-Paippalāda 5.21.1.

192. See Dunkel 1988–90.

193. See Eliade 1992: 55.

194. The otherwise isolated Vedic mytheme *rodasī* (heaven and earth) may well be based on *rud* (to cry), if we take into account the Polynesian (Maori) version of the separation of Father Heaven and Mother Earth by the *toko* (pole).

195. Cf. the discussion by Baumann (1986: 143 sqq.).

196. See Heissig 1980: 47 sqq. (Father Heaven and Mother Earth).

197. Guillemoz 1983: 192 sqq., 197.

198. See discussion by Puett (2002: 48 sqq.).

199. Huainan zi, in Mathieu 1989: 27.

200. The female sun is called "daytime moon" (*tōno chuh*), and the moon is "dark moon" (*kunne chuh*). They are aspects of the *same* female deity, who is called *chuh kamuy* (cf. Jpn. *kami*, "deity"), who "possesses the sky." She is worshipped twice per year in a special ritual; her main role is that of mediator with other deities (Ohnuki-Thierney 1974: 103). This remarkably non-Laurasian concept and other aspects of Ainu myth need more detailed study to discover similarities, if any, with Gondwana myths.

201. For example, with the Dayak of Borneo (Baumann 1986: 130; Schärer 1946), with Mahatara (Heaven) and Djata/Putir (Earth), who are also represented by a male hornbill bird and a female water serpent who form a unit but also are in periodic competition. Cf. also Baumann 1986: 252 sq.; §2, n. 115; §6, n. 17.

202. See http://www.maori.org.nz/korero/?d=page&pid=sp37&parent=36. It continues: "At length the offspring of Ranginui and Papatuanuku, worn out with continual darkness, met together to decide what should be done about their parents that man might arise. 'Shall we kill our parents, shall we slay them, our father and our mother, or shall we separate them?' they asked. And long did they consider in the darkness....

"And long did they consider further. At the end of a time no man can measure they decided that Ranginui and Papatuanuku must be forced apart, and they began by turns to attempt this deed....

"So then it became the turn of Tanemahuta. Slowly, slowly as the kauri tree did Tanemahuta rise between the Earth and Sky. At first he strove with his arms to move them, but with no success. And so he paused, and the pause was an immense period of time. Then he placed his shoulders against the Earth, his mother, and his feet against the Sky. Soon, and yet not soon, for the time was vast, the Sky and Earth began to yield.

"The parents of the children cried out and asked them, '*why are you doing this crime, why do you wish to slay your parents' love?*'

"Great Tanemahuta thrust with all his strength, which was the strength of growth. Far beneath him he pressed the Earth. Far above he thrust the Sky, and held him there. The sinews that bound them were stretched, taunt. Tumatauenga sprang up and slashed at the bonds that bound his parents and the blood spilt red on the earth. Today this is the *kokowai*, the sacred red earth that was created when the first blood was spilt at the dawn of time. As soon as Tanemahuta work was finished the multitude of creatures were uncovered whom Ranginui and Papatuanuku had begotten, and who had never known light."

203. Sumerian An, his wife, is the earth, Ki; see Jacobsen 1976: 95; Kramer 1963: 118, 285.

204. For a political analysis of the Sumerian version of this myth, see Jacobsen 1976: 184.

205. Kuiper 1983; Witzel 1984b.

206. See §3, nn. 66, 547, on Bushongo myth. However, note that the animal faces of many deities may just represent their qualities. They are representations of the *character*, *power, etc.* of the gods (Ions 1990), as a sort of visual representation of what the Vedic poets use in similes, and metaphors, such as Indra = bull.

207. To be dealt with below: §3.6 and §2.5.2, on the Four/Five Ages.

208. Cf. the Vedic myth of the blemishes of the sun and of Apālā.

209. Soisson and Soisson 1987: 97 sqq.

210. Cf. the Hittite myth of Upelluri and Ullikummi and the Japanese Izanagi/Izanami stone worship at Shingu, Kii Peninsula, Japan; see §3, n. 122.

211. "And she has left us a token in all the temples...in the form of dances and songs" (Eliade 1992: 16, quoting Paul Radin's *Monotheism among Primitive Peoples*).

212. Cf. Goodchild 1991: 104. Another form of "(Father) Heaven" is well known under the name Manitou, though this term includes many other aspects, somewhat like the Japanese *kami*: among Algonkin-speaking people the spirits are led by the great Manitou (Kitchi-manitou). Other Amerindians use different terms. Note the origin of humans from stone in Taiwan, Melanesia, etc.

213. See §1, n. 88; §3, nn. 35, 178.

214. See http://www.maori.org.nz/korero/; Eliade 1992.

215. Baumann (1936: 174 sqq., cf. 243 sq.) explains the isolated pockets of the myth of the world parents as motifs brought from the Sahel north; in the area south of the Niger bend to the Guinea coast, in eastern Nigeria; from the Lower Niger area (Yoruba, Edo, Mossi, Baule) northward toward Lake Chad; and similarly by import from these areas to a small pocket near the mouth of the Congo as well as another small pocket near the Upper Zambezi (Luyi/Rotse). He regards another area stretching from the east coast of Lake Victoria toward southern Ethiopia as exhibiting influence from Indian trade relations. (However, Sudanic/ Nilotic influence may be tested.)

216. Baumann (1986: 345 sqq.) sees this development as late. He rather stresses the "antagonism" between the two sexes. Baumann (1986: 361) sees the myth of the egg that is divided into two parts as creating the male and female parts of the universe; cf. Gimbutas 1991: 213 sqq., with illustrations.

217. Most prominent in Papua societies (Baumann 1986: 347); see also §5.3.3.

218. For the Toradja of Sulawesi, see Koubi 1982: 24. For Kédang Lembata/Lomblen, an island east of Flores, see Barnes 1974: 109: at first "the sky was close" to the earth, in inces- tual condition, "when the earth was new"; they were separated for an unknown reason. Formerly access to the sky was possible via the banyan tree, now seen in the moon.

219. It may stand in for the penis of Heaven that was severed from Earth upon their separation.

220. The Milky Way is also seen as a rainbow snake, an old motif found in Africa, India (Munda), and Australia.

221. Lesky 1950: 137–36. Cf. also Tièche 1945: 67 sqq.

222. Hesiod, *Theogony* 507 sqq. Apparently he also rises from the primordial ocean (Homer, *Odyssey* 1.52 sqq.).

223. See Mathieu 1989.

224. For the full myth, see http://www.maori.org.nz/korero/?d=page&pid=sp37&pare
nt=36 and the various publications by G. Grey (1855/1956), in English and in the original
Maori.

225. The Hawai'ian version is given by P. Colum (1937); see Leonard and McClure
2004: 286–89. Interestingly, before lifting up the sky, Tanemahuta is strengthened by a
certain drink, just as Indra is by the soma drink before he can slay the dragon.

226. Ponette 1968: 13. Note also the appearance in other southern traditions: see the
map in Berezkin 2007; and note Thompson 1993: Motif A665.6. Serpent supports sky, S.
Am. (Yuracare). It is also found in Africa, the Andamans, Australia, etc. For southern
Australia, see Smith 1996: 22, 182. For Africa, see Baumann 1936: 77 (Kanioka), 116 (Uelle
Pygmies), 197 (Kikuyu), 212 sq. (Ewe), 218 sq. (Hausa), 324; cf. Zuesse 1979: 45 for the
Pygmies. See further Berezkin 2007; Campbell 1988: I.2: 141; Nikonov 1980. The motif
likely is very old, of Pan-Gaean origin.

227. Thompson 1993: Motifs A652. World-tree. Tree extending from lowest to highest
world (cf. A878), Irish, Norse, Babylonian, N. A. Indian; A665.4. Tree supports sky; A665.4
(cf. A652.1; F54. Tree to upper world; A665.4); A878. Earth-tree; D950 Magic tree; E90.
Tree of life; F162.3.1. Tree of Life in otherworld; details: A652.3. Tree in upper world,
Iroquois; A652.4. Sky as overshadowing tree. Shadowing the earth, Egyptian; A714.2. Sun
and moon placed in top of tree. Hero makes the sun and moon and fastens them to the top of
the "World Tree" (cf. A652), but they give no light at first, Finnish; D1576.1. Magic song
causes tree to rise to sky. Has moon and Great Bear in its branches. Note also the motif of the
tree rising from the navel of the Virgin Mary; see Campbell 1989: II.1: cover; and cf. the
Zoroastrian world tree *vīspō.biš* in the middle of "Lake" Vouru.kaša (Witzel 1984b), as well as
the Himorogi offering platform in Japanese ritual, with a tree as artificial center of the ritual,
or a pole (*yūpa*) in Vedic ritual (cf. Naumann 1988: 101).

228. Cf. the data in Walter and Fridman 2004: 263–64 (India, Persia, Maya, Indonesia,
Siberia, Iceland, Buryat, Lolo, Ireland, Mongolia). See Staudacher 1942. The Chinese version
has a revolt by Zhong and Li (Yang and An 2005: 66), whence the connection between
Heaven and Earth was ordered to be cut.

229. Eight is the number favored in Japan and Polynesia, which is different for the Near
East, with the number 7, and in North Asia, with 9.

230. Thompson 1993: Motif A878.1. Stream of paradise from roots of world-tree,
Iceland; cf. world tree in India, Plakṣa Prasravaṇa; Witzel 1984b. Thompson 1993: Motifs
F162.2.1. The four rivers of paradise; A878.1.1. Other streams from roots of earth-tree,
Iceland; A941.7.1. Spring from beneath world-tree, Iceland, Jewish; A652. World-tree;
A941.7.2. Spring from roots of sacred tree when arrow is shot into it, Fiji: Beckwith, Myth
317.

231. Thompson 1993: Motifs A878.1.2. Three wells under the three roots of earth-tree,
Iceland; A878.2. Lake of milk by tree of life, Siberian.

232. From Indo-European *smer*, Sanskrit *smar*, Latin *me-mor–* (to remember).

233. Which, however, according to one tradition was situated in Heaven itself.

234. Note that Germanic Norns spin there, while in Japanese myth, weaving is done in
Amaterasu's heaven; note also the concept of the life thread woven by them and the Vedic
concept of "cutting off" the life thread. See further the idea of day and night weaving the
threads/cloth of day and night in Ṛgvedic mythology.

235. Where he is discovered by the Sea god's servant and eventually marries his daughter
Toyotama Hime. There are several such myths, such as the one about Urashima Taro. In all
cases, it is the sea god's daughters who marry humans. There also is a similar story from China

in the Hou Han Shu, eastern barbarians section: "In the sea, there is a women's country, without men, and there is a heavenly well; when one looks at it, then a child is conceived." These stories deal with a beautiful young woman from the sea, who goes to this world to follow or marry a human; she lives with him for a while, gives birth to a child, and finally goes back. (Cf. Purūravas and Urvaśī, Ṛgveda 10.95; and see §3, nn. 468, 509, 554.)

236. See See §2, p. 40.

237. Witzel 1984b.

238. Dṛṣadvatī means "Having rocks, large stones, mill stones."

239. See Witzel 1984b: n. 101, and 1972: n. 56 (Jaiminīya Br. and Vādhūla Pitṛmedha Sūtra); further, Jaiminīya Upaniṣad Brāhmaṇa 4.6.12.

240. As the texts normally speak of selecting a treeless place for burial, which is placed under a low, man-high mound. The older custom of simply leaving dead bodies on trees, just as the Amerindians and some Siberians do, is found in the Ṛgveda as well.

241. First mentioned in Śatapatha Brāhmaṇa 13.8.1 as "eastern" custom; for Ise, see Naumann 1988: 61.

242. Cf. also the research by John Irwin (1973, 1983) on Ashokan pillars.

243. Cf. the results of the Svayambhunath project; Kölver 1992, 1996.

244. Cf. Allen 1997.

245. See Kuiper 1983; cf. Thompson 1993: Motif A652.2. Tree hanging from sky. A tree hangs upside down in the sky. By its branches men pass back and forth to the upper world, Indonesia, Micronesian. Cf., for Germanic tribes, §3, n. 576; §6, n. 22.

246. Witzel 1984b; cf. churning of the ocean in epic Indian myth (§3.5.3).

247. Thompson 1993: Motif A652.1. India.

248. Thompson 1993: Motif A652.1. Tree to heaven, Lithuanian, Lettish, Finnish: Kalevala.

249. Thompson 1993: Motifs A652.1. N. A. Indian; S. Am. Indian (Chaco); A652. World tree; C621.1. Tree of knowledge forbidden; D950. Magic tree; E90. Tree of life; F162.3.1. Tree of life in otherworld. An outcome of this is Thompson 1993: Motif A814.4. Earth from tree grown in primeval water, Tungus: Holmberg Siberian 329. Cf. the Iranian myth of the *vīspō.biš* tree in the midst of "Lake Vouru.kaša," along with the fish Kara. Note also Thompson 1993: Motifs A878.3. Animals at earth-tree; A878.3.1. Snake at roots of earth-tree, Iceland, Siberian. (See also Thompson 1993: s.v. *world tree Motifs A652, A878*.)

250. Beckwith 1987: 279 sqq. (a cornucopia tree); Tregear 1891/1969: 58. In Hawai'i (Tregear 1891/1969: 57)—which is one of the old names of *Sawaiki, the ancient homeland of origins of the Polynesians—it is also called "the dark mountain," which is described as paradise. Tradition says: "It was a sacred land: a man must be righteous to attain to it; if faulty, he cannot go there; if he prefers his family, he will not enter into Paliuli." (The myth of paradise is very similar to that of the Bible—though other Polynesian versions are not— and to that of Yama in Vedic myth.) Note that the paradise is described as a dark mountain, which again coincides with Vedic/Iranian (stone sky) and Japanese (Kojiki) evidence.

251. The tree Kien-mu, without branches but with nine sections (*yu ki chu*); see Münke 1976: 335.

252. The ten suns and moons are children of Di Jun and his two wives, Xihe and Changxi. The suns live on the Fusang tree (and nine are later on shot down by the great archer Yi); see Mathieu 1989: Myth no. 47; Yang and An 2005: 66. The Austronesian-speaking Atayal of Taiwan tell of two primordial suns, one of which was shot down.

253. Details in Evans 1923: 148, 156; Schebesta 1952: 152, 156 sqq. The Semang have a High God, Tata Ta Pedn, and the spirits (*chenoi, cenoi*) are mediators. Cf. on the problem of

the High God as a typical Gondwana trait, §5.3.6; note, however, Gusinde 1977: 496 sqq. on the High God (Tẹmáụkel) of the Selk'nam Fuegans.

254. For southern Australia, see the illustration in Smith 1996: 175; for the Arunta tribe, cf. also Lawlor 1991: 75 and maybe 226, 361. Cf. the use of the double *tjurunga*. Cf. §2, n. 144; §7, n. 134.

255. Note that such shamanistic ceremonies are found far in the south, for example, with the Nepalese Magars (Oppitz 1991).

256. Thompson 1993: Motifs A665.2. Pillar supporting sky, Siberian; Norse; A665.2.0.1. Pillars supporting sky, Tahiti; Eskimo; A841. World columns: two (four); F58. Tower (column) to upper world. Cf. F. B. J. Kuiper's *Varuṇa and Viduṣaka* (1978); cf. Biardeau 1989.

257. Thompson 1993: Motif A984. Pillars of Hercules at Gibraltar set up by Herakles (cf. A901), Greek.

258. §3.3; Thompson 1993: Eskimo.

259. See an Aztec painting in Soisson and Soisson 1987:79; cf. §3, nn. 266, 274.

260. Cf. Naumann 1971; in the Kujiki (Sendai-kuji-hongi), Izanagi and Izanami's spear is inserted into the earth and turned into the heavenly prop (Naumann 1988: 59).

261. See again, on the Mexican voladores, §3, n. 270. The same connection, viewed as a "string" (*tantu*), is visible in ritual in general: the god of Fire, Agni, reestablishes this connection with the gods by his leaping flames and even more so by his column of smoke, which drifts up toward the gods, as in the biblical myth of Abraham's sacrifice.

262. It also occurs in certain rituals (Lakṣahoma, as in the 1976 two-week celebration at Bhaktapur, Nepal).

263. Cf. Biardeau 1989; Thompson 1993: Motif A992.1. Origin of sacred post (placed there by ancestral culture hero), India.

264. Falk 1986: 86. Other ways to conceive from a deceased and the ancestors (*pitṛ*) include drinking the remnants of a libation to the ancestors.

265. Paippalāda Saṃhitā 18.74.5.

266. Their important central pole, which had been kept at the Peabody Museum at Harvard University for about a hundred years, has recently been returned to the Lakota.

267. Thompson 1993: Motifs A665.2.1.3. Sky extended by means of pillars, Tahiti: Henry 342; A984; A665.2.0.1. Pillars supporting sky, Tahiti: Henry 342; A665.2.1. Four sky-columns. Four columns support the sky.—Cook Zeus II 140ff.; Frobenius Erdteile VI 165ff.—Egyptian; A665.2.1.1. Four gods at world-quarters support the sky, India, Aztec; A665.2.1.2. Four dwarfs support the sky, Iceland.

268. Wai-ora-ta, in which the moon renews herself every month.

269. Mostly, he also is regarded as creator of man. Sometimes this is Tiki.

270. A fifth man stays on top of the pole, plays the flute, and dances. Cf. the Aztec painting in Soisson and Soisson 1987: 79: the leader, *k'ohal*, sits—turned eastward—on top of the pillar; he is dressed in a blue and red toga; he calls out to the deities like an eagle and offers them a drink; he turns to the four directions, beating his wings. Incidentally, in Nepal we have a horizontal version of this with a four-sided Ferris wheel; it is used at the beginning of the New Year (in October). Other implements are the swing that was used in the Vedic Mahāvrata (New Year) festival and the "big swing" that still can be seen in central Bangkok and that is used for the same purpose.

271. This points to avoidance of contact with the fertile female element/blood—as the pillar is regarded as male: *wo-bashira* (and, in other circumstances, as fire drill, see below).

272. See below on the Hittite Upelluri.

273. Indeed, when visiting the shrine in February 1990, at the occasion of the yearly fire festival—see the foreword—in which the newly churned fire is carried down from the hill by males only while the town's women wait below to receive the new fire, an old women pointed me to a niche inside the rock as the main place of worship, marked by white pebbles to indicate the sacredness.

274. Note that in Kojiki 1.2 there also is another counterpart, Kuni.no Toko-tachi.no Kami, which means "Mundane eternally standing god," whose function may be that of the world pillar; perhaps this is the world tree/pole on earth, in opposition to that of heaven (Ama.no Toko-tachi.no Kami)?

275. Indian myth shows that the world tree of daytime is reversed at night, its roots pointing upward, while being held by the god Varuṇa; see above, §3, n. 97; Kuiper 1978, 1983; Witzel 1984b; cf. Feddersen 1881.

276. Kojiki I 1 leaves out the very beginning and starts with the first generation of gods: the names of the deities that were born ("became") in the High Plain of High Heaven (Takama.no Hara) were Ame.no mi-naka-nushi.no kami (Master of the august center of Heaven [polestar?]) etc.

277. Thompson 1993: Motifs 841. World columns: two (four); F58.

278. Thompson 1993: Motifs A841. World columns: two (four) (cf. F58. Tower [column] to upper world); A841. Four world-columns; A665.2.1. Four sky-columns. Four columns support the sky, Egyptian; A665.2.1.3. Sky extended by means of pillars, Tahiti.

279. For Africa, see Frobenius 1925–29: 165 ff. Also found with the aboriginal (*bumiputra*) Semang of Malaya (Eliade 1954b: 268).

280. Thompson 1993: Motifs A842. Atlas. A man supports the earth on his shoulders, Greek; N. A. Indian; Chibcha; A665.2.1.1. Four gods at world-quarters support the sky, India, Aztec; A665.2.1.2. Four dwarfs support the sky, Iceland.

281. Thompson 1993: Motifs A842. Atlas; A665.3. Mountain supports sky, India; Siberian; A665.3.1. Four mountains support sky; cf. also A841.3. Twelve iron pillars steady the earth, India.

282. Thompson 1993: Motif A984. Pillars of Hercules at Gibraltar set up by Herakles (cf. A901), Greek.

283. See §2, n. 167; §3, n. 89.

284. Cf. Thompson 1993: Motifs A841.4. Four earth-nails, India (cf. also on support of the earth by an underground tortoise [India, China]); A842.1. Goddess standing on her head supports earth, India; A842.2. Old woman supports earth on her head, India.

285. Or on Kailāśa in Tibet, in the case of Śiva. Thompson 1993: Motifs A151.1. Home of gods on high mountain; F132. Otherworld on lofty mountain.

286. Eliade 1954b: 255 sq.

287. See Rundle Clark 1959.

288. Such as in the Hebrew Bible (Job) and in various other versions (Sarasvatī; cf. Bāmistūn in Manichaeism etc.; Witzel 1984b; in fairy tales: "Jack and the Beanstalk"). Thompson 1993: Motifs A666. Ladder to heaven (applied to saint), Irish; A666.1. Eight (symbolical) steps of the ladder of heaven, Irish; A666.2. Rodent gnaws away ladder to other world and thus ghosts remain on earth, S. Am. Indian (Brazil).

289. Ṛgveda 1.19.7 etc.; Maitrāyaṇī Saṃhitā 1.10.13; Kaṭha Saṃhitā 36.7 (see above, §2, n. 167; §3, n. 283. Note that both the stemming part and the fixing of the Earth occur much later in mythological time than that of Heaven and Earth. Indra is a descendant of the second generation of deities. If we count the Asuras or Titans as the third generation, they are in fact the cousins of the "fourth" generation, to which Indra belongs. In Japan, the feature of pre-

paring the land for habitation occurs again later on (cf. Aston 1972: 59). Probably in both traditions, myths were restructured and attributed to the most important gods.

290. See Puhvel 1987: 39, 146.

291. Mathieu 1989: 40 and esp. 73 sq. In a myth of southeastern China, she escaped the Great Flood in a calabash. Nugua is one of the three sovereigns of primordial age (Mathieu 1989: 30), is usually feminine, and is associated with Fuxi, her brother and husband, in Tang texts. Earlier, in Han time, she had a human head and a serpent body surrounding that of Fuxi. She created humans and invented the flute.

292. Mathieu 1989: 40. The tortoise also appears in Indian, other Eurasian, and North American myths; the black dragon represents excess water; the nine provinces mean that the earth is square; heaven covers it in round form. See Huainan zi, chap. 1. Cf. Thompson 1993: Motifs A843. Earth supported on post. The post has an old woman as guardian. When she is hungry the post shakes, causing earthquakes, Finno-Ugric; N. A. Indian (Tlingit, Hare); A843.1. Earth supported on cross of wood, S. Am. Indian (Guarani, Apapocuvá).

293. According to Aston 1972: 7 sqq.: 1. Ame.no mi-naka-nushi.no mikoto (Heaven middle master) and Umashi-ashi-kabi hikoji.no mikoto (Sweet reed-shoot prince elder); 2. Kuni.no toko-tachi.no mikoto (Land eternal stand) and Toyo-kuni-nushi.no mikoto (Rich land master); 3. Tsuno-gui.no mikoto (Horn stake) and Iku-gui.no mikoto (Live stake, his wife or sister); 4. U-hiji-ni.no mikoto (Mud earth) and Su-hiji-ni.no mikoto (Sand earth, his younger sister or wife); 5. Oho-toma-hiko.no mikoto (Great mat prince) and Oho-toma-he. no mikoto (Great mat place, his wife or younger sister); 6. Awo-kashiki no.no mikoto (Green awful) and Aya-kashiki no.no mikoto (Ah! Awful, his wife or younger sister); 7. Izanagi and Izanami (his wife or younger sister). Cf. Naumann 1988: 58.

294. This island is not located with certainty, but it may be thought that it is connected with the famous maelstrom between Awaji-shima and Shikoku. On Onogoro, they erect the heavenly pillar (Ame.no mi-hashira; see above, on the tree/pillar). We have two representations of the central pillar: the spear and the *mi-hashira* pillar. Cf. Naumann 1988: 59, 63: in the Kujiki (Sendai-kuji-hongi), their spear is inserted into the earth and turned into the heavenly prop.

295. For Izumo and Ise, see Ōbayashi 1982; cf. Naumann 1988: 92 sq. on Ōnamuji and Sukuna-biko.

296. For the primordial shaky earth, cf. §3, nn. 89, 289.

297. Note the Ainu concept of the sky, which constantly closes and opens, at the end of the world, so that birds can migrate; and cf. the Vedic Indian text, Bṛhad Araṇyaka Upaniṣad 3.9, as well as Berezkin's (2007) maps for a moving sky.

298. Also in Egypt: all will revert to Nun; see Ions 1990: 22. Note the following motifs in Thompson 1993: Motifs A1000. World catastrophe; A1010. Deluge; A1020. Escape from deluge; A1030. World fire; A1040. Continuous winter destroys the race; A1050. Heavens break up at end of world; A1060. Earth-disturbances at end of world; A1030. World-fire. A conflagration destroys the earth. Details in §2.5.2, §3.9, §5.7.2.

299. Detailed discussion in Witzel 2005b, of which only a summary is given here.

300. Thompson 1993: Motifs A710–39, esp. A734. Sun hides; A734.1. Sun hides in cave; A713. Sun and moon from cave; A721.0.2. Sun shut up in pit; A721. Sun kept in box; A721.0.1. Sun and moon kept in pots; A1411.1. Light kept in a box; A721.1. Theft of sun; A1411. Theft of light; A260.1. Goddess of light; A270. God of dawn; A270.1. Goddess of dawn.

301. See Ōbayashi 1960; Witzel 2005b. For another interpretation of the myth as the central part of the Susa.no Wo cycle, see Naumann 1988: 68 sq., for a noncosmic interpretation of the emergence of Amaterasu from the cave, 84 sq.

302. As most historical data in the text refer to the last five generations before the end of the Ṛgveda period, a date between c. 1200 and 1000 BCE is not unreasonable. It coincides with the archaeologically attested, linguistically slightly older Indian names in the Mitanni records of northern Iraq of c. 1400 BCE, which mention the Vedic Indian gods Mitra, Varuṇa, and Indra and the Nāsatyas (Aśvin).

303. For possible links in early Central Asia at c. 2000 BCE, see Witzel 2005b.

304. In the Mahābhārata, the "demon" Vala was killed; it is found only in the Aśvin hymn imitating Ṛgveda poetry of Mahābhārata 1.3.60 sqq., cf. also 5.149.22, 6.91.54, 8.63.10, 13.19.23. Similarly the demon (*daitya*) Vṛtra, appears only in the late sections of the Mahābhārata, 12.272–73, 12.270.13, and 14.11.6–20, cf. also 9.42 (Brockington 1998: 232–33). A curiosity is the recent on-line paper by the Kashmir-born Louisiana scientist S. Kak, who retells the influence of post-Vedic Indian myth on Japan that actually came with the introduction of Buddhism in the mid–first millennium CE. These well-known facts are presented as another novel proof of previous Indian cultural and scientific dominance. He overlooks the multifarious evidence of millennia of mutual give and take between the various Eurasian cultures (http://www.ece.lsu.edu/kak/VedicJapan.pdf).

305. There are some versions elsewhere that see the creation of light differently: there was no sun, or it had to be released from the netherworld (Maya etc.). The Indian and Japanese versions presuppose the existence of light/sun. However, another old version found in the Veda has eternal daylight, and the gods first had to create the night (Yama/Yamī; Maitrāyaṇī Saṃhitā 1.4). There also is a modern Czech version of the myth, written for children, that is very close to the Indian version.

306. It is matched in more "southern" civilizations by a myth of a "midday standstill of the sun." See the Hebrew Bible: Joshua (cf. §2, n. 172); Polynesia: held by a cord in Maui; Incas: the sun is bound to a sacred rock near the cave of the emergence of the sun, to which the sun is tied (cf. Lévi-Strauss 1973: 168, M. 416 [Yabarana]); Aztecs: the sun is generally immobile but moved by blood offerings.

307. Etymologically = Greek *Eōs*; and cf. Latin *Aurorā*, Germanic *Ostera*, Engl. *Easter*. Cf., however, the motif of the Lithuanian Sáule and Latvian Saule.

308. For the myth, see Schmidt 1968.

309. Cf. Greek *angelos* (messenger) and the Persian loanword *angaros* (mail rider).

310. Vedic *dhī* is connected by popular etymology with *dhenu* (milch cow) and in Old Iranian with *daenā* (thought > religion); cf. further Witzel 1991.

311. See Ṛgveda 3.31.9.

312. Very clear in Iranian and Vedic texts; see Kuiper 1983.

313. In addition, the Vala/Vara pen for cows can easily be explained, in real life, as a stable that is necessary for the cows to survive the cold northern winters. Indeed, similar structures have been found in Bactria, dating from the third millennium BCE (Oxus/Bactria-Margiana Archaeological Complex [BMAC] culture) up to the Achaemenid period, and are reflected in the Avesta (Vīdēvdād 2).

314. Cf. Eliade 1954b.

315. For a good account of this yearly period, see Schärer 1946, 1963, on the Dayak in Borneo. Note that their carnival period at year's end surprisingly lasts for two months; this apparently "northern" custom is continued in the tropics.

316. Note the Aśvin's attack on Uṣas's chariot and Dyaus's pursuit of Uṣas. Further Indian motifs include Indra and the cave, the five Indras (mentioned in Ṛgveda 1.2.87, cf. 5.80.22); cf. the also the somewhat parallel Ṛgvedic myth of the "hiding Agni," who flees as he does not want to become the (sacrificial) fire.

317. Apparently, not done even by Japanese scholars of the Veda or vice versa, by Western Indologists who know Japanese.

318. Instead of his brother Tsuku-Yomi, who early on disappeared, as in many Eurasian mythologies, from the further Kiki accounts. Cf. Naumann 1988: 66 sq., 73 sq.; Ōbayashi 1975.

319. Note the Grimms' (2003) fairy tale Snow White and the seven dwarves: the motifs of long sleep, the mirror, her rescue by a "prince," etc.

320. Still used in private houses and shrines at New Year. It expresses the irreversibility of the deliverance of the sun (cf. below on Amerindian myths, §2.5); cf. the opposite summer solstice custom of tying the sun to a rock in Maui, in the Inca realm, and with the Yabarana (Orinoco); cf. §2, n. 171; §3 n. 306; 360. Note also the Korean *kumjul* or *kumsaeq*, the "string of interdiction"; discussion in Guillemoz 1983: 120 sq.

321. See Witzel 2005b.

322. Witzel 2005b: tables.

323. For the Iranian Vara and the primordial winter, cf. also Allen 2000.

324. Cf. Frau Holle in the Grimms' (2003) fairy tales and the self-illuminated subterranean realms of the dwarfs or of the Indian Nāgas.

325. See the work of K. Jettmar (1975) and Georg Buddruss (Prasun Nuristani texts and trans., planned for the Harvard Oriental Series). Cf. further the sources and literature quoted by Allen (2000).

326. Katičić 2001, 2003; Katičić et al. 1992. For the Iranian Vara, cf. also Allen 2000.

327. Katičić 2001, 2003.

328. In Latvian wedding songs, when a bride comes in her new husband's house, the husband's relative (Dievs, "God"; Laima, "Fortune") cuts a cross in the doorpost with the same intention.

329. Greimas 1985.

330. Etymologically connected with Uṣas, Lat. *Aurora*, Germanic *Ostera*; cf. Greimas 1985.

331. Puhvel 1987: 223, according to the contemporary report by a Bohemian monk, Hieronymus.

332. Haudry 1987: 263; cf. Egypt: where the sun moves back to its rising point in the east in a boat on the river below the earth.

333. Archaeologists have recently dug up replicas of these mythological boats in Japan, see *Nihon Keizai Shimbun*, April 11, 2004. Note also the newly found Xinjiang mummies, buried in boat-like tree stems; see *Nihon Keizai Shimbun*, January 2005; http://www.nhk.or.jp/silkroad/digital/index.html, http://www.nhk.or.jp/silkroad/50.html, no. 21/3. Otherwise, the Indo-European sun god moves about in a horse-drawn chariot during daytime. Cf. Burkert 1982: 83 sqq.

334. The cattle of Geryon (son of Chrysaor by Callirrhoe, daughter of Okeanos), on an island in the Atlantic Ocean, now Gadira (after crossing the Gibraltar Strait?). Geryon has three bodies grown together; the cattle are watched over by the two-headed dog Orthus and the herder Eurytion; the cattle are red (as in India); Menoetes (herder of the cattle of Hades) tells Geryon, who battles with Herakles on the River Anthemus; Herakles kills both and travels back with the cows to Greece. Discussed in detail by Burkert (1982: 83 sqq.).

335. Herakles (= Alkides), son of Zeus and Alkmena, is born as a twin (his brother Phicles has a human father); he kills the Hydra with nine heads (cf. the Japanese dragon, Yamata.no Orochi).

336. A concept prominent in Japanese myth as *tokoyo*; also found in Polynesian and other mythologies. Cf. Burkert 1982: 179 n. 2; Matsumura 2006a.

337. Burkert (1982: 80 sqq.) compares Mesopotamian and Levant parallels but also discusses the accumulation of various traditions that resulted in the Greek versions.

338. A. Yoshida (1961–62, 1974) has often compared Indo-European mythology with Japanese mythology (cf. also Ōbayashi 1989) and has discovered many, obviously not accidental similarities between Japanese and Indo-European (Scythian, Ossete, Greek) mythology. For example, Izanami's stay in the netherworld, which is similar to the Orpheus myth; also, it may be added, the Indian myths of Naciketas in the Kaṭha Upaniṣad, the Sāvitrī/Satyavant story of the Mahābhārata (3.277–83), the Polynesian story of Hinuitepo, and the Cherokee myth quoted above (§2.5). However, unlike Persephone, Eurydice went back on her own free will. The reason for Persephone's fetter to Hades is that she had eaten his food (as in Kaṭha Upaniṣad and with Izanami). Note that the Greek story has the same motif of curiosity as the Japanese one: looking (back) curiously results in being bound to the netherworld forever; similarly in the Cherokee tale, it is human curiosity that killed the daughter of the Sun; cf. also the mytheme of the curiosity of Lot's wife in the Hebrew Bible, which likewise kills her.

339. See Dunkel 1988–90; for Demeter/Damater, cf. Burkert 1985: 159.

340. Cf. Kaṭha Upaniṣad 1.9. Note the opposite concept in the connection of eating the biblical apple in Paradise with mortality: just as one belongs to Hades after eating its fruit, so one is thrown out of paradise after eating its fruit; heavenly fruits are only for "heavenly" beings, not for humans. Cf. the similar Polynesian version (Tregear 1891/1969: 56 sqq.); cf. also the West African Bassari myth about Unumbotte below, §6.1 (see Campbell 1988: I.1: 14; Frobenius 1924: 75–76). See §2, n. 179; §5, nn. 299, 368; §6, n. 30; cf. also §3, nn. 414, 523.

341. In Virgil's *Aeneid*. Cf. Burkert (1982: 84); he (1982: 86 sq.) regards this Italic myth as pre-Greek and, in this context, as a simple herder's myth, though counterbalanced by the Vedic Indra and the Pylian Melampus myths. He goes on to compare all of this with the evidence from shamanism.

342. Note the backward skinning of the piebald horse of the sun in the Kiki, probably that of the (white) sun horse, in other words, killing and mutilating the sun itself. Just like Cacus pulls in the sun cows by their tails, Susa.no Wo pulls the (skin of) the sun horse backward. Naumann (1988: 74 sq.) takes it as general act of "inverted" magic. For a detailed discussion of the Roman, Greek, and Indian myths, see Burkert 1982: 85 sqq., as a "likely candidate for Indo-European mythology." However, he also traces their roots in the shamanistic hunter's magic of the Upper Paleolithic (1982: 88 sqq., 94 sqq.), visible in the cave paintings of Stone Age Europe (1982: 90 sqq.); see detailed discussion below, §4.4.1.

343. See Philippi 1979: 81 n. 3. Note the Grimms' (2003) fairy tale of Snow White. The Sun is female also with the Yukagir in northeastern Siberia ("Mother Sun"), the Samoyed on the Yenesei ("Mother of the world," who was born from the right eye of the creator god Num, the Cheremis ("Mother Sun"), and the Turkish peoples ("Mother Sun," as opposed to Father/Uncle Moon); but see Matsumura 1998: 64 for Japan; and cf. §2, n. 176; §3, n. 202.

344. See Philippi 1979: 82 n. 8. For the red crown of the rooster, see also Ṛgveda Khila 5.22.

345. Note the corresponding Old Chinese myth of shooting down nine of the tens suns (archer Yi); cf. the great archer Apollo; and cf. below on Amerindian myths, §2.5. Note also the Avestan and Vedic archers (§3, nn. 333, 346) and the n. bow shooting in the Vedic Pravargya

myth: Rudra is killed by the severed string of his bow, which cuts off his head, which becomes the blazing sun (Witzel 2004a).

346. Like several famous Old Chinese myths (such as that of the world giant, Pangu) it may have an origin among the Austric peoples. Cf. other archer myths in Iran, Hindu Kush, India, the Indus civilization, and Mesoamerica; see §3, nn. 252, 367, 490.

347. Maenche-Helffen thought that this variant of the myth of the hiding sun resembles the Japanese one, including the mirror etc., and that Susa.no Wo was born from Izanami's *misogi* (purification): he and Amaterasu are siblings. However, cf. also the Mesoamerican myths (Kekchi etc.) above, §2.5. For other Southeast Asian variants, see Ōbayashi 1960. In Hawai'i, the sun is kept by Ka-oha-lei, angered by Niheu; the land remains in darkness until Kana visits a far eastern land and receives the sun, the stars, and the rooster that announces the dawn. As in the Indra myths, this is done by trickery (Beckwith 1987: 50 sq.). In Tahiti, it is Maui who steps on the disk of the sun until it is cracked; see Beckwith 1987: 452.

348. Yoshida 1961–62, 1974, 2006.

349. Cf., however, the deliberations by J. Colarusso (2006: 48), who sees an opposition between Indo-European *hens-iyo/hens-uro* (Norse *Æsir*; Skt. *Asura*; Avestan *Ahura*; Hittite *hanš*, "to favor"), thus, those who are favored/grant favor, and *deywo* (the shining ones, Skt. *deva*).

350. Witzel 2004a.

351. Beckwith 2004.

352. See Keally 2004.

353. Or much earlier, in some recent scenarios: see Valverde finds in Chile, now dated around 14,000 years ago. There also are new theories of immigration by boat along the west coast of North America (Chatters 2001; Thomas and Colley 2001). Note also the thesis by von Sadovszky (1978) about Uralic-speaking Wintu in the California Valley, as well as the Aurignacian immigration of the people represented by sites in Virginia and Pennsylvania, from Western Europe via the ice sheet, Iceland, and Greenland; see Lemonick and Dorfman 2006. For a genetic update, see §4, n. 211.

354. Cf. Berezkin 1996–97.

355. Erdosi and Ortiz 1984: 152.

356. For the motif, cf. Berezkin 1996–97.

357. See Farmer et al. 2002; Witzel 1992.

358. Details in Witzel 2005b.

359. Mathieu 1989: Myth no. 11: Xihe is the mother of ten suns (ten days per decade) and 12 moons (months). Xihe bathes the ten suns in the "Sweet Springs" behind the sea of the southeast. According to Mathieu (1989: Myth no. 12, Shanhai Jing), there is a mulberry tree on a mountain in the north, on an island in the middle of the ocean (for which cf. the *vīspō-biš* tree in the middle of "Lake" Vouru.kaša, in the Avesta; cf. Mathieu 1989: Myth no. 17, on the island of Dushuo and its tree, according to Shanhai Jing). Nine suns are on its lower branches, and one is on its higher branches. Out of the ten suns, nine are shot down by the archer Yi; see Mathieu 1989: Myth nos. 13, 47.

360. Lévi-Strauss 1973: 168, M. 416 (Yabarana). It is important to note that the original myth must have been widespread in Amazonia.

361. Bierhorst 1992: 183; Soisson and Soisson 1987: 97 sqq.

362. Cf. the Huichol myth of the sun and the fire; Bierhorst 1992.

363. Cf. the motif in a Vedic myth where the sun likewise had to be pushed up; Pañcaviṃśa Brāhmaṇa 25.10; see above, §2.6, on the "bent" Milky Way/Sarasvatī.

364. Finally, the wind god Ecatl (a form of Quetzalcoatl) blew the Sun on its course. Humans, too, were flawed: Quetzalcoatl robbed the bones of the ancestors from the nether-

world, but some demons caught him and threw him down into the abyss, where he died but rose again and escaped with the bones. With the help of a female companion, he re-created humans, but he did not quite know how.

365. Tedlock 1985; for a detailed philological translation, see Schultze Jena 1944.

366. Tedlock 1985: 73.

367. Tedlock 1985: 90.

368. Tedlock 1985: 153. The five days refer to the 5¼ "extra" days at the end of the year. Note that, as in Indo-European, the twins "belong to the sun" (*-yo suffix); they are not *the* sun (Sanskrit *sūr-ya*, Greek *hēl-ios*). The Hawai'ians have a similar concept: The divine "Eyeball of the sun" (Ka-onohi-o-ka-la) lives in the sun but comes down to earth in human nature. (For the concept of a link between eye and sun, see the Vedic texts, where this is found from R̥gveda 10.90 onward; and cf. the concept of the wandering eye of the Sun in Old Egypt.)

369. R̥gveda, Jaiminīya Brāhmaṇa 3.233–35.

370. Lehmann 1938: 340.

371. Schultze Jena 1944: 187.

372. Kuiper 1950.

373. Bierhorst 1992: 112, taken from Shaw's *According to Our Ancestors*.

374. Berezkin (1996–97) holds the same opinion.

375. The motif of the emergence of humans from below is mixed with the emergence from a tree, which is prominently found in Iceland (*askr* and *embla*), Japanese folktales (Kaguyahime), and Austronesian Taiwan and Amerindian myths, but also in Australia and Central Africa (Baumann 1936). This seems to be one of the oldest motifs of human mythology, much older than Laurasian myth; see §6.

376. An exception is the Hopi, who tell of a flood that was avoided, after two previous destructions; cf. Thompson 1993: Motif A1018.

377. Farmer et al. 2002.

378. Witzel 2005a, presentation given at a Conference at Tainan, Taiwan, in October 2005. This section relies, to some extent, on Witzel 2005a, 2007b, 2008, 2009b.

379. Philippi 1968: 88 n. 2.

380. Cf. J. Shaw (2006: 155 sqq.) for the opinion of Benveniste that the Iranian version is more conservative than the Indian one. However, the Iranian version in the Avesta is clearly and strongly influenced by pre-Indo-Iranian, local BMAC mythology; see Witzel 2004b.

381. We may also compare Thor's and Tyr's killing of the giants. For the Germanic myths, see Mizuno 2003.

382. Puhvel 1987: 226 sq.

383. Katičić 2001.

384. Watkins 1995. Also, see Fontenrose 1980; Katičić 2001; and the many Indo-European comparisons made by V. Ivanov and V. N. Toporov (1974). Note also the Hittite myth of Illuyankaš (Eel-snake), which tells of the fight of the Storm God with a giant snake, who steals the god's heart and eyes but is finally killed.

385. Eliade 1992: 96 sq.

386. Münke 1976: 90 sqq., 219 sqq. (Kung Kung), cf. 247 sq.; Yang and An 2005: 124 sqq.

387. Or at Nihon Shoki 1.54: on the Upper River Ye in Aki (Hiroshima Prefecture); at Nihon Shoki 1.56 Susa.no Wo with his son Iso-takeru ("50 courageous") goes down to Shiragi (Korea), at Soshimori (*mori* = Kor. *moi*, "mountain" [Aston 1972]), saying, "I will not dwell in this land," takes a clay(!) boat, and crosses over to Mt. Tori-kamu.no Take at the

Upper Hi River in Izumo. (At Nihon Shoki I 58 the opposition with Yamato is mediated: Susa.no Wo pulled out his hairs, which become trees. His child Isotakeru planted trees and lived on the Kii Peninsula next to and just south of Yamato; note the etymology: *ki*, "tree"; his other children moved to Kii as well.) Then, Susa.no Wo dwelt on Mt. Kuma-nari (Mt. Kumano in Izumo? near Suga) and finally went to Hades. Cf. Naumann 1988: 81 sq.

388. See the similar description of the three-headed monster in the Avesta; Witzel 2004b.

389. With the typical Japanese preference for the number 8, not 7 as in the Near East or 9 as in Siberia. Eight is also found in Polynesia. On numbers in Japan, see Naumann 2000: 115: number 3 is preferred in Jōmon art, but she also finds 5 and 7; this is remarkably different from the later Japanese preference for 8 (Naumann 1988: 60) and the North Asian "shamanic" number 9. Cf. also Blažek 1999: III, with archaeological evidence for Magdalenian counting, and 132, on Japanese numbers.

390. Cf. the myth of Perseus and his killing of the Gorgon Medusa; see Graves 1955: 238.

391. See §2.5.1 for areal features of Laurasian mythology; Witzel 2005b.

392. The influence of this region can be expanded by many more examples; see, for example, the extensive work of A. Yoshida (1961–62 etc.). Examples include the "misdeed" of the primordial parents and the birth of their first, deformed child (Hirugo versus Mārtāṇda), the visit to the netherworld in search of the departed wife (Orpheus motif), the delivery of sunlight from the cave (Vala motif), marriage with a sea princess, the Pandora motif, the Milky Way, offerings of horses and humans at burials of Scythian kings, the custom of placing *haniwa* figures, etc.

393. Yašt 5.33–35, 19.38–40; Yasna 9.7–8, 11.

394. Benveniste and Renou 1934.

395. Francfort 1994.

396. Falk 1997; Vajracharya 1997.

397. Compare the Armenian myth and epic of David of Sassoun (Sasuntsʻi Dawitʻ); Shalian 1964; Tchavouchian 2003.

398. For further details on the BMAC, Iranian, and Indian dragon, see Witzel 2004a.

399. At his temple, located at Pytho, at Crisa, below the Parnassos Mountain.

400. Translation by Evelyn-White (1977).

401. Kadmos founded the castle of Kadmeia, the later Thebes. He killed a dragon, descended from Ares, with stones. He broke off the teeth of the monster and sowed them into the earth. Immediately, fully armed men arose from it, the ancestors of the Theban nobility.

402. Cf. Colarusso 2006: 32 (for reflections in the Nart myths of the western Caucasus); Katz 2005. The same Storm God kills Illuyankaš only in a second battle with the help of the goddess In(a)ra (cf. Indra; Colarusso 2006: 35). The same is true in Hurrian myth. One is reminded of Indra, who, according to post-Ṛgvedic myth, is clinically awestruck by mortal fear (*apvā*) upon seeing the dragon and is only released from this state of shock when his Marut allies accidentally run their chariot into the back of his knee (Hoffmann 1992).

403. Dalley 1989: 250 sqq.

404. Next to the unicorn (*lin*), the phoenix (*feng*), and the tortoise (*kuei*). See Münke 1976: 90 sqq.; cf. Chang 1983 on the art forms of the dragon and background.

405. Cf. above, §3, n. 19. See Mathieu 1989: 40 and esp. 73 sq.; Yang and An 2005.

406. Mathieu 1989: 40. Cf. E. W. Lai, personal communication, February 29, 2004, for the dragon-slayer myth; see Lai 1984, focusing on the legendary Hsia anthropogonic figure Emperor K'ung-chia.

407. Other texts see it as an uprising; Liehtzu (Liezi), chap. 5: *t'ang-wen*.

408. Huainan zi, chap. 6: Lanming; see Lai 1984; Yang and An 2005: 74, 124 sqq. For the disaster of floods following the breaking of one of the four heavenly pillars, the northwestern one (Mt. Buzhou), and its repair by Nüwa, see Mathieu 1989: 38; Yang and An 2005: 75. Because of the breaking of this pillar, the stars and the sun incline toward the northwest/ southeast.

409. Lai 1984. He sees the archer Yi of the east coastal region as belonging to the historic Shang, whose totem is the sun-bird. The prehistoric/legendary Hsia is in the center, and its totem is the snake-fish Dragon complex.

410. The sign for Pa is that of a snake.

411. E. W. Lai, personal communication, February 29, 2004; see §3, n. 410.

412. Maori Mokomoko, Mokoroa; Haw. Mo'o; Tregear 1891/1969: 249.

413. See Tregear 1891/1969: 57, s.v. *Hawaiki.*

414. Cf. also "paradise" myths of the West African Bassari, §3.7; and for the southern Australian concept of the "Perfect Land," transported to the Milky Way after the flood, see Smith 1996: 22, 182.

415. Zolbrod 1984: 171 sqq.: the twins, descendants of the only pair of humans that had survived in this, the Fifth World, kill Déélgééd, the Horned Monster (Zolbrod 1984: 189), and many others. The Navajo myths have been brought southward from the Athapascan homeland in Alaska and the Yukon; see Bierhorst 1986: 68.

416. See Suárez 2005.

417. Campbell 1989: II.1: 41, ill. 78.

418. The motif of a dragon or giant snake is also prominent in New Guinea; see §5.3.3; Kamma 1978: 121–66. It seems to have spread from New Guinea eastward toward the Solomons and, during the last Ice Age, over the land bridge to northern and central Australia; see §5.3.2. Its age and origin in Sahul Land must be investigated separately and also must be compared with the apparently ancient motif of the rainbow snake.

419. See Witzel 2005a, 2008, 2009b.

420. Thompson 1993: Motifs A1415. Theft of fire (cf. K300. Thefts and cheats); cf. also A721.1. Theft of the sun; A1411. Theft of light. The theft of fire is less common in North America (southeastern United States and Rocky Mountains).

421. Thompson 1993: Motif Q501.4. Punishment of Prometheus.

422. Kuiper 1983. Humans are also punished for theft: Thompson 1993: Motifs A1346.1. Man must work as punishment for theft of fire, Greek; A1031.2. World-fire after theft of fire, India; A1031.5. World-fire because of man's arrogance, African (Fang).

423. Patton 1992, making use of my *On Ritual* (Witzel 1985).

424. Thompson 1993: Hdwb. d. März. II 109b nn. 14–15, Greek, Hindu.

425. Kagu-Tsuchi.no Kami etc.; Kojiki I 8.

426. Thompson 1993: Finnish, Polynesia, Maori, Chatham Is., Marquesas, Hawaii, Micronesia, Woodlark Is., Tonga, Indonesia; Eskimo; N. A. Indian, S. Am. Indian (Baikairi, Amazon, Caingang, Botocudo, Tucuna, Nimuendajú, Tenethara, Guarani, Guarporé, Tapirape, Chamacoco, Choco [Western Colombia], Apapocuvú-Guarani); also: Melanesia.

427. Thompson 1993: Motif A1414.4. Origin of fire—gift from god (supernatural person), India, Maori, Isabel Is., Hawaii; S. Am. Indian (Sherente, Cashiba, Chamacoco, Warrau, Caviña, Tumupasa, Chiriguano, Toba); Africa (Bushongo, Congo); cf. also A1414. Origin of fire, Irish, Persian; Micronesian; N. A. Indian (Kaska, Tahltan, Sinkyone, Shasta, Calif. Indian, Aztec), S. Am. Indian (Jibaro [Peru], Tropical Forest, Chiriguano). Contrast the Gondwana mytheme of the origin of fire from a man's own body (see below) or acci- dental discovery by a water rat in southern Australia (Smith 1996: 69).

428. Witzel 1990a etc.; Thompson 1993: Motifs A712. Sun as fire rekindled every morning, Australia; A714.3. Sun from fire flung into sky, Siberian; A1414.6. Bird as guardian of primordial fire, S. Am. Indian (Apapocuvú-Guaraní). Similarly, in Tasmania, see §5.3.2.1.

429. E. W. Lai, personal communication, February 29, 2004. In a popular Chinese myth, Suirenshi (Sir flint-man) imitates a bird pecking at a tree, which produces sparks; Suirenshi uses a fire drill instead; see Mathieu 1989: Myth no. 91; Yang and An 2005: 71. Similarly, when fire is discovered in southern Australia, the secret is taken by force by a totem animal, the Eagle Hawk (Smith 1996: 68 sq.).

430. Thompson 1993: Motif A1414.2. Origin of fire—found in person's own body, Australia, New Guinea, Torres Str., Massim (British New Guinea). Note, however, that the same myth is also found in Polynesia and South America (Thompson 1993: Motif A1414.2. Marquesas, S. Am. Indian [Warrau]).

431. Thompson 1993: Theft of fire, African: Frobenius Atlantis XII 80, Bushongo, Congo. Cf. the Finnish, the Motu, and the Massim of British New Guinea, Australia. The Andamanese also have a myth about the theft of fire from Prawn, by Kingfisher (Man 1883); for Australia, see the last note.

432. Roth 1899: 84 sq., app. H, xxxVIII–IX.

433. Thompson 1993: Motifs A1428. Acquisition of wine, Greek, India, Chinese; Africa (Tshi, Fang); A1427. Acquisition of spirituous liquors, India, Buddhist; S. Am. Indian (Guarayu). For a discussion of other Indo-European accounts (Germanic, Iranian: from a god's spittle/blood), see Lincoln 1986: 196 n. 7.

434. Thompson 1993: Motifs A1426.2.2. Origin of rice-beer, India; A1428. Acquisition of wine, Greek, India, Chinese; Africa (Tshi, Fang).

435. Apparently first attested in an Atharvaveda hymn, Paippalāda Saṃhitā 8.12, where this popular, plant-based alcohol is called *surā*. It is clearly distinguished from the ritualistic, sacred drink soma, which does not lead to drunkenness, sexual banter, and boasting. See Thompson 1993: Motifs A1427. Acquisition of spirituous liquors, India, Buddhist, S. Am. Indian (Guarayu); A1456. Origin of distilling. For *surā* in the Paippalāda Saṃhitā of the Atharvaveda, see Oort 2002.

436. Thompson 1993: Motif A153. Food of the gods. Ambrosia, Hindu/India, Greek, Hawaii, Iceland, Irish.

437. Thompson 1993: Motifs A153.1. Theft of ambrosia; A153.1. Theft of ambrosia. Food of the gods stolen.

438. Doht 1974; Thompson 1993: Motifs A154.2. Theft of magic mead by Odin, Iceland; A661.1.0.2. Goat (Heidrún) in Valhalla gives mead, Iceland; M234.1. Life spared in return for poetic mead.

439. Cf. Eliade 1992: 246, 279, for (dated) translations of typical soma hymns.

440. The Ṛgveda says that it comes from Mt. Mūjavant (Maujavant), which seems to reflect the modern (Kirgiz-named) Mt. Muzh Tagh Ata, on the Tajik–Chinese border. Another mountain with the same name is situated in northern-most Kashmir. See Staal 2004; Thompson 2003; Witzel 1999a, 2004a.

441. For details, see Witzel 2004b.

442. Mathieu 1989: Myth no. 19.

443. Antoni 1988; the book contains a brief comparison with soma (206–9); cf. Naumann 1988: 92.

444. Thompson 1993: Motifs A2686.3.1. Origin of kava plant, Tonga; A2751.4.6. Why kava plant is grey, Tonga.

445. Thompson 1993: Motif A1428. Acquisition of wine, Greek, Chinese.

446. Thompson 1993: Motif A481. God of intoxication (or of wine), Greek, Hindu/India, S. Am. Indian (Chibcha).

447. Witzel 2004a.

448. In China, see Thompson 1993: Motif A1428. Acquisition of wine. However, the tales from Africa must be counterchecked, even though they may deal with palm "wine": Thompson 1993: Tshi, Fang; Motifs A2681.12. Origin of palm-wine tree, Africa (Bushongo); A920.1.16. Lake originally filled with palm wine, Africa (Bushongo).

449. Bierhorst (1992: 129 sqq.), however, takes the myths of the Four or Five Ages as "myths in sequence" that individual populations in Mesoamerica created on their own, such as what he calls the "repeated myth" of the Aztec, Maya, Yucatec, Tzotzil, Tarascans, Totonac, and Tarahumara. This loses sight of their occurrence in South America and other Laurasian areas.

450. For the Indo-European "Mother Earth" as the wife of Heaven, see RV 1.89.4, 6.51.5, etc.; Ṛgveda Khila 5.5.5. Cf. Oberlies 1998: 265 sqq.; various congruent Polynesian myths.

451. These concepts are perhaps best seen in Ṛgveda 3.38 (a hymn later assigned to Indra): the androgynous "older bull" Asura (cf. Iranian myth), the "great hoary" bull, gives birth to/creates the world; he is in part identified with Heaven and Earth (Rodasī), who were later separated; the (*younger) bull, Heaven/Sun, is also called Asura Viśvarūpa (a demon); Mitra and Varuṇa(?), the grandsons of Heaven, reign, served by the wind-haired Gandharvas.

452. Cf. also the more complicated case of the biblical angels and the devil, which is closer to the Zoroastrian opposition of the Good and the Evil Spirit, after Zaraϑuštra's reform of Indo-Iranian religion.

453. Dumézil 1934; Staudacher 1942 ("world wide spread").

454. Cf. also the Gigantomachia of Cl. Claudianus (370–404 ce); see above, §3.3.

455. Gurney 1976: 190 sqq.; Hunger 1984: 408; Lesky 1950: 137 sqq.

456. The Japanese counterpart, Izanagi, just dies and is buried in Awaji.

457. Frazer 1963: 348 sqq.

458. Cf. Colarusso 2006: 35 for a Caucasian parallel.

459. See Matsumura 1998.

460. See Matsumura 2006b; cf. Ōbayashi 1977, 1982.

461. Cf. above, §3.6; cf. also Thor and the giants in Norse myth.

462. The son is called Ō-ana-muchi in the Nihon Shoki and Ō-kuni-mitama in the Kojiki.

463. Cf. Ōbayashi 1977, 1982.

464. See immediately below; cf. §8.5.

465. Cf. Matsumura 2006a.

466. For quick reference, see the table in Rotermund 2000: 117. For the symbolism, cf. Naumann 1988: 83.

467. And most interestingly, it is the goddess of the sea who is the mother of one of the greatest Greek heroes, Achilles—a fact reflected in the parentage of Jimmu.

468. Similarly, the descent of the Indian gods' descendants to reign on earth takes place only in the third generation after the sun god. Aditi's son Vivasvant has the children: Manu, the first real man, and Yamī and her twin brother, the god Yama (who mysteriously dies—like Yima in Iranian myth—and becomes lord of Hades). Manu's son, the third-generation Nābhānediṣṭha, is a shadowy figure, but his grandson Purūravas is well known in mythology as a mundane "king," who is temporarily "married" to a nymph, the Apsaras Urvaśī. Similarly,

in Japan, the third-generation descendant of the Sun goddess, Ninigi, marries a lovely young women he met at Cape Kasasa, daughter of Ō-Yama.tsu mi-no kami, a *tsuchi-kami* (mundane deity), who was a child of Izanagi and Izanami. Just like Purūravas, he married outside his own group. Purūravas is told (Ṛgveda 10.95.18) that he will ultimately rejoice in heaven and that his son will go on to fight for the gods. Indeed, the son, Āyu, has become the ancestor of all future Indian kings (*āyava*) of the "solar line" (*sūryavaṃśa*)—just as Jimmu does in Japan. For a political and mythological interpretation, see Naumann 1988: 89 sq., 93 sq.

469. Kuiper 1983.

470. Witzel 2004a. One should consider whether this state of affairs is reflected in the New Year period in Japan, when Amaterasu hides in her cave, the gods have a carnival outside, and the emperor has to perform special rituals. Preceding this, during the tenth lunar month (now November), all the gods are invited as *marebito* visitors from across the sea and assemble at Izumo for the Kamiarisai rituals. Does this reflect a return to the original state of things, before the victory of Amaterasu's children?

471. Bek-Pedersen (2003) tries out several models, including the Æsir :: Vanir one.

472. Kott *art'a* (true, veritable) from Indo-Iranian **ṛta/arta*, the underlying universal force behind the Deva/Asura conflict; see Witzel 2004a; §2.1.2. Mordwin *azoro* (lord), Vogul *ātər* (prince), from Indo-Iran. **asura* (lord); Witzel 2004b; §3, n. 144.

473. Granet 1988.

474. Schärer 1946, 1963.

475. Or Tagaro (opposed by Suqe) in the New Hebrides or Qat (opposed by the spider Marawa) in the Banks Islands; see Beckwith 1972: 61; cf. also Eliade 1954b: 345 sq.

476. Note the role of the spider (Ananse) in African (and Amerind) myths, §5.3.5.2 sqq.

477. For the Aztecs, see Soisson and Soisson 1987: 97 sqq.

478. Tedlock 1985: 86 sqq. The mytheme of the scorpion at the foot of the tree where Seven Macaw sits has baffled interpreters. However, if the appearance of the early sun and its destruction is correlated with the theory of precession (cf. Barber and Barber 2004: 206), this would not be surprising. The early sun (belonging to the ancient Near Eastern asterism Taurus) is slain by Mithras, while a scorpion is attacking him or his testicles from below or behind. In astronomy, Scorpio and Taurus are asterisms on opposite ends of the sky, representing the summer and winter solstice. In spite of *Hamlet's Mill*, the question, certainly, remains how the Maya could have had the same concept as the people of the ancient Near East. The scorpion is obviously not an animal that would have been known to Bering Land ancestors of the Maya; it would have been substituted by the Mayas for an earlier northern-latitude animal.

479. With the Aztec, east = white, south = blue, west = red, north = black (Lehmann 1953: 42 sq.). The Hopi and Navajo, however, have red/copper/east, blue/silver/south, yellow/gold/ west, and yellowish-white/mixed mineral *sikyápala*/north (see §2, n. 262). The Navajo also have black as the fourth color (north); see Locke 2004: 58; §2, n. 262. On the other hand, the Chinese and Old Iranian colors for the directions of the sky are different: east = blue/green, south = red, west = white, and north = black (Witzel 1972). The traditional colors for the three or four classes of the Indo-Europeans are white for the priesthood, red for the nobility, blue/green for the "people," and sometimes, a fourth class (black) is added; for their interpretation, see Lyle 1990: 41–47.

480. Sullivan 1996.

481. Barber and Barber 2004: 201–2, 208 sqq. They (2004: 210) have a useful table of the Babylonian, Hittite/Hurrian, Phoenician, Greek, and Norse myths, which leaves out, however, Iran, India, the Aztecs, the Mayas, etc.

482. For a structural interpretation, a pentadic scheme, of the Four–Five Ages, see Allen 2000.

483. Cf. Puhvel 1987: 21 sqq.; and the myths and stories in Rotermund 2000: 45 sqq.

484. Some tribes agree with the Eurasian myths about the creation of light/sun that took place soon after initial creation (see above, §3.1), for example, even the South American Yabarana on the Orinoco; Lévi-Strauss 1973: 168, M. 416.

485. See Mathieu 1989: Myth nos. 13–14; Yang and An 2005: 73, 75. The myth is found with many other ethnic groups in what is now China (Miao, Naxi, etc.). The Austronesian Atayal of Taiwan have a myth about two original suns, one of which was shot down. The Maya myth seems to go back to such Asian origins. Note the importance of the number 10 in connection with the sun and decade count of days, cf. on the decades Lévi-Strauss 1973; note also that in the Old Japanese Kujiki (ninth–tenth century) Uzume counts up to ten on her upturned tub; see Aston 1972: 44.

486. This recalls the Iranian myth of the great archer Ɜrəxša (Yašt 8.6) or of Rudra (Śiva) shooting at Father Heaven (Dyaus, visible as a deer, Mṛga [Orion]), who pursued his daughter, Dawn. Cf. the parallel Maori myth of Rangaroa (Ocean), who pierced Rangi (Heaven) with a spear as he had committed adultery with Papa (Earth), the wife of his father, Te-more-tu (Tregear 1891/1969: 463).

486. A similar myth may have existed even earlier in India, as an archer appears in already in Indus iconography (2600–1900 BCE). However, the idea of shooting at the new sun(s) is also found in Central America, for example with the Maya (see above) or with the Huichol of Mexico, where the new sun is shot at. The Baltic myth of the three suns (Saule) may provide another clue. Here, it is the three aspects of the sun that are meant: the morning sun at dawn, the hot midday sun, and the evening sun at dusk. In India, we find similar appellations of the sun.

487. On the other hand, the Chinese and Iranian colors for the directions of the sky are different: east = blue/green, west = white, north = black, and south = red; see §3, n. 479. For the Four–Five Ages in Iran, cf. Allen 2000.

488. This is retained in the Indian Bhagavadgītā, chap. 11, in Kṛṣṇa's devouring the world in his epiphany.

489. The exception is the Hopi, whose relation to immigrant groups from the north needs to be investigated. For the Four/Five Ages in South America, note the flood, which is found, for example, in Tierra del Fuego or with the Yanomami (Sullivan 1988: 63); see Roe's (1982) detailed discussion of Amazonia. For the Makiritare, see Sullivan 1988: 69; for Patagonia, where the Tehuelche have four eras related to the actions of a culture hero, see Sullivan 1988: 52; cf. Casamiquela 1982. There also are four destructions in the Gran Chaco. For a complete list and discussion of South America, see Sullivan 1988: 49 sqq.; for a short bibliography on flood myth, see Dundes 1988: 221.

490. Schultze Jena 1944: 101.

491. Baumann 1936; Frobenius 1904; see §1, n. 56.

492. However, cf., on pre-Columbian chicken import to South America, Storey et al. 2007; cf. Carter 1971.

493. Cf. Herbig 1988: 264 sqq.

494. Cf. §7, n. 286.

495. Ions 1990: 13, 21, esp. 117; Murray 1963: 110; Simpson 1973: 270. Cf. Blumenthal 1978, on the denial of divinity of the pharaoh, which has been controversially discussed; see G. Posener (1992).

496. Jacobsen 1976: 181.

497. Witzel 1987b.

498. Hoffmann 1992.

499. Puhvel 1987.

500. In Kati (Nuristani) myth, the primordial pair, Wrok and Brok, produced children; see Allen 2000.

501. Cf. the (Buddhist) Mongolian fire goddess next to an older male fire deity. Cf. Munro 1963: 15, 16 sqq., 55 sqq., etc.

502. After Tanaka, in Walter and Fridman 2004: 658 sq.

503. Tanaka, in Walter and Fridman 2004: 659. For the similar myths, albeit with some-what torturous etymologies, of the assimilated Ainu in northernmost Honshu (Tsugaru), see Tanaka, in Walter and Fridman 2004: 700.

504. Beckwith 1987: 46, 307 sqq., with a discussion of the various Hawai'ian and other versions; Grey 1855/1956: 11.

505. However, just as in India and the Near East, there also is a weather god, Illapa, and an earth mother, Pachamana.

506. Witzel 2005b.

507. The pattern of spread along a belt from Europe/North Africa via Iran and India to Southeast Asia and Japan, and across the Polynesian Pacific has been interpreted by H. Baumann (1986: 9, 250, 374 sq.) as gradual diffusion from "archaic high cultures" between the Nile and the Indus. However, see discussion on diffusion above, §1.2.

508. Philippi 1968: 61 sqq.

509. Aston 1972: 30. Cf. Naumann 1988: 62 sq. The myth has echoes of the Purūravas tale; Ṛgveda 10.95.

510. Some relic versions let humans be produced from clay or from trees, as in the Bible (clay), in Old Egypt (clay, with beer), with the Kafirs (clay), among the Mayas (from maize), etc. It will be obvious that the latter is a later version; see §3, n. 520. Similarly, see descent from trees (Kaguyahime in Japanese folktales, Askr/Embla, Austronesian Taiwan, which is a Gondwana relic); see below, §5.

511. Lists in Tregear 1891/1969: 667 sqq.; for the Toradja of Sulawesi, see Koubi 1982: 24: their noble lineages derive from the gods.

512. See §5.3.5; Baumann 1936: 206–13, 242–53.

513. Baumann 1936: 243 sqq.

514. Baumann 1936: 386.

515. Additionally, a few more or less related myths may be indicated: Thompson 1993: Motifs A114.4. Deity born from tree, Hawaii: Beckwith, Myth 279, 284.—So. Am. Indian (Tembé); A115.7. Gods emerge from hole in tree, India (as does Kaguyahime, the princess of the moon, in a Jpn. fairy tale). Animals, too, emerge from a tree; A1793. Hawaii: Beckwith, Myth 287; S. Am. Indian (Warrau).

516. Rundle Clark 1959: 20. Note that, after the slaying by Hat-Thor of humankind, beer is made, and red ochre is added (which looks like human blood); Re pours out the beer at the spot in the desert of the slaying; the goddess drinks of it and spares the rest of the humans. Or humans are made from the tears of the primordial god Re.

517. From mud and blood. Note also the creation of humans from the slain Kingu and his blood; Jacobsen 1976: 181.

518. Campbell 1988: I.1: 14, from Frobenius 1924: 75–76.

519. From the Sun; Yang and An 2005: 67 sq. They mention many other origin myths from what is now China: humans were made by gods, e.g., by Nuwa, from yellow earth (cf. Mathieu 1989: Myth no. 24), spat out from the mouth of gods, made from a plant, made from a cave or a stone or gourd, etc. The question is how far such mythemes reflect earlier Gondwana concepts, dating back to the earliest settlement of China around 40 kya.

520. Tana-compta, the first man, was modeled of red clay (Tregear 1891/1969: 315); he gave birth to a daughter who propped up the sky, which rather looks like the common Gondwana myth of a woman pushing up the sky with a pole or a pestle; see §5, n. 269; this is unlike the Laurasian myth about Indra etc.

521. Tregear 1891/1969: 57.

522. Fornander, *Collection* (1916–19), quoted in Beckwith 1987: 43.

523. Cf. also the African version of the myth, with the Bassari in Togo (Frobenius 1924: 75–76; see Campbell 1988: I.1: 14). Cf. §2, nn. 113, 179, §3, nn. 340, 414, 523; §5, nn. 113, 299, 368; §6, n. 30.

524. See http://www.maori.org.nz/korero/?d=page&pid=sp41&parent=36.

525. Cf. http://www.archaeology.org/interactive/tiwanaku/history.html. In Maya myth, however, humans are created from maize (Popol Vuh [Schultze Jena 1944: 101]), according to a change typical in later, agricultural societies; cf. §7.2.

526. The location, right in front of the old gate, was symbolically used on January 21, 2006, for the inauguration of the new, indigenous president of Bolivia.

527. The origin of the Inca dynasty on Lake Titicaca in Bolivia and their underground "march" northward to Cuzco is one of the many founding myths that involves a "prestigious" arrival from the outside, such as the Hebrew Exodus from Egypt (and the earlier one of Abraham from Ur in Mesopotamia, thus linking the Hebrews with both the Mesopotamians and the Egyptians!) and their crossing of the River Jordan, the Japanese myth of the eastward march of Jimmu from Kyushu to Yamato (in the Asuka/Nara area), the myth of the Latin people's arrival from Troy in Virgil's *Aeneid*, and various Irish migration myths. Other origin myths, however, such as the northern origin of the Aztecs, do *not* feature a prestigious origin area; the Maya case ("from Tulan") is complex. As for Gondwana examples, see below, §5.2 sqq.; Baumann 1936: 202 sqq.; and compare the travels of the Aborigines' totem ancestors across Australia along their "song lines." The motif as such is very old, as will be seen later (§6).

528. Shaw 2006: 160.

529. The Austronesian-speaking, high mountain Tsou tribe has a myth of the origin of a handsome boy from a banana tree; see Tung 1964: 327, 381. The Tsou themselves derive from leaves shaken down by a god in primordial times; Tung 1964: 287.

530. Baumann 1936: 224 sqq.; for Taiwan, see the previous note.

531. Echoes of this are found in tenth-century China (Barrett 1995: 75 sq.), including the myth of the ancient hero Yi Yin, created from a hollow mulberry tree (Birrell 1993: chap. 5, 128 n. sq.), and less related tales from ancient Szechuan, the Uighurs, and the Vietnamese. The Szechuan tale is closest to the Kaguyahime myth, in that a boy child was born from a bamboo log. Note also the African, Australian (Howitt 1904: 458), and Tasmanian tree burial; below §5.

532. Schultze Jena 1944: 101; Tedlock 1985: 164. Similarly, see the Pueblo cultures (Bierhorst 1986: 82); cf. the Mexican illustration in Campbell 1989: II.1: 159.

533. See Witzel 2006a.

534. A primordial egg is produced in the empty sky, and a man (Warma Nyinya) with many animal features and magical powers emerges from it; a Bön version is given by Van Over (1980: 373 sq.); see Snellgrove and Richardson 1968: 55 sqq.

535. Beckwith 2004; Chang 1983: 10; see below, §3.1.7; cf. Granet 1989: 81.

536. See below, §3.1.6; Witzel 2004a. The egg motif is also found in Africa: see Baumann 1986: 268 sqq., map 4. However, it occurs along the Nigerian and Cameroon coast as well as in the Sahel belt: northern influence (including from Old Egypt) seems likely.

537. Eliade 1992: 190. With the Eastern Shawnee they live on the little stars of the Milky Way or with the Chinook, in the sun, in daylight; otherwise (Eliade 1992: 189) they dwell in

a house in the forest or some other place, usually, however, in the netherworld, which is the same as the land of the dead. With the Mayan or Pueblo people, however, the netherworld is the original home of mankind, a place for renewal of life, realm of the dead, and place of the unborn.

538. Indian myth also places the origin of humans after two trial creations of birds (who walk on two feet like men) and snakes—egg-laying creatures (who are thus "reborn" just like human males during initiation); see Śatapatha Brāhmaṇa 2.5.1.1 sqq. The text clearly says that by now "three generations have passed."

539. An idea also found in Australia: stepping on rocks that embody an ancestor makes a wife pregnant.

540. Echoing the abandonment of Vivasvant as a misshaped egg. On a whim the gods take pity and carve him into shape; see Hoffmann 1992.

541. Chang 1983: 15.

542. Chang 1983: 15.

543. For a brief discussion of Chinese myths about gourd origins, see Barrett 1995: 74, including a reference to a Korean founder figure, P'ogong (Sir Gourd; in the Sanguk Yusa; Ha and Mintz 1972: 55).

544. Berger 1959.

545. For possible connections between Indian myths and those of Austric and some East Asian populations, see Sergent 1997: 369–96.

546. Kristina Lindell, Jan-Ojvind Swahn, and Damrong Tayanin, in Dundes 1988: 265–80, esp. 276. Discussion in Yamada 2003.

547. Rivers 1906: 203 sqq. Additionally, a few myths about the creation (of humans) by vomiting may be mentioned; see §3, n. 119. In medieval Kashmir, Śiva creates the world by vomiting it; in Old Egypt, it is vomited by Atum; in ancient Tibet King Sron tsan sgam po is created from the saliva of the Bodhisattva. For Africa, see Baumann 1936: 423, s.v. *Menschenerbrechen*. With the Bushongo, the primordial god Bumba vomited the sun, moon, earth, plants, and animals and then humanity. (Cf. §2, n. 180; §3, nn. 66, 68, 119.) The myth may be of Gondwana age.

548. In the Laurasian area we occasionally find the birth of humans from a rock: with Taiwan Aborigines such as the Atayal (Rimuy Aki et al. 2002: 18 sqq.) and with the Dayaks. For the Nepalese Kham Magar, see Oppitz 1991: 115, 117, 119; cf. also the Hittite myth of Ullikummi. The ancestors of some Chinese dynasties are born from rocks; see Granet 1989: 81 sq. For the Toradja of Sulawesi, see Koubi 1982: 23, where a variation is seen: a goddess emerges from a rock and then creates humans. This seems to be a Gondwana motif; see §5.3.3 sqq.; and cf. §6 for a scenario of its retention in Laurasian mythology.

549. Cf. Eliade 1958: 134 sq., cf. 124 sqq. Strangely, Eliade restricts sun worship basically to "Egypt, Asia, and primitive Europe," which leaves out the Americas (de la Garza 2005) and more recent imports into Africa (Baumann 1936).

550. On the status of the Japanese emperor as a deity (*kami*), see Ohnuki-Thierney 1991.

551. Most interestingly, it is the goddess of the sea who is the mother of one of the greatest Greek heroes, Achilles—a fact reflected in the parents of Jimmu as well. Cf. §3, nn. 235, 467, 551.

552. Cf. Naumann 1988: 103 (including parallels with Korean royal myths); Philippi 1968: 163. His progress follows the "way of the sun" (see Matsumura 2006a) along the 34°32' North latitude line from Ise to Awaji. But in Jimmu's case this occurs in reverse order, from west to east (Witzel 2009b, which points to a solar myth: he is the descendant of the sun deity

Amaterasu, and just like her, he travels back to the east during the night, and he has to emerge victoriously in the east—as Jimmu indeed does, from the southeast of Yamato. For an impression, see the photo in Witzel 2005b: it shows the *central* "heavenly" mountain (Ama.no Kaguyama) in the Yamato Plain, north of the grave of Jimmu; the photo is taken from the southeast, near to the entry point of Jimmu.

553. Beckwith 2004.

554. The background of this myth is given in Witzel 2008, 2009b. Cf. the closely parallel Maori myth of Tawhaki (Tregear 1891/1969: 496), who is searched out by Tango-tango, one of the heavenly nymphs; she visits him every night and gives birth to his child, whom she takes with her. Tawhaki, like Purūravas, longs for her and finally goes to heaven via a vine, just as Purūravas is promised Heaven (Ṛgveda 10.05.18).

555. Witzel 2005b.

556. See §2, n. 214; Naumann 1988: 95 (as cosmic mantle of the emperor; cf. the trefoil mantle in the Veda); Ōbayashi 1984; Waida 1973.

557. Ōbayashi 1984, 1991a. See Harva 1938.

558. Unless we want to understand the destruction by Susa.no Wo of the dams of the heavenly rice fields as such. However, the myth occurs in folktales as the breaking of a dam of a mountain lake, as also found in Kashmir, Nepal, and Khotan (Allen 1997).

559. An ancient *haniwa* clay replica has recently been found in Mie-Ken; see *Nihon Keizai Shimbun*, April 11, 2004 (with photo). This *haniwa* has been interpreted as a ship guiding the soul of the deceased to the otherworld. A few others are known, one with a (soul) bird on the boat (quite similar to some Indo-European artworks; see Gotō 2006). Also, cf. the expression, still used for the imperial burial, *funa-kan*. See above on the similar Ainu concept; §3, n. 73, cf. n. 387.

560. Cf. §2.3; Witzel 2005b. This precedes later Iranian ("Scythian") ones; see Yoshida 2006 on Central Asian influences via Korea.

561. The flood myth itself, which is found in a Japanese folktale as flowing from a lake, will be treated in the next section; cf. also §5.6.

562. Witzel 1984b.

563. The motif of humans created from stone is also found in Austronesian Taiwan, Polynesia, and Central and South America. Thompson 1993: Motif A1245. Man created from stones. Hdwb. d. Abergl. I 463, Greek, Nauru, Tonga, Samoa, Melanesia, Indonesia; Central America, S. Am. Indian (Inca, Paressi). Or humans come from a mountain: Thompson 1993: Motifs A1245.5. Man born from mountains, India; A1234.2. Mankind emerges from mountain, Pijaos (Colombia). Cf. §2, n. 177; §5, n. 319; §6, n. 20. Humans may be born from rocks, with the Greek motif of stones thrown over the shoulders; cf. Thompson 1993: Motif A1254.1. New race from seeds thrown over head after deluge (cf. A1245.1; A1006), Tamanac (Carib).

564. See the translations of the relevant Vedic and Iranian myths and the discussion in Hoffmann 1992.

565. Chang 1983: 10.

566. Chang 1983:10. Other early monarchs were born from a stone etc.; see Mathieu 1989: Myth nos. 51–58.

567. Chang 1983.

568. Beckwith 2004.

569. Bierhorst 1986: 192.

570. The flood is just one of the several ways that the early earth and (proto)humans have been wiped out several times (see Mesoamerica, in §2.5.2, §3.11) or will be wiped out in the

future: by water, ice, fire, wind, devouring, etc. See the discussions in Day 1984: 400 sqq.; Dundes 1988; Yamada 2003 (especially on South China and Southeast Asia).

571. Itself adapted from the myth of Atrahasis (or Ziusudra), a Sumerian text believed to have been translated from the Akkadian version; see Kovacs 1985: 97 n. 1.

572. Dalley 1989; Gardner and Maier 1984; Heidel 1963; Kovacs 1985 etc. Detailed version by Pettinato (2002), with the first complete translation on new materials, discovered in a royal tomb in 1999 by the Italian archaeological mission at Me-Turan, between Djala and Tigri. It has a new end of the Gilgamesh saga, of c. 1700 BCE, much older than the Ninive text. Pettinato has been publishing on the new texts since 2001.

573. For recent work on the flood myth, see Allen 2000 (also on the age of the motif; he excludes a Near Eastern origin for the pentadic Indo-European motif); Gonda 1978; Etter 1989; Magnone 1999, 2000.

574. Atrahasis II SBV iv; Dalley 1989: 23 sqq.

575. See §5.7.2 for the Pan-Gaean topic of retribution and revenge; Smith 1996: 35, 151 sqq.

576. Tregear 1891/1969: 558, 222. According to Vedic myth, the earth turned upside down every night; see Kuiper 1983; Witzel 1984b. Another Polynesian myth has Tane jumping on heaven until it cracks. For the Hawai'ian version, see Beckwith 1987: 315. In some versions, Christian influence is seen. For other Oceanic versions, see Beckwith 1987: 315 sqq.

577. Tregear 1891/1969: 560; for this, cf. §3.7.

578. See http://www.maori.org.nz/korero/?d=page&pid=sp40&parent=36. The myth continues: "This is the narrative about the generations of the ancestors of men from the beginning of the Po, and therefore we, the people of this land, carefully preserved these traditions of old times as a thing to be taught to the generations that come after us. So we repeat them in our *karakia* [invocation] and whenever we relate the deeds of the ancestors from whom each *iwi* [bone] and family is descended, and on other similar occasions."

579. Though in some areas with its "reverse" version, that of a flooding caused by a great lake or pond, which laid the Kathmandu and Kashmir Valley dry but briefly flooded nearby areas; see Allen 1997.

580. Thompson 1993: Motif A1010. Deluge. Inundation of whole world or section, Irish, Greek, Egyptian, Persian, Hindu/India, Chinese, Korean, Indo-Chinese, Indonesian, Philippine (Tinguian), Polynesian (Samoan, Hawaii), Siberian, Eskimo, N. A. Indian (Pima, Walapai, Sia, Hopi, Sinkyone, Calif. Indian, Maya, Mixtec), S. Am. Indian (Carib, Chibcha, Amazon tribes, Jivaro, Yugua, Cubeo, Aymara, Zaparoans, Pebans, Bacairi, Nambicuara, Guaporé, Caingang, Eastern Brazil).

581. See Mathieu 1989: Myth nos. 39–41; Yang and An 2005: 74. A new creation of humans occurs by the marriage of a brother and sister after all humans had been wiped out by a disaster (flood, fire, snow, etc.); this myth is found with the Han and some 40 other ethnic groups (as well as in the Philippines). In some versions, the first child is abnormal due to a mistake in the "marriage" procedure (as in Japan), resulting in a spherically shaped child, a gourd or stone, all of which has echoes in Indo-Iranian and Japanese myth (Mārtāṇḍa, Hirugo); see Yang and An 2005: 68, 73 sq.

582. In a different version found with the Mundas; see Ponette 1968: 99: a rain of fire sent as punishment by the supreme god Siṃboṅga.

583. See Yamada 2003: the gourd motif is fairly prominent. The paper contains a careful discussion of various mythemes and subtypes of the flood myth in this area: "brother and sister survive the flood," classified as 1. Primordial flood, 2. Cosmic antagonists, 3. Cosmic flood, 4. Flood caused by "sin." The gourd appears in versions 2 and 4.

584. Eugenio 1993; Shi 2006.

585. Such as at Taitung in southeastern Taiwan. The Taiwan Austronesian tribes have several versions of the flood myth; see Witzel 2006a; Yamada 2003.

586. Campbell 1988: I.2: 259; Gusinde 1977.

587. Cf. also the Inca tale reported in Barber and Barber 2004: 202 sq.; Sullivan 1996: 16. It dates back (in two versions) to the 16th century. See further Bierhorst 1988: 79 sq. for Guyana, 142 sq. for the Gran Chaco, 164 sq. for Tierra del Fuego.

588. Gusinde 1977; Wilbert 1977: 25–30.

589. Witzel 2001a. Cf. also Yamada 2003: 1.

590. See Dundes 1988: 115; Yamada 2003.

591. Dundes 1988: 2.

592. Erich Kolig, in Dundes 1988: 241 sqq.

593. For a fairly comprehensive listing, see http://www.talkorigins.org/faqs/flood-myths.html.

594. Keller 1956. Or the recent theories of a Northwest Coast Amerindian Ice Age refuge and spread after the meltdown, not to speak of more idiosyncratic explanations such as that of an astronomical myth, found with the Inca (Sullivan 1996). A similar kind of mythological explanation would provide for a big flood in the subterranean (= heavenly) ocean of night (cf. the myth of the sun's progress through the underground waters in Egypt etc.) or a flood in the "yearly" night, at the time of winter solstice, if the Milky Way would stop turning: it would remain "flattened out" as ocean surrounding and flooding the world; see illustrations in Witzel 1984b.

595. Dundes 1988: 151–65. See *Habil.-Schrift* by A. Etter (1989) and other Indologists such as Gonda (1978), Magnone (1999, 2000), etc.

596. Thompson 1993: Motif A1010: Melanesian, Australian, African. See Witzel 2010.

597. Ragin 1987: 164–65, cf. 55.

598. Nagy 1979; Raglan 1934; Segal et al. 1990; Vielle 1997.

599. Propp 1958.

600. Ježić 2005.

601. Raglan 1956.

602. See Eliade 1963: 54 sqq., with many examples. Sometimes the destruction is seen in the motif of the previous four generations of the gods or the Four/Five Ages of the world, notably in the Americas, where the ages ("Suns") are increasingly better than the earlier trial creations. The question whether this "optimistic" American scheme is older than the pessimistic view of the Four Ages in the West has been discussed earlier; §2.5.2; see, however, below.

603. A brief Buddhist version is found in Saṃyutta-Nikāya 22.99 (Pali Text Soc., vol. 3, 149 sq.): "there will be a time when the great ocean will dry up,...the king of mountains, Sineru [= Sumeru], will disappear,...the great earth will be burnt up." Note the revelation to Arjuna of the absorption of the universe in Kṛṣṇa's mouth (Bhagavadgītā 11).

604. Such as in the Bhagavadgītā 11 or in Mesoamerican myths.

605. Atum says to Osiris (Book of the Dead, chap. 175): "You will live for more than millions of years, an era of millions, but in the end I will destroy everything that I have created; the earth will become again part of the Primeval Ocean, like the abyss of waters in their original state. Then I will be what will remain, just I and Osiris, when I will have changed myself back into the Old Serpent who knew no man and saw no god" (Eliade 1992: 26; cf. Ions 1990: 22 on Nun).

606. Winter (Iceland and elsewhere: see §2, n. 196; 208; §5, n. 417), Kṛṣṇa in the Gītā (see §3, n. 603 sq.), various types in Maya/Aztec/Inca myths. The (then "misplaced")

biblical/Manu's/Gilgamesh's flood would be a piece of "Maya-type" myth retained before reordering the scheme toward a final destruction at the end of the world. Note that these particular flood myths all are Near Eastern and from surrounding areas. However, other flood myths are found worldwide; see §5.7.2.

607. All will revert to Nun; see Ions 1990: 22; §3, n. 610.

608. The Hopi and Navajo know of not just five but even seven or more future worlds, to emerge after the end of the present fifth one.

609. For the theory of the Four Ages in Indian texts, see González-Reimann 2002. There are hints of several ages (*yuga*) even in the oldest Indian text, the Ṛgveda, and in the early Zoroastrian texts. See §2.5.2 for "the earlier/later Yuga" (Ṛgveda 7.87.4) and the Zoroastrian account (Vīdēvdād 2) of the creation of the world and its expansion three times (cf. Varuna's actions in Ṛgveda 4.42); and cf. Allen 2000 for Nuristani and Kalash versions.

610. Cf. Eliade 1963.

611. S. Thompson (1993) lists the following motifs: A1000. World catastrophe; A1010. Deluge; A1020. Escape from deluge; A1030. World fire; A1040. Continuous winter destroys the race; A1050. Heavens break up at end of world; A1060. Earth-disturbances at end of world; A1070. Fettered monster's escape at end of world; A1080. Battle at end of world; A1090. World calamities—miscellaneous motifs.—For Fire: A622. Universe created out of fire world, Iceland; A1006.9. After world-fire life recreated from tree, Africa (Fang); A1009.1. First race of men perishes when sun first rises, S. Am. Indian (Aymara, Chibaya). A1030. World-fire. A conflagration destroys the earth. Sometimes (as with the flood legends) the tradition is somewhat local and does not refer to an actual destruction of the whole earth; sometimes the fire marks the end of the world, Iceland, Greek, Lithuanian, Jewish, Babylonian, Siberian, Hindu/India, Chinese, Maori, N. Am. Indian S. Am. Indian (Yuracare, W. Brazil, Araucanian, Chaco, Tupinamba, Apapocuva-Guarani, Tembé, Shipaya, Carajá, Mura, Cashinawa, Witoto, Arawak, Yuracare, Mataco, Toba, Tucuna, Nimuendajú, Bacairi).

612. See Yang and An 2005: 73.

613. There may be a connection with the Chinese motif of ten suns of, nine of which had to be shot down (like the fake sun, Seven Macaw, in Maya myth). This must be contrasted with the "eternal" sun in Melanesian and other Gondwana myths.

614. For additional (structural) reasons for the schema of 4 + 1 ages in Proto-Indo-European, see Allen 2000.

615. For a limited view on serial creation, see Bierhorst 1992: 129 sqq.; cf. §2, n. 193.

616. But not so with their neighbors, the Hopi and their *Pueblo* mythology.

617. Sullivan 1988: 744 n. 78.

618. A universal conflagration and the flood; see Campbell 1988: I.2: 259, based on Gusinde 1977: II: 1145 sq., 1155 sq., 1232 sq., trans. Wilbert 1977; cf. Sullivan 1988: 49, 66–72, 81; see Thompson 1993: Motif A1030.

■ Chapter 4

1. Cavalli-Sforza 1991; Cavalli-Sforza and Cavalli-Sforza 1994; Cavalli-Sforza et al. 1994.

2. See Cavalli-Sforza 1991.

3. Note the Kafiri/Kalash case in northeastern Afghanistan and northwestern Pakistan, where the Kalash speak an archaic Indo-Aryan dialect, while the neighboring Nuristanis speak several languages that belong to the third branch of Indo-Iranian, Nuristani (formerly called Kafiri). However, the mythology of both populations overlaps to a very large degree

(Jettmar 1975). Or cf. the overlaps between Ainu and other northeastern Asian mythologies; or the large amount of overlaps between the mythology of the Navajo/Apache, late Na-Dene-speaking newcomers from the Alaskan and Canadian north, and that of their Amerindian-speaking neighbors in the southwestern United States (Pueblo); or the well-attested, ancient relationship between Hittite and Hatti myths and rituals.

4. See Robert McMahon (2004).

5. It is also found in Africa (see Baumann 1936) and Southeast Asia (Bahnars in Central Vietnam; see Yamada 2003: 5).

6. Bopp 1816. A good overview of the comparative method is found in Ruhlen 1994a: 284–90.

7. In linguistics, reconstructed words are marked by an asterisk, thus *diēus*.

8. In this special case, even the reverse is true: Engl. *hound* :: German *Hund* (dog).

9. For explanations of such semantic relationships, based on a theory of the meaning of smallest components carrying meaning (*noemes*) underlying the aggregate of meaning represented by a certain word, and on etymologies, see Hoffmann 1992.

10. Cf. in another Italic dialect, Oscan: *Iu-pater*. The Latin form is now understood as the outcome of a fairly rare development, the "*littera* rule," which explains doubling of long vowel + single consonant as in *lītera > littera*, **Iū-piter > Iuppiter*, etc.; see Meiser 1998: 77. The earlier alternative explanation was that it was taken from the emphatic vocative form: "oh, Father Heaven."

11. And quite a number of other verbs belonging to the same category, such as *i* (to go).

12. Beekes 1995.

13. Ehret 1995.

14. Décsy 1990.

15. Scholarship tends to fluctuate between two extremes every few decades; after the unifying positions personified by N. Poppe and S. Starostin versus splitters in the sixties that included G. Clauson and G. Doerfer, some have started to doubt the very existence of the Altaic family again; see A. Vovin (2003). Proof for Altaic is given by Robbeets (2005).

16. Called Tibeto-Burman by some, notably van Driem (2006 etc.). For a brief overview, see van Driem 2006; his "Tibeto-Burman" includes Chinese as a northern outlier. For a discussion of current views, see Sagart et al. 2005.

17. Cf. also Benedict's (1990) proposal of a Japanese-Austro-Tai family. See further, for Austro-Tai, Benedict 1975. For a brief overview, see Anderson 2001, 2007; Diffloth 2001, 2005; van Driem 2006. On genetics, see van Driem 2006: 173 sq.

18. Also including, according to some, Miao/Hmong and some other languages in South China, such as Tai-Kadai, which includes Thai. For their classification, see Bengtson 2006; cf. Benedict 1976; and the recent discussions in Sagart et al. 2005 by Ostapirat, Reid, Sagart, and Starosta.

19. See the recent updates in Black 2006; Foley 1986; Pawley and Ross 1995; Whitehouse 2006; Wurm 1982.

20. Clendon 2006; Dixon 2002; Wurm 1972.

21. Bender 1996; Ehret 2001; Heine 2000.

22. Nurse and Philippson 2003; Williamson and Blench 2000.

23. Semitic: Akkadian (Babylonian, Assyrian), Hebrew, Aramaic, Phoenician, Arabic; further: Old Egyptian/Coptic, Berber, Kushitic (Somali, Oromo), Hausa, etc. See Ehret 1995.

24. Some common grammatical and syntactical features of this area have been discovered by Masica (1976); the close, still enigmatic relationship of areal linguistic features that

exist between South Asia and Ethiopia is part of Masica's linguistic area and of the Nostratic area.

25. If carried out in uncritical fashion, this give rise to problems, as the meanings of words change, e.g., the name of the beech tree has become the word for "oak" in Greek and British Engl. *corn* (wheat) is the American word for "maize"; see Zimmer 1990.

26. See Caries et al. 1997; Powell 2005; cf. Gollan 1985.

27. See the convenient word list by Mark Kaiser (1989); the collections and correlations by Ch. Graves (1997) are omnicomparativist and can be neglected.

28. Witzel 1992; also in *$Hoṭa$ (fire) seen in Indo-European *$hwet-(r)$, Avest. *atar* (Kaiser 1989).

29. Typical for the oldest Indian text (Ṛgveda, c. 1200–1000 BCE) is the fire :: water symbolism; fire resides in and emerges from (primordial) water; for example, Ṛgveda 2.1.1, 3.9.2, 4.40.5, 10.91.6, etc.

30. Masica 1976.

31. However, see below on connections with genetics, mtDNA haplogroup M (§4.3).

32. Abbi 2006: 95.

33. Witzel 2005b, 2009a.

34. Witzel 2005b, 2009a.

35. For details, see Witzel 2005b. Japanese myth (in its recorded form, of 712 CE), goes back at least to the first half of the first millennium CE and has no direct or indirect connections with Vedic India (1500–500 BCE) before the introduction of Buddhism around 500 CE.

36. Just as in Indo-Iranian and Indo-European mythologies. See Witzel 2005b.

37. However, the feature of showing the breasts has been explained by ethologists as a general human motif of pacification and acquiescence; see Wunn 2005; §4.4.1. If universally correct, this example must be abandoned.

38. See Usher 2002; and cf. §5.3.2.1.

39. Whitehouse et al. 2004; cf. Rana 2002, 2006; Watters 2005.

40. Greenberg 1987b.

41. Greenberg 2000–2002.

42. Greenberg thought that "the Eurasiatic-Amerind family represents a relatively recent expansion (circa 15,000 BP) into territory opened up by the melting of the Arctic ice cap" (2000–2002: 2).

43. Ragin 1987.

44. Bengtson 1990.

45. Bengtson 1991. For recent linguistic data, see Bengtson 2010; Vajda 2008.

46. Bengtson and Ruhlen 1994.

47. Or Pulleyblank's (1993) proposal to link Chinese with Indo-European; see Beckwith 2004; and the discussion in Sagart et al. 2005 by van Driem and the late Stanley Starosta, who derives all language families involved (Sino-Tibetan, Hmong-Mien, Austro-Asiatic, and Austronesian) from a common Proto–East Asian superfamily.

48. For possible connections between Indian myths and those of Austric and some East Asian populations, see Sergent 1997: 369–96.

49. See discussion in §4.3, end.

50. See the summary by N. Saitou (2006) and by P. Manning (2006), following Greenberg. Saitou assumes a two-pronged eastward movement via Central Asia (100–50 kya) and an early move to Europe at 90 kya. See the discussion in Sagart et al. 2005.

51. Note that Lieberman (2006, 2007; cf. Devlin 2006) improbably even denies current "fully vocalized" speech to humans before 50 kya; see §4.4.

52. For example, via the scriptless western Central Asian region; see Witzel 2004a, 2004b. A similar idea is maintained by Manning (2006: 155).

53. Mehdi et al. 1999. Cf., however, Ayub et al. 2003; Underhill et al. 2000.

54. Successfully attempted by J. Bengtson (1990, 2003) for what he calls the Macro-Caucasian family (Basque, North Caucasian, Burushaski).

55. McMahon 2004: 9. He requires that linguists must provide "numerically tractable hierarchical classifications" both within and between language families and reports on several new strategies (obviously derived from recent biological models of cladistics and stemmatics) based on various types of linguistic data, such as (1) "recurrence metrics" quantifying the comparative method by using cladistic clustering or new phonetic comparisons, (2) improving "traditional" lexico-statistic use of word lists and developing new non-tree-like analysis based on them, and (3) developing new estimates of "inter-language-based" distances "calculated from phonetics and morpho-syntactic data." Most of this has obviously been done over the past 200 years of course, albeit not in the strictly quantified fashion that McMahon desires. Cf. also Dunn et al. 2005; Gray and Atkinson 2003; Nakhleh et al. 2005—though with linguistically and culturally dubious results.

56. Note the projects under way at the Santa Fe Institute (http://ehl.santafe.edu/intro1.htm) and the Rosetta Project (http://www.rosettaproject.org/).

57. Cavalli-Sforza and Cavalli-Sforza 1994: 112, 118, 372.

58. Cavalli-Sforza and Cavalli-Sforza 1994: 115; italics mine.

59. W. W. Howell's research, cited in Cavalli-Sforza and Cavalli-Sforza 1994: 117.

60. Cavalli-Sforza and Cavalli-Sforza 1994: 116.

61. See Wade 2007.

62. For a short description of this kind of analysis, see §4.3.

63. Alain Froment (1992) made use of nine measurements: length, breadth, and height of the skull; the distance between basion and nasion and between nasion and prosthion (both of which allow one to measure prognathism); the breadth and height of the face; and the breadth and height of the nose (see Table 4.1, below). See the discussion by Stock et al. (2007: 245 sqq.).

64. Cavalli-Sforza et al. 1994; Day 1977; Kennedy 1995; Sergent 1997; Stock et al. 2007; Tobias et al. 2001.

65. For example, based on dentochronological data the date for the Out of Africa migration has been set at 60,000 ± 6,100 years (Turner 1986), which is close to that of genetics (§4.3). Further, the distinction between Sundadont (in Southeast Asia) and Sinodont (East Asia) has been well established (Pietrusewsky 2005, with a dendogram of 63 Asian and Oceanic populations; Scott and Turner 1997), which again agrees with the division made by genetics. Further results derive from the study of fingerprints; cf. the discussion by J. Stock et al. (2007: 245 sqq.).

66. Kennedy 2000; Sergent 1997; contrast with Stock et al. 2007.

67. Froment (1992) and Sergent (1997: 43) believe that the number of "European" immigrants into South Asia was minor in relation to the original exodus from Africa; this is contradicted by recent genetic research based on autosomal data (Patterson et al. 2008).

68. In Cavalli-Sforza and Cavalli-Sforza 1994: 116–18.

69. However, it is interesting to note that the Dravidian, Vedda (Sri Lanka), and Indus data range about ±0. For the ancient remnant population, the Veddas, one would perhaps expect a

much more "southern" location, such as that of some of the Africans (and the Papuans, Australians, Pygmies, and Bushmen; see Howells, in Cavalli-Sforza and Cavalli-Sforza 1994: 117).

70. Masica 1976.

71. There is continuity, as has been underlined by several anthropologists (paleontologists), between the pre-Indus (c. 2600 BCE) and post-Indus (c. 1900 BCE) osteological record. Based on limited skeletal data, no trace of a (substantial) "foreign" influx has been found for the second millennium BCE, according to Kennedy (1995); see his (2000) very detailed discussion of South Asia; and cf. the discussion by Stock et al. (2007: esp. 245 sqq.).

72. Witzel 1995, 1999a, 2001b, etc.

73. Oppenheimer 2006.

74. Cavalli-Sforza et al. 1994: 19. Cavalli-Sforza continues to stress that there is only *one* human species and that "no single gene is sufficient for classifying human populations into systematic categories," and in further trying to classify humans, the boundaries between clusters become less and less clear. He sums up that "because the geographic differentiation of humans is recent...there has...been too little time for the accumulation of a substantial divergence." In sum, the differences between human groups are small when compared with those occurring *within* major groups or those *within* a single group.

75. Cavalli-Sforza and Cavalli-Sforza 1994: 123 sq.

76. Cavalli-Sforza and Cavalli-Sforza 1994: 228 sq.; cf. McEvoy et al. 2006; Relethford 2002.

77. Wade 2007a. Chris Stringer and Robin McKie have summed up the debate: "some of the oldest *Homo sapiens* relics, like those 100,000-year-old fossils from Qafzeh and Skhul,...do not have the kind of differentiation that distinguish races today....[Some of] the Cro-Magnons, the presumed ancestors of modern Europeans...were more like present-day Australians or Africans,...as is the case with some early modern skulls from Upper Cave at Zhoukoudian in China [42–39 kya]....[R]acial differences were still developing relatively recently....[H]umanity's modern African origin does not imply derivation from people like current Africans, because these populations must also have changed through the impact of evolution over the past 100,000 years" (1996: 154).

78. Kennedy 1995: 61; similarly Cavalli-Sforza and Cavalli-Sforza 1994.

79. Compared with mtDNA, nonrecombinant Y (NRY) therefore "is ordinarily sharper than that coming from mitochondrial DNA" (Cavalli-Sforza 2002: 84).

80. The combination of research into the fairly stable NRY haplotypes with that into rapidly changing microsatellites provides an effective system to evaluate time scales (Underhill 2003b, citing de Knijff et al.).

81. NRY changes are relatively fewer than those found at other genetic loci; see Digitale 2008; Underhill 2003a, citing Shen et al., 2000. They result in the typical high rate of correlation of NRY with geographical spread.

82. Underhill 2003a: 71. He stresses that combining it with the study of mtDNA data and the analysis of the principal components of classical genetic markers (Cavalli-Sforza et al. 1994) "provides the most detailed roadmap of human affinity, diversification and migration yet from a genetic perspective."

83. One assumes one mutation per c. 7,000 years (Chaubey et al. 2006: 92, citing Kivisild et al.). The error bars for the time of the exodus still are huge: Forster and Renfrew (2002: 92) give 54,200 ± 11,400 years for haplogroup M and 53,400 ± 11,700 years for N. (Hudjashov et al. [2007] give M at 54,900 ± 7,600 ya; N at 49,700 ± 6800; R at 55,700 ± 8,200; and P at 48,800 ± 5,600 ya.) Furthermore, the exact rate of change is still open to dispute. It is correlated with the split, assessed by fossil finds, between early hominids and early chimpanzees,

put at either 5 or 7 mya (cf. Brooks 2006). This would result, as per Brooks, in the earliest possible Out of Africa event at 77 or even 100 kya. Cf. §2, n. 311; §4, nn. 97, 126, 276, 287; §7, n. 22. For a date of split at c. 5.4 mya, see Patterson et al. 2006, http://www.broad.mit.edu/cgi-bin/news/display_news.cgi?id=1003.

84. See the discussion by Underhill (2003a: 67).

85. See the map in Forster and Renfrew 2002: 94.

86. For the spread, at 65 kya, from an East African origin (mtDNA L2, L3) to an arrival in West Africa at 30 kya, see Forster and Renfrew 2002: 95; Watson et al. 1997.

87. For popular online scenarios, see http://www.bradshawfoundation.com/journey/; https://genographic.nationalgeographic.com/genographic/lan/en/atlas.html.

88. Metspalu et al. 2006, which includes an important review of the relevant paleoclimate; cf. Jonathan Adams, Oak Ridge National Laboratory, http://www.esd.ornl.gov/projects/qen/nercEURASIA.html. See also below, §4.4.

89. See Abbi 2006; cf. http://www.andamanese.net/.

90. For Papuan genetics, see Forster and Renfrew 2002: 92 sqq.; Hudjashov et al. 2007. For Australia, see Hudjashov et al. 2007: Australian genetic signatures (mtDNA M, N derived) are most closely related to Papuas'; both come from the same initial settlement around 50 kya; both were then isolated from the rest of Asia. Note that the skeletal specimen from Lake Mungo 3 has been dated archaeologically to 62/46 kya. It has yielded DNA material that seems to be an ancient mtDNA type that was later on replaced by more modern types, worldwide (Adcock et al. 2001). On the robust characteristics of early specimens, see Hudjashov et al. 2007.

After the initial settlement only one additional migration occurred, that of mtDNA haplogroup Q, from New Guinea during the last Ice Age, before 8 kya (Redd and Stoneking 1999; Redd et al. 2002). This migration has long been suspected by mythologists and anthropologists (see §5.3.2). However, a still more recent connection with India (as in Redd and Stoneking 1999; Redd et al. 2002) is denied by Hudjashov. The numerous linguistic links between Dravidian and Australian, brought forward and discussed by V. Blažek (2006), are based on an Australian substrate in India.

91. Endicott et al. 2003; Thangaraj 2003.

92. Stressed for Australia and New Guinea by Hudjashov et al. (2007), on the basis of both mtDNA and NRY analysis. Sahul Land genetics point to a quick dispersal from Africa, without much genetic change, within some 5,200 years. Settlement of Sahul Land, including Melanesia, was effected by a single founder group around 50 kya (56 ± 8 kya). Here also belongs mtDNA P, which is as old. Hudjashov et al. also detect a new haplogroup, mtDNA S (a derivative of N), which is some 25,400 years old.

93. Forster and Renfrew 2002: 92. They give 2.481 ± 0.5232 mutations = 54,200 ± 11,400 years for M and 2.4512 ± 0.5463 mutations = 53,400 ± 11,700 years for N; on the other hand, they date the first expansion in Eurasia at 65 ± 23 kya(!) based on Papua data; the dentochronological data result in 60,000 ± 6,100 years (Turner 1986). The authors stress that the rate of mutations from the African ancestral female is about ten mutations, while that of the earliest ex-Africa haplogroups (after L3), M and N, is only two mutations, which indicates a genetically close-knit group.

94. For a pathbreaking case, that of an overlap of archaeology with genetics, see King and Underhill 2002. The appearance of M172-related lineages is correlated with that of Neolithic figurines (88% accuracy) and of painted pottery (80% accuracy).

95. Early examples of investigations of an overlap with genetics include Villems 2005, for a variant of the northern Siberian diver myth.

96. For data, see Cavalli-Sforza 2001, 2002; note also the extensive linguistic area, discussed by Masica (1976): it includes South, Central, and North Asia as well as Korea and Japan; the data transgress both language boundaries and those of language families.

97. Error bars are based on the molecular clock; see immediately below. As pointed out earlier, the time frame of the reconstructed haplotypes is based on an assumption, the speed of the molecular clock and the split of the primate pedigree into humans and chimpanzees. If this is set earlier or later, it results in an Out of Africa move at 77 kya, not c. 65 kya (see §2, n. 311). Furthermore, all such dates have large error bars (see §4, n. 83), just like the 14C dates of archaeology. For dates around 10 kya the error bars still are estimated at ±3,000 years, and for those around 54 kya, they are 11 kya.

98. Villems 2005.

99. New methods, announced by Noonan et al. (2006), promise that we can make more use of ancient DNA; see §4, n. 115.

100. Krings et al. 1997; Ovchinnikov et al. 2000; Schrenk and Müller 2005: 103 sqq.; cf. §4, n. 115.

101. For later and recent regional genetic developments such as lactose tolerance, white skin color, malaria resistance, salt retention, and even hearing and brain function (microcephaline gene, such as DAB1), see the summary by N. Wade (2007); cf. McEvoy et al. 2006; Relethford 2002.

102. Cavalli-Sforza 1991, 2001; Cavalli-Sforza et al. 1990, 1994; Ruhlen 1994b.

103. Ruhlen 1994b.

104. On the general problem of comparing linguistic and genetic data, see Cavalli-Sforza 2001, 2002: 87; Cavalli-Sforza et al. 1988; Penny et al. 1993.

105. Cf. Cavalli-Sforza et al. 1994.

106. W. Allman, in *U.S. News and World Report* (1990); R. Wright, in *The Atlantic* (1991); Ph. Ross, in *Scientific American* (1991); L. L. Cavalli-Sforza, in *Scientific American* (1991). The recent stress, much hyped and overvalued, on some "horizontal" (non-tree-like) spread of genes and the transmission of some linguistic features between (un)related languages does not invalidate their underlying tree structures. Such horizontal transmissions have been well studied in the stemmata of manuscripts ("contamination") since Johannes Schmidt (*Wellentheorie*, 1872), with reference to the spread of features within Indo-European, and as areal features (*Sprachbund*) shared by unrelated languages such as the Pueblo, Balkan, and South Asian ones.

107. For an accessible introduction, see Cavalli-Sforza and Cavalli-Sforza 1994.

108. Cavalli-Sforza and Cavalli-Sforza 1994: 106–14.

109. Cavalli-Sforza and Cavalli-Sforza 1994: 118 sqq.

110. On Robert Dorit, who examined a stretch of the Y chromosome, see Stringer and McKie 1996: 133. In addition, autosomal DNA can also be studied, a field that is taking off only now; cf. Patterson et al. 2006; Patterson et al. 2008.

111. Brown 1980: "Homo sapiens could have speciated or passed through a severe population constriction as recently as 180,000 years ago."

112. Depending on the time of the split between the lineages of chimpanzees and early humans (see §2, n. 310; §4, nn. 83, 97, 126, 276, 288; §7, n. 22).

113. The African Eve scenario, however, was initially challenged by some researchers, such as Alan Templeton, who claimed that out of a number of possible computer programs only one has been used by the proponents of the African Eve theory while others have been neglected. According to this now muted rival model, *Homo erectus* gradually evolved into anatomically modern *Homo sapiens sapiens*/Crô Magnon at various locations in Africa, Europe, and Asia, in other words, with a number of points of origin. Templeton and others have

charged that the great diversity of sub-Saharan mtDNA types could also be due to a larger population size than in subsequently settled areas. (The reliability of the speed of mtDNA change also has been doubted.) He has slightly modified his views since. Multilocal origin still has some support, as in China (and elsewhere), further instigated by the recent find of a c. 100,000-year-old skeleton "with heavy browridges" that still needs to be studied in detail.

114. See Torroni et al. 2006 for a review of advancements.

115. For Neanderthal DNA, see Culotta 2007; Krause et al. 2007; Krings et al. 1997; Noonan et al. 2006; Schmitz 2003; Schmitz et al. 2002; Serre et al. 2004. Research of ancient DNA has greatly been facilitated as DNA strings can now be duplicated indefinitely by the polymerase chain reaction and as DNA can also be taken from hard tissues, bone marrow, and even rock-art pigment. Old DNA can be tested only if samples are not contaminated by later intrusions; see Noonan et al. 2006.

116. Semino et al. 2000; Underhill et al. 2001.

117. Underhill 2006.

118. Underhill and Kivisild 2007: see figs. 10, 13–14.

119. Cavalli-Sforza and Cavalli-Sforza 1994: 147; cf. above, §2.1.

120. Cavalli-Sforza and Cavalli-Sforza 1994: 156.

121. Witzel 2003.

122. An overview of the major principle components indicates the following:
- The 1st PC is centered in Africa, Arabia, and Europe, while Papua–Australia are outliers.
- The 2nd PC centers in Papua–Australia and has Brazil and Peru at the rim.
- The 3rd PC centers in South Africa and has Europe at the rim.
- The 4th PC (maybe climatically caused) centers in northwestern Europe and has West/Central Africa, and South America at the rim.
- The 5th PC centers in Southeast Asia and Brazil and has northwestern North America as its rim.
- The 6th PC has its center in the American Arctic and Southeast Asia, with northwestern Europe at the rim.
- The 7th PC has its center in South Africa with the Bushmen and Khoi-San, and its rim on both sides of the Red Sea, and North Africa. (Cavalli-Sforza et al. 1994: 135)

123. Cavalli-Sforza and Cavalli-Sforza 1994: 145, map; Relethford 2002; Wade 2007a.

124. Cavalli-Sforza and Cavalli-Sforza 1994: 144–45.

125. However, Cavalli-Sforza et al. have also warned about "the distinction between genetic evidence from *gene frequencies for polymorphic genes,* ... and *mutational changes* observed *between individuals*" (in mtDNA), as the first "considers *populations* and the second considers *single individuals* or groups of them, which cannot be equated to populations" (1994: 322; my italics). These two approaches are frequently confused in popular literature.

126. See the overview by Mellars (2006); however, according to Brooks, the "oldest possible age for 'out-of-Africa' is c. 77 kyr (?or 100 kyr if the date of the chimp–human divergence is 7mya instead of 5mya)" (2006; cf. §4, nn. 1, 110, 151, 322). See S. Jones (2007: 173 sqq.) for mid-Paleolithic *archaeological* data from South India, before and after the Toba explosion of c. 74 kya; and cf. J. Harrod, http://www.originsnet.org.

127. Cavalli-Sforza and Cavalli-Sforza (1994: 121) sum up that the oldest *Homo sapiens sap.* remnants come from Africa, the birthplace of *Homo sapiens sapiens,* and from the Middle East, at c. 100,000 years ago, while those in Australia and New Guinea are some 55,000–65,000 years old. Cavalli-Sforza notes that genetic distance between the Oceanian (= Sahul) Aborigines and the Southeast Asians is about half that between Africans and non-Africans.

128. Cf. also Cavalli-Sforza et al. 1994: 253. For demic diffusion in general, see Cavalli-Sforza 2002, as opposed to a simplistic "migrationist" approach.

129. Metspalu et al. 2006; see §4.4.

130. For the spread of humans into northern China in Paleolithic times, see Underhill 2003a: 73; and cf. the recent find at Zhoukoudian, dated at c. 42–39 kya; see Hong Shang et al. 2007.

131. Cavalli-Sforza and Cavalli-Sforza (1994: 149) still assumed that only some 100,000 people settled the Near East and Europe. One now thinks of 2,000–10,000 African emigrants.

132. Palestine, Lebanon, etc.; see Bar-Yosef 1998; O. Bar-Yosef, in Shaw 2001; §4, nn. 244, 247.

133. Chris Stringer and Robin McKie summed up the then current evidence from Asia: "There is little evidence of any Homo sapiens prevalence [anywhere outside Africa] (apart from the Levant) until about 40,000 years ago. We catch glimpses of their presence at contemporary sites like K'sar Akil in Lebanon and Darra-i-Kur in Afghanistan; and in Sri Lanka about 30,000 years ago; in China about 25,000 years ago and in Japan about 17,000 years before present" (1996: 149). Some earlier dates for North China, Okinawa, and Borneo have been added since.

134. Stringer and McKie 1996: 51.

135. See S. Oppenheimer (2003), according to whom a Southeast Asian volcanic (Toba) explosion of c. 74 kya would have destroyed nearly all earlier humans in South Asia, and this region would have been repopulated from Southeast Asia, his "Eden in the East." Cf. also Chaubey et al. 2006: 91. However, this is now also contradicted by the Middle Paleolithic data from South India that come from before and soon after the explosion (Petraglia et al. 2007), as the layer of Toba ashes is much smaller there than assumed; see the discussion by S. Jones (2007: 173 sqq.); cf. §2, n. 310; §4, nn. 83, 97, 112, 126; §7, n. 22. Note also the survival of still another human species, *Homo floresiensis*, in eastern Indonesia, down to some 18,000 years ago (Schrenk and Müller 2005: 115).

136. Note, however, several areas of early rock art along the Central Indian Narmada Valley (see below, §4.4.1) and the recent discovery of Paleolithic tools in Tamil Nadu, before and after the Toba explosion (Petraglia et al. 2007).

137. Birdsell 1977; Flood 1983; Roberts et al. 1994; Thorne et al. 1980, 1999.

138. Cavalli-Sforza still uses the term *Australoid* for all these early Asian groups; however, all such terminology employed in traditional anthropological and archaeological literature is confusing and should be avoided. One still finds terms such as *Veddoid*, *Proto-Australoid*, *pseudo-Australoid*, *(Proto-)Mediterranean*, *Proto-Nordic*, and a "mixture" of these groups. As has been pointed out above, also by Cavalli-Sforza, any definition of assumed "races" remains very fuzzy.

Cavalli-Sforza classifies the small surviving tribes of Andamanese hunter-gatherers as Negritos. One of the four major Andamanese groups, the Great Andamanese, were indirectly destroyed through peaceful contact by disease and alcoholism, so at the time of writing (1994) only 29 survived of an estimated 3,500 persons in 1858. The other Andamanese groups (except for the elusive Jarawa and Sentinel, that is) also have dwindled (see Abbi 2006). Cavalli-Sforza describes the Jarawa on the South and Middle Andaman, the Onge on Little Andaman, and (the rarely contacted) Sentinelese as having "small stature, very dark skin, and peppercorn hair; the women have fairly high steatopygia" (Cavalli-Sforza et al. 1994: 213). He adds that the Andamanese perhaps represent the relics of the exodus, of 70 or 60 kya, from Africa to Australia; however, for further information, see Abbi 2006, with refs.; http://www.andaman.org/; Usher 2006. For their genetic background, see Endicott et al. 2003; Thangaraj et al. 2005. We can now add recent data (shared NRY D) for them, the South Indian Kurumba, and the northeastern Indian Rajbanshis, on the Bengal/Nepal border. See §4, nn. 142, 169, 230; §5, nn. 238, 247, 251; §7, n. 219.

139. See Watson et al. 1997 for their early spread in Africa, based on genetic data. For the Pygmy substrate language, see Bahuchet 2006; Blench 1999.

140. See http://www.andaman.org/ on language; and Anvita Abbi (2006), who compares Great Andamanese, Jarawa, and Onge, based on recent field trips; cf. http://www.andaman.org/BOOK/reviews/reviews-books/abbi2007.htm. For a comparison of all Great Andamanese data published until 2006, see the presentation of T. Usher (2006) at the Association for the Study of Language in Prehistory/Harvard conference of October 2006, published in *Mother Tongue* 11.

141. Cavalli-Sforza et al. 1994: 242.

142. Endicott et al. 2003; Thangaraj 2003. To be added are the data on the Kurumba and Rajbanshis (Thangaraj et al. 2005); see §7, n. 219.

143. Metspalu et al. 2006. All mtDNA branches outside Africa are derived from the M or N haplogroups.

144. Cavalli-Sforza et al. (1994: 212) sum up the population statistics of South Asian tribal groups.

145. Metspalu et al. 2006.

146. Semino et al. 2000; Underhill et al. 2001.

147. See table of the Y Chromosome Consortium, http://ycc.biosci.arizona.edu/nomenclature_system/fig1.pdf.

148. Semino et al. 2000.

149. Sengupta et al. 2006.

150. R1a1-M198 is dated at 14 kya for its entry into India; see Gayden et al., who nevertheless stress "that multiple events resulting from subsequent migrations from southwestern Asia may also have contributed" (2007, quoting Sengupta et al. 2006). For Indo-European (Indo-Aryan) connections, see Quintana-Murci et al. 2001.

151. Chaubey et al. 2006; Sahoo et al. 2006; Sengupta et al. 2006.

152. Chaubey et al. 2006: 95.

153. For early resistance against the model (Alan Templeton etc.), see §4, n. 113. He has slightly modified his stance since. There also was some remigration into North Africa: mtDNA M1, U6.

154. Metspalu et al. 2006; Underhill and Kivisild 2007: 542.

155. Metspalu et al. 2006.

156. For a northern Asian route of expansion to East Asia via Central Asia, see Forster and Renfrew 2002: 94 and the following note.

157. The preceding paragraph is based on Metspalu et al. 2006. Note that Wells's (2002) assertion of a Central Asian origin of European and East Asian populations (and still maintained in his *National Geographic* website, https://genographic.nationalgeographic.com/genographic/lan/en/atlas.html, for 50 kya) is diametrically opposed to these results and not supported by new, firm data.

158. Metspalu et al. 2006; Underhill and Kivisild 2007.

159. See §4, n. 221; §7, nn. 123, 124; in spite of two recent finds of early shaman women's graves in central Europe and Israel. Shamanism is not restricted to men, though they dominate numerically.

160. Semino et al. 2000; Underhill et al. 2001.

161. Y Chromosome Consortium 2002; see next note.

162. See http://ycc.biosci.arizona.edu/nomenclature_system/fig1.html.

163. Jobling and Tyler-Smith 2003; Underhill and Kivisild 2007.

164. For a summary, see Metspalu et al. 2006; Underhill and Kivisild 2007, with refs. A few new haplogroups derive from N –> R: B/R11, R 9 (and F); many others derive from M. Southeast Asia, too, has some "autochthonous" lineages that are not found north of this area (Metspalu et al. 2006).

165. See immediately below, §4, n. 168.

166. Kuiper (1962) lists *ape* (fire), *seta* (dog), and *saroq* (monkey); cf. see further *Mother Tongue* 2 (1996), 3 (1997), 11 (2006), with other proposals for the linguistic affiliation of Ainu. The manifold Austric connections have recently been listed and discussed by Bengtson (2006; http://jdbengt.net/articles.htm; cf. the Austric superfamily: Benedict 1976; Blust 1996). For the genetic origins of the Ainu, see Tajima et al. 2004; and for genetic data on Japan, see Maruyama et al. 2003; Tanaka et al. 2004; cf. http://www.kahaku.go.jp/special/past/japanese/ipix/; and the next note.

167. According to Tajima et al. (2004), about half of the mtDNA sequence types are unique to the Ainu, with their closest relatives being the Nivkhi in northern Sakhalin. As for NRY, 87.5% of the Ainu have Asian YAP+ lineages (NRY haplogroups D-M55*, D-M125) but *not* the non-D (D2-M55) haplogroups commonly found in Japanese and Okinawans (C-M8, O-M175*, O-M122*). (As indicated, capital letters with asterisks indicate haplogroups that have not yet been sufficiently investigated yet.) Further, Tajima finds the NRY haplogroup C-M217* of North Asia and Sakhalin, summing up that the Ainu have high affinities with Japanese and Nivkhi populations. Haplogroup D is also common in Tibetans but not in Tamangs and Newars of the Kathmandu Valley; the latter have a strong Indian component (Gayden et al. 2007); see §4, n. 230 sq.

168. Tibetans have 50.6% of D1-M15, while in Japan a much older version, D2-M55, is prevalent. The date for D1 is Neolithic, while D2 is Paleolithic and clearly a remnant of the first exodus (in Tibet, D1-M15 is dated at c. 5 kya, and D3-P47, at c. 11 kya). Concurrently, D*-M174 is also found in the Andamans in high proportion with the Onge and Jarawa, again a remnant of the exodus (Gayden et al. 2007). A later subclade of D is found with the Rajbanshis in northwestern Bengal and eastern Nepal and with the Kurumba in the South Indian Nilgiris; see §5, n. 238.

169. Note Lin et al. 2005. For the Todas and other Nilgiri tribes and their linguistic substrate, see Zvelebil 1990; and contrast nontribal Dravidian-speaking populations: Zvelebil 1982. Note also the traces of early Australian substrates in Dravidian, as per Blažek 2006.

170. For the spread of humans into northern China in Paleolithic times, see Li and Su 2000; Su et al. 1999; Underhill 2003a: 73. And cf. the recent find at Zhoukoudian, dated at c. 42–39 kya (Hong Shang et al. 2007); and Jonathan Adams, at http://www.esd.ornl.gov/projects/qen/nercEURASIA.html.

171. See §4.4.1, §7.1–2. If one would follow Lieberman (2006, 2007; cf. Devlin 2006), one might add the current form of human language, as defined by him.

172. On their genetics, see the summary by van Driem (2006: 173 sq., citing the work of Ashma, Banerjee, Cordeaux, Debnath, Kashyap, Kivisild, Krithika, Kumar, Maity, Sahoo, Singh, Su, Tomas, and Watkins, among many others). Van Driem, Sahoo et al. (2006), and Chaubey et al. (2006: 95–96) derive Austro-Asiatic languages, based on genetics (especially NRY O2), from Southeast Asia; however, the assignment of Austro-Asiatic to mtDNA M2 is strongly criticized by Chaubey et al. (2006: 94) on the basis of wrong data on the part of Basu

et al. (2003). Contrast P. Donegan and D. Stampe (2004; not mentioned by these authors), who show strong linguistic data indicating an East Indian homeland of Austro-Asiatic. Cf. also the literature in van Driem 2006 (Diffloth 2001, 2005; Peiros 1998; etc.); and the discussions in Sagart et al. 2005. In sum, the current picture still is not yet settled and remains unclear.

173. Also in rare inscriptions from the Picts' Scotland to Gibraltar; see Sverdrup 2002. Farther east we find the Hatti among the Hittites, the various Caucasus languages, and Burushaski in the Pamirs.

174. Due to regional effects (§2.3, cf. 2.5) they can also be discovered in those of neighboring peoples; note, for example, old Scythian folklore preserved by both their descendants, the Ossetes, and various nonrelated North Caucasus peoples (Colarusso 2006) or Mesoamerican/Pueblo myths with the newly arrived Navajo and Apache. In the Macro-Caucasian case one would have to look at North Caucasian (Macro-Caucasian) myths and rituals found with the Kartvelians (Georgians, Svans, etc.; see the work of K. Tuite [1996, 1998, etc.]) or note the myths and rituals of the (Indo-Aryan-speaking) Kalash in the Chitral area of northwestern Pakistan who have preserved much of their pre-Islamic beliefs (Witzel 2004a; the Macro-Caucasian-speaking Burushos, much less so). Note that the Kalash also are genetically isolated.

175. Bengtson 1995 sqq.; see http://jdbengt.net/articles.htm; note Bengtson 2003.

176. Witzel 2003.

177. Mehdi et al. 1999; cf., however, Ayub et al. 2003; Underhill et al. 2000.

178. Athapascans, Navajo, Apache, with the genetic inheritance RPS4Y-T, M45b; see Schurr and Sherry 2004. For recent linguistic data, see Bengtson 2010; Vajda 2008.

179. Tajima et al. 2004.

180. Apparently the link between western South Asia and Southwest Asia that is seen in mtDNA haplogroups R2, U7, and W was interrupted by the expanding deserts at this time (Metspalu et al. 2006).

181. Forster and Renfrew 2002.

182. The expansion from six clusters in this area is put after 17 kya (Forster and Renfrew 2002: 95); from there they moved northward.

183. From where latecomers (Na-Dene and Inuit) settled in North America; they have the mtDNA haplogroup A2, while earlier Amerindians have B, just like the Central Asians (Forster and Renfrew 2002: 95).

184. Forster and Renfrew 2002: 94; see the popular animation at http://www.bradshaw-foundation.com/stephenoppenheimer/. Cf. S. Wells, https://genographic.nationalgeo-graphic.com/genographic/atlas.html.

185. Semino et al. 2000; Underhill 2003a: 68.

186. Cf. Cavalli-Sforza (2002: 84), who points to the NRY haplotype Eu 18 (now part of NRY haplogroup R); Semino et al. 2000. H and V make up more than 50% of western European genes (Forster and Renfrew 2002: 95).

187. Underhill 2003a: 74, citing Cavalli-Sforza et al. 1994 and Passarino et al..

188. See Cavalli-Sforza and Cavalli-Sforza 1994: 115 on face and skin color; Relethford 2002 and Wade 2007a on the recent mutation to white skin in Europe and, independently, in East Asia.

189. Chaubey et al. 2006.

190. Theoretically, this might have allowed the spread of Laurasian mythology northward into present-day China, perhaps with the expansion of speakers of Tibeto-Burmese/Chinese northward (Forster and Renfrew 2002: 95), if G. van Driem's (2006) model is correct. Note also Cordaux et al. 2004. See, however, the discussions in Sagart et al. 2005. For a vivid impression of the Southern Silk Road, see Lu 2002.

191. Cf. Watson et al. 1997.

192. Summary by Brooks (2006) and Connah (2004).

193. For Papuan genetics (mainly NRY P1, Q), see Forster and Renfrew 2002: 92 sqq. They give a date of minimally 33 kya and maximally 51 ± 17 kya for the settlement of New Guinea. Cf. Forster et al. 2001; see Hudjashov et al. 2007, with dates ranging between 54 and 48 kya (± 11,700/± 5600); cf. §4, nn. 90, 65, 83, 93.

194. Hudjashov et al. 2007.

195. See §5.3.2.1; and Usher 2002, on the connection of the Tasmanian languages with those in Melanesia, especially Solomonic. Nevertheless, there is some minor overlap with southeastern Australian (Victoria), probably loanwords.

196. Presser et al. 2007; see §5.3.2.1.

197. For the genetic pattern, see Forster and Renfrew 2002: 95. Amerindians mainly have the mtDNA haplogroup B, just like the Central Asians, and, for example, a variant of A, unlike that of the Na-Dene and Inuit; cf. §4, n. 183.

198. But also the so-called European gene, mtDNA X2b, is found in the Upper Midwest and especially in the Northeast. However, the haplogroup X2a in America is different from European X2b, and the American X2a does not have close relatives in Eurasia (including Siberia). Bifurcation apparently took place early on, during the expansion and spread of X2 from the Near East, around or after the Last Glacial Maximum (Reidla et al. 2003). Contrast this with the (European) Solutrean tools found in the eastern Mid-Atlantic states (Topper, Cactus Hill, Meadowcroft), dated to c. 15,200–14,250 BP. See §4, n. 211; and cf. §2, n. 326; §4, n. 322; §7, nn. 214, 215; Jones 2004.

199. Note the work by Yuri Berezkin (2002 etc.).

200. Underhill and Kivisild 2007.

201. Metspalu et al. 2006.

202. In addition, there are admixture zones (with over 20% of admixture) between the three domains; importantly, Central Asia is the biggest admixture zone, where the mtDNA pools of West and East Asia, and much less so, those of South Asia, intermix. See Metspalu et al. 2006.

203. As well as S, O, P, and Q in New Guinea/Australia for the Gondwana myth area.

204. Chaubey et al. 2006: 93.

205. See Forster and Renfrew 2002: 94.

206. Van Binsbergen puts a similar question with regard to his concept of a "dead end" of the Out of Africa move in Australia and New Guinea and a "considerable delay (15 ka) before [his] Route B successfully made inroads into Asia" (2006a: 30; for details, see 2006b). However, this movement is merely a function of climate: only after the end of the second-to-last ice age was northward movement successful; note that *Homo sapiens sapiens* was at Beijing already at 42/39 kya (see next note). Van Binsbergen's second "remaining question," why "route B was so successful," is answered by the same point and by the existence of Laurasian mythology by then (cf. §8).

207. For the spread of humans into northern China in Paleolithic times, see Underhill 2003a: 73; and cf. the recent find at Zhoukoudian, dated at c. 42–39 kya. For the general situation in East and Southeast Asia, see Poloni et al. 2005; Sanchez-Mazas et al. 2005; Underhill 2005.

208. Forster and Renfrew 2002: 94.

209. Cf. Bellwood and Renfrew 2002; Benedict 1975, 1976; van Driem 2006; and the overview by Sagart et al. (2005).

210. See Mehdi et al. 1999 on Pakistani NRY genetics. Cf., however, Ayub et al. 2003; Underhill et al. 2000.

211. As for recent Amerindian DNA data: some want to see just one entry of Amerindians around 21 kya (Silva et al. 2002), based on mtDNA haplotypes A, B, C, and also D; many others, such as Bortolini et al. (2003, based on NRY), see a more complex population history, with two different major (male) migrations to North and South America, dated around 14 kya, from southern/central Siberia (the second migration being restricted to North America); both share ancestors in Central Asia (Underhill 2003a: 74). Four mtDNA lineages (A–D) have commonly been mentioned (Wallace and Torroni 1992), with two distinct migrations for Amerindian and Na-Dene-speaking populations, while the Amerind populations are estimated as being about four times older than the Na-Dene. Similarly, Bonatto and Salzano see an early migration (mtDNA A–D), with beginning ancestral-population differentiation at c. 30,000–40,000 BP with a "95%-confidence-interval lower bound of approximately 25,000 ybp" (1997: 1413 and passim).

Another recent summary (Schurr and Sherry 2004) maintains an initial migration (mtDNA A–D and NRY P-M45a and Q-242/Q-M3) at 20,000–15,000 BP, which took place, due to the continental ice sheets, along the coastal route. It reached South America by 12,500 BP (Monte Verde). A second migration, after the opening of the corridor between the Canadian Cordillera and Laurentian shields, brought mtDNA haplogroup X and NRY haplogroups P-M45b, C-M130, and R1a1-M17 to North and Central America. (For X, see above, §4, n. 198.) Third, two Beringian populations expanded into northern North America after the Ice Age (LGM), the Eskimo-Aleuts and Na-Dene Amerindians. These migrations, one from central/southern Siberia (where the Jōmon people of Japan also originated), the other one from the Okhotsk/Amur area, are also maintained by Lell et al. Tamm et al. (2007) maintain a Beringian standstill and then a rapid, continuous migration, all the way down to Tierra del Fuego, involving mtDNA A2, B2, C1, and D1. The C1 subclades are dated at 13.9 kya.

In sum, we have two major Siberian occurrences of exodus: the first started in southern middle Siberia with the founding haplotype M45a and moved via Beringia, (with its descendant, the predominant Amerindian M3 lineage). A second exodus started in the Lower Amur/Sea of Okhkotsk region (RPS4Y-T, M45b) and contributed to the modern genetic pool of the Na-Dene and Amerinds of North and Central America. This scenario is supported by studies of ancient DNA (Stone and Stoneking 1999). Data from a 700-year-old population of central Illinois showed the four major Amerindian mtDNA haplogroups and a fifth that too "associates with Mongolian sequences and hence is probably authentic" (Stone and Stoneking 1999: 153).

212. Cavalli-Sforza 2002.

213. Where they could have arrived during the warm period 45–25 kya, while their western section (Macro-Caucasian) spread westward into the Caucasus and Europe.

214. For a northern (Asian) track via southern Siberia, see Forster and Renfrew 2002: 94; Oppenheimer 2003; Tanaka et al. 2004; Maca-Meyer et al. 2001; Wells et al. 2001, cited by Metspalu et al. 2006. The latter two articles oppose this model. Southern Siberia and Central Asia have mixed pools of western and eastern haplogroups; they are not at their root. This spread must be distinguished from a (hypothetical) still earlier one, starting from the Near East around 100 kya.

215. For the Neolithic and early historical period, cf. the genetic observations by van Driem (2006: 172); and for the linguistic situation, see Witzel 2003, 2004a. We concur in the fact that present (western) Central Asia is heavily layered. Linguistically speaking, we have to reckon with the late Turkic migration, an earlier Iranian cultural spread (around 1000 BCE), an Indo-Iranian level (around 2000 BCE), and the pre-Indo-European local language(s) (before c. 3000 BCE), probably of Macro-Caucasian nature (Witzel 2003).

216. Metspalu et al. 2006.

217. And their earliest subclades; Metspalu et al. 2006 with refs.

218. Forster and Renfrew 2002. The transmission of Laurasian mythology to East and Southeast Asia is discussed below.

219. Metspalu et al. 2006.

220. See example of Australia, where men and women maintain separate spiritual identities but share mainly the same general mythological background. Cf. §1, n. 82.

221. See §6.1, §7.1; the Grimms' introduction to their *Fairy Tales* (Rölleke 2003: 16); Gusinde 1977: 568 sqq., 858 sqq., 874, on the manner and faithfulness of the Selk'nam Fuegians as they retold their myths; Maskarinec 1998, 2008, on Nepalese shaman traditions; and a similar observation by van Driem (2006) on the transmission of language. In general, on oral literature and its transmission (in response to Jack Goody's theories of literacy and its effect on rational thinking), see Falk 1990.

222. Excluding those haplogroups representing Melanesians (Q, P) and Australians (new haplogroup S < N; see Hudjashov et al. 2007) and also C3 (with Melanesians). I leave open, for the moment, the link between NRY E (= III), an early "cousin" of F, and mythology. NRY E is well represented in the Near East and Europe but also in Africa. It may well be that this haplogroup is connected with pre-Laurasian or very early Laurasian mythologies. In order to decide the question, close study of the remnant languages of Europe (Basque, Caucasus) as well as Burushaski (and beyond: Ket etc.) and of the vestiges of their old myths and rituals is required, which cannot be done here. Cf., however, §5, 384, §4, n. 445, on the Lady of the Animals (Tuite 2007).

223. Forster and Renfrew 2002: 94.

224. Masica 1976.

225. Some include even highland Ethiopia, which was settled late by Semitic speakers from South Arabia; see Masica 1976; §4.1.

226. Metspalu et al. 2006.

227. Masica 1976.

228. Metspalu et al. 2006.

229. Van Driem 2005, 2006. Gayden et al. (2007), however, use recent genetic data (O3a5a-M134, at c. 8.1 kya) to indicate a more recent, Neolithic northern (Yellow River Basin) homeland of Tibeto-Burman speakers inside Tibet. Historically, but of course much later, these were called the Di-Qiang tribes in Chinese records. This migration was preceded by an earlier dispersal from Southeast Asia (O3a5a-M117, c. 25 kya, and O3a5a-M134, c. 22 kya) to the Himalayas before the Neolithic period (Su et al. 2000). M117 may be at the root of the Tibeto-Burman language family. Su et al. link this early migration to that of the Baric group of Tibeto-Burman (i.e., the Bodo-Garo of Assam, not to be confused with the Bodic one, to which Tibetan belongs). The earlier settlement of the Tibetan area is archaeologically dated at c. 33 kya in central Qaidam and 21.7 kya near Lhasa (Gayden et al. 2007). The ancient haplogroup D (also very prominent in Japan, with the South Asian Kurumba and Rajbanshis) is likewise abundantly found, though in later versions (of c. 11 and 5 kya) among Tibetans; see §4, nn. 167, 168, 230.

230. Both the Tibetans and the Tamang of Nepal (dated at 10.8 ± 5.6 kya for NRY O3a5-M134) have strong Southeast Asian NRY influx (60.4 and 66.2%, respectively), less from Central Asia (26.2 and 28.7%) and from Northeast Asia (8.9 and 5.1%); see Gayden et al. 2007. Among the Newars of the Kathmandu Valley, both Central Asian and Indian influences are pronounced (56.6 and 43.4%, respectively).

231. For the genetics of southern China, see the summary by van Driem (2006: 180, citing the work of Wen et al.), which shows mtDNA B, F, R9a, R9b, and N9a (even 55% with Southern Han). Compare the rather heuristic map of Bellwood 2005: 26.

232. Forster and Renfrew 2002: 94.

233. For accounts of earlier populations in South China and along the coast, see Lacouperie 1970; Luo 1999; Sagart et al. 2005; Suwa 1989.

234. There are many data in the Chinese language, mostly unused by Western scholars, found in Chinese archives; they have been collected over the past few decades. Cf. Yang and An 2005: 253–58.

235. Trejaut et al. 2005. This probably is due to matrilineal and matrilocal preferences, as the NRY evidence indicates the participation of Australo-Melanesians in the colonization of Polynesia (Underhill 2003a: 73). Indeed, the typical Polynesian Lapita culture spread eastward along the northern coast of New Guinea. Some Polynesian coastal bridgeheads are still found on that island.

236. Such as origin from rocks, which seems to be an archaic Gondwana feature. However, their highland Tsou neighbors have a flood myth (Tung 1964: 271, 351, 377, 397), just like the lowland tribes, the Ami and others, who have closer links with typical Austronesian mythology. They also maintain the typical Laurasian feature of a sacred language reserved for the gods and priests (oral information, Taitung, Taiwan, October 2005). For the genetic differences between lowland and highland tribes, see Lin et al. 2005: esp. 242.

237. The following section dealing with early *Homo sapiens* heavily relies on the summary given by H. Fleming in *Long Ranger* (2003, http://www.people.fas.harvard.edu/~witzel/MTLR-34b.htm).

238. See Balter 2007b; Junker 2006; Schrenk and Müller 2005. On their tools, see Hopkins 2006.

239. For an account of the discovery of Neanderthal Man, early interpretations, and the now largely vanished idyllic surroundings near Düsseldorf, Germany, see the work of Ernst J. Kahrs (1876–1948), the first director of the Ruhrland Museum at Essen and one of the first archaeologists in this area. He reported about the history of the discovery of the Neanderthal skeleton (1942: 10–11, 33 sqq.), as well as on his new finds of tools made there in 1927–28 (1942: 34 sqq.) among the rubble of the Neanderthal chalk formation, which had been destroyed and discarded by industry. These investigations have remained unknown to Ralph Schmitz (Schmitz et al. 2002; cf. Schmitz and Thissen 2002; Schrenk and Müller 2005: 14), who claims to have rediscovered the original site. Schmitz recently once more reinvestigated all of the rubble, which has yielded more fragments of the original Neanderthal skeleton that have also successfully been tested for DNA (Schmitz et al. 2002).

240. For example, *Homo neanderthalensis* at Arago in the Pyrenees at c. 400,000 BCE; tent posts for a Neanderthal camp site found at Terra Armata near Nice, France (Wunn 2005: 56); and a preserved, 1.5-meter-long wooden spear of c. 400,000 BCE at Schöningen near Helmstedt, Germany (Wunn 2005: 59).

241. For the investigation of ancient DNA by using the polymerase chain reaction, see Noonan et al. 2006.

242. Noonan et al. 2006.

243. Akazawa and Bar-Yosef 1998; cf. Shaw 2001, http://www.harvard-magazine.com/on-line/09016.html.

244. See §4, n. 132.

245. Lieberman 2006, 2007 (cf. Devlin 2006); Schrenk and Müller 2005; Wunn 2005: 106.

246. Bar-Yosef, in Shaw 2001.

247. See last note; and cf. Schrenk and Müller 2005: 81.

248. Schrenk and Müller 2005: 65 sq.

249. Junker 2006: 99 sqq.; Lieberman 2006; Schrenk and Müller 2005.

250. Krause et al. 2007; Trinkhaus 2007. Cf. the summary by Mithen (2005: 249 sq.). However, the relevance of this gene for the original development of language has recently been questioned, even by its co-discoverer, Simon Fisher. It is not "*the* language gene" but one of many involved in speech, and it has been present in mammals for 70 million years, such as in mice or bats, just as it is in orangutans and chimpanzees, all of which do not use spoken language. S. Fisher straightforwardly denies a "language gene": "Genes do not specify behaviours or cognitive processes; they make regulatory factors, signaling molecules, receptors, enzymes, and so on.... [M]uch of the data on FOXP2 from molecular and developmental biology confounds any expectations that one might have for a hypothetical 'language gene'" (2006: 288). Alec MacAndrew (2002) sums up that the development of language did not rely just on a single mutation in FOXP2 and that many other changes were involved, such as anatomical ones of the supralaryngeal tract (which differs markedly from that of other mammals, in that the descent of the larynx provides a resonant channel for speech; cf. Lieberman 2006, 2007). He stresses that all of this did not occur over just 100,000 years. Further, in addition to somatic changes, the genetic basis for language "involved many more genes that influence both cognitive and motor skills.... Ultimately, we will find great insight from further unraveling the evolutionary roots of human speech—in contrast to Noam Chomsky's lack of interest in this subject" (MacAndrew 2002). More emphasis is given to this gene by Lieberman (2006, 2007).

251. Schrenk and Müller 2005: 112. However, other forms of contact, such as silent trading or exchanges based on very limited faculty of speech (cf. Lieberman 2006, 2007), may also have taken place, as is seen at Vindija in Croatia (see §4, n. 263).

252. Cf. also Bar-Yosef, quoted in Shaw 2001.

253. Schrenk and Müller 2005: 96 sqq., 108; summary by Wunn (2005: 112).

254. The insertion of flowers into Neanderthal graves is a modern myth (Schrenk and Müller 2005). The famous Shanidar grave in northern Iraq has been shown to be contaminated. The pollen of flowers found there were brought down to these levels by rats (Schrenk and Müller 2005: 80); van Binsbergen (2006b) still uses the flower argument.

255. There are also some indications of incipient Neanderthal use of grave goods and of the application of ochre in France, Crimea, etc. See Schrenk and Müller 2005: 80, esp. 96 sqq.

256. Campbell 1988: I.1: 55. The existence of the Neanderthal bear cult has been disputed by Wunn (2005). However, she (2005: 71) correctly regards Neanderthals as different in anatomy and behavior from modern humans.

257. Cf. Ōbayashi and Klaproth 1966 for Sakhalin; Paulson 1965.

258. Noonan et al. 2006.

259. Unless one wants to make a case for a very early Levant origin of Laurasian mythology (up to 100 kya), where the attested interleafing occupations could have favored such a transmission. The exact (Southwest Asian) area of its origin, however, is still unclear (§4.3 on the genetic links). Cf. Sagart et al. 2005.

260. Noonan et al. (2006) give the date of the last common ancestor of Neanderthals and pre–anatomically modern humans at c. 706 kya and the date of split between the two groups at 370 kya. First there was the European form of *Homo erectus* (*Homo heidelbergensis*) at c. 800–375 kya, then early Neanderthals (*Homo steinheimensis*) at c. 350–180 kya, and then

Homo neanderthalensis at 90–27 kya, as per Schrenk and Müller 2005: 28, 118; cf. S. Atreya, in Petraglia and Allchin 2007: 137 sqq.

261. For example, at Peştera cu Oase, near Anina, Romania, with various finds, at c. 42–35 kya.

262. In Goram's Cave at Gibraltar until 28–24 kya; see http://news.bbc.co.uk/2/hi/science/nature/5343266.stm. Other late, c. 30,000-year-old sites include Figueira Brava in Portugal (31 kya), Zafarraya in southern Spain (32–28 kya), and Vindija in Croatia (28 kya), the latter with Mousterian and Aurignacian(!) tools, which points to contact with *Homo sapiens sapiens*; see Schrenk and Müller 2005: 112; cf. also http://www.The-Neanderthal-Tools.org.

263. For lack of genetic evidence, see Schmitz 2003; Schrenk and Müller 2005: 110; cf. Culotta 2007; Noonan et al. 2006. The supposedly interbred Neanderthal/*Homo sapiens* child from Lagar Velho in Portugal had some modern characteristics in its inner ear bones (Schrenk and Müller 2005: 108 sq.). See Serre et al. 2004, http://www.ncbi.nlm.nih.gov/sites/entrez?cmd=Retrieve&db=PubMed&list_uids=15024415&dopt=Citation. This showed, on average, 27 divergences with modern humans. As for the study of ancient DNA in general, a major problem remains, that of intrusions of modern materials—though apparently not in this case. Cf. Schrenk and Müller 2005: 107 sq.

264. About which the excavators, Tim White et al., note: "the Herto crania, both metrically and non-metrically, lack any derived affinity with modern African crania or with any other modern group.... Instead, the closest approximations among modern individuals to the overall morphology, size, and facial robusticity are found in some Australian and Oceanic individuals, although these are also clearly distinct from the Herto hominids" (2003: 744; cf. Stringer and McKie 1996: 154). Ann Gibbons (2007: 377) gives 195–160 kya for *Homo sapiens*.

265. For African archaeology, see the summaries by Connah (2004) and Phillipson (2005).

266. See summary in Fleming 2003. See also the literature in Mellars 2006: nos. 1–11.

267. Akazawa and Bar-Yosef 1998.

268. For a recent overview of the archaeology and the religion of the these early emigrants, see J. Harrod (2006); he supports the southern trail of the Out of Africa movement but also asserts a northern trail. For the (genetically unsupported) theory of a parallel expansion via Central Asia eastward, the northern (Asian) route (Wells 2002; Wells et al. 2001), see below.

269. As was the case even earlier with *Homo erectus*. See the overview by Metspalu et al. (2006); see the summary by Harrod, http://www.originsnet.org.

270. Mellars 2006.

271. See Mellars 2006, referring to recent papers by P. Forster, Kivisild et al., Endicott et al., Metspalu et al., Quintana-Murti, Oppenheimer, and Mellars. He gives a vague date of "sometime before 50,000 YBP." See also Mellars 2006: 797, citing work by Forster and Matsumura, Macauly, Stringer.

272. The Persian Gulf was nonexistent then, and the migrants would have followed a direct path from Oman northward toward Baluchistan.

273. Mellars 2006: 796, citing Forster and Matsumura 2005, Macaulay et al. 2005, and Thangaraj et al. 2005. Mellars thinks that the early dates of 65–60 kya may have been overestimates.

274. See the Niah Cave Project report, http://www.le.ac.uk/archaeology/research/projects/niah/index.html.

275. Jerimalai Cave, recently excavated by O'Connor; see Balter 2007a, http://www.sciencemag.org/content//318/5849/388.full.

276. Hong Shang et al. 2007. Bones were found at Tianyuan Cave, Zhoukoudian, Beijing, in 2003.

277. Hong Shang et al. 2007.

278. Recent excavations have yielded dates from 35 to 40 kya (Weber 2006), and surveys have shown 15 examples of rock art.

279. Mellars 2006: 797, citing work by C. B. Stringer, J. F. O'Connell and J. Allen, J. M. Bowler et al., and J. Mulvaney and J. Kaminga. Anatomically modern humans are represented by a skull at Lake Mungo 3, in southern Australia. For the claim of an early settlement of Australia by 60–50 kya, see Thorne et al. 1999.

280. Nevertheless, early humans traveled by boat to the islands north of New Guinea: 180 kilometers to Buka at 28,000 years ago and 230 kilometers to Manus at 21,000 years ago; see Balter 2007a.

281. Metspalu et al. 2006.

282. Cf. Harrod 2006.

283. As mentioned (§4, n. 141), according to Brooks, the "oldest possible age for 'out-of-Africa' is c. 77 kyr (?or 100 kyr)" (2006).

284. That would have eradicated all humans in India due to the "nuclear" winter that followed the huge amount of ash expelled by the Toba eruption; see Oppenheimer 1998, 2003, http://www.bradshawfoundation.com/stephenoppenheimer/. This would have caused a secondary spread out of his "Eden in the East"; but see discussions by K. Pandayya (in Petraglia and Allchin 2007: 97 sqq.), S. Jones (2007: 173 sqq.), and H. James (2007: 201 sqq.) for continued occupation in South India before and after the Toba explosion.

285. Mellars 2006: 797.

286. Petraglia et al. 2007.

287. Cf. Connah 2004: 18. The Howieson's Poort assembly (c. 70 kya) is an interruption of the long-standing occupation at Klasies River (120–1 kya) with a flake and blade industry. Howieson's Poort shows "spears barbed with microliths, and possibly even bows and microlith-barbed arrows" (Connah 2004: 18; cf. Petraglia and Allchin 2007: 450, map). Other early sites in Africa include Haua Fteah on the Libyan coast, c. 70 kya, where a more developed industry appeared at c. 40 kya, and Kalambi Falls in northern Zambia, c. 100–80 kya (Connah 2004: 18 sq.).

288. Unless, as J. Harrod pointed out to me, this was "simply a parallel development, moved out of Africa at an earlier date, which would be mid–Middle Paleolithic" (personal communication, August 2007). See Harrod's database and Harrod 2006.

289. Lahr and Foley 1994; Mellars 2006: 797.

290. With a Levallois discoidal core. Harrod thinks that they were "probably inland hunter subsistence people, including North African Aterians, Tabun C (Skhul-Qafzeh), etc. that spread across North Africa into Near East and on into India, especially across the Narmada-Son Valley site" (personal communication, August 2007). Cf. §4, n. 295. For a detailed discussion, see Mellars 2006: 797 sqq.

291. Wells 2002.

292. Mellars 2006: 797; Metspalu et al. 2006; see §4.3. The northern route (before the later Pleistocene) via the Nile Valley and the Sinai Peninsula to some adjacent parts of Asia is supported by R. Derricourt, July 7, 2006, http://www.springerlink.com/content/3833776l28145713. See Oppenheimer 2003; Wells et al. 2001; cf. also Forster and Renfrew 2002: 94; Schrenk and Müller 2005: 102.

293. Mellars 2006: 797 sqq.

294. Mellars 2006: 798 sq.

295. Witzel 2006a, based on a talk given at the Tokyo symposium "Generalized Sciences" (Sciences généralizées), organized by H. Nakatani of the Asia–Africa Institute of the Tokyo University of Foreign Studies, March 2005.

296. Weber 2006: chap. 24.

297. Caution is advised, however, as far as Neanderthal tools are concerned. The Recent research as shown that *both* Neanderthals and *Homo sapiens sapiens* (Crô Magnon) have been found with late Middle Paleolithic and late Paleolithic tools. *Both* produced Aurignacian tools. At the end of the Middle Paleolithic, there existed a large variety of cultural features and newly invented tools in Europe, even before anatomically modern humans appeared there (Wunn 2005: 69). "Almost all features of evolution such as tool industry, communication, social behavior, brain structure and body constitution are already found prepared.... [H]owever, the cultural progress increased steadily.... Both with the Neanderthals and modern humans, the overlapping and synergy effect of various factors of biological and cultural evolution takes effect" (Schrenk 1997: 121; my translation).

298. See §4, n. 275.

299. For other dates around 77 kya and earlier, see Harrod, http://www.originsnet.org; Brooks 2006 (cf. §2, n. 310).

300. Mellars 2006: 797, citing work by Forster and Matsumura, Macauly, and Stringer.

301. Or 40 kya; there is a debate about even earlier dates such as 50–60 kya; cf. Harrod 2006. Kimberley rock art is available at http://www.bradshawfoundation.com/. For a map, see Campbell 1988: I.2: 138.

302. G. Weber, http://www.Andaman.org, according to data from New Guinea.

303. Situated at Bhiyanpura village on the Bhopal-Hoshangabad road near Abedullaganj, a little north of the Narmada Valley.

304. See http://www.OriginsNet.org; illustrations for various periods have been made available at http://www.bradshawfoundation.com/india.

305. At c. 62 or 45 kya; Thorne et al. 1999. The Bradshaw paintings are older than 17,000 years, as indicated by archaeological data; see http://www.bradshawfoundation.com/india.

306. Mellars 2006: 797, citing work by C. B. Stringer, J. F. O'Connell and J. Allen, J. M. Bowler et al., and J. Mulvaney and J. Kaminga. A route from Bali to the Kimberleys, west of Arnhem Land, would have necessitated eight crossings around 50,000 BCE, according to Birdsell (1977), of 87, 29, 19, and the rest less than 10 kilometers. Cf. Butlin 1989. Recent excavations have yielded dates from 40 to 35 kya (Weber 2006); see http://donsmaps.com/timorcave.html. Anatomically modern humans are represented by a skull at Lake Mungo 3, in southern Australia. Cf. Mellars 2006 also for claims of an early settlement of Australia by 60–50 kya.

307. See map in Leitner 2006: 12 sq.

308. See the Niah Cave Project report, http://www.le.ac.uk/archaeology/research/projects/niah/index.html. This would have involved ten crossings, the longest one of 93 kilometers (Birdsell 1977).

309. Dixon 2002: 7–9.

310. Usher 2002, on linguistic grounds.

311. Glover and Presland 1985.

312. Dixon 2002: 11; Gollan 1985.

313. Blažek 2006, for an Australian substrate in Dravidian, which would agree with the southern expansion route of early humans.

314. Dixon 2002: 11.

315. Other cultural features, such as the curved boomerang, were still in the process of spreading (Dixon 2002: 13) when Europeans arrived in the late 18th century; cf. also the spread of a particular ceremony after 1893 (Dixon 2002: 18).

316. For Papuan genetics, see Forster and Renfrew 2002: 92 sqq.

317. For an entertaining account of human spread and culture after the last Ice Age (20,000–5000 BCE), see Mithen 2004.

318. See Schrenk and Müller 2005. The last Neanderthals have been found at Gibraltar, c. 28–24 kya:, http://news.bbc.co.uk/2/hi/science/nature/5343266.stm.

319. Hong Shang et al. 2007.

320. Wells 2002.

321. Underhill et al. 2001; cf. Metspalu et al. 2006.

322. However, excavations at Topper in South Carolina, Cactus Hill in Virginia, and Meadowcroft in Pennsylvania, from around 14,250–15,200 BP, are claimed to have western European (Solutrean) remains. Other early Amerindian remains include those at Monte Verde at 12,500 BP and Pedra Furada, northeastern Brazil, at 47,000 BP(?); see below. And there also is the discussion of a sea route, of Ainu-like people from Asia along the American west coast, perhaps at 30,000 BP; cf. Lemonick and Dorfman 2006; cf. for Paleoamerican origins, Smithsonian Institute, http://www.si.edu/Encyclopedia_SI/nmnh/origin.htm. See §2, n. 108.

323. Note also the supposedly Ob-Ugrian (Uralic) language of the Wintun in the San Francisco Bay area; see von Sadovszky 1978, 1996.

324. Similarly, for North America: see the common mythological characteristics in Siberia and North America, while South America has preserved older traits that are found in Southeast Asia (pointed out by Y. Berezkin [2002, 2005b]).

325. Leaving apart the alleged similarities between Jōmon and Ecuadorian pottery, dismissed by Antoni (1977); Campbell's (1988: I.2: 195) map maintains such diffusions. However, note the presentations at the VIIth International Conference on Easter Island and the Pacific Islands, Visby, 2007; cf. below, §4, n. 333. See Chang 1983; cf. Campbell 1988: I.2: 194, with illustrations.

326. Stanford and Bradley 2004.

327. According to "New Archaeology," with its deterministic, materialistic, and hypothesis/deduction-based method, one should study humans, their behavior, and their history, making use of the sciences such as physics, biology, geography, and linguistics, as it is *their* laws—to be discovered by archaeology—that determine human behavior and thus, history (Lorblanchet 2000: 131, citing P. Courbin, 1982).

328. Cf. Fleming 2003; among those who favor strictly local development for South Asia are Shaffer and Lichtenstein (1999) and M. Kenoyer (1998). In contrast, note C. Renfrew's (1987) problematic model of agricultural spread from the Near East for the European Neolithic and his—more likely—elite dominance model for India. Similarly Bellwood 2005; Bellwood and Renfrew 2002, for Southeast Asia and the Pacific. Cf. also Schuster 1951; Sorenson and Johannessen 2006.

329. Where the stance is due to nationalist tendencies: *any* outside or "foreign" influence on the formation of the "eternal" (*sanātana*) Indian civilization is disallowed. Multilocal origin is also popular in some Chinese circles.

330. Speakers at the VIIth International Conference on Easter Island and the Pacific Islands at Visby picked up, among others, the topic of the import of Polynesian chicken to South America and of the export of the sweet potato (and its designation) to Polynesia. See http://mainweb.hgo.se/Conf/Conference2007.nsf/(§all)/D83A53EDC96E6759C125718 8003331F7?OpenDocument. Cf. Schuster 1951; Sorenson and Johannessen 2006.

331. Neither reached the isolated Tasmania.

332. Metspalu et al. 2006, citing the work of Kivisild et al., Lahr and Foley 1994, Quintana-Murci et al. 1999, and Stringer. Cf. Forster and Renfrew 2002: 94; Oppenheimer 2003.

333. For alleged trans-Pacific contacts, see §4, nn. 325, 328.

334. See Campbell 1988: I.1: 34 sqq., I.2: 166.

335. As mentioned above (§4, n. 254), flowers in Neanderthal graves are a modern myth (Schrenk and Müller 2005); however, Neanderthal grave goods and the use of ochre existed in France, the Crimea, etc.

336. Of c. 24,500 BP; Schrenk and Müller 2005: 108, cf. 97 sq.

337. Lewis-Williams 2002. Compare, for example, the detailed methodology used by J. Harrod (2006) for analyzing early art and spirituality, and cf. his exposition at http://www.originsnet.org/glossmeth.html. For early art, since 350 kya (at Bilzingsleben, Germany; Makapansgat Cave, South Africa; Bacho Kiro, Bulgaria), see Bednarik, quoted in van Binsbergen 2006a: 8, 2006b; cf. Harrod 2006. We probably have to reckon with a very gradual development of the symbolic faculty in early humans and thus, of art. The question remains, from what point in time can we speak of the fully developed symbolic function and, therefore, art, speech—and thus, mythology? (For the emergence of anatomically modern human behavior, see also James 2007: 204 sqq.) The data provided in the present book point to a date *before* the exodus from Africa, c. 65 kya (cf. §4, nn. 65, 168, 248–250, on Neanderthal speech).

338. Connah 2004: 34 sqq. Saharan art is usually divided into four phases: Bubaline phase, with paintings of the extinct bubalus buffalo, 8–5 kya, and the contemporary Round Head phase; Bovidian phase, with cattle herds, 5–3 kya; Horse phase, 3–2 kya; and Camel phase, 2 kya until the present. This scheme has to some extent been modified, notably taking into account regional variations and with dates slightly revised, the Bubaline phase starting at only 6 kya (Connah 2004: 25 sqq.). In this section I will frequently refer to J. Campbell (1988) because of the large amount of illustrations, maps, and diagrams in his *Atlas*.

339. Huyge et al. (2007) think of dates around 15 kya.

340. Campbell 1988: I.1: 64, map.

341. Brooks et al. 1976; Pandey 1993; Wanke 1974, 1977. See also Chakravarty 1984; Christie 1978; Lal and Gupta 1984. New finds were recently made in the Bhimbetka area in January 2007. Cf. http://www.bradshawfoundation.com.

342. For New Guinea/Irian, see Chakravarty 1984: 182; Kosasih 1991: 76 sqq. (he discusses Ceram, Sulawesi, Timor, etc., as well).

343. Bullen 1991; Franklin 1991; McDonald 1991; Rosenfeld 1991. For the Kimberleys at 40 kya, depicting humans, weapons, animals, yams, and fishes, see Leitner 2006: 57; for Tasmania, see Brown 1991.

344. Connah 2004: 27 sqq. For the new finds in South Africa, at 26,000 BP, see also Wendt 1976. For other engravings, see Campbell 1988: I.1: 88, no. 157: Capsian style. However, these paintings extend from the beginning of our era to the early 19th century. Those at the Wonderwerk Cave in interior South Africa date from 10 to 4 kya; some of the artists seem to have been shamans (Connah 2004: 29 sqq.). Some 19th-century folklore reported from their Bantu neighbors, the local Sotho, described them to have lived in caves, where they drew pictures on cave walls during a trance; they were also reputed to be good rainmakers.

345. See, however, Brooks 2006; note the finds of shells as decorations at Pinnacle Point (South Africa) at 164 kya, Shkul (Israel) at 130–100 kya, beads in Algeria at c. 90 kya, etc. See §4, n. 366; cf. http://www.originsnet.org.

346. See Campbell 1988: I.2: xiv sq., xxi (cf. xxiii), at c. 40,000 BCE.

347. Gibbons 2007.

348. Vanhaeren et al. 2006.

349. Van Binsbergen (2006a: 12, 14; 2006b) adduces the ochre block found in the Blombos Cave (South Africa, in 2002), dated to c. 70,000 BCE, as representing his "Lightning bird" motif; however, it rather seems to be an example of the worldwide string patterns ("cat's cradle," "Jacob's ladder"); see illustrations in Campbell 1988: I.1: 101, I.2: 139, 185. Modern local interpretations of the design, however, vary greatly.

350. Brooks 2006; Connah 2004.

351. Mellars 2006: 799.

352. For the archaeology and spirituality of these migrants, see the detailed survey by Harrod (2006).

353. Not, as genetics now indicate, via Central Asia (Kazakhstan) but, rather, along the general southern path of the Out of Africa emigrants, via Arabia and South Asia.

354. However, most of it is totemistic (Walter and Fridman 2004: 219); a shamanistic tradition is seen in some paintings of northern Australia (Walter and Fridman 2004: 222). Even then, the probable remnants of earlier (Tasmanian?) myth traditions in southeastern Australia and Tasmania (§5.3.2) would have to be checked against this scenario.

355. Recent surveys have shown 15 examples of rock art (Weber 2006); see *Past Worlds. The Times Atlas of Archaeology* (1995).

356. See http://www.bradshawfoundation.com.

357. See Watson et al. 1997 for an early expansion in Africa based on genetic data; cf. Walter and Fridman 2004: 219 sq. Note, however, that early art is dated at 27,000 BCE in modern San territory (Walter and Fridman 2004: 222) and at 26 kya at the Apollo 11 Cave in Namibia (Connah 2004: 29). This is much earlier that the immigration of the Khoi-San from East Africa around 6000 BCE (Brooks 2006). San rock art from over the past 2,000 years is found in some marginal mountain and desert areas, such as in the open rock shelters of the Drakenberg Mountains; they depict shamanistic trance and its experiences (pictures in Campbell 1988: I.1: 91, 98 sqq., cf., however, 86, ill. 153). This art is dominated, as per D. Whitley (in Walter and Fridman 2004: 210), by shamanistic images: the eland, "flying bucks," and other half-human beings (cf. Lascaux etc.); humans with ritual implements; and rituals (shamanistic dance, rainmaking). It thus provides a catalog of San practices; cf. §4, n. 344.

358. The last common genetic ancestor of the Hadza/Sandawe and Khoi-San (Jun/wasi) is dated at c. 40 kya; Brooks 2006.

359. Wunn 2005, cf. also 2000, for the earlier part of the period; contrast this, for example, with the detailed methodology used by J. Harrod (2006) for analyzing early art and spirituality, and cf. his exposition at http://www.originsnet.org/glossmeth.html.

360. Wunn 2005: 71.

361. Bellah 1973.

362. Wunn 2005: 71 sqq.

363. Wunn 2005: 109 sqq., 133.

364. Wunn 2005: 84, 162 sqq., 174, 183.

365. Though they might have been regarded as entry points to the netherworld by Neolithic times (as per Wunn 2005).

366. Brooks 2006. As mentioned, they include objects in South Africa at 160 kya, Algeria at 90 kya, etc. (see §4, n. 345).

367. Wunn 2005: 110.

368. Wunn 2005: 111 sqq.

369. Wunn 2005: 113; contrast Harrod 2006, http://www.originsnet.org/glossmeth. html.

370. As an example Wunn (2005: 127) cites the Old Egyptian depiction of the human body with its strangely aligned separate parts: the body is not seen as a natural unit. In sum: abstractions, too, form art. Note that even chimpanzees have various differing cultures (Lycett et al. 2007), and so do whales (song dialects) and even monkeys (Japanese macaques with locally developed, inherited techniques).

371. Wunn 2005: 113.

372. Illustration in Campbell 1988: I.1: 65.

373. See, for example, Campbell 1988: I.1: 80 sqq.

374. Cf. the frequency chart in Lorblanchet 2000: 59.

375. Wunn 2005: 131.

376. Wunn 2005: 115.

377. Breuil, the pioneer of cave art studies, perceived hunting and fertility magic in the Franco-Cantabrian cave paintings. His sketches and paintings of cave art have recently been criticized as incomplete, idealizing, and idiosyncratic (Lorblanchet 2000: 81 sqq.; Wunn 2005: 122; see §7, n. 185, for details). However, most subsequent interpretations rest on his drawings, which continue to be used uncritically.

378. Leroi-Gourhan used a structural method, discovering an organized universe with a fixed "syntax": all motifs are male/female symbols (Lorblanchet 2000: 83). Similarly, Annette Laming-Emperaire (1962; Lorblanchet 2000: 83) rather sees themes with a sexual background. Later, Leroi-Gourhan shifted from sexual interpretations to that of the cave as a sanctuary.

379. Wunn 2005: 116 sqq.; cf. Leonard and McClure 2004: 185 sq.

380. Eliade 1978: 28.

381. Illustration in Campbell 1988: I.1: 76.

382. For depictions of such shaman-like figures, see Campbell 1988: I.1: 74, 78, I.2: 156; Gimbutas 1991: 176. Leonard and McClure (2004: 186) have a current photo of the "sorcerer," juxtaposed next to Breuil's sketch; the figure is attributed to 13,000 BCE. For another, still older photo of c. 1960, see Langen 1963: 129.

383. Illustration in Campbell 1988: I.1: 65.

384. Breuil 1952: 144–46; Maringer 1956: 130.

385. Campbell 1988; Eliade 1954b, 1989; Kirchner 1952.

386. Dickson 1990: 215; Mithen 1996: 164–67. However, see the motif collected by Berezkin (2007: Chthonic canine as guard of the netherworld in N. Central and S. America [Andes, Guyana, etc.]).

387. Ucko 1977.

388. Lorblanchet 2000: 209 sqq.

389. Lorblanchet 2000: 189.

390. Lorblanchet 2000: 65 sq.; Wunn 2005: 122.

391. Lorblanchet 2000: 138, 189 sqq.

392. Lorblanchet 2000: 139, 150.

393. Lorblanchet 2000: 139, 150.

394. Wunn 2005: 128 sq. Such pictures, generated by the eye itself, are discussed in detail by Nicholson (2002, 2006). The connections between shamanism and purely entoptic experiences is denied by some scholars (debate in Wallis 2002; Walter and Fridman 2004: 25, 27).

395. Lewis-Williams and Dowson 1988, 1996.

396. Lorblanchet 2000: 209 sqq.; for a different interpretation of dots in Arnhem Land rock art, that is, as depictions of "some intangible power" in visionary experiences, comparable to modern Australian shamans ("clever men"), see Chippindale et al. 2000.

397. Warburg 1938–39.

398. Wunn 2005: 127. The development of human perception, instinctive action, and learning disposition influences us and even other primates in our artistic expression (Wunn 2005: 128).

399. Eibl-Eibesfeldt 1997.

400. Wunn 2005: 129. Léon Pales (between 1969 and 1989; see Lorblanchet 2000: 83 sq.) even says that modern humans have no direct access to such paintings: "only one of a thousand drawn lines can be deciphered."

401. Wunn 2005: 129.

402. Lorblanchet 2000: 64 sqq.

403. Wunn 2005: 130 sq. Following Victor Turner, she believes that the fantastic human/ animal depictions were used, as in Ndembu art (southeastern Africa), to school the intellect and to think about human/animal relations.

404. See §7.2; Campbell 1988: I.1; Gimbutas 1991: 176. For depictions of such shaman-like figures, see Campbell 1988: I.1: 74–78, I.2: 156.

405. Wunn 2005: 131; my translation.

406. Wunn 2005: 36; my translation.

407. Wunn 2005: 132 sq.

408. Wunn 2005: 140 sqq.

409. For the (misplaced) interpretation of Stone Age paintings and sculptures as "art"— as we understand it today—and for the required stress on the individual social context, see also R. J. Wallis, in Walter and Fridman 2004: 22.

410. Wunn 2005: 132; my translation. She complains that this kind of approach has hardly entered the debate so far: incidental selection of motives and old ideas of prehistoric religion prevail.

411. Harrod 2006 and "Researching the Origins of Art, Religion and Mind," http://www.originsnet.org/glossmeth.html.

412. Bellah 1973; Herbig 1988; Wunn 2005.

413. Wunn 2005: 32–36. Clearly, echoes are heard, in both Wunn's and Bellah's work, of Herbert Spencer's (Darwinian-based) beliefs in the origins of religion from the worship of ancestors and a constant development to "higher" forms of religion.

414. Note early instances of art; see Connah 2004; §4, n. 287.

415. Cf. Burkert 1982: 88 sqq. For a detailed discussion, see Lewis-Williams 2002; and below, §7.2.

416. Wunn 2005: 134.

417. See map in Lorblanchet 2000: 54–55.

418. Cf. Campbell 1988: I.1: 62, 67, cf. 91 on Khoi-San (Bushmen) culture, and see I.2: xxi. Cf. also Gimbutas 1991; a *Spiegel* report (April 4, 2005) on new finds near Leipzig, Germany, of male/female sculptured pieces fitting each other in a sexual position; they are about 7,200 years old.

419. Cf. Gimbutas 1991: 213 sqq., with illustrations.

420. Campbell 1988: I.1: 46 sq., 66.

421. Cf., however, Wunn 2005: 155.

422. Lorblanchet 2000: 54 sq.; Wunn 2005: 141 sqq.; see illustrations in Campbell 1988: I.1: 67 sqq.

423. Conkey and Tringham 1995: 212–13; Leonard and McClure 2004: 109 sqq.; Wunn 2005: 140 sqq.

424. An early sculpture at Montespan (Campbell 1988: I.1: 62); and later, at 14 kya: at Tuc d'Audoubert (Pyrenees) of two copulating clay bison (Campbell 1988: I.1: 77 n. 134).

425. Lorblanchet 2000: 56, 318.

426. As Wunn (2005: 120) herself admits.

427. Illustration of bison in Campbell 1988: I.1: 77, ill. 134. For lion man, see Lorblanchet 2000: 26. The figure nevertheless has the head of a female lion, which has been interpreted as a symbol of power because it is the female lions that hunt; cf. Campbell 1988: I.1: 79. See also Wunn 2005: 134, 136 sqq., with further interpretations given by others, such as that of a shaman. Note the recent discovery of a 35,000-year-old figure of a mammoth, discovered near Ulm (Germany); *Spiegel*, February 2, 2007.

428. Wunn 2005: 134, which again points to unknown periods in the development of art (for example, in tropical climates) that have not survived or have not yet been surveyed.

429. On early music, cf. Mithen 2005.

430. Marshak 1971.

431. For the Andamans and Papuas, see Witzel 2002a. A similar tallying system exists in southeastern Australia (Howitt 1904: 697 sq.). The Andaman system employs individually named body parts (not numbers), from the little finger (1) to the top of the head (15) and down again on the other side of the body, and thus counts items 1–32; cf. §7, n. 130.

432. Cf. Barber and Barber 2004: 178.

433. See §4, n. 345, 366; §7, n. 308; cf. Brooks 2006; Harrod, http://www.originsnet.org. Even some Neanderthal objects would fit this category; see immediately below; and cf. two objects in Campbell 1988: I.1: 57.

434. Schrenk and Müller 2005: 94 sqq.

435. If it indeed is from a Neanderthal level, as is now suggested by the recent find of a Neanderthaloid skull. Cf. also the Sungir find (see §4, n. 341), with use of 3,000 beads.

436. Herbig 1988: 64; my translation.

437. Leroi-Gourhan 1965, 1967; see J. Harrod's website, http://www.originsnet.org/ glossmeth.html, and also the rich materials at http://www.originsnet.org. One may look, as an example, at an interpretation of the Australian *tjuringa*; see Campbell 1988: I.2: 145 sq.

438. It is only at this point that Wunn (2005: 131) brings in ethnographic comparison that, in the spirit of her caveat, "might help" in the interpretation of cave art.

439. However, see following note.

440. In the Chauvet Cave in France; see Arnold et al. 2003.

441. For discussions of earlier Paleolithic art, around 90,000 bce, 160 kya, see Brooks 2006; Harrod 2006. See §4, nn. 345, 366; and Schrenk and Müller 2005 on Neanderthal art.

442. Wunn 2005: 111 sqq.

443. Much less, so far, through reconstruction of the vocabulary of linguistic superfamilies; see §4.1. Even reconstructed Nostratic vocabulary is sketchy so far in this regard (see above, §4.1).

444. As Wunn, relying on the interpretation of preserved archaeological objects, reconstructs with Bellah (1973) a fairly simple, "archaic" Paleolithic and Mesolithic religion (see above, §1.6, §4.4.1).

445. For depictions of such shaman-like figures, see Campbell 1988: I.1; Gimbutas 1991: 176.

446. The idea was launched by Stanner (1959: 108 sqq.).

447. See pictures in Campbell 1988: I.2: 144.

448. Cf. Burkert 1983.

449. Campbell 1988: I.1: 65, see illustration 105; http://www.lascaux.culture.fr/#/
fr/02_07_00.xml.

450. This tradition is found even in early attested religions, such as in Greece, where the
entrails of animals were offered to the gods, and in Vedic India, where the omentum of cows
was offered. Even today, in the Tantric ritual of Nepal, only the head and the tail of a ritually
killed buffalo are offered among the Newars. (The head is ritually divided and eaten by important members of the offering community.)

451. Cf. Wunn 2005: 160. Note also the recent development of horse sacrifice, described
by Ch. Darwin (1839–43: 87), among the tribes in the Rio Negro Valley of Patagonia,
Argentina: there was a famous sacred tree, inhabited by the god Walleechu, where horses
were sacrificed in large number, along with alcohol and smoke.

452. Campbell 1988: I.1: 62, I.2: xiii; Harrod, http://www.originsnet.org/glossmeth.
html; Lorblanchet 2000: 59; Wunn 2005: 117. Note, however, the critique of extreme structuralist approaches such as that of Leroi-Gourhan (above).

453. Paraphrasing Bar-Yosef, in Shaw 2001; see also Bar-Yosef 1998. For early China,
Forster and Renfrew (2002: 95) give a date for rice cultivation in the Yangtze Valley at 11.5
kya and 8 kya. See Sagart et al. 2005; Sato 2006.

454. See the settlement maps, §4.3: NRY chromosome F: G–J: M89, 35.

455. Fuller 1999, 2006, 2007; and D. Fuller, in Petraglia and Allchin 2007: 93 sqq.

456. Sato 2006.

457. Fuller 2006.

458. Bar-Yosef 1998; Bar-Yosef, in Shaw 2001.

459. Witzel 2003; see above, §4.1, and below, 4.4.5.

460. For illustrations, see Campbell 1988, 1989.

461. Wunn 2005.

462. See the discussion by Eliade (1958: 265 sqq., 331 sqq.).

463. Caland 1990: 116–19, a passage from the late Vedic Vādhūla Anvākhyāna/Sūtra.
For a discussion of other Indo-European accounts, see Lincoln 1986: 66 sqq.

464. For Ōgetsu, see §2, n. 284; §3, n. 119; cf. §4, n. 464. Note Naumann 1988: 88 sq.,
2000: 223; cf. §7 intro., especially 7.2.

465. "Originating in SE Asia," according to Carl O. Sauer (1969: 28–29). Note the
linguistic similarity of the Indo-European and Chinese words and those of Ainu and Nahali
(Central India), among others (see the complete table for Laurasia/Africa by Ruhlen in
§4.4.4). New genetic data now put dog domestication at 15 kya (Caries et al. 1997; Morell
1997; Powell 2005; Savolainen et al. 2002).

466. Ruhlen 1994: 302.

467. Note that the San (Bushmen) migrated from northern East Africa to their current
home in South Africa only some 6,000 years ago; see Brooks 2006.

468. Before the San migration south from Tanzania. This agrees with the genetic origins
in East Africa.

469. See Mortensen 2003. Note the prominent role of the three-legged "crow" (actually
a raven) in Japanese myth, acting as a messenger and as sun bird (as in China); there are no
crows in Japan (just as in the South Indian Nilgiris).

470. Meisig 1995.

471. Thompson 1993: Motif A673. Hound of hell. Cerberus (monstrous dog) guards
the bridge to the lower world.—Encyc. Rel. Ethics, Greek, Norse, Persian and Hindu,
Eskimo.

472. Cf. Mortensen 2003, on the Eurasian and Laurasian raven; Thompson 1993: Motif A2232.8. Dog's embassy to Zeus chased forth; etc. (cf. A2471.1).

473. Meisig 1995;for details see Witzel 1997b.

474. Campbell 1988: I.2: 167, with illustration.

475. Campbell 1988: I.2: 175.

476. David Anthony, http://users.hartwick.edu/anthonyd/ritual.html.

477. With the Kalash, see Witzel 2004a. Note also the Chinese and North American Indian fox fairies.

478. Around 7,000 years ago, in the Near East; cf. MacHugh 1998; Stokstad 2002.

479. American bull riding at rodeos is still another echo of such prehistoric rites, though with no obvious direct links.

480. Brighenti 2003; also with the Yi in Yunnan and on the Okinawa islands of Japan.

481. Campbell 1988: I.1: 82, no. 144, where a lion is seen as well, just as in Lascaux; see illustration in Lorblanchet 2000: 26, of the lion (wo)man of Hohlenstein-Stadel, 35–30 kya. Note also the older find of the body of a shaman woman in the Czech Republic (Tedlock 2005) and another recently in Israel (Grosman et al. 2008). The question is how much weight to give to and what to make of these stray archaeological finds coming from one region of the world. We know that both male and female shamans are historically attested, though the preponderance is on male shamans, in both the Gondwana and the Laurasian worlds; see §7.1.1.

482. Ions 1990: 124.

483. For the history of pigs, see Seward 2007; and contrast an earlier study by Larsen et al. (2005).

484. Witzel 2004a.

485. Puhvel 1987; Witzel 1997, 1999a, 2004a.

486. Witzel 2003.

487. See the collection of data in Campbell 1989: II.1: 58 sqq.

488. Mair 2007.

489. Also seen, for example, in some rituals of the Trobriand Islanders and of the Hopi ("smothering" eagles).

490. Bierhorst 1986.

491. The Lakota moved into the prairies from a more eastern locality during the medieval "Little Ice Age" and gave up agriculture. Thus, their "original" mythology would not have had the buffalo as a central figure.

492. Cf. §4, n. 451, with Darwin's (1839–43) report on the Rio Negro area of Argentina.

493. See Siegel et al. 2006.

494. At Socrates's death; see Plato's *Phaedo* 118.

495. Witzel 2005b.

496. Which incidentally is another indication of the introduction of Vedic mythology from Central Asia.

497. Thompson 1993: Motif A2494.4.11. Enmity between dog and rooster, Duala.

498. Campbell 1989: II.1: 13, 18, cf. 1988: I.2: 195; Sorenson and Johannessen 2006; and the presentations at the VIIth International Conference on Easter Island and the Pacific Islands in 2007 (cf. §1, n. 65 sqq.; §2, n. 109; §4, nn. 325, 333, 501, 509; §5, n. 413).

499. See Campbell 1989: II.1: 18; Carter 1971, citing Erland Nordenskiøld (1922).

500. See Tregear 1891/1969: 56 on Hawaiki; note the island of Sawai in Samoa and, obviously, Hawai'i. In the Marquesas the mythical journey from *Sawaiki has 17 steps, one of them in Tonga. For the Hawai'ians, the home is in Kahiki(-ku) (Tahiti).

501. See Sorenson and Johannessen 2006 and note the recent genetic data (Gichuki et al. 2003; Hurles et al. 2003), which indeed point to the introduction of the sweet potato from South America. The case of some South American Indian NRY in Polynesia, however, seems related to recent slave trade (Hurles et al. 2003); see §1, nn. 64, 67.

502. Bernhard 1967.

503. Such faithfulness can transcend the mere beginnings of stories and rhymes, as the Brothers Grimm discussed in the introduction to their *Fairy Tales*. One major informant, Viehmännin from N. Hesse, a woman of over 50 years of age who died in 1816, "told [her stories] circumspectly, surely, extremely lively, while taking delight in it herself.... Those who—as a rule—believe in easy falsification of tradition, carelessness in preservation, and therefore in the impossibility of long term [tradition], should have heard how exactly she always retained the story and was eager for its correctness; when repeating it, she never changed material facts and she corrected a mistake in mid-story, as soon as she noticed it" (Rölleke 2003: 16; my translation). For a similar account about the telling of myths with the Fuegan Selk'nam, see Gusinde 1977.

504. For illustrations, see Campbell 1988: I.1: 101, I.2: 139, 185. In Australia, they are made of human hair, and each strand represents a cosmological myth (Lawlor 1991).

505. Such as the Grimms' (2003) "Rotkäppchen" (Red Riding Hood) and "Snow White" or "Jack and Jill" and "Jack and the Beanstalk"; for hero folktales in Russia and their Indian counterpart in the Rāmāyaṇa, see Ježić 2005.

506. For its supposed early origins, see Mithen 2005.

507. See, however, Merriam 1977; Netti 2005; Rice 1987; Stone 2008.

508. Note Lorblanchet 2000 on inferred music in the Paleolithic caves; some ancient flutes have indeed been found.

509. Puhvel (1987) compares the traditional Indo-European colors used for the three (or four) classes.

510. Say, the red, white, and blue of the Saami dress.

511. That is already in use at Chauvet, c. 33 kya.

512. Cf. Mithen 2005: 154 sqq.

513. Aboudan and Beattie 1996.

514. Where one tilts the head left and right in doing so.

515. Widespread in the Mediterranean area (*corna*).

516. Campbell 1988: I.1: 59, no. 90, 66, no. 106.

517. Campbell 1988: I.1: 66, no. 107. See Smith 1996: 187 n. 1.

518. Which may be used as hunting magic in dance; see Campbell 1988: I.1: 93, no. 170.

519. Wunn 2005: 24–29; cf. Mithen 2005: 154 sqq. See Eibl-Eibesfeldt 1997; Lorenz 1963; Tinbergen 1962.

520. An example is in Campbell 1988: I.1: 61; see discussion by Wunn (2005). The gesture degenerated in Neolithic times to a simple M-like design. The original, provoking human gesture can still be found at certain Indian sacred places in the form of statues, as well as in Palau and in some medieval Celtic-area churches.

521. See earlier discussion (§2 n. 46, §4 n. 37) of the goddess Uṣas and the corresponding Gilyak custom.

522. Not noticed and misinterpreted by M. Gimbutas (1991: 19).

523. Such as carried out by the members of our Harvard Round Tables since 1999 (see above, foreword). Note also the programmatic title of Berezkin 1996–97: "The Fourth Source of Data." Independently of each other, we both have thought and worked on the same problem for the past two decades or so, before we first met in 2005.

524. The exact boundaries are not clear. However, since Macro-Caucasian spread from northern Pakistan across Afghanistan to western Central Asia (Witzel 2003), the Caucasus, and Europe (Basque), one probably has to think of the Persian Gulf area (then above water), Baluchistan, Pakistan, and maybe beyond.

525. Cf. the provisional synthesis by P. Manning (2006).

526. As discussed in great detail by Wunn (2005).

527. See the Association for the Study of Language in Prehistory and its journal, *Mother Tongue*, http://www.people.fas.harvard.edu/%7Ewitzel/aslip.html; http://www.aslip.org.

528. See above; Underhill and Kivisild 2007, Figure 4.1.

529. For recent genetic data, see §4, n. 211.

530. Bierhorst 1986: 59, 135, 154.

531. Petraglia et al. 2007.

532. See Berezkin 1996–97, esp. 2002: 91, etc.; cf. http://www.ruthenia.ru/folklore/berezkin. He notes (1996–97: 61) that several themes characteristic for Central America do not penetrate deeply into South America, where, on the other hand, some old Sahul motifs have been retained. This has to be contrasted, however, with S. Thompson's findings that c. 150 South American myths, from primeval chaos to world fire, are found throughout the world; see Bierhorst 1988: 14 sq.

533. Though incidental late contact between South America and Polynesia has now been established by genetics, that is, import of the sweet potato from South America and of chicken from Polynesia; see Storey et al. 2007.

534. A similar case may be that of Hawai'i, which apparently was reached by a ship-wrecked Japanese warrior bearing steel arms; see §1, n. 66. This has left no visible impression in Hawai'ian mythology.

535. For example, we must check whether there is enough evidence, outside the great civilizations, among the isolated tribes of South America to establish the Four/Five Ages: four separate destructions are indeed found among the isolated Gran Chaco tribes, and less than the full set exists with the equally isolated Amazonian Yanomami and the Fuegans of Tierra del Fuego; see §3, n. 489. Cf. also the discussion of the Four/Five Ages by N. Allen (2000).

536. Each of these fields has its own problems of data collection and interpretation, but they nevertheless support each other in the present case.

537. And, according to some, with the development of true human speech; Lieberman 2006, 2007 (cf. Devlin 2006). Note, however, the discovery of a c. 60,000-year-old Neanderthal hyoid bone at Kebara II (Israel, found in 1983); see Schrenk and Müller 2005: 81 sq.

▓ Chapter 5

1. Dundes 1988; Thompson 1993.

2. Witzel 2001a.

3. See van Binsbergen 2007.

4. Cf. Cavalli-Sforza and Cavalli-Sforza 1994: 198 sq.

5. Ragin 1987: 164; my italics. See Witzel 2001a (erroneously) on the alleged absence of flood myths for Africa. The flood myth and similar concepts do not disprove the theory but refine it and lead to the discovery of new intermediate, regional levels, such as the Near Eastern, Greek, the ancient Central Asian one or the Central American/Pueblo one.

6. Rasmus Rask, Franz Bopp (1816).

7. Brugmann 1886–1900.

8. For the various versions from 1868 up to 2007, see http://en.wikipedia.org/wiki/Schleicher's_fable.

9. On theory and procedure, see Ragin 1987.

10. Smith 1982: 19–35, reprinted in Patton and Ray 2000: esp. 27–29.

11. Farmer et al. 2002.

12. See, for example, Rundle Clark 1959: 264.

13. Dundes 1988.

14. Dundes 1988: 249 sqq.

15. Dundes 1988: 241 sqq.

16. See Dundes 1988: 115, 249. However, on Africa, see Baumann 1936: 307–18, with some 20–30 cases, most of them from the Niger-Congo-speaking peoples and some brought about by missionaries. And in China and the Himalayas we find the "reverse" of the flood, the draining of a lake or pond from which the waters rush out. This myth is attested early on in literature for Khotan, Kashmir, and the Kathmandu Valley, but it is found all over the eastern Himalayas as well (Allen 1997) and has echoes in Chinese myth and in a Japanese folktale.

17. Baumann 1936; Witzel 2005a, 2010.

18. For a large collection of flood myths from around the globe, see http://www.talkorigins.org/faqs/flood-myths.html; cf. the brief list in Dundes 1988: 221.

19. Witzel 2001b.

20. The same would apply to the claim that Africa does not have female witches of Eurasian type. The African "shamans" mostly are possessed witch doctors, which includes females; though some inroads of Eurasian shamanism have been stated since Frobenius (1998: 296). See W. van Binsbergen's experiences in Zambia (as per his recordings; in Dutch, see http://www.shikanda.net/) and learning from a female "witch doctor" in Zambia; this included ecstatic practices and blood drinking (like the Nava Durga dancers in Bhaktapur, Nepal) as well as targeted killing. In all these cases we do not deal with Laurasian shamans and the power of the secret/sacred word that they control (Witzel 2011).

21. Such as the detailed discussion by L. Sullivan (1988) of South American myths or by Wilbert (1997 [trans. of Gusinde 1977]).

22. As, for example, in Japan, with its basic "continental" mythology derived from Manchuria and Central Asia (Witzel 2005b; Yoshida 1961–62) but influenced, during the first millennium CE, by Chinese motifs and myths; see, for example, Matsumura 2006b; cf. §3.5.1–2.

23. Either by northern Iranians/Saka or perhaps early Tocharians, but even direct Indo-European influences on early China are not excluded; see Beckwith 2004.

24. Granet 1989: 29; Münke 1976: 219 sqq.; Yang and An 2005: 124 sqq.

25. In the Shi Ji there is a tale about the descent of the Emperor Gau Zu of the Han dynasty who appeared as a dragon. He was born from a human mother who had dreamed about a dragon. In Indian mythological history, many dynasties, from Kashmir to Cambodia, are descendants of unions of humans and Nāga (snakelike beings). I will deal with this motif in a future publication (*The Nāgas of Kashmir*). The link between humans and snakes appears from later Vedic literature (Brāhmaṇas) onward.

26. Cf. Ōbayashi 1960, 1990, 1991a, 1991c. See Yoshida 2006 on Scythian influences via Korea, cf. 1974.

27. See Matsumura 2006b.

28. Raglan's *The Hero* (1956).

29. Note that Campbell (1988) is a diffusionist when it suits him, while he otherwise mainly follows Jungian explanations.

30. Except, for example, in Na-Dene (Athapascan) lands (where we find the dog husband); note also Thompson 1993: Motif A522.1.1. Dog as culture hero, Aztec.

31. Probably in East Asia. See Caries et al. 1997; Savolainen et al. 2002; cf. also Powell 2005.

32. If domestication is from the period around 15,000 BCE, reasons are obvious for the relative absence of the dog in American myth, except for the Na-Dene. In South America it is rarely found. See Sullivan: with the Yupa, a dog acts as guide in travel across the river in the world of the dead (1988: 537); the other two cases concern killing of dogs at funerals— Kaingáng (1988: 491) and Tehuelche (1988: 494). All these cases may easily be late, medieval additions to myth and ritual.

33. See the collection of data in Campbell 1989: II.1: 18 sq., 58 sqq.

34. Chicken are mentioned in the Avesta (*kahrka*), though not yet in the R̥gveda (c. 1000 BCE), and in post-R̥gveda texts (*kr̥ka-vāku*); both words look onomatopoetic. Cf. §7, n. 153. For the ancient dispersion of chicken in North India and South China, see D. Fuller (in Petraglia and Allchin 2007: 400 sq.), who argues for domestication in Central China during the fifth millennium BCE.

35. Their—very interesting and promising—study requires a detailed investigation of the remnants of their old mythology, which has been influenced by neighboring populations to a larger or lesser degree. This cannot be carried out in this book; cf., however, §5.3.3.1.

36. See van Binsbergen 2006a, 2006b; note also the genetic theories of a reflux into North Africa based on NRY III/C and mtDNA M1.

37. Cf. Day 1984: 365, in unspecific terms: "some archaic societies have no myths about the creation of the earth, nonchalantly presuming that the earth has always abided."

38. Hochegger 2005; see above, §3, n. 187; cf. also Wiredu 1996: 84 sqq.

39. Leenhardt 1979: 28 sq. For details on *bao* (frequently, "deified ancestors"), see Leenhardt 1979: 27 sqq.

40. Bastide 1967: 270; Baumann 1936: intro.

41. Zahan 1970: 4. However, Zahan quite erroneously regards and treats all of sub-Saharan Africa as *one* unit: "To speak of the multiplicity of religions in black Africa is likewise to demonstrate our ignorance of African spirituality. In this regard Africans are no more divided than Muslims or Christians.... [T]he essence of African spirituality lies in the feeling man has of being at once image, model, and integral part of the world in whose cyclical life he senses himself deeply and necessarily engaged." One look at the complex religious/mythological situation of Kenya would convince of the opposite: the multiplicity of religions; cf. §5, n. 348.

42. Bastide 1967: 270 sq.; my translation.

43. It is important to note that Leenhardt (1979: xviii sq.) writes in the tradition of Lévy-Bruhl's analysis of the "primitive" mind (cf. Day 1984: 294) but goes beyond him in asserting the role of myth as lived in this world and the linguistic system from which it emerged.

44. Leenhardt 1979: 17. For details on this concept, which is strongly reflected in local language, see Leenhardt 1979: 16–23.

45. Leenhardt 1979: 60: "There is no distance between people and things; the object adheres to the subject.... The eye ... sees only in two dimensions" (cf. 1979: 175–76).

46. Leenhardt 1979: 175.

47. Leenhardt 1979: 191.

48. "Mythic languages cannot be clear if we know nothing of the deep myth which inspires it. Its images are rapidly expressed." Leenhardt (1979: 171) claims that such myths are increasingly less found in southern Melanesian areas; cf. Leenhardt 1979: 44 sq. Northern art (tridimensional) also differs from southern art (bidimensional) (Leenhardt 1979: 176 sq.). Clearly, the early settlement and mythological development of the various parts of Melanesia are in urgent need of further study.

49. See, for example, Leenhardt 1979: 29 sq.

50. See Farmer et al. 2002; Witzel 1979.

51. However, as Malinowski (1922: 406 sqq., 428 sqq.) shows, this is also typical for Trobriand/Melanesian sorcery: "the voice of the reciter transfers [the power]." The use of archaic wording of well-structured spells aligns them with Laurasian sorcery, as opposed to that in sub-Saharan Africa. However, the seafaring Trobriand Islanders, off southeastern New Guinea and in spite of their Melanesian culture, are part of Austronesian-speaking peoples and their Laurasian mythology; their interactions must be compared closely so as to determine any (mutual) influences.

52. Leenhardt 1979: 132.

53. Leenhardt 1979: 34 sqq. This is similar to the West African Dogons' use of *so* (parole; Leenhardt 1979: xx).

54. Bastide 1967: 271; all of which is not unlike the Vedic system of correlations (Farmer et al. 2002). Leroi-Gourhan (1965, 1967) wants to discover, in structuralist fashion, such oppositions and dualism already in late Paleolithic cave paintings. See also J. Harrod, http://www.originsnet.org, and the Marind of Irian for even more complex systems.

55. Farmer et al. 2002.

56. See the work of William Pietz (1985, 1987, 1988); http://proteus.brown.edu/materialworlds/1878.

57. For ancient India (and Iran), see Witzel 2004a; cf. http://www.people.fas.harvard.edu/%7Ewitzel/vedica.pdf. For ancient Egypt, see Rundle Clark 1959: 264; for Old Japan, see Rotermund 2000: 86 sq., esp. 90 (*kotoage*, *kotodama*); for the ancient Mayas, see the Popol Vuh (Tedlock 1985: 73, 78). The power of the spoken word is also found, for example, with Aboriginal Austronesians in Taiwan (the Ami tribe's special priestly language) or the Trobriand Islanders (see §5, n. 51). Note further the use of mantras in Hinduism and Buddhism, the proper ritual formulas in Rome, etc.

58. See §3.1.1, §8.5. Cf. Kojiki I 13.4, 17.3, where the mountains, trees, etc. make noise but cannot really speak; similarly for early creation described in the Popol Vuh; and cf. for Greece, §2, n. 85.

59. Witzel 1979, 2004a.

60. Malinowski 1926.

61. For Papuan genetics, see Forster and Renfrew 2002: 92 sqq.

62. See below for details; Endicott et al. 2003; Thangaraj 2003; §5.3.1.

63. The Monte Verde finds in Chile were at first claimed to be 35,000 years old, but now they are dated around 12,500 BP; see Lemonick and Dorfman 2006 for a popular account. Note also the recent discovery at Topping, Va., at 15,200 BCE, Cactus Hill, Va., at 15,070 BCE; and Meadowcroft, Pa., at 14,250 BCE; and the controversial remains of Kennewick Man. See §2, n. 108; §7, n. 285.

64. For recent genetic and linguistic data, see below: on indications of links with India and with Dravidian (Dixon 1980), see Redd et al. 2002; and note the Australian linguistic substrate in South Indian Dravidian languages; see Blažek 2006. Dravidian influence on Australia is denied by Hudjashov et al. (2007); for late Papua influence on Australia, see Hudjashov et al. 2007: mtDNA haplogroup Q, which is typically Papuan and Melanesian, occurs in northern Australia, however, at a deep level of c. 30,400 ± 9,300 year ago, which is attributed to settlers from New Guinea before the land bridge disappeared around 8 kya.

There was, however, also an earlier land bridge during the second-to-last Ice Age, before 40 kya, that would have been long gone before the last Ice Age, c. 25 kya. Perhaps we rather have to take the lower date, c. 21 kya, of Hudyashov's data, which would fit perfectly well with the Last Glacial Maximum.

65. See diagram in van Binsbergen 2006b: 331 sqq.

66. Redd et al. 2002. See Blažek 2006; Dixon 1980, 2002; Whitehouse 2006; Wurm 1972.

67. Gollan 1985.

68. Glover and Presland 1985.

69. Evans 2003; Evans and Jones 1997.

70. Dixon 1980.

71. Redd et al. 2002: 676; see Blažek 2006.

72. Redd et al. 2002: 676.

73. Hudjashov et al. 2007.

74. Whitehouse et al. 2004.

75. For linguistic means to separate southeast Australia from the rest, see Wurm 1979: 578 sqq.

76. For some differentiation between Australian populations, see, however, the steep boundary west of the Aranda language group (based on blood types [Dixon 2002: 12]) as well as, reportedly, the pygmoid population in the Cairns area of York (Tindale and Birdsell 1941). Studies of population genetics will further differentiate this in the near future.

77. Dixon 2002.

78. Dixon 2002: 7, 690.

79. This scenario is denied by Dixon (2002: xvii sqq., 690 sqq.), who favors an old pan-Australian linguistic area, established after the first settlement and modified by numerous independent trends that followed each other and spread in wave fashion across the continent over the past 40,000 years. All of which would not allow for a tree model (Dixon 2002: 699). Clendon (2006) sees the Pama-Nyungan languages as spreading westward, out of the northeast coastal area, after the end of the Ice Age, around 4000 BCE.

80. Safe for some retreat areas, as in the Caucasus, Pyrenees, Pamirs, Himalayas, etc.

81. In the Kimberleys; see Dundes 1988: 241 sqq.

82. Howitt 1904: 493 sqq. Note the isolation of the Victorian Kurnai tribe from others (Howitt 1904: 505).

83. See Campbell 1988: I.2: 145; Eliade 1992: 3 sqq., 287 sqq.; Howitt 1904: 491 sq. After he went to heaven, he is now seen as a star, Formalhaut or Altair. With other southeast tribes, around Maryborough in Queensland, Kohin (Coin) lives in the Milky Way (Howitt 1904: 498).

84. The early American ethnographer Horatio Hale was one of the first to report on Bajaume/Baiame from Wellington (New South Wales) in 1846, based on his observations made in 1839 during a Navy expedition to the Pacific. He reports from the Wellington Lake near Bairnsdale, Victoria: "The Wellington tribe, at least, believe in the existence of a deity called Baiamai, who lives on an island beyond the great sea to the east.... Some of the natives consider him the maker of all things, while others attribute the creation of the world to his son Burampin" (1846: 110); see, in detail, Howitt 1904: 488 sqq.

85. Panoff 1967: 241 sqq. See Eliade 1992: 4 sq.

86. For example, in "race," myth, rock art, etc. Typical is a dreamlike power, male and female, human or rainbow snake. On the Papuan dragon/snake, see §5.3.3. Note that the western Papuan snake myth later on also spread eastward into the Melanesian Islands, except for their southern parts (§5.3.3).

87. Dixon 2002.

88. Note also the report of a Papuan pygmy tribe in northeastern Australia, near Cairns; see Tindale and Birdsell 1941. Around 50,000 BCE there was a land bridge between New Guinea and Australia, across the Torres Strait (cf. §5, n. 64), and during the Last Glacial Maximum, again, around 25,000 years ago, across the Arafura Sea and the Torres Strait; Dixon 2002: 7.

89. Clendon 2006.

90. Cf. also the change in climate and animal habitat by intentional burning of vegetation from the Stone Age onward; see the report of BBC Science, July 8, 2005, http://news. bbc.co.uk/1/hi/sci/tech/4660691.stm.

91. Clendon (2006) believes that the origin of the split between the Pama-Nyungan and the other (northwest) languages of Australia is due to postglacial migrations of groups that represented an ancient *Sprachbund*.

92. Dixon 2002: 7.

93. Huxley 1870: 404.

94. Gollan 1985.

95. Glover and Presland 1985. This, however, may just be influence by contact or trade with Indonesia, such as from Makassar until early in the 20th century; the same applies to dingoes: note how eagerly the isolated Tasmanians took over British dogs! See Robinson 1966.

96. Mulvaney and Kamminga 1999. For linguistic relationships with India, see Blažek 2006 on Australian substrate words in Dravidian.

97. Hudjashov et al. 2007.

98. Clendon 2006.

99. The case then would be similar to the complex situation in Africa: old traits were preserved in isolated areas (Bantus of the rain forest etc.) but were heavily altered in West Africa by Sahel influence and in the East African belt by northern influences (e.g., heavenly kingship); see Frobenius 1998: 203; van Binsbergen 2006a, 2006b.

100. Capell 1979; Wurm 1972: 156. Examples include the initial consonant clusters in the southeastern languages of Kurnai, Kulin, and Narrinueric (Victoria), which are also typical for Tasmanian; cf. Dixon 2002.

101. Anthropologists and linguists alike regard some of the features preserved by southeast tribes as archaic; see Baumann 1986: 344 n. 2 on the Kurnai; and cf. below, §5.3.2.1, on their relationship with the Tasmanians.

102. See Eliade 1992: 5; Howitt 1904: 500. For the All-Father in southeastern Australia, the absence of missionary influence on this concept, and the isolation of the Kurnai tribe from others in Australia, see Howitt 1904: 488 sqq., 501, 504–5.

103. This has—too rashly—been attributed either to "Malay thought," as Makassar Malays were clearly visiting northwestern Australia until the early 20th century, as archaeological remnants indicate, or to Western New Guinea influences (Campbell 1988: I.2: 139).

104. Jaiminīya Brāhmaṇa 3.233–35, as an aberrant version of the Vala myth (see §3.5.1).

105. One cannot a priori exclude, in the more accessible southeastern parts of the country, the influence of or the reporting by missionaries who automatically stressed the topic of a primordial god. This is, however, contradicted by the early report of Hale (1846). Further, the congruence between the southeast Australians and the isolated Tasmanians speaks for preservation of an old myth rather than late European influence.

106. Campbell 1988: I.2: 141. A Rainbow Snake is also found, per Eliade (1954b: 135 sq.), during the initiation of a medicine man in the area of Forrest River.

107. See §6; Berezkin 2007.

108. Campbell 1988: I.2: 141.

109. Campbell 1988: I.2: 142; cf. for Africa Baumann 1936: 77 (Kanioka), 116 (Uelle Pygmies), 197 (Kikuyu), 212 sq. (Ewe), 218 sq. (Hausa), 324.

110. Cf. Campbell 1988: I.2: 143.

111. Strehlow 1978: 11 sqq. In the notes I will give the variants found in the generally similar version from the coast of southern Australia (Nullarbor Plain); it was told by a Karraryu woman called Kardin-nilla. Though Smith (1996: intro.) claims that he has not changed the text materially, his language is intentionally Victorian and sometimes romantic. Incredibly, he even speaks of the "chariot of light" of the Sun deity (1996: 30). Cf. also the myth and ritual account from the northern Aranda in Campbell 1988: I.2: 137 n. 241, which includes primordial darkness and a decorated sacred pole, an illustration of which is at 146.

112. Cf. Smith 1996: 173. He sent a "prophet," Nurunderi, who taught people about this deity as their Great Father and about culture.

113. From a southern Australian myth about a perfect land of paradise, reserved for birds, insects, and plants; it can, however, be reached via a narrow ledge of rock guarded by a good and an evil snake; troubled and sick people try to reach this land; one meets friends, relatives, and other tribes there; finally the Land of Perfection is destroyed by a flood and moved by the Father Spirit to the Milky Way (Smith 1996: 182). See also Smith 1996: 174 sqq.

114. It was imagined as a giant tree or was represented by a spear (Strehlow 1978: 12).

115. This is where Smith picks up the myth: "a great darkness covered all space … in it the earth dwelt cold and lifeless" (1996: 23).

116. Called variously Sun Goddess, Young Goddess, Mother, Sun Mother, and Goddess of Light and Life (Smith 1996: 23).

117. As well as forms of lives, in caves (Smith 1996: 23).

118. At first the Sun Goddess is awakened by the "great Father Spirit" (Smith 1996: 24); later he becomes a demiurge, after sending a flood (Smith 1996: 35). She floods the world with light and stirs, successively, vegetation, insects, snakes and lizards, birds, and finally, animals (i.e., "mammals"). Seasonal changes and the night emerge as well (Smith 1996: 25–26).

119. They were of human form and intelligence and could intermarry; however, they wanted to change form and abode (to their present state [Smith 1996: 31, 45, 55]), which is finally granted by the Sun deity. The creation of man and woman is elaborately told (Smith 1996: 40, 56 sqq.). She also creates a "brother" for them, the female moon (Smith 1996: 28 sqq.).

120. Smith 1996: 30: "The moon descended on the earth and became the wife of the morning star." Their children "multiplied in the form of the human race." Stars are children of the morning star and the moon, too: "Bajjara and Arna, the prophets of the Spirit world, said: "You … shall not seek to change your state like the animals" (etc.); "you and your children will all return to the Great All Father, the Eternal Spirit" (Smith 1996: 30 sq.; for copious details, see Howitt 1904: 488 sqq.). For star myths of southern Australia, see Smith 1996: 22; cf. the evidence from Tasmania (§5.3.2.1).

121. Cf. Smith 1996: 33.

122. Strehlow 1978: 11–19. See above, Smith 1996: 30. On death and tree burial, see Howitt 1904: 458; Smith 1996: 59, 61.

123. That is found only sporadically in sub-Saharan Africa; see Baumann 1936: 227, 234, 324, 378.

124. See http://www.Andaman.org.

125. See http://www.bradshawfoundation.com/bradshaws/.

126. However, an earlier, Indo-Pacific and even Gondwana mythological trait can be distinguished that links the San, Andamanese, and Australians (e.g., the heat in the spinal cord of shamans; see §7, n. 112; Witzel 2011).

127. See the bibliography by Plomley (1969).

128. Tasmania was earlier connected to Australia around 50 kya but separated by 30 kya, to be reconnected in another ice age by c. 22,000 and 18,000 kya, when the plain that is now the Bass Straight was settled (Brown 1991: 98).

129. Brown 1991: 96; Dixon 2002: 9, 39. Earlier dates given were closer to 23,000 years ago (Dixon 2002: 7; Plomley 1993: x, 76 sq.). See Brown 1991 for a summary of the subsequent settlement history: first in the south, after 11,600 BCE in the north, and eventually spreading to the whole island again.

130. Brown 1991: 98. Similar Pleistocene rock art is found in Arnhem Land and southern and southwestern Australia.

131. Brown 1991; Clark 1983: 23–24; Plomley 1993: 62 sqq.

132. Some 19th-century authors alleged that the Tasmanians could not produce fire but relied on that produced by lightning strikes etc.; however, other reports clearly speak of the use of flint stones, and Roth (1899: 82) reproduces a fire drill and socket. There also is a legend of the origin of fire, linking it with the stars (Roth 1899: 84 sq., app. H: lxxxviii sq.).

133. Crowley and Dixon 1981: 419 sq.; Wurm 1972: 168–74.

134. Crowley and Dixon 1981; Wurm 1972: 156.

135. Wurm 1972: 174.

136. Usher 2002.

137. Nevertheless, some minor overlap with southeastern Australian (Victoria) remains, also discussed by Usher (2002); they probably are loanwords.

138. Greenberg 1971. His proposal of an Indo-Pacific family is variously judged—even called "outrageous" by Crowley and Dixon (1981: 420). However, see Whitehouse et al. 2004 on the link of the Himalayan isolate Kusunda with Indo-Pacific; further update by Usher (2006).

139. Tindale and Birdsell 1941.

140. Crowley and Dixon 1981: 419; discussion in Dixon 2002: 36 sqq.; see Usher 2006.

141. Plomley 1993: 61; Roth 1899: 53 sq. Cf. also Worms 1960 for the etymologies of 12 mythological terms.

142. Only from the central eastern language. Based on our limited knowledge of the Tasmanian languages, one may guess that *marrabona* means "one-downward (to us)." Worms (1960: 5 sqq.) takes it, following W. Schmidt's (1952) reconstructions, as ⁺Digana Mara Bona, "Twilight man": *diga-na*, "dim, dark, shadowy"; *mara*, "light"; *bona*, "man." Other etymologies are possible.

143. Schmidt 1952: 468 sq. Pater W. Schmidt, the author of a multivolume work (1912–55) on the (Stone Age) origins of the idea of a (monotheistic) God, can be suspected to have a monotheistic bias.

144. Plomley 1966: 837. The transcription of Tasmanian words by Robinson heavily depends on the English pronunciation current in the 1820s. Thus *–pannner* is [pana], *oo* [u:], *ee* [i:], etc. For details, see Plomley 1966; Schmidt 1952.

145. Plomley 1966: 63.

146. Plomley 1976: 243: "may be the name of the Ben Lomond tribe."

147. Plomley 1966: 281.

148. Plomley 1976: 242 sq.

149. Plomley 1976: 243: "may be no more than *noieanh* '(kind of) face.'"

150. Still, Plomley (1976: 242 sq.) comments that the existence of "God" or a "good spirit" is not absolutely certain due to the Christian bias of Robinson's notes but that, nevertheless, the words quoted do not show any connections with those for the evil spirits (or "devils," see below). However, there is no connection with the words for "heaven" and "sky" (see Plomley 1976: 393).

151. Otherwise, *tarner*, the "boomer kangaroo," made *lymeene*, i.e., the "lagoons"; Plomley 1966: 374.

152. Pumpermehowle (Pumperneowlle) and Pineterrinner. However, it was not believed by the Bruny Island tribe that they are the creator spirits. Other names of Moihernee are Moilnee, Laller, and perhaps also Tarner (see below).

153. Plomley 1966: 373–74.

154. Plomley 1966: 373–74, 376–77.

155. Plomley 1966: 373–74.

156. Plomley 1966: 402–3, 470 n. 252.

157. Plomley 1966: 373–74, 376–77.

158. Plomley 1966: 373–74.

159. Plomley 1966: 373.

160. Plomley 1966: 373–74: "Droemerdeene made kangaroorat, which some natives say was asleep when this animal made its appearance and that the rat came and threw stones at the natives and that the natives partly awoke and again slept, when he came again and threw more stones and repeated these visits till at length the natives caught him and put him on the ground, and that by and by he came out and stopped in the bush and that afterwards the natives eat him."

161. Plomley 1966: 402–3, cf. 567.

162. The western tribes have Numma, a white spirit being that created the badger.

163. Plomley 1966: 567, 837.

164. Plomley 1966: 641.

165. Plomley 1966: 861, 1976: 408 sq.

166. Plomley 1966: 464 n. 188.a.

167. Plomley 1966: 402, 1976: 408.

168. Plomley 1966: 892–3. For *lowtin*, see Plomley 1976: 409.

169. Plomley 1966: 399. Worms (1960: 15 sq.) adds a name for the Sun, *Buga Nubrana, "The man's Eye," based on his etymology as *ba/bu-ga*, "man"; *nu–*, a possessive pronoun (in body parts); and *–brana* (*bere, meri*, etc.), "eye."

170. See Schmidt 1952: 292: *lūne*, "woman."

171. Roth 1899: 55. Worms (1960: 11) adds *Wara Wana, "Spirit Being," from *wara, wura*, "shadow, spirit of dead, echo; sky," and *wana*, "man, being."

172. Due to their distance often called "England" in conversations with the British. This is obviously due to the identification of white people with the white-colored spirits of the dead (as is common in Melanesia, too). See also Worms 1960: 11 sqq., s.v. *Tini Drini* (*Teeny Dreeny*), "The Island of the Dead," from *tini* (*teeny* etc.), "bone," and *drini* (*dreeny*), "stone, island." He quotes Robinson (from Ling Roth [1899: 55]) with the Tasmanian saying, "Man here dead fire, goes road England, plenty natives England." Note also *Kana Tana, "Bone Man," "appearance of a departed one, spirit of the dead" (Worms 1960: 14); for Western Tasmanian, *kana*, "man," and *tana* (*tane, teni, tina*), "bone, skeleton."

173. Cf. Roth 1899: 55.

174. Clark 1983: 28; Plomley 1993: 65–66, 887; Roth 1899: 56; cf. Worms 1960: 12.

175. See above, Roth 1899: 56 sq.

176. Plomley 1966: 641.

177. Plomley 1966: 892.

178. The name Moihernee may be connected with *moi*, "death," or **moi–*, "water."

179. Or Ragoo wrapper, or Namma, etc. Worms (1960: 7 sq.) translates ⁺Ragi Roba as "Revered Spirit" and derives it from *ragi*, "ghost, white (deceased)," and *roba*, "dreaded."

180. Clark 1983: 28; Roth 1899: 55. Worms (1960: 10) adds ⁺Mura Bugana Luwana (*murrumbuckannya lowana*) as "Bright Spirit of the Night."

181. Plomley 1966: 403.

182. Plomley 1966: 249.

183. Plomley 1966: 281.

184. Plomley 1966: 374: "Worrady says that here is a large tree at Recherche Bay on which is cut the head of a man in large size and also children that the natives call Wrageowraper and that the children cry when they see it that the native men destroyed it, and that this was done by the first white men."

185. Plomley 1966: 403.

186. Schmidt 1952: *komtena, náma, Namme bura.k/Namberi.k, Rágarópa/Rígarópa* (also "thunder, lightning"), *rīt'e/ret'e, ria(na), wiña/wine, tiananga wine, talba*, and *patanīla*. In addition, there are the spirits of the deceased, *wö'rawe(na)*, and of elves or fairies, *nöngiña/nönxīna* (Worms 1960: 14 sq.: ⁺Nangina, "the Ghost," from *nuna/nana*, "darkness, shadow, ghost," and nominal suffix *–gina*); *noilowana*, who are evil but a friend of children and who dance on the hills; and finally, the "swamp light, will-o'-the-wisp," *pökarīt'e/pökarea*. Plomley (1976: 200 sq.) lists *driewerrowwenner, karpennueyouhenner, kormtenner, krottomien-toneack, mienginnya* (or ⁺*maiengiña*; Schmidt 1952; see Worms 1960: 9, Maian Ginja, "The Killer," from *mai*, "dead," and *gana*, "to put"), *namneberick* (Worms [1960: 7] translates ⁺Nama Burag as "spirit of the thunderstorm"), *nanginnya, noilowanah, nowhummer, patteneele, powwenne, prarmmeneannar, preolenna, raegeowropper, rutyer, talba, winnya*, and *wyerkartenner*. He comments that there are too many names to refer to a single "devil" but that there is nothing to point out the differences between these beings. A related name is ⁺Laga Rabana (*larguerroperne*), which Worms (1960: 8) interprets as "awe-ful spirit of the dead" (*laga-na* from *loga-na*, "to sleep," and *raba*, "bad, awful"). Worms (1960: 10) further adds ⁺Mura Bugana Luwana (*murrumbuckannya lowana*) as "Bright Spirit of the Night." Another spirit was ⁺Badanela, "Shadow Man" (Worms 1960: 13 sq.), listed as *patanela, pawtening-eelye* (Schmidt 1952: no. 807), from *ba*, "man," and W. Tasm. *danela* (*deina-lia, deia-lia*), "dark, dim, ghost."

187. Plomley 1966: 249.

188. Plomley 1966: 616.

189. Plomley 1966: 791.

190. Plomley 1993: 61–62.

191. Plomley 1993: 62; Roth 1899: 55.

192. Cf. above, Parledee as one of the original spirits.

193. This is echoed in the belief of some western tribes, who allegedly had no idea of a future existence after death but nevertheless described themselves as kangaroos (Roth 1899: 57).

194. Clark 1983: 28.

195. For a brief discussion of the Tasmanian languages, see Cowley and Dixon 1981; Plomley 1976. For connections with Kusunda, see Whitehouse et al. 2004. Unfortunately, so

far we only have one brief, not very informative myth about the origin of the Kusunda and their Tibeto-Burmese and Indo-Aryan-speaking neighbors.

196. Leenhardt 1979: 28. He continues: "But this entire etiological role diminishes as we move south in Melanesia, which may be evidence that it belongs to imported folklore." He sees several waves of immigration into Melanesia; cf. below.

197. Trompf 1991: 17.

198. Walter and Fridman 2004: 875.

199. Trompf 1991: 13, 16.

200. Trompf 1991: 13.

201. Trompf 1991: 17.

202. Wirz 1925. See also Nevermann 1957; he reports many myths. For the Dema, see Nevermann 1957: 13 sq.

203. The elders (*samb-anim*) are responsible for the preservation of myths within their own extended families (Nevermann 1957: 13).

204. Wirz 1925.

205. Summarized, with Wirz's painting, in Campbell 1989: II.1: 68–71. The "husband and wife" (Ezam, Uzum) festival involved human sacrifice and cannibalism.

206. It is reported from the island of Bonarua that there is a supreme being in the sky, Yabwahine, "the god of plants, land, seas and all creation … and that Yabwahine punished the wrongdoer" (Trompf 1991: 9, cf. 51 sqq. on retribution).

207. Trompf 1991: 13.

208. Reschke 1935: 68.

209. Kamma 1978: 129 sq.

210. Kamma 1978: 135.

211. Kamma 1978: 141.

212. Trompf 1991: 19.

213. Leenhardt 1979: 44: In northern Melanesia, "Indonesian serpent mythology led to a confusion with a totemic serpent." For such snakes or dragons in Western New Guinea, see Kamma 1978: 121–66.

214. Panoff 1967: 232. A hint of this myth is also found with the highland tribe of Taiwan, the Tsou; see Tung 1964: 299, cf. also 399.

215. Kamma 1978: 122.

216. Panoff 1967: 231.

217. Nevermann 1957: 15 sqq. Note that the Austronesian Tsou (highland Taiwan) have preserved a version of this myth: a piece of floating wood, put into a pocket, makes a fishing woman pregnant; see Tung 1964: 334 sq.

218. Trompf 1991: 41, 45.

219. Lawlor 1991: 345.

220. Trompf 1991: 44 sqq.

221. F. Barth (1987) provides a useful account of the multiplicity of mythologies that have developed in a linguistically and culturally closely related group of people, the Ok, living in a fairly small area of central New Guinea.

222. For a survey of Melanesia, see Reschke 1935: 14 sqq.

223. Reschke (1935: 164 sqq.), on the contrary, sees eastern Melanesian influence in New Guinea.

224. Evans 1923: 154.

225. Thus Evans 1923: 147.

226. Evans 1923: 156.

227. Evans 1923: 148. There are variants of this myth; see Evans 1923: 149.

228. Evans 1923: 154 sq.

229. Evans 1923: 155.

230. Evans 1923: 192 sq.

231. Evans 1923: 195.

232. Evans 1923: 153, cf. further 210 sqq. for detailed descriptions. The shaman is claimed to be able to turn into a were-tiger.

233. Evans 1923: 157.

234. Evans 1923: 158 sq. Evans also provides the words for some chants. Note that they vary each time, as would be expected in Gondwana traditions.

235. Also (abusively) called Pugut or Pugot by their neighbors.

236. De Silva 1972.

237. For a brief overview of the language and its peculiarities, see Nara and Bhaskararao 2001, 2003.

238. Rivers 1906: 183 sqq. Cf. Zvelebil 1990, 2001. Though they speak a form of Dravidian now, their language seems to contain indications of a local substrate (Witzel 1999a). Note also that their neighbors, the Dravidian-speaking Kurumba, belong, together with the Rajbanshi and Andamanese, to an old haplogroup of 60/26 kya (NRY D); see §4.3 (cf. §4, nn. 138, 142, 169, 230; §5, nn. 247, 251; §7, n. 219).

239. Rivers 1906: 231 sqq.

240. Such as Teikirzi's husband, Teipakh, and their children Mazo-Mazo, Korateu (who was born from afterbirth), and Kulinkars (Teikhars), who is married to Notirzi; further, Puzi, who gave birth to a son, Kurindo, who immediately became fire but is restored to a boy; and the three sisters Kwoten, Teikuteidi, and Elnākhum. Many legends are told about Kwoten. Further there is Kwoto or Melitars, who was born from a gourd; about him too many stories are told. There are many other deities (Rivers 1906: 210 sqq.).

241. See W. Crooke, in Hastings 1922–28: 1–20, s.v. *Dravidians (North India)*. The essay actually deals with many other pre-Hindu tribes and castes of North India as well and thus provides a useful impression of what local religion may have been before medieval Hinduism formed an overlay. By contrast, the following chapter by R. W. Frazer on Dravidians (South India [in Hastings 1922–28: 221–28]) deals almost exclusively with Hinduism and thus yields nothing for the current purpose.

242. Crooke, in Hastings 1922–28: 5: "formerly the sky lay close down upon the earth. One day an old woman happened to be sweeping, and when she stood up, she knocked her head against the sky. Enraged, she put up her broom and pushed the sky away, when it rose up above the earth, and has ever since remained there." Similar myths are told in Southeast Asia and Africa; see §5, n. 269.

243. Hastings 1922–28: 13.

244. Hastings 1922–28: 502 (F. Hahn and W. Crooke).

245. However, the time most likely for first settlement would be that of the lowest sea level at c. 15 kya, when the northern tip of the then much extended Andamans was close to the mainland. A similar situation must have obtained during the second-to-last Ice Age, before c. 40 kya.

246. Mellars 2006: 796.

247. The Andamanese languages are frequently regarded as isolated, though Greenberg links them to Papuan and Whitehouse et al. (2004) also link them to Kusunda. See the overview by Abbi (2006). For their genetics, see Endicott et al. 2003; Thangaraj 2003; Thangaraj et al. 2005. Their closest genetic "relatives" are the Rajbanshi on the Bengal/Nepali border and the Kurumba in the South Indian Nilgiris, sharing NRY D; see §4.3.

248. Excavations in the Andamans by Lidio Capriani (1952) at Bee Hive Hill (now Goal Pohar); see Cooper 2002; and the summary of Andamanese archaeology by George Weber, http://www.andaman.org/BOOK/chapter24/text24.htm.

249. Campbell 1988: I.1: 122.

250. Cooper 2002; http://www.andaman.org/BOOK/chapter24/text24.htm.

251. Endicott et al. 2003; Thangaraj 2003; Thangaraj et al. 2005. They have close genetic, though no longer linguistic, "relatives" in the Rajbanshi of northern Bengal and the Kurumba of the South Indian Nilgiris, who split off some 46,000–45,000 years ago. The little-studied, non-Austro-Asiatic Shompen in the neighboring Nicobar Islands should be investigated further; see Blench 2007; Rizvi 1990; cf. http://www.andaman.org/NICOBAR/book/Shompen/Shompen.htm.

252. Man 1883; Radcliffe-Brown 1933; cf. Campbell 1988: I.1: 118 sqq.

253. Reflected in archaeology; Campbell 1988: I.1: 121–22 sqq.

254. Cf. Abbi 2006; for the Sentinelese, Pandit 1990; as well as a short film made by one of the Indian government's contact missions, now completely abandoned. The Sentinel Island now is off limits to everybody, officials included. Cf. http://www.andaman.org/BOOK/chapter8/text8.htm#sentineli; http://www.andaman.org/BOOK/reprints/goodheart/rep-goodheart.htm.

255. Radcliffe-Brown 1933: the Aka-Jeru, however, believed that the sun in the shape of a man made the earth and created humans. The Aka-Kol and A-Pucikwar had the monitor lizard who married a civet cat as ancestor of humans. Meanwhile E. Man (mostly dealing with south Andamanese [1883]) has Puluga as the main deity who created all. However, Radcliffe-Brown (mostly dealing with north Andamanese [1933]) underlines that he is but one of several important deities.

256. Disputed by Radcliffe-Brown. For a complex tale about the "creator," Puluga, the first man, Tomo, and the flood, artificially assembled by H. Man, see http://www.andaman.org/BOOK/chapter23/text23.htm.

257. Campbell 1988: I.1: 121; Radcliffe-Brown 1933: 192. Note the tree origin of humans in Iceland, Taiwan, the Philippines, and Japan. The parallel in Taiwan is from the aboriginal Austronesian tribes; the Philippine one is from the Tagalog; the Japanese is preserved in a folktale (Kaguyahime). The concept is also found in Africa: the Zulu assume origin from a reed, and the southwest African Herero, from a tree; cf. Day 1984: 365. In another Andamanese version, the first man cohabited with an ant nest (that is, the tall termite structures with deep holes) and begot many children; or he made a woman from the clay of an ant nest (Radcliffe-Brown 1933: 192).

258. Cf. also in Old Egypt, from clay with the help of beer; the Bible; and the pagan Kalasha in northwestern Pakistan. Or from the root of a tree, as in the creation of humans from the maize deity in Mesoamerica (cf. §2, n. 177; §4, nn. 510, 525). Or in the Andaman Islands: created by the southwest monsoon or by Lady Crab (Campbell 1988: I.1: 121); or for the A-Pucikwar, a monitor lizard bit off the genitals of a man and made him into a woman.

259. Radcliffe-Brown 1933: 191.

260. Campbell 1988: I.1: 124; Radcliffe-Brown 1933: 220.

261. Campbell 1988: I.1: 124 sq.; Radcliffe-Brown 1933: 200 sq.

262. Campbell 1988: I.1: 125; Radcliffe-Brown 1933: 216 sq.

263. Campbell 1988: I.1: 122.

264. Campbell 1988: I.1: 123.

265. Note that many early written or orally fixed myths (as in early Vedic prose in the Yajurveda Saṃhitās) are of the same type; they have extremely short sentences that are in need of a lot of background information in order to understand them.

266. Radcliffe-Brown 1933: 189.

267. Radcliffe-Brown 1933; cf. G. Weber, http://www.andaman.org/BOOK/chapter23/text23.htm.

268. Cf. the many animal myths in Campbell 1988: I.1: 124 sq.; Radcliffe-Brown 1933.

269. Campbell 1988: I.1: 124; Radcliffe-Brown 1933: 199–200. The myth is also similar to that found in Africa (see Baumann 1936: 417, s.v. *Himmel–Erde, Trennung*), where a woman hit the sky with a stick. In the Andamanese version, the sky was close to the earth, just above the trees, and Porokul made a large bow whose tip struck heaven, and it moved up to its current position; see §5, n. 242.

270. Campbell 1988: I.1: 123; Radcliffe-Brown 1933: 207–8. The flood myth is told in several versions.

271. For the connection, see Campbell 1988: I.1: 122.

272. Cf. the tale of the jackal and the hunter in the medieval Indian text Pañcatantra, also met with in Melanesia, where in both cases the tusks = moon, an idea also found in Ireland.

273. Campbell 1988: I.1: 121–22.

274. Campbell 1988: I.1: no. 220.

275. Berezkin 2007.

276. A. Motingea, personal communication, University of Kinshasa, August 2005.

277. H. Fleming, personal communication, 2006.

278. According to Knight et al. (2003), Hadza NRY is mainly B2b (52%), like that of the Pygmies (Mbuti). Strong "Bantu" influence is seen in E3a (30%), and the rest is mostly E as well. However, mtDNA show the very old haplogroups L2 (Pygmies too have L2a1) and L3 (mainly the East African L3g). Importantly, as with NRY, these are *not* found with the San, who have L0d/L0k. The Hadza, thus, originally seem to have had NRY B2b and mtDNA L2a1, which was interfered with by East African and "Bantu" lineages.

279. Brooks 2006.

280. On their genetic relations, see Tishkoff 2007; note, however, that she missed the "Yellow Sandawe" as per H. Fleming (personal communication, 2006); hence, the "Black Sandawe" do not show much difference with the surrounding African populations including the Pygmies.

281. Brooks 2006; Connah 2004. Cf. also the rather schematic maps in Campbell 1988: I.1: 43 (following the outdated classification of Carleton Coon).

282. The Hottentots' mythology is mixed with that of the San; note that the Pygmies of the Congo Basin also have a High God. The Damara god Gamab is in heaven above the sky; he lives there with the souls of the dead who have reached him across a deep abyss; they are living under the shade of the heavenly tree and do not have children anymore (all of which reads like a description of Vedic eschatology!), but they also eat the bodies of dead persons; see Bastide 1967: 252. The Herero nomads are influenced by Bantu mythology. Important for them is the first man (as with Nilotic or Zulu people), and they have a High God.

283. Walter and Fridman 2004: 891.

284. Cf. Bastide 1967: 252.

285. Following Noah Butler and Frank Salamone (in Walter and Fridman 2004: 891 sq.), who base their account on Lee 2003: 125 sqq.

286. D. N. Lee and H. C. Woodhouse/Pager, in Campbell 1988: I.1: 99, no. 178.

287. In Eastern Free State and in Lesotho, local Sotho folklore of the 19th century and later describes the San as living in caves, where they drew wall pictures during shamanic trances; they were also known as good rainmakers. For examples, see illustrations in Campbell 1988: I.1: 98 sq.; cf. http://www.bradshawfoundation.com/rari/index.php; and the "Rosetta

stone" image of a shaman and an eland at http://www.bradshawfoundation.com/rari/bushman.php. Van Binsbergen (2006a: 16, 2006b) adduces an undated representation in rock art from Chad, which would point to the Capsian origin of the antelope motif (and that of the San?).

288. This interpretation follows that of Lewis-Williams and Dawson, quoted in Walter and Fridman 2004: 220.

289. Bastide 1967: 252. All of this actually reminds one very much of Ṛgveda mythology (see §5, n. 282).

290. Based in part on Brauer 1925.

291. Campbell 1988: I.1: 106.

292. See Watson et al. 1997 for their early spread in Africa, based on genetic data.

293. Campbell 1988: I.1: 106.

294. Campbell 1988: I.1: 106. This idea is not uniform in all Pygmy tribes; see Schebesta 1936.

295. Campbell 1988: I.1: 109.

296. See summary by Baumann (1936: 385 sq.).

297. Campbell 1988: I.1: 111.

298. Campbell 1988: I.1: 108; Schebesta 1936: 177 sqq. The myth echoes the biblical motif of the punishment of Eve.

299. Schebesta (1936: 180) underlines that (just as in the Bassari creation myth reported by Baumann [1936: 265 sqq.; Frobenius 1924]; see the actual text in §6.1) the Pygmy tribe (at Maseda) had no knowledge of biblical matters. Cf. Campbell 1988: I.1: 109. The myth was also recorded by another missionary. Obviously, one does not need to interpret such data in the fashion of P. W. Schmidt (1912–55) as remnants of tales connected with his ur-monotheism.

300. Zuesse 1979: 45.

301. Baumann 1936: 386.

302. Such as the Tere/Tule (Tore) complex in the rain forest, the exchange of Heaven/ Earth (Ituri Pygmies), the origin from an egg with the Gabon Pygmies, Imama elements with the Kivupy, and the Rainbow Snake of the Ituri Pygmies.

303. Campbell (1988: I.1: 112) adds some speculative notes on the origin of myth and on different levels of psyche, which would exclude the (typical Laurasian) question of how and from where the world evolved.

304. See §1.3 on archetypes.

305. Baumann (1936: 385), based on the *Kulturkreis* classification, wants to distinguish between the Pygmies as representatives of an older hunter and gatherer culture, as opposed to the San, who would belong to a "higher" Eurafrican hunter and gatherer tradition.

306. On a similar concept, see Frobenius 1998: 169 sq.; van Binsbergen 2006a, 2006b, with map. Further, see Frobenius 1998: 296 on the intrusive influence of North African and Indian Ocean shamanism.

307. Baumann 1936, 1986; Frobenius 1998: 203 sqq.

308. Motingea 2004. A study of the substrate language(s) in the Bantu Pygmy languages is of high priority; see Bahuchet 2006; §4, n. 139.

309. Baumann 1936: 185 sq. For example, with the Kamba or Yao. Baumann (1936: 185) reduces the lack of true creation myths and the preponderance of myths dealing with fashioning a preexistent earth and of humans to the "manistic" form of typical African mythology: stress on ancestors and human origins.

310. Baumann 1936: 1; my translation.

311. Cf. also Thomas et al. 1969: 86: "In Black Africa, one hesitates to qualify as myths certain accounts of creation or of the origin of the world. It rather seems that the actual myths treat the creation of man. When an ethnic group is asked, in prolonged fashion, about the creation of the world, several elements of the account may be mystic, but others incontestably reveal a classification effort of the facts of nature, a cosmogony obtained by reduction of experience to first explicatory principles" (my translation). Wiredu (1996: 84 sqq., cf. 49) discusses the problem along linguistic and philosophical lines, mostly for the Akan language of Ghana and the Luo language of Kenya (following the work of Okot p'Bitek [1970]). Wiredu concludes, "The Akan, then, would seem to be like the Luo in not having a concept of a creation out of nothing" (1996: 87). He (1996: 91) continues to show how ridiculous translations of the Bible into Luo/Akan and then back into English would look: The Word was God –> *Lok Aye ceng Lubanga* –> News was Hunchback Spirit (Luo) or: The Word was God –> *Na Asem no ye Onyame* –> The piece of discourse was God (Akan). Cf. Whorf 1956.

312. Hochegger 2005; my italics. Cf. §3, n. 187; §5, n. 38.

313. And with the Herero in central Namibia; for examples of Africa-wide "creation" myths, see Radin 1983: 25 sqq.

314. Baumann 1936: 96 sqq. Some authors, such as Opoku (1978: 14 sqq.) or worse, Mbiti (1970: 5), turn this into an all-African "God" with quasi-Abrahamic traits. Opoku holds that West African religion is not polytheistic as God "is outside the Pantheon of gods. He is the eternal Creator of all the other gods, and of men and the universe" (1978: 4). Mbiti even says: "Every African people recognizes one God" (1970: 29). Similarly, see Idowu 1973: 146. For a discussion of the Akan (Ghana) concept of the High God and the lack of his worship versus other gods, see Wiredu 1996: 47 sqq. For the sky god in general, see Eliade 1958: 38 sqq.

315. In the Congo, with the Ngombe, there is a creator acting like a potter (Parrinder 1972: 31).

316. Baumann 1936: 108. From *umba*, "to create, to form"; *nya/nsa/nza/nya* is a verbal adjective that forms nouns.

317. For the High God as creator, see Mbiti 1970: 46 sqq.; Opoku 1978: 19 sqq.; Thomas et al. 1969: 8, 47 sq. For the High God as father, see Mbiti 1970: 92 sqq.; Thomas et al. 1969: 48. For his son and children, see Mbiti 1970: 115 sqq.; on other deities, see Thomas et al. 1969: 49 sqq.

318. For the creation of man, see Mbiti 1970: 161 sqq.

319. Additional cases in Baumann 1936: 224. Related myths are also found in central Angola; see Baumann 1936: 95; cf. Eliade 1957: 343 sqq. Baumann (1936: 185) lists the following types of the origin of humans: from clay (203), from wood (205), from trees (224; note: tree grave [235]), from heaven (206), from excrements (214, etc.; note also: humans as center [215]), from termite hills and from caves and rocks (219); from knee (221; earlier humans [240] destroyed by fire); see also origin of women (239) and origin of animals (201).

320. See Mbiti 1970: 173 sqq.

321. See Baumann 1936: 327 sqq.

322. Sproul 1991: 49 sqq.

323. Baumann 1936: 386 sq.

324. A feature that is also typical for India, from early on: Ṛgveda 10.129 (c. 1000 BCE) and other creation hymns stress this. Differently from the Near East, it is not a god who "creates"; rather, the world merely "emerges": from the late Ṛgveda onward, the world "emerges" (*sṛj*) from Prajāpati, "the lord of progeny." The question to be investigated is whether we can

see here the workings of the Gondwana substrate that permeates much of later Vedic and Indian thought. This question has not even been engaged seriously, though Indologists have talked about vague "aboriginal" influences for more than a century (see, however, Berger 1959). The establishment of Laurasian and Gondwana mythology offers us the chance to test this point step by step.

325. Details in Baumann 1936: 185 sqq.

326. Griaule 1948; Parin et al. 1962.

327. For West African religion in general, see Opoku 1978.

328. Griaule 1948; Parin et al. 1962.

329. Frobenius 1998: 169 sq.

330. Van Binsbergen 2006b: 331 sqq.

331. Parrinder 1972: 20 sq.

332. Old Mother Earth in the underworld where the dead are buried "in her pocket" (Parrinder 1972: 31). Parrinder (1972: 26) discerns mixed ideas of theism, spirits, and dynamics.

333. Note the different role of the spider (Marawa) in Polynesia, who gets things wrong; see §3, n. 475; contrast the role of the spider (Ananse) in West Africa, Australia, and the Americas.

334. Baumann 1936: 241.

335. Against a generalization of fetishes as typical for African religion, see Opoku 1978: 4.

336. Parrinder 1972: 31.

337. Villems 2005; see §3.1.

338. Cf. the role of the "sacred insider," below; see van Binsbergen 2003, 2006a, 2006b. Note the kingless societies of the Ibo, Ewe, Kikuyu, Nuer, Maasai, etc. I prefer not to follow such writers as Frobenius and Baumann who wanted to link mythologies too closely with economic development, for example, in linking "hoe-type" mythologies with patriarchal or matriarchal societies.

339. Note the early observation by Frobenius (1998) on various influences in this belt, though he did not always attribute them to a straightforward north–south movement but also took into account (like Baumann 1936) influence emanating from the coast.

340. Ehret 1995, and importantly, 2002.

341. Baumann 1936: 56 sqq. He stresses the dualistic nature of Maasai religion.

342. Baumann (1936: 60) indeed underlines that this primordial dragon is not found "anywhere else" (in Africa). The dragon is still supposed to live near Mt. Kilimanjaro where he kills passersby.

343. Parrinder 1972: 31.

344. Baumann 1936: 80–90.

345. Zuesse 1979.

346. The hoe culture has female cultivators, while plowing is done by men. However, in the West African savanna, men carry out agriculture with hoes: patrilineal descent is more common; see Zuesse 1979: 79.

347. Zuesse 1979: 103 and passim.

348. Zuesse 1979: 104 n. 2. In light of the above, it is difficult to see why some writers such as Zahan regard all of Africa as a unit: "To speak of the multiplicity of religions in black Africa is likewise to demonstrate our ignorance of African spirituality. In this regard Africans are no more divided than Muslims or Christians. . . . The essence of African spirituality lies in the feeling man has of being at once image, model, and integral part of the world in whose cyclical life he senses himself deeply and necessarily engaged" (1970: 4; cf. Mbiti 1970).

Again, as mentioned above, one look at the complex religious situation in Kenya would result in a different approach; cf. §5, nn. 38, 314.

349. Frobenius 1998: 169 sq.; van Binsbergen 2006a: 31 sqq., 2006b; see last section.

350. Parrinder 1972: 31. See Baumann 1936; Mbiti 1970; Opoku 1978; Thomas et al. 1969.

351. Parrinder 1972: 38.

352. For a discussion of the "lost paradise," see Baumann 1936: 265 sqq. The myth is also found in eastern Gondwana mythologies; see above, §5, n. 113 (Australia).

353. Parrinder 1972: 43.

354. Parrinder 1972: 57.

355. Parrinder 1972: 67.

356. Parrinder 1972: 71.

357. For Africa, see the listings by Baumann (1936: 224 sqq.).

358. For the Aeta (Agta/Ata), see Beyer 1918– etc.

359. One may compare the Inca idea that the dark spots in the Milky Way represent animals; see Witzel 1984. For illustrations, see Sullivan 1996: figs. 2.9A and 3.5. In Tahiti, the Milky Way (Vai-ora-o-Tane) is above the highest heaven and is called "the water for the gods to lap up into their mouths" (see Beckwith 1987: 4). For southern Australia, see Smith 1996: 22, 182.

360. Note that in many Laurasian myths, trees (and grass) could talk in the beginning, such as in Japanese (Kojiki 1.14, Nihon Shoki 1.29) and in Mesoamerican myth; see §2, n. 85.

361. Baumann 1936: 224 sqq.; also in Austronesian Taiwan, the Philippines, Japan (Kaguyahime). In Africa: the Zulu, Herero from a tree; cf. Day 1984: 365. See above, §2, n. 177; §3, nn. 375, 510; §5, n. 257.

362. Baumann 1936: 235 sqq. See §5.4, §6.1; for India, see the burial at the root of a tree in a *stūpa*; for Tasmania, see §5.3.2.1; for Africa, see Baumann 1936: 235 sqq.; for Australia, cf. the use of trees in burial.

363. Sproul 1991: 114 sq.

364. Baumann 1936: 235 sqq.; this includes customs of the Pygmies.

365. In the middle to late Vedic text, Jaiminīya Brāhmaṇa 3.233–35, describing the emergence of females (Apsaras, nymphs), next to cows (§3.5.1).

366. Baumann 1936: 268 sqq.

367. See van Binsbergen 2006a, 2006b.

368. Campbell 1988: I.1: 14. Frobenius asserted that the Bassari in Togo had never been visited by Christian or Islamic missionaries. See above, §5, n. 299.

369. Such as at Lascaux (Leroi-Gourhan 1965). On this topic, see, however, Lorblanchet 2000; Wunn 2005.

370. Farmer et al. 2002.

371. Note, however, that dualities are also found in the Andaman Islands and in the South Indian Nilgiri Mountains, where we find two primordial deities: Ön and his sister Teikirzi, from whom the preexisting world develops (Rivers 1906).

372. Horton points out for the Congo that the local *Weltanschauung* establishes unity underlying apparent diversity, using analogy between observations and already familiar phenomena, so that "only a limited aspect of such phenomena...is incorporated into the resulting model. Other aspects...are irrelevant" (1975: 342). Similarly, in Vedic India; see Witzel 1979, 2004b.

373. Denham et al. 2004.

374. Jensen 1978. For the relationship between Ceram and West Africa, Congo, see Jensen 1948: 178; on Hainuwele, see Jensen 1948: 14, 34.

375. Gollan 1985. Depending on the age of dog bones found in Australia, (some of) it may also have been due to some recent Malay trading posts, as seen in archaeology; see §5, nn. 95, 377.

376. Redd et al. 2002.

377. Though some contact with Makassar (Indonesia) existed, due to visits of Makassar boats that stopped only in 1907; see §5, n. 95.

378. Another one existed along the Guinea coast, from Sierra Leone in the west to Cameroon in the east, that is, an area settled by various Niger-Congo-speaking peoples, to whom the Bantus belong.

379. Ehret 2002: 168; see below, §5.6.1; Connah 2004: 40–50, 131 sqq.

380. See van Binsbergen 2006a, 2006b.

381. Capriani (1952) dates it to c. 3000 BCE.

382. Witzel 1990a.

383. Mehdi et al. 1999. Cf., however, Ayub et al. 2003; Underhill et al. 2000.

384. Jettmar 1975; Tuite 2007: 25; cf. also Tuite 1996, 1998.

385. Witzel 2004a on the Kalasha. See also the work of J. Colarusso (1985a, 1985b, 1987, 2002) and G. Charachidzé on the connections of Caucasus myths with those of neighboring groups such as the Iranian-speaking Ossetes and vice versa.

386. Cf. Carrín 2008; Vincente and Valle 2003; cf. *El Rey, La Diosa y el Orden Cósmico*, 2004, http://www.celtiberia.net/articulo.asp?id=1020.

387. Ehret 2002: 168.

388. The earlier border line was central north of Lake Tanganyika; west, north, and east of Lake Victoria; and then more or less eastward to north of Galana River in Kenya and up to the ocean. See map in Ehret 2002: 167.

389. Note the interpretation as sacred insider by W. van Binsbergen, http://www.shi-kanda.net/; cf. van Binsbergen 2006a, 2006b.

390. Baumann 1936: 189.

391. Baumann 1936: 142.

392. Baumann 1936: 200.

393. Baumann 1936: 190.

394. Baumann 1936: 190; cf. Eliade 1992: 91 sq.

395. Baumann 1936: 190.

396. Baumann 1936: 190, cf. 196 sqq.

397. An area in which the establishment of kingdoms (such as Monomotapa/Zimbabwe) furthered trade and import of East African ideas.

398. Baumann 1936: 191 sq.

399. Baumann 1936: 192.

400. Baumann 1936: 191.

401. See §3.3; Baumann 1936: 191.

402. Cf. §3.5.2; Baumann 1936: 193 sqq.

403. See §5.7.2; Baumann 1936: 193 sq.

404. Baumann 1936: 174 sqq., cf. 243 sq.

405. Baumann 1936.

406. Witzel 2006c.

407. "Oceanic *guggulu*" or bdellium is mentioned in the second-oldest Indian text, the Atharvaveda (19.38.2), next to the local kind: apparently it was brought from the Near East.

408. If indeed the (unlikely) migration of Sunda Land tribes (of ultimately Indian origins) took place as late as just some 3,000–5,000 years ago (Redd et al. 2002), a close comparison of the oldest Tamil documents (Sangam texts) and the lore of the isolated Toda tribe of the Nilgiris would be of great importance; cf. Zvelebil 1982, 1990.

409. See above, §5.3.2 on pronouns; in Wurm 1979, with map; for genetics, see Hudjashov et al. 2007.

410. Such as the mythological figure of Cpt. Cook.

411. For details of Tasmanian mythology, see §5.3.2.1. Some mixed bands, descendants of Tasmanian women and British men, survive on the northern Tasmanian islands; they are now trying to revive their long-lost native language: http://www.fatsilc.org.au/languages/language-of-the-month/lotm-1996-to-2000/1999-dec---lynne-spotswood-?.

412. See http://www.ruthenia.ru/folklore/berezkin.

413. This does *not* mean that Australia and South America have experienced regular late interchanges, via Polynesia; for the contrary position, see Schuster 1951; Sorenson and Johannessen 2006. Cf., however, Storey et al. 2007 for chicken import into Chile. See §1, nn. 67, 68; cf. §5, n. 377.

414. Baumann 1936: 174 sqq.

415. Berezkin 2002.

416. Lieberman 2006, 2007. Note, however, the discovery of a Neanderthal hyoid bone found at Kebara (Schrenk and Müller 2005).

417. Thompson 1993: **Motif A1010**. The Flood (presented here in abbreviated form); A1011.1. Flood partially caused by breaking forth of springs, Irish, India (cf. A941.6. Breaking forth of springs partial cause of flood); A1011.2. Flood caused by rising of river, S. A. Indian (Chiriguano); **A1012**. Flood from fluids of the body; 1012.2. Flood from urine. (Koryak, Eskimo, Athapascan Indians); **A1015**. Flood caused by gods or other superior beings (cf. A1018), Babylonian, Marquesas, S. Am. Indian (Tupinamba, Yuracare); A1015.3. Flood caused by deity stamping on floor of heavens, Maori; A1016. Pseudo-scientific explanations of the flood; **A1016.3**. Flood caused by melting of ice after great spell of cold, N. Am. Indian (Déné), S. Am. Indian (Gusinde); A1016.6. Moon falls into sea and causes flood by overflowing, S. Am. Indian (Fuegians); **A1017.2**. Flood caused by prayer, Maori; A1017.3. Flood caused by curse, S. Am. Indian (Chiriguano); **A1018**. Flood as punishment. Old Testament, Spanish. Cole: Australian (cf. B91.6. Serpent causes flood), Jewish, Greek, Babylonian, India, Buddhist myth, Society Is., Hawaiian, Maori, Marquesas; N. Am. Indian (Calif., Pomo, Wishosk, Apache, Hopi, Zuñi); Caribbean (Cuan); S. Am. Indian (Chaco, Cubeo, Toba, Inca)—see also references to "Sintflut" in A1010 and A1015, where in nearly all cases the gods produce the flood as punishment (cf. Q200. Deeds punished; Q552.19.6. Flood as punishment for murder); A1018.1. Flood as punishment for breaking tabu, Fiji, Tahiti, Maori, Andaman; S. Am. Indian (Toba, Mataco, Lengua); A1018.2. Flood as punishment for incest, American Indian (Namba; cf. Incest punished; T410); A1018.3. Flood brought as revenge for injury, Tuamotu; N. Am. Indian (Carrier, Ts'etsaut, North Pacific Tribes, Haida, Kwakiutl, Mono, Shasta, Pima, Ojibwa, Menomini); Central and S. Am. Indian (Cahita, Bororo, Tupinamba); **A1019**. Deluge: miscellaneous; A1019.3. Flood because earth has become too thickly populated, India; A1019.4. Flood puts out world-fire (cf. A1030), S. Am. Indian (Tupinamba, Tucuna, Nimuendajá, Cubeo); **A1020**. Escape from deluge; **A1021**. Deluge: escape in boat (ark), Irish, Icelandic, Spanish, Greek, Hebrew: Genesis, ch. 6, 7, 8; Jewish, Babylonian, Hindu/India/Buddhist myth, Chinese, Siberian, Pelew Is. (Micronesia), Maori; Eskimo, American Indian (Carrier, Chipewyan, Coos, Kathlamet, Nootka, Chimariko, Salishan, Crow, Cochiti, White Mountain Apache, Ojibwa,

Choctaw, Shawnee, Natchez, Aztec, Arawak, Carib, Mbaya, Mura, Nimuendajú, Taulipang, Camara ["selections only"]; cf. Z356. Unique survivor); A1021.0.2. Escape from deluge in wooden cask (drum), Chinese, S.A. Indian (Guaporé); A1021.0.3. Deluge: escape in gourd, India; A1021.0.4. Deluge: escape on floating tree, Korean; A1021.0.5. Deluge: escape in hollow tree trunk, American Indian (Seneca, Mexican); A1021.0.6. Deluge: escape on floating building, American Indian (Tlingit, Cahita); A1021.1. Pairs of animals in ark. Seed of all beings put into ark to escape destruction—see references to "Sintflutsage" in A1010, Irish, Hebrew: Genesis 6: 19, Babylonian, Hindu; Aztec; A1021.2. Bird scouts sent out from ark, Irish, Hebrew, Babylonian; **A1022**. Escape from deluge on mountain, Greek, Hebrew, Hindu/India, Philippines, Borneo, West Caroline Is.; Polynesian, Cook Group, Hawaii; N. Am. Indian (Bella-Bella, Tahltan, Luiseño, Shasta, Blackfoot, Chiricahua Apache, Zuñi); S. Am. Indian (Araucanian, Inca, Yunca, [Peru], Caingang, Amazon ["only a selection of references for North and South America."]). Australian; **A1023**. Escape from deluge on tree, India; American Indian (Paiute, Plains Cree, Fox, Catawba, Ackawoi, Caingang, Guayaki, Maina; cf. R311. Tree refuge); **A1024**. Escape from deluge in cave, Andaman Is.; American Indian (Cheyenne, Arawak, Antis, Yuracare); **A1025**. Escape from deluge on island, Society Is.; **A1026**. Escape from deluge on foot, Chinese; **A1027**. Rescue from deluge by fish, Hindu (cf. B551. Fish carries man across water); **A1028**. Bringing deluge to end; A1028.1. Trickster sticks spear in ground and leads water to sea, ending deluge, S. Am. Indian (Chaco); A1028.2. Birds fill sea with dirt and overcome flood, S. Am. Indian (Caingang); **A1029**. Miscellaneous; A1029.3. Escape from deluge in pot or jar, S. Am. Indian (Chiriguano, Guarayu); A1029.4. Flood: refuge in huge gourds with seven rooms in each, India; A1029.5. Escape from deluge in box or basket, American Indian (Thompson River, Apache, Guarayu, Cubeo, Chaco); A1029.6. Survivors of flood establish homes, S. Am. Indian (Chiriguano). For other world catastrophes, see below: Fire, winter, etc.; **A1030**. World-fire. A conflagration destroys the earth. Sometimes (as with the flood legends) the tradition is somewhat local and does not refer to an actual destruction of the whole earth; sometimes the fire marks the end of the world, Iceland, Greek, Lithuanian, Jewish, Babylonian, Siberian, Hindu/Indian, Chinese; Maori; N. Am. Indian, S. Am. Indian (Yuracare, W. Brazil, Araucanian, Chaco, Tupinamba, Apapocuva-Guarani, Tembé, Shipaya, Carajá, Mura, Cashinawa, Witoto, Arawak, Yuracare, Mataco, Toba, Tucuna, Nimuendajú, Bacairi); **A1031**. Causes of world-fire (cf. C984.6. General conflagration from violation of tabu); A1031.2. World-fire after theft of fire, India; A1031.3. Evil demons set world on fire, S. Am. Indian (Yuracare, Tupinamba, Arawak); A1031.4. Fall of sun causes world-fire, S. Am. Indian (Toba, Mataco, Lengua, Mocovi); A1031.4.1. All countries burned while the wife of sun god pours fire from a small bowl, India; 1031.5. World-fire because of man's arrogance, African (Fang); A1031.6. Miscellaneous reasons for world-fire, S. Am. Indian (Witoto, Apapocuva-Guarani, Toba, Inca); A1035. Quenching the world-fire; **A1035.1**. Rain invoked to destroy world-fire, Maori, Melanesian; A1035.2. Creator puts out world-fire with his staff, S. A. Indian (Inca; cf. **A1036**. Earth recreated after world-fire, S. Am. Indian [Munderucú]); **A1038**. Men hide from world-fire and renew race (cf. A1006.1); cf. 1045 Swiss: Wallis; India; S. Am. Indian (Toba, Arawak, Mura, Yuracare, Tupinamba, Chiriguano), African (Fang); A1039. Miscellaneous; A1039.1. Vulture sent out as scout to see whether earth has cooled from world-fire (cf. A1021.2); **A1040**. Continuous winter destroys the race. Spoken of as "Fimbulwinter." It ushers in the end of the world, Iceland, Persian; S. Am. Indian (Toba, Pilagá, Tierra del Fuego, Chaco); **A1045**. One pair escapes continuous winter and renews race (cf. A1006.1, A1038); **A1046**. Continuous world-eclipse, India; S. Am. Indian (Toba, Mocovi, Mataco, Choroti, Tupinamba, Guarani); (Various motifs): A1046.1. World-eclipse ended by bat making sun smile, India; **A1050**. Heavens break up at end of world; **A1051**. Behavior of stars at end of world; A1051.1. Stars fall down at end of world, Irish; A1051.2. End of world when stars in one constellation overtake those in another, Siberian; **A1052**. Behavior of sun at end of world; A1052.1. Sun devoured by monster at end of world; A1052.2. Sun shining at night as sign of Doomsday, Jewish (M307.1); A1052.3. End of world when four (seven) suns appear in sky, Buddhist; **A1053**. Behavior of moon at end of world; A1053.1. Moon shining by day as sign of Doomsday (cf. A1002), Jewish; A1057. Seven days silence in whole universe at the end of the world, Jewish (M307.10); **A1058**. End of world when culture hero removes one of the world-props, S. Am. Indian (Guaraní); **A1060**. Earth-disturbances at end of world, Irish, Jewish; A1002. Doomsday; **A1061**. Earth sinks into sea at end of world; A1061.1. Earthquakes at the end of the world, Jewish (M307.12); S. Am. Indian (Chiriguano); **A1062**. Mountains fall together at end of world; **A1063**. Water-disturbances at end of world; A1063.1. Sea makes extraordinary noise and throws out fishes at end of world, Jewish (M307.6); A1063.2. Sea water mixes with fresh water at end of the world, Jewish (M307.8); **A1065**. Continuous drought at end of world, Buddhist; S. Am. Indian (Chiriguano); **A1066**. Sun will lock moon in deep ditch in earth's bottom and will eat up stars at end of world, Africa (Fang); **A1067**. Extraordinary wind at end of the world, Jewish (M307.15); **A1068**. Sun thrown on fire: period of darkness, rain, Calif. Indian; **A1069**. Flow of molten metal at end of world, Persian.

418. In this short review of motifs, the actual texts cannot be presented. For a large selection, see http://www.talkorigins.org/faqs/flood-myths.html. For a review of the restricted materials available to Frazer (1963) and Hastings (1922–28 [and an update until 1951]), see Dundes 1988: 113–16. Van Binsbergen (2006a: 18, 2006b) regards the spread of the motif in Africa as occasioned by diffusion from Austronesian Madagascar into East Africa. This should even have reached West Africa by maritime means. However, his map of African occurrences overlaps only partially with that of Baumann (1936: 307 sqq.); see further below. For worldwide flood myths, see Witzel 2010.

419. Now confirmed by genetics; see Hudjashov et al. 2007.

420. On linguistic means to separate southeastern Australia from the rest, see Wurm 1979: 578 sqq.

421. For southern Australia (Nullarbor Plain), see also Smith 1996: 35, 151 sqq. The flood is sent by the "Father of All Spirits" after the animals changed to their present form. Some survive in a big cave made for this purpose by the Sun deity. Or the frilled lizard family, who are in charge of lightning, rain, and wind, send the flood to destroy their enemies, the platypus family, "who have become too numerous" (echoing Mesopotamian and later myths; cf. Allen 2000). Some of the totem animals survive on a mountaintop (Smith 1996: 154 sq.).

422. Hudjashov et al. 2007.

423. The same is also said of the southeastern Australian supreme deity, Bundjel; see Dundes 1988: 130.

424. Cf. also Kamma 1978; Thompson 1993: Motif A1010. Melanesian. For some additional Melanesian myths, see Hans Kelsen, in Dundes 1988: 130 sq.

425. Gaster 1958: 103–4.

426. Endicott et al. 2003; Thangaraj 2003.

427. Gaster 1958: 104–5. Another version (Beckwith 1987: 319) has a great storm killing many people and turning them into fishes and birds; the water rose above the trees; Minni Cara and Minni Kota took the fire in a cooking pot to a cave on top of a hill where it was kept until the flood receded. Cf. the Nuristan evidence in Allen 2000.

428. Cf. van Binsbergen 2006a: 18, 2006b. He explains all African occurrences by north–south diffusion (see §3.3.5 out of the Sahel and East Africa). However, at least some of the occurrences in Frobenius's/van Binsbergen's (2006a: 24). Atlantic/southwestern "African core area" would point to an older, Gondwana layer in Africa.

429. The flood myth has been discussed at length by Baumann (1936: 307 sqq.); he criticizes the then (as today) prevailing opinion that the flood myth is hardly found in Africa (Doniger 1991). Instead, it is basically spread, in pockets, all over sub-Saharan Africa, with some variants. (For an English summary of Baumann's observations, see Kelsen, in Dundes 1988: 136–37.) See also Thompson 1993: Motif A1010. African; cf. §5, n. 417.

430. Cf. the appearance of the rainbow in biblical myth, after the flood.

431. W. van Binsbergen, personal communication, the Second International Conference on Comparative Mythology, Ravenstein, the Netherlands, August 2008; see http://www.compmyth.org/.

■ Chapter 6

1. For the theoretical observation on reconstructing a common *Urkultur* of all humans, see Bornemann 1967: 83. The question had been put as early as 1928 by Montandon.

2. Sanskrit *pra-math* means "to steal" and thus provides an Indo-European etymology for *Prometheus*, different from the fanciful Greek ones.

3. Vādhūla Sūtra, ed. and trans. Caland (1990: 116–19). For a discussion of other Indo-European accounts, see Lincoln 1986: 63 sqq.

4. Jensen 1978.

5. This echoes the tales about the Waq-Waq Islands in the *Arabian Nights*. Later, the 15th-century writer Ibn al-Wardi reports that on Waq-Waq, there are "trees that bear women as fruit: shapely, with bodies, eyes,... and when they feel the wind and sun, they shout 'Waq Waq.'" This looks like the typical trader's tale, picked up near the spice islands, the Moluccas, but it is ultimately based on local myth; however, also found in S.E. Asia.

6. At conferences held at Leiden in 2003 and Harvard in 2004 ("Long-Range Mythical Continuities across Asia and Africa: Linguistic and Iconographic Evidence Concerning Leopard Symbolism"), Kyoto in 2005 ("A Preliminary Attempt to Situate Sub-Saharan African 'Creation' Myths within a Long-Range Intercontinental Comparative Perspective"), Beijing in 2006 ("Further Steps towards an Aggregative Diachronic Approach to World Mythology Starting from the African Continent"), and Edinburgh in 2007. I will quote from his Edinburgh handout, which to some extent overlaps with his chapter in Osada 2006, of which it is an update. Comparative mythology was explored at the fourth and subsequent Harvard Round Tables, where I gave a preview of this book in 2005–6. Y. Berezkin presented his views at the Seventh Round Table at Kyoto, at the Eighth at Beijing, and at the Tenth at Edinburgh (2007).

7. See van Binsbergen 2006a, 2006b, and discussion above.

8. Van Binsbergen 2006a: 22, 2006b. As I will also try to do in §7.2, he perceives a link between the development of myth and the Neolithic mode of production; however, I will establish a link backward to Paleolithic forms of thinking. At any rate, a simple Durkheimian/Marxist correlation between society/production and myth is excluded, as the Paleolithic roots of later (and modern) thinking can be discerned clearly.

9. Berezkin (2002, 2007) shows the origins of some South American myths that have retained, unlike North American ones, some vestiges of their African origins; cf. also his (2002, 2005a, 2005b, 2005d) essays on Siberian–American links and a forthcoming one on Eurasian and Pacific links.

10. See http://www.ruthenia.ru/folklore/berezkin.

11. For the procedures, strategies, and patterns involved in "rewriting"—better: the constant reformulation of local mythology, often based on inner tensions and contradictions—see below, §8.

12. Schmidt 1912–55. For the High God of the Austronesian Tsou (highland Taiwan), see Tung 1964: 363 etc., s.v. *Hícu ta pépe*, "god of heaven."

13. Africa: Baumann 1936: 327 sqq.; or, after the flood, southeastern Australia.

14. Apparently even in Tasmania; see §5.3.2.1.

15. Importantly, this seems to be the case also in Tasmania, which has been isolated from Australia for some 8,000 years (see above, §5.3.2.1). Only in some cases, he directly creates humans himself, though a persistent Pan-Gaean myth speaks of human origins from trees or by emerging through the core of trees, from underground, from the Netherworld.

16. Schmidt 1912–55.

17. A similar dualistic concept seems to have been retained(?) or newly developed by the Austronesian Dayak of Borneo: the opposition between two moieties, upperworld and underworld, Hornbill and Watersnake. See Schärer 1963: 27, 153; cf. §2, n. 115; §3, n. 201.

18. In Austronesian Taiwan, this frequently is the first human instead. Note also the Dayak (Borneo) motif of two primeval mountains that clash and produce beings; see Schärer 1946, 1963; that of a large primordial rock (Hittite Ullikummi) is not far off.

19. For the Dogon, is its made by the god Amma; see Sproul 1991: 50 sq.

20. The myths about several ancestors of Chinese dynasties include people born from rocks; see Granet 1989: 81 sq.

21. Sometimes the humans were born or emerge from primordial spirits, as in isolated Tasmanian myth (§3.5.2.1) and in parts of Africa.

22. As for the tree motif: so far, I have not yet seen a Paleo-/Mesolithic picture of the world tree or paintings indicating the "sacred" number 9 (see Eliade 1954b: 259 sqq.); see below on the "Siberia/Altaic" origin of the world tree, which was transmitted to the Americas as well. The idea is old and central to Laurasian cosmography (not treated to any extent in this book; see Kuiper 1983; Lyle 1990; Witzel 1984b). However, it does not seem to be central in Gondwana myths, though there are some Australian data, such as the world tree as world axis with the central Australian Aranda tribe (illustration in Lawlor 1991: 75, 227). Connected is the use of elongated (male/female) double *tjuringas* in Australian initiation rituals (Campbell 1988: I.2: 137). If this particular idea of male/female union is old, we can compare the Stone Age sculpture of Laussel in France; see Campbell 1988: I.1: 67. Similarly, in West Africa (Dogon Land); see Frobenius 1998: 156.

23. The topic of the belief in (automatic) rebirth cannot be treated at length here. Suffice it to say that it is much more widespread than commonly thought: it is widespread in the Indo-European area (Witzel 1984a, 1987a, 1987c; cf. http://www.people.fas.harvard.edu/~witzel/vedica.pdf) but also in Australia, the Americas, West Africa (Obeyesekere 1980, 2002), etc. The Indian version, just like the Greek one, involves personal responsibility and morality, while the older forms represent an automatic return, often to one's own family after three–four generations; hence, repeated names within a family after three–four generations, best seen in the names of the Achaemenid kings of ancient Persia.

24. Witzel 2005b.

25. See §2, n. 85; §5, n. 360: trees (or grass) could talk in the beginning.

26. The linking idea may have been that of a wooden splinter or branch. Note also the Hainuwele myth (see immediately below) and the Waq-Waq Islands myths (*Arabian Nights*) of humans growing on trees.

27. Jensen 1978.

28. Berezkin 2007.

29. See discussion of this and similar myths in Africa by Baumann (1936: 265 sqq.).

30. Frobenius 1924: 75–76; my translation. See Campbell 1988: I.1: 14; cf. Baumann 1936: 265 sqq. Though Frobenius asserted that the Bassari had never been visited by missionaries, the question of nearby Soninke and Islamic influence must still be investigated; cf. §5, n. 368.

31. Schultze Jena 1944: 47; Tedlock 1985: 113 sq.

32. This topic was treated at some length at the Second International Conference of the International Association for Comparative Mythology, at Ravenstein, the Netherlands; see http://www.compmyth.org/action.php?conf02., published by van Binsbergen and Venbrux (2010).

33. Vala myth; see Witzel 2005b; §3.5.1.

34. See map in Campbell 1988: I.1: 40.

35. Campbell 1988: I.1: 122.

36. Eliade 1954: 356; Witzel 2011.

37. Walter and Fridman 2004.

38. Mortensen 2003.

39. See http://www.talkorigins.org/faqs/flood-myths.html.

40. Leenhardt 1979: 29.

41. Berezkin 1996–97 etc.; for data, see http://www.ruthenia.ru/folklore/berezkin.

42. Graves 1955.

43. Schärer 1963.

44. The death ritual (*tantalok matei*) alone has some 386 pages in Ngaju Dayak with German translation, thus some 193 pages in Dayak (Schärer 1963: 443–829).

45. Barth 1987.

46. Beckwith 1987: 301 sqq.

47. In addition, we have the large post-Ṛgvedic "theological" and ritualistic literature of the other Veda Saṃhitās, Brāhmaṇas, Āraṇyakas, Upaniṣads, and Sūtras that constitute multiples of the size of the Ṛgveda and were orally transmitted (and still are!) by various specialists just the same. An estimate of the combined size of the Vedas would not be very far off from that of combined Dayak myths and ritual texts.

48. Witzel 2005b.

49. However, see §5, n. 64, on how northern Australian has been influenced by Papua traits; and cf. Campbell 1988: I.2: 142.

50. In contrast, van Binsbergen's (2006a: 22, 2006b) seven major "contexts of intensified transformation and innovation" would include the original (African) mythical package with his (original) nos. 4. The lightening bird, 9. The moon, 10. The earth as primary, 12. From under the tree, 13. The cosmic/rainbow snake, and 15. The spider (and female arts). Obviously, there is some, but sparingly little, overlap with the motifs given above. However, van Binsbergen is more positive about our general congruences: "Witzel's Gondwana complex corresponds with the NCs emerging in Africa in the Middle Palaeolithic ... whereas his Laurasian traits contain a selection of NCs developed in the subsequent course of the history of world mythology" (2006a: 27, 2006b). This is indeed what I propose in this book: Laurasian mythology is an early offshoot of Gondwana mythology.

51. For the (late) development of speech, see Lieberman 2006, 2007; cf., however, Schrenk and Müller 2005: 81 sq. See §4, nn. 51, 171, 250, 337; §6, n. 52; §7, n. 17 and, in detail, n. 19. As discussed above (§4.4), we have only sparse Neanderthal graves with some grave goods, such as tools, and the use of ochre color.

52. Different from the archaeologically and speculative theory–based dates of Wunn (2005), a combination of Bellah's evolutionary scheme and her use of archaeological data recovered so far; see above, §2.6, §4.4.1; and below, §7.1.2. Also, the dating of human speech has to be sorted out. Lieberman (2006, 2007) puts the faculty of speech of anatomically modern humans only at c. 50,000 BCE, while the exodus from Africa is usually dated about 15,000 or more years earlier. It is not likely that humans developed full speech (and hence, myth) only *after* the exodus and, given the various types of mythology (as well as language families) discussed in this section, *independently* of each other. Lieberman's dates are too low.

▪ Chapter 7

1. Note the contrary opinion of Wunn (2005): myth and religion developed only in the Upper Mesolithic (see §1.6).

2. For supposed earlier forms of religious awakening in early hominids (*Australopithecus* etc.), see Wunn 2005: 41 sqq. Wunn (2005: 49) concludes that Eliade's idea of a "mystical solidarity" between hunter and hunted animal is not sustained by archaeology for these early periods: early stone tools were not used for hunting but for scavenging. The same applies to the use of fire attested for some 1.5 million years among *Homo erectus*; it remained sporadic for a long time (2005: 50 sq.). She also doubts "real" religious thought for *Homo erectus* (2005: 61), who—though having better tools—mostly relied on animals killed by carnivores or otherwise deceased (2005: 60 sq.). As for Neanderthals (2005: 62 sqq.), whose early forms are attested around 400,000 BCE (see §4.4) but whose development speeded up around 200,000 BCE (Levallois culture with locally adjusted tools), some scholars think that they still were not planning ahead for hunting and food preservation; others deny this (based on finds at Kebera in Israel, 65,000–40,000 BCE [2005: 68]). However, according to Lewis Binford, men and women already divided their work: women stayed near the camp, and men hunted farther away (2005: 67). However, even late Neanderthals and their contemporary *Homo sapiens sapiens* neighbors did not differ in tools and settlement pattern (2005: 68). As for religion, Wunn (2005: 71) concludes, following her correlation between observed cultural remnants and thought: accumulation in cultural knowledge, tools, techniques, etc. reached a preliminary culmination with the Neolithic. Religion's first vague beginnings can be observed in the Middle Paleolithic but must have been much more simple. Reconstruction based on uncritical comparisons with modern surviving hunter cultures are impossible. They are divided less by intellectual abilities than by several tens of thousands of years of cultural evolution (see above, §2.6, §4.4.1).

3. Gusinde 1977; Wilbert 1975, 1977.

4. Bachofen 1861. This applies to his epigones. Bachofen (1861) himself had a much more limited scheme in mind, a reconstruction of an early, pre-Greek mother goddess ("Aphrodite"), a creating and destroying force; see the discussion in Wunn 2005: 197 sq. It cannot be denied, however, that during the Stone Age, just as in various parts of Asia today, female shamans existed next to male ones; see the evidence in Grosman et al. 2008; Tedlock 2005.

5. Junker 2006.

6. Cf. §1, n. 160.

7. Bellah 1973; Wunn 2005; see above, §1.6.

8. See Farmer et al. 2002: once a dominant myth (or frame of mind) has been established, it tends to perpetuate.

9. Farmer et al. 2002.

10. Durkheim 1925; see §1.2.

11. Denied by Wunn (2005: 32 sq.).

12. Schrenk and Müller 2005.

13. Lieberman 2006; Schrenk and Müller 2005; Wunn 2005: 106. For a new theory of major, rather recent changes of the human brain, see Hawks et al. 2007.

14. Cf. Wunn 2005: 71 sq.

15. However, see Wunn 2005: 173, with arguments against this use. Wunn stresses the use of ochre in coloring clothes or regular painting of the body; some ochre coloring is even due to regular decomposition processes: "The ideas of Maringer and Eliade about a symbolic meaning of ochre thus are, at least, problematic" (2005: 173).

16. See below, §7.1.2; Wunn (2005: 84, 132) denies it.

17. See, for example, Bickerton 1990; Lieberman 2006.

18. Noonan et al. (2006) give a date for the split between the two branches at 370 kya; Schmitz et al. (2002), Serre et al. (2004), and Krings et al. (1997) do not provide any data speaking for interbreeding (now see, however, Introduction p. xviii).

19. Cf. earlier, §4.3, 4.4.1.

20. Lieberman 2006. A related scenario with similar dates (c. 40 kya) is presented by Hawks et al. (2007) with regard to supposed recent acceleration of human evolution; however, there is no initial consensus (Wade 2007b). Lieberman's approach is based, apart from neurological data, on a study of the superlaryngeal tract, which would not have allowed early humans and Neanderthals to produce basic vowels (such as *a, i, u*) but just the rather undifferentiated schwa vowel (ə), as heard in the pronunciation of *a* in *about*, the *e* in *bulletin*, and the *i* in *tangible*. This overlooks the fact that there are languages that use other vowels, such as *r* in Croatian *Krk* and Sanskrit *vṛka* and *l* as in Engl. *bottle* or Czech (and that Kabardian in the Caucasus has been alleged to have no vowels, probably wrongly). Thus, one can produce words of the type *txk* (with the vowel *x*), Croation *krk*, and Czech *vlk*, which is perfectly enough for regular communication. If indeed early humans down to Shkul V (Middle Paleolithic) could not produce vowels other than ə, they would merely have spoken an "earlier" form of human language (with words such as *bək, gbə, tkx*, etc.), which could have transmitted their thoughts and mythology just as well as more "modern" languages. It should also be noted that we still occasionally communicate with clicks (disgust, urging on a horse, etc.) that are part of regular speech only in San, Hadza, and Sandawe (and the San-influenced languages of South Africa). Early human language thus may have looked quite different from the one Lieberman assumes for periods before 50 kya, for which he thinks it probable "that fully human syntactic and cognitive abilities were also present" (2006: 59). This would also have been necessary for the development of both the Gondwana and Laurasian mythologies several tens of thousands of years earlier. For a recent discussion of the FOXP2 gene, see §4, n. 60; for the emergence of anatomically modern human behavior, see James 2007: 204 sqq.

21. See §4, nn. 51, 171, 250; §7, n. 20.

22. As mentioned (§2, n. 310; §4, nn. 97, 126, 286), according to Brooks, the "oldest possible age for 'out-of-Africa' is c. 77 kyr" (2006).

23. Bar-Yosef 1998; cf. O. Bar-Yosef, in Shaw 2001.

24. Junker 2006; cf. Schrenk and Müller 2005: 115.

25. Helen Briggs, BBC, May 31, 2006, http://news.bbc.co.uk/1/hi/sci/tech/5021214.stm.

26. Yamada 2007.

27. Cf. Beckwith 1987: 324 sq., and as ancestors, 42, 321, 337, etc.; Westervelt 1987: 205 sqq.

28. Campbell 1988: I.1: 46, 66 sqq.; cf. Arvidsson 2006: 166 (about J. Harrison); Gimbutas 1991; but see the critique in Wunn 2005: 33, 140 sqq., and also on Bachofen, 197 sq. See Lorblanchet 2000: 26, of a human with a female lion head, c. 35,000–30,000 BCE, found in southwestern Germany; Wunn 2005: 136 sqq. See §4, nn. 433, 481.

29. Bellah 1973; Wunn 2005.

30. Wunn 2005: 132 sq.

31. Wunn 2005: 132; my translation. She complains that old ideas of prehistoric religion prevail; see above, §4, n. 413.

32. Wunn 2005: 115.

33. Campbell 1988: I.1: 67.

34. Cf. Campbell 1988: I.1: 62, 67, cf. 91 on Bushmen culture, and I.2: xxi; cf. also Gimbutas 1991: 316 sqq. Note the *Spiegel* report (April 4, 2005) on such a sculpture that is about 7,200 years old (see §4, n. 427).

35. Eliade 1992: 87 (Society Islands).

36. Cf. Gimbutas 1991: 213 sqq., with illustrations. Note that the naked woman with pendulous breasts who holds a horn (reminiscent of the moon) in her right hand would point, with Campbell (1988: I.1: 67), to the lunar and menstrual cycle. Interestingly, the horn has some 13 incisions, close to the half-moon period; cf. above, §4.4.1.

37. Frobenius 1998: 153–57.

38. Campbell 1988.

39. Campbell 1988: I.1: 46 sq., 66.

40. Campbell 1988: I.1: 77; Lorblanchet 2000: 21,71.

41. An early sculpture at Montespan (Campbell 1988: I.1: 62); later, c. 14 kya, at Tuc d'Audoubert (Pyrenees; Campbell 1988: I.1: 77 n. 134): two copulating clay bison; cf. §4, n. 429.

42. Cf. the detailed interpretation as shamanistic by Campbell (1988: I.1: 64 sq.); see §7.2; http://www.lascaux.culture.fr/#/fr/02_07.xml.

43. Cf. Wunn 2005: 134. One may speculate, with Campbell and others, that materials like wood had been used before that have left no traces in tropical climates, such as in parts of Africa.

44. Lorblanchet 2000: 26.

45. For example, Gimbutas 1991: 316 sq.; cf. also Conkey and Tringham 1995: 212–13; Leonard and McClure 2004: 109 sqq. See Wunn 2005: 140 sqq.

46. Wunn (2005: 145) again denies that attributes of a religious specialist have been found or that shamanic practices were part of religious actions. She admits, however, that the existence of shamans cannot be excluded; see the summary in Wunn 2005: 132.

47. For depictions of such shaman-like figures, see Campbell 1988: I.1: 78, I.2: 156; Gimbutas 1991: 176.

48. Campbell 1988: I.1: 76, nos. 131–32. See also the discussion by Wunn (2005: 132, 145). In any case, it certainly is not a male deity, as Gimbutas (1991: 175) maintains.

49. See Lorblanchet 2000: 83. As discussed in detail in §4.4, §5.3 sqq., and §7.2. Leonard and McClure (2004: 185 sqq.) and Langen (1963: 129) show recent photos that differ markedly from the sketch made by Abbé Breuil (see §4, nn. 377, 382; §7, n. 185). It is unclear whether this difference is due to deterioration of the painting or to the imagination of Breuil; note also the detailed criticism and experiments to replicate Breuil's drawings by several students, described by Layton (1991: 26–30).

50. Campbell 1988: I.1: 74–75, no. 131, 78, no. 135.

51. Wunn 2005. For depictions of such shaman-like figures, see Campbell 1988: I.1; Gimbutas 1991: 176; http://www.lascaux.culture.fr/#/fr/02_07.xml.

52. Campbell 1988: I.1: 65, no. 105.

53. Breuil 1952: 144–46; Maringer 1956: 130.

54. Kirchner et al. 1988: 310. Shamanism in cave art has also been asserted by Dickson (1990: 215); see Mithen 1996: 164–67.

55. Wunn 2005: 117, 121.

56. See Campbell 1988: I.1: 2, I.2: 140; cf. discussion in §7.1.2.

57. Wunn 2005.

58. Lewis-Williams, Dickson, Eliade, Campbell; see Wunn 2005: 117 sq.

59. One might think, as an example, of an interpretation of the Australian *tjuringa* (Campbell 1988: I.2: 145). For many depictions of Stone Age art, see http://www.originsnet. org/home.html.

60. The latter is also admitted by Herbig (1988), as far as *general* conclusions are concerned.

61. Cf. earlier, §4.4.1 on cave art; and Witzel 2006a.

62. Eliade 1946, 1954b, 1974. See the encyclopedic volumes by Namba Walter and Neumann Fridman (2004), including the entry by M. Winkelman, "Cross-Cultural Perspectives on Shamans" (2004: 61–70). He finds that healing practitioners of the hunter-gatherers etc. of Eurasia, the Americas, and Africa "are more similar to one another than to other magico-religious practitioners in the same region" as they are dependent on a nomadic lifestyle and on small local communities. This phenomenon is not spread by diffusion, and shamans had an independent origin in each society (Winkelman 2004: 63). Otherwise, Winkelman follows the common pattern of an altered state of consciousness, initiation, healing, etc.; it includes a scheme of transformation from hunter-gatherer shamans to sorcerers/ witches, mediums, and priests in agricultural and state societies (Winkelman 1990, 2004: 67–68); cf. the discussion below, §7.2. For Eurasian shamanism (and Greek myths), see Burkert 1982: 88 sqq.; Ōbayashi 1991b; Oppitz 1991 (with a detailed study of Kham Magar shamanism of Nepal); Vitebsky 1995. See Maskarinec 1995 for the neighboring area of central Nepal. A history of the study of shamanism is given by Francfort et al. (2004: 142–47). Cf. §7, nn. 135, 138.

63. See Walter and Fridman 2004: XIX; Witzel 2011.

64. See, for example, the typical traits of Yamana (Tierra del Fuego) initiation of shamans (Eliade 1954b: 63, following Gusinde [see 1977]).

65. Eliade 1954b: 60 sq. He (1954b: 357) excludes a discussion of African shamanism, awaiting better materials.

66. Eliade 1954b: 61. For the myths about the first shaman from the Kham Magar, see Oppitz 1991: 174 sqq., and for his successors, 392 sqq.

67. Eliade 1954b: 62. In light of recent work by Y. Berezkin, South America may preserve some archaic data that otherwise are found only in New Guinea and Australia, while North America has subsequently been heavily influenced from Siberia. If so, the trait of inserted crystals would have been brought in around 20 kya.

68. Eliade 1954b: 60.

69. Campbell 1988: I.2: 170 sq.

70. The typical shamanistic frame drum is attested in Sumerian finds of c. 2000 BCE, with the Hittites, and among the Egyptians (c. 950–730 BCE); see Walter and Fridman 2004: 101 sqq.; and note Witzel 2003, 2004b, on the Central Asian and Indus versions: these are depicted on seals of the Bactria-Margiana Archaeological Complex about 2000 BCE. A similar scene is found in the contemporary Indus civilization. A neighboring modern specimen is found with the Kalasha in northwestern Pakistan (Witzel 2004a). Drumming is

not strictly necessary to produce the shamanistic altered state of mind—note the San's drumless music (some elements of such music go back to our primate ancestors); cf. Walter and Fridman 2004: 100, 189.

71. This may be connected with the climbing of the (world) tree during the initiation of a shaman; for illustrations, see Campbell 1988: I.2: 159 (Mapuche in central Chile); Oppitz 1991: 375; Vitebsky 1995: 62. The concept is retained in the solemn Vedic *vājapeya* ritual, where husband (and wife) have to climb a tall pole and a priest sits on a wheel (symbol of the turning of the sun and nighttime sky), while they are pelted with salt bags; cf. Witzel 1984b.

72. See Eliade 1954b: 356; Witzel 2011.

73. Eliade 1954b: 438 sqq.; cf. Campbell 1988: I.2: 165.

74. Walter and Fridman 2004: XVII sqq., esp. XXI sq.

75. Note the neurobiological critique by Winkelman (2002); and in Walter and Fridman 2004: 187 sqq.

76. Basilov 1999: 39. Cf. Walter and Fridman 2004: XXI. The classical definition by Shirokogoroff for Tungus shamans is similar, if more concise:

(1) A shaman is a master of spirits, who has

(2) mastered a group of spirits;

(3) a shaman commands a recognized array of techniques and paraphernalia that have been transmitted from elders;

(4) s/he possesses a theoretical justification for the shamanistic process;

(5) the shaman occupies a special position. (1999: 268 sq.)

(Note Maskarinec 2004: 767; F. Smith, in Walter and Fridman 2004: 780.)

77. Linguistically attested at least since Nostratic times (see Illich-Svitych 1971–; see Mark Kaiser's [1989] summary in English), which means since well before 10,000 BCE; some put Nostratic at a much earlier date. This is indeed required by the deep time depth of one of its members, Afrasian; see Ehret 1995.

78. On the initiation of shamans, see Walter and Fridman 2004: 153 sqq.

79. This is to be distinguished from (involuntary) spirit possession, which is more typical for Africa and parts of India; see discussion in Walter and Fridman 2004: 228–34; Witzel 2011; cf. Winkelman 2004: 61 sqq. and passim on various African populations.

80. Basilov 1999: 39.

81. See Walter and Fridman 2004: XIX.

82. Eliade 1954b; Hamayon 1990. Recent updates are found in Campbell 1988: I.1: 73 sqq., 90 sqq., I.2: 156 sqq.; in Mastromattei and Rigopulos 1999; and notably in the encyclopedic collection edited by Walter and Fridman (2004). Early Chinese forms have been studied by K. C. Chang (1983), and early Indian ones in the Ṛgveda, by Oguibénine (1968), Meisig (1995), Filippi (1999), Torcinovich (1999), and G. Thompson (2003).

83. For a brief summary, see Connah 2004: 30 sq.

84. Campbell 1988: I.2: 171.

85. Campbell 1988: I.2: 167.

86. See characterization by Edith Turner, in Walter and Fridman 2004: 886–89. For possession, see Walter and Fridman 2004: 951 sqq.; similarly, including sacrifice, perhaps the West African Igbo (2004: 925 sqq.).

87. Eliade 1954b: 66; Maskarinec 1998, 2004, 2008.

88. See Walter and Fridman 2004: 16–25, 219–23. Note the recently discovered Chauvet Cave in the Ardèche region of France, of c. 33,000 BCE (which already has paintings with

perspective; see Arnold et al. 2003; Geneste 2005; Wunn 2005: 124); see Lewis-Williams 2002.

89. Note especially the pointing sticks or horns attached to heads as in Lascaux, with the Australians and Bushmen: Campbell 1988: I.1: 66, nos. 106–7, 93, no. 170; cf. above, §4.5 (*corna* gestures).

90. Maskarinec 1998, 2004; Walter and Fridman 2004: 747–50, 767–72, 775–78.

91. See Campbell 1988: I.2; or, since the 1930s, disappearance of priests and recently of shamans, with the pagan Kalash of northwestern Pakistan.

92. Cf., however, Barnes 1974; Davis 1984; Eugenio 1993; Koubi 1982; Yang 2006, 2007; and similar works.

93. Campbell 1988: I.1: 55; Paulson 1965. Wunn (2005: 84, 132) denies its existence.

94. For a short discussion, see W. Burkert, in Narby and Huxley 2001: 223–26.

95. Fleming recalls what he was told by his friend Willard Park, who was then interviewing an old shaman (probably Paiute) with the help of an interpreter. Park asked him whether his tribe followed a particular custom. The shaman "spoke eloquently for half an hour in response to the question. So what did he say, asked Willard of the interpreter. He said 'yes,' was the answer. Very disappointed was my friend who did, however, learn that English might not be the vehicle for probing the complexity of shamanly thought" (2003, http://www.people.fas.harvard.edu/~witzel/MTLR-34b.htm); note also the "retelling" of Andaman myths by Radcliffe-Brown and H. Man (§5.3.4) and those of other civilizations.

96. Cf. Harvey 2002.

97. Campbell 1988: I.1: 94; Connah 2004: 30 sq.; Walter and Fridman 2004: 219–20, 981–94. See Narby and Huxley 2001: 131–34, with a pregnant description of !Kung shamanism and dancing by Lorna Marshall; virtually all men can act as healers.

98. Walter and Fridman 2004: 24.

99. Walter and Fridman 2004: 893.

100. Walter and Fridman 2004: 24.

101. Lewis-Williams 2002.

102. Brooks 2006; Connah 2004.

103. At the Apollo 11 Cave, Namibia, belonging to the Upper Paleolithic. This concerns "a painted plaquette of a feline with plantigrade rear feet, suggesting...continuity of belief throughout the Late Stone age" (Walter and Fridman 2004: 20; see Lewis-Williams 1984).

104. See Dempwolf 1916; Kagaya 1993; Tishkoff 2007.

105. F. Marlowe, 2002, http://www.fas.harvard.edu/~hbe-lab/acrobatfiles/why%20the%20hadza%20are%20still%20hunter-gatherers.pdf.

106. Campbell 1988: I.1: 118 sqq.; Radcliff-Brown 1933: 175 sqq.

107. The Andamanese also knew of an axis mundi (the *Dipterocarpus* tree), which raises the interesting possibility of lost shamanic practices (moving up the tree, as in later Siberian-style shamanism?) or, simply, lack of recording their practices and beliefs by Radcliffe-Brown (1933).

108. Radcliffe-Brown 1933: 186.

109. Abbott 1984.

110. Walter and Fridman 2004: 865–69, 874–79; cf. Trompf 1991: 127, 132, 136 n. 73, cf. 96 sq.

111. Eliade 1954b: 346. He attributes the lack of an "actual shamanistic tradition" to the prevalence of secret societies and their initiation rituals.

112. Eliade 1954b: 347, cf. 356 on shamanistic heat in general. Cf. §5, n. 126.

113. Eliade 1954b: 438.

114. Eliade 1954b: 356, 438.

115. The term *shaman* is not frequently used for them; instead "medicine man," "clever man," "man of high degree," etc. (locally, *karajji, wireenan/ walamira, wingirin, kuldukke, banmanm/barnmarn, mabarn, marrngitj, margidjbu, mekigar,* "one who sees," etc.). Some women also act as shamans. Some scholars do not regard the "clever men" as shamans at all, as some aspects of Siberian shamanism are missing. See Eliade 1954b: 135; L. Hume, in Walter and Fridman 2004: 860–65.

116. A similar concept is found with the Mayas: the vision serpent (and the double-headed serpent bat), as a path of communication between the two worlds (earth and the Otherworld; see Walter and Fridman 2004: 20). This is, however, a widespread Gondwana concept. One can jump on a rainbow snake and fly upward and reach heaven. In central Australia the snake is identified with the Milky Way. Note that Pygmies, too, have a concept of a rainbow serpent (Zuesse 1979: 45). Baumann (1936: 386) regards this motif as well as some others as having drifted in from their neighbors. Further, the rainbow snake is found with the Austro-Asiatic Munda people (see Ponette 1968: 13) and also in South America (see the map in Berezkin 2007; and note Thompson 1993: Motif A665.6. Serpent supports sky, S. Am. [Yuracare]). It is also found in Africa, the Andamans, Australia, etc. See Berezkin 2007; Campbell 1988: I.2: 141; Nikonov 1980. For Africa, see Baumann 1936: 77 (Kanioka), 116 (Uelle Pygmies), 197 (Kikuyu), 212 sq. (Ewe), 218 sq. (Hausa), 324.

117. Detailed discussion in Eliade 1954b: 54 sqq.; cf. quotes in Lawlor 1991: 374.

118. In the northern Kimberley area, the incipient shaman is swallowed by the Rainbow Snake or scum from the snake's pool is inserted (as snake egg) into his navel and grows inside him.

119. The mytheme of the many-colored rainbow snake is expressed in myth by the primordial snake in a multicolored ocean. The concept of the rainbow snake is also found with the Negrito Semang of Malaya and in some South American tribes; see Eliade 1954b: 62.

120. Campbell 1988: I.2: 172; Walter and Fridman 2004: 532–652.

121. Cf. Thor's ram (in the Gylfaginning) and in the ancient Indian text, Bṛhadāraṇyaka Upaniṣad, about the gods who best like to "eat humans."

122. Campbell 1988: I.2: 167.

123. Campbell 1988: I.2: 173.

124. Among the northern (Kham) Magar of Nepal this is not necessary, as both male and female shamans are found, frequently in alternating lineage, from male to female to male; see Oppitz 1991.

125. See Ōbayashi 1991b.

126. Campbell 1988: I.1: 65, 74, 76.

127. Walter and Fridman 2004: 893.

128. See examples in Indo-European, in Japan, and with the Taiwan Ami tribe; note that any hunters' language is archaic. See §2, n. 235; §7, nn. 235, 242; cf. also the Indian "truth sorcery" (*satyakriyā*).

129. Cf. Maskarinec 1998, 2004, for central Nepal.

130. Note the various designs used by various populations: medieval and Tibetan "memory palaces," Vedic Indians' mental designs to keep a fixed order of the 1,028 hymns of the oldest text, the Ṛgveda, and the Polynesian method of using the skeleton of a fish on whose bones certain data are "stored" (Witzel 1996). The Papuan and Andamanese (and southeastern Australian) ways of counting, or rather, tallying, also closely resemble each other; see Witzel 2002a; §4, n. 431.

131. See Burkert, in Narby and Huxley 2001: 223–26.

132. See discussion in Campbell 1988: I.1: 72 sqq.; Wunn 2005: 156 sqq., 159, also 150.

133. Burkert 1983; and Burkert, in Narby and Huxley 2001: 223–26. He stresses the connection with hunting; cf. also §4.4.3. Cf. Frobenius 1998: 280 for the San. Cf. §1, n. 134; §4, n. 444; §7, nn. 94, 138.

134. Who do not seem to have animal sacrifice; the case of "sacrifice" discussed by Stanner (1959; cf. §4, n. 452; §7, n. 142) merely involves the offering of men's own blood to the new initiates, in other words, *self-sacrifice*, the "oldest" form of sacrifice, before this was substituted by animal slaughter. Such self-induced bloodletting is also found with the Maya (to make the sun move); it was substituted by human sacrifice with the Aztec; cf. also §4, n. 452.

135. On the sacrifice and shamanism in Siberia, see Eliade 1954b: 193 sqq.

136. Rundle Clark 1959: 103.

137. Jacobsen 1976: 181.

138. On the violent Stone Age origins of sacrifice, see Burkert 1983; cf. Burkert 1987.

139. For the horse sacrifice, especially with the Altai Turks, see Eliade 1954b: 185–92; for the Indian version, see Witzel 1997a; for East Asia, see Mair 2007.

140. Vādhūla Sūtra; Caland 1990: 116–19.

141. Campbell 1988: I.1: 79; Frobenius 1998: 66.

142. See Campbell 1988: I.1: 79, ill. 138, 82, ill. 143; Frobenius 1998: 66.

143. Campbell 1988: I.1: 128 sq.; Frobenius 1998: 99 sqq., ill. 110 sqq.

144. Campbell 1988: I.2: 147 sqq. Wunn (2005: 84, 132) denies an ancient bear cult.

145. Van Binsbergen 2006a, 2006b.

146. It is not very prominent in Amerindian myth, except with late immigrants, the Na-Dene (Athapascan), where we find the myth of the dog husband; exceptionally, also with the Aztecs; see Thompson 1993: Motif A522.1.1. Dog as culture hero (Aztec); see above, §5.1.4, n. 30. Cf. §2, n. 102; http://users.hartwick.edu/anthonyd/ritual.html.

147. For the Near East, as in the biblical account of Genesis 2.32. Cf. also the Mosaic scapegoat; and Campbell 1988: I.1: 82, ill. 144. For the Old Egyptian and modern African (Sudan, Sahel, Berber) representation of the sun as ram, or a (Hottentot) connection, see Baumann 1936: 275. For South Asia, note goat sacrifice at Mehrgarh in southwestern Pakistan at c. 6500 BCE.

148. Campbell 1989: II.1: 58. Therefore, the relative absence of pigs in Laurasian mythology surprises, though pigs occur in some local mythologies.

149. See F. Brighenti (2003, http://www.svabhinava.org/friends/FrancescoBrighenti/index.php).

150. See further details on Amerindian and Indian buffalo myths at http://tech.groups.yahoo.com/group/IndiaArchaeology/message/4075.

151. Note, however, the use of tortoise shells and deer scapulas for divination in early China; see Puett 2002. Also, for the concept of turning ancestor spirits into "gods," see Puett 2002: 50 sqq.

152. As mentioned above (§3.2 sqq., 3.8; §5.1.4), the myth of the hidden sun does not yet employ horses in its Southeast and East Asia forms (and, obviously, not in the Americas). Similarly, when the asterism of the Great Bear(s) (Ursa Maior) was replaced by the four-wheeled Great Wagon/ wain (or still later, the two-wheeled chariot carrying the Sun), this concept did not make it into eastern Eurasian myth, while it is found—even in Proto-Indo-European poetic collocation as "the wheel of the Sun" (an oxcart)—in Greek, early Indian, and Germanic texts and myth.

153. They are more prominent in Southeast Asian and East Asian myths (see the myth of the hidden sun, above, §3.5.1). Chicken are attested in Old Iranian (in Avestan) as *kahrka* (modern Persian *kark*) and the second-oldest Indian text, the Atharvaveda, as *kṛkavāku*; see §5, n. 17.

154. Campbell 1988: I.1: 88 sqq.

155. The mantis, however, has a rather human-looking (some say, even a Bushman-like) face, and its raised arms add to the humanlike impression. The mantis can change into an antelope; see the story reported by Frobenius (1998: 232); cf. the role of the mantis with the Sandawe.

156. Which is, however, often used as clan animal, for example, with the Hopi.

157. Cf. Lincoln 1991.

158. Burkert 1983; Caland 1990: 116 sqq.; Campbell 1988: I.1: 122.

159. In the Dema rituals of New Guinea (Campbell 1988: I.1: 70 sqq.; Wirz 1925); note also the cases of Idi Amin or Sierra Leone (reported to me, for the early seventies, by a diplomat stationed there: some such witch doctors were imprisoned and simply starved to death; cf. Arens 1979: 90 sqq.). Cannibalism is conveniently denied by Arens; see, however, his map of recent "blood sacrifice" (Arens 1979: 15).

160. Caland 1990: 416–19.

161. Vādhūla Sūtra; Caland 1990: 116 sqq.

162. Similarly, the Andamanese tell that hunted animals had at first been men; Campbell 1988: I.1: 122.

163. Vādhūla Sūtra; see Witzel 1987b, cf. 1987a.

164. This practice has recently been revived at Kāmākhyā (Assam) by the offering of a six-foot human, though in effigy: it is made, just like its Vedic *piṣṭapaśu* predecessors, out of vegetable materials, as reported on April 3, 2002, by the BBC (http://news.bbc.co.uk/2/hi/south_asia/1908706.stm).

165. For the earliest South African Stone Age art, c. 27,000 BP, see Lewis-Williams 2002; Walter and Fridman 2004: 20.

166. Andamanese myths include some Laurasian motifs, probably due to continental influence around 3000 BCE, but still lack its well-structured story line (cf. Sreenathan 2010). However, recent archaeological excavations have found some simple pottery even from the first millennium CE.

167. Campbell 1988: I.1: 122.

168. Campbell 1988: I.2: no. 220.

169. Campbell 1988: I.1: 122, cf. 1989: II.1: 58, with a map of the global occurrence of pig sacrifice.

170. See Ōbayashi 1991b.

171. Bogoras 1907: 450–57; Campbell 1988: I.2: 175.

172. See http://users.hartwick.edu/anthonyd/ritual.html.

173. Campbell 1988: I.2: 152 sqq.; Walter and Fridman 2004: 667 sqq., 700 sqq.; cf. Ōbayashi and Klaproth 1966 for Sakhalin. Wunn (2005: 84, 132), as usual, denies an ancient cult. Note that the bear was connected with the netherworld in Siberian shamanism (Walter and Fridman 2004: 255) and that he ("the dog of the gods") is substituted by a fox with the Kalasha (Witzel 2004b).

174. See detailed description of the Sakhalin and Hokkaido ritual (*kamuy oka inkara*, "sending the deity off," which includes the sacrifice of two male dogs) by Ohnuki-Tierney (1974: 90 sqq.); cf. Campbell 1988: I.2: 150. In addition to the reindeer-herding Saami (and many Siberian peoples), the settled Saami also retain much of this bear folklore and elaborate rituals, such as killing the bear by spear, positioning a bear head on a high tree, as is still done

in Finland, and asking him to return to his ancestors and report favorably on the humans etc. See Kalevala 46; and cf. Fromm and Fromm 1985: 585 sqq. on the bear festivals, well reported in Finland since 1675. The Ainu also have a similar, though abbreviated, ritual for foxes that they rear and then kill (Ohnuki-Tierney 1974: 97). Note also the rearing and "smothering" of eagles with the Hopi.

175. Campbell 1988: I.1: 56 sq., I.2: 150, cf. for later periods 154 sq. Wunn (2005: 84, 132) denies this.

176. Campbell 1988: I.1: 55, no. 82.

177. Campbell 1988: I.1: 62.

178. Bahn 1991; Wunn 2005: 76 sqq., 80–84.

179. Lorblanchet 2000: 71, 318, with statistics about the number of animal species depicted; http://www.metmuseum.org/toah/hd/chav/hd_chav.htm.

180. Lewis-Williams 2002; http://genre.homo.over-blog.com/album-160242.html; http://www.metmuseum.org/toah/hd/chav/hd_chav.htm; http://donsmaps.com/chauvet-cave.html.

181. Lewis-Williams 2002; Walter and Fridman 2004: 16–25; criticized by Wunn (2005: 121).

182. Wunn 2005.

183. Cf. Winkelman (2002), who attributes shamanistic universals to our underlying neurobiological structures; for details, see Winkelman, in Walter and Fridman 2004: 187–95.

184. Lewis-Williams 2002.

185. Campbell 1988: I.1: 76, nos. 131–32. See also the discussion by Wunn (2005: 121, 132); Leonard and McClure 2004: 185 sqq., especially the photo, which differs markedly from the sketch made by Abbé Breuil. For another recent photo, see Langen 1963: 129; §7, n. 49. It is unclear whether this difference is due to deterioration of the painting or to the imagination of Breuil. In any case, it certainly is not a male deity, as Gimbutas (1991: 175) maintains.

186. Campbell 1988: I.1: 74–77, no. 131.

187. Campbell 1988: I.1: 78, no. 135.

188. See also Leeming and Page 1996: 12–14.

189. Only ranked 11th out of commonly hunted animals; Lorblanchet 2000: 59 sq. Note that the numerical representation of animals in the South African San paintings of the past few centuries, too, does *not* agree with the extent of their archaeological remains (Campbell 1988: I.1: 60, 90 sq.). Clearly, even recently, a selection was made for such paintings, obviously on religious or ritual grounds. The same may have applied in Paleolithic times. Interestingly such cultural selection is also seen in that of the major predator fought by the culture hero: leopard in the Bactria-Margiana civilization, tiger in the Indus civilization (but lion in the R̥gveda, in the northern part of this culture), and lion in Mesopotamia/Persia—though the habitat of all animals overlapped; even the tiger was found in the Oxus area until a few decades ago.

190. The selection of animals and the mixture of motifs have even been interpreted as representing images and hallucinations in trance (Lewis-Williams and Dowson 1988, cf. 1993). In some cases, such as in 6,000-year-old European and 10,000-year-old North American finds, a link to a hallucinogenic, drug-induced state of mind has been suggested (Walter and Fridman 2004: 18).

191. The oldest datable reference of such drums known to me is from the Bactria-Margiana Archaeological Complex of southwestern Central Asia, c. 2400–1600 BCE; see §7, n. 70; §8, n. 25. There may be older forms in Eurasian rock art.

192. Campbell 1988: I.1: 44 sq., no. 131.

193. Campbell 1988: I.1: 65, no. 105; http://www.lascaux.culture.fr/#/fr/02_07.xml.

194. Stone Age art at Lascaux also shows a connection with the new invention, the spear-thrower, bull roarers, and "totemism," as perhaps indicated by animal pictures (Campbell 1988: I.1: 65).

195. Cf. the *corna* sign in Mediterranean (Italian/Turkish etc.) customs; cf. Wunn 2005: 24 sqq. on such gestures.

196. Campbell 1988: I.1: 98, ill. 176, 100, ill. 179.

197. Campbell 1998: I.1: 65.

198. Examples of representations of a hunter's erect penis are found in Campbell 1988: I.1: 98–100. Note also the imposing and threatening penis sheets of the Papuas (now forbidden by Indonesian law).

199. See Campbell 1988: I.1: 66, nos. 106–7, 93, 90 (at Lascaux and in Australia).

200. Wunn 2005: 221.

201. The image of an erect phallus therefore is also used to ward off evil, such as at the borders of ancient Greek townships (cf. Wunn 2005: 25) and on the back of Japanese Jizō statues, which are meant to protect deceased children. Aston (1972: 11 sq.) gives examples of a phallic procession in Japan in 1868 and connected data.

202. Cf. Frobenius 1998: 280 sq.

203. The animal has to shake its head, the Greek and Indian way to agree: this is effected by pouring some water on its head, which the animal then shakes off. With the Nakhi, too, a horse that is to accompany the deceased to the land of the ancestors has to shake its head (again, induced by pouring water on it); see Oppitz and Hsu 1998: 135. Similarly the *iomante* bear is asked by the Ainu if it may be killed; cf. Ōbayashi and Klaproth 1966. Similar ideas are found in Vedic India, in Ṛgveda 1.162–63, dealing with the horse sacrifice; cf. Ṛgveda 4.38–39.

204. Campbell 1988: I.1: 65.

205. See the observations of Leroi-Gourhan (1967: 316).

206. Campbell 1988: I.1: 66.

207. Campbell 1988: I.1: 66. Cf. also Burkert 1982: 88 sqq.; he (1982: 90 sqq.; see §4.4.1) traces the roots of some Greek myths (Herakles) back to the shamanistic hunter's magic of the Upper Paleolithic and sees the early myths represented in the cave paintings of Stone Age Europe.

208. Farmer et al. 2002; Judge 2007; Witzel 1979.

209. On sacrifice and shamanism in Siberia, see Eliade 1954b: 193 sqq.

210. Campbell l988: I.1: 62, ill. 94.

211. This is controversially discussed by Bahn (1991), who does not reject Paleolithic hunting magic but denies that it had a dominant role and calls for much more caution in the interpretation of Paleolithic art. But note the recent find of a bear skull on an "altar" in the undisturbed Chauvet Cave, 32,000 BP.

212 Campbell 1988: I.1: 54 sq. Immediately below, in the next section, Campbell (1988: I.1: 55, no. 82) interprets it, in Vedic fashion, as an offering of himself to himself. On this point, cf. Ṛgveda 1.164. 50 and Odin's rune song in the elder Edda, http://noadi.cywh.com/runesong.htm.

213. Wunn (2005: 84) denies it for Neanderthal people.

214. Campbell 1988: I.2: 147 sqq.

215. Campbell 1988: I.2: 150–52; Fromm and Fromm 1985: 585 sqq.; Ohnuki-Tierney 1981; Walter and Fridman 2004: 660 sq.; etc. Cf. Ōbayashi and Klaproth 1966 for Sakhalin.

216. Campbell 1988: I.2: 147 sqq.

217. This practice is visible even today, for example, in German hunters' language: blood = *Schweiss* (sweat), tail (of a hare) = *Lampe* (lamp), tail of hare or fox = *Blume* (flower), eyes = *Lichter* (lights), *Losung* (animal's feces), etc.; http://de.wikipedia.org/ wiki/Jägersprache. In northern Japan, hunters have a traditional *matagi* language (cf. §2, n. 235; §7, n. 222); cf. Taguchi's 1992, 1994, and 1999 work at http://ja.wikipedia.org/ wiki/田口洋美#.E5.A4.96. E9.83.A8.E3.83.AA.E3.83.B3.E3.82.AF.

218. Campbell 1988: I.2: 150 sq.

219. Campbell 1988: I.2: 149. For the Saami (Lapp), see also Wunn 2005: 83.

220. Pictures in Campbell 1988: I.2: 151 sqq.

221. Campbell 1988: I.2: 151. For the Oroken in Sakhalin, see Ōbayashi and Klaproth 1966.

222. Campbell 1988: I.2: 152 sqq.; Walter and Fridman 2004: 660 sq.; Wunn 2005: 81.

223. Walter and Fridman 2004: 700 sq. They use a peculiar hunting language (*matagi*); see above, §7, n. 217.

224. For North American examples (Ojibwa), see Wunn 2005: 83. However, following her usual procedure, unlike with the Saami, Ainu, and Ojibwa, she does not find remains of Middle Paleolithic art that would indicate that the same ideas were prevalent at that period.

225. For visitor deities who come to visit only once per year, note the Japanese *marebito* deities visiting Izumo once per year (*kamiarisai* festival), the Indr (Balumain) of the Kalash of the Hindu Kush (Jettmar 1975), and Indra at New Year in Vedic India (Witzel 1997b); compare the visits of the Katsina deities of the Hopi, who descend from the high mountains in winter and spring, just as the Shuchi goddesses of the Kalash do during this period.

226. Cf. Campbell's (1988: I.1: 55) characterization of a Drachenloch bear skull with his own (?) long bone put in his mouth, which reminded him, though not stated, of these parallels.

227. A common feature, in Vedic *atirātra* (overnight) rites (still performed in Kerala) or in the Japanese coronation ritual (*taikanshiki*).

228. Originally even of horses, now substituted by pictures of horses (*ema*); nevertheless there still is the contemporary offering of a hare in Nagano Prefecture; see §7, n. 246.

229. The etymology of Artemis's name is unclear; see Burkert 1985: 149, 407 n. 2. Some indeed connect it with *arktos* (bear). She is called the Lady of the Animals (*potniā therōn*) in *Iliad* 21.470.

230. See summary in Campbell 1988: I.2: 165 sq. I observed an Indian man with his "dancing bear" in the Nepalese hills east of Kathmandu in 1976.

231. Scherer 1953.

232. It appears under different images in other parts of the world; see Witzel 1999b. For example, in Kédang and other parts of Indonesia, its four major stars are called the "Boat star"; see Barnes 1974: 116.

233. Campbell 1988: I.2: 150 sq., ill. 259.

234. Campbell 1988: I.1: 55.

235. For the Paleolithic great cave bear, see Campbell 1998: I.1: 54 sqq.; Wunn 2005: 72 sqq.; popularized by Jean Auel's (mostly factually based) novels.

236. Campbell 1988: I.1: 92 sq. Some see the eland as a representation of Kaggen; see above, §5.3.5.1; cf. §4, n. 357; §5, n. 287; Frobenius 1998: 280 sq.

237. Herbig (1988: 84 sq., 90 sq.), taking his cue from the northwestern Amazon Desana, detects a sexual relationship between the hunter and the hunted animal. (The hunter increases his sexual potency by abstinence.) Indeed, hunters are often depicted in Stone Age paintings in ithyphallic fashion; however, this can also be understood as a power gesture (on ethological grounds). Cf. §7, n. 208.

238. Cf., however, the discussion by Baumann (1986: 143 sqq.). Cf. also the biblical Cain and Abel and the planned sacrifice of Abraham's son Isaac, as well as the parallel Vedic offering of Śunaḥśepa (in Aitareya Brāhmaṇa).

239. Campbell 1988: I.1: 122.

240. Cf. Wunn 2005: 201 sqq.

241. Farmer et al. 2002.

242. It would be an interesting project for a sociologist or anthropologist to investigate the methods used in murder and in (terror) killing in the various regions of the world. It can be predicted that even here the pathway dependencies of the local cultures—and religions—involved will become apparent.

243. The pagan Romans, certainly, were well aware of the concept and generated propaganda myths, for example, that the early Christians sacrificed babies.

244. Typically, the Buddha never answers when he is invited for lunch, and the founder of Jainism, Mahāvīra, is reported to have eaten pigeons—killed by a cat. Certain Hindu ascetics will eat only fruits that have fallen from a tree and thus are "dead."

245. Such as the Honmoku Jinja in Yokohama (observed in 2005).

246. See, for example, Nihon Shoki for the year 642 CE; Aston 1972: 174. Animal sacrifices are still carried out occasionally, for example, at the Suwa shrine in Nagano Prefecture: hare, boar, and deer have been offered; and a white hare is still offered on a spit.

247. Wirz 1925.

248. Wirz 1925; Campbell (1989: II.1: 68–71), illustrated); Wirz has been criticized since.

249. Some substitutions were made in late Vedic texts; see Witzel 1987a.

250. The sun, which is weak at first, is fed by blood; see Lehmann 1953: 42 sqq.

251. See §7, n. 182.

252. Frazer's *Totemism and Exogamy* (1910)—worldwide. However, the widely discussed and exploited topic of totemism (see *Encyclopaedia of Religion and Ethics* [Hastings 1922–28]) is now viewed in a new light. For example, Central Indian tribes are divided into four animal totem lineages, of which only A and C, and B and D, but not A and B etc., may intermarry; see Pfeffer 1982.

253. For post-Ṛgvedic versions of the mytheme, see Lincoln 1986: 65 sqq. and esp. 73, 86. However, for the great bull in a cosmogonic context, and the (younger) bull, Heaven/ Sun, see Ṛgveda 3.38; see above, §3.1.5.

254. See also the map in Baumann 1986: Karte IV.

255. Lorna Marshall (1962), quoted in Walter and Fridman 2004: 197.

256. For details on (the offer of) domesticated animals, see §4.4.5. For sacrifice in shamanism, see Schiller 2004.

257. Schiller 2004: 199.

258. Schiller 2004: 199. (Cf. J. Hubert and M. Mauss's *Sacrifice* [see Hubert 1964].)

259. For a detailed study, see F. Brighenti, "Buffalo Sacrifice and Tribal Mortuary Rituals" (2003, http://www.svabhinava.org/friends/FrancescoBrighenti/index.php); or at the same Web site, in a longer version: Brighenti's *Sacrificio di bovini, rituale funerario e culto degli antenati nelle culture tribali dell'India e del sudest asiatico* (2005).

260. The horns or skulls of the sacrificed bovines are installed on these monuments or on houses or Nepali and other Himalayan temples. This can also take the form of forked posts, shaped as a pair of bovine horns.

261. As well as with social status: such as with the Naga of northeastern India (who also stress the ancestor cult), the Gadaba and Hill Saora of Orissa and in Indonesia, the Toraja of Sulawesi, and the tribes of Sumba; as well as at graves in Austronesian Madagascar.

262. Widespread over Assam, Burma, and especially Indonesia, where tribal longhouses are decorated with real or wooden buffalo horns or with buffalo heads made of straw. Note also the still current Toda custom of killing buffaloes at the cremation of a deceased person (though they do not consume its meat and the head and horns are abandoned). Incidentally, note the still current Low Saxony custom (and Lithuanian) of decorating the gable section of houses with two wooden horse heads, reminiscent of the *dios kouroi*, Hengist and Horsa, the mythical conquerors of England. Horse sacrifice was common, as Tacitus reports.

263. As Stanner (1959) maintains for an initiation ritual.

264. Stanner 1959.

265. Campbell 1989: II.1: 58–71.

266. Baumann (1986) sees these developments connected with the "bisexual" (androgynous) world myth that he discerns.

267. Herbig 1988: 150 sqq.

268. Bierhorst 1986: 18.

269. "The Maize Stalk Drinking Blood" or "Nine Grass"; Campbell 1989: II.1: 36, ill. 69, from the Codex Borgia, cf. 41, ill. 78: the primordial sacrifice.

270. Compare, for example, the closely staged exchanges of food in myth and ritual (Lopez 1997) among the pastoralist Vedic tribes of the early first millennium BCE.

271. Or by Ukemochi.no ōkami, just from her mouth, in the Nihon Shoki I 26, cf. I 15, III 19.

272. Naumann 2000: 223.

273. Vādhūla Sūtra; Caland 1990: 116–19.

274. For Samoa, see Dixon 1916: 17.

275. Jacobsen 1976: 181; cf., however, the discussion by Baumann (1986: 143 sqq.).

276. See Beckwith 1987: 154 sqq. about the dark pit of Milu at the western end of the islands.

277. Witzel 1995, 1997a.

278. C. I. Beckwith, personal communication, Tokyo, 2006. For the development of the early Chinese concepts of spirits and ancestors, see Puett 2002.

279. Add Herbig's (1988: 449 sqq.) characterization of early Egyptian versus Mesopotamian or Mesoamerican mind-sets, where stability is constantly threatened by the emergence of a new (fifth or sixth) age.

280. *Pace* Schuster 1951; Sorenson and Johannessen 2006. As far as chicken and sweet potato import is concerned, see Carter 1971; Storey et al. 2007. Cf. §1, n. 67; §2, n. 326; §4, n. 501.

281. Farmer et al. 2002.

282. See Campbell 1989: II.1: 36, 41 (cf. above); for the Maize deity "First Father," Nun-Nal-Ye, "First Tree Precious (or yellow)," also depicted as a tree, see Freidel et al. 1993: 53 sqq.

283. See Brooks 2006; van Binsbergen 2005, 2006a, 2006b.

284. The early dates around 35,000 BCE, proposed after the initial discovery of Monte Verde in Chile, are no longer supported; the site is now set at 12.5 kya; and similarly, dates for Fort Liard (Yukon), Santa Rosa Island (Calif.), Levi (Tex.) and Meadowcroft Rockshelters (Pa.), Valsequillo (Puebla, Mexico), Pikimachay Cave (Ayacucho, Peru), and Tagua-Tagua (Chile; see Campbell 1988: I.1: 34 sqq.). The longtime consensus for the earliest date for immigration, that of Clovis Man (Tex.) at c. 11.5 kya, is now superseded. These dates point to the time of the loss of sustained contact with Asia (the Inuit and the northwestern Na-Dene tribes excepted).

285. There also is the much debated case of the 9,400-year-old Kennewick Man found on the Columbia River in Washington State, which was at first reported to have a "Caucasoid" skull, while in fact it is more like that of the Ainus or Polynesians and South Asians (Lemonic and Dorfman 2006: 48); there are indeed early sites along the Pacific coast all the way down to Chile (Monte Verde, 12,500 BP; Palli Aike in Tierra del Fuego, 8640 BP), as well as one site in northeastern Brazil that is even put at an unlikely 47,000 BP. In addition, there is the (European) Aurignacoid (Solutrean) culture found, e.g., at Topper, Va., of 15,200 BP; cf. also Campbell 1988: I.1: 34 sqq.

286. See Walter and Fridman 2004: 275 sqq.

287. See Lemonic and Dorfman 2006. For a survey of recent Amerindian DNA studies, see §4, n. 211.

288. Cf. also the intriguing case of the Wintu language in the Bay Area of California, which has been attributed to a rather late Uralic immigration by boat (von Sadovszky 1978, 1996). Note that Uralic is indeed spoken as far east as the coast of northeastern Siberia (Yukhagir).

289. If the affiliation of Na-Dene with the Macro-Caucasian languages is accepted (see §4.1), an early date around 40 kya for their own, original mythology is likely; cf. discussion above, §4.3.

290. For Australian and New Guinea myths, see Berezkin 2002.

291. Berezkin 2002.

292. See Berezkin's (2007) map of principal components.

293. Berezkin 2002, 2005b.

294. See above, §4.4; Metspalu et al. 2006.

295. Dixon 2002: 7.

296. Hudjashov et al. 2007.

297. Cf. also its archaeology and paleontology in Campbell 1988: I.1: 30 sqq.

298. Blažek 2006; Wells 2002.

299. Kumarasamy Thangaraj, personal communication, November 2007. The Andamanese have the mtDNA haplogroup M31a (in two subgroups, M31a1a/b), distributed between the Onge/Jarawa and Great Andamans (Endicott et al. 2003); the Rajbanshi have M31b, and the Kurumba, M32 (cf. Palanichamy et al. 2006; see §4, n. 168; §5, n. 238). NRY D*-M174 is found with the Onge and Jarawa in high proportion, a remnant of the exodus (Gayden et al. 2007).

300. Which may have been confirmed by recent excavations in South India that point to c. 75 kya (Petraglia et al. 2007).

301. For a brief summary, see Witzel 1999a.

302. Hong et al. 2007; cf. Li and Su 2000.

303. Differently from Oppenheimer's Toba explosion theory (*Eden in the East* [1998]).

304. As described above (§5.2) for dualism; some scholars such as Leroi-Gourhan (1965, 1967) want to see such structured oppositions already in the cave paintings of Franco-Cantabria, such as at Lascaux; for well-founded opposition to this structuralistic interpretation, see Lorblanchet 2000.

305. See Baumann 1936; van Binsbergen 2006a, 2006b.

306. Such as the NRY haplogroups J1 and K and the mtDNA group M1.

307. Summary by Fleming (2003).

308. See §4, nn. 345, 366, on South Africa and in Algeria.

309. I have done some preliminary studies of Toda (Nilgiri), Austronesian Taiwanese, and Ainu myth, and I have prepared large parts of a work on Japanese myth "seen from the outside" that I hope to publish next.

■ **Chapter 8**

1. Cf. Barth's (1987: 67) myth as metaphor; similarly, see Witzel 1979 for Indian (Brāhmaṇa-time) sacrificial myths.

2. Cf. Wunn 2005; see §4.3.1.

3. Allen 2006.

4. See Barth 1987: 67; §5, n. 221; §8, n. 9.

5. See Farmer et al. 2002. Note that some scholars regard the worldview of its apparent authors, Stone Age shamanism, as a body-based cosmology and some of its aspects, such as soul flight, as symbolism that presents the experiences of dreams. (Shamanism could then be a symbolic system that even predates language.) See Walter and Fridman 2004: 188.

6. Such as rituals, poems, epics, sculptures, paintings, and music.

7. Farmer et al. 2002; Graham-Rowe 2007; Lévi-Strauss 1995: 316 sqq.: he restricted the binary mode to *some* societies (those dealt with by him in the Americas).

8. The anthropocentric tendency is seen in all humans, worldwide, and is evident even in small children who see (and paint) eyes and faces on all sorts of inanimate objects. This sets in soon after birth, when babies get fixed on the triangle of eyes and mouth in their mother's and other's faces. One may therefore speculate on the connections made with the "face" of the mantis in San and Sandawe myth, as well as "extraterrestrials" in contemporary space myths.

9. Also into ritual; see discussion on the myth and ritual school, §1.5; cf. Barth 1987: 75 on metaphor and ritual.

10. See, for example, the work of M. M. Merzenich, http://lib.bioinfo.pl/auth:Merzenich,MM.

11. Witzel 1979.

12. Rudy 1962: 213. For the Ainu, see Ohnuki-Tierney 1974: 97 sq.

13. Cf. Mortensen 2003.

14. Or as Xenophanes of Colophon (c. 560–478 BCE) is said to have written: "If oxen and horses had hands and could draw pictures, … they would draw pictures of gods like horses and oxen."

15. It would be interesting to investigate the origin of animal fables (in Greece, India) at length and to compare them with the frequent totemic fables found in many cultures, such as in Australia, New Guinea, and Central India, as well as similar tales in North America.

16. Or whole (imperial) courts of people among the Daoists. Cf. Burkert 1982: 78 sqq.

17. Vārāha Gṛhya Parisiṣṭa, ed. and trans. by Rolland (1975).

18. Perhaps seen in Stone Age sculpture, at Laussel in France and in Dogon Land in West Africa. See §4.4; cf. §2, n. 166; §3, n. 188; §7, n. 37. Cf. also Baumann 1986: 130 for the Dayak.

19. Note also the widespread belief in personal rebirth; see §2, n. 200; §6, n. 23.

20. Which connection he denied (Lévi-Strauss 1995: 316). See §1, n. 153.

21. Lévi-Strauss 1995: 316.

22. Typical for the Newars of the Kathmandu Valley.

23. Primordial misdeed or "sin" of Adam and Eve for Christians (and some other Abrahamic religions); primordial obligation to the gods in Hinduism, where one of its early deities, Mārtāṇḍa Vivasvant, is the outcome of Aditi's, his mother's, mistake of eating too early; Vivasvant's son Yama, too, made some sort of mistake (never clearly enunciated) and had to die; humans are descendants of his brother Manu (Man; Germanic Mannus, as Tacitus has it) and follow Yama into his realm of the dead. In Shintō it is the primordial mistake of the equivalent of Aditi, Izanami, who makes the mistake of speaking too early; humans are the descendant of her daughter Amaterasu and are always plagued by pollution

(*kegare*) and evil (*tsumi*). For some other cases, see Melanesia (§5.3.3), Africa (Unumbotte myth; §6.1), etc.

24. The Greek *tritopatores*, or three ancestors, in India and Russia symbolized by rice balls (meatballs in Kashmir) or dumplings in ancestor ritual.

25. The Bible does not follow up on this theme: while humans were created in God's image, their behavior is not attributed or likened to the character of the deity that created them. Nevertheless, the God of the Hebrew Bible can be an angry and vengeful figure, just like his "children." From a Laurasian and a Gondwana point of view, Adam and Eve are of course the *actual* children of the gods (*elohīm*).

26. This is especially seen in China and India, since Bronze Age times; cf. Beckwith 2004.

27. See my *On Ritual* (Witzel 1985), an unpublished paper that has, however, been used by several colleagues; see Patton 1992. For Africa, see Baumann 1936: 408, s.v. *Ahnen-kult*, and 24, 31, etc. The situation in early China is slightly different: there is not *do ut des*, but offerings make the spirits manageable (Puett 2002: 41 sqq.).

28. Farmer et al. 2002.

29. Farmer et al. 2002; Witzel 1979.

30. Witzel 1996.

31. Cf. Lincoln 1999.

32. Last dealt with by me (Witzel 2011) and R. Hamayon (1990). See the discussions in Walter and Fridman 2004: xx, 161 sqq., 228 sqq., 271 sqq.

33. See Herbig 1988.

34. Is this an outcome of the Laurasian stress on story line texts? Note the well-reconstructed Indo-European poetic speech (Watkins 1995), its rhetoric questions about mythology, and its catalogs of questions and answers (Witzel 1987b), emulated in the Vedic speech contests, especially at New Year (Kuiper 1983), and in the Upaniṣadic *brahmodyas*.

35. See, for example, the cases of faithful transmission mentioned by Maskarinec (1998) for central Nepal. More comparable data from other central Nepalese regions are included in his (2008) second installment in the Harvard Oriental Series (with video).

36. Lévi-Strauss 1995: xii–xiii. For a short summary of his views, see Narby and Huxley 2001: 245–47; see also Yalman 1996.

37. Witzel 1996; see also Barber and Barber 2004.

38. Farmer et al. 2002.

39. It would be an interesting investigation, however, to see how far the older Laurasian or Gondwana structures are maintained in each individual culture, e.g., the Kalash, Saami, Hopi, Ainu, Toda, Semang, Aeta, Australian, Papua, and Andaman ones; cf. §5.6.

40. Such as the age of ancient Indian texts (exceeding their commonly agreed dates by several millennia), ascribing technical advances (such as spoke-wheeled chariots) to cultures earlier than actually attested, interpreting ancient texts so as to show that all things Indian are indigenous, etc. Similar claims have been made by various (nation-)states, for example, by the Nazis and Soviets, and this is continued in other (especially newly emerging) states today.

41. That is, all knowledge, all technology, was known to the Vedic ancestors but has subsequently been stolen by Westerners, notably "Max Müller and the Germans," who "took away sacred texts, studied them, and with that knowledge built airplanes and atomic bombs"—as I heard everywhere from Benares to Madras. A further parallel to New Guinea is that the members of political parties espousing such ideas during the struggle for independence indeed took over the government. In India this finally occurred between 1998–99 and 2004. During this period, the government championed several projects to "take back" history and

to use traditional knowledge, including projects of finding long-lost quasi-mythical rivers (Sarasvatī) or alleged sunken cities (Gulf of Cambay), teaching astrology in the universities, and even preparing modern military implements and weapons based on 2,000-year-old texts (such as the Arthaśāstra). Among them were soldiers' boots allowing them to run for seven days (as in Grimms' *Fairy Tales*) and an eye ointment that would allow its user perfect night vision: it was to be prepared from ... an *owl* extract—a perfect example of archaic correlation (Farmer et al. 2002).

42. Burkert 1982: 142.

43. For Beowulf and other Germanic heroes, see Mizuno 2003.

44. See Nagy 1979.

45. Or the Dalmatian Vlaho (Blasius). He was identified with the Old Slavic god Veles/ Volos, who is associated with dragons.

46. Ježić 2005.

47. Propp 1958.

48. Ježić 2005.

49. For folktales, see Propp 1958; Raglan 1934, 1956. Note that, for a change, *anti*heroes were popular in the eighties in American TV series.

50. The 78-episode series ran on Sundays from January 25, 1987, to July 31, 1988.

51. His spirit appears to his family as a giant white bird, whom they follow, and then they build Yamato Takeru's grave where it stops (Kojiki II 88: 29).

52. Broadcast by Nippon Hōsō Kyōkai, the independent national TV company, in 2005.

53. See, for example, Wagner 1990.

54. In addition to several series of invented legends (again mostly Hollywood productions) and British-inspired films such as *The Lord of the Rings, Harry Potter*, etc.

55. See Dawkins 2006; Hübner 1985; Schatz and Spatzenegger 1986. Cf. also Jaspert 1991 on de-mytholization; McKee 2005, http://www.newscientist.com/article.ns?id=dn7147. James Randerson, in *Guardian Unlimited* (September 4, 2006), reports that Bruce Hood, a professor at Bristol University, discovered that magical and supernatural beliefs are hardwired in humans and that religions are simply using this psychological feature. According to Hood, "It is pointless to think that we can get people to abandon their belief systems because they are operating at such a fundamental level. No amount of rational evidence is going to be taken on board to get people to abandon those ideas." This has recently been echoed by other psychologists, who have stressed the utility of religion and myth in establishing and maintaining social relations and hierarchies beyond the actual presence of the people involved. In addition, religious thought is regarded as the way of "least resistance" for our cognitive system.

56. See Wunn 2005 for Stone Age religion; and cf. above, §2.6, §4.4.1, §7.1.

57. See McKee 2005.

58. McKee 2005.

59. For the ebb and flow of various religious explanations, see Ausloos and Petroni 2007. They maintain that evolutionary models widely used in other scientific fields can be applied to historical studies of the rise and fall of religious systems. Their mathematical approach is now widely applied in economics, neurobiology, etc.; so why not to broader cultural forms as well?

60. Hübner 1985: 349.

61. See Rosenberg 1982.

62. Cassirer 1946: 235.

63. Cf. Hübner 1985: 362 sqq.

64. Cassirer 1946: 235–36.

65. Or the transformation of old myths into new Marxist ones or the transformation of historical facts of the October Revolution into new myths, such as by the prominent poet Vladimir V. Mayakovski (Gottschalk 1979: 34).

66. Hochgeschwender 2007.

67. See §2.4; cf. §2, n. 197; §8, n. 67 on state societies. I leave apart the other strongly myth-based beliefs of the Evangelicals (Hochgeschwender 2007), notably their literal understanding of the biblical flood myth (Gould 1988).

68. See John O'Sullivan, in Sanford 1974; further see Pratt 1933.

69. See John Winthrop (1995) for "American exceptionalism"; Rutman 1975.

70. See, for example, the amusing account of the American class system by Paul Fussell (1983).

71. Witzel 2001b, 2006c. Notably in the 2005–6 California schoolbook affair, about which I will report separately.

72. Lévi-Strauss 1995: 13.

73. Hübner 1985.

74. Hübner 1985: 410: the philosopher Leszek Kolakowski sees the contemporaneous presence of myth even in the (natural) sciences, as they, too, reflect the human wish to find meaning in life. Similarly, the biologist Adolf Portmann (1897–1982) regarded both science and myth as two human attempts at ordering experience: myth by analogy, science by true statements, both of which might someday be integrated (Gottschalk 1979: 28, 31 sq.). Cf. also Campbell 1977; Van Over 1980: 12. Note also comparable current projects on religion and science such as those by the Templeton Foundation, which has supported a range of scientific, philosophical, historical, educational, and theological programs on the theme of science and religion. See http://www.templeton.org/.

75. Hübner 1985: 410.

76. Cf. Herbig 1988: 466 sqq., with a description of the critiques of modern science, ecology, technology, and "progress" in general, as well as the underlying social conditions.

77. See Witzel 2001b, 2002b.

78. For the "pure polytheistic manifestation of Shintō," see Kato 1988: 15 sqq. On the deities of Shintō, see Havens and Inoue 2001; Hirafuji 2004; Inoue 1998; Kitagawa 1987; Mori 1999; Swanson and Chilson 2006.

79. Some of it may go back to the old "mountain religion" that is also seen with the Burushos, who live just north of the Kalash and the, until recently, pagan Nuristani; see above, §5.6.1, on Macro-Caucasian (Burusho and Caucasus) similarities; cf. §2, n. 268; §5, nn. 384, 385.

80. In the Engishiki (Bock 1970).

81. In Hawai'i, similarly, a formula was used to invite each and every deity, by saying: "Invoke we now the 40,000 gods, the 400,000 gods, the 4,000 gods"; see Beckwith 1987: 82. Note the Greek idea to offer to the "unknown" deity, as reported in the New Testament (Paul's Letters).

82. See Thomas et al. 1969: 347 sqq., with Christian and Muslim examples, from the Bwiti-fan of Gabon, Wolof, Lebu, Ivory Coast, Congo, Central Africa, Kikuyu, etc.

83. See Lorenz's (1963) and Tinbergen's (1962) studies of ethology.

84. Cf. Hübner 1985: 325.

85. Note the more immediate pursuit of one's somatic ancestors: witness the many services in America for tracing one's (immigrated) ancestors or the recent fashion of getting one's DNA tested to find more remote ancestors; see, for example, http://www.familytreedna.com/genographic-project.aspx; or for Britain, http://www.ethnoancestry.com/.

86. In modern science fiction and in the widespread beliefs in the existence of extraterrestrials; see Lewis 1995; Partridge 2003; Sutcliffe 2004.

87. Whether this takes the fifties version of a communist- or capitalist-inspired threat from the outside or an alien threat from Mars; or the more recent version of friendly, cooperative aliens (à la Spielberg's *ET*); or with the late C. Sagan, one that says that we are not yet ready for contact. Note the various SETI projects.

88. Lewis 1995; Partridge 2003.

89. See Rothstein 1995.

90. As science fiction writers habitually assume but which many American nationalists surprisingly choose to regard as a viable threat.

91. See Huntingdon 1993.

92. Witzel 2001b, 2002b.

93. Though one would certainly not look for the traditional, feudalistic variant of Confucianism.

94. Obviously the last 400 years of Confucian influence since the beginning of the Edo period followed a traditional, rigid pattern, not appropriate for today's society.

95. Shaped during in the Meiji period of the 19th century and including nationalism and European humanism. For the current problem of defining the self, see Ohnuki-Tierney 1990; cf. Roland 1988.

96. Except perhaps for some forms of Buddhism; the number of its adherents is increasing rapidly in the Chinese population, now more than one billion strong.

97. Note the cargo cults, current Indian reimagining of the past in a mythical fashion, syncretistic religions such as Cao Dai in Vietnam and others in Africa and Brazil, cults involving UFOs and extraterrestrial Others, and the recent Chinese attempt (Hu 2002) to finally come up with a contiguous origin myth. Rather, see, for the fragmentary nature (and dates) of ancient Chinese myths, Bodde 1961: 403–7; Mathieu 1989.

■ BIBLIOGRAPHY

Aarne, Antti, and Stith Thompson. *The types of the folktale*. FF Communications No. 184. Helsinki: Academia Scientiarum Fennica, 1973.

Abbi, Anvita. *Endangered languages of the Andaman Islands*. Munich: Lincom, 2006.

Abbott, John. *Indian ritual and belief. The keys of power*. Delhi: Usha, 1984. (Originally: *The Keys of Power*, 1932.)

Aboudan, R., and G. Beattie. Cross cultural similarities in gestures: The deep relationship between gestures and speech which transcend language barriers. *Semiotica* 111 (1996): 269–94.

Adcock, G. J., et al. Mitochondrial DNA sequences in ancient Australians: Implications for modern human origins. *Proceedings of the National Academy of Sciences of the United States of America* 98 (2001): 537–42.

Aiken, M. J., et al., eds. *The origin of modern humans and the impact of chronometric dating: A discussion*. Princeton: Princeton University Press, 1993.

Akazawa, T., and Ofer Bar-Yosef, eds. *Neandertals and modern humans in Western Asia*. New York: Plenum Press, 1998.

Allen, N. And the lake drained away: An essay in Himalayan comparative mythology. In *Mandala and landscape*, ed. A. W. Macdonald, 435–51. New Delhi: D. K. Printworld, 1997.

———. Imra, Pentads and catastrophes. *Ollodagos* [Brussels] 14 (2000): 278–308.

———. Indo-European epics and comparative methods: Pentadic structure in Homer and the Mahābhārata. In Osada 2006: 243–52.

Allen, S. *The shape of the turtle: Myth, art and cosmos in early China*. Albany: State University of New York Press, 1991.

Allman, Wiliam F. The mother tongue. Linguists are working back from modern speech to re-create the first language of the human race. *U.S. News and World Report*, November 5, 1990: 60–70.

Anderson, Gregory D. S. *The Munda verb: Typological perspectives*. Berlin: Mouton de Gruyter, 2007.

———. Recent advances in Proto-Munda and Proto-Austroasiatic reconstruction. Presentation at the Third Harvard Round Table on the Prehistory of Central and South Asia, Cambridge, Mass., May 2001.

Anthony, David. *The horse, the wheel, and language: How Bronze-Age riders from the Eurasian steppes shaped the modern world*. Princeton: Princeton University Press, 2007.

Antoni, Klaus. *Der weiße Hase von Inaba—Vom Mythos zum Märchen. Analyse eines "Mythos der ewigen Wiederkehr" vor dem Hintergrund altchinesischen und zirkumpazifischen Denkens*. Wiesbaden: Münchener Ostasiatische Studien Bd. 28, 1982.

———. *Miwa—Der heilige Trank. Zur Geschichte und religiösen Bedeutung des alkoholischen Getränkes (sake) in Japan*. Stuttgart: Steiner, 1988.

———. Zur Herkunft der Valdivia-Keramik in Ekuador (Jômon-Valdivia). *Baessler-Archiv*, NF 25 (1977): 401–20.

Anttila, R. *Historical and comparative linguistics*. Amsterdam: John Benjamins, 1989.

Aoki, Michiko Y. *Records of wind and earth. A translation of Fudoki with introduction and commentaries.* Ann Arbor: Association for Asian Studies, 1997.

Arens, W. *The man-eating myth: Anthropology and anthropophagy.* New York: Oxford University Press, 1979.

Arieti, Silvano. *The intrapsychic self; feeling, cognition, and creativity in health and mental illness.* New York: Basic Books, [1967].

Arnold, M., et al. *Chauvet Cave: The art of earliest times.* Dir. Jean Clottes; trans. Paul G. Bahn. Salt Lake City: University of Utah Press, 2003.

Arvidsson, S. *Aryan Idols. Indo-European mythology as ideology and science.* Chicago: University of Chicago Press, 2006.

Aston, W. G. *Nihongi. Chronicles of Japan from the earliest times to* A.D. 697. Rutland: Tuttle, 1972 [1896].

Ausloos, M., and F. Petroni. Statistical dynamics of religions and adherents. *Europhysics Letters* 77 (2007): 38002.

Ayub, Q., et al. Reconstruction of human evolutionary tree using polymorphic autosomal microsatellites. *American Journal of Physical Anthropology* 122 (2003): 259–68.

Bachofen, Johann J. *Das Mutterrecht. Eine Untersuchung über die Gynaikokratie der alten Welt nach ihrer religiösen und rechtlichen Natur. Mit 9 Steindruck-Tafeln und einem ausführlichen Sachregister.* Stuttgart: Krais und Hoffman, 1861.

Bächtold-Stäubli, Hanns. *Handwörterbuch des deutschen Aberglaubens; herausgegeben von Hanns Bächtold-Stäubli unter Mitwirkung von Eduard Hoffmann-Krayer, mit einem Vorwort von Christoph Daxelmüller.* Berlin: W. de Gruyter, 1987 [1930].

Bahn, Paul G. Where is the beef? The myth of hunting magic in Paleolithic art. In Bahn and Rosenfeld 1991: 1–13.

Bahn, Paul G., and A. Rosenfeld. Rock art and prehistory. In Bahn and Rosenfeld 1991.

Bahn, Paul, and Andrée Rosenfeld, eds. *Rock art and prehistory. Papers presented to Symposium G of the AURA Congress, Darwin 1988.* Oxford: Oxbow Monograph 10, 1991.

Bahuchet, Serge. Languages of the Central African rainforest "Pygmy" hunter-gatherers. Hunter-Gatherer Workshop, 2006, http://lingweb.eva.mpg.de/HunterGatherer Workshop2006/Bahuchet.pdf.

Balter, Michael. In search of the world's most ancient mariners. *Science* 318, no. 5849 (October 19, 2007a): 388–89.

———. Small brains, big fight: "Hobbits" called new species. *Science Magazine* 315, no. 5812 (February 2, 2007b), http://www.sciencemag.org/content/vol315/issue5812/news-summaries.dtl.

Bamshad, Michael J., and Steve E. Olson. Does race exist? If races are defined as genetically discrete groups, no. But researchers can use some genetic information to group individuals into clusters with medical relevance. *Scientific American,* November 10, 2003.

Bandelt, Hans-Jürgen, et al. *Human mitochondrial DNA and the evolution of* Homo sapiens. Berlin: Springer, 2006.

Bantly, F. C. Archetypes of selves: Study of the Chinese mytho-historical process. In Patton and Doniger 1996: 177–207.

Barber, E. J. W., and P. T. Barber. *When they severed earth from sky: How the human mind shapes myth.* Princeton: Princeton University Press, 2004.

Barnes, R. H. *Kédang. A study of the collective thought of an eastern Indonesian people.* Oxford: Clarendon, 1974.

Barrett, T. H. Comparison and Chinese mythology. *Cosmos* 11 (1995): 69–78.

Barth, F. *Cosmologies in the making. A generative approach to cultural variation in Inner New Guinea*. Cambridge: Cambridge University Press, 1987.

Bar-Yosef, Ofer. On the nature of transitions: The Middle to Upper Paleolithic and the Neolithic revolution. *Cambridge Archaeological Journal* 8 (1998): 141–63.

Basilov, V. N. Cosmos as everyday reality in shamanism: An attempt to formulate a more precise definition of shamanism. In Mastromattei and Rigopulos 1999: 17–39.

Bastian, Adolf. *Der Menschheitsgedanke durch Raum und Zeit*. Berlin: Dümmler, 1901.

———. *Der Völkergedanke im Aufbau einer Wissenschaft vom Menschen und seine Begründung auf ethnologischen Sammlungen*. Berlin: F. Dümmler, 1881.

Bastide, Roger. Die Mythologie der Afrikaner. In Pierre Grimal, *Mythen der Völker*, Bd. III, 249–79. Hamburg: Fischer, 1967. (Originally: Paris, 1963.)

Basu, A., N. Mukherjee, S. Roy, S. Sengupta, S. Banerjee, et al. Ethnic India: A genomic view, with special reference to peopling and structure. *Genome Research* 13 (2003): 2277–90.

Baumann, Hermann. *Das doppelte Geschlecht*. Berlin: Reimer, 1986 [1955].

———. *Schöpfung und Urzeit der Menschen im Mythos der afrikanischen Völker*. Berlin, 1936.

Beckwith, C. I. *Koguryo: The language of Japan's continental relatives*. Leiden: Brill, 2004.

Beckwith, M. *Hawaiian mythology*. Honolulu: University of Hawai'i Press, 1987. (Originally: *Hawaiian myth*. New Haven: Yale University Press, 1940.)

———. *The Kumulipo. A Hawaiian creation chant*. Honolulu: University of Hawaii Press, 1972 [1951].

Beekes, R. S. P. *Comparative Indo-European linguistics: An introduction*. Amsterdam: J. Benjamins, 1995.

———. The Pre-Greek loans in Greek. 3rd version, January 2007, http://www.ieed.nl/ied/pdf/pre-greek.pdf.

Bek-Pedersen, Karen. Opposites and mediators in Norse mythology. *Cosmos* 17 (2003): 37–58.

Bell, D. *Daughters of the Dreaming*. Sydney: Allen and Unwin, 1983.

Bellah, R. N. Religiöse Evolution. In *Religion und gesellschaftliche Entwicklung*, ed. Constans Seyfarth and Walter M. Sprondel. Frankfurt (am Main): Suhrkamp, 1973. (Originally: Religious evolution. *American Sociological Review* 29 [1964]: 358–74.)

Bellwood, P. Formosan prehistory and Austronesian dispersal. In *Austronesian Taiwan. Linguistics, history, ethnology and prehistory*, ed. D. Blundell, 337–65. Berkeley, 2000.

Bellwood, Peter. *First farmers: The origins of agricultural societies*. Malden, Mass.: Blackwell, 2005.

———. Lexicostatistics/glottochronology: From Swadesh to Sankoff to Starostin to future horizons. In *Time depth in historical linguistics*, ed. Colin Renfrew, April McMahon, and Larry Trask. Cambridge: McDonald Institute for Archaeological Research, 2000.

Bellwood, P., and C. Renfrew, eds. *Examining the farming/language dispersal hypothesis*. Cambridge: McDonald Institute for Archaeological Research, University of Cambridge, 2002.

Benedict, Paul K. Austro-Thai and Austroasiatic. In *Austroasiatic studies, pt. I*, ed. Philip N. Jenner, Laurence C. Thompson, and Stanley Starosta, 1–36. Honolulu: University of Hawai'i Press, 1976.

———. *Austro-Tai: Language and culture, with a glossary of roots*. New Haven: HRAF Press, 1975.

———. *Japanese/Austro-Thai*. Ann Arbor: Karoma, 1990.

Bender, M. L. *The Nilo-Saharan languages: A comparative essay.* Munich: Lincom Europa, 1996.

Bengtson, John D. Burushaski, Yeniseian, and the Karasuk culture. Presentation at the 14th Harvard Round Table on the Ethnogenesis of South and Central Asia, October 4–5, 2010, http://www.fas.harvard.edu/~sanskrit/2010/oct4-5/papers/(1)RT2010JDBengt.pdf.

————. Dene-Sino-Caucasian languages. In E. Vajda, *Yeneseian peoples and languages,* 130–41. Bochum: Brockmeyer, 1991.

————. An end to splendid isolation: The Macro-Caucasian phylum. *Mother Tongue/Long Ranger [Newsletter]* 10 (1990).

————. *Macro-Caucasian cultural vocabulary (Basque, Burushaski, Caucasian).* 2003, http://jdbengt.net/articles.htm.

————. A multilateral look at Greater Austric. *Mother Tongue* 11 (2006): 219–58.

Bengtson, John D., and Merritt Ruhlen. Global etymologies. In Ruhlen 1994a: 277–336, http://jdbengt.net/articles.htm.

Benveniste, E., and L. Renou. *Vṛtra et Vṛthragna. Etude de mythologie indo-iranienne.* Paris, 1934.

Berezkin, Yuri. The assessment of the probable age of Eurasian–American mythological links. *Archaeology, Ethnology and Anthropology of Eurasia* 1, no. 21 (2005a): 146–51.

————. Continental Eurasian and Pacific links in American mythologies and their possible time-depth. *Latin American Indian Literatures Journal* 21 (2005b): 99–115.

————. Cosmic hunt: Variants of a Siberian–North American myth. *Archaeology, Ethnology and Anthropology of Eurasia* 2, no. 22 (2005c): 141–50.

————. Dwarfs and cranes. Baltic Finnish mythologies in Eurasian and American perspective. 70 years after V. Toivonen. *Electronic Journal of Folklore* 36 (2007): 67–88, http://haldjas.folklore.ee/folklore/vol36/berezkin.pdf.

————. The fourth source of data. Amerindian oral literatures and the peopling of Central and South America. *Arx* 2–3 (1996–97): 53–63.

————. O putiax zaseleniia novogo sveta: Nekotoryie rezultaty sravnitel'nogo izucheniia amerikanskix i sibirskix mifologii. *Archeologicheskie Vesti* 10 (2003a): 228–89 [English summary: Peopling of the New World: Results of comparative study of American and Siberian mythologies, 281–89].

————. Otsenka drevnosti Evraziiskogo-Amerikanskix sviazeii v oblasti mifologiia. *Archaeology, Ethnology and Anthropology of Eurasia* 1, no. 21 (2005d): 146–51.

————. Review of Th. A. Gregor and D. Tuzin, ed., *Gender in Amazonia and Melanesia. An Exploration of the Comparative Method.* Berkeley: University of California Press, 2001. *Latin American Indian Literatures Journal* 18, no. 1 (2002): 84–91.

————. Siberian myths about the origin of death in the global perspective. Offprint, n.d.

————. Southern Siberian–North American links in mythology. *Archaeology, Ethnology and Anthropology of Eurasia* 2, no. 14 (2003b): 94–105.

Berger, H. Deutung einiger alter Stammesnamen der Bhil aus der vorarischen Mythologie des Epos und der Purāṇa. *Wiener Zeitschrift für die Kunde Süd- und Ostasiens* 3 (1959): 34–82.

————. *Die Burushaski-Sprache von Hunza und Nagar,* vols. 1–3. Wiesbaden: Harrassowitz, 1988.

Bernal, Martin. *Black Athena: The Afroasiatic roots of classical civilization.* London: Free Association Books, 1987.

————. *Black Athena writes back: Martin Bernal responds to his critics.* Ed. David Chioni Moore. Durham: Duke University Press, 2001.

Bernhard, Franz. Zur Entstehung einer Dhāraṇī. *Zeitschrift der Deutschen Morgenländischen Gesellschaft* 117 (1967): 148–68.

Beyer, Henry Otley. *Ethnography of the Negrito-Aeta peoples; a collection of original sources.* Manila, 1918–.

Biardeau, Madeleine. *Histoires de Poteaux.* Paris: EFEO, 1989.

Bickerton, Derek. *Language and species.* Chicago: University of Chicago Press, 1990.

Bierhorst, J. *The mythology of Mexico and Central America.* New York: Quill, 1992 [1990].

———. *The mythology of North America.* New York: William Morrow, 1986.

———. *The mythology of South America.* New York: William Morrow, 1988.

Binford, Lewis Roberts. *Die Vorzeit war ganz anders.* Munich, 1984 [1983].

———. *In pursuit of the past: Decoding the archaeological record.* With the editorial collaboration of John F. Cherry and Robin Torrence. New York: Thames and Hudson, 1983.

Birdsell, J. B. The recalibration of a paradigm of the first peopling of Australia. In *Sunda and Sahul: Prehistoric studies in Southeast Asia,* ed. J. Allen, J. Golson, and R. Jones, 113–67. London: Academic Press, 1977.

Birrell, Anne. *Chinese mythology: An introduction.* Baltimore: Johns Hopkins University Press, 1993.

Black, Paul. Outside relationships of Australian languages. *Mother Tongue* 11 (2006): 259–61.

Blacker, Carmen. *The catalpa bow: A study of shamanic practices in Japan.* London: Allen and Unwin, 1986 [1975].

Blažek, V. *Numerals. Comparative-etymological analyses of numeral systems and their implications (Saharan, Nubian, Egyptian, Berber, Kartvelian, Uralic, Altaic and Indo-European languages).* Brno: Masarykova Univerzita v Brně, 1999.

———. Was there an Australian substratum in Dravidian? *Mother Tongue* 12 (2006): 275–94.

Blench, Roger M. Are the African pygmies an ethnographic fiction? In *Central African hunter-gatherers in a multi-disciplinary perspective: Challenging elusiveness,* ed. Karen Biesbrouck, Stephan Elders, and Gerda Rossel, 41–60. Leiden: Centre for Non-Western Studies, 1999.

———. The language of the Shom Pen. A language isolate in the Nicobar Islands. *Mother Tongue* 12 (2007): 179–202.

Blumenthal, Elke. Zur Göttlichkeit des regierenden Königs in Ägypten. *Orientalische Literaturzeitung* 73, no. 6 (1978): 534–41.

Blust, Robert. Beyond the Austronesian homeland: The Austric hypothesis and its implications for archaeology. In *Prehistoric settlement of the Pacific,* ed. Ward H. Goodenough, 117–37. Transactions of the American Philosophical Society 86, no. 5. Collingdale, Pa.: DIANE Publishing Co., 1996.

Bock, Felicia Gressit. *Engi-shiki; procedures of the Engi Era. Translated with introduction and notes.* Tokyo: Sophia University, 1970.

Bodde, D. Myths of ancient China. In S. N. Kramer, *Mythologies of the ancient world,* 367–408. New York: Doubleday, 1961.

Bogoras, W. *The Chukchee. Reports of the Jesup North Pacific Expedition.* New York: Memoirs of the American Museum of Natural History 11, 1907.

Bonatto, S. L., and F. M. Salzano. Diversity and age of the four major mtDNA haplogroups, and their implications for the peopling of the New World. *American Journal of Human Genetics* 61, no. 6 (December 1997): 1413–23.

Bopp, Franz. *Über das Conjugationssystem der Sanskritsprache: In Vergleichung mit jenem der griechischen, lateinischen, persischen und germanischen Sprache.* Frankfurt am Main: Andreäische, 1816.

Bornemann, F. Chronologie, Kulturkreis und Urkultur in der kulturhistorischen Methode. In *Historische Völkerkunde*, ed. C. A. Schmitz, 79–120. Frankfurt: Akademische Verlagsgesellschaft, 1967.

Bortolini, M. C., et al. Y-chromosome evidence for differing ancient demographic histories in the Americas. *American Journal of Human Genetics* 73 (2003): 524–39.

Bosch, F. D. K. *The golden germ: An introduction to Indian symbolism.* 's Gravenhage: Mouton, 1960.

Botto, Oscar. *Atti del nono Convegno nazionale di studi sanscriti: Genova, 23–24 ottobre 1997.* Torino: ETS, 1999.

Brauer, E. *Religion der Herero.* Leipzig, 1925.

Brednich, Rolf Wilhelm, et al., eds. *Enzyklopädie des Märchens. Handwörterbuch zur historischen und vergleichenden Erzählforschung.* Berlin, 1977–.

Breuil, Henri. *Four hundred centuries of cave art.* Montignac: Centre d'Etudes et Documentations Préhistoriques, 1952.

Brighenti, F. Buffalo sacrifice and tribal mortuary rituals. 2003, http://www.svabhinava.org/friends/FrancescoBrighenti/index.php.

———. *Sacrificio di bovini, rituale funerario e culto degli antenati nelle culture tribali dell'India e del sudest asiatico.* 2005, http://www.svabhinava.org/friends/FrancescoBrighenti/SacrificioBovini-frame.html.

Brockington, John. *The Sanskrit epics.* Leiden: Brill, 1998.

Brookes, More. *Ovid's Metamorphoses: Translation in blank verse.* Francestown, N.H.: Marshall Jones, 1978.

Brooks, Alison. Why East Africa is the homeland of modern humans. Presentaition at the 9th Round Table/ASLIP Conference, Cambridge, Mass., October 2006 (summary by H. Fleming). *Mother Tongue* 11 (2006): 85–90.

Brooks, Robert R., et al. *Stone Age painting in India.* New Haven: Yale University Press, 1976.

Brown, S. Art and Tasmanian prehistory: Evidence for changing cultural traditions in a changing environment. In Bahn and Rosenfeld 1991: 96–108.

Brown, W. M. Polymorphism in mitochondrial DNA of humans as revealed by restriction endonuclease analysis. *Proceedings of the National Academy of Sciences of the United States of America* 77, no. 6 (June 1980): 3605–9.

Brugmann, Karl. *Grundriss der vergleichenden Grammatik der indogermanischen Sprachen.* Strasbourg: Trübner, 1886–1900.

Bullen, E. An interpretation of women in the rock art of northern Australia. In Bahn and Rosenfeld 1991: 53–57.

Burkert, W. *Greek religion. Archaic and classical.* London: Blackwell, 1985.

———. *Homo Necans: The anthropology of ancient Greek sacrificial ritual and myth.* Berkeley: University of California Press, 1983 [1972].

———. The problem of ritual killing. In *Violent origins: Walter Burkert, René Girard, and Jonathan Z. Smith on ritual killing and cultural formation*, ed. R. Hammerton-Kelly, 149–76. Stanford: Stanford University Press, 1987.

———. *Structure and history in Greek mythology and ritual.* Berkeley: University of California Press, 1982 [1979].

Butlin, N. G. The paeleoeconomic history of aboriginal migration. *Australian Economic History Review* 29 (1989): 1–57.

Cacopardo, A. Shamans and the sphere of the "pure" among the Kalasha of the Hindu Kush. In Mastromattei and Rigopulos 1999: 57–71.

Cahill, Th. *Sailing the wine-dark sea. Why the Greeks matter.* New York: Anchor Books 2003.

Caland, W. *Kleine Schriften.* Ed. M. Witzel. Stuttgart, 1990.

Campbell, J. *The hero with a thousand faces.* Princeton: Princeton University Press, 1972. (Originally: New York: Meridian, 1956.)

———. *Historical atlas of world mythology: The way of the animal powers: Mythologies of the primitive hunter and gatherers,* vol. I, pts. 1–2. New York: Harper and Row, 1988.

———. *Historical atlas of world mythology,* vol. II, pts. 1–3. New York: Harper and Row, 1989.

———. *The meaning of myths.* New York: Bantam Boos, 1977.

———. *Myths to live by.* London: Paladin, 1985. (Originally: New York: Viking, 1972.)

———. *Primitive mythology.* New York: Penguin, 1991 [1987].

Campbell, J., with M. Toms. *An open life.* Ed. J. M. Hare and D. Briggs. Burdett: Larson, 1989.

Capell, A. History of Australia languages. A first approach. In *Australian linguistic studies,* ed. S. A. Wurm, 419–619. Canberra: Department of Linguistics, Research School of Pacific Studies, Australian National University, 1979.

Capriani, Lidio. Excavations in Andamanese kitchen middens. In *Actes du IVe Congrès International des Sciences Anthropologiques et Etnologiques,* tome 2, 250–53. Vienna, 1952.

Caries, Vila, et al. Multiple and ancient origins of the domestic dog. *Science* 276 (1997): 1687–89.

Carrín, Cristobo de Milio. *La creación del mundo y otros mitos asturianas.* Oviedo: C. de Milio, 2008.

Carrasco, David. *Quetzalcoatl and the irony of empire: Myths and prophecies in the Aztec tradition.* Chicago: University of Chicago Press, 1982.

Carter, G. F. Pre-Columbian chickens in S. America. In *Man across the sea,* ed. C. L. Riley, J. C. Kelley, C. W. Pennington, and T. L. Rands. Austin: University of Texas Press, 1971.

Casamiquela, R. Tehuelches, araucanos y otros en los últimos 500 años de poblamiento del ámbito patagónico. *Síntomas* 4 (1982): 17–29.

Cassirer, Ernst. *The myth of the state.* New Haven: Yale University Press, 1946.

———. *The philosophy of symbolic forms.* Trans. Ralph Manheim. Preface and intro. by Charles W. Hendel. New Haven: Yale University Press, 1953–96 [1925].

Cavalli-Sforza, Luigi L. Demic diffusion as the basic process of human expansions. In Bellwood and Renfrew 2002: 79–88.

———. Genes, peoples and languages. *Scientific American,* November 1991: 104–9.

———. *Genes, peoples, and languages.* New York: Farrar, Straus and Giroux, 2001.

Cavalli-Sforza, Luigi L., and Francesco Cavalli-Sforza. *The great human diasporas: The history of diversity and evolution.* Trans. from Italian by Sarah Thorne. Reading, Mass.: Addison-Wesley; and Cambridge, Mass.: Perseus Books, 1994.

Cavalli-Sforza, Luigi L., Francesco Cavalli-Sforza, et al. Reconstruction of human evolution: Bringing together genetic, archeological and linguistic data. *Proceedings of the National Academy of Sciences of the United States of America* 85 (1988): 6002–6.

Cavalli-Sforza, Luigi L., Paolo Menozzi, and Alberto Piazza. *The history and geography of human genes.* Princeton: Princeton University Press, 1994.

Chakravarty, K. K., ed. *Rock-art of India. Painting and engraving.* New Delhi: Arnold-Heinemann, 1984.

Chamberlain, Basil Hall. *The Kojiki. Records of ancient matters.* Rutland: Tuttle, 1981 [1882].

———. *The language, mythology, and geographical nomenclature of Japan viewed in the light of Aino studies. Including "An Ainu grammar"... and a catalogue of books relating to Yezo and the Ainos.* Tokyo: Imperial University, 1887.

Chang, K. C. *Art, myth and ritual. The path to political authority in ancient China.* Cambridge: Harvard University Press, 1983.

Chappell, J. Sea level changes forced ice breakouts in the last glacial cycle: New results from coral terraces. *Quarternary Science Review* 21 (2002): 1229–40.

Charachidzé, Georges. *La mémoire indo-européenne du Caucase.* Paris: Hachette, 1987.

Chatters, J. *Ancient encounters: Kennewick Man and the first Americans.* New York: Simon and Schuster, 2001.

Chaubey, G., et al. Peopling of South Asia: Investigating the caste–tribe continuum in India. *BioEssays* 20 (2006): 91–100.

Cheek, Charles D., and Balaji Mundkur. On the alleged diffusion of Hindu symbols to Mesoamerica. *Current Anthropology* 20, no. 1 (March 1979): 167–71.

Chiaroni, Jacques, Peter A. Underhill, and Luca L. Cavalli-Sforza. Y chromosome diversity, human expansion, drift, and cultural evolution. *Proceedings of the National Academy of Sciences of the United States of America* 106, no. 48 (December 1, 2009): 20174–79.

Chippindale, Christopher, et al. Visions of dynamic power: Archaic rock-paintings, altered states of consciousness and "clever men" in western Arnhem Land (NT), Australia. *Cambridge Archaeological Journal* 10 (2000): 63–101.

Christie, Anthony. Review of *Stone Age Painting in India* by Robert R. R. Brooks, Vishnu S. Wakankar. *Bulletin of the School of Oriental and African Studies, University of London* 41, no. 3 (1978): 614–15.

Cipriani, Lidio. *The Andaman Islanders.* Ed. and trans. D. Taylor Cox. London: Weidenfeld and Nicholson; and New York: F. A. Praeger, 1966.

———. Excavations in Andamanese kitchen-middens. In *Actes du IVᵉ congrès international des sciences anthropologiques,* tome 2, 250–53. Vienna, 1952.

———. On the origin of the Andamanese. *Census of India 1951.* Delhi: Government of India, 1951.

Clark, J. *The Aboriginal people of Tasmania.* Hobart: Tasmanian Museum and Art Gallery, 1983.

Clendon, Mark. Reassessing Australia's linguistic prehistory. *Current Anthropology* 47 (2006): 673–77.

Clooney, F. *Divine mother, blessed mother.* New York: Oxford University Press, 2006.

Colarusso, J. Affinities of the Northwest Caucasian Nart sagas. Presentation at the Second Conference on the Cultures of the Caucasus, University of Chicago, May 1985a.

———. The Functions revisited. A Nart god of war and three Nart heroes. *Journal of Indo-European Studies* 34 (2006): 27–54.

———. *Nart sagas from the Caucasus: Myths and legends from the Circassians, Abazas, Abkhaz, and Ubykhs.* Assembled, trans., and annotated by John Colarusso, with the assistance of B. George Hewitt et al. Princeton: Princeton University Press, 2002.

———. Parallels between the Circassian Nart sagas, the *RgVeda* and Germanic mythology. In *South Asian horizons, I: Culture and philosophy,* ed. V. S. Pendakar, 1–28. Ottawa: Canadian Asian Studies Association, 1985b.

———. Some interesting women of the Circassian Nart sagas: Lady Tree and Amazon, the Forest Mother. Presentation at the Third Conference on the Cultures of the Caucasus, University of Chicago, May 1987.

Colopano, J. The interpreter. Has a remote Amazonian tribe upended our understanding of language? *The New Yorker,* April 16, 2007: 119–37.

Colum, P. *Legends of Hawaii.* New Haven: Yale University Press, 1937.

Conkey, Margaret W., and Ruth E. Tringham. Archaeology and the goddess: Exploring the contours of feminist archaeology. In *Feminisms in the academy,* ed. D. C. Stanton and A. J. Stewart, 199–247. Ann Arbor: University of Michigan Press, 1995.

Connah, G. *Forgotten Africa: An introduction to its archaeology.* London: Routledge, 2004.

Cooper, Zarine. *Archaeology and history—Early settlements in the Andaman Islands.* New Delhi: Oxford University Press, 2002.

Cordaux, Richard, et al. The northeast Indian passageway: A barrier or corridor for human migrations? *Molecular Biology and Evolution* 21 (2004): 1525–33.

Crowley, T., and R. M. W. Dixon. Tasmanian. In *Handbook of Australian languages,* ed. R. M. W. Dixon and B. J. Blake, 394–427. Canberra: Australian National University Press, 1981.

Culotta, Elizabeth. Ancient DNA reveals Neandertals with red hair, fair complexion. *Science* 318 (October 26, 2007): 546–47.

Dalley, S. *Myths from Mesopotamia. Creation, the flood, Gilgamesh and others.* Oxford: Oxford University Press, 1989.

Dammann, E. *Die Religionen Afrikas.* Stuttgart, 1963.

Darwin, Charles. *The zoology of the voyage of H.M.S. Beagle, under the command of Captain Fitzroy, R.N., during the years 1832 to 1836. Published with the approval of the Lords Commissioners of Her Majesty's Treasury.* Ed. and superintended by Charles Darwin. London: Smith, Elder and Co., 1839–43.

Davis, Richard B. *Muang methaphysiscs. A study of northern Thai myth and ritual.* Bangkok: Pandora, 1984.

Dawkins, Richard. *The God delusion.* Boston: Houghton Mifflin, 2006.

———. *Unweaving the rainbow: Science, delusion and the appetite for wonder.* Boston: Houghton Mifflin, 1998.

Day, Michael H. *Guide to fossil man: A handbook of human palaeontology.* 3rd ed., completely rev. and enlarged. Chicago: University of Chicago Press, 1977.

Day, M. S. *The many meanings of myth.* Lanham, Md.: University Press of America, 1984.

Décsy, Gyula. The Uralic protolanguage: A comprehensive reconstruction. *Etude descriptive générale du proto-ouralien et glossaires proto-ouralien-anglais. Ural-altaische Jahrbücher* 62 (1990): 9–147.

de Heusch, L. *Le roi ivre, ou l'origine de l'état. Mythes et rites Bantous.* Paris, 1972.

de la Garza, Mercedes. The solar god in Maya religion. Presentation at the 19th World Congress of the International Association for the History of Religions, Tokyo, March 2005.

Dempwolf, Otto. *Die Sandawe: Linguistisches und ethnographisches Material aus Deutsch-Ostafrika.* Hamburg: L. Friederichsen, 1916.

Denham, Tim, et al. New evidence and revised interpretations of early agriculture in highland New Guinea. *Antiquity* 78 (2004): 839–57.

de Santillana, G., and H. von Dechend. *Hamlet's mill. An essay on myth and the frame of time.* Boston: Godine, 1977.

de Saussure, Ferdinand. *Course in general linguistics.* Trans. Wade Baskin. New York: Philosophical Library, 1959.

Deshpande, Madhav. What to do with the Anaryas? In *Aryan and non-Aryan in South Asia: Evidence, interpretation and ideology,* ed. Johannes Bronkhorst and Madhav M. Deshpande, 107–27. Cambridge: Department of Sanskrit and Indian Studies, Harvard University, 1999.

De Silva, M. W. Sugathapala. *Vedda language of Ceylon; texts and lexicon.* Münchener Studien zur Sprachwissenschaft. Beiheft n.F. 7. Munich: R. Kitzinger, 1972.

Devlin, Joseph T. Language: Are we dancing apes? *Science* 314 (November 10, 2006): 926–27.

de Vries, Jan. *Betrachtungen zum Märchen, besonders in seinem Verhältnis zu Heldensage und Mythos.* Helsinki: Suomalainen Tiedeakatemia, 1954.

Dharmadāsa, K. N. O., and S. W. R. de A. Samarasinghe, eds. *The vanishing aborigines: Sri Lanka's Veddas in transition.* New Delhi: International Centre for Ethnic Studies, in association with NORAD and Vikas Pub. House, 1990.

Dickson, D. Bruce. *The dawn of belief: Religion in the Upper Palaeolithic of southwestern Europe.* Tuscon: University of Arizona Press, 1990.

Diffloth, Gérard. The contribution of linguistic palaeontology to the homeland of Austroasiatic. In Sagart et al. 2005: 77–80.

———. Tentative calibration of time depths of Austroasiatic branches. Presentation at "Perspectives sur la Phylogénie des Langues d'Asie Orientales," Périgueux, France, August 30, 2001.

Digitale, Erin. Genetic evidence traces ancient African migration. 2008, http://news.stanford.edu/news/2008/august6/med-ychrome-080608.html.

Dixon, R. *Oceanic mythology.* Boston: Marshall Jones, 1916.

Dixon, R. M. W. *Australian languages. Their nature and development.* Cambridge: Cambridge University Press, 2002.

———. *The languages of Australia.* New York: Cambridge University Press, 1980.

Doht, Renate. *Der Rauschtrank im germanischen Mythos.* Vienna, 1974.

Dolgopolsky, Aharon, et al. *The Nostratic macrofamily and linguistic palaeontology.* Intro. by Colin Renfrew. Cambridge: McDonald Institute for Archaelogical Research, 1998.

Donegan, Patricia, and David Stampe. Rhythm and the synthetic drift of Munda. In *The yearbook of South Asian languages and linguistics 2004*, ed. Rajendra Singh, 3–36. Berlin: Mouton de Gruyter, 2004.

Doniger, Wendy. *The implied spider: Politics and theology in myth.* New York: Columbia University Press, 1998.

———. *The origins of evil in Hindu mythology.* Berkeley: University of California Press, 1976.

———. Review of C. Ginsburg, *Deciphering the Witches' Sabbath.* Translated by Raymond Rosenthal. Illustrated. 399 pp. New York: Pantheon Books. *New York Times Book Review*, July 14, 1991: 3, 26.

Doty, W. *Mythography. The study of myths and rituals.* Tuscaloosa: University of Alabama Press, 2000 [1986].

Dumézil, Georges. *Mythe et Epopée*, vols. 1–3. Paris: Gallimard, 1995 [1968].

———. *Ouranos–Váruṇa.* Paris, 1934.

Dundes, A., ed. *The flood myth.* Berkeley: University of California Press, 1988.

Dunkel, G. Vater Himmels Gattin. *Die Sprache* 34 (1988–90): 1–26.

Dunn, Michael, et al. Structural phylogenetics and the reconstruction of ancient language history. *Science Magazine* 309 (2005): 2072–75.

Durkheim, Emile. *The elementary forms of the religious life: A study in religious sociology.* Trans. from French by Joseph Ward Swain. London: G. Allen and Unwin; and New York: Macmillan, 1915. (Originally: *Formes élémentaires de la vie religieuse.*)

———. *Les formes élémentaires de la vie religieuse: Le système totémique en Australie.* 2d ed. rev. Paris: F. Alcan, 1925.

Eberhard, W. Die Kultur und Siedlung der Randvölker Chinas nach modernen Gesichtspunkten. *T'oung Pao*, suppl. 36 (1942).

———. *The local cultures of South and East China.* Leiden: Brill, 1968.

Ehret, C. *A historical-comparative reconstruction of Nilo-Saharan.* Cologne, 2001.

———. Language family expansions: Broadening our understandings of cause from an African perspective. In Bellwood and Renfrew 2002: 163–76.

————. *Reconstructing Proto-Afroasiatic (Proto-Afrasian). Vowels, tone, consonants and vocabulary.* Berkeley: University of California Press, 1995.

————. Testing the expectations of glottochronology against the correlations of language and archaeology in Africa. In *Time depth in historical linguistics*, ed. Colin Renfrew, April McMahon, and Larry Trask. Cambridge: McDonald Institute for Archaeological Research, 2000.

Eibl-Eibesfeldt, I. *Die Biologie des menschlichen Verhaltens. Grundriss der Humanethologie.* Weyarn, 1997.

Eliade, Mircea. *Chamanisme et les techniques archaïques de l'extase* [Shamanism: archaic techniques of ecstasy]. Trans. from French by Willard R. Trask. London: Arkana, 1989.

————. *Das Heilige und das Profane: Vom Wesen des Religiösen.* Hamburg: Rowohlt, 1957. (Originally: *Le sacré et la profane.*)

————. *Die Religionen und das Heilige.* Frankfurt: Insel, 1998 [1949]. (Originally: *Traité d'histoire des Religions.*)

————. *Dreams and mysteries.* New York: Harper and Row, 1960.

————. *Essential sacred writings from around the world.* Repr. San Francisco: Harper, 1992. (Originally: *From primitives to Zen.* New York: Harper and Row, 1967.)

————. *Geschichte der religiösen Ideen*, 1. Freiburg: Herder, 2009 [1978]. (Originally: *Histoire des croyances et des idées religieuses 1. De l'âge de la pierre aux mystères d'Eleusis.* Paris, 1970.)

————. Le problem du chamanisme. *Revue de l'Histoire des Religions* 131 (1946): 5–52.

————. *Méphistophélès et l'androgyne.* Paris, 1962.

————. *Myth and reality.* Harper Torch Book, 1963.

————. *Mythe de l'éternel retour* [The myth of the eternal return]. Trans. from French by Willard R. Trask. New York: Pantheon Books, 1954a.

————. *Patterns in comparative religion.* London: Routledge and Kegan Paul, 1958.

————. *Schamanismus und archaische Ekstasetechnik.* Zurich: Rascher, 1954b. (Originally: *Le chamanisme et les techniques archaiques de l'extase.* Paris: Payot, 1951; trans.: *Shamanism: Archaic techniques of ecstacy.* New York: Pantheon Books, 1964.)

————. Shamanism. In *Forgotten religions*, ed. Vergilius Fer, 299–308. Princeton: Princeton University Press, 1974. (Originally: New York: Philosophical Library, 1949.)

Ellwood, R. *The politics of myth: A study of C. G. Jung, Mircea Eliade, and Joseph Campbell.* Issues in the Study of Religion Series. Albany: State University of New York Press, 1999.

Endicott, Phillip, et al. The genetic origins of the Andaman Islanders. *American Journal of Human Genetics* 72 (2003): 1590–93.

Enzyklopädie des Märchens. Handwörterbuch zur historischen und vergleichenden Erzählforschung. Ed. Rolf Wilhelm Brednich et al. Berlin, 1977–.

Erdosi, R., and A. Ortiz. *American Indian myths and legends.* New York: Pantheon, 1984.

Etter, A. *Die Flut-Sage.* Habilitations-Schrift. Zurich, 1989.

Eugenio, Damiana L. *Philippine folk literature. The myths.* Diliman, Quezon City: University of the Philippines Press, 1993.

Evans, Ivor H. N. *Studies in religion, folk-lore and custom in British North-Borneo and the Malay Pensinsula.* Cambridge: Cambridge University Press, 1923.

Evans, Nicholas. *The non-Pama-Nyungan languages of northern Australia: Comparative studies of the continent's most linguistically complex region.* Canberra: Pacific Linguistics, Research School of Pacific and Asian Studies, Australian National University, 2003.

Evans, Nicholas, and R. Jones. The cradle of the Pama-Nyungans: Archaeological and linguistic speculations. In *Archaeology and linguistics: Aboriginal Australia in global per-*

spective, ed. P. McConvell and N. Evans, 385–417. Oxford: Oxford University Press, 1997.

Evelyn-White, Hugh G. *Hesiod. The Homeric Hymns and Homerica.* Loeb Classical Library. Cambridge: Harvard University Press, 1977.

Everett, Dan. Cultural constraints on grammar and cognition in Piranhā. *Cultural Anthropology* 46, no. 4 (August 2005): 621–46.

Falk, Harry. *Bruderschaft und Würfelspiel.* Freiburg: Hedwig Falk, 1986.

———. Goodies for India. Literacy, orality and Vedic culture. In *Erscheinungsformen kultureller Prozesse: Jahrbuch 1988 des Sonderforschungsbereichs "Übergänge und Spannungsfelder zwischen Mündlichkeit und Schriftlichkeit,"* ed. Wolfgang Raible, 103–20. Tübingen: Narr, 1990.

Farmer, Steve. The neurobiological origins of primitive religion. In van Binsbergen and Venbrux 2010: 279–314.

Farmer, S., J. B. Henderson, and M. Witzel. Neurobiology, layered texts, and correlative cosmologies: A cross-cultural framework for premodern history. *Bulletin of the Museum of Far Eastern Antiquities* 72 (2002 [2000]): 48–90.

Feddersen, Arthur. To Mosefund. *Aarböger for nordisk Oldkyndighed og Historie,* 1881: 368–89.

Feldman, B., and R. D. Richardson. *The rise of modern mythology 1680–1860.* Indiana University Press, 1972.

Filippi, G. G. The celestial ride. In Mastromattei and Rigopulos 1999: 73–87.

Findeisen, H. *Dokumente urtümlicher Weltanschauung der Völker Nordasiens.* Oosterhout: Anthropological Publications, 1970.

Fisher, Simon. Tangled webs: Tracing the connections between genes and cognition. *Cognition* 101 (2006): 270–97.

Fleming, Harold. [Editorial.] *Long Ranger* 34b (2003), http://www.people.fas.harvard.edu/~witzel/MTLR-34b.htm.

Flood, Josephine. *Archaeology of the Dreamtime.* Honolulu: University of Hawai'i Press, 1983.

Foley, William A. *The Papuan languages of New Guinea.* Cambridge: Cambridge University Press, 1986.

Fontenrose, Joseph Eddy. *Python.* Berkeley: University of California Press, 1980 [1959].

Fornander, A., trans. *An account of the Polynesian race; its origins and migrations, and the ancient history of the Hawaiian people to the times of Kamehameha I.* 3 vols. Rutland: Tuttle, 1969. (Originally: London: Trübner, 1879–85.)

Forster, P., and S. Matsumura. Did early huamns go north or south? Where Out-of-Africa humans entered Asia. *Science* 3008 (2005): 965–66.

Forster, P., and C. Renfrew. The DNA chronology of prehistoric human dispersals. In Bellwood and Renfrew 2002: 89–97.

Forster, P., et al. Phylogenetic star contraction applied to Asian and Papuan mtDNA evolution. *Molecular Biology and Evolution* 18 (2001): 1864–81.

Francfort, H.-P. The Central Asian dimension of the symbolic system in Bactria and Margiana. *Antiquity* 68 (1994): 406–18.

Francfort, H.-P., R. N. Hamayon, and P. G. Bahn, eds. *The concept of shamanism: Uses and abuses.* Budapest: Akadémiai Kiadó, 2001.

Franklin, N. Explorations of the Panaramite style. In Bahn and Rosenfeld 1991: 120–35.

Frazer, James George. *The golden bough: A study in magic and religion.* 3rd ed. London: Macmillan; and New York: St. Martin's Press, 1963 [1890].

————. *Totemism and exogamy: A treatise on certain early forms of superstition and society.* London: Macmillan, 1910.

Freidel, D., L. Schele, and J. Parker. *Maya cosmos. Three thousand years on the shaman's path.* New York: Quill/William Morrow, 1993.

Freud, Sigmund. *Collected papers.* Authorized trans. under the supervision of Joan Riviere. New York: Basic Books, 1959.

Frobenius, L. *Atlantis. Volskmärchen und Volksdichtungen Afrikas.* Repr. Nendeln: Kraus, 1978.

————. *Kulturgeschichte Afrikas.* Frankfurt: Hammer, 1998. (Originally: Vienna, 1933; Zurich: Phaidon, 1954.)

————. *Monumenta Africana. Erlebte Erdteile; Ergebnisse eines deutschen Forscherlebens.* Frankfurt/Main: Frankfurter Societätsdruckerei, 1925–29.

————. *Volksdichtungen aus Oberguinea, vol. 1. Fabuleien dreier Völker.* Jena: Diederichs, 1924.

————. *Vom Kulturreich des Festlandes.* Berlin, 1923.

————. *Zeitalter des Sonnengottes.* Berlin, 1904.

Froment, Alain. La différenciation morphologique de l'homne moderne. Congruence entre forme du crâne et répartition géographique du peuplement. *Comptes rendues de l'Académie des sciences* 315, série 3 (1992): 323–29.

Fromm, L., and H. Fromm. *Kalevala. Das finnische Eops des Elias Lönrot.* Stuttgart: Reclam, 1985.

Fuller, Dorian Q. Contrasting patterns in crop domestication and domestication rates: Recent archaeobotanical insights from the Old World. *Annals of Botany,* AOB *Preview,* May 10, 2007, doi:10.1093/aob/mcm048.

————. The emergence of agricultural societies in South India: Laying a foundation. Ph.D. dissertation, University of Cambridge, Cambridge, 1999.

————. Silence before sedentism and the advent of cash-crops: A status report and early agriculture in South Asia from plant domestication to the development of political economies (with an excursus on the problem of semantic shift among millets and rice). In Osada 2006: 175–213.

Fuller, D., R. Korisettar, P. C. Vankatasubbaiah, and M. K. Jones. Early plant domestications in southern India: Some preliminary archaeobotanical results. *Vegetation History and Archaeobotany* 13 (2004): 115–29.

Fussell, Paul. *Class.* New York: Ballantine, 1983.

Gardner, J. and J. Maier. *Gilgamesh, with the assistance of R. A. Henshaw. Translated from the Sîn-Leqi-Unninnī version.* New York: Random, 1984.

Gaster, Theodor Herzl. *The oldest stories in the world: Originally translated and retold, with comments.* New York: Viking Press, 1958 [1952].

Gayden, Tenzin, et al. The Himalayas as directional barrier to gene flow. *American Journal of Human Genetics* 80 (2007): 884–94.

Geneste, J. *La grotte Chauvet à Vallon-Pont-d'Arc: Un bilan des recherches pluridisciplinaires: Actes de la scéance de la Société préhistorique française, 11 et 12 octobre 2003, Lyon [sous la direction de Jean-Michel Geneste].* [Paris]: Société préhistorique française, 2005.

Gibbons, Ann. Coastal artifacts suggest early beginnings for modern behavior. *Science* 318, no. 5849 (October 19, 2007): 377.

Gichuki, S. T., et al. Genetic diversity in sweetpotato (*Ipomoea batatas* [L.] Lam.) in relationship to geographic sources as assessed with RAPD marker. *Genetic Resources and Crop Evolution* 50 (2003): 429–37.

Gilmore, Donald Y., and Linda S. McElroy, eds. *Across before Columbus? Evidence for transoceanic contact with the Americas prior to 1492.* Edgecomb, Me.: New England Antiquities Research Association, NEARA Publications, 1998.

Gimbutas, M. *The language of the goddess: Unearthing the hidden symbols of Western civilization*. New York: Harper San Francisco, 1991. (Originally: Thames and Hudson, 1989.)

Glover, I. C., and G. Presland. Microliths in Indonesian flaked stone industries. In *Recent advances in Indo-Pacific prehistory*, ed. V. N. Misra and P. Bellwood, 185–95. New Delhi: Oxford University Press and IBH, 1985.

Gollan, K. Prehistoric dogs in Australia: An Indian origin? In *Recent advances in Indo-Pacific prehistory*, ed. V. N. Misra and P. Bellwood, 439–43. New Delhi: Oxford University Press and IBH, 1985.

González-Reimann, Luis. *The Mahābhārata and the Yugas: India's great epic poem and the Hindu system of world ages*. New York: Peter Lang, 2002.

Goodchild, Peter. *Raven tales*. Chicago: Chicago Review Press, 1991.

Goodwin, William, and Igor Ovchinnikov. Ancient DNA and the Neanderthals. In Bandelt et al. 2006.

Gonda, Jan. De indische zondvlooet-mythe. *Verhandelingen der Koninklijke Nederlandse Akademie van Wetenschappen, Afdeling Letterkunde, NR deel* 41, no. 2 (1978): 27–46.

Gotō, Toshifumi. Aśvin and Nāsatya in the Ṛgveda and their prehistoric background. In Osada 2006: 253–83.

Gottschalk, Herbert. *Lexikon der Mythologie*. Munich: Heyne, 1979.

Gould, Richard A. The mystery of the prehistoric "Chinese anchors": Toward research designs. In *Shipwreck anthropology*, ed. Richard A. Gould. Los Angeles: University of New Mexico Press, 1983a.

Gould, Richard A., ed. *Shipwreck anthropology*. Albuquerque: University of New Mexico Press, 1983b.

Gould, Stephen Jay. Creationism vs. geology. In *The flood myth*, ed. A. Dundes, 427–37. Berkeley: University of California Press, 1988.

Graham-Rowe, D. A working brain model. A computer simulation could eventually allow neuroscience to be carried out in silico. *Technology Review* [MIT], November 28, 2007, http://www.technologyreview.com/Biotech/19767/?nlid=692.

Granet, Marcel. *La pensée chinoise*. Repr. Paris: Albin Michel, 1988. (Originally: Paris: La Renaissance du livre, 1934.)

———. *La religion des Chinois*. Paris: Imago, 1989.

Graves, Charles. *Old Eurasian and Amerindian onomastics*. Bochum: Brockmeyer, 1997.

———. *Proto-religions in Central Asia*. Bochum: Brockmeyer, 1994.

Graves, R. *Greek myths*. Baltimore: Penguin Books, 1955.

Gray, Russel D., amd Quentin D. Atkinson. Language-tree divergence times support the Anatolian theory of Indo-European origin. *Nature* 426 (2003): 435–39.

Greenberg, Joseph H. *Indo-European and its closest relatives: The Eurasiatic language family, vol. I: Grammar*. Stanford: Stanford University Press, 1987a.

———. *Indo-European and its closest relatives: The Eurasiatic language family, vol. II: Lexicon*. Stanford: Stanford University Press, 2000–2002.

———. The Indo-Pacific hypothesis. In *Current trends in linguistics VIII*, ed. Thomas Sebeok, 807–71. The Hague: Mouton, 1971.

———. *Language in the Americas*. Stanford: Stanford University Press, 1987b.

———. *The languages of Africa*. Indiana University Press, 1963.

Greimas, Algirdas J. *Of gods and men. Studies in Lithuanaian mythology*. Trans. Milda Newman. Bloomington: Indiana University Press, 1985. (Originally: *Apie dievus ir žmones; Des dieux et des hommes*. Paris.)

Grey, George. *Polynesian mythology and ancient traditional history of the New Zealand race, as furnished by their priests and chiefs.* Christchurch: Whitcomb and Tombs, 1956 [1855]. (Originally: In Maori, 1854.)

Griaule, M. *Dieu d' Eau. Entretiens avec Ogotemmêli.* Paris: du Chêne, 1948.

Grimm, Wilhelm, and Ludwig Grimm. *Kinder- und Hausmärchen gesammelt durch die Brüder Grimm. Vollständige Ausgabe auf der Grundlage der dritten Auflage* (1837) [*Grimm's Märchen*]. Ed. Heinz Rölleke. Frankfurt: Deutscher Klassiker Verlag, 2003.

Grosman, Leore, et al. Skeleton of 12,000-year-old shaman discovered buried with leopard, 50 tortoises and human foot. *Science Daily*, November 8, 2008.

Guillemoz, A. *Les algues, les anciens, les dieux. La vie et la religion d'un village de pêcheurs-agriculteurs coreens.* Paris: Léopard d'Or, 1983.

Gurney, O. R. *The Hittites.* Harmondsworth, England: Penguin, 1976 [1952].

———. *Some aspects of Hittite religion.* Oxford: Oxford University Press, 1977.

Gusinde, Martin. *Die Feuerland Indianer; Ergebnisse meiner vier Forschungsreisen in den Jahren 1918 bis 1924. Unternommen im Auftrage des Ministerio de Instrucción pública de Chile; in drei Bänden herausgegeben von Martin Gusinde, Bd. 1: Die Selk'nam; vom Leben und Denken eines Jägervolkes auf der grossen Feuerlandinsel, Bd. 2: Die Yamana; vom Leben und Denken der Wassernomaden am Kap Hoorn, Bd. 3: T. 1. Die Halakwulup.* Trans. J. Wilbert. Folk Literature of the Yamana Indians. Los Angeles: University of California Press (Latin American Studies), 1977 [1975]. (Originally: Mödling bei Wien: Verlag der Internationalen Zeitschrift "Anthropos," 1931–.).

Ha, Tae-Hung, and Grafton Mintz. *Samguk Yusa: Legends and history of the Three Kingdoms of ancient Korea.* Seoul: Yonsei University Press, 1972.

Haas, V. *Hethitische Berggötter und hurritische Steindämonen: Riten, Kulte und Mythen: eine Einführung in die altkleinasiatischen religiösen Vorstellungen.* Mainz: Zabern, 1982.

Haguenauer, Charles. *Origines de la civilisation japonaise. Introduction à l'étude de la préhistoire du Japon.* Paris: Klincksiek, 1956.

Hale, Horatio. *Ethnography and philology.* Philadelphia: Lea and Blanchard, 1846.

Hamayon, R. *La chasse à l'âme: Esquisse d'une théorie du chamanisme sibérien.* Nanterre: Société d'ethnologie, 1990.

———. Le chamanisme siberien: Reflexion sur un medium. *La Recherche* 26 (1990): 417–22.

Hamilton, A. Dual social systems: Technology, labour and women's rights in eastern Western Desert of Australia. *Oceania* 51 (1980): 4–19.

Handwörterbuch des deutschen Aberglaubens. Berlin: de Gruyter, 1987.

Harich, Wolgang. *Nicolai Hartmann: Leben, Werk, Wirkung, hrsg. von Martin Morgenstern.* Würzburg: Königshausen und Neumann, 2000.

Harrod, J. Periods of globalization over "the southern route" in human evolution (Africa, Southwest Asia, Southern Asia, Southeast Asia, and Sahul and the Far East). A meta-review of archaeology and evidence for symbolic behavior. *Mother Tongue* 11 (2006): 23–84.

Hartmann, Nicolai. *Anthropologie.* Goeschen, 1960.

Harva, Uno. *Die religiösen Vorstellungen der altaischen Völker.* Helsinki: FF Communications 125, 1938.

Harvey, G. *Shamanism, a reader.* London: Routledge, 2002.

Hastings, J., ed. *Encyclopaedia of religion and ethics, edited by James Hastings. With the assistance of John A. Selbie and other scholars.* Edinburgh: T. and T. Clark; and New York: Scribner, 1922–28.

Hatt, G. The corn mother in America and Indonesia. *Anthropos* 46 (1951): 853–914.

Haudry, Jean. *La religion cosmique des Indo-Européens.* Milan: Archè; and Paris: Les Belles Lettres, 1987 [1986].

Havens, Norman, and Nobutaka Inoue. *An encyclopedia of Shinto (Shintō Jiten), vol.* 1: *Kami.* Tokyo: Institute for Japanese Culture and Classics, Kokugakuin University, 2001.

Hawks, John, et al. Recent acceleration of human adaptive evolution. *Proceedings of the National Academy of Sciences of the United States of America* 104 (2007): 20753–58.

Head, Lyndsay F. Land, authority and the forgetting of being in early colonial Maori history. Ph.D. dissertation, University of Canterbury, 2006.

Hegedüs, I., and P. Sidwell, eds. *Nostratic Centennial Conference: The Pécs papers.* Pécs: Lingua Franca Group, 2004.

Heidel, A. *The Gilgamesh Epic and Old Testament parallels. A translation and interpretation of the Gilgamesh Epic and related Babylonian and Assyrian documents.* Chicago: University of Chicago Press, 1963 [1946].

Heine, Bernd. *African languages: An introduction.* Ed. Bernd Heine and Derek Nurse. Cambridge: Cambridge University Press, 2000.

Heissig, W. *The religions of Mongolia.* Berkeley: University of California Press, 1980.

Herbert, J. *La cosmogonie japonaise.* Paris: Hervy, 1977.

Herbig, J. *Nahrung für die Götter.* Munich, 1988.

Hillebrandt, Alfred. Vedic mythology. Trans. from German by Sreeramula Rajeswara Sarma (1927). 1st English language ed. Delhi: Motilal Banarsidass, 1980–81.

Hiltebeitel, A. Rama and Gilgamesh: The sacrifices of the water buffalo and the bull of heaven. *History of Religions* 19 (1980): 187–223.

Hirafuji, Kikuko. *Shinwagaku to Nihon no Kamigami* [Mythography and the Japanese deities]. Tokyo: Koubundo, 2004.

Hirth, Friedrich, and W. W. Rockhill. *Chau Ju-kua: His work on the Chinese and Arab trade in the twelfth and thirteenth centuries, entitled Chu-fan-chi.* Taipeh: Ch'eng-Wen Publishing Co., 1970 [1911].

Hochegger, Hermann. *Congolese myths about beginnings. Variations from 1906 to 1994.* Trans. from French by Timothy D. Stabell. Mödling: Antenne d'Autriche, 2005, http://www. ceeba.at/myth/myths_of_the_beginnings.htm.

Hochgeschwender, M. *Amerikanische Religion. Evangekalismus, Pfingstlertum und Fundamentalismus.* Frankfurt: Verlag der Weltreligionen, 2007.

Hock, H. H. *Principles of historical linguistics.* Berlin: Mouton de Gruyter, 1986.

Hoffmann, K. Mārtāṇḍa und Gayōmart. Repr. In *Aufsätze zur Indoiranistik,* ed. S. Glauch et al., 715–32. Wiesbaden, 1992. (Originally: *Münchener Studien zur Sprachwissenschaft* 11 [1957]: 85–103.)

Holmberg, (Harva) Uno. *Finno-Ugric, Siberian [mythology].* New York: Cooper Square Publishers, 1964. (Originally: Boston, 1927.)

Hong Shang, et al. An early modern human from Tianyuan Cave, Zhoukoudian, China. *Proceedings of the National Academy of Sciences of the United States of America* 104, no. 16 (April 17, 2007): 6573–78.

Hopkins, Michael. Old tools shed light on hobbit origins. *Nature* 441, no. 559 (June 1, 2006): 559.

Horowitz, Wayne. The Babylonian map of the world. *Iraq* 50 (1988): 147–65.

Horton, Robin. African traditional thought and Western science. In *Witchcraft and sorcery,* ed. Max Marwick, 342–68. Harmondsworth, England: Penguin, 1975.

Howitt, A. W. *The native tribes of southeast Australia.* London: Macmillan, 1904.

Hu, Chongjun. *Hei an zhuan* [The story of darkness]. In Chinese. Wuhan: Changjiang Art Publishing House, 2002.

Hubert, Henri. *Essai sur la Nature et la Fonction du Sacrifice* [Essays on the nature and function of sacrifice]. Trans. W. D. Halls. Foreword by E. E. Evans-Pritchard. Chicago: University of Chicago Press, 1964. (Originally: Pt. 2 in *Mélanges d'histoire des religions*, ed. H. Hubert and M. Mauss. Paris: F. Alcan, 1909.)

Hübner, Kurt. *Die Wahrheit des Mythos*. Munich: Beck, 1985.

Hudjashov, Georgi, et al. Revealing the prehistoric settlement of Australia, Y-chromosome and mtDNA analysis. *Proceedings of the National Academy of Sciences of the United States of America* 104, no. 21 (May 22, 2007): 8726–30.

Hunger, H. *Lexikon der griechischen und römischen Mythologie*. Hamburg: Rohwolt, 1984.

Huntingdon, Samuel P. The clash of civilizations? *Foreign Affairs* 72 (1993): 22–49.

Hurles, Matthew E., et al. Native American Y chromosomes in Polynesia: The genetic impact of the Polynesian slave trade. *American Journal of Human Genetics* 72 (2003): 1282–87.

Huxley, T. H. On the geographcial distribution of the chief modifications of mankind. *Journal of the Ethnological Society of London* 2 (1870): 404–12.

Huyge, D., et al. Lascaux along the Nile: Late Pleistocene rock art in Egypt. *Antiquity* 81, no. 313 (September 2007), http://antiquity.ac.uk/projgall/huyge/index.html.

Idowu, E. Bọlaji. *African traditional religion: A definition*. Maryknoll, N.Y.: Orbis Books, 1973.

Illich-Svitych, Vladislav Markovich. *Opyt sravneniia nostraticheskikh iazykov: semitokhamitskii, kartvel'skii, indoevropeiskii, ural'skii, dvadidiiskii, altaiskii*. Moscow: Nauka, 1971–.

Inoue, Nobutaka, ed. *Kami*. Contemporary Papers on Japanese Religion, 4. Tokyo: Institute for Japanese Culture and Classics, Kokugakuin University, 1998.

Ions, V. *Egyptian mythology*. Library of the World's Myths and Legends, 1990 [1982].

Irwin, J. "Asokan" pillars: A reassessment of the evidence. *Burlington Magazine* 115, no. 848 (November 1973): 706–20.

———. The sacred anthill and the cult of the primordial mound. *History of Religions* 22, no. 2 (1982): 339–60.

———. The true chronology of Asokan pillars. *Artibus Asiae* 44, no. 4 (1983): 247–65.

Ivanov, V., and V. N. Toporov. *Issledovaniia v oblasti slavianskix drevnostei. Leksicheskie i frazeologicheskie voprosy rekonstrukcii tekstov*. Moscow, 1974.

Jacobsen, Thorkild. *The treasures of darkness. A history of Mesopotamian religion*. New Haven: Yale University Press, 1976.

James, Hannah V. A. The emergence of modern behavior in South Asia: A review of the current evidence and discussion of its possible implications. In Petraglia and Allchin 2007: 204–27.

Jaspert, B., ed. *Bibel und Mythos: Fünfzig Jahre nach R. Bultmanns Entmythologisierungsprogramm*. Stuttgart, 1991.

Jensen, Ad. E. *Die drei Ströme*. Leipzig: Harrassowitz, 1948.

———. *Die getötete Gottheit*. Stuttgart: Kohlhammer, 1968.

———. *Hainuwele*. New York: Arno Press, 1978. (Originally: Frankfurt: Klostermann, 1939.)

———. *Mythos und Kult bei Naturvölkern. Religionswissenschaftliche Betrachtungen*. Wiesbaden: Steiner, 1951.

Jettmar, K. *Die Religionen des Hindukusch*. Stuttgart: Kohlhammer, 1975.

Ježić, Mislav. Can a monkey play a bitch? In *Epics, Khilas, and Purāṇas. Continuities and ruptures. Proceedings of the Third Dubrovnik International Conference on the Sanskrit Epics and Purāṇas. September 2002*, ed. P. Koskikallio, 255–93. Zagreb: Croatian Academy of Sciences and the Arts, 2005.

Jiroft. Fabuleuse Découverte en Iran. In *Dossiers d'Archéologie*. Dijon: Editions Faton, October 2003.

Jobling, M. A., and C. Tyler-Smith. The human Y chromosome: An evolutionary marker comes of age. *Nature* 4 (August 2003): 598–612.

Jomon vs Yayoi. Tokyo: National Science Museum, 2005.

Jones, Peter N. *American Indian mtDNA, Y chromosome genetic data, and the peopling of North America*. Boulder: Bäuu Institute, 2004.

Jones, Sacha C. The Toba supervolcanic eruption: Tephra-fall deposits in India and palaeoanthropological implications. In Petraglia and Allchin 2007: 173–200.

Jongewaard, C. Woven time in Andean textiles. Presentation at the Colloquium on Andean Indigenous Cultures Today, Centre for Latin American Linguistic Studies, St. Andrews, 1986.

Judge, A. Theories of correspondences and potential equivalences between them in correlative thinking (draft). 2007, http://www.laetusinpraesens.org/docs00s/corresp.php#corr.

Jung, Carl Gustav. *The basic writings of C. G. Jung*. Ed. with an intro. by Violet Staub de Laszlo. New York: Modern Library, 1959.

Junker, Thomas. *Die Evolution des Menschen*. Munich: Beck, 2006.

Kagaya, Ryohei. *A classified vocabulary of the Sandawe language*. Tokyo: Institute for the Study of Languages and Cultures of Asia and Africa, 1993.

Kahrs, Ernst. *Die Höhlen des Neandertals*. Mitteilung aus dem Museum der Stadt Essen, No. 49. Essen: Museum, 1933.

———. Vom Naturschutzgebiet Neanderthal. In *Die Natur am Niederrhein* 18, 1–11, 31–40. Krefeld: Kleinsche Druckerei, 1942.

Kaiser, Mark. V. M. Illic-Svityc's early reconstructions of Nostratic. Trans. and arranged by Mark Kaiser. In *Reconstructing languages and cultures*, ed. Vitaly Shevoroshkin, 125–76. Bochum: Brockmeyer, 1989.

Kalakaua. *The legends and myths of Hawaii. The fables and folk-lore of a strange people by His Hawaiian Majesty King David Kalakaua, edited with an introduction by Hon. R. M. Dagget*. Foreword by Glen Grant. Honolulu: Mutual Publishing, 1990 [1888].

Kamei, T. *Chinese borrowings in prehistoric Japanese*. Tokyo: Yoshikawa Kobunkan, 1954.

Kamma, F. C. *Religious texts of the oral tradition from Western New-Guinea (Irian Jaya) part B. The threat to life and its defence against "natural" and "supernatural" phenomena*. Leiden: Brill, 1978.

Kant, I. *Kritik der reinen Vernunft*. Würzburg: Meiner, 1956 [1781].

Karlgren, Bernhard. Legends and cults in ancient China. *Bulletin of the Museum of Far Eastern Antiquities* 18 (1946): 199–365.

Katičić, Radoslav. *Auf den Spuren sakraler Dichtung des slawischen und des baltischen Heidentums*. Wiesbaden: Westdeutscher Verlag, 2001.

———. *Die Hauswirtin am Tor: Auf den Spuren der grossen Göttin in Fragmenten slawischer und baltischer sakraler Dichtung*. Frankfurt am Main: Lang, 2003.

Katičić, Radoslav, et al. *Zweitausend Jahre schriftlicher Kultur in Kroatien*. Zagreb: Muzejsko galerijski centar, 1992.

Kato, Genichi. *A historical study of the religious development of Shintō*. New York: Greenwood Press, 1988.

Katz, J. To turn a blind eel. In *Proceedings of the Sixteenth Annual UCLA Indo-European Conference, Los Angeles, Nov. 5–6, 2004*, ed. K. Jones-Bley, M. E. Huld, A. della Volpe, and M. R. Dexter. Washington, D.C.: Journal of Indo-European Monograph Series, No. 50, 2005.

Kaye, A. S. Review of: Patrick R. Bennett: *Comparative Semitic Linguistics: A Manual. Bulletin of the American Schools of Oriental Research* 315 (1999a): 92–96.

———. Review of Dolgopolsky (1988). *Language* 75 (1999b): 627–28.

Keally, Charles T. Bad science and the distortion of history: Readiocarbon dating in Japanese archaeology. *Sophia International Review*, February/May 2004, http://www.t-net.ne.jp/~keally/Reports/sir2004.html.

Keller, Werner. *Und die Bibel hat doch recht* [The Bible as history: A confirmation of the Book of Books]. Trans. William Neil. New York: W. Morrow, 1956. (Originally: Düsseldorf: Econ-Verlag, 1955.)

Kennedy, K. A. R. *God-apes and fossil men: Paleoanthropology of South Asia.* Ann Arbor: University of Michigan Press, 2000.

———. Have Aryans been identified in the prehistoric skeletal record from South Asia? Biological anthropology and concepts of ancient races. In *The Indo-Aryans of ancient South Asia*, ed. George Erdosy, 32–66. Berlin: de Gruyter, 1995.

Kenoyer, J. M. *Ancient cities of the Indus Valley civilization.* Oxford: Oxford University Press/ American Institute of Pakistan Studies, 1998.

Kidder, J, Edward. *Himiko and Japan's elusive chiefdom of Yamatai: Archaeology, history, and mythology.* Honolulu: University of Hawai'i Press, 2007.

King, R., and P. Underhill. Congruent distribution of Neolithic painted pottery and ceramic figurines with Y-chromsome lineages. *Antiquity* 76 (2002): 707–14.

Kinoshita, Iwao. *Kojiki. Aelteste japanische Reichsgeschichte. Band III. Deutsche Übersetzung.* Fukuoka: Kashiigû Hôsaikai, 1976.

Kirchner, Horst. Ein archäologischer Beitrag zur Urgeschichte des Schamanismus. *Anthropos* 47 (1952): 244–86.

Kirk, G. S. *Myth. Its meaning and functions in ancient and other cultures.* London: Cambridge University Press; and Berkeley and Los Angeles: University of California Press, 1970.

———. *The nature of Greek myths.* London: Penguin, 1974.

Kitagawa, Joseph M. *On understanding Japanese religion.* Princeton: Princeton University Press, 1987.

Knauer, E. R. The Queen Mother of the West. A study of the influences of Western prototypes on the iconography of a Taoist deity. In Mair 2006: 62–115.

Knight, A., et al. African Y chromosome and mtDNA divergence provides insight into the history of click languages. *Current Biology* 13 (2003): 464–73.

Kölver, Bernhard. *Constructing pagodas according to traditional Nepalese drawings.* Berlin: Akademie Verlag, 1996.

———. *Re-building a* stūpa: *Architectural drawings of the Svayaṃbhūnāth.* Bonn: VGH Wissenschaftsverlag, 1992.

Kosasih, E. A. Rock art in Indonesia. In Bahn and Rosenfeld 1991: 65–77.

Koubi, Jeanine. *Rambu Solo', la fumée descend. La culte des morts chez les Toradja du Sud.* Paris: Edition Centre National de la Recherche Scientifique, 1982.

Kovacs, M. G. *The epic of Gilgamesh.* Stanford: Stanford University Press, 1985.

Kramer, S. N. *Mythologies of the ancient world.* New York: Doubleday, 1961.

———. *The Sumerians. Their history, culture, and character.* Chicago: University of Chicago Press, 1963.

Krause, J., et al. The derived FOXP variant of modern humans was shared with Neanderthals. *Current Biology* 17, no. 21 (2007): 1908–12.

Krings, M., et al. Neandertal DNA sequences and the origin of modern humans. *Cell* 90 (July 11, 1997): 19–30.

Kroeber, A. L. *Cultural and natural areas of native North America*. Berkeley: University of California Press, 1939.

Kuiper, F. B. J. *Ancient Indian cosmology*. Ed. J. Irwin. Delhi: Vikas, 1983.

———. *Aryans in the Rigveda*. Amsterdam: Rodopi, 1991.

———. *An Austro-Asiatic myth in the RV*. Amsterdam: Noord-Hollandsche Uitgevers Maatschappij, 1950.

———. *Nahali. A comparative study*. Amsterdam: Noord-Hollandsche Uitgevers Maatschappij, 1962.

———. *Varuṇa and Vidūṣaka*. Amsterdam: North-Holland Pub. Co., 1978.

Kumulipo. An account of the creation of the world according to Hawaiian tradition. Trans. Queen Liliuokalani. Boston: Lee and Shepard, 1897.

Lacarrière, J. *Au Coeur des mythologiques. En suivant les dieux*. Paris: Ph. Lebaud, 1998.

Lacouperie, Terrien de. *The languages of China before the Chinese*. Repr. Taipei: Ch'eng-wen Publishing Co., 1970. (Originally: London: Nutt, 1887.)

Lahr, M. M., and R. Foley. Multiple dispersals and modern human origin. *Evolutionary Anthropology* 3 (1994): 48–60.

Lai, E. Whalen. Symbolism of evil in China. *History of Religions*, 1984: 316–43.

Lal, B. B., and S. P. Gupta. *Frontiers of the Indus civilisation*. Delhi: Books and Books, 1984.

Laming-Emperaire, A. *La signification de l'art rupestre paléolitique*. Paris, 1962.

Langen, Dietrich. *Archaische Ekstase und asiatische Meditation mit ihren Beziehungen zum Abendland*. Stuttgart: Hippokrates, 1963.

Larsen, Gregor, et al. Worldwide phylogeography of wild boar reveals multiple centers of pig domestication. *Science* 307 (2005): 1618 sqq.

Lawlor, Robert. *Voices of the first day. Awakening in the aboriginal Dreamtime*. Rochester, Vt.: Inner Traditions, 1991.

Layton, R. L. *Australian rock art: A new synthesis*. Cambridge: Cambridge University Press, 1992.

———. Figure, motif and symbol in the hunter-gatherer rock art of Europe and Australia. In Bahn and Rosenfeld 1991: 23–38.

———. *Uluru: An Aboriginal history of Ayers Rock*. Canberra: Australian Institute of Aboriginal Studies, 1986.

Leach, Edmund R. Genesis as myth. In John Middleton, *Myth and cosmos. Readings in mythology and symbolism*, 1–13. Austin: University of Texas Press, 1977 [1967].

Lee Ki-moon [Yi, Ki-mun]. *Geschichte der koreanischen Sprache*. Ed. Bruno Lewin. Wiesbaden: Reichert, 1977.

Lee, R. *The Dobe Ju/'hoansi*. 2nd ed. Toronto: Wadsworth, 2003. (Originally: *The Dobe!Kung*. Toronto: Wadsworth, 1984.)

Leeming, D., with Margaret A. Leeming. *A dictionary of creation myths*. Oxford: Oxford University Press, 1995.

Leeming, D., and J. Page. *Goddess. Myths of the female divine*. New York: Oxford University Press, 1994.

Leeming, D., and J. Page, eds. *God. Myths of the male divine*. New York: Oxford University Press, 1996.

Leenhardt, Maurice. *Do kamo. Person and myth in the Melanesian world*. Chicago: University of Chicago Press, 1979. (Originally: *Do Kamo. La personne et le mythe dans le monde mélanésien*, 1947.)

Lefkowitz, Mary R., and Guy MacLean Rogers, ed. *Black Athena revisited*. Chapel Hill: University of North Carolina Press, 1996.

Lehmann, Henri. *Les civilisations précolombiennes*. Paris: Presses universitaires des France, 1953.

Lehmann, W. *Die Geschichte des Königreiches von Colhuacan und Mexiko. Quellenwerke zur alten Geschichte Amerikas, aufgezeichnet in den Sprachen der Eingeborenen*. Stuttgart: Ibero-Amerikanisches Institut, 1938.

Lehmann-Nitsche, R. *Studien zur südamerikanischen Mythologie, die ätiologischen Motive*. Hamburg: Friederichsen, de Gruyter, 1939.

Leitner, G. *Die Aborigines Australiens*. Munich: Beck, 2006.

Lell, J. T. The dual origin and Siberian affinities of Native American Y chromosomes. *American Journal of Human Genetics* 70, no. 5 (May 2002): 1377–80.

Lemonick, Michael D., and Andrea Dorfman. Who were the first Americans? *Time*, March 13, 2006: 41–48.

Leonard, S., and M. McClure. *Myth and knowing. An introduction to world mythology*. Boston: McGraw-Hill, 2004.

Leroi-Gourhan, André. *Préhistoire de l'art occidental*. Paris: Éditions d'art L. Mazenod, 1965.

———. *Préhistoire de l'art occidental* [Treasures of prehistoric art]. New York: H. N. Abrams, 1967.

Lesky, S. A. Hethitische Texte und griechischer Mythos, Anzeiger der Oesterreichischen Akademie der Wissenschaften, philosophisch-historische. *Klasse* 87 (1950).

Lévi-Strauss, Claude. *Der Ursprung der Tischsitten*. Frankfurt: Suhrkamp, 1973. (Originally: *Mythologica III. L'origine des manières de table*. Paris: Plon, 1968.)

———. *Mythologiques, vol. 1: Le cru et le cuit*. Paris: Plon, 1964.

———. Note sur les versions americaines de l'histoire du lièvre blanc d'Inaba. In *Mythes symboles literature*, ed. Shinoda Chiwaki. Nagoya: Rakurō Shoin, 2002, http://opac.ndl.go.jp/recordid/000003582433/jpn.

———. The story of Asdiwal. In *The structural study of myth and totemism*, ed. Edmund Leach, 1–47. London: Tavistock Publications, 1967.

———. *The story of Lynx*. Trans. Catherine Tihanyi. Chicago: University of Chicago Press, 1995. (Originally *L'histoire des lynx*, 1991.)

Lewis, I. M. Is there a shaman cosmology? In Mastromattei and Rigopulos 1999: 117–27.

Lewis, J., ed. *The gods have landed: New religions from other worlds*. Albany: State University of New York Press, 1995.

Lewis-Williams, J. D. *The mind in the cave. Consciousness and the origins of art*. London: Thames and Hudson, 2002.

Lewis-Williams, J. David. Ideological continuities in prehistoric southern Africa: The evidence of rock art. In *Past and present in hunter-gatherer studies*, ed. C. Schrire, 225–52. New York: Academic Press, 1984.

———. *The shamans of prehistory: Trance and magic in the painted caves*. New York: Abrams, 1996.

———. The signs of all times: Entopic phenomena in Upper Paleolithic rock art. *Current Anthropology* 29 (1988): 201–45.

Lewis-Williams, J. David, and Th. A. Dowson. On vision and power in the Neolithic: Evidence from the decorated monuments. *Current Anthropology* 34 (1993): 55–65.

Li, Jin, and Bing Su. Modern human origin in East Asia. *Nature Reviews* 126 (2000): 126–33.

Lieberman, Philip. The evolution of human speech. Its anatomical and neural bases. *Current Anthropology* 48, no. 1 (February 2007): 39.

———. *Toward an evolutionary biology of language*. Cambridge: Harvard University Press, 2006.

Lièvre, Viviane, and Jean-Yves Loude. *Le chamanisme des Kalash du Pakistan: Des montagnards polythéistes face à l'islam*. Preface by Roberte N. Hamayon; with iconography by Hervé Nègre. Paris: Editions Recherche sur les Civilisations, 1990.

Lin, Marie, et al. Genetic diversity of Taiwan's indigenous peoples. Possible relationship with insular Southeast Asia. In Sagart et al. 2005: 232–45.

Lincoln, B. *Death, war, and sacrifice: Studies in ideology and practice*. Chicago: University of Chicago Press, 1991.

———. *Myth, cosmos, and society*. Cambridge: Harvard University Press, 1986.

———. *Theorizing myth: Narrative, ideology and scholarship*. Chicago: University of Chicago Press, 1999.

Lindstrom, L. *Cargo cult. Strange stories of desire from Melanesia and beyond*. Honolulu: University of Hawai'i Press, 1993.

Locke, Raymond Friday. *The book of the Navajo*. Los Angeles: Mankind, 2004 [1976].

Long, Ch. A. *The myths of creation*. New York: George Braziller, 1963.

Lopez, C. Food and immortality in the Veda: A gastronomic theology? *Electronic Journal of Vedic Studies* 3, no. 3 (1997), http://www.ejvs.laurasianacademy.com/ejvs0303/ejvs0303article.pdf.

Lorblanchet, Michel. AURA Congress. Symposium A (2nd: 1992: Cairns, Qld.). In *Rock art studies: The post-stylistic era, or, Where do we go from here? Papers presented in Symposium A of the 2nd AURA Congress, Cairns 1992*, ed. Michel Lorblanchet and Paul G. Bahn. Oxford: Oxbow Books, 1993.

———. AURA Congress, Symposium C. State of the art: Regional rock art studies in Australia and Melanesia. In *Proceedings of Symposium C, "Rock Art Studies in Australia and Oceania," and Symposium D, "The Rock Art of Northern Australia," of the First AURA Congress held in Darwin in 1988*, ed. Jo McDonald and Ivan P. Haskovec. Melbourne: Australian Rock Art Research Association, 1992.

———. *Höhlenmalerei: Ein Handbuch*. Herausgegeben, mit einem Vorwort und einem Beitrag zur Wandkunst im Ural von Gerhard Bosinski; Aus dem Französischen übertragen von Peter Nittmann. 2, aktualisierte Auflage. Stuttgart: J. Thorbecke, 2000. (Originally: *Grottes ornées de la préhistoire. Nouveaux regards*. Paris: Éditions Errance, 1995.)

Lorblanchet, M., and P. G. Bahn, eds. *Rock art studies: The post-stylistic era, or, Where do we go from here? Papers presented in Symposium A of the 2nd AURA Congress, Cairns 1992*. Oxford: Oxbow Books, 1993.

Lorenz, Conrad. *Das sogenannte Böse. Zur Naturgeschichte der Aggression*. Vienna, 1963.

Lu, Zh. *China's southwestern Silk Road*. Beijing: Foreign Language Press, 2002.

Luo, Chia-li. Costal culture and religion in early China. Ph.D. dissertation, Indiana University, 1999.

Lycett, Stephen J., Mark Collard, and William C. McGrew. Phylogenetic analyses of behavior support existence of culture among wild chimpanzee. *Proceedings of the National Academy of Sciences of the United States of America* 104, no. 45 (November 6, 2007): 17588–92.

Lyle, Emily. *Archaic cosmos. Polarity, space and time*. Edinburgh: Polygon, 1990.

Lynch, J. *Pacific languages. An introduction*. Honolulu: University of Hawai'i Press, 1998.

Maas, P. *Textual criticism*. Oxford, 1968. (Originally: *Textkritik*, trans., in *Einleitung in die Altertumswissenschaft*, ed. A. Gercke and E. Norden. Leipzig: B. G. Teubner, 1922.)

Maca-Meyer, Nicole, et al. Major genomic mitochondrial lineages delineate early human expansions. *BMC Genetics* 2, no. 13 (2001), http://www.biomedcentral.com/1471-2156/2/13.

MacAndrew, Alec. FOXP2 and the evolution of language. *Molecular Biology*, 2002, http://www.evolutionpages.com/FOXP2_language.htm.

Macaulay, Vincent, et al. Single, rapid coastal settlement of Asia revealed by analysis of complete mitochondrial genomes. *Science* 308 (2005): 1034–36.

MacHugh, D. Molecular biogeography and genetic structure of domesticated cattle. Thesis, Smurfit Institute of Genetics, Trinity College, Dublin, April 15, 1998.

Maclagan, David. *Creation myths. Man's introduction to the world.* London: Thames and Hudson, 1977.

Magnone, P. Floodlighting the deluge: Traditions in comparison. *Studia Indologiczne* 7 (2000): 233–44, http://www.jambudvipa.net/quodlibet.htm.

———. Matsyavatara: Scenari indiani del diluvio [Matsyāvatāra: Indian scenarios of the flood]. In *Atti del Nono Convegno Nazionale di Studi Sanscriti (Genova, 23–24 ottobre 1997)*, ed. S. Sani and O. Botto, 125–36. Pisa, 1999.

Mair, V. *Canine conundrums: Eurasian dog ancestor myths in historical and ethnic perspective.* Philadelphia: Sino-Platonic Papers 87, 1998a.

———. Horse sacrifices and sacred groves among the north(western) peoples of East Asia. *Eurasian Studies* 6 (2007): 22–52.

Mair, V., ed. *The Bronze Age and early Iron Age peoples of eastern Central Asia.* JIES Monograph 26. Washington, D.C.: Institute for the Study of Man; and Philadelphia: University of Pennsylvania Museum Publications, 1998b.

———. *Contact and exchange in the ancient world.* Honolulu: University of Hawai'i Press, 2006.

Malinowski, B. *Argonauts of the western Pacific. An account of native enterprise and adventure in the archipelagoes of Melanesian New Guinea.* New York: Dutton, 1922.

———. *Myth in primitive psychology.* New York: W. W. Norton and Co.; and London: K. Paul, Trench, Trubner and Co., 1926.

Malo, David. *Hawaiian antiquities. Moolelo Hawaii.* Honolulu: Bernice P. Bishop Museum, 1997. (Originally: In Hawai'ian, trans. by Nathaniel B. Emerson, 1898.)

Man, Edward Horace. *On the aboriginal inhabitants of the Andaman Islands; with report of researches into the language of the South Andaman Islands, by A. J. Ellis.* London: Trübner, 1883.

Manning, Patrick. *Homo sapiens* populates the earth: A provisional synthesis, privileging linguistic evidence. *Journal of World History* 17 (2006): 115–58.

Maringer, Johannes. *Vorgeschichtliche Religion. Religionen im steinzeitlichen Europa.* Zurich, 1956.

Markmann, R. H., and P. T. Markmann. *The Flayed God: The Meso-American mythological tradition: Sacred texts and images from pre-Columbian Mexico and Central America.* San Francisco: Harper Collins, 1992.

Marshak, A. *The roots of civilization.* New York: McGraw Hill, 1971.

Marshall, Lorna. !Kung bushman religious beliefs. *Africa* 39 (1962): 347–81.

Martin, Samuel Elmo. *Consonant lenition in Korean and the Macro-Altaic question.* Honolulu: Center for Korean Studies, University of Hawai'i, 1996.

———. *The Japanese language through time.* New Haven: Yale University Press, 1987.

Maruyama, S., et al. Sequence polymorsphisms of the mitochondrial DNA control region and phylogenetic analysis of mtDNA lineages in the Japanese population. *International Journal of Legal Medicine* 117 (2003): 218–25.

Masica, Colin. *Defining a linguistic area: South Asia.* Chicago: University of Chicago Press, 1976.

Maskarinec, G. *Nepalese shaman oral texts.* Ed., trans., and annotated. Cambridge: Harvard University Press, 1998.

———. *Nepalese shaman oral texts. II: Texts of the Bhují Valley; including material collected by John T. Hitchcock.* Cambridge: Harvard University Press, 2008.

———. Nepalese shamans. In Walter and Fridman 2004: 766–72.

———. *The rulings of the night: An ethnography of Nepalese shaman oral texts.* Madison: University of Wisconsin Press, 1995.

Maspero, M. H. Légendes mythologiques dans le Chou King. *Journal asiatique* 204 (1924): 65.

Mastromattei, Romano, and Antonio Rigopulos, eds. *Shamanic cosmos—From India to the North Pole Star.* New Delhi: Venetian Academy of Indian Studies/D. K. Printworld, 1999.

Mathieu, R. *Anthologie des mythes et légendes de la Chine ancienne.* Paris: Gallimard, 1989.

Matsumoto, N. *Essai sur la mythologie japonaise.* Paris, 1928.

———. *Nihon shinwa no kenkyū* [Study of Japanese mythology]. Tokyo: Shibundo, 1956.

Matsumura, Kazuo. "Alone among women." A comparative mythic analysis of the development of Amaterasu theology. In *Kami*, ed. I. Nobutaka, trans. Norman Havens, 42–71. Tokyo: Institute for Japanese Culture and Classics, Kokugakuin University, 1998.

———. Ancient Japan and religion. In *Nanzan guide to Japanese religions*, ed. Paul L. Swanson and Clark Chilson, 131–43. Honolulu: University of Hawai'i Press, 2006a.

———. Birth of mythology in the Victorian British Empire. *Celtic Forum: The Annual Reports of Japan Celtic Society* 4–5 (2004): 83–85.

———. The influence of Chinese thought on the formation of Japanese mythology. Presentation at the Conference on Comparative Mythology of Harvard and Peking Universities, Beijing, May 10–13, 2006b.

———. Myth theories and war. Presentation at the 19th World Congress of the International Association for the History of Religions, Tokyo, 2005.

Mayr, E. *What evolution is.* New York: Basic Books, 2001.

Mbiti, John S. *Concepts of god in Africa.* London: SPCK, Holy Trinity Church, 1970.

McCaskill, D., ed. *Amerindian cosmology.* Brandon, Manitoba: Canadian Journal of Native Studies, 1987.

McCrea, Lawrence. *The teleology of poetics in medieval Kashmir.* Harvard Oriental Series 71. Cambridge: Harvard University Press, 2008.

McDonald, J. Archeology and art in the Sydney region: Context and theory in the analysis of a dual-medium art style. In Bahn and Rosenfeld 1991: 78–85.

McEvoy, Brian, Sandra Beleza, and Mark D. Shriver. The genetic architecture of normal variation in human pigmentation: An evolutionary perspective and model. *Human Molecular Genetics* 15, no. 2 (2006): R176–81.

McKee, Maggie. Genes contribute to religious inclination. *New Scientist*, March 16, 2005, http://www.newscientist.com/article.ns?id=dn7147.

McMahon, Robert. Genes and languages. *Community Genetics* 7 (2004): 2–13. (Originally: *American Journal Human Genetics* 72 [2003]: 1282.)

Mehdi, S. Q., et al. The origins of Pakistani populations. Evidence from Y chromosome markers. In *Genomic diversity: Applications in human population genetics*, ed. S. Papiha, R. Deka, and R. Chakraborty, 83–90. New York: Kluwer/Plenum, 1999.

Meiser, G. *Historische Laut- und Formenlehre der lateinischen Sprache.* Darmstadt: Wissenschaftliche Buchgesellschaft, 1998.

Meisig, Marion. Eine schamanistische Seance im Rgveda (RV 10.108). *Mitteilungen für Anthropologie und Religionsgeschichte* 10 (1995): 119–42.

Mellars, Paul. Going east: New genetic and archaeological perspectives on the modern humans colonization of Eurasia. *Science* 313 (2006): 796–800.

Menas Orea. *Siṅboṅgā. Oṛoḥ eṭaaḥ eṭaaḥ boṅgāko. Singbonga and the spirit world of the Mundas.* Ed. and trans. P. Ponette, S.J. Ranchi: Catholic Press, 1968.

Menzies, Gavin. *1421: The year China discovered America.* 1st U.S. ed. [New York]: William Morrow, 2003.

Merriam, A. P. Definitions of "comparative musicology" and "ethnomusicology": An historical-theoretical perspective. *Ethnomusicology* 21 (1977): 189–204.

Metspalu, M., et al. The pioneer settlement of modern humans in Asia. In Bandelt et al. 2006: 181–99.

Miller, Roy Andrew. *Japanese and the other Altaic languages.* Chicago: University of Chicago Press, 1971.

Mishra, Nihar Ranjan. *Kamakhya, a socio-cultural study.* New Delhi: D. K. Printworld, 2004.

Mithen, Steven. *After the ice. A global human history, 20,000–5000 BC.* Cambridge: Harvard University Press, 2004.

―――. *The prehistory of the mind: A search for the origins of art, religion, and science.* London: Thames and Hudson, 1996.

―――. *The singing Neanderthals. The origins of music, language, mind and body.* London: Weidenfels and Nicholson, 2005.

Mizuno, Tomoaki. The dragon conquest as holy combat for the stranger: Focussing on Beowulf and Thor. *Iris* 25 (2003): 105–34.

Moerenhout, J. A. *An account of the Polynesian race; its origins and migrations.* Trans. A. Fornander. London, 1880. (Originally: *Voyage aux Iles du Grand Océan.* Paris, 1837.)

Montandon, G. *L'Ologénèse Humaine.* Paris, 1923.

Morell, Virginia. The origin of dogs: Running with the wolves. *Science* 276 (June 13, 1997): 1647–48.

Morford, Mark P. O., and Robert J. Leanardon. *Classical mythology.* New York: Oxford University Press, 2003.

Morgenstierne, G. *The Kalasha language.* Compiled by K. Kristiansen and I. Ross. Oslo: Universitetsforlaget, 1973.

Mori, Shozo. The idea of *kami*: A study of the Japanese concept of deity. M.A. thesis, Harvard University, 1999.

Mortensen, Eric. Raven augury in Tibet, northwest Yunnan, Inner Asia, and circumpolar regions; a study in comparative folklore and religion. Ph.D. dissertation, Harvard University, 2003.

Motingea, M. Parlers minoritaires du basin central du Congo et le Bantou commun. Presentation at Institute for the Study of Languages and Cultures of Asia and Africa, October 2004.

Mulvaney, D. J., and J. Kamminga. *Prehistory of Australia.* Washington, D.C.: Smithsonian Institution Press, 1999.

Münke, Wolfgang. *Die klassische chinesische Mythologie.* Stuttgart: Klett, 1976.

Munro, N. G. *Ainu. Creed and cult.* Ed. with a preface and additional chap. by B. Z. Seligman; intro. by H. Watanabe. New York: Columbia University Press, 1963.

Murray, Margaret A. *The splendour that was Egypt.* London: Book Club Associates, 1963.

Nagy, Gregory. *The best of the Achaeans: Concepts of the hero in Archaic Greek poetry*. Baltimore: Johns Hopkins University Press, 1979.

———. Can myth be saved? In *Myth. A new symposium*, ed. G. Schrempp and W. Hansen, 240–48. Bloomington: Indiana University Press, 2002.

———. *Poetry as performance. Homer and beyond*. Cambridge: Cambridge University Press, 1996.

Nakhleh, Luay, et al. A comparison of phylogenetic reconstruction methods on an Indo-European dataset. *Transactions of the Philological Society* 103 (2005): 171–92.

Nara, Tsuyoshi, and Peri Bhaskararao, eds. *Songs of the Toda. Text. Translation and sound files*. Osaka: Osaka Gakuin University, Endangered Languages of the Pacific Rim, 2003.

———. *Toda vocabulary. A preliminary list*. Osaka: Osaka Gakuin University, Endangered Languages of the Pacific Rim, 2001.

Narby, Jeremy, and Francis Huxley. *Shamans through time. 500 years on the path to knowledge*. London: Thames and Hudson, 2001.

Naumann, N. *Das Umwandeln des Himmelspfeilers. Ein japanischer Mythos und seine kulturhistorische Einordnung*. Tokyo: AFS Monograph 5, 1971.

———. *Die einheimische Religion Japans. Teil 1. Bis zum Ende der Heian-Zeit*. Leiden: Brill, 1988.

———. *Japanese prehistory. The material and spiritual culture of the Jōmon period*. Asien- und Afrika-Studien der Humboldt Universität zu Berlin, Vol. 6. Wiesbaden: Harrassowitz, 2000.

———. Zur ursrünglichen Bedeutung des *harahe. Bonner Zeitschrift für Japanologie* 1 (1979): 169–90.

Netti, Bruno. *The study of ethnomusicology: Thirty-one issues and concepts*. New ed. Urbana: University of Illinois Press, 2005.

Nevermann, Hans. *Söhne des tötenden Vaters. Dämonen- und Kopfjägergeschichten aus Neuguinea*. Eisenach und Kassel: Erich Röth, 1957.

Nevins, Andrew Ira, David Pesetsky, and Cilene Rodrigues. [Piraha exceptionality: A reassessment]. March 12, 2007, http://ling.auf.net/lingBuzz/000411.

Nichols, J. The epicentre of the Indo-European linguistic spread. In *Archaeology and language I*, ed. R. Blench and M. Spriggs, 122–48. London, 1997.

———. The Eurasian spread zone and the Indo-European dispersal. In *Archaeology and language II. Correlating archaeological and linguistic hypotheses*, ed. R. Blench and M. Spriggs, 220–66. London, 1999.

Nicholson, Philip T. Light visions: Shamanic control fantasies and the creation of myth. Presentation at the International Conference on Comparative Mythology, Beijing, May 11–13, 2006.

———. The soma code: Luminous visions in the Rig Veda. *Electronic Journal of Vedic Studies* 8, no. 3 (2002).

Nikonov, V. A. Geografiia nazvanii Mlechnogo Puti. In *Onomastika Vostoka*, ed. E. M. Murzaev, V. A. Nikonov, and V. V. Tsybul'skii, 242–61. Moscow: Nauka, 1980.

Nilsson, M. N. *The Mycenaean origin of Greek mythology*. Berkeley: University of California Press, 1972 [1932].

Noonan, J. P., et al. Sequencing and analysis of Neanderthal genomic DNA. *Science*, 314, no. 5802 (November 17, 2006): 1113, http://www.sciencemag.org/cgi/content/abstract/314/5802/1113?etoc.

Nordal, Sigurdur. *Völuspá*. Darmstadt: Wissenschaftliche Buchgesellschaft, 1980.

Nordenskiøld, Erland. Deductions suggested by the geographical distribution of some post-Columbian words used by the Indians of South America. In *Comparative ethnographic studies*, vol. 5, 1–46. Gøteborg, 1922.

Nurse, Derek, and Gérard Philippson. *The Bantu languages*. London: Routledge, 2003.

Ōbayashi, Taryō. The ancient myths of Korea and Japan. In "The Formation of Japan's Ethnic Culture: Comparative Approaches," ed. Ōbayashi Taryō, *Acta Asiatica: Bulletin of the Institute of Eastern Culture* 61 (1991a): 68–82.

———. Die Amaterasu-Mythe im alten Japan und die Sonnenfinsternismythe in Südostasian. *Ethnos* 25 (1960): 20–43.

———. Ise und Izumo, Die Schreine des Schintoismus. In *Die Welt der Religionen*, Bd. 6. Freiburg: Herder, 1982.

———. Japanese myths of descent from heaven and their Korean parallels. *Asian Folklore Studies* 43 (1984): 171–84.

———. La partition trifonctionelle dans la mythologie japonaise. Rivalité triangulaire entre trois divinités: Amaterasu, Susanowo et Ohokuninushi. In *Georges Dumézil in Memoriam*, III. Etudes indo-europénnes 8. Lyon: L'Institut d'etudes Indo-Européennes, 1989.

———. *Nihon Shinwa no Kigen* [The origin of Japanese mythology]. Tokyo: Tokuma Shoten, 1990. (Originally: Kadokawa Shoten, 1961; 2nd expanded ed., 1973.)

———. *Nihon Shinwa no Kōzō* [The structure of Japanese myths]. Tokyo: Kōbundō, 1975.

———. The origins of the universe. *The East* 12, nos. 1–2 (1976): 8–15, 9–13.

———. The shaman's role in the hunting rituals of northern peoples. In *Hunting rituals of northern peoples: 5th International Abashiri Symposium*, ed. Hokkaido Museum of Northern Peoples, 1–10. Abashiri: Association for Northern Cultural Promotion, 1991b.

———. *Shinwa no keifu. Nihon shinwa no genryū wo sagaru* [Genealogy of myths. Investigations in the origin of Japanese mythology]. Tokyo: Kōdansha, 1991c. (Originally: Seidosha, 1986.)

———. The structure of the pantheon and the concept of sin in ancient Japan. *Diogenes* 98 (1977): 117–32.

Ōbayashi, Taryō, and Hans-Joachim R. Klaproth. Das Bärenfest der Oroken auf Sachalin. *Zeitschrift für Ethnologie* 91 (1966): 211–36.

Oberlies, Thomas. *Die Relion des Ṛgveda*. Vienna: Institut für Indologie der Universität Wien, 1998.

Obeyesekere, Gananath. *Imagining karma: Ethical transformation in Amerindian, Buddhist, and Greek rebirth*. Berkeley: University of California Press, 2002.

———. Rebirth eschatology and its transformations: A contribution to the sociology of early Buddhism. In *Karma and rebirth in classical Indian traditions*, ed. Wendy Doniger O'Flaherty, 137–64. Sponsored by the Joint Committee on South Asia of the Social Science Research Council and the American Council of Learned Societies. Berkeley: University of California Press, 1980.

Oda, Junichi. Description of structure of the folktale: Using a bioinformatics multiple alignment program. In *Cultural change in the Arab world*, ed. Tetsuo Nishio, 153–74. Senri Ethnological Studies 55. Osaka: National Museum of Ethnology, 2001.

———. Description of structure of the folktale I: From bioinformatics to text theory [In Japanese]. In *Genesis of narrative*, ed. Junichi Oda, 67–92. Tokyo: Institute for the Study of Languages and Cultures of Asia and Africa, 1995.

————. Structure du narration du fabliau: Essai d'un reclassement des pièces par Cluster-Analysis. *Mathematical Linguistics* 14, no. 7 (1984): 281–303.

Ogawa, N., and Erin Asai. *Gengo ni yoru Taiwan Takasagozoku densetsushū* [The myths and traditions of the Formosan native tribes (texts and notes)]. Tokyo: Tōkō Shōin, Shōwa 10, [1935].

Oguibénine, B. Sur le symbolisme du type chamanique dans le Rgveda. *Uchenyie Zapiski Tartuskogo Gosudarstvennogo universiteta* 201 (1968): 149–50.

Ohnuki-Thierney, Emiko. *The Ainu of the northwest coast of southern Sakhalin*. New York: Holt, Rinehart and Wiston, 1974.

————. The ambivalent self of the contemporary Japanese. *Cultural Anthropology* 5 (1990): 197–216.

————. The emperor of Japan as a deity (*kami*). *Ethnology* 30 (1991): 199–215.

————. *Illness and healing among the Sakhalin Ainu: A symbolic interpretation*. Cambridge: Cambridge University Press, 1981.

Oort, Marianne S. Surā in the Paippalāda Saṃhitā of the Atharvaveda. "Indic and Iranian Studies in Honor of Stanley Insler on His Sixty-Fifth Birthday," *Journal of the American Oriental Society* 122, no. 2 (April–June 2002): 355–60.

Opie, Iona Archibald. *The Oxford nursery rhyme book*. Assembled by Iona Opie and Peter Opie; illustrations by Joan Hassall. Oxford: Clarendon Press; and London: Oxford University Press, 1955.

Opie, Iona Archibald, and Peter Opie, eds. *The Oxford dictionary of nursery rhymes*. Oxford: Clarendon Press, 1951.

Opoku, Kofi Asare. *West African tradition religion*. Accra: FEP International, 1978.

Oppenheimer, Stephen. *Eden in the East: The drowned continent of Southeast Asia*. London: Weidenfeld and Nicolson, 1998.

————. *The origins of the British: A genetic detective story*. London: Constable, 2006.

————. *The peopling of the world*. London: Constable, 2003, http://www.bradshawfounda-tion.com/stephenoppenheimer/.

Oppitz, Michael. *Onkels Tochter, keine sonst: Heiratsbündnis und Denkweise in einer Lokalkultur des Himalaya*. Frankfurt/Main: Suhrkamp, 1991.

Oppitz, Michael, and Eliabeth Hsu. *Naxi and Moso ethnography. Kin, rites, pictographs*. Zurich: Völkerkundemuseum, 1998.

Orans, M. *The Santal. A tribe in search of a great tradition*. Detroit: Wayne State University Press, 1965.

Osada, Toshiki, ed. *Proceedings of the pre-symposium of RHIN and 7th ESCA Harvard–Kyoto Round Table*. Kyoto: Research Institute for Humanity and Nature, 2006.

Osada, Toshiki, and A. Vovin, eds., with K. Russel. *Perspectives on the origins of the Japanese language*. Kyoto: International Center for Japanese Studies, 2003.

Ovchinnikov, I. V., et al. Molecular analysis of Neanderthal DNA from the Northern Caucasus. *Nature* 404 (2000): 490–93.

Pache, Alois. *Die religiösen Vorstellungen in den Mythen der formosanischen Bergstämme*. Vienna: Verlag der Missionsdruckerei St. Gabriel, 1964.

Palanichamy, Mallia Gounder, et al. Comment on "Reconstructing the Origin of the Andaman Islanders." *Science* 311 (2006): 468.

Pandey, S. K. *Indian rock art*. New Delhi: Aryan Books International, 1993.

Pandit, T. N. *The Sentinelese*. Calcutta: Seagull Books/Anthropological Survey of India, 1990.

Panoff, M. Die Mythologie der Ozeanier. In Pierre Grimal, *Mythen der Völker*, Bd. III, 215–48. Hamburg: Fischer, 1967. (Originally: Paris, 1963.)

Parin, O., F. Morgenthaler, and G. Parin-Matthey. *Die Weißen denken zu viel. Psychoanalytische Untersuchungen in Westafrika*. Munich: Kindler, 1962.

Parrinder, Geoffrey. *African traditional religion*. London, 1972 [1954].

Partridge, Ch., ed. *UFO religions*. London: Routledge, 2003.

Past worlds: The Times atlas of archaeology. London: Times Books, 1995 [1988].

Patterson, N., et al. Genetic evidence for complex speciation of humans and chimpanzees. *Nature*, 2006, http://www.broad.mit.edu/cgi-bin/news/display_news.cgi?id=1003.

Patterson, N., et al. Genetic insights into the mixture history of South Asian populations. Presentation at the 11th Round Table on the Ethnogenesis of South and Central Asia, Harvard University, May 8, 2008, http://www.people.fas.harvard.edu/~witzel/RT2008.htm.

Patton, K. C. When the High Gods pour out wine: A paradox of ancient Greek iconography in comparative context. Ph.D. dissertation, Harvard University, 1992.

Patton, K. C., and B. C. Ray, eds. *A magic still dwells*. Berkeley: University of California Press, 2000.

Patton, L. L., and W. Doniger, eds. *Myth and method*. Charlottesville: University Press of Virginia, 1996.

Paulson, Ivar. Die rituelle Erhebung des Bärenschädels bei arktischen und subarktischen Völkern. *Minzokugaku Kenkyū/Japanese Journal for Ethnology* 29 (1965): 191–205.

Pawley, A., and M. Ross. The prehistory of Oceanic languages: A current view. In *The Austronesians: Historical and comparative perspectives*, ed. Peter Bellwood et al., 43–80. Canberra: Department of Anthropology, as part of the Comparative Austronesian Project, Research School of Pacific and Asian Studies, Australian National University, 1995.

p'Bitek, Okot. *African religions in Western scholarship*. Nairobi: East African Literature Bureau, 1970.

Peiros, Ilia. *Comparative linguistics in Southeast Asia*. Canberra: Pacific Linguistics, 1998.

Penny, D., et al. Trees from genes and languages are very similar. *Systematic Biology* 42 (1993): 382–92.

Petraglia, Michael D., and Bridget Allchin, eds. *The evolution and history of human populations in South Asia. Inter-disciplinary studies in archaeology, biological anthropology, linguistics and genetics*. Dordrecht, 2007.

Petraglia, Michael D., et al. Middle Paleolithic assemblages from the Indian Subcontinent before and after the Toba super-eruption. *Science* 317 (2007): 114–16.

Pettinato, Giovanni. *La saga di Gilgamesh*. Milano, 1992.

Pfeffer, Georg. *Status and affinity in Middle India*. Wiesbaden: F. Steiner, 1982.

Philippi, D. L. *Kojiki. Translated with an introduction and notes*. Tokyo: University of Tokyo Press, 1968.

Philippi, Donald L. *Norito. A translation of the ancient Japanese ritual prayers*. Princeton: Princeton University Press, 1990.

———. *Songs of gods, songs of humans: The epic tradition of the Ainu*. Foreword by Gary Snyder. Princeton: Princeton University Press, 1979.

Phillipson, David W. 2005 *African archaeology*. 3rd ed. Cambridge: Cambridge University Press, 2005.

Pietrusewsky, Michael. The physical anthropology of the Pacific, East Asia and Southeast Asia. A multivariate craniometric analysis. In Sagart et al. 2005: 201–29.

Pietz, William. The problem of the fetish. Part I. *Res* 9 (1985): 5–17.

———. The problem of the fetish. Part II. *Res* 13 (1987): 23–45.

————. The problem of the fetish. Part III. *Res* 16 (1988): 105–23.

Plato. *Phaedo*. In *Plato [works] in twelve volumes, with an English translation*. Loeb Series 36. London: Heinemann; and Cambridge: Harvard University Press, 1963.

Plomley, Norman James Brian. *An annotated bibliography of the Tasmanian Aborigines*. London: Royal Anthropological Institute of Great Britain and Ireland, 1969.

————. *Friendly mission. The Tasmanian journals and papers of George Augustus Robinson 1829–1834*. Hobart: Tasmanian Historical Research Association, 1966.

————. *The Tasmanian Aborigines*. Launceton: Plomley, 1993.

————. *A word-list of the Trasmanian Aborigines*. Launceston: N. Plomley in association with the Government of Tasmania, 1976.

Poloni, Estella S., et al. Comparing linguistic and genetic relationships among East Asian populations. A study of the RH and GM polymorphisms. In Sagart et al. 2005: 252–72.

Ponette, P., ed. and trans. *Menas Oṛea, Siṅboṃga, Oṛoh eṭaah eṭaah boṃgāko. Singbonga and the spirit world of the Mundas*. Ranchi: Catholic Press, 1968.

Posener, G. *La divinité du pharaon*. Paris: Quirke, 1992.

Poppe, N. N. *Vergleichende Grammatik der altaischen Sprachen. 1. Vergleichende Lautlehre*. Wiesbaden: O. Harrassowitz, 1960.

Powell, Alvin. Dog genome latest DNA to be fully sequenced. *Harvard Gazette*, December 8, 2005: 1, 10.

Pratt, Charles Henry. The gold problem. A.B. thesis, Harvard University, 1933.

Presser, J. C., et al. Tasmanian Aborigines and DNA. *Papers and Proceedings of the Royal Society of Tasmania* 136 (2007): 35–38.

Propp, Vladimir Y. *The mythology of the folktale*. Philadelphia: American Folklore Society, 1958. (Originally: *Morfologiia skazki*, 1928.)

Puett, Michael J. *To become a god. Cosmology, sacrifice, and self-divinization in early China*. Cambridge: Harvard University Press, 2002.

Puhvel, J. *Comparative mythology*. Baltimore: Johns Hopkins University Press, 1987.

Pulleyblank, Edwin. The typology of Indo-European. *Journal of Indo-European Studies*, 1993: 106–7.

Quintana-Murci, L., et al. Y-chromosome lineages trace diffusion of people and languages in southwestern Asia. *American Journal of Human Genetics* 68 (2001): 537–42.

Radcliffe-Brown, Alfred Reginald. *The Andaman Islanders: A study in social anthropology*. 2nd printing (enlarged). Cambridge: Cambridge University Press, 1933 [1906].

Radin, P. *The road of life and death. A ritual drama of the American Indians*. Princeton: Princeton University Press, 1991.

Radin, P., ed. *African folktales*. New York: Schocken, 1983.

Raffetta, P. On the creation of domestic animals in Proto-Indo-European mythology. Presentation at "Pecus: Man and Animal in Antiquity," Swedish Institute, Rome, September 2002, http://www.svabhinava.org/friends/PaolaRaffetta/CreationDomesticAnimals-frame.html.

Ragin, F. *The comparative method. Moving beyond qualitative and quantitative strategies*. Berkeley: University of California Press, 1987.

Raglan, Lord. *The hero. A study in tradition, myth, and drama*. New York: Vintage Books, 1956. (Originally: London: Methuen, 1936.)

————. The hero of tradition. *Folklore* 45 (1934): 212–31.

Rana, B. K. New materials on the Kusunda language. Presentation at the Fourth Harvard Round Table on the Ethnogenesis of South and Central Asia, Harvard University, May 11–13, 2002, http://www.fas.harvard.edu/%7Esanskrit/RoundTableSchedule.html

————. Significance of the Kusundas and their language in the trans-Himalayan region. *Mother Tongue* 11 (2006): 212–18.

Redd, A., and M. Stoneking. Peopling of Sahul: mtDNA variation in aboriginal Australian and Papua New Guinean populations. *American Journal of Human Genetics* 65 (1999): 808–28.

Redd, A., et al. Gene flow from the Indian Subcontinent to Australia: Evidence from the Y chromosome. *Current Biology* 12 (April 16, 2002): 673–77.

Reidla, Maere, et al. Origin and diffusion of mtDNA haplogroup X. *Human Genetics* 73, no. 5 (November 2003): 1178–90.

Relethford, John H. Apportionment of global human genetic diversity based on craniometrics and skin color. *American Journal of Physical Anthropology* 118, no. 4 (2002): 393–98.

Renfrew, Colin. *Archaeology and language: The puzzle of Indo-European origins.* London: J. Cape, 1987.

Renfrew, Colin, April McMahon, and Larry Trask, eds. *Time depth in historical linguistics.* Cambridge: McDonald Institute for Archaeological Research, 2000.

Renfrew, Colin, and Daniel Nettle, eds. *Nostratic: Examining a linguistic macrofamily.* Cambridge: McDonald Institute of Archeological Research, 1999.

Reschke, Heinz. *Linguistische Untersuchung der Mythologie und Initiation in Neuguinea.* Münster: Aschendorfsche Verlagsbuchhandlung, 1935.

Rice, T. Toward the remodeling of ethnomusicology. *Ethnomusicology* 31, no. 3 (1987): 469–88.

Rimuy Aki, Meimei Masow, and Robin J. Winkler. *The Rainbow's judgment: Stories of the Atayal tribe* [In Chinese and English]. Taipeh: Third Nature Publishing, 2002.

Rivers, William Halse. *The Todas.* London: Macmillan, 1906.

Rizvi, S. N. H. *The Shompen: A vanishing tribe of the Great Nicobar Island.* Calcutta: Seagull Books, on behalf of the Anthropological Survey of India, 1990.

Robbeets, Martine Irma. *Is Japanese related to Korean, Tungusic, Mongolic and Turkic?* Wiesbaden: Harrassowitz, 2005.

Roberts, R. G., et al. The human colonisation of Australia: Optical dates of 53,000 and 60,000 years bracket human arrival at Deaf Adder Gorge, Northern Territory. *Quaternary Science* 13 (1994): 575–83.

Robinson, George Augustus. *Friendly mission; the Tasmanian journals and papers of George Augustus Robinson, 1829–1834.* Ed. N. J. B. Plomley. Hobart: Tasmanian Historical Research Association, 1966.

Rockhill, W. W. *The land of the Lama: Notes of a journey through China, Mongolia and Tibet with maps and illustrations.* London: Longmans, 1891.

Roe, Peter. *The cosmic zygote: Cosmology in the Amazon Basin.* New Brunswick, N.J.: Rutgers University Press, 1982.

Roland, A. *In search of self in India and Japan. Toward a cross-cultural psychology.* Princeton: Princeton University Press, 1988.

Rolland, Pierre, ed. and trans. *Vārāha Gṛhyapuruṣa Parisiṣṭa.* Aix: Éditions de l'Université de Provence, 1975.

Rölleke, Heinz, ed. *Kinder- und Hausmärchen gesammelt durch die Brüder Grimm. Vollständige Ausgabe auf der Grundlage der dritten Auflage.* Frankfurt: Deutscher Klassiker Verlag, 2003 [1837].

Rosenberg, A. *Mythus des 20. Jahrhunderts.* English trans. Torrance: Noontide Press, 1982 [1933].

Rosenfeld, A. Panaramitee: Dead or alive? In Bahn and Rosenfeld 1991: 136–44.

Ross, Ph. E. Hard words. *Scientific American*, April 1991: 138–47.

Rotermund, Hartmut O. *Religions, croyances et traditions populaires du Japon. I. Aux temps où arbres et plantes disaient des choses*. With Jean-Pierre Berthon, Laurence Caillet, and François Macé. Paris: Maisonneuve et Larose, 2000 [1988].

Roth, H. L. *The Aborigines of Tasmania*. Halifax, England, 1899.

Rothstein, Mikael. Science and religion in the new religions. In *The gods have landed: New religions from other worlds*, ed. J. Lewis, 99–118. Albany: State University of New York Press, 1995.

Rudy, Zvi. *Ethnosoziologie sowjetischer Völker. Wege und Richtlinien*. Bern: Francke, 1962.

Ruhlen, M. *On the origin of languages, studies in linguistic taxonomy*. Stanford: Stanford University Press, 1994a.

———. *The origin of language: Tracing the evolution of the mother tongue*. New York: Wiley, 1994b.

Rühmkorf, P. *Über das Volkvermögen. Exkurse in den literarischen Untergrund*. Reinbek: Rowohlt, 1969.

Rundle Clark, R. T. *Myth and symbol in ancient Egypt*. London: Thames and Hudson, 1959.

Rutman, Darret. *John Winthrop's decision for America, 1629*. Philadelphia: Lippincott, 1975.

Ryan, W. B., and W. C. Pitman. *Noah's flood: The new scientific discoveries about the event that changed history*. Ill. by Anastasia Sotiropoulos; maps by William Haxby. New York: Simon and Schuster, 1998.

Sagart, Laurent, et al., eds. *The peopling of East Asia: Putting together archaeology, linguistics, and genetics*. London: Routledge, 2005.

Sahlins, M. *Stone Age economics*. New York: Routledge, 2004. (Originally: New York: Aldine Publishing Co., 1972.)

Sahoo, Sanghamitra, et al. A prehistory of Indian Y chromosomes: Evaluating demic diffusion scenarios. *Proceedings of the National Academy of Sciences of the United States of America* 103, no. 4 (January 24, 2006): 843–48.

Saitou, N. Relationship between genetic and linguistic differentiation of people in Eurasia. In Osada 2006: 220–21.

Sanchez-Mazas, Alicia, et al. HLA genetic diversity and linguistic variation in East Asia. In Sagart et al. 2005: 273–96.

Sanford, C. L. *Manifest Destiny and the imperialism question*. New York: John Wiley and Sons, 1974.

Sato, Y. I. Domestication of crops: What is common and what is different?—Fudo and agriculture. In Osada 2006: 73–78.

Sauer, Carl O. *Seeds, spades, hearths and herds*. Cambridge: MIT Press, 1969. (Originally: *Agricultural origins and dispersals*. New York: American Geographical Society, 1952.)

Savolainen, Peter, et al. Genetic evidence for an East Asian origin of domestic dogs. *Science* 298, no. 5598 (November 22, 2002): 1610–13.

Schärer, H. *Die Gottesidee der Ngadju Dajak in Borneo*. Leiden: Brill, 1946.

———. *Ngaju religion, the conception of god among a South Borneo people*. The Hague: Nijhoff, 1963.

Schatz, Oskar, and Hans Spatzenegger, eds. *Wovon werden wir morgen geistig leben? Mythos, Religion und Wissenschaft in der "Postmoderne."* Salzburg, 1986.

Schebesta, Paul. *Les pygmées du Congo belge. Traduit de l'allemand par Henri Plard*. Bruxelles, 1952.

———. *Les Pygmées. Traduit de l'allemand par François Berge*. Paris: Gallimard, 1940.

———. *Revisiting my Pygmy hosts.* Trans. from German by Gerald Griffin. London: Hutchinson, 1936.

Scherer, A. *Gestirnnamen bei den indogermanischen Völkern.* Heidelberg: Winter, 1953.

Schiller, Anne. Offerings and sacrifice in shamanism. In Walter and Fridman 2004: 197–200.

Schmidt, Hanns-Peter. *Br̥haspati und Indra; Untersuchungen zur vedischen Mythologie und Kulturgeschichte.* Wiesbaden: Harassowitz, 1968.

Schmidt, P. Wilhelm. *Der Ursprung der Gottesidee. I, Historisch-kritischer Teil: Eine historisch-kritische und positive Studie,* 12 vols. Münster: Aschendorffsche Verlagsbuchhandlung, 1912–55.

———. *Die Tasmanischen Sprachen.* Utrecht-Anvers: Spectrum, 1952.

———. *Endsynthese der Religionen der Urvölker Amerikas, Asiens, Australiens, Afrikas.* Münster: Aschendorffsche Verlagsbuchhandlung, 1935.

Schmidt, R. A. Shamans in northern cosmology: The direct historical approach to Mesolithic sexuality. In *Archaeologies of sexuality,* ed. R. A. Schmidt and B. L. Voss, 220–35. New York: Routledge.

Schmitz, C. A., ed. *Historische Völkerkunde.* Frankfurt: Akademische Verlagsgesellschaft, 1967.

Schmitz, Ralph W. Interdisziplinäre Untersuchungen an den Neufunden aus dem Neandertal. Johann Carl Fuhlrott (1803–1877) gewidmet. *Mitteilungen der Gesellschaft für Urgeschichte* 12 (2003): 25, http://www.urgeschichte.uni-tuebingen.de/fileadmin/ downloads/GfU/2003/gfu12_3.pdf.

Schmitz, Ralph W., and J. Thissen. *Neanderthal. Die Geschichte geht weiter.* Heidelberg: Spektrum, 2002.

Schmitz, Ralph W., et al. The Neandertal type site revisited: Interdisciplinary investigations of skeletal remains from the Neander Valley, Germany. *Proceedings of the National Academy of Sciences of the United States of America* 99, no. 20 (October 1, 2002): 13342–47, http://www.pnas.org/cgi/content/abstract/99/20/13342.

Schrenk, F. *Die Frühzeit des Menschen. Der Weg zum Homo sapiens.* Munich, 1997.

Schrenk, F., and Stephanie Müller. *Die Neanderthaler.* With Christine Hemm. Munich: Beck, 2005.

Schultze Jena, L. *Popol Vuh. Das heilige Buch der Quiché-Indianer von Guatemala. Nach einer wiedergefundenen alten Handschrift neu übersetzt und erläutert.* Stuttgart: Kohlhammer, 1944.

Schurr, T. G., and S. T. Sherry. Mitochondrial DNA and Y chromosome diversity and the peopling of the Americas: Evolutionary and demographic evidence. *American Journal of Human Biology* 16, no. 4 (July–August 2004): 420–39.

Schuster, Karl. *Joint marks. A possible index of cultural contact between America, Oceania, and the Far East.* Amsterdam: Royal Tropical Institute, 1951.

Scott, George Richard, and Christy G. Turner. *The anthropology of modern human teeth: Dental morphology and its variation in recent human populations.* Cambridge: Cambridge University Press, 1997.

Segal, R. A. Does myth have a future? In Patton and Doniger 1996: 82–106.

———. *Jospeh Campbell: An introduction.* New York: New American Library, 1990.

———. *Myth. Critical concepts in literary and cultural studies.* 4 vols. London: Routledge, 2007.

———. *The myth and ritual theory.* Oxford: Blackwell, 1998.

———. The myth and ritual theory. *Cosmos* 17 (2001): 141–62.

Segal, R. A., et al. *In quest of the hero.* Princeton: Princeton University Press, 1990.

Semino, Ornella, et al. The genetic legacy of Paleolithic *Homo sapiens sapiens* in extant Europeans: A Y chromosome perspective. *Science Magazine* 290, no. 5494 (2000): 1155–59.

Sengupta, S., et al. Polarity and temporality of high-resolution Y-chromosome distributions in India identify both indigenous and exogenous expansions and reveal minor genetic influence of central Asian pastoralists. *American Journal of Human Genetics* 78 (2006): 202–21.

Sergent, Bernard. *Genèse de l'Inde.* Paris: Payot, 1997.

Serre, D., et al. No evidence of Neandertal mtDNA contribution to early modern humans. *PLoS Biology* 2, no. 3 (2004), http://www.ncbi.nlm.nih.gov/sites/entrez?cmd=Retri eve&db=PubMed&list_uids=15024415&dopt=Citation.

Seward, Liz. Pig DNA reveals farming history. 2007, http://news.bbc.co.uk/2/hi/science/nature/6978203.stm.

Shaffer, Jim G., and Diane A. Lichtenstein. Migration, philology, and South Asian archaeology. In *Aryans and Non-Aryans: Evidence, interpretation and ideology*, ed. J. Bronkhorst and M. Deshpande, 239–60. Cambridge: Harvard Oriental Series, Opera Minora 3, 1999.

Shalian, Artin K. *David of Sassoun; the Armenian folk epic in four cycles. The original text translated with an introd. and notes.* Athens: Ohio University Press, 1964.

Shaw, Jonathan. Origins: Technological revolutions—not simple biology—led to the emergence of modern humans. *Harvard Magazine*, September/October 2001, http://www.harvard-magazine.com/on-line/09016.html.

Shaw, John. Indo-European dragon-slayers and healers, and the Irish account of Dian Cécht and Méiche. *Journal of Indo-European Studies* 34 (2006): 153–81.

Sherbondy, J. El regadio, los lagos y los mitos de origen. *Allpanchis* 17, no. 20 (1982): 3–32.

Sherrat, A. The trans-Eurasian exchange. The prehistory of Chinese relations with the West. In Mair 2006: 30–61.

Shevoroshkin, V., and P. Sidwell, eds. *Languages and their speakers in ancient Eurasia. Dedicated to Professor Aharon Dolgopolsky on his 70th birthday.* AHL Studies in the Science and History of Language 5. Canberra: Association for the History of Language, 2002.

Shirokogoroff, S. M. *Psychomental complex of the Tungus.* Berlin: Schletzer, 1999 [1935].

Siegel, P., et al. Progress from chicken genetics to the chicken genome. *Poultry Science* 85, no. 12 (2006): 2050–60.

Sienkewicz, Thomas J. *World mythology. An annotated guide to collections and anthologies.* Lanham, Md.: Scarecrow Press, 1996.

Silva, W. A., et al. Mitochondrial genome diversity of Native Americans supports a single early entry of founder populations into America. *American Journal of Human Genetics* 71 (2002): 187–92.

Simpson, William K., ed. *The literatures of ancient Egypt. An anthology of stories, instruction and poetry.* New Haven: Yale University Press, 1973.

Simrock, K., and H. Kuhn. *Götterlieder der älteren Edda.* Stuttgart: Reclam, 1966.

Smith, C. E. Female artists: The unrecognized factor in sacred rock art production. In Bahn and Rosenfeld 1991: 45–52.

Smith, G. Elliott. *The evolution of the dragon.* London, 1919.

Smith, J. Z. The "end" of comparison. In *A magic still dwells*, ed. K. C. Patton and B. C. Ray, 237–41. Berkeley: University of California Press, 2000a.

———. *Imagining religion: From Babylon to Jonestown.* Chicago: University of Chicago Press, 1982.

———. In comparison a magic dwells. In *A magic still dwells*, ed. K. C. Patton and B. C. Ray, 23–44. Berkeley: University of California Press, 2000b. (Originally: in Smith 1982: chap. 2.)

Smith, William Ramsey. *Aborigine myths and legends*. London: Random, 1996 [1930].

Snellgrove, David, and Hugh Richardson. *A cultural history of Tibet*. Praeger Publications, 1968.

Soisson, P., and J. Soisson. *La vie des Aztèques dans l'ancien Mexique*. Paris: Minerva, 1987.

Sorenson, J. L., and C. L. Johannessen. Biological evidence for Pre-Columbian transoceanic voyages. In Mair 2006: 238–97.

Sproul, Barbara C. *Primal myths. Creation myths around the world*. San Francisco: Harper, 1991.

Sreenathan, M., and V. R. Rao. Andamanese mythical signatures linking Gondwana mythology with the Laurasian cluster. *Mother Tongue* 13 (2010): 249–64.

Staal, J. F. Three mountains and seven rivers. In *Three mountains and seven rivers: Prof. Musashi Tachikawa's felicitation volume*, ed. Shoun Hino and Toshihiro Wada. Delhi: Motilal Banarsidass Publishers, 2004.

Stanford, Dennis, and Bruce Bradley. The North Atlantic Ice-Edge Corridor: A possible Palaeolithic route to the New World. *World Archaeology* 36, no. 4 (2004): 459–78.

Stanner, W. E. H. On aboriginal religion. I. The lineaments of sacrifice. *Oceania* 30 (1959): 108–27.

———. On aboriginal religion. II. Sacramentalism, rite and myth. *Oceania* 30 (1960): 245–78.

Starostin, S. *Of long-range comparison*. 2002, http://starling.rinet.ru/Texts/method.pdf.

Staudacher, Willibald. *Die Trennung von Himmel und Erde: Ein vorgriechischer Schöpfungsmythus bei Hesiod und den Orphikern*. Tübingen, 1942.

Steinbauer, F. *Melanesische Cargo-Kulte. Neureligiöse Heilsbewegungen in der Südsee*. Munich: Delp'sche Verlagsbuchhandlung, 1971.

Stengel, M. K. The diffusionists have landed. *Atlantic Monthly*, 2000.

Stock, Jay T., et al. Cranial diversity in South Asia relative to modern human dispersals and global patterns of human variation. In Petraglia and Allchin 2007: 245–70.

Stokstad, Erik. Early cowboys herded cattle in Africa. *Science* 296, no. 5566 (April 12, 2002).

Stone, A. C., and M. Stoneking. Analysis of ancient DNA from a prehistoric Amerindian cemetery. *Philosophical Transactions of the Royal Society B: Biological Sciences* 354, no. 1379 (January 29, 1999): 153–59.

Stone, Ruth M. *Theory for ethnomusicology*. Upper Saddle River, N.J.: Pearson Prentice Hall, 2008.

Storey, Alice A., et al. Radiocarbon and DNA evidence for a pre-Columbian introduction of Polynesian chickens to Chile. *Proceedings of the National Academy of Sciences of the United States of America* 104, no. 25 (June 19, 2007): 10335–39.

Strehlow, T. G. H. *Central Australian religion. Personal monototemism in a polytotemic community*. Bedford Park: Australian Association for the Study of Religions, 1978.

Strensky, I. The rise of ritual and the hegemony of myth. Sylvain Lévy, the Durkheimians, and Max Müller. In Patton and Doniger 1996: 52–81.

Stringer, Chris, and Robin McKie. *African exodus*. London: Cape 1996.

Su, B., et al. Y chromosome haplotypes reveal prehistorical migrations to the Himalayas. *Human Genetics*, 2000: 582–90.

Su, Bing, et al. Y-chromsome evidence for a northward migration of modern humans into eastern Asia during the last Ice Age. *American Journal of Human Genetics* 65 (1999): 1718–24.

Suárez, Tomás Pérez. Images of "Olmec Dragon" in the Mayan area. Presentation at the 19th World Congress of the International Association for the History of Religions, Tokyo, March 2005.

Sullivan, L. E. *Icanchu's drum. An orientation in meaning in South American religions*. New York: Macmillan, 1988.

Sullivan, W. *The secret of the Incas. Myth, astronomy, and the war against time*. New York: Three Rivers Press, 1996.

Sutcliffe, S. Review of Partridge 2003. *Cosmos* 20 (2004): 261–63.

Suwa, Tetsuo. *Two essays on the formation of the East Asian ethnic world*. Tokyo: Institute for the Study of Languages and Cultures of Asia and Africa, 1989.

Sverdrup, Harald. Exploring properties of the Rhaetian (Rhaetic) language. In *Languages and their speakers in ancient Eurasia. Dedicated to Professor Aharon Dolgopolsky on his 70th birthday*, ed. Vitaly Shevoroshkin and Paul Sidwell, 85–114. Canberra: AHL Studies in the Science and History of Languages 5, 2002.

Swadesh, Morris. Towards greater accuracy in lexicostatistic dating. *International Journal of American Linguistics* 21 (1955): 121–37.

———. What is glottochronology? In *The origin and diversification of languages*, 271–84. London: Routledge and Kegan Paul, 1972.

Swanson, Paul L., and Clark Chilson, eds. *Nanzan guide to Japanese religions*. Honolulu: University of Hawai'i Press, 2006.

Tajima, A., et al. Genetic origins of the Ainu inferred from combined DNA analyses of maternal and paternal lineages. *Japan Society of Human Genetics* 49 (2004): 187–93.

Talon, Philippe. *The standard Babylonian creation myth. Enuma Eliš*. Helsinki, 2005.

Tamm, Erika, et al. Beringian standstill and spread of Native American founders. *PLos* 9 (September 2007): e829.

Tanaka, M., et al. Mitochondrial genome variation in eastern Asia and the peopling of Japan. *Genome Research* 14 (2004): 1832–50.

Tchavouchian, Benjamin. *David de Sassoun: Troisième branche de l'épopée nationale arménienne; d'après Hov. Toumanian; version française de Benjamin Tchavouchian; illustrations de Claude Tchavouch*. Yerevan: Zangak-97, 2003.

Tedlock, Barbara. *The woman in the shaman's body. Reclaiminig the feminine in religion and medicine*. New York: Bantam, 2005.

Tedlock, D. *Popol Vuh. The Mayan book of the dawn of life*. New York: Touchstone, 1985.

Thangaraj, Kumarasamy. Genetic affinities of the Andaman Islanders, a vanishing human population. *Current Biology* 13 (January 21, 2003): 86–93.

Thangaraj, Kumarasamy, et al. Reconstructing the origin of the Andamanese Islanders. *Science* 308 (2005): 996.

Thomas, D. H., and S. Colley. *Skull wars: Kennewick Man, archaeology, and the battle for native identity*. New York: Basic Books, 2001.

Thomas, Louis-Vincent, René Luneau, and J.-L. Doneux. *Les religions d'Afrique Noire, texts et traditions sacrés*. Paris: Fayard, 1969.

Thompson, George. Shamanism in the R̥gveda and its Central Asian antecedents. Presentation at the 5th Harvard Round Table, May 9–12, 2003, http://www.people.fas.harvard.edu/~witzel/Thompson.pdf.

Thompson, Stith. *The folktale*. Berkeley: University of California Press, 1977.

———. *Motif index of folk-literature. A classification of narrative elements in folk-tales, ballads, myths, fables, mediaeval romances, exempla, fabliaux, jest-books, and local legends*. Bloomington: Indiana University Press; and Clayton: InteLex Corp., 1993. (Originally: Bloomington, Ind., 1932–36; 2nd ed., 1966.)

———. *The types of the folk-tale: Anti Aarne "Verzeichnis der Märchentypen" translated and enlarged.* FF Communications 74. Helsinki: Suomalainen Tiedeakatemia, 1971.

Thorne, A., et al. Australia's oldest human remains: Age of the Lake Mungo 3 skeleton. *Journal of Human Evolution* 36 (1999): 591–612.

———. The longest link: Human evolution in Southeast Asia and the settlement of Australia. In *Indonesia: Australian perspectives.* Canberra: Research School of Pacific Studies, Australian National University, 1980.

Tièche, Edouard. Atlas als Personifikation der Weltachse. *Museum Helveticum* 2 (1945): 65–86.

Tinbergen, Niko. On aims and methods in ethology. *Zeitschrift für Tierpsychologie* 20 (1963): 410–33.

———. *Social behavior in animals, with special reference to vertebrates.* London: Methuen; and New York: Wiley, 1962.

Tindale, N. B., and J. B. Birdsell. Tasmanoid tribes in northern Queensland. *Records of the South Australian Museum* 7 (1941): 1–9.

Ting, Nai-tung. *A type index of Chinese folktales: In the oral tradition and major works of non-religious classical literature.* Helsinki: Suomalainen Tiedeakatemia, Academia Scientiarum Fennica, 1978.

Tishkoff, Sara A. History of click-speaking populations of Africa inferred from mtDNA and Y chromosome genetic variation. *Molecular Biology and Evolution* 24 (July 26, 2007): 2180–95.

Tobias, Phillip V., et al. *Humanity from African naissance to coming millennia: Colloquia in human biology and palaeoanthropology.* Firenze: Firenze University Press; and Johannesburg: Witwatersrand University Press, 2001.

Torcinovich, G. The horse and the journey to heaven of the shamans and of the Vedic sacrificer. In Mastromattei and Rigopulos 1999: 237–49.

Torroni, Antonio, et al. Harvesting the fruit of the human mtDNA tree. *Trends in Genetics* 22 (2006): 339–45.

Tregear, E. *The Malayo-Polynesian comparative dictionary.* Repr. Oosterhout: Anthropologcial Publications, 1969. (Originally: Wellington, 1891.)

Trejaut, J. A., et al. Traces of archaic mitochondrial lineages persist in Austronesian-speaking Formosan populations. *PLoS Biology* 3, no. 8 (2005): e247.

Trinkhaus, E. Human evolution: Nenderthal geme speaks out. *Current Biology* 17, no. 21 (2007): R917–19.

Trompf, G. W. *Melanesain religion.* Cambridge: Cambridge University Press, 1991.

Tucker, M. *Dreaming with open eyes: The shamanic spirit in contemporary art and culture.* London: Harper Collins, 1992.

Tuite, Kevin. Achilles and the Caucasus. 2007: 1–66, http://www.mapageweb.umontreal.ca/tuitekj/publications/Tuite_Achilles.pdf.

———. Der Kaukasus und der Hindu-Kush: Eine neue Betrachtung des Beweismaterials über frühe Verbindungen. *Georgica* 19 (1996): 92–108.

———. Evidence for prehistoric links between the Caucasus and Central Asia: The case of the Burushos. In *The Bronze Age and early Iron Age peoples of eastern Central Asia,* ed. Victor H. Mair, 448–75. Washington, D.C.: Institute for the Study of Man, 1998.

Tung, T'ung-ho. *A descriptive study of the Tsou language, Formosa.* With the assistance of S. H. Wang et al. Taipei: Institute of History and Philology, Academia Sinica, 1964.

Turner, C. G. Dentochronological seperation estimates for Pacific Rim populations. *Science* 232 (1986): 1140–42.

Ucko, P. *Form in indigenous art, schematization in the art of aboriginal Australia and prehistoric Europe.* Canberra: Australian Institute of Aboriginal Studies, 1977.

Underhill, Peter A. Inference of Neolithic population histories using Y-chromosome haplotypes. In *Examining the farming/language dispersal hypothesis,* ed. P. Bellwood and C. Renfrew, 65–78. Cambridge: McDonald Institute for Archaeological Research, 2003a.

———. Inferring human history: Clues from Y-chromosome haplotypes. *Cold Spring Harbor Symposia on Quantitative Biology* 68 (2003b): 487–93.

———. The peopling of Eurasia. A Y chromosome perspective. Presentation at the Ninth Harvard Round Table on the Ethnogenesis of South and Central Asia, October 21–22, 2006.

———. A synopsis of extant Y chromosome diversity on East Asia and Oceania. In Sagart et al. 2005: 297–313.

Underhill, P. A., and Toomas Kivisild. Use of Y chromosome and mitochondrial DNA population structure in tracing human migrations. *Annual Review of Genetics* 41 (2007): 539–64.

Underhill, P. A., et al. The phylogeography of Y chromosome binary haplotypes and the origins of modern human populations. *Annals of Human Genetics* 63 (2001): 43–62.

———. Y chromosome sequence variation and the history of human populations. *Nature Genetics* 26 (2000): 358–61.

Unterberger, Gerald. *Die Kosmologie der Dogon: Die Mystik von der Himmelsstütze und dem Verkehrten Weltbaum in kulturgeschichtlichem Vergleich.* Vienna: Afro-Pub., 2001.

Usher, T. Great Andamanese reconstruction underway; a condensed handout with tentative remarks on Papuan and Australian vis-a-vis external language families. *Mother Tongue* 11 (2006): 295–98.

———. The origin of the Tasmanian languages. *Mother Tongue* 7 (2002): 65–84.

Vajda, Edward. The Siberian origins of Na-Dene languages. Paper presented at the Dene-Yeniseic Work Session, Fairbanks, February 26–27, 2008, and at the Annual Meeting of the Alaskan Anthropological Society, Anchorage, February 28, 2008.

Vajracharya, G. V. The adaptation of monsoonal culture by Ṛgvedic Aryans: A further study of the frog hymn. *Electronic Journal of Vedic Studies* 3, no. 2 (1997).

van Binsbergen, Wim M. J. Mythological archaeology: Reconstructing humankind's oldest discourse. Presentation at the International Conference on Comparative Mythology, Beijing, 2006a, http://shikanda.net/ancient_models/mythical_archaeology/mythology.htm.

———. Mythological archaeology. Situating sub-Saharan African cosmogonic myths within a long-range intercontinental comparative perspective. 2006b. In Osada 2006: 319–49.

———. Rupture and fusion in the approach to myth. Presentation at the Conference "Myth and the Disciplines," Leiden, December 12, 2003.

———. Rupture and fusion in the approach to myth. 2005, http://www.shikanda.net/ancient_models/myth%20mineke%20defdefdef.pdf.

———. Transcontinental mythological patterns in prehistory. *Cosmos* 23 (2007): 29–80. (Also: *On Bernal's Black Athena,* http://www.shikanda.net/.)

van Binsbergen, Wim M. J., and Eric Venbrux. *New perspectives on myth. Proceedings of the Second Annual Conference of the International Association for Comparative Mythology, Ravenstein (the Netherlands), 19–21 August, 2008.* Papers in Intercultural Philosophy and Transcontinental Studies 5. Haarlem, 2010.

van Driem, G. The prehistory of Tibeto-Burman and Austroasiatic in the light of emergent population genetic studies. *Mother Tongue* 11 (2006): 160–211.

———. Tibeto-Burman vs Indo-Chinese: Implications for population genetics, archeologists, and prehistorians. In Sagart et al. 2005: 81–106.

Vanhaeren, Marian, et al. Middle Palaeolithic shell beads in Israel and Algeria. *Science* 312, no. 5781 (June 23, 2006): 1785–88.

Van Over, Raymond. *Sun songs: Creation myths from around the world.* New York: New American Library, 1980.

Varenne, Jean. *Cosmogonies védiques.* Paris: Les belles lettres, 1982.

Vico, Giambattista. *Principi di una scienza nuova* [The new science of Giambattista Vico] (1725). Rev. trans. of 3rd ed. (1774) by Thomas Goddard Bergin and Max Harold Fisch. Ithaca: Cornell University Press, 1968.

Vielle, Christophe. *Le mytho-cycle héroïque dans l'aire indoeuropéenne.* Louvain-la-Neuve: Peeters, 1997.

Villems, R. Genetics and mythology—An unexplored field. Presentation at the Seventh Ethnogenesis of South and Central Asia Round Table, Kyoto, June 8, 2005.

Vincente, Xuan Xosé Sánchez, and Xesús Cañedo Valle. *El gran libro de la Mitología Asturiana* [Traducción del asturiano]. Oviedo: Trabe, 2003.

Vitebsky, Pierce. *The shaman. Voyages of the soul. Trance, exstasy, and healing from Siberia to the Amazon.* London: DBP, Macmillan, 1995.

von Sadovszky, Otto J. *Demonstration of a close genetic relationship between the Wintun languages of northern California and the Ob-Ugrian languages of north-western Siberia: A preliminary report.* Fullerton, Calif., 1978.

———. *The discovery of California: A Cal-Ugrian comparative study.* Budapest: Akadémiai Kiadó; and Los Angeles: International Society for Trans-oceanic Research, 1996.

Vovin, A. Introduction. In *Perspectives on the origins of the Japanese language,* ed. T. Osada and A. Vovin, with K. Russel, 421–28. Kyoto: International Center for Japanese Studies, 2003.

Wade, N. Humans have spread globally, and evolved locally. *New York Times,* June 26, 2007a, http://www.nytimes.com/2007/06/26/science/26human.html?ei=5087%0A&em=&en=4ee6fee/1dbf69961&ex=1183003200&pagewanted=all.

———. Selection spurred recent evolution, researchers say. *New York Times,* December 11, 2007b.

Wagner, Rudolf G. *The contemporary Chinese historical drama: Four studies.* Berkeley: University of California Press, 1990.

Waida, Manabu. Symbolism of "descent" in Tibetan sacred kingship and some East Asian parallels. *Numen* 20, no. 1 (1973): 60–78.

Wallace, D. C., and A. Torroni. American Indian prehistory as written in the mitochondrial DNA: A review. *Human Biology* 64, no. 3 (June 1992): 403–16.

Wallis, J. *The social production of art.* London: Macmillan, 2002.

Walter, Mariko Namba, and E. J. Neumann Fridman, eds. *Shamanism.* Santa Barbara: ABC Clio, 2004.

Wang, Aihe. *Cosmology and political culture in early China.* Cambridge: Cambridge University Press, 2000.

Wanke, Lothar. *Indische Felsbilder als Urkunden einer weltweiten Frühreligion.* Icking: ORA Verlag, 1974.

———. *Zentralindische Felsbilder.* Graz, 1977.

Warburg, Aby. A serpent ritual. *Journal of the Warburg Institute* 2 (1938–39): 222–92.

Waters, Frank. *Book of the Hopi.* New York: Penguin Books, 1977 [1963].

Watkins, C. *How to kill a dragon: Aspects of Indo-European poetics.* New York: Oxford University Press, 1995.

Watson, E., et al. Mitochondrial footprints of human expansions in Africa Americans. *Journal of Human Genetics* 61 (1997): 691–704.

Watters, D. E. *Notes on Kusunda (a language isolate of Nepal)*. Kathmandu: National Foundation for the Development of Indigenous Nationalities, 2005.

Weber, George. Lonely island. The Andamanese and other Negrito people and the Out-of-Africa story of the human race. March 2006, http://www.andaman.org/.

Wehmeyer, Ann. *Kojiki-den, book 1. by Motoori Norinaga. Introduced, translated, and annotated*. Ithaca: East Asia Program, Cornell Universtity, 1997.

Weigle, Marta. *Creation and procreation: Feminist reflections on mythologies of cosmogony and parturition*. Philadelphia: University of Pennsylvania Press, 1989.

Wells, R. S., et al. The Eurasian heartland: A Continental perspective on Y-chromosome diversity. *Proceedings of the National Academy of Sciences of the United States of America* 98 (2001): 10244–49.

Wells, S. *The journey of man: A genetic odyssey*. Princeton: Princeton University Press, 2002.

Wendt, W. E. "Art Mobilier" from the Apollo 11 Cave, South West Africa: Africa's oldest dated works of art. *South African Archaeological Bulletin* 5 (1976): 5–11.

Werner, E. C. T. *A dictionary of Chinese mythology*. Shanghai, 1932.

Werner, M., and Bénédicte Zimmermann. Beyond comparison: *Histoire croisée* and the challenge of reflexivity (draft). N.d., http://www.iue.it/HEC/ResearchTeaching/20042005-Spring/Werner.pdf.

West, M. L. Ancient Near Eastern myths in classical Greek religious thought. In J. M. Sasson, *Civilizations of the ancient Near East*, 4 vols., 33–42. New York: Scribner, 1995.

———. *The east face of Helicon*. Oxford: Oxford, 1997.

Westervelt, W. D. *Myths and legends of Hawaii. Ancient lore retold, selected and edited by A. Grove Day*. Honolulu: Mutual Publishing Co., 1987.

Westgate, J., et al. All Toba tephra occurrences across peninsular India belong to the 75,000 yr BP eruption. *Quarternary Research* 50 (1998): 107–12.

White, Tim D., et al. Pleistocene *Homo sapiens* from Middle Awash, Ethiopia. *Nature* 423 (June 12, 2003): 742–47.

Whitehouse, Paul. The "lost" paper: A belated conference postscript. *Mother Tongue* 11 (2006): 262–74.

Whitehouse, Paul, Timothy Usher, and Merritt Ruhlen. Kusunda: An Indo-Pacific language in Nepal. *Proceedings of the National Academy of Sciences of the United States of America* 101, no. 15 (April 13, 2004): 5692–95, http://www.pnas.org_cgi_doi_10.1073_pnas.0400233101,http://www.pnas.org_cgi_doi_10.1073_pnas.0400233101, http://www.pnas.org/cgi/reprint/101/15/5692.pdf.

Whorf, B. L. *Language, thought and reality*. Ed. J. B. Carroll. Cambridge: MIT Press, 1956.

Wilbert, J. *Folk literature of the Selknam Indians: Martin Gusinde's collection of Selknam narratives*. Los Angeles: University of California Press, 1975.

———. *Folk literature of the Yamana Indians*. Los Angeles: University of California Press, 1977.

Williamson, Kay, and Roger Blench. Niger-Congo. In *African languages—An introduction*, ed. Bernd Heine and Derek Nurse, 11–42. Cambridge: Cambridge University Press, 2000.

Winkelman, M. Cross-cultural perspectives on shamans. In Walter and Fridman 2004: 61–70.

———. Shaman and other "magico-religious" healers? A cross-cultural study of their origins, nature, and social transformation. *Ethos* 18 (1990): 308–52.

————. Shamanism and cognitive evolution. *Cambridge Archaeological Journal* 12 (2002): 71–101.

Winthrop, John. A model of Christian charity (1630). In *Norton anthology of American literature*. Shorter 4th ed. New York: W. W. Norton, 1995.

Wiredu, Kwasi. *Cultural universals and articulars: An African perspective*. Bloomington: Indiana University Press, 1996.

Wirz, P. *Die Marind-Amin von Holländisch-Süd–Neu-Guinea*. Hamburg: Friedrichsen 1925 [1922].

Witzel, Michael. Autochthonous Aryans? The evidence from Old Indian and Iranian texts. *Electronic Journal of Vedic Studies* 7, no. 3 (2001a), http://www.ejvs.laurasianacademy. com/ejvs0703/ejvs0703article.pdf.

————. Canon and continuing innovation: Indian approaches to the classics. In *Classics as a basis of creativity. Proceeedings of the 7th International Symposium on the Reconstitution of Classical Studies (ISRCS)*, September 22–23, Kyoto, 2002 *[Heisei 14]*, ed. H. Nakatani, 46–55, 2002a, http://www.classics.jp/RCS/index.html.

————. The case of the shattered head. Festschrift für W. Rau. *Studien zur Indologie und Iranistik* 13–14 (1987a): 363–415.

————. Chuo Ajia Shinwa to Nihon Shinwa [Central Asian mythology and Japanese mythology]. In Japanaese. *Annual Report of the Institute for Japanese Culture and Classics, Kokugakuin University*, Heisei 21 (September 2009a): 85–96.

————. Comparison and reconstruction: Language and mythology. *Mother Tongue* 6 (2001b): 45–62.

————. The coronation rituals of Nepal, with special reference to the coronation of King Birendra in 1975. In *Heritage of the Kathmandu Valley. Proceedings of an international conference in Lübeck, June 1985*, ed. Niels Gutschow and Axel Michaels, 417–67. St. Augustin, Germany: VGH Wissenschaftsverlag, 1987b.

————. Dragon myths. Presentation at the first conference of the International Society for Comparative Mythology, "Deep History of Stories," Edinburgh, August 2007a.

————. Dragons. Presentation at a conference at Tainan, Taiwan, October 2005a.

————. The earliest form of the concept of rebirth in India (summary). In *31st CISHAAN (Tokyo-Kyoto), proceedings*, ed. T. Yamamoto, 145–46. Tokyo, 1984a.

————. Early Sanskritization. Origins and development of the Kuru state. *Electronic Journal of Vedic Studies* 1, no. 4 (December 1995), http://www.ejvs.laurasianacademy.com. (Revised: Early sanskritization. Origins and development of the Kuru state. In *Recht, Staat und Verwaltung im klassischen Indien* [The state, the law, and administration in classical India], ed. B. Kölver, 27–52. Munich: R. Oldenbourg, 1997.)

————. Early sources for South Asian substrate languages. *Mother Tongue*, extra number (1999a).

————. How to enter the Vedic mind? Strategies in translating a Brāhmaṇa text. In *Translating, translations, translators from India to the West*, ed. E. Garzilli. Opera Minora 1. Cambridge: Harvard Oriental Series, 1996, http://www.people.fas.harvard. edu/~witzel/How-to-Enter.pdf.

————. Jungavestisch apāxəδra im System der avestischen Himmelsrichtungsbezeichnungen. *Münchener Studien zur Sprachwissenschaft* 30 (1972): 163–91.

————. *Kaṭha Āraṇyaka*. Critical ed. with a trans. into German and an intro. Cambridge: Harvard Oriental Series 65, 2004a.

————. Kumano kara Woruga made [From Kumano to the Volga]. In Japanese. *Zinbun* 36 (1990a): 4–5.

————. Linguistic evidence for cultural exchange in prehistoric western Central Asia. *Sino-Platonic Papers* 129 (2003).

————. Macrocosm, mesocosm, and microcosm: The persistent nature of "Hindu" beliefs and symbolic forms. *International Journal of Hindu Studies* 1 (December 1997a): 501–43.

————. Meaningful ritual. Structure, development and interpretation of the Tantric *agnihotra* ritual of Nepal. In *Ritual, state and history in South Asia. Essays in honour of J. C. Heesterman*, ed. A. W. van den Hoek et al., 774–827. Leiden, 1992.

————. Myths and consequences. Review of Stefan Arvidsson, *Indo-European Mythology as Ideology and Science*, Chicago University Press 2006. *Science* 317 (September 28, 2007b): 1868–69, http://www.sciencemag.org/cgi/content/full/317/5846/1868?ijkey=vNHCuWdIhTviU&keytype=ref&siteid=sci.

————. The numeral system of Jarawa Andamanese. *Mother Tongue* 7 (2002b): 265–72.

————. On Indian historical writing: The case of the Vaṃśāvalīs. *Journal of the Japanese Association for South Asian Studies* 2 (1990b): 1–57, http://www.people.fas.harvard.edu/~witzel/vamsa.pdf.

————. *On magical thought in the Veda*. Leiden: Universitaire Pers, 1979.

————. *On ritual*. Unpublished MS, Kathmandu, 1985.

————. On the origin of the literary device of the "frame story" in Old Indian literature. In *Hinduismus und Buddhismus, Festschrift für U. Schneider*, ed. H. Falk, 380–414. Freiburg, 1987c.

————. Out of Africa: The journey of the oldest tales of humankind. Presentation given at the Conference on Generalized Sciences: Peaceful World and Enriching Lives. Tokyo, March 17, 2006a.

————. Out of India: Classical values for today and tomorrow. In *Reconstitution of classical studies*, ed. H. Nakatani, September 10–13, 2001c, http://www.classics.jp/RCS/index.html.

————. Pan-Gaean flood myths. Gondwana myths—and beyond. In van Binsbergen and Venbrux 2010: 225–42.

————. *Prajātantu*. In *Harānandalaharī. Volume edited in honour of Professor Minoru Hara on his seventieth birthday*, ed. Ryutaro Tsuchiyama and Albrecht Wezler, 457–80. Reinbek: Inge Wezler, 2000.

————. Rama's realm: Indocentric rewritings of early South Asian archaeology and history. In *Archaeological fantasies. How pseudoarchaeology misrepresents the past and misleads the public*, ed. G. G. Fagan, 203–32. London: Routledge, 2006b.

————. Releasing the sun at midwinter and slaying the dragon at midsummer: A Laurasian myth complex. *Cosmos. The Journal of the Traditional Cosmology Society* 23 (2009b [2007]): 203–44.

————. Review of *Zur Schulzugehörigkeit von Werken der Hinayana-Literatur, zweiter Teil* by Heinz Bechert. *Journal of the American Oriental Society* 111 (1991): 581–83.

————. The R̥gvedic religious system and its Central Asian and Hindukush antecedents. In *The Vedas: Texts, language and ritual*, ed. Arlo Griffiths and Jan E. M. Houben, 581–636. Groningen: Forsten, 2004b.

————. Sapta r̥ṣayaḥ—The Big Dipper (Ursa Maior). Reconstitution of Classical Studies, no. 4, ed. H. Nakatani. *Heisei* 11 [1999b]: 36, http://www.kotengaku.bun.kyoto-u.ac.jp.

————. Saramā and the Paṇis. Origins of prosimetric exchange in archaic India. In *Prosimetrum: Crosscultural perspectives on narrative in prose and verse*, ed. Joseph Harris and Karl Reichl, 397–409. Cambridge: D. S. Brewer, 1997b.

———. Shamanism in northern and southern Eurasia: Their distinctive methods of change of consciousness. *Social Science Information/Information sur les Sciences Sociales* 50 (2011): 39–61.

———. Slaying the dragon across Eurasia. In *In hot pursuit of language in prehistory. Essays in the four fields of anthropology. In honor of Harold Crane Fleming*, ed. John D. Bengtson, 263–86. Amsterdam: John Benjamin's Publishing Co., 2008.

———. South Asian agricultural vocabulary. In Osada 2006c: 96–120.

———. Sur le chemin du ciel. *Bulletin des Etudes indiennes* 2 (1984b): 213–79.

———. Vala and Iwato. The myth of the hidden sun in India, Japan, and beyond. *Electronic Journal of Vedic Studies* 12, no. 1 (2005b): 1–69, http://www.ejvs.laurasianacademy.com/ejvs1201/ejvs1201article.pdf.

———. The Vedas and the epics: Some comparative notes on persons, lineages, geography, and grammar. In *Epics, Khilas, and Purāṇas. Continuities and ruptures. Proceedings of the Third Dubrovnik International Conference on the Sanskrit Epics and Purāṇas. September 2002*, ed. P. Koskikallio, 21–80. Zagreb: Croatian Academy of Sciences and the Arts, 2005c.

Wölfel, J. D. *Die Religion des vorindogermanischen Europa*. Vienna, 1951.

Worms, E. A. Tasmanian mythological terms. *Anthropos* 55 (1960): 1–16.

Wright, Robert. Quest for the mother tongue. *The Atlantic* 267, no. 4 (April 1991): 39–68.

Wundt, Wilhelm Max. *Völkerpsychologie: Eine Untersuchung der Entwicklungsgesetze von Sprache, Mythus und Sitte*. Leipzig: W. Engelmann, 1900–20.

Wunn, Ina. Beginning of religion. *Numen* 47 (2000): 417–52.

———. *Die Religionen in vorgeschichtlicher Zeit*. Stuttgart: Kohlhammer, 2005.

———. *Götter, Mütter, Ahnenkult. Religionsentwicklung in der Jungsteinzeit*. Beiheft, Archäologische Mitteilungen aus Nordwestdeutschland, No. 36. Rahden: Leidorf, 2001.

Wurm, S. A. *Australian linguistic studies*. Canberra: Department of Linguistics, Research School of Pacific Studies, Australian National University, 1979.

———. *Languages of Australia and Tasmania*. The Hague: Mouton, 1972.

———. *New Guinea area languages and language study, vol. 1: Papuan languages and the New Guinea linguistic scene*. Pacific Linguistics, Research School of Pacific and Asian Studies, Australian National University. Canberra: Australian National University, 1977.

———. *Papuan languages of Oceania*. Tübingen: Narr, 1982.

Wurm, S. A., and D. C. Laycock, eds. *Pacific linguistic studies in honour of Arthur Capell*. Canberra: Linguistic Circle of Canberra, 1970.

[Y Chromosome Consortium]. A nomenclature system for the tree of human Y-chromosome binary haplogroups, Cold Spring Harbor Laboratory Press. *Genome Research* 12 (2002): 339–48, http://www.genome.org/cgi/doi/10.1101/gr.217602.

Yalman, N. Lévi-Strauss in wonderland. *American Ethnologist* 23 (1996): 901–3.

Yamada, H. The gourd in South Chinese and Southeast Asian flood myths. Presentation at the International Symposium on *fudaraku tokai. Nara*, July 19–20, 2003: 1–14.

———. Mythical little people in Taiwan: Do they imply the existence of Negritos? Presentation at the First Conference of the International Society for Comparative Mythology, "Deep History of Stories," Edinburgh, August 2007.

Yang, Lihui, and Deming An, with Jesssica Anderson Turner. *Handbook of Chinese mythology*. Santa Barbara: ABC Clio, 2005.

Yang, Shi. The flood as meaningful rebirth, the symbolism of Mangyan Filipinos' flood myth. Presentation at the Conference on Comparative Mythology, Beijing, 2006.

———. Myth among the Alangan-Mangyan of the Philippines. *Cosmos* 23 (2007): 111–22.

Ye, Shuxian. Totem and the origin of bear myths in Euro-Asia. Presentation at the Conference on Comparative Mythology, Beijing, June 2006.

Yoshida, Atsuhiko. Dumézil and comparative studies of Eurasian myths. In Osada 2006: 236–42.

———. *Girisha shinwa to nihon shinwa. Hikaku shinwagaku no kokoromi* [Greek myths and Japanese myths. An attempt at comparative mythology]. Tokyo: Misuzu Shobō, 1974.

———. La mythologie japonaise: Essai d'interpretation structurale. III. Susanō, l'orage et la foudre. *Revue de l'histoire des religions* 160–61 (1961–62): 47–66, 25–44.

Zahan, Dominique. *The religion, spirituality and thought of traditional Africa.* Chicago, 1970. (Originally: *Religion, spiritualité, et pensée africaines.* Paris.)

Zimmer, S. On Europeanization. *Journal of Indo-European Studies* 18 (1990): 141–55.

Zolbrod, Paul G. *Diné bahane'. The Navajo creation story.* Albuquerque: University of New Mexico Press, 1984.

Zuesse, Evan M. *Ritual cosmos. The sanctification of life in African religions.* Athens: Ohio University Press, 1979.

Zvelebil, Kamil. Creation and origin myths of some Nilgiri tribes. *Temenos* 26 (1990): 159–71.

———. Mythologie der Tamilen und anderer drawidisch sprechender Völker. In *Wörterbuch der Mythologie,* ed. H. W. Haussig, 827–950. Stuttgart: Klett-Cotta, 1982.

———. *Nilgiri areal studies.* Ed. Jaroslav Vacek and Jan Dvořak. Prague: Charles University, Karolinum Press, 2001.

■ INDEX

Abel and Cain, 118, 168, 169
Abhaya mudrā, 272
Aboriginals, 5, 15, 30, 249
    comparison of myths, 78–79
    countercheck to Laurasian theory, 297,
        300–302, 310, 324, 340
    historical development of Laurasian
        mythology, 382, 384, 408
    Pan-Gaean period, 362–363
Abrahamic religions, 9, 263, 436, 437, 439
    comparative mythology, 58, 92
    historical development of Laurasian
        theory, 409
    see also Christianity; Islam; Judaism
Accusative markers, 193
Achilles, 79, 180, 431
Ad quem, 410, 411, 413
Adam and Eve, 3, 23
    countercheck to Laurasian theory, 339
    Pan-Gaean period, 363–365
    see also African Adam; African Eve
Aden, Strait of, 210, 245
Aditi, 176
Āditya, 163, 176
Adonai, 360
Adstrate influences, 73, 81, 91, 98
Aegean area, comparative mythology, 70
Æsir, 164, 181
Aeta people, 308, 324
    historical development of Laurasian
        mythology, 375, 414, 419
Aether, 108
Afghanistan, 118, 338, 402
Afrasian language family, 191
Africa, 6, 15, 28, 31, 33
    within Gondwana mythological system, *xi*
    exodus from. *See* Out of Africa
        movement
    linking language families, 191
    mythologies of. *See* African mythologies
    "Old African" culture, 317
    syncretistic cults, 436
    see also particular people and places in Africa

African Adam (common male ancestor),
    212, 221, 224
African Eve (common female ancestor), 2,
    3, 6, 23, 179, 185
    comparison of myths, 47, 58, 59
    countercheck to Laurasian theory, 355
    historical development of Laurasian
        mythology, 400, 416
    other sciences contributing to mythology
        reconstruction, 208, 210, 212, 221,
        232
    Pan-Gaean period, 372
    table of descendants, 221
African mythologies
    within Gondwana mythological system, *xi*
    comparative mythology, 52, 61, 80–81
    countercheck to Laurasian theory, 289,
        290, 317
    creation myths, 124, 171, 172, 178
    "forest of tales," 430
    lives of gods and humans, 427
    other sciences contributing to mythology
        reconstruction, 233, 264
    Pan-Gaean period, 358, 366–367
    simplified scheme of flood myths, 354, 355
    tricksters Pan-Gaean period, 366
African North-South Highway, 293, 316,
    318, 319
    see also Out of Africa movement
Afro-Asiatic people and languages, 19,
    191–195
    countercheck to Laurasian theory, 288,
        319, 321, 343
    Nostratic subfamily, 194–195
Afro-Australian myths, 202, 295, 371
    see also Gondwana
Afterlife, 243, 422–423
    Pan-Gaean period, 366–367
    see also Heaven
Age of myths, 6, 20, 104
Ages, Four. *See* Four Ages
Aghoris, 395
Aging and eternal youth, 297

CPSIA information can be obtained at www.ICGtesting.com
Printed in the USA
BVOW04s0107020414

349496BV00002B/4/P